Less managing. More teaching. Greater learning.

INSTRUCTORS...

Would you like your **students** to show up for class **more prepared**?
(Let's face it, class is much more fun if everyone is engaged and prepared...)

Want an **easy way to assign** homework online and track student **progress**?
(Less time grading means more time teaching...)

Want an **instant view** of student or class performance relative to learning objectives? *(No more wondering if students understand...)*

Need to **collect data and generate reports** required for administration or accreditation? *(Say goodbye to manually tracking student learning outcomes...)*

Want to **record and post your lectures** for students to view online?

With **McGraw-Hill's** *Connect®* **Plus Business Statistics,**

INSTRUCTORS GET:

- Simple **assignment management**, allowing you to spend more time teaching.
- **Auto-graded** assignments, quizzes, and tests.
- **Detailed Visual Reporting** where student and section results can be viewed and analyzed.
- Sophisticated **online testing** capability.
- A **filtering and reporting** function that allows you to easily select Excel-based homework problems, as well as assign and report on materials that are correlated to accreditation standards, learning outcomes, and Bloom's taxonomy.
- An easy-to-use **lecture capture** tool.
- The option to **upload course documents** for student access.

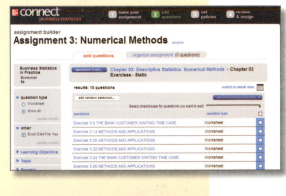

Want an online, **searchable version** of your textbook?

Wish your textbook could be **available online** while you're doing your assignments?

 Connect® Plus Business Statistics eBook

If you choose to use *Connect® Plus Business Statistics*, you have an affordable and searchable online version of your book integrated with your other online tools.

Connect® Plus Business Statistics eBook offers features like:

- Topic search
- Direct links from assignments
- Adjustable text size
- Jump to page number
- Print by section
- Highlight
- Take notes
- Access instructor highlights/notes

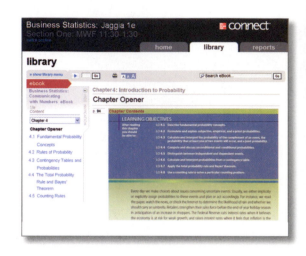

 Want to get more **value** from your textbook purchase?

Think learning business statistics should be a bit more **interesting**?

 Check out the STUDENT RESOURCES section under the *Connect®* Library tab.

Here you'll find a wealth of resources designed to help you achieve your goals in the course. You'll find things like **quizzes, guided examples, narrated PowerPoints, and Internet activities** to help you study. Every student has different needs, so explore the STUDENT RESOURCES to find the materials best suited to you.

BUSINESS STATISTICS

BUSINESS STATISTICS

Communicating with Numbers

Sanjiv Jaggia
*California Polytechnic
State University*

Alison Kelly
Suffolk University

BUSINESS STATISTICS: COMMUNICATING WITH NUMBERS

2 3 4 5 6 7 8 9 0 RJE/RJE 1 0 9 8 7 6 5 4 3 2

ISBN 978-0-07-337366-9
MHID 0-07-337366-4

Vice president and editor-in-chief: *Brent Gordon*
Publisher: *Tim Vertovec*
Executive editor: *Steve Schuetz*
Executive director of development: *Ann Torbert*
Senior development editor: *Wanda J. Zeman*
Vice president and director of marketing: *Robin J. Zwettler*
Marketing director: *Brad Parkins*
Marketing manager: *Dean Karampelas*
Vice president of editing, design, and production: *Sesha Bolisetty*
Lead project manager: *Christine A. Vaughan*
Senior buyer: *Michael R. McCormick*
Senior designer: *Mary Kazak Sander*
Senior photo research coordinator: *Keri Johnson*
Photo researcher: *Robin Sand*
Lead media project manager: *Daryl Horrocks*
Media project manager: *Balaji Sundararaman*
Interior Design: *Laurie Entringer*
Cover Design: *Gino Cieslik*
Cover images: *© Ruth Black/Alamy, © Alistair Laming/Alamy, © Tony Cordoza/Alamy, © Martin Thomas Photography/Alamy, © Bob Pardue/Alamy, © 2010 Getty Images, Ryan McVay/Getty Images, Getty Images, Courtesy of The Home Depot*
Typeface: *10.5/12 Times LT Std Roman*
Compositor: *MPS Limited, a Macmillan Company*
Printer: *R. R. Donnelley*

Library of Congress Cataloging-in-Publication Data

Jaggia, Sanjiv, 1960-
    Business statistics : communicating with numbers / Sanjiv Jaggia, Alison Kelly.
        p. cm.
    Includes index.
    ISBN-13: 978-0-07-337366-9 (alk. paper)
    ISBN-10: 0-07-337366-4 (alk. paper)
    1. Commercial statistics. I. Hawke, Alison Kelly. II. Title.
HF1017.J34 2013
519.5—dc23   2011037378

www.mhhe.com

Sanjiv Jaggia

Sanjiv Jaggia is a professor of economics and finance at California Polytechnic State University in San Luis Obispo, California. After earning a Ph.D. from Indiana University, Bloomington, in 1990, Dr. Jaggia spent 17 years at Suffolk University, Boston. In 2003 he became a Chartered Financial Analyst (CFA®). Dr. Jaggia's research interests include empirical finance, statistics, and econometrics. He has published extensively in research journals, including the *Journal of Empirical Finance, Review of Economics and Statistics, Journal of Business and Economic Statistics*, and *Journal of Econometrics*. Dr. Jaggia's ability to communicate in the classroom has been acknowledged by several teaching awards. In 2007, he traded one coast for the other and now lives in San Luis Obispo, California, with his wife and daughter. In his spare time, he enjoys cooking, hiking, and listening to a wide range of music.

Alison Kelly

Alison Kelly is a professor of economics at Suffolk University in Boston, Massachusetts. She received her B.A. degree from Holy Cross in Worcester, Massachusetts, her M.A. degree from the University of Southern California in Los Angeles, and her Ph.D. from Boston College in Chestnut Hill, Massachusetts. Dr. Kelly has published in highly regarded journals such as the *American Journal of Agricultural Economics, Journal of Macroeconomics, Review of Income and Wealth, Applied Financial Economics*, and *Contemporary Economic Policy*. She is a Chartered Financial Analyst (CFA®) and regularly teaches review courses in quantitative methods to candidates preparing to take the CFA exam. Each summer Dr. Kelly also teaches an introductory statistics course at Boston College. She resides in Hamilton, Massachusetts, with her husband and two children.

A unique emphasis on communicating with numbers . . .

Today's business students face a highly competitive and global job market that will demand the most of their analytical abilities. Vast amounts of data are available to everyone, but there is a big difference between having data and making good decisions based on that data. This generation of future business managers will need to process relevant data, recognize and implement correct statistical methods, and most important, interpret the results and incorporate them into the larger decision problem. Our motivation for writing *Business Statistics: Communicating with Numbers* was that we saw a fairly wide gap between a student's ability to number crunch and then to relay the meaning of those numbers. By incorporating the perspective of professional users of statistics in this text, it has been our goal to make the subject matter more relevant and the presentation of material more straightforward for students.

We have written a textbook that is intellectually stimulating, practical, and visually attractive, from which students can learn and instructors can teach. Throughout the book, we have presented the material in an accessible way by using timely business applications to which students can relate. Although the text is application-oriented, it is also mathematically sound and uses notation that is generally accepted for the topic being covered.

*This is probably the **best book** I have seen in terms of explaining concepts.*
Brad McDonald, *Northern Illinois University*

*The book is **well written, more readable and interesting than most stats texts,** and effective in explaining concepts. The examples and cases are particularly good and effective teaching tools.*
Andrew Koch, *James Madison University*

Thorough, complete coverage, with good chapter exercises.
Dane Peterson, *Missouri State University*

makes business statistics relevant to students

Key Features

Key to this text's positive reception are six core features around which this text is built.

Integrated Introductory Cases. Realistic introductory cases that students can relate to introduce each chapter topic and form the basis of several examples in the chapters.

Writing with Statistics. Interpreting results and conveying information effectively is critical to effective decision making in a business environment. Students are taught how to take the data, apply it, and convey the information in a meaningful way.

Unique Coverage of Regression Analysis. Extensive coverage of regression without repetition is an important hallmark of this text.

Written as Taught. Topics are presented the way they are taught in class, beginning with the intuition and explanation and concluding with the application.

Integration of Microsoft® Excel. Students are taught to develop an understanding of the concepts and how to derive the calculation; then Excel is used as a tool to perform the cumbersome calculations.

Connect Business Statistics. Connect is an online system that gives students the tools they need to be successful in the course. Through guided examples and LearnSmart adaptive study tools, students receive guidance and practice to help them master the topics.

*I really like the case studies and the **emphasis on writing**. We are making a big effort to incorporate more business writing in our core courses so that meshes well.*

Elizabeth Haran, *Salem State University*

*For a statistical analyst, your analytical skill is only as good as your communication skill. Writing with statistics **reinforces the importance of communication** and provides students with concrete examples to follow.*

Jun Liu, *Georgia Southern University*

Integrated Introductory Cases

Each chapter opens with a real-life case study that forms the basis for several examples within the chapter. The questions included in the examples create a roadmap for mastering the most important learning outcomes within the chapter. We present a synopsis of each chapter's introductory case when the last of these examples has been discussed. Instructors of distance learners may find these introductory cases particularly useful.

INTRODUCTORY CASE

Investment Decision

Rebecca Johnson works as an investment counselor at a large bank. Recently, an inexperienced investor asked Johnson about clarifying some differences between two top-performing mutual funds from the last decade: Vanguard's Precious Metals and Mining fund (henceforth, Metals) and Fidelity's Strategic Income Fund (henceforth, Income). The investor shows Johnson the return data he has accessed over the Internet, but the investor has trouble interpreting the data. Table 3.1 shows the return data for these two mutual funds for the years 2000–2009; the data, labeled **Fund Returns**, can also be found on the text website.

SYNOPSIS OF INTRODUCTORY CASE

Vanguard's Precious Metals and Mining fund (Metals) and Fidelity's Strategic Income fund (Income) were two top-performing mutual funds for the years 2000 through 2009. An analysis of annual return data for these two funds provides important information for any type of investor. Over the past 10 years, the Metals fund posts the higher values for both the mean return and the median return, with values of 24.65% and 33.83%, respectively. Extreme values are often present when the mean differs dramatically from the median. On the other hand, the mean return and the median return for the Income fund are quite comparable at 8.51% and 7.34%, respectively.

In all of these chapters, **the opening case leads directly into the application questions** that students will have regarding the material. Having a strong and related case will certainly provide more benefit to the student, as context leads to improved learning.

Alan Chow, *University of South Alabama*

This is an excellent approach. The student gradually gets the idea that he can look at a problem—one which might be fairly complex—and break it down into root components. He learns that a little bit of math could go a long way, and even more math is even more beneficial to evaluating the problem.

Dane Peterson, *Missouri State University*

and build skills to communicate results

Writing with Statistics

One of our most important innovations is the inclusion of a sample report within every chapter (except Chapter 1). Our intent is to show students how to convey statistical information in written form to those who may not know detailed statistical methods. For example, such a report may be needed as input for managerial decision making in sales, marketing, or company planning. Several similar writing exercises are provided at the end of each chapter. Each chapter also includes a synopsis that addresses questions raised from the introductory case. This serves as a shorter writing sample for students. Instructors of large sections may find these reports useful for incorporating writing into their statistics courses.

WRITING WITH STATISTICS

Callie Fitzpatrick, a research analyst with an investment firm, has been asked to write a report summarizing the weekly stock performance of Home Depot and Lowe's. Her manager is trying to decide whether or not to include one of these stocks in a client's portfolio and the average stock performance is one of the factors influencing their decision. Callie decides to use descriptive measures to summarize stock returns in her report, as well as provide confidence intervals for the average return for Home Depot and Lowe's. She collects weekly returns for each firm for the first eight months of 2010. A portion of the return data is shown in Table 8.4; the complete data is available.

 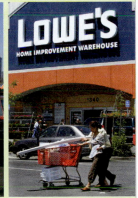

Sample Report—Weekly Stock Performance: Home Depot vs. Lowe's

Grim news continues to distress the housing sector. On August 24, 2010, Reuters reported that the sales of previously owned U.S. homes took a record plunge in July to the slowest pace in 15 years. Combine this fact with the continued fallout from the subprime mortgage debacle, a sluggish economy, and high unemployment, and the housing sector appears quite unstable. Have these unfavorable events managed to trickle down and harm the financial performance of Home Depot and Lowe's, the two largest home improvement retailers in the U.S.?

One way to analyze their financial stability is to observe their stock performance during this period. In order to make valid statements concerning the reward of holding these stocks, weekly return data for each firm were gathered from January through August of 2010. Table 8.A summarizes the important descriptive statistics.

TABLE 8.A Descriptive Statistics for Weekly Returns of Home Depot and Lowe's ($n = 34$)

	Home Depot	Lowe's
Mean	0.00%	−0.33%
Median	0.76%	−0.49%
Minimum	−8.08%	−7.17%
Maximum	5.30%	7.71%
Standard deviation	3.59%	3.83%
Margin of error with 95% confidence	1.25%	1.34%

Unique coverage and presentation . . .

Unique Coverage of Regression Analysis

Our coverage of regression analysis is more extensive than that of the vast majority of texts. This focus reflects the topic's growing use in practice. We combine simple and multiple regression in the first regression chapter, which we believe is a seamless grouping and eliminates needless repetition. However, for those instructors who prefer to cover only simple regression, doing so is still an option. Three more in-depth chapters cover statistical inference, nonlinear relationships, and dummy variable and binary choice models.

Chapter 14: Regression Analysis
Chapter 15: Inference with Regression Models
Chapter 16: Regression Models for Nonlinear Relationships
Chapter 17: Regression Models with Dummy Variables

Inclusion of Important Topics

In our teaching outside the classroom, we have found that several fundamental topics important to business are not covered by the majority of traditional texts. For example, most books do not integrate the geometric mean and mean-variance analysis with descriptive statistics. Similarly, the discussion of probability concepts generally does not include odds ratios, risk aversion, and the analysis of portfolio returns. We cover these important topics throughout the text. Overall, our text contains material that practitioners use on a regular basis.

> *. . . having regression explained in multiple* chapters **will allow** *students and instructors to better focus on each regression topic*
>
> Alicia Graziosi Strandberg, *Temple University*

> *The inclusion of material used on a regular basis by investment professionals adds real-world credibility to the text and course and better prepares students for the real world.*
>
> Bob Gillette, *University of Kentucky*

THE SHARPE RATIO

The **Sharpe ratio** measures the extra reward per unit of risk. The Sharpe ratio for an investment I is computed as:

$$\frac{\overline{x}_I - \overline{R}_f}{s_I}$$

where $\overline{x}_I$ is the mean return for the investment, $\overline{R}_f$ is the mean return for a risk-free asset such as a Treasury bill (T-bill), and s_I is the standard deviation for the investment.

Written as Taught

We introduce topics just the way we teach them; that is, the relevant tools follow the opening application. Our roadmap for solving problems is

1. start with intuition
2. introduce mathematical rigor, and
3. produce computer output that confirms results.

We use worked examples throughout the text to illustrate how to apply concepts to solve real-world problems.

> *This is **easy for students to follow** and I do get the feeling . . . the sections are spoken language.*
>
> Zhen Zhu, *University of Central Oklahoma*

that make the content more effective

Integration of Microsoft® Excel

We prefer that students first focus on and absorb the statistical material before replicating their results with a computer. We feel that solving each application manually provides students with a deeper understanding of the relevant concept. However, we recognize that, primarily due to cumbersome calculations or the need for statistical tables, the embedding of computer output is necessary. Microsoft Excel® is the primary software package used in this text and it is integrated within each chapter. We chose Excel over other statistical packages—such as JMP, Minitab, SPSS, and (freely available) R—based on reviewer feedback and the fact that students benefit from the added spreadsheet experience. We use Minitab in a few places where Excel is not adequate. Directions for JMP, Minitab, and SPSS are provided on the text website.

Constructing a Histogram from a Set of Raw Data

A. **FILE** Open the *Mission Viejo Houses* data (Table 2.1) from the text website into an Excel spreadsheet.

B. In a column next to the data, enter the values of the upper limits of each class, or in this example, 400, 500, 600, 700, and 800; label this column "Class Limits." The reason for these entries is explained in the next step. The house-price data and the class limits (as well as the resulting frequency distribution and histogram) are shown in Figure 2.9.

FIGURE 2.9 Constructing a histogram from raw data with Excel

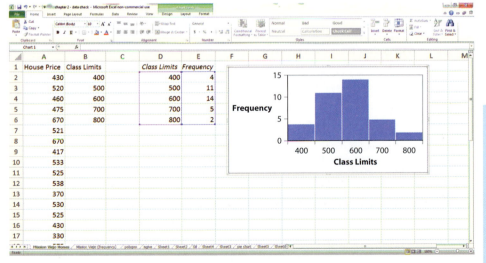

> I like the Excel incorporated within the chapter so that you **get right to the task of how to apply** the statistical procedure in Excel, which all of my students have available.
>
> Alan Chow, *University of South Alabama*

Real-world exercises and case studies that reinforce the material

Conceptual and Applied Exercises

Chapter exercises are a well-balanced blend of conceptual, computational-type problems followed by more ambitious, interpretive-type problems. We have found that simpler drill problems tend to build students' confidence prior to tackling more difficult applied problems. Moreover, we repeatedly use many data sets—including house prices, rents, stock returns, salaries, and debt—in the text. For instance, students first use these real data to calculate summary measures and then continue on to make statistical inferences with confidence intervals and hypothesis tests and perform regression analysis.

Applied exercises from *The Wall Street Journal, Kiplinger's, Fortune, The New York Times, USA Today*; various websites —Census.gov, Zillow.com, Finance.yahoo.com, ESPN.com; and more.

a. Construct the 80% confidence interval of the population mean.

Construct the 90% confidence interval of the population

What happens to the margin of error as the confidence increases from 80% to 90%?

...ons

... weight loss program claims that with its ...mended healthy diet regimen, users lose significant ... within a month. In order to estimate the mean ...ht loss of all customers, a nutritionist takes a sample ... dieters and records their weight loss one month after ...ining the program. He computes the sample mean and the standard deviation of weight loss as 12.5 pounds and 9.2 pounds, respectively. He believes that weight loss is likely to be normally distributed.

a. Calculate the margin of error with 95% confidence.

b. Compute the 95% confidence interval of the population mean.

25. The manager of The Cheesecake Factory in Boston reports that on six randomly selected weekdays, the number of customers served was 120, 130, 90, 205, 185, and 220. She believes that the number of customers served on weekdays follows a normal distribution. Construct a 90% confidence interval of the average number of customers served on weekdays.

26. According to a recent survey, high school girls average 100 text messages daily (*The Boston Globe*, April 21, 2010). Assume that the survey was based on a random sample of 36 high school girls. The sample standard deviation is computed as 10 text messages daily.

a. Calculate the margin of error with 99% confidence.

b. What is the 99% confidence interval of the population mean texts that all high school girls send daily?

a. Derive a 99% confidence interval of the average time taken by a college student to solve a *Sudoku* puzzle.

b. What assumption is necessary to make this inference?

29. Executive compensation has risen dramatically beyond the rising levels of an average worker's wage over the years. Sarah is an MBA student who decides to use her statistical skills to estimate the mean CEO compensation in 2010 for all large companies in the United States. She takes a random sample of six CEO compensations.

Firm	Compensation (in $ millions)
Intel	8.20
Coca-Cola	2.76
Wells Fargo	6.57
Caterpillar	3.88
McDonald's	6.56
U.S. Bancorp	4.10

Source: http://finance.yahoo.com.

a. How will Sarah use the above information to provide a 90% confidence interval of the mean CEO compensation of all large companies in the United States?

b. What assumption did Sarah make for deriving the interval estimate?

c. How can Sarah reduce the margin of error reported in the above interval estimate?

30. A price-earnings ratio or P/E ratio is calculated as a firm's share price compared to the income or profit earned by the firm per share. Generally, a high P/E ratio suggests that investors are expecting higher earnings growth in the future compared to companies with a lower P/E ratio. The following table shows the P/E ratios for a sample of firms in the

*I especially like the introductory cases, the **quality of the end-of-section problems**, and the writing examples.*

Dave Leupp, *University of Colorado at Colorado Springs*

*Plenty of application **exercises** and case studies.*

Mostafa Aminzadeh, *Towson University*

Features that go beyond the typical

Conceptual Review

At the end of each chapter, we provide a conceptual review that provides a more holistic approach to reviewing the material. This section revisits the learning outcomes and provides the most important definitions, interpretations, and formulas.

Conceptual Review

LO 6.1   **Describe a continuous random variable.**

A **continuous random variable** is characterized by (infinitely) uncountable values and can take on any value within an interval. The probability that a continuous random variable X assumes a particular value x is zero, that is, $P(X = x) = 0$. Thus, for a continuous random variable, we calculate the probability within a specified interval. Moreover, the following equalities hold: $P(a \leq X \leq b) = P(a < X < b) = P(a \leq X < b) = P(a < X \leq b)$.

The **probability density function** $f(x)$ of a continuous random variable X describes the relative likelihood that X assumes a value within a given interval. The probability $P(a \leq X \leq b)$ is the area under $f(x)$ between points a and b.

For any value x of the random variable X, the **cumulative distribution function** $F(x)$ is defined as $F(x) = P(X \leq x)$.

LO 6.2   **Describe a continuous uniform distribution and calculate associated probabilities.**

The **continuous uniform distribution** describes a random variable that has an equally likely chance of assuming a value within a specified range. The probability is essentially the area of a rectangle, which is the base times the height, or the length of a specified interval times the probability density function $f(x) = \frac{1}{b - a}$, where a and b are the lower and upper bounds of the interval, respectively.

Most texts basically list what one should have learned but don't add much to that. You do a good job of reminding the reader of what was covered and what was most important about it.

Andrew Koch, *James Madison University*

*They have gone beyond the typical [summarizing formulas] and I like the structure. This is a **very strong feature** of this text.*

Virginia M. Miori, *St. Joseph's University*

What technology connects students . . .

McGraw-Hill *Connect*® *Business Statistics*

McGraw-Hill *Connect Business Statistics* is an online assignment and assessment solution that connects students with the tools and resources they'll need to achieve success through faster learning, higher retention, and more efficient studying. It provides instructors with tools to quickly select content for assignments according to the topics and learning objectives they want to emphasize.

Online Assignments. *Connect Business Statistics* helps students learn more efficiently by providing practice material and feedback when they are needed. *Connect* grades homework automatically and provides instant feedback on any problems that students are challenged to solve.

Integration of Excel Data Sets. A convenient feature is the inclusion of an Excel data file link in many problems using data files in their calculation. The link allows students to easily launch into Excel, work the problem, and return to *Connect* to key in the answer and receive feedback on their results.

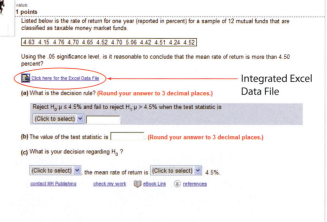

Student Resource Library. The *Connect Business Statistics* Student Library is the place for students to access additional resources. The Student Library provides quick access to recorded lectures, practice materials, the eBooks, data files, PowerPoint files, and more.

to success in business statistics?

Guided Examples. These narrated video walkthroughs provide students with step-by-step guidelines for solving selected exercises similar to those contained in the text. The student is given personalized instruction on how to solve a problem by applying the concepts presented in the chapter. The narrated voiceover shows the steps to take to work through an exercise. Students can go through each example multiple times if needed.

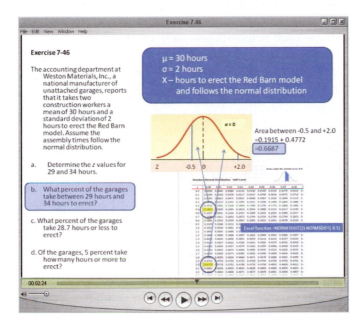

LearnSmart. LearnSmart adaptive self-study technology in *Connect Business Statistics* helps students make the best use of their study time. LearnSmart provides a seamless combination of practice, assessment, and remediation for every concept in the textbook. LearnSmart's intelligent software adapts to students by supplying questions on a new concept when students are ready to learn it. With LearnSmart students will spend less time on topics they understand and instead focus on the topics they need to master.

What technology connects students . . .

Simple Assignment Management and Smart Grading. When it comes to studying, time is precious. *Connect Business Statistics* helps students learn more efficiently by providing feedback and practice material when they need it, where they need it. When it comes to teaching, your time also is precious. The grading function enables you to:

- Have assignments scored automatically, giving students immediate feedback on their work and the ability to compare their work with correct answers.
- Access and review each response; manually change grades or leave comments for students to review.

Student Reporting. *Connect Business Statistics* keeps instructors informed about how each student, section, and class is performing, allowing for more productive use of lecture and office hours. The progress-tracking function enables you to:

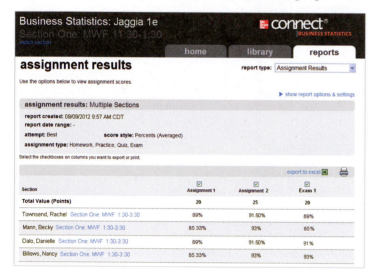

- View scored work immediately and track individual or group performance with assignment and grade reports.
- Access an instant view of student or class performance relative to topic and learning objectives.
- Collect data and generate reports required by many accreditation organizations, such as AACSB.

Instructor Library. The *Connect Business Statistics* Instructor Library is your repository for additional resources to improve student engagement in and out of class. You can select and use any asset that enhances your lecture. The *Connect Business Statistics* Instructor Library includes:

- eBook
- PowerPoint presentations
- Test Bank
- Instructor's Solutions Manual
- Digital Image Library

to success in business statistics?

McGraw-Hill CONNECT® PLUS BUSINESS STATISTICS

Connect® Plus Business Statistics includes a seamless integration of an eBook and *Connect Business Statistics*, with rich functionality integrated into the product.

Integrated Media-Rich eBook. An integrated media-rich eBook allows students to access media in context with each chapter. Students can highlight, take notes, and access shared instructor highlights/notes to learn the course material.

Dynamic Links. Dynamic links provide a connection between the problems or questions you assign to your students and the location in the eBook where that problem or question is covered.

Powerful Search Function. A powerful search function pinpoints and connects key concepts in a snap. This state-of-the-art, thoroughly tested system supports you in preparing students for the world that awaits. For more information about *Connect,* go to www.mcgrawhillconnect.com or contact your local McGraw-Hill sales representative.

Tegrity Campus: Lectures 24/7

Tegrity Campus is integrated in *Connect* to help make your class time available 24/7. With Tegrity, you can capture each one of your lectures in a searchable format for students to review when they study and complete assignments using connect. With a simple one-click start-and-stop process, you can capture everything that is presented to students during your lecture from your computer, including audio. Students can replay any part of any class with easy-to-use browser-based viewing on a PC or Mac.

Educators know that the more students can see, hear, and experience class resources, the better they learn. In fact, studies prove it. With *Tegrity Campus*, students quickly recall key moments by using *Tegrity Campus*'s unique search feature. This search helps students efficiently find what they need, when they need it, across an entire semester of class recordings. Help turn all your students' study time into learning moments immediately supported by your lecture. To learn more about *Tegrity*, watch a two-minute Flash demo at http://tegritycampus.mhhe.com.

What software is available with this text?

MegaStat® for Microsoft Excel® 2003, 2007 and 2010 (and Excel: Mac 2011)

CD ISBN: 0077496442 *Note: The CD-ROM is for Windows users only.*

Access Card ISBN: 0077426274 *Note: Best option for both Windows and Mac users.*

MegaStat® by J. B. Orris of Butler University is a full-featured Excel add-in that is available three ways—on CD, through access card packaged with the text, and on the *MegaStat* website at www.mhhe.com/megastat. It works with Excel 2003, 2007, and 2010 (and Excel: Mac 2011). On the website, students have 10 days to successfully download and install *MegaStat* on their local computer. Once installed, *MegaStat* will remain active in Excel with no expiration date or time limitations. The software performs statistical analyses within an Excel workbook. It does basic functions, such as descriptive statistics, frequency distributions, and probability calculations as well as hypothesis testing, ANOVA, and regression. *MegaStat* output is carefully formatted and its ease-of-use features include Auto Expand for quick data selection and Auto Label detect. Since *MegaStat* is easy to use, students can focus on learning statistics without being distracted by the software. *MegaStat* is always available from Excel's main menu. Selecting a menu item pops up a dialog box. Screencam tutorials are included that provide a walkthrough of major business statistics topics. Help files are built in, and an introductory user's manual is also included.

Minitab®/SPSS®/JMP®

Minitab® Student Version 14 ISBN: 007305237X

SPSS® Student Version 18.0 ISBN: 0077327144

JMP® Student Edition Version 8 ISBN: 007739030X

These software tools are available to help students solve the business statistics exercises in the text. Each can be packaged with any McGraw-Hill business statistics text. SPSS SV18 is both Windows and Mac compatible. The software expires 13 months after installation. JMP SV8 is also Windows and Mac compatible. It expires 12 months after installation. The software is current as of the publication of this text.

Please check with your local rep for updates.

What resources are available for instructors?

Online Learning Center   www.mhhe.com/jaggiakelly

The Online Learning Center (OLC) provides the instructor with a complete Instructor's Solutions Manual in Word format, the complete Test Bank in both Word files and computerized EZ Test Online format, Instructor PowerPoint slides, text art files, an introduction to ALEKS®, an introduction to McGraw-Hill *Connect*® Business Statistics, and more.

All test bank questions are available in an EZ Test online. Included are a number of multiple choice, true/false, and short-answer questions and problems. The answers to all questions are given, along with a rating of the level of difficulty, chapter goal the question tests, Bloom's taxonomy question type, and the AACSB knowledge category.

Online Course Management   The **Best** of **Both Worlds**

McGraw-Hill Higher Education and Blackboard have teamed up. What does this mean for you?

1. **Single sign-on.** Now you and your students can access McGraw-Hill's *Connect*® and Create™ right from within your Blackboard course—all with one single sign-on.

2. **Deep integration of content and tools.** You get a single sign-on with *Connect* and Create, and you also get integration of McGraw-Hill content and content engines right into Blackboard. Whether you're choosing a book for your course or building *Connect* assignments, all the tools you need are right where you want them—inside of Blackboard.

3. **One grade book.** Keeping several grade books and manually synchronizing grades into Blackboard is no longer necessary. When a student completes an integrated *Connect* assignment, the grade for that assignment automatically (and instantly) feeds your Blackboard grade center.

4. **A solution for everyone.** Whether your institution is already using Blackboard or you just want to try Blackboard on your own, we have a solution for you. McGraw-Hill and Blackboard can now offer you easy access to industry leading technology and content, whether your campus hosts it, or we do. Be sure to ask your local McGraw-Hill representative for details.

Connect Packaging Options

Connect with LearnSmart 2 Semester Access Card: 0073361615

Connect Plus with LearnSmart 2 Semester Access Card: 0077600363

What resources are available for students?

CourseSmart
ISBN: 0077501381

CourseSmart is a convenient way to find and buy eTextbooks. CourseSmart has the largest selection of eTextbooks available anywhere, offering thousands of the most commonly adopted textbooks from a wide variety of higher-education publishers. Course Smart eTextbooks are available in one standard online reader with full text search, notes and highlighting, and e-mail tools for sharing notes between classmates. Visit **www.CourseSmart.com** for more information on ordering.

ALEKS

ALEKS is an assessment and learning program that provides individualized instruction in Business Statistics, Business Math, and Accounting. Available online in partnership with McGraw-Hill/Irwin, ALEKS interacts with students much like a skilled human tutor, with the ability to assess precisely a student's knowledge and provide instruction on the exact topics the student is most ready to learn. By providing topics to meet individual students' needs, allowing students to move between explanation and practice, correcting and analyzing errors, and defining terms, ALEKS helps students to master course content quickly and easily.

ALEKS also includes a new instructor module with powerful, assignment-driven features and extensive content flexibility. ALEKS simplifies course management and allows instructors to spend less time with administrative tasks and more time directing student learning. To learn more about ALEKS, visit **www.aleks.com**.

Online Learning Center   www.mhhe.com/jaggiakelly

The Online Learning Center (OLC) provides students with the following content:

- Quizzes—self grading to access knowledge of the material
- PowerPoint—gives an overview of the chapter content
- Data Files—import into Excel for quick calculation and analysis
- Appendixes—quick lookup when the text isn't available

Assurance of Accuracy

Dear Colleague,

As textbook authors, and more importantly, as instructors of business statistics, we recognize the great importance placed on accuracy. With this in mind, we have taken the following steps to ensure that *Business Statistics: Communicating with Numbers* is error-free:

1. We received detailed feedback from over 150 instructor reviews, starting with first draft manuscript through the final draft submitted to the publisher. Each review contributed in significant ways to the accuracy of the content.

2. We personally class-tested the manuscript with our students in various drafts, continually improving the accuracy of the material.

3. Each of us wrote, reviewed, and carefully checked all of the end-of-chapter material.

4. A developmental editor went through each sentence to ensure that our language was as clear as possible.

5. Multiple accuracy checkers reviewed each chapter and its accompanying end-of-chapter material—once when the final manuscript was submitted to the publisher, and again when our final formatted pages were completed.

6. A copyeditor checked the grammar of the final manuscript.

7. A proofreader reviewed each page to ensure no errors remained.

8. Our Solutions Manual and Test Bank were reviewed by multiple independent accuracy checkers.

Given the steps taken above, we have the utmost confidence that you and your students will have a great experience using *Business Statistics: Communicating with Numbers*.

CONTACT INFORMATION We would be grateful to hear from any and all users of this text and its supplements. Send your comments and suggestions to sjaggia@calpoly.edu or akelly@suffolk.edu.

Sincerely,

Sanjiv Jaggia   Alison Kelly

ACKNOWLEDGMENTS

We could not have developed our approach to teaching business statistics in isolation. Many thanks go to a multitude of people for helping us make our idea come to fruition. First and foremost, we would like to thank our families and friends for their support, feedback, and patience throughout what has been an arduous, but rewarding, project. We are especially grateful to Chandrika, Minori, John, Megan, and Matthew for bearing with us on a daily basis.

We thank Scott Isenberg for believing that we could write this text before a single chapter was written; Fr. James Woods (Boston College) for providing a jump-start to Chapter 1; David Chelton for excellent assistance as a content editor; and Chandrika Jaggia for invaluable assistance with the initial format of the book. We are indebted to Jerzy Kamburowski (University of Toledo) for his outstanding accuracy check and his insistence on mathematical precision and consistency. Preliminary editions of our book were used at Suffolk University, Boston College, Cal Poly San Luis Obispo, and the University of Kentucky, and we thank the many students and instructors who provided comments and suggestions. Special thanks go to Timothy Lambie-Hanson, Kossi Makpayo, and Sara Shorba. Thanks too to Minitab, Inc. for the use of their software.

The editorial staff of McGraw-Hill/Irwin are deserving of our gratitude for their guidance throughout this project, especially Wanda Zeman, Steve Schuetz, Tim Vertovec, Ann Torbert, Dean Karampelas, Christine Vaughan, Michael McCormick, Mary Kazak Sander, Keri Johnson, and Daryl Horrocks.

Reviewers

The text has benefited immensely from reviewers' helpful suggestions, keen insights, and constructive criticisms. We are very grateful to the following professors for taking the time to provide valuable feedback throughout the development process:

Mehdi Afiat
College of Southern Nevada

Mohammad Ahmadi
University of Tennessee–Chattanooga

Sung Ahn
Washington State University

Mostafa Aminzadeh
Towson University

Ardavan Asef-Vaziri
California State University

Scott Bailey
Troy University

Douglas Barrett
University of North Alabama

John Beyers
University of Maryland

Arnab Bisi
Purdue University–West Lafayette

Randy Boan
Aims Community College

Matthew Bognar
University of Iowa

Juan Cabrera
Ramapo College of New Jersey

Kathleen Campbell
St. Joseph's University

Michael Cervetti
University of Memphis

Gary Huaite Chao
University of Pennsylvania–Kutztown

Sangit Chatterjee
Northeastern University

Anna Chernobai
Syracuse University

Alan Chesen
Wright State University

Alan Chow
University of South Alabama

Bruce Christensen
Weber State University

Howard Clayton
Auburn University

Robert Collins
Marquette University

Tom Davis
University of Dayton

Matthew Dean
University of Maine

Jason Delaney
University of Arkansas–Little Rock

Joan Donohue
University of South Carolina

David Doorn
University of Minnesota

Luca Donno
University of Miami

Mike Easley
University of New Orleans

Erick Elder
University of Arkansas–Little Rock

Ashraf ELHoubi
Lamar University

Grace Esimai
University of Texas Arlington

Priya Francisco
Purdue University

Vickie Fry
*Westmoreland County
Community College*

Ed Gallo
Sinclair Community College

Robert Gillette
University of Kentucky

Mark Gius
Quinnipiac University

Don Gren
Salt Lake Community College

Robert Hammond
*North Carolina State
University*

Elizabeth Haran
Salem State University

Paul Hong
University of Toledo

Ping-Hung Hsieh
Oregon State University

Robin James
Harper College

Molly Jensen
University of Arkansas

Craig Johnson
*Brigham Young
University–Idaho*

Janine Sanders Jones
University of St. Thomas

Jerzy Kamburowski
University of Toledo

Krishna Kasibhatla
*North Carolina A&T State
University*

Ronald Klimberg
St. Joseph's University

Andrew Koch
James Madison University

Brandon Koford
Weber University

Randy Kolb
St. Cloud State University

Vadim Kutsyy
San Jose State University

Francis Laatsch
*University of Southern
Mississippi*

David Larson
*University of South
Alabama*

John Lawrence
*California State
University–Fullerton*

Radu Lazar
University of Maryland

David Leupp
*University of Colorado–
Colorado Springs*

Carel Ligeon
*Auburn University–
Montgomery*

Carin Lightner
*North Carolina A&T State
University*

Jun Liu
Georgia Southern University

Salvador Lopez
University of West Georgia

John Loucks
St. Edward's University

Cecilia Maldonado
*Georgia Southwestern State
University*

Farooq Malik
*University of Southern
Mississippi*

Bradley McDonald
Northern Illinois University

Elaine McGivern
Duquesne University

John Miller
*Sam Houston State
University*

Virginia Miori
St. Joseph's University

Joseph Mollick
*Texas A&M University–
Corpus Christi*

James Moran
Oregon State University

Khosrow Moshirvaziri
*California State University–
Long Beach*

Tariq Mughal
University of Utah

Patricia Mullins
*University of
Wisconsin–Madison*

Anthony Narsing
Macon State College

Robert Nauss
*University of Missouri–
St. Louis*

Thang Nguyen
*California State University–
Long Beach*

Satish Nayak
*University of Missouri–
St. Louis*

Mohammad Oskoorouchi
*California State University–
San Marcos*

Barb Osyk
University of Akron

Scott Paulsen
Illinois Central College

Norman Pence
*Metropolitan State College
of Denver*

Dane Peterson
Missouri State University

Joseph Petry
*University of Illinois–
Champaign*

Courtney Pham
Missouri State University

Jan Pitera
Broome Community College

Hamid Pourmohammadi
*California State University–
Dominguez Hills*

Tammy Prater
Alabama State University

Michael Racer
University of Memphis

Srikant Raghavan
*Lawrence Technological
University*

Bharatendra Rai
*University of
Massachusetts–Dartmouth*

Tony Ratcliffe
James Madison University

Darlene Riedemann
Eastern Illinois University

Carolyn Rochelle
*East Tennessee State
University*

Alfredo Romero
*North Carolina A&T State
University*

Ann Rothermel
University of Akron

Deborah Rumsey
Ohio State University

Stephen Russell
Weber State University

William Rybolt
Babson College

Fati Salimian
Salisbury University

Samuel Sarri
College of Southern Nevada

Jim Schmidt
*University of Nebraska–
Lincoln*

Patrick Scholten
Bentley University

Pali Sen
University of North Florida

Soheil Sibdari
*University of
Massachusetts–Dartmouth*

Harvey Singer
George Mason University

Harry Sink
*North Carolina A&T State
University*

Don Skousen
Salt Lake Community College

Robert Smidt
*California Polytechnic State
University*

Gary Smith
Florida State University

Arun Kumar Srinivasan
*Indiana University–
Southeast*

Alicia Strandberg
Temple University

Bedassa Tadesse
University of Minnesota

Roberto Duncan Tarabay
*University of
Wisconsin–Madison*

Deborah Tesch
Xavier University

Patrick Thompson
University of Florida

Satish Thosar
University of Redlands

Ricardo Tovar-Silos
Lamar University

Elzbieta Trybus
*California State
University–Northridge*

Fan Tseng
*University of
Alabama–Huntsville*

Silvanus Udoka
*North Carolina A&T State
University*

Raja Velu
Syracuse University

Holly Verhasselt
University of Houston–Victoria

Rachel Webb
Portland State University

Alan Wheeler
*University of Missouri–
St. Louis*

Mary Whiteside
*University of Texas–
Arlington*

Jan Wolcott
Wichita State University

Ali Zargar
San Jose State University

Eugene Zhang
Midwestern State University

Ye Zhang
*Indiana University-Purdue
University–Indianapolis*

Yi Zhang
*California State
University–Fullerton*

Yulin Zhang
San Jose State University

Wencang Zhou
Baruch College

Zhen Zhu
*University of Central
Oklahoma*

BRIEF CONTENTS

CONTENTS

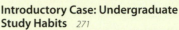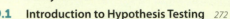

Statistical Inference Concerning Variance 334

Chi-Square Tests 360

Analysis of Variance 386

Regression Analysis 422

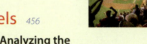

BUSINESS STATISTICS

1

Statistics and Data

LEARNING OBJECTIVES

After reading this chapter you should be able to:

LO **1.1** Describe the importance of statistics.

LO **1.2** Differentiate between descriptive statistics and inferential statistics.

LO **1.3** Explain the need for sampling and discuss various data types.

LO **1.4** Describe variables and various types of measurement scales.

Every day we are bombarded with data and claims. The analysis of data and the predictions made from data are part of the field of statistics. Virtually every phase of human activity incorporates statistics, yet most people do not know they are using it. In this first chapter, we are going to introduce some important terms that will help us describe different aspects of statistics and their practical importance. We will be using these terms frequently throughout the rest of the book. You are probably familiar with some of these ideas already, from reading or hearing about opinion polls, surveys, and the all-pervasive product ads. Our goal in this chapter is to place what you already know about these uses of statistics within a framework of terms and descriptions that we can then use for explaining where they came from and what they really mean. A proper understanding of statistical ideas and concepts can help you understand what politicians or advertisers are really saying, or not saying. But it can also help you understand more of the real world around us, including business, finance, health, social interactions—just about any area of contemporary human activity.

Tween Survey

Luke McCaffrey owns a ski resort two hours outside Boston, Massachusetts, and is in need of a new marketing manager. He is a fairly tough interviewer and believes that the person in this position should have a basic understanding of data fundamentals, including some background with statistical methods. Luke is particularly interested in serving the needs of the "tween" population (children aged 8 to 12 years old). He believes that tween spending power has grown over the past few years, and he wants their skiing experience to be memorable so that they want to return. At the end of last year's ski season, Luke asked 20 tweens four specific questions.

Q1. On your car drive to the resort, which radio station was playing?

Q2. On a scale of 1 to 4, rate the quality of the food at the resort (where 1 is poor, 2 is fair, 3 is good, and 4 is excellent).

Q3. Presently, the main dining area closes at 3:00 pm. What time do you think it should close?

Q4. How much of your *own* money did you spend at the lodge today?

The responses to these questions are shown in Table 1.1; these data are also found on the text website and are labeled **Tween Survey**.

TABLE 1.1 Tween Responses to Skylark Valley Resort Survey FILE

Tween	Q1	Q2	Q3	Q4	Tween	Q1	Q2	Q3	Q4
1	JAMN94.5	4	5:00 pm	20	11	JAMN94.5	3	3:00 pm	0
2	MIX104.1	2	5:00 pm	10	12	JAMN94.5	4	4:00 pm	5
3	KISS108	2	4:30 pm	10	13	KISS108	2	4:30 pm	5
4	JAMN94.5	3	4:00 pm	0	14	KISS108	2	5:00 pm	10
5	KISS108	1	3:30 pm	0	15	KISS108	3	4:00 pm	5
6	JAMN94.5	1	6:00 pm	25	16	JAMN94.5	3	6:00 pm	20
7	KISS108	2	6:00 pm	15	17	KISS108	2	5:00 pm	15
8	KISS108	3	5:00 pm	10	18	MIX104.1	4	6:00 pm	15
9	KISS108	2	4:30 pm	10	19	KISS108	1	5:00 pm	25
10	KISS108	3	4:30 pm	20	20	KISS108	2	4:30 pm	10

Luke asks each job applicant to use the information to:

1. Classify the tween responses into the appropriate measurement scale.

2. Compare and contrast the type of information that can be extracted from each measurement scale.

3. Given the results of the survey, provide management with suggestions for improvement.

A synopsis from the job applicant with the best answers is provided at the end of Section 1.3.

1.1 The Relevance of Statistics

LO **1.1**

Describe the importance of statistics.

In order to make intelligent decisions in a world full of uncertainty, we all have to understand statistics—the language of data. Unfortunately, many people avoid learning statistics because they believe (incorrectly!) that statistics simply deals with incomprehensible formulas and tedious calculations, and that it has no use in real life. This type of thinking is far from the truth because we encounter statistics *every day* in real life. We must understand statistics or risk making uninformed decisions and costly mistakes. While it is true that statistics incorporates formulas and calculations, it is logical reasoning that dictates how the data are collected, the calculations implemented, and the results communicated. A knowledge of statistics also provides the necessary tools to differentiate between sound statistical conclusions and questionable conclusions drawn from an insufficient number of data points, "bad" data points, incomplete data points, or just misinformation. Consider the following examples.

Example 1. After Washington, DC, had record amounts of snow in the winter of 2010, the headline of a newspaper stated "What global warming?"

Problem with conclusion: The existence or nonexistence of climate change cannot be based on one year's worth of data. Instead, we must examine long-term trends and analyze decades' worth of data.

Example 2. A gambler predicts that his next roll of the dice will be a lucky 7 because he did not get that outcome on the last three rolls.

Problem with conclusion: As we will see later in the text when we discuss probability, the probability of rolling a 7 stays constant with each roll of the dice. It does not become more likely if it did not appear on the last roll or, in fact, any number of preceding rolls.

Example 3. On January 10, 2010, nine days prior to a special election to fill the U.S. Senate seat that was vacated due to the death of Ted Kennedy, a *Boston Globe* poll gave the Democratic candidate Martha Coakley a 15-point lead over the Republican candidate Scott Brown. On January 19, 2010, Brown won 52% of the vote compared to Coakley's 47% and became a U.S. senator for Massachusetts.

Problem with conclusion: Critics accused the *Globe*, which had endorsed Coakley, of purposely running a bad poll to discourage voters from coming out for Brown. In reality, by the time the *Globe* released the poll, it contained old information from January 2–6, 2010. Even more problematic was that the poll included people who said that they were unlikely to vote!

Example 4. Starbucks Corp., the world's largest coffee-shop operator, reported that sales at stores open at least a year climbed 4% at home and abroad in the quarter ended December 27, 2009. Chief Financial Officer Troy Alstead said that "the U.S. is back in a good track and the international business has similarly picked up. . . . Traffic is really coming back. It's a good sign for what we're going to see for the rest of the year" (http://www.bloomberg.com, January 20, 2010).

Problem with conclusion: In order to calculate same-store sales growth, which compares how much each store in the chain is selling compared with a year ago, we remove stores that have closed. Given that Starbucks closed more than 800 stores over the past few years to counter large sales declines, it is likely that the sales increases in many of the stores were caused by traffic from nearby, recently closed stores. In this case, same-store sales growth may overstate the overall health of Starbucks.

Example 5. Researchers at the University of Pennsylvania Medical Center found that infants who sleep with a nightlight are much more likely to develop myopia later in life (*Nature*, May 1999).

Problem with conclusion: This example appears to commit the *correlation-to-causation fallacy*. Even if two variables are highly correlated, one does not necessarily cause the other. *Spurious correlation* can make two variables appear closely related when no causal relation exists. Spurious correlation between two variables is not based on any demonstrable relationship, but rather on a relation that arises in the data solely because each of those variables is related to some third variable. In a follow-up study, researchers at The Ohio State University found no link between infants who sleep with a nightlight and the development of myopia (*Nature*, March 2000). They did, however, find strong links between parental myopia and the development of child myopia, and between parental myopia and the parents' use of a nightlight in their children's room. So the cause of both conditions (the use of a nightlight and the development of child myopia) is parental myopia.

Note the diversity of the sources of these examples—the environment, psychology, polling, business, and health. We could easily include others, from sports, sociology, the physical sciences, and elsewhere. Data and data interpretation show up in virtually every facet of life, sometimes spuriously. All of the above examples basically misuse data to add credibility to an argument. A solid understanding of statistics provides you with tools to react intelligently to information that you read or hear.

1.2 What Is Statistics?

LO **1.2**

Differentiate between descriptive statistics and inferential statistics.

In the broadest sense, we can define the study of statistics as the methodology of extracting useful information from a data set. Three steps are essential for doing good statistics. First, we have to find the right data, which are both complete and lacking any misrepresentation. Second, we must use the appropriate statistical tools, depending on the data at hand. Finally, an important ingredient of a well-executed statistical analysis is to clearly communicate numerical information into written language.

We generally divide the study of statistics into two branches: descriptive statistics and inferential statistics. **Descriptive statistics** refers to the summary of important aspects of a data set. This includes collecting data, organizing the data, and then presenting the data in the forms of charts and tables. In addition, we often calculate numerical measures that summarize, for instance, the data's typical value and the data's variability. Today, the techniques encountered in descriptive statistics account for the most visible application of statistics—the abundance of quantitative information that is collected and published in our society every day. The unemployment rate, the President's approval rating, the Dow Jones Industrial Average, batting averages, the crime rate, and the divorce rate are but a few of the many "statistics" that can be found in a reputable newspaper on a frequent, if not daily, basis. Yet, despite the familiarity of descriptive statistics, these methods represent only a minor portion of the body of statistical applications.

The phenomenal growth in statistics is mainly in the field called inferential statistics. Generally, **inferential statistics** refers to drawing conclusions about a large set of data—called a **population**—based on a smaller set of **sample** data. A population is defined as all members of a specified group (not necessarily people), whereas a sample is a subset of that particular population. In most statistical applications we must rely on sample data in order to make inferences about various characteristics of the population. For example, a 2010 survey of 1,208 registered voters by a USA TODAY/Gallup Poll found that President Obama's job performance was viewed favorably by only 41% of those polled, his lowest rating in a USA TODAY/Gallup Poll since he took office in January 2009 (*USA TODAY*, August 3, 2010). Researchers use this sample result, called a **sample statistic**, in an attempt to estimate the corresponding unknown **population parameter**. In this case, the parameter of interest is the percentage of *all* registered voters that view the President's job performance favorably. It is generally not feasible to obtain population data and calculate the relevant parameter directly due to prohibitive costs and/or practicality, as discussed next.

The Need for Sampling

A major portion of inferential statistics is concerned with the problem of estimating population parameters or testing hypotheses about such parameters. If we have access to data that encompasses the entire population, then we would know the values of the parameters. Generally, however, we are unable to use population data for two main reasons.

- **Obtaining information on the entire population is expensive**. Consider how the monthly unemployment rate in the United States is calculated by the Bureau of Labor Statistics (BLS). Is it reasonable to assume that the BLS counts every unemployed person each month? The answer is a resounding NO! In order to do this, every home in the country would have to be contacted. Given that there are over 150 million individuals in the labor force, not only would this process cost too much, it would take an inordinate amount of time. Instead, the BLS conducts a monthly sample survey of about 60,000 households to measure the extent of unemployment in the United States.

- **It is impossible to examine every member of the population**. Suppose we are interested in the average length of life of a Duracell© AAA battery. If we tested the duration of each Duracell© AAA battery, then in the end, all batteries would be dead and the answer to the original question would be useless.

Types of Data

Sample data are generally collected in one of two ways. **Cross-sectional data** refers to data collected by recording a characteristic of many subjects at the same point in time, or without regard to differences in time. Subjects might include individuals, households, firms, industries, regions, and countries. The tween data presented in Table 1.1 in the introductory case is an example of cross-sectional data because it contains tween responses to four questions at the end of the ski season. It is unlikely that all 20 tweens took the questionnaire at exactly the same time, but the differences in time are of no relevance in this example. Other examples of cross-sectional data include the recorded scores of students in a class, the sale prices of single-family homes sold last month, the current price of gasoline in different states in the U.S., and the starting salaries of recent business graduates from The Ohio State University.

Time series data refers to data collected by recording a characteristic of a subject over several time periods. Time series can include daily, weekly, monthly, quarterly, or annual observations. Examples of time series data include the monthly sales of cars at a dealership in 2010, the daily price of IBM stock in the first quarter of 2010, the weekly exchange rate between the U.S. dollar and the euro, and the annual growth rate of India in the last decade. Figure 1.1 shows a plot of the real (inflation-adjusted) GDP growth rate of the United States from 1980 through 2010. The average growth rate for this period is 2.7%, yet the plot indicates a great deal of variability in the series. It exhibits a wavelike movement, spiking downward in 2008 due to the economic recession before rebounding in 2010.

Figure 1.1 Real GDP growth rate from 1980 through 2010

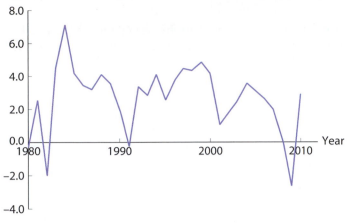

Source: Bureau of Economic Analysis.

> **Cross-sectional data** contain values of a characteristic of many subjects at the same point in time or without regard to differences in time. **Time series data** contain values of a characteristic of a subject over time.

Getting Started on the Web

As you can imagine, there is an abundance of data on the Internet. We accessed much of the data in this text by simply using a search engine like Google. These search engines often directed us to the same data-providing sites. For instance, the U.S. federal government publishes a great deal of economic and business data. The Bureau of Economic Analysis (BEA), the Bureau of Labor Statistics (BLS), the Federal Reserve Economic Data (FRED), and the U.S. Census Bureau provide data on inflation, unemployment, gross domestic product (GDP), and much more. Zillow.com is a real estate site that supplies data such as recent home sales, monthly rent, and mortgage rates. Finance.yahoo.com is a financial site that lists data such as stock prices, mutual fund performance, and international market data. *The Wall Street Journal*, *The New York Times*, *USA Today*, *The Economist*, and *Fortune* are all reputable publications that provide all sorts of data. Finally, espn.com offers comprehensive sports data on both professional and college teams. We list these sites in Table 1.2 and summarize *some* of the data that are available.

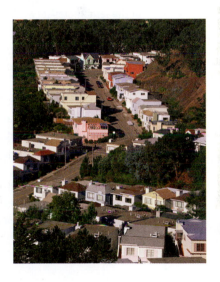

TABLE 1.2 Select Internet Data Sites

Internet Site	Select Data Availability
Bureau of Economic Analysis (BEA)	National and regional data on gross domestic product (GDP) and personal income, international data on trade in goods and services.
Bureau of Labor Statistics (BLS)	Inflation rates, unemployment rates, employment, pay and benefits, spending and time use, productivity.
Federal Reserve Economic Data (FRED)	Banking, business/fiscal data, exchange rates, reserves, monetary base.
U.S. Census Bureau	Economic indicators, foreign trade, health insurance, housing, sector-specific data.
zillow.com	Recent home sales, home characteristics, monthly rent, mortgage rates.
finance.yahoo.com	Historical stock prices, mutual fund performance, international market data.
The New York Times, *USA Today*, *The Wall Street Journal*, *The Economist*, and *Fortune*	Poverty, crime, obesity, and plenty of business-related data.
espn.com	Professional and college teams' scores, rankings, standings, individual player statistics.

EXERCISES 1.2

1. It came as a big surprise when Apple's touch screen iPhone 4, considered by many to be the best smartphone ever, was found to have a problem (*The New York Times*, June 24, 2010). Users complained of weak reception, and sometimes even dropped calls, when they cradled the phone in their hands in a particular way. A quick survey at a local store found that 2% of iPhone 4 users experienced this reception problem.

   a. Describe the relevant population.

   b. Does 2% denote the population parameter or the sample statistic?

2. Many people regard video games as an obsession for youngsters, but in fact, the average age of a video game player is 35 years (Reuters.com, August 21, 2009). Is the value 35 likely the actual or the estimated average age of the population? Explain.

3. An accounting professor wants to know the average GPA of the students enrolled in her class. She looks up information on Blackboard about the students enrolled in her class and computes the average GPA as 3.29.

   a. Describe the relevant population.

   b. Does the value 3.29 represent the population parameter or the sample statistic?

4. Business graduates in the U.S. with a marketing concentration earn high salaries. According to the Bureau of Labor Statistics, the average annual salary for marketing managers was $104,400 in 2007.

   a. What is the relevant population?

   b. Do you think the average salary of $104,400 was computed from the population? Explain.

5. Recent research suggests that depression significantly increases the risk of developing dementia later in life (*BBC News*, July 6, 2010). In a study involving 949 elderly persons, it was reported that 22% of those who had depression went on to develop dementia, compared to only 17% of those who did not have depression.

   a. Describe the relevant population and the sample.

   b. Do the numbers 22% and 17% represent the population parameters or the sample statistics?

6. Go to http://www.finance.yahoo.com/ to get a current stock quote for Google, Inc. (ticker symbol = GOOG). Then, click on historical prices to record the monthly adjusted close price of Google stock in 2010. Create a table that uses this information. What type of data do these numbers represent? Comment on the data.

7. Ask 20 of your friends whether they live in a dormitory, a rental unit, or other form of accommodation. Also find out their approximate monthly lodging expenses. Create a table that uses this information. What type of data do these numbers represent? Comment on the data.

8. Go to http://www.zillow.com/ and find the sale price data of 20 single-family homes sold in Las Vegas, Nevada, in the last 30 days. You must include in the data set the sale price, the number of bedrooms, the square footage, and the age of the house. What type of data do these numbers represent? Comment on the data.

9. The Federal Reserve Bank of St. Louis is a good source for downloading economic data. Go to http://research.stlouisfed.org/fred2/ to extract quarterly data on gross private saving (GPSAVE) from 2007 to 2010 (16 observations). Create a table that uses this information. Plot the data over time and comment on the savings trend in the U.S.

10. Another good source of data is the U.S. Census Bureau. Go to http://www.census.gov/ and extract the most recent state median income by family size (total) for Alabama, Arizona, California, Florida, Georgia, Indiana, Iowa, Maine, Massachusetts, Minnesota, Mississippi, New Mexico, North Dakota, and Washington. What type of data do these numbers represent? Comment on the regional differences in income.

1.3 Variables and Scales of Measurement

LO 1.4

Describe variables and various types of measurement scales.

When we conduct a statistical investigation, we invariably focus on people, objects, or events with particular characteristics. When a characteristic of interest differs in kind or degree among various observations, then the characteristic can be termed a **variable**. For instance, the 2010 Census asked each respondent to indicate gender on the form. Each respondent chose either male or female. In general, a variable that is described verbally rather than numerically is called a **qualitative variable**. Other examples of qualitative variables include race, profession, type of business, the manufacturer of a car, and so on.

On the other hand, a variable that assumes meaningful numerical values is called a **quantitative variable**. Quantitative variables, in turn, are either discrete or continuous. A **discrete variable** assumes a countable number of distinct values. Consider the number of children in a family or the number of points scored in a basketball game. We may observe distinct values such as 3 children in a family or 90 points being scored in a basketball game, but we will not observe 1.3 children or 92.5 scored points. Note that the distinct values need not be whole numbers. For instance, another example of a discrete variable is the price of a stock for a particular firm. The stock price may take on a value of $20.37 or $20.38, but it cannot take on a value between these two points.

A **continuous variable** is characterized by infinitely uncountable values and can take on any value within an interval. Weight, height, time, and investment return are all examples of continuous variables. For example, an unlimited number of values occur between the weights of 100 and 101 pounds, such as 100.3, 100.625, 100.8342, and so on. In practice, however, continuous variables may be measured in discrete values. We may report a newborn's weight (a continuous variable) in discrete terms as 6 pounds 10 ounces and another newborn's weight in similar discrete terms as 6 pounds 11 ounces, yet we implicitly understand that an infinite number of values exist between these two weights.

QUALITATIVE VARIABLES VERSUS QUANTITATIVE VARIABLES

A **variable** is the general characteristic being observed on a set of people, objects, or events, where each observation varies in kind or degree. Values corresponding to a **qualitative variable** are typically expressed in words but may be coded into numbers later on for purposes of data processing. A **quantitative variable** assumes meaningful numerical values, and can be further categorized as either **discrete** or **continuous**. A discrete variable takes on individually distinct values, whereas a continuous variable can take on any value within an interval.

In order to choose the appropriate statistical methods for summarizing and analyzing data, we need to distinguish between different measurement scales. All data measurements can be classified into one of four major categories: nominal, ordinal, interval, and ratio. Nominal and ordinal scales are used for qualitative variables, whereas interval and ratio scales are used for quantitative variables. We discuss these scales in ascending order of sophistication.

The Nominal Scale

The **nominal scale** represents the least sophisticated level of measurement. If we are presented with nominal data, all we can do is categorize or group the data. The values in the data set differ merely by name or label. Consider the following example.

Each company listed in Table 1.3 is a member of the Dow Jones Industrial Average (DJIA). The DJIA is a stock market index that shows how 30 large, publicly owned companies based in the United States have traded during a standard trading session in the stock market. Table 1.3 also shows where stocks of these companies are traded: either on the National Association of Securities Dealers Automated Quotations (Nasdaq) or the New York Stock Exchange (NYSE). These data are classified as nominal scale, since we are simply able to group or categorize them. Specifically, only three stocks are traded on Nasdaq, whereas the remaining 27 are traded on the NYSE.

Often we substitute *numbers* for the particular qualitative characteristic or trait that we are grouping. One reason why we do this is for ease of exposition; always referring to the National Association of Securities Dealers Automated Quotations, or even Nasdaq, becomes awkward and unwieldy. In addition, as we will see later in the text, computer statistical analysis is greatly facilitated by using numbers instead of names. For example, we might use the number 0 to show that a company's

TABLE 1.3 Companies of the DJIA and Exchange Where Stock Is Traded

Company	Exchange	Company	Exchange
3M (MMM)	NYSE	Intel (INTC)	Nasdaq
Alcoa (AA)	NYSE	IBM (IBM)	NYSE
American Express (AXP)	NYSE	Johnson & Johnson (JNJ)	NYSE
AT&T (T)	NYSE	JPMorgan Chase (JPM)	NYSE
Bank of America (BAC)	NYSE	Kraft Foods (KFT)	NYSE
Boeing (BA)	NYSE	McDonald's (MCD)	NYSE
Caterpillar (CAT)	NYSE	Merck (MRK)	NYSE
Chevron Corp. (CVX)	NYSE	Microsoft (MSFT)	Nasdaq
Cisco Systems (CSCO)	Nasdaq	Pfizer (PFE)	NYSE
Coca-Cola (KO)	NYSE	Procter & Gamble (PG)	NYSE
DuPont (DD)	NYSE	Travelers (TRV)	NYSE
ExxonMobil (XOM)	NYSE	United Tech. Corp. (UTX)	NYSE
General Electric (GE)	NYSE	Verizon Comm. (VZ)	NYSE
Hewlett-Packard (HPQ)	NYSE	Wal-Mart (WMT)	NYSE
Home Depot (HD)	NYSE	Walt Disney (DIS)	NYSE

SOURCE: http://www.finance.yahoo.com.

stock is traded on Nasdaq and the number 1 to show that a company's stock is traded on NYSE. In tabular form:

Exchange	Number of Companies Trading on Exchange
0	3
1	27

The Ordinal Scale

Compared to the nominal scale, the **ordinal scale** reflects a stronger level of measurement. With ordinal data we are able both to *categorize* and *rank* the data with respect to some characteristic or trait. The weakness with ordinal-scaled data is that we cannot interpret the difference between the ranked values because the actual numbers used are arbitrary. For example, suppose you are asked to classify the service at a particular hotel as excellent, good, fair, or poor. A standard way to record the ratings is

Excellent	4	Fair	2
Good	3	Poor	1

Here the value attached to excellent (4) is higher than the value attached to good (3), indicating that the response of excellent is preferred to good. However, another representation of the ratings might be

Excellent	100	Fair	70
Good	80	Poor	40

Excellent still receives a higher value than good, but now the difference between the two categories is 20 (100 − 80), as compared to a difference of 1 (4 − 3) when we use the first classification. In other words, *differences between categories are meaningless with ordinal data*. (We should also note that we could reverse the ordering so that, for instance, excellent equals 40 and poor equals 100; this renumbering would not change the nature of the data.)

EXAMPLE 1.1

In the introductory case, four questions were posed to tweens. The first question (Q1) asked tweens to name the radio station that they listened to on the ride to the resort, and the second question (Q2) asked tweens to rate the food quality at the resort on a scale of 1 to 4. The tweens' responses to these questions are shown in Table 1.1 in the introductory case.

a. What is the scale of measurement of the radio station data?

b. How are the data based on the ratings of the food quality similar to the radio station data? How are the data different?

c. Summarize the tweens' responses to Q1 and Q2 in tabular form. How can the resort use the information from these responses?

SOLUTION:

a. When asked which radio station played on the car ride to the resort, tweens responded with one of the following answers: JAMN94.5, MIX104.1, or KISS108. These are nominal data—the values in the data differ merely in name or label.

b. Since we can both categorize and rank the food quality data, we classify these responses as ordinal data. Ordinal data are similar to nominal data in the sense that we can categorize the data. The main difference between ordinal and nominal data is that the categories of ordinal data are ranked. A rating of 4 is better than a rating of 3. With the radio station data, we cannot say that KISS108 is ranked higher than MIX104.1; some tweens may argue otherwise, but we simply categorize nominal data without ranking.

c. With respect to the radio station data (Q1), we can assign 1 to JAMN94.5, 2 to MIX104.1, and 3 to KISS108. Counting the responses that fall into each category, we find that six tweens listened to 1, two listened to 2, and 12 listened to 3, or in tabular form:

Radio Station	Number of Tweens Listening to Radio Station
1	6
2	2
3	12

Twelve of the 20 tweens, or 60%, listened to KISS108. This information could prove useful to the management of the resort as they make decisions as to where to allocate their advertising dollars. If the resort could only choose to advertise at one radio station, it would appear that KISS108 would be the wise choice.

Given the food quality responses (Q2), we find that three of the tweens rated food quality with a 4, six tweens rated food quality with a 3, eight tweens rated food quality with a 2, and three tweens rated food quality with a 1. In tabular form:

Rating	Number of Tweens
4	3
3	6
2	8
1	3

The food quality results may be of concern to management. Just as many tweens rated the food quality as excellent as compared to poor. Moreover, the majority $[(8 + 3)/20 = 55\%]$ felt that the food was, at best, fair. Perhaps a more extensive survey that focuses solely on food quality would reveal the reason for their apparent dissatisfaction.

As mentioned earlier, nominal and ordinal scales are used for *qualitative variables*. Values corresponding to a qualitative variable are typically expressed in words but are coded into numbers for purposes of data processing. When summarizing the results of a qualitative variable, we typically count the number or calculate the percentage of persons or objects that fall into each possible category. With a qualitative variable, we are unable to perform meaningful arithmetic operations, such as adding and subtracting.

The Interval Scale

With data on an **interval scale**, not only can we categorize and rank the data, but we are also assured that the differences between scale values are equal. Thus, the arithmetic operations of addition and subtraction are meaningful. The Fahrenheit scale for temperatures is an example of an interval scale. Not only is 60 degrees hotter than 50 degrees, but the same difference of 10 degrees exists as between 90 and 80 degrees Fahrenheit.

The main drawback of data on an interval scale is that the value of zero is arbitrarily chosen; the zero point of an interval scale does not reflect a complete absence of what is being measured. No specific meaning is attached to zero degrees Fahrenheit other than to say it is 10 degrees colder than 10 degrees Fahrenheit. With an arbitrary zero point, meaningful ratios cannot be constructed. For instance, it is senseless to say that 80 degrees is twice as hot as 40 degrees; in other words, the ratio 80/40 has no meaning.

The Ratio Scale

The **ratio scale** represents the strongest level of measurement. Ratio-scaled data have all the characteristics of interval-scaled data as well as a true zero point as the origin. A ratio scale is used to measure many types of data in business analysis. Variables such as sales, profits, and inventory levels are expressed as ratio-scaled data. Measurements such as weight, time, and distance are also measured on a ratio scale, since zero is meaningful.

Unlike qualitative data, arithmetic operations are valid on interval- and ratio-scaled data. In later chapters, we will calculate summary measures for the typical value and variability of quantitative variables; we cannot calculate these measures if the variable is qualitative in nature.

EXAMPLE 1.2

In the last two questions from the introductory case's survey (Q3 and Q4), the 20 tweens were asked: "What time should the main dining area close?" and "How much of your *own* money did you spend at the lodge today?" Their responses appear in Table 1.1 in the introductory case.

a. How are the time data classified? In what ways do the time data differ from ordinal data? What is a potential weakness of this measurement scale?

b. What is the measurement scale of the money data? Why is it considered the strongest form of data?

c. In what ways is the information from Q3 and Q4 useful for the resort?

SOLUTION:

a. Clock time responses, such as 3:00 pm and 3:30 pm, or 5:30 pm and 6:00 pm, are on an interval scale. Interval data are a stronger measurement scale than ordinal data because differences between interval-scaled values are meaningful. In this particular example, we can say that 3:30 pm is 30 minutes later than 3:00 pm and 6:00 pm is 30 minutes later than 5:30 pm. The weakness with interval-scaled data is that the value of zero is arbitrary. Here, with the clock time responses, we have no apparent zero point; however, we could always arbitrarily define a zero point, say, at 12:00 am. Thus, although differences are comparable with interval-scaled data, ratios are meaningless due to the arbitrariness of the zero point. In other words, it is senseless to form the ratio 6:00 pm/3:00 pm and conclude that 6:00 pm is twice as long a time period as 3:00 pm.

b. Since the tweens' responses are in dollar amounts, this is ratio-scaled data. The ratio scale is the strongest form of data because we can categorize and rank values as well as calculate meaningful differences. Moreover, since there is a natural zero point, valid ratios can also be calculated. For example, the data show that three tweens spent $20. These tweens spent four times as much as the three tweens that spent $5 ($20/$5 = 4).

c. A review of the clock time responses (Q3) in Table 1.1 shows that the vast majority of the tweens would like the dining area to remain open later. In fact, only one tween feels that the dining area should close at 3:00 pm. An inspection of the money responses (Q4) in Table 1.1 indicates that only three of the 20 tweens did not spend any of his/her own money. This is very important information. It does appear that the discretionary spending of this age group is significant. The resort would be wise to cater to some of their preferences.

SYNOPSIS OF INTRODUCTORY CASE

A preliminary survey of tween preferences conducted by the management of a ski resort two hours outside Boston, Massachusetts, revealed some interesting information.

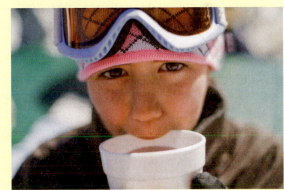

- Tweens were first asked to name the radio station that they listened to on the way to the resort. Even though their responses are in the form of nominal data, the least sophisticated form of measurement, useful information can still be extracted from it. For instance, the responses show that 60% of the tweens listened to KISS108. If the resort wishes to contact tweens using this media, it may want to direct its advertising dollars to this station.

- Next, the tweens were asked to rate the food quality at the resort on a scale of 1 to 4 (where 1 is poor, 2 is fair, 3 is good, and 4 is excellent). Their responses to food quality were ordinal in nature; that is, the responses can be categorized and ranked. The survey results with respect to food quality are disturbing. The majority of the tweens, 55% (11/20), felt that the food was, at best, fair. A more extensive study focusing on food quality appears necessary.

- Tweens were then asked what time the main dining area should close, given a present closing time of 3:00 pm. Their clock-time responses reflect the interval scale. The interval scale is stronger than the nominal and ordinal scales, implying that more can be extracted from the data than mere percentages; however, data on the interval scale have an arbitrary zero point, so meaningful ratios cannot be constructed. The data suggest that the vast majority of the tweens (19 out of 20) would like the dining area to remain open later.

- Finally, the tweens were asked to report the amount of their *own* money they spent at the lodge. Responses in dollar amounts reflect the ratio scale, the strongest form of measurement. The ratio scale has all the characteristics of the interval scale, but valid ratios can also be calculated. The resort is likely pleased with the responses to the last question, since 17 of the 20 tweens spent their own money at the lodge. The answers to the last question appear to support the belief that tween spending is growing.

11. Which of the following variables are qualitative and which are quantitative? If the variable is quantitative, then specify whether the variable is discrete or continuous.

    a. Points scored in a football game.

    b. Racial composition of a high school classroom.

    c. Heights of 15-year-olds.

12. Which of the following variables are qualitative and which are quantitative? If the variable is quantitative, then specify whether the variable is discrete or continuous.

    a. Colors of cars in a mall parking lot.

    b. Time it takes each student to complete a final exam.

    c. The number of patrons who frequent a restaurant.

13. In each of the following scenarios, define the type of measurement scale.

    a. A kindergarten teacher marks whether each student is a boy or a girl.

    b. A ski resort records the daily temperature during the month of January.

    c. A restaurant surveys its customers about the quality of its waiting staff on a scale of 1 to 4, where 1 is poor and 4 is excellent.

14. In each of the following scenarios, define the type of measurement scale.

    a. An investor collects data on the weekly closing price of gold throughout a year.

    b. An analyst assigns a sample of bond issues to one of the following credit ratings, given in descending order of credit quality (increasing probability of default): AAA, AA, BBB, BB, CC, D.

    c. The dean of the business school at a local university categorizes students by major (i.e., accounting, finance, marketing, etc.) to help in determining class offerings in the future.

15. In each of the following scenarios, define the type of measurement scale.

    a. A meteorologist records the amount of monthly rainfall over the past year.

    b. A sociologist notes the birth year of 50 individuals.

    c. An investor monitors the daily stock price of BP following the 2010 oil disaster in the Gulf of Mexico.

16. A professor records the majors of her 30 students as follows:

Accounting	Economics	Undecided	Finance	Management
Marketing	Finance	Marketing	Economics	Management
Marketing	Finance	Marketing	Accounting	Finance
Finance	Undecided	Management	Undecided	Economics
Economics	Accounting	Management	Undecided	Economics
Accounting	Economics	Management	Accounting	Economics

    a. What is the measurement scale of these data?

    b. Summarize the results in tabular form.

    c. What information can be extracted from the data?

17. **FILE** The accompanying table shows a portion of the 30 companies that comprise the Dow Jones Industrial Average (DJIA); the full data set can be found on the text website and is labeled **DOW Characteristics**. The second column shows the year that the company joined the DJIA (Year). The third column shows each company's Morningstar rating (Rating). (Five stars is the best rating that a company can receive, indicating that the company's stock price is undervalued and thus a very good buy. One star is the worst rating a company can be given, implying that the stock price is overvalued and a bad buy.) Finally, the fourth column shows each company's stock price as of June 30, 2010 (Stock Price).

Company	Year	Rating	Stock Price
3M (MMM)	1976	*****	$78.99
Alcoa (AA)	1959	****	10.03
⋮	⋮	⋮	⋮
Walt Disney (DIS)	1991	***	31.50

SOURCE: Morningstar ratings retrieved from http://www.morningstar.com on June 30, 2010; stock prices retrieved from http://www.finance.yahoo.com.

    a. What is the measurement scale of the Year data? What are the strengths of this type of data? What are the weaknesses?

    b. What is the measurement scale of Morningstar's star-based rating system? Summarize Morningstar's star-based rating system for the companies in tabular form. Let 5 denote *****, 4 denote ****, and so on. What information can be extracted from this data?

    c. What is the measurement scale of the Stock Price data? What are its strengths?

Conceptual Review

LO 1.1   Describe the importance of statistics.

A proper understanding of statistical ideas and concepts helps us understand more of the real world around us, including issues in business, finance, health, and social interactions. We must understand statistics or risk making bad decisions and costly mistakes. A knowledge of statistics also provides the necessary tools to differentiate between sound statistical conclusions and questionable conclusions drawn from an insufficient number of data points, "bad" data points, incomplete data points, or just misinformation.

LO 1.2 Differentiate between descriptive statistics and inferential statistics.

The study of statistics is generally divided into two branches: descriptive statistics and inferential statistics. **Descriptive statistics** refers to the summary of a data set in the form of tables, graphs, or the calculation of numerical measures. **Inferential statistics** refers to extracting useful information from a **sample** to draw conclusions about a **population**.

A **population** consists of the complete collection of items with the characteristic we wish to understand. A **sample** is a subset of the population of interest.

LO 1.3 Explain the need for sampling and discuss various data types.

In general, we use sample data rather than population data for two main reasons: (1) obtaining information on the entire population is expensive, and/or (2) it is impossible to examine every item of the population.

Cross-sectional data contain values of a characteristic of many subjects at the same point in time or without regard to differences in time. **Time series data** contain values of a characteristic of a subject over time.

LO 1.4 Describe variables and various types of measurement scales.

A **qualitative variable** is normally described in words rather than numerically. A **quantitative variable** assumes meaningful numerical values, and can be further categorized as either **discrete** or **continuous**. A discrete variable assumes a countable number of distinct values, whereas a continuous variable can take on any value within an interval.

All data measurements can be classified into one of four major categories.

- The **nominal scale** represents the least sophisticated level of measurement. The values in nominal data differ merely by name or label, and the values are then simply categorized or grouped by name.

- The values of data on an **ordinal scale** can be categorized *and* ranked; however, differences between the ranked values are meaningless.

- The **interval scale** is a stronger measurement scale as compared to nominal and ordinal scales. Values on the interval scale can be categorized and ranked, and differences between scale values are valid. The main drawback of the interval scale is that the value of zero is arbitrarily chosen; this implies that ratios constructed from interval-scaled values bear no significance.

- The **ratio scale** represents the strongest level of measurement. Ratio-scaled data have all the characteristics of interval-scaled data as well as a true zero point as the origin; thus, as its name implies, meaningful ratios can be calculated with values on the ratio scale.

Nominal and ordinal scales are used for qualitative variables. Values corresponding to qualitative data are typically expressed in words but are coded into numbers later on for purposes of data processing. When summarizing the results of qualitative data, we typically count the number or calculate the percentage of persons or objects that fall into each possible category. Interval and ratio scales are used for quantitative variables. Unlike qualitative variables, arithmetic operations are valid on quantitative variables.

2

Tabular and Graphical Methods

LEARNING OBJECTIVES

After reading this chapter you should be able to:

LO 2.1 Summarize qualitative data by forming frequency distributions.

LO 2.2 Construct and interpret pie charts and bar charts.

LO 2.3 Summarize quantitative data by forming frequency distributions.

LO 2.4 Construct and interpret histograms, polygons, and ogives.

LO 2.5 Construct and interpret a stem-and-leaf diagram.

LO 2.6 Construct and interpret a scatterplot.

People often have difficulty processing information provided by data in its raw form. A useful way of interpreting data effectively is to condense the data with some kind of visual or numerical summary. In this chapter we present several tabular and graphical tools that can help you organize and present data. We first deal with qualitative data by constructing frequency distributions. We can visualize these frequency distributions by constructing pie charts and bar charts. For quantitative data, we again make frequency distributions. In addition to giving us an overall picture of where the data tend to cluster, frequency distributions using quantitative data also show us how the data are spread out from the lowest value to the highest value. For visual representations of quantitative data, we examine histograms, polygons, ogives, and stem-and-leaf diagrams. Finally, we show how to construct a scatterplot, which graphically depicts the relationship between two quantitative variables. We will find that a scatterplot is a very useful tool when conducting correlation and regression analysis, topics discussed in depth later in the text.

House Prices in Southern California

Mission Viejo, a city located in Southern California, was named the safest city in California and the third-safest city in the nation (CQPress.com, November 23, 2009). Matthew Edwards, a relocation specialist for a real estate firm in Mission Viejo, often relays this piece of information to clients unfamiliar with the many benefits that the city offers. Recently, a client from Seattle, Washington, asked Matthew for a summary of recent sales. The client is particularly interested in the availability of houses in the $500,000 range. Table 2.1 shows the sale price for 36 single-family houses in Mission Viejo during June 2010; the data are also available on the text website and are labeled **Mission Viejo Houses**.

TABLE 2.1 Recent Sale Price of Houses in Mission Viejo, CA, for June 2010 (data in $1000s)

FILE

$430	670	530	521	669	445
520	417	525	350	660	412
460	533	430	399	702	735
475	525	330	560	540	537
670	538	575	440	460	630
521	370	555	425	588	430

Source: http://www.zillow.com.

Matthew wants to use the sample information to:

1. Make summary statements concerning the range of house prices.
2. Comment on where house prices tend to cluster.
3. Calculate appropriate percentages in order to compare house prices in Mission Viejo, California, to those in Seattle, Washington.

We provide a synopsis of this case at the end of Section 2.2.

2.1 Summarizing Qualitative Data

LO 2.1

Summarize qualitative data by forming frequency distributions.

As we discussed in Chapter 1, nominal and ordinal data are types of qualitative data. Nominal data typically consist of observations that represent labels or names; information related to gender or race are examples. Nominal data is considered the least sophisticated form of data, since all we can do with the data is categorize it. Ordinal data is stronger in the sense that we can categorize and order the data. Examples of ordinal data include the ratings of a product or a professor, where 1 represents the worst and 4 represents the best. In order to organize qualitative data, it is often useful to construct a frequency distribution.

> **FREQUENCY DISTRIBUTION FOR QUALITATIVE DATA**
>
> A **frequency distribution** for qualitative data groups data into categories and records the number of observations that fall into each category.

To illustrate the construction of a frequency distribution with nominal data, Table 2.2 shows the weather for the month of February (2010) in Seattle, Washington.

TABLE 2.2 Seattle Weather, February 2010

Sunday	Monday	Tuesday	Wednesday	Thursday	Friday	Saturday
	1 Rainy	2 Rainy	3 Rainy	4 Rainy	5 Rainy	6 Rainy
7 Rainy	8 Rainy	9 Cloudy	10 Rainy	11 Rainy	12 Rainy	13 Rainy
14 Rainy	15 Rainy	16 Rainy	17 Sunny	18 Sunny	19 Sunny	20 Sunny
21 Sunny	22 Sunny	23 Rainy	24 Rainy	25 Rainy	26 Rainy	27 Rainy
28 Sunny						

SOURCE: www.wunderground.com.

We first note that the weather in Seattle is categorized as cloudy, rainy, or sunny. The first column in Table 2.3 lists these categories. Initially, we use a "tally" column to record the number of days that fall into each category. Since the first eight days of February were rainy days, we place the first eight tally marks in the rainy category; the ninth day of February was cloudy, so we place one tally mark in the cloudy category, and so on. Finally, we convert each category's total tally count into its respective numerical value in the frequency column. Since only one tally mark appears in the cloudy category, we record the value 1 as its frequency. Note that if you sum the frequency column, you obtain the sample size. A frequency distribution in its final form does not include the tally column.

TABLE 2.3 Frequency Distribution for Seattle Weather, February 2010

Weather	Tally	Frequency
Cloudy	I	1
Rainy	HHH HHH HHH HHH	20
Sunny	HHH II	7
		Total = 28 days

From the frequency distribution, we can now readily observe that the most common type of day in February was rainy, since this type of day occurs with the highest frequency. In many applications we want to compare data sets that differ in size. For example, we might want to compare the weather in February to the weather in March. However, February has 28 days (except during a leap year) and March has 31 days. In this instance, we would convert the frequency distribution to a **relative frequency distribution**. We calculate each category's relative frequency by dividing the respective category's frequency by the total number of observations. The sum of the relative frequencies should equal one, or a value very close to one due to rounding.

Table 2.4 shows the frequency distribution in Table 2.3 converted into a relative frequency distribution. In addition, we also show the relative frequency distribution for the month of March. March had 3 cloudy days, 10 sunny days, and 18 rainy days. Each of these frequencies was then divided by 31, the number of days in the month of March.

TABLE 2.4 Relative Frequency Distribution for Seattle Weather

Weather	February 2010: Relative Frequency	March 2010: Relative Frequency
Cloudy	1/28 = 0.036	3/31 = 0.097
Rainy	20/28 = 0.714	18/31 = 0.581
Sunny	7/28 = 0.250	10/31 = 0.323
	Total = 1	Total = 1 (approximately)

Source: www.wunderground.com.

We can easily convert relative frequencies into percentages by multiplying by 100. For instance, the percent of cloudy days in February and March equal 3.6% and 9.7%, respectively. From the relative frequency distribution, we can now conclude that the weather in Seattle in both February and March was predominantly rainy. However, the weather in March was a bit nicer in that approximately 32% of the days were sunny, as opposed to only 25% of the days in February.

CALCULATING RELATIVE AND PERCENT FREQUENCIES

The **relative frequency** of each category equals the proportion (fraction) of observations in each category. A category's relative frequency is calculated by dividing the frequency by the total number of observations. The sum of the relative frequencies should equal one.

The **percent frequency** is the percent (%) of observations in a category; it equals the relative frequency of the category multiplied by 100%.

EXAMPLE 2.1

In Adidas' Online Annual Report 2009, net sales were reported in four regions of the world for the years 2000 and 2009 as shown in Table 2.5. Convert each region's net sales to its respective proportion for that year. Have the proportions of Adidas' net sales in each region remained the same over this 10-year period? Explain.

TABLE 2.5 Adidas' Net Sales by Region (in millions of euros, €)

Region	2000	2009
Europe	2,860	4,384
North America	1,906	2,360
Asia	875	2,614
Latin America	171	1,006
	Total = 5,812	Total = 10,364

SOLUTION: Over the 10-year period, Adidas' total net sales have almost doubled. However, it appears that the increase in net sales within each region has varied dramatically. In order to calculate the proportions of Adidas' net sales for each region, we take each region's net sales and divide by the year's total sales, as shown in Table 2.6.

TABLE 2.6 Proportion of Adidas' Net Sales by Region

Region	2000	2009
Europe	2,860/5,812 = 0.492	4,384/10,364 = 0.423
North America	1,906/5,812 = 0.328	2,360/10,364 = 0.228
Asia	875/5,812 = 0.151	2,614/10,364 = 0.252
Latin America	171/5,812 = 0.029	1,006/10,364 = 0.097
	Total = 1	Total = 1

Once we convert the data to proportions, we see significant changes in the proportion of net sales allocated to each region. In 2009, Europe still has the highest percentage of net sales at 42.3%; however, this percentage has fallen over the 10-year period. A large decline took place in the percentage of net sales in North America, from 32.8% to 22.8%, compared to significant increases in the percentages of net sales in Asia, from 15.1% to 25.2%, and in Latin America, from 2.9% to 9.7%. In short, there has been considerable movement in the percentage of Adidas' net sales allocated to each region over the 10-year period. This type of information can help Adidas when making important marketing decisions.

Picturing Frequency Distributions for Qualitative Data

LO **2.2**

Construct and interpret pie charts and bar charts.

We can visualize the information found in frequency distributions by constructing various graphs. Graphical representations often portray the data more dramatically, as well as simplify interpretation. A **pie chart** and a **bar chart** are two widely used pictorial representations of qualitative data.

> **GRAPHICAL DISPLAY OF QUALITATIVE DATA: PIE CHARTS**
>
> A **pie chart** is a segmented circle whose segments portray the relative frequencies of the categories of some qualitative variable.

In order to construct a pie chart, first draw a circle. Then cut the circle into slices, or sectors, such that each sector is proportional to the size of the category you wish to display. For instance, Table 2.6 shows that Europe accounted for 49.2% of Adidas' net sales in 2000. Since a circle contains 360 degrees, the portion of the circle representing Europe encompasses 0.492 × 360 = 177.1 degrees; thus, almost half of the circle should reflect Europe's contribution to sales. Similar calculations for the other three regions in 2000 yield:

North America: 0.328 × 360 = 118.1 degrees
Asia: 0.151 × 360 = 54.4 degrees
Latin America: 0.029 × 360 = 10.4 degrees

The same methodology can be used to calculate each region's contribution to net sales for the year 2009. Figure 2.1 shows the resulting pie charts.

FIGURE 2.1
Pie charts for Adidas' net sales.

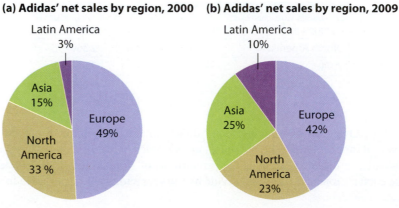

(a) Adidas' net sales by region, 2000   **(b) Adidas' net sales by region, 2009**

Using Excel to Construct a Pie Chart

Excel offers various options for displaying a pie chart. To replicate the pie chart in Figure 2.1a, follow these steps:

A. **FILE** Open the ***Adidas Sales*** data (Table 2.5) from the text website into an Excel spreadsheet.

B. Select the categorical names and respective frequencies from the year 2000. Leave out the heading (top row); see Figure 2.2 below.

C. From the menu choose **Insert** > **Pie** > **2-D Pie**. From the options given, choose the graph on the top left.

D. In order to give the pie chart category names and their respective percentages, from the menu choose **Layout** > **Data Labels** > **More Data Label Options**. Under *Label Options*, deselect "Value" and select "Category Name" and "Percentage."

FIGURE 2.2 Constructing a pie chart with Excel

Another way to graphically depict qualitative data is to construct a **bar chart**. When constructing a bar chart, first place each category on the horizontal axis and then mark the vertical axis with an appropriate range of values for either frequency or relative frequency. The height of each bar is equal to the frequency or the relative frequency of the corresponding category. Typically, you should leave space between categories to improve clarity.

> **GRAPHICAL DISPLAY OF QUALITATIVE DATA: BAR CHARTS**
>
> A **bar chart** depicts the frequency or the relative frequency for each category of the qualitative data as a bar rising vertically from the horizontal axis.

Figure 2.3 shows a relative frequency bar chart for the Adidas net sales example. It is particularly useful because we can group net sales by region, emphasizing the rise in the proportion of sales in Asia and Latin America versus the fall in the proportion of sales in Europe and North America over the 10-year period.

Using Excel to Construct a Bar Chart

Excel provides many options for showing a bar chart. To replicate the bar chart in Figure 2.3, follow these steps:

A. **FILE** Open the ***Proportion of Adidas Sales*** data (Table 2.6) from the text website into an Excel spreadsheet.

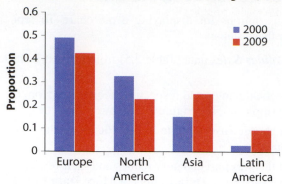

FIGURE 2.3 The proportion of Adidas' net sales in four regions, 2000 versus 2009

B. Select the categorical names and respective relative frequencies for the years 2000 and 2009. Leave out the heading (top row); see Figure 2.4.

C. Choose **Insert > Column > 2-D Column**. From the options given, choose the graph on the top left. (This will create a vertical bar chart. If you want to construct a horizontal bar chart, choose **Insert > Bar > 2-D Bar**.)

D. In the legend to the right of the bar chart, Excel labels the data for the year 2000 as "Series 1" and the data for the year 2009 as "Series 2" by default. In order to edit the legend, select the legend and choose **Design > Select Data**. From the *Legend Entries*, select "Series 1," then select *Edit*, and under *Series Name*, type the new name of 2000. Follow the same steps to rename "Series 2" to 2009.

FIGURE 2.4 Constructing a bar chart with Excel

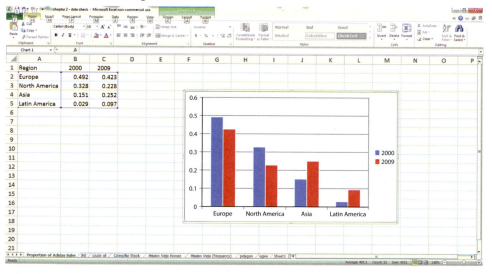

Cautionary Comments when Constructing or Interpreting Charts or Graphs

As with many of the statistical methods that we examine throughout this text, the possibility exists for unintentional, as well as purposeful, distortions of graphical information. As a careful researcher, you should follow these basic guidelines:

- The simplest graph should be used for a given set of data. Strive for clarity and avoid unnecessary adornments.

- Axes should be clearly marked with the numbers of their respective scales; each axis should be labeled.

FIGURE 2.5 Misleading scales on vertical axes

(a) Vertical axis with high upper limit

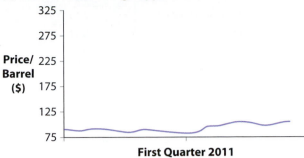

Price/ Barrel ($)

First Quarter 2011

Source: U.S. Energy Information Administration.

(b) Stretched vertical axis

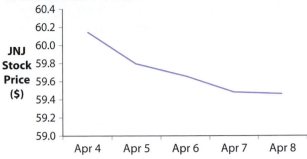

JNJ Stock Price ($)

Source: http://www.finance.yahoo.com.

- The scale on the vertical axis should begin at zero. Moreover, the vertical axis should not be given a very high value as an upper limit. In these instances, the data may appear compressed so that an increase (or decrease) of the data is not as apparent as it perhaps should be. Conversely, the axis should not be stretched so that an increase (or decrease) of the data appears more pronounced than warranted. For example, Figure 2.5(a) plots the daily price for a barrel of crude oil for the first quarter of 2011 (the data labeled **Crude Oil** are available on the text website). Due to Middle East unrest, the price of crude oil rose from a low of $83.13 per barrel to a high of $106.19 per barrel, or approximately 28% $\left(= \frac{106.19 - 83.13}{83.13} \right)$. However, since Figure 2.5(a) uses a high value as an upper limit on the vertical axis ($325), the rise in price appears dampened. Figure 2.5(b) charts the daily closing stock price for Johnson & Johnson (JNJ) for the week of April 4, 2011 (the data labeled **JNJ** are available on the text website). It is true that the stock price declined over the week from a high of $60.15 to a low of $59.46; this amounts to a $0.69 decrease or an approximate 1% decline. However, since the vertical axis is stretched, the drop in stock price appears more dramatic.

- When creating a bar chart, each bar should be of the same width. Increasing (or decreasing) bar widths creates distortions. The same principle holds in the next section when we discuss histograms.

EXERCISES 2.1

1. A local restaurant is committed to providing its patrons with the best dining experience possible. On a recent survey, the restaurant asked patrons to rate the quality of their entrées. The responses ranged from 1 to 5, where 1 indicated a disappointing entrée and 5 indicated an exceptional entrée. The results of the survey are as follows:

3	5	4	4	3	2	3	3	2	5	5	5
5	3	3	2	1	4	5	5	4	2	5	5
5	4	4	3	1	5	2	1	5	4	4	4

a. Construct a frequency and a relative frequency distribution that summarizes the survey's results.
b. Are patrons generally satisfied with the quality of their entrées? Explain.

2. First-time patients at North Shore Family Practice are required to fill out a questionnaire that gives the doctor an overall idea of each patient's health. The first question is: "In general, what is the quality of your health?" The patient chooses Excellent, Good, Fair, or Poor. Over the past month, the responses to this question from first-time patients were:

Fair	Good	Fair	Excellent
Good	Good	Good	Poor
Excellent	Excellent	Poor	Good
Fair	Good	Good	Good
Good	Poor	Fair	Excellent
Excellent	Good	Good	Good

a. Construct a frequency and a relative frequency distribution that summarizes the responses to the questionnaire.
b. What is the most common response to the questionnaire? How would you characterize the health of first-time patients at this medical practice?

3. A survey asked chief executives at leading U.S. firms the following question: "Where do you expect the U.S. economy

to be 12 months from now?" A representative sample of their responses appears below:

Same	Same	Same	Better	Worse
Same	Same	Better	Same	Worse
Same	Better	Same	Better	Same
Worse	Same	Same	Same	Worse
Same	Same	Same	Better	Same

a. Construct a frequency and a relative frequency distribution that summarizes the responses to the survey. Where did most chief executives expect the U.S. economy to be in 12 months?

b. Construct a pie chart and a bar chart to summarize your results.

4. AccuWeather.com reported the following weather delays at these major U.S. airline hubs for July 21, 2010:

City	Delay	City	Delay
Atlanta	PM Delays	Mpls./St. Paul	None
Chicago	None	New York	All Day Delays
Dallas/Ft. Worth	None	Orlando	None
Denver	All Day Delays	Philadelphia	All Day Delays
Detroit	AM Delays	Phoenix	None
Houston	All Day Delays	San Francisco	AM Delays
Las Vegas	All Day Delays	Salt Lake City	None
Los Angeles	AM Delays	Seattle	None
Miami	AM Delays	Washington	All Day Delays

a. Construct a frequency and a relative frequency distribution that summarizes the delays at major U.S. hubs. What was the most common type of delay? Explain.

b. Construct a pie chart and a bar chart to summarize your results.

5. Fifty pro-football rookies were rated on a scale of 1 to 5, based on performance at a training camp as well as on past performance. A ranking of 1 indicated a poor prospect whereas a ranking of 5 indicated an excellent prospect. The following frequency distribution was constructed.

Rating	Frequency
1	4
2	10
3	14
4	18
5	4

a. How many of the rookies received a rating of 4 or better? How many of the rookies received a rating of 2 or worse?

b. Construct the corresponding relative frequency distribution. What percent received a rating of 5?

c. Construct a bar chart for these data.

6. A recent survey asked 5,324 individuals: "What's most important to you when choosing where to live?" The responses are shown in the following relative frequency distribution.

Response	Relative Frequency
Good jobs	0.37
Affordable homes	0.15
Top schools	0.11
Low crime	0.23
Things to do	0.14

Source: CNNMoney.com, July 13, 2010.

a. Construct the corresponding frequency distribution. How many of the respondents chose "low crime" as the most important criteria when choosing where to live?

b. Construct a bar chart for these data.

7. What is the perfect summer trip? A National Geographic Kids survey (*AAA Horizons*, April 2007) asked this question to 316 children ages 8 to 14. Their responses are given in the following frequency distribution.

Top Vacation Choice	Frequency
Cruises	140
Beaches	68
Amusement Parks	68
Big Cities	20
Lakes	12
Summer Camp	8

a. Construct a relative frequency distribution. What percentage of the responses cited "Cruises" as the perfect summer trip?

b. Construct a bar chart for these data.

8. The following table lists U.S. revenue (in $ billions) of the major car-rental companies.

Car-Rental Company	Revenue in 2009
Enterprise	$10.7
Hertz	4.7
Avis Budget	4.0
Dollar Thrifty	1.5
Other	1.0

Source: *The Wall Street Journal*, July 30, 2010.

a. Construct a relative frequency distribution.

b. Hertz accounted for what percentage of sales?

c. Construct a pie chart for these data.

9. A survey conducted by CBS News asked 829 respondents which of the following events will happen first. The responses are summarized in the following table:

Cure for cancer found	40%
End of dependence on oil	27%
Signs of life in outer space	12%
Peace in Middle East	8%
Other	6%
None will happen	7%

Source: *Vanity Fair*, December 2009.

a. Construct a bar chart and a pie chart for these data.

b. How many people think that a cure for cancer will be found first?

10. A 2010 poll conducted by NBC asked respondents who would win Super Bowl XLV in 2011. The responses by 20,825 people are summarized in the following table.

Team	Number of Votes
Atlanta Falcons	4,040
New Orleans Saints	1,880
Houston Texans	1,791
Dallas Cowboys	1,631
Minnesota Vikings	1,438
Indianapolis Colts	1,149
Pittsburgh Steelers	1,141
New England Patriots	1,095
Green Bay Packers	1,076
Others	

a. How many responses were for "Others"?

b. The Green Bay Packers won Super Bowl XLV, defeating the Pittsburgh Steelers by the score of 31-25. What proportion of respondents felt that the Green Bay Packers would win?

c. Construct a bar chart for these data using relative frequencies.

11. The accompanying figure plots the monthly stock price of Caterpillar, Inc., from July 2009 through March 2011. The stock has experienced tremendous growth over this time period, almost tripling in price. Does the figure reflect this growth? If not, why not?

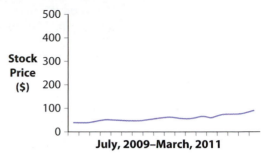

12. Annual sales at a small pharmaceutical firm have been rather stagnant over the most recent five-year period, exhibiting only 1.2% growth over this time frame. A research analyst prepares the accompanying graph for inclusion in a sales report.

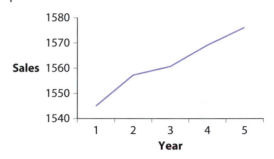

Does this graph accurately reflect what has happened to sales over the last five years? If not, why not?

2.2 Summarizing Quantitative Data

With quantitative data, each value is a number that represents a meaningful amount or count. The number of patents held by pharmaceutical firms (count) and household incomes (amount) are examples of quantitative data. Although different in nature from qualitative data, we still use frequency distributions to summarize quantitative data.

Before discussing the mechanics of constructing a frequency distribution, we find it useful to first examine one in its final form, using the house-price data from Table 2.1. We converted the raw data (the actual values) from Table 2.1 into a frequency distribution with five intervals or **classes**, each of width 100, as shown in Table 2.7. We see, for instance, that four houses sold in the first class, where prices ranged from $300,000 up to $400,000. The data are more manageable using a frequency distribution, but some detail is lost because we no longer see the actual values.

LO **2.3**

Summarize quantitative data by forming frequency distributions.

TABLE 2.7 Frequency Distribution for House-Price Data

Class (in $1000s)	Frequency
300 up to 400	4
400 up to 500	11
500 up to 600	14
600 up to 700	5
700 up to 800	2
	Total = 36

It turns out that reading and understanding a frequency distribution is actually easier than forming one. When we constructed a frequency distribution with qualitative data, the raw data could be categorized in a well-defined way. With quantitative data, we must make certain decisions about the number of classes, as well as the width of each class. We do not apply concrete rules when we define the classes in Table 2.7; however, we are able to follow several guidelines.

Guidelines for Constructing a Frequency Distribution

- *Classes are mutually exclusive.* In other words, classes do not overlap. Each observation falls into one, and only one, class. For instance, suppose a value of 400 appeared in Table 2.1. Given the class divisions in Table 2.7, we would have included this observation in the second class interval. Mathematically, the second class interval is expressed as $400 \leq \text{Price} < 500$. Alternatively, we can define the second interval as $400 < \text{Price} \leq 500$, in which case the value 400 is included in the previous class interval. In short, no matter the specification of the classes, the observation is included in only one of the classes.

- *Classes are exhaustive.* The total number of classes covers the entire sample (or population). In Table 2.7, if we had left off the last class, 700 up to 800, then we would be omitting two observations from the sample.

- *The total number of classes in a frequency distribution usually ranges from 5 to 20.* Smaller data sets tend to have fewer classes than larger data sets. Recall that the goal of constructing a frequency distribution is to summarize the data in a form that accurately depicts the group as a whole. If we have too many classes, then this advantage of the frequency distribution is lost. For instance, suppose we create a frequency distribution for the house-price data with 17 classes, each of width 25, as shown in Table 2.8.

  Technically, this is a valid frequency distribution, but the summarization advantage of the frequency distribution is lost because there are too many class intervals. Similarly, if the frequency distribution has too few classes, then considerable accuracy and detail are lost. Consider a frequency distribution of the house-price data with three classes, each of width 150, as shown in Table 2.9.

TABLE 2.8 Too Many Classes in a Distribution

Class (in $1000s)	Frequency
325 up to 350	2
350 up to 375	1
375 up to 400	1
400 up to 425	3
425 up to 450	5
450 up to 475	3
475 up to 500	0
500 up to 525	5
525 up to 550	5
550 up to 575	3
575 up to 600	1
600 up to 625	0
625 up to 650	1
650 up to 675	4
675 up to 700	0
700 up to 725	1
725 up to 750	1
	Total = 36

TABLE 2.9 Too Few Classes in a Distribution

Class (in $1000s)	Frequency
300 up to 450	12
450 up to 600	17
600 up to 750	7
	Total = 36

Again, this is a valid frequency distribution. However, we cannot tell whether the 17 houses that sold for $450,000 up to $600,000 fall closer to the price of $450,000, fall closer to the price of $600,000, or are evenly spread within the interval. With only three classes in the frequency distribution, too much detail is lost.

- Once we choose the number of classes for a raw data set, we can then *approximate the width of each class* by using the formula

$$\frac{\text{Largest value} - \text{Smallest value}}{\text{Number of classes}}.$$

Generally, the width of each class is the same for each class interval. If the class width varied, comparisons between the numbers of observations in different intervals would be misleading. Moreover, it is preferable to define class limits that are easy to recognize and interpret.

Suppose we conclude, as we do in Table 2.7, that we should have five classes in the frequency distribution for the house-price data. Applying the class-width formula with the largest value of 735 and the smallest value of 330 (from Table 2.1) yields $\frac{735 - 330}{5} = 81$. Table 2.10 shows the frequency distribution with five classes and a class width of 81.

TABLE 2.10 Cumbersome Class Width in a Distribution

Class (in $1000s)	Frequency
330 up to 411	4
411 up to 492	11
492 up to 573	12
573 up to 654	3
654 up to 735	6
	Total = 36

Again, this is a valid frequency distribution, but it proves unwieldy. Recall that one major goal in forming a frequency distribution is to provide more clarity in interpreting the data. Grouping the data in this manner actually makes analyzing the data more difficult. In order to facilitate interpretation of the frequency distribution, it is best to define class limits with ease of recognition in mind. To this end, and as initially shown in Table 2.7, we set the lower limit of the first class at 300 (rather than 330) and obtain the remaining class limits by successively adding 100 (rather than 81).

Once we have clearly defined the classes for a particular data set, the next step is to count and record the number of data points that fall into each class. As we did with the construction of a qualitative frequency distribution, we usually include a tally column to aid in counting (see Table 2.11), but then we remove this column in the final presentation of the frequency distribution. For instance, in Table 2.1, the first data point, 430, falls in the second class, so we place a tally mark in the second class; the next value of 520 falls in the third class, so we place a tally mark in the third class, and so on. The frequency column shows the numerical value of the respective tally count. Since four tally marks appear in the first class, we record the value 4 as its frequency—the number of observations that fall into the first class. One way to ensure that we have included all the data points in the frequency distribution is to sum the frequency column. This sum should always equal the population or sample size.

TABLE 2.11 Constructing Frequency Distributions for the House-Price Data

Class (in $1000s)	Tally	Frequency	Cumulative Frequency
300 up to 400	IIII	4	4
400 up to 500	HH HH I	11	4 + 11 = 15
500 up to 600	HH HH IIII	14	4 + 11 + 14 = 29
600 up to 700	HH	5	4 + 11 + 14 + 5 = 34
700 up to 800	II	2	4 + 11 + 14 + 5 + 1 = 36
		Total = 36	

A frequency distribution indicates how many observations (in this case house prices) fall within some range. However, we might want to know how many observations fall below the upper limit of a particular class. In these cases, our needs are better served with a cumulative frequency distribution.

The last column of Table 2.11 shows values for cumulative frequency. The cumulative frequency of the first class is the same as the frequency of the first class, that is, the value 4. However, the interpretation is different. With respect to the frequency column, the value 4 tells us that four of the houses sold in the $300,000 up to $400,000 range. For the cumulative frequency column, the value 4 tells us that four of the houses sold for less than $400,000. To obtain the cumulative frequency for the second class, we add its frequency, 11, with the preceding frequency, 4, and obtain 15. This tells us that 15 of the houses sold for less than $500,000. We solve for the cumulative frequencies of the remaining classes in a like manner. Note that the cumulative frequency of the last class is equal to the sample size of 36. This indicates that all 36 houses sold for less than $800,000.

> ### FREQUENCY AND CUMULATIVE FREQUENCY DISTRIBUTIONS FOR QUANTITATIVE DATA
>
> For quantitative data, a **frequency distribution** groups data into intervals called **classes**, and records the number of observations that falls into each class.
>
> A **cumulative frequency distribution** records the number of observations that falls below the upper limit of each class.

EXAMPLE 2.3

Using Table 2.11, how many of the houses sold in the $500,000 up to $600,000 range? How many of the houses sold for less than $600,000?

SOLUTION: From the frequency distribution, we find that 14 houses sold in the $500,000 up to $600,000 range. In order to find the number of houses that sold for less than $600,000, we use the cumulative frequency distribution. We readily observe that 29 of the houses sold for less than $600,000.

Suppose we want to compare house prices in Mission Viejo, California, to house prices in another region of the United States. Just as for qualitative data, when making comparisons between two quantitative data sets—especially if the data sets are of different sizes—a relative frequency distribution tends to provide more meaningful information as compared to a frequency distribution.

The second column of Table 2.12 shows the construction of a relative frequency distribution from the frequency distribution in Table 2.11. We take each class's frequency and divide by the total number of observations. For instance, we observed four houses that sold in the lowest range of $300,000 up to $400,000. We take the class frequency of 4 and divide by the sample size, 36, and obtain 0.11. Equivalently, we can say 11% of the houses sold in this price range. We make similar calculations for each class and note that when we sum the column of relative frequencies, we should get a value of one (or, due to rounding, a number very close to one).

TABLE 2.12 Constructing Relative Frequency Distributions for House-Price Data

Class (in $1000s)	Relative Frequency	Cumulative Relative Frequency
300 up to 400	4/36 = 0.11	0.11
400 up to 500	11/36 = 0.31	0.11 + 0.31 = 0.42
500 up to 600	14/36 = 0.39	0.11 + 0.31 + 0.39 = 0.81
600 up to 700	5/36 = 0.14	0.11 + 0.31 + 0.39 + 0.14 = 0.95
700 up to 800	2/36 = 0.06	0.11 + 0.31 + 0.39 + 0.17 + 0.06 ≈ 1
	Total = 1 (approximately)	

The last column of Table 2.12 shows cumulative relative frequency. The cumulative relative frequency for a particular class indicates the proportion or fraction of the observations that fall below the upper limit of that particular class. We can calculate the cumulative relative frequency of each class in one of two ways: (1) we can sum successive relative frequencies, or (2) we can divide each class's cumulative frequency by the sample size. In Table 2.12 we show the first way. The value for the first class is the same as the value for its relative frequency, that is, 0.11. For the second class we add 0.31 to 0.11 and obtain 0.42; this value indicates that 42% of the house prices were less than $500,000. We continue calculating cumulative relative frequencies in this manner until we reach the last class. Here, we get the value one, which means that 100% of the houses sold for less than $800,000.

RELATIVE AND CUMULATIVE RELATIVE FREQUENCY DISTRIBUTIONS

For quantitative data, a **relative frequency distribution** identifies the proportion (or the fraction) of values that fall into each class, that is,

$$\text{Class relative frequency} = \frac{\text{Class frequency}}{\text{Total number of values}}.$$

A **cumulative relative frequency distribution** records the proportion (or the fraction) of values that fall below the upper limit of each class.

EXAMPLE 2.4

Using Table 2.12, what percent of the houses sold for at least $500,000 but not more than $600,000? What percent of the houses sold for less than $600,000? What percent of the houses sold for $600,000 or more?

SOLUTION: The relative frequency distribution indicates that 39% of the houses sold for at least $500,000 but not more than $600,000. Further, the cumulative relative frequency distribution indicates that 81% of the houses sold for less than $600,000. This result implies that 19% sold for $600,000 or more.

Visualizing Frequency Distributions for Quantitative Data

LO **2.4**

Construct and interpret histograms, polygons, and ogives.

Histograms and **polygons** are graphical depictions of frequency and relative frequency distributions. The advantage of a visual display is that we can quickly see where most of the observations tend to cluster, as well as the spread and shape of the data. For instance, histograms and polygons may reveal whether or not the distribution is symmetrically shaped.

GRAPHICAL DISPLAY OF QUANTITATIVE DATA: HISTOGRAMS

A **histogram** is a series of rectangles where the width and height of each rectangle represent the class width and frequency (or relative frequency) of the respective class.

For quantitative data, a histogram is essentially the counterpart to the bar chart we use for qualitative data. When constructing a histogram, we mark off the class limits along the horizontal axis. The height of each bar represents either the frequency or relative frequency for each class. No gaps appear between the interval limits. Figure 2.6 shows a histogram for the frequency distribution of house prices shown in Table 2.7. A casual inspection of the histogram reveals that the selling price of houses in this sample ranged from $300,000 to $800,000; however, most house prices fell in the $500,000 to $600,000 range.

FIGURE 2.6 Frequency histogram for house prices

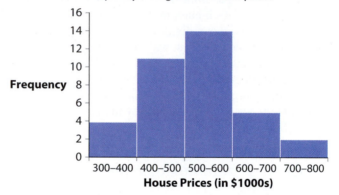

The only difference between a frequency histogram and a relative frequency histogram is the unit of measurement on the vertical axis. For the frequency histogram, we use the frequency of each class to represent the height; for the relative frequency histogram we use the proportion (or the fraction) of each class to represent the height. In a relative frequency histogram, the area of any rectangle is proportional to the relative frequency of observations falling into that class. Figure 2.7 shows the relative frequency histogram for house prices.

FIGURE 2.7 Relative frequency histogram for house prices

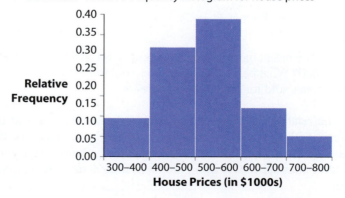

In general, the shape of most data distributions can be categorized as either symmetric or skewed. A symmetric distribution is one that is a mirror image of itself on both sides of its center. That is, the location of values below the center correspond to those above the center. As we will see in later chapters, the smoothed histogram for many data sets approximates a bell-shaped curve, which indicates the well-known normal distribution. If the distribution is not symmetric, then it is either positively skewed or negatively skewed, as shown in Figure 2.8.

FIGURE 2.8 Histograms with differing shapes

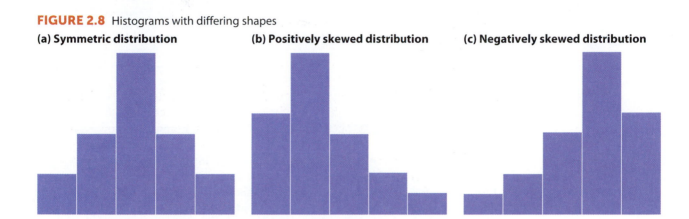

(a) Symmetric distribution **(b) Positively skewed distribution** **(c) Negatively skewed distribution**

The histogram in Figure 2.8(a) shows a symmetric distribution. If the edges were smoothed, this histogram would approximate the bell-shaped normal distribution. In Figure 2.8(b), the histogram shows a positively skewed, or skewed to the right, distribution with a long tail extending to the right. This attribute reflects the presence of a small number of relatively large values. Finally, the histogram in Figure 2.8(c) indicates a negatively skewed, or skewed to the left, distribution since it has a long tail extending off to the left. Data that follow a negatively skewed distribution have a small number of relatively small values.

Though not nearly as skewed as the data exhibited in Figure 2.8(b), the house-price data in Figure 2.7 exhibit slight positive skew. This is the result of a few, relatively expensive homes in the city. It is common for distributions of house prices and incomes to exhibit positive skewness.

Using Excel to Construct a Histogram

In general, Excel offers two different ways to construct a histogram, depending on whether we have access to the raw data or the frequency distribution. In either case, we need to have the classes clearly defined. We will first construct a histogram for house prices using the raw data from Table 2.1, and then show a histogram for the house prices from the frequency distribution from Table 2.7.

Constructing a Histogram from a Set of Raw Data

A. FILE Open the *Mission Viejo Houses* data (Table 2.1) from the text website into an Excel spreadsheet.

B. In a column next to the data, enter the values of the upper limits of each class, or in this example, 400, 500, 600, 700, and 800; label this column "Class Limits." The reason for these entries is explained in the next step. The house-price data and the class limits (as well as the resulting frequency distribution and histogram) are shown in Figure 2.9.

FIGURE 2.9 Constructing a histogram from raw data with Excel

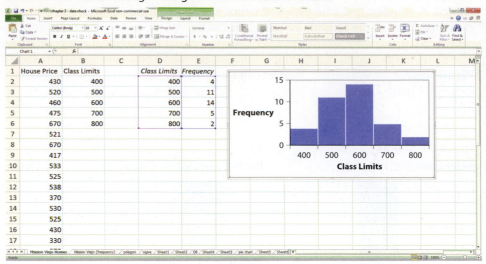

C. From the menu choose **Data** > **Data Analysis** > **Histogram** > **OK**. (*Note:* If you do not see the **Data Analysis** option under **Data**, you must *add-in* this option. Go to the **Office Button** and choose **Excel Options** > **Add-Ins**. Then choose the box to the left of **Analysis Toolpak**, choose **Go**, and then click **OK**. If you have installed this option properly, you should now see **Data Analysis** under **Data**.)

D. In the *Histogram* dialog box (see Figure 2.10), under *Input Range*, select the data. Excel uses the term "bins" for the class limits. If we leave the *Bin Range* box empty, Excel creates evenly distributed intervals using the minimum and maximum values of the input range as end points. This methodology is rarely satisfactory. In order to construct a histogram that is more informative, we use the upper limit of each class as the bin values. Under *Bin Range*, we select the *Class Limits* data. (Check the *Labels* box if you have included the names House Price and Class Limits as part of the selection.) Under *Output Options* we choose **Chart Output**, then click **OK**.

FIGURE 2.10 Excel's dialog box for a histogram

E. Since Excel leaves spaces between the rectangles, we right-click on any of the rectangles, choose **Format Data Series** and change the *Gap Width* to 0, then choose **Close**. In the event that the given class limits do not include all the data points, Excel automatically adds another interval labeled "More" to the resulting frequency distribution and histogram. Since we observe zero observations in this interval for this example, we delete this interval for expositional purposes. Excel also defines its classes by excluding the value of the lower limit and including the value of the upper class limit for each interval. For example, if the value 400 appeared in the house-price data, Excel would have accounted for this observation in the first class. If any upper-limit value appeared in the house-price data, we would have adjusted the class limits in the *Bin Range* to 399, 499, etc., so that Excel's frequency distribution and histogram would be consistent with those that we constructed in Table 2.11 and Figure 2.6. Further formatting regarding colors, axes, grids, etc. can be done by selecting **Layout** from the menu.

Constructing a Histogram from a Frequency Distribution

Suppose we do not have the raw data for house prices, but we have the frequency distribution reported in Table 2.7.

A. **FILE** Open the *Mission Viejo (frequency)* data (Table 2.7) from the text website into an Excel spreadsheet.

B. Select the classes and respective frequencies. See Figure 2.11 below.

C. From the menu choose **Insert** > **Column** > **2-D Column**. From the options given, choose the graph on the top left.

D. In order to remove the spaces between the rectangles, right-click on any of the rectangles, choose **Format Data Series** and change the *Gap Width* to 0, then choose **Close**.

E. Further formatting regarding colors, axes, grids, etc. can be done by selecting **Layout** from the menu.

FIGURE 2.11 Constructing a histogram from a frequency distribution with Excel

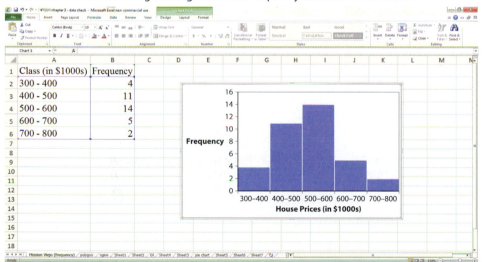

A **polygon** provides another convenient way of depicting a frequency distribution. It too gives a general idea of the shape of a distribution. In order to construct a polygon, we plot the midpoint of each interval on the horizontal axis and the frequency (or relative frequency) for that interval on the vertical axis. We then connect neighboring points with a straight line.

> ### GRAPHICAL DISPLAY OF QUANTITATIVE DATA: POLYGONS
>
> A **polygon** connects a series of neighboring points where each point represents the midpoint of a particular class and its associated frequency or relative frequency.

If we choose to construct a polygon for the house-price data, we first calculate the midpoint of each interval; thus, the midpoint for the first interval is $\frac{300 + 400}{2} = 350$ and similarly, the midpoints for the remaining intervals are 450, 550, 650, and 750. We treat each midpoint as the x-coordinate and the respective frequency (or relative frequency) as the y-coordinate. After plotting the points, we connect neighboring points. In order to close off the graph at each end, we add one interval below the lowest interval (so, 200 up to 300 with midpoint 250) and one interval above the highest interval (so, 800 up to 900 with midpoint 850) and assign each of these classes zero frequencies. Table 2.13 shows the relevant coordinates for plotting a polygon using the house-price data. We chose to use relative frequency to represent the y-coordinate.

TABLE 2.13 Coordinates for Plotting Relative Frequency Polygon

Classes	x-coordinate (midpoints)	y-coordinate (relative frequency)
(Lower end)	250	0
300–400	350	0.11
400–500	450	0.31
500–600	550	0.39
600–700	650	0.14
700–800	750	0.06
(Upper end)	850	0

Figure 2.12 plots a relative frequency polygon for the house-price data. Here the distribution appears to approximate the bell-shaped distribution discussed earlier. Only a careful inspection of the right tail suggests that the data are slightly positively skewed.

FIGURE 2.12 Polygon for the house-price data

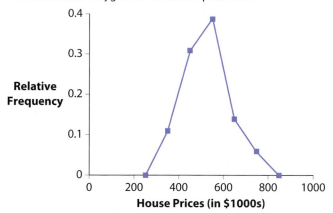

Using Excel to Construct a Polygon

A. To construct a polygon, input the appropriate x- and y-coordinates into an Excel spreadsheet. We use the data from Table 2.13.

B. Select the x- and the y-coordinates (as shown in Figure 2.13) and choose **Insert > Scatter**. Select the box on the middle right.

C. Further formatting regarding colors, axes, grids, etc. can be done by selecting **Layout** from the menu.

FIGURE 2.13 Constructing a polygon with Excel

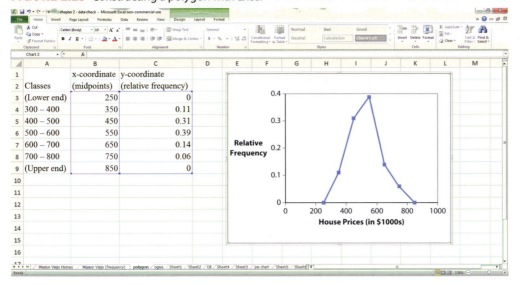

In many instances, we might want to convey information by plotting an ogive (pronounced "ojive").

GRAPHICAL DISPLAY OF QUANTITATIVE DATA: OGIVES

An **ogive** is a graph that plots the cumulative frequency or the cumulative relative frequency of each class against the upper limit of the corresponding class.

An ogive differs from a polygon in that we use the upper limit of each class as the x-coordinate and the cumulative frequency or cumulative relative frequency of the corresponding class as the y-coordinate. After plotting the points, we connect neighboring points. Lastly, we close the ogive only at the lower end by intersecting the x-axis at the lower limit of the first class. Table 2.14 shows the relevant coordinates for plotting an ogive using the house-price data. We choose to use cumulative relative frequency as the y-coordinate. The use of cumulative frequency would not change the shape of the ogive, just the unit of measurement on the y-axis.

TABLE 2.14 Coordinates for an Ogive

Classes	x-coordinate (upper limit)	y-coordinate (cumulative relative frequency)
(Lower end)	300	0
300–400	400	0.11
400–500	500	0.42
500–600	600	0.81
600–700	700	0.95
700–800	800	1

Figure 2.14 plots the ogive for the house-price data. In general, we can use an ogive to approximate the proportion of values that are less than a specified value on the horizontal axis. Consider an application to the house-price data in Example 2.5.

FIGURE 2.14 Ogive for the house-price data

EXAMPLE 2.5

Using Figure 2.14, approximate the percentage of houses that sold for less than $550,000.

SOLUTION: Draw a vertical line that starts at 550 and intersects the ogive. Then follow the line to the vertical axis and read the value. You can conclude that approximately 60% of the houses sold for less than $550,000.

Using Excel to Construct an Ogive

A. To construct an ogive, input the appropriate x- and the y-coordinates into an Excel spreadsheet. We use the data from Table 2.14.

B. Select the x- and the y-coordinates (as shown in Figure 2.15) and choose **Insert > Scatter**. Select the box on the middle right.

C. Further formatting regarding colors, axes, grids, etc. can be done by selecting **Layout** from the menu.

FIGURE 2.15 Constructing an ogive with Excel

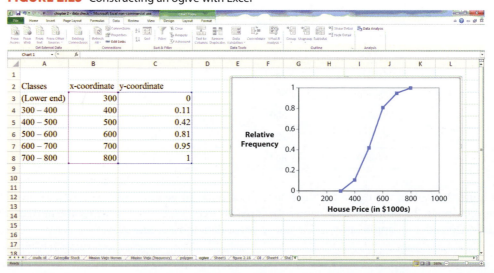

SYNOPSIS OF INTRODUCTORY CASE

During June 2010, Matthew Edwards reviewed the selling prices of 36 home sales in Mission Viejo, California for a client from Seattle, Washington. After constructing various frequency distributions, he is able to make the following summary conclusions. House prices ranged from $300,000 up to $800,000 over this time period. Most of the houses (14) sold in the $500,000 up to $600,000 range, which is, more or less, the client's price range. Twenty-nine of the houses sold for less than $600,000. Converting the data into percentages so the client can make comparisons with home sales in the Seattle area, Matthew found that 39% of the houses sold for $500,000 up to $600,000. Further, 81% of the houses sold for less than $600,000, which implies that 19% sold for $600,000 or more.

EXERCISES 2.2

Concepts

13. Consider the following data set:

4	10	8	7	6	10	11	14	13	14
3	9	8	5	7	6	10	3	11	11
8	8	4	5	5	12	12	3	8	8

a. Construct a frequency distribution using classes of 3 up to 5, 5 up to 7, etc.

b. Construct relative frequency, cumulative frequency, and cumulative relative frequency distributions.

c. How many of the observations are at least 7 but less than 9? How many of the observations are less than 9?

d. What percent of the observations are at least 7 but less than 9? What percent of the observations are less than 9?

e. Graph a relative frequency histogram.

f. Graph an ogive.

14. Consider the following data set:

4	10	8	7	6	10	11	14	13	14
3	9	8	5	7	6	10	3	11	11
8	8	4	5	5	12	12	3	8	8
10	−9	28	14	−5	9	11	5	8	−3
33	−4	2	3	22	25	5	29	26	0
−8	−5	0	15	−4	35	21	15	19	23
4	6	−2	12	24	36	15	3	−5	2

a. Construct a frequency distribution using classes of −10 up to 0, 0 up to 10, etc. How many of the observations are at least 10 but less than 20?

b. Construct a relative frequency distribution and a cumulative relative frequency distribution. What percent of the observations are at least 10 but less than 20? What percent of the observations are less than 20?

c. Graph a relative frequency polygon. Is the distribution symmetric? If not, then how is it skewed?

15. Consider the following frequency distribution:

Class	Frequency
10 up to 20	12
20 up to 30	15
30 up to 40	25
40 up to 50	4

a. Construct a relative frequency distribution. Graph a relative frequency histogram.

b. Construct a cumulative frequency distribution and a cumulative relative frequency distribution.

c. What percent of the observations are at least 30 but less than 40? What percent of the observations are less than 40?

16. Consider the following frequency distribution:

Class	Frequency
1000 up to 1100	2
1100 up to 1200	7
1200 up to 1300	3
1300 up to 1400	4

   a. Construct a relative frequency distribution. What percent of the observations are at least 1100 but less than 1200?
   b. Construct a cumulative frequency distribution and a cumulative relative frequency distribution. How many of the observations are less than 1300?
   c. Graph a frequency histogram.

17. Consider the following cumulative frequency distribution:

Class	Cumulative Frequency
15 up to 25	30
25 up to 35	50
35 up to 45	120
45 up to 55	130

   a. Construct a frequency distribution. How many observations are at least 35 but less than 45?
   b. Graph a frequency histogram.
   c. What percent of the observations are less than 45?

18. Consider the following relative frequency distribution:

Class	Relative Frequency
−20 up to −10	0.04
−10 up to 0	0.28
0 up to 10	0.26
10 up to 20	0.22
20 up to 30	0.20

   a. Suppose this relative frequency distribution is based on a sample of 50 observations. Construct a frequency distribution. How many of the observations are at least −10 but less than 0?
   b. Construct a cumulative frequency distribution. How many of the observations are less than 20?
   c. Graph a relative frequency polygon.

19. Consider the following cumulative relative frequency distribution.

Class	Cumulative Relative Frequency
150 up to 200	0.10
200 up to 250	0.35
250 up to 300	0.70
300 up to 350	1

   a. Construct a relative frequency distribution. What percent of the observations are at least 250 but less than 300?
   b. Graph an ogive.

Applications

20. *Kiplinger's* (August 2007) lists the assets (in billions of $) for the 20 largest stock mutual funds (ranked by size) as follows:

$99.8	49.7	86.3	109.2	56.9
88.2	44.1	58.8	176.7	49.9
61.4	128.8	53.6	95.2	92.5
55.0	96.5	45.3	73.0	70.9

   a. Construct a frequency distribution using classes of 40 up to 70, 70 up to 100, etc.
   b. Construct the relative frequency distribution, the cumulative frequency distribution, and the relative cumulative frequency distribution.
   c. How many of the funds had assets of at least $100 but less than $130 (in billions)? How many of the funds had assets less than $160 (in billions)?
   d. What percent of the funds had assets of at least $70 but less than $100 (in billions)? What percent of the funds had assets less than $130 (in billions)?
   e. Construct a histogram. Comment on the shape of the distribution.

21. The numbers of texts sent by 25 13-year-olds over the past month were as follows:

630	516	892	643	627	510	937	909	654
817	760	715	605	975	888	912	952	701
744	793	852	504	562	670	685		

   a. Construct a frequency distribution using classes of 500 up to 600, 600 up to 700, etc.
   b. Construct the relative frequency distribution, the cumulative frequency distribution and the relative cumulative frequency distribution.
   c. How many of the 13-year-olds sent at least 600 but less than 700 texts? How many sent less than 800 texts?
   d. What percent of the 13-year-olds sent at least 500 but less than 600 texts? What percent of the 13-year-olds sent less than 700 texts?
   e. Construct a polygon. Comment on the shape of the distribution.

22. AccuWeather.com listed the following high temperatures (in degrees Fahrenheit) for 33 European cities on July 21, 2010.

75	92	81	85	90	73	94	95	81	64	85
62	84	85	81	86	90	79	74	90	91	95
88	87	81	73	76	86	90	83	75	92	83

   a. Construct a frequency distribution using classes of 60 up to 70, 70 up to 80, etc.
   b. Construct the relative frequency, the cumulative frequency, and the relative cumulative frequency distributions.
   c. How many of the cities had high temperatures less than 80°?

d. What percent of the cities had high temperatures of at least 80° but less than 90°? What percent of the cities had high temperatures less 90°?

e. Construct a polygon. Comment on the shape of the distribution.

23. **FILE** The following table lists a portion of the average math SAT scores for each state for the year 2009. The complete data set can be found on the text website and is labeled *Math SAT 2009*.

State	SAT
Alabama	552
Alaska	516
⋮	⋮
Wyoming	568

SOURCE: www.collegeboard.com.

a. Construct a frequency distribution using classes of 450 to 500, 501 to 550, etc. How many of the states had scores between 551 and 600?

b. Construct the relative frequency, the cumulative frequency, and the relative cumulative frequency distributions.

c. How many of the states had math SAT scores of 550 or less?

d. What percent of the states had math SAT scores between 551 and 600? What percent of the states had mean SAT scores of 550 or less?

e. Construct a histogram. Comment on the shape of the distribution.

24. Fifty cities provided information on vacancy rates (in percent) in local apartments in the following frequency distribution.

Vacancy Rate (in percent)	Frequency
0 up to 3	5
3 up to 6	10
6 up to 9	20
9 up to 12	10
12 up to 15	5

a. Construct the corresponding relative frequency distribution, cumulative frequency distribution, and cumulative relative frequency distribution.

b. How many of the cities had a vacancy rate less than 12%? What percent of the cities had a vacancy rate of at least 6% but less than 9%? What percent of the cities had a vacancy rate of less than 9%?

c. Construct a histogram. Comment on the shape of the distribution.

25. The following relative frequency distribution summarizes the ages of women who had a child in the last year.

Ages	Relative Frequency
15 up to 20	0.10
20 up to 25	0.25
25 up to 30	0.28
30 up to 35	0.24
35 up to 40	0.11
40 up to 45	0.02

SOURCE: *The Statistical Abstract of the United States, 2010.*

a. Assume the relative frequency distribution is based on a sampling of 2,000 women. Construct the corresponding frequency distribution, cumulative frequency distribution, and cumulative relative frequency distribution.

b. What percent of the women were at least 25 but less than 30 years old? What percent of the women were younger than 35 years old?

c. Construct a relative frequency polygon. Comment on the shape of the distribution.

d. Construct an ogive. Using the graph, approximate the age of the middle 50% of the distribution.

26. The manager of a nightclub near a local university recorded the ages of the last 100 guests in the following cumulative frequency distribution.

Ages	Cumulative Frequency
18 up to 22	45
22 up to 26	70
26 up to 30	85
30 up to 34	96
34 up to 38	100

a. Construct the corresponding frequency, relative frequency, and cumulative relative frequency distributions.

b. How many of the guests were at least 26 but less than 30 years old? What percent of the guests were at least 22 but less than 26 years old? What percent of the guests were younger than 34 years old? What percent were 34 years or older?

c. Construct a histogram. Comment on the shape of the distribution.

2.3 Stem-and-Leaf Diagrams

John Tukey (1915–2000), a well-known statistician, provided another visual method for displaying quantitative data. A **stem-and-leaf diagram** is often a preliminary step when analyzing a data set. It is useful in that it gives an overall picture of where the data are centered and how the data are dispersed from the center.

LO **2.5**

Construct and interpret a stem-and-leaf diagram.

A **stem-and-leaf diagram** is constructed by separating each value of a data set into two parts: a *stem*, which consists of the leftmost digits, and a *leaf*, which consists of the last digit.

The best way to explain a stem-and-leaf diagram is to show an example.

EXAMPLE 2.6

Table 2.15 shows the ages of the 25 wealthiest people in the world; these data labeled *Wealthiest People* are also available on the text website. Construct and interpret a stem-and-leaf diagram.

TABLE 2.15 Wealthiest People in the World, 2010

FILE

Name	Age	Name	Age
Carlos Slim Helu	70	Li Ka-shing	81
William Gates III	54	Jim Walton	62
Warren Buffet	79	Alice Walton	60
Mukesh Ambani	52	Liliane Bettencourt	87
Lakshmi Mittal	59	S. Robson Walton	66
Lawrence Ellison	65	Prince Alwaleed Alsaud	54
Bernard Arnault	61	David Thomson	52
Eike Batista	53	Michael Otto	66
Amancio Ortega	74	Lee Shau Kee	82
Karl Albrecht	90	Michael Bloomberg	68
Ingvar Kamprad	83	Sergey Brin	36
Christy Walton	55	Charles Koch	74
Stefan Persson	62		

Source: www.forbes.com/lists/2010.

SOLUTION: For each age we first decide that the number in the tens spot will denote the stem, thus leaving the number in the ones spot as the leaf. We then identify the lowest and highest values in the data set. Sergey Brin is the youngest member of this group at 36 years of age (stem: 3, leaf: 6) and Karl Albrecht is the oldest at 90 years of age (stem: 9, leaf: 0). These values give us the first and last values in the stem. This means our stems will be 3, 4, 5, 6, 7, 8, and 9, as shown in Panel A of Table 2.16.

TABLE 2.16 Constructing a Stem-and-Leaf Diagram for Example 2.6

Panel A		Panel B		Panel C	
Stem	**Leaf**	**Stem**	**Leaf**	**Stem**	**Leaf**
3		3	6	3	6
4		4		4	
5		5	4 2 9 3 5 4 2	5	2 2 3 4 4 5 9
6		6	5 1 2 2 0 6 6 8	6	0 1 2 2 5 6 6 8
7	0	7	0 9 4 4	7	0 4 4 9
8		8	3 1 7 2	8	1 2 3 7
9		9	0	9	0

We then begin with the wealthiest man in the world, Carlos Slim Helu, whose age of 70 gives us a stem of 7 and a leaf of 0. We place a 0 in the row corresponding to a stem of 7, as shown in Panel A of the table. We continue this process with all the other ages and obtain the values in Panel B. Finally, in Panel C we arrange each individual leaf row in ascending order. Panel C is the actual stem-and-leaf display.

The stem-and-leaf diagram (Panel C) presents the original 25 values in a more organized form. From the diagram we can readily observe that the ages range from 36 to 90. Wealthy individuals in their sixties make up the greatest group in the sample with eight members, while those in their fifties place a close second, accounting for seven members. We also note that the distribution is not perfectly symmetric. A stem-and-leaf diagram is similar to a histogram turned on its side with the added benefit of retaining the original values.

Concepts

27. Consider the following data set:

5.4	4.6	3.5	2.8	2.6	5.5	5.5	2.3	3.2	4.2
4.0	3.0	3.6	4.5	4.7	4.2	3.3	3.2	4.2	3.4

Construct a stem-and-leaf diagram. Is the distribution symmetric? Explain.

28. Consider the following data set:

−64	−52	−73	−82	−85	−80	−79	−65	−50	−71
−80	−85	−75	−65	−77	−87	−72	−83	−73	−80

Construct a stem-and-leaf diagram. Is the distribution symmetric? Explain.

Applications

29. A sample of patients arriving at Overbrook Hospital's emergency room recorded the following body temperature readings over the weekend:

100.4	99.6	101.5	99.8	102.1	101.2	102.3	101.2	102.2	102.4
101.6	101.5	99.7	102.0	101.0	102.5	100.5	101.3	101.2	102.2

Construct and interpret a stem-and-leaf diagram.

30. Suppose the following high temperatures were recorded for major cities in the contiguous United States for a day in July.

84	92	96	91	96	94	93	82	81	76
90	95	84	90	84	98	94	90	83	78
88	96	106	78	92	98	91	84	80	94
94	93	107	87	77	99	94	73	74	92

Construct and interpret a stem-and-leaf diagram.

31. A police officer is concerned with excessive speeds on a portion of Interstate 90 with a posted speed limit of 65 miles per hour. Using his radar gun, he records the following speeds for 25 cars and trucks:

66	72	73	82	80	81	79	65	70	71
80	75	75	65	67	67	72	73	73	80
81	78	71	70	70					

Construct a stem-and-leaf diagram. Are the officer's concerns warranted?

32. Spain was the winner of the 2010 World Cup, beating the Netherlands by a score of 1–0. The ages of the players from both teams were as follows:

Spain									
29	25	23	30	32	25	29	30	26	29
21	28	24	21	27	22	25	21	23	24
Netherlands									
27	22	26	30	35	33	29	25	27	25
35	27	27	26	23	25	23	24	26	39

Construct a stem-and-leaf diagram for each country. Comment on similarities and differences between the two data sets.

2.4 Scatterplots

All of the tabular and graphical tools presented thus far have focused on describing one variable. However, in many instances we are interested in the relationship between two variables. People in virtually every quantitative discipline examine

LO **2.6**

Construct and interpret a scatterplot.

how one variable may systematically influence another variable. Consider, for instance, how

- Incomes vary with education.
- Sales vary with advertising expenditures.
- Stock prices vary with corporate profits.
- Crop yields vary with the use of fertilizer.
- Cholesterol levels vary with dietary intake.
- Weight varies with exercise.

SCATTERPLOTS

A **scatterplot** is a graphical tool that helps in determining whether or not two variables are related in some systematic way. Each point in the diagram represents a pair of known or observed values of the two variables.

When constructing a scatterplot, we generally refer to one of the variables as x and represent it on the horizontal axis and the other variable as y and represent it on the vertical axis. We then plot each pairing: (x_1, y_1), (x_2, y_2), etc. Once the data are plotted, the graph may reveal that

- A linear relationship exists between the two variables;
- A curvilinear relationship exists between the two variables; or
- No relationship exists between the two variables.

For example, Figure 2.16(a) shows points on a scatterplot clustered together in a straight, upward-sloping line; we infer that the two variables have a positive linear relationship. Part (b) depicts a positive curvilinear relationship; as x increases, y tends to increase at an increasing rate. The points in part (c) are scattered with no apparent pattern; thus, there is no relationship between the two variables.

FIGURE 2.16 Scatterplots depicting relationships between two variables

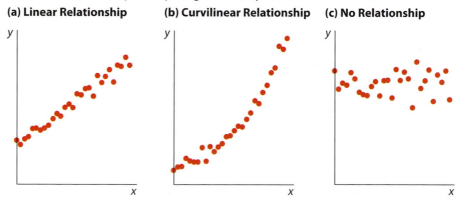

(a) Linear Relationship **(b) Curvilinear Relationship** **(c) No Relationship**

In order to illustrate a scatterplot, consider the following example.

EXAMPLE 2.7

A social scientist wants to analyze the relationship between educational attainment and salary. He collects the following data, where "education" refers to years of higher education and "income" is the individual's annual salary in thousands of dollars. Construct and interpret a scatterplot.

Individual	Education	Income
1	3	45
2	4	56
3	6	85
4	2	35
5	5	55
6	4	48
7	8	100
8	0	38

SOLUTION: We let x and y denote education and income, respectively. We plot the first individual's pairing as (3, 45), the second individual's pairing as (4, 56), and so on. The graph should resemble Figure 2.17.

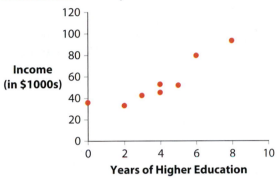

FIGURE 2.17 Scatterplot of education versus income

As expected, we observe a positive relationship between the two variables; that is, when education increases, income tends to increase.

Using Excel to Construct a Scatterplot

A. To construct a scatterplot, input the appropriate x- and y-coordinates into an Excel spreadsheet. Here we use the data from Example 2.7.

B. As shown in Figure 2.18, select the x- and y-coordinates and choose **Insert > Scatter**. Select the graph on the top left.

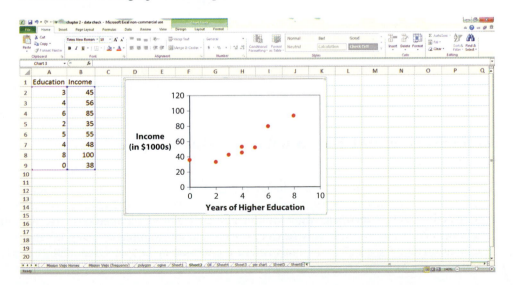

FIGURE 2.18
Constructing a scatterplot with Excel

EXERCISES 2.4

Concepts

33. Construct a scatterplot with the following data. Categorize the relationship between x and y.

x	3	7	12	5	6
y	22	10	5	14	12

34. Construct a scatterplot with the following data. Does a linear relationship exist between x and y?

x	10	4	6	3	7
y	3	2	6	6	4

35. Construct a scatterplot with the following data. Categorize the relationship between x and y.

x	1	2	3	4	5	6	7	8
y	22	20	18	10	5	4	3	2

Applications

36. A statistics instructor wants to examine whether a relationship exists between the hours a student spends studying for the final exam (Hours) and a student's grade on the final exam (Grade). She takes a sample of 8 students.

Hours	8	2	3	8	10	15	25	5
Grade	75	47	50	80	85	88	93	55

Construct a scatterplot. What conclusions can you draw from the scatterplot?

37. A recent study offers evidence that the more weight a woman gains during pregnancy, the higher the risk of having a high-birth-weight baby, defined as 8 pounds, 13 ounces, or 4 kilograms (*The Wall Street Journal*, August 5, 2010). High-birth-weight babies are more likely to be obese in adulthood. The weight gain (in kilograms) of seven mothers and the birth weight of their newborns (in kilograms) is recorded below.

Mother's Weight Gain	Newborn's Birth Weight
18	4.0
7	2.5
8	3.0
22	4.5
21	4.0
9	3.5
8	3.0
10	3.5

Construct a scatterplot. Do the results support the findings of the study?

38. In order to diversify risk, investors are often encouraged to invest in assets whose returns have either a negative relationship or no relationship. The annual return data on two assets is shown below.

Return A	Return B
−20%	8%
−5	5
18	−1
15	−2
−12	2

Construct a scatterplot. For diversity purposes, would the investor be wise to include these assets in her portfolio? Explain.

39. In an attempt to determine whether a relationship exists between the price of a home and the number of days it takes to sell the home, a real estate agent collects data on the recent sales of eight homes.

Price (in $1,000s)	Days to Sell Home
265	136
225	125
160	120
325	140
430	145
515	150
180	122
423	145

Construct a scatterplot. What can the realtor conclude?

WRITING WITH STATISTICS

The tabular and graphical tools introduced in this chapter are the starting point for most studies and reports that involve statistics. They can help you organize data so you can see patterns and trends in the data, which can then be analyzed by the methods described in later chapters of this book. In this section, we present an example of using tabular and graphical methods in a sample report. Each of the remaining chapters contains a sample report incorporating the concepts developed in that respective chapter.

Camilla Walford is a newly hired journalist for a national newspaper. One of her first tasks is to analyze gas prices in the United States during the week of the Fourth of July holiday. She collects average gas prices for the 48 contiguous states and the District of Columbia (DC), a portion of which is shown in Table 2.17. The complete data set can be found on the text website and is labeled **Gas Prices, Summer 2010**.

TABLE 2.17 U.S. Gas Prices, July 2, 2010

FILE

State	Average Price ($ per gallon)
Alabama	$2.59
Arkansas	2.60
⋮	⋮
Wyoming	2.77

SOURCE: *AAA's Daily Fuel Gauge Report*, July 2, 2010.

Camilla wants to use the sample information to:

1. Construct frequency distributions to summarize the data.
2. Make summary statements concerning gas prices.
3. Convey the information from the distributions into graphical form.

Sample Report—Gas Prices across the United States

Historically, in the United States, many people choose to take some time off during the Fourth of July holiday period and travel to the beach, the lake, or the mountains. The roads tend to be heavily traveled, making the cost of gas a concern. The following report provides an analysis of gas prices across the nation over this holiday period.

The analysis focuses on the average gas price for the 48 contiguous states and the District of Columbia (henceforth, referenced as 49 states for ease of exposition). The range of gas prices is from a low of $2.52 per gallon (South Carolina) to a high of $3.15 per gallon (California). To find out how gas prices are distributed between these extremes, the data have been organized into several frequency distributions as shown in Table 2.A. For instance, most states (17 of the 49) have an average gas price from $2.70 up to $2.80 per gallon. Equivalently, looking at the relative frequency column, 35% of the states have an average price in this range. The cumulative frequency column indicates that 35 states (out of a total of 49) have an average price less than $2.80 per gallon. Finally, the last column shows that the average price in 72% of the states (approximately three-quarters of the sample) is less than $2.80 per gallon.

TABLE 2.A Frequency Distributions for Gas Prices in the United States, July 2, 2010

Average Price ($ per gallon)	Frequency	Relative Frequency	Cumulative Frequency	Cumulative Relative Frequency
2.50 up to 2.60	5	0.10	5	0.10
2.60 up to 2.70	13	0.27	18	0.37
2.70 up to 2.80	17	0.35	35	0.72
2.80 up to 2.90	8	0.16	43	0.88
2.90 up to 3.00	4	0.08	47	0.96
3.00 up to 3.10	1	0.02	48	0.98
3.10 up to 3.20	1	0.02	49	1.00
	Sample Size = 49			

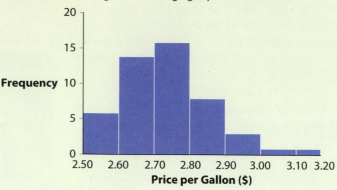

FIGURE 2.A Histogram of average gas prices nationwide

Figure 2.A shows a histogram for gas prices, which graphs the frequency distribution from Table 2.A. This graph reinforces the fact that the average price of gas nationwide is between $2.60 and $2.90 per gallon. Moreover, gas prices are positively skewed since the distribution runs off to the right; only two states (California and Washington) have gas prices that are more than $3.00 per gallon.

Another useful visual representation of the data is an ogive, shown in Figure 2.B. The ogive graphs the cumulative relative frequency distribution from Table 2.A. The ogive is useful for approximating the "middle" price. If we draw a horizontal line on the ogive at the 0.5 relative frequency mark, it intersects the plot at a point corresponding on the horizontal axis to a "middle price" of approximately $2.75. This indicates that gas stations in approximately half of the states charged below this price and half charged above it.

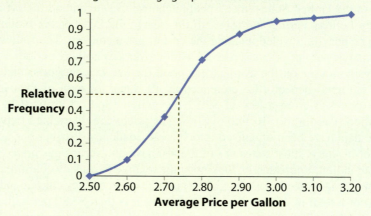

FIGURE 2.B Ogive of average gas prices nationwide

Conceptual Review

LO **2.1**   **Summarize qualitative data by forming frequency distributions.**

For **qualitative data,** a **frequency distribution** groups data into categories and records the number of observations that fall into each category. A **relative frequency distribution** shows the proportion (or the fraction) of observations in each category.

LO **2.2**   **Construct and interpret pie charts and bar charts.**

Graphically, we can show a frequency distribution for qualitative data by constructing a **pie chart** or a **bar chart**. A pie chart is a segmented circle that clearly portrays the sectors of some qualitative variable. A bar chart depicts the frequency or the relative frequency of each category as a bar rising vertically from the horizontal axis.

LO 2.3 Summarize quantitative data by forming frequency distributions.

For quantitative data, a **frequency distribution** groups data into intervals called **classes**, and records the number of observations that fall into each class. A **cumulative frequency distribution** records the number of observations that fall below the upper limit of each class. A **relative frequency distribution** identifies the proportion (or the fraction) of observations that fall into each class. A **cumulative relative frequency distribution** shows the proportion (or the fraction) of observations that fall below the upper limit of each class.

LO 2.4 Construct and interpret histograms, polygons, and ogives.

Histograms and **polygons** are graphical representations of frequency distributions. A casual inspection of these graphs reveals where most of the observations tend to cluster, as well as the general shape and spread of the data. An **ogive** is a graphical representation of a cumulative frequency distribution.

LO 2.5 Construct and interpret a stem-and-leaf diagram.

A **stem-and-leaf diagram** is another visual method of displaying quantitative data. It is constructed by separating each value of a data set into a *stem*, which consists of the leftmost digits, and a *leaf*, which consists of the last digit. Like histograms and polygons, stem-and-leaf diagrams give an overall picture of where the data are centered and how the data are dispersed from the center.

LO 2.6 Construct and interpret a scatterplot.

A **scatterplot** is a graphical tool that helps in determining whether or not two variables are related in some systematic way. Each point in the diagram represents a pair of observed values of the two variables.

Additional Exercises and Case Studies

Exercises

40. A 2003 survey by the Centers for Disease Control and Prevention concluded that smoking is forbidden in nearly 75% of U.S. households (*Boston Globe*, May 25, 2007). The survey gathered responses from at least 900 households in each state. When residents of Utah were asked whether or not smoking was allowed in their households, a representative sample of responses was as follows:

No	No	No	No	No	No	Yes	No	No	No
No	Yes	No	No	No	No	No	No	No	No

When a similar survey was taken in Kentucky, a representative sample of responses was as follows:

No	No	Yes	No	Yes	No	Yes	Yes	No	No
No	Yes	Yes	No	Yes	No	No	Yes	Yes	No

a. Construct a relative frequency distribution that summarizes the responses of residents from Utah and Kentucky. Comment on the results.

b. Construct a bar chart that summarizes the results for each state.

41. Patrons at a local restaurant were asked to rate their recent experience at the restaurant with respect to its advertised atmosphere of upbeat, comfortable, and clean. Possible responses included Outstanding, Good, OK, and Please Get Help. The following table shows the responses of 28 patrons:

Please Get Help	OK	Please Get Help	Please Get Help
OK	OK	Please Get Help	Please Get Help
Please Get Help	OK	Please Get Help	Good
Please Get Help	Good	Good	Good
Please Get Help	OK	Please Get Help	OK
Good	Good	Please Get Help	Good
Please Get Help	OK	Please Get Help	Good

a. Construct a relative frequency distribution that summarizes the responses of the patrons. Briefly summarize your findings. What recommendations would you make to the owner of the restaurant?

b. Construct a pie chart and a bar chart for these data.

42. A survey conducted by CBS News asked parents about the professions they would want their children to pursue. The results are summarized in the following table.

Profession	Parents' Preference
Doctor, banker, lawyer, or president	65%
Internet mogul	13
Humanitarian-aid worker	6
Athlete	9
Movie star, rock star	2
Other	5

Source: *Vanity Fair*, December 2009.

a. Construct a bar chart and a pie chart for these data.

b. How many parents wanted their children to become athletes if the above results were based on 550 responses?

43. The one-year return (in %) for 24 mutual funds is as follows:

−14.5	−5.0	−3.7	2.5	−7.9	−11.2
4.8	−16.8	9.0	6.5	8.2	5.3
−12.2	15.9	18.2	25.4	3.4	−1.4
5.5	−4.2	−0.5	6.0	−2.4	10.5

a. Construct a frequency distribution using classes of −20 up to −10, −10 up to 0, etc.

b. Construct the relative frequency, the cumulative frequency, and the relative cumulative frequency distributions.

c. How many of the funds had returns of at least 0% but less than 10%? How many of the funds had returns of 10% or more?

d. What percent of the funds had returns of at least 10% but less than 20%? What percent of the funds had returns less than 20%?

44. *The Statistical Abstract of the United States, 2010* provided the following frequency distribution of the number of people who live below the poverty level by region.

Region	Number of People (in 1,000s)
Northeast	6,166
Midwest	7,237
South	15,501
West	8,372

a. Construct a relative frequency distribution. What percent of people who live below the poverty level live in the Midwest?

b. Construct a pie chart and a bar chart for these data.

45. *Money* magazine (January 2007) reported that an average of 77 million adults in the U.S. make financial resolutions at the beginning of a new year. Consider the following frequency distribution, which reports the top financial resolutions of 1,026 Americans (Source: MONEY/ICR poll conducted November 8–12, 2006).

Financial Resolution	Frequency
Saving more	328
Paying down debt	257
Making more income	154
Spending less	133
Investing more	103
Saving for a large purchase	41
Don't know	10

a. Construct a relative frequency distribution for these data. What percent of the sample indicated that paying down debt was their top financial resolution?

b. Construct a bar chart.

46. A recent poll of 3,057 individuals asked: "What's the longest vacation you plan to take this summer?" The following relative frequency distribution summarizes the results.

Response	Relative Frequency
A few days	21%
A few long weekends	18%
One week	36%
Two weeks	25%

a. Construct a frequency distribution of these data. How many people are going to take a one-week vacation this summer?

b. Construct a pie chart.

47. A survey conducted by CBS News asked 1,026 respondents: "What would you do with an unexpected tax refund?" The responses are summarized in the following table.

Pay off debts	47%
Put it in the bank	30%
Spend it	11%
I never get a refund	10%
Other	2%

Source: *Vanity Fair*, June 2010.

a. Construct a bar chart for these data.

b. How many people will spend the tax refund?

48. The following table lists the U.S. sales (in $ millions) of prescription drugs used to treat seizure disorders.

Drug	Sales in 2006
Topamax	$1,825.4
Lamictal	1,684.3
Depakote	770.4
Lyrica	727.8
Keppra	710.5

Source: *The Wall Street Journal*, July 13, 2007.

a. Construct a relative frequency distribution.

b. For what percentage of sales did Lamictal account?

c. Construct a pie chart.

49. The manager at a water park constructed the following frequency distribution to summarize attendance in July and August.

Attendance	Frequency
1000 up to 1250	5
1250 up to 1500	6
1500 up to 1750	10
1750 up to 2000	20
2000 up to 2250	15
2250 up to 2500	4

a. Construct the corresponding relative frequency, cumulative frequency, and cumulative relative frequency distributions.

b. What is the most likely attendance range? How many times was attendance less than 2000 people?

c. What percent of the time was attendance at least 1750 but less than 2000 people? What percent of the time was attendance less than 1750 people? What percent of the time was attendance 1750 or more?

d. Construct a histogram. Comment on the shape of the distribution.

50. A researcher conducts a mileage economy test involving 80 cars. The frequency distribution describing average miles per gallon (mpg) appears in the following table.

Average mpg	Frequency
15 up to 20	15
20 up to 25	30
25 up to 30	15
30 up to 35	10
35 up to 40	7
40 up to 45	3

a. Construct the corresponding relative frequency, cumulative frequency, and cumulative relative frequency distributions.

b. How many of the cars got less than 30 mpg? What percent of the cars got at least 20 but less than 25 mpg? What percent of the cars got less than 35 mpg? What percent got 35 mpg or more?

c. Construct a histogram. Comment on the shape of the distribution.

51. *The Wall Street Journal* (August 28, 2006) asked its readers: "Ideally, how many days a week, if any, would you work from home?" The following relative frequency distribution summarizes the responses from 3,478 readers.

Days Working from Home	Relative Frequency
0	0.12
1	0.18
2	0.30
3	0.15
4	0.07
5	0.19

Construct a pie chart and a bar chart to summarize the data.

52. **FILE** The accompanying table lists a portion of the ages and net worth of the wealthiest people in America; the complete data set can be found on the text website and is labeled *Wealthiest Americans*.

Name	Age	Net Worth ($ billions)
William Gates III	53	50.0
Warren Buffet	79	40.0
⋮	⋮	⋮
Philip Knight	71	9.5

Source: *Forbes*, Special Report, September 2009.

a. What percent of the wealthiest people in America had net worth more than $20 billion?

b. What percent of the wealthiest people in America had net worth between $10 billion and $20 billion?

c. Construct a stem-and-leaf diagram on age. Comment on the shape of the distribution and how it compares with the one for 2010 in Table 2.16.

53. **FILE** The price-to-earnings growth ratio, or PEG ratio, is the market's valuation of a company relative to its earnings prospects. A PEG ratio of 1 indicates that the stock's price is in line with growth expectations. A PEG ratio less than 1 suggests that the stock of the company is undervalued (typical of value stocks), whereas a PEG ratio greater than 1 suggests the stock is overvalued (typical of growth stocks). The accompanying table shows a portion of PEG ratios of companies listed on the Dow Jones Industrial Average; the complete data set can be found on the text website and is labeled *DOW PEG Ratios*.

Company	PEG Ratio
3M (MMM)	1.4
Alcoa (AA)	0.9
⋮	⋮
Walt Disney (DIS)	1.2

Source: www.finance.yahoo, data retrieved April 13, 2011.

Construct a stem-and-leaf diagram on the PEG ratio. Interpret your findings.

54. The following table lists the sale price and type of 20 recently sold houses in New Jersey.

Price	Type	Price	Type
$305,000	Ranch	$568,000	Colonial
$450,000	Colonial	$385,000	Other
$389,000	Contemporary	$310,000	Contemporary
$525,000	Other	$450,000	Colonial
$300,000	Ranch	$400,000	Other
$330,000	Contemporary	$359,000	Ranch
$355,000	Contemporary	$379,000	Ranch
$405,000	Colonial	$509,000	Colonial
$365,000	Ranch	$435,000	Colonial
$415,000	Ranch	$510,000	Other

a. Construct a pie chart and a bar chart on types of houses sold in New Jersey. Interpret your findings.

b. Construct a frequency distribution using seven classes, with the first class starting from $300,000.

c. Use a histogram and an ogive to summarize the data.

55. A manager of a local retail store analyzes the relationship between advertising (in $100s) and sales (in $1,000s) by reviewing the store's data for the previous six months. Construct a scatterplot and comment on whether or not a relationship exists.

Advertising (in $100s)	Sales (in $1,000s)
20	15
25	18
30	20
22	16
27	19
26	20

56. The following table lists the National Basketball Association's (NBA's) leading scorers, their average minutes per game (MPG), and their average points per game (PPG) for 2008:

Player	MPG	PPG
D. Wade	38.6	30.2
L. James	37.7	28.4
K. Bryant	36.1	26.8
D. Nowitzki	37.3	25.9
D. Granger	36.2	25.8
K. Durant	39.0	25.3
C. Paul	38.5	22.8
C. Anthony	34.5	22.8
C. Bosh	38.0	22.7
B. Roy	37.2	22.6

Source: www.espn.com.

Construct and interpret a scatterplot of PPG against MPG. Does a relationship exist between the two variables?

CASE STUDIES

Case Study 2.1

In its 2000 and 2009 Annual Reports, Nike, Inc., reported the following net revenues, in millions of dollars, in four distinct regions of the world:

Data for Case Study 2.1 Net Revenue of Nike in 2000 and 2009

Region	2000	2009
U.S. Region	$4,732.1	$6,542.9
EMEA Region[a]	2,350.9	5,512.2
Asia Pacific Region	955.1	3,322.0
Americas Region	550.2	1,284.7
	Total = 8,588.3	Total = 16,661.8

[a]EMEA Region consists of Europe, the Middle East, and Africa.

In a report, use the sample information to:

1. Convert each region's net revenues to its respective proportion for that year. Have the proportions of Nike's net sales in each region remained the same over this 10-year period? Discuss any trends that you see.

2. Compare and contrast your findings concerning Nike's net revenues with those of Adidas, found in Table 2.6. What similarities and differences do you detect?

Case Study 2.2

When reviewing the overall strength of a particular firm, financial analysts typically examine the net profit margin. This statistic is generally calculated as the ratio of a firm's net profit after taxes (net income) to its revenue, expressed as a percentage. For example, a 20% net profit margin means that a firm has a net income of $0.20 for each dollar of sales. A net profit margin can even be negative if the firm has a negative net income. In general, the higher the net profit margin, the more effective the firm is at converting revenue into actual profit. The net profit margin serves as a good way of comparing firms in the same industry, since such firms generally are subject to the same business conditions. However, financial analysts also use the net profit margin to compare firms in different industries in order to gauge which firms are relatively more profitable. The accompanying table shows a portion of net profit margins for a sample of clothing retailers; the complete data set can be found on the text website and is labeled **Net Profit Margins**.

Data for Case Study 2.2 Net Profit Margin for Clothing Retailers

Firm	Net Profit Margin (in percent)	FILE
Abercrombie & Fitch	1.58	
Aéropostale	10.64	
⋮	⋮	
Wet Seal	16.15	

Source: www.finance.yahoo.com, data retrieved July 2010.

In a report, use the sample information to:

1. Provide a brief definition of net profit margin and explain why it is an important statistic.

2. Construct appropriate tables and graphs that summarize the clothing industry's net profit margin.

3. Discuss where the data tend to cluster and how the data are spread from the lowest value to the highest value.

4. Comment on the net profit margin of the clothing industry, as compared to the beverage industry's net profit margin of approximately 10.9% (Source: biz.yahoo, July 2010).

Case Study 2.3

The following table lists a portion of U.S. median housing prices for 2005 for the 50 states; the full data set is on the text website and is labeled **Median Housing Prices**.

Data for Case Study 2.3 Median Housing Prices by State, 2005

State	Median	FILE
California	$477,700	
Hawaii	453,600	
⋮	⋮	
Mississippi	82,700	

Source: U.S. Census Bureau, *2005 American Community Survey*.

In a report, use the sample information to:

1. Construct appropriate tables and graphs that summarize the median housing prices in the U.S.

2. Discuss where the data tend to cluster and how the data are spread from the lowest value to the highest value.

3. Comment on the shape of the distribution.

3

Numerical Descriptive Measures

C H A P T E R

In Chapter 2 we learned how to summarize data by using tables and graphs so that we can extract meaningful information. In this chapter we focus on numerical descriptive measures. These measures provide precise, objectively determined values that are easy to calculate, interpret, and compare with one another. We first calculate several measures of central location, which attempt to find a typical or central value for the data. In addition to analyzing the center, we need to know how the data vary around the center. Measures of spread or dispersion gauge the underlying variability of the data. We use measures of central location and dispersion to introduce some popular applications, including the Sharpe ratio and the empirical rule. Finally, we discuss measures that examine the linear relationship between two variables. These measures assess whether two variables have a positive linear relationship, a negative linear relationship, or no linear relationship.

Investment Decision

Rebecca Johnson works as an investment counselor at a large bank. Recently, an inexperienced investor asked Johnson about clarifying some differences between two top-performing mutual funds from the last decade: Vanguard's Precious Metals and Mining fund (henceforth, Metals) and Fidelity's Strategic Income Fund (hence-forth, Income). The investor shows Johnson the return data he has accessed over the Internet, but the investor has trouble interpreting the data. Table 3.1 shows the return data for these two mutual funds for the years 2000–2009; the data, labeled **Fund Returns**, can also be found on the text website.

TABLE 3.1   Returns (in percent) for the Metals and the Income Funds, 2000–2009

FILE

Year	Metals	Income	Year	Metals	Income
2000	−7.34	4.07	2005	43.79	3.12
2001	18.33	6.52	2006	34.30	8.15
2002	33.35	9.38	2007	36.13	5.44
2003	59.45	18.62	2008	−56.02	−11.37
2004	8.09	9.44	2009	76.46	31.77

Source: http://www.finance.yahoo.com.

Rebecca would like to use the above sample information to:

1. Determine the typical return of the mutual funds.

2. Evaluate the investment risk of the mutual funds.

A synopsis of this case is provided at the end of Section 3.4.

3.1 Measures of Central Location

LO **3.1**

Calculate and interpret the arithmetic mean, the median, and the mode.

The term *central location* relates to the way quantitative data tend to cluster around some middle or central value. Measures of central location attempt to find a typical or central value that describes the data. Examples include finding a typical value that describes the return on an investment, the number of defects in a production process, the salary of a business graduate, the rental price in a neighborhood, the number of customers at a local convenience store, and so on.

The Arithmetic Mean

The **arithmetic mean** is the primary measure of central location. Generally, we refer to the "arithmetic mean" as simply the "mean." Shortly, we will calculate and interpret another type of mean called the geometric mean; both the arithmetic mean and the geometric mean are considered averages—one is an arithmetic average, whereas the other is a multiplicative average.

In order to calculate the arithmetic mean of a data set, we simply add up the values of all the data points and divide by the number of data points in the population or sample.

EXAMPLE 3.1

Let's use the data in Table 3.1 in the introductory case to calculate and interpret the mean return of the Metals fund and the mean return of the Income fund.

SOLUTION: Let's start with the mean return for the Metals fund. We first add all the returns and then divide by the number of returns as follows:

$$\text{Metals fund mean return} = \frac{-7.34 + 18.33 + \cdots + 76.46}{10} = \frac{246.54}{10} = 24.65\%.$$

Similarly, we calculate the mean return for the Income fund as:

$$\text{Income fund mean return} = \frac{4.07 + 6.52 + \cdots + 31.77}{10} = \frac{85.14}{10} = 8.51\%.$$

Thus, over the 10-year period 2000–2009, the mean return for the Metals fund was greater than the average return for the Income fund, or equivalently, $24.65\% > 8.51\%$. These arithmetic means represent typical annual returns resulting from a one-year investment. Later we will discuss the geometric mean to describe the annual return resulting from a multi-year investment.

All of us have calculated a mean before. What might be new for some of us is the notation used to express the mean as a formula. For instance, when calculating the mean return for the Metals fund, we let $x_1 = -7.34$, $x_2 = 18.33$, and so on, and let n represent the number of observations in the sample. So our calculation for the mean can be written as

$$\text{Mean} = \frac{x_1 + x_2 + \cdots + x_{10}}{n}.$$

The mean of the sample is referred to as $\bar{x}$ (pronounced x-bar). Also, we can denote the numerator of this formula using summation notation, which yields the following compact formula for the **sample mean**: $\bar{x} = \frac{\Sigma x_i}{n}$. We should also point out that if we had all the return data for this mutual fund, instead of just the data for the past 10 years, then we would have been able to calculate the **population mean** μ as $\mu = \frac{\Sigma x_i}{N}$, where μ is the Greek letter mu (pronounced as "mew"), and N is the number of observations in the population.

For sample values, $x_1, x_2, \ldots, x_n$, the **sample mean** $\bar{x}$ is computed as

$$\bar{x} = \frac{\sum x_i}{n}.$$

For population values, $x_1, x_2, \ldots, x_N$, the **population mean** μ is computed as

$$\mu = \frac{\sum x_i}{N}.$$

The calculation method is identical for the sample mean and the population mean except that the sample mean uses n observations and the population mean uses N observations, where $n < N$. In later chapters we will refer to the population mean as a **parameter** and the sample mean as a **statistic**. Since the population mean is generally unknown, we often use the sample mean to estimate the population mean.

The arithmetic mean is used extensively in statistics. However, it can give a misleading description of the center of the distribution in the presence of extremely small or large values.

The arithmetic mean is the most commonly used measure of central location. One weakness of this measure is that it is unduly influenced by **outliers**, that is, extremely small or large values.

Example 3.2 highlights the main weakness of the arithmetic mean.

EXAMPLE 3.2

Seven people work at Acetech, a small technology firm in Seattle. Their salaries over the past year are listed in Table 3.2. Compute the mean salary for this firm and discuss whether it accurately indicates a typical value.

TABLE 3.2 Salaries of Employees at Acetech

Title	Salary
Administrative Assistant	$40,000
Research Assistant	40,000
Computer Programmer	65,000
Senior Research Associate	90,000
Senior Sales Associate	145,000
Chief Financial Officer	150,000
President (and owner)	550,000

SOLUTION: Since all employees of Acetech are included, we calculate the population mean as:

$$\mu = \frac{\sum x_i}{N} = \frac{40,000 + 40,000 + \cdots + 550,000}{7} = \$154,286.$$

It is true that the mean salary for this firm is $154,286, but this value does not reflect the typical salary at this firm. In fact, six of the seven employees earn less than $154,286. This example highlights the main weakness of the mean, that is, it is very sensitive to extreme observations (extremely large or extremely small values), or outliers.

The Median

Since the mean can be affected by outliers, we often also calculate the **median** as a measure of central location. The median is the middle value of a data set. It divides the data in half; an equal number of observations lie above and below the median. Many government publications and other data sources publish both the mean and the median in order to accurately portray a data set's typical value. If the values of the mean and the median differ significantly, then it is likely that the data set contains outliers. For instance, in 2007 the United States Census Bureau determined that the median income for American households was $46,326, whereas the mean income was $63,344. It is well documented that a small number of households in the U.S. have income considerably higher than the typical American household income. As a result, these top-earning households influence the mean by pushing its value significantly above the value of the median.

THE MEDIAN

The **median** is the middle value of a data set. We arrange the data in ascending (or descending) order and calculate the median as

- The middle value if the number of observations is odd, or
- The average of the two middle values if the number of observations is even.

The median is especially useful when outliers are present.

EXAMPLE 3.3

Use the data in Table 3.2 to calculate the median salary of employees at Acetech.

SOLUTION: In Table 3.2, the data are already arranged in ascending order. We reproduce the salaries along with their relative positions.

Position:	1	2	3	4	5	6	7
Value:	$40,000	40,000	65,000	90,000	145,000	150,000	550,000

Given seven salaries, the median occupies the 4th position. Thus, the median is $90,000. Three salaries are less than $90,000 and three salaries are greater than $90,000. As compared to the mean income of $154,286, the median in this case better reflects the typical salary.

EXAMPLE 3.4

Use the data in Table 3.1 in the introductory case study to calculate and interpret the median returns for the Metals and the Income funds.

SOLUTION: Let's start with the median return for the Metals fund. We first arrange the data in ascending order:

Position:	1	2	3	4	5	6	7	8	9	10
Value:	−56.02	−7.34	8.09	18.33	33.35	34.30	36.13	43.79	59.45	76.46

Given 10 observations, the median is the average of the values in the 5th and 6th positions. These values are 33.35 and 34.30, so the median is $\frac{33.35 + 34.30}{2} = 33.83\%$. Over the period 2000–2009, the Metals fund had a median return of 33.83%, which indicates that 5 years had returns less than 33.83% and 5 years had returns greater than 33.83%. A comparison of the median return (33.83%) and the mean return (24.65%) reveals a mean that is less than the median by almost 10 percentage points, which means that the Metals data are affected by outliers. Thus, in order to give a more transparent description of a data's center, it is wise to report both the mean and the median.

Similarly we can find the median for the Income fund as 7.34%. In this case, the median return of 7.34% does not appear to deviate drastically from the mean return of 8.51%. This is not surprising, since a casual inspection reveals that the relative magnitude of outliers is weaker in the Income fund data.

Note that the mean and the median suggest that a typical annual return for the Metals fund is much higher than the Income fund. Then why would anyone want to invest in the Income fund? We will come back to this question later in this chapter, when we explore the risk associated with these funds.

The Mode

The **mode** of a data set is the value that occurs most frequently. A data set can have more than one mode, or even no mode. For instance, if we try to calculate the mode return for either the Metals fund or the Income fund in Table 3.1, we see that no value in either fund occurs more than once. Thus, there is no mode value for either fund. If a data set has one mode, then we say it is unimodal. If two modes exist, then the data set is bimodal; if three modes exist, then it is trimodal. Generally, the mode's value as a measure of central location tends to diminish with data sets that have more than three modes.

THE MODE

The **mode** is the most frequently occurring value in a data set. A data set may have no mode or more than one mode. The mode is the only meaningful measure of central location that can be used to summarize qualitative data.

EXAMPLE 3.5

Use the data in Table 3.2 to calculate the mode salary of employees at Acetech.

SOLUTION: The salary $40,000 is earned by two employees. Every other salary occurs just once. So $40,000 is the mode salary. Just because a value occurs with the most frequency does not guarantee that it best reflects the center of the data. It is true that the mode salary at Acetech is $40,000, but most employees earn considerably more than this amount.

In the preceding examples we used measures of central location to describe quantitative data. However, in many instances we want to summarize qualitative data, where the mode is the only meaningful measure of central location.

EXAMPLE 3.6

Kenneth Forbes is a manager at the University of Wisconsin campus bookstore. There has been a recent surge in the sale of women's sweatshirts, which are available in three sizes: Small (S), Medium (M), and Large (L). Kenneth notes that the campus bookstore sold 10 sweatshirts over the weekend in the following sizes:

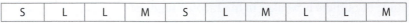

| S | L | L | M | S | L | M | L | L | M |

Comment on the data set and use the appropriate measure of central location that best reflects the typical size of a sweatshirt.

SOLUTION: This data set is an example of ordinal data (qualitative data). Here, the mode is the only relevant measure of central location. The mode size is L since it appears 5 times as compared to S and M that appear 2 and 3 times, respectively. Often, when examining issues relating to the demand for a product, such as replenishing stock, the mode tends to be the most relevant measure of central location.

Using Excel to Calculate Measures of Central Location

In general, Excel offers a couple of ways to calculate most of the descriptive measures that we discuss in this chapter. The easiest way to calculate the mean, the median, and the mode is presented below.

A. Open the data labeled *Fund Returns* (Table 3.1) from the text website into an Excel spreadsheet.

B. From the menu choose **Data** > **Data Analysis** > **Descriptive Statistics** > **OK**. (Note: As mentioned in Chapter 2, if you do not see **Data Analysis** under **Data**, you must *Add-in* the Analysis Toolpak option.)

C. See Figure 3.1. In the *Descriptive Statistics* dialog box, click on the box next to *Input Range*, then select the data. If you included the fund names when you highlighted the data, make sure you click on the option next to *Labels in First Row*. Click the box in front of *Summary Statistics*. Then click **OK**.

FIGURE 3.1 Descriptive statistics dialog box.

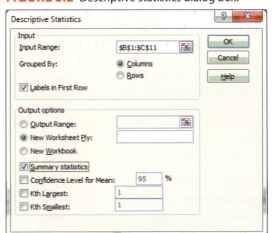

D. Table 3.3 presents the Excel output. If the output is difficult to read, highlight the data and choose **Home** > **Format** > **Column** > **Autofit Selection**. Note that Excel provides numerous descriptive statistics. We have put the measures of central location in boldface. (Measures of dispersion are also in boldface; we analyze these measures in more detail shortly.)

TABLE 3.3 Excel Output Using Descriptive Statistics Dialog Box

Metals		Income	
Mean	**24.654**	**Mean**	**8.514**
Standard Error	11.7414004	Standard Error	3.4997715
Median	**33.825**	**Median**	**7.335**
Mode	**#N/A**	**Mode**	**#N/A**
Standard Deviation	**37.1295681**	**Standard Deviation**	**11.067249**
Sample Variance	**1378.60483**	**Sample Variance**	**122.484**
Kurtosis	1.668701	Kurtosis	2.3615757
Skewness	−1.0076169	Skewness	0.5602496
Range	**132.48**	**Range**	**43.14**
Minimum	−56.02	Minimum	−11.37
Maximum	76.46	Maximum	31.77
Sum	246.54	Sum	85.14
Count	10	Count	10

Note that there is no unique mode as no return in either fund occurs more than once; Excel reports it as #NA. We would also like to comment on the numerical measures of **skewness** and (excess) **kurtosis** that Excel reports, even though we have not discussed their calculations. A skewness coefficient of zero indicates the data values are relatively evenly distributed on both sides of the mean. A positive skewness coefficient implies that extreme values are concentrated in the right tail of the distribution, pulling the mean up, and the bulk of values lie to the left of the mean. Similarly, a negative skewness coefficient implies that extreme values are concentrated in the left tail of the distribution, pulling the mean down, and the bulk of values lie to the right of the mean. We find that the returns are negatively skewed (Skewness = −1.0076) for the Metals fund and positively skewed (Skewness = 0.5602) for the Income fund. A (excess) kurtosis coefficient measures whether or not a distribution is more peaked with fatter tails (kurtosis > 0) or less peaked with thinner tails (kurtosis < 0) than a normal distribution. As we discuss in later chapters, the normal distribution, with the skewness and kurtosis coefficients of zero, is a widely used distribution for statistical analysis. The kurtosis coefficient is positive for the Metals as well as the Income returns, indicating that the return distributions are more peaked and have fatter tails than the normal distribution. In other words, there is a higher likelihood of outliers as compared to the normal distribution.

EXERCISES 3.1

Concepts

1. Given the following observations from a sample, calculate the mean, the median, and the mode.

8	10	9	12	12

2. Given the following observations from a sample, calculate the mean, the median, and the mode.

−4	0	−6	1	−3	−4

3. Given the following observations from a population, calculate the mean, the median, and the mode.

150	257	55	110	110	43	201	125	55

4. Given the following observations from a population, calculate the mean, the median, and the mode.

20	15	25	20	10	15	25	20	15

Applications

5. The following table shows the retail price for a box of 12 Titleist Pro golf balls from around the world; the data, labeled *Titleist*, can also be found on the text website.

City	Retail Price in U.S.$	City	Retail Price in U.S.$
Seoul	$65.45	Hong Kong	$55.26
New York	48.77	Brussels	65.53
Tokyo	52.81	Paris	69.55
Kuala Lumpur	73.92	Rome	69.55
Singapore	72.61	Frankfort	76.23
Manila	64.54	London	69.72
Sydney	75.33	Taipei	48.37

Source: *The Wall Street Journal*, April 10, 2007.

a. In what city are golf balls most expensive? Least expensive?

b. Calculate the mean price, the median price, and the modal price for this sample.

6. The following table shows the 10 highest-paid chief executive officers of the last decade.

Name	Firm	Compensation (in millions)
Lawrence Ellison	Oracle	$1,835.7
Barry Diller	IAC, Expedia	1,142.9
Ray Irani	Occidental Petroleum	857.1
Steve Jobs	Apple	748.8
Richard Fairbank	Capital One	568.5
Angelo Mozilo	Countrywide	528.6
Eugene Isenberg	Nabors Industries	518.0
Terry Semel	Yahoo	489.6
Henry Silverman	Cendant	481.2
William McGuire	UnitedHealth Group	469.3

Source: *The Wall Street Journal*, July 27, 2010.

a. Calculate the mean compensation for the 10 highest-paid chief executive officers.

b. Does the mean accurately reflect the center of the data? Explain.

7. **FILE** The following table shows Fortune 500's rankings of America's 10 largest corporations for 2010. Next to each corporation is its market capitalization (in billions of dollars as of March 26, 2010) and its total return to investors for the year 2009. These data, labeled **Largest Corporations**, are also available on the text website.

Company	Mkt. Cap. (in $ billions)	Total Return
Walmart	$209	−2.7%
Exxon Mobil	314	−12.6
Chevron	149	8.1
General Electric	196	−0.4
Bank of America	180	7.3
ConocoPhillips	78	2.9
AT&T	155	4.8
Ford Motor	47	336.7
JP Morgan Chase	188	19.9
Hewlett-Packard	125	43.1

Source: money.cnn.com, May 3, 2010.

a. Calculate the mean and the median for market capitalization.

b. Calculate the mean and the median for total return.

c. For each variable (market capitalization and total return), comment on which measure best reflects central location.

8. The Massachusetts Department of Public Health reported the following prevalent causes of death in the state.

Cause of Death	Deaths per Day	Cause of Death	Deaths per Day
Cancer	36	Alzheimer's	5
Heart Disease	35	Diabetes	3
Respiratory	14	HIV/AIDS	1
Injury	8	Infant Death	1
Stroke	7		

Source: Massachusetts Department of Health, *Massachusetts Deaths 2007*.

Which measure of central location is most useful in making staffing decisions at Massachusetts' hospitals? Explain.

9. **FILE** One important statistic in baseball is a pitcher's earned run average, or ERA. This number represents the average number of earned runs given up by the pitcher per nine innings. The following table lists a portion of the ERAs for pitchers playing for the New York Yankees and the Baltimore Orioles as of July 22, 2010; the complete data, labeled **ERA**, are available on the text website.

New York Yankees	ERA	Baltimore Orioles	ERA
Sabathia	3.13	Guthrie	4.58
Pettitte	2.88	Millwood	5.77
⋮	⋮	⋮	⋮

Source: www.mlb.com.

a. Calculate the mean and the median ERA for the New York Yankees.

b. Calculate the mean and the median ERA for the Baltimore Orioles.

c. Based solely on your calculations above, which team is likely to have the better winning record? Explain.

10. **FILE** The following table shows a portion of the sale price (in $1000s) for 36 homes sold in Mission Viejo, CA, during June 2010; the complete data, labeled ***Mission Viejo Houses***, are also available on the text website.

Number	Sale Price (in $1000s)
1	$430
2	520
⋮	⋮
36	430

a. Calculate the mean, the median, and the mode.

b. Given the values calculated in part (a), which measure do you think best reflects central location? Why?

3.2 Percentiles and Box Plots

As discussed earlier, the median is a measure of central location that divides the data in half; that is, half of the data points fall below the median and half fall above that value. The median is also called the 50th percentile. In many instances, we are interested in a **percentile** other than the 50th percentile. Here we discuss calculating and interpreting percentiles. Generally, percentiles are calculated for large data sets; for ease of exposition, we show their use with small data sets. In addition, we construct a box plot, which is, more or less, a visual representation of particular percentiles.

Percentiles provide detailed information about how data are spread over the interval from the smallest value to the largest value. You have probably been exposed to percentiles. For example, the SAT is the most widely used test in the undergraduate admissions process. Scores on the math portion of the SAT range from 200 to 800. Suppose you obtained a raw score of 650 on this section of the test. It may not be readily apparent how you did relative to other students that took the same test. However, if you know that the raw score corresponds to the 75th percentile, then you know that approximately 75% of students had scores lower than your score and approximately 25% of students had scores higher than your score.

LO **3.2**

Calculate and interpret percentiles and a box plot.

PERCENTILES

In general, the pth **percentile** divides a data set into two parts:

- Approximately p percent of the observations have values less than the pth percentile;

- Approximately $(100 - p)$ percent of the observations have values greater than the pth percentile.

Calculating the pth percentile

A. First arrange the data in ascending order.

B. Locate the approximate position of the percentile by calculating L_p:

$$L_p = (n + 1)\frac{p}{100},$$

where L_p indicates the location of the desired percentile p and n is the sample size. For the population percentile, replace n by N. We set $p = 50$ for the median as it is the 50th percentile.

C. Once you find the value for L_p, observe whether or not L_p is an integer:

- If L_p is an integer, then L_p denotes the location of the pth percentile. For instance, if L_{20} is equal to 2, then the 20th percentile is equal to the second observation in the ordered data set.
- If L_p is not an integer, we need to interpolate between two observations to approximate the desired percentile. So if L_{20} is equal to 2.25, then we need to interpolate 25% of the distance between the second and third observations in order to find the 20th percentile.

EXAMPLE 3.7

Consider the information presented in the introductory case of this chapter. Calculate and interpret the 25th and the 75th percentiles for the Metals fund.

SOLUTION: The first step is to arrange the data in ascending order:

Position:	1	2	3	4	5	6	7	8	9	10
Value:	−56.02	−7.34	8.09	18.33	33.35	34.30	36.13	43.79	59.45	76.46

For the 25th percentile: $L_{25} = (n + 1)\frac{p}{100} = (10 + 1)\frac{25}{100} = 2.75$. So, the 25th percentile is located 75% of the distance between the second and third observations; it is calculated as

$$-7.34 + 0.75(8.09 - (-7.34)) = -7.34 + 11.57 = 4.23.$$

Thus, 25% of the returns were less than 4.23% and 75% of the returns were greater than 4.23%.

For the 75th percentile: $L_{75} = (n + 1)\frac{p}{100} = (10 + 1)\frac{75}{100} = 8.25$. So, the 75th percentile is located 25% of the distance between the eighth and ninth observations; it is calculated as

$$43.79 + 0.25(59.45 - 43.79) = 43.79 + 3.92 = 47.71.$$

Thus, 75% of the returns were less than 47.71% and 25% of the returns were greater than 47.71%.

Earlier we calculated the median or the 50th percentile for the Metals fund and obtained a value of 33.83%. When we calculate the 25th, the 50th, and the 75th percentiles for a data set, we have effectively divided the data into four equal parts, or quarters. Thus, the 25th percentile is also referred to as the first quartile (Q1), the 50th percentile is referred to as the second quartile (Q2), and the 75th percentile is referred to as the third quartile (Q3).

We can define other dividing lines that split the data into smaller parts:

- **Quintiles** divide the data set into fifths.
- **Deciles** divide the data set into tenths.
- **Percentiles** divide the data set into hundredths.

A **box plot**, also referred to as a box-and-whisker plot, is a convenient way to graphically display the smallest value (S), the quartiles (Q1, Q2, and Q3), and the largest value (L) of a data set. Box plots are particularly useful when comparing data sets; they are also an effective tool for identifying outliers. Using our results from the Metals fund, Table 3.4 summarizes the five values that we will plot:

TABLE 3.4 Summary Values for the Metals Fund

S	Q1	Q2	Q3	L
−56.02%	4.23%	33.83%	47.71%	76.46%

The values in Table 3.4 are often referred to as the five-number summary for the data set. We follow these steps to construct a box plot and also to detect outliers.

A. Plot the five-number summary values in ascending order on the horizontal axis.

B. Draw a box encompassing the first and third quartiles.

C. Draw a dashed line in the box at the median.

D. To determine if a given observation is an outlier, first calculate the difference between Q3 and Q1. This difference is called the **interquartile range** or IQR. The IQR represents the middle half of the data. Draw a line ("whisker") that extends from Q1 to the smallest data value that is not farther than 1.5 × IQR from Q1. Similarly, draw a line that extends from Q3 to the largest data value that is not farther than 1.5 × IQR from Q3.

E. Use an asterisk to indicate points that are farther than 1.5 × IQR from the box. These points are considered outliers.

EXAMPLE 3.8

Construct the box plot for the Metals fund.

SOLUTION: Based on the information in Table 3.4, we calculate the IQR as the difference between Q3 and Q1 or 47.71% − 4.23% = 43.48%. We then calculate 1.5 × IQR or 1.5 × 43.48% = 65.22%. The distance between Q1 and the smallest value, 4.23 − (−56.02%) = 60.25%, is within the limit of 65.22%; thus, the line will extend to the smallest value of −56.02% on the left side of the box plot (Figure 3.2). Similarly, the distance between the largest value and Q3, 76.46% − 47.71% = 28.75, is also well within the limit of 65.22%; here the line will extend to the right up to the largest value of 76.46%. Given the criteria for constructing a box plot, there are no outliers in this data set.

FIGURE 3.2 Box plot for the Metals Fund

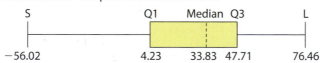

From this box plot we can quickly grasp several points concerning the distribution of returns for the *Metals* fund. First, returns range from −56.02% to 76.46%, with about half being less than 33.83% and half being greater than 33.83%. We make two further observations: (1) the median is off-center within the box, being located to the right of center, and (2) the left whisker is longer than the right whisker. This indicates that the distribution is negatively skewed. If the median is left of center and the right whisker is longer than the left whisker, then the distribution is positively skewed. If the median is in the center of the box and the left and right whiskers are equidistant from their respective quartiles, then the distribution is symmetric.

EXERCISES 3.2

Concepts

11. Calculate the 20th, 50th, and 80th percentiles for the following data set:

| 120 | 215 | 187 | 343 | 268 | 196 | 312 |

12. Calculate the 20th, 40th, and 70th percentiles for the following data set:

| −300 | −257 | −325 | −234 | −297 | −362 | −255 |

13. Consider the following data set:

| 12 | 9 | 27 | 15 | 58 | 35 | 21 | 32 | 22 |

   a. Calculate and interpret the 25th, 50th, and 75th percentiles.
   b. Construct a box plot. Are there any outliers?

14. Consider the following data set:

| 0.04 | 0.10 | −0.05 | −0.02 | 0.08 | 0.15 | −0.09 |

   a. Calculate and interpret the 25th, 50th, and 75th percentiles.
   b. Construct a box plot. Are there any outliers?

Applications

15. Scores on the final in a statistics class are as follows.

| 75 | 25 | 75 | 62 | 80 | 85 | 80 | 99 | 90 | 60 |
| 86 | 92 | 40 | 74 | 72 | 65 | 87 | 70 | 85 | 70 |

   a. Calculate and interpret the 25th, 50th, and 75th percentiles.
   b. Construct a box plot. Are there any outliers? Is the distribution symmetric? If not, comment on its skewness.

16. Consider the return data (in percent) for the Income fund in Table 3.1.
   a. Calculate and interpret the 25th, 50th, and 75th percentiles.
   b. Construct a box plot. Are there any outliers?
   c. Is the distribution symmetric? If not, comment on its skewness.

17. FILE A price-earnings ratio or P/E ratio is calculated as a firm's share price compared to the income or profit earned by the firm per share. Generally, a high P/E ratio suggests that investors are expecting higher earnings growth in the future compared to companies with a lower P/E ratio. The accompanying table shows a portion of 26 companies that comprise the Dow Jones Industrial Average and their P/E ratios as of July 23, 2010 (at the time data were retrieved, data on four firms were not available). The complete data, labeled **PE Ratio** are available on the text website.

Company	P/E Ratio
3M (MMM)	17
American Express (AXP)	22
⋮	⋮
Wal-Mart (WMT)	14

   a. Calculate and interpret the 25th, 50th, and 75th percentiles.
   b. Construct a box plot. Are there any outliers? Is the distribution symmetric? If not, comment on its skewness.

3.3 The Geometric Mean

LO **3.3**
Calculate and interpret a geometric mean return and an average growth rate.

The geometric mean is a multiplicative average, as opposed to an additive average (the arithmetic mean). It is the relevant measure when evaluating investment returns over several years. It is also the relevant measure when calculating average growth rates.

The Geometric Mean Return

Suppose you invested $1,000 in a stock that had a 10% return in 2009 and a −10% return in 2010. The arithmetic mean suggests that by the end of year 2010, you would be right back where you started with $1,000 worth of stock. It is true that the arithmetic mean return over the two-year period is 0% $\left(\bar{x} = \frac{0.10 + (-0.10)}{2} = 0\right)$; however, the arithmetic mean ignores the effects of compounding. As shown in Table 3.5, the value of your investment at the end of two years is $990, a loss of $10. The geometric mean accurately captures a negative annual return from the two-year investment period.

TABLE 3.5 End of Year Holdings Given an Initial Investment of $1,000

Year	Return	Value at the End of Year
2009	10 percent	$1,000 + 1,000(0.10) = $1,100
2010	−10 percent	$1,100 + 1,100(−0.10) = $990

For multiperiod returns $R_1, R_2, \ldots, R_n$, the **geometric mean return** G_R is computed as

$$G_R = \sqrt[n]{(1 + R_1)(1 + R_2) \cdots (1 + R_n)} - 1,$$

where n is the number of multiperiod returns.

Let us revisit the above case where you invested $1,000 in a stock that had a 10% return in 2009 and a -10% return in 2010. The geometric mean is computed as

$$G_R = \sqrt[2]{(1 + 0.10)(1 + (-0.10))} - 1 = ((1.10)(0.90))^{1/2} - 1 = -0.005, \text{ or } -0.5\%.$$

We interpret the geometric mean return as the **annualized return**, that you will earn from a two-year investment period. Table 3.6 shows that with the computed annualized return of -0.5%, the end investment value is the same as shown in Table 3.5.

TABLE 3.6 End of Year Holdings Given an Initial Investment of $1,000

Year	Annualized Return	Value at the End of Year
2009	-0.5%	$1,000 + 1,000(-0.005) = $995
2010	-0.5%	$995 + 995(-0.005) = $990

EXAMPLE 3.9

Use the data in Table 3.1 to calculate the geometric mean for the Metals and the Income funds.

SOLUTION:

Metals Fund: $G_R = \sqrt[10]{(1 - 0.0734)(1 + 0.1833) \cdots (1 + 0.7646)} - 1$

$$= (5.1410)^{1/10} - 1 = 0.1779, \text{ or } 17.79\%.$$

Income Fund: $G_R = \sqrt[10]{(1 + 0.0407)(1 + 0.0652) \cdots (1 + 0.3177)} - 1$

$$= (2.1617)^{1/10} - 1 = 0.0801, \text{ or } 8.01\%.$$

Therefore, for the 10-year period, the annualized return for the Metals fund is higher than that of the Income fund, $17.79\% > 8.01\%$. However, the magnitude of the difference is relatively smaller than that of the arithmetic means, which for the Metals and Income funds are 24.65% and 8.51%, respectively. This shows that the geometric mean is not as sensitive to extreme values as is the arithmetic mean. The arithmetic mean for the Metals fund is unduly influenced by the extreme return of 76.46% in 2009.

An issue that begs for explanation is the relevance of the arithmetic mean and the geometric mean as summary measures for financial returns. Both means are relevant descriptive measures for annual return; however, each has a different interpretation. The arithmetic mean is appropriate for analyzing a one-year investment, whereas the geometric mean is appropriate for analyzing a multi-year investment. In Example 3.9, the arithmetic mean of 24.65% is the average annual return for summarizing returns with an investment horizon of one year. The geometric mean of 17.79% is the average annual return when the investment horizon is 10 years. For illustration, we can think of the arithmetic mean as the relevant metric for an investor who is saving/investing to buy a house in about a year's time. The geometric mean is the relevant metric for an investor who is saving for retirement.

The Average Growth Rate

We also use the geometric mean when we calculate average growth rates.

> **FORMULA FOR THE AVERAGE GROWTH RATE**
>
> For growth rates $g_1, g_2, \ldots, g_n$, the **average growth rate** G_g is computed as:
>
> $$G_g = \sqrt[n]{(1 + g_1)(1 + g_2) \cdots (1 + g_n)} - 1$$
>
> where n is the number of multiperiod growth rates.

EXAMPLE 3.10

Table 3.7 shows sales for Adidas (in millions of €) for the years 2005 through 2009.

TABLE 3.7 Sales for Adidas (in millions of €), 2005–2009

Year	2005	2006	2007	2008	2009
Sales	6,636	10,084	10,299	10,799	10,381

Calculate the growth rates for 2005–2006, 2006–2007, 2007–2008, and 2008–2009 and use them to compute the average growth rate.

SOLUTION: The growth rates for Adidas for four years are computed as:

- 2005–2006: $\dfrac{10,084 - 6,636}{6,636} = 0.5196$

- 2006–2007: $\dfrac{10,299 - 10,084}{10,084} = 0.0213$

- 2007–2008: $\dfrac{10,799 - 10,299}{10,299} = 0.0485$

- 2008–2009: $\dfrac{10,381 - 10,799}{10,799} = -0.0387$

Therefore,

$$G_g = \sqrt[4]{(1 + 0.5196)(1 + 0.0213)(1 + 0.0485)(1 - 0.0387)} - 1$$

$$= \sqrt[4]{(1.5196)(1.0213)(1.0485)(0.9613)} = 1.5643^{1/4} - 1 = 0.1184, \text{ or } 11.84\%.$$

Sales for Adidas from 2005 to 2009 had an average growth rate of 11.84% per year.

There is a simpler way to compute the average growth rate when the underlying values of the series are given. In the above example, it is cumbersome to first calculate the relevant growth rates and then use them to compute the average growth rate.

AN ALTERNATIVE FORMULA FOR THE AVERAGE GROWTH RATE

For observations $x_1, x_2, \ldots, x_n$, the **average growth rate** G_g is computed as:

$$G_g = \sqrt[n-1]{\frac{x_n}{x_{n-1}} \frac{x_{n-1}}{x_{n-2}} \frac{x_{n-2}}{x_{n-3}} \cdots \frac{x_2}{x_1}} - 1 = \sqrt[n-1]{\frac{x_n}{x_1}} - 1$$

where $n - 1$ is the number of distinct growth rates. Note that only the first and last observations are needed in the time series due to cancellations in the formula.

EXAMPLE 3.11

Calculate the average growth rate for Adidas directly from the sales data in Table 3.7.

SOLUTION: Using the first and last observations from the time series consisting of five observations, we calculate

$$G_g = \sqrt[n-1]{\frac{x_n}{x_1}} - 1 = \sqrt[5-1]{\frac{10,381}{6,636}} - 1 = 1.5643^{1/4} - 1 = 0.1184, \text{ or } 11.84\%$$

which is the same as in Example 3.10.

EXERCISES 3.3

Concepts

18. Calculate the average growth rate return of the following data set:

4%	8%	−5%	6%

19. Calculate the geometric mean return of the following data set:

−3%	2%	−5%	2.7%	3.1%

20. The returns for a pharmaceutical firm are 10% in Year 1, 5% in Year 2, and −15% in Year 3. What is the annualized return for the period?

21. The returns from an investment are 2% in Year 1, 5% in Year 2, and 1.8% in the first half of Year 3. Calculate the annualized return for the entire period.

22. The returns for an auto firm are 5% in Year 1 and 3% in the first quarter of Year 2. Calculate the annualized return for the period.

23. Consider the following observations of a series:

Year 1	Year 2	Year 3	Year 4
90	110	150	160

   a. Calculate the growth rates for Year 1–Year 2, Year 2–Year 3, and Year 3–Year 4.
   b. Calculate the average growth rate.

24. Consider the following observations of a time series:

Year 1	Year 2	Year 3	Year 4
1,200	1,280	1,380	1,520

   a. Calculate the growth rates for Year 1–Year 2, Year 2–Year 3, and Year 3–Year 4.
   b. Calculate the average growth rate.

25. Calculate the average growth rate from the following growth rates.

2.5%	3.6%	1.8%	2.2%	5.2%

Applications

26. Suppose at the beginning of 2006 you decide to invest $1,000 in Vanguard's European Stock Index mutual fund. The following table shows the returns for the years 2006–2009.

Year	Annual Return
2006	33.42 percent
2007	13.82 percent
2008	−44.73 percent
2009	31.91 percent

Source: http://www.finance.yahoo.com.

   a. Calculate and interpret the arithmetic mean return.
   b. Calculate and interpret the geometric mean return.
   c. How much money would you have accumulated by the end of 2009?

27. Suppose at the beginning of 2005 you decide to invest $20,000 in Driehaus' Emerging Markets Growth mutual fund. The following table shows the returns for the years 2005–2009.

Year	Annual Return
2005	0.2585 percent
2006	0.2755 percent
2007	0.2747 percent
2008	−0.4702 percent
2009	0.7575 percent

Source: http://www.finance.yahoo.com.

a. Calculate and interpret the arithmetic mean return.
b. Calculate and interpret the geometric mean return.
c. How much money would you have accumulated by the end of 2009?

28. Home Depot and Lowe's are the two largest home improvement retailers in the U.S. The following table shows the total revenue (in billions) for each retailer for the years 2008–2010.

Year	Home Depot	Lowe's
2008	$77.35	$48.28
2009	71.29	48.23
2010	66.18	47.22

Source: Annual Reports of Home Depot, Inc., and Lowe's Companies Inc.

a. Calculate the growth rate for 2008–2009 and 2009–2010 for each retailer.
b. Calculate the average growth rate for each retailer.

29. The following table shows the total revenue (in billions of $) for Walmart Stores, Inc. and Target Corp. for the years 2008–2010.

Year	2008	2009	2010
Walmart	379.8	404.3	408.2
Target	63.4	65.0	65.3

Source: Annual Reports of Walmart Stores, Inc., and Target Corp.

a. Calculate the average growth rate for each firm.
b. Which firm had the higher growth rate over the 2008–2010 period?

30. The following table shows sales for Nike (in millions of $) for the years 2005 through 2009.

Year	2005	2006	2007	2008	2009
Sales	13,740	14,955	16,326	18,627	19,176

Source: Annual Reports of Nike, Inc.

a. Use the growth rates for 2005–2006, 2006–2007, 2007–2008, and 2008–2009 to calculate the average growth rate.
b. Calculate the average growth rate directly from sales.

3.4 Measures of Dispersion

LO 3.4

Calculate and interpret the range, the mean absolute deviation, the variance, the standard deviation, and the coefficient of variation.

In the previous sections we focused on measures of central location, in an attempt to find a typical or central value that describes the data. It is also important to analyze how the data vary around the center. Recall that over the 10-year period 2000–2009, the average returns for the Metals and Income funds were 24.65% and 8.51%, respectively. As an investor you might ask why anyone would put money in the Income fund when, on average, this fund has a lower return. The answer to this question will become readily apparent once we analyze measures of variability or dispersion.

Table 3.8 shows each fund's minimum and maximum returns, as well as each fund's average return, over this time period. Note that the average return for the Income fund is relatively closer to its minimum and maximum returns as compared to the Metals fund. The comparison of the funds illustrates that the average is not sufficient when summarizing a data set; that is, it fails to describe the underlying variability of the data.

TABLE 3.8 Select Measures for the Metal and Income Funds, 2000–2009

	Minimum Return	Average Return	Maximum Return
Metals fund	−56.02%	24.65%	76.46%
Income fund	−11.37%	8.51%	31.77%

We now discuss several measures of dispersion that gauge the variability of a data set. Each measure is a numerical value that equals zero if all data values are identical, and increases as data values become more diverse.

Range

The **range** is the simplest measure of dispersion; it is the difference between the maximum and the minimum values in a data set.

> **Range** = Maximum Value − Minimum Value.

EXAMPLE 3.12

Use the data in Table 3.8 to calculate the range for the Metals and the Income funds.

SOLUTION:

$$\text{Metals fund: } 76.46\% - (-56.02\%) = 132.48\%$$
$$\text{Income fund: } 31.77\% - (-11.37\%) = 43.14\%$$

The Metals fund has the higher value for the range, indicating that it has more dispersion with respect to its minimum and maximum values.

The range is not considered a good measure of dispersion because it focuses solely on the extreme values and ignores every other observation in the data set. While the interquartile range, IQR = Q3 − Q1, discussed in Section 3.2, does not depend on the extreme values, this measure still does not incorporate all the data.

The Mean Absolute Deviation

A good measure of dispersion should consider differences of all observations from the mean. If we simply average all differences from the mean, the positives and the negatives will cancel out, even though they both contribute to dispersion, and the resulting average will equal zero. The **mean absolute deviation** (MAD) is an average of the absolute differences between the observations and the mean.

> ### THE MEAN ABSOLUTE DEVIATION (MAD)
> For sample values, $x_1, x_2, \ldots, x_n$, the **sample MAD** is computed as
> $$\text{Sample MAD} = \frac{\Sigma |x_i - \bar{x}|}{n}.$$
> For population values, $x_1, x_2, \ldots, x_n$, the **population MAD** is computed as
> $$\text{Population MAD} = \frac{\Sigma |x_i - \mu|}{N}.$$

EXAMPLE 3.13

Use the data in Table 3.1 to calculate MAD for the Metals and the Income funds.

SOLUTION: We first compute the MAD for the Metals fund. The second column in Table 3.9 shows differences from the sample mean, $\bar{x} = 24.65$. As mentioned above, the sum of these differences equals zero (or a number very close to zero due to rounding). The third column shows the absolute value of each deviation from the mean. Summing these values yields the numerator for the MAD formula.

TABLE 3.9 MAD Calculations for the Metals Fund

x_i	$x_i - \bar{x}$	$|x_i - \bar{x}|$
−7.34	$-7.34 - 24.65 = -31.99$	31.99
18.33	$18.33 - 24.65 = -6.32$	6.32
⋮	⋮	⋮
76.46	$76.46 - 24.65 = 51.81$	51.81
	Total = 0 (approximately)	Total = 271.12

For the Metals fund: $\text{MAD} = \dfrac{\Sigma|x_i - \bar{x}|}{n} = \dfrac{271.12}{10} = 27.11$.

Similar calculations for the Income fund yield: $\text{MAD} = \dfrac{\Sigma|x_i - \bar{x}|}{n} = \dfrac{70.30}{10} = 7.03$.

The Income fund has a smaller value for MAD than the Metals fund, again indicating a less dispersed data set.

The Variance and the Standard Deviation

The **variance** and the **standard deviation** are the two most widely used measures of dispersion. Instead of calculating the average of the absolute differences from the mean, as in MAD, we calculate the average of the squared differences from the mean. The squaring of differences from the mean emphasizes larger differences more than smaller ones; MAD weighs large and small differences equally.

The variance is defined as the average of the squared differences between the observations and the mean. The formula for the variance differs depending on whether we have a sample or a population. Variance squares the original units of measurement. In order to return to the original units of measurement, we take the positive square root of variance, which gives us the standard deviation.

> **THE VARIANCE AND THE STANDARD DEVIATION**
>
> For sample values, $x_1, x_2, \ldots, x_n$, the **sample variance** s^2 and the **sample standard deviation** s are computed as
>
> $$s^2 = \frac{\Sigma(x_i - \bar{x})^2}{n - 1} \qquad \text{and} \qquad s = \sqrt{s^2}.$$
>
> For population values, $x_1, x_2, \ldots, x_N$, the **population variance** σ^2 and the **population standard deviation** σ are computed as
>
> $$\sigma^2 = \frac{\Sigma(x_i - \mu)^2}{N} \qquad \text{and} \qquad \sigma = \sqrt{\sigma^2}.$$
>
> *Note:* The sample variance uses $n - 1$ rather than n in the denominator; the reason is discussed in Chapter 8.

EXAMPLE 3.14

Use the data in Table 3.1 to calculate the sample variance and the sample standard deviation for the Metals and the Income funds. Express the answers in the correct units of measurement.

SOLUTION: We will show the calculations for the Metals fund with the mean return of 24.65 percent. The second column in Table 3.10 shows each return less the mean.

The third column shows the square of each deviation from the mean. Summing these values yields the numerator for the sample variance formula.

TABLE 3.10 Sample Variance Calculation for the Metals Fund

x_i	$x_i - \bar{x}$	$(x_i - \bar{x})^2$
−7.34	$-7.34 - 24.65 = -31.99$	$(-31.99)^2 = 1{,}023.36$
18.33	$18.33 - 24.65 = -6.32$	$(-6.32)^2 = 39.94$
⋮	⋮	⋮
76.46	$76.46 - 24.65 = 51.81$	$(51.81)^2 = 2{,}684.28$
	Total = 0 (approximately)	Total = 12,407.44

For the Metals fund: $s^2 = \dfrac{\Sigma(x_i - \bar{x})^2}{n - 1} = \dfrac{12{,}407.44}{10 - 1} = 1{,}378.60(\%)^2$.

Note that the units of measurement are squared. The sample standard deviation is

$$s = \sqrt{1{,}378.60} = 37.13(\%).$$

Similar calculations for the Income fund yield

$$s^2 = \frac{\Sigma(x_i - \bar{x})^2}{n - 1} = \frac{1{,}102.34}{10 - 1} = 122.48(\%)^2 \text{ and } s = \sqrt{122.48} = 11.07(\%).$$

Based on all measures of dispersion discussed thus far, we can conclude that the Income fund is less dispersed than the Metals fund. With financial data, standard deviation tends to be the most common measure of risk. Therefore the investment risk of the Income fund is lower than that of the Metals fund.

Some people prefer to use a shortcut formula for computing the variance.

SHORTCUT FORMULA FOR THE VARIANCE

$$s^2 = \frac{\Sigma x_i^2}{n - 1} - \frac{n\bar{x}^2}{n - 1}$$

$$\sigma^2 = \frac{\Sigma x_i^2}{N} - \mu^2$$

We recommend that you use the shortcut formula to replicate the results of Example 3.14.

The Coefficient of Variation

In some instances, analysis entails comparing two or more data sets that have different means or units of measurement. The **coefficient of variation (CV)** serves as a relative measure of dispersion and adjusts for differences in the magnitudes of the means. Calculated by dividing a data set's standard deviation by its mean, CV is a unitless measure that allows for direct comparisons of mean-adjusted dispersion across different data sets.

THE COEFFICIENT OF VARIATION (CV)

$$\text{Sample CV} = \frac{s}{\bar{x}}$$

$$\text{Population CV} = \frac{\sigma}{\mu}$$

Calculate and interpret the coefficient of variation for the Metals and Income funds.

SOLUTION: We use the sample means and the standard deviations computed earlier.

$$\text{For the Metals fund: } CV = \frac{s}{\bar{x}} = \frac{37.13\%}{24.65\%} = 1.51.$$

$$\text{For the Income fund: } CV = \frac{s}{\bar{x}} = \frac{11.07\%}{8.51\%} = 1.30.$$

Since 1.51 is greater than 1.30, we can conclude that the data for the Metals fund has more relative dispersion than the Income fund.

Using Excel to Calculate Measures of Dispersion

As discussed in Section 3.1, the easiest way to calculate many of the measures of dispersion in Excel is to select the relevant data and then choose **Data** > **Data Analysis** > **Descriptive Statistics** > **OK**. Section 3.1 outlines the directions you should use in the *Descriptive Statistics* dialog box. For measures of variability, Excel treats the data as a sample and returns the range, the sample variance, and the sample standard deviation; these measures are in bold face in Table 3.3. Excel offers several built-in functions that we can use to compute other summary measures. For example, since the output using the **Descriptive Statistics** option does not provide the value for MAD, we can obtain MAD as follows.

A. Open the data labeled *Fund Returns* (Table 3.1) from the text website into an Excel spreadsheet.

B. Choose **Formulas** > **Insert Function**.

C. In the *Insert Function* dialog box, choose **All** under *Select a Category*. Under *Select a Function*, choose **AVEDEV**. Click **OK**.

D. In the AVEDEV dialog box as shown in Figure 3.3, click on the box to the right of *Number 1*. Select the Metals data. Click **OK**. You should see the value 27.11, which equals the MAD value that we calculated manually. Repeat these steps to calculate the MAD for the Income fund.

FIGURE 3.3 Excel's dialog box for MAD

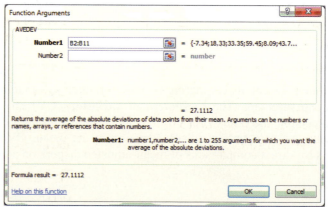

Similarly, we can compute the population variance by using the **VAR.P** function in Excel. Alternatively, we can compute the population variance by simply multiplying the sample variance that Excel provides by $\frac{N-1}{N}$.

SYNOPSIS OF INTRODUCTORY CASE

Vanguard's Precious Metals and Mining fund (Metals) and Fidelity's Strategic Income fund (Income) were two top-performing mutual funds for the years 2000 through 2009. An analysis of annual return data for these two funds provides important information for any type of investor. Over the past 10 years, the Metals fund posts the higher values for both the mean return and the median return, with values of 24.65% and 33.83%, respectively. Extreme values are often present when the mean differs dramatically from the median. On the other hand, the mean return and the median return for the Income fund are quite comparable at 8.51% and 7.34%, respectively.

While measures of central location typically represent the reward of investing, these measures do not incorporate the risk of investing. Standard deviation tends to be the most common measure of risk with financial data. Since the standard deviation for the Metals fund is substantially greater than the standard deviation for the Income fund (37.13% > 11.07%), the Metals fund is likelier to have returns far above as well as far below its mean. Also, the coefficient of variation—a relative measure of dispersion—for the Metals fund is greater than the coefficient of variation for the Income fund. These two measures of dispersion indicate that the Metals fund is the riskier investment. These funds provide credence to the theory that funds with higher average returns often carry higher risk.

Concepts

31. Consider the following population data:

36	42	12	10	22

   a. Calculate the range.
   b. Calculate MAD.
   c. Calculate the population variance.
   d. Calculate the population standard deviation.

32. Consider the following population data:

0	−4	2	−8	10

   a. Calculate the range.
   b. Calculate MAD.
   c. Calculate the population variance.
   d. Calculate the population standard deviation.

33. Consider the following sample data:

40	46	32	52	38	42

   a. Calculate the range.
   b. Calculate MAD.
   c. Calculate the sample variance.
   d. Calculate the sample standard deviation.

34. Consider the following sample data:

−10	12	−8	−2	4	8

   a. Calculate the range.
   b. Calculate MAD.
   c. Calculate the sample variance.
   d. Calculate the sample coefficient of variation.

Applications

35. The Department of Transportation (DOT) fields thousands of complaints about airlines each year. The DOT categorizes and tallies complaints, and then periodically publishes rankings of airline performance. The following table presents the 2006 results for the 10 largest U.S. airlines.

Airline	Complaints*	Airline	Complaints*
Southwest Airlines	1.82	Northwest Airlines	8.84
JetBlue Airways	3.98	Delta Airlines	10.35
Alaska Airlines	5.24	American Airlines	10.87
AirTran Airways	6.24	US Airways	13.59
Continental Airlines	8.83	United Airlines	13.60

SOURCE: Department of Transportation.
*per million passengers.

   a. Which airline fielded the least amount of complaints? Which airline fielded the most? Calculate the range.

b. Calculate the mean and median number of complaints from this sample.

c. Calculate the variance and standard deviation.

36. The monthly closing stock prices (rounded to the nearest dollar) for Starbucks Corp. and Panera Bread Co. for the first six months of 2010 are reported in the following table.

Month	Starbucks Corp.	Panera Bread Co.
January 2010	$22	$71
February 2010	23	73
March 2010	24	76
April 2010	26	78
May 2010	26	81
June 2010	24	75

Source: http://www.finance.yahoo.com.

a. Calculate the sample variance and sample standard deviation for each firm's stock price.

b. Which firm's stock price had greater variability as measured by standard deviation?

c. Which firm's stock price had the greater relative dispersion?

37. FILE While the housing market is in recession and is not likely to emerge anytime soon, real estate investment in college towns continues to promise good returns (*The Wall Street Journal*, September 24, 2010). Marcela Treisman works for an investment firm in Michigan. Her assignment is to analyze the rental market in Ann Arbor, which is home to the University of Michigan. She gathers data on monthly rent for 2011 along with the square footage of 40 homes. A portion of the data is shown in the accompanying table; the complete data, labeled **Ann Arbor Rental**, can be found on the text website.

Monthly Rent	Square Footage
645	500
675	648
⋮	⋮
2400	2700

Source: www.zillow.com.

a. Use Excel to calculate the mean and standard deviation for monthly rent.

b. Use Excel to calculate the mean and standard deviation for square footage.

c. Which variable has greater relative dispersion?

38. FILE Go to the text website and access the data labeled **Largest Corporations**. It shows the Fortune 500 rankings of America's largest corporations for 2010. Next to each corporation are its market capitalization (in billions of dollars as of March 26, 2010) and its total return to investors for the year 2009.

a. Calculate the coefficient of variation for market capitalization.

b. Calculate the coefficient of variation for total return.

c. Which variable has greater relative dispersion?

3.5 Mean-Variance Analysis and the Sharpe Ratio

LO 3.5

Explain mean-variance analysis and the Sharpe ratio.

In the introduction to Section 3.4, we asked why any rational investor would invest in the Income fund over the Metals fund, since the average return for the Income fund over the 2000–2009 period was approximately 9%, whereas the average return for the Metals fund was close to 25%. It turns out that investments with higher returns also carry higher risk. Investments include financial assets such as stocks, bonds, and mutual funds. The average return represents an investor's reward, whereas variance, or equivalently standard deviation, corresponds to risk. That is, the higher the average associated with the return on a particular stock, bond, or mutual fund, the higher is the reward. Similarly, the higher the variance, the higher is the level of risk.

According to mean-variance analysis, we can measure performance of any risky asset solely on the basis of the average and the variance of its returns.

MEAN-VARIANCE ANALYSIS

Mean-variance analysis postulates that we measure the performance of an asset by its rate of return and evaluate this rate of return in terms of its reward (mean) and risk (variance). In general, investments with higher average returns are also associated with higher risk.

Consider Table 3.11, which summarizes the mean and variance for the Metals and Income funds.

TABLE 3.11 Mean-Variance Analysis of Two Mutual Funds, 2000–2009

Fund	Mean Return	Variance
Metals fund	24.65%	1,378.61(%)^2
Income fund	8.51%	122.48(%)^2

It is true that the Metals fund provided an investor with a higher reward over the 10-year period, but this same investor encountered considerable risk compared to an investor who invested in the Income fund. Table 3.11 shows that the variance of the Metals (1,378.61(%)^2) fund is significantly greater than the variance of the Income fund (122.48(%)^2). If we look back at Table 3.1 and focus on the Metals fund, we see returns far above the average return of 24.65% (for example, 59.45% and 76.46%), but also returns far below the average return of 24.65% (for example, −7.34% and −56.02%). Repeating this same analysis for the Income fund, the returns are far closer to the average return of 8.51%; thus, the Income fund provided a lower return, but also far less risk.

A discussion of mean-variance analysis seems almost incomplete without mention of the **Sharpe ratio**. Nobel Laureate William Sharpe developed what he originally referred to as the "reward-to-variability" ratio. However, academics and finance professionals prefer to call it the "Sharpe ratio." The Sharpe ratio is used to characterize how well the return of an asset compensates for the risk that the investor takes. Investors are often advised to pick investments that have high Sharpe ratios.

The Sharpe ratio is defined with the reward specified in terms of the population mean and the variability specified in terms of the population variance. However, we often compute the Sharpe ratio in terms of the sample mean and sample variance, where the return is usually expressed as a percent and not a decimal.

THE SHARPE RATIO

The **Sharpe ratio** measures the extra reward per unit of risk. The Sharpe ratio for an investment I is computed as:

$$\frac{\bar{x}_I - \bar{R}_f}{s_I}$$

where $\bar{x}_I$ is the mean return for the investment, $\bar{R}_f$ is the mean return for a risk-free asset such as a Treasury bill (T-bill), and s_I is the standard deviation for the investment.

The numerator of the Sharpe ratio measures the extra reward that investors receive for the added risk taken—this difference is often called excess return. The higher the Sharpe ratio, the better the investment compensates its investors for risk.

EXAMPLE 3.16

Calculate and interpret the Sharpe ratios for the Metals and Income funds given that the return on a 1-year T-bill is 4%.

SOLUTION: Since the return on a 1-year T-bill is 4%, $\bar{R}_f = 4$. Plugging in the values of the relevant means and standard deviations into the Sharpe ratio yields:

Sharpe ratio for the Metals fund: $\dfrac{\bar{x}_I - \bar{R}_f}{s_I} = \dfrac{24.65 - 4}{37.13} = 0.56.$

Sharpe ratio for the Income fund: $\dfrac{\bar{x}_I - \bar{R}_f}{s_I} = \dfrac{8.51 - 4}{11.07} = 0.41.$

We had earlier shown that the Metals fund had a higher return, which is good, along with a higher variance, which is bad. We can use the Sharpe ratio to make a valid comparison between the funds. The Metals fund provides the higher Sharpe ratio than the Income fund (0.56 > 0.41); therefore, the Metals fund offered more reward per unit of risk compared to the Income fund.

EXERCISES 3.5

Concepts

39. Consider the following data for two investments, A and B:

Investment A:	$\bar{x} = 8$ and $s = 5$
Investment B:	$\bar{x} = 10$ and $s = 7$

a. Which investment provides the higher return? Which investment provides the least risk? Explain.

b. Given a risk-free rate of 2%, calculate the Sharpe ratio for each investment. Which investment provides the higher reward per unit of risk? Explain.

40. Consider the following data for two investments, A and B:

Investment A:	$\bar{x} = 10$ and $s = 5$
Investment B:	$\bar{x} = 15$ and $s = 10$

a. Which investment provides the higher return? Which investment provides the least risk? Explain.

b. Given a risk-free rate of 1.4%, calculate the Sharpe ratio for each investment. Which investment provides the higher reward per unit of risk? Explain.

41. Consider the following returns for two investments, A and B:

Investment 1:	2%	8%	−4%	6%
Investment 2:	6%	12%	−8%	10%

a. Which investment provides the higher return?

b. Which investment provides the least risk?

c. Given a risk-free rate of 1.2%, calculate the Sharpe ratio for each investment. Which investment has performed better? Explain.

Applications

42. The following table shows the annual returns (in percent) and summary measures for the Vanguard Energy Fund and the Vanguard Health Care Fund from 2005 through 2009.

Year	Energy	Health Care
2005	44.60	15.41
2006	19.68	10.87
2007	37.00	4.43
2008	−42.87	−18.45
2009	38.36	20.96
	$\bar{x}_{Energy} = 19.35$	$\bar{x}_{Health} = 6.64$
	$s_{Energy} = 35.99$	$s_{Health} = 15.28$

SOURCE: http://www.finance.yahoo.com.

a. Which fund had the higher average return?

b. Which fund was riskier over this time period?

c. Given a risk-free rate of 3%, which fund has the higher Sharpe ratio? What does this ratio imply?

43 The following table shows the annual returns (in percent) and summary measures for the Fidelity Latin America Fund and the Fidelity Canada Fund from 2005 through 2009.

Year	Latin America	Canada
2005	55.17	27.89
2006	44.33	15.04
2007	43.71	35.02
2008	−54.64	−42.64
2009	91.60	39.63

SOURCE: http://www.finance.yahoo.com.

a. Which fund had the higher average return?

b. Which fund was riskier over this time period?

c. Given a risk-free rate of 3%, which fund has the higher Sharpe ratio? What does this ratio imply?

3.6 Chebyshev's Theorem and the Empirical Rule

LO 3.6

Apply Chebyshev's Theorem and the empirical rule.

We have discussed several different measures of central location and dispersion for data. Unlike measures of central location, it is not always easy to interpret measures of dispersion intuitively. All we can say is that a low value of standard deviation indicates that the data points are close to the mean, while a high standard deviation indicates that the data are spread out. We will use Chebyshev's theorem and the empirical rule to make more precise statements regarding the percentage of data values that fall within a specified number of standard deviations from the mean.

Chebyshev's Theorem

As we will see in more detail in later chapters, it is important to be able to use the standard deviation to make statements about the proportion of observations that fall within certain intervals. Fortunately, a Russian mathematician Pavroty Chebyshev (1821–1894) found bounds for the proportion of the data that lie within a specified number of standard deviations from the mean.

CHEBYSHEV'S THEOREM

For any data set, the proportion of observations that lie within k standard deviations from the mean is at least $1 - 1/k^2$, where k is any number greater than 1.

This theorem holds both for a sample and for a population.

EXAMPLE 3.17

A large lecture class has 280 students. The professor has announced that the mean score on an exam is 74 with a standard deviation of 8. At least how many students scored within 58 and 90?

SOLUTION: The score 58 is two standard deviations below the mean, ($\bar{x} - 2s = 74 - (2 \times 8) = 58$), while the score 90 is two standard deviations above the mean, ($\bar{x} + 2s = 74 + (2 \times 8) = 90$). Using Chebyshev's Theorem and $k = 2$, we have $1 - 1/2^2 = 0.75$. In other words, Chebyshev's Theorem asserts that at least 75% of the scores will fall within 58 and 90. Therefore, at least 75% of 280 students, or $0.75(280) = 210$ students, scored within 58 and 90.

The application of Chebyshev's Theorem results in conservative bounds for the percentage of observations falling in a particular interval. The actual percentage of observations lying in the interval may in fact be much larger.

The Empirical Rule

If we know that our data are drawn from a relatively symmetric and bell-shaped distribution—perhaps by a visual inspection of its histogram or polygon—then we can make more precise statements about the percentage of observations that fall within certain intervals. Symmetry and bell-shape are characteristics of the normal distribution, a topic that we discuss in Chapter 6. The normal distribution is often used as an approximation for many real-world applications. The **empirical rule** is illustrated in Figure 3.4. It provides the approximate percentage of observations that fall within 1, 2, or 3 standard deviations from the mean.

THE EMPIRICAL RULE

Given a sample mean $\bar{x}$, a sample standard deviation s, and a relatively symmetric and bell-shaped distribution:

- Approximately 68% of all observations fall in the interval $\bar{x} \pm s$,
- Approximately 95% of all observations fall in the interval $\bar{x} \pm 2s$, and
- Almost all observations fall in the interval $\bar{x} \pm 3s$.

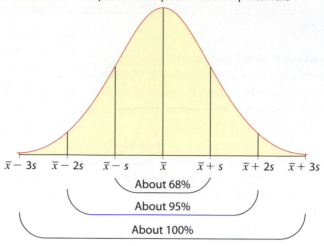

FIGURE 3.4 Graphical description of the empirical rule

$\bar{x} - 3s$ $\bar{x} - 2s$ $\bar{x} - s$ $\bar{x}$ $\bar{x} + s$ $\bar{x} + 2s$ $\bar{x} + 3s$

About 68%

About 95%

About 100%

EXAMPLE 3.18

Let's revisit Example 3.17 regarding a large lecture class with 280 students with a mean score of 74 and a standard deviation of 8. Assume that the distribution is symmetric and bell-shaped.

a. Approximately how many students scored within 58 and 90?

b. Approximately how many students scored more than 90?

SOLUTION:

a. As shown in Example 3.17, the score 58 is two standard deviations below the mean while the score 90 is two standard deviations above the mean. The empirical rule states that approximately 95% of the observations fall within two standard deviations of the mean. Therefore about 95% of 280 students, or 0.95(280) = 266 students, scored within 58 and 90.

b. We know that the score 90 is two standard deviations above the mean. Since approximately 95% of the observations fall within two standard deviations of the mean, we can infer that 5% of the observations fall outside the interval. Therefore, about half of 5%, or 2.5%, of 280 students scored above 90. Equivalently, about 7 students (0.025 × 280) scored above 90 on the exam. If the professor uses a cutoff score above 90 for an A, then only seven students in the class are expected to get an A.

The main difference between Chebyshev's Theorem and the empirical rule is that Chebyshev's Theorem applies to all data sets whereas the empirical rule is appropriate when the distribution is symmetric and bell-shaped.

The empirical rule also provides us with a rough approximation for the standard deviation of the data if we only have information on the range of the data. Since the empirical rule tells us that 95% of the observations fall within two standard deviations of the mean, the resulting interval encompasses approximately $4 \times s$ of the observations. Thus, the range = $4 \times s$, or analogously, $s = \frac{\text{range}}{4}$. Keep in mind that this formula provides only a rough estimate for the sample standard deviation.

Concepts

44. A data set has a mean of 80 and a standard deviation of 5.
    a. Using Chebyshev's Theorem, what percentage of the observations fall between 70 and 90?
    b. Using Chebyshev's Theorem, what percentage of the observations fall between 65 and 95?

45. A data set has a mean of 1500 and a standard deviation of 100.
    a. Using Chebyshev's Theorem, what percentage of the observations fall between 1300 and 1700?
    b. Using Chebyshev's Theorem, what percentage of the observations fall between 1100 and 1900?

46. A data set has a mean of 500 and a standard deviation of 25.
    a. Using Chebyshev's Theorem, find the interval that encompasses at least 75% of the data.
    b. Using Chebyshev's Theorem, find the interval that encompasses at least 89% of the data.

47. Data are drawn from a relatively symmetric and bell-shaped distribution with a mean of 20 and a standard deviation of 2.
    a. What percentage of the observations fall between 18 and 22?
    b. What percentage of the observations fall between 16 and 24?
    c. What percentage of the observations are less than 16?

48. Consider a symmetric and bell-shaped distribution with a mean of 750 and a standard deviation of 50. There are 500 observations in the data set.
    a. What percentage of the observations are less than 700?
    b. Approximately how many observations are less than 700?

49. Data are drawn from a symmetric and bell-shaped distribution with a mean of 25 and a standard deviation of 4. There are 1000 observations in the data set.
    a. What percentage of the observations are less than 33?
    b. Approximately how many observations are less than 33?

50. Data are drawn from a relatively symmetric and bell-shaped distribution with a mean of 5 and a range of 10.
    a. What is the rough estimate of the standard deviation?
    b. What percentage of the observations are positive?
    c. What percentage of the observations are not positive?

51. Data with 250 observations are drawn from a relatively symmetric and bell-shaped distribution with a mean of 50 and a range of 48.
    a. What is the rough estimate of the standard deviation?
    b. Approximately how many observations are more than 74?

Applications

52. A sample of the salaries of assistant professors on the business faculty at a local university revealed a mean income of $72,000 with a standard deviation of $3,000.
    a. Using Chebyshev's Theorem, what percentage of the faculty earns at least $66,000 but no more than $78,000?
    b. Using Chebyshev's Theorem, what percentage of the faculty earns at least $63,000 but no more than $81,000?

53. The historical returns on a portfolio had an average return of 8 percent and a standard deviation of 12 percent. Assume that returns on this portfolio follow a bell-shaped distribution.
    a. What percentage of returns were greater than 20 percent?
    b. What percentage of returns were below −16 percent?

54. It is often assumed that IQ scores follow a bell-shaped distribution with a mean of 100 and a standard deviation of 16.
    a. What percentage of scores are between 84 and 116?
    b. What percentage of scores are less than 68?
    c. What percentage of scores are more than 116?

55. An investment strategy has an expected return of 8 percent and a standard deviation of 6 percent. Assume investment returns are bell shaped.
    a. How likely is it to earn a return between 2 percent and 14 percent?
    b. How likely is it to earn a return greater than 14 percent?
    c. How likely is it to earn a return below −4 percent?

56. Average talk time between charges of a given cell phone is advertised as 4 hours. Let the standard deviation be 0.8 hours.
    a. Use Chebyshev's Theorem to approximate the proportion of cell phones that will have talk time between 2.4 hours and 5.6 hours.
    b. Assume a bell-shaped distribution to approximate the proportion of cell phones that will have talk time between 2.4 hours and 5.6 hours.

3.7 Summarizing Grouped Data

The mean and the variance are the most widely used descriptive measures in statistics. However, the preceding formulas apply to ungrouped or raw data. In many instances we access data that are in the form of a frequency distribution or grouped data. This is especially true of secondary data, such as data we obtain from government publications.

LO **3.7**

Calculate the mean and the variance for grouped data.

When data are grouped or aggregated, the formulas for the mean and the variance must be modified.

> ## CALCULATING THE MEAN AND THE VARIANCE FOR A FREQUENCY DISTRIBUTION
>
> **Sample:**
>
> Mean: $\bar{x} = \dfrac{\sum m_i f_i}{n}$
>
> Variance: $s^2 = \dfrac{\sum (m_i - \bar{x})^2 f_i}{n - 1}$
>
> **Population:**
>
> Mean: $\mu = \dfrac{\sum m_i f_i}{N}$
>
> Variance: $\sigma^2 = \dfrac{\sum (m_i - \mu)^2 f_i}{N}$,
>
> where m_i and f_i are the midpoint and the frequency of the ith class, respectively. The standard deviation is the positive square root of the variance.

Note that by aggregating, some of the data information is lost. Therefore, unlike in the case of raw data, we can only compute approximate values of the summary measures with grouped data.

EXAMPLE 3.19

Recall the frequency distribution of house prices we constructed in Chapter 2.

Class (in $1000s)	Frequency
300 up to 400	4
400 up to 500	11
500 up to 600	14
600 up to 700	5
700 up to 800	2

a. Calculate the average house price.

b. Calculate the sample variance and the sample standard deviation.

SOLUTION: Table 3.12 shows the frequencies f_i and the midpoint of each class m_i in the second and third columns, respectively.

TABLE 3.12 The Sample Mean and the Sample Variance Calculation for Grouped Data

Class (in $1,000s)	f_i	m_i	$m_i f_i$	$(m_i - \bar{x})^2 f_i$
300 up to 400	4	350	1,400	$(350 - 522)^2 \times 4 = 118{,}336$
400 up to 500	11	450	4,950	$(450 - 522)^2 \times 11 = 57{,}024$
500 up to 600	14	550	7,700	$(550 - 522)^2 \times 14 = 10{,}976$
600 up to 700	5	650	3,250	$(650 - 522)^2 \times 5 = 81{,}920$
700 up to 800	2	750	1,500	$(750 - 522)^2 \times 2 = 103{,}968$
Total	36		18,800	372,224

a. For the mean, we multiply each class's midpoint by its respective frequency, as shown in the fourth column of Table 3.12. Finally, we sum the fourth column and divide by the sample size. Or,

$$\bar{x} = \frac{\sum m_i f_i}{n} = \frac{18{,}800}{36} = 522.$$ The average house price is thus $522,000.

b. For the sample variance, we first calculate the sum of the weighted squared differences from the mean. The fifth column in Table 3.12 shows the appropriate calculations for each class. Summing the values in the fifth column yields the numerator for the variance formula:

$$s^2 = \frac{\Sigma(m_i - \bar{x})^2 f_i}{n - 1} = \frac{372{,}224}{36 - 1} = 10{,}635(\$)^2.$$

The standard deviation is simply the positive square root of the sample variance, or, $s = \sqrt{10{,}635} = 103.13(\$)$. The standard deviation is $103.13.

As in the case of raw data, some people prefer to use a shortcut formula for computing the variance.

SHORTCUT FORMULA FOR THE VARIANCE

$$s^2 = \frac{\Sigma m_i^2 f_i}{n - 1} - \frac{n\bar{x}^2}{n - 1}$$

$$\sigma^2 = \frac{\Sigma m_i^2 f_i}{N} - \mu^2$$

We recommend that you use the shortcut formula to replicate the results of Example 3.19.

Many times the data from secondary sources are distributed in the form of a relative frequency distribution rather than a frequency distribution. In order to use the formulas for the mean and variance for grouped data, first convert the relative frequency distribution into a frequency distribution, as discussed in Section 2.2 of Chapter 2.

The sample mean calculated with grouped data can be thought of as a **weighted mean** where the relative frequency f_i/n is treated as a weight for the midpoint. The more general formula for the weighted mean is given below.

THE WEIGHTED MEAN

Let $w_1, w_2, \ldots, w_n$ denote the weights of the sample observations $x_1, x_2, \ldots, x_n$ such that $w_1 + w_2 + \cdots + w_n = 1$. The **weighted mean** for the sample is computed as

$$\bar{x} = \Sigma w_i x_i.$$

The weighted mean for the population is computed similarly.

EXAMPLE 3.20

A student scores 60 on Exam 1, 70 on Exam 2, and 80 on Exam 3. What is the student's average score for the course if Exams 1, 2, and 3 are worth 25%, 25%, and 50% of the grade, respectively?

SOLUTION: We define the weights as $w_1 = 0.25$, $w_2 = 0.25$, and $w_3 = 0.50$. We compute the average score as $\bar{x} = \Sigma w_i x_i = 0.25(60) + 0.25(70) + 0.50(80) = 72.50$. Note that the unweighted mean is only 70 as it does not incorporate the higher weight given to the score on Exam 3.

EXERCISES 3.7

Concepts

57. Consider the following frequency distribution.

Class	Frequency
2 up to 4	20
4 up to 6	60
6 up to 8	80
8 up to 10	20

a. Calculate the population mean.
b. Calculate the population variance and the population standard deviation.

58. Consider the following frequency distribution.

Class	Frequency
50 up to 60	10
60 up to 70	15
70 up to 80	8
80 up to 100	2

a. Calculate the sample mean.
b. Calculate the sample variance and the sample standard deviation.

59. The following relative frequency distribution was constructed from a population of 200. Calculate the population mean, the population variance, and the population standard deviation.

Class	Relative Frequency
−20 up to −10	0.35
−10 up to 0	0.25
0 up to 10	0.40
10 up to 20	0.05

60. The following relative frequency distribution was constructed from a sample of 50. Calculate the sample mean, the sample variance, and the sample standard deviation.

Class	Relative Frequency
0 up to 2	0.34
2 up to 4	0.20
4 up to 6	0.40
6 up to 8	0.06

Applications

61. Fifty cities provided information on vacancy rates (in percent) in local apartments in the following frequency distribution.

Vacancy Rate (in percent)	Frequency
0 up to 3	5
3 up to 6	5
6 up to 9	10
9 up to 12	20
12 up to 15	10

a. Calculate the average vacancy rate.
b. Calculate the variance and the standard deviation for this sample.

62. A local hospital provided the following frequency distribution summarizing the weights of babies delivered over the month of January.

Weight (in pounds)	Number of Babies
2 up to 4	3
4 up to 6	8
6 up to 8	25
8 up to 10	30
10 up to 12	4

a. Calculate the mean weight.
b. Calculate the variance and the standard deviation for this sample.

63. An investor bought common stock of Microsoft Corporation on three occasions at the following prices.

Date	Price Per Share	Number of Shares
January 2009	$19.58	70
July 2009	$24.06	80
December 2009	$29.54	50

Calculate the average price per share at which the investor bought these shares.

64. A researcher conducts a mileage economy test involving 80 cars. The frequency distribution describing average miles per gallon (mpg) appears below.

Average MPG	Frequency
15 up to 20	15
20 up to 25	30
25 up to 30	15
30 up to 35	10
35 up to 40	7
40 up to 45	3

a. Calculate the mean mpg.
b. Calculate the variance and the standard deviation.

65. The Boston Security Analysts Society, Inc. (BSAS) is a nonprofit association that serves as a forum for the exchange of ideas for the investment community. Suppose the ages of its members are based on the following frequency distribution.

Age	Frequency
21–31	11
32–42	44
43–53	26
54–64	7

a. Calculate the mean age.
b. Calculate the sample variance and the sample standard deviation.

66. The National Sporting Goods Association (NSGA) conducted a survey of the ages of people that purchased athletic footwear in 2009. The ages are summarized in the following relative frequency distribution.

Age of Purchaser	Percent
Under 14 years old	19
14 to 17 years old	6
18 to 24 years old	10
25 to 34 years old	13
35 to 44 years old	14
45 to 64 years old	25
65 years old and over	13

Suppose the survey was based on 100 individuals. Calculate the average age of this distribution. Calculate the sample standard deviation. Use 10 as the midpoint of the first class and 75 as the midpoint of the last class.

67. You score 90 on the midterm, 60 on the final, and 80 on the class project. What is your average score if the midterm is worth 30%, the final is worth 50% and the class project is worth 20%?

68. An investor bought common stock of Dell Inc. Corporation on three occasions at the following prices.

Date	Price Per Share
January 2009	$10.34
July 2009	$13.98
December 2009	$14.02

a. What is the average price per share if the investor had bought 100 shares in January, 60 in July, and 40 in December?

b. What is the average price per share if the investor had bought 40 shares in January, 60 in July, and 100 in December?

3.8 Covariance and Correlation

LO **3.8**

Calculate and interpret the covariance and the correlation coefficient.

In Chapter 2, we introduced the idea of a scatterplot to visually assess whether two variables had some type of linear relationship. In this section we present two numerical measures that quantify the existence and strength of a particular relationship between two variables, x and y.

An objective numerical measure that reveals the direction of the linear relationship between two variables is called the **covariance**. We use s_{xy} to refer to a sample covariance and σ_{xy} to refer to a population covariance.

THE COVARIANCE

For values $(x_1, y_1), (x_2, y_2), \ldots, (x_n, y_n)$, the **sample covariance** s_{xy} is computed as

$$s_{xy} = \frac{\Sigma(x_i - \bar{x})(y_i - \bar{y})}{n - 1}.$$

For values $(x_1, y_1), (x_2, y_2), \ldots, (x_N, y_N)$, the **population covariance** σ_{xy} is computed as

$$\sigma_{xy} = \frac{\Sigma(x_i - \mu_x)(y_i - \mu_y)}{N}.$$

Note: As in the case of the sample variance, the sample covariance uses $n - 1$ rather than n in the denominator.

- A positive value of covariance indicates a positive linear relationship between the two variables; on average, if x is above its mean, then y tends to be above its mean, and vice versa.

- A negative value of covariance indicates a negative linear relationship between the two variables; on average, if x is above its mean, then y tends to be below its mean, and vice versa.

- The covariance is zero if y and x have no linear relationship.

The covariance, like the variance earlier, is difficult to interpret because it is sensitive to the units of measurement. That is, the covariance between two variables might be 100 and the covariance between another two variables might be 1,000; yet all we can conclude is that both sets of variables are positively related. We cannot comment on the strength of the relationships. An easier measure to interpret is the **correlation coefficient**; it describes both the direction and strength of the relationship between x and y. We use r_{xy} to refer to a sample correlation coefficient and ρ_{xy} (the Greek letter rho) to refer to a population correlation coefficient.

THE CORRELATION COEFFICIENT

Sample Correlation Coefficient: $r_{xy} = \dfrac{s_{xy}}{s_x s_y}$

Population Correlation Coefficient: $\rho_{xy} = \dfrac{\sigma_{xy}}{\sigma_x \sigma_y}$

The correlation coefficient is unit free since the units in the numerator cancel with those in the denominator. The value of the correlation coefficient falls between -1 and 1. A perfect positive relationship exists if it equals 1, and a perfect negative relationship exists if it equals -1. Other values for the correlation coefficient must be interpreted with reference to -1, 0, or 1. For instance, a correlation coefficient equal to -0.80 indicates a strong negative relationship, whereas a correlation coefficient equal to 0.12 indicates a weak positive relationship.

EXAMPLE 3.21

Calculate the covariance and the correlation coefficient for the Metals (x) and Income (y) funds. Interpret these values. Recall that $\bar{x} = 24.65$, $s_x = 37.13$, $\bar{y} = 8.51$, and $s_y = 11.07$.

SOLUTION: As a first step, Figure 3.5 shows a scatterplot of the return data for the Metals and Income funds. It appears that there is a positive linear relationship between the two fund returns.

FIGURE 3.5 Scatterplot of return data for the Metals and Income funds

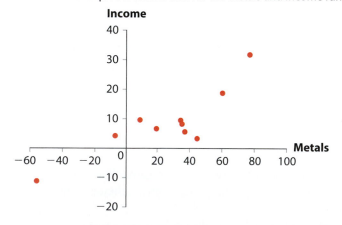

Table 3.13 shows the return data for each fund in the first two columns. The third column shows the product of differences from the mean.

Summing the values in the third column yields the numerator for the covariance formula. Thus, we calculate the covariance as:

$$s_{xy} = \frac{\Sigma(x_i - \bar{x})(y_i - \bar{y})}{n - 1} = \frac{3{,}165.55}{10 - 1} = 351.73.$$

TABLE 3.13 Covariance Calculation for the Metals and Income Funds

x_i	y_i	$(x_i - \bar{x})(y_i - \bar{y})$
−7.34	4.07	$(-7.34 - 24.65)(4.07 - 8.51) = 142.04$
18.33	6.52	$(18.33 - 24.65)(6.52 - 8.51) = 12.58$
⋮	⋮	⋮
76.46	31.77	$(76.46 - 24.65)(31.77 - 8.51) = 1{,}205.10$
		Total = 3,165.55

The covariance of 351.73 indicates that the variables have a positive linear relationship. In other words, on average, when one fund's return is above its mean, the other fund's return is above its mean, and vice versa. The covariance is used to compute the correlation coefficient as:

$$r_{xy} = \frac{s_{xy}}{s_x s_y} = \frac{351.73}{(37.13)(11.07)} = 0.86.$$

The correlation coefficient of 0.86 indicates a strong positive linear relationship. In order to diversify the risk in an investor's portfolio, an investor is often advised to invest in assets (such as stocks, bonds, and mutual funds) whose returns are not strongly correlated. If asset returns are not strongly correlated, then if one investment does poorly, the other may still do well.

Using Excel to Calculate Covariance and the Correlation Coefficient

We can use Excel to replicate the results that we arrived at by hand.

A. FILE Open the *Fund Returns* data (Table 3.1) from text website into an Excel spreadsheet.

B. Choose **Formulas > Insert Function > COVARIANCE.S**. (If you have population data choose COVAR or COVARIANCE.P.) Click **OK**.

C. Figure 3.6 shows Excel's COVARIANCE.S dialog box. Click on the box to the right of *Array 1*. Select the Metals data. Then, click on the box to the right of *Array 2*. **Select** the Income data. Click **OK**. You should see the value 351.73, which is the value that we calculated manually.

FIGURE 3.6 Excel's dialog box for the covariance

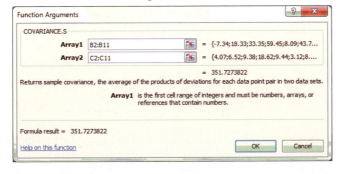

D. In order to calculate the sample correlation coefficient, choose **Formulas > Insert Function > CORREL**. This command is appropriate for both sample and population data. Select the data as you did in part C. Excel returns the value 0.86, again matching the value that we calculated manually.

EXERCISES 3.8

Concepts

69. Consider the following sample data:

x	12	18	20	22	25
y	15	20	25	22	27

a. Calculate the covariance between the variables.
b. Calculate and interpret the correlation coefficient.

70. Consider the following sample data:

x	−2	0	3	4	7
y	−2	−3	−8	−9	−10

a. Calculate the covariance between the variables.
b. Calculate and interpret the correlation coefficient.

Applications

71. The following table shows the annual returns (in percent) for the T-Rowe Price's Value and International Stock funds for the time period 2005–2009.

Year	Value Fund	International Fund
2005	6.30	16.27
2006	19.75	19.26
2007	0.75	13.43
2008	−39.76	−48.02
2009	37.15	52.20

a. Calculate and interpret the covariance between returns.
b. Calculate and interpret the coefficient of correlation.

72. In an attempt to determine whether a linear relationship exists between the price of a home and the number of days it takes to sell the home, a real estate agent collected the following data from recent sales in his city.

Price (in $1,000s)	Days to Sell Home	Price (in $1,000s)	Days to Sell Home
265	136	430	145
225	125	515	121
160	120	180	122
325	140	423	145

a. Calculate the covariance. What kind of linear relationship exists?
b. Calculate the coefficient of correlation. Comment on the strength of the linear relationship.

73. The director of graduate admissions at a local university is analyzing the relationship between scores on the Graduate Record Examination (GRE) and subsequent performance in graduate school, as measured by a student's grade point average (GPA). She uses a sample of 10 students who graduated within the past five years.

GRE	GPA
1500	3.4
1400	3.5
1000	3.0
1050	2.9
1100	3.0
1250	3.3
800	2.7
850	2.8
950	3.2
1350	3.3

a. Calculate and interpret the covariance.
b. Calculate and interpret the coefficient of correlation. Does an applicant's GRE score seem to be a good indicator of subsequent performance in graduate school?

74. A social scientist wants to analyze the relationship between educational attainment and salary. He collects the following sample of data where "Education" refers to years of higher education and "Salary" is the person's annual salary in thousands of dollars.

Education	3	4	6	2	5	4	8	0
Salary	$40	53	60	35	55	50	80	35

a. Calculate the covariance. What kind of linear relationship exists?
b. Calculate the coefficient of correlation. Comment on the strength of the linear relationship.

WRITING WITH STATISTICS

Many environmental groups and politicians are suggesting a return to the federal 55-mile-per-hour (mph) speed limit on America's highways. They argue that not only will a lower national speed limit reduce greenhouse emissions, it will also increase traffic safety.

Cameron Grinnell believes that a lower speed limit will not increase traffic safety. He believes that traffic safety is based on the variability of the speeds with which people are driving, rather than the average speed. The person who drives 20 mph below the pace of traffic is often as much a safety menace as the speeder. Cameron gathers the speeds of 40 cars from a highway with a speed limit of 55 mph (Highway 1) and the speeds of 40 cars from a highway with a speed limit of 65 mph (Highway 2). A portion of the data is shown in Table 3.14; the complete data, labeled **Highway Speeds**, are available on the text website.

TABLE 3.14 Speed of Cars from Highway 1 and Highway 2

Highway 1 (55-mph limit)	Highway 2 (65-mph limit)
60	70
55	65
⋮	⋮
52	65

Cameron would like to use the above sample information to:

1. Compute and interpret the typical speed on these highways.
2. Compute and interpret the variability of speed on these highways.
3. Discuss if the reduction in the speed limit to 55 mph would increase safety on the highways.

Sample Report— Analyzing Speed Limits

Recently, many concerned citizens have lobbied for a return to the federal 55-mile-per-hour (mph) speed limit on America's highways. The reduction may lower gas emissions and save consumers on gasoline costs, but whether it will increase traffic safety is not clear. Many researchers believe that traffic safety is based on the variability of the speed rather than the average speed with which people are driving—the more variability in speed, the more dangerous the roads. Is there less variability in speed on a highway with a 55-mph speed limit as opposed to a 65-mph speed limit?

To compare average speeds, as well as the variability of speeds on highways, the speeds of 40 cars were recorded on a highway with a 55-mph speed limit (Highway 1) and a highway with a 65-mph speed limit (Highway 2). Table 3.A shows the most relevant descriptive measures for the analysis.

TABLE 3.A Summary Measures for Highway 1 and Highway 2

	Highway 1 (55-mph speed limit)	Highway 2 (65-mph speed limit)
Mean	57	66
Median	56	66
Mode	50	70
Minimum	45	60
Maximum	74	70
Standard deviation	7.0	3.0
Coefficient of variation	0.12	0.05
Number of Cars	40	40

The average speed of a car on Highway 1 was 57 mph, as opposed to 66 mph on Highway 2. On Highway 1, half of the 40 cars drove faster than 56 mph and half drove slower than 56 mph, as measured by the median; the median for Highway 2 was 66 mph. The mode shows that the most common speeds on Highway 1 and Highway 2 were 50 mph and 70 mph, respectively. Based on each measure of central location, Highway 2 experiences higher speeds as compared to Highway 1.

While measures of central location typically represent where the data clusters, these measures do not relay information about the variability in the data. Given the minimum and maximum speeds of 45 mph and 74 mph, respectively, the range of speeds is 29 mph for Highway 1 as compared to a range of just 10 mph for Highway 2. Generally, standard deviation is a more credible measure of dispersion, since range is based entirely on the minimum and the maximum values. The standard deviation for Highway 1 is substantially greater than the standard deviation for Highway 2 (7.0 mph > 3.0 mph). Therefore, the speeds on Highway 1 are more variable than the speeds on Highway 2. Even adjusting for differences in the magnitudes of the means by calculating the coefficient of variation, the speeds on Highway 1 are still more dispersed than Highway 2 (0.12 > 0.05).

On average, it is true that the speeds on Highway 2 are higher than the speeds on Highway 1; however, the variability of speeds is greater on Highway 1. If traffic safety improves when the variability of speeds declines, then the data suggest that a return to a federal 55-mph speed limit may not enhance the well-being of highway travelers.

Conceptual Review

LO 3.1 Calculate and interpret the arithmetic mean, the median, and the mode.

The **sample mean**, $\bar{x} = \frac{\Sigma x_i}{n}$, and the **population mean**, $\mu = \frac{\Sigma x_i}{N}$, are the **arithmetic averages** of the data set. The mean is the most widely used measure of central location. One weakness of the mean is that it is unduly influenced by **outliers**—extremely small or large values.

The **median** is the middle value of a data set and is especially useful when outliers are present or when the distribution is skewed. We arrange the data in ascending (or descending) order and find the median as

- The middle value if the number of observations is odd, or

- The average of the two middle values if the number of observations is even.

The **mode** is the value in the data set that occurs with the most frequency. A data set may have no mode or more than one mode. If the data are qualitative, then the mode is the only meaningful measure of central location.

LO 3.2 Calculate and interpret percentiles and a box plot.

Percentiles provide detailed information about how the data are spread over the interval from the smallest value to the largest value. In general, the *p*th percentile divides the data set into two parts, where approximately *p* percent of the observations have values less than the *p*th percentile and the rest have values greater than the *p*th percentile. The 25th percentile is also referred to as the first quartile (Q1), the 50th percentile is referred to as the second quartile (Q2), and the 75th percentile is referred to as the third quartile (Q3).

A **box plot** displays the five-number summary (the smallest value, Q1, Q2, Q3, and the largest value) for the data set. Box plots are particularly useful when comparing similar information gathered at another place or time; they are also an effective tool for identifying outliers.

LO 3.3 Calculate and interpret a geometric mean return and an average growth rate.

The **geometric mean** is the multiplicative average of a data set. In general, the geometric mean is smaller than the arithmetic mean and is less sensitive to outliers. The geometric mean is relevant when summarizing financial returns over several years.

For multiperiod returns $R_1, R_2, \ldots, R_n$, the **geometric mean return** is computed as $G_R = \sqrt[n]{(1 + R_1)(1 + R_2) \cdots (1 + R_n)} - 1$, where n is the number of multiperiod returns.

The geometric mean is also used when summarizing **average growth rates**. For growth rates $g_1, g_2, \ldots, g_n$, the average growth rate is computed as $G_g = \sqrt[n]{(1 + g_1)(1 + g_2) \cdots (1 + g_n)} - 1$, where n is the number of multiperiod growth rates. When the underlying values of the series are given, there is a simpler way to compute the average growth rate. For observations $x_1, x_2, \ldots, x_n$, the average growth rate is computed as $G_g = \sqrt[n-1]{\dfrac{x_n}{x_1}} - 1$.

LO 3.4 **Calculate and interpret the range, the mean absolute deviation, the variance, the standard deviation, and the coefficient of variation.**

The **range** is the difference between the maximum and the minimum values in a data set.

The **mean absolute deviation** (MAD) is an average of the absolute differences between the observations and the mean of a data set. The sample MAD and the population MAD are computed as $\text{MAD} = \dfrac{\Sigma|x_i - \bar{x}|}{n}$ and $\text{MAD} = \dfrac{\Sigma|x_i - \mu|}{N}$, respectively.

The **variance** and **standard deviation**, which are based on squared differences from the mean, are the two most widely used measures of dispersion. The sample variance s^2 and the sample standard deviation s are computed as $s^2 = \dfrac{\Sigma(x_i - \bar{x})^2}{n - 1} = \dfrac{\Sigma x_i^2}{n - 1} - \dfrac{n\bar{x}^2}{n - 1}$ and $s = \sqrt{s^2}$, respectively. The population variance σ^2 and the population standard deviation σ are computed as $\sigma^2 = \dfrac{\Sigma(x_i - \mu)^2}{N} = \dfrac{\Sigma x_i^2}{N} - \mu^2$ and $\sigma = \sqrt{\sigma^2}$, respectively. Variance squares the original units of measurement; by calculating the standard deviation, we return to the original units of measurement.

The **coefficient of variation CV** is a relative measure of dispersion. The CV allows comparisons of variability between data sets with different means or different units of measurement. The sample CV and the population CV are computed as $\text{CV} = \dfrac{s}{\bar{x}}$ and $\text{CV} = \dfrac{\sigma}{\mu}$, respectively.

LO 3.5 **Explain mean-variance analysis and the Sharpe ratio.**

Mean-variance analysis postulates that we measure the performance of an asset by its rate of return and evaluate this rate of return in terms of its reward (mean) and risk (variance). In general, investments with higher average returns are also associated with higher risk.

The **Sharpe ratio** measures extra reward per unit of risk. The Sharpe ratio for an investment, I, is computed as $\dfrac{\bar{x}_I - \bar{R}_f}{s_I}$, where $\bar{R}_f$ denotes the return on a risk-free asset. The higher the Sharpe ratio, the better the investment compensates its investors for risk.

LO 3.6 **Apply Chebyshev's Theorem and the empirical rule.**

Chebyshev's Theorem dictates that for any data set, the proportion of observations that lie within k standard deviations from the mean will be at least $1 - 1/k^2$, where k is any number greater than 1.

Given a sample mean $\bar{x}$, a sample standard deviation s, and a relatively symmetric and bell-shaped distribution, the **empirical rule** dictates that:

- Approximately 68% of all observations fall in the interval $\bar{x} \pm s$,

- Approximately 95% of all observations fall in the interval $\bar{x} \pm 2s$, and

- Almost all observations fall in the interval $\bar{x} \pm 3s$.

Calculate the mean and variance for grouped data.

When analyzing **grouped data**, the formulas for the mean and variance are modified as follows:

- The sample mean and the population mean are computed as $\bar{x} = \frac{\Sigma m_i f_i}{n}$ and $\mu = \frac{\Sigma m_i f_i}{N}$, respectively.

- The sample variance and the population variance are computed as $s^2 = \frac{\Sigma(m_i - \bar{x})^2 f_i}{n-1} = \frac{\Sigma m_i^2 f_i}{n-1} - \frac{n\bar{x}^2}{n-1}$ and $\sigma^2 = \frac{\Sigma(m_i - \mu)^2 f_i}{N} = \frac{\Sigma m_i^2 f_i}{N} - \mu^2$, respectively. As always the standard deviation is calculated as the positive square root of the variance.

Calculate and interpret the covariance and the correlation coefficient.

The **covariance** and the **correlation coefficient** are measures that assess the existence and strength of a linear relationship between two variables, x and y.

The sample covariance s_{xy} and the population covariance σ_{xy} are computed as $s_{xy} = \frac{\Sigma(x_i - \bar{x})(y_i - \bar{y})}{n-1}$ and $\sigma_{xy} = \frac{\Sigma(x_i - \mu_x)(y_i - \mu_y)}{N}$, respectively.

The sample correlation coefficient r_{xy} and the population correlation coefficient ρ_{xy} are computed as $r_{xy} = \frac{s_{xy}}{s_x s_y}$ and $\rho_{xy} = \frac{\sigma_{xy}}{\sigma_x \sigma_y}$, respectively.

Additional Exercises and Case Studies

75. Annual growth rates for individual firms in the toy industry tend to fluctuate dramatically, depending on consumers' tastes and current fads. Consider the following growth rates (in percent) for two companies in this industry, Hasbro and Mattel.

Year	2005	2006	2007	2008	2009
Hasbro	3.0	2.1	21.8	4.8	1.2
Mattel	1.5	9.1	5.7	−0.1	−8.2

Source: Annual Reports for Hasbro, Inc., and Mattel Inc.

a. Use the geometric mean to calculate the average growth rates for each firm.

b. Use the standard deviation to evaluate the variability for each firm.

c. Which company had the higher average growth rate? Which company's growth rate had greater variability?

76. The following table lists the sales (in millions of dollars) of the top Italian restaurant chains in 2009.

Restaurant	Sales (millions)
Olive Garden	$3,300
Carrabba's Italian Grill	629
Romano's Macaroni Grill	583
Maggiano's	366
Carino's Italian Grill	356
Buca di Beppo	220
Bertucci's	210

Source: *The Boston Globe*, July 31, 2010.

Calculate the mean, the median, and the mode. Which measure of central tendency best reflects typical sales? Explain.

77. The following table shows the annual returns (in percent) for Fidelity's Electronic and Utilities funds.

Year	Electronic	Utilities
2005	13.23	9.36
2006	1.97	32.33
2007	2.77	21.03
2008	−50.00	−35.21
2009	81.65	14.71

Source: http://www.finance.yahoo.com.

a. Calculate the sample mean, the sample variance, and the sample standard deviation for each fund.

b. Which fund had the higher average return?

c. Which fund was riskier over this time period? Use both standard deviation and the coefficient of variation in your explanation.

d. Given a risk-free rate of 4%, which fund has the higher Sharpe ratio? What does this ratio imply?

78. The following table shows the revenues (in millions of dollars) for The Gap, Inc., and American Eagle Outfitters, Inc., for the years 2008–2010.

Year	Gap	American Eagle
2008	$15.73	$3.06
2009	14.53	2.99
2010	14.20	2.99

Source: Annual Reports for Gap, Inc., and American Eagle Outfitters, Inc.

a. Calculate the average growth rate for each firm.

b. Which firm had the higher growth rate over the 2008–2010 period?

79. Monthly stock prices for two competing firms are as follows.

Month	Firm A	Firm B
January	$28	$21
February	31	24
March	32	24
April	35	27
May	34	25
June	28	20

a. Calculate the sample mean, the sample variance, and the sample standard deviation for each firm's stock price.

b. Which firm had the higher stock price over the time period?

c. Which firm's stock price had greater variability as measured by standard deviation? Which firm's stock price had the greater relative dispersion?

80. The manager at a water park constructed the following frequency distribution to summarize attendance for 60 days in July and August.

Attendance	Frequency
1,000 up to 1,250	5
1,250 up to 1,500	6
1,500 up to 1,750	10
1,750 up to 2,000	20
2,000 up to 2,250	15
2,250 up to 2,500	4

a. Calculate the mean attendance.

b. Calculate the variance and the standard deviation.

81. The National Sporting Goods Association (NSGA) conducted a survey of the ages of individuals that purchased skateboarding footwear. The ages of this survey are summarized in the following relative frequency distribution.

Age of User	Percent
Under 14 years old	35
14 to 17 years old	41
18 to 24 years old	15
25 to 34 years old	4
35 to 44 years old	4
45 to 64 years old	1

Suppose the survey was based on a sample of 200 individuals. Calculate the mean and standard deviation of the age of individuals that purchased skateboarding shoes. Use 10 as the midpoint of the first class.

82. The following table shows the annual returns (in percent) for two of Putnam's mutual funds: the Voyager Growth Fund and the George Putnam Fund of Boston.

Year	Growth Fund	Fund of Boston
2002	−26.43	−8.42
2003	24.71	17.40
2004	4.80	8.32
2005	5.50	4.04
2006	5.23	12.25

Source: http://www.finance.yahoo.com.

a. Calculate and interpret the covariance.

b. Calculate the correlation coefficient. Comment on the strength of the linear relationship.

83. A manager of a local retail store analyzes the relationship between advertising and sales by reviewing the store's data for the previous six months.

Advertising (in $100s)	Sales (in $1,000s)
20	15
25	18
30	20
22	16
27	19
26	20

a. Calculate the mean of advertising and the mean of sales.

b. Calculate the standard deviation of advertising and the standard deviation of sales.

c. Calculate and interpret the covariance between advertising and sales.

d. Calculate and interpret the correlation coefficient.

84. FILE An economist wishes to summarize sample data from 26 metropolitan areas in the U.S. The following table lists each area's 2010–2011 median income as well as the monthly unemployment rate and average consumer debt for August 2010; the complete data set can be found on the text website and is labeled **Debt Payments**.

Metropolitan Area	Income (in $1,000s)	Unemployment	Debt
Washington, D.C.	$103.50	6.3%	$1,285
Seattle	81.70	8.5	1,135
⋮	⋮	⋮	⋮
Pittsburgh	63.00	8.3	763

Source: eFannieMae.com reports 2010–2011 area median incomes; www.bls.gov gives monthly unemployment rates for August 2010; Experian.com collected average monthly consumer debt payments in August 2010 and published the data in November 2010.

Use Excel to compute the summary measures of income, the monthly unemployment rate, and average consumer debt. Interpret these summary measures.

85. FILE American football is the highest paying sport on a per-game basis. Given that the quarterback is considered the most important player on an NFL team, he is typically well-compensated. Consider a portion of the following quarterback salary data in 2009; the complete data set labeled **Quarterback Salaries** can be found on the text website.

Name	Salary (in $ millions)
Philip Rivers	25.5566
Jay Cutler	22.0441
⋮	⋮
Tony Romo	0.6260

SOURCE: http://www.nfl.com.

a. Use Excel to compute and interpret the mean and median salary of a quarterback.

b. Use Excel to compute and interpret the range and the standard deviation of quarterback salaries.

CASE STUDIES

Case Study 3.1

An article in *The Wall Street Journal* (July 11, 2008) outlined a number of reasons as to why the 16 teams in Major League Baseball's National League (NL) are inferior to the 14 teams in the American League (AL). One reason for the imbalance pointed to the disparity in opening-day payrolls: the average AL payroll is greater than the NL average. A portion of the data showing opening-day payroll for each team is in the accompanying table; the complete data, labeled **MLB Salaries**, can be found on the text website.

Data for Case Study 3.1 Major League Baseball's Opening-Day Payrolls, 2010

FILE

American League	Payroll	National League	Payroll
New York Yankees	$206,333,389	Chicago Cubs	$146,609,000
Boston Red Sox	162,447,333	Philadelphia Phillies	141,928,379
⋮	⋮	⋮	⋮

SOURCE: http://www.bizofbaseball.com.

In a report, use the sample information to:

1. Discuss the mean and median of AL and NL opening-day salaries and comment on skewness.

2. Compare the range and standard deviation of AL and NL opening-day salaries.

3. Use these summary measures to comment on the findings in *The Wall Street Journal*.

Case Study 3.2

Five years after graduating from college, Lucia Li feels that she is finally ready to invest some of her earnings. She has eliminated her credit card debt and has established an emergency fund. Her parents have been pleased with the performance of their mutual fund investments with Janus Capital Group. She has narrowed her search down to two mutual funds:

The Janus Balanced Fund: This "core" fund consists of stocks and bonds and its goal is diversification. It has historically produced solid long-term returns through different market cycles.

The Janus Overseas Fund: This fund invests in overseas companies based on their individual merits instead of their geography or industry sector.

The following table reports the annual returns (in percent) of these two funds over the past 10 years; these data, labeled **Janus Funds**, are also available on the text website.

Data for Case Study 3.2 Returns (in percent) for Janus Funds

FILE

Year	Janus Balanced Fund	Janus Overseas Fund	Year	Janus Balanced Fund	Janus Overseas Fund
2000	−2.16	−18.57	2005	7.75	32.39
2001	−5.04	−23.11	2006	10.56	47.21
2002	−6.56	−23.89	2007	10.15	27.76
2003	13.74	36.79	2008	−15.22	−52.75
2004	8.71	18.58	2009	24.28	78.12

SOURCE: http://www.finance.yahoo.com.

In a report, use the sample information to:

1. Calculate measures of central location to describe the similarities and the differences in these two funds' returns.
2. Calculate measures of dispersion to assess the risk of each fund.
3. Calculate measures of correlation between the two funds.

Case Study 3.3

Nike's Online Annual Report provides total revenues (in millions of $) for the Asian and Latin American regions for the years 2005 through 2009 as follows:

Nike Revenues in Asia and Latin America (in millions of $)

	2005	2006	2007	2008	2009
Asia	1,897	2,054	2,296	2,888	3,322
Latin America	696	905	967	1,165	1,285

Adidas' Online Annual Report provides total revenues (in millions of €) for the Asian and Latin American regions for the years 2005 through 2009 as follows:

Adidas Revenues in Asia and Latin America (in millions of €)

	2005	2006	2007	2008	2009
Asia	1,523	2,020	2,254	2,662	2,614
Latin America	319	499	657	893	1,006

In a report, use the sample information to:

1. Summarize the growth rates in Asia and Latin America for Nike.
2. Summarize the growth rates in Asia and Latin America for Adidas.
3. Discuss the similarities and the differences of the growth rates in the two companies.

Case Study 3.4

Due to a crisis in subprime lending, obtaining a mortgage has become difficult even for people with solid credit. In a report by the *Associated Press* (August 25, 2007), sales of existing homes fell for a 5th consecutive month, while home prices dropped for a record 12th month in July 2007. Mayan Horowitz, a research analyst for QuantExperts, wishes to study how the mortgage crunch has impacted the once booming market of Florida. He collects data on the sale prices (in $1,000s) of 25 single-family homes in Fort Myers, Florida, in January 2007 and collects another sample in July 2007. For a valid comparison, he samples only three-bedroom homes, each with 1,500 square feet or less of space on a lot size of 10,000 square feet or less. A portion of the data is given below; the complete data, labeled **Ft. Myers Sales**, are available on the text website.

Data for Case Study 3.4 Home Prices (in $1,000s) in January 2007 and July 2007

Number	January	July
1	$100	$136
2	190	235
⋮	⋮	⋮
25	200	180

Source: www.zillow.com.

In a report, use the sample information to:

1. Compare the mean, median, and mode in each of the two sample periods.
2. Compare the standard deviation and coefficient of variation in each of the two sample periods.
3. Discuss significant changes in the housing market in Fort Myers over the 6-month period.

4

Introduction to Probability

LEARNING OBJECTIVES

After reading this chapter you should be able to:

LO 4.1 Describe fundamental probability concepts.

LO 4.2 Formulate and explain subjective, empirical, and a priori probabilities.

LO 4.3 Calculate and interpret the probability of the complement of an event, the probability that at least one of two events will occur, and a joint probability.

LO 4.4 Calculate and interpret a conditional probability.

LO 4.5 Distinguish between independent and dependent events.

LO 4.6 Calculate and interpret probabilities from a contingency table.

LO 4.7 Apply the total probability rule and Bayes' theorem.

LO 4.8 Use a counting rule to solve a particular counting problem.

Every day we make choices about issues concerning uncertain events. Usually, we either implicitly or explicitly assign probabilities to these events and plan or act accordingly. For instance, we read the paper, watch the news, or check the Internet to determine the likelihood of rain and whether we should carry an umbrella. Retailers strengthen their sales force before the end-of-year holiday season in anticipation of an increase in shoppers. The Federal Reserve cuts interest rates when it believes the economy is at risk for weak growth, and raises interest rates when it feels that inflation is the greater risk. By figuring out the chances of various uncertain events, we are better prepared to make the more desirable choices. This chapter presents the essential probability tools needed to frame and address many real-world issues involving uncertainty. Uncertainty describes a situation where a variety of events are possible. Probabilities tell us how often we can anticipate observing certain events given assumptions about the situation. Probability theory turns out to be the very foundation for statistical inference, and numerous concepts introduced in this chapter are essential for understanding later chapters.

Sportswear Brands

Annabel Gonzalez is chief retail analyst at Longmeadow Consultants, a marketing firm. One aspect of her job is to track sports-apparel sales and uncover any particular trends that may be unfolding in the industry. Recently, she has been following Under Armour, Inc., the pioneer in the compression-gear market. Compression garments are meant to keep moisture away from a wearer's body during athletic activities in warm and cool weather. Under Armour has experienced exponential growth since the firm went public in November 2005. However, Nike, Inc., and Adidas Group, with 18% and 10% market shares, respectively, have aggressively entered the compression-gear market (*The Wall Street Journal*, October 23, 2007).

As part of her analysis, Annabel would first like to examine whether the age of the customer matters when buying compression clothing. Her initial feeling is that the Under Armour brand attracts a younger customer, whereas the more established companies, Nike and Adidas, draw an older clientele. She believes this information is relevant to advertisers and retailers in the sporting-goods industry as well as to some in the financial community. She collects data on 600 recent purchases in the compression-gear market. She cross-classifies the data by age group and brand name, as shown in Table 4.1.

TABLE 4.1 Purchases of Compression Garments Based on Age and Brand Name

Age Group	Brand Name		
	Under Armour	Nike	Adidas
Under 35 years	174	132	90
35 years and older	54	72	78

Annabel wants to use the sample information to:

1. Calculate and interpret relevant probabilities.
2. Determine whether the age of a customer is independent of his/her brand choice.

A synopsis of this case is provided at the end of Section 4.3.

4.1 Fundamental Probability Concepts

LO 4.1

Describe fundamental probability concepts.

Since many choices we make involve some degree of uncertainty, we are better prepared for the eventual outcome if we can use probabilities to describe which events are likely and which are unlikely.

> A **probability** is a numerical value that measures the likelihood that an uncertain event occurs. This value is between zero and one, where a value of zero indicates *impossible* events and a value of one indicates *definite* events.

In order to define an event and assign the appropriate probability to it, it is useful to first establish some terminology and impose some structure on the situation.

An **experiment** is a trial that results in any one of several possible outcomes. The diversity of the outcomes of an experiment is due to the uncertainty of the real world. When you purchase a new computer, there is no guarantee as to how long it will last before any repair work is needed. It may need repair in the first year, in the second year, or after two years. You can think of this as an experiment because the actual outcome will be determined only over time. Other examples of an experiment include whether a roll of a fair die will result in a value of 1, 2, 3, 4, 5, or 6; whether the toss of a coin results in heads or tails; whether a project is finished early, on time, or late; whether the economy will improve, stay the same, or deteriorate; whether a ball game will end in a win, loss, or tie.

A **sample space**, denoted by S, of an experiment records all possible outcomes of the experiment. For example, suppose the sample space representing the letter grade in a course is given by $S = \{A, B, C, D, F\}$. If the teacher also gives out an I (incomplete) grade, then S is not valid because all outcomes of the experiment are not included in S. The sample space for an experiment need not be unique. For example, in the above experiment, we can also define the sample space with just P (pass) and F (fail) outcomes, or $S = \{P, F\}$.

> An **experiment** is a trial that results in one of several uncertain outcomes. A **sample space**, denoted S, of an experiment contains all possible outcomes of the experiment.

EXAMPLE 4.1

A snowboarder competing in the Winter Olympic Games is trying to assess her probability of winning a medal in her event, the ladies' halfpipe. Construct the appropriate sample space.

SOLUTION: The athlete's attempt to predict her chances of medaling is an experiment because, until the Winter Games occur, the outcome is unknown. We formalize an experiment by constructing its sample space. The athlete's competition has four possible outcomes: gold medal, silver medal, bronze medal, and no medal. We formally write the sample space as $S = \{$gold, silver, bronze, no medal$\}$.

Events

An **event** is a subset of the sample space. A simple event consists of just one of the possible outcomes of an experiment. Getting an A in a course is an example of a simple event. An event may also be a subset of outcomes of an experiment. For example, we can define an event as getting a passing grade in a course; this event is formed by the subset of outcomes, A, B, C, and D.

An **event** is a subset of the sample space. It can be a simple event consisting of one outcome or it can be a subset of several outcomes.

Let us define two events from Example 4.1, where one event represents "earning a medal" and the other denotes "failing to medal." These events are **exhaustive** because they include all outcomes in the sample space. In other words, they exhaust the entire sample space. This contrasts with the earlier grade-distribution example, where the events of getting grades A and B are not exhaustive because they do not include many feasible grades in the sample space. However, the events P and F, defined as pass and fail, respectively, are exhaustive.

Another important probability concept concerns **mutually exclusive** events. Suppose we define the two events "at least earning a silver medal" (outcomes of gold and silver) and "at most earning a silver medal" (outcomes of silver, bronze, no medal). These two events are exhaustive because no outcome of the random experiment is omitted. However, in this case, the events are not mutually exclusive because the outcome "silver" appears in both events. For two mutually exclusive events, the occurrence of one event precludes the occurrence of the other. Going back to the grade-distribution example, while the events of getting grades A and B are not exhaustive, they are mutually exclusive, since you cannot possibly get an A as well as a B in the same course. However, getting grades P and F are exhaustive and mutually exclusive. Similarly, the events defined as "at least earning a silver medal" and "at most earning a bronze medal" are exhaustive and mutually exclusive.

Events are **exhaustive** if all possible outcomes of a random experiment are included in the events.

has to be = 1 or 0

Events are **mutually exclusive** if they do not share any common outcome of a random experiment.

Given a sample space consisting of simple events, we can define events and then combine events to form new events. The **union** of two events, denoted $A \cup B$, is the event consisting of all outcomes in A or B. A useful way to illustrate these concepts is through the use of a Venn diagram, named after the British mathematician John Venn (1834–1923). Figure 4.1 shows a Venn diagram where the rectangle represents the sample space S and the two circles represent events A and B. The union $A \cup B$ is the portion in the Venn diagram that is included in either A or B.

FIGURE 4.1 The union of two events, $A \cup B$

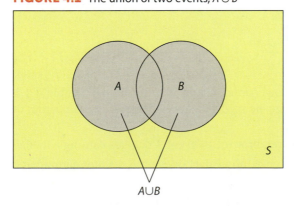

The **intersection** of two events, denoted $A \cap B$, is the event consisting of all outcomes in A and B. Figure 4.2 depicts the intersection of two events A and B. The intersection $A \cap B$ is the portion in the Venn diagram that is included in both A and B.

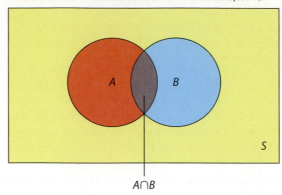

FIGURE 4.2 The intersection of two events, $A \cap B$

$A \cap B$

The **complement** of event A, denoted A^c, is the event consisting of all outcomes in the sample space S that are not in A. In Figure 4.3, A^c is everything in S that is not included in A.

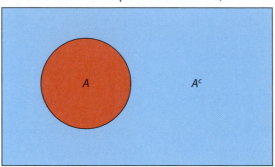

FIGURE 4.3 The complement of an event, A^c

COMBINING EVENTS

- The **union** of two events, denoted $A \cup B$, is the event consisting of all outcomes in A *or* B.
- The **intersection** of two events, denoted $A \cap B$, is the event consisting of all outcomes in A *and* B.
- The **complement** of event A, denoted A^c, is the event consisting of all outcomes in the sample space S that are not in A.

EXAMPLE 4.2

Recall that the snowboarder's sample space from Example 4.1 is defined as $S =$ {gold, silver, bronze, no medal}. Now suppose the snowboarder defines the following three events:

- $A =$ {gold, silver, bronze} or event A denotes earning a medal;
- $B =$ {silver, bronze, no medal} or event B denotes earning at most a silver medal; and
- $C =$ {no medal} or event C denotes failing to medal.

a. Find $A \cup B$ and $B \cup C$.

b. Find $A \cap B$ and $A \cap C$.

c. Find B^c.

SOLUTION:

a. The union of A and B denotes all outcomes common to A or B; here, the event $A \cup B = \{\text{gold, silver, bronze, no medal}\}$. Note that there is no double counting of the outcomes "silver" or "bronze" in $A \cup B$. Similarly, we have the event $B \cup C = \{\text{silver, bronze, no medal}\}$.

b. The intersection of A and B denotes all outcomes common to A and B; here, the event $A \cap B = \{\text{silver, bronze}\}$. The event $A \cap C = \varnothing$, where $\varnothing$ denotes the null (empty) set; no common outcomes appear in both A and C.

c. The complement of B denotes all outcomes in S that are not in B; here, the event $B^c = \{\text{gold}\}$.

Assigning Probabilities

LO **4.2**

Formulate and explain subjective, empirical, and a priori probabilities.

Now that we have described a valid sample space and the various ways in which we can define events from that sample space, we are ready to assign probabilities. When we arrive at a probability, we generally are able to categorize the probability as a *subjective probability*, an *empirical probability*, or an *a priori probability*.

Suppose the snowboarder from Example 4.1 believes that there is a 0.10 chance that she will win a gold medal, a 0.15 chance that she will win a silver medal, a 0.20 chance that she will win a bronze medal, and a 0.55 chance that she will not medal at all. She has assigned a **subjective probability** to each of the simple events. She made a personal assessment of these probabilities without referencing any data.

The snowboarder believes that the most likely outcome is failing to earn a medal since she gives that outcome the greatest chance of occurring at 0.55. When formally writing out the probability that an event occurs, we generally construct a probability statement. Here, the probability statement might take the form: $P(\{\text{no medal}\}) = 0.55$, where $P(\text{"event"})$ represents the probability that a certain event occurs. Table 4.2 summarizes each simple event and its respective subjective probability.

TABLE 4.2 Snowboarder's Subjective Probabilities

Event	Probability
Gold	0.10
Silver	0.15
Bronze	0.20
No medal	0.55

Reading from the table we can readily see, for instance, that the athlete assesses that there is a 15% chance that she will earn a silver medal, or $P(\{\text{silver}\}) = 0.15$. We should note that all the probabilities are between the values of zero and one, and when we sum the probabilities of these simple events we obtain the value one. This example demonstrates the two defining properties of probability.

THE TWO DEFINING PROPERTIES OF A PROBABILITY

1. The probability of any event A is a value between 0 and 1, $0 \le P(A) \le 1$.

2. The sum of the probabilities of any list of mutually exclusive and exhaustive events equals 1.

Suppose the snowboarder wants to calculate the probability of earning a medal. In Exercise 4.2 we defined "earning a medal" as event A, so the probability statement takes the form $P(A)$. We calculate this probability by summing the probabilities of the outcomes in A, or equivalently,

$$P(A) = P(\{\text{gold}\}) + P(\{\text{silver}\}) + P(\{\text{bronze}\}) = 0.10 + 0.15 + 0.20 = 0.45.$$

EXAMPLE 4.3

Given the events in Example 4.2 and the probabilities in Table 4.2, calculate the following probabilities.

a. $P(B \cup C)$

b. $P(A \cap C)$

c. $P(B^c)$

SOLUTION:

a. The probability that event B or event C occurs is

$$P(B \cup C) = P(\{\text{silver}\}) + P(\{\text{bronze}\}) + P(\{\text{no medal}\})$$
$$= 0.15 + 0.20 + 0.55 = 0.90.$$

b. The probability that event A and event C occur is

$$P(A \cap C) = 0; \text{ recall that there are no common outcomes in } A \text{ and } C.$$

c. The probability that the complement of B occurs is

$$P(B^c) = P(\{\text{gold}\}) = 0.10.$$

In many instances we calculate probabilities by referencing data. We estimate an **empirical probability** by calculating the relative frequency with which an event occurs. Relationships have to be stable through time for empirical probabilities to be accurate.

CALCULATING AN EMPIRICAL PROBABILITY

We use the relative frequency to calculate the empirical probability of event A as

$$P(A) = \frac{\text{the number of outcomes in } A}{\text{the number of outcomes in } S}.$$

EXAMPLE 4.4

The frequency distribution in Table 4.3 summarizes the ages of the richest 400 Americans. Suppose we randomly select one of these individuals.

a. What is the probability that the individual is between 50 to 60 years old?

b. What is the probability that the individual is younger than 60 years old?

c. What is the probability that the individual is at least 80 years old?

TABLE 4.3 Frequency Distribution of Ages of 400 Richest Americans

Ages	Frequency
30 up to 40	7
40 up to 50	47
50 up to 60	90
60 up to 70	109
70 up to 80	93
80 up to 90	45
90 up to 100	9

Source: www.forbes.com.

SOLUTION: In Table 4.3a, we first label each outcome with letter notation; for instance, the outcome "30 up to 40" is denoted as event A. Next we calculate the relative frequency of each event and use the relative frequency to denote the probability of the event.

TABLE 4.3a Relative Frequency Distribution of Ages of 400 Richest Americans

Ages	Event	Frequency	Relative Frequency
30 up to 40	A	7	7/400 = 0.0175
40 up to 50	B	47	0.1175
50 up to 60	C	90	0.2250
60 up to 70	D	109	0.2725
70 up to 80	E	93	0.2325
80 up to 90	F	45	0.1125
90 up to 100	G	9	0.0225

a. The probability that an individual is between 50 and 60 years old is
$$P(C) = \frac{90}{400} = 0.225.$$

b. The probability that an individual is younger than 60 years old is
$$P(A \cup B \cup C) = \frac{7 + 47 + 90}{400} = 0.360.$$

c. The probability that an individual is at least 80 years old is
$$P(F \cup G) = \frac{45 + 9}{400} = 0.135.$$

In a more narrow range of well-defined problems, we can sometimes deduce probabilities by reasoning about the problem. The resulting probability is an **a priori probability**. A priori probabilities are often used in games of chance. Later in this chapter we will discuss counting rules that are particularly important when calculating an a priori probability.

EXAMPLE 4.5

Suppose our random experiment consists of rolling a six-sided die. Then we can define the appropriate sample space as $S = \{1, 2, 3, 4, 5, 6\}$.

a. What is the probability that we roll a 2?

b. What is the probability that we roll a 2 or 5?

c. What is the probability that we roll an even number?

SOLUTION: Here we recognize that each outcome is equally likely. So with 6 possible outcomes, each outcome has a 1/6 chance of occurring.

a. The probability that we roll a 2, $P(\{2\})$, is thus 1/6.

b. The probability that we roll a 2 or 5, $P(\{2\}) + P(\{5\})$, is $1/6 + 1/6 = 1/3$.

c. The probability that we roll an even number, $P(\{2\}) + P(\{4\}) + P(\{6\})$, is $1/6 + 1/6 + 1/6 = 1/2$.

Probabilities Expressed as Odds

Even though we tend to report the probability of an event occurring as a number between 0 and 1, alternative approaches to expressing probabilities include percentages and odds. Specifically, in wagering it is common to state probabilities in terms of odds. For instance, at the start of the 2008–2009 football season, the Pittsburgh Steelers were not one of the strong favorites to win the Super Bowl, with odds for winning of 1:24 (*Betfair* website). In other words, an individual who bet $1 on the Steelers' winning the Super Bowl prior to the season would have won $24 in profits. Since the bettor also receives the original stake back, for every $1 staked in the wager, he/she would have gotten back $25. We can convert the odds ratio into a probability by using the following generalization:

Thus, with odds for winning the Super Bowl of 1:24, we can solve for the probability of the Steelers' winning as: $1/(1 + 24) = 1/25$ or 0.04. Moreover, the bet's anticipated profit is $0 because (0.04 probability of winning) $\times$ ($24 profit if the wager is won) + (0.96 probability of losing) $\times$ (−$1 if the wager is lost) = 0.96 + (−0.96) = 0.

This is an example of an expected value calculation, which we discuss further in Chapter 5. We would also like to point out that sports betting odds are usually displayed in various formats, including American, British, or European formats; the details are beyond the scope of this chapter.

EXAMPLE 4.6

Days prior to the 2009 Super Bowl, the Pittsburgh Steelers' odds for beating the Arizona Cardinals increased to approximately 2:1. What was the probability of the Steelers' winning just prior to the Super Bowl?

SOLUTION: The probability that the Steelers would win the Super Bowl rose to

$$\frac{a}{a+b} = \frac{2}{2+1} = 0.67.$$

(Note: The Steelers did win the Super Bowl, but just barely, scoring the winning touchdown with 35 seconds left in the game.)

Similarly, we can convert a probability to an odds ratio using the following generalization:

> ### CONVERTING A PROBABILITY TO AN ODDS RATIO
> If $P(A)$ denotes the probability of an event A occurring, and $P(A)$ does not equal zero or one, then:
>
> $$\text{The odds } for \text{ } A \text{ occurring equal } \frac{P(A)}{1 - P(A)}, \text{ and}$$
>
> $$\text{The odds } against \text{ } A \text{ occurring equal } \frac{1 - P(A)}{P(A)}.$$

EXAMPLE 4.7

The summer of 2008 proved to be another difficult period for travelers. New York's Kennedy Airport topped the list with the lowest on-time arrival rate: the likelihood that a plane arrived on-time occurred only 56% of the time (*The Wall Street Journal*, September 9, 2008). Travelers at Atlanta's Airport fared a bit better, where the on-time arrival rate was 74%.

a. Calculate the odds for a plane arriving on-time at New York's Kennedy Airport.
b. Calculate the odds for a plane arriving on-time at Atlanta's Airport.

SOLUTION:

a. First, given an on-time arrival probability of 0.56 for New York's Kennedy Airport we find

$$\frac{P(\{\text{on-time}\})}{1 - P(\{\text{on-time}\})} = \frac{0.56}{1 - 0.56} = \frac{0.56}{0.44} = 1.27$$

or, we would report the odds for arriving on-time as 1.27 to 1. Note that given an odds for arriving on-time as 1.27:1, we can deduce $P(\{\text{on-time}\})$ as

$$\frac{1.27}{2.27} = 0.56.$$

b. We calculate the odds for on-time arrival at Atlanta's Airport given a probability of 0.74 as

$$\frac{P(\{\text{on-time}\})}{1 - P(\{\text{on-time}\})} = \frac{0.74}{1 - 0.74} = \frac{0.74}{0.26} = 2.85 \text{ to } 1.$$

EXERCISES 4.1

Concepts

1. Determine whether the following probabilities are best categorized as subjective, empirical, or a priori probabilities.

   a. Before flipping a fair coin, Sunil assesses that he has a 50% chance of obtaining tails.

   b. At the beginning of the semester, John believes he has a 90% chance of receiving straight A's.

   c. A political reporter announces that there is a 40% chance that the next person to come out of the conference room will be a Republican, since there are 60 Republicans and 90 Democrats in the room.

2. Express each of the probabilities in the preceding question as

   a. odds assessed by Sunil for obtaining tails.

   b. odds assessed by John for receiving straight A's.

   c. odds assessed by the reporter for a Republican coming out of the room.

3. A sample space S yields five equally likely events, A, B, C, D, and E.

   a. Find $P(D)$.

   b. Find $P(B^c)$.

   c. Find $P(A \cup C \cup E)$.

4. You roll a die with the sample space, $S = \{1, 2, 3, 4, 5, 6\}$. You define A as $\{1, 2, 3\}$, B as $\{1, 2, 3, 5, 6\}$, C as $\{4, 6\}$, and D as $\{4, 5, 6\}$. Determine which of the following events are exhaustive and/or mutually exclusive.

   a. A and B
   b. A and C
   c. A and D
   d. B and C

5. A sample space, S, yields four simple events, A, B, C, and D, such that $P(A) = 0.35$, $P(B) = 0.10$, and $P(C) = 0.25$.

   a. Find $P(D)$.
   b. Find $P(C^c)$.
   c. Find $P(A \cup B)$.

Applications

6. You apply for a position at two firms. Let event A represent the outcome of getting an offer from the first firm and event B represent the outcome of getting an offer from the second firm.

   a. Explain why events A and B are not exhaustive.
   b. Explain why events A and B are not mutually exclusive.

7. An alarming number of U.S. adults are either overweight or obese. The distinction between overweight and obese is made on the basis of body mass index (BMI), expressed as weight/height². An adult is considered overweight if the BMI is 25 or more but less than 30. An obese adult will have a BMI of 30 or greater. According to the 2003–2004 National Health and Nutrition Examination Survey, 34.1% of the adult population in the U.S. is overweight and 32.2% is obese. Use this information to answer the following questions.

   a. What is the probability that a randomly selected adult is either overweight or obese?
   b. What is the probability that a randomly selected adult is neither overweight nor obese?
   c. Are the events "overweight" and "obese" exhaustive?
   d. Are the events "overweight" and "obese" mutually exclusive?

8. Many communities are finding it more and more difficult to fill municipal positions such as town administrators, finance directors, and treasurers. The following table shows the percentage of municipal managers by age group in the United States for the years 1971 and 2006.

Age	1971	2006
Under 30	26%	1%
30 to 40	45%	12%
41 to 50	21%	28%
51 to 60	5%	48%
Over 60	3%	11%

Source: The International City-County Management Association.

   a. In 1971, what was the probability that a municipal manager was 40 years old or younger? In 2006, what was the probability that a municipal manager was 40 years old or younger?
   b. In 1971, what was the probability that a municipal manager was 51 years old or older? In 2006, what was the probability that a municipal manager was 51 years old or older?
   c. What trends in ages can you detect from municipal managers in 1971 versus municipal managers in 2006?

9. At four community health centers on Cape Cod, Massachusetts, 15,164 patients were asked to respond to questions designed to detect depression (The Boston Globe, June 11, 2008). The survey produced the following results.

Diagnosis	Number
Mild	3,257
Moderate	1,546
Moderately Severe	975
Severe	773
No Depression	8,613

   a. What is the probability that a randomly selected patient suffered from mild depression?
   b. What is the probability that a randomly selected patient did not suffer from depression?
   c. What is the probability that a randomly selected patient suffered from moderately severe to severe depression?
   d. Given that the national figure for moderately severe to severe depression is approximately 6.7%, does it appear that there is a higher rate of depression in this summer resort community? Explain.

10. On Sunday, July 11, 2010, Spain and the Netherlands played in the 2010 World Cup Final in Johannesburg. On the eve of the final, many betting lines were offering Spain's odds for winning at 15:8 (Oddschecker website).

   a. Spain won the World Cup. Suppose you had bet $1,000 on Spain. What was your net gain? If Spain had lost, what would have been your net loss?
   b. What was the implied probability of Spain winning the final?

11. Prior to the Academy Awards ceremony in 2009, the United Kingdom bookmaker Ladbrokes reported the following odds for winning an Oscar in the category of best actress (The Wall Street Journal, February 20, 2009).

Best Actress	Movie	Odds
Anne Hathaway	Rachel Getting Married	2:11
Angelina Jolie	Changeling	1:20
Melissa Leo	Frozen River	1:33
Meryl Streep	Doubt	3:10
Kate Winslet	The Reader	5:2

   a. Express the odds for each actress winning as a probability.
   b. According to your calculations, which actress was most likely to win an Oscar? Kate Winslet won her first Oscar on February 22, 2009. Was your prediction realized?

4.2 Rules of Probability

Once we have determined the probabilities of simple events, we have various rules to calculate the probabilities of more complex, related events.

LO 4.3

Calculate and interpret the probability of the complement of an event, the probability that at least one of two events will occur, and a joint probability.

The Complement Rule

The complement rule follows from one of the defining properties of probability: The sum of probabilities assigned to simple events in a sample space must equal one. Note that since S is a collection of all possible outcomes of the experiment (nothing else can happen), $P(S) = 1$. Let's revisit the sample space that we constructed when we rolled a six-sided die: $S = \{1, 2, 3, 4, 5, 6\}$. Suppose event A is defined as an even-numbered outcome or $A = \{2, 4, 6\}$. We then know that the complement of A, A^c, is the set consisting of $\{1, 3, 5\}$. Further, we can deduce that $P(A) = 1/2$ and $P(A^c) = 1/2$, so $P(A) + P(A^c) = 1$. We obtain the complement rule by subtracting $P(A)$ from each side of the equation, or $P(A^c) = 1 - P(A)$.

> ### THE COMPLEMENT RULE
>
> The **complement rule** states that the probability of the complement of an event, $P(A^c)$, is equal to one minus the probability of the event, or equivalently, $P(A^c) = 1 - P(A)$.

The complement rule is quite straightforward and rather simple, but it is widely used and powerful.

EXAMPLE 4.8

In 2007, 45% of women ages 25 to 34 had a college degree, compared with 36% of young men (*The Wall Street Journal*, May 29, 2008).

a. What is the probability that a randomly selected woman between the ages of 25 to 34 does not have a college degree?

b. What is the probability that a randomly selected man between the ages of 25 to 34 does not have a college degree?

SOLUTION:

a. Let's define event A as the event that a randomly selected woman between the ages of 25 to 34 has a college degree, thus $P(A) = 0.45$. In this problem we are interested in the complement of A or $P(A^c)$. So $P(A^c) = 1 - P(A) = 1 - 0.45 = 0.55$.

b. Similarly, we define event B as the outcome that a randomly selected man between the ages of 25 to 34 has a college degree, so $P(B) = 0.36$. Thus, $P(B^c) = 1 - P(B) = 1 - 0.36 = 0.64$.

The Addition Rule

The addition rule allows us to find the probability of the union of two events. Suppose we want to find the probability that either A occurs or B occurs, or in probability terms, $P(A \cup B)$. We reproduce the Venn diagram, used earlier in Figure 4.1, to help in exposition. Figure 4.4 shows a sample space S with the two events A and B. Recall that the union, $A \cup B$, is the portion in the Venn diagram that is included in either A *or* B. The intersection, $A \cap B$, is the portion in the Venn diagram that is included in both A *and* B.

If we try to obtain $P(A \cup B)$ by simply summing $P(A)$ with $P(B)$, then we overstate the probability because we double-count the probability of the intersection of A and B,

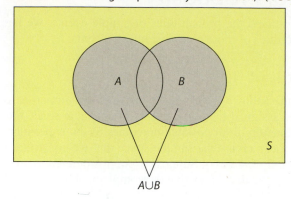

FIGURE 4.4 Finding the probability of the union, $P(A \cup B)$

$A \cup B$

$P(A \cap B)$. When implementing the addition rule, we sum $P(A)$ and $P(B)$ and then subtract $P(A \cap B)$ from this sum.

THE ADDITION RULE

The **addition rule** states that the probability that A or B occurs, or that at least one of these events occurs, is equal to the probability that A occurs, plus the probability that B occurs, minus the probability that both A and B occur, or equivalently,

$$P(A \cup B) = P(A) + P(B) - P(A \cap B).$$

EXAMPLE 4.9

Anthony feels that he has a 75% chance of getting an A in Statistics and a 55% chance of getting an A in Managerial Economics. He also believes he has a 40% chance of getting an A in both classes.

a. What is the probability that he gets an A in at least one of these courses?

b. What is the probability that he does not get an A in either of these courses?

SOLUTION:

a. Let $P(A_S)$ correspond to the probability of getting an A in Statistics and $P(A_M)$ correspond to the probability of getting an A in Managerial Economics. Thus, $P(A_S) = 0.75$ and $P(A_M) = 0.55$. In addition, there is a 40% chance that Anthony gets an A in both classes, or $P(A_S \cap A_M) = 0.40$. In order to find the probability that he receives an A in at least one of these courses, we calculate:

$$P(A_S \cup A_M) = P(A_S) + P(A_M) - P(A_S \cap A_M) = 0.75 + 0.55 - 0.40 = 0.90.$$

b. The probability that he does not receive an A in either of these two courses is actually the complement of the union of the two events or $P((A_S \cup A_M)^c)$. We calculated the union in part a, so using the complement rule we have

$$P((A_S \cup A_M)^c) = 1 - P(A_S \cup A_M) = 1 - 0.90 = 0.10.$$

An alternative expression that correctly captures the required probability is $P((A_S \cup A_M)^c) = P(A_S^c \cap A_M^c)$. A common mistake is to calculate the probability as $P((A_S \cap A_M)^c) = 1 - P(A_S \cap A_M) = 1 - 0.40 = 0.60$, which simply indicates that there is a 60% chance that Anthony will not get an A in both courses. This is clearly not the required probability that Anthony does not get an A in either course.

The Addition Rule for Mutually Exclusive Events

Mutually exclusive events are those events that cannot take place at the same time. Figure 4.5 shows the Venn diagram for two mutually exclusive events; note that the circles do not intersect.

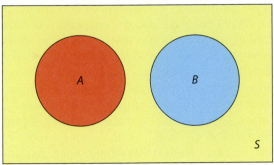

FIGURE 4.5 Mutually exclusive events

For mutually exclusive events A and B, the probability of their intersection is zero, $P(A \cap B) = 0$. We need not concern ourselves with double-counting, and therefore, the probability of the union is simply the sum of the two probabilities.

THE ADDITION RULE FOR MUTUALLY EXCLUSIVE EVENTS

If A and B are mutually exclusive events, then $P(A \cap B) = 0$ and, therefore, the addition rule simplifies to $P(A \cup B) = P(A) + P(B)$.

EXAMPLE 4.10

Samantha Greene, a college senior, contemplates her future immediately after graduation. She thinks there is a 25% chance that she will join the Peace Corps and teach English in Madagascar for the next 27 months. Alternatively, she believes there is a 35% chance that she will enroll in a full-time law school program in the United States.

a. What is the probability that she joins the Peace Corps or enrolls in law school?

b. What is the probability that she does not choose either of these options?

SOLUTION:

a. We can write the probability that Samantha joins the Peace Corps as $P(A) = 0.25$ and the probability that she enrolls in law school as $P(B) = 0.35$. Immediately after college, Samantha cannot choose both of these options. This implies that these events are mutually exclusive, so $P(A \cap B) = 0$. Thus, when solving for the probability that Samantha joins the Peace Corps or enrolls in law school, $P(A \cup B)$, we can simply sum $P(A)$ and $P(B)$: $P(A \cup B) = P(A) + P(B) = 0.25 + 0.35 = 0.60$.

b. In order to find the probability that she does not choose either of these options, we need to recognize that this probability is the complement of the union of the two events, or $P((A \cup B)^c)$. Therefore, using the complement rule, we have

$$P((A \cup B)^c) = 1 - P(A \cup B) = 1 - 0.60 = 0.40.$$

Conditional Probability

In business applications, the probability of interest is often a conditional probability. Examples include the probability that the housing market will improve conditional on the Federal Reserve taking remedial actions; the probability of making a six-figure salary conditional on getting an MBA; the probability that a company's stock price will go up conditional on higher-than-expected profits; the probability that sales will improve conditional on the firm launching a new innovative product.

Let's use an example to illustrate the concept of conditional probability. Suppose the probability that a recent business college graduate finds a suitable job is 0.80. The probability of finding a suitable job is 0.90 if the recent business college graduate has prior work experience. This type of probability is called a **conditional probability**, where the probability of an event is conditional on the occurrence of another event. If A represents "finding a job" and B represents "prior work experience," then $P(A) = 0.80$ and the conditional probability is denoted as $P(A|B) = 0.90$. The vertical mark | means "given that" and the conditional probability is typically read as "the probability of A given B." In the above example, the probability of finding a suitable job increases from 0.80 to 0.90 when conditioned on prior work experience. In general, the conditional probability, $P(A|B)$, is greater than the **unconditional (marginal) probability**, $P(A)$, if B exerts a positive influence on A. Similarly, $P(A|B)$ is less than $P(A)$ when B exerts a negative influence on A. Finally, if B exerts no influence on A, then $P(A|B)$ equals $P(A)$.

As we will see later, it is important that we write the event that has already occurred after the vertical mark, since in most instances $P(A|B) \neq P(B|A)$. In the above example $P(B|A)$ would represent the probability of prior work experience conditional on having found a job.

UNCONDITIONAL VERSUS CONDITIONAL PROBABILITIES

An **unconditional (marginal) probability** refers to the probability of an event without any restriction; it might even be thought of as a stand-alone probability. A **conditional probability** is the probability of an event given that another event has already occurred.

We again rely on the Venn diagram in Figure 4.6 to explain the conditional probability.

FIGURE 4.6 Finding the conditional probability, $P(A|B)$

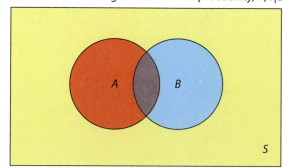

Since $P(A|B)$ represents the probability of A conditional on B (B has occurred), the relevant portion of the sample space reduces to B. The conditional probability $P(A|B)$ is based on the portion of A that is included in B. It is derived as the ratio of the intersection (of A and B) to B.

EXAMPLE 4.11

Economic globalization is defined as the integration of national economies into the international economy through trade, foreign direct investment, capital flows, migration, and the spread of technology. Although globalization is generally viewed favorably, it also increases the vulnerability of a country to economic conditions of the other country. An economist predicts a 60% chance that country A will perform poorly and a 25% chance that country B will perform poorly. There is also a 16% chance that both countries will perform poorly.

a. What is the probability that country A performs poorly given that country B performs poorly?

b. What is the probability that country B performs poorly given that country A performs poorly?

c. Interpret your findings.

SOLUTION: We first write down the available information in probability terms. Defining A as "country A performing poorly" and B as "country B performing poorly," we have the following information: $P(A) = 0.60$, $P(B) = 0.25$, and $P(A \cap B) = 0.16$.

a. $P(A|B) = \dfrac{P(A \cap B)}{P(B)} = \dfrac{0.16}{0.25} = 0.64.$

b. $P(B|A) = \dfrac{P(A \cap B)}{P(A)} = \dfrac{0.16}{0.60} = 0.27.$

c. It appears that globalization has definitely made these countries vulnerable to the economic woes of the other country. The probability that country A performs poorly increases from 60% to 64% when country B has performed poorly. Similarly, the probability that country B performs poorly increases from 25% to 27% when conditioned on country A performing poorly. In this example, event B has a positive influence on event A and event A has a positive influence on event B, since both probabilities increase when conditioned on the other event.

Independent and Dependent Events

LO **4.5**

Distinguish between independent and dependent events.

Of particular interest to researchers is whether or not two events influence one another. Two events are **independent** if the occurrence of one event does not affect the probability of the occurrence of the other event. Let's revisit the earlier example where the probability of finding a job is 0.80 and the probability of finding a job given prior work experience is 0.90. Prior work experience exerts a positive influence on finding a job because the conditional probability, $P(A|B) = 0.90$, exceeds the unconditional probability, $P(A) = 0.80$. Now consider the probability of finding a job given that your neighbor has bought a red car. Obviously, your neighbor's decision to buy a red car has no influence on your probability of finding a job, which remains at 0.80.

Events are considered **dependent** if the occurrence of one is related to the probability of the occurrence of the other. We generally test for the independence of two events by comparing the conditional probability of one event, for instance $P(A|B)$, to its unconditional probability, $P(A)$. If these two probabilities are the same, we say that the two events, A and B, are independent; if the probabilities differ, the two events are dependent.

> **INDEPENDENT VERSUS DEPENDENT EVENTS**
>
> Two events, A and B, are **independent** if and only if $P(A|B) = P(A)$ or, equivalently, $P(B|A) = P(B)$. Otherwise, the events are **dependent**.

EXAMPLE 4.12

Suppose that for a given year there is a 2% chance that your desktop computer will crash and a 6% chance that your laptop computer will crash. Further, there is a 0.12% chance that both computers will crash. Is the reliability of the two computers independent of each other?

SOLUTION: Let event D represent the outcome that your desktop crashes and event L represent the outcome that your laptop crashes. Therefore, $P(D) = 0.02$, $P(L) = 0.06$, and $P(D \cap L) = 0.0012$. The reliability of the two computers is independent because

$$P(D|L) = \frac{P(D \cap L)}{P(L)} = \frac{0.0012}{0.06} = 0.02 = P(D).$$

In other words, if your laptop crashes, it does not alter the probability that your desktop also crashes. Equivalently,

$$P(L|D) = \frac{P(D \cap L)}{P(D)} = \frac{0.0012}{0.02} = 0.06 = P(L).$$

The Multiplication Rule

In some situations, we are interested in finding the probability that two events, A and B, both occur, or $P(A \cap B)$. This is also referred to as a **joint probability**—the likelihood of the occurrence of two events, A and B. This probability is zero for events that are mutually exclusive. In order to obtain a joint probability, we can rewrite the formula for conditional probability and solve for $P(A \cap B)$. For instance, from $P(A|B) = \frac{P(A \cap B)}{P(B)}$, we can easily derive $P(A \cap B) = P(A|B)P(B)$. Similarly, from $P(B|A) = \frac{P(A \cap B)}{P(A)}$, we derive $P(A \cap B) = P(B|A)P(A)$. Since we calculate the product of two probabilities to find the joint probability, the resulting equations are called the **multiplication rule** for probabilities.

> **THE MULTIPLICATION RULE**
>
> The **multiplication rule** states that the probability that A and B both occur, a **joint probability**, is equal to the probability that A occurs given that B has occurred times the probability that B occurs, that is, $P(A \cap B) = P(A|B)P(B)$. Equivalently, we can also arrive at the joint probability as $P(A \cap B) = P(B|A)P(A)$.

EXAMPLE 4.13

A stockbroker knows from past experience that the probability that a client owns stocks is 0.60 and the probability that a client owns bonds is 0.50. The probability that the client owns bonds if he/she already owns stocks is 0.55.

a. What is the probability that the client owns both of these securities?

b. Given that the client owns bonds, what is the probability that the client owns stocks?

SOLUTION:

a. Let event A denote the outcome that a client owns stocks and event B as the outcome that a client owns bonds. Thus, the unconditional probabilities that the client owns stocks and that the client owns bonds are $P(A) = 0.60$ and $P(B) = 0.50$, respectively. The conditional probability that the client owns bonds given that he/she owns stocks is $P(B|A) = 0.55$. We calculate the probability that the client owns both of these securities as $P(A \cap B) = P(B|A)P(A) = 0.55 \times 0.60 = 0.33$.

b. We need to calculate the conditional probability that the client owns stocks given that he/she owns bonds, or $P(A|B)$. Using the formula for conditional probability and the answer from part (a), we find $P(A|B) = \dfrac{P(A \cap B)}{P(B)} = \dfrac{0.33}{0.50} = 0.66$.

The Multiplication Rule for Independent Events

We know that two events, A and B, are independent if $P(A|B) = P(A)$ or if $P(B|A) = P(B)$. With independent events, the multiplication rule $P(A \cap B) = P(A|B)P(B)$ simplifies to $P(A \cap B) = P(A)P(B)$. We can use this rule to determine whether or not two events are independent. That is, two events are independent if the joint probability $P(A \cap B)$ equals the product of their unconditional probabilities, $P(A)P(B)$. In Example 4.12, we were given the probabilities $P(D) = 0.02$, $P(L) = 0.06$, and $P(D \cap L) = 0.0012$. Consistent with the earlier result, events D and L are independent because $P(D \cap L) = 0.0012$ equals $P(D)P(L) = 0.02 \times 0.06 = 0.0012$.

> **THE MULTIPLICATION RULE FOR INDEPENDENT EVENTS**
>
> The **multiplication rule for independent events** dictates that the joint probability of A and B equals the product of the individual probabilities of A and B, or $P(A \cap B) = P(A)P(B)$.

EXAMPLE 4.14

The probability of passing the Level 1 CFA (Chartered Financial Analyst) exam is 0.50 for John Campbell and 0.80 for Linda Lee. The prospect of John's passing the exam is completely unrelated to Linda's success on the exam.

a. What is the probability that both John and Linda pass the exam?

b. What is the probability that at least one of them passes the exam?

SOLUTION:

We can write the unconditional probabilities that John passes the exam and that Linda passes the exam as $P(J) = 0.50$ and $P(L) = 0.80$, respectively.

a. Since we are told that John's chances of passing the exam are not influenced by Linda's success at the exam, we can conclude that these events are independent, so $P(J) = P(J|L) = 0.50$ and $P(L) = P(L|J) = 0.80$. Thus, when solving for the probability that both John and Linda pass the exam, we calculate the product of the unconditional probabilities or $P(J \cap L) = P(J) \times P(L) = 0.50 \times 0.80 = 0.40$.

b. We calculate the probability that at least one of them passes the exam as:
$P(J \cup L) = P(J) + P(L) - P(J \cap L) = 0.50 + 0.80 - 0.40 = 0.90$.

EXERCISES 4.2

Concepts

12. Let $P(A) = 0.65$, $P(B) = 0.30$, and $P(A|B) = 0.45$.
    a. Calculate $P(A \cap B)$.
    b. Calculate $P(A \cup B)$.
    c. Calculate $P(B|A)$.

13. Let $P(A) = 0.55$, $P(B) = 0.30$, and $P(A \cap B) = 0.10$.
    a. Calculate $P(A|B)$.
    b. Calculate $P(A \cup B)$.
    c. Calculate $P((A \cup B)^c)$.

14. Let A and B be mutually exclusive with $P(A) = 0.25$ and $P(B) = 0.30$.
    a. Calculate $P(A \cap B)$.
    b. Calculate $P(A \cup B)$.
    c. Calculate $P(A|B)$.

15. Let A and B be independent with $P(A) = 0.40$ and $P(B) = 0.50$.
    a. Calculate $P(A \cap B)$.
    b. Calculate $P((A \cup B)^c)$.
    c. Calculate $P(A|B)$.

16. Let $P(A) = 0.65$, $P(B) = 0.30$, and $P(A|B) = 0.45$.
    a. Are A and B independent events? Explain.
    b. Are A and B mutually exclusive events? Explain.
    c. What is the probability that neither A nor B takes place?

17. Let $P(A) = 0.15$, $P(B) = 0.10$, and $P(A \cap B) = 0.05$.
    a. Are A and B independent events? Explain.
    b. Are A and B mutually exclusive events? Explain.
    c. What is the probability that neither A nor B takes place?

18. Consider the following probabilities: $P(A) = 0.25$, $P(B^c) = 0.40$, and $P(A \cap B) = 0.08$. Find:
    a. $P(B)$
    b. $P(A|B)$
    c. $P(B|A)$

19. Consider the following probabilities: $P(A^c) = 0.30$, $P(B) = 0.60$, and $P(A \cap B^c) = 0.24$. Find:
    a. $P(A|B^c)$
    b. $P(B^c|A)$
    c. Are A and B independent events? Explain.

20. Consider the following probabilities: $P(A) = 0.40$, $P(B) = 0.50$, and $P(A^c \cap B^c) = 0.24$. Find:
    a. $P(A^c|B^c)$
    b. $P(A^c \cup B^c)$
    c. $P(A \cup B)$

Applications

21. The probabilities that stock A will rise in price is 0.40 and that stock B will rise in price is 0.60. Further, if stock B rises in price, the probability that stock A will also rise in price is 0.80.

    a. What is the probability that at least one of the stocks will rise in price?
    b. Are events A and B mutually exclusive? Explain.
    c. Are events A and B independent? Explain.

22. Despite government bailouts and stimulus money, unemployment in the U.S. had not decreased significantly as economists had expected (*US News and World Report,* July 2, 2010). Many analysts predicted only an 18% chance of a reduction in unemployment. However, if Europe slipped back into a recession, the probability of a reduction in U.S. unemployment would drop to 0.06.
    a. What is the probability that there is not a reduction in unemployment?
    b. Assume there is an 8% chance that Europe slips back into a recession. What is the probability that there is not a reduction in U.S. unemployment and that Europe slips into a recession?

23. Dr. Miriam Johnson has been teaching accounting for over 20 years. From her experience she knows that 60% of her students do homework regularly. Moreover, 95% of the students who do their homework regularly generally pass the course. She also knows that 85% of her students pass the course.
    a. What is the probability that a student will do homework regularly and also pass the course?
    b. What is the probability that a student will neither do homework regularly nor will pass the course?
    c. Are the events "pass the course" and "do homework regularly" mutually exclusive? Explain.
    d. Are the events "pass the course" and "do homework regularly" independent? Explain.

24. Records show that 5% of all college students are foreign students who also smoke. It is also known that 50% of all foreign college students smoke. What percent of the students at this university are foreign?

25. An analyst estimates that the probability of default on a seven-year AA rated bond is 0.06, while that on a seven-year A rated bond is 0.13. The probability that they will both default is 0.04.
    a. What is the probability that at least one of the bonds defaults?
    b. What is the probability that neither the seven-year AA rated bond nor the seven-year A rated bond defaults?
    c. Given that the seven-year AA rated bond defaults, what is the probability that the seven-year A rated bond also defaults?

26. In general, shopping online is supposed to be more convenient than going to stores. However, according to a recent Harris Interactive poll, 87% of people have experienced problems with an online transaction (*The Wall Street Journal,* October 2, 2007). Forty-two percent of people who experienced a problem abandoned the transaction or

switched to a competitor's website. Fifty-three percent of people who experienced problems contacted customer-service representatives.

a. What percentage of people did not experience problems with an online transaction?

b. What percentage of people experienced problems with an online transaction and abandoned the transaction or switched to a competitor's website?

c. What percentage of people experienced problems with an online transaction and contacted customer-service representatives?

27. Christine Wong has asked Dave and Mike to help her move into a new apartment on Sunday morning. She has asked them both in case one of them does not show up. From past experience, Christine knows that there is a 40% chance that Dave will not show up and a 30% chance that Mike will not show up. Dave and Mike do not know each other and their decisions can be assumed to be independent.

a. What is the probability that both Dave and Mike will show up?

b. What is the probability that at least one of them will show up?

c. What is the probability that neither Dave nor Mike will show up?

28. According to a recent survey by two United Nations agencies and a nongovernmental organization, two in every three women in the Indian capital of New Delhi are likely to face some form of sexual harassment in a year (*BBC World News*, July 9, 2010). The study also reports that women who use public transportation are especially vulnerable. Suppose the corresponding probability of harassment for women who use public transportation is 0.82. It is also known that 28% of women use public transportation.

a. What is the probability that a woman takes public transportation and also faces sexual harassment?

b. If a woman is sexually harassed, what is the probability that she had taken public transportation?

29. Since the fall of 2008, millions of Americans have lost jobs due to the economic meltdown. A recent study shows that unemployment has not impacted white collar and blue collar workers equally (*Newsweek*, April 20, 2009). According to the Bureau of Labor Statistics report, while the national unemployment rate is 8.5%, it is only 4.3% for those with a college degree. It is fair to assume that 27% of people in the labor force are college educated. You have just heard that another worker in a large firm has been laid off. What is the probability that the worker is college educated?

30. A recent study challenges the media narrative that foreclosures are dangerously widespread (*New York Times*, March 2, 2009). According to this study, 62% of all foreclosures were centered in only four states, namely, Arizona, California, Florida, and Nevada. The national average rate of foreclosures in 2008 was 0.79%. What percent of the homes in the United States were foreclosed in 2008 and also centered in Arizona, California, Florida or Nevada?

31. According to results from the Spine Patient Outcomes Research Trial, or SPORT, surgery for a painful, common back condition resulted in significantly reduced back pain and better physical function than treatment with drugs and physical therapy (*The Wall Street Journal*, February 21, 2008). SPORT followed 803 patients, of whom 398 ended up getting surgery. After two years, of those who had surgery, 63% said they had a major improvement in their condition, compared with 29% among those who received nonsurgical treatment.

a. What is the probability that a patient had surgery? What is the probability that a patient did not have surgery?

b. What is the probability that a patient had surgery and experienced a major improvement in his or her condition?

c. What is the probability that a patient received nonsurgical treatment and experienced a major improvement in his or her condition?

4.3 Contingency Tables and Probabilities

We learned in Chapter 2 that, when organizing qualitative data, it is often useful to construct a frequency distribution. A frequency distribution is a useful tool when we want to sort one variable at a time. However, in many instances we want to examine or compare two qualitative variables. On these occasions, a **contingency table** proves very useful. Contingency tables are widely used in marketing and biomedical research, as well as in the social sciences.

LO **4.6**

Calculate and interpret probabilities from a contingency table.

A CONTINGENCY TABLE

A **contingency table** generally shows frequencies for two qualitative or categorical variables, x and y, where each cell represents a mutually exclusive combination of the pair of x and y values.

Table 4.4, first presented in the introductory case study of this chapter, is an example of a contingency table where the qualitative variables of interest, x and y, are "age group" and "brand name," respectively. Age group has two possible outcomes: (1) under 35 years and (2) 35 years and older; brand name has three possible outcomes: (1) Under Armour, (2) Nike, and (3) Adidas.

TABLE 4.4 Purchases of Compression Garments Based on Age and Brand Name

Age Group	Brand Name		
	Under Armour	Nike	Adidas
Under 35 years	174	132	90
35 years and older	54	72	78

Each cell in Table 4.4 represents a frequency; for example, 174 customers under the age of 35 purchased an Under Armour product, whereas 54 customers at least 35 years old purchased an Under Armour product. Recall that we estimate an empirical probability by calculating the relative frequency of the occurrence of the event. To make calculating these probabilities less cumbersome, it is often useful to denote each outcome with letter notation and calculate totals for each column and row as follows:

TABLE 4.4a A Contingency Table Labeled Using Event Notation

Age Group	Brand Name			Total
	B_1	B_2	B_3	
A	174	132	90	396
A^c	54	72	78	204
Total	228	204	168	600

Thus, events A and A^c represent the outcomes "under 35 years" and "Under Armour," "Nike," and "Adidas" "35 years and older," respectively; events B_1, B_2, and B_3 stand for the outcomes, respectively. In addition, after calculating row totals, it is now easier to recognize that 396 of the customers were under 35 years old and 204 of the customers were at least 35 years old. Similarly, column totals indicate that 228 customers purchased Under Armour, 204 purchased Nike, and 168 purchased Adidas. Finally, the frequency corresponding to the cell in the last column and the last row is 600. This value represents the sample size, or the possible outcomes in the sample space. We arrive at this value by either summing the values in the last column (396 + 204) or summing the values in the last row (228 + 204 + 168).

The following example illustrates how to calculate probabilities when the data are presented in the form of a contingency table.

EXAMPLE 4.15

Using the data in Table 4.4a, answer the following questions.

a. What is the probability that a randomly selected customer is younger than 35 years old?

b. What is the probability that a randomly selected customer purchases an Under Armour garment?

c. What is the probability that a customer is younger than 35 years old and purchases an Under Armour garment?

d. What is the probability that a customer is either younger than 35 years old or purchases an Under Armour garment?

e. What is the probability that a customer is under 35 years of age, given that the customer made an Under Armour purchase?

SOLUTION:

a. $P(A) = \dfrac{\text{the number of outcomes in } A}{\text{the number of outcomes in } S} = \dfrac{396}{600} = 0.66$; there is a 66% chance that a randomly selected customer is less than 35 years old.

b. $P(B_1) = \dfrac{\text{the number of outcomes in } B_1}{\text{the number of outcomes in } S} = \dfrac{228}{600} = 0.38$; there is a 38% chance that a randomly selected customer purchases an Under Armour garment.

c. $P(A \cap B_1) = \dfrac{\text{the number of outcomes in } A \text{ and } B_1}{\text{the number of outcomes in } S} = \dfrac{174}{600} = 0.29$; there is a 29% chance that a randomly selected customer is younger than 35 years old and purchases an Under Armour garment.

d. $P(A \cup B_1) = \dfrac{\text{the number of outcomes in } A \text{ or } B_1}{\text{the number of outcomes in } S} = \dfrac{174 + 132 + 90 + 54}{600} = \dfrac{450}{600} = 0.75$; there is a 75% chance that a randomly selected customer is either younger than 35 years old or purchases an Under Armour garment. Alternatively, we can use the addition rule to solve this problem as $P(A \cup B_1) = P(A) + P(B_1) - P(A \cap B_1) = 0.66 + 0.38 - 0.29 = 0.75$.

e. We wish to calculate the conditional probability, $P(A \mid B_1)$. When the data are in the form of a contingency table, calculating a conditional probability is rather straightforward. We are given the information that the customer has already purchased an Under Armour product, so the relevant number of outcomes shrinks from 600 to 228. We can ignore all customers that made Nike or Adidas purchases, or all outcomes in events B_2 and B_3. Thus, of the 228 customers who made an Under Armour purchase, 174 of them are under 35 years of age. Therefore, the probability that a customer is under 35 years of age given that the customer makes an Under Armour purchase is calculated as $P(A \mid B_1) = \dfrac{174}{228} = 0.76$. Alternatively, we can use the conditional probability formula to solve the problem as $P(A \mid B_1) = \dfrac{P(A \cap B_1)}{P(B_1)} = \dfrac{0.29}{0.38} = 0.76$.

Arguably, a more convenient way of calculating relevant probabilities is to convert the contingency table to a **joint probability table**. The frequency in each cell is divided by the number of outcomes in the sample space, which in this example is 600 customers. Table 4.4b shows the results.

TABLE 4.4b Converting a Contingency Table to a Joint Probability Table

Age Group	Brand Name			
	B_1	B_2	B_3	Total
A	0.29	0.22	0.15	0.66
A^c	0.09	0.12	0.13	0.34
Total	0.38	0.34	0.28	1.00

All the probabilities in the interior of the table represent joint probabilities. For instance, the probability that a randomly selected person is under 35 years of age and makes an Under Armour purchase, denoted $P(A \cap B_1)$, is 0.29. Similarly, we can readily read from this table that 12% of the customers purchase a Nike garment and are at least 35 years old, or $P(A^c \cap B_2) = 0.12$.

The probabilities on the periphery of Table 4.4b represent unconditional probabilities. For example, the probability that a randomly selected customer is under 35 years of age, $P(A)$ is simply 0.66. Also, the probability of purchasing a Nike garment, $P(B_2)$, is 0.34.

Note that the conditional probability is basically the ratio of a joint probability to an unconditional probability. Since $P(A \mid B_1) = \dfrac{P(A \cap B_1)}{P(B_1)}$, the numerator is a joint probability,

$P(A \cap B_1)$, and the denominator is an unconditional probability, $P(B_1)$. Let's refer back to the probability that we calculated earlier; that is, the probability that a customer is under 35 years of age, given that the customer already purchased an Under Armour product. As shown earlier, the conditional probability is easily computed as

$$P(A|B_1) = \frac{P(A \cap B_1)}{P(B_1)} = \frac{0.29}{0.38} = 0.76.$$

EXAMPLE 4.16

Given the data in Table 4.4b, what is the probability that a customer purchases an Under Armour product, given that the customer is under 35 years of age?

SOLUTION: Now we are solving for $P(B_1|A)$. So

$$P(B_1|A) = \frac{P(A \cap B_1)}{P(A)} = \frac{0.29}{0.66} = 0.44.$$

Note that $P(B_1|A) = 0.44 \neq P(A|B_1) = 0.76$.

EXAMPLE 4.17

Determine whether the age of a customer is independent of the brand name of the product purchased.

SOLUTION: In order to answer this question, we compare the event's conditional probability to its unconditional probability. As discussed before, events A and B are independent if $P(A|B) = P(A)$. In the Under Armour example, we have already found that $P(A|B_1) = 0.76$. In other words, there is a 76% chance that a customer is under 35 years old given that the customer already purchased an Under Armour product. We compare this conditional probability to its unconditional probability, $P(A) = 0.66$. Since these probabilities differ, the events age and brand name are not independent events. We could have compared $P(B_1|A)$ to $P(B_1)$ and found that $0.44 \neq 0.38$, which leads us to the same conclusion that the events are dependent. As discussed in the preceding section, an alternative approach to test for independence is to compare the joint probability with the product of the two unconditional probabilities. Events are independent if $P(A \cap B_1) = P(A)P(B_1)$. In the above example, $P(A \cap B_1) = 0.29$ does not equal $P(A)P(B_1) = 0.66 \times 0.38 = 0.25$, so the two events are not independent.

SYNOPSIS OF INTRODUCTORY CASE

After careful analysis of the contingency table representing customer purchases of compression garments based on age and brand name, several interesting remarks can be made. From a sample of 600 customers, it appears that the majority of the customers who purchase these products tend to be younger: 66% of the customers were younger than 35 years old, whereas 34% were at least 35 years old. It is true that more customers chose to purchase Under Armour garments (with 38% of purchases) as compared to Nike or Adidas garments (with 34% and 28% of purchases, respectively). However, given that Under Armour was the pioneer in the compression-gear market, this company should be concerned with the competition posed by Nike and Adidas. Further inspection of the contingency table reveals that if a customer was at least 35 years old, the chances of the customer purchasing an Under Armour garment drops to about 26%. This result indicates that the age of a customer seems to influence the brand name purchased. In other words, 38% of the customers choose to buy Under Armour products, but as soon as the sample is confined to those customers who are at least 35 years old, the likelihood of a purchase from Under Armour drops to 26%. This information is relevant not only for Under Armour and how the firm may focus its advertising efforts, but also to competitors and retailers in the compression garment market.

Concepts

32. Consider the following contingency table.

	B	B^c
A	26	34
A^c	14	26

a. Convert the contingency table into a joint probability table.
b. What is the probability that A occurs?
c. What is the probability that A and B occur?
d. Given that B has occurred, what is the probability that A occurs?
e. Given that A^c has occurred, what is the probability that B occurs?
f. Are A and B mutually exclusive events? Explain.
g. Are A and B independent events? Explain.

33. Consider the following joint probability table.

	B_1	B_2	B_3	B_4
A	9%	22%	15%	20%
A^c	3%	10%	9%	12%

a. What is the probability that A occurs?
b. What is the probability that B_2 occurs?
c. What is the probability that A^c and B_4 occur?
d. What is the probability that A or B_3 occurs?
e. Given that B_2 has occurred, what is the probability that A occurs?
f. Given that A has occurred, what is the probability that B_4 occurs?

Applications

34. According to an online survey by Harris Interactive for job site CareerBuilder.com, more than half of IT (information technology) workers say they have fallen asleep at work (*InformationWeek*, September 27, 2007). Sixty-four percent of government workers admitted to falling asleep on the job. Consider the following contingency table that is representative of the survey results.

	Job Category	
Slept on the Job?	IT Professional	Government Professional
Yes	155	256
No	145	144

a. Convert the contingency table into a joint probability table.
b. What is the probability that a randomly selected worker is an IT professional?
c. What is the probability that a randomly selected worker slept on the job?
d. If a randomly selected worker slept on the job, what is the probability that he/she is an IT professional?
e. If a randomly selected worker is a government professional, what is the probability that he/she slept on the job?
f. Is job category independent of whether or not a worker slept on the job? Explain using probabilities.

35. A recent poll asked 16- to 21-year-olds whether or not they are likely to serve in the U.S. military. The following table, cross-classified by gender and race, reports the percentage of those polled who responded that they are likely or very likely to serve in the active-duty military.

	Race		
Gender	Hispanic	Black	White
Male	33.5%	20.5%	16.5%
Female	14.5%	10.5%	4.5%

Source: Defense Human Resources Activity telephone poll of 3,228 Americans conducted October through December 2005.

a. What is the probability that a randomly selected respondent is female?
b. What is the probability that a randomly selected respondent is Hispanic?
c. Given that a respondent is female, what is the probability that she is Hispanic?
d. Given that a respondent is white, what is the probability that the respondent is male?
e. Is gender independent of race? Explain using probabilities.

36. Merck & Co. conducted a study to test the promise of its experimental AIDS vaccine (*The Boston Globe*, September 22, 2007). Volunteers in the study were all free of the human immunodeficiency virus (HIV), which causes AIDS, at the start of the study, but all were at high risk for getting the virus. Volunteers were either given the vaccine or a dummy shot: 24 of 741 volunteers who got the vaccine became infected with HIV, whereas 21 of 762 volunteers who got the dummy shot became infected with HIV. The following table summarizes the results of the study.

	Vaccinated	Dummy Shot
Infected	24	21
Not Infected	717	741

a. Convert the contingency table into a joint probability table.
b. What is the probability that a randomly selected volunteer got vaccinated?
c. What is the probability that a randomly selected volunteer became infected with the HIV virus?
d. If the randomly selected volunteer was vaccinated, what is the probability that he/she got infected?
e. Is whether or not a volunteer became infected with HIV independent of getting vaccinated? Explain using probabilities. Given your answer, is it surprising that Merck & Co. ended enrollment and vaccination of volunteers in the study? Explain.

37. More and more households are struggling to pay utility bills given a shaky economy and high heating costs (*The Wall Street Journal*, February 14, 2008). Particularly hard hit are households with homes heated with propane or heating oil. Many of these households are spending twice as much to stay warm this winter compared to those who heat with natural gas or electricity. A representative sample of 500 households was taken to investigate if the type of heating influences whether or not a household is delinquent in paying its utility bill. The following table reports the results.

Delinquent in Payment?	Type of Heating			
	Natural Gas	Electricity	Heating Oil	Propane
Yes	50	20	15	10
No	240	130	20	15

a. What is the probability that a randomly selected household uses heating oil?
b. What is the probability that a randomly selected household is delinquent in paying its utility bill?
c. What is the probability that a randomly selected household uses heating oil and is delinquent in paying its utility bill?
d. Given that a household uses heating oil, what is the probability that it is delinquent in paying its utility bill?
e. Given that a household is delinquent in paying its utility bill, what is the probability that the household uses electricity?
f. Is a household's delinquency in paying its utility bill independent of type of heating? Explain using probabilities.

38. The research team at a leading perfume company is trying to test the market for its newly introduced perfume. In particular the team wishes to look for gender and international differences in the preference for this perfume. They sample 2,500 people internationally and each person in the sample is asked to try the new perfume and list his/her preference. The following table reports the results.

Preference	Gender	America	Europe	Asia
Like it	Men	210	150	120
	Women	370	310	180
Don't like it	Men	290	150	80
	Women	330	190	120

a. What is the probability that a randomly selected man likes the perfume?
b. What is the probability that a randomly selected Asian likes the perfume?
c. What is the probability that a randomly selected European woman does not like the perfume?
d. What is the probability that a randomly selected American man does not like the perfume?
e. Are there gender differences in the preference for the perfume in (i) America, (ii) Europe, (iii) Asia? Explain using probabilities.
f. Are there international differences in the preference for the perfume for men and women? Explain using probabilities.

4.4 The Total Probability Rule and Bayes' Theorem

LO 4.7

Apply the total probability rule and Bayes' theorem.

In this section we present two important rules in probability theory: the total probability rule and Bayes' theorem. The **total probability rule** is a useful tool for breaking the computation of a probability into distinct cases. **Bayes' theorem** uses this rule to update a probability of an uncertain outcome that has been affected by a new piece of evidence.

The Total Probability Rule

Sometimes the unconditional (marginal) probability of an event is not readily apparent, even if we have information on its conditional or joint probability. The total probability rule explains the unconditional probability of an event in terms of conditional probabilities. Let $P(A)$ denote the unconditional probability of an event of interest. We can express this probability as the sum of its intersections with some mutually exclusive and exhaustive events corresponding to an experiment. For instance, consider event B and its complement B^c. Figure 4.7 shows the sample space partitioned entirely into these two mutually exclusive and exhaustive events. The circle, representing event A, consists entirely of its intersections with B and B^c. According to the total probability rule, $P(A)$ equals the sum of $P(A \cap B)$ and $P(A \cap B^c)$.

FIGURE 4.7 The total probability rule: $P(A) = P(A \cap B) + P(A \cap B^c)$

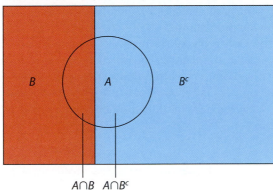

$A \cap B \quad A \cap B^c$

Oftentimes the joint probabilities needed to compute the total probability are not explicitly specified. Therefore, we use the multiplication rule to derive these probabilities from the conditional probabilities as $P(A \cap B) = P(A|B)P(B)$ and $P(A \cap B^c) = P(A|B^c)P(B^c)$.

> **THE TOTAL PROBABILITY RULE CONDITIONAL ON TWO OUTCOMES**
>
> The **total probability rule** expresses the unconditional probability of an event, $P(A)$, in terms of probabilities conditional on various mutually exclusive and exhaustive events. The total probability rule conditional on two events, B and B^c, is
>
> $$P(A) = P(A \cap B) + P(A \cap B^c),$$
>
> or equivalently,
>
> $$P(A) = P(A|B)P(B) + P(A|B^c)P(B^c).$$

An intuitive way to express the total probability rule is with the help of a **probability tree**. Whenever a random experiment can be broken down into stages, with a different aspect of the result observed at each stage, we can use a probability tree to represent the various possible sequences of observations. Both the addition and multiplication rules can be illustrated with a probability tree. Later, we will use an alternative method to systematically solve for an unconditional probability based on the total probability rule with the help of a **probability table**. The following example illustrates the mechanics of a probability tree and table.

EXAMPLE 4.18

Even though a certain statistics professor does not require attendance as part of a student's overall grade, she has noticed that those who regularly attend class have a higher tendency to get a final grade of A. The professor calculates that there is an

80% chance that a student attends class regularly. Moreover, given that a student attends class regularly, there is a 35% chance that the student receives an A grade; however, if a student does not attend class regularly, there is only a 5% chance of an A grade. Use this information to answer the following questions.

a. What is the probability that a student does not attend class regularly?

b. What is the probability that a student attends class regularly and receives an A grade?

c. What is the probability that a student does not attend class regularly and receives an A grade?

d. What is the probability that a student receives an A grade?

SOLUTION: We first denote event A as the simple event corresponding to the outcome that a student receives an A grade and event R as the simple event corresponding to the outcome that a student attends class regularly. From the above information, we then have the following probabilities: $P(R) = 0.80$, $P(A|R) = 0.35$, and $P(A|R^c) = 0.05$. Figure 4.8 shows a probability tree that consists of nodes (junctions) and branches (lines) where the initial node O is called the origin. The branches emanating from O represent the possible outcomes that may occur at the first stage. Thus, at stage 1 we have outcomes R and R^c originating from O. These outcomes become the nodes at the second stage. The sum of the probabilities coming from any particular node is equal to one.

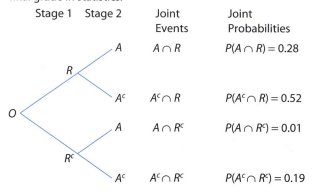

FIGURE 4.8 Probability tree for class attendance and final grade in statistics.

a. Using the complement rule, if we know that there is an 80% chance that a student attends class regularly, $P(R) = 0.80$, then the probability that a student does not attend class regularly is 0.20, or $P(R^c) = 1 - P(R) = 1 - 0.80 = 0.20$.

In order to arrive at a subsequent stage, and deduce the corresponding probabilities, we use the information obtained from the previous stage. For instance, given that a student attends class regularly, there is a 35% chance that the student receives an A grade, $P(A|R) = 0.35$. We then deduce that given that a student regularly attends class, the likelihood of not receiving an A grade is 65%, or $P(A^c|R) = 1 - P(A|R) = 0.65$. Similarly, given $P(A|R^c) = 0.05$, we calculate $P(A^c|R^c) = 1 - P(A|R^c) = 1 - 0.05 = 0.95$. Any path through branches of the tree from the origin to a terminal node defines the intersection of the earlier two events. Thus, following the top branches, we arrive at the joint event $A \cap R$, or the outcome that a student attends class regularly and receives an A grade. The probability of this event is the product of the probabilities attached to the branches forming that path; here we are simply applying the multiplication rule. Now we are prepared to answer parts b and c.

b. Multiplying the probabilities attached to the top branches we obtain $P(A \cap R) = P(A|R)P(R) = 0.35 \times 0.80 = 0.28$; there is a 28% chance that a student attends class regularly and receives an A grade.

c. In order to calculate the probability that a student does not attend class regularly and receives an A grade, we compute $P(A \cap R^c) = P(A|R^c)P(R^c) = 0.05 \times 0.20 = 0.01$.

d. An unconditional probability is found by summing the relevant joint probabilities. The probability that a student receives an A grade, $P(A)$, is not explicitly given in Example 4.18. However, we have calculated the relevant joint probabilities in parts b and c that can be summed to obtain this unconditional probability:

$$P(A) = P(A \cap R) + P(A \cap R^c) = 0.28 + 0.01 = 0.29.$$

An alternative method uses the tabular representation of probabilities. Table 4.5, referred to as a probability table, contains all relevant probabilities that are directly or indirectly specified in Example 4.18.

TABLE 4.5 Probability Table for Class Attendance and Final Grade in Statistics

Attendance Probability	Conditional Probability	Joint Probability
$P(R) = 0.80$	$P(A|R) = 0.35$	$P(A \cap R) = 0.28$
$P(R^c) = 0.20$	$P(A|R^c) = 0.05$	$P(A \cap R^c) = 0.01$
$P(R) + P(R^c) = 1$		$P(A) = 0.29$

As we saw earlier, each joint probability is computed as a product of its conditional probability and the corresponding attendance probability. For instance, $P(A \cap R) = P(A|R)P(R) = 0.35 \times 0.80 = 0.28$. Similarly, $P(A \cap R^c) = P(A|R^c)P(R^c) = 0.05 \times 0.20 = 0.01$. Therefore, $P(A) = P(A \cap R) + P(A \cap R^c) = 0.29$.

Bayes' Theorem

The total probability rule is also needed to derive Bayes' theorem, developed by the Reverend Thomas Bayes (1702–1761). Bayes' theorem is a procedure for updating probabilities based on new information. The original probability is an unconditional probability called a **prior probability** in the sense that it reflects only what we know now before the arrival of any new information. On the basis of new information, we update the prior probability to arrive at a conditional probability called a **posterior probability**.

Suppose we know that 99% of the individuals who take a lie detector test tell the truth. Therefore, the prior probability of telling the truth is 0.99. Suppose an individual takes the lie detector test and the results indicate that the individual lied. Bayes' theorem updates a prior probability to compute a posterior probability, which in the above example is essentially a conditional probability based on the information that the lie detector has detected a lie.

Let $P(B)$ denote the prior probability and $P(B|A)$ the posterior probability. Note that the posterior probability is conditional on event A, representing new information. In a sense, we can think of Bayes' theorem as a special case of a conditional probability. Recall the conditional probability formula from Section 4.2:

$$P(B|A) = \frac{P(A \cap B)}{P(A)}.$$

In some instances we may have to evaluate $P(B|A)$, but we do not have explicit information on $P(A \cap B)$ or $P(A)$. However, given information on $P(B)$, $P(A|B)$ and

$P(A|B^c)$, we can use the total probability rule and the multiplication rule to solve for $P(B|A)$ as follows:

$$P(B|A) = \frac{P(A \cap B)}{P(A)} = \frac{P(A \cap B)}{P(A \cap B) + P(A \cap B^c)} = \frac{P(A|B)P(B)}{P(A|B)P(B) + P(A|B^c)P(B^c)}.$$

BAYES' THEOREM

Given a set of prior probabilities for an event of interest, upon the arrival of new information, the rule for updating the probability of the event is **Bayes' theorem**. Here $P(B)$ is the prior probability and $P(B|A)$ is the posterior probability:

$$P(B|A) = \frac{P(A \cap B)}{P(A \cap B) + P(A \cap B^c)},$$

or equivalently,

$$P(B|A) = \frac{P(A|B)P(B)}{P(A|B)P(B) + P(A|B^c)P(B^c)}.$$

EXAMPLE 4.19

In a lie-detector test, an individual is asked to answer a series of questions, while connected to a polygraph (lie detector). This instrument measures and records several physiological responses of the individual on the basis that false answers will produce distinctive measurements. Assume that 99% of the individuals who go in for a polygraph test tell the truth. These tests are considered to be 95% reliable. In other words, there is a 95% chance that the test will detect a lie if an individual actually lies. Let there also be a 0.5% chance that the test erroneously detects a lie even when the individual is telling the truth. An individual has just taken a polygraph test and the test has detected a lie. What is the probability that the individual was actually telling the truth?

SOLUTION: First we define some events and their associated probabilities. Let D denote the simple event corresponding to the outcome that the polygraph detects a lie and T represent the simple event corresponding to the outcome that an individual is telling the truth. We are given that $P(T) = 0.99$, implying that $P(T^c) = 1 - 0.99 = 0.01$. In addition, we formulate $P(D|T^c) = 0.95$ and $P(D|T) = 0.005$. We need to solve for $P(T|D)$ when we are not explicitly given $P(D \cap T)$ and $P(D)$. We can use Bayes' theorem to calculate:

$$P(T|D) = \frac{P(D \cap T)}{P(D \cap T) + P(D \cap T^c)} = \frac{P(D|T)P(T)}{P(D|T)P(T) + P(D|T^c)P(T^c)}$$

Although we can use this formula to solve the problem directly, it is often easier to solve it systematically with the help of a probability tree or a probability table; we will use the probability table shown in Table 4.6 for calculations.

TABLE 4.6 Probability Table for Example 4.19

Prior Probability	Conditional Probability	Joint Probability	Posterior Probability
$P(T) = 0.99$	$P(D|T) = 0.005$	$P(D \cap T) = 0.00495$	$P(T|D) = 0.34256$
$P(T^c) = 0.01$	$P(D|T^c) = 0.95$	$P(D \cap T^c) = 0.00950$	$P(T^c|D) = 0.65744$
$P(T) + P(T^c) = 1$		$P(D) = 0.01445$	$P(T|D) + P(T|D^c) = 1$

The first column presents prior probabilities and the second column shows related conditional probabilities. We first compute the denominator of Bayes' theorem by using the total probability rule, $P(D) = P(D \cap T) + P(D \cap T^c)$. Joint probabilities are calculated as products of conditional probabilities with their corresponding prior probabilities. For instance, in Table 4.6, in order to obtain $P(D \cap T)$, we multiply $P(D|T)$ with $P(T)$, which yields $P(D \cap T) = 0.005 \times 0.99 = 0.00495$. Similarly, we find $P(D \cap T^c) = 0.95 \times 0.01 = 0.00950$. Thus, according to the total probability rule, $P(D) = 0.00495 + 0.00950 = 0.01445$. Finally, $P(T|D) = \dfrac{P(D \cap T)}{P(D \cap T) + P(D \cap T^c)} = \dfrac{0.00495}{0.01445} = 0.34256$. The prior probability of an individual telling the truth is 0.99. However, given the new information that the polygraph detected the individual telling a lie, the posterior probability of this individual telling the truth is now revised downward to 0.34256.

So far we have used the total probability rule as well as Bayes' theorem based on two mutually exclusive and exhaustive events, namely, B and B^c. We can easily extend the analysis to include n mutually exclusive and exhaustive events, $B_1, B_2, \ldots, B_n$.

EXTENSIONS OF THE TOTAL PROBABILITY RULE AND BAYES' THEOREM

Let a sample space be partitioned into n mutually exclusive and exhaustive events, $B_1, B_2, \ldots, B_n$.

The total probability rule is:

$$P(A) = P(A \cap B_1) + P(A \cap B_2) + \cdots + P(A \cap B_n),$$

or equivalently,

$$P(A) = P(A|B_1)P(B_1) + P(A|B_2)P(B_2) + \cdots + P(A|B_n)P(B_n).$$

Similarly, **Bayes' theorem,** for any $i = 1, 2, \ldots, n$, is:

$$P(B_i|A) = \frac{P(A \cap B_i)}{P(A \cap B_1) + P(A \cap B_2) + \cdots + P(A \cap B_n)},$$

or equivalently,

$$P(B_i|A) = \frac{P(A|B_i)P(B_i)}{P(A|B_1)P(B_1) + P(A|B_2)P(B_2) + \cdots + P(A|B_n)P(B_n)}.$$

EXAMPLE 4.20

Scott Myers is a security analyst for a telecommunications firm called Webtalk. Although he is optimistic about the firm's future, he is concerned that its stock price will be hugely affected by the condition of credit flow in the economy. He believes that the probability is 0.20 that credit flow will improve significantly, 0.50 that it will improve only marginally, and 0.30 that it will not improve at all. He also estimates that the probability that the stock price of Webtalk will go up is 0.90 with significant improvement in credit flow in the economy, 0.40 with marginal improvement in credit flow in the economy, and 0.10 with no improvement in credit flow in the economy.

a. Based on Scott's estimates, what is the probability that the stock price of Webtalk goes up?

b. If we know that the stock price of Webtalk has gone up, what is the probability that credit flow in the economy has improved significantly?

SOLUTION: As always, we first define the relevant events and their associated probabilities. Let S, M, and N denote significant, marginal, and no improvement in credit flow, respectively. Then $P(S) = 0.20$, $P(M) = 0.50$, and $P(N) = 0.30$. In addition, allow G to denote an increase in stock price, we formulate $P(G|S) = 0.90$,

$P(G|M) = 0.40$, and $P(G|N) = 0.10$. We need to calculate $P(G)$ in part (a) and $P(S|G)$ in part (b). Table 4.7 aids in assigning probabilities.

TABLE 4.7 Probability Table for Example 4.20

Prior Probabilities	Conditional Probabilities	Joint Probabilities	Posterior Probabilities
$P(S) = 0.20$	$P(G|S) = 0.90$	$P(G \cap S) = 0.18$	$P(S|G) = 0.4390$
$P(M) = 0.50$	$P(G|M) = 0.40$	$P(G \cap M) = 0.20$	$P(M|G) = 0.4878$
$P(N) = 0.30$	$P(G|N) = 0.10$	$P(G \cap N) = 0.03$	$P(N|G) = 0.0732$
$P(S) + P(M) + P(N) = 1$		$P(G) = 0.41$	$P(S|G) + P(M|G) + P(N|G) = 1$

a. In order to calculate, $P(G)$, we use the total probability rule, $P(G) = P(G \cap S) + P(G \cap M) + P(G \cap N)$. The joint probabilities are calculated as a product of conditional probabilities with their corresponding prior probabilities. For instance, in Table 4.7, $P(G \cap S) = P(G|S)P(S) = 0.90 \times 0.20 = 0.18$. Therefore, the probability that the stock price of Webtalk goes up equals $P(G) = 0.18 + 0.20 + 0.03 = 0.41$.

b. According to Bayes' theorem, $P(S|G) = \dfrac{P(G \cap S)}{P(G \cap S) + P(G \cap M) + P(G \cap N)}$. Note that the denominator is simply the total probability, $P(G)$. As seen in Table 4.7, $P(S|G) = \dfrac{P(G \cap S)}{P(G)} = \dfrac{0.18}{0.41} = 0.4390$. Therefore, the prior probability of a significant improvement in credit flow is revised upward from 0.20 to a posterior probability of 0.4390.

EXERCISES 4.4

Concepts

39. Let $P(A) = 0.70$, $P(B|A) = 0.55$, and $P(B|A^c) = 0.10$. Use a probability tree to calculate the following probabilities:

    a. $P(A^c)$

    b. $P(A \cap B)$ and $P(A^c \cap B)$

    c. $P(B)$

    d. $P(A|B)$

40. Let $P(B) = 0.60$, $P(A|B) = 0.80$, and $P(A|B^c) = 0.10$. Calculate the following probabilities:

    a. $P(B^c)$

    b. $P(A \cap B)$ and $P(A \cap B^c)$

    c. $P(A)$

    d. $P(B|A)$

41. Complete the following probability table.

Prior Probability	Conditional Probability	Joint Probability	Posterior Probability
$P(B) = 0.85$	$P(A|B) = 0.05$	$P(A \cap B) =$	$P(B|A) =$
$P(B^c) =$	$P(A|B^c) = 0.80$	$P(A \cap B^c) =$	$P(B^c|A) =$
Total $=$		$P(A) =$	Total $=$

42. Let a sample space be partitioned into three mutually exclusive and exhaustive events, B_1, B_2, and B_3. Complete the following probability table.

Prior Probabilities	Conditional Probabilities	Joint Probabilities	Posterior Probabilities
$P(B_1) = 0.10$	$P(A|B_1) = 0.40$	$P(A \cap B_1) =$	$P(B_1|A) =$
$P(B_2) =$	$P(A|B_2) = 0.60$	$P(A \cap B_2) =$	$P(B_2|A) =$
$P(B_3) = 0.30$	$P(A|B_3) = 0.80$	$P(A \cap B_3) =$	$P(B_3|A) =$
Total $=$		$P(A) =$	Total $=$

Applications

43. Christine has always been weak in mathematics. Based on her performance prior to the final exam in Calculus, there is a 40% chance that she will fail the course if she does not have a tutor. With a tutor, her probability of failing decreases to 10%. There is only a 50% chance that she will find a tutor at such short notice.

    a. What is the probability that Christine fails the course?

    b. Christine ends up failing the course. What is the probability that she had found a tutor?

44. An analyst expects that 20% of all publicly traded companies will experience a decline in earnings next year. The analyst has developed a ratio to help forecast this decline. If the company is headed for a decline, there is a 70% chance that this ratio will be negative. If the company is not headed for a decline, there is a 15% chance that the ratio will be negative. The analyst randomly selects a company and its ratio is

negative. What is the posterior probability that the company will experience a decline?

45. The State Police are trying to crack down on speeding on a particular portion of the Massachusetts Turnpike. To aid in this pursuit, they have purchased a new radar gun that promises greater consistency and reliability. Specifically, the gun advertises ± one-mile-per-hour accuracy 98% of the time; that is, there is a 0.98 probability that the gun will detect a speeder, if the driver is actually speeding. Assume there is a 1% chance that the gun erroneously detects a speeder even when the driver is below the speed limit. Suppose that 95% of the drivers drive below the speed limit on this stretch of the Massachusetts Turnpike.
    a. What is the probability that the gun detects speeding and the driver was speeding?
    b. What is the probability that the gun detects speeding and the driver was not speeding?
    c. Suppose the police stop a driver because the gun detects speeding. What is the probability that the driver was actually driving below the speed limit?

46. A crucial game of the Los Angeles Lakers basketball team depends on the health of their key player. According to his doctor's report, there is a 40% chance that he will be fully fit to play, a 30% chance that he will be somewhat fit to play, and a 30% chance that he will not be able to play at all. The coach has estimated the chances of winning at 80% if the player is fully fit, 60% if he is somewhat fit, and 40% if he is unable to play.
    a. What is the probability that the Lakers will win the game?
    b. You have just heard that the Lakers won the game. What is the probability that the key player had been fully fit to play in the game?

47. An analyst thinks that next year there is a 20% chance that the world economy will be good, a 50% chance that it will be neutral, and a 30% chance that it will be poor. She also predicts probabilities that a start-up firm, Creative Ideas, will be good, neutral, or poor for each of the economic states of the world economy. The following table presents probabilities for three states of the world economy and the corresponding conditional probabilities for Creative Ideas.

State of the World Economy	Probability of Economic State	Performance of Creative Ideas	Conditional Probability of Creative Ideas
Good	0.20	Good	0.6
		Neutral	0.3
		Poor	0.1
Neutral	0.50	Good	0.4
		Neutral	0.3
		Poor	0.3
Poor	0.30	Good	0.2
		Neutral	0.3
		Poor	0.5

   a. What is the probability that the performance of the world economy will be neutral and that of creative ideas will be poor?
   b. What is the probability that the performance of Creative Ideas will be poor?
   c. The performance of Creative Ideas was poor. What is the probability that the performance of the world economy had also been poor?

4.5 Counting Rules

In several areas of statistics, including the binomial distribution discussed in the next chapter, the calculation of probabilities involves defining and counting outcomes. Here we discuss principles and shortcuts for counting. Specifically, we explore the factorial, combination, and permutation notations.

When we are interested in counting the arrangements of a given set of n items, we calculate **n factorial**, denoted $n!$. In other words, given n items, there are $n!$ ways of arranging them. We apply the factorial when there are no groups—we are only arranging a given set of n items.

LO **4.8**

Use a counting rule to solve a particular counting problem.

THE FACTORIAL FORMULA

The number of ways to assign every member of a group of size n to n slots is calculated using the **factorial formula**:

$$n! = n \times (n-1) \times (n-2) \times (n-3) \times \cdots \times 1$$

By definition, $0! = 1$.

EXAMPLE 4.21

A little-league coach has nine players on his team and he has to assign each of the players to one of nine positions (pitcher, catcher, first base, etc.). In how many ways can the assignments be made?

SOLUTION: The first player may be assigned to nine different positions. Then eight positions remain. The second player can be assigned to eight different positions. The third player can be assigned to seven different positions, and so on, until the ninth and last player can be assigned in only one way. The total number of different assignments is equal to $9! = 9 \times 8 \times \cdots \times 1 = 362,880$.

The **combination** and **permutation formulas** apply to two groups of predetermined size. We apply the combination formula when the order of the arrangement does not matter, whereas we use the permutation formula when the order is important. Generally, we look for a specific reference to "order" being important when employing the permutation formula.

THE COMBINATION FORMULA

The number of ways to choose x objects from a total of n objects, where the order in which the x objects are listed *does not matter*, is calculated using the **combination formula**:

$$_nC_x = \binom{n}{x} = \frac{n!}{(n-x)!x!}$$

EXAMPLE 4.22

The little-league coach from Example 4.21 recruits three more players so that his team has backups in case of injury. Now his team totals 12. In how many ways can the coach select nine players from the 12-player roster?

SOLUTION: This is a combination problem because we are simply interested in placing 9 players on the field. We have no concern, for instance, as to whether a player pitches, catches, or plays first base. In other words, the order in which the players are selected is not important. We make use of the combination formula as follows:

$$_{12}C_9 = \binom{12}{9} = \frac{12!}{(12-9)! \times 9!} = \frac{12 \times 11 \times \cdots \times 1}{(3 \times 2 \times 1) \times (9 \times 8 \times \cdots \times 1)} = 220.$$

THE PERMUTATION FORMULA

The number of ways to choose x objects from a total of n objects, where the order in which the x objects is listed *does matter*, is calculated using the **permutation formula**:

$$_nP_x = \frac{n!}{(n-x)!}$$

EXAMPLE 4.23

Now suppose the little league coach from Example 4.22 recognizes that the nine positions of baseball are quite different. It matters whether one player is pitching or whether that same player is in the outfield. The teammates that this player plays with in any particular inning also matters. In how many ways can the coach assign his 12-player roster to the nine different positions?

SOLUTION: This is a permutation problem because the order in which the coach assigns the positions matters; that is, in one inning a player may catch, but in another inning this same player may pitch. Even though the player is participating in the two innings, the player's position changes, thus it is a different arrangement. We calculate the answer as follows:

$$_{12}P_9 = \frac{12!}{(12-9)!} = \frac{12 \times 11 \times \cdots \times 1}{3 \times 2 \times 1} = 79,833,600.$$

Comparing the answers we obtained from Examples 4.22 and 4.23, we see there is a big difference between the number of arrangements when the position of the player does not matter versus the number of arrangements when the position is important.

EXERCISES 4.5

Concepts

48. Calculate the following values.
    a. 8! and 6!
    b. $_8C_6$
    c. $_8P_6$

49. Calculate the following values.
    a. 7! and 3!
    b. $_7C_3$
    c. $_7P_3$

Applications

50. At a local elementary school, a principal is making random class assignments for her 8 teachers. Each teacher must be assigned to exactly one job. In how many ways can the assignments be made?

51. Twenty cancer patients volunteer for a clinical trial. Ten of the patients will receive a placebo and 10 will receive the trial drug. In how many different ways can the researchers select 10 patients to receive the trial drug from the total of 20?

52. There are 10 players on the local basketball team. The coach decides to randomly pick 5 players for the game.
    a. In how many different ways can the coach select 5 players to start the game if order does not matter?
    b. In how many different ways can the coach select 5 players to start the game if order (the type of position, i.e., point guard, center, etc.) matters?

53. David Barnes and his fiancée Valerie Shah are visiting Hawaii. At the Hawaiian Cultural Center in Honolulu, they are told that 2 out of a group of 8 people will be randomly picked for a free lesson of a Tahitian dance.
    a. What is the probability that both David and Valerie get picked for the Tahitian dance lesson?
    b. What is the probability that Valerie gets picked before David for the Tahitian dance lesson?

WRITING WITH STATISTICS

A University of Utah study examined 7,925 severely obese adults who had gastric bypass surgery and an identical number of people who did not have the surgery (*The Boston Globe*, August 23, 2007). The study wanted to investigate whether or not losing weight through stomach surgery prolonged the lives of severely obese patients, thereby reducing their deaths from heart disease, cancer, and diabetes.

Over the course of the study, 534 of the participants died. Of those who died, the cause of death was classified as either a disease death (such as heart disease, cancer, and

diabetes) or a nondisease death (such as suicide or accident). Lawrence Plummer, a research analyst, is handed Table 4.8 a contingency table that summarizes the study's findings:

TABLE 4.8 Deaths Cross-Classified by Cause and Method of Losing Weight

Cause of Death	Method of Losing Weight	
	No Surgery	Surgery
Death from disease	285	150
Death from nondisease	36	63

Lawrence wants to use the sample information to:

1. Calculate and interpret relevant probabilities for the cause of death and the method of losing weight.

2. Determine whether the method of losing weight is independent of the cause of death.

Sample Managerial Report— Linking Cause of Death with the Method of Losing Weight

Numerous studies have documented the health risks posed to severely obese people—those people who are at least 100 pounds overweight. Severely obese people, for instance, typically suffer from high blood pressure and are more likely to develop diabetes. A University of Utah study examined whether the manner in which a severely obese person lost weight influenced a person's longevity. The study followed 7,925 patients who had stomach surgery and an identical number who did not have the surgery. Of particular interest in this report are the 534 participants who died over the course of the study.

The deceased participants were cross-classified by the method in which they lost weight and by the cause of their death. The possible outcomes for the method of losing weight were either "no surgery" or "surgery," and the possible outcomes for the cause of death were either "disease death" (such as heart disease, cancer, and diabetes) or a "nondisease death" (such as suicide or accident). Table 4.A shows the joint probability table.

TABLE 4.A Joint Probability Table of Deaths Cross-Classified by Cause and Method of Losing Weight

Cause of Death	Method of Losing Weight		Total
	No Surgery	Surgery	
Death from disease	0.53	0.28	0.81
Death from nondisease	0.07	0.12	0.19
Total	0.60	0.40	1.00

The unconditional probabilities reveal that 0.60 of the deceased participants in the study did not have surgery, while 0.40 of those who died had opted for the stomach surgery. Of the 534 participants that died, the vast majority, 0.81, died from disease, whereas the cause of death for the remainder was from a nondisease cause.

Joint probabilities reveal that the probability that a deceased participant had no surgery and died from disease was 0.53; yet the probability that a deceased participant had surgery and died from disease was only 0.28. Using the unconditional probabilities and the joint probabilities, it is possible to calculate conditional probabilities. For example, given that a participant's cause of death was from disease, the probability that the participant did not have surgery was 0.65 (= 0.53/0.81). Similarly, of those participants who opted for no surgery, the likelihood that their death was from disease was 0.88 (= 0.53/0.60).

A comparison of the conditional probabilities with the unconditional probabilities can reveal whether or not the method of losing weight is independent of the cause of death. For instance, there is an 81% chance that a randomly selected obese person dies from disease. However, given that an obese person chooses to lose weight without surgery, the likelihood that he/she dies from disease jumps to 88%. Thus, this initial research appears to suggest that a participant's cause of death is not independent of his/her method of losing weight.

Conceptual Review

LO 4.1 **Describe fundamental probability concepts.**

In order to assign the appropriate probability to an uncertain event, it is useful to establish some terminology. An **experiment** is a trial that results in one of several possible outcomes. A **sample space**, denoted S, of an experiment contains all possible outcomes of the experiment. An **event** is any subset of outcomes of an experiment, and is called a simple event if it consists of a single outcome. Events are considered **exhaustive** if all possible outcomes of an experiment are included in the events. Events are considered **mutually exclusive** if they do not share any common outcome of an experiment.

A **probability** is a numerical value that measures the likelihood that an uncertain event occurs. It assumes a value between zero and one where a value zero indicates an impossible event and a value one indicates a definite event. The **two defining properties of a probability** are (1) the probability of any event A is a value between 0 and 1, $0 \le P(A) \le 1$, and (2) the sum of the probabilities of any list of mutually exclusive and exhaustive events equals 1.

LO 4.2 **Formulate and explain subjective, empirical, and a priori probabilities.**

We generally categorize a probability as either **subjective** or **objective**. A subjective probability is calculated by drawing on personal and subjective judgment. **Empirical probabilities** and **a priori probabilities** are considered objective because they do not vary from person to person. An empirical probability is calculated from data as a relative frequency of occurrence. An a priori probability is based on logical analysis rather than on observation or personal judgment.

LO 4.3 **Calculate and interpret the probability of the complement of an event, the probability that at least one of two events will occur, and a joint probability.**

Rules of probability allow us to calculate the probabilities of more complex events. The **complement rule** states that the probability of the complement of an event can be found by subtracting the probability of the event from one: $P(A^c) = 1 - P(A)$. We calculate the probability that at least one of two events occurs by using the **addition rule**: $P(A \cup B) = P(A) + P(B) - P(A \cap B)$. Since $P(A \cap B) = 0$ for mutually exclusive events, the addition rule simplifies to $P(A \cup B) = P(A) + P(B)$. Finally, to find the probability that two events both occur, we apply the **multiplication rule**, that is, $P(A \cap B) = P(A|B)P(B)$ or $P(A \cap B) = P(B|A)P(A)$.

LO 4.4 **Calculate and interpret a conditional probability.**

The probability of event A, denoted $P(A)$, is referred to as an **unconditional (marginal) probability**. It is the probability that A occurs without any additional information. A **joint probability** of two events A and B, denoted $P(A \cap B)$, indicates the likelihood of the occurrence of the two events. The probability that A occurs given that B has already occurred, denoted $P(A|B)$, is a **conditional probability**. A conditional probability is calculated as the ratio of a joint probability to an unconditional probability, that is, $P(A|B) = \frac{P(A \cap B)}{P(B)}$.

Distinguish between independent and dependent events.

Two events, A and B, are **independent** if and only if $P(A|B) = P(A)$, or if $P(B|A) = P(B)$. Otherwise, the events are **dependent**. For independent events, the multiplication rule simplifies to $P(A \cap B) = P(A)P(B)$.

LO **4.6**

Calculate and interpret probabilities from a contingency table.

A **contingency table** generally shows frequencies for two qualitative or categorical variables, x and y, where each cell represents a mutually exclusive combination of x-y values. Empirical probabilities are easily calculated as the relative frequency of the occurrence of the event.

LO **4.7**

Apply the total probability rule and Bayes' theorem.

The **total probability rule** explains the unconditional probability of an event A in terms of probabilities conditional on two mutually exclusive and exhaustive events, B and B^c:

$$P(A) = P(A \cap B) + P(A \cap B^c) = P(A|B)P(B) + P(A|B^c)P(B^c).$$

We can extend the above rule where the sample space is partitioned into n mutually exclusive and exhaustive events, $B_1, B_2, \ldots, B_n$. The total probability rule is: $P(A) = P(A \cap B_1) + P(A \cap B_2) + \cdots + P(A \cap B_n)$, or equivalently, $P(A) = P(A|B_1)P(B_1) + P(A|B_2)P(B_2) + \cdots + P(A|B_n)P(B_n)$.

Bayes' theorem is a procedure for updating probabilities based on new information. Let $P(B)$ be the prior probability and $P(B|A)$ be the posterior probability based on new information provided by A. Then:

$$P(B|A) = \frac{P(A \cap B)}{P(A \cap B) + P(A \cap B^c)} = \frac{P(A|B)P(B)}{P(A|B)P(B) + P(A|B^c)P(B^c)}.$$

For the extended total probability rule, Bayes' theorem, for any $i = 1, 2, \ldots, n$, is:

$$P(B_i|A) = \frac{P(A \cap B_i)}{P(A \cap B_1) + P(A \cap B_2) + \cdots + P(A \cap B_n)}, \text{ or}$$

equivalently, $P(B_i|A) = \dfrac{P(A|B_i)P(B_i)}{P(A|B_1)P(B_1) + P(A|B_2)P(B_2) + \cdots + P(A|B_n)P(B_n)}$.

LO **4.8**

Use a counting rule to solve a particular counting problem.

Shortcut rules for counting include the **factorial**, the **combination**, and the **permutation** formulas. When we are interested in arranging a given set of n items, we calculate n factorial as: $n! = n \times (n-1) \times \cdots \times 1$. The combination and permutation formulas apply to two groups of predetermined size. We apply the combination formula when the order of the arrangement does not matter: $_nC_x = \binom{n}{x} = \frac{n!}{(n-x)!x!}$. We use the permutation formula when the order of the arrangement is important: $_nP_x = \frac{n!}{(n-x)!}$.

Additional Exercises and Case Studies

54. Henry Chow is a stockbroker working for Merrill Lynch. He knows from past experience that there is a 70% chance that his new client will want to include U.S. equity in her portfolio and a 50% chance that she will want to include foreign equity. There is also a 40% chance that she will want to include both U.S. equity and foreign equity in her portfolio.

a. What is the probability that the client will want to include U.S. equity if she already has foreign equity in her portfolio?

b. What is the probability that the client decides to include neither U.S. equity nor foreign equity in her portfolio?

55. The following frequency distribution shows the ages of India's 40 richest individuals. One of these individuals is selected at random.

Ages	Frequency
30 up to 40	3
40 up to 50	8
50 up to 60	15
60 up to 70	9
70 up to 80	5

Source: www.forbes.com.

a. What is the probability that the individual is between 50 and 60 years of age?
b. What is the probability that the individual is younger than 50 years of age?
c. What is the probability that the individual is at least 60 years of age?

56. AccuScore calculated an 84% chance that there would be a fight during the game between the Anaheim Ducks and the Chicago Blacks, two of the National Hockey League's most pugnacious teams (*The Wall Street Journal*, March 3, 2009). What are the odds for a fight occurring?

57. Anthony Papantonis, owner of Nauset Construction, is bidding on two projects, A and B. The probability that he wins project A is 0.40 and the probability that he wins project B is 0.25. Winning Project A and winning Project B are independent events.
a. What is the probability that he wins project A or project B?
b. What is the probability that he does not win either project?

58. Since the fall of 2008, millions of Americans have lost jobs due to the economic meltdown. A recent study shows that unemployment has not impacted males and females in the same way (*Newsweek*, April 20, 2009). According to a Bureau of Labor Statistics report, 8.5% of those who are eligible to work are unemployed. The unemployment rate is 8.8% for eligible men and only 7.0% for eligible women. Suppose 52% of the eligible workforce in the U.S. consists of men.
a. You have just heard that another worker in a large firm has been laid off. What is the probability that this worker is a man?
b. You have just heard that another worker in a large firm has been laid off. What is the probability that this worker is a woman?

59. How much you smile in your younger days can predict your later success in marriage (msnbc.com, April 16, 2009). The analysis is based on the success rate in marriage of people over age 65 and their smiles when they were only 10 years old. Researchers found that only 11% of the biggest smilers had been divorced, while 31% of the biggest frowners had experienced a broken marriage.

a. Suppose it is known that 2% of the people are the biggest smilers at age 10 and divorced in later years. What percent of people are the biggest smilers?
b. If 25% of people are considered to be the biggest frowners, calculate the probability that a person is the biggest frowner at age 10 and divorced later in life.

60. A recent study in the *Journal of the American Medical Association* (February 20, 2008) found that patients who go into cardiac arrest while in the hospital are more likely to die if it happens after 11 pm. The study investigated 58,593 cardiac arrests that occurred during the day or evening. Of those, 11,604 survived to leave the hospital. There were 28,155 cardiac arrests during the shift that began at 11 pm, commonly referred to as the graveyard shift. Of those, 4,139 survived for discharge. The following contingency table summarizes the results of the study.

	Survived for Discharge	Did not Survive for Discharge	
Day or Evening Shift	11,604	46,989	58,593
Graveyard Shift	4,139	24,016	28,155
	15,743	71,005	86,748

a. What is the probability that a randomly selected patient experienced cardiac arrest during the graveyard shift?
b. What is the probability that a randomly selected patient survived for discharge?
c. Given that a randomly selected patient experienced cardiac arrest during the graveyard shift, what is the probability the patient survived for discharge?
d. Given that a randomly selected patient survived for discharge, what is the probability the patient experienced cardiac arrest during the graveyard shift?
e. Is whether or not a patient survives independent of the timing of the cardiac arrest? Explain using probabilities. Given your answer, what type of recommendations might you give to hospitals?

61. It has been reported that women end up unhappier than men later in life, even though they start out happier (*Yahoo News*, August 1, 2008). Early in life, women are more likely to fulfill their family life and financial aspirations, leading to greater overall happiness. However, men report a higher satisfaction with their financial situation and family life, and are thus happier than women in later life. Suppose the results of the survey of 300 men and 300 women are presented in the following table.

Response to the question "Are you satisfied with your financial and family life?"

	Age		
Response by Women	**20 to 35**	**35 to 50**	**Over 50**
Yes	73	36	32
No	67	54	38

Response by Men	Age		
	20 to 35	35 to 50	Over 50
Yes	58	34	38
No	92	46	32

a. What is the probability that a randomly selected woman is satisfied with her financial and family life?

b. What is the probability that a randomly selected man is satisfied with his financial and family life?

c. Does the above survey suggest that, for a woman, satisfaction with life depends on age? Explain.

d. Does the above survey suggest that, for a man, satisfaction with life depends on age? Explain.

62. An analyst predicts that there is a 40% chance that the U.S. economy will perform well. If the U.S. economy performs well, then there is an 80% chance that Asian countries will also perform well. On the other hand, if the U.S. economy performs poorly, the probability of Asian countries performing well goes down to 30%.

a. What is the probability that both the U.S. economy and the Asian countries will perform well?

b. What is the unconditional probability that the Asian countries will perform well?

c. What is the probability that the U.S. economy will perform well, given that the Asian countries perform well?

63. Apparently, depression significantly increases the risk of developing dementia later in life (*BBC News*, July 6, 2010). In a recent study it was reported that 22% of those who had depression went on to develop dementia, compared to only 17% of those who did not have depression. Suppose 10% of all people suffer from depression.

a. What is the probability of a person developing dementia?

b. If a person has developed dementia, what is the probability that the person suffered from depression earlier in life?

CASE STUDIES

Case Study 4.1

Ever since the introduction of New Coke failed miserably in the 1980s, most food and beverage companies have been cautious about changing the taste or formula of their signature offerings. In an attempt to attract more business, Starbucks recently introduced a new milder brew, Pike Place Roast, as its main drip coffee at the majority of its locations nationwide. The idea was to offer a more approachable cup of coffee with a smoother finish. However, the strategy also downplayed the company's more established robust roasts; initially, the milder brew was the only option for customers after noon. Suppose on a recent afternoon, 100 customers were asked whether or not they would return in the near future for another cup of Pike Place Roast. The following contingency table (cross-classified by type of customer and whether or not the customer will return) lists the results:

Data for Case Study 4.1

Return in Near Future?	Customer Type	
	First-time Customer	Established Customer
Yes	35	10
No	5	50

In a report, use the sample information to:

1. Calculate and interpret unconditional probabilities.

2. Calculate the probability that a customer will return given that the customer is an established customer.

3. Determine whether the type of customer is independent of his/her choice to return. Shortly after the introduction of Pike Place Roast, Starbucks decided to offer its bolder brew again in the afternoon at many of its locations. Do your results support Starbucks' decision? Explain.

Case Study 4.2

It is common to ignore the thyroid gland of women during pregnancy (*New York Times,* April 13, 2009). This gland makes hormones that govern metabolism, helping to regulate body weight, heart rate, and a host of other factors. If the thyroid malfunctions, it can produce too little or too much of these hormones. Hypothyroidism, caused by an untreated underactive thyroid in pregnant women, carries the risk of impaired intelligence in the child. According to one research study, 62 out of 25,216 pregnant women were identified with hypothyroidism. Nineteen percent of the children born to women with an untreated underactive thyroid had an I.Q. of 85 or lower, compared with only 5% of those whose mothers had a healthy thyroid. It was also reported that if mothers have their hypothyroidism treated, their children's intelligence would not be impaired.

In a report, use the sample information to:

1. Find the likelihood that a woman suffers from hypothyroidism during pregnancy and later has a child with an I.Q. of 85 or lower.

2. Determine the number of children in a sample of 100,000 that are likely to have an I.Q. of 85 or lower if the thyroid gland of pregnant women is ignored.

3. Compare and comment on your answer to part b with the corresponding number if all pregnant women are tested and treated for hypothyroidism.

Case Study 4.3

In 2008, it appeared that rising gas prices had made Californians less resistant to offshore drilling. A Field Poll survey showed that a higher proportion of Californians supported the idea of drilling for oil or natural gas along the state's coast than in 2005 (*The Wall Street Journal*, July 17, 2008). Assume that random drilling for oil only succeeds 5% of the time.

An oil company has just announced that it has discovered new technology for detecting oil. The technology is 80% reliable. That is, if there is oil, the technology will signal "oil" 80% of the time. Let there also be a 1% chance that the technology erroneously detects oil, when in fact no oil exists.

In a report, use the sample information to:

1. Prepare a probability table.

2. Solve for the probability that, on a recent expedition, oil actually existed but the technology detected "no oil" in the area.

5

Discrete Probability Distributions

LEARNING OBJECTIVES

After reading this chapter you should be able to:

LO 5.1 Distinguish between discrete and continuous random variables.

LO 5.2 Describe the probability distribution of a discrete random variable.

LO 5.3 Calculate and interpret summary measures for a discrete random variable.

LO 5.4 Differentiate among risk neutral, risk averse, and risk loving consumers.

LO 5.5 Compute summary measures to evaluate portfolio returns.

LO 5.6 Describe the binomial distribution and compute relevant probabilities.

LO 5.7 Describe the Poisson distribution and compute relevant probabilities.

LO 5.8 Describe the hypergeometric distribution and compute relevant probabilities.

In this chapter we extend our discussion about probability by introducing the concept of a random variable. A random variable summarizes the results of an experiment in terms of numerical values. It can be classified as discrete or continuous depending on the range of values that it assumes. A discrete random variable assumes a countable number of distinct values, whereas a continuous random variable is characterized by infinitely uncountable values. In this chapter, we focus on discrete random variables. Examples include the number of credit cards carried by consumers, the number of foreclosures in a sample of 100 households, and the number of cars lined up at a toll booth. Once we define the range of possible values that a random variable assumes, we construct a probability distribution to compute the probabilities associated with these different values. We also calculate summary measures for a random variable, including its mean, variance, and standard deviation. Finally, we discuss three widely used discrete probability distributions: the binomial, the Poisson, and the hypergeometric distributions.

Available Staff for Probable Customers

In addition to its previous plan to shut 100 stores, Starbucks announced plans in 2008 to close 500 more U.S. locations (*The Wall Street Journal*, July 9, 2008). Executives claimed that a weak economy and higher gas and food prices led to a drop in domestic store traffic. Others speculate that Starbucks' rapid expansion produced a saturated market. The locations that will close are not profitable, are not expected to be profitable, and/or are located near an existing company-operated Starbucks.

Anne Jones, a manager at a local Starbucks, has been reassured by headquarters that her store will remain open. She is concerned about how other nearby closings might affect business at her store. Anne knows that a typical Starbucks customer visits the chain between 15 and 18 times a month, making it among the nation's most frequented retailers. She believes that her loyal Starbucks customers, along with displaced customers, will average 18 visits to the store over a 30-day month. To decide staffing needs, Anne knows that she needs a solid understanding about the probability distribution of customer arrivals. If too many employees are ready to serve customers, some employees will be idle, which is costly to the store. However, if not enough employees are available to meet demand, this could result in losing angry customers who choose not to wait for service.

Anne wants to use the above information to:

1. Calculate the expected number of visits from a typical Starbucks customer in a specified time period.
2. Calculate the probability that a typical Starbucks customer visits the chain a certain number of times in a specified time period.

We provide a synopsis of this case at the end of Section 5.5.

5.1 Random Variables and Discrete Probability Distributions

LO **5.1**

Distinguish between discrete and continuous random variables.

We often have to make important decisions in the face of uncertainty. For example, a car dealership has to determine the number of cars to hold on its lot when the actual demand for cars is unknown. Similarly, an investor has to select a portfolio when the actual outcomes of investment returns are not known. This uncertainty is captured by what we call a **random variable**. A random variable summarizes outcomes of an experiment with numerical values.

> A **random variable** is a function that assigns numerical values to the outcomes of a random experiment.
>
> Following the usual convention in statistics, we denote **random variables** by **upper-case letters** and particular **values** of the random variables by the corresponding **lower-case letters**.

We generally use the letter X to denote a random variable. A **discrete random variable** assumes a countable number of distinct values such as x_1, x_2, x_3 and so on. It may assume either a finite number of values, or an infinite sequence of values. A **continuous random variable**, on the other hand, is characterized by (infinitely) uncountable values. In other words, a continuous random variable can take on any value within an interval or collection of intervals.

> A **discrete random variable** assumes a countable number of distinct values, whereas a **continuous random variable** is characterized by (infinitely) uncountable values within any interval.

Recall from Chapter 4, the sample space is a set of all outcomes of a random experiment. Whenever some numerical values are assigned to these outcomes, a random variable X is defined. Consider the following experiments, and some examples of discrete random variables (with their possible values) that are associated with the experiments:

Experiment 1. Rolling a six-sided die; sample space = {1, 2, 3, 4, 5, 6}.

Let X = the number rolled; possible values: {1, 2, 3, 4, 5, 6}

Let X = the odd number rolled; possible values = {1, 3, 5}

Experiment 2. Two shirts are selected from the production line and each can be defective (D) or non-defective (N); sample space = {(D,D), (D,N), (N,D), (N,N)}.

Let X = the number of defective shirts; possible values = {0, 1, 2}

Let X = the proportion of defective shirts; possible values = {0, 1/2, 1}

Experiment 3. Reviewing a single mortgage application and deciding whether the client gets approved (A) or denied (D); sample space = {A, D}.

Let X = 1 for A and 0 for D; possible values = {1, 0}

Let X = 1 for A and −1 for D; possible values = {1, −1}

Experiment 4. Reviewing multiple mortgage applications and, for each client, deciding whether the client gets approved (A) or denied (D); sample space = the set of all possible infinite sequences whose elements are A or D.

Let X = the number of approvals; possible values = {0, 1, 2, 3. . . .}

Let X = the squared number of approvals; possible values = {0, 1, 4, 9, . . .}

The random variables defined for Experiments 1, 2 and 3 have finite numbers of values, while the two random variables defined for Experiment 4 have infinite but countable numbers of values.

Sometimes, we can define a random variable *directly* by identifying its values with some numerical outcomes. For example, we may be interested in the number of students who get financial aid out of the 100 students who applied. Then the set of possible values of the random variable, equivalent to the sample space, is {0, 1, . . . , 100}. In a similar way, we can define a discrete random variable with an infinite number of values that it may take. For example, consider the number of cars that cross the Brooklyn Bridge between 9:00 am and 10:00 am on a Monday morning. Here the discrete random variable takes an infinite but countable number of values from {0, 1, 2, . . .}. It is possible that no cars cross the bridge in this time period; perhaps, due to an accident, the bridge is temporarily closed. Note that we cannot specify an upper bound on the observed number of cars.

Although, we explore discrete random variables in this chapter, random variables can also be continuous. For example, the time taken by a student to complete a 60-minute exam may assume any value between 0 and 60 minutes. Thus, the set of such values is uncountable; that is, it is impossible to put all real numbers from the interval [0, 60] in a sequence. Here, the random variable is continuous because the outcomes are (infinitely) uncountable. Some students may think that time in the above example is countable in seconds; however, this is not the case once we consider fractions of a second. We will discuss the details of continuous random variables in the next chapter.

The Discrete Probability Distribution

LO **5.2**

Every random variable is associated with a **probability distribution** that describes the variable completely. It is common to define discrete random variables in terms of their **probability mass function** and continuous random variables in terms of their **probability density function**. Both variables can also be defined in terms of their **cumulative distribution function**.

Describe the probability distribution of a discrete random variable.

> The **probability mass function** of a discrete random variable X is a list of the values of X with the associated probabilities, that is, the list of all possible pairs $(x, P(X = x))$.
>
> The **cumulative distribution function** of X is defined as $P(X \leq x)$.

For convenience, in this chapter, we will use terms like "probability distribution" and "distribution" for the probability mass function. We will do the same in the next chapter for the probability density function. In both chapters, we will use "cumulative probability distribution" for the cumulative distribution function.

You can view a discrete probability distribution in several ways, including tabular, algebraic, and graphical forms. Example 5.1 shows one of two tabular forms. In general, we can construct a table in two different ways. The first approach directly specifies the probability that the random variable assumes a specific value.

EXAMPLE 5.1

Refer back to Experiment 1 of rolling a six-sided die, with the random variable defined as the number rolled. Present the probability distribution in a tabular form.

SOLUTION: A probability distribution for rolling a six-sided die is shown in Table 5.1.

TABLE 5.1 Probability Distribution for Example 5.1

x	1	2	3	4	5	6
P(X = x)	1/6	1/6	1/6	1/6	1/6	1/6

From Table 5.1, we can deduce, for instance, that $P(X = 5)$ equals 1/6. For that matter, the probability that X assumes any of the six possible values is 1/6.

The probability distribution defined in Example 5.1 illustrates two components of all discrete probability distributions.

The second tabular view of a probability distribution is based on the cumulative probability distribution.

The cumulative probability representation is convenient when we are interested in finding the probability over a range of values rather than a specific value. For the random variable defined in Example 5.1, the cumulative probability distribution is shown in Table 5.2.

TABLE 5.2 Cumulative Probability Distribution for Example 5.1

x	1	2	3	4	5	6
$P(X \le x)$	1/6	2/6	3/6	4/6	5/6	6/6

If we are interested in finding the probability of rolling a four or less, $P(X \le 4)$, we see from the cumulative probability distribution that this probability is 4/6. With the earlier probability representation, we would add up the probabilities to compute $P(X \le 4)$ as

$$P(X = 1) + P(X = 2) + P(X = 3) + P(X = 4) = \frac{1}{6} + \frac{1}{6} + \frac{1}{6} + \frac{1}{6} = \frac{4}{6}.$$

At the same time, we can use the cumulative probability distribution to find the probability that the random variable assumes a specific value. For example, $P(X = 3)$ can be found as $P(X \le 3) - P(X \le 2) = 3/6 - 2/6 = 1/6$.

In many instances we can express a probability distribution by applying an algebraic formula. A formula representation of the probability distribution of the random variable defined in Example 5.1 is:

$$P(X = x) = \begin{cases} 1/6 & \text{if } x = 1, 2, 3, 4, 5, 6 \\ 0 & \text{otherwise.} \end{cases}$$

Thus, from the formula we can ascertain that $P(X = 5) = 1/6$ and $P(X = 7) = 0$.

In order to graphically depict a probability distribution, we place all values x of X on the horizontal axis and the associated probabilities $P(X = x)$ on the vertical axis. We then draw a line segment that emerges from each x and ends where its height equals $P(X = x)$. Figure 5.1 graphically illustrates the probability distribution of the random variable defined in Example 5.1.

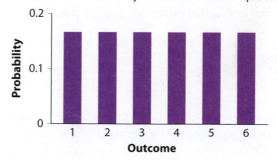

FIGURE 5.1 Probability distribution for Example 5.1

The probability distribution in Figure 5.1 is an example of a **discrete uniform distribution**, which has the following characteristics:

- The distribution has a finite number of specified values.
- Each value is equally likely.
- The distribution is symmetric.

EXAMPLE 5.2

Bankrate.com provided the probability distribution in Table 5.3, which reflects the number of credit cards that its readers carry:

TABLE 5.3 Data for Example 5.2

Number of Credit Cards	Percentage
0	2.5%
1	9.8
2	16.6
3	16.5
4*	54.6

*denotes 4 or more credit cards.

SOURCE: www.bankrate.com, Financial Literacy Series, 2007.

a. Is this a valid probability distribution?

b. What is the probability that a reader carries no credit cards?

c. What is the probability that a reader carries less than two credit cards?

d. What is the probability that a reader carries at least two credit cards?

e. Graphically depict the probability distribution and comment on its symmetry/skewness.

SOLUTION:

a. We first note that the random variable X denotes the number of credit cards that a bankrate.com reader carries. This variable assumes the values 0 through 4. The probability distribution is valid because it satisfies the following two conditions: (1) all percentages fall between 0 and 100, or equivalently, the probabilities fall between 0 and 1; and (2) the percentage sum totals 100 (2.5% + 9.8% + · · · + 54.6% = 100%), or equivalently, the probability sum totals 1 (0.025 + 0.098 + · · · + 0.546 = 1).

b. In order to find the probability that no bankrate.com readers carry a credit card, we first write the question using the appropriate probability statement notation. We find $P(X = 0) = 0.025$.

c. We express the appropriate probability statement and then sum the respective probabilities: $P(X < 2) = P(X = 0) + P(X = 1) = 0.025 + 0.098 = 0.123$.

d. We again write the probability statement and then sum the respective probabilities: $P(X \geq 2) = P(X = 2) + P(X = 3) + P(P = 4^*) = 0.166 + 0.165 + 0.546 = 0.877$.

Note that since the sum of the probabilities over all values of X equals 1, we can also find the above probability as $P(X \geq 2) = 1 - P(X < 2) = 1 - 0.123 = 0.877$.

e. The graph in Figure 5.2 shows that the distribution is not symmetric, rather it is skewed to the left. There are small chances of low values, namely carrying no more than one credit card. The most likely value by far is carrying four or more credit cards, with a likelihood of 54.6%.

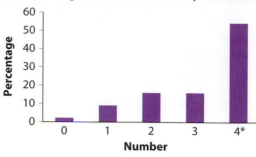

FIGURE 5.2 Percentage of Credit Cards Held by Bankrate.com Readers

EXERCISES 5.1

Concepts

1. Consider the following discrete probability distribution.

x	15	22	34	40
P(X = x)	0.14	0.40	0.26	0.20

a. Is this a valid probability distribution? Explain.
b. Graphically depict this probability distribution.
c. What is the probability that the random variable X is less than 40?
d. What is the probability that the random variable X is strictly between 10 and 30?
e. What is the probability that the random variable X is greater than 20?

2. Consider the following discrete probability distribution.

x	−25	−15	10	20
P(X = x)	0.35	0.10		0.10

a. Complete the probability distribution.
b. Graphically depict the probability distribution and comment on the symmetry of the distribution.
c. What is the probability that the random variable X is negative?
d. What is the probability that the random variable X is greater than −20?
e. What is the probability that the random variable X is less than 20?

3. Consider the following cumulative probability distribution.

x	0	1	2	3	4	5
P(X ≤ x)	0.15	0.35	0.52	0.78	0.84	1

a. Calculate $P(X \leq 3)$.
b. Calculate $P(X = 3)$.
c. Calculate $P(2 \leq X \leq 4)$.

4. Consider the following cumulative probability distribution.

x	−25	0	25	50
P(X ≤ x)	0.25	0.50	0.75	1

a. Calculate $P(X \leq 0)$.
b. Calculate $P(X = 50)$.
c. Is this a discrete uniform distribution? Explain.

Applications

5. India is the second most populous country in the world, with a population of over 1 billion people. Although the government has offered various incentives for population control, some argue that the birth rate, especially in rural India, is still too high to be sustainable. A demographer computes the following probability distribution of the household size in India.

Household Size	Probability
1	0.05
2	0.09
3	0.12
4	0.24
5	0.25
6	0.12
7	0.07
8	0.06

a. What is the probability that there are less than 5 members in a typical household in India?

b. What is the probability that there are 5 or more members in a typical household in India?

c. What is the probability that the number of members in a typical household in India is strictly between 3 and 6?

d. Graphically depict this probability distribution and comment on its symmetry.

6. A financial analyst creates the following probability distribution for the performance of an equity income mutual fund.

Performance	Probability
Very poor	0.14
Poor	0.43
Neutral	0.22
Good	0.16
Very good	0.05

a. Use 1 = very poor, 2 = poor, . . . , 5 = very good to depict the above probability distribution graphically. Comment on the optimism or pessimism depicted in the analyst's estimates.

b. Convert the above probability distribution to a cumulative probability representation.

c. What is the probability that this mutual fund will do well?

7. A basketball player is fouled while attempting to make a basket and receives two free throws. The opposing coach believes there is a 55% chance that the player will miss both shots, a 25% chance that he will make one of the shots, and a 20% chance that he will make both shots.

a. Construct the appropriate probability distribution.

b. What is the probability that he makes no more than one of the shots?

c. What is the probability that he makes at least one of the shots?

d. In a tight game, should the opposing team's coach have his players foul this player? Explain why or why not. (A regular basketball shot is worth two points, but each free throw is worth only one point.)

8. In early 2010, leading U.S. stock markets tumbled more than 2.5% as U.S. consumer confidence fell to its lowest level since August 2009 (*BBC News,* July 16, 2010). Given fresh economic data, an economist believes there is a 35% chance that consumer confidence will fall below 62 and only a 25% chance that it will rise above 65.

a. According to the economist, what is the probability that consumer confidence will be between 62 and 65?

b. According to the economist, what is the probability that consumer confidence will not fall below 62?

9. Professor Sanchez has been teaching Principles of Economics for over 25 years. He uses the following scale for grading.

Grade	Probability
A	0.10
B	0.30
C	0.40
D	0.10
F	0.10

a. Use A = 4, B = 3, C = 2, D = 1, and F = 0 to depict the above probability distribution graphically. Comment on whether or not the probability distribution is symmetric.

b. Convert the above probability distribution to a cumulative probability representation.

c. What is the probability of earning at least a B in Professor Sanchez's course?

d. What is the probability of passing Professor Sanchez's course?

5.2 Expected Value, Variance, and Standard Deviation

The analysis of probability distributions is useful because it allows us to calculate various probabilities associated with the different values that the random variable assumes. In addition, it helps us calculate summary measures for a random variable. These summary measures include the mean, the variance, and the standard deviation.

LO 5.3

Calculate and interpret summary measures for a discrete random variable.

Expected Value

One of the most important probabilistic concepts in statistics is that of the **expected value**, also referred to as the **population mean**. The expected value of the discrete random variable X, denoted by $E(X)$ or simply μ, is a weighted average of all possible values of X. Before we present its definition, we would like to point out that the expected value of a random variable should not be confused with its most probable value. As we will see later, the expected value is, in general, not even one of the possible values of the random variable. We can think of the expected value as the long-run average value of the random variable over infinitely many independent repetitions of an experiment. Consider a simple experiment with a fair coin, where you win $10 if it is heads and lose $10 if it is tails. If you flip the coin many times, the expected gain is $0, which is neither of the two possible values of the gain, namely $10 or −$10.

> ### EXPECTED VALUE OF A DISCRETE RANDOM VARIABLE
>
> For a discrete random variable X with values $x_1, x_2, x_3, \ldots$ that occur with probabilities $P(X = x_i)$, the **expected value** of X is calculated as
>
> $$E(X) = \mu = \Sigma x_i P(X = x_i).$$

Variance and Standard Deviation

The mean μ of the random variable X provides us with a measure of the central location of the distribution of X, but it does not give us information on how the various values are dispersed from μ. We need a measure that indicates whether the values of X are clustered about μ or widely scattered from μ.

> ### VARIANCE AND STANDARD DEVIATION OF A DISCRETE RANDOM VARIABLE
>
> For a discrete random variable X with values $x_1, x_2, x_3, \ldots$ that occur with probabilities $P(X = x_i)$, the **variance** of X is calculated as
>
> $$\text{Var}(X) = \sigma^2 = \Sigma (x_i - \mu)^2 P(X = x_i) = \Sigma x_i^2 P(X = x_i) - \mu^2.$$
>
> The **standard deviation** of X is
>
> $$SD(X) = \sigma = \sqrt{\sigma^2}.$$

EXAMPLE 5.3

Brad Williams is the owner of a large car dealership in Chicago. Brad decides to construct an incentive compensation program that equitably and consistently compensates employees on the basis of their performance. He offers an annual bonus of $10,000 for superior performance, $6,000 for good performance, $3,000 for fair performance and $0 for poor performance. Based on prior records, he expects an employee to perform at superior, good, fair, and poor performance levels with probabilities 0.15, 0.25, 0.40, and 0.20, respectively. Table 5.4 lists the bonus amount, performance type, and the corresponding probabilities.

TABLE 5.4 Data for Example 5.3

Bonus (in $1,000s)	Performance Type	Probability
$10	Superior	0.15
$6	Good	0.25
$3	Fair	0.40
$0	Poor	0.20

a. Calculate the expected value of the annual bonus amount.

b. Calculate the variance and standard deviation of the annual bonus amount.

c. What is the total annual amount that Brad can expect to pay in bonuses if he has 25 employees?

SOLUTION:

a. Let the random variable X denote the bonus amount (in \$1,000s) for an employee. The first and second columns of Table 5.5 show the probability distribution of X. The calculations of the mean are provided in the third column. We weigh each outcome by its respective probability, $x_i P(X = x_i)$, and then sum these weighted values. Thus, as shown at the bottom of the third column, $E(X) = \mu = \Sigma x_i P(X = x_i) = 4.2$, or 4,200. Note that the expected value is not one of the possible values of X; that is, none of the employees will earn a bonus of 4,200. This outcome reinforces the interpretation of expected value as a long-run average.

TABLE 5.5 Calculations for Example 5.3

Value, x_i	Probability, $P(X = x_i)$	Weighted Value, $x_i P(X = x_i)$	Weighted Squared Deviation, $(x_i - \mu)^2 P(X = x_i)$
10	0.15	$10 \times 0.15 = 1.5$	$(10 - 4.2)^2 \times 0.15 = 5.05$
6	0.25	$6 \times 0.25 = 1.5$	$(6 - 4.2)^2 \times 0.25 = 0.81$
3	0.40	$3 \times 0.40 = 1.2$	$(3 - 4.2)^2 \times 0.40 = 0.58$
0	0.20	$0 \times 0.20 = 0$	$(0 - 4.2)^2 \times 0.20 = 3.53$
		Total $= 4.2$	Total $= 9.97$

b. We use the formula, $\sigma^2 = \Sigma (x_i - \mu)^2 P(X = x_i)$ to calculate the variance; we recommend that you replicate the result with the alternate formula, $\sigma^2 = \Sigma x_i^2 P(X = x_i) - \mu^2$. The last column of Table 5.5 shows the calculation for the variance. We first calculate each x_i's squared difference from the mean $(x_i - \mu)^2$, weigh each value by the appropriate probability $(x_i - \mu)^2 P(X = x_i)$, and then sum these weighted squared differences. Thus, as shown at the bottom of the fourth column, $Var(X) = \sigma^2 = \Sigma (x_i - \mu)^2 P(X = x_i) = 9.97$, or 9.97 (in \$1,000s)^2. The standard deviation is the positive square root of the variance, $SD(X) = \sigma = \sqrt{9.97} = 3.158$, or \$3,158.

c. Note that the expected bonus of an employee is \$4,200. Since Brad has 25 employees, he can expect to pay \$4,200 $\times$ 25 $=$ \$105,000 in bonuses.

Risk Neutrality and Risk Aversion

LO 5.4

Differentiate among risk neutral, risk averse, and risk loving consumers.

An important concept in economics, finance, and psychology relates to the behavior of consumers under uncertainty. It is well documented that, in general, consumers are **risk averse**. Consider a seemingly fair gamble where you flip a coin and get \$10 if it is heads and lose \$10 if it is tails, resulting in an expected gain of zero ($10 \times 0.5 - 10 \times 0.5 = 0$). For a risk averse consumer, the pain associated with losing \$10 is more than the pleasure of winning \$10. Therefore, the consumer will not want to participate in this seemingly fair gamble because there is no reward to compensate for the risk. Researchers have used this argument to explain why the expected return from stocks is more than the risk-free T-bills rate. The explanation provided is that investors want a higher expected return to compensate for the risk involved in stock investment. Example 5.4 expands on this type of consumer behavior.

You have a choice of receiving $1,000 in cash or receiving a beautiful painting from your grandmother. The actual value of the painting is uncertain. You are told that the painting has a 20% chance of being worth $2,000, a 50% chance of being worth $1,000, and a 30% chance of being worth $500. What should you do?

SOLUTION: Let the random variable X represent the worth of the painting. Given the above information, we define the probability distribution as shown in Table 5.6.

TABLE 5.6 Probability Distribution for Example 5.4

x	$P(X = x)$
$2,000	0.20
$1,000	0.50
$500	0.30

We calculate the expected value as

$$E(X) = \Sigma x_i P(X = x_i) = \$2,000 \times 0.20 + \$1,000 \times 0.50 + \$500 \times 0.30$$
$$= \$1,050$$

Since the expected value of the painting is more than $1,000, it may appear that the right choice is to pick the painting over $1,000 in cash. This choice, however, is based entirely on the expected value of the painting, ignoring the risk completely. While the expected value of $1,050 is more than $1,000, the painting entails some risk. For instance, there is a 30% chance that it may be worth only $500. The decision to pick the painting makes no allowance for risk. In fact, with the above logic, you would choose the painting over cash even if the risk were significantly higher.

In general, a **risk averse consumer** demands a positive expected gain as compensation for taking risk. This compensation increases with the level of risk taken and the degree of risk aversion. A **risk neutral consumer**, on the other hand, completely ignores risk and makes his/her decisions solely on the basis of expected values.

> In general, consumers are **risk averse** and expect a reward for taking risk. A **risk averse consumer** may decline a risky prospect even if it offers a positive expected gain. A **risk neutral consumer** completely ignores risk and always accepts a prospect that offers a positive expected gain. Finally, a **risk loving consumer** may accept a risky prospect even if the expected gain is negative.

In Example 5.4, a risk neutral consumer will take the painting because its expected value exceeds the risk-free cash value of $1,000. This consumer is not concerned with risk, as measured by the standard deviation. A risk lover will be thrilled to take the painting. For a risk averse consumer, however, the decision is not clear cut. It depends on the risk involved in picking the painting and how much he/she wants to be compensated for this risk. One way we resolve this issue is to define the utility function of the consumer, which in essence conveys the degree of risk aversion. A risk averse consumer will pick the risky prospect if the expected utility (not the expected money) of the risky prospect exceeds the utility of a risk-free alternative. Further details are beyond the scope of this book.

Concepts

10. Calculate the mean, variance, and standard deviation of the following discrete probability distribution.

x	5	10	15	20
P(X = x)	0.35	0.30	0.20	0.15

11. Calculate the mean, variance, and standard deviation of the following discrete probability distribution.

x	−23	−17	−9	−3
P(X = x)	0.50	0.25	0.15	0.10

Applications

12. An analyst has developed the following probability distribution of the rate of return for a common stock.

Scenario	Probability	Rate of Return
1	0.30	−5%
2	0.45	0%
3	0.25	10%

   a. Calculate the expected rate of return.
   b. Calculate the variance and standard deviation of this probability distribution.

13. Organizers of an outdoor summer concert in Toronto are concerned about the weather conditions on the day of the concert. They will make a profit of $25,000 on a clear day and $10,000 on a cloudy day. They will make a loss of $5,000 if it rains. The weather channel has predicted a 60% chance of rain on the day of the concert. Calculate the expected profit from the concert if the likelihood is 10% that it will be sunny and 30% that it will be cloudy.

14. Mark Underwood is a professor of Economics at Indiana University. He has been teaching Principles of Economics for over 25 years. Professor Underwood uses the following scale for grading.

Grade	Probability
A	0.10
B	0.30
C	0.40
D	0.10
F	0.10

   Calculate the expected numerical grade in Professor Underwood's class using 4.0 for A, 3.0 for B, etc.

15. You are considering buying insurance for your new laptop computer, which you have recently bought for $1,500. The insurance premium for three years is $80. Over the three-year period there is an 8% chance that your laptop computer will require work worth $400, a 3% chance that it will require work worth $800, and a 2% chance that it will completely

break down with a scrap value of $100. Should you buy the insurance (assume risk neutrality)?

16. Four years ago, Victor Consuelo purchased a very reliable automobile (as rated by a reputable consumer advocacy publication). His warranty has just expired, but the manufacturer has just offered him a 5-year, bumper-to-bumper warranty extension. The warranty costs $3,400. Consuelo constructs the following probability distribution with respect to anticipated costs if he chooses not to purchase the extended warranty.

Cost (in $)	Probability
1,000	0.25
2,000	0.45
5,000	0.20
10,000	0.10

   a. Calculate Victor's expected cost.
   b. Given your answer in part (a), should Victor purchase the extended warranty (assume risk neutrality)? Explain.

17. Market observers are quite uncertain whether the stock market has bottomed out from the economic meltdown that began in 2008. In an interview on March 8, 2009, CNBC interviewed two prominent economists who offered differing views on whether the U.S. economy was getting stronger or weaker. An investor not wanting to miss out on possible investment opportunities considers investing $10,000 in the stock market. He believes that the probability is 0.30 that the market will improve, 0.40 that it will stay the same, and 0.30 that it will deteriorate. Further, if the economy improves, he expects his investment to grow to $15,000, but it can also go down to $8,000 if the economy deteriorates. If the economy stays the same, his investment will stay at $10,000.

   a. What is the expected value of his investment?
   b. What should the investor do if he is risk neutral?
   c. Is the decision clear cut if he is risk averse? Explain.

18. You are considering two mutual funds for your investment. The possible returns for the funds are dependent on the state of the economy and are given in the accompanying table.

State of the Economy	Fund 1	Fund 2
Good	20%	40%
Fair	10%	20%
Poor	−10%	−40%

   You believe that the likelihood is 20% that the economy will be good, 50% that it will be fair, and 30% that it will be poor.

   a. Find the expected value and the standard deviation of returns for Fund 1.
   b. Find the expected value and the standard deviation of returns for Fund 2.
   c. Which fund will you pick if you are risk averse? Explain.

19. Investment advisors recommend risk reduction through international diversification. International investing allows you to take advantage of the potential for growth in foreign economies, particularly in emerging markets. Janice Wong is considering investment in either Europe or Asia. She has studied these markets and believes that both markets will be influenced by the U.S. economy, which has a 20% chance for being good, a 50% chance for being fair, and a 30% chance for being poor. Probability distributions of the returns for these markets are given in the accompanying table.

State of the U.S. Economy	Returns in Europe	Returns in Asia
Good	10%	18%
Fair	6%	10%
Poor	−6%	−12%

a. Find the expected value and the standard deviation of returns in Europe and Asia.

b. What will Janice pick as an investment if she is risk neutral?

c. Discuss Janice's decision if she is risk averse.

5.3 Portfolio Returns

LO 5.5

Compute summary measures to evaluate portfolio returns.

As discussed in Chapter 3, we often evaluate investment opportunities using expected return as a measure of reward, and variance or standard deviation of return as a measure of risk. Consider two assets where Asset A is expected to have a return of 12% and Asset B is expected to have a return of 8% for the year. While Asset A is attractive in terms of its reward, an investor may still choose Asset B over Asset A if the risk associated with Asset A is too high. In other words, both reward as well as risk are relevant for evaluating the investment.

So far we have considered assets separately. However, most investors hold a **portfolio** of assets, where a portfolio is defined as a collection of assets such as stocks and bonds. As in the case of an individual asset, an investor is concerned about the reward as well as the risk of a portfolio. The derivation of the expected return and the variance of a portfolio depend on some important results regarding the joint distribution of random variables.

Let X and Y represent two random variables of interest, denoting, say, the returns of two assets. Since an investor may have invested in both assets, we would like to evaluate the portfolio return formed by a linear combination of X and Y. The following properties of random variables are useful in evaluating portfolio returns.

Properties of Random Variables

Given two random variables X and Y, the expected value of their sum, $E(X + Y)$, is equal to the sum of their individual expected values, $E(X)$ and $E(Y)$, or

$$E(X + Y) = E(X) + E(Y).$$

Using algebra, it can be shown that the variance of the sum of two random variables, $Var(X + Y)$, yields

$$Var(X + Y) = Var(X) + Var(Y) + 2Cov(X, Y),$$

where Cov is the covariance between the random variables X and Y.

For given constants a and b, the above results are extended as:

$$E(aX + bY) = aE(X) + bE(Y), \text{ and}$$
$$Var(aX + bY) = a^2 Var(X) + b^2 Var(Y) + 2abCov(X, Y).$$

Expected Return, Variance, and Standard Deviation of Portfolio Returns

We are now in a position to derive the expected return and the variance of a portfolio based on the above properties. For the sake of simplicity, consider a portfolio consisting of only two assets, Asset A and Asset B. These assets, for instance, may represent stocks and bonds. Following popular notation in finance, let R_A and R_B be the random variables of interest, representing the returns of assets A and B, respectively. Further, a portfolio is described not only by its assets but also by its **portfolio weights**. Consider a portfolio with a total value of $5,000, with $1,000 invested in Asset A and $4,000 in Asset B. The portfolio weights are derived as

$$w_A = \frac{1,000}{5,000} = 0.20 \quad \text{and} \quad w_B = \frac{4,000}{5,000} = 0.80.$$

Note that the portfolio weights add up to one, that is, $w_A + w_B = 0.20 + 0.80 = 1$. We then define the portfolio return R_p as a linear combination of the individual returns,

$$R_p = w_A R_A + w_B R_B.$$

PORTFOLIO EXPECTED RETURN

Given a portfolio with two assets, Asset A and Asset B, the **expected return of the portfolio** $E(R_p)$ is computed as

$$E(R_p) = w_A E(R_A) + w_B E(R_B),$$

where w_A and w_B are the **portfolio weights** ($w_A + w_B = 1$) and $E(R_A)$ and $E(R_B)$ are the expected returns on assets A and B, respectively.

EXAMPLE 5.5

Consider an investment portfolio of $40,000 in Stock A and $60,000 in Stock B. Calculate the expected return of this portfolio based on the information in Table 5.7.

TABLE 5.7 Data for Example 5.5

Stock A	Stock B
$E(R_A) = \mu_A = 9.5\%$	$E(R_B) = \mu_B = 7.6\%$
$SD(R_A) = \sigma_A = 12.93\%$	$SD(R_B) = \sigma_B = 8.20\%$
$Cov(R_A, R_B) = \sigma_{AB} = 18.60\%$	

SOLUTION: First we compute the portfolio weights. Since $40,000 is invested in Stock A and $60,000 in Stock B, we compute

$$w_A = \frac{40,000}{100,000} = 0.40 \quad \text{and} \quad w_B = \frac{60,000}{100,000} = 0.60.$$

Thus, using the formula for portfolio expected return, we solve:

$$E(R_p) = (0.40 \times 9.5\%) + (0.60 \times 7.6\%) = 3.80\% + 4.56\% = 8.36\%.$$

Note that the portfolio expected return of 8.36% is lower than the expected return of investing entirely in Stock A with an expected return of 9.5%, yet higher than the expected return of investing entirely in Stock B with an expected return of 7.6%.

The risk of the portfolio depends not only on the individual risks of the assets but also on the interplay between the asset returns. For example, if one asset does poorly, the second asset may serve as an offsetting factor to stabilize the risk of the overall portfolio. This result will work as long as the return of the second asset is not perfectly correlated with the return of the first asset. Similar to the covariance $Cov(x, y) = \sigma_{xy}$ introduced in Chapter 3, the covariance $Cov(R_A, R_B) = \sigma_{AB}$ helps determine whether the linear relationship between the asset returns is positive, negative, or zero. Recall that an easier measure to interpret is the correlation coefficient ρ which describes both the direction and the strength of the linear relationship between two random variables. The value of the correlation coefficient falls between -1 and 1. The closer the value is to 1, the stronger is the positive relationship between the variables. Similarly, the closer the value is to -1, the stronger is the negative relationship between the variables. Let $\rho_{AB} = \frac{\sigma_{AB}}{\sigma_A \sigma_B}$ denote the correlation coefficient between the returns R_A and R_B.

With information on either the covariance or the correlation coefficient of the two returns, we can now determine the portfolio variance of return.

PORTFOLIO VARIANCE

The **portfolio variance**, $Var(R_p) = Var(w_A R_A + w_B R_B)$, is calculated as

$$Var(R_p) = w_A^2 \sigma_A^2 + w_B^2 \sigma_B^2 + 2w_A w_B \sigma_{AB}$$

or, equivalently,

$$Var(R_p) = w_A^2 \sigma_A^2 + w_B^2 \sigma_B^2 + 2w_A w_B \rho_{AB} \sigma_A \sigma_B$$

where σ_A^2 and σ_B^2 are the variances of the returns for Asset A and Asset B, respectively, σ_{AB} is the covariance between the returns for Asset A and Asset B, and ρ_{AB} is the correlation coefficient between the returns for Asset A and Asset B.

The **standard deviation of return** $SD(R_p)$ is then calculated as the positive square root of the portfolio variance.

EXAMPLE 5.6

Using the information in Example 5.5, answer the following questions.

a. Calculate and interpret the correlation coefficient between the returns on Stocks A and B.

b. Calculate the portfolio variance using both formulas.

c. Calculate the portfolio standard deviation.

d. Comment on the findings.

SOLUTION:

a. We calculate the correlation coefficient as $\rho_{AB} = \frac{\sigma_{AB}}{\sigma_A \sigma_B} = \frac{18.60}{12.93 \times 8.20} = 0.1754$. This value implies that the returns have a positive linear relationship, though the magnitude of the relationship is weak (ρ_{AB} is well below 1).

b. Using the first formula for portfolio variance, we calculate

$$\begin{aligned} Var(R_p) &= w_A^2 \sigma_A^2 + w_B^2 \sigma_B^2 + 2w_A w_B \sigma_{AB} \\ &= (0.40)^2(12.93)^2 + (0.60)^2(8.20)^2 + 2(0.40)(0.60)(18.60) \\ &= 26.75 + 24.21 + 8.93 \\ &= 59.89. \end{aligned}$$

Using the alternative formula for portfolio variance, we calculate

$$\begin{aligned} Var(R_p) &= w_A^2 \sigma_A^2 + w_B^2 \sigma_B^2 + 2w_A w_B \rho_{AB} \sigma_A \sigma_B \\ &= (0.40)^2(12.93)^2 + (0.60)^2(8.20)^2 \\ &\quad + 2(0.40)(0.60)(0.1754)(12.93)(8.20) \\ &= 26.75 + 24.21 + 8.93 \\ &= 59.89. \end{aligned}$$

Using either formula, the variance of portfolio return is 59.89 $(\%)^2$.

c. The portfolio standard deviation is $SD(R_p) = \sqrt{59.89} = 7.74$, or 7.74%.

d. We note how the portfolio standard deviation of 7.74%, a measure of risk, is lower than the risk of 12.93% of investing entirely in Stock A as well as the risk of 8.20% of investing entirely in Stock B. This occurs because the returns of Stock A and Stock B have a correlation of only 0.1754. This example highlights the benefits of properly diversifying your portfolio in order to reduce risk. In general, the benefits of diversification depend on the correlation between the assets: the lower the correlation, the larger the benefit.

EXERCISES 5.3

20. What are the portfolio weights for a portfolio that has 100 shares of Stock X that sell for $20 per share and 200 shares of Stock Y that sell for $12 per share?

21. You own a portfolio that has $4,400 invested in stocks and $5,600 invested in bonds. What is the expected return of the portfolio if stocks and bonds are expected to yield a return of 9% and 5%, respectively?

22. A portfolio has $200,000 invested in Asset X and $300,000 in Asset Y. Consider the summary measures in the following table.

Measures	Asset X	Asset Y
Expected Return (%)	8	12
Standard deviation (%)	12	20
Correlation		0.40

a. Calculate the portfolio weights for assets X and Y.
b. Calculate the expected return of the portfolio.
c. Calculate the standard deviation of the portfolio.

23. An analyst has predicted the following returns for Stocks A and B in three possible states of the economy.

State	Probability	A	B
Boom	0.3	0.15	0.25
Normal	0.5	0.10	0.20
Recession	?	0.02	0.01

a. What is the probability of a recession?
b. Calculate the expected return of Stocks A and B.
c. Calculate the expected return of a portfolio that is invested 55% in A and 45% in B.

24. A pension fund manager is considering three mutual funds for investment. The first one is a stock fund, the second is a bond fund and the third is a money market fund. The money market fund yields a risk-free return of 4%. The inputs for the risky funds are given below.

Fund	Expected Return	Standard Deviation
Stock fund	14%	26%
Bond fund	8%	14%

The correlation coefficient between the stock and bond funds is 0.20.

a. What is the expected return and the variance of a portfolio that invests 60% in the stock fund and 40% in the bond fund?
b. What is the expected return and the variance of a portfolio that invests 60% in the stock fund and 40% in the money market fund? [*Hint: Note that the correlation between any asset and the risk-free T-bills is zero.*]
c. Compare the portfolios in parts a and b with a portfolio that is invested entirely in the bond fund.

25. You have $400,000 invested in a well-diversified portfolio. You inherit a house that is presently worth $200,000. Consider the summary measures in the following table:

Investment	Expected Return	Standard deviation
Old portfolio	6%	16%
House	8%	20%

The correlation coefficient between your portfolio and the house is 0.38.

a. What is the expected return and standard deviation of your portfolio comprising your old portfolio and the house?
b. Suppose you decide to sell the house and use the proceeds of $200,000 to buy risk-free T-bills that promise a 3% rate of return. Calculate the expected return and standard deviation of the resulting portfolio.

5.4 The Binomial Probability Distribution

Different types of experiments generate different probability distributions. In the next three sections, we discuss three special cases: the binomial, the Poisson, and the hypergeometric probability distributions. Here we focus on the binomial distribution. Before we can discuss the binomial distribution, we first must ensure that the experiment satisfies the conditions of a **Bernoulli process**, which is a particular type of experiment

LO **5.6**

Describe the binomial distribution and compute relevant probabilities.

named after the person who first described it, the Swiss mathematician James Bernoulli (1654–1705).

> A **Bernoulli process** consists of a series of n independent and identical trials of an experiment such that on each trial:
>
> - There are only two possible outcomes, conventionally labeled success and failure; and
> - Each time the trial is repeated, the probabilities of success and failure remain the same.

We use p to denote the probability of success, and therefore $1 - p$ is the probability of failure. For simplicity, we denote the probability of failure, $1 - p$, as q.

A **binomial random variable** is defined as the number of successes achieved in the n trials of a Bernoulli process. The possible values of a binomial random variable include $0, 1, \ldots, n$. Many random experiments fit the conditions of a Bernoulli process. For instance:

- A bank grants or denies a loan to a mortgage applicant.
- A consumer either uses or does not use a credit card.
- An employee travels or does not travel by public transportation.
- A life insurance policy holder dies or does not die.
- A drug is either effective or ineffective.
- A college graduate applies or does not apply to graduate school.

Our goal is to attach probabilities to various outcomes of a Bernoulli process. The result is a **binomial probability distribution**.

> A **binomial random variable** X is defined as the number of successes achieved in the n trials of a Bernoulli process. A **binomial probability distribution** shows the probabilities associated with the possible values of the binomial random variable.

We will eventually arrive at a general formula that helps us derive a binomial probability distribution. First, however, we will use a specific example and construct a **probability tree** in order to illustrate the possible outcomes and their associated probabilities.

EXAMPLE 5.7

From past experience, a manager of an upscale shoe store knows that 85% of her customers will use a credit card when making purchases. Suppose three customers are in line to make a purchase.

a. Does this example satisfy the conditions of a Bernoulli process?

b. Construct a probability tree that delineates all possible values and their associated probabilities.

c. Using the probability tree, derive the binomial probability distribution.

SOLUTION:

a. This example satisfies the conditions of a Bernoulli process because a customer either uses a credit card (labeled success), with an 85% likelihood, or does not use a credit card (labeled failure), with a 15% likelihood. Moreover, given a large number of customers, these probabilities of success and failure do not change from customer to customer.

b. In Figure 5.3, we let S denote the outcome that a customer uses a credit card and F denote the outcome that a customer does not use a credit card. Starting from the unlabeled node on the left, each branch reflects the probability of that branch outcome's occurring. For instance, there is an 85% chance that customer 1 uses a credit card. The branches emanating from customer 1 denote conditional probabilities of customer 2 using a credit card, given whether customer 1 used a credit card. However, since we assume that the trials of a Bernoulli process are independent, the conditional probability of the branch outcome's occurring is the same as its unconditional probability. In other words, customer 2 has an 85% chance of using a credit card and a 15% chance of not using one. The same holds for the probabilities for customer 3. The fourth column shows that there are eight possible outcomes at the conclusion of this experiment. We are able to obtain relevant probabilities by using the multiplication rule for independent events. For instance, following the top branches throughout the probability tree, we calculate the probability that all three customers use a credit card as $(0.85)(0.85)(0.85) = 0.614$. The probabilities for the remaining outcomes are found in a similar manner.

FIGURE 5.3 Probability tree for Example 5.7.

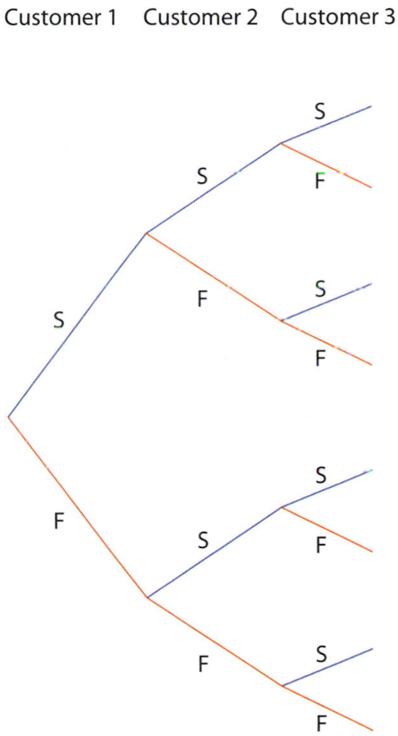

Customer 1	Customer 2	Customer 3	Events	Customers using credit card, x	Probabilities
		S	SSS	3	$(0.85)(0.85)(0.85)$ $= 0.614$
	S	F	SSF	2	$(0.85)(0.85)(0.15)$ $= 0.108$
	F	S	SFS	2	$(0.85)(0.15)(0.85)$ $= 0.108$
S		F	SFF	1	$(0.85)(0.15)(0.15)$ $= 0.019$
	S	S	FSS	2	$(0.15)(0.85)(0.85)$ $= 0.108$
		F	FSF	1	$(0.15)(0.85)(0.15)$ $= 0.019$
F	F	S	FFS	1	$(0.15)(0.15)(0.85)$ $= 0.019$
		F	FFF	0	$(0.15)(0.15)(0.15)$ $= 0.003$

c. Since we are not interested in identifying the particular customer who uses a credit card, but rather the number of customers who use a credit card, we can combine events with the same number of successes, using the addition rule for mutually exclusive events. For instance, in order to find the probability that one customer uses a credit card, we add the probabilities that correspond to the outcome $x = 1$ (see shaded areas in table): $0.019 + 0.019 + 0.019 = 0.057$. Similarly, we calculate the remaining probabilities corresponding to the other values of X and construct the probability distribution shown in Table 5.8. Note that in many solved problems, the probabilities do not add up to 1 due to rounding.

TABLE 5.8 Binomial Probabilities for Example 5.7

x	P(X = x)
0	0.003
1	0.057
2	0.324
3	0.614
	Total = 1 (approximately)

Fortunately we do not have to construct a binomial probability tree each time we want to find a binomial probability distribution. We can use the following formula for calculating the probability associated with a binomial random variable.

THE BINOMIAL PROBABILITY DISTRIBUTION

For a **binomial random variable** X, the probability of x successes in n Bernoulli trials is

$$P(X = x) = \binom{n}{x} p^x q^{n-x} = \frac{n!}{x!(n-x)!} p^x q^{n-x}$$

for $x = 0, 1, 2, \ldots, n$. By definition, $0! = 1$.

The formula consists of two parts:

- The first term, $\binom{n}{x} = \frac{n!}{x!(n-x)!}$, tells us how many sequences with x successes and $n - x$ failures are possible in n trials. We discussed this combination formula in Chapter 4; here we call it the binomial coefficient. For instance, in order to calculate the number of sequences that contain exactly 1 credit card user in 3 trials, we substitute $x = 1$ and $n = 3$ into the formula and calculate $\binom{n}{x} = \frac{n!}{x!(n-x)!} = \frac{3!}{1!(3-1)!} = \frac{3 \times 2 \times 1}{(1) \times (2 \times 1)} = 3$. So there are three outcomes having exactly 1 success—we can verify this result with Figure 5.3.

- The second part of the equation, $p^x q^{n-x}$, represents the probability of any particular sequence with x successes and $n - x$ failures. For example, we can obtain the probability of 1 success in 3 trials from rows 4, 6, or 7 on the last column of the probability tree as (see shaded areas):

$$\left.\begin{array}{l} \text{row 4: } 0.85 \times 0.15 \times 0.15 \\ \text{row 6: } 0.15 \times 0.85 \times 0.15 \\ \text{row 7: } 0.15 \times 0.15 \times 0.85 \end{array}\right\} \quad \text{or} \quad (0.85)^1 \times (0.15)^2 = 0.019$$

In other words, each sequence consisting of 1 success in 3 trials has a 1.9% chance of occurring.

In order to obtain the overall probability of getting 1 success in 3 trials, we then multiply the binomial coefficient by the probability of obtaining the particular sequence, or here, $3 \times 0.019 = 0.057$. This is precisely the probability that we found for $P(X = 1)$ using the probability tree.

Further, we could use the formulas shown in Section 5.2 to calculate the expected value, the variance, and the standard deviation of any binomial random variable. Fortunately, for the binomial distribution, these formulas simplify to $E(X) = np$ and $Var(X) = npq$. The simplified formula for expected value is rather intuitive in that if we know the probability of success p of a random experiment and we repeat the experiment n times, then on average, we expect np successes.

For instance, for the binomial probability distribution assumed in Example 5.7, we can derive the expected value with the earlier general formula as

$$E(X) = \Sigma x_i P(X = x_i) = (0 \times 0.003) + (1 \times 0.057) + (2 \times 0.324) + (3 \times 0.614) = 2.55.$$

However, an easier way is to use $E(X) = np$ and thus calculate the expected value as $3 \times 0.85 = 2.55$. Similarly, the variance can be easily calculated as

$$Var(X) = npq = 3 \times 0.85 \times 0.15 = 0.38.$$

EXAMPLE 5.8

Approximately 20% of U.S. workers are afraid that they will never be able to retire (bankrate.com, June 23, 2008). Suppose 10 workers are randomly selected.

a. What is the probability that none of the workers is afraid that they will never be able to retire?

b. What is the probability that at least two of the workers are afraid that they will never be able to retire?

c. What is the probability that no more than two of the workers are afraid that they will never be able to retire?

d. Calculate the expected value, the variance, and the standard deviation of this binomial probability distribution.

SOLUTION: First, this problem satisfies the conditions of a Bernoulli process. Here, a worker is either afraid that he/she will never be able to retire, with probability $p = 0.20$, or is not afraid, with probability $q = 1 - 0.20 = 0.80$. In addition, the random selection of 10 workers, $n = 10$, fulfills the requirement that the probability that a worker fears that he/she will never be able to retire stays the same from worker to worker.

a. We let $x = 10$ and find

$$P(X = 0) = \frac{10!}{0!(10 - 0)!} \times (0.20)^0 \times (0.80)^{10}$$

$$= \frac{10 \times 9 \times \cdots \times 1}{(1) \times (10 \times 9 \times \cdots \times 1)} \times 1 \times (0.80)^{10} = 1 \times 1 \times 0.1074$$

$$= 0.1074.$$

In other words, there is a 10.74% chance that none of the workers is afraid that they will never be able to retire.

b. The phrase "at least two workers" leads to the following probability statement:

$$P(X \geq 2) = P(X = 2) + P(X = 3) + \cdots + P(X = 10).$$

We can solve this problem by first calculating each of the nine probabilities, from $P(X = 2)$ to $P(X = 10)$. A simpler method uses one of the key properties of a probability distribution, which states that the sum of the probabilities over all values of X equals 1. Therefore, $P(X \geq 2)$ can be written as $1 - [P(X = 0) + P(X = 1)]$, where we need to calculate only two probabilities, $P(X = 0)$ and $P(X = 1)$, to solve the problem. We know from part (a) that $P(X = 0) = 0.1074$. Similarly, we can calculate $P(X = 1)$:

$$P(X = 1) = \frac{10!}{1!(10 - 1)!} \times (0.20)^1 \times (0.80)^9 = 0.2684.$$

Therefore, $P(X \geq 2) = 1 - [0.1074 + 0.2684] = 0.6242$, or a 62.42% likelihood.

c. The phrase "no more than two workers" leads to the following probability statement:

$$P(X \leq 2) = P(X = 0) + P(X = 1) + P(X = 2).$$

We have already found $P(X = 0)$ from part a and $P(X = 1)$ from part b. So we now compute $P(X = 2)$:

$$P(X = 2) = \frac{10!}{2!(10 - 2)!} \times (0.20)^2 \times (0.80)^8 = 0.3020.$$

Next we sum the three relevant probabilities and obtain

$$P(X \leq 2) = 0.1074 + 0.2684 + 0.3020 = 0.6778.$$

d. We use the simplified formulas for these summary measures and obtain:

$$E(X) = np = 10 \times 0.20 = 2 \text{ workers,}$$

$$Var(X) = npq = 10 \times 0.20 \times 0.80 = 1.60 \text{ (workers)}^2, \text{ and}$$

$$SD(X) = \sqrt{1.60} = 1.26 \text{ workers.}$$

Using Excel to Obtain Binomial Probabilities

As you may have noticed, at times it is somewhat tedious and cumbersome to solve binomial distribution problems using the formulas. This issue becomes even more pronounced when we encounter large values for n and we wish to determine probabilities where X assumes a wide range of values. Some textbooks include probability tables to help with the calculations for important discrete probability distributions. We will rely on Excel to solve cumbersome binomial probabilities. Consider the following problem.

EXAMPLE 5.9

In 2007 approximately 4.7% of the households in the Detroit metropolitan area were in some stage of foreclosure, the highest foreclosure rate in the nation (*The Associated Press*, February 13, 2008). Suppose we sample 100 mortgage-holding households in the Detroit area.

a. What is the probability that exactly 5 of these households are in some stage of foreclosure?

b. What is the probability that no more than 5 of these households are in some stage of foreclosure?

c. What is the probability that more than 5 households are in some stage of foreclosure?

SOLUTION:

a. It is possible to use the binomial formula and solve this problem as $P(X = 5) = \frac{100!}{5!95!} \times (0.047)^5 \times (0.953)^{95}$, but we would quickly find the arithmetic quite unwieldy. Using the binomial function on Excel (**Formulas** > **Insert Function** > **BINOM.DIST**), we supply the following four arguments in the dialog box, as shown in Figure 5.4.

- **Number_s** is the number of successes in *n* trials. We enter 5.
- **Trials** is the number of independent trials. We enter 100.
- **Probability_s** is the probability of success on each trial. We enter 0.047.
- **Cumulative** is a logical value. If we enter the value 1 or TRUE, Excel will return a cumulative probability, or in this case $P(X \leq 5)$. Since we want $P(X = 5)$, which is a probability mass function, we enter 0 or FALSE.

FIGURE 5.4 Computing binomial probabilities with Excel (Example 5.9a)

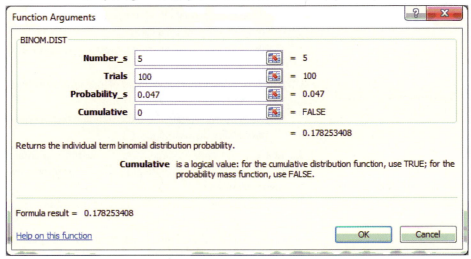

Excel returns the formula result as 0.1783; thus, $P(X = 5) = 0.1783$.

b. We write the probability that no more than 5 of these households are in some stage of foreclosure as $P(X \leq 5)$. Using Excel we input data as shown in Figure 5.5.

FIGURE 5.5 Computing cumulative binomial probabilities with Excel (Example 5.9b)

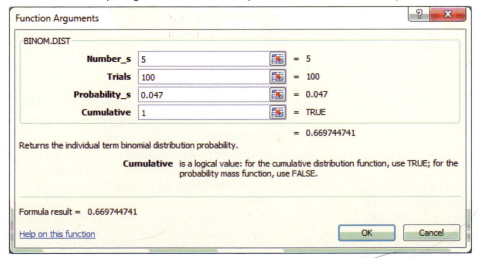

In this case, the only value that changes is for **Cumulative**. Here, we enter 1 for cumulative because we are solving for a cumulative probability. Excel returns the probability 0.6697; thus, $P(X \leq 5) = 0.6697$.

c. The probability that more than five households are in some stage of foreclosure is written as $P(X > 5)$. Using the information in part b, we solve this as $P(X > 5) = 1 - P(X \leq 5) = 1 - 0.6697 = 0.3303$.

EXERCISES 5.4

Concepts

26. Assume that X is a binomial random variable with $n = 5$ and $p = 0.35$. Calculate the following probabilities.
    a. $P(X = 0)$
    b. $P(X = 1)$
    c. $P(X \leq 1)$

27. Assume that X is a binomial random variable with $n = 6$ and $p = 0.68$. Calculate the following probabilities.
    a. $P(X = 5)$
    b. $P(X = 4)$
    c. $P(X \geq 4)$

28. Assume that X is a binomial random variable with $n = 8$ and $p = 0.32$. Calculate the following probabilities.
    a. $P(3 < X < 5)$
    b. $P(3 < X \leq 5)$
    c. $P(3 \leq X \leq 5)$

29. Let the probability of success on a Bernoulli trial be 0.30. In five Bernoulli trials, what is the probability that there will be (a) 4 failures, (b) more than the expected number of failures?

30. (Use computer) Let X represent a binomial random variable with $n = 150$ and $p = 0.36$. Find the following probabilities.
    a. $P(X \leq 50)$
    b. $P(X = 40)$
    c. $P(X > 60)$
    d. $P(X \geq 55)$

31. (Use computer) Let X represent a binomial random variable with $n = 200$ and $p = 0.77$. Find the following probabilities.
    a. $P(X \leq 150)$
    b. $P(X > 160)$
    c. $P(155 \leq X \leq 165)$
    d. $P(X = 160)$

Applications

32. According to a report from the Center for Studying Health System Change, 20% of Americans delay or go without medical care because of concerns about cost (*The Wall Street Journal*, June 26, 2008). Suppose eight individuals are randomly selected.

a. What is the probability that none will delay or go without medical care?
b. What is the probability that no more than two will delay or go without medical care?
c. What is the probability that at least seven will delay or go without medical care?
d. What is the expected number of individuals who will delay or go without medical care?
e. Calculate the variance and the standard deviation for this probability distribution.

33. At a local commuter college, 40% of students who enter the college as freshmen go on to graduate. Ten freshmen are randomly selected.
    a. What is the probability that none of them graduates from the local university?
    b. What is the probability that at most nine will graduate from the local university?
    c. What is the expected number that will graduate?

34. The percentage of Americans who have confidence in U.S. banks dropped to 23% in June 2010, which is far below the pre-recession level of 41% reported in June 2007 (gallup.com).
    a. What is the probability that fewer than half of 10 Americans in 2010 have confidence in U.S. banks?
    b. What would have been the corresponding probability in 2007?

35. In recent analyses of Census figures, one in four American counties have passed or are approaching the tipping point where black, Hispanic, and Asian children constitute a majority of the under-20 population (*New York Times*, August 6, 2008). Racial and ethnic minorities now account for 43% of Americans under 20.
    a. What is the expected number of under-20 whites in a random sample of 5,000 Americans? What is the corresponding standard deviation?
    b. What is the expected number of racial and ethnic minorities in a random sample of 5,000 under-20 Americans? What is the corresponding standard deviation?
    c. If you randomly sample six American counties, what is the probability that for the under-20 population, whites have a clear majority in all of the counties?

36. Approximately 76% of baby boomers aged 43 to 61 are still in the workforce (*The Boston Globe*, July 10, 2008). Six baby boomers are selected at random.
   a. What is the probability that exactly one of the baby boomers is still in the workforce?
   b. What is the probability that at least five of the baby boomers are still in the workforce?
   c. What is the probability that less than two of the baby boomers are still in the workforce?
   d. What is the probability that more than the expected number of the baby boomers are still in the workforce?

37. Sikhism, a religion founded in the 15th century in India, is going through turmoil due to a rapid decline in the number of Sikh youths who wear turbans (*Washington Post,* March 29, 2009). The tedious task of combing and tying up long hair and a desire to assimilate has led to approximately 25% of Sikh youths giving up the turban.
   a. What is the probability that exactly two in a random sample of five Sikh youths wear a turban?
   b. What is the probability that two or more in a random sample of five Sikh youths wear a turban?
   c. What is the probability that more than the expected number of Sikh youths wear a turban in a random sample of five Sikh youths?
   d. What is the probability that more than the expected number of Sikh youths wear a turban in a random sample of 10 Sikh youths?

38. According to the U.S. Census, roughly half of all marriages in the United States end in divorce. Researchers from leading universities have shown that the emotions aroused by one person's divorce can transfer like a virus, making divorce contagious (*CNN,* June 10, 2010). A splitup between immediate friends increases a person's own chances of getting divorced from 36% to 63%, an increase of 75%. Use these findings to answer the following questions.
   a. Compute the probability that more than half of four randomly selected marriages will end in divorce.
   b. Redo part a if it is known that the couple's immediate friends have split up.
   c. Redo part a if it is known that none of the couple's immediate friends have split up.

39. (Use computer) Suppose 40% of recent college graduates plan on pursuing a graduate degree. Fifteen recent college graduates are randomly selected.
   a. What is the probability that no more than four of the college graduates plan to pursue a graduate degree?
   b. What is the probability that exactly seven of the college graduates plan to pursue a graduate degree?
   c. What is the probability that at least six but no more than nine of the college graduates plan to pursue a graduate degree?

40. (Use computer) At the University of Notre Dame Mendoza College of Business, 40% of the students seeking a master's degree specialize in finance (*Kiplinger's Personal Finance,* March 2009). Twenty master's degree students are randomly selected.
   a. What is the probability that exactly 10 of the students specialize in finance?
   b. What is the probability that no more than 10 of the students specialize in finance?
   c. What is the probability that at least 15 of the students specialize in finance?

41. (Use computer) The Washington, D.C., region has one of the fastest-growing foreclosure rates in the nation, as 15,613 homes went into foreclosure during the one-year period ending in February 2008 (*The Washington Post*, June 19, 2008). Over the past year, the number of foreclosures per 10,000 is 131 for the Washington area, while it is 87 nationally. In other words, the foreclosure rate is 1.31% for the Washington area and 0.87% for the nation. Assume that the foreclosure rates remain stable.
   a. What is the probability that in a given year, fewer than 2 out of 100 houses in the Washington area will go up for foreclosure?
   b. What is the probability that in a given year, fewer than 2 out of 100 houses in the nation will go up for foreclosure?
   c. Comment on the above findings.

5.5 The Poisson Probability Distribution

Another important discrete probability distribution is the Poisson probability distribution, named after the French mathematician Simeon Poisson (1781–1849). It is particularly useful in problems that deal with time or space, where space refers to area or region.

LO **5.7**

Describe the Poisson distribution and compute relevant probabilities.

> A binomial random variable counts the number of successes in a fixed number of Bernoulli trials, whereas a **Poisson random variable** counts the number of successes over a given interval of time or space.

We first must ensure that our random experiment satisfies the conditions of a **Poisson process**.

A random experiment satisfies a **Poisson process** if:

- The number of successes within a specified time or space interval equals any integer between zero and infinity.
- The numbers of successes counted in nonoverlapping intervals are independent.
- The probability that success occurs in any interval is the same for all intervals of equal size and is proportional to the size of the interval.

For a Poisson process, we define the number of successes achieved in a specified time or space interval as a Poisson random variable. Like the Bernoulli process, many random experiments fit the conditions of a Poisson process, for instance:

Examples of Poisson Random Variables with Respect to Time

- The number of cars that cross the Brooklyn Bridge between 9:00 am and 10:00 am on a Monday morning.
- The number of customers that use a McDonald's drive-thru in a day.
- The number of bankruptcies that are filed in a month.
- The number of homicides that occur in a year.

Examples of Poisson Random Variables with Respect to Space

- The number of defects in a 50-yard roll of fabric.
- The number of schools of fish in 100 square miles.
- The number of leaks in a specified stretch of a pipeline.
- The number of bacteria in a specified culture.

We use the following formula for calculating the probability associated with a Poisson random variable.

THE POISSON PROBABILITY DISTRIBUTION

For a **Poisson random variable** X, the probability of x successes over a given interval of time or space is

$$P(X = x) = \frac{e^{-\mu}\mu^x}{x!},$$

for $x = 0, 1, 2, \ldots$, where μ is the mean number of successes and $e \approx 2.718$ is the base of the natural logarithm.

As with the binomial random variable, we have simplified formulas to calculate the variance and standard deviation of a Poisson random variable. An interesting fact is that the mean of the Poisson random variable is equal to the variance.

EXPECTED VALUE, VARIANCE, AND STANDARD DEVIATION OF A POISSON RANDOM VARIABLE

If X is a Poisson random variable, then

$$E(X) = \mu,$$
$$Var(X) = \sigma^2 = \mu, \quad \text{and}$$
$$SD(X) = \sigma = \sqrt{\mu}.$$

EXAMPLE 5.10

We can now address questions first posed by Anne Jones in the introductory case of this chapter. Recall that Anne is concerned about staffing needs at the Starbucks that she manages. She has specific questions about the probability distribution of customer arrivals at her store. Anne believes that the typical Starbucks customer averages 18 visits to the store over a 30-day month. She wants answers to the following probabilities:

a. How many visits should Anne expect in a 5-day period from a typical Starbucks customer?

b. What is the probability that a customer visits the chain five times in a 5-day period?

c. What is the probability that a customer visits the chain no more than two times in a 5-day period?

d. What is the probability that a customer visits the chain at least three times in a 5-day period?

SOLUTION: In applications of the Poisson distribution, we first determine the mean number of successes in the relevant time or space interval. We use the Poisson process condition that the probability that success occurs in any interval is the same for all intervals of equal size and is proportional to the size of the interval. Here, the relevant mean will be based on the rate of 18 visits over a 30-day month.

a. Given the rate of 18 visits over a 30-day month, we can write the mean for the 30-day period as $\mu_{30} = 18$. For this problem, we compute the proportional mean for a 5-day period as $\mu_5 = 3$ because $\frac{18 \text{ visits}}{30 \text{ days}} = \frac{3 \text{ visits}}{5 \text{ days}}$.
In other words, on average, a typical Starbucks customer visits the store 3 times over a 5-day period.

b. We find the probability $P(X = 5)$ as

$$P(X = 5) = \frac{e^{-3}3^5}{5!} = \frac{(0.0498)(243)}{120} = 0.1008$$

c. For the probability that a customer visits the chain no more than two times in a 5-day period, we express the appropriate probability statement as $P(X \leq 2)$. Since this probability is equivalent to $P(X = 0) + P(X = 1) + P(X = 2)$, we first must calculate these individual probabilities and then find the sum:

$$P(X = 0) = \frac{e^{-3}3^0}{0!} = \frac{(0.0498)(1)}{1} = 0.0498,$$

$$P(X = 1) = \frac{e^{-3}3^1}{1!} = \frac{(0.0498)(3)}{1} = 0.1494, \quad \text{and}$$

$$P(X = 2) = \frac{e^{-3}3^2}{2!} = \frac{(0.0498)(9)}{2} = 0.2241.$$

Thus, $P(X \leq 2) = 0.0498 + 0.1494 + 0.2241 = 0.4233$. There is approximately a 42% chance that a customer visits the chain no more than two times in a 5-day period.

d. We write the probability that a customer visits at least three times in a 5-day period as $P(X \geq 3)$. Initially, we might attempt to solve this problem by evaluating $P(X \geq 3) = P(X = 3) + P(X = 4) + P(X = 5) + \cdots$. However, we cannot solve a Poisson problem this way. Here, we find $P(X \geq 3)$ as $1 - [P(X = 0) + P(X = 1) + P(X = 2)]$. Based on the probabilities in part c, we have $P(X \geq 3) = 1 - [0.0498 + 0.1494 + 0.2241] = 1 - 0.4233 = 0.5767$. Thus, there is about a 58% chance that a customer will frequent the chain at least 3 times in a 5-day period.

SYNOPSIS OF INTRODUCTORY CASE

Anne Jones, the manager of a Starbucks store, is concerned about how other nearby store closings might affect foot traffic at her store. A solid understanding of the likelihood of customer arrivals is necessary before she can make further statistical inference. Historical data allow her to assume that a typical Starbucks customer averages 18 visits to a Starbucks store over a 30-day month. With this information and the knowledge that she can model customer arrivals using the Poisson distribution, she deduces that a typical customer averages three visits in a 5-day period. The likelihood that a typical customer frequents her store five times in a 5-day period is approximately 10%. Further, there is approximately a 42% chance that a typical customer goes to Starbucks no more than two times, while the chances that this customer visits the chain at least three times is approximately 58%. These preliminary probabilities will prove vital as Anne plans her future staffing needs.

Using Excel to Obtain Poisson Probabilities

Like the binomial formula, the manual use of the Poisson formula can become quite cumbersome, especially when the values of x and μ become large. Excel again proves useful when calculating Poisson probabilities, as the next example shows.

EXAMPLE 5.11

Last year, even as a recession gripped the country, 114 microbreweries and brewpubs opened in the United States (*The Wall Street Journal*, March 18, 2009). Assume this number represents an average and remains constant over time. Solve the following probabilities with Excel.

a. What is the probability that no more than 100 microbreweries or brewpubs open in a given year?

b. What is the probability that exactly 115 microbreweries or brewpubs open in a given year?

SOLUTION:

a. We wish to determine the probability that no more than 100 microbreweries or brewpubs open in a given year, that is, $P(X \leq 100)$. Using the Poisson function on Excel (**Formulas > Insert Function > POISSON. DIST**), we supply three arguments in the **POISSON** dialog box as shown in Figure 5.6.

- **X** is the number of successes over some interval. We enter 100.

- **Mean** is the expected value and it must be a positive value. We enter 114.

- **Cumulative** is a logical value. If we enter the value 1 or TRUE, Excel will return a cumulative probability or in this case $P(X \leq 100)$; If we enter the value 0 or FALSE, Excel will return a probability mass function or in this case $P(X = 100)$. We enter 1.

Excel returns the formula result as 0.1012; thus, there is approximately a 10% chance that no more than 100 microbreweries or brewpubs will open in any given year.

FIGURE 5.6 Computing Poisson probabilities with Excel (Example 5.11a)

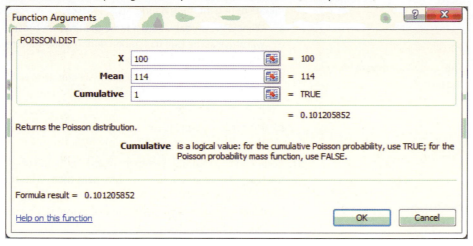

b. Here we wish to find $P(X = 115)$ or the probability that exactly 115 microbreweries or brewpubs open in any given year. We input the value 115 for **X**, 114 for **Mean**, and 0 for **Cumulative** and Excel returns the data in Figure 5.7.

FIGURE 5.7 Computing Poisson probabilities with Excel (Example 5.11b)

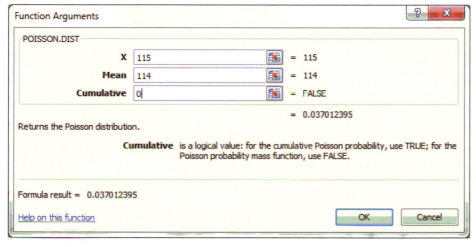

Thus, there is a 3.7% chance that exactly 115 microbreweries or brewpubs will open in any given year.

EXERCISES 5.5

Concepts

42. Assume that X is a Poisson random variable with $\mu = 1.5$. Calculate the following probabilities.
    a. $P(X = 1)$
    b. $P(X = 2)$
    c. $P(X \geq 2)$

43. Assume that X is a Poisson random variable with $\mu = 4$. Calculate the following probabilities.
    a. $P(X = 4)$
    b. $P(X = 2)$
    c. $P(X \leq 1)$

44. Let the mean success rate of a Poisson process be 8 successes per hour.
    a. Find the expected number of successes in a half-hour period.
    b. Find the probability of at least 2 successes in a given half-hour period.
    c. Find the expected number of successes in a two-hour period.
    d. Find the probability of 10 successes in a given two-hour period.

45. (Use computer) Assume that X is a Poisson random variable with $\mu = 15$. Calculate the following probabilities.

a. $P(X \leq 10)$

b. $P(X = 13)$

c. $P(X > 15)$

d. $P(12 \leq X \leq 18)$

46. (Use computer) Assume that X is a Poisson random variable with $\mu = 20$. Calculate the following probabilities.

a. $P(X < 14)$

b. $P(X \geq 20)$

c. $P(X = 25)$

d. $P(18 \leq X \leq 23)$

Applications

47. A textile manufacturing process finds that on average, two flaws occur per every 50 yards of material produced.

a. What is the probability of exactly 2 flaws in a 50-yard piece of material?

b. What is the probability of no more than two flaws in a 50-yard piece of material?

c. What is the probability of no flaws in a 25-yard piece of material?

48. A tollbooth operator has observed that cars arrive randomly at an average rate of 360 cars per hour.

a. Find the probability that 2 cars arrive during a specified 1-minute period.

b. Find the probability that at least 2 cars arrive during a specified 1-minute period.

c. Find the probability that 40 cars arrive between 10:00 am and 10:10 am.

49. Airline travelers should be ready to be more flexible as airlines once again cancel thousands of flights this summer. The Coalition for Airline Passengers Rights, Health, and Safety averages 400 calls a day to help stranded travelers deal with airlines (seattlepi.com, July 10, 2008). Suppose the hotline is staffed for 16 hours a day.

a. Calculate the average number of calls in a one-hour interval; 30-minute interval; 15-minute interval.

b. What is the probability of exactly 6 calls in a 15-minute interval?

c. What is the probability of no calls in a 15-minute interval?

d. What is the probability of at least two calls in a 15-minute interval?

50. Motorists arrive at a Gulf gas station at the rate of two per minute during morning hours.

a. What is the probability that more than two motorists will arrive at the Gulf gas station during a one-minute interval in the morning?

b. What is the probability that exactly six motorists will arrive at the Gulf gas station during a five-minute interval in the morning?

c. How many motorists can an employee expect in her three-hour morning shift?

51. According to a recent government report, the aging of the U.S. population is translating into many more visits to doctors' offices and hospitals (*USA Today*, August 7, 2008). It is estimated that an average person makes four visits a year to doctors' offices and hospitals.

a. What is the mean and standard deviation of an average person's number of monthly visits to doctors' offices and hospitals?

b. What is the probability that an average person does not make any monthly visits to doctors' offices and hospitals?

c. What is the probability that an average person makes at least one monthly visit to doctors' offices and hospitals?

52. (Use computer) On average, 400 people a year are struck by lightning in the United States (*The Boston Globe*, July 21, 2008).

a. What is the probability that at most 425 people are struck by lightning in a year?

b. What is the probability that at least 375 people are struck by lightning in a year?

53. (Use computer) In the fiscal year that ended September 30, 2008, there were 24,584 age-discrimination claims filed with the Equal Employment Opportunity Commission, an increase of 29% from the previous year (*The Wall Street Journal*, March 7–8, 2009). Assume there were 260 working days in the fiscal year by which a worker could file a claim.

a. Calculate the average number of claims filed on a working day.

b. What is the probability that exactly 100 claims were filed on a working day?

c. What is the probability that no more than 100 claims were filed on a working day?

5.6 The Hypergeometric Probability Distribution

LO **5.8**

Describe the hypergeometric distribution and compute relevant probabilities.

In Section 5.3 we defined a binomial random variable X as the number of successes in the n trials of a Bernoulli process. The trials, according to a Bernoulli process, are independent and the probability of success does not change from trial to trial. The **hypergeometric probability distribution** is appropriate in applications where we cannot assume the trials are independent.

Consider a box full of production items, of which 10% are known to be defective. Let success be labeled as the draw of a defective item. The probability of success may not be the same from trial to trial; it will depend on the size of the population and whether the sampling was done with or without replacement. Suppose the box consists of 20 items of which 10%, or 2, are defective. The probability of success in the first draw is 0.10 (= 2/20). However, the probability of success in subsequent draws will depend on the outcome of the first draw. For example, if the first item was defective, the probability of success in the second draw will be 0.0526 (= 1/19), while if the first item was not defective, the probability of success in the second draw will be 0.1053 (= 2/19). Therefore, the binomial distribution is not appropriate because the trials are not independent and the probability of success changes from trial to trial.

> We use the hypergeometric distribution in place of the binomial distribution when we are sampling **without replacement** from a population whose size N is not significantly larger than the sample size n.

In the above example, we assumed sampling without replacement; in other words, after an item is drawn, it is not put back in the box for subsequent draws. The binomial distribution would be appropriate if we sample with replacement since, in that case, for each draw there will be 20 items of which 2 are defective, resulting in an unchanging probability of success. Further, the dependence of the trials can be ignored if the population size is very large relative to the sample size. For instance, if the box consists of 10,000 items of which 10%, or 1,000, are defective, then the probability of success in the second draw will be either 999/9,999 or 1,000/9,999, which are both approximately equal to 0.10.

THE HYPERGEOMETRIC PROBABILITY DISTRIBUTION

For a **hypergeometric random variable** X, the probability of x successes in a random selection of n items is

$$P(X = x) = \frac{\binom{S}{x}\binom{N-S}{n-x}}{\binom{N}{n}},$$

for $x = 0, 1, 2, \ldots, n$ if $n \leq S$ or $x = 0, 1, 2, \ldots, S$ if $n > S$, where N denotes the number of items in the population of which S are successes.

The formula consists of three parts:

- The first term in the numerator, $\binom{S}{x} = \frac{S!}{x!(S-x)!}$, represents the number of ways x successes can be selected from S successes in the population.
- The second term in the numerator, $\binom{N-S}{n-x} = \frac{(N-S)!}{(n-x)!(N-S-n+x)!}$, represents the number of ways $(n - x)$ failures can be selected from $(N - S)$ failures in the population.
- The denominator, $\binom{N}{n} = \frac{N!}{n!(N-n)!}$, represents the number of ways a sample of size n can be selected from the population of size N.

As with the binomial and Poisson distributions, simplified formulas can be used to calculate the mean, the variance, and the standard deviation of a hypergeometric random variable.

EXPECTED VALUE, VARIANCE, AND STANDARD DEVIATION OF A HYPERGEOMETRIC RANDOM VARIABLE

If X is a hypergeometric random variable, then

$$E(X) = \mu = n\left(\frac{S}{N}\right),$$

$$Var(X) = \sigma^2 = n\left(\frac{S}{N}\right)\left(1 - \frac{S}{N}\right)\left(\frac{N-n}{N-1}\right), \quad \text{and}$$

$$SD(X) = \sigma = \sqrt{n\left(\frac{S}{N}\right)\left(1 - \frac{S}{N}\right)\left(\frac{N-n}{N-1}\right)}.$$

EXAMPLE 5.12

Wooden boxes are commonly used for the packaging and transportation of mangoes. A convenience store in Morganville, New Jersey, regularly buys mangoes from a wholesale dealer. For every shipment, the manager randomly inspects five mangoes from a box containing 20 mangoes for damages due to transportation. Suppose the chosen box contains exactly 2 damaged mangoes.

a. What is the probability that one out of five mangoes used in the inspection are damaged?

b. If the manager decides to reject the shipment if one or more mangoes are damaged, what is the probability that the shipment will be rejected?

c. Calculate the expected value, variance, and standard deviation of the number of damaged mangoes used in the inspection.

SOLUTION: The hypergeometric distribution is appropriate because the probability of finding a damaged mango changes from mango to mango (sampling is without replacement and the population size N is not significantly more than the sample size n). We use the following values to answer the questions: $N = 20$, $n = 5$, $S = 2$.

a. The probability that one out of five mangoes is damaged is $P(X = 1)$. We calculate

$$P(X = 1) = \frac{\binom{2}{1}\binom{20-2}{5-1}}{\binom{20}{5}} = \frac{\left(\frac{2!}{1!1!}\right)\left(\frac{18!}{4!14!}\right)}{\left(\frac{20!}{5!15!}\right)} = \frac{(2)(3060)}{15,504} = 0.3947.$$

Therefore, the likelihood that exactly one out of five mangoes is damaged is 39.47%.

b. Note that $P(X \geq 1) = 1 - P(X = 0)$ where

$$P(X = 0) = \frac{\binom{2}{0}\binom{20-2}{5-0}}{\binom{20}{5}} = \frac{\left(\frac{2!}{0!2!}\right)\left(\frac{18!}{5!13!}\right)}{\left(\frac{20!}{5!15!}\right)} = \frac{(1)(8568)}{15504} = 0.5526.$$

Therefore, the probability that the shipment will be rejected equals $P(X \geq 1) = 1 - P(X = 0) = 1 - 0.5526 = 0.4474$.

c. We use the simplified formulas to obtain

$$E(X) = n\left(\frac{S}{N}\right) = 5\left(\frac{2}{20}\right) = 0.50,$$

$$Var(X) = n\left(\frac{S}{N}\right)\left(1 - \frac{S}{N}\right)\left(\frac{N-n}{N-1}\right) = 5\left(\frac{2}{20}\right)\left(1 - \frac{2}{20}\right)\left(\frac{20-5}{20-1}\right) = 0.3553, \text{ and}$$

$$SD(X) = \sqrt{0.3553} = 0.5960$$

Using Excel to Obtain Hypergeometric Probabilities

It is tedious and cumbersome to solve hypergeometric distribution problems using the formula. Fortunately, Excel provides a function to solve hypergeometric probabilities.

We solve Example 5.12a using the hypergeometric function provided by Excel (**Formulas > Insert Function > HYPGEOM.DIST**) by supplying the following five arguments in the **HYPGEOM.DIST** dialog box as shown in Figure 5.8.

- **Sample_s** is the number of successes in the sample. We enter 1.
- **Number_sample** is the size of the sample. We enter 5.
- **Population_s** is the number of successes in the population. We enter 2.
- **Number_pop** is the size of the population. We enter 20.
- **Cumulative** is a logical value. If we enter the value 1 or TRUE, Excel will return a cumulative probability; if we enter the value 0 or FALSE, Excel will return a probability mass function. We enter 0 since we wish to solve for $P(X = 1)$.

FIGURE 5.8 Computing hypergeometric probabilities with Excel (Example 5.12a)

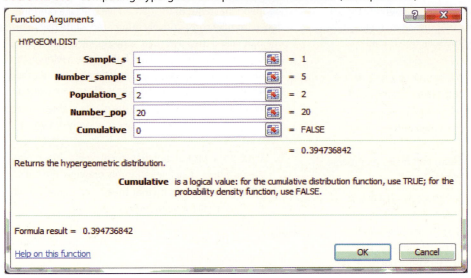

Excel returns the formula result 0.3947 for $P(X = 1)$, which is the value that we obtained manually.

EXERCISES 5.6

Concepts

54. Assume that X is a hypergeometric random variable with $N = 25$, $S = 3$, and $n = 4$. Calculate the following probabilities.
    a. $P(X = 0)$
    b. $P(X = 1)$
    c. $P(X \leq 1)$

55. Assume that X is a hypergeometric random variable with $N = 15$, $S = 4$, and $n = 3$. Calculate the following probabilities.
    a. $P(X = 1)$
    b. $P(X = 2)$
    c. $P(X \geq 2)$

56. Compute the probability of no success in a random sample of 3 items obtained from a population of 12 items that contains 2 successes. What are the expected number and the standard deviation of successes from the sample?

57. (Use computer) Assume that X is a hypergeometric random variable with $N = 50$, $S = 20$, and $n = 5$. Calculate the following probabilities.
    a. $P(X = 2)$
    b. $P(X \geq 2)$
    c. $P(X \leq 3)$

58. (Use computer) Compute the probability of at least 8 successes in a random sample of 20 items obtained from a population of 100 items that contains 25 successes. What are the expected number and the standard deviation of successes?

Applications

59. Despite the repeated effort by the government to reform how Wall Street pays its executives, some of the nation's

biggest banks are continuing to pay out bonuses nearly as large as those in the best years before the crisis (*The Washington Post,* January 15, 2010). It is known that 10 out of 15 members of the board of directors of a company were in favor of a bonus. Suppose three members were randomly selected by the media.
    a. What is the probability that all of them were in favor of a bonus?
    b. What is the probability that at least two members were in favor of a bonus?

60. Many programming teams work independently at a large software company. The management has been putting pressure on these teams to finish a project on time. The company currently has 18 large programming projects, of which only 12 are likely to finish on time. Suppose the manager decides to randomly supervise three such projects.
    a. What is the probability that all three are likely to finish on time?
    b. What is the probability that at least two are likely to finish on time?

61. David Barnes and his fiancée Valerie Shah are visiting Hawaii. There are 20 guests registered for orientation. It is announced that 12 randomly selected registered guests will receive a free lesson of the Tahitian dance.
    a. What is the probability that both David and Valerie get picked for the Tahitian dance lesson?
    b. What is the probability that neither of them gets picked for the Tahitian dance lesson?

62. The National Science Foundation is fielding applications for grants to study climate change. Twenty universities

apply for a grant, and only 4 of them will be awarded. If Syracuse University and Auburn University are among the 20 applicants, what is the probability that these two universities will receive a grant? Assume that the selection is made randomly.

63. (Use computer) A committee of 40 members consists of 24 men and 16 women. A subcommittee consisting of 10 randomly selected members will be formed.
    a. What are the expected number of men and women in the subcommittee?
    b. What is the probability that at least half of the members in the subcommittee will be women?

64. (Use computer) Powerball is a jackpot game with a grand prize starting at $20 million and often rolling over into the hundreds of millions. In 2006, the jackpot was $365 million. The winner may choose to receive the jackpot prize paid over 29 years or as a lump sum payment. For $1 the player selects six numbers for the base game of Powerball. There are two independent stages of the game. Five balls are randomly drawn from 59 consecutively numbered white balls. Further, one ball, called the Powerball, is randomly drawn from 39 consecutively numbered red balls. To be a winner, the numbers selected by the player must match the numbers on the randomly drawn white balls as well as the Powerball.
    a. What is the probability that the player is able to match the numbers of two out of five randomly drawn white balls?
    b. What is the probability that the player is able to match the numbers of all five randomly drawn white balls?
    c. What is the probability that the player is able to match the Powerball for a randomly drawn red ball?
    d. What is the probability of winning the jackpot? [*Hint: Remember that the two stages of drawing white and red balls are independent.*]

WRITING WITH STATISTICS

Senior executives at Skyhigh Construction, Inc., participate in a pick-your-salary plan. They choose salaries in a range between $125,000 and $150,000. By choosing a lower salary, an executive has an opportunity to make a larger bonus. If Skyhigh does not generate an operating profit during the year, then no bonuses are paid. Skyhigh has just hired two new senior executives, Allen Grossman and Felicia Arroyo. Each must decide whether to choose *Option* 1: a base pay of $125,000 with a possibility of a large bonus, or *Option* 2: a base pay of $150,000 with a possibility of a bonus, but the bonus would be one-half of the bonus under Option 1.

Grossman, 44 years old, is married with two young children. He bought his home at the height of the market and has a rather large monthly mortgage payment. Arroyo, 32 years old, just completed her M.B.A. at a prestigious Ivy League university. She is single and has no student loans due to a timely inheritance upon entering graduate school. Arroyo just moved to the area so has decided to rent an apartment for at least one year. Given their personal profile, inherent perception of risk, and subjective view of the economy, Grossman and Arroyo construct their individual probability distributions with respect to bonus outcomes shown in Table 5.9.

TABLE 5.9 Grossman's and Arroyo's Probability Distributions

Bonus (in $)	Probability	
	Grossman	Arroyo
0	0.35	0.20
50,000	0.45	0.25
100,000	0.10	0.35
150,000	0.10	0.20

Jordan Lake, an independent human resource specialist, is asked to summarize the payment plans with respect to each executive's probability distribution.

Jordan would like to use the above probability distributions to:

1. Compute expected values to evaluate payment plans for Grossman and Arroyo.
2. Help Grossman and Arroyo decide whether to choose Option 1 or Option 2 for his/her compensation package.

Skyhigh Construction, Inc., has just hired two new senior executives, Allen Grossman and Felicia Arroyo, to oversee planned expansion of operations. As senior executives, they participate in a pick-your-salary plan. Each executive is given two options for compensation:

Option 1: A base pay of $125,000 with a possibility of a large bonus.

Option 2: A base pay of $150,000 with a possibility of a bonus, but the bonus would be one-half of the bonus under Option 1.

Grossman and Arroyo understand that if the firm does not generate an operating profit in the fiscal year, then no bonuses are paid. Each executive has constructed a probability distribution given his/her personal background, underlying risk preferences, and subjective view of the economy.

Given the probability distributions and with the aid of expected values, the following analysis will attempt to choose the best option for each executive. Grossman, a married father with two young children, believes that Table 5.A best reflects his bonus payment expectations.

TABLE 5.A Calculating Grossman's Expected Salary

Bonus (in $)	Probability	Weighted Value, $x_i P(x_i)$
0	0.35	$0 \times 0.35 = 0$
50,000	0.45	$50,000 \times 0.45 = 22,500$
100,000	0.10	$100,000 \times 0.10 = 10,000$
150,000	0.10	$150,000 \times 0.10 = 15,000$
		Total = $47,500

Expected bonus, $E(X)$, is calculated as a weighted average of all possible bonus values and is shown at the bottom of the third column of Table 1. Grossman's expected bonus is $47,500. Using this value for his bonus, his salary options are:

Option 1: $125,000 + $47,500 = $172,500

Option 2: $150,000 + (1/2 \times $47,500) = $173,750

Grossman should choose *Option 2* as his salary plan.

Arroyo is single with few financial constraints. Table 5.B shows the expected value of her bonus given her probability distribution.

TABLE 5.B Calculating Arroyo's Expected Salary

Bonus (in $)	Probability	Weighted Value, $x_i P(x_i)$
0	0.20	$0 \times 0.20 = 0$
50,000	0.25	$50,000 \times 0.25 = 12,500$
100,000	0.35	$100,000 \times 0.35 = 35,000$
150,000	0.20	$150,000 \times 0.20 = 30,000$
		Total = $77,500

Arroyo's expected bonus amounts to $77,500. Thus, her salary options are:

Option 1: $125,000 + $77,500 = $202,500

Option 2: $150,000 + (1/2 \times $77,500) = $188,750

Arroyo should choose *Option 1* as her salary plan.

Conceptual Review

LO **5.1**

Distinguish between discrete and continuous random variables.

A **random variable** summarizes outcomes of an experiment with numerical values. A random variable is either discrete or continuous. A **discrete random variable** assumes a countable number of distinct values, whereas a **continuous random variable** is characterized by (infinitely) uncountable values within any interval.

LO **5.2**

Describe the probability distribution of a discrete random variable.

The **probability distribution function** of a discrete random variable X is a list of the values of X with the associated probabilities, that is, the list of all possible pairs $(x, P(X = x))$.

The **cumulative distribution function** of X is defined as $P(X \leq x)$.

A **discrete uniform distribution** is a symmetric distribution where the random variable assumes a finite number of specified values and each value is equally likely.

LO **5.3**

Calculate and interpret summary measures for a discrete random variable.

For a discrete random variable X with values $x_1, x_2, x_3, \ldots$ that occur with probabilities $P(X = x_i)$, the **expected value** of X is calculated as $E(X) = \mu = \Sigma x_i P(X = x_i)$. We interpret the expected value as the long-run average value of the random variable over infinitely many independent repetitions of an experiment. Measures of dispersion indicate whether the values of X are clustered about μ or widely scattered from μ. The **variance** of X is calculated as $Var(X) = \sigma^2 = \Sigma(x_i - \mu)^2 P(X = x_i) = \Sigma x_i^2 P(X = x_i) - \mu^2$. The **standard deviation** of X is $SD(X) = \sigma = \sqrt{\sigma^2}$.

LO **5.4**

Differentiate among risk neutral, risk averse, and risk loving consumers.

In general, a **risk averse consumer** expects a reward for taking risk. A risk averse consumer may decline a risky prospect even if it offers a positive expected gain. A **risk neutral consumer** completely ignores risk and always accepts a prospect that offers a positive expected gain. Finally, **a risk loving consumer** may accept a risky prospect even if the expected gain is negative.

LO **5.5**

Compute summary measures to evaluate portfolio returns.

Portfolio return R_p is represented as a linear combination of the individual returns. With two assets, $R_p = w_A R_A + w_B R_B$, where R_A and R_B represent asset returns and w_A and w_B are the corresponding portfolio weights. The **expected return** and the **variance** of the portfolio are $E(R_p) = w_A E(R_A) + w_B E(R_B)$ and $Var(R_p) = w_A^2 \sigma_A^2 + w_B^2 \sigma_B^2 + 2w_A w_B \sigma_{AB}$, or equivalently, $Var(R_p) = w_A^2 \sigma_A^2 + w_B^2 \sigma_B^2 + 2w_A w_B \rho_{AB} \sigma_A \sigma_B$.

LO **5.6**

Describe the binomial distribution and compute relevant probabilities.

A **Bernoulli process** is a series of n independent and identical trials of a random experiment such that on each trial there are only two possible outcomes, conventionally labeled "success" and "failure." The probabilities of success and failure, denoted p and $q = 1 - p$, remain constant from trial to trial.

For a **binomial random variable** X, the probability of x successes in n Bernoulli trials is $P(X = x) = \binom{n}{x} p^x q^{n-x} = \frac{n!}{x!(n-x)!} p^x q^{n-x}$ for $x = 0, 1, 2, \ldots, n$.

The **expected value**, **variance**, and **standard deviation** of a binomial random variable are $E(X) = np$, $Var(X) = \sigma^2 = npq$, and $SD(X) = \sigma = \sqrt{npq}$, respectively.

The Poisson probability distribution is appropriate in problems that deal with time or space. A binomial random variable counts the number of successes in a fixed number of Bernoulli trials, whereas a **Poisson random variable** counts the number of successes over a given interval of time or space. For a Poisson random variable X, the probability of x successes over a given interval of time or space is $P(X = x) = \dfrac{e^{-\mu}\mu^{x}}{x!}$ for $x = 0, 1, 2, \ldots$, where μ is the mean number of successes and $e \approx 2.718$ is the base of the natural logarithm. The **expected value**, the **variance**, and the **standard deviation** of a Poisson probability distribution are $E(X) = \mu$, $Var(X) = \sigma^2 = \mu$, and $SD(X) = \sigma = \sqrt{\mu}$, respectively.

The hypergeometric probability distribution is appropriate in applications where the trials are not independent and the probability of success changes from trial to trial. We use it in place of the binomial distribution when we are sampling **without replacement** from a population whose size N is not significantly larger than the sample size n. For a **hypergeometric random variable** X, the probability of x successes in a random selection of n items is $P(X = x) = \dfrac{\binom{S}{x}\binom{N-S}{n-x}}{\binom{N}{n}}$ for $x = 0, 1, 2, \ldots, n$ if $n \le S$ or $x = 0, 1, 2, \ldots, S$ if $n > S$, where N denotes the number of items in the population of which S are successes. The **expected value**, the **variance**, and the **standard deviation** of a hypergeometric probability distribution are $E(X) = n\left(\frac{S}{N}\right)$, $Var(X) = \sigma^2 = n\left(\frac{S}{N}\right)\left(1 - \frac{S}{N}\right)\left(\frac{N-n}{N-1}\right)$, and $SD(X) = \sigma = \sqrt{n\left(\frac{S}{N}\right)\left(1 - \frac{S}{N}\right)\left(\frac{N-n}{N-1}\right)}$, respectively.

Additional Exercises and Case Studies

65. Facing the worst economic climate since the dot-com bust in the early 2000s, high-tech companies in the U.S. search for investment opportunities with cautious optimism (*USA Today*, February 17, 2009). Suppose the investment team at Microsoft is considering an innovative start-up project. According to its estimates, Microsoft can make a profit of $5 million if the project is very successful and $2 million if it is somewhat successful. It also stands to lose $4 million if the project fails. Calculate the expected profit or loss for Microsoft if the probabilities that the project is very successful and somewhat successful are 0.10 and 0.40, respectively, with the remaining amount being the failure probability.

66. An analyst developed the following probability distribution for the rate of return for a common stock.

Scenario	Probability	Rate of Return
1	0.25	−15%
2	0.35	5%
3	0.40	10%

a. Calculate the expected rate of return.
b. Calculate the variance and the standard deviation of this probability distribution.

67. Consider the following information on the expected return of companies X and Y.

Economy	Probability	X	Y
Boom	0.20	30%	10%
Neutral	0.50	10%	20%
Poor	0.30	−30%	5%

a. Calculate the expected value and the standard deviation of returns of companies X and Y.
b. Calculate the correlation coefficient if the covariance between X and Y is 88.

68. An investor owns a portfolio consisting of two mutual funds, A and B, with 35% invested in A. The following table lists the inputs for these funds.

Measures	Fund A	Fund B
Expected Value	10	5
Variance	98	26
Covariance	22	

a. Calculate the expected value of the portfolio return.
b. Calculate the standard deviation of the portfolio return.

69. Forty-four percent of consumers with credit cards carry balances from month to month (bankrate.com, February 20, 2007). Four consumers with credit cards are randomly selected.
   a. What is the probability that all consumers carry a credit card balance?
   b. What is the probability that fewer than two consumers carry a credit card balance?
   c. Calculate the expected value, variance, and standard deviation of this binomial probability distribution.

70. According to the Department of Transportation, 27% of domestic flights were delayed last year (*Money*, May 2008). At New York's John F. Kennedy Airport, five flights are randomly selected.
   a. What is the probability that all five flights are delayed?
   b. What is the probability that all five are on time?

71. (Use computer) Twenty percent of U.S. mortgages are "underwater" (*The Boston Globe*, March 5, 2009). A mortgage is considered underwater if the value of the home is less than what is owed on the mortgage. Suppose 100 mortgage holders are randomly selected.
   a. What is the probability that exactly 15 of the mortgages are underwater?
   b. What is the probability that more than 20 of the mortgages are underwater?
   c. What is the probability that at least 25 of the mortgages are underwater?

72. (Use computer) According to a survey by consulting firm Watson Wyatt, approximately 19% of employers have eliminated perks or plan to do so in the next year (*Kiplinger's Personal Finance*, February 2009). Suppose 30 employers are randomly selected.
   a. What is the probability that exactly 10 of the employers have eliminated or plan to eliminate perks?
   b. What is the probability that at least 10 employers, but no more than 20 employers, have eliminated or plan to eliminate perks?
   c. What is the probability that at most 8 employers have eliminated or plan to eliminate perks?

73. Studies have shown that bats can consume an average of 10 mosquitoes per minute (berkshiremuseum.org).
   a. Calculate the average number of mosquitoes that a bat consumes in a 30-second interval.
   b. What is the probability that a bat consumes 4 mosquitoes in a 30-second interval?
   c. What is the probability that a bat does not consume any mosquitoes in a 30-second interval?
   d. What is the probability that a bat consumes at least one mosquito in a 30-second interval?

74. (Use computer) Despite the fact that home prices seem affordable and mortgage rates are at historic lows, real estate agents say they are showing more homes, but not selling more (*The Boston Globe*, March 7, 2009). A real estate company estimates that an average of five people show up at an open house to view a property. There is going to be an open house on Sunday.
   a. What is the probability that at least five people will show up to view the property?
   b. What is the probability that fewer than five people will show up to view the property?

75. A professor has learned that three students in her class of 20 will cheat on the exam. She decides to focus her attention on four randomly chosen students during the exam.
   a. What is the probability that she finds at least one of the students cheating?
   b. What is the probability that she finds at least one of the students cheating if she focuses on six randomly chosen students?

76. (Use computer) Many U.S. households still do not have Internet access. Suppose 20 out of 80 households in a small southern town do not have Internet access. A company that provides high speed Internet has recently entered the market. As part of the marketing campaign, the company decides to randomly select 10 households and offer them free laptops along with a brochure that describes their services. The aim is to build goodwill and, with a free laptop, tempt nonusers into getting Internet access.
   a. What is the probability that 6 laptop recipients do not have Internet access?
   b. What is the probability that at least five laptop recipients do not have Internet access?
   c. What is the probability that two or fewer laptop recipients do not have Internet access?
   d. What is the expected number of laptop recipients who do not have Internet access?

CASE STUDIES

Case Study 5.1

An extended warranty is a prolonged warranty offered to consumers by the warranty administrator, the retailer, or the manufacturer. A recent report in *The New York Times* (November 23, 2009) suggests that 20.4% of laptops fail over three years. Roberto D'Angelo is interested in an extended warranty for his laptop. A good extended warranty is being offered at Compuvest.com for $74. It will cover any repair job that his laptop may need in the next three years. Based on his research, he determines that the likelihood of a repair job in the next three years is 13% for a minor repair, 8% for a major repair, and

3% for a catastrophic repair. The extended warranty will save him $80 for a minor repair, $320 for a major repair, and $500 for a catastrophic repair. These results are summarized in the following probability distribution.

Data for Case Study 5.1 Probability Distribution for Repair Cost

Type of Repair	Probability	Repair Cost
None	0.76	$0
Minor	0.13	$80
Major	0.08	$320
Catastrophic	0.03	$500

In a report, use the above information to:

1. Calculate and interpret the expected value of the repair cost.

2. Analyze the expected gain or loss for a consumer who buys the above extended warranty.

3. Determine what kind of a consumer (risk neutral, risk averse, or both) will buy this extended warranty.

Case Study 5.2

According to figures released by the New York City government, smoking amongst New York City teenagers is on a decline, continuing a trend that began more than a decade ago (*The New York Times*, January 2, 2008). According to the New York City Youth Risk Behavior Survey, the teenage smoking rate dropped to 8.5% in 2007 from about 17.6% in 2001 and 23% in 1997. City officials attribute the lower smoking rate to factors including a cigarette tax increase, a ban on workplace smoking, and television and subway ads that graphically depict tobacco-related illnesses.

In a report, use the above information to:

1. Calculate the probability that at least one in a group of 10 New York City teenagers smoked in 2007.

2. Calculate the probability that at least one in a group of 10 New York City teenagers smoked in 2001.

3. Calculate the probability that at least one in a group of 10 New York City teenagers smoked in 1997.

4. Comment on the smoking trend between 1997 and 2007.

Case Study 5.3

Disturbing news regarding Scottish police concerns the number of crashes involving vehicles on operational duties (*BBC News*, March 10, 2008). Statistics showed that Scottish forces' vehicles had been involved in traffic accidents at the rate of 1,000 per year. The statistics included vehicles involved in 999 calls (the equivalent of 911 in the U.S.) and pursuits. Fire service and ambulance vehicles were not included in the figures.

In a report, use the above information to:

1. Calculate and interpret the expected number of traffic accidents per day involving vehicles on operational duties.

2. Use this expected value to compute and plot the probability distribution table that lists the probability of 0, 1, 2, . . . , 10 traffic accidents per day.

6

Continuous Probability Distributions

CHAPTER

In the preceding chapter, we defined a random variable and discussed its numerical outcomes. We then classified the random variable as a discrete or a continuous random variable, depending on the range of numerical values that it can assume. A discrete random variable assumes a countable number of distinct values, such as the number of credit cards carried by consumers, the number of foreclosures in a sample of 100 households, and the number of cars lined up at a toll booth. A continuous random variable, on the other hand, is characterized by (infinitely) uncountable values, such as the investment return on a mutual fund, the waiting time at a toll booth, and the amount of soda in a cup. In this chapter we focus our attention on continuous random variables. Most of this chapter is devoted to the discussion of the normal distribution, which is the most extensively used continuous probability distribution and is the cornerstone of statistical inference. Other important continuous distributions discussed in the chapter are the uniform, the exponential, and the lognormal distributions.

Demand for Salmon

Akiko Hamaguchi is the manager of a small sushi restaurant called Little Ginza in Phoenix, Arizona. As part of her job, Akiko has to purchase salmon every day for the restaurant. For the sake of freshness, it is important that she buys the right amount of salmon daily. Buying too much may result in wastage and buying too little may disappoint some customers on high demand days.

Akiko has estimated that the daily consumption of salmon is normally distributed with a mean of 12 pounds and a standard deviation of 3.2 pounds. She has always bought 20 pounds of salmon every day. Lately, she has been criticized by the owners because this amount of salmon was too often resulting in wastage. As part of cost cutting, Akiko is considering a new strategy. She will buy salmon that is sufficient to meet the daily demand of customers on 90% of the days.

Akiko wants to use the above information to:

1. Calculate the proportion of days that demand for salmon at Little Ginza was above her earlier purchase of 20 pounds.

2. Calculate the proportion of days that demand for salmon at Little Ginza was below 15 pounds.

3. Determine the amount of salmon that should be bought daily so that it meets demand on 90% of the days.

We provide a synopsis of this case at the end of Section 6.3.

6.1 Continuous Random Variables and the Uniform Probability Distribution

LO 6.1

Describe a continuous random variable.

As discussed in Chapter 5, a discrete random variable X assumes a countable number of distinct values such as x_1, x_2, x_3, and so on. A **continuous random variable**, on the other hand, is characterized by infinitely uncountable values and can take on any value within an interval. Unlike the case of a discrete random variable, we cannot describe the possible values of a continuous random variable X with a list $x_1, x_2, \ldots$ because the outcome $(x_1 + x_2)/2$, not in the list, might also be possible.

For a discrete random variable, we can compute the probability that it assumes a particular value x, or written as a probability statement, $P(X = x)$. For instance, for a binomial random variable, we can calculate the probability of exactly one success in n trials, that is, $P(X = 1)$. We cannot make this calculation with a continuous random variable. The probability that a continuous random variable assumes a particular value x is zero, that is, $P(X = x) = 0$. This occurs because we cannot assign a nonzero probability to each of infinitely uncountable values and still have the probabilities sum to one. Thus, for a continuous random variable it is only meaningful to calculate the probability that the value of the random variable falls within some specified interval. Therefore, for a continuous random variable, $P(a \leq X \leq b) = P(a < X < b) = P(a \leq X < b) = P(a < X \leq b)$ since $P(X = a)$ and $P(X = b)$ are both zero.

For a continuous random variable, the counterpart to the probability mass function is called the **probability density function**, denoted by $f(x)$. As mentioned in Chapter 5, in this book we often use the term "probability distribution" to refer to both functions. The graph of $f(x)$ approximates the relative frequency polygon for the population. Unlike the discrete probability distribution, $f(x)$ does not provide probabilities directly. The probability that the variable assumes a value within an interval, say $P(a \leq X \leq b)$, is defined as the area under $f(x)$ between points a and b. Moreover, the entire area under $f(x)$ over all values of x must equal one; this is equivalent to the fact that, for discrete random variables, the probabilities add up to one.

THE PROBABILITY DENSITY FUNCTION

The probability density function $f(x)$ of a continuous random variable X describes the relative likelihood that X assumes a value within a given interval, where

- $f(x) > 0$ for all possible values x of X, and
- the area under $f(x)$ over all values of x equals one.

As in the case of discrete random variables, we can use the **cumulative distribution function**, denoted by $F(x)$, to compute probabilities for continuous random variables. For a value x of the random variable X, $F(x) = P(X \leq x)$ is simply the area under the probability density function $f(x)$ up to the value x.

THE CUMULATIVE DISTRIBUTION FUNCTION

For any value x of the random variable X, the cumulative distribution function $F(x)$ is computed as

$$F(x) = P(X \leq x).$$

If you are familiar with calculus, then you will recognize that this cumulative probability is the integral of $f(x)$ in the range below x. Similarly, $P(a \leq X \leq b) = F(b) - F(a)$ is the integral of $f(x)$ between points a and b. Fortunately, we do not necessarily need the knowledge of integral calculus to compute probabilities with the continuous random variables discussed in this text.

The Continuous Uniform Distribution

LO 6.2

Describe a continuous uniform distribution and calculate associated probabilities.

One of the simplest continuous probability distributions is called the **continuous uniform distribution**. This distribution describes a random variable that has an equally likely chance of assuming a value within a specified range. For example, suppose you are informed that your new refrigerator will be delivered between 2:00 pm and 3:00 pm. Let the random variable X denote the delivery time of your refrigerator. This variable is bounded below by 2:00 pm and above by 3:00 pm for a total range of 60 minutes. It is reasonable to infer that the probability of delivery between 2:00 pm and 2:30 pm equals 0.50 ($=30/60$), as does the probability of delivery between 2:30 pm and 3:00 pm. Similarly, the probability of delivery in any 15-minute interval equals 0.25 ($=15/60$), and so on.

Figure 6.1 depicts the probability density function of the continuous uniform random variable. The values a and b on the horizontal axis represent its lower and upper limits, respectively. The continuous uniform distribution is symmetric around its mean μ computed as $\frac{a+b}{2}$. In the refrigerator delivery example, the mean is computed as $\mu = \frac{2+3}{2} = 2.5$, implying that you expect the delivery at 2:30 pm. The standard deviation σ of a continuous uniform variable equals $\sqrt{(b-a)^2/12}$.

FIGURE 6.1 Continuous uniform probability density function $f(x)$

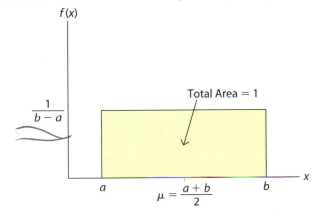

It is important to emphasize that the height of the probability density function $f(x)$ does not directly represent a probability. As in the case of all continuous random variables, it is the area under $f(x)$ that corresponds to probability. For the continuous uniform distribution, the probability is essentially the area of a rectangle, which is the base times the height. Therefore, the probability is easily computed by multiplying the length of a specified interval (base) with $f(x) = \frac{1}{b-a}$ (height).

THE CONTINUOUS UNIFORM DISTRIBUTION

A random variable X follows the **continuous uniform distribution** if its probability density function is

$$f(x) = \begin{cases} \dfrac{1}{b-a} & \text{for } a \leq x \leq b, \text{ and} \\ 0 & \text{for } x < a \text{ or } x > b, \end{cases}$$

where a and b represent the lower and upper limits of values, respectively, that the random variable assumes.

The expected value and the standard deviation of X are computed as

$$E(X) = \mu = \frac{a+b}{2} \quad \text{and} \quad SD(X) = \sigma = \sqrt{(b-a)^2/12}.$$

EXAMPLE 6.1

A manager of a local drugstore is projecting next month's sales for a particular cosmetic line. She knows from historical data that sales follow a continuous uniform distribution with a lower limit of $2,500 and an upper limit of $5,000.

a. What are the mean and standard deviation of this uniform distribution?

b. What is the probability that sales exceed $4,000?

c. What is the probability that sales are between $3,200 and $3,800?

SOLUTION:

a. With a value for the lower limit of $a = $2,500 and a value for the upper limit of $b = $5,000, we calculate the mean and standard deviation of this continuous uniform distribution as

$$\mu = \frac{a + b}{2} = \frac{\$2,500 + \$5,000}{2} = \$3,750, \text{ and}$$

$$\sigma = \sqrt{(b - a)^2/12} = \sqrt{(5,000 - 2,500)^2/12} = \$721.69.$$

b. We find $P(X > 4,000)$, which is the area between $4,000 and $5,000 in the graph of the distribution (see Figure 6.2). The base of the rectangle equals $5,000 - 4,000 = 1,000$ and the height equals $\frac{1}{5,000 - 2,500} = 0.0004$. Thus $P(X > 4,000) = 1,000 \times 0.0004 = 0.40$.

FIGURE 6.2 Area to the right of 4,000 (Example 6.1b)

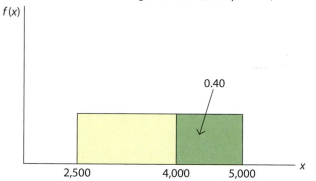

c. We find $P(3,200 \leq X \leq 3,800)$. Using the same methodology as in part b, we multiply the base times the height of the rectangle in the graph of the distribution (see Figure 6.3), or $(3,800 - 3,200) \times 0.0004$ and obtain an area or a probability of 0.24.

FIGURE 6.3 Area between 3,200 and 3,800 (Example 6.1c)

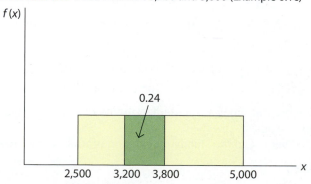

Concepts

1. The cumulative probabilities for a continuous random variable X are $P(X \leq 10) = 0.42$ and $P(X \leq 20) = 0.66$. Calculate the following probabilities.
   a. $P(X > 10)$
   b. $P(X > 20)$
   c. $P(10 < X < 20)$

2. For a continuous random variable X with an upper bound of 4, $P(0 \leq X \leq 2.5) = 0.54$ and $P(2.5 \leq X \leq 4) = 0.16$. Calculate the following probabilities.
   a. $P(X < 0)$
   b. $P(X > 2.5)$
   c. $P(0 \leq X \leq 4)$

3. For a continuous random variable X, $P(20 \leq X \leq 40) = 0.15$ and $P(X > 40) = 0.16$. Calculate the following probabilities.
   a. $P(X < 40)$
   b. $P(X < 20)$
   c. $P(X = 40)$

4. A random variable X follows the continuous uniform distribution with a lower bound of 5 and an upper bound of 35.
   a. What is the height of the density function $f(x)$?
   b. What is the mean and the standard deviation of the distribution?
   c. Calculate $P(X > 10)$.

5. A random variable X follows the continuous uniform distribution with a lower bound of -2 and an upper bound of 4.
   a. What is the height of the density function $f(x)$?
   b. What are the mean and the standard deviation of the distribution?
   c. Calculate $P(X \leq -1)$.

6. A random variable X follows the continuous uniform distribution with a lower limit of 10 and an upper limit of 30.
   a. Calculate the mean and standard deviation of the distribution.
   b. What is the probability that X is greater than 22?
   c. What is the probability that X is between 15 and 23?

7. A random variable X follows the uniform distribution with a lower limit of 750 and an upper limit of 800.
   a. Calculate the mean and standard deviation of this distribution.
   b. What is the probability that X is less than 770?

Applications

8. Suppose the average price of electricity for a New England customer follows the continuous uniform distribution with a lower bound of 12 cents per kilowatt-hour and an upper bound of 20 cents per kilowatt-hour.
   a. Calculate the average price of electricity for a New England customer.
   b. What is the probability that a New England customer pays less than 15.5 cents per kilowatt-hour?
   c. A local carnival is not able to operate its rides if the average price of electricity is more than 14 cents per kilowatt-hour. What is the probability that the carnival will need to close?

9. The arrival time of an elevator in a 12-story dormitory is equally likely at any time range during the next 4 minutes.
   a. Calculate the expected arrival time.
   b. What is the probability that an elevator arrives in less than 1½ minutes?
   c. What is the probability that the wait for an elevator is more than 1½ minutes?

10. The Netherlands is one of the world leaders in the production and sale of flowers. Suppose the heights of the tulips in the greenhouse of Rotterdam's Fantastic Flora follow a continuous uniform distribution with a lower bound of 7 inches and an upper bound of 16 inches. You have come to the greenhouse to select a bouquet of tulips, but only tulips with a height greater than 10 inches may be selected. What is the probability that a randomly selected tulip is tall enough to pick?

11. The scheduled arrival time for a daily flight from Boston to New York is 9:25 am. Historical data show that the arrival time follows the continuous uniform distribution with an early arrival time of 9:15 am and a late arrival time of 9:55 am.
    a. Calculate the mean and standard deviation of the distribution.
    b. What is the probability that a flight arrives late?

6.2 The Normal Distribution

The **normal distribution** is the familiar **symmetric** and **bell-shaped distribution**. It is the most extensively used probability distribution in statistical work. One reason for this common use is that the normal distribution closely approximates the probability distribution of a wide range of random variables of interest. Examples of random variables that closely follow a normal distribution include:

- Heights and weights of newborn babies
- Scores on the SAT
- Cumulative debt of college graduates

- Advertising expenditure of firms
- Rate of return on an investment

In this chapter we focus on the probabilities associated with a normally distributed random variable. The computation of these probabilities is easy and direct. Another important function of the normal distribution is that it serves as the cornerstone of statistical inference. Recall from Chapter 1 that the study of statistics is divided into two branches: descriptive statistics and inferential statistics. Statistical inference is generally based on the assumption of the normal distribution and serves as the major topic in the remainder of this text.

LO **6.3**

Explain the characteristics of the normal distribution.

Characteristics of the Normal Distribution

- The normal distribution is **symmetric** around its mean. In other words, the mean, the median, and the mode are all equal for a normally distributed random variable.
- The normal distribution is **completely described by two parameters**—the population mean μ and the population variance σ^2. The population mean describes the central location and the population variance describes the dispersion of the distribution.
- The normal distribution is **asymptotic** in the sense that the tails get closer and closer to the horizontal axis, but never touch it. Thus, theoretically, a normal random variable can assume any value between minus infinity and plus infinity.

The following definition mathematically expresses the probability density function of the normal distribution.

THE NORMAL DISTRIBUTION

A random variable X with mean μ and variance σ^2 follows the **normal distribution** if its probability density function is

$$f(x) = \frac{1}{\sigma\sqrt{2\pi}}\exp\left(-\frac{(x-\mu)^2}{2\sigma^2}\right)$$

where π equals approximately 3.14159 and $\exp(x) = e^x$ is the exponential function where $e \approx 2.718$ is the base of the natural logarithm.

A graph depicting the normal probability density function is often referred to as the **normal curve** or the **bell curve**. The following example relates the normal curve to the location and the dispersion of the normally distributed random variable.

EXAMPLE 6.2

Suppose we know that the ages of employees in Industries A, B, and C are normally distributed. We are given the following information on the relevant parameters:

Industry A	Industry B	Industry C
$\mu = 42$ years	$\mu = 36$ years	$\mu = 42$ years
$\sigma = 5$ years	$\sigma = 5$ years	$\sigma = 8$ years

Graphically compare the ages of employees in Industry A with Industry B. Repeat the comparison with Industry A versus Industry C.

SOLUTION: Figure 6.4 illustrates the difference in location given that the mean age of employees of Industry A is greater than that of Industry B. Both distributions show the same dispersion since the standard deviation is the same. Figure 6.5

compares the dispersion given that the standard deviation of age in Industry A is less than that of Industry C. Here, the peak of Industry A is higher than the peak of Industry C, reflecting the fact that an employee's age is likelier to be closer to the mean age in Industry A. These graphs also serve to point out that we can capture the entire distribution of any normally distributed random variable based on its mean and variance (or standard deviation).

FIGURE 6.4 Normal probability density function for two values of μ along with $\sigma = 5$

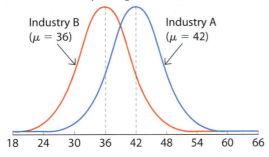

FIGURE 6.5 Normal probability density function for two values of σ along with $\mu = 42$

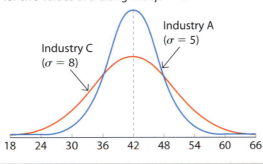

We generally use the cumulative distribution function $F(x)$ to compute probabilities for a normally distributed random variable, where $F(x) = P(X \leq x)$ is simply the area under $f(x)$ up to the value x. As mentioned earlier, we do not necessarily need the knowledge of integral calculus to compute probabilities with the normal distribution. Instead, we rely on a table to compute probabilities. We can also compute probabilities with Excel and other statistical packages. The specifics of how to use the table are delineated next.

The Standard Normal Variable

A **standard normal distribution** is a special case of the normal distribution with a mean equal to zero and a standard deviation (or variance) equal to one. Using the letter Z to denote a random variable with a standard normal distribution, we have $E(Z) = 0$ and $SD(Z) = 1$. As usual, we use the lowercase letter z to denote the value that the random variable Z may assume.

All introductory statistics texts include a **standard normal table**, also referred to as the **z table**, to provide areas (probabilities) under the z curve. However, the format of these probabilities is sometimes different. In this book the z table provides cumulative probabilities $P(Z \leq z)$; this table appears on two pages in Appendix A and is labeled Table 1. The left-hand page provides cumulative probabilities for z values less than or equal to zero. The right-hand page shows cumulative probabilities for z values greater than or equal to zero. Given the symmetry of the normal distribution and the fact that the

LO 6.4

Use the standard normal table or the z table.

area under the entire curve is one, other probabilities can be easily computed. We can also use the table to compute z values for given cumulative probabilities.

> ### STANDARD NORMAL DISTRIBUTION
>
> A standard normal random variable Z is a normal random variable with $E(Z) = 0$ and $SD(Z) = 1$. The z table provides cumulative probabilities $P(Z \le z)$ for positive and for negative values of z.

We first focus on reading the z table. In the next section, we will show that any normal distribution is equivalent to a standard normal distribution when the unit of measurement is changed to measure standard deviations from the mean. Therefore, while most real-world normally distributed variables are not standard normal, we can always transform them into standard normal and use the z table to compute the relevant probabilities.

Figure 6.6 represents a standard normal or z distribution. Since the random variable Z is symmetric around its mean of zero, $P(Z < 0) = P(Z > 0) = 0.5$. As is the case with all continuous random variables, we can also write the probabilities as $P(Z \le 0) = P(Z \ge 0) = 0.5$.

FIGURE 6.6 Standard normal probability density function

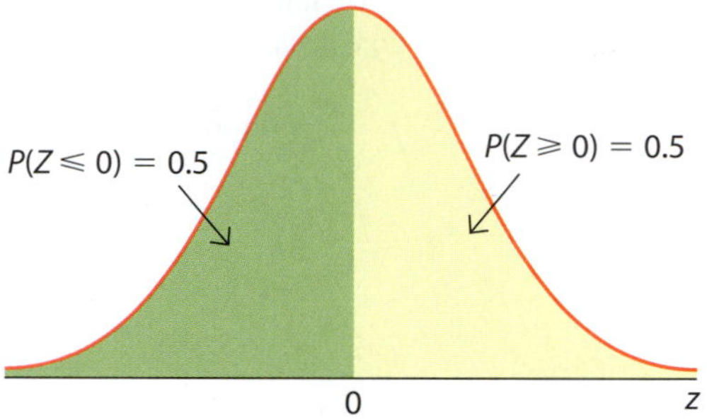

$P(Z \le 0) = 0.5$
$P(Z \ge 0) = 0.5$

Finding a Probability for a Given z Value

As mentioned earlier, the z table provides cumulative probabilities $P(Z \le z)$ for a given z. Consider, for example, a cumulative probability $P(Z \le 1.52)$ where $z = 1.52$. Since z is a positive value, we can look up this probability from the right-hand page of the z table provided in Table 1 of Appendix A; Table 6.1 shows a portion of the table.

TABLE 6.1 Portion of the Right-Hand Page of the z Table

z	0.00	0.01	0.02
0.0	0.5000	0.5040	↓
0.1	0.5398	0.5438	↓
⋮	⋮	⋮	⋮
1.5	→	→	0.9357

The first column of the table, denoted as the z column, shows values of z up to the tenth decimal point, while the first row of the table, denoted as the z row, shows hundredths values. Thus, for $z = 1.52$, we match 1.5 on the z column with 0.02 on the z row to find a corresponding probability of 0.9357. The arrows in Table 6.1 indicate that $P(Z \le 1.52) = 0.9357$.

In Figure 6.7, the cumulative probability corresponding to $z = 1.52$ is highlighted. Note that $P(Z \le 1.52) = 0.9357$ represents the area under the z curve to the left of 1.52. Therefore, the area to the right of 1.52 can be computed as $P(Z > 1.52) = 1 - P(Z \le 1.52) = 1 - 0.9357 = 0.0643$.

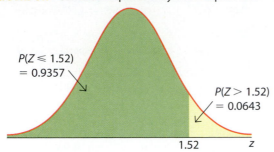

FIGURE 6.7 Cumulative probability with respect to $z = 1.52$

$P(Z \leq 1.52)$
$= 0.9357$

$P(Z > 1.52)$
$= 0.0643$

1.52 z

Similarly, suppose we want to find $P(Z \leq -1.96)$. Since z is a negative value, we can look up this probability from the left-hand page of the z table provided in Table 1 of Appendix A; Table 6.2 shows a portion of the table with arrows indicating that $P(Z \leq -1.96) = 0.0250$. Figure 6.8 highlights the corresponding probability. As before, the area to the right of -1.96 can be computed as $P(Z > -1.96) = 1 - P(Z \leq -1.96) = 1 - 0.0250 = 0.9750$.

TABLE 6.2 Portion of the Left-Hand Page of z Table

z	0.00	0.01	0.02	0.03	0.04	0.05	0.06
−3.9	0.0000	0.0000	0.0000	0.0000	0.0000	0.0000	↓
−3.8	0.0001	0.0001	0.0001	0.0001	0.0001	0.0001	↓
⋮	⋮	⋮	⋮	⋮	⋮	⋮	⋮
−1.9	→	→	→	→	→	→	0.0250

FIGURE 6.8 Cumulative probability with respect to $z = -1.96$

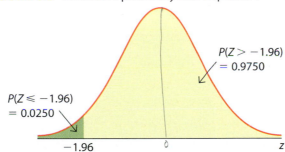

$P(Z > -1.96)$
$= 0.9750$

$P(Z \leq -1.96)$
$= 0.0250$

−1.96   0 z

EXAMPLE 6.3

Find the following probabilities for a standard normal random variable Z.

a. $P(0 \leq Z \leq 1.96)$

b. $P(1.52 \leq Z \leq 1.96)$

c. $P(-1.52 \leq Z \leq 1.96)$

d. $P(Z > 4)$

SOLUTION: It always helps to start by highlighting the relevant probability in the z graph.

a. As shown in Figure 6.9, the area between 0 and 1.96 is equivalent to the area to the left of 1.96 minus the area to the left of 0. Therefore, $P(0 \leq Z \leq 1.96) = P(Z \leq 1.96) - P(Z < 0) = 0.9750 - 0.50 = 0.4750$.

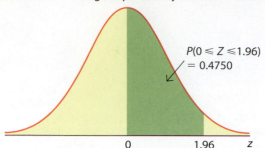

FIGURE 6.9 Finding the probability between 0 and 1.96

$P(0 \leq Z \leq 1.96)$
$= 0.4750$

b. As in part a and shown in Figure 6.10, $P(1.52 \leq Z \leq 1.96) = P(Z \leq 1.96) - P(Z < 1.52) = 0.9750 - 0.9357 = 0.0393$.

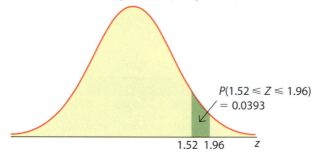

FIGURE 6.10 Finding the probability between 1.52 and 1.96

$P(1.52 \leq Z \leq 1.96)$
$= 0.0393$

c. From Figure 6.11, $P(-1.52 \leq Z \leq 1.96) = P(Z \leq 1.96) - P(Z < -1.52) = 0.9750 - 0.0643 = 0.9107$.

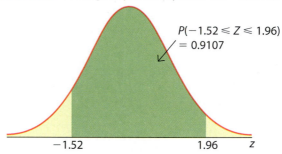

FIGURE 6.11 Finding the probability between −1.52 and 1.96

$P(-1.52 \leq Z \leq 1.96)$
$= 0.9107$

d. $P(Z > 4) = 1 - P(Z \leq 4)$. However, the z table only goes up to 3.99 with $P(Z \leq 3.99) = 0.9999$. For any z value greater than 3.99, it is acceptable to treat $P(Z \leq z) = 1.0$. Therefore, $P(Z > 4) = 1 - P(Z \leq 4) = 1 - 1 = 0$ (approximately).

Finding a *z* Value for a Given Probability

So far we have computed probabilities for given z values. Now we will evaluate z values for given probabilities.

EXAMPLE 6.4

For a standard normal variable Z, find the z values that satisfy the following.
a. $P(Z \leq z) = 0.6808$
b. $P(Z \leq z) = 0.90$

c. $P(Z \leq z) = 0.0643$

d. $P(Z > z) = 0.0212$

e. $P(-z \leq Z \leq z) = 0.95$

SOLUTION: As always, we use a graph to set up a problem. As mentioned earlier, the z table lists z values along with the corresponding cumulative probabilities. Noncumulative probabilities can be evaluated using symmetry.

a. Since the probability is already in a cumulative format, that is, $P(Z \leq z) = 0.6808$, we simply look up 0.6808 from the body of the table (right-hand side) to find the corresponding z value from the row/column of z. Table 6.3 shows the relevant portion of the z table and Figure 6.12 depicts the corresponding area. Therefore, $z = 0.47$.

TABLE 6.3 Portion of the z Table for Exercise 6.4a

z	0.00	0.01	0.02	0.03	0.04	0.05	0.06	0.07
0.0	0.5000	0.5040	0.5080	0.5120	0.5160	0.5199	0.5239	↑
0.1	0.5398	0.5438	0.5478	0.5517	0.5557	0.5596	0.5636	↑
⋮	⋮	⋮	⋮	⋮	⋮	⋮	⋮	⋮
0.4	←	←	←	←	←	←	←	0.6808

FIGURE 6.12 Finding z given $P(Z \leq z) = 0.6808$

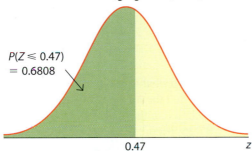

$P(Z \leq 0.47)$
$= 0.6808$

0.47 z

b. When deriving z for $P(Z \leq z) = 0.90$, we find that the z table (right-hand side) does not contain the cumulative probability 0.90. In such cases, we use the closest cumulative probability to solve the problem. Therefore, z is approximately equal to 1.28, which corresponds to a cumulative probability of 0.8997. Figure 6.13 shows this result graphically.

FIGURE 6.13 Finding z given $P(Z \leq z) = 0.90$

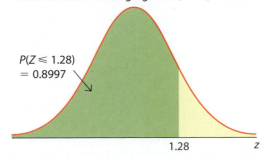

$P(Z \leq 1.28)$
$= 0.8997$

1.28 z

c. As shown in Figure 6.14, the z value that solves $P(Z \leq z) = 0.0643$ must be negative because the probability to its left is only 0.0643 (less than 0.50). We look up the cumulative probability 0.0643 (left-hand side) to get $z = -1.52$.

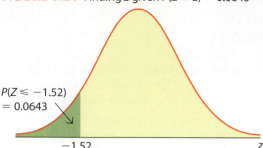

FIGURE 6.14 Finding z given $P(Z \leq z) = 0.0643$

$P(Z \leq -1.52)$
$= 0.0643$

-1.52 z

d. We have to find a z value such that the probability to the right of this value is 0.0212. Since the table states cumulative probabilities, we look up $P(Z \leq z) = 1 - 0.0212 = 0.9788$ in the table (right-hand side) to get $z = 2.03$. Figure 6.15 shows the results.

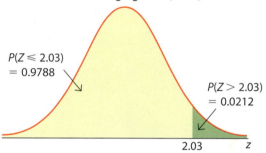

FIGURE 6.15 Finding z given $P(Z > z) = 0.0212$

$P(Z \leq 2.03)$
$= 0.9788$

$P(Z > 2.03)$
$= 0.0212$

2.03   z

e. Since we know that the total probability under the curve equals one, and we want to find $-z$ and z such that the area between the two values equals 0.95, we can conclude that the area in either tail is 0.025, that is, $P(Z < -z) = 0.025$ and $P(Z > z) = 0.025$. Figure 6.16 shows these results. We then use the cumulative probability, $P(Z \leq z) = 0.975$, to find $z = 1.96$.

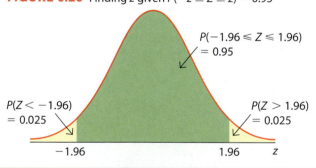

FIGURE 6.16 Finding z given $P(-z \leq Z \leq z) = 0.95$

$P(-1.96 \leq Z \leq 1.96)$
$= 0.95$

$P(Z < -1.96)$
$= 0.025$

$P(Z > 1.96)$
$= 0.025$

-1.96 1.96   z

Revisiting the Empirical Rule

In Section 3.6 we discussed useful probability statements about the dispersion of values in a data set. The **empirical rule** gives the approximate percentage of values that fall within 1, 2, or 3 standard deviations of the mean. Approximate percentages are appropriate for many real-world applications where the normal distribution is used only as an approximation. For normally distributed random variables, these percentages are exact.

The empirical rule, in the context of a normal distribution, is shown in Figure 6.17. Given a normal random variable X with mean μ and standard deviation σ:

- 68.26% of the values fall within 1 standard deviation of the mean, that is, $P(\mu - \sigma \le X \le \mu + \sigma) = 0.6826$,
- 95.44% of the values fall within 2 standard deviations of the mean, that is, $P(\mu - 2\sigma \le X \le \mu + 2\sigma) = 0.9544$, and
- 99.72% of the values fall within 3 standard deviations of the mean, that is, $P(\mu - 3\sigma \le X \le \mu + 3\sigma) = 0.9972$.

FIGURE 6.17 Graphical description of the empirical rule

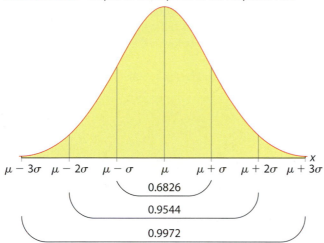

For a standard normal variable Z, $P(-1 \le Z \le 1)$ refers to the probability within 1 standard deviation of the mean since $\mu = 0$ and $\sigma = 1$. From the z table, we can show that $P(-1 \le Z \le 1)$ equals $P(Z \le 1) - P(Z \le -1) = 0.8413 - 0.1587 = 0.6826$. Therefore, the exact probability that Z falls within 1 standard deviation of the mean is 0.6826. Similarly, the exact probabilities that Z falls within 2 and 3 standard deviations of the mean are $P(-2 \le Z \le 2) = 0.9544$ and $P(-3 \le Z \le 3) = 0.9972$, respectively. These exact probabilities hold true for all normally distributed random variables.

EXAMPLE 6.5

An investment strategy has an expected return of 4% and a standard deviation of 6%. Assume that investment returns are normally distributed. Use the empirical rule to answer the following questions.

a. What is the probability of earning a return greater than 10%?

b. What is the probability of earning a return less than −8%?

SOLUTION: We use the empirical rule with $\mu = 4$ and $\sigma = 6$ to solve these questions.

a. A return of 10% is one standard deviation above the mean, or $10 = 4 + 6$. Since about 68% of observations fall within one standard deviation of the mean, 32% (100% − 68%) of the observations are outside the range. Using symmetry, we conclude that 16% (half of 32%) of the observations are greater than 10% (see Figure 6.18).

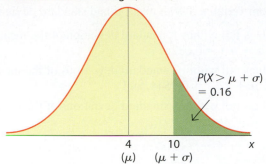

FIGURE 6.18 Finding $P(X > 10)$

$P(X > \mu + \sigma)$
$= 0.16$

4   10   x
(μ)   ($\mu + \sigma$)

b. A return of -8% is two standard deviations below the mean, or $-8 = 4 - (2 \times 6)$. Since about 95% of the observations fall within two standard deviations of the mean, only 2.5% (half of 5%) are below -8% (see Figure 6.19).

FIGURE 6.19 Finding $P(X < -8)$

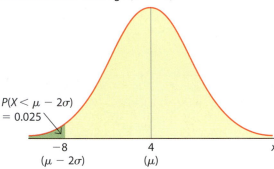

$P(X < \mu - 2\sigma)$
$= 0.025$

−8   4   x
($\mu - 2\sigma$)   (μ)

EXERCISES 6.2

Concepts

12. Find the following probabilities based on a standard normal variable Z.
    a. $P(Z > 1.32)$
    b. $P(Z \leq -1.32)$
    c. $P(1.32 \leq Z \leq 2.37)$
    d. $P(-1.32 \leq Z \leq 2.37)$

13. Find the following probabilities based on a standard normal variable Z.
    a. $P(Z > 0.74)$
    b. $P(Z \leq -1.92)$
    c. $P(0 \leq Z \leq 1.62)$
    d. $P(-0.90 \leq Z \leq 2.94)$

14. Find the following probabilities based on a standard normal variable Z.
    a. $P(-0.67 \leq Z \leq -0.23)$
    b. $P(0 \leq Z \leq 1.96)$
    c. $P(-1.28 \leq Z \leq 0)$
    d. $P(Z > 4.2)$

15. Find the following z values for the standard normal variable Z.
    a. $P(Z \leq z) = 0.9744$
    b. $P(Z > z) = 0.8389$
    c. $P(-z \leq Z \leq z) = 0.95$
    d. $P(0 \leq Z \leq z) = 0.3315$

16. Find the following z values for the standard normal variable Z.
    a. $P(Z \leq z) = 0.1020$
    b. $P(z \leq Z \leq 0) = 0.1772$
    c. $P(Z > z) = 0.9929$
    d. $P(0.40 \leq Z \leq z) = 0.3368$

Applications

17. The historical returns on a balanced portfolio have had an average return of 8% and a standard deviation of 12%. Assume that returns on this portfolio follow a normal distribution. Use the empirical rule to answer the following questions.
    a. What percentage of returns were greater than 20%?
    b. What percentage of returns were below −16%?

18. Assume that IQ scores follow a normal distribution with a mean of 100 and a standard deviation of 16. Use the empirical rule to answer the following questions.

    a. What percentage of people score between 84 and 116?

    b. What percentage of people score less than 68?

19. The average rent in a city is $1,500 per month with a standard deviation of $250. Assume rent follows the normal distribution. Use the empirical rule to answer the following questions.

    a. What percentage of rents are between $1,250 and $1,750?

    b. What percentage of rents are less than $1,250?

    c. What percentage of rents are greater than $2,000?

20. A professional basketball team averages 80 points per game with a standard deviation of 10 points. Assume points per game follow the normal distribution. Use the empirical rule to answer the following questions.

    a. What percentage of scores are between 60 and 100 points?

    b. What percentage of scores are more than 100 points? If there are 82 games in a regular season, in how many games will the team score more than 100 points?

6.3 Solving Problems with Normal Distributions

In the preceding section, we found probabilities for a standard normal distribution, which is a normal distribution with mean zero and standard deviation one. For other normal distributions, we found probabilities using the empirical rule. However, in many applications, the underlying distribution is not standard normal and the interval for computing a probability cannot be expressed within one, two, or three standard deviations of the mean. In this section we examine problems in these situations.

LO **6.5**

Calculate and interpret probabilities for a random variable that follows the normal distribution.

The Normal Transformation

The importance of the standard normal distribution arises from the fact that any normal random variable can be transformed into the standard normal random variable to derive the relevant probabilities. In other words, any normally distributed random variable X with mean μ and standard deviation σ can be transformed, or standardized, into the standard normal variable Z with mean zero and standard deviation one. We transform X into Z by subtracting from X its mean and dividing by its standard deviation.

> **THE NORMAL TRANSFORMATION: CONVERTING X INTO Z**
>
> Any normally distributed random variable X with mean μ and standard deviation σ can be transformed into the standard normal random variable Z as
>
> $$Z = \frac{X - \mu}{\sigma}.$$
>
> This normal transformation implies that any value x of X has a corresponding value z of Z given by
>
> $$z = \frac{x - \mu}{\sigma}.$$

By construction, $E(Z) = 0$ and $SD(Z) = 1$. As illustrated in Figure 6.20, if the x value is $x = \mu$, then the corresponding z value is $z = \frac{\mu - \mu}{\sigma} = 0$, implying that $E(Z) = 0$. Similarly for $x = \mu + \sigma$, $z = \frac{\mu + \sigma - \mu}{\sigma} = 1$, implying that $SD(Z) = 1$. Furthermore, any

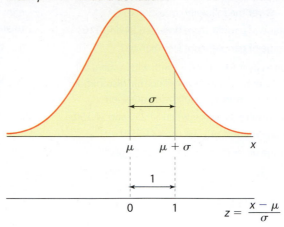

$$z = \frac{x - \mu}{\sigma}$$

z value has a simple interpretation. It specifies by how many standard deviations the corresponding *x* value falls above ($z > 0$) or below ($z < 0$) the mean μ. In particular:

- A positive *z* indicates by how many standard deviations the corresponding *x* lies above μ.
- A zero *z* indicates that the corresponding *x* equals μ.
- A negative *z* indicates by how many standard deviations the corresponding *x* lies below μ.

EXAMPLE 6.6

Scores on a management aptitude exam are normally distributed with a mean of 72 and a standard deviation of 8.

a. What is the probability that a randomly selected manager will score above 60?
b. What is the probability that a randomly selected manager will score between 68 and 84?

SOLUTION: Let *X* represent scores with $\mu = 72$ and $\sigma = 8$. We will use the normal transformation $z = \frac{x - \mu}{\sigma}$ to solve these problems.

a. The probability that a manager scores above 60 is $P(X > 60)$. Figure 6.21 shows the probability as the shaded area to the right of 60. We transform $x = 60$ into $z = \frac{60 - 72}{8} = -1.5$. Therefore, $P(X > 60) = P(Z > -1.5)$. Since $P(Z > -1.5) = 1 - P(Z \le -1.5)$, we look up -1.50 in the *z* table (left-hand side) to get this probability as $1 - 0.0668 = 0.9332$.

FIGURE 6.21 Finding $P(X > 60)$

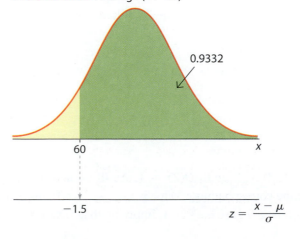

$$z = \frac{x - \mu}{\sigma}$$

b. Here, we find $P(68 \leq X \leq 84)$. The shaded area in Figure 6.22 shows this probability. We transform $x = 68$ into $z = \frac{68 - 72}{8} = -0.5$ and $x = 84$ into $z = \frac{84 - 72}{8} = 1.5$. Therefore, $P(68 \leq X \leq 84) = P(-0.5 \leq Z \leq 1.5)$. We compute this probability using the z table as $P(Z \leq 1.5) - P(Z < -0.5)$ $= 0.9332 - 0.3085 = 0.6247$.

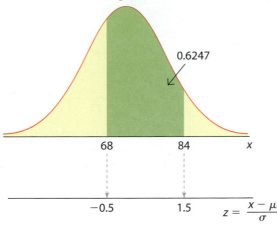

FIGURE 6.22 Finding $P(68 \leq X \leq 84)$

The Inverse Transformation

So far we have used the normal transformation to compute probabilities for given x values. We can use the inverse transformation, $x = \mu + z\sigma$, to compute x values for given probabilities.

THE INVERSE TRANSFORMATION: CONVERTING Z INTO X

A standard normal variable Z can be transformed to the normally distributed random variable X with mean μ and standard deviation σ as $X = \mu + Z\sigma$.

Therefore any value z of Z has a corresponding value x of X given by $x = \mu + z\sigma$.

EXAMPLE 6.7

Scores on a management aptitude examination are normally distributed with a mean of 72 and a standard deviation of 8.

a. What is the lowest score that will place a manager in the top 10% (90th percentile) of the distribution?

b. What is the highest score that will place a manager in the bottom 25% (25th percentile) of the distribution?

SOLUTION: Let X represent scores on a management aptitude examination with $\mu = 72$ and $\sigma = 8$. We will use the inverse transformation to solve these problems, where $x = \mu + z\sigma$.

a. The 90th percentile is a numerical value x such that $P(X < x) = 0.90$. We look up 0.90 (or the closest value to 0.90) in the z table (right-hand side) to get $z = 1.28$ and use the inverse transformation to find $x = 72 + 1.28 \times 8 = 82.24$. Therefore, a score of 82.24 or higher will place a manager in the top 10% of the distribution (see Figure 6.23).

FIGURE 6.23 Finding *x* given $P(X < x) = 0.90$

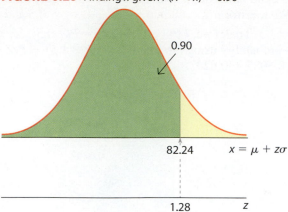

0.90

82.24 $x = \mu + z\sigma$

1.28   *z*

b. We find *x* such that $P(X < x) = 0.25$. Using the *z* table (left-hand side), we find the corresponding *z* value that satisfies $P(Z < z) = 0.25$ as -0.67. We then solve $x = 72 - 0.67 \times 8 = 66.64$. Therefore, a score of 66.64 or lower will place a manager in the bottom 25% of the distribution. (see Figure 6.24).

FIGURE 6.24 Finding *x* given $P(X < x) = 0.25$

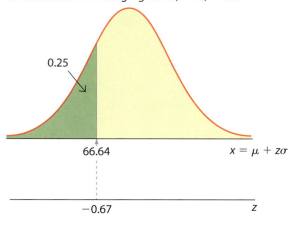

0.25

66.64 $x = \mu + z\sigma$

-0.67 *z*

EXAMPLE 6.8

We can now answer the questions first posed by Akiko Hamaguchi in the introductory case of this chapter. Recall that Akiko is concerned about buying the right amount of salmon for daily consumption at Little Ginza. Akiko has estimated that the daily consumption of salmon is normally distributed with a mean of 12 pounds and a standard deviation of 3.2 pounds. She wants to answer the following questions:

a. What proportion of days was the demand at Little Ginza above her earlier purchase of 20 pounds?

b. What proportion of days was the demand at Little Ginza below 15 pounds?

c. How much salmon should she buy so that it meets customer demand on 90% of the days?

SOLUTION: Let *X* denote consumer demand for salmon at the restaurant. We know that *X* is normally distributed with $\mu = 12$ and $\sigma = 3.2$.

a. $P(X > 20) = P\left(Z > \dfrac{20 - 12}{3.2}\right) = P(Z > 2.50) = 1 - 0.9938 = 0.0062.$

b. $P(X < 15) = P\left(Z < \dfrac{15 - 12}{3.2}\right) = P(Z < 0.94) = 0.8264.$

c. In order to compute the required amount of salmon, we solve for x in $P(X \leq x) = 0.90$. Since $P(X \leq x) = 0.90$ is equivalent to $P(Z \leq z) = 0.90$, we first derive $z = 1.28$. Given $x = \mu + z\sigma$, we find $x = 12 + 1.28(3.2) = 16.10$. Therefore, Akiko should buy 16.10 pounds of salmon daily to ensure that customer demand is met on 90% of the days.

SYNOPSIS OF INTRODUCTORY CASE

Akiko Hamaguchi is a manager at a small sushi restaurant called Little Ginza in Phoenix, Arizona. She is aware of the importance of purchasing the right amount of salmon daily. While purchasing too much salmon results in wastage, purchasing too little can disappoint customers who may choose not to frequent the restaurant in the future. In the past, she has always bought 20 pounds of salmon daily. A careful analysis of her purchasing habits and customer demand reveals that Akiko is buying too much salmon. The probability that the demand for salmon would exceed 20 pounds is very small at 0.0062. Even a purchase of 15 pounds satisfies customer demand on 82.64% of the days. In order to execute her new strategy of meeting daily demand of customers on 90% of the days, Akiko should purchase approximately 16 pounds of salmon daily.

Using Excel for the Normal Distribution

In order to illustrate the use of Excel for calculating normal probabilities, we revisit Example 6.8. We know that the daily consumption of salmon at Little Ginza is normally distributed with a mean of 12 pounds and a standard deviation of 3.2 pounds. We first solve Example 6.8a. Assuming that X denotes consumer demand for salmon at Little Ginza, we need to find $P(X > 20)$. When the goal is to calculate a probability using the normal distribution, we select **Formulas > Insert Function > NORM.DIST** from Excel's menu. In the dialog box shown in Figure 6.25, we supply four arguments:

- **X** is the value for which you want to find the cumulative probability. We enter 20.

- **Mean** is the mean of the distribution. We enter 12.

FIGURE 6.25 Using Excel to compute a normal cumulative probability for a given x

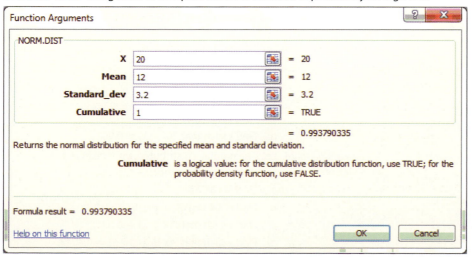

- **Standard_dev** is the standard deviation of the distribution. We enter 3.2.
- **Cumulative** is a logical value. When we enter the value 1 or TRUE, Excel returns a cumulative probability.

Excel returns a cumulative probability, or in this case $P(X \le 20) = 0.9938$. Since we want $P(X > 20)$, we compute $1 - 0.9938 = 0.0062$.

In order to compute the required amount of salmon that is needed to satisfy demand on 90% of the days (Example 6.8c), we select **Formulas** > **Insert Function** > **NORM.INV** from Excel's menu. In the dialog box shown in Figure 6.26, we supply three arguments in the **NORM.INV** dialog box:

- **Probability** is a cumulative probability associated with the normal distribution. We enter 0.90.
- **Mean** is the mean of the distribution. We enter 12.
- **Standard_dev** is the standard deviation of the distribution. We enter 3.2.

FIGURE 6.26 Using Excel to compute x for a given normal cumulative probability

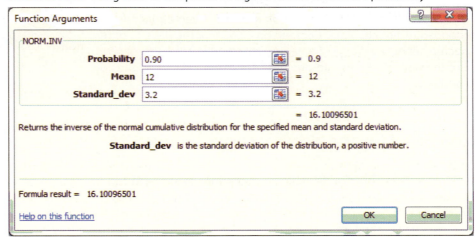

Excel returns the value 16.10. In other words, 16.10 pounds of salmon are needed to meet customer demand on 90% of the days.

EXERCISES 6.3

Concepts

21. Let X be normally distributed with mean $\mu = 10$ and standard deviation $\sigma = 6$.
    a. Find $P(X \le 0)$.
    b. Find $P(X > 2)$.
    c. Find $P(4 \le X \le 10)$.
    d. Find $P(6 \le X \le 14)$.

22. Let X be normally distributed with mean $\mu = 10$ and standard deviation $\sigma = 4$.
    a. Find $P(X \le 0)$.
    b. Find $P(X > 2)$.
    c. Find $P(4 \le X \le 10)$.
    d. Find $P(6 \le X \le 14)$.

23. Let X be normally distributed with mean $\mu = 120$ and standard deviation $\sigma = 20$.
    a. Find $P(X \le 86)$.
    b. Find $P(80 \le X \le 100)$.
    c. Find x such that $P(X \le x) = 0.40$.
    d. Find x such that $P(X > x) = 0.90$.

24. Let X be normally distributed with mean $\mu = 2.5$ and standard deviation $\sigma = 2$.
    a. Find $P(X > 7.6)$.
    b. Find $P(7.4 \le X \le 10.6)$.
    c. Find x such that $P(X > x) = 0.025$.
    d. Find x such that $P(x \le X \le 2.5) = 0.4943$.

25. Let X be normally distributed with mean $\mu = 2500$ and standard deviation $\sigma = 800$.
   a. Find x such that $P(X \le x) = 0.9382$.
   b. Find x such that $P(X > x) = 0.025$.
   c. Find x such that $P(2500 \le X \le x) = 0.1217$.
   d. Find x such that $P(X \le x) = 0.4840$.

26. The random variable X is normally distributed. Also, it is known that $P(X > 150) = 0.10$.
   a. Find the population mean μ if the population standard deviation $\sigma = 15$.
   b. Find the population mean μ if the population standard deviation $\sigma = 25$.
   c. Find the population standard deviation σ if the population mean $\mu = 136$.
   d. Find the population standard deviation σ if the population mean $\mu = 128$.

Applications

27. The average high-school teacher annual salary is $43,000 (Payscale.com, August 20, 2010). Let teacher salary be normally distributed with a standard deviation of $18,000.
   a. What percent of high school teachers make between $40,000 and $50,000?
   b. What percent of high school teachers make more than $80,000?

28. Americans are increasingly skimping on their sleep (National Geographic News, February 24, 2005). A health expert believes that American adults sleep an average of 6.2 hours on weekdays with a standard deviation of 1.2 hours. To answer the following questions, assume that sleep time on weekdays is normally distributed.
   a. What percent of American adults sleep more than 8 hours on weekdays?
   b. What percent of American adults sleep less than 6 hours on weekdays?
   c. What percent of American adults sleep between 6 to 8 hours on weekdays?

29. The weight of turkeys is normally distributed with a mean of 22 pounds and a standard deviation of 5 pounds.
   a. Find the probability that a randomly selected turkey weighs between 20 and 26 pounds.
   b. Find the probability that a randomly selected turkey weighs below 12 pounds.

30. According to the Bureau of Labor Statistics, it takes an average of 22 weeks for someone over 55 to find a new job, compared with 16 weeks for younger workers (The Wall Street Journal, September 2, 2008). Assume that the probability distributions are normal and that the standard deviation is 2 weeks for both distributions.
   a. What is the probability that it takes a worker over the age of 55 more than 19 weeks to find a job?
   b. What is the probability that it takes a younger worker more than 19 weeks to find a job?
   c. What is the probability that it takes a worker over the age of 55 between 23 and 25 weeks to find a job?
   d. What is the probability that it takes a younger worker between 23 and 25 weeks to find a job?

31. Loans that are 60 days or more past due are considered seriously delinquent. The Mortgage Bankers Association reported that the rate of seriously delinquent loans has an average of 9.1% (The Wall Street Journal, August 26, 2010). Let the rate of seriously delinquent loans follow a normal distribution with a standard deviation of 0.80%.
   a. What is the probability that the proportion of seriously delinquent loans is above 8%?
   b. What is the probability that the proportion of seriously delinquent loans is between 9.5% and 10.5%?

32. The time required to assemble an electronic component is normally distributed with a mean and standard deviation of 16 minutes and 8 minutes, respectively.
   a. Find the probability that a randomly picked assembly takes between 10 and 20 minutes.
   b. It is unusual for the assembly time to be above 24 minutes or below 6 minutes. What proportion of assembly times fall in these unusual categories?

33. Recent research suggests that Americans make an average of 10 phone calls per day (CNN, August 26, 2010). Let the number of calls be normally distributed with a standard deviation of 3 calls.
   a. What is the probability that an average American makes between 4 and 12 calls per day?
   b. What is the probability that an average American makes more than 6 calls per day?
   c. What is the probability that an average American makes more than 16 calls per day?

34. The manager of a night club in Boston stated that 95% of the customers are between the ages of 22 and 28 years. If the age of customers is normally distributed with a mean of 25 years, calculate its standard deviation.

35. An estimated 1.8 million students take on student loans to pay ever-rising tuition and room and board (New York Times, April 17, 2009). It is also known that the average cumulative debt of recent college graduates is about $22,500. Let the cumulative debt among recent college graduates be normally distributed with a standard deviation of $7,000. Approximately how many recent college graduates have accumulated a student loan of more than $30,000?

36. Scores on a marketing exam are known to be normally distributed with mean and standard deviation of 60 and 20, respectively.
   a. Find the probability that a randomly selected student scores between 50 and 80.
   b. Find the probability that a randomly selected student scores between 20 and 40.
   c. The syllabus suggests that the top 15% of the students will get an A in the course. What is the minimum score required to get an A?
   d. What is the passing score if 10% of the students will fail the course?

37. Average talk time between charges of a cell phone is advertised as 4 hours. Assume that talk time is normally distributed with a standard deviation of 0.8 hour.

    a. Find the probability that talk time between charges for a randomly selected cell phone is below 3.5 hours.

    b. Find the probability that talk time between charges for a randomly selected cell phone is either more than 4.5 hours or below 3.5 hours.

    c. Twenty-five percent of the time, talk time between charges is below the 1st quartile value. What is this value?

38. A young investment manager tells his client that the probability of making a positive return with his suggested portfolio is 90%. What is the risk (standard deviation) that this investment manager has assumed in his calculation if it is known that returns are normally distributed with a mean of 5.6%?

39. A construction company in Naples, Florida, is struggling to sell condominiums. In order to attract buyers, the company has made numerous price reductions and better financing offers. Although condominiums were once listed for $300,000, the company believes that it will be able to get an average sale price of $210,000. Let the price of these condominiums in the next quarter be normally distributed with a standard deviation of $15,000.

    a. What is the probability that the condominium will sell at a price (i) below $200,000?, (ii) above $240,000?

    b. The company is also trying to sell an artist's condo. Potential buyers will find the unusual features of this condo either pleasing or objectionable. The manager expects the average sale price of this condo to be the same as others at $210,000, but with a higher standard deviation of $20,000. What is the probability that this condo will sell at a price (i) below $200,000?, (ii) above $240,000?

40. You are considering the risk-return profile of two mutual funds for investment. The relatively risky fund promises an expected return of 8% with a standard deviation of 14%. The relatively less risky fund promises an expected return and standard deviation of 4% and 5%, respectively. Assume that the returns are approximately normally distributed.

    a. Which mutual fund will you pick if your objective is to minimize the probability of earning a negative return?

    b. Which mutual fund will you pick if your objective is to maximize the probability of earning a return above 8%?

6.4 Other Continuous Probability Distributions

As discussed earlier, the normal distribution is the most extensively used probability distribution in statistical work. One reason that this occurs is because the normal distribution accurately describes numerous random variables of interest. However, there are applications where other continuous distributions are more appropriate.

LO 6.6

Calculate and interpret probabilities for a random variable that follows the exponential distribution.

The Exponential Distribution

A useful nonsymmetric continuous probability distribution is the **exponential distribution**. The exponential distribution is related to the Poisson distribution, even though the Poisson distribution deals with discrete random variables. Recall from Chapter 5 that the Poisson random variable counts the number of occurrences of an event over a given interval of time or space. For instance, the Poisson distribution is used to calculate the likelihood of a specified number of cars arriving at a McDonald's drive-thru over a particular time period or the likelihood of a specified number of defects in a 50-yard roll of fabric. Sometimes we are less interested in the *number* of occurrences over a given interval of time or space, but rather in the time that has elapsed or space encountered *between* such occurrences. For instance, we might be interested in the length of time that elapses between car arrivals at the McDonald's drive-thru or the distance between defects in a 50-yard roll of fabric. We use the exponential distribution for describing these times or distances.

    The exponential distribution is also used in modeling lifetimes or failure times. For example, an electric bulb with a rated life of 1,000 hours is expected to fail after about 1,000 hours of use. However, the bulb may burn out either before or after 1,000 hours. Thus, the lifetime of an electric bulb is a random variable with an expected value of 1,000. A noted feature of the exponential distribution is that it is "memoryless," thus implying a constant failure rate. In the electric bulb example, it implies that the probability that the bulb will burn out on a given day is independent of whether the bulb has already been used for 10, 100, or 1,000 hours. The exponential random variable is nonnegative and is bounded from below by 0.

> ### THE EXPONENTIAL DISTRIBUTION
>
> A random variable X follows the **exponential distribution** if its probability density function is
>
> $$f(x) = \lambda e^{-\lambda x} \quad \text{for } x \geq 0,$$
>
> where λ is a rate parameter and $e \approx 2.718$ is the base of the natural logarithm.
>
> The mean and the standard deviation of X are equal: $E(X) = SD(X) = \frac{1}{\lambda}$. The **cumulative distribution function** of X is
>
> $$P(X \leq x) = 1 - e^{-\lambda x}.$$

The exponential distribution is based entirely on one parameter, $\lambda > 0$ (λ is the Greek letter lambda), which is often called the *rate parameter*. The graphs in Figure 6.27 show the shapes of the exponential distribution based on various values of λ.

FIGURE 6.27 Exponential probability density function for various values of λ

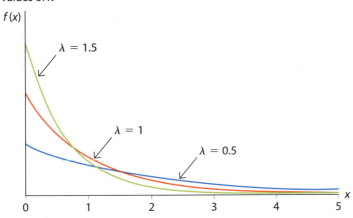

EXAMPLE 6.9

Let the time between e-mail messages during work hours be exponentially distributed with a mean of 25 minutes.

a. Calculate the rate parameter λ.

b. What is the probability that you do not get an e-mail for more than one hour?

c. What is the probability that you get an e-mail within 10 minutes?

SOLUTION:

a. Since the mean $E(X)$ equals $\frac{1}{\lambda}$, we compute $\lambda = \frac{1}{E(X)} = \frac{1}{25} = 0.04$.

b. The probability that you do not get an e-mail for more than an hour is $P(X > 60)$. Since $P(X \leq x) = 1 - e^{-\lambda x}$, we have $P(X > x) = 1 - P(X \leq x) = e^{-\lambda x}$. Therefore, $P(X > 60) = e^{-0.04(60)} = e^{-2.40} = 0.0907$. The probability of not getting an e-mail for more than one hour is 0.0907.

c. Here, $P(X \leq 10) = 1 - e^{-0.04(10)} = 1 - e^{-0.40} = 1 - 0.6703 = 0.3297$. The probability of getting an e-mail within 10 minutes is 0.3297.

Using Excel for the Exponential Distribution

Let's revisit the problem in Example 6.9b to illustrate how to use Excel for exponential distribution calculations. We already computed the rate parameter as $\lambda = \frac{1}{E(X)} = \frac{1}{25} = 0.04$. In order to calculate $P(X > 60)$, we select **Formulas > Insert Function > EXPON.DIST** from Excel's menu. In the EXPON.DIST dialog box (see Figure 6.28), we supply three arguments:

- **X** is the nonnegative value for which you want to find the cumulative probability. We enter 60.
- **Lambda** λ is the parameter value, a positive number. We enter 0.04.
- **Cumulative** is a logical value. When we enter the value 1 or TRUE, Excel returns a cumulative probability.

FIGURE 6.28 Using Excel to compute an exponential cumulative probability for a given x

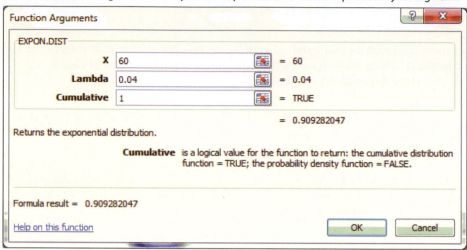

Excel's formula result indicates that $P(X \leq 60) = 0.9093$. Thus, $P(X > 60) = 1 - 0.9093 = 0.0907$.

The Lognormal Distribution

LO **6.7**

Calculate and interpret probabilities for a random variable that follows the lognormal distribution.

The **lognormal distribution** is defined with reference to the normal distribution. However, unlike the normal distribution, the lognormal distribution is defined for a positive random variable and it is also positively skewed. Thus, it is useful for describing variables such as income, real estate values, and asset prices. Unlike the exponential distribution whose failure rate is constant, the failure rate of the lognormal distribution may increase or decrease over time. This flexibility has led to broad applications of the lognormal distribution ranging from modeling the failure time of new equipment to the lifetime of cancer patients. For instance, in the break-in period of new equipment, the failure rate is high. However, if it survives this initial period, the subsequent failure rate is greatly reduced. The same is true for cancer survivors.

A random variable Y is lognormal if its natural logarithm $X = \ln(Y)$ is normally distributed. Alternatively, if X is a normal random variable, the lognormal variable is defined as $Y = e^X$.

THE LOGNORMAL DISTRIBUTION

Let X be a normally distributed random variable with mean μ and standard deviation σ. The random variable $Y = e^X$ follows the **lognormal distribution** with a probability density function as

$$f(y) = \frac{1}{y\sigma\sqrt{2\pi}}\exp\left(-\frac{(\ln(y) - \mu)^2}{2\sigma^2}\right) \quad \text{for } y > 0,$$

where π equals approximately 3.14159, $\exp(x) = e^x$ is the exponential function, and $e \approx 2.718$ is the base of the natural logarithm.

The graphs in Figure 6.29 show the shapes of the lognormal density function based on various values of σ. The lognormal distribution is clearly positively skewed for $\sigma > 1$. For $\sigma < 1$, the lognormal distribution somewhat resembles the normal distribution.

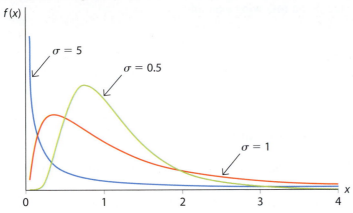

FIGURE 6.29 Lognormal probability density function for various values of σ along with $\mu = 0$

The mean and the variance of the lognormal random variable Y are related to the mean and the standard deviation of the corresponding normal random variable X.

EXPECTED VALUES AND STANDARD DEVIATIONS OF THE LOGNORMAL AND NORMAL DISTRIBUTIONS

Let X be a normal random variable with mean μ and standard deviation σ and let $Y = e^X$ be the corresponding lognormal variable. The mean μ_Y and standard deviation σ_Y of Y are derived as

$$\mu_Y = \exp\left(\frac{2\mu + \sigma^2}{2}\right) \quad \text{and} \quad \sigma_Y = \sqrt{(\exp(\sigma^2) - 1)\exp(2\mu + \sigma^2)}.$$

Equivalently, the mean and standard deviation of the normal variable $X = \ln(Y)$ are derived as

$$\mu = \ln\left(\frac{\mu_Y^2}{\sqrt{\mu_Y^2 + \sigma_Y^2}}\right) \quad \text{and} \quad \sigma = \sqrt{\ln\left(1 + \frac{\sigma_Y^2}{\mu_Y^2}\right)}.$$

EXAMPLE 6.10

Compute the mean and standard deviation of a lognormal random variable if the mean and the standard deviation of the underlying normal random variable are as follows:

a. $\mu = 0, \sigma = 1$

b. $\mu = 2, \sigma = 1$

c. $\mu = 2, \sigma = 1.5$

SOLUTION: Since X is normal, $Y = e^X$ is lognormal with mean $\mu_Y = \exp\left(\frac{2\mu + \sigma^2}{2}\right)$ and standard deviation $\sigma_Y = \sqrt{(\exp(\sigma^2) - 1)\exp(2\mu + \sigma^2)}$.

a. We compute $\mu_Y = \exp\left(\frac{0 + 1^2}{2}\right) = 1.65$ and $\sigma_Y = \sqrt{(\exp(1^2) - 1)\exp(0 + 1^2)} = 2.16$.

b. Here $\mu_Y = \exp\left(\frac{4 + 1^2}{2}\right) = 12.18$ and $\sigma_Y = \sqrt{(\exp(1^2) - 1)\exp(4 + 1^2)} = 15.97$.

c. Here $\mu_Y = \exp\left(\frac{4 + 1.5^2}{2}\right) = 22.76$ and $\sigma_Y = \sqrt{(\exp(1.5^2) - 1)\exp(4 + 1.5^2)} = 66.31$.

The popularity of the lognormal distribution is also due to the fact that the probabilities of a lognormal random variable are easily evaluated by reference to the normal distribution. This is illustrated in the following example.

EXAMPLE 6.11

Let $Y = e^X$ where X is normally distributed with mean $\mu = 5$ and standard deviation $\sigma = 1.2$.

a. Find $P(Y \leq 200)$.

b. Find the 90th percentile of Y.

SOLUTION: We solve these problems by first converting them into the corresponding normal distribution problems.

a. Note that $P(Y \leq 200) = P(\ln(Y) \leq \ln(200)) = P(X \leq 5.30)$. We transform $x = 5.30$ in the usual way to get $z = \frac{5.30 - 5}{1.2} = 0.25$. From the z table, we get $P(Z \leq 0.25) = 0.5987$. Therefore, $P(Y \leq 200) = P(X \leq 5.30) = P(Z \leq 0.25) = 0.5987$.

b. The 90th percentile is a value y such that $P(Y < y) = 0.90$. We first note that $P(Y < y) = 0.90$ is equivalent to $P(\ln(Y) < \ln(y)) = P(X < x) = 0.90$ where $x = \ln(y)$. We look up the cumulative probability of 0.90 in the z table to get $z = 1.28$. We use the inverse transformation to derive $x = \mu + z\sigma = 5 + 1.28(1.2) = 6.54$. Finally, we compute $y = e^x = e^{6.54} = 692.29$. Therefore, the 90th percentile of the distribution is 692.29.

Using Excel for the Lognormal Distribution

Let's first revisit Example 6.11a to illustrate the use of Excel with lognormal distributions. In particular, recall that we let $Y = e^X$ where X is normally distributed with mean $\mu = 5$ and standard deviation $\sigma = 1.2$. In order to evaluate $P(Y \leq 200)$, we select **Formulas > Insert Function > LOGNORM.DIST** from Excel's menu. In the LOGNORM.DIST dialog box (see Figure 6.30), we supply four arguments:

- **X** is the nonnegative value for which you want to find the cumulative probability. We enter 200.

- **Mean** is the mean of the normal distribution. We enter 5.

FIGURE 6.30 Using Excel to compute a lognormal cumulative probability for a given x

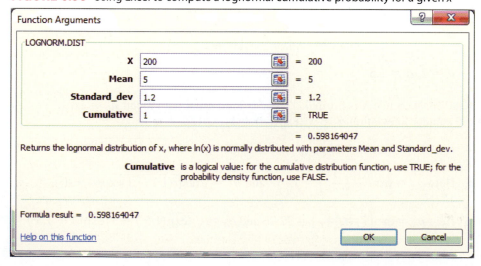

- **Standard_dev** is the standard deviation of the normal distribution. We enter 1.2.
- **Cumulative** is a logical value. When we enter the value 1 or TRUE, Excel returns a cumulative probability.

Thus, $P(Y \le 200) = 0.5982$. Note that the earlier calculations were slightly off due to rounding.

In order to find the 90th percentile of Y using Excel (Exercise 6.11b), we select **Formulas > Insert Function > LOGNORM.INV** from Excel's menu. In the LOGNORM.INV dialog box, we supply three arguments (see Figure 6.31):

- **Probability** is a cumulative probability associated with the normal distribution. We enter 0.90.
- **Mean** is the mean of the normal distribution. We enter 5.
- **Standard_dev** is the standard deviation of the normal distribution. We enter 1.2.

FIGURE 6.31 Using Excel to compute y for a given lognormal cumulative probability

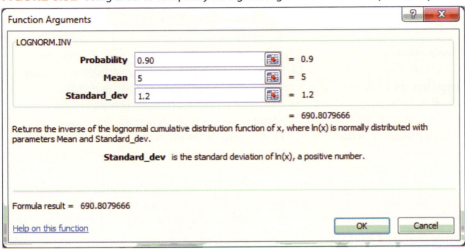

Thus, the 90th percentile is 690.81. Again, the earlier calculations were slightly off due to rounding.

EXERCISES 6.4

Concepts

41. A random variable X is exponentially distributed with a mean of 0.1.
    a. What is the rate parameter λ? What is the standard deviation of X?
    b. Compute $P(X > 0.20)$.
    c. Compute $P(0.10 \le X \le 0.20)$.

42. A random variable X is exponentially distributed with an expected value of 25.
    a. What is the rate parameter λ? What is the standard deviation of X?
    b. Compute $P(20 \le X \le 30)$.
    c. Compute $P(15 \le X \le 35)$.

43. A random variable X is exponentially distributed with a probability density function of $f(x) = 5e^{-5x}$. Calculate the mean and the standard deviation of X.

44. Compute the mean and the variance of a lognormal variable $Y = e^X$ where X is normally distributed with the following mean and variance:
    a. $\mu = 3, \sigma^2 = 2$
    b. $\mu = 5, \sigma^2 = 2$
    c. $\mu = 5, \sigma^2 = 3$

45. Let $Y = e^X$, where X is normally distributed. Compute the mean and the variance of X given the following information.
    a. $\mu_Y = 14, \sigma_Y^2 = 22$
    b. $\mu_Y = 20, \sigma_Y^2 = 22$
    c. $\mu_Y = 20, \sigma_Y^2 = 120$

46. Let $Y = e^X$ where X is normally distributed with $\mu = 1.8$ and $\sigma = 0.80$. Compute the following values.
    a. $P(Y \le 7.5)$
    b. $P(8 < Y < 9)$
    c. The 90th percentile of Y

47. Let Y have the lognormal distribution with mean 82.8 and variance 156.25. Compute the following probabilities.
a. $P(Y > 100)$
b. $P(80 < Y < 100)$

Applications

48. Customers make purchases at a convenience store, on average, every six minutes. It is fair to assume that the time between customer purchases is exponentially distributed. Jack operates the cash register at this store.
a. What is the rate parameter λ? What is the standard deviation of this distribution?
b. Jack wants to take a five-minute break. He believes that if he goes right after he has serviced a customer, he will lower the probability of someone showing up during his five-minute break. Is he right in this belief?
c. What is the probability that a customer will show up in less than five minutes?
d. What is the probability that nobody shows up for over half an hour?

49. When crossing the Golden Gate Bridge, traveling into San Francisco, all drivers must pay a toll. Suppose the amount of time drivers wait in line to pay the toll follows an exponential distribution with a probability density function of $f(x) = 0.2e^{-2x}$.
a. What is the mean waiting time that drivers face when entering San Francisco via the Golden Gate Bridge?
b. What is the probability that a driver spends more than the average time to pay the toll?
c. What is the probability that a driver spends more than 10 minutes to pay the toll?
d. What is the probability that a driver spends between 4 and 6 minutes to pay the toll?

50. The Bahamas is a tropical paradise made up of 700 islands sprinkled over 100,000 square miles of the Atlantic Ocean. According to the figures released by the government of the Bahamas, the mean household income in the Bahamas is $39,626 and the median income is $33,600. A demographer decides to use the lognormal random variable to model this nonsymmetric income distribution. Let Y represent household income, where for a normally distributed X, $Y = e^X$. Further, suppose the standard deviation of household income is $10,000. Use this information to answer the following questions.
a. Compute the mean and the standard deviation of X.
b. What proportion of the people in the Bahamas have household income above the mean?
c. What proportion of the people in the Bahamas have household income below $20,000?
d. Compute the 75th percentile of the income distribution in the Bahamas.

51. It is well documented that a typical washing machine can last anywhere between 5 to 12 years. Let the life of a washing machine be represented by a lognormal variable, $Y = e^X$ where X is normally distributed. Furthermore, let the mean and standard deviation of the life of a washing machine be 8 years and 4 years, respectively.
a. Compute the mean and the standard deviation of X.
b. What proportion of the washing machines will last for more than 10 years?
c. What proportion of the washing machines will last for less than 6 years?
d. Compute the 90th percentile of the life of the washing machines.

WRITING WITH STATISTICS

Professor Lang is a professor of Economics at Salem State University. She has been teaching a course in Principles of Economics for over 25 years. Professor Lang has never graded on a curve since she believes that relative grading may unduly penalize (benefit) a good (poor) student in an unusually strong (weak) class. She always uses an absolute scale for making grades, as shown in the two left columns of Table 6.4.

TABLE 6.4 Grading Scales with Absolute Grading versus Relative Grading

Absolute Grading		Relative Grading	
Grade	Score	Grade	Probability
A	92 and above	A	0.10
B	78 up to 92	B	0.35
C	64 up to 78	C	0.40
D	58 up to 64	D	0.10
F	Below 58	F	0.05

A colleague of Professor Lang's has convinced her to move to relative grading, since it corrects for unanticipated problems. Professor Lang decides to experiment with grading based on the relative scale as shown in the two right columns of Table 6.4. Using this relative grading scheme, the top 10% of students will get As, the next 35% Bs, and so on. Based on her years of teaching experience, Professor Lang believes that the scores in her course follow a normal distribution with a mean of 78.6 and a standard deviation of 12.4.

Professor Lang wants to use the above information to:

1. Calculate probabilities based on the absolute scale. Compare these probabilities to the relative scale.

2. Calculate the range of scores for various grades based on the relative scale. Compare these ranges to the absolute scale.

3. Determine which grading scale makes it harder to get higher grades.

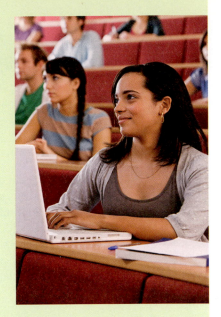

Many teachers would confess that grading is one of the most difficult tasks of their profession. Two common grading systems used in higher education are relative and absolute. Relative grading systems are norm referenced or curve based, in which a grade is based on the student's relative position in class. Absolute grading systems, on the other hand, are criterion referenced, in which a grade is related to the student's absolute performance in class. In short, with absolute grading, the student's score is compared to a predetermined scale whereas with relative grading, the score is compared to the scores of other students in the class.

Let X represent the grade in Professor Lang's class, which is normally distributed with a mean of 78.6 and a standard deviation of 12.4. This information is used to derive the grade probabilities based on the absolute scale. For instance, the probability of receiving an A is derived as $P(X \geq 92) = P(Z \geq 1.08) = 0.14$. Other probabilities, derived similarly, are presented in Table 6.A.

TABLE 6.A Probabilities Based on Absolute Scale and Relative Scale

Grade	Probability Based on Absolute Scale	Probability Based on Relative Scale
A	0.14	0.10
B	0.38	0.35
C	0.36	0.40
D	0.07	0.10
F	0.05	0.05

The second column of Table 6.A shows that 14% of students are expected to receive As, 38% Bs, and so on. Although these numbers are generally consistent with the suggested relative scale shown in the third column of Table 6.A, it appears that the suggested relative scale makes it harder for students to get higher grades. For instance, 14% get As with the absolute scale compared to only 10% with the suggested relative scale.

Alternatively, we can compare the two grading methods on the basis of the range of scores for various grades. The second column of Table 6.B restates the range of scores based on absolute grading. In order to obtain the range of scores based on relative grading, it is once again necessary to apply concepts from the normal distribution. For instance, the minimum score required to earn an A with relative grading is derived by solving for x in $P(X \geq x) = 0.10$. Since $P(X \geq x) = 0.10$ is equivalent to $P(Z \geq z) = 0.10$, it follows that $z = 1.28$. Inserting the proper values of the mean, the standard deviation, and z into $x = \mu + z\sigma$ yields a value of x equal to 94.47. Ranges for other grades, derived similarly, are presented in the third column of Table 6.B.

TABLE 6.B Range of Scores with Absolute Grading versus Relative Grading

Grade	Range of Scores Based on Absolute Grading	Range of Scores Based on Relative Grading
A	92 and above	94.47 and above
B	78 up to 92	80.21 up to 94.47
C	64 up to 78	65.70 up to 80.21
D	58 up to 64	58.20 up to 65.70
F	Below 58	Below 58.20

Once again comparing the results in Table 6.B, the use of the relative scale makes it harder for students to get higher grades in Professor Lang's courses. For instance, in order to receive an A with relative grading, a student must have a score of at least 94.47 versus a score of at least 92 with absolute grading. Both absolute and relative grading methods have their merits and teachers often make the decision on the basis of their teaching philosophy. However, if Professor Lang wants to keep the grades consistent with her earlier absolute scale, she should base her relative scale on the probabilities computed in the second column of Table 6.A.

Conceptual Review

LO 6.1   Describe a continuous random variable.

A **continuous random variable** is characterized by (infinitely) uncountable values and can take on any value within an interval. The probability that a continuous random variable X assumes a particular value x is zero, that is, $P(X = x) = 0$. Thus, for a continuous random variable, we calculate the probability within a specified interval. Moreover, the following equalities hold: $P(a \leq X \leq b) = P(a < X < b) = P(a \leq X < b) = P(a < X \leq b)$.

The **probability density function** $f(x)$ of a continuous random variable X describes the relative likelihood that X assumes a value within a given interval. The probability $P(a \leq X \leq b)$ is the area under $f(x)$ between points a and b.

For any value x of the random variable X, the **cumulative distribution function** $F(x)$ is defined as $F(x) = P(X \leq x)$.

LO 6.2   Describe a continuous uniform distribution and calculate associated probabilities.

The **continuous uniform distribution** describes a random variable that has an equally likely chance of assuming a value within a specified range. The probability is essentially the area of a rectangle, which is the base times the height, or the length of a specified interval times the probability density function $f(x) = \dfrac{1}{b - a}$, where a and b are the lower and upper bounds of the interval, respectively.

LO 6.3   Explain the characteristics of the normal distribution.

The **normal distribution** is the most extensively used continuous probability distribution and is the cornerstone of statistical inference. It is the familiar bell-shaped distribution, which is symmetric around the mean with one side of the mean being just the mirror image of the other side. The normal distribution is completely described by two parameters: the population mean μ and the population variance σ^2.

A **standard normal distribution,** also referred to as the z **distribution**, is a special case of the normal distribution, with mean zero and standard deviation (or variance) one.

LO 6.4 | Use the standard normal table or the z table.

The **standard normal table** or the **z table** provides **cumulative probabilities** $P(Z \le z)$; this table appears on two pages in Table 1 of Appendix A. The left-hand page provides cumulative probabilities for z values less than or equal to zero. The right-hand page shows cumulative probabilities for z values greater than or equal to zero. We also use the table to compute z values for given cumulative probabilities.

LO 6.5 | Calculate and interpret probabilities for a random variable that follows the normal distribution.

Any normally distributed random variable X with mean μ and standard deviation σ can be transformed into the standard normal random variable Z as $Z = \frac{X - \mu}{\sigma}$. This normal transformation implies that any value x of X has a corresponding value z of Z given by $z = \frac{x - \mu}{\sigma}$.

A standard normal variable Z can be transformed to the normally distributed random variable X with mean μ and standard deviation σ as $X = \mu + Z\sigma$. This inverse transformation implies that any value z of Z has a corresponding value x of X given by $x = \mu + z\sigma$.

LO 6.6 | Calculate and interpret probabilities for a random variable that follows the exponential distribution.

A useful nonsymmetric continuous probability distribution is the **exponential distribution**. A random variable X follows the exponential distribution if its probability density function is $f(x) = \lambda e^{-\lambda x}$ for $x \ge 0$, where λ is a rate parameter and $e \approx 2.718$ is the base of the natural logarithm. The mean and the standard deviation of the distribution are both equal to $\frac{1}{\lambda}$. For a given λ, the **cumulative probabilities** are computed as $P(X \le x) = 1 - e^{-\lambda x}$.

LO 6.7 | Calculate and interpret probabilities for a random variable that follows the lognormal distribution.

The **lognormal distribution** is another useful positively skewed distribution. Let X be a normal random variable with mean μ and variance σ^2 and let $Y = e^X$ be the corresponding lognormal variable. The mean μ_Y and standard deviation σ_Y of Y are derived as $\mu_Y = \exp\left(\frac{2\mu + \sigma^2}{2}\right)$ and $\sigma_Y = \sqrt{(\exp(\sigma^2) - 1)\exp(2\mu + \sigma^2)}$, respectively. Equivalently, the mean and standard deviation of the normal variable $X = \ln(Y)$ are derived as $\mu = \ln\left(\frac{\mu_Y^2}{\sqrt{\mu_Y^2 + \sigma_Y^2}}\right)$ and $\sigma = \sqrt{\ln\left(1 + \frac{\sigma_Y^2}{\mu_Y^2}\right)}$, respectively. Probabilities for a lognormal random variable are easily evaluated by reference to the normal distribution.

Additional Exercises and Case Studies

Exercises

52. A florist makes deliveries between 1:00 pm and 5:00 pm daily. Assume delivery times follow the continuous uniform distribution.

    a. Calculate the mean and variance of this distribution.

    b. Determine the percentage of deliveries that are made after 4:00 pm.

    c. Determine the percentage of deliveries that are made prior to 2:30 pm.

53. A worker at a landscape design center uses a machine to fill bags with potting soil. Assume that the quantity put in each bag is a uniformly distributed random variable that ranges from 10 to 12 pounds.

    a. Calculate the expected value and standard deviation of this distribution.

    b. Find the probability that the weight of a randomly selected bag is no more than 11 pounds.

    c. Find the probability that the weight of a randomly selected bag is at least 10.5 pounds.

54. The revised guidelines from the National High Blood Pressure Education Program define normal blood pressure as readings below 120/80 millimeters of mercury (*The New York Times*, May 14, 2003). Prehypertension is suspected when the top number (systolic) is between 120 to 139 or when the bottom number (diastolic) is between 80 to 90. A recent survey reported that the mean systolic reading of Canadians is 125 with a standard deviation of 17 and the mean diastolic

reading is 79 with a standard deviation of 10. Assume that diastolic as well as systolic readings are normally distributed.

a. What proportion of Canadians are suffering from prehypertension caused by high diastolic readings?

b. What proportion of Canadians are suffering from prehypertension caused by high systolic readings?

55. U.S. consumers are increasingly viewing debit cards as a convenient substitute for cash and checks. The average amount spent annually on a debit card is $7,790 (*Kiplinger's*, August 2007). Assume that the average amount spent on a debit card is normally distributed with a standard deviation of $500.

a. A consumer advocate comments that the majority of consumers spend over $8,000 on a debit card. Find a flaw in this statement.

b. Compute the 25th percentile of the amount spent on a debit card.

c. Compute the 75th percentile of the amount spent on a debit card.

d. What is the interquartile range of this distribution?

56. On St. Patrick's Day, men spend an average of $43.87 while women spend an average of $29.54 (*USA Today*, March 17, 2009). Assume the standard deviations of spending for men and women are $3 and $11, respectively, and that both distributions are normally distributed.

a. What is the probability that men spend over $50 on St. Patrick's Day?

b. What is the probability that women spend over $50 on St. Patrick's Day?

c. Are men or women more likely to spend over $50 on St. Patrick's Day?

57. Lisa Mendes and Brad Lee work in the sales department of an AT&T Wireless Store. Lisa has been signing in an average of 48 new cell phone customers every month with a standard deviation of 22, while Brad signs in an average of 56 new customers with a standard deviation of 17. The store manager offers both Lisa and Brad a $100 incentive bonus if they can sign in more than 100 new customers in a month. Assume a normal distribution to answer the following questions.

a. What is the probability that Lisa will earn the $100 incentive bonus?

b. What is the probability that Brad will earn the $100 incentive bonus?

c. Are you surprised by the results? Explain.

58. On a particularly busy section of the Garden State Parkway in New Jersey, police use radar guns to detect speeders. Assume the time that elapses between successive speeders is exponentially distributed with a mean of 15 minutes.

a. Calculate the rate parameter λ.

b. What is the probability of a waiting time less than 10 minutes between successive speeders?

c. What is the probability of a waiting time in excess of 25 minutes between successive speeders?

59. According to the Federal Bureau of Investigation, there is a violent crime in the U.S. every 22 seconds (*ABC News*, September 25, 2007). Assume that the time between violent crimes is exponentially distributed.

a. What is the probability that there is a violent crime in the U.S. in the next one minute?

b. If there has not been a violent crime in the previous minute, what is the probability that there will be a violent crime in the subsequent minute?

60. The relief time provided by a standard dose of a popular children's allergy medicine averages six hours with a standard deviation of two hours.

a. Determine the percentage of children who experience relief for less than four hours if the relief time follows a normal distribution.

b. Determine the percentage of children who experience relief for less than four hours if the relief time follows a lognormal distribution.

c. Compare the results based on these two distributions.

61. The mileage (in thousands of miles) that car owners get with a certain kind of radial tire is a random variable Y having a lognormal distribution such that $Y = e^X$ where X is normally distributed. Let the mean and the standard deviation of the life of a radial tire be 40,000 miles and 5,000 miles, respectively.

a. Compute the mean and standard deviation of X.

b. What proportion of the tires will last for more than 50,000 miles?

c. What proportion of the tires will last for no more than 35,000 miles?

d. Compute the 95th percentile of the life distribution of the tire.

CASE STUDIES

Case Study 6.1

Body Mass Index (BMI) is a reliable indicator of body fat for most children and teens. BMI is calculated from a child's weight and height and is used as an easy-to-perform method of screening for weight categories that may lead to health problems. For children and teens, BMI is age- and sex-specific and is often referred to as BMI-for-age.

The Center for Disease Control and Prevention (CDC) reports BMI-for-age growth charts for girls as well as boys to obtain a percentile ranking. Percentiles are the most commonly used indicator to assess the size and growth patterns of individual children in the United States.

The following table provides weight status categories and the corresponding percentiles and BMI ranges for 10-year-old boys in the United States.

Weight Status Category	Percentile Range	BMI Range
Underweight	Less than 5th	Less than 14.2
Healthy Weight	Between 5th and 85th	Between 14.2 and 19.4
Overweight	Between 85th and 95th	Between 19.4 and 22.2
Obese	More than 95th	More than 22.2

Health officials of a midwestern town are concerned about the weight of children in their town. For example, they believe that the BMI of their 10-year-old boys is normally distributed with mean 19.2 and standard deviation 2.6.

In a report, use the sample information to:

1. Compute the proportion of 10-year-old boys in this town that are in the various weight status categories given the BMI ranges.

2. Discuss whether the concern of health officials is justified.

Case Study 6.2

In the introductory case of Chapter 3 we discussed Vanguard's Precious Metals and Mining fund (Metals) and Fidelity's Strategic Income fund (Income), which were two top-performing mutual funds for the years 2000 through 2009. An analysis of annual return data for these two funds provided important information for any type of investor. Over the past 10 years, the Metals fund posted a mean return of 24.65% with a standard deviation of 37.13%. On the other hand, the mean and the standard deviation of return for the Income fund were 8.51% and 11.07%, respectively. It is reasonable to assume that the returns of the Metals and the Income funds are both normally distributed, where the means and the standard deviations are derived from the 10-year sample period.

In a report, use the sample information to compare and contrast the Metals and Income funds from the perspective of an investor whose objective is to:

1. Minimize the probability of earning a negative return.

2. Maximize the probability of earning a return between 0% to 10%.

3. Maximize the probability of earning a return greater than 10%.

Case Study 6.3

A variety of packaging solutions exist for products that must be kept within a specific temperature range. A cold chain distribution is a temperature-controlled supply chain. An unbroken cold chain is an uninterrupted series of storage and distribution activities that maintain a given temperature range. Cold chains are particularly useful in the food and pharmaceutical industries. A common suggested temperature range for a cold chain distribution in pharmaceutical industries is between 2 and 8 degrees Celsius.

Gopal Vasudeva works in the packaging branch of Merck & Co. He is in charge of analyzing a new package that the company has developed. With repeated trials, Gopal has determined that the mean temperature that this package is able to maintain during its use is 5.6°C with a standard deviation of 1.2°C. He is not sure if the distribution of temperature is symmetric or skewed to the right.

In a report, use the sample information to:

1. Calculate the probability that temperature goes (a) below 2°C and (b) above 8°C using a normal distribution approximation.

2. Calculate the probability that temperature goes (a) below 2°C and (b) above 8°C using a lognormal distribution approximation.

3. Compare the results from the two distributions used in the analysis.

7

Sampling and Sampling Distributions

LEARNING OBJECTIVES

After reading this chapter you should be able to:

LO 7.1 Differentiate between a population parameter and a sample statistic.

LO 7.2 Explain common sample biases.

LO 7.3 Describe simple random sampling.

LO 7.4 Distinguish between stratified random sampling and cluster sampling.

LO 7.5 Describe the properties of the sampling distribution of the sample mean.

LO 7.6 Explain the importance of the central limit theorem.

LO 7.7 Describe the properties of the sampling distribution of the sample proportion.

LO 7.8 Use a finite population correction factor.

LO 7.9 Construct and interpret control charts for quantitative and qualitative data.

In the last few chapters we were given the population parameters, such as the population mean and the population proportion, for the analysis of discrete and continuous random variables. In many instances we do not have information on the parameters, so we make inferences on the basis of sample statistics. Although sample statistics represent only a portion of the population, they contain useful information to estimate the unknown characteristics of the population. The credibility of any statistical inference depends on the quality of the sample on which it is based. In this chapter we discuss various ways to draw a good sample and also highlight cases in which the sample misrepresents the population. It is important to note that any given situation involves only one population, but many possible samples from which a statistic can be derived. Therefore, while the population parameter is a constant, the sample statistic is a random variable whose value depends on the choice of the random sample. We will discuss how to evaluate the properties of sample statistics. In particular, we will study the probability distributions of the sample mean and the sample proportion based on simple random sampling. Finally, we will use these distributions to construct control charts, which are popular statistical tools for monitoring and improving quality.

Marketing Iced Coffee

Although hot coffee is still Americans' drink of choice, the market share of iced coffee is growing steadily. Thirty percent of coffee drinkers had at least one iced, frozen, or blended coffee drink in 2009, up from 28% in 2008 (*The Boston Globe*, April 6, 2010). In response to this growing change in taste, the coffee chains have ramped up their offerings: Starbucks recently introduced an upgraded Frappuccino; Dunkin' Donuts launched a new iced dark roast; and McDonald's unveiled new blended coffee iced drinks and smoothies.

In order to capitalize on this trend, Starbucks advertised a Happy Hour from May 7 through May 16 whereby customers enjoyed a half-price Frappuccino beverage between 3 pm and 5 pm (starbucks.com). Anne Jones, a manager at a local Starbucks (see the Chapter 5 introductory case), wonders how this marketing campaign has affected her business. She knows that women and teenage girls comprise the majority of the iced-coffee market, since they are willing to spend more on indulgences. In fact, Anne reviews her records prior to the promotion and finds that 43% of iced-coffee customers were women and 21% were teenage girls. She also finds that customers spent an average of $4.18 on iced coffee with a standard deviation of $0.84.

One month after the marketing period ends, Anne surveys 50 of her iced-coffee customers and finds that they had spent an average of $4.26. Further, 23 (46%) of the customers were women and 17 (34%) were teenage girls. Anne wants to determine if the marketing campaign has had a lingering effect on the amount of money customers spend on iced coffee and on the proportion of customers who are women and teenage girls. Anne wonders if Starbucks would have gotten such business if it had chosen not to pursue the marketing campaign.

Anne wants to use the above survey information to:

1. Calculate the probability that customers spend an average of $4.26 or more on iced coffee.
2. Calculate the probability that 46% or more of iced-coffee customers are women.
3. Calculate the probability that 34% or more of iced-coffee customers are teenage girls.

We provide a synopsis of this case at the end of Section 7.3.

7.1 Sampling

LO **7.1**

Differentiate between a population parameter and a sample statistic.

A major portion of statistics is concerned with inferential statistics, where we examine the problem of estimating population parameters or testing hypotheses about such parameters. Recall that a population consists of all items of interest in the statistical problem. If we had access to data that encompass the entire population, then the values of the parameters would be known and no statistical inference would be needed. Since it is generally not feasible to gather data on an entire population, we use a subset of the population, or a sample, and use this information to make statistical inference. We can think of a census and survey data as representative of population and sample data, respectively. While a census captures almost everyone in the country, a survey captures a small number of people who fit a particular category. We regularly use survey data to analyze government and business activities.

> **POPULATION VERSUS SAMPLE**
>
> A **population** consists of all items of interest in a statistical problem, whereas a **sample** is a subset of the population. We use a calculated **sample statistic**, or simply **statistic**, to make inferences about the unknown population **parameter**.

In later chapters we explore estimation and hypothesis testing, which are based on sample information. It is important to note that no matter how sophisticated the statistical methods are, the credibility of statistical inference depends on the quality of the sample on which it is based. A primary requisite for a "good" sample is that it be representative of the population we are trying to describe. When the information from a sample is not typical of information in the population in a systematic way, we say that **bias** has occurred.

> **Bias** refers to the tendency of a sample statistic to systematically over- or under-estimate a population parameter.

LO **7.2**

Explain common sample biases.

Classic Case of a "Bad" Sample: The *Literary Digest* Debacle of 1936

In theory, drawing conclusions about a population based on a good sample sounds logical; however, in practice, what constitutes a "good" sample? Unfortunately, there are many ways to collect a "bad" sample. One way is to inadvertently pick a sample that represents only a portion of the population. The *Literary Digest*'s attempt to predict the 1936 presidential election is a classic example of an embarrassingly inaccurate poll.

In 1932 and amidst the Great Depression, Herbert Hoover was voted out of the White House, and Franklin Delano Roosevelt (FDR) was elected the 32nd President of the United States. Although FDR's attempts to end the Great Depression within four years were largely unsuccessful, he retained the general public's faith. In 1936, FDR ran for reelection against Alf Landon, the Governor of Kansas and the Republican nominee. The *Literary Digest,* an influential, general interest weekly magazine, wanted to predict the next U.S. President, as it had done successfully five times before.

After conducting the largest poll in history, the *Literary Digest* predicted a landslide victory for Alf Landon: 57% of the vote to FDR's 43%. Further, the *Literary Digest* claimed that its prediction would be within a fraction of 1% of the actual vote. Instead, FDR won in a landslide: 62% to 38%. So what went wrong?

The *Literary Digest* sent postcards to 10 million people (one-quarter of the voting population at the time) and received responses from 2.4 million people. The response rate of 24% (2.4 million/10 million) might seem low to some, but in reality it is a reasonable response rate given this type of polling. What was atypical of the poll is the manner in which the *Literary Digest* obtained the respondents' names. The *Literary Digest* randomly sampled its own subscriber list, club membership rosters, telephone directories, and automobile registration rolls. This sample reflected predominantly middle- and upper-class people; that is, the vast majority of those polled were wealthier people who were more inclined to vote for the Republican candidate. Back in the 1930s, owning a phone, for instance, was far from universal. Only 11 million residential phones were in service in 1936 and these homes were disproportionately well-to-do and in favor of Landon. The sampling methodology employed by the *Literary Digest* suffered from **selection bias**. Selection bias occurs when portions of the population are excluded from the sample. FDR's support came from lower-income classes whose opinion was not reflected in the poll. The sample, unfortunately, misrepresented the general electorate.

> **Selection bias** refers to a systematic exclusion of certain groups from consideration for the sample.

In addition to selection bias, the *Literary Digest* survey also had a great deal of **nonresponse bias**. This occurs when those responding to a survey or poll differ systematically from the nonrespondents. In the survey, a larger percentage of educated people mailed back the questionnaires. During that time period, the more educated tended to come from affluent families that again favored the Republican candidate. Problems with nonresponse bias persist today. Most people do not want to spend time carefully reading and responding to polls conducted by mail. Only those who care a great deal about an election or a particular issue take the time to read the instructions, fill out the questionnaire, and mail it back. Those who do respond may be atypical of the population as a whole.

> **Nonresponse bias** refers to a systematic difference in preferences between respondents and nonrespondents to a survey or a poll.

What should the *Literary Digest* have done differently? At a minimum, most would agree that names should have been obtained from voter registration lists rather than telephone directory lists and car registrations. However, generating a sample by randomly selecting names from voter registration lists also has possible shortcomings, especially with respect to selection bias.

Sampling Methods

LO **7.3**

Describe simple random sampling.

As mentioned earlier, a primary requisite for a "good" sample is that it be representative of the population you are trying to describe. The basic type of sample that can be used to draw statistically sound conclusions about a population is a **simple random sample**.

> ### SIMPLE RANDOM SAMPLE
>
> A **simple random sample** is a sample of *n* observations which has the same probability of being selected from the population as any other sample of *n* observations. Most statistical methods presume simple random samples.

EXAMPLE 7.1

A recent analysis shows a dramatic decline in studying time among today's college students (*The Boston Globe*, July 4, 2010). In 1961, students invested 24 hours per week in their academic pursuits, whereas today's students study an average of 14 hours per week. A dean at a large university in California wonders if this trend is reflective of the students at her university. The university has 20,000 students and the dean would like a sample of 100. Use Excel to draw a simple random sample of 100 students.

SOLUTION: Excel offers a useful tool to aid in randomly selecting 100 students from the list of 20,000 students. Simply choose **Formulas > Insert function > RANDBETWEEN** and input the number 1 for **Bottom** and the number 20,000 for **Top**, as shown in Figure 7.1.

FIGURE 7.1 The dialog box for Excel's RANDBETWEEN function

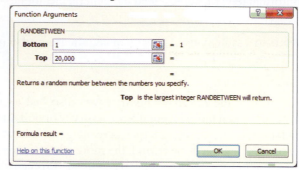

The RANDBETWEEN function will return a random number between these limits, perhaps the value 6,319. The dean can then choose the 6,319th student from the list. In order to generate the remaining 99 random numbers, we can select the cell with the value 6,319, drag it down 99 cells, and then from the menu choose **Home > Fill > Down**.

LO 7.4

Distinguish between stratified random sampling and cluster sampling.

While a simple random sample is the most commonly used sampling method, in some situations other sampling methods have an advantage over simple random samples. Two alternative methods for forming a sample are stratified random sampling and cluster sampling.

Political pollsters often employ **stratified random sampling** in an attempt to ensure that each area of the country, each ethnic group, each religious group, and so forth, is appropriately represented in the sample. With stratified random sampling, the population is divided into groups (strata) based on one or more classification criteria. Simple random samples are then drawn from each stratum in sizes proportional to the relative size of each stratum in the population. These samples are then pooled.

STRATIFIED RANDOM SAMPLING

In stratified random sampling, the population is first divided up into mutually exclusive and collectively exhaustive groups, called *strata*. A stratified sample includes randomly selected observations from each stratum, which are proportional to the stratum's size.

Stratified random sampling has two advantages. First, it guarantees that the population subdivisions of interest are represented in the sample. Second, the estimates of parameters produced from stratified random sampling have greater precision than estimates obtained from simple random sampling.

Even stratified random sampling, however, can fall short with its predictive ability. One of the nagging mysteries of the 2008 Democratic presidential primaries was: Why were the polls so wrong in New Hampshire? All nine major polling groups predicted that

Barack Obama would beat Hillary Clinton in the New Hampshire primary by an average of 8.3 percentage points. When the votes were counted, Clinton won by 2.6%. Several factors contributed to the wrong prediction by the polling industry. First, pollsters overestimated the turnout of young voters, who overwhelmingly favored Obama in exit polls but did not surge to vote as they had in the Iowa caucus. Second, Clinton's campaign made a decision to target women Democrats, especially single women. This focus did not pay off in Iowa, but it did in New Hampshire. Finally, on the eve of the primary, a woman in Portsmouth asked Clinton: "How do you do it?" Clinton's teary response was powerful and warm. Voters, who rarely saw Clinton in such an emotional moment, found her response humanizing and appealing. Most polls had stopped phoning voters over the weekend, too soon to catch the likely voter shift.

Cluster sampling is another method for forming a representative sample. A cluster sample is formed by dividing the population into groups (clusters), such as geographic areas, and then selecting a sample of the groups for the analysis. The technique works best when most of the variation in the population is within the groups and not between the groups. In such instances, a cluster is a miniversion of the population.

CLUSTER SAMPLING

In cluster sampling, the population is first divided up into mutually exclusive and collectively exhaustive groups, called *clusters*. A cluster sample includes observations from randomly selected clusters.

In general, cluster sampling is cheaper as compared to other sampling methods. However, for a given sample size, it provides less precision than either simple random sampling or stratified sampling. Cluster sampling is useful in applications where the population is concentrated in natural clusters such as city blocks, schools, and other geographic areas. It is especially attractive when constructing a complete list of population elements is difficult and/or costly. For example, since it may not be possible to create a full list of customers that go to Walmart, we can form a sample that includes customers only from selected stores.

STRATIFIED VERSUS CLUSTER SAMPLING

In stratified sampling, the sample consists of elements from each group, whereas in cluster sampling, the sample consists of elements from the selected groups. Stratified sampling is preferred when the objective is to increase precision and cluster sampling is preferred when the objective is to reduce costs.

The Special Election to Fill Ted Kennedy's Senate Seat

On January 19, 2010, Scott Brown, the Republican candidate, beat Martha Coakley, the Democratic candidate, in a special election to fill the U.S. Senate seat for Massachusetts that had been vacated with the death of Senator Ted Kennedy. Given that Kennedy, the "Liberal Lion," had held the seat for over 40 years, the election was one of the biggest upsets in Massachusetts' political history. Nine days prior to the election, a *Boston Globe* poll gave Coakley, the state's attorney general, a 15-point lead over Brown. Critics accused the *Globe*, which had endorsed Coakley, of purposely running a bad poll to discourage voters from coming out for Brown. In reality, by the time the *Globe* released the poll, it contained old information from January 2–6. In addition, the *Globe* partnered with the University of New Hampshire for the poll, and unfortunately included people in the poll who said that they were unlikely to vote! Eighty years after the *Literary Digest* fiasco, pollsters are still making predictions based on samples with a great deal of selection bias.

The first poll that foretold Brown's stunning victory over Coakley was released by Suffolk University on January 14. The poll had Brown ahead by 50% to Coakley's 46%, approximately one percentage point off the Election Day results (52% to 47%). How did Suffolk University arrive at its findings? It conducted a statewide poll, and in addition, implemented a form of cluster sampling. As mentioned earlier, the technique works best when most of the variation in the population is within the groups and not between the groups. The pollsters from Suffolk University selected three bellwethers, or towns that would indicate the way that the state would vote. In choosing the bellwethers, the pollsters spent enormous amounts of time examining the results of similar elections over many years. Figure 7.2 shows a map of Massachusetts and the three bellwethers: Gardner, Fitchburg, and Peabody. The statewide poll and the results from the bellwethers were reported separately but yielded the same results.

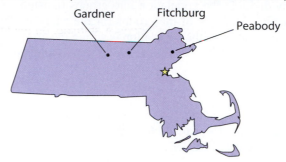

FIGURE 7.2 Map of Massachusetts with three bellwethers (towns)

In practice, it is extremely difficult to obtain a truly random sample that is representative of the underlying population. As researchers, we need to be aware of the population from which the sample was selected and then limit our conclusions to that population. For the remainder of the text, we assume that the sample data is void of "human error"; that is, we have sampled from the correct population (no selection bias); we have no response bias; and, we have collected, analyzed, and reported the data properly.

EXERCISES 7.1

1. In 2010, Apple introduced the iPad, a tablet-style computer that its former CEO Steve Jobs called a "a truly magical and revolutionary product" (*CNN*, January 28, 2010). Suppose you are put in charge of determining the age profile of people who purchased the iPad in the U.S. Explain in detail the following sampling strategies that you could use to select a representative sample.
   a. Simple random sampling
   b. Stratified random sampling
   c. Cluster sampling

2. A marketing firm opens a small booth at a local mall over the weekend, where shoppers are asked how much money they spent at the food court. The objective is to determine the average monthly expenditure of shoppers at the food court. Has the marketing firm committed any sampling bias? Discuss.

3. Natalie Min is a business student in the Haas School of Business at Berkeley. She wishes to pursue an MBA from Berkeley and wants to know the profile of other students who are likely to apply to the Berkeley MBA program. In particular, she wants to know the GPA of students with whom she might be competing. She randomly surveys

40 students from her accounting class for the analysis. Discuss in detail whether or not Natalie's analysis is based on a representative sample.

4. Vons, a large supermarket in Grover Beach, California, is considering extending its store hours from 7:00 am to midnight, seven days a week, to 6:00 am to midnight. Discuss the sampling bias in the following sampling strategies:
   a. Mail a prepaid envelope to randomly selected residents in the Grover Beach area, asking for their preference for the store hours.
   b. Ask the customers who frequent the store in the morning if they would prefer an earlier opening time.
   c. Place an ad in the local newspaper, requesting people to submit their preference for store hours on the store's website.

5. In the previous question regarding Vons' store hours, explain how you can obtain a representative sample based on the following sampling strategies:
   a. Simple random sampling.
   b. Stratified random sampling.
   c. Cluster sampling.

7.2 The Sampling Distribution of the Sample Mean

As mentioned earlier, we are generally interested in the characteristics of the population. For instance, a student is interested in the average starting salary (population mean) of college graduates. Similarly, a banker is interested in the default probability (population proportion) of mortgage holders. Recall that the population mean and the population proportion are the parameters that describe quantitative and qualitative data, respectively. Since it is cumbersome or impossible to analyze the entire population, we generally make inferences about the characteristics of the population on the basis of a random sample drawn from the population.

It is important to note that there is only one population, but many possible samples of a given size can be drawn from the population. Therefore, a population parameter is a constant, even though its value may be unknown. A statistic, on the other hand, is a random variable whose value depends on the particular sample that is randomly drawn from the population.

> A **parameter** is a **constant**, although its value may be unknown. A **statistic**, such as the sample mean or the sample proportion, is a **random variable** whose value depends on the chosen random sample.

Consider the starting salary of a business graduate from a Big Ten school as the variable of interest. If you decide to make inferences about the population mean on the basis of a random draw of 38 recent graduates from a Big Ten school, then the sample mean $\overline{X}$ is the relevant statistic. However, the value of $\overline{X}$ will change if you choose a different random sample of 38 Big Ten students. The sample mean is commonly referred to as the estimator of the population mean.

> **ESTIMATOR AND ESTIMATE**
>
> When a statistic is used to estimate a parameter, it is referred to as an **estimator**. A particular value of the estimator is called an **estimate**.

We continue to follow the convention introduced in earlier chapters where random variables are denoted by upper-case letters and particular values of the random variables are denoted by the corresponding lower-case letters. In the above example, the sample mean $\overline{X}$ is the estimator of the mean starting salary of Big Ten students. If the average derived from a specific sample is $54,000, then $\overline{x} = 54,000$ is the estimate of the population mean. Similarly, if the variable of interest is the default probability of mortgage holders, then the sample proportion of defaults, denoted by $\overline{P}$, from a random sample of 80 mortgage holders is the estimator of the population proportion. If 10 out of 80 mortgage holders in a given sample default, then $\overline{p} = 10/80 = 0.125$ is the estimate of the population proportion.

In this section we will focus on the probability distribution of the sample mean $\overline{X}$, which is commonly referred to as the **sampling distribution** of $\overline{X}$. Since $\overline{X}$ is a random variable, its sampling distribution is simply the probability distribution derived from all possible samples of a given size from the population. Consider, for example, a mean derived from a sample of n observations. Another mean can similarly be derived from a different sample of n observations. If we repeat this process a very large number of times, then the frequency distribution of the sample means can be thought of as its sampling distribution. In particular, we will discuss the expected value and the standard deviation of the sample mean. We will also study the conditions under which the sampling distribution of the sample mean is normally distributed.

LO **7.5**

Describe the
properties of the
sampling distribution
of the sample mean.

The Expected Value and the Standard Deviation of the Sample Mean

Let the random variable X represent a certain characteristic of a population under study. Here X is a selected element of the population. Furthermore, for convenience, we refer to X as the population of interest with an expected value, $E(X) = \mu$, and a variance, $Var(X) = \sigma^2$. Let the sample mean $\overline{X}$ be based on a random sample of n observations from the population. It is easy to derive the expected value and the variance of $\overline{X}$ (see Appendix 7.1 at the end of the chapter for the derivations).

The **expected value** of $\overline{X}$ is the same as the expected value of the individual observation, or $E(\overline{X}) = E(X) = \mu$. In other words, if we were to sample repeatedly from a given population, the average value of the sample means will equal the population mean from the underlying population. This result holds irrespective of whether the sample mean is based on a small or a large sample. We will elaborate on this desirable property of an estimator in Chapter 8 on estimation.

The **variance** of $\overline{X}$, $Var(\overline{X}) = \frac{\sigma^2}{n}$, is smaller than the variance of the individual observation $Var(X) = \sigma^2$. This is an intuitive result, suggesting that averages have less variation than individual observations. Since each sample is likely to contain both high and low observations, the highs and lows cancel one another, making the variability between sample means smaller than the variability between individual observations. As usual, the **standard deviation** of the sampling distribution of $\overline{X}$ is calculated as the positive square root of the variance, or $SD(\overline{X}) = \sqrt{\frac{\sigma^2}{n}} = \frac{\sigma}{\sqrt{n}}$. We often have to estimate this standard deviation. The estimate is called the standard error of $\overline{X}$, referred to as $SE(\overline{X})$.

EXPECTED VALUE AND STANDARD DEVIATION OF THE SAMPLE MEAN

The expected value of $\overline{X}$ equals the population mean, or $E(\overline{X}) = \mu$. The standard deviation of $\overline{X}$ equals the population standard deviation divided by the square root of the sample size, or $SD(\overline{X}) = \frac{\sigma}{\sqrt{n}}$.

EXAMPLE 7.2

The chefs at a local pizza chain in Cambria, California, strive to maintain the suggested size of their 16-inch pizzas. Despite their best efforts, they are unable to make every pizza exactly 16 inches in diameter. The manager has determined that the size of the pizzas is normally distributed with a mean of 16 inches and a standard deviation of 0.8 inch.

a. What is the expected value and the standard deviation of the sample mean derived from a random sample of 2 pizzas?

b. What is the expected value and the standard deviation of the sample mean derived from a random sample of 4 pizzas?

c. Compare the expected value and the standard deviation of the sample mean with those of an individual pizza.

SOLUTION: We know that the population mean $\mu = 16$ and the population standard deviation $\sigma = 0.8$. We use $E(\overline{X}) = \mu$ and $SD(\overline{X}) = \frac{\sigma}{\sqrt{n}}$ to calculate the following results.

a. With the sample size $n = 2$, $E(\overline{X}) = 16$ and $SD(\overline{X}) = \frac{0.8}{\sqrt{2}} = 0.57$.

b. With the sample size $n = 4$, $E(\overline{X}) = 16$ and $SD(\overline{X}) = \frac{0.8}{\sqrt{4}} = 0.40$.

c. The expected value of the sample mean for both sample sizes is identical to the expected value of the individual pizza. However, the standard deviation of the sample mean with $n = 4$ is lower than the one with $n = 2$. For both sample sizes, the standard deviation of the sample mean is lower than that of the individual pizza. This result confirms that averaging reduces variability.

Sampling from a Normal Population

An important feature of the sampling distribution of the sample mean $\overline{X}$ is that, irrespective of the sample size n, $\overline{X}$ is normally distributed if the population X from which the sample is drawn is normal. In other words, if X is normal with expected value μ and standard deviation σ, then $\overline{X}$ is also normal with expected value μ and standard deviation $\sigma/\sqrt{n}$.

SAMPLING FROM A NORMAL POPULATION

For any sample size n, the sampling distribution of $\overline{X}$ is **normal** if the population X from which the sample is drawn is normally distributed.

If $\overline{X}$ is normal we can transform it into the **standard normal random variable** as:

$$Z = \frac{\overline{X} - E(\overline{X})}{SD(\overline{X})} = \frac{\overline{X} - \mu}{\sigma/\sqrt{n}}.$$

Therefore any value $\bar{x}$ on $\overline{X}$ has a corresponding value z on Z given by $z = \frac{\bar{x} - \mu}{\sigma/\sqrt{n}}$.

EXAMPLE 7.3

Use the information in Example 7.2 to answer the following questions:

a. What is the probability that a randomly selected pizza is less than 15.5 inches?

b. What is the probability that 2 randomly selected pizzas average less than 15.5 inches?

c. What is the probability that 4 randomly selected pizzas average less than 15.5 inches?

d. Comment on the computed probabilities.

SOLUTION: Since the population is normally distributed, the sampling distribution of the sample mean is also normal. Figure 7.3 depicts the shapes of the three distributions based on the population mean $\mu = 16$ and the population standard deviation $\sigma = 0.8$. We use the transformations $Z = \frac{X - \mu}{\sigma}$ and $Z = \frac{\overline{X} - \mu}{\sigma/\sqrt{n}}$ to answer these questions.

FIGURE 7.3 Normal distribution of the sample means

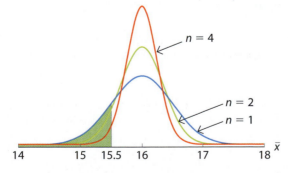

Note that when the sample size $n = 1$, the sample mean $\bar{x}$ is the same as the individual observation x.

a. In order to find $P(X < 15.5)$, we transform $x = 15.5$ into $z = \frac{15.5 - 16}{0.8} = -0.63$. Therefore, $P(X < 15.5) = P(Z < -0.63) = 0.2643$. There is a 26.43% chance that an individual pizza is less than 15.5 inches.

b. Here we find $P(\overline{X} < 15.5)$. We transform $\bar{x} = 15.5$ into $z = \frac{15.5 - 16}{0.8/\sqrt{2}} = -0.88$. Therefore, $P(\overline{X} < 15.5) = P(Z < -0.88) = 0.1894$. In a random sample of 2 pizzas, there is an 18.94% chance that the average size is less than 15.5 inches.

c. Again we find $P(\overline{X} < 15.5)$, but now $n = 4$. We transform $\bar{x} = 15.5$ into $z = \frac{15.5 - 16}{0.8/\sqrt{4}} = -1.25$. Therefore $P(\overline{X} < 15.5) = P(Z < -1.25) = 0.1056$. In a random sample of 4 pizzas, there is a 10.56% chance that the average size is less than 15.5 inches.

d. The probability that the average size is under 15.5 inches, for 4 randomly selected pizzas, is less than half of that for an individual pizza. This is due to the fact that while X and $\overline{X}$ have the same expected value of 16, the variance of $\overline{X}$ is less than that of X.

LO **7.6**

Explain the importance of the central limit theorem.

The Central Limit Theorem

For making statistical inferences, it is essential that the sampling distribution of $\overline{X}$ is normally distributed. So far we have only considered the case where $\overline{X}$ is normally distributed because the population X from which the sample is drawn is normal. What if the underlying population is not normal? Here we present the **central limit theorem** (**CLT**), which perhaps is the most remarkable result of probability theory. The CLT states that the sum or mean of a large number of independent observations from the same underlying distribution has an approximate normal distribution. The approximation steadily improves as the number of observations increases. In other words, irrespective of whether or not the population X is normal, the sample mean $\overline{X}$ computed from a random sample of size n will be approximately normally distributed as long as n is sufficiently large.

> **THE CENTRAL LIMIT THEOREM FOR THE SAMPLE MEAN**
>
> For any population X with expected value μ and standard deviation σ, the sampling distribution of $\overline{X}$ will be **approximately normal if the sample size n is sufficiently large.** As a general guideline, the normal distribution approximation is justified when $n \geq 30$.
>
> As before, if $\overline{X}$ is approximately normal, then we can transform it to $Z = \frac{\overline{X} - \mu}{\sigma/\sqrt{n}}$.

Figure 7.3, discussed in Example 7.3, is not representative of the CLT principle because for a normal population, the sampling distribution of $\overline{X}$ is normal irrespective of the sample size. Figures 7.4 and 7.5, however, illustrate the CLT by using random samples of various sizes drawn from nonnormal populations. The relative frequency polygon of $\overline{X}$,

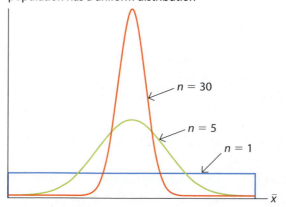

FIGURE 7.4 Sampling distribution of $\overline{X}$ when the population has a uniform distribution

which essentially represents its distribution, is generated from repeated draws (computer simulations) from the continuous uniform distribution (Figure 7.4) and the exponential distribution (Figure 7.5). Both of these nonnormal distributions were discussed in Chapter 6.

FIGURE 7.5 Sampling distribution of $\bar{X}$ when the population has an exponential distribution

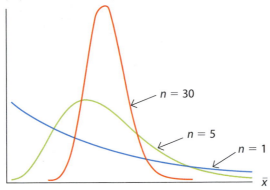

Note that when the sample size $n = 1$, the sample mean is the same as the individual observation (population) with the familiar uniform and exponential shapes. With $n = 5$, the sampling distribution of $\bar{X}$ begins to resemble the shape of the normal distribution. With $n = 30$, the shapes of the sampling distribution of $\bar{X}$ are approximately normal with the uniform as well as the exponential population distributions. The CLT can similarly be illustrated with other distributions of the population. How large a sample is necessary for normal convergence depends on the magnitude of the departure of the population from normality. As mentioned above, practitioners often use the normal distribution approximation when $n \geq 30$.

EXAMPLE 7.4

Consider the information presented in the introductory case of this chapter. Recall that Anne wants to determine if the marketing campaign has had a lingering effect on the amount of money customers spend on iced coffee. Before the campaign, customers spent an average of $4.18 on iced coffee with a standard deviation of $0.84. Anne reports that the average amount, based on 50 customers sampled after the campaign, is $4.26. She wants to calculate the probability that customers spend an average of $4.26 or more on iced coffee.

SOLUTION: If Starbucks did not pursue the marketing campaign, spending on iced coffee would still have mean $\mu = 4.18$ and standard deviation $\sigma = 0.84$. Anne needs to calculate the probability that the sample mean is at least 4.26, that is, $P(\bar{X} \geq 4.26)$. The population from which the sample is drawn is not known to be normal. However, since $n \geq 30$, from the central limit theorem, we know that $\bar{X}$ is approximately normal. Therefore, we transform $\bar{x} = 4.26$ into $z = \frac{4.26 - 4.18}{0.84/\sqrt{50}} = 0.67$. As shown in Figure 7.6, $P(\bar{X} \geq 4.26) = P(Z \geq 0.67) = 1 - 0.7486 = 0.2514$. It is quite plausible (probability = 0.2514) that in a sample of 50 customers, the sample mean is $4.26 or more even if Starbucks did not pursue the marketing campaign.

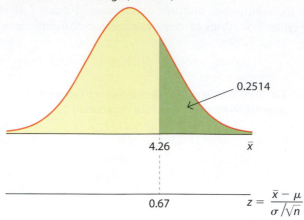

FIGURE 7.6 Finding $P(\bar{X} \geq 4.26)$

0.2514

4.26

$\bar{x}$

0.67

$z = \dfrac{\bar{x} - \mu}{\sigma/\sqrt{n}}$

EXERCISES 7.2

Concepts

6. A random sample is drawn from a normally distributed population with mean $\mu = 12$ and standard deviation $\sigma = 1.5$.
   a. Comment on the sampling distribution of the sample mean with $n = 20$ and $n = 40$.
   b. Can you use the standard normal distribution to calculate the probability that the sample mean is less than 12.5 for both sample sizes?
   c. Report the probability if you answered yes to the previous question for either sample size.

7. A random sample is drawn from a population with mean $\mu = 66$ and standard deviation $\sigma = 5.5$.
   a. Comment on the distribution of the sample mean with $n = 16$ and $n = 36$.
   b. Can you use the standard normal distribution to calculate the probability that the sample mean falls between 66 and 68 for both sample sizes?
   c. Report the probability if you answered yes to the previous question for either sample size.

8. A random sample of size $n = 100$ is taken from a population with mean $\mu = 80$ and standard deviation $\sigma = 14$.
   a. Calculate the expected value and the standard deviation for the sampling distribution of the sample mean.
   b. What is the probability that the sample mean falls between 77 and 85?
   c. What is the probability that the sample mean is greater than 84?

9. A random sample of size $n = 50$ is taken from a population with mean $\mu = -9.5$ and standard deviation $\sigma = 2$.
   a. Calculate the expected value and the standard deviation for the sampling distribution of the sample mean.
   b. What is the probability that the sample mean is less than -10?
   c. What is the probability that the sample mean falls between -10 and -9?

Applications

10. According to a recent survey, high school girls average 100 text messages daily (*The Boston Globe*, April 21, 2010). Assume the population standard deviation is 20 text messages. Suppose a random sample of 50 high school girls is taken.
    a. What is the probability that the sample mean is more than 105?
    b. What is the probability that the sample mean is less than 95?
    c. What is the probability that the sample mean is between 95 and 105?

11. Beer bottles are filled so that they contain 330 ml of beer in each bottle. Suppose that the amount of beer in a bottle is normally distributed with a standard deviation of 4 ml.
    a. What is the probability that a randomly selected bottle will have less than 325 ml of beer?
    b. What is the probability that a randomly selected 6-pack of beer will have a mean amount less than 325 ml?
    c. What is the probability that a randomly selected 12-pack of beer will have a mean amount less than 325 ml?
    d. Comment on the sample size and the corresponding probabilities.

12. Despite its nutritional value, seafood is only a tiny part of the American diet, with the average American eating just 16 pounds of seafood per year. Janice and Nina both work in the seafood industry and they decide to create their own random samples and document the average seafood diet in their sample. Let the standard deviation of the American seafood diet be 7 pounds.
    a. Janice samples 42 Americans and finds an average seafood consumption of 18 pounds. How likely is it to get an average of 18 pounds or more if she had a representative sample?
    b. Nina samples 90 Americans and finds an average seafood consumption of 17.5 pounds. How likely is it

to get an average of 17.5 pounds or more if she had a representative sample?

c. Which of the two women is likely to have used a more representative sample? Explain.

13. The weight of people in a small town in Missouri is known to be normally distributed with a mean of 180 pounds and a standard deviation of 28 pounds. On a raft that takes people across the river, a sign states, "Maximum capacity 3,200 pounds or 16 persons." What is the probability that a random sample of 16 persons will exceed the weight limit of 3,200 pounds?

14. The weight of turkeys is known to be normally distributed with a mean of 22 pounds and a standard deviation of 5 pounds.

   a. Discuss the sampling distribution of the sample mean based on a random draw of 16 turkeys.

b. Find the probability that the mean weight of 16 randomly selected turkeys is more than 25 pounds.

c. Find the probability that the mean weight of 16 randomly selected turkeys is between 18 and 24 pounds.

15. A small hair salon in Denver, Colorado, averages about 30 customers on weekdays with a standard deviation of 6. It is safe to assume that the underlying distribution is normal. In an attempt to increase the number of weekday customers, the manager offers a $2 discount on 5 consecutive weekdays. She reports that her strategy has worked since the sample mean of customers during this 5 weekday period jumps to 35.

   a. How unusual would it be to get a sample average of 35 or more customers if the manager had not offered the discount?

   b. Do you feel confident that the manager's discount strategy has worked? Explain.

7.3 The Sampling Distribution of the Sample Proportion

Our discussion thus far has focused on the population mean, but many business, socio-economic, and political matters are concerned with the population proportion. For instance, a banker is interested in the default probability of mortgage holders; a superintendent may note the proportion of students suffering from the H1N1 flu when determining whether to keep school open; an incumbent up for reelection cares about the proportion of constituents that will ultimately cast a vote for him/her. In all of these examples, the parameter of interest is the population proportion p. However, analogous to our discussion concerning the mean, we almost always make inferences about the population proportion on the basis of sample data. Here, the relevant statistic (estimator) is the sample proportion, $\overline{P}$; a particular value (estimate) is denoted by $\overline{p}$. Since $\overline{P}$ is a random variable, we need to discuss properties of the sampling distribution of $\overline{P}$.

LO 7.7

Describe the properties of the sampling distribution of the sample proportion.

The Expected Value and the Standard Deviation of the Sample Proportion

We first introduced the population proportion p in Chapter 5, when we discussed the binomial distribution. It turns out that the sampling distribution of $\overline{P}$ is closely related to the binomial distribution. Recall that the binomial distribution describes the total number of successes X in n independent trials where p is the probability of success on one particular trial; thus, $\overline{P} = \frac{X}{n}$ is the total number of successes X divided by the sample size n. In addition, the expected value and the variance of the binomial variable X are $E(X) = np$ and $Var(X) = np(1 - p)$, respectively. We use these results to derive the expected value and the variance of the sampling distribution of $\overline{P}$ as $E(\overline{P}) = p$ and $Var(\overline{P}) = \frac{p(1 - p)}{n}$, respectively (see Appendix 7.1 at the end of the chapter for the derivations). The standard deviation is simply the positive square root of the variance, that is, $SD(\overline{P}) = \sqrt{\frac{p(1 - p)}{n}}$. We often have to estimate this standard deviation. The estimate is called the standard deviation of $\overline{P}$, referred to as $SE(\overline{P})$.

EXPECTED VALUE AND STANDARD DEVIATION OF THE SAMPLE PROPORTION

The expected value of $\overline{P}$ equals the population proportion, or $E(\overline{P}) = p$.

The standard deviation of $\overline{P}$ equals $SD(\overline{P}) = \sqrt{\frac{p(1 - p)}{n}}$.

EXAMPLE 7.5

Many people apply for jobs to serve as paramedics or firefighters, yet they cannot complete basic physical fitness standards. A recent study found that 77% of all candidates for paramedic and firefighter positions were overweight or obese (*Obesity*, March 19, 2009).

a. What is the expected value and the standard deviation of the sample proportion derived from a random sample of 100 candidates for paramedic or firefighter positions?

b. What is the expected value and the standard deviation of the sample proportion derived from a random sample of 200 candidates for paramedic or firefighter positions?

c. Comment on the value of the standard deviation as the sample size gets larger.

SOLUTION: Given that $p = 0.77$, we can derive the expected value and the standard deviation as follows.

a. With $n = 100$, $E(\overline{P}) = 0.77$ and $SD(\overline{P}) = \sqrt{\dfrac{p(1 - p)}{n}} = \sqrt{\dfrac{0.77(1 - 0.77)}{100}} = 0.042$.

b. With $n = 200$, $E(\overline{P}) = 0.77$ and $SD(\overline{P}) = \sqrt{\dfrac{p(1 - p)}{n}} = \sqrt{\dfrac{0.77(1 - 0.77)}{200}} = 0.030$.

c. As in the case of the sample mean, while the expected value of the sample proportion is unaffected by the sample size, the standard deviation of the sample proportion is reduced as the sample size increases.

It is essential that the sampling distribution of $\overline{P}$ is approximately normal for making statistical inferences about the population proportion. Again, we use the CLT, which states that the normal distribution approximation of $\overline{P}$ is valid as long as n is sufficiently large.

THE CENTRAL LIMIT THEOREM FOR THE SAMPLE PROPORTION

For any population proportion p, the sampling distribution of $\overline{P}$ is **approximately normal if the sample size n is sufficiently large**. As a general guideline, the normal distribution approximation is justified when $np \geq 5$ and $n(1 - p) \geq 5$.

If $\overline{P}$ is normal, we can transform it into the **standard normal random variable** as

$$Z = \frac{\overline{P} - E(\overline{P})}{SD(\overline{P})} = \frac{\overline{P} - p}{\sqrt{\dfrac{p(1 - p)}{n}}}.$$

Therefore any value $\overline{p}$ on $\overline{P}$ has a corresponding value z on Z given by

$$z = \frac{\overline{p} - p}{\sqrt{\dfrac{p(1 - p)}{n}}}.$$

According to the CLT, the sampling distribution of $\overline{P}$ approaches the normal distribution as the sample size increases. However, as the population proportion deviates from $p = 0.50$, we need a larger sample size for the approximation. We illustrate these results by generating the sampling distribution of $\overline{P}$ from repeated draws from a population with various values of the population proportion and sample sizes. As in the case of $\overline{X}$, we use the relative frequency polygon to represent the distribution of $\overline{P}$. The simulated sampling distribution of $\overline{P}$ is based on the population proportion $p = 0.10$ (Figure 7.7) and $p = 0.30$ (Figure 7.8).

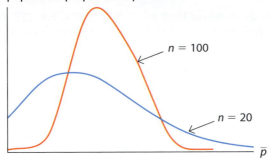

FIGURE 7.7 Sampling distribution of $\bar{P}$ when the population proportion is $p = 0.10$

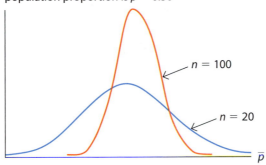

FIGURE 7.8 Sampling distribution of $\bar{P}$ when the population proportion is $p = 0.30$

When $p = 0.10$, the sampling distribution of $\bar{P}$ does not resemble the shape of the normal distribution with $n = 20$ since the approximation condition $np \geq 5$ and $n(1 - p) \geq 5$ is not satisfied. However, the curve becomes close to normal with $n = 100$. When $p = 0.30$, the shape of the sampling distribution of $\bar{P}$ is approximately normal since the approximation condition is satisfied with both sample sizes. In empirical work, it is common to work with large survey data, and as a result, the normal distribution approximation is justified.

EXAMPLE 7.6

Consider the information presented in the introductory case of this chapter. Recall that Anne Jones wants to determine if the marketing campaign has had a lingering effect on the proportion of customers who are women and teenage girls. Prior to the campaign, 43% of the customers were women and 21% were teenage girls. Based on a random sample of 50 customers after the campaign, these proportions increase to 46% for women and 34% for teenage girls. Anne has the following questions.

a. If Starbucks chose not to pursue the marketing campaign, how likely is it that 46% or more of iced-coffee customers are women?

b. If Starbucks chose not to pursue the marketing campaign, how likely is it that 34% or more of iced-coffee customers are teenage girls?

SOLUTION: If Starbucks had not pursued the marketing campaign, the proportion of customers would still be $p = 0.43$ for women and $p = 0.21$ for teenage girls. With $n = 50$, the normal approximation of the sample proportion is justified for both population proportions.

a. In order to calculate $P(\overline{P} \geq 0.46)$, we transform $\overline{p} = 0.46$ into $z = \dfrac{0.46 - 0.43}{\sqrt{\dfrac{0.43(1 - 0.43)}{50}}} = 0.43$. Therefore, as shown in Figure 7.9, $P(\overline{P} \geq 0.46) = P(Z \geq 0.43) = 1 - 0.6664 = 0.3336$.

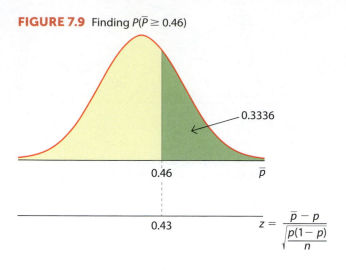

FIGURE 7.9 Finding $P(\overline{P} \geq 0.46)$

With a likelihood of 33.36%, it is quite plausible that the proportion of iced coffee purchased by women is at least 0.46 even if Starbucks did not pursue the marketing campaign.

b. Here we find $P(\overline{P} \geq 0.34)$. We transform $\overline{p} = 0.34$ into $z = \dfrac{0.34 - 0.21}{\sqrt{\dfrac{0.21(1 - 0.21)}{50}}} = 2.26$.

Therefore, as shown in Figure 7.10, $P(\overline{P} \geq 0.34) = P(Z \geq 2.26) = 1 - 0.9881 = 0.0119$.

FIGURE 7.10 Finding $P(\overline{P} \geq 0.34)$

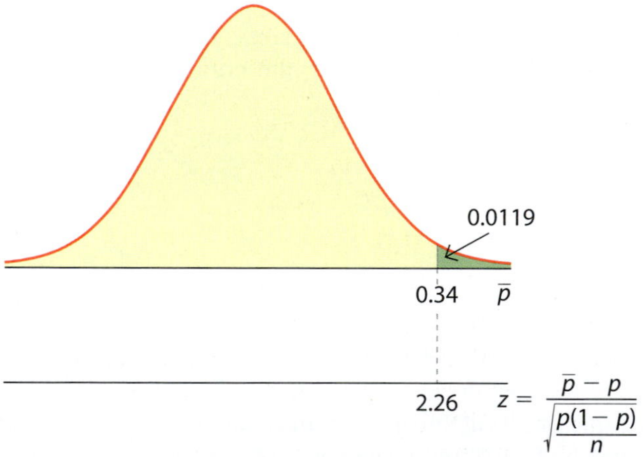

With only a 1.19% chance, it is unlikely that the proportion of iced coffee purchased by teenage girls is at least 0.34 if Starbucks did not pursue the marketing campaign.

Therefore, Anne can use this sample information to infer that the increase in the proportion of iced-coffee sales to women may not necessarily be due to the marketing campaign. However, the marketing campaign seems to have been successful in increasing the proportion of iced-coffee sales to teenage girls.

Iced coffee, traditionally a warm-weather and warm-region drink, has broadened its appeal over the years. According to a May 13, 2010, report in *Bloomberg Businessweek*, the number of servings of iced coffee surged from 300 million in 2001 to 1.2 billion in 2009. Large corporations have taken notice and have engaged in various strategies to capitalize on the growing trend. Starbucks, for instance, recently promoted a happy hour where customers paid half-price for a Frappuccino beverage between 3:00 pm and 5:00 pm for a 10-day period in May. One month after the marketing period ended, Anne Jones, the manager at a local Starbucks, surveys 50 of her customers. She reports an increase in spending in the sample, as well as an

increase in the proportion of customers who are women and teenage girls. Anne wants to determine if the increase is due to chance or due to the marketing campaign. Based on an analysis with probabilities, Anne finds that higher spending in a sample of 50 customers is plausible even if Starbucks had not pursued the marketing campaign. Using a similar analysis with proportions, she infers that while the marketing campaign may not have necessarily increased the proportion of women customers, it seems to have attracted more teenage girls. The findings are consistent with current market research, which has shown that teenage girls have substantial income of their own to spend and often purchase items that are perceived as indulgences.

EXERCISES 7.3

Concepts

16. Consider a population proportion $p = 0.68$.
    a. Calculate the expected value and the standard deviation of $\bar{P}$ with $n = 20$. Is it appropriate to use the normal distribution approximation for $\bar{P}$? Explain.
    b. Calculate the expected value and the standard deviation of $\bar{P}$ with $n = 50$. Is it appropriate to use the normal distribution approximation for $\bar{P}$? Explain.

17. Consider a population proportion $p = 0.12$.
    a. Discuss the sampling distribution of the sample proportion with $n = 20$ and $n = 50$.
    b. Can you use the normal approximation to calculate the probability that the sample proportion is between 0.10 and 0.12 for both sample sizes?
    c. Report the probabilities if you answered yes to the previous question.

18. A random sample of size $n = 200$ is taken from a population with population proportion $p = 0.75$.
    a. Calculate the expected value and the standard deviation for the sampling distribution of the sample proportion.
    b. What is the probability that the sample proportion is between 0.70 and 0.80?
    c. What is the probability that the sample proportion is less than 0.70?

Applications

19. A recent study by Allstate Insurance Co. finds that 82% of teenagers have used cell phones while driving (*The Wall Street Journal*, May 5, 2010). Suppose a random sample of 100 teen drivers is taken.
    a. Discuss the sampling distribution of the sample proportion.
    b. What is the probability that the sample proportion is less than 0.80?
    c. What is the probability that the sample proportion is within ± 0.02 of the population proportion?

20. According to a recent FCC survey, one in six cell phone users have experienced "bill shock" from unexpectedly high cell phone bills (*Tech Daily Dose,* May 26, 2010).
    a. Discuss the sampling distribution of the sample proportion based on a sample of 200 cell phone users. Is it appropriate to use the normal distribution approximation for the sample proportion?
    b. What is the probability that more than 20% of cell phone users in the sample have experienced "bill shock"?

21. A car manufacturer is concerned about poor customer satisfaction at one of its dealerships. The management decides to evaluate the satisfaction surveys of its next 40 customers. The dealer will be fined if fewer than

26 customers report favorably and the dealership will be dissolved if fewer than 22 report favorably. It is known that 70% of the dealer's customers report favorably on satisfaction surveys.

a. What is the probability that the dealer will be fined?

b. What is the probability that the dealership will be dissolved?

22. Europeans are increasingly upset at their leaders for making deep budget cuts to many social programs that are becoming too expensive to sustain. For instance, the popularity of President Nicolas Sarkozy of France has plummeted, giving him an approval rating of just 26% (*The Wall Street Journal*, July 2, 2010).

a. What is the probability that fewer than 60 of 200 French people give President Sarkozy a favorable rating?

b. What is the probability that more than 150 of 200 French people give President Sarkozy an *unfavorable* rating?

23. At a new exhibit in the Museum of Science, people are asked to choose between 50 or 100 random draws from

a machine. The machine is known to have 60 green balls and 40 red balls. After each draw, the color of the ball is noted and the ball is put back for the next draw. You win a prize if more than 70% of the draws result in a green ball. Would you choose 50 or 100 draws for the game? Explain.

24. After years of rapid growth, illegal immigration into the United States has declined, perhaps owing to the recession and increased border enforcement by the U.S. (*Los Angeles Times*, September 1, 2010). While its share has declined, California still accounts for 23% of the nation's estimated 11.1 million undocumented immigrants.

a. In a sample of 50 illegal immigrants, what is the probability that more than 20% live in California?

b. In a sample of 200 illegal immigrants, what is the probability that more than 20% live in California?

c. Comment on the reason for the difference between the computed probabilities in parts a and b.

7.4 The Finite Population Correction Factor

LO 7.8

Use a finite population correction factor.

One of the implicit assumptions we have made thus far is that the sample size n is much smaller than the population size N. In many applications, the size of the population is not even known. For instance, we do not have information on the total number of pizzas made at a local pizza chain in Cambria (Examples 7.2 and 7.3) or the total number of customers at the local Starbucks store (Example 7.6). If the population size is relatively small (finite) and has a known value, then it is preferable to use a correction factor in the standard deviation of the estimators, which accounts for the added precision gained by sampling a larger percentage of the population. As a general guideline, we use the finite factor correction when the sample constitutes at least 5% of the population, that is, $n \geq 0.05N$.

THE FINITE POPULATION CORRECTION FACTOR FOR THE SAMPLE MEAN

We use the **finite population correction factor** to reduce the sampling variation of $\overline{X}$. The resulting standard deviation is $SD(\overline{X}) = \frac{\sigma}{\sqrt{n}}\left(\sqrt{\frac{N-n}{N-1}}\right)$. The transformation of $\overline{X}$ to Z is made accordingly.

Note that the correction factor is always less than one; when N is large relative to n, the correction factor is close to one and the difference between the formulas with and without the correction is negligible.

EXAMPLE 7.7

A large introductory marketing class has 340 students. The class is divided up into 10 groups for the final course project. Connie is in a group of 34 students. These students had averaged 72 on the midterm, when the class as a whole had an average score of 73 with a standard deviation of 10. Connie is concerned that her group is not very good.

a. Calculate the expected value and the standard deviation of the sample mean.

b. How likely is it that a random sample of 34 students will average 72 or lower?

SOLUTION: The population mean is $\mu = 73$ and the population standard deviation is $\sigma = 10$.

a. The expected value of the sample mean is $E(\overline{X}) = \mu = 73$. We use the finite population correction factor because the sample size $n = 34$ is more than 5% of the population size $N = 340$. Therefore, the standard deviation of the sample mean is $SD(\overline{X}) = \frac{\sigma}{\sqrt{n}}\left(\sqrt{\frac{N-n}{N-1}}\right) = \frac{10}{\sqrt{34}}\left(\sqrt{\frac{340-34}{340-1}}\right) = 1.63$. Note that without the correction factor, the standard deviation would be higher at $SD(\overline{X}) = \frac{\sigma}{\sqrt{n}} = \frac{10}{\sqrt{34}} = 1.71$.

b. In order to calculate $P(\overline{X} \le 72)$, we use $Z = \frac{\overline{X} - E(\overline{X})}{SD(\overline{X})}$ to transform $\bar{x} = 72$ into $z = \frac{72-73}{1.63} = -0.61$. Therefore, $P(\overline{X} \le 72) = P(Z \le -0.61) = 0.2709$. That is, the likelihood of 34 students averaging 72 or lower is 27.09%.

We can use a similar finite population correction factor for a sample proportion when the sample size is more than 5% of the population size.

> ### THE FINITE POPULATION CORRECTION FACTOR FOR THE SAMPLE PROPORTION
>
> We use the **finite population correction factor** to reduce the sampling variation of the sample proportion $\overline{P}$. The resulting standard deviation of $\overline{P}$ is $SD(\overline{P}) = \sqrt{\frac{p(1-p)}{n}}\left(\sqrt{\frac{N-n}{N-1}}\right)$. The transformation of $\overline{P}$ to Z is made accordingly.

EXAMPLE 7.8

The home ownership rate during 2009 declined to approximately 67% and is now comparable to the rate in early 2000 (*U.S. Census Bureau News*, February 2, 2010). A random sample of 80 households is taken from a small island community with 1,000 households. The home ownership rate on the island is equivalent to the national home ownership rate of 67%.

a. Calculate the expected value and the standard deviation for the sampling distribution of the sample proportion. Is it necessary to apply the finite population correction factor? Explain.

b. What is the probability that the sample proportion is within 0.02 of the population proportion?

SOLUTION:

a. We must apply the finite population correction factor because the sample size $n = 80$ is more than 5% of the population size $N = 1,000$. Therefore, $E(\overline{P}) = p = 0.67$ and

$$SD(\overline{P}) = \sqrt{\frac{p(1-p)}{n}}\left(\sqrt{\frac{N-n}{N-1}}\right) = \sqrt{\frac{0.67(1-0.67)}{80}}\left(\sqrt{\frac{1,000-80}{1,000-1}}\right) = 0.0505.$$

b. The probability that the sample proportion is within 0.02 of the population proportion is $P(0.65 \le \overline{P} \le 0.69)$. We transform $\bar{p} = 0.65$ into $z = \frac{0.65-0.67}{0.0505} = -0.40$. Similarly, we transform $\bar{p} = 0.69$ into $z = 0.40$. Therefore, $P(0.65 \le \overline{P} \le 0.69) = P(-0.40 \le Z \le 0.40) = 0.6554 - 0.3446 = 0.3108$. The likelihood of getting a home ownership rate within 0.02 of the population proportion is 31.08%.

EXERCISES 7.4

Concepts

25. A random sample of size $n = 100$ is taken from a population of size $N = 2,500$ with mean $\mu = -45$ and variance $\sigma^2 = 81$.

    a. Is it necessary to apply the finite population correction factor? Explain. Calculate the expected value and the standard deviation of the sample mean.

    b. What is the probability that the sample mean is between -47 and -43?

    c. What is the probability that the sample mean is greater than -44?

26. A random sample of size $n = 70$ is taken from a finite population of size $N = 500$ with mean $\mu = 220$ and variance $\sigma^2 = 324$.

    a. Is it necessary to apply the finite population correction factor? Explain. Calculate the expected value and the standard deviation of the sample mean.

    b. What is the probability that the sample mean is less than 210?

    c. What is the probability that the sample mean lies between 215 and 230?

27. A random sample of size $n = 100$ is taken from a population of size $N = 3,000$ with a population proportion of $p = 0.34$.

    a. Is it necessary to apply the finite population correction factor? Explain. Calculate the expected value and the standard deviation of the sample proportion.

    b. What is the probability that the sample proportion is greater than 0.37?

28. A random sample of size $n = 80$ is taken from a population of size $N = 600$ with a population proportion $p = 0.46$.

    a. Is it necessary to apply the finite population correction factor? Explain. Calculate the expected value and the standard deviation of the sample proportion.

    b. What is the probability that the sample mean is less than 0.40?

Applications

29. The issues surrounding the levels and structure of executive compensation have gained added prominence in the wake of the financial crisis that erupted in the fall of 2008. Based on the 2006 compensation data obtained from the Securities and Exchange Committee (SEC) website, it was determined that the mean and the standard deviation of compensation for the 500 highest paid CEOs in publicly traded U.S. companies is \$10.32 million and \$9.78 million, respectively. An analyst randomly chooses 32 CEO compensations for 2006.

    a. Is it necessary to apply the finite population correction factor? Explain.

    b. Is the sampling distribution of the sample mean normally distributed? Explain.

    c. Calculate the expected value and the standard deviation of the sample mean.

    d. What is the probability that the sample mean is more than \$12 million?

30. Suppose in the previous question the analyst had randomly chosen 12 CEO compensations for 2006.

    a. Is it necessary to apply the finite population correction factor? Explain.

    b. Is the sampling distribution of the sample mean normally distributed? Explain.

    c. Calculate the expected value and the standard deviation of the sample mean.

    d. Can you use the normal approximation to calculate the probability that the sample mean is more than \$12 million? Explain.

31. Given the recent economic downturn, only 60% in a graduating class of 250 will find employment in the first round of a job search. You have 20 friends who have recently graduated.

    a. Discuss the sampling distribution of the sample proportion of your friends who will find employment in the first round of a job search.

    b. What is the probability that less than 50% of your friends will find employment in the first round of a job search?

32. Despite the recession, companies are setting aside a large chunk of their IT spending for green technology projects (*BusinessWeek*, March 5, 2009). Two out of three of the large companies surveyed by Deloitte said they have at least 5% of their IT budget earmarked for green IT projects. Suppose that the survey was based on 1,000 large companies. What is the probability that more than 75 of 120 large companies will have at least 5% of their IT expenditure earmarked for green IT projects?

LO **7.9**

Construct and
interpret control
charts for quantitative
and qualitative data.

7.5 Statistical Quality Control

Now more than ever, a successful firm must focus on the quality of the products and services it offers. Global competition, technological advances, and consumer expectations are all factors contributing to the quest for quality. In order to ensure the production of high-quality goods and services, a successful firm implements some form of quality control. In this section we give a brief overview of the field of **statistical quality control**.

> **Statistical quality control** involves statistical techniques used to develop and maintain a firm's ability to produce high-quality goods and services.

In general, two approaches are used for statistical quality control. A firm uses **acceptance sampling** if it produces a product (or offers a service) and at the completion of the production process, the firm then inspects a portion of the products. If a particular product does not conform to certain specifications, then it is either discarded or repaired. The problems with this approach to quality control are, first, it is costly to discard or repair a product. Second, the detection of all defective products is not guaranteed. Defective products may be delivered to customers, thus damaging the firm's reputation.

A preferred approach to quality control is the **detection approach**. A firm using the detection approach inspects the production process and determines at which point the production process does not conform to specifications. The goal is to determine whether the production process should be continued or adjusted before a large number of defects are produced. In this section we focus on the detection approach to quality control.

In general, no two products or services are identical. In any production process, variation in the quality of the end product is inevitable. Two types of variation occur. **Chance variation**, or common variation, is caused by a number of randomly occurring events that are part of the production process. This type of variation is not generally considered under the control of the individual worker or machine. For example, suppose a machine fills one-gallon jugs of milk. It is unlikely that the filling weight of each jug is exactly 128 ounces. Very slight differences in the production process lead to minor differences in the weights of one jug to the next. Chance variation is expected and is not a source of alarm in the production process so long as its magnitude is tolerable and the end product meets acceptable specifications.

The other source of variation is referred to as **assignable variation**, or specially caused variation. This type of variation in the production process is caused by specific events or factors that can usually be identified and eliminated. Suppose in the milk example that the machine is "drifting" out of alignment. This causes the machine to overfill each jug—a costly expense for the firm. This is the type of variation in the production process that the firm wants to identify and correct.

Control Charts for Quantitative Data

Walter A. Shewhart, a researcher at Bell Telephone Laboratories during the 1920s, is often credited as being the first to apply statistics to improve the quality of output. He developed the **control chart**—a tool used to monitor the behavior of a production process.

THE CONTROL CHART

The most commonly used statistical tool in quality control is the **control chart**, a plot of calculated statistics of the production process over time. If the calculated statistics fall in an expected range, then the production process is in control. If the calculated statistics reveal an undesirable trend, then adjustment of the production process is likely necessary.

We first focus on quantitative data and examine the $\bar{x}$ **chart**, which monitors the central tendency of a production process. We then move to qualitative data and construct the $\bar{p}$ **chart**, which assesses a process by showing the proportion of defectives (or some other characteristic) in a series of samples. We use the following example to elaborate on the $\bar{x}$ chart.

EXAMPLE 7.9

A firm that produces one-gallon jugs of milk wants to ensure that the machine is operating properly. Every two hours, the company samples 25 jugs and calculates the following sample mean filling weights (in ounces):

128.7	128.4	128.0	127.8	127.5	126.9

Assume that when the machine is operating properly, $\mu = 128$ and $\sigma = 2$, and that filling weights follow the normal distribution. Can the firm conclude that the machine is operating properly? Should the firm have any concerns with respect to this machine?

SOLUTION: To answer these questions, we construct an $\bar{x}$ chart. This chart relies on the normal distribution for the sampling distribution of the sample mean $\bar{X}$. Recall that if we are sampling from a normal population, then $\bar{X}$ is normally distributed even for small sample sizes. In this example, we are told that filling weights follow the normal distribution, a common assumption in the literature on quality control.

Each $\bar{x}$ chart contains a **centerline** and control limits. The centerline is the mean when the process is under control. Here, we know that $\mu = 128$. Above the centerline is the **upper control limit** and below the centerline is the **lower control limit**. If the sample means fall randomly within the upper and lower control limits, then the production process is deemed "under control." The control limits are generally set at three standard deviations from the centerline. As we observed in Chapter 6, the area under the normal curve that corresponds to ±3 standard deviations from the mean is 0.9974. Thus, there is only a $1 - 0.9974 = 0.0026$ chance that the sample means will fall outside the limit boundaries. If a sample mean falls outside the limit boundaries, then the production process is deemed "out of control." Since the standard deviation of the sample mean (the statistic we are tracking) is $\frac{\sigma}{\sqrt{n}}$, we define the control limits as follows:

$$\text{Upper Control Limit, UCL:} \quad \mu + 3\frac{\sigma}{\sqrt{n}}$$

$$\text{Lower Control Limit, LCL:} \quad \mu - 3\frac{\sigma}{\sqrt{n}}$$

In the given example, the upper control limit is $128 + 3\frac{2}{\sqrt{25}} = 129.2$ and the lower control limit is $128 - 3\frac{2}{\sqrt{25}} = 126.8$. Figure 7.11 shows the centerline and the control limits as well as the sample means for Example 7.9.

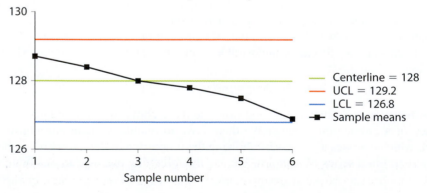

FIGURE 7.11 Mean chart for milk production process

All of the sample means fall within the upper control and the lower control limits, which indicates, at least initially, that the production process is in control. However, the sample means should be randomly spread between these limits; there should be no pattern. One indication of a process that is potentially heading out of control is unusually long runs above or below the center line. Another possible problem is any evidence of a trend within the control limits. Here, there is clearly a downward trend in the sample means. It appears as though the machine is beginning to underfill the one-gallon jugs. So even though none of the sample means lies beyond the control limits, the production process is likely veering out of control and the firm would be wise to inspect the machine sooner rather than later.

Using Excel to Create a Control Chart

It is relatively easy to obtain a control chart using Excel. In order to replicate Figure 7.11, follow these steps.

- Enter Headings for the Centerline, UCL, LCL, and Sample Mean as shown in the first row of the Excel spreadsheet in Figure 7.12.

- Enter the relevant values under each of the headings. For columns with many repeated values (Centerline, UCL, and LCL), it is useful to select the respective value, drag it down a certain number of cells, and then from the menu choose **Home > Fill > Down**. For instance, for the Centerline value of 128, select 128, drag the cursor down five more cells (since we want it repeated six times), and choose **Home > Fill > Down**.

- After all the data have been entered into the spreadsheet, select all the data with the headings and choose **Insert > Line > 2-D Line** (choose the option on the top left). Figure 7.12 shows the embedded control chart.

- Formatting regarding colors, axes, grids, etc. can be done by selecting **Layout** from the menu.

FIGURE 7.12 Using Excel to create a control chart

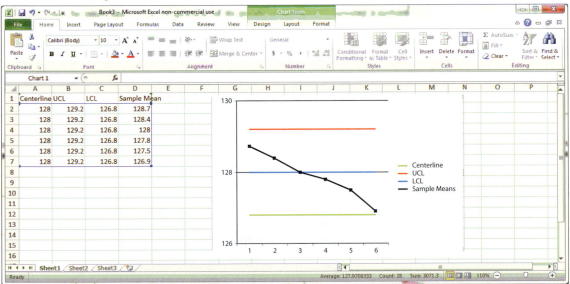

Control Charts for Qualitative Data

A firm may be interested in the proportion of its goods or services possessing a certain attribute or characteristic. For example, most firms strive to produce high-quality goods (or services) and thus hope to keep the proportion of defects at a minimum. When a production process is to be assessed based on sample proportions—here, the proportion of defects—then a $\bar{p}$ chart proves quite useful. Since the primary purpose of the $\bar{p}$ chart is to track the proportion of defects in a production process, it is also referred to as a fraction defective chart or a percent defective chart.

This chart relies on the central limit theorem for the normal approximation for the sampling distribution of the sample proportion $\bar{P}$. Recall that so long as np and $n(1 - p)$ are ≥ 5, then the sampling distribution of $\bar{P}$ is approximately normally distributed. Analogous to the $\bar{x}$ chart, the $\bar{p}$ chart contains a centerline, an upper control limit, and a lower control limit. The control limits are again set at three standard deviations from the centerline. If the sample proportions fall within the control limits, then the production process is under control; otherwise, it is out of control. Since the standard deviation of the sample proportion is $\sqrt{\frac{p(1 - p)}{n}}$, we define the control limits as follows:

$$\text{Upper Control Limit, UCL:} \quad p + 3\sqrt{\frac{p(1 - p)}{n}}$$

$$\text{Lower Control Limit, LCL:} \quad p - 3\sqrt{\frac{p(1 - p)}{n}}$$

If the UCL equation provides a value greater than one, we reset UCL to one in the control chart. Similarly, if the LCL equation provides a negative value for LCL, we reset LCL to zero in the control chart.

EXAMPLE 7.10

In a 2010 automotive quality study conducted by J.D. Power & Associates, Toyota Motor Corp. was rated below average, falling to 21st place from 7th the year before (*The Wall Street Journal*, June 18, 2010). Toyota's reputation suffered due to massive recalls in late 2009 and early 2010 related to defects that could cause the company's cars to accelerate on their own. Moreover, the company was criticized for its delay in responding to the problem. Suppose that from past experience, Toyota expects complaints from 5% of new car buyers each month. For each of the last six months, the company surveys 500 new car buyers and asks if the owner has any complaints about the car. The following sample proportions are obtained:

0.065	0.075	0.082	0.086	0.090	0.092

a. Construct a $\bar{p}$ chart. Plot the sample proportions on the $\bar{p}$ chart.

b. Based on the results, should Toyota have any concerns? Explain.

SOLUTION:

a. Since historical data indicate that 5% of new car buyers lodge some type of complaint, we set the centerline at $p = 0.05$. We then calculate the upper control limit and lower control limit as follows:

$$\text{UCL:} \, p + 3\sqrt{\frac{p(1 - p)}{n}} = 0.05 + 3\sqrt{\frac{0.05(1 - 0.05)}{500}} = 0.079$$

$$\text{LCL:} \, p - 3\sqrt{\frac{p(1 - p)}{n}} = 0.05 - 3\sqrt{\frac{0.05(1 - 0.05)}{500}} = 0.021$$

Plotting the values for the centerline, UCL, and LCL, as well as the sample proportions, yields Figure 7.13.

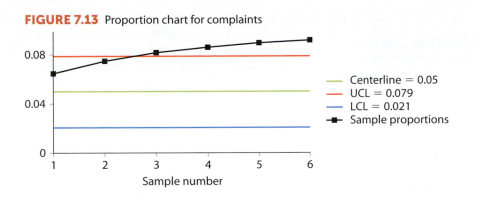

FIGURE 7.13 Proportion chart for complaints

Centerline = 0.05
UCL = 0.079
LCL = 0.021
Sample proportions

b. Four of the most recent sample proportions fall above the upper control limit. The proportion of complaints far surpasses what Toyota expects from past experience. Based on the given sample information, the company needs to seriously address the complaints to avoid further harm to its reputation.

In order to construct a $\bar{p}$ chart using Excel, you would follow the same steps as those outlined earlier for the $\bar{x}$ chart.

EXERCISES 7.5

Concepts

33. Consider a population with mean $\mu = 80$ and standard deviation $\sigma = 14$.
    a. Construct the centerline and the upper and lower control limits for the $\bar{x}$ chart if samples of size 5 are used.
    b. Repeat the analysis with samples of size 10.
    c. Discuss the effect of the sample size on the control limits.

34. A random sample of size $n = 25$ is taken from a population with mean $\mu = 20$ and standard deviation $\sigma = 10$.
    a. Construct the centerline and the upper and lower control limits for the $\bar{x}$ chart.
    b. Suppose six more samples of size 25 were drawn producing the following sample means: 18, 16, 19, 24, 28, and 30. Plot these values on the $\bar{x}$ chart.
    c. Are any points outside the control limits? Does it appear that the process is under control? Explain.

35. A random sample of size $n = 36$ is taken from a population with mean $\mu = 150$ and standard deviation $\sigma = 42$.
    a. Construct the centerline and the upper and lower control limits for the $\bar{x}$ chart.
    b. Suppose five more samples of size 36 were drawn, producing the following sample means: 133, 142, 150, 165, and 169. Plot these values on the $\bar{x}$ chart.
    c. Are any points outside the control limits? Does it appear that the process is under control? Explain.

36. A random sample is taken from a population with $p = 0.04$.
    a. Construct the centerline and the upper and lower control limits for the $\bar{p}$ chart if a random sample of size $n = 250$ is used.
    b. Repeat the analysis with $n = 150$.
    c. Discuss the effect of the sample size on the control limits.

37. A random sample of size $n = 400$ is taken from a population with $p = 0.10$.
    a. Construct the centerline and the upper and lower control limits for the $\bar{p}$ chart.
    b. Suppose six more samples of size 400 were drawn, producing the following sample proportions: 0.06, 0.11, 0.09, 0.08, 0.14, and 0.16. Plot these values on the $\bar{p}$ chart.
    c. Is the production process under control? Explain.

38. A random sample of size $n = 500$ is taken from a population with $p = 0.34$.
    a. Construct the centerline and the upper and lower control limits for the $\bar{p}$ chart.
    b. Suppose six more samples of size 500 were drawn, producing the following sample proportions: 0.28, 0.30, 0.33, 0.34, 0.37, and 0.39. Plot these values on the $\bar{p}$ chart.
    c. Are any points outside the control limits? Does it appear that the process is under control? Explain.

Applications

39. A production process is designed to fill boxes with an average of 14 ounces of cereal. The population of filling weights is normally distributed with a standard deviation of 2 ounces. Inspectors take periodic samples of 10 boxes. The following sample means are obtained.

13.7	14.2	13.9	14.1	14.3	13.9

   a. Construct an $\bar{x}$ chart. Plot the sample means on the $\bar{x}$ chart.
   b. Can the firm conclude that the production process is operating properly? Explain.

40. Major League Baseball Rule 1.09 states that "the baseball shall weigh not less than 5 or more than 5¼ ounces" (www.mlb.com). Use these values as the lower and the upper control limits, respectively. Assume the centerline equals 5.125 ounces. Periodic samples of 50 baseballs produce the following sample means:

5.05	5.10	5.15	5.20	5.22	5.24

   a. Construct an $\bar{x}$ chart. Plot the sample means on the $\bar{x}$ chart.
   b. Are any points outside the control limits? Does it appear that the process is under control? Explain.

41. **FILE** Fast bowling, also known as pace bowling, is an important component of the bowling attack in the sport of cricket. The objective is to bowl at high speed and make the ball turn in the air and off the ground so that it becomes difficult for the batsman to hit it cleanly. Kalwant Singh is a budding Indian cricketer in a special bowling camp. While his coach is happy with Kalwant's average bowling speed, he feels that Kalwant lacks consistency. He records his bowling speed on the next four overs, where each over consists of six balls; the data labeled **Cricket** is also available on the text website.

Over 1	Over 2	Over 3	Over 4
96.8	99.2	88.4	98.4
99.5	100.2	97.8	91.4
88.8	90.1	82.8	85.5
81.9	98.7	91.2	87.6
100.1	96.4	94.2	90.3
96.8	98.8	89.8	85.9

   It is fair to assume that Kalwant's bowling speed is normally distributed with a mean and standard deviation of 94 and 2.8 miles per hour, respectively.

   a. Construct the centerline and the upper and lower control limits for the $\bar{x}$ chart. Plot the average speed of Kalwant's four overs on the $\bar{x}$ chart.
   b. Is there any pattern in Kalwant's bowling that justifies his coach's concerns that he is not consistent in bowling? Explain.

42. A firm produces computer chips for personal computers. From past experience, the firm knows that 4% of the chips are defective. The firm collects a sample of the first 500 chips manufactured at 1:00 pm for the past two weeks. The following sample proportions are obtained:

0.044	0.052	0.060	0.036	0.028	0.042	0.034	0.054	0.048	0.025

   a. Construct a $\bar{p}$ chart. Plot the sample proportions on the $\bar{p}$ chart.
   b. Can the firm conclude that the process is operating properly?

43. A manufacturing process produces steel rods in batches of 1,000. The firm believes that the percent of defective items generated by this process is 5%.

   a. Construct the centerline and the upper and lower control limits for the $\bar{p}$ chart.
   b. An engineer inspects the next batch of 1,000 steel rods and finds that 6.2% are defective. Is the manufacturing process under control? Explain.

44. The college admissions office at a local university usually admits 750 students and knows from previous experience that 25% of these students choose not to enroll at the university. Assume $p = 0.25$.

   a. Construct the centerline and the upper and lower control limits for the $\bar{p}$ chart.
   b. Assume that this year the university admits 750 students and 240 choose not to enroll at the university. Should the university be concerned? Explain.

45. Following customer complaints about the quality of service, Dell stopped routing corporate customers to a technical support call center in Bangalore, India (*USA Today*, November 24, 2003). Suppose Dell's decision to direct customers to call centers outside of India was based on consumer complaints in the last six months. Let the number of complaints per month for 80 randomly selected customers be given below.

Month	Number of Complaints
1	20
2	12
3	24
4	14
5	25
6	22

   a. Construct the centerline and the upper and lower control limits for the $\bar{p}$ chart if management allows a 15% complaint rate.
   b. Can you justify Dell's decision to direct customers to call centers outside of India?

WRITING WITH STATISTICS

Barbara Dwyer, the manager at Lux Hotel, makes every effort to ensure that customers attempting to make phone reservations wait an average of only 60 seconds to speak with a reservations specialist. She knows that this is likely to be the customer's first impression of the hotel and she wants the initial interaction to be a positive one. Since the hotel accepts phone reservations 24 hours a day, Barbara wonders if this quality service is consistently maintained throughout the day. She takes six samples of $n = 4$ calls during each of four shifts over one 24-hour period and records the wait time of each call. A portion of the data, in seconds, is presented in Table 7.1; the complete data, labeled *Lux Hotel*, are available on the text website.

TABLE 7.1 Wait times for phone reservations

Shift	Sample	Wait Time (in seconds)				Sample Mean, $\bar{x}$
Shift 1:	1	67	48	52	71	60
12:00 am–6:00 am	2	57	68	60	66	63
	3	37	41	60	41	45
	4	83	59	49	66	64
	5	82	63	64	83	73
	6	87	53	66	69	69
⋮	⋮	⋮	⋮	⋮	⋮	⋮
Shift 4:	19	6	11	8	9	9
6:00 pm–12:00 am	20	10	8	10	9	9
	21	11	7	14	7	10
	22	8	9	9	12	10
	23	9	12	9	14	11
	24	5	8	15	11	10

Barbara relays to the quality control engineer that the mean wait time is 60 seconds with a standard deviation of 30 seconds. She instructs the quality control engineer to use the sample information to:

1. Prepare a control chart for the wait time for a customer.
2. Use the control chart to determine whether the quality service is consistently maintained throughout the day.

When a potential customer phones Lux Hotel, it is imperative for the reservations specialist to set a tone that relays the high standard of service that the customer will receive if he/she chooses to stay at the Lux. For this reason, management at the Lux strives to minimize the time that elapses before a potential customer speaks with a reservations specialist; however, management also recognizes the need to use its resources wisely. If too many reservations specialists are on duty, then resources are wasted due to idle time; yet if too few reservations specialists are on duty, the result might mean angry first-time customers, or worse, lost customers. In order to ensure customer satisfaction as well as an efficient use of resources, a study is conducted to determine whether a typical customer waits an average of 60 seconds to speak with a reservations specialist. Before data are collected, a control chart is constructed. The upper control limit (UCL) and the lower control limit (LCL) are set three standard deviations from the desired average of 60 seconds. In Figure 7.A, the desired average of 60 seconds is denoted as the centerline and the upper and lower

Sample Report— Customer Wait Time

control limits amount to 105 seconds and 15 seconds $\left(\mu \pm 3\frac{\sigma}{\sqrt{n}} = 60 \pm 3\frac{30}{\sqrt{4}} = 60 \pm 45\right)$, respectively. The reservation process is deemed under control if the sample means fall randomly within the upper and lower control limits; otherwise the process is out of control and adjustments should be made.

FIGURE 7.A Sample mean wait times

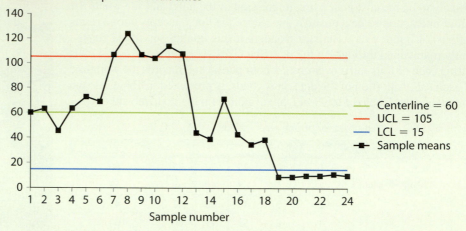

During each of four shifts, six samples of $n = 4$ calls are randomly selected over one 24-hour period and the average wait time of each sample is recorded. All six sample means from the first shift (1st shift: 12:00 am–6:00 am, sample numbers one through six) fall within the control limits, indicating that the reservation process is in control. However, five sample means from the second shift (2nd shift: 6:00 am–12:00 pm, sample numbers seven through 12) lie above the upper control limit. Customers calling during the second shift are waiting too long before they speak with a specialist. In terms of quality standards, this is unacceptable from the hotel's perspective. All six sample means from the third shift fall within the control limits (3rd shift: 12:00 pm–6:00 pm, sample numbers 13 through 18), yet all sample means for the fourth shift fall below the lower control limit (4th shift: 6:00 pm–12:00 am, sample numbers 19 through 24). Customers are waiting for very short periods of time to speak with a reservations specialist, but reservations specialists may have too much idle time. Perhaps one solution is to shift some reservations specialists from shift four to shift two.

Conceptual Review

LO **7.1** **Differentiate between a population parameter and a sample statistic.**

The numerical measure of a population is called a **population parameter**, or simply a **parameter**. A parameter is a **constant** even though its value may be unknown. The numerical measure of a sample is called a **sample statistic**, or simply a **statistic**. A statistic, such as the sample mean or the sample proportion, is a **random variable** whose value depends on the chosen random sample.

LO **7.2** **Explain common sample biases.**

A sampling **bias** occurs when the information from a sample is not typical of that in the population in a systematic way. **Selection bias** refers to a systematic exclusion of certain groups from consideration for the sample. **Nonresponse bias** refers to a systematic difference in preferences between respondents and nonrespondents to a survey or a poll.

LO 7.3 | **Describe simple random sampling.**

A **simple random sample** is a sample of n observations which has the same probability of being selected from the population as any other sample of n observations. Most statistical methods presume simple random samples.

LO 7.4 | **Distinguish between stratified random sampling and cluster sampling.**

A **stratified random sample** is formed when the population is divided into groups (strata) based on one or more classification criteria. A stratified random sample includes randomly selected observations from each stratum, which are proportional to the stratum's size. A **cluster sample** is formed when the population is divided into groups (clusters) based on geographic areas. Whereas a stratified random sample consists of elements from each group, a cluster sample includes observations from randomly selected clusters. Stratified random sampling is preferred when the objective is to **increase precision** and cluster sampling is preferred when the objective is to **reduce costs**.

LO 7.5 | **Describe the properties of the sampling distribution of the sample mean.**

Since the sample mean is a random variable, its sampling distribution is the probability distribution of sample means derived from all possible samples of a given size from the population. The expected value of the sample mean $\overline{X}$ equals $E(\overline{X}) = \mu$ and the standard deviation equals $SD(\overline{X}) = \frac{\sigma}{\sqrt{n}}$. For any sample size, the sampling distribution of $\overline{X}$ is normal if the **population is normally distributed**.

A normally distributed $\overline{X}$ can be transformed into a **standard normal random variable** as $Z = \frac{\overline{X} - \mu}{\sigma/\sqrt{n}}$. Therefore, any value $\overline{x}$ on $\overline{X}$ has a corresponding value z on Z given by $z = \frac{\overline{x} - \mu}{\sigma/\sqrt{n}}$.

LO 7.6 | **Explain the importance of the central limit theorem.**

The **central limit theorem** (**CLT**) is used when it is not known whether or not the random sample is derived from a normal population. It states that for any population X with expected value μ and standard deviation σ, the sampling distribution of $\overline{X}$ is approximately normal if the sample size n **is sufficiently large**. As a general guideline, the normal distribution approximation is justified when $n \geq 30$.

LO 7.7 | **Describe the properties of the sampling distribution of the sample proportion.**

The **expected value** and the **standard deviation** of the sample proportion $\overline{P}$ are $E(\overline{P}) = p$ and $SD(\overline{P}) = \sqrt{\frac{p(1-p)}{n}}$. The **central limit theorem** states that for any population proportion p, the sampling distribution of $\overline{P}$ is approximately normal if the sample size n **is sufficiently large**. As a general guideline, the normal distribution approximation is justified when $np \geq 5$ and $n(1-p) \geq 5$. If we assume $\overline{P}$ to be normal, it can be transformed into a standard normal random variable as $Z = \frac{\overline{P} - p}{\sqrt{\frac{p(1-p)}{n}}}$. Therefore, any value $\overline{p}$ on $\overline{P}$ has a corresponding value z on Z given by $z = \frac{\overline{p} - p}{\sqrt{\frac{p(1-p)}{n}}}$.

LO 7.8 | **Use a finite population correction factor.**

If the population size is relatively small (finite) and its value is known, then it is preferable to use the correction factor in the standard deviation of the estimators. As a general guideline, we use the finite correction factor when the sample constitutes at least 5% of the population, or $n \geq 0.05N$. With the correction factor, $SD(\overline{X}) = \frac{\sigma}{\sqrt{n}}\left(\sqrt{\frac{N-n}{N-1}}\right)$ and $SD(\overline{P}) = \sqrt{\frac{p(1-p)}{n}}\left(\sqrt{\frac{N-n}{N-1}}\right)$. The transformation to Z is made accordingly.

Construct and interpret control charts for quantitative and qualitative data.

Statistical quality control involves statistical techniques used to develop and maintain a firm's ability to produce high-quality goods and services. The most commonly used statistical tool in quality control is the **control chart**. A control chart specifies a centerline as well as an upper control limit (UCL) and a lower control limit (LCL). In general, the UCL and the LCL are set within three standard deviations of the centerline.

The upper and lower control limits for the $\bar{x}$ **chart** are defined as $\mu + 3\frac{\sigma}{\sqrt{n}}$ and $\mu - 3\frac{\sigma}{\sqrt{n}}$, respectively. For the $\bar{p}$ **chart**, these limits are defined as $p + 3\sqrt{\frac{p(1-p)}{n}}$ and $p - 3\sqrt{\frac{p(1-p)}{n}}$, respectively. If the sample means, or the sample proportions, fall within the control limits, then generally the process is under control. However, the sample means, or the sample proportions, must be randomly spread between the control limits. If there is a trend or unusually long runs above or below the center line, then the process may be veering out of control.

Additional Exercises and Case Studies

46. A seminal study conducted by scientists at the University of Illinois found evidence of improved memory and reasoning for those who took three vigorous 40-minute walks a week over six months (*Newsweek,* June 28–July 5, 2010). As an assistant manager working for a public health institute based in Florida, you would like to estimate the proportion of adults in Miami, Florida, who follow such a walking regimen. Discuss the sampling bias in the following strategies where people are asked if they walk regularly:
    a. Randomly selected adult beachgoers in Miami.
    b. Randomly selected Miami residents are requested to disclose the information in prepaid envelopes.
    c. Randomly selected Miami residents are requested to disclose the information on the firm's website.
    d. Randomly selected adult patients at all hospitals in Miami.

47. In the previous question regarding walking regimens of the residents of Miami, explain how you can obtain a representative sample based on the following sampling strategies:
    a. Simple random sampling.
    b. Stratified random sampling.
    c. Cluster sampling.

48. According to the Bureau of Labor Statistics it takes an average of 22 weeks for someone over 55 to find a new job, compared with 16 weeks for younger workers (*The Wall Street Journal,* September 2, 2008). Assume that the probability distributions are normal and that the standard deviation is 2 weeks for both distributions.
    a. What is the probability that 8 workers over the age of 55 take an average of more than 20 weeks to find a job?
    b. What is the probability that 20 younger workers average less than 15 weeks to find a job?

49. While starting salaries have fallen for college graduates in many of the top hiring fields, there is some good news for business undergraduates with concentrations in accounting and finance (*Bloomberg Businessweek,* July 1, 2010). According to the National Association of Colleges and Employers' Summer 2010 Salary Survey, accounting graduates commanded the second highest salary at $50,402, followed by finance graduates at $49,703. Let the standard deviation for accounting and finance graduates be $6,000 and $10,000, respectively.
    a. What is the probability that 100 randomly selected accounting graduates will average more than $52,000 in salary?
    b. What is the probability that 100 randomly selected finance graduates will average more than $52,000 in salary?
    c. Comment on the above probabilities.

50. An automatic machine in a manufacturing process is operating properly if the length of an important subcomponent is normally distributed with a mean $\mu = 80$ cm and standard deviation $\sigma = 2$ cm.
    a. Find the probability that the length of one randomly selected unit is less than 79 cm.
    b. Find the probability that the average length of 10 randomly selected units is less than 79 cm.
    c. Find the probability that the average length of 30 randomly selected units is less than 79 cm.

51. Trader Joe's is a privately held chain of specialty grocery stores in the U.S. Starting out as a small chain of convenience stores, it has expanded to over 340 stores as of June 2010 (Traderjoe .com). It has developed a reputation as a unique grocery store selling products such as gourmet foods, beer and wine, bread, nuts, cereal, and coffee. One of their best-selling nuts is Raw California Almonds, which are priced at $4.49 for 16 ounces. Since it is impossible to pack exactly 16 ounces in each packet, a researcher has determined that the weight of almonds in each packet is normally distributed with a mean and standard deviation equal to 16.01 and 0.08 ounces, respectively.

a. Discuss the sampling distribution of the sample mean based on any given sample size.

b. Find the probability that a random sample of 20 bags of almonds will average less than 16 ounces.

c. Suppose your cereal recipe calls for no less than 48 ounces of almonds. What is the probability that three packets of almonds will meet your requirement?

52. The average college graduate has a student loan debt of $23,186 (*The Boston Globe*, June 8, 2010). Assume the population standard deviation is $5,000. Suppose you take a random sample of 50 college graduates.

a. What is the probability that the sample mean debt is more than $25,000?

b. What is the probability that the sample mean debt is less than $22,000?

c. What is the probability that the sample mean debt is within $2,500 of the population mean?

53. Data from the Bureau of Labor Statistics' Consumer Expenditure Survey (CE) show that annual expenditures for cellular phone services per consumer unit increased from $210 in 2001 to $608 in 2007. Let the standard deviation of annual cellular expenditure be $48 in 2001 and $132 in 2007.

a. What is the probability that the average expenditure of 100 cellular customers in 2001 exceeded $200?

b. What is the probability that the average expenditure of 100 cellular customers in 2007 exceeded $600?

54. According to a recent report, scientists in New England say they have identified a set of genetic variants that predicts extreme longevity with 77% accuracy (*New York Times*, July 1, 2010). Assume 150 patients decide to get their genome sequenced.

a. If the claim by scientists is accurate, what is the probability that more than 120 patients will get a correct diagnosis for extreme longevity?

b. If the claim by scientists is accurate, what is the probability that fewer than 70% of the patients will get a correct diagnosis for extreme longevity?

55. American workers are increasingly planning to delay retirement (*US News & World Report*, June 30, 2010). According to a Pew Research Center comprehensive survey, 35% of employed adults of age 62 and older say they have pushed back their retirement date.

a. What is the probability that in a sample of 100 employed adults of age 62 and older, more than 40% have pushed back their retirement date?

b. What is the probability that in a sample of 200 employed adults of age 62 and older, more than 40% have pushed back their retirement date?

c. Comment on the difference between the two estimated probabilities.

56. Presidential job approval is the most-watched statistic in American politics. According to the June 2010 NBC/*Wall*

Street Journal public opinion poll, President Barack Obama has reached his lowest approval rating since taking office in January of 2009. The poll showed that 48% of people disapprove of the job Obama is doing as President of the United States, while only 45% approve. Experts attribute the drop in approval ratings to a poor economy and the government's reaction to the massive oil spill in the Gulf of Mexico. Assume the above approval and disapproval ratings in June 2010 to answer the following questions.

a. What is the probability that President Obama gets a majority support in a random sample of 50 Americans?

b. What is the probability that President Obama gets a majority disapproval in a random sample of 50 Americans?

57. The producer of a particular brand of soup claims that its sodium content is 50% less than that of its competitor. The food label states that the sodium content measures 410 milligrams per serving. Assume the population of sodium content is normally distributed with a standard deviation of 25 milligrams. Inspectors take periodic samples of 25 cans and measure the sodium content. The following sample means are obtained.

| 405 | 412 | 399 | 420 | 430 | 428 |

a. Construct an $\bar{x}$ chart. Plot the sample means on the $\bar{x}$ chart.

b. Can the inspectors conclude that the producer is advertising the sodium content accurately? Explain.

58. **FILE** A variety of packaging solutions exist for products that must be kept within a specific temperature range. Cold chain distribution is particularly useful in the food and pharmaceutical industries. A packaging company strives to maintain a constant temperature for its packages. It is believed that the temperature of its packages follows a normal distribution with a mean of 5 degrees Celsius and a standard deviation of 0.3 degree Celsius. Inspectors take weekly samples for 5 weeks of eight randomly selected boxes and report the following temperatures in degrees Celsius. A portion of the data are given below; the complete data, labeled *Packaging*, are available on the text website.

Week 1	Week 2	Week 3	Week 4	Week 5
3.98	5.52	5.79	3.98	5.14
4.99	5.52	6.42	5.79	6.25
⋮	⋮	⋮	⋮	⋮
4.95	4.95	5.44	5.95	4.28

a. Construct an $\bar{x}$ chart for quality control. Plot the five weekly sample means on the $\bar{x}$ chart.

b. Are any points outside the control limits? Does it appear that the process is in control? Explain.

59. Acceptance sampling is an important quality control technique, where a batch of data is tested to determine if the proportion of units having a particular attribute exceeds a given percentage. Suppose that 10% of produced items are

known to be nonconforming. Every week a batch of items is evaluated and the production machines are adjusted if the proportion of nonconforming items exceeds 15%.

a. What is the probability that the production machines will be adjusted if the batch consists of 50 items?

b. What is the probability that the production machines will be adjusted if the batch consists of 100 items?

60. In the previous question, suppose the management decides to use a $\bar{p}$ chart for the analysis. As noted earlier, 10% of produced items are known to be nonconforming. The firm analyzes a batch of production items for 6 weeks and computes the following percentages of nonconforming items.

Week	Nonconforming Percentage
1	5.5%
2	13.1%
3	16.8%
4	13.6%
5	19.8%
6	2.0%

a. Suppose weekly batches consisted of 50 items. Construct a $\bar{p}$ chart and determine if the machine needs adjustment in any of the weeks.

b. Suppose weekly batches consisted of 100 items. Construct a $\bar{p}$ chart and determine if the machine needs adjustment in any of the weeks.

CASE STUDIES

Case Study 7.1

The significant decline of savings in the United States from the 1970s and 1980s to the 1990s and 2000s has been widely discussed by economists (money.cnn.com, June 30, 2010). According to the Bureau of Economic Analysis, the savings rate of American households, defined as a percentage of the disposable personal income, was 4.20% in 2009. The reported savings rate is not uniform across the country. A public policy institute conducts two of its own surveys to compute the savings rate in the Midwest. In the first survey, a sample of 160 households is taken and the average savings rate is found to be 4.48%. Another sample of 40 households finds an average savings rate of 4.60%. Assume that the population standard deviation is 1.4%.

In a report, use the above information to:

1. Compute the probability of obtaining a sample mean that is at least as high as the one computed in each of the two surveys.

2. Use these probabilities to decide which of the two samples is likely to be more representative of the United States as a whole.

Case Study 7.2

According to a report, college graduates in 2010 were likely to face better job prospects than 2009 graduates (*The New York Times,* May 24, 2010). Many employers who might have been pessimistic at the start of the 2009–2010 academic year were making more offers than expected. Despite the improvement in job prospects, the Bureau of Labor Statistics reported that the current jobless rate for college graduates under age 25 was still 8%. For high school graduates under age 25 who did not enroll in college, the current jobless rate was 24.5%. Cindy Chan works in the sales department of a trendy apparel company and has recently been relocated to a small town in Iowa. She finds that there are a total of 220 college graduates and 140 high school graduates under age 25 who live in this town. Cindy wants to gauge the demand for her products by the number of youths in this town who are employed.

In a report, use the above information to:

1. Compute the expected number of college and high school graduates who are employed.

2. Report the probabilities that at least 200 college graduates and at least 100 high school graduates under age 25 are employed.

Case Study 7.3

Hockey pucks used by the National Hockey League (NHL) and other professional leagues weigh an average of 163 grams (5.75 ounces). A quality inspector monitors the manufacturing process for hockey pucks. She takes eight samples of $n = 10$. Measured in grams, the weights appear in the table below. It is fair to assume that when the production process is in control, $\mu = 163$ and $\sigma = 7.5$. A portion of the data are shown below; the complete data labeled **Hockey Puck** are available on the text website.

Data for Case Study 7.3 Hockey Puck Samples

	#1	#2	#3	#4	#5	#6	#7	#8
FILE	162.2	165.8	156.4	165.3	168.6	167.0	186.8	178.3
	159.8	166.2	156.4	173.3	175.8	171.4	160.4	163.0
	⋮	⋮	⋮	⋮	⋮	⋮	⋮	⋮
	160.3	160.6	152.2	166.4	168.2	168.4	176.8	171.3

In a report, use the above information to:

1. Prepare a control chart that specifies a centerline as well as an upper control limit (UCL) and a lower control limit (LCL).

2. Use the control chart to determine whether the process is in control.

7.A1 Appendix

Derivation of the Properties of the Sample Mean

Let the expected value and the variance of the population X be denoted by $E(X) = \mu$ and $Var(X) = \sigma^2$, respectively. The sample mean $\overline{X}$ based on a random draw of n observations, $X_1, X_2, \ldots, X_n$, from the population is computed as $\overline{X} = \frac{X_1 + X_2 + \cdots + X_n}{n}$.

We use the properties of the sum of random variables to derive

$$E(\overline{X}) = E\left(\frac{X_1 + X_2 + \cdots + X_n}{n}\right) = \frac{E(X_1) + E(X_2) + \cdots + E(X_n)}{n}$$

$$= \frac{\mu + \mu + \cdots + \mu}{n} = \frac{n\mu}{n} = \mu.$$

Since the sample mean is based on n independent draws from the population, the covariance terms drop out and the variance of the sample mean is thus derived as:

$$Var(\overline{X}) = Var\left(\frac{X_1 + X_2 + \cdots + X_n}{n}\right) = \frac{1}{n^2} Var(X_1 + X_2 + \cdots + X_n)$$

$$= \frac{1}{n^2}(Var(X_1) + Var(X_2) + \cdots + Var(X_n))$$

$$= \frac{\sigma^2 + \sigma^2 + \cdots + \sigma^2}{n^2} = \frac{n\sigma^2}{n^2} = \frac{\sigma^2}{n}.$$

Derivation of the Properties of the Sample Proportion

Let X be a binomial random variable representing the number of successes in n trials. Recall from Chapter 5 that $E(X) = np$ and $Var(X) = np(1 - p)$ where p is the probability of success. For the sample proportion $\overline{P} = \frac{X}{n}$,

$$E(\overline{P}) = E\left(\frac{X}{n}\right) = \frac{E(X)}{n} = \frac{np}{n} = p, \quad \text{and}$$

$$Var(\overline{P}) = Var\left(\frac{X}{n}\right) = \frac{Var(X)}{n^2} = \frac{np(1 - p)}{n^2} = \frac{p(1 - p)}{n}.$$

8 Estimation

In earlier chapters we made a distinction between the population parameters, such as the population mean and the population proportion, and the corresponding sample statistics. The sample statistics are used to make statistical inferences regarding the unknown values of the population parameters. In general, two basic methodologies emerge from the inferential branch of statistics: estimation and hypothesis testing. In this chapter we focus on estimation. A point estimator is a function of the random sample that produces a single value as an estimate of the unknown population parameter of interest. A confidence interval, on the other hand, is a range of values that is likely to include the unknown parameter. We first discuss point estimators and their desirable properties. We then use point estimates to develop and interpret the confidence intervals of the population mean and the population proportion. Since obtaining a sample is one of the first steps in making statistical inferences, we also learn how an appropriate sample size is determined in order to achieve a certain level of precision in the estimates.

Fuel Usage of "Ultra-Green" Cars

A car manufacturer advertises that its new "ultra-green" car obtains an average of 100 miles per gallon (mpg) and, based on its fuel emissions, is one of the few cars that earns an A+ rating from the Environmental Protection Agency. Pinnacle Research, an independent consumer advocacy firm, obtains a sample of 25 cars for testing purposes. Each car is driven the same distance in identical conditions. Pinnacle Research provides Jared Beane, a journalist at a reputable automobile magazine, with each car's mpg as shown in Table 8.1; these data labeled **MPG** are also available on the text website.

TABLE 8.1   MPG for a Sample of 25 "Ultra-Green" Cars

97	117	93	79	97
87	78	83	94	96
102	98	82	96	113
113	111	90	101	99
112	89	92	96	98

Jared has already used tabular and graphical methods to summarize the data in his article. He would like to make statistical inference regarding key population parameters. In particular, he wants to use the above sample information to:

1. Estimate the mean mpg of all ultra-green cars with 90% confidence.

2. Estimate the proportion of all ultra-green cars that obtain over 100 mpg with 90% confidence.

3. Determine the sample size that will enable him to achieve a specified level of precision in his mean and proportion estimates.

We provide a synopsis of this case at the end of Section 8.5.

8.1 Point Estimators and Their Properties

In the introductory case, Jared Beane is provided with the mpg for a sample of 25 ultra-green cars. We can use the sample information in Table 8.1 to compute the mean mpg of the cars. As discussed in Chapter 3, we compute the sample mean as $\bar{x} = \frac{\Sigma x_i}{n} = \frac{2413}{25} = 96.52$ mpg. We can also use the sample information to compute the proportion of cars with mpg greater than 100. Since there are seven cars in the sample with mpg greater than 100, we compute the sample proportion as $\bar{p} = \frac{x}{n} = \frac{7}{25} = 0.28$. These descriptive measures indicate that the mean mpg of ultra-green cars is 96.52 mpg. In addition, 28% of the cars recorded more than 100 mpg.

The above descriptive measures represent the values of the statistics $\bar{X}$ and $\bar{P}$, respectively. Since they are based on a sample of 25 cars, they are likely to vary between samples. For instance, the values will change if another sample of 25 cars is used. What Jared really wishes to estimate are the descriptive measures (parameters) of all ultra-green cars (population), not just of those in the sample. Although sample statistics represent only a portion of the overall population, they contain useful information for estimating the unknown population parameters. In this chapter we focus on estimating two population parameters: the population mean and the population proportion.

The sample statistics $\bar{X}$ and $\bar{P}$ are the **point estimators** of their population counterparts μ and p. These statistics are called point estimators because each of them provides a single value—*a point*—as an estimate of the unknown population parameter. The sample mean is a point estimator of the population mean and the sample proportion is a point estimator of the population proportion.

POINT ESTIMATORS AND POINT ESTIMATES

A **point estimator** is a function of the random sample used to make inferences about the value of an unknown population parameter. A **point estimate** is the value of the point estimator derived from a given sample.

In the above example, $\bar{x} = 96.5$ mpg is a point estimate of the mean mpg for all ultra-green cars and $\bar{p} = 0.28$ is a point estimate of the proportion of all ultra-green cars that obtain over 100 mpg.

EXAMPLE 8.1

A statistics section at a large university has 100 students. The scores of 10 randomly selected final exams are:

66	72	40	85	75	90	92	60	82	38

Calculate the point estimate for the population mean.

SOLUTION: We calculate $\bar{x} = \frac{66 + 72 + \cdots + 38}{10} = \frac{700}{10} = 70$. Therefore, a score of 70 is a point estimate of the population mean.

Properties of Point Estimators

We generally discuss the performance of an estimator in terms of its statistical properties. Some of the desirable properties of a point estimator include unbiasedness, consistency, and efficiency. An estimator is **unbiased** if, based on repeated sampling from the population, the average value of the estimator equals the population parameter. In other words, for an unbiased estimator, the expected value of the point estimator equals the population parameter.

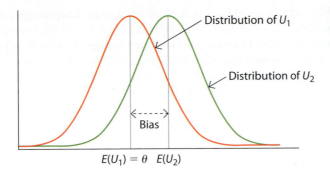

FIGURE 8.1 The distributions of unbiased (U_1) and biased (U_2) estimators

Figure 8.1 shows the sampling distributions for two estimators U_1 and U_2, which are assumed to be normally distributed. Let θ (the Greek letter read as theta) be the true parameter value of the population. Estimator U_1 is unbiased because its expected value $E(U_1)$ equals θ. Estimator U_2 is biased because $E(U_2) \neq \theta$; the amount of bias is given by the difference between $E(U_2)$ and θ.

Recall from Chapter 7 that $E(\bar{X}) = \mu$ and $E(\bar{P}) = p$; therefore, $\bar{X}$ and $\bar{P}$ are the unbiased estimators of μ and p, respectively. This property is independent of the sample size. For instance, the expected value of the sample mean is equal to the population mean irrespective of the sample size.

We often compare the performance of the unbiased estimators in terms of their relative **efficiency**. An estimator is deemed efficient if its variability between samples is smaller than that of other unbiased estimators. Recall that the variability is often measured by the standard error of the estimator, where the standard error is the estimated standard deviation of the estimator. For an unbiased estimator to be efficient, its standard error must be lower than that of other unbiased estimators. It is well documented that the estimators $\bar{X}$ and $\bar{P}$ are not only unbiased, but also efficient.

Figure 8.2 shows the sampling distributions for two unbiased estimators V_1 and V_2 for the true population parameter θ. Again, for illustration, V_1 and V_2 follow the normal distribution. While both V_1 and V_2 are unbiased ($E(V_1) = E(V_2) = \theta$), V_1 is more efficient because it has less variability.

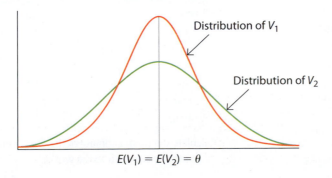

FIGURE 8.2 The distributions of efficient (V_1) and less efficient (V_2) estimators

Another desirable property, which is often considered a minimum requirement for an estimator, is **consistency**. An estimator is consistent if it approaches the population parameter of interest as the sample size increases. Consistency implies that we will get the inference right if we take a large enough sample. The estimators $\overline{X}$ and $\overline{P}$ are not only unbiased, but also consistent. For instance, the sample mean collapses to the population mean ($\overline{X} \to \mu$) as the sample size approaches infinity ($n \to \infty$). An unbiased estimator is consistent if its standard deviation, or its standard error, collapses to zero as the sample size increases.

CONSISTENCY

An estimator is **consistent** if it approaches the unknown population parameter being estimated as the sample size grows larger.

The consistency of $\overline{X}$ is illustrated in Figure 8.3.

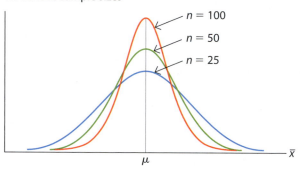

FIGURE 8.3 The distribution of a consistent estimator $\overline{X}$ for various sample sizes

As the sample size n increases, the variability of $\overline{X}$ decreases. In particular as $n \to \infty$, $SD(\overline{X}) = \sigma/\sqrt{n} \to 0$, thus implying that $\overline{X}$ is a consistent estimator of μ.

EXERCISES 8.1

Concepts

1. A random sample produced the following data:

135	120	127	132	123	130

Calculate the point estimate of the population mean.

2. A random sample produced the following data:

0	−10	−8	−4	2	6

Calculate the point estimate of the population mean.

3. A random sample of 50 observations results in 20 successes.
   a. Calculate the point estimate of the population proportion of successes.
   b. Calculate the point estimate of the population proportion of failures.

4. A random sample of 400 observations results in 300 successes.
   a. Calculate the point estimate of the population proportion of successes.
   b. Calculate the point estimate of the population proportion of failures.

Applications

5. A random sample of eight drugstores shows the following prices (in $) of a popular pain reliever:

2.99	3.25	2.75	3.05	3.10	2.95	2.99	3.25

Calculate the point estimate of the population mean price for the pain reliever.

6. As reported by tradingeconomics.com in 2011, the unemployment rates (in %) in major economies around the world are as follows:

Country	Unemployment Rate (in %)
France	9.6
India	9.4
United States	9.1
United Kingdom	7.9
Canada	7.3
Germany	6.6
Australia	5.3

Calculate the point estimate of the unemployment rate in major economies around the world.

7. A recent survey asked 5,324 individuals: What's most important to you when choosing where to live? The responses are shown by the following frequency distribution.

Response	Frequency
Good jobs	1,969
Affordable homes	799
Top schools	586
Low crime	1,225
Things to do	745

Source: CNNMoney.com, July 13, 2010.

a. Calculate the point estimate of the population proportion of those who believe that low crime is most important.

b. Calculate the point estimate of the population proportion of those who believe that good jobs or affordable homes are most important.

8. A survey conducted by CBS News asked 1,026 respondents: "What would you do with an unexpected tax refund?" The responses are summarized in the following table.

Response	Frequency
Pay off debts	482
Put it in the bank	308
Spend it	112
I never get a refund	103
Other	21

Source: *Vanity Fair*, June 2010.

a. Calculate the point estimate of the population proportion of those who would put the tax refund in the bank.

b. Calculate the point estimate of the population proportion of those who never get a refund.

8.2 Confidence Interval of the Population Mean When σ Is Known

LO 8.2

Explain an interval estimator.

So far we have only discussed point estimators. Often it is more informative to provide a range of values—an **interval**—rather than a single point estimate of the unknown population parameter. This range of values is called a **confidence interval**, also referred to as an **interval estimate**, of the population parameter.

CONFIDENCE INTERVAL

A **confidence interval** provides a range of values that, with a certain level of confidence, contains the population parameter of interest.

In order to construct a confidence interval for the population mean μ or the population proportion p, it is essential that the distributions of $\overline{X}$ and $\overline{P}$ follow, or approximately follow, a normal distribution. Recall from Chapter 7 that $\overline{X}$ follows a normal distribution when the underlying population is normally distributed; this result holds irrespective of the sample size n. If the underlying population is not normally distributed, then by the central limit theorem, the sampling distribution of $\overline{X}$ will be approximately normally distributed if the sample size is sufficiently large, or when $n \geq 30$. Similarly, the sampling distribution of $\overline{P}$ is approximately normally distributed if the sample size is sufficiently large, or when $np \geq 5$ and $n(1 - p) \geq 5$.

A confidence interval is generally associated with a **margin of error** that accounts for the variability of the estimator and the desired confidence level of the interval.

It is common to construct a confidence interval as: Point estimate $\pm$ Margin of error.

An analogy to a simple weather example is instructive. If you feel that the outside temperature is about 50 degrees, then perhaps you can, with a certain level of confidence, suggest that the actual temperature is between 40 and 60 degrees. In this example, 50 degrees is analogous to a point estimate of the actual temperature and 10 degrees is the margin of error that is added to and subtracted from this point estimate.

We know from the introductory case study that the point estimate of the population mean mpg of all ultra-green cars is 96.5 mpg; that is, $\bar{x} = 96.5$. We can construct a confidence interval by using the point estimate as a base to which we add and subtract the margin of error.

The symmetry of the normal distribution implies that the same margin of error will be added to and subtracted from the point estimate. Since numerous samples of size n can be drawn from the underlying population, the variability of the estimator is captured by its standard deviation, or its standard error. The margin of error incorporates this important information along with the desired confidence level of the interval.

LO **8.3**

Calculate a confidence interval for the population mean when the population standard deviation is known.

Constructing a Confidence Interval for μ When σ Is Known

Consider a standard normal random variable Z. Using the symmetry of Z, we can compute $P(Z \geq 1.96) = P(Z \leq -1.96) = 0.025$; see Figure 8.4. Remember that $z = 1.96$ is easily determined from the z table given the probability of 0.025 in the upper-tail of the distribution. Therefore, we formulate the probability statement $P(-1.96 \leq Z \leq 1.96) = 0.95$.

FIGURE 8.4 Graphical depiction of $P(-1.96 \leq Z \leq 1.96) = 0.95$

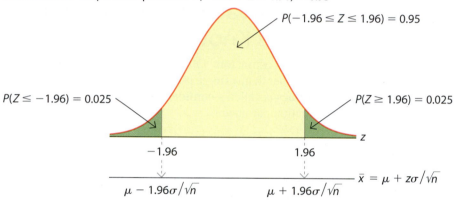

Since $Z = \frac{\bar{X} - \mu}{\sigma/\sqrt{n}}$, for a normal $\bar{X}$ with mean μ and standard deviation $\sigma/\sqrt{n}$, we get

$$P\left(-1.96 \leq \frac{\bar{X} - \mu}{\sigma/\sqrt{n}} \leq 1.96\right) = 0.95.$$

Finally, we multiply by $\sigma/\sqrt{n}$ and add μ to obtain

$$P(\mu - 1.96\sigma/\sqrt{n} \leq \bar{X} \leq \mu + 1.96\sigma/\sqrt{n}) = 0.95.$$

This equation (see also the lower portion of Figure 8.4) implies that there is a 0.95 probability that the sample mean $\bar{X}$ will fall between $\mu - 1.96\sigma/\sqrt{n}$ and $\mu + 1.96\sigma/\sqrt{n}$, or within the interval $\mu \pm 1.96\sigma/\sqrt{n}$. In other words, if samples of size n are drawn repeatedly from a given population, 95% of the computed sample means, $\bar{x}$'s, will fall within the interval and the remaining 5% will fall outside the interval.

We do not know the population mean μ, and therefore cannot determine if a particular $\bar{x}$ falls within the interval or not. However, we do know that $\bar{x}$ will fall within the interval $\mu \pm 1.96\sigma/\sqrt{n}$ if and only if μ falls within the interval $\bar{x} \pm 1.96\sigma/\sqrt{n}$. This will happen 95% of the time given how the interval is constructed. Therefore, we call the interval $\bar{x} \pm 1.96\sigma/\sqrt{n}$ a 95% confidence interval for the population mean, where $1.96 \frac{\sigma}{\sqrt{n}}$ is its margin of error.

Confidence intervals are often misinterpreted; you need to exercise care in characterizing them. For instance, the above 95% confidence interval does *not* imply that the probability that μ falls in the interval is 0.95. Remember that μ is a constant, although its value is not known. It either falls in the interval (probability equals one) or does not fall in the interval (probability equals zero). The randomness comes from $\bar{X}$, not μ, since many possible sample means can be derived from a population. Therefore, it is incorrect to say that the probability that μ falls in the $\bar{x} \pm 1.96\sigma/\sqrt{n}$ interval is 0.95. A 95% confidence interval simply implies that if numerous samples of size n are drawn from a given population, then 95% of the intervals formed by the above formula will contain μ. Keep in mind that we only use one sample to derive the estimates. Since there are many possible samples, we will be right 95% of the time, thus giving us 95% confidence.

EXAMPLE 8.2

A sample of 25 cereal boxes of Granola Crunch, a generic brand of cereal, yields a mean weight of 1.02 pounds of cereal per box. Construct a 95% confidence interval of the mean weight of all cereal boxes. Assume that the weight is normally distributed with a population standard deviation of 0.03 pound.

SOLUTION: Note that the normality condition of $\bar{X}$ is satisfied since the underlying population is normally distributed. A 95% confidence interval of the population mean is computed as

$$\bar{x} \pm 1.96\sigma/\sqrt{n} = 1.02 \pm 1.96\frac{0.03}{\sqrt{25}} = 1.02 \pm 0.012.$$

With 95% confidence, we can report that the mean weight of all cereal boxes falls between 1.008 and 1.032 pounds.

While it is common to report a 95% confidence interval, in theory we can construct an interval of any level of confidence ranging from 0 to 100%. Let's now extend the analysis to include intervals of any confidence level. Let the Greek letter α (alpha) denote the probability of error, also known as the level of significance. This is the allowed probability that the estimation procedure will generate an interval that does not contain μ. The **confidence coefficient** $(1 - \alpha)$ is interpreted similarly. The probability of error α and the confidence level are related as

- $\alpha = 1 -$ confidence coefficient, and
- Confidence level $= 100(1 - \alpha)\%$.

For example, a confidence coefficient of 0.95 implies that the probability of error α equals $1 - 0.95 = 0.05$ and the confidence level equals $100(1 - 0.05)\% = 95\%$. Similarly, for a 90% confidence interval, $\alpha = 1 - 0.90 = 0.10$. The following statement generalizes the construction of a confidence interval for μ when σ is known.

CONFIDENCE INTERVAL FOR μ WHEN σ IS KNOWN

A $100(1 - \alpha)\%$ confidence interval of the population mean μ when the population standard deviation σ is known is computed as

$$\bar{x} \pm z_{\alpha/2}\frac{\sigma}{\sqrt{n}} \quad \text{or} \quad \left[\bar{x} - z_{\alpha/2}\frac{\sigma}{\sqrt{n}}, \bar{x} + z_{\alpha/2}\frac{\sigma}{\sqrt{n}}\right].$$

The notation $z_{\alpha/2}$ is the z value associated with the probability of $\alpha/2$ in the upper-tail of the standard normal probability distribution, or $P(Z > z_{\alpha/2}) = \alpha/2$. In other words, if Z is a standard normal random variable and α is any probability, then $z_{\alpha/2}$ represents a z value such that the area under the z curve to the right of $z_{\alpha/2}$ is $\alpha/2$. Figure 8.5 depicts the notation $z_{\alpha/2}$.

FIGURE 8.5 Graphical depiction of the notation $z_{\alpha/2}$

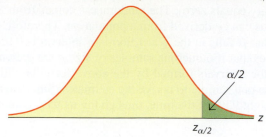

As discussed earlier, for a 95% confidence interval, $\alpha = 0.05$ and $\alpha/2 = 0.025$. Therefore, $z_{\alpha/2} = z_{0.025} = 1.96$. Similarly, we can derive the following:

- For a 90% confidence interval, $\alpha = 0.10$, $\alpha/2 = 0.05$ and $z_{\alpha/2} = z_{0.05} = 1.645$.
- For a 99% confidence interval, $\alpha = 0.01$, $\alpha/2 = 0.005$ and $z_{\alpha/2} = z_{0.005} = 2.575$.

LO 8.4

Describe the factors that influence the width of a confidence interval.

The Width of a Confidence Interval

The margin of error used in the computation of the confidence interval of the population mean, when the population standard deviation is known, is $z_{\alpha/2}\frac{\sigma}{\sqrt{n}}$. Since we are basically adding and subtracting this quantity from $\bar{x}$, the width of the confidence interval is two times the margin of error. In Example 8.2, the margin of error for a 95% confidence interval is 0.012 and the width of the interval is $1.032 - 1.008 = 2(0.012) = 0.024$. Now let's examine how the width of a confidence interval is influenced by various factors.

> I. For a given confidence level $100(1 - \alpha)\%$ and sample size n, the width of the interval is wider, the greater the population standard deviation σ.

EXAMPLE 8.2b

Let the standard deviation of the population in Example 8.2 be 0.05 instead of 0.03. Compute a 95% confidence interval based on the same sample information.

SOLUTION: We use the same formula as before, but we substitute 0.05 for the standard deviation instead of 0.03:

$$1.02 \pm 1.96\frac{0.05}{\sqrt{25}} = 1.02 \pm 0.020.$$

The width has increased from 0.024 to $2(0.020) = 0.040$.

> II. For a given confidence level $100(1 - \alpha)\%$ and population standard deviation σ, the width of the interval is wider, the smaller the sample size n.

EXAMPLE 8.2c

Instead of 25 observations, let the sample in Example 8.2 be based on 16 observations. Compute a 95% confidence interval using the same sample mean of 1.02 pounds and the same population standard deviation of 0.03.

SOLUTION: Again we use the same formula as before, but this time we substitute 16 for n instead of 25:

$$1.02 \pm 1.96\frac{0.03}{\sqrt{16}} = 1.02 \pm 0.015.$$

The width has increased from 0.024 to $2(0.015) = 0.030$.

III. For a given sample size n and population standard deviation σ, the width of the interval is wider, the greater the confidence level $100(1 - \alpha)\%$.

EXAMPLE 8.2d

Compute a 99%, instead of a 95%, confidence interval based on the information in Example 8.2.

SOLUTION: Now we use the same formula and substitute the value 2.575 for $z_{\alpha/2}$ instead of 1.96:

$$1.02 \pm 2.575 \frac{0.03}{\sqrt{25}} = 1.02 \pm 0.015.$$

The width has increased from 0.024 to $2(0.015) = 0.030$.

The precision is directly linked with the width of the confidence interval—the wider the interval, the lower is its precision. Continuing with the weather analogy, a temperature estimate of 40 to 80 degrees is imprecise because the interval is too wide to be of value. Examples 8.2b and 8.2c suggest that the estimate will be less precise if the variability of the underlying population is high (σ is high) or a small segment of the population is sampled (n is small). Example 8.2d relates the width with the confidence level. For a given sample information, the only way we can gain confidence is by making the interval wider. If you are 95% confident that the outside temperature is between 40 and 60, then you can increase your confidence level to 99% only by using a wider range, say between 35 and 65. This result also helps us understand the difference between precision (width of the interval) and the confidence level. There is a trade-off between the amount of confidence we have in an interval and its width.

EXAMPLE 8.3

IQ tests are designed to yield results that are approximately normally distributed. Researchers think that the population standard deviation is 15. A reporter is interested in estimating the average IQ of employees in a large high-tech firm in California. She gathers the IQ information on 22 employees of this firm and records the sample mean IQ as 106.

a. Compute 90% and 99% confidence intervals of the average IQ in this firm.

b. Use these results to infer if the mean IQ in this firm is significantly different from the national average of 100.

SOLUTION:

a. For a 90% confidence interval, $z_{\alpha/2} = z_{0.05} = 1.645$. Similarly, for a 99% confidence interval, $z_{\alpha/2} = z_{0.005} = 2.575$.

The 90% confidence interval is $106 \pm 1.645 \frac{15}{\sqrt{22}} = 106 \pm 5.26$.

The 99% confidence interval is $106 \pm 2.575 \frac{15}{\sqrt{22}} = 106 \pm 8.23$.

Note that the 99% interval is wider than the 90% interval.

b. The reporter wishes to determine if the mean IQ in this firm is significantly different from the national average of 100. With 90% confidence, she can infer that the average IQ of this firm's employees differs from the national average, since the value 100 falls outside the 90% confidence interval, [100.74, 111.26]. However, she cannot infer the same result with 99% confidence, since the wider range of the interval, [97.77, 114.23], includes the value 100. We will study the link between estimation and testing in more detail in the next chapter.

EXERCISES 8.2

Concepts

9. Find $z_{\alpha/2}$ for each of the following confidence levels used in estimating the population mean.
   a. 90%
   b. 98%
   c. 88%

10. Find $z_{\alpha/2}$ for each of the following confidence levels used in estimating the population mean.
    a. 89%
    b. 92%
    c. 96%

11. A simple random sample of 25 observations is derived from a normally distributed population with a known standard deviation of 8.2.
    a. Is the condition that $\bar{X}$ is normally distributed satisfied? Explain.
    b. Compute the margin of error with 80% confidence.
    c. Compute the margin of error with 90% confidence.
    d. Which of the two margins of error will lead to a wider interval?

12. Consider a population with a known standard deviation of 26.8. In order to compute an interval estimate of the population mean, a sample of 64 observations is drawn.
    a. Is the condition that $\bar{X}$ is normally distributed satisfied?
    b. Compute the margin of error at a 95% confidence level.
    c. Compute the margin of error at a 95% confidence level based on a larger sample of 225 observations.
    d. Which of the two margins of error will lead to a wider confidence interval?

13. Discuss the factors that influence the margin of error of the confidence interval of the population mean. What can a practitioner do to reduce the margin of error?

Applications

14. The average life expectancy for Bostonians is 78.1 years (*The Boston Globe*, August 16, 2010). Assume that this average was based on a sample of 50 Bostonians and that the population standard deviation is 4.5 years.
    a. What is the point estimate of the population mean?
    b. At 90% confidence, what is the margin of error?
    c. Construct a 90% confidence interval for the population average life expectancy of Bostonians.

15. In order to estimate the mean 30-year fixed mortgage rate for a home loan in the United States, a random sample of 28 recent loans is taken. The average calculated from this sample is 5.25%. It can be assumed that 30-year fixed mortgage rates are normally distributed with a standard deviation of 0.50%. Compute a 90% and a 99% confidence interval for the population mean 30-year fixed mortgage rate.

16. An article in the *National Geographic News* ("U.S. Racking Up Huge Sleep Debt," February 24, 2005) argues that Americans are increasingly skimping on their sleep. A researcher in a small Midwestern town wants to estimate the mean weekday sleep time of its adult residents. He takes a random sample of 80 adult residents and records their weekday mean sleep time as 6.4 hours. Assume that the population standard deviation is fairly stable at 1.8 hours.
    a. Calculate a 95% confidence interval of the population mean weekday sleep time of all adult residents of this Midwestern town.
    b. Can we conclude with 95% confidence that the mean sleep time of all adult residents in this Midwestern town is not 7 hours?

17. A family is relocating from St. Louis, Missouri, to California. Due to an increasing inventory of houses in St. Louis, it is taking longer than before to sell a house. The wife is concerned and wants to know when it is optimal to put their house on the market. They ask their realtor friend for help and she informs them that the last 26 houses that sold in their neighborhood took an average time of 218 days to sell. The realtor also tells them that based on her prior experience, the population standard deviation is 72 days.
    a. What assumption regarding the population is necessary for making an interval estimate of the population mean?
    b. Construct a 90% confidence interval of the mean sale time for all homes in the neighborhood.

18. U.S. consumers are increasingly viewing debit cards as a convenient substitute for cash and checks. The average amount spent annually on a debit card is $7,790 (*Kiplinger's*, August 2007). Assume that this average was based on a sample of 100 consumers and that the population standard deviation is $500.
    a. At 99% confidence, what is the margin of error?
    b. Construct a 99% confidence interval of the population mean amount spent annually on a debit card.

8.3 Confidence Interval of the Population Mean When σ Is Unknown

So far we have considered confidence intervals for the population mean where the population standard deviation σ is known. In reality, σ is rarely known. Recall from Chapter 3 that the population variance and the standard deviation are calculated as $\sigma^2 = \frac{\Sigma(x_i - \mu)^2}{N}$ and $\sigma = \sqrt{\sigma^2}$, respectively. It is highly unlikely that σ is known when μ is not. However, there are instances when the population standard deviation is considered fairly stable, and therefore, can be determined from prior experience. In these cases the population standard deviation is treated as known.

As discussed earlier, the margin of error in a confidence interval depends on the standard deviation, or the standard error, of the estimator and the desired confidence level. With σ unknown, the standard deviation of $\overline{X}$, given by $\sigma/\sqrt{n}$, can be conveniently estimated by the standard error $s/\sqrt{n}$, where s denotes the sample standard deviation. Given access to sample data, we can easily compute $s = \sqrt{s^2}$ where $s^2 = \frac{\Sigma(x_i - \bar{x})^2}{n - 1}$.

The t Distribution

LO 8.5

Discuss features of the t distribution.

As discussed earlier, in order to derive a confidence interval of μ, it is essential that $\overline{X}$ be normally distributed. A normally distributed $\overline{X}$ is standardized as $Z = \frac{\overline{X} - \mu}{\sigma/\sqrt{n}}$ where Z follows a standard normal distribution, that is, the z distribution. Another standardized statistic, which uses the estimator S in place of σ, is computed as $T = \frac{\overline{X} - \mu}{S/\sqrt{n}}$. The random variable T follows the Student's t distribution, more commonly known as the t distribution.[1]

> **THE t DISTRIBUTION**
>
> If repeated samples of size n are taken from a normal population with a finite variance, then the statistic $T = \frac{\overline{X} - \mu}{S/\sqrt{n}}$ follows the t distribution with $(n - 1)$ degrees of freedom, df.

The t distribution is actually a family of distributions, which are similar to the z distribution in that they are all bell-shaped and symmetric around zero. However, the t distribution has slightly broader tails than does the z distribution. Each t distribution is identified by the **degrees of freedom**, or simply df. The degrees of freedom determine the extent of the broadness of the tails of the distribution; the fewer the degrees of freedom, the broader the tails. Since the t distribution is defined by the degrees of freedom, it is common to refer to it as the t_{df} distribution.

Specifically, the degrees of freedom refer to the number of independent pieces of information that go into the calculation of a given statistic, and in this sense, can be "freely chosen." Consider the number of independent observations that enter into the calculation of the sample mean. If it is known that $\bar{x} = 20$ and three of the observations have values of $x_1 = 16$, $x_2 = 24$, and $x_3 = 18$, then there is no choice but for the fourth observation to have a value of 22. In other words, three degrees of freedom are involved in computing $\bar{x} = 20$ if $n = 4$; in effect, one degree of freedom is lost.

Summary of the t_{df} Distribution

- Like the z distribution, the t_{df} distribution is bell-shaped and symmetric around 0 with asymptotic tails (the tails get closer and closer to the horizontal axis, but never touch it).

---

[1] William S. Gossett (1876–1937) published his research concerning the t distribution under the pen name "Student" because his employer, the Guinness Brewery, did not allow employees to publish their research results.

- The t_{df} distribution has slightly broader tails than the z distribution.
- The t_{df} distribution consists of a family of distributions where the actual shape of each one depends on the degrees of freedom df. As df increases, the t_{df} distribution becomes similar to the z distribution; it is identical to the z distribution when df approaches infinity.

From Figure 8.6 we note that the tails of the t_2 and t_5 distributions are broader than the tails of the t_{50} distribution. For instance, for t_2 and t_5, the area exceeding a value of 3, or $P(T_{df} > 3)$, is greater than that for t_{50}. In addition, the t_{50} resembles the z distribution.

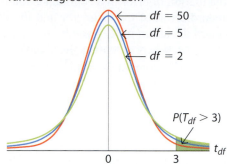

FIGURE 8.6 The t_{df} distribution with various degrees of freedom

Locating t_{df} Values and Probabilities

Table 8.2 lists t_{df} values for selected upper-tail probabilities and degrees of freedom df. Table 2 of Appendix A provides a more complete table. Since the t_{df} distribution is a family of distributions identified by the df parameter, the t table is not as comprehensive as the z table. It only lists probabilities corresponding to a limited number of values. Also, unlike the cumulative probabilities in the z table, the t table provides the probabilities in the upper-tail of the distribution.

TABLE 8.2 Portion of the t Table

df	\multicolumn{5}{c}{Area in Upper Tail, α}
	0.10	0.05	0.025	0.01	0.005
1	3.078	6.314	12.706	31.821	63.657
⋮	⋮	⋮	⋮	⋮	⋮
10	1.372	**1.812**	2.228	2.764	3.169
⋮	⋮	⋮	⋮	⋮	⋮
∞	1.282	1.645	1.960	2.326	2.576

We use the notation $t_{\alpha,df}$ to denote a value such that the area in the upper-tail equals α for a given df. In other words, for a random variable T_{df}, the notation $t_{\alpha,df}$ represents a value such that $P(T_{df} \geq t_{\alpha,df}) = \alpha$. Similarly, $t_{\alpha/2,df}$ represents a value such that $P(T_{df} \geq t_{\alpha/2,df}) = \alpha/2$. Figure 8.7 illustrates the notation.

FIGURE 8.7 Graphical depiction of $P(T_{df} \geq t_{\alpha,df}) = \alpha$

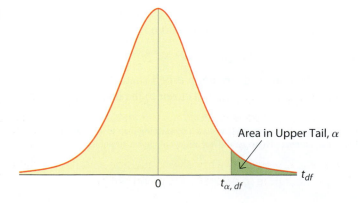

Area in Upper Tail, α

When determining the value $t_{\alpha,df}$, we need two pieces of information: (a) the sample size n, or analogously, $df = n - 1$; and (b) α. For instance, suppose we want to find the value $t_{\alpha,df}$ with $\alpha = 0.05$ and $df = 10$, that is, $t_{0.05,10}$. Using Table 8.2, we look at the first column labeled df and find the row 10. We then continue along this row until we reach the column $\alpha = 0.05$. The value 1.812 suggests that $P(T_{10} \geq 1.812) = 0.05$. Due to the symmetry of the t distribution, we also get $P(T_{10} < -1.812) = 0.05$. Figure 8.8 shows these results graphically. Also, since the area under the entire t_{df} distribution sums to one, we deduce that $P(T_{10} < 1.812) = 1 - 0.05 = 0.95$, which also equals $P(T_{10} \geq -1.812)$.

FIGURE 8.8 Graph of the probability $\alpha = 0.05$ on both sides of T_{10}

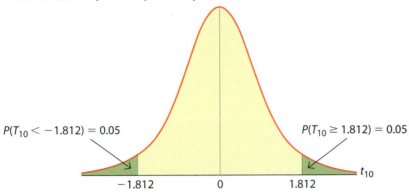

$P(T_{10} < -1.812) = 0.05$ $P(T_{10} \geq 1.812) = 0.05$

-1.812 0 1.812 t_{10}

Sometimes the exact probability cannot be determined from the t table. For example, given $df = 10$, the exact probability $P(T_{10} \geq 1.562)$ is not included in the table. However, this probability is between 0.05 and 0.10 because the value 1.562 falls between 1.372 and 1.812. Similarly, $P(T_{10} < 1.562)$ is between 0.90 and 0.95. We can use Excel and other statistical packages to compute exact probabilities.

EXAMPLE 8.4

Compute $t_{\alpha,df}$ for $\alpha = 0.025$ using 2, 5, and 50 degrees of freedom.

SOLUTION:

- For $df = 2$, $t_{0.025,2} = 4.303$.
- For $df = 5$, $t_{0.025,10} = 2.571$.
- For $df = 50$, $t_{0.025,60} = 2.009$.

Note that the t_{df} values change with the degrees of freedom. Further, as df increases, the t_{df} distribution begins to resemble the z distribution. In fact with $df = \infty$, $t_{0.025,\infty} = 1.96$, which is identical to the corresponding z value; recall that $P(Z \geq 1.96) = 0.025$.

Constructing a Confidence Interval for μ When σ Is Unknown

LO 8.6

Calculate a confidence interval for the population mean when the population standard deviation is not known.

We can never stress enough the importance of the requirement that $\overline{X}$ follows a normal distribution in estimating the population mean. Recall that $\overline{X}$ follows the normal distribution when the underlying population is normally distributed or when the sample size is sufficiently large ($n \geq 30$). We still construct the confidence interval for μ as: Point estimate $\pm$ Margin of error. However, when the population standard deviation is unknown, we now use the t_{df} distribution to calculate the margin of error.

As before, $100(1 - \alpha)\%$ is the confidence level and $t_{\alpha/2,df}$ is the t_{df} value associated with the probability $\alpha/2$ in the upper-tail of the distribution with $df = n - 1$. In other words, $P(T_{df} > t_{\alpha/2,df}) = \alpha/2$.

EXAMPLE 8.5

In the introductory case of this chapter, Jared Beane wants to estimate the mean mpg of all ultra-green cars. Table 8.1 lists the mpg of a sample of 25 cars. Use this information to construct a 90% confidence interval of the population mean. Assume that mpg follows a normal distribution.

SOLUTION: The condition that $\overline{X}$ follows a normal distribution is satisfied since we assumed that mpg is normally distributed. Thus, we construct the confidence interval as $\bar{x} \pm t_{\alpha/2,df} \frac{s}{\sqrt{n}}$. This is a classic example where a statistician has access only to sample data. Since the population standard deviation is not known, the sample standard deviation has to be computed from the sample. From the sample data in Table 8.1, we find that $\bar{x} = \frac{\Sigma x_i}{n} = \frac{2413}{25} = 96.52$ mpg and $s = \sqrt{\frac{\Sigma(x_i - \bar{x})^2}{n - 1}} = \sqrt{\frac{2746.24}{25 - 1}} = 10.70$; alternatively, we can use Excel to find these values. For a 90% confidence interval, $\alpha = 0.10$, $\alpha/2 = 0.05$ and given $n = 25$, $df = 25 - 1 = 24$. Thus, $t_{0.05,24} = 1.711$.

A 90% confidence interval of μ is computed as

$$\bar{x} \pm t_{\alpha/2,df} \frac{s}{\sqrt{n}} = 96.52 \pm 1.711 \frac{10.70}{\sqrt{25}} = 96.52 \pm 3.66.$$

Thus, Jared concludes with 90% confidence that the average mpg of all ultra-green cars is between 92.86 mpg and 100.18 mpg. Note that the manufacturer's claim that the ultra-green car will average 100 mpg cannot be rejected by the sample data, since the value 100 falls within the 90% confidence interval.

Using Excel to Construct Confidence Intervals

In general, Excel offers a couple of ways to construct confidence intervals. One way is to calculate each value in the formula independently using **Formulas > Insert Function > "relevant value."** The easiest way to estimate the mean when the population standard deviation is unknown is as follows.

A. Open the *MPG* data (Table 8.1) from the text website into an Excel spreadsheet.

B. From the menu choose **Data > Data Analysis > Descriptive Statistics > OK**.

C. See Figure 8.9. In the *Descriptive Statistics* dialog box, click on the box next to *Input Range*, then select the data. If you include the label "MPG" when you select the data, then click the box next to *Labels in first row*. Click the box in front of *Summary statistics* as well as the box in front of *Confidence Level for Mean*. By default, Excel provides a 95% confidence interval. Since we want to calculate a 90% confidence interval, we enter the value 90. Finally, click **OK**.

FIGURE 8.9 Descriptive statistics dialog box

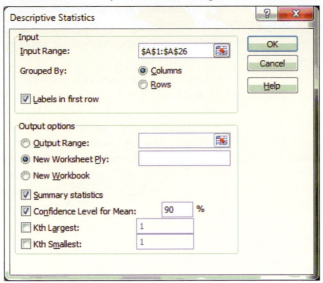

D. Table 8.3 presents the relevant Excel output. As mentioned in Chapter 3, Excel provides numerous numerical measures; however, we only include the point estimate (Mean) and the margin of error (see the value next to Confidence Level (90.0%)), or 96.52 ± 3.66, which is essentially the interval that we calculated manually in Example 8.5.

TABLE 8.3 Confidence Interval for MPG Using Excel

Mean	96.52
⋮	⋮
Confidence Level (90.0%)	3.66

EXERCISES 8.3

Concepts

19. Find $t_{\alpha,df}$ from the following information.
    a. $\alpha = 0.025$ and $df = 12$
    b. $\alpha = 0.10$ and $df = 12$
    c. $\alpha = 0.025$ and $df = 25$
    d. $\alpha = 0.10$ and $df = 25$

20. We use the t distribution for the statistical inference of the population mean when the underlying population standard deviation is not known. Under the assumption that the population is normally distributed, find $t_{\alpha/2,df}$ for the following scenarios.
    a. A 90% confidence level and a sample of 28 observations.
    b. A 95% confidence level and sample of 28 observations.
    c. A 90% confidence level and a sample of 15 observations.
    d. A 95% confidence level and a sample of 15 observations.

21. A random sample of 24 observations is used to estimate the population mean. The sample mean and the sample standard deviation are calculated as 104.6 and 28.8, respectively. Assume that the population is normally distributed.

a. Construct a 90% confidence interval of the population mean.
b. Construct a 99% confidence interval of the population mean.
c. Use your answers to discuss the impact of the confidence level on the width of the interval.

22. Consider a normal population with an unknown population standard deviation. A random sample results in $\bar{x} = 48.68$ and $s^2 = 33.64$.
a. Compute a 95% confidence interval for μ if $\bar{x}$ and s^2 were obtained from a sample of 16 observations.
b. Compute a 95% confidence interval for μ if $\bar{x}$ and s^2 were obtained from a sample of 25 observations.
c. Use your answers to discuss the impact of the sample size on the width of the interval.

23. Let the following sample of 8 observations be drawn from a normal population with unknown mean and standard deviation: 22, 18, 14, 25, 17, 28, 15, 20.
a. Calculate the sample mean and the sample standard deviation.

b. Construct the 80% confidence interval of the population mean.

c. Construct the 90% confidence interval of the population mean.

d. What happens to the margin of error as the confidence level increases from 80% to 90%?

Applications

24. A popular weight loss program claims that with its recommended healthy diet regimen, users lose significant weight within a month. In order to estimate the mean weight loss of all customers, a nutritionist takes a sample of 18 dieters and records their weight loss one month after joining the program. He computes the sample mean and the standard deviation of weight loss as 12.5 pounds and 9.2 pounds, respectively. He believes that weight loss is likely to be normally distributed.

a. Calculate the margin of error with 95% confidence.

b. Compute the 95% confidence interval of the population mean.

25. The manager of The Cheesecake Factory in Boston reports that on six randomly selected weekdays, the number of customers served was 120, 130, 90, 205, 185, and 220. She believes that the number of customers served on weekdays follows a normal distribution. Construct a 90% confidence interval of the average number of customers served on weekdays.

26. According to a recent survey, high school girls average 100 text messages daily (*The Boston Globe*, April 21, 2010). Assume that the survey was based on a random sample of 36 high school girls. The sample standard deviation is computed as 10 text messages daily.

a. Calculate the margin of error with 99% confidence.

b. What is the 99% confidence interval of the population mean texts that all high school girls send daily?

27. The Chartered Financial Analyst (CFA®) designation is fast becoming a requirement for serious investment professionals. Although it requires a successful completion of three levels of grueling exams, it also entails promising careers with lucrative salaries. A student of finance is curious about the average salary of a CFA® charterholder. He takes a random sample of 36 recent charterholders and computes a mean salary of $158,000 with a standard deviation of $36,000. Use this sample information to determine the 95% confidence interval of the average salary of a CFA® charterholder.

28. The *Sudoku* puzzle has recently become very popular all over the world. It is based on a 9 × 9 grid and the challenge is to fill in the grid so that every row, every column, and every 3 × 3 box contains the digits 1 through 9. A researcher is interested in estimating the average time taken by a college student to solve the puzzle. He takes a random sample of 8 college students and records their solving times as 14, 7, 17, 20, 18, 15, 19, 28 minutes.

a. Derive a 99% confidence interval of the average time taken by a college student to solve a *Sudoku* puzzle.

b. What assumption is necessary to make this inference?

29. Executive compensation has risen dramatically beyond the rising levels of an average worker's wage over the years. Sarah is an MBA student who decides to use her statistical skills to estimate the mean CEO compensation in 2010 for all large companies in the United States. She takes a random sample of six CEO compensations.

Firm	Compensation (in $ millions)
Intel	8.20
Coca-Cola	2.76
Wells Fargo	6.57
Caterpillar	3.88
McDonald's	6.56
U.S. Bancorp	4.10

Source: http://finance.yahoo.com.

a. How will Sarah use the above information to provide a 90% confidence interval of the mean CEO compensation of all large companies in the United States?

b. What assumption did Sarah make for deriving the interval estimate?

c. How can Sarah reduce the margin of error reported in the above interval estimate?

30. A price-earnings ratio or P/E ratio is calculated as a firm's share price compared to the income or profit earned by the firm per share. Generally, a high P/E ratio suggests that investors are expecting higher earnings growth in the future compared to companies with a lower P/E ratio. The following table shows the P/E ratios for a sample of firms in the footwear industry:

Firm	P/E Ratio
Brown Shoe Co., Inc.	20.54
Collective Brands, Inc.	9.33
CROCS Inc.	22.63
DSW Inc.	14.42
Nike Inc.	18.68
Skechers USA Inc.	9.35
Timberland Co.	14.93

Source: http://biz.yahoo.com; data retrieved August 23, 2010.

Let these ratios represent a random sample drawn from a normally distributed population. Derive a 90% confidence interval of the mean P/E ratio for the entire footwear industry.

31. The monthly closing stock prices (rounded to the nearest dollar) for Panera Bread Co. for the first six months of 2010 are reported in the following table.

Month	Closing Stock Price
January 2010	$71
February 2010	73
March 2010	76
April 2010	78
May 2010	81
June 2010	75

SOURCE: http://finance.yahoo.com.

a. Calculate the sample mean and the sample standard deviation.

b. Compute the 90% confidence interval of the mean stock price of Panera Bread Co., assuming that the stock price is normally distributed.

c. What happens to the margin of error if a higher confidence level is used for the interval estimate?

32. The following table shows the annual returns (in percent) for Fidelity's Electronic and Utilities funds.

Year	Electronic	Utilities
2005	13.23%	9.36%
2006	1.97	32.33
2007	2.77	21.03
2008	−50.55	−35.21
2009	81.65	14.71

SOURCE: http://finance.yahoo.com.

a. Derive 99% confidence intervals for the mean return of Fidelity's Electronic and Utilities funds.

b. What did you have to assume to make the above inferences?

33. FILE A recent study found that consumers are making average monthly debt payments of $983 (Experian.com, November 11, 2010). The accompanying table shows a portion of average debt payments for 26 metropolitan areas. The complete data set is on the text website and is labeled **Debt Payments**.

City	Debt Payments
Washington, D.C.	$1,285
Seattle	1,135
⋮	⋮
Pittsburgh	763

SOURCE: www.Experian.com, November 11, 2010.

a. Use Excel to calculate the mean and standard deviation for debt payments.

b. Construct a 90% and a 95% confidence interval for the population mean. Comment on the width of the intervals.

8.4 Confidence Interval of the Population Proportion

Sometimes the parameter of interest describes a population that is qualitative rather than quantitative. Recall that while the population mean μ and population variance σ^2 describe quantitative data, the population proportion p is the essential descriptive measure when the data type is qualitative. The parameter p represents the proportion of successes in the population, where success is defined by a particular outcome. Examples of population proportions include the proportion of women students at a university, the proportion of defective items in a manufacturing process, and the default probability on a mortgage loan.

As in the case of the population mean, we estimate the population proportion on the basis of its sample counterpart. In particular, we use the sample proportion $\overline{P}$ as the point estimator of the population proportion p. As discussed earlier, $\overline{P}$ is an unbiased, efficient, and consistent estimator of p. Also, although the sampling distribution of $\overline{P}$ is based on a binomial distribution, we can approximate it by a normal distribution for large samples, according to the central limit theorem. This approximation is valid when the sample size n is such that $np \geq 5$ and $n(1 - p) \geq 5$.

For a normally distributed $\overline{P}$ with $E(\overline{P}) = p$ and $SD(\overline{P}) = \sqrt{p(1 - p)/n}$, we can derive

$$Z = \frac{\overline{P} - p}{\sqrt{p(1 - p)/n}}, \text{ and therefore, } P\left(-z_{\alpha/2} \leq \frac{\overline{P} - p}{\sqrt{p(1 - p)/n}} \leq z_{\alpha/2}\right) = 1 - \alpha.$$

Analogously to the derivation of the confidence interval of the population mean, a $100(1 - \alpha)\%$ confidence interval of the population proportion is

$$\overline{p} \pm z_{\alpha/2}\sqrt{\frac{p(1 - p)}{n}} \quad \text{or} \quad \left[\overline{p} - z_{\alpha/2}\sqrt{\frac{p(1 - p)}{n}}, \overline{p} + z_{\alpha/2}\sqrt{\frac{p(1 - p)}{n}}\right].$$

LO **8.7**

Calculate a confidence interval for the population proportion.

This confidence interval is theoretically sound; however, it cannot be implemented because it uses p in the derivation, which is unknown. Since we always use large samples for the normal distribution approximation, we can also conveniently replace p with its estimate $\bar{p}$ in the construction of the interval. This substitution yields a feasible confidence interval of the population proportion.

CONFIDENCE INTERVAL FOR p

A $100(1 - \alpha)\%$ confidence interval of the population proportion p is computed as

$$\bar{p} \pm z_{\alpha/2}\sqrt{\frac{\bar{p}(1 - \bar{p})}{n}} \quad \text{or} \quad \left[\bar{p} - z_{\alpha/2}\sqrt{\frac{\bar{p}(1 - \bar{p})}{n}}, \bar{p} + z_{\alpha/2}\sqrt{\frac{\bar{p}(1 - \bar{p})}{n}}\right]$$

EXAMPLE 8.6

In the introductory case of this chapter, Jared Beane wants to estimate the proportion of all ultra-green cars that obtain over 100 mpg. Use the information in Table 8.1 to construct a 90% and a 99% confidence interval of the population proportion.

SOLUTION: As shown in Table 8.1, seven of the 25 cars obtain over 100 mpg; thus the point estimate of the population proportion is $\bar{p} = x/n = 7/25 = 0.28$. Note that the normality condition is satisfied since $np \geq 5$ and $n(1 - p) \geq 5$, where p is evaluated at $\bar{p} = 0.28$. With a 90% confidence level, $\alpha/2 = 0.10/2 = 0.05$; thus we find $z_{\alpha/2} = z_{0.05} = 1.645$. Substituting the appropriate values into $\bar{p} \pm z_{\alpha/2}\sqrt{\frac{\bar{p}(1 - \bar{p})}{n}}$ yields

$$0.28 \pm 1.645\sqrt{\frac{0.28(1 - 0.28)}{25}} = 0.28 \pm 0.148.$$

With 90% confidence, Jared reports that the percentage of cars that obtain over 100 mpg is between 13.2% and 42.8%.

If Jared had wanted a 99% confidence level, we would use $\alpha/2 = 0.01/2 = 0.005$ and $z_{\alpha/2} = z_{0.005} = 2.575$ to obtain

$$0.28 \pm 2.575\sqrt{\frac{0.28(1 - 0.28)}{25}} = 0.28 \pm 0.231.$$

At a higher confidence level of 99%, the interval for the percentage of cars that obtain over 100 mpg becomes 4.9% to 51.1%. Given the current sample size of 25 cars, Jared can gain confidence (from 90% to 99%) at the expense of precision, as the corresponding margin of error increases from 0.148 to 0.231.

EXERCISES 8.4

Concepts

34. A random sample of 100 observations results in 40 successes.
    a. What is the point estimate of the population proportion of successes?
    b. Construct a 90% confidence interval of the population proportion.
    c. Construct a 99% confidence interval of the population proportion.

35. A random sample of 80 observations results in 50 successes.
    a. Construct a 95% confidence interval of the population proportion of successes.
    b. Construct a 95% confidence interval of the population proportion of failures.

36. Assume $\bar{p} = 0.6$ in a sample size of $n = 50$.
    a. Construct a 95% confidence interval of the population proportion.
    b. What happens to the margin of error if the above sample proportion is based on $n = 200$ instead of $n = 50$?

37. A sample of 80 results in 30 successes.
    a. Calculate the point estimate of the population proportion of successes.
    b. Construct a 90% and a 99% confidence interval of the population proportion.
    c. Can we conclude at 90% confidence that the population proportion differs from 0.5?
    d. Can we conclude at 99% confidence that the population proportion differs from 0.5?

38. In a sample of 30 observations the number of successes equals 18.
    a. Construct an 88% confidence interval of the population proportion of successes.
    b. Construct a 98% confidence interval of the population proportion of successes.
    c. What happens to the margin of error as you move from an 88% confidence interval to a 98% confidence interval?

Applications

39. A survey of 1,026 people asked: "What would you do with an unexpected tax refund?" Forty-seven percent responded that they would pay off debts (*Vanity Fair*, June 2010).
    a. At 95% confidence, what is the margin of error?
    b. Construct a 95% confidence interval of the population proportion of people who would pay off debts with an unexpected tax refund.

40. A recent poll of 1,079 adults finds that 51% of Americans support Arizona's stringent new immigration enforcement law, even though it may lead to racial profiling (*New York Times/CBS News*, April 28–May 2, 2010). Use the sample information to compute a 95% confidence interval of the population parameter of interest.

41. An economist reports that 560 out of a sample of 1,200 middle-income American households actively participate in the stock market.
    a. Construct a 90% confidence interval of the proportion of middle-income Americans who actively participate in the stock market.
    b. Can we conclude that the proportion of middle-income Americans that actively participate in the stock market is not 50%?

42. In a CNNMoney.com poll conducted on July 13, 2010, a sample of 5,324 Americans were asked about what matters most to them in a place to live. Thirty-seven percent of the respondents felt job opportunities matter most.
    a. Construct a 90% confidence interval of the proportion of Americans who feel that good job opportunities matter most in a place to live.
    b. Construct a 99% confidence interval of the proportion of Americans who feel that good job opportunities matter most in a place to live.
    c. Which of the above two intervals has a higher margin of error? Explain why.

43. In a recent poll of 760 homeowners in the United States, one in five homeowners report having a home equity loan that they are currently paying off. Using a confidence coefficient of 0.90, derive an interval estimate of the proportion of all homeowners in the United States that hold a home equity loan.

44. In an *NBC News/Wall Street Journal* poll of 1,000 American adults conducted on August 5–9, 2010, 44% of respondents approved of the job that Barack Obama was doing in handling the economy.
    a. Compute a 90% confidence interval of the proportion of Americans who approved of Barack Obama's handling of the economy.
    b. What is the resulting margin of error?
    c. Compute the margin of error associated with a 99% confidence level.

45. Obesity is generally defined as 30 or more pounds over a healthy weight. A recent study of obesity reports 27.5% of a random sample of 400 adults in the United States to be obese.
    a. Use this sample information to compute a 90% confidence interval of the adult obesity rate in the United States.
    b. Is it reasonable to conclude with 90% confidence that the adult obesity rate in the United States is not 30%?

46. An accounting professor is notorious for being stingy in giving out good letter grades. In a large section of 140 students in the fall semester, she gave out only 5% As, 23% Bs, 42% Cs, and 30% Ds and Fs. Assuming that this was a representative class, compute a 95% confidence interval of the probability of getting at least a B from this professor.

47. One in five 18-year-old Americans has not graduated from high school (*The Wall Street Journal*, April 19, 2007). A mayor of a northeastern city comments that its residents do not have the same graduation rate as the rest of the country. An analyst from the Department of Education decides to test the mayor's claim. In particular, she draws a random sample of 80 18-year-olds in the city and finds that 20 of them have not graduated from high school.
    a. Compute the point estimate of the proportion of 18-year-olds who have graduated from high school in this city.
    b. Use this point estimate to derive a 95% confidence interval of the population proportion.
    c. Can the mayor's comment be justified at 95% confidence?

8.5 Selecting a Useful Sample Size

So far we have discussed how a confidence interval provides useful information on a given unknown population parameter. We compute the confidence interval by adding and subtracting the margin of error to/from the point estimate. If the margin of error is very large, the confidence interval becomes too wide to be of much value. For instance, little useful information can be gained from a confidence interval that suggests that the

LO **8.8**

Select a sample size to estimate the population mean and the population proportion.

average annual starting salary of a business graduate is between $16,000 and $64,000. Similarly, an interval estimate that 10% to 60% of business students pursue an MBA is not very informative.

Statisticians like precision in their interval estimates, which is implied by a low margin of error. If we are able to increase the size of the sample, the larger n reduces the margin of error for the interval estimates. How large should the sample size be for a given margin of error? We will now examine the required sample size, for a desired margin of error, in the confidence intervals of the population mean μ and the population proportion p. In order to be conservative in our estimate, we always round up non-integer values of the required sample size.

Selecting n to Estimate μ

Consider a confidence interval for μ with a known population standard deviation σ. In addition, let D denote the desired margin of error. In other words, you do not want the sample mean to deviate from the population mean by more than D, for a given level of confidence. Since $D = z_{\alpha/2} \frac{\sigma}{\sqrt{n}}$, we rearrange this equation to derive the formula for the required sample size as $n = \left(\frac{z_{\alpha/2} \sigma}{D} \right)^2$. The sample size can be computed if we specify the population standard deviation σ, the value of $z_{\alpha/2}$ based on the confidence level $100(1 - \alpha)\%$, and the desired margin of error D.

This formula is based on a knowledge of σ. However, in most cases σ is not known and therefore, has to be estimated. In such cases, we replace σ with its reasonable estimate $\hat{\sigma}$.

> ### THE REQUIRED SAMPLE SIZE WHEN ESTIMATING THE POPULATION MEAN
>
> For a desired margin of error D, the minimum sample size n required to estimate a $100(1 - \alpha)\%$ confidence interval of the population mean μ is
>
> $$n = \left(\frac{z_{\alpha/2} \hat{\sigma}}{D} \right)^2,$$
>
> where $\hat{\sigma}$ is a reasonable estimate of σ in the planning stage.

If σ is known, we replace $\hat{\sigma}$ with σ. Note that the sample standard deviation s is not a feasible choice for $\hat{\sigma}$ because s can be computed only after a sample of size n has been selected. Sometimes we use the sample standard deviation from a preselected sample as $\hat{\sigma}$ in the planning stage. Another choice for $\hat{\sigma}$ is to use an estimate of the population standard deviation from prior studies. Finally, if the lowest and highest possible values of the population are available, a rough approximation for the population standard deviation is given by $\hat{\sigma} = \text{range}/4$.

EXAMPLE 8.7

Let us revisit Example 8.5, where Jared Beane wants to construct a 90% confidence interval of the mean mpg of all ultra-green cars. Suppose Jared would like to constrain the margin of error to within 2 mpg. Further, Jared knows that the lowest mpg in the population is 76 mpg, whereas the highest is 118 mpg. How large a sample does Jared need to compute the 90% confidence interval of the population mean?

SOLUTION: For a 90% confidence level, Jared computes $z_{\alpha/2} = z_{0.05} = 1.645$. He estimates the population standard deviation as $\hat{\sigma} = \text{range}/4 = (118 - 76)/4 = 10.50$. Given $D = 2$, the required sample size is

$$n = \left(\frac{z_{\alpha/2}\hat{\sigma}}{D}\right)^2 = \left(\frac{1.645 \times 10.50}{2}\right)^2 = 74.58$$

which is rounded up to 75. Therefore, Jared needs a random sample of at least 75 ultra-green cars to provide a more precise interval estimate of the mean mpg.

Selecting n to Estimate p

The margin of error D of the confidence interval of the population proportion p is $D = z_{\alpha/2}\sqrt{\frac{\bar{p}(1-\bar{p})}{n}}$, where $\bar{p}$ represents the sample proportion. By rearranging, we derive the formula for the required sample size as $n = \left(\frac{z_{\alpha/2}}{D}\right)^2 \bar{p}(1 - \bar{p})$. Note that this formula is not feasible because it uses $\bar{p}$, which cannot be computed unless a sample of size n has already been selected. We replace $\bar{p}$ with a reasonable estimate $\hat{p}$ of the population proportion p.

> **THE REQUIRED SAMPLE SIZE WHEN ESTIMATING THE POPULATION PROPORTION**
>
> For a desired margin of error D, the minimum sample size n required to estimate a $100(1 - \alpha)\%$ confidence interval of the population proportion p is
>
> $$n = \left(\frac{z_{\alpha/2}}{D}\right)^2 \hat{p}(1 - \hat{p}),$$
>
> where $\hat{p}$ is a reasonable estimate of p in the planning stage.

Sometimes we use the sample proportion from a preselected sample as $\hat{p}$ in the planning stage. Once the optimal sample size is determined, the final sample is selected for estimating the population proportion. Another choice for $\hat{p}$ is to use an estimate of the population proportion from prior studies. If no other reasonable estimate of the population proportion is available, we can use $\hat{p} = 0.5$ as a conservative estimate to derive the optimal sample size; note that the required sample is the largest when $\hat{p} = 0.5$.

> ### EXAMPLE 8.8
>
> Recall Example 8.6, where Jared Beane wants to construct a 90% confidence interval of the proportion of all ultra-green cars that obtain over 100 mpg. Jared does not want the margin of error to be more than 0.10. How large a sample does Jared need for his analysis of the population proportion?
>
> **SOLUTION:** For a 90% confidence level, Jared computes $z_{\alpha/2} = z_{0.05} = 1.645$. Since no estimate for the population proportion is readily available, Jared uses a conservative estimate of $\hat{p} = 0.50$. Given $D = 0.10$, the required sample size is
>
> $$n = \left(\frac{z_{\alpha/2}}{D}\right)^2 \hat{p}(1 - \hat{p}) = \left(\frac{1.645}{0.10}\right)^2 0.50(1 - 0.50) = 67.65,$$
>
> which is rounded up to 68. Therefore, Jared needs to find another random sample of at least 68 ultra-green cars to provide a more precise interval estimate of the proportion of all ultra-green cars that obtain over 100 mpg.

Jared Beane, a journalist at a reputable automobile magazine, prepares to write an article on the new ultra-green car that boasts an average of 100 mpg. Based on a sample of 25 cars, Jared reports with 90% confidence that the average mpg of all ultra-green cars is between 92.86 mpg and 100.18 mpg. Jared also constructs a 90% confidence interval for the proportion of cars that obtain more than 100 mpg and obtains an interval estimate of 0.132 to 0.428. Jared wishes to increase the precision of his confidence intervals by reducing the margin of error. If his desired margin of error is 2 mpg for the population mean, he must use a sample of at least 75 cars for the analysis. Jared also wants to reduce the margin of error to 0.10 for the proportion of cars that obtain more than 100 mpg. Using a conservative estimate, he calculates that a sample of at least 68 cars is needed to achieve this goal. Thus, in order to gain precision in the interval estimate of both the mean and the proportion with 90% confidence, Jared's sample must contain at least 75 cars.

EXERCISES 8.5

Concepts

48. What is the minimum sample size n required to estimate μ with 90% confidence if the desired margin of error is $D = 1.2$? The population standard deviation is estimated as $\hat{\sigma} = 3.5$. What happens to n if the desired margin of error decreases to $D = 0.7$?

49. The lowest and highest observations in a population are 20 and 80, respectively. What is the minimum sample size n required to estimate μ with 80% confidence if the desired margin of error is $D = 2.6$? What happens to n if you decide to estimate μ with 95% confidence?

50. Find the required sample size for estimating the population mean in order to be 95% confident that the sample mean is within 10 units of the population mean. Assume that the population standard deviation is 40.

51. You need to compute a 99% confidence interval of the population mean. How large a sample should you draw to ensure that the sample mean does not deviate from the population mean by more than 1.2? (Use 6.0 as an estimate of the population standard deviation from prior studies.)

52. What is the minimum sample size n required to estimate p with 95% confidence if the desired margin of error $D = 0.08$? The population proportion is estimated as $\hat{p} = 0.36$ from prior studies. What happens to n if the desired margin of error increases to $D = 0.12$?

53. In the planning stage, a sample proportion is estimated as $\hat{p} = 40/50 = 0.80$. Use this information to compute the minimum sample size n required to estimate p with 99% confidence if the desired margin of error $D = 0.12$.

What happens to n if you decide to estimate p with 90% confidence?

54. You wish to compute a 95% confidence interval of the population proportion. How large a sample should you draw to ensure that the sample proportion does not deviate from the population proportion by more than 0.06? No prior estimate of the population proportion is available.

Applications

55. An analyst from an energy research institute in California wishes to precisely estimate a 99% confidence interval of the average price of unleaded gasoline in the state. In particular, she does not want the sample mean to deviate from the population mean by more than $0.06. What is the minimum number of gas stations that she should include in her sample if she uses the standard deviation estimate of $0.32, as reported in the popular press?

56. An analyst would like to construct 95% confidence intervals of the mean returns of two mutual funds. Fund A is a high-risk fund with a known population standard deviation of 20.6%, whereas the Fund B is a lower-risk fund with a known population standard deviation of 12.8%.

   a. What is the minimum sample size required by the analyst if she wants to restrict the margin of error to 4% for Fund A?

   b. What is the minimum sample size required by the analyst if she wants to restrict the margin of error to 4% for Fund B?

   c. Why do the above results differ if they use the same margin of error?

57. The manager of a pizza chain in Albuquerque, New Mexico, wants to determine the average size of their advertised 16-inch pizzas. She takes a random sample of 25 pizzas and records their mean and standard deviation as 16.10 and 1.8 inches, respectively. She subsequently computes a 95% confidence interval of the mean size of all pizzas as [15.36, 16.84]. However, she finds this interval to be too broad to implement quality control and decides to re-estimate the mean based on a bigger sample. Using the standard deviation estimate of 1.8 from her earlier analysis, how large a sample must she take if she wants the margin of error to be under 0.5 inch?

58. Mortgage lenders often use FICO® scores to check the credit worthiness of consumers applying for real estate loans. In general, FICO scores range between 300 and 850 with higher scores representing a better credit profile. A lender in a Midwestern town would like to estimate the mean credit score of its residents. What is the required number of sample FICO scores needed if the lender does not want the margin of error to exceed 20, with 95% confidence?

59. A survey by the AARP (*Money*, June 2007) reported that approximately 70% of people in the 50 to 64 age bracket have tried some type of alternative therapy (for instance, acupuncture or the use of nutrition supplements). Assume this survey was based on a sample of 400 people.

a. Identify the relevant parameter of interest for these qualitative data and compute its point estimate as well as the margin of error with 90% confidence.

b. You decide to redo the analysis with the margin of error reduced to 2%. How large a sample do you need to draw? State your assumptions in computing the required sample size.

60. Subprime lending was big business in the United States in the mid-2000s, when lenders provided mortgages to people with poor credit. However, subsequent increases in interest rates coupled with a drop in home values necessitated many borrowers to default. Suppose a recent report finds that two in five subprime mortgages are likely to default nationally. A research economist is interested in estimating default rates in Illinois with 95% confidence. How large a sample is needed to restrict the margin of error to within 0.06, using the reported national default rate?

61. A student of business is interested in estimating a 99% confidence interval of the proportion of students who bring laptops to campus. He wishes a precise estimate and is willing to draw a large sample that will keep the sample proportion within five percentage points of the population proportion. What is the minimum sample size required by this student, given that no prior estimate of the population proportion is available?

WRITING WITH STATISTICS

Callie Fitzpatrick, a research analyst with an investment firm, has been asked to write a report summarizing the weekly stock performance of Home Depot and Lowe's. Her manager is trying to decide whether or not to include one of these stocks in a client's portfolio and the average stock performance is one of the factors influencing their decision. Callie decides to use descriptive measures to summarize stock returns in her report, as well as provide confidence intervals for the average return for Home Depot and Lowe's. She collects weekly returns for each firm for the first eight months of 2010. A portion of the return data is shown in Table 8.4; the complete data, labeled *Weekly Returns*, are available on the text website.

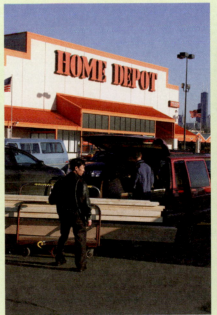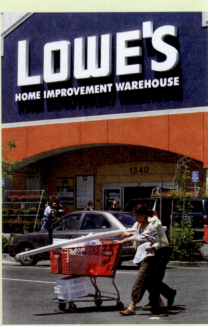

TABLE 8.4 Weekly Returns for Home Depot and Lowe's

Date	Home Depot	Lowe's
1/11/2010	−1.44	−1.59
1/19/2010	−2.98	−3.53
⋮	⋮	⋮
8/30/2010	−2.61	−3.89

Source: http://finance.yahoo.com.

Callie would like to use the sample information to:

1. Summarize weekly returns of Home Depot and Lowe's.
2. Provide confidence intervals for the average weekly returns.
3. Make recommendations for further analysis.

Sample Report—Weekly Stock Performance: Home Depot vs. Lowe's

Grim news continues to distress the housing sector. On August 24, 2010, Reuters reported that the sales of previously owned U.S. homes took a record plunge in July to the slowest pace in 15 years. Combine this fact with the continued fallout from the subprime mortgage debacle, a sluggish economy, and high unemployment, and the housing sector appears quite unstable. Have these unfavorable events managed to trickle down and harm the financial performance of Home Depot and Lowe's, the two largest home improvement retailers in the U.S.?

One way to analyze their financial stability is to observe their stock performance during this period. In order to make valid statements concerning the reward of holding these stocks, weekly return data for each firm were gathered from January through August of 2010. Table 8.A summarizes the important descriptive statistics.

TABLE 8.A Descriptive Statistics for Weekly Returns of Home Depot and Lowe's ($n = 34$)

	Home Depot	Lowe's
Mean	0.00%	−0.33%
Median	0.76%	−0.49%
Minimum	−8.08%	−7.17%
Maximum	5.30%	7.71%
Standard deviation	3.59%	3.83%
Margin of error with 95% confidence	1.25%	1.34%

Over the past 34 weeks, Home Depot posted both the higher average return and median return of 0.00% and 0.76%, respectively. Lowe's return over the same period was negative, whether the central tendency was measured by its mean (−0.33%) or its median (−0.49%). In terms of dispersion, Lowe's return data had the higher standard deviation (3.83% > 3.59%). In terms of descriptive measures, the investment in Home Depot's stock not only provided higher returns, but was also less risky than the investment in Lowe's stock.

Table 8.A also shows the margins of error for 95% confidence intervals for the mean returns. With 95% confidence, the mean return for Home Depot fell in the range [−1.25%, 1.25%], while that for Lowe's fell in the range [−1.67%, 1.01%]. Given that these two intervals overlap, one cannot conclude that Home Depot delivered the higher reward over this period—a conclusion one may have arrived at had only the point estimates been evaluated. It is not possible to recommend one stock over the other for inclusion in a client's portfolio based solely on the mean return performance. Other factors, such as the standard deviation of the returns and the correlation between the stock and the existing portfolio, must be analyzed before this decision can be made.

Conceptual Review

LO 8.1 | **Discuss point estimators and their desirable properties.**

The sample mean $\overline{X}$ is the **point estimator** of the population mean μ and the sample proportion $\overline{P}$ is the point estimator of the population proportion p. Sample values of the point estimators represent the **point estimates** of the population parameter of interest; $\overline{x}$ and $\overline{p}$ are the point estimates of μ and p, respectively.

Some of the desirable properties of point estimators are **unbiasedness, efficiency**, and **consistency**. Unbiasedness indicates that no systematic bias appears against the unknown population parameter of interest; in other words, the expected value of the estimator equals the true value of the population parameter. An unbiased estimator is deemed efficient if its variability is less than that of other unbiased estimators. Consistency implies that the estimator approaches the population parameter as the sample size gets very large. It is well documented that $\overline{X}$ and $\overline{P}$ are the unbiased, efficient, and consistent estimators of μ and p, respectively.

LO 8.2 | **Explain an interval estimator.**

While a point estimator provides a single value or a point that approximates the value of the unknown parameter, a **confidence interval**, or an **interval estimate**, provides a range of values that, with a certain level of confidence, will contain the population parameter of interest.

Often, we construct a confidence interval as: point estimate $\pm$ margin of error. The **margin of error** accounts for the variability of the estimator and the desired confidence level of the interval.

In order to construct a confidence interval for μ or p, it is essential that the sampling distributions of $\overline{X}$ and $\overline{P}$ follow a normal distribution. The sampling distribution of $\overline{X}$ is normal when either the underlying population is normally distributed or when the sample size $n \geq 30$. The sampling distribution of $\overline{P}$ is approximately normal when the sample size is sufficiently large such that $np \geq 5$ and $n(1 - p) \geq 5$.

LO 8.3 | **Calculate a confidence interval for the population mean when the population standard deviation is known.**

A $100(1 - \alpha)\%$ confidence interval of the population mean μ when the population standard deviation σ is known is computed as $x \pm z_{\alpha/2}\frac{\sigma}{\sqrt{n}}$, where $z_{\alpha/2}\frac{\sigma}{\sqrt{n}}$ is the margin of error.

LO 8.4 | **Describe the factors that influence the width of a confidence interval.**

The **precision** of a confidence interval is directly linked with the **width** of the interval: the wider the interval, the lower is its precision. A confidence interval is wider (a) the greater the population standard deviation σ, (b) the smaller the sample size n, and (c) the greater the confidence level.

LO 8.5 | **Discuss features of the t distribution.**

The **t distribution** is a family of distributions that are similar to the z distribution, in that they are all symmetric and bell-shaped around zero with asymptotic tails. However, the t distribution has broader tails than does the z distribution. Each t distribution is identified by a parameter known as the **degrees of freedom df**. The df determines the extent of broadness—the smaller the df, the broader the tails. Since the t distribution is defined by the degrees of freedom, it is common to refer to it as the t_{df} distribution.

LO 8.6 **Calculate a confidence interval for the mean when the population standard deviation is not known.**

A $100(1 - \alpha)\%$ confidence interval of the population mean μ when the population standard deviation σ is not known is computed as $\bar{x} \pm t_{\alpha/2,df} \frac{s}{\sqrt{n}}$, where s is the sample standard deviation.

LO 8.7 **Calculate a confidence interval for the population proportion.**

A $100(1 - \alpha)\%$ confidence interval of the population proportion p is computed as $\bar{p} \pm z_{\alpha/2} \sqrt{\frac{\bar{p}(1 - \bar{p})}{n}}$, where $\bar{p} = x/n$ is the sample proportion.

LO 8.8 **Select a sample size to estimate the population mean and the population proportion.**

For a desired margin of error D, the minimum n required to estimate μ with $100(1 - \alpha)\%$ confidence is $n = \left(\frac{z_{\alpha/2}\,\hat{\sigma}}{D}\right)^2$, where $\hat{\sigma}$ is a reasonable estimate of σ in the planning stage. If σ is known, we replace $\hat{\sigma}$ with σ. Other choices for $\hat{\sigma}$ include an estimate from a preselected sample, prior studies, or $\hat{\sigma} = \text{range}/4$. For a desired margin of error D, the minimum n required to estimate p with $100(1 - \alpha)\%$ confidence is $n = \left(\frac{z_{\alpha/2}}{D}\right)^2 \hat{p}(1 - \hat{p})$, where $\hat{p}$ is a reasonable estimate of p in the planning stage. Choices for $\hat{p}$ include an estimate from a preselected sample or prior studies; a conservative estimate of $\hat{p} = 0.5$ is used when no other reasonable estimate is available.

Additional Exercises and Case Studies

62. Over a 10-year sample period, the mean return and standard deviation of annual returns on a portfolio you are analyzing were 10% and 15%, respectively. You assume that returns are normally distributed. Construct a 95% confidence interval of the population mean.

63. **FILE** A realtor in Mission Viejo, California, wants to estimate the average price of a house in the city.
    a. Open the **Mission Viejo (raw)** data from the text website into an Excel spreadsheet (data are in $1,000s). Assume the population standard deviation is $100 (in $1,000s).
    b. Construct a 90% and a 99% confidence interval for the average house price. Comment on the corresponding widths of the intervals.

64. A hair salon in Cambridge, Massachusetts, reports that on seven randomly selected weekdays, the number of customers who visited the salon were 40, 30, 28, 22, 36, 16, and 50. It can be assumed that weekday customer visits follow a normal distribution.
    a. Construct a 90% confidence interval of the average number of customers who visit the salon on weekdays.
    b. Construct a 99% confidence interval of the average number of customers who visit the salon on weekdays.
    c. What happens to the width of the interval as the confidence level increases?

65. Recently, six single-family homes in San Luis Obispo County in California sold at the following prices (in $1,000s): $549, $449, $705, $529, $639, $609.
    a. Construct a 95% confidence interval for the mean sale price in San Luis Obispo County.

b. What assumption have you made when constructing this confidence interval?

66. According to data from the Organization for Economic Cooperation and Development, the average U.S. worker takes 16 days of vacation each year (*The Wall Street Journal*, June 20, 2007). Assume that these data were based on a sample of 225 workers and that the sample standard deviation is 12 days.
    a. Construct a 95% confidence interval of the population mean.
    b. At a 95% confidence level, can we conclude that the average U.S. worker does not take 14 days of vacation each year?

67. A machine that is programmed to package 1.20 pounds of cereal is being tested for its accuracy. In a sample of 36 cereal boxes, the sample mean filling weight is calculated as 1.22 pounds. The population standard deviation is known to be 0.06 pound.
    a. Identify the relevant parameter of interest for these quantitative data and compute its point estimate as well as the margin of error with 95% confidence.
    b. Can we conclude that the packaging machine is operating properly?
    c. How large a sample must we take if we wish to contain the margin of error below 0.01 pound with 95% confidence?

68. The SAT is the most widely used test in the undergraduate admissions process. Scores on the math portion of the SAT are believed to be normally distributed and range from

200 to 800. A researcher from the admissions department at the University of New Hampshire is interested in estimating the mean math SAT scores of the incoming class with 90% confidence. How large a sample should she take to ensure that the margin of error is below 15?

69. A recent study by Allstate Insurance Co. finds that 82% of teenagers have used cell phones while driving (*The Wall Street Journal*, May 5, 2010). Suppose this study was based on a random sample of 50 teen drivers.
    a. Construct a 99% confidence interval for the proportion of all teenagers that have used cell phones while driving.
    b. What is the margin of error with 99% confidence?

70. The following table shows the annual returns (in percent) for the Vanguard Energy Fund.

Year	Return
2005	44.60
2006	19.68
2007	37.00
2008	−42.87
2009	38.36

SOURCE: http://finance.yahoo.com.

    a. Calculate the point estimate for μ.
    b. Construct a 95% confidence interval for μ.
    c. What assumption did you make when constructing the interval?

71. **FILE** While the housing market is in the tank and is not likely to emerge anytime soon, real estate investment in college towns continues to promise good returns (*The Wall Street Journal*, September 24, 2010). Marcela Treisman works for an investment firm in Michigan. Her assignment is to analyze the rental market in Ann Arbor, which is home to the University of Michigan. She gathers data on monthly rents for 2011 along with the square footage of 40 homes. A portion of the data is shown below; the complete data, labeled **Ann Arbor Rental**, can be found on the text website.

Monthly Rent	Square Footage
645	500
675	648
⋮	⋮
2400	2700

SOURCE: www.zillow.com.

    a. Use Excel to calculate the mean and standard deviation for monthly rent.
    b. Use Excel to calculate the mean and standard deviation for square footage.
    c. Use Excel to construct 90% confidence intervals for the mean rent and the mean square footage of all homes in Ann Arbor, Michigan.

72. According to a survey of 1,235 businesses by IDC, a market-research concern in Framingham, Massachusetts, 12.1% of sole proprietors are engaging in e-commerce (*The Wall Street Journal*, July 26, 2007).
    a. What is the margin of error in estimating with 95% confidence the proportion of sole proprietors that engage in e-commerce?
    b. Construct a 95% confidence interval of the population proportion.

73. A Monster.com poll of 3,057 individuals asked: "What's the longest vacation you plan to take this summer?" The following relative frequency distribution summarizes the results.

Response	Relative Frequency
A few days	21%
A few long weekends	18%
One week	36%
Two weeks	22%

SOURCE: *The Boston Globe*, June 12, 2007.

    a. Construct a 95% confidence interval for the proportion of people who plan to take a one-week vacation this summer.
    b. Construct a 99% confidence interval for the proportion of people who plan to take a one-week vacation this summer.
    c. Which of the two confidence intervals is wider?

74. Linda Barnes has learned from prior studies that one out of five applicants gets admitted to top MBA programs in the country. She wishes to construct her own 90% confidence interval of the acceptance rate in top MBA programs. How large a sample should she take if she does not want the acceptance rate of the sample to deviate from that of the population by more than five percentage points? State your assumptions in computing the required sample size.

75. According to a recent report by the PEW Research Center, 85% of adults under 30 feel optimistic about the economy, but the optimism is shared by only 45% of those who are over 50 (*Newsweek*, September 13, 2010). A research analyst would like to construct 95% confidence intervals for the proportion patterns in various regions of the country. She uses the reported rates by the PEW Research Center to determine the sample size that would restrict the margin of error to within 0.05.
    a. How large a sample is required to estimate the proportion of adults under 30 who feel optimistic about the economy?
    b. How large a sample is required to estimate the proportion of adults over 50 who feel optimistic about the economy?

Case Study 8.1

Texas is home to more than one million undocumented immigrants and most of them are stuck in low-paying jobs. Meanwhile, the state also suffers from a lack of skilled workers. The Texas Workforce Commission estimates that 133,000 jobs are currently unfilled, many because employers cannot find qualified applicants (*The Boston Globe*, September 29, 2011). Texas was the first state to pass a law that allows children of undocumented immigrants to pay in-state college tuition rates if they have lived in Texas for three years and plan to become permanent residents. The law passed easily back in 2001 because most legislators believed that producing college graduates and keeping them in Texas benefits the business community. In addition, since college graduates earn more money, they also provide the state with more revenue. Carol Capaldo wishes to estimate the mean hourly wage of workers with various levels of education. She collects a sample of the hourly wages of 30 Texas workers with a bachelor's degree or higher, 30 Texas workers with only a high school diploma, and 30 Texas workers who did not finish high school. A portion of the data is shown in the accompanying table; the full data set is on the text website, labeled ***Texas Wages***.

Data for Case Study 8.1 Hourly Wages of Texas Workers by Education Level (in $)

FILE

Bachelor's Degree or Higher	High School Diploma	No High School Diploma
$22.50	$12.68	$11.21
19.57	11.23	8.54
⋮	⋮	⋮
21.44	7.47	10.27

In a report, use the above information to:

1. Use descriptive statistics to compare the hourly wages of the three education levels.
2. Construct and interpret 95% confidence intervals of the mean hourly wage at each education level.

Case Study 8.2

The following table presents the returns of two mutual funds offered by the investment giant Fidelity. The *Fidelity Select Automotive Fund* invests primarily in companies engaged in the manufacturing, marketing, or sales of automobiles, trucks, specialty vehicles, parts, tires, and related services. The *Fidelity Gold Fund* invests primarily in companies engaged in exploration, mining, processing or dealing in gold and, to a lesser degree, in other precious metals and minerals. A portion of the annual return data is shown below; the full data set is available on the text website, labeled ***Fidelity Returns***.

Data for Case Study 8.2 Annual Total Return (%) History

FILE

Year	Annual Total Return (%) History	
	Fidelity Select Automotive Fund	Fidelity Select Gold Fund
2001	22.82	24.99
2002	−6.48	64.28
⋮	⋮	⋮
2009	122.28	38.00

Source: http://finance.yahoo.com.

In a report, use the above information to:

1. Use descriptive statistics to compare the returns of the mutual funds.
2. Assess reward by constructing and interpreting 95% confidence intervals for the population mean return. What assumption did you make for the interval estimates?

Case Study 8.3

The information gathered from opinion polls and political surveys is becoming so increasingly important for candidates on the campaign trail that it is hard to imagine an election that lacks extensive polling. An NBC News/*Wall Street Journal* survey (August 5–9, 2010) of 1,000 adults asked people's preferences on candidates and issues prior to the midterm 2010 elections. Some of the responses to the survey are shown below, as well as responses from prior surveys.

Question: In general, do you approve or disapprove of the way Barack Obama is handling the aftermath of the Gulf Coast oil spill in August 2010 (and George W. Bush's handling of Katrina in March 2006)?

	August 2010	March 2006
Approve	50%	36%
Disapprove	38%	53%
Not sure	12%	11%

Question: Which are more important to you in your vote for Congress this November: domestic issues such as the economy, health care, and immigration; or international issues such as Afghanistan, Iran, and terrorism?

	August 2010	September 2006
Domestic issues	73%	43%
International issues	12%	28%
Both equally important	15%	28%

In a report, construct 95% confidence intervals of the relevant population proportions to:

1. Compare the approval rates of President Obama's handling of the Gulf Coast oil spill and President George W. Bush's handling of the Hurricane Katrina crisis.
2. Compare the importance of domestic issues in August 2010 and in September 2006.

Hypothesis Testing

CHAPTER 9

In Chapter 8, we learned how to estimate an unknown population parameter of interest using point estimates and confidence intervals. In this chapter, we will focus on the second major area of statistical inference, called hypothesis testing. We use a hypothesis test to challenge the status quo, or some belief about an underlying population parameter, based on sample data. For instance, we may wish to test whether the average age of MBA students in the U.S. is less than 30 years. Since we do not have access to the ages of all MBA students in the country, we have to perform statistical inference on the basis of limited sample information. Suppose that a sample of 40 MBA students reveals a mean age of 29 years. Although the sample mean is less than 30, it does not guarantee that the mean age of all MBA students in the population is less than 30. We may be able to justify the lower sample mean by pure chance. In this chapter, we will discuss how to determine whether the conclusion from the sample can be deemed real (that is, the mean age is less than 30) or due to chance (that is, the mean age is not less than 30).

Undergraduate Study Habits

Are today's college students studying hard or hardly studying? A recent study asserts that over the past five decades the number of hours that the average college student studies each week has been steadily dropping (*The Boston Globe*, July 4, 2010). In 1961, students invested 24 hours per week in their academic pursuits, whereas today's students study an average of 14 hours per week.

Susan Knight is a dean at a large university in California. She wonders if the study trend is reflective of the students at her university. She randomly selects 35 students and asks their average study time per week (in hours). The responses are shown in Table 9.1; the data set is also on the text website and is labeled **Study Hours**.

TABLE 9.1 Average Hours Studied per Week for a Sample of 35 College Students

25	17	8	14	17	7	11
19	16	9	15	12	17	19
26	14	22	17	14	35	24
11	21	6	20	27	17	6
29	10	10	4	25	13	16

Summary measures: $\bar{x} = 16.37$ hours and $s = 7.22$ hours.

Susan wants to use the sample information to:

1. Determine if the mean study time of students at her university is below the 1961 national average of 24 hours per week.
2. Determine if the mean study time of students at her university differs from today's national average of 14 hours per week.

We provide a synopsis of this case at the end of Section 9.3.

9.1 Introduction to Hypothesis Testing

We use hypothesis testing to resolve conflicts between two competing opinions (hypotheses) on a particular population parameter of interest. We refer to one hypothesis as the **null hypothesis**, denoted H_0, and the other as the **alternative hypothesis**, denoted H_A. We can think of a null hypothesis as corresponding to a presumed default state of nature or status quo. An alternative hypothesis, on the other hand, contradicts the default state or status quo. In other words, only one of the two hypotheses is true and the hypotheses cover all possible values of the population parameter.

> **NULL HYPOTHESIS VERSUS ALTERNATIVE HYPOTHESIS**
>
> When constructing a hypothesis test, we define a **null hypothesis**, denoted H_0, and an **alternative hypothesis**, denoted H_A. We conduct a hypothesis test to determine whether or not sample evidence contradicts H_0.

In statistics we use sample information to make inferences regarding the unknown population parameters of interest. In this chapter our goal is to determine if the null hypothesis can be rejected in favor of the alternative hypothesis. An analogy can be drawn with applications in the medical and legal fields, where we can define the null hypothesis as "an individual is free of disease" or "an accused is innocent." In both cases the verdict is based on limited evidence, which in statistics translates into making a decision based on limited sample information.

The Decision to "Reject" or "Not Reject" the Null Hypothesis

The hypothesis testing procedure enables us to make one of two decisions. If sample evidence is inconsistent with the null hypothesis, we reject the null hypothesis. Conversely, if sample evidence is not inconsistent, then we do not reject the null hypothesis. It is not correct to conclude that "we accept the null hypothesis" because while the sample data may not be inconsistent with the null hypothesis, it does not necessarily prove that the null hypothesis is true.

> On the basis of sample information, we either **"reject the null hypothesis"** or **"do not reject the null hypothesis."**

Consider the example just referenced where the null is defined as "an individual is free of disease." Suppose a particular medical procedure does not detect the disease. On the basis of this limited information, we can only conclude that we are unable to detect the disease (do not reject the null hypothesis). It does not necessarily prove that the person does not have the disease (accept the null hypothesis). Similarly, in the court example where the null hypothesis is defined as "an accused is innocent," we can conclude that the person is guilty (reject the null hypothesis) or that there is not enough evidence to convict (do not reject the null hypothesis).

Defining the Null Hypothesis and the Alternative Hypotheses

As mentioned earlier, we use a hypothesis test to contest the status quo, or some belief about an underlying population parameter, based on sample data. A very crucial step concerns the formulation of the two competing hypotheses, since the conclusion of the test depends on how the hypotheses are stated. As a general guideline, whatever we wish to establish is placed in the alternative hypothesis whereas the null hypothesis includes the status quo. If we are unable to reject the null hypothesis, then we maintain the status quo or "business as usual." However, if we reject the null hypothesis, this establishes that the alternative hypothesis is true, which may require that we take some kind of action. For instance, if we reject the null hypothesis that an individual is free of disease, then we conclude that the person is sick, for which treatment may be prescribed. Similarly, if we reject that an accused is innocent, we conclude that the person is guilty and should be suitably punished.

Another requirement in hypothesis testing is that some form of the equality sign appears in the null hypothesis. (The justification for the equality sign will be provided later.) Any of the three signs "=", "≤", or "≥" are valid statements for the null hypothesis. Given that the alternative hypothesis states the opposite of the null hypothesis, the alternative hypothesis is then specified with a "≠", ">", or "<" sign.

> As a general guideline, we use the alternative hypothesis as a vehicle to establish something, or contest the status quo, for which a corrective action may be required. In general, the null hypothesis regarding a particular population parameter of interest is specified with one of the following signs: =, ≤, or ≥; the corresponding alternative hypothesis is then specified with one of the competing signs: ≠, >, or <.

A hypothesis test can be **one-tailed** or **two-tailed**. A two-tailed test is defined when the null hypothesis states a specific value for the population parameter of interest. For example, $H_0: \mu = \mu_0$ versus $H_A: \mu \neq \mu_0$ and $H_0: p = p_0$ versus $H_A: p \neq p_0$ are two-tailed tests, where μ_0 and p_0 represent hypothesized values of the population mean and the population proportion, respectively. If the null hypothesis is rejected, it suggests that the true parameter does not equal the hypothesized value.

A one-tailed test, on the other hand, involves a null hypothesis that can only be rejected on one side of the hypothesized value. For example, consider $H_0: \mu \leq \mu_0$ versus $H_A: \mu > \mu_0$. Here we can reject the null hypothesis only when there is substantial evidence that the population mean is greater than μ_0. It is also referred to as a **right-tailed test** since rejection of the null hypothesis occurs on the right side of the hypothesized mean. Another example is a **left-tailed test**, $H_0: \mu \geq \mu_0$ versus $H_A: \mu < \mu_0$, where the null hypothesis can only be rejected on the left side of the hypothesized mean. One-tailed tests for the population proportion are defined similarly.

> ### ONE-TAILED VERSUS TWO-TAILED HYPOTHESIS TESTS
>
> Hypothesis tests can be **one-tailed** or **two-tailed**. In a **one-tailed test** we can reject the null hypothesis only on one side of the hypothesized value of the population parameter. In a **two-tailed test**, we can reject the null hypothesis on either side of the hypothesized value of the population parameter.

In general, we follow three steps when formulating the competing hypotheses:

- Identify the relevant population parameter of interest.
- Determine whether it is a one- or a two-tailed test.
- Include some form of the equality sign in the null hypothesis and use the alternative hypothesis to establish a claim.

The following examples highlight one- and two-tailed tests of the population mean and the population proportion. In each example we want to state the appropriate competing hypotheses.

EXAMPLE 9.1

A trade group predicts that back-to-school spending will average $606.40 per family this year. A different economic model is needed if the prediction is wrong. Specify the null and the alternative hypotheses to determine if a different economic model may be needed.

SOLUTION: Given that we are examining average back-to-school spending, the parameter of interest is the population mean. Since we want to be able to determine if the population mean differs from $606.40 ($\mu \neq 606.40$), we need a two-tailed test and formulate the null and alternative hypotheses as

$$H_0: \mu = 606.40$$

$$H_A: \mu \neq 606.40$$

The trade group is advised to use a different economic model if the null hypothesis is rejected.

EXAMPLE 9.2

An advertisement for a popular weight-loss clinic suggests that participants in its new diet program lose, on average, more than 10 pounds. A consumer activist wants to determine if the advertisement's claim is valid. Specify the null and the alternative hypotheses to validate the advertisement's claim.

SOLUTION: The advertisement's claim concerns average weight loss, thus the parameter of interest is again the population mean. This is an example of a one-tailed test because we want to determine if the mean weight loss is more than 10 pounds ($\mu > 10$). We specify the competing hypotheses as

$$H_0: \mu \leq 10 \text{ pounds}$$

$$H_A: \mu > 10 \text{ pounds}$$

The underlying claim that the mean weight loss is more than 10 pounds is true if our decision is to reject the null hypothesis. Conversely, if we do not reject the null hypothesis, we infer that the claim is not supported by the sample data.

EXAMPLE 9.3

A television research analyst wishes to test a claim that more than 50% of the households will tune in for a TV episode. Specify the null and the alternative hypotheses to test the claim.

SOLUTION: This is an example of a one-tailed test regarding the population proportion p. Given that the analyst wants to determine whether $p > 0.50$, this claim is placed in the alternative hypothesis, whereas the null hypothesis is just its opposite.

$$H_0: p \leq 0.50$$

$$H_A: p > 0.50$$

The claim that more than 50% of the households will tune in for a TV episode is valid only if the null hypothesis is rejected.

EXAMPLE 9.4

It is generally believed that at least 0.60 of the residents in a small town in Texas are happy with their lives. A sociologist is concerned about the lingering economic crisis and wants to determine whether the crisis has adversely affected the happiness level in this town. Specify the null and the alternative hypotheses to determine if the sociologist's concern is valid.

SOLUTION: This is also a one-tailed test regarding the population proportion p. While the population proportion has been at least 0.60 ($p \geq 0.60$), the sociologist wants to establish that the current population proportion is below 0.60 ($p < 0.60$). Therefore, the hypotheses are formulated as

$$H_0: p \geq 0.60$$

$$H_A: p < 0.60$$

In this case, the sociologist's concern is valid if the null hypothesis is rejected. Nothing new is established if the null hypothesis is not rejected.

Type I and Type II Errors

LO 9.2

Distinguish between Type I and Type II errors.

Since the decision of a hypothesis test is based on limited sample information, we are bound to make errors. Ideally, we would like to be able to reject the null hypothesis when the null hypothesis is false and not reject the null hypothesis when the null hypothesis is true. However, we may end up rejecting or not rejecting the null hypothesis erroneously. In other words, sometimes we reject the null hypothesis when we should not, or choose not to reject the null hypothesis when we should.

We consider two types of errors in the context of hypothesis testing: a **Type I error** and a **Type II error**. A Type I error is committed when we reject the null hypothesis when the null hypothesis is actually true. On the other hand, a Type II error is made when we do not reject the null hypothesis and the null hypothesis is actually false. We denote the probability of a Type I error by α and the probability of a Type II error by β. We can lower both of these errors only if we have access to increased sample evidence for making a decision. In other words, as the sample size n increases, both α and β tend to decrease. However, for a given sample size, any attempt to reduce the likelihood of one error will increase the likelihood of the other error. For a given n, α can be reduced only at the expense of a higher β. Similarly, the only way to reduce β is to accept a higher value of α. The optimal choice of α and β depends on the cost of these two types of errors, and determining these costs is not always easy. Typically, the decision regarding the optimal use of Type I and Type II errors is made by the management of a firm where the job of a statistician is to conduct the hypothesis test for a chosen value of α.

TYPE I AND TYPE II ERRORS

A **Type I error** is committed when we reject the null hypothesis when the null hypothesis is true. A **Type II error** is made when we do not reject the null hypothesis when the null hypothesis is false. The probability of a Type I error is denoted by α and the probability of a Type II error is denoted by β. For a given sample size n, a decrease in α will increase β and vice versa. Both α and β decrease as n increases.

EXAMPLE 9.5

Consider the following hypotheses that relate to the medical example mentioned earlier.

$$H_0: \text{A person is free of disease}$$

$$H_A: \text{A person has disease}$$

Suppose a person takes a medical test that attempts to detect the disease. Discuss the consequences of a Type I error and a Type II error.

SOLUTION: A Type I error occurs when the medical test indicates that the person has the disease (reject H_0), but in reality, the person is free of the disease. We often refer to this type of result as a false positive. If the medical test shows that the person is free of the disease (do not reject H_0) when the person actually has the disease, then a Type II error occurs. We often call this type of result a false negative.

EXAMPLE 9.6

Consider the following competing hypotheses that relate to the court of law.

$$H_0: \text{An accused person is innocent}$$

$$H_A: \text{An accused person is guilty}$$

Suppose the accused person is judged by a jury of her peers. Discuss the consequences of a Type I error and a Type II error.

SOLUTION: A Type I error is a verdict that finds that the accused is guilty (reject H_0) when she is actually innocent. A Type II error is due to a verdict that concludes the accused is innocent (do not reject H_0) when in reality, she is guilty. For given evidence, we cannot reduce either of these two errors without increasing the other. Moreover, as mentioned earlier, it is not always easy to determine which of the two errors is more costly to society.

Table 9.2 summarizes the circumstances surrounding Type I and Type II errors. Two correct decisions are possible: not rejecting the null hypothesis when the null hypothesis is true, and rejecting the null hypothesis when the null hypothesis is false. Conversely, two incorrect decisions (errors) are also possible: rejecting the null hypothesis when the null hypothesis is true (Type I error), and not rejecting the null hypothesis when the null hypothesis is false (Type II error).

TABLE 9.2 Type I and Type II Errors

Decision	Null hypothesis is true	Null hypothesis is false
Reject the null hypothesis	Type I error	Correct decision
Do not reject the null hypothesis	Correct decision	Type II error

As we will see in later sections, a hypothesis test is based on the chosen level of the Type I error α. We want the test to have the ability to reject the null hypothesis when the null hypothesis is false. The **power of the test** is defined as the probability of rejecting the null hypothesis when the null hypothesis is false. Since β is the probability of a Type II error, the power of the test is defined as $1 - \beta$. In more advanced statistics, we learn how to compare various types of tests on the basis of their size and power, where the size denotes the actual proportion of rejections when the null is true and the power denotes the actual proportion of rejections when the null is false. These analyses are based on computer simulations.

1. Explain why the following hypotheses are not constructed correctly.
   a. $H_0: \mu \leq 10; H_A: \mu \geq 10$
   b. $H_0: \mu \neq 500; H_A: \mu = 500$
   c. $H_0: p \leq 0.40; H_A: p > 0.42$
   d. $H_0: \bar{X} \leq 128; H_A: \bar{X} > 128$

2. Which of the following statements are valid null and alternative hypotheses? If they are invalid hypotheses, explain why.
   a. $H_0: \bar{X} \leq 210; H_A: \bar{X} > 210$
   b. $H_0: \mu = 120; H_A: \mu \neq 120$
   c. $H_0: p \leq 0.24; H_A: p > 0.24$
   d. $H_0: \mu < 252; H_A: \mu > 252$

3. Explain why the following statements are not correct.
   a. "With my methodological approach, I can reduce the Type I error with the given sample information without changing the Type II error."
   b. "I have already decided how much of the Type I error I am going to allow. A bigger sample will not change either the Type I or Type II errors."
   c. "I can reduce the Type II error by making it difficult to reject the null hypothesis."
   d. "By making it easy to reject the null hypothesis, I am reducing the Type I error."

4. Which of the following statements are correct? Explain if incorrect.
   a. "I accept the null hypothesis since sample evidence is not inconsistent with the null hypothesis."
   b. "Since sample evidence cannot be supported by the null hypothesis, I reject the null hypothesis."
   c. "I can establish a given claim if sample evidence is consistent with the null hypothesis."
   d. "I cannot establish a given claim if the null hypothesis is not rejected."

5. Construct the null and the alternative hypotheses for the following tests:
   a. Test if the mean weight of cereal in a cereal box differs from 18 ounces.
   b. Test if the stock price increases on more than 60% of the trading days.
   c. Test if Americans get an average of less than seven hours of sleep.

6. Define the consequences of Type I and Type II errors for each of the tests considered in the preceding question.

7. Construct the null and alternative hypotheses for the following claims:
   a. "I am going to get the majority of the votes to win this election."
   b. "I suspect that your 10-inch pizzas are, on average, less than 10 inches in size."
   c. "I will have to fine the company since its tablets do not contain an average of 250 mg of ibuprofen as advertised."

8. Discuss the consequences of Type I and Type II errors for each of the claims considered in the preceding question.

9. A polygraph (lie detector) is an instrument used to determine if the individual is telling the truth. These tests are considered to be 95% reliable. In other words, if an individual lies, there is a 0.95 probability that the test will detect a lie. Let there also be a 0.005 probability that the test erroneously detects a lie even when the individual is actually telling the truth. Consider the null hypothesis, "the individual is telling the truth," to answer the following questions.
   a. What is the probability of Type I error?
   b. What is the probability of Type II error?
   c. Discuss the consequences of Type I and Type II errors.
   d. What is wrong with the statement, "I can prove that the individual is telling the truth on the basis of the polygraph result."

10. The screening process for detecting a rare disease is not perfect. Researchers have developed a blood test that is considered fairly reliable. It gives a positive reaction in 98% of the people who have that disease. However, it erroneously gives a positive reaction in 3% of the people who do not have the disease. Answer the following questions using the null hypothesis as "the individual does not have the disease."
   a. What is the probability of Type I error?
   b. What is the probability of Type II error?
   c. Discuss the consequences of Type I and Type II errors.
   d. What is wrong with the nurse's analysis, "The blood test result has proved that the individual is free of disease."

9.2 Hypothesis Test of the Population Mean When σ Is Known

In Chapter 8 we discussed that the population standard deviation σ is rarely known. There are instances when σ is considered fairly stable, and therefore, can be determined from prior experience. In such cases the population standard deviation is treated as known. We use the case of a known population standard deviation to introduce the basic methodology for hypothesis testing, a technique we will use throughout the remainder of the book.

A hypothesis test regarding the population mean μ is based on the sampling distribution of the sample mean $\overline{X}$. In particular, it uses the fact that $E(\overline{X}) = \mu$ and $SD(\overline{X}) = \sigma/\sqrt{n}$. Also, in order to implement the test, it is essential that the sampling distribution of $\overline{X}$ follows a normal distribution. Recall that $\overline{X}$ is normally distributed when the underlying population is normally distributed. If the underlying population is not normally distributed, then by the central limit theorem, $\overline{X}$ is approximately normally distributed if the sample size is sufficiently large, or when $n \geq 30$.

The hypothesis testing procedure simply enables us to determine whether sample evidence is inconsistent with what is hypothesized under the null hypothesis. Consider the hypotheses, $H_0: \mu = \mu_0$ versus $H_A: \mu \neq \mu_0$, where μ_0 is the hypothesized value of the population mean. If the given value of the sample mean $\overline{x}$ differs from μ_0, it does not necessarily suggest that the sample evidence is inconsistent with the null hypothesis. Perhaps the difference can be explained by pure chance. Remember that even when the true population mean equals μ_0 (H_0 is true), $\overline{X}$ is still a random variable with a 50% chance that it is more than μ_0 and a 50% chance that it is less than μ_0. We can make a compelling case for rejecting the null hypothesis only when the discrepancy between $\overline{x}$ and μ_0 is significant.

The basic principle of hypothesis testing is to first assume that the null hypothesis is true and then determine if sample evidence contradicts this assumption. This principle is analogous to the scenario in the court of law where the null hypothesis is defined as "the individual is innocent" and the decision rule is best described by "innocent until proven guilty."

We follow a four-step procedure when implementing a hypothesis test. We make a distinction between two equivalent methods—the **p-value approach** and the **critical value approach**—for hypothesis testing. The four-step procedure with the two approaches is valid for one-tailed and two-tailed tests regarding the population mean, the population proportion, or any other population parameter of interest.

LO **9.3**

Explain the steps of a
hypothesis test using
the p-value approach.

The p-Value Approach

Suppose a sociologist wants to establish that the mean retirement age is greater than 67 ($\mu > 67$). It is assumed that retirement age is normally distributed with a known population standard deviation σ of 9 years. We can investigate the sociologist's belief by a test of the population mean where we specify the competing hypotheses as

$$H_0: \mu \leq 67$$
$$H_A: \mu > 67$$

Let a random sample of 25 retirees produce an average retirement age of 71, or $\overline{x} = 71$. This sample evidence casts doubt on the validity of the null hypothesis, since the sample mean is greater than the hypothesized value, $\mu_0 = 67$. However, as discussed earlier, the discrepancy between $\overline{x}$ and μ_0 does not necessarily imply that the null hypothesis is false. It is common to evaluate this discrepancy in terms of the appropriate test statistic.

TEST STATISTIC FOR μ WHEN σ IS KNOWN

The value of the **test statistic** for the hypothesis test of **the population mean μ** when the **population standard deviation σ is known** is computed as $z = \dfrac{\overline{x} - \mu_0}{\sigma/\sqrt{n}}$, where μ_0 is the hypothesized mean value.

Note that the value of the test statistic z is evaluated at $\mu = \mu_0$, which explains why we need some form of the equality sign in the null hypothesis. Given that the population is normally distributed with a known standard deviation, $\sigma = 9$, we compute the value of the test statistic as $z = \dfrac{\overline{x} - \mu_0}{\sigma/\sqrt{n}} = \dfrac{71 - 67}{9/\sqrt{25}} = 2.22$. Therefore, comparing $\overline{x} = 71$ with 67 is identical to comparing $z = 2.22$ with 0, where 67 and 0 are the means of the unstandardized normal distribution and the standard normal distribution, respectively.

We now compute the **p-value**, which is the likelihood of obtaining a sample mean that is at least as extreme as the one derived from the given sample, under the assumption that the null hypothesis is true. Since in the above example $\bar{x} = 71$, we define the extreme value as a sample mean of 71 or higher, and use the z table to compute the p-value as $P(\bar{X} \geq 71) = P(Z \geq 2.22) = 1 - 0.9868 = 0.0132$. Figure 9.1 shows the computed p-value.

FIGURE 9.1 The p-value for a right-tailed test with $z = 2.22$

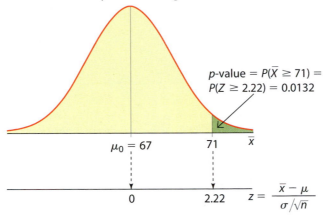

Note that when the population mean equals 67, there is only a 1.32% chance that $\bar{X}$ will be 71 or more. Therefore, if we decide to reject the null hypothesis, there is a 1.32% chance that our decision will be erroneous. In order to make a decision, we need to determine if the p-value is deemed small enough to reject the null hypothesis.

Remember that a Type I error occurs when we reject the null hypothesis when the null hypothesis is true. The allowed probability of making a Type I error is α, which is also referred to as the **significance level** of the test. We choose a value for α before implementing a hypothesis test. Most hypothesis tests are conducted using a significance level of 1, 5, or 10%, using $\alpha = 0.01, 0.05,$ or 0.10, respectively. The decision rule is to reject the null hypothesis when the p-value $< \alpha$ and not reject the null hypothesis when p-value $\geq \alpha$.

Suppose we choose $\alpha = 0.05$ to conduct the above test. Therefore, we reject the null hypothesis because $0.0132 < 0.05$. This means that the sample data support the sociologist's claim that the average retirement age is greater than 67 years old. Individuals may be working past the normal retirement age of 67 either because their savings have been depleted due to the financial crisis and/or the fact that this generation is expected to outlive any previous generation and needs a job to pay the bills.

In the retirement age example of a right-tailed test, we calculated the p-value as $P(Z \geq z)$. Analogously, for a left-tailed test the p-value is given by $P(Z \leq z)$. For a two-tailed test, the extreme values exist on both sides of the distribution of the test statistic. Given the symmetry of the z distribution, the p-value for a two-tailed test is twice that of the p-value for a one-tailed test. It is calculated as $2P(Z \geq z)$ if $z > 0$ or as $2P(Z \leq z)$ if $z < 0$.

THE p-VALUE APPROACH

Under the assumption that $\mu = \mu_0$, the p-value is the likelihood of observing a sample mean that is at least as extreme as the one derived from the given sample. Its calculation depends on the specification of the alternative hypothesis.

Alternative Hypothesis	p-value
$H_A: \mu > \mu_0$	Right-tail probability: $P(Z \geq z)$
$H_A: \mu < \mu_0$	Left-tail probability: $P(Z \leq z)$
$H_A: \mu \neq \mu_0$	Two-tail probability: $2P(Z \geq z)$ if $z > 0$ or $2P(Z \leq z)$ if $z < 0$

The decision rule: Reject H_0 if p-value $< \alpha$.

Figure 9.2 shows the three different scenarios of determining the *p*-value depending on the specification of the competing hypotheses.

FIGURE 9.2 The *p*-values for one- and two-tailed tests

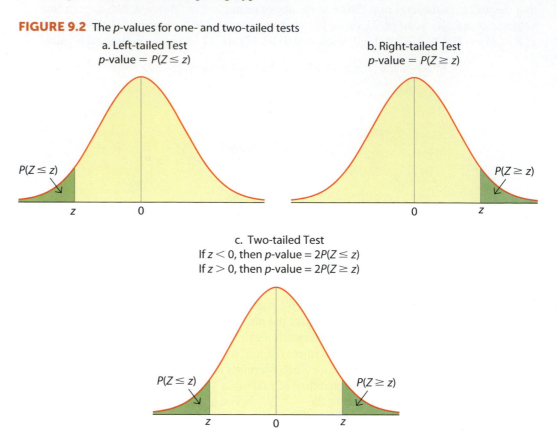

a. Left-tailed Test
p-value = $P(Z \leq z)$

$P(Z \leq z)$

b. Right-tailed Test
p-value = $P(Z \geq z)$

$P(Z \geq z)$

c. Two-tailed Test
If $z < 0$, then *p*-value = $2P(Z \leq z)$
If $z > 0$, then *p*-value = $2P(Z \geq z)$

$P(Z \leq z)$

$P(Z \geq z)$

Figure 9.2a shows the *p*-value for a left-tailed test. Since the appropriate test statistic follows the standard normal distribution, we calculate the *p*-value as $P(Z \leq z)$. When calculating the *p*-value for a right-tailed test (see Figure 9.2b), we find the area to the right of the value of the test statistic *z* or equivalently, $P(Z \geq z)$. We should note here that if $z \geq 0$ for a left-tailed test or if $z \leq 0$ for a right-tailed test, then H_0 can never be rejected. Figure 9.2c shows the *p*-value for a two-tailed test, calculated as $2P(Z \leq z)$ when $z < 0$ or as $2P(Z \geq z)$ when $z > 0$.

We will now summarize the four-step procedure using the *p*-value approach.

THE FOUR-STEP PROCEDURE USING THE *p*-VALUE APPROACH

Step 1. Specify the null and the alternative hypotheses. We identify the relevant population parameter of interest, determine whether it is a one- or a two-tailed test and, most importantly, include some form of the equality sign in the null hypothesis and place whatever we wish to establish in the alternative hypothesis.

Step 2. Specify the test statistic and compute its value. When the population standard deviation σ is known, the value of the test statistic $z = \frac{\bar{x} - \mu_0}{\sigma/\sqrt{n}}$, where μ_0 is the hypothesized value of the population mean.

Step 3. Calculate the *p*-value. Since the test statistic is assumed to follow the *z* distribution, the *p*-value for a right-tailed test is $P(Z \geq z)$. Analogously, the *p*-value for a left-tailed test is $P(Z \leq z)$. The *p*-value for a two-tailed test is $2P(Z \geq z)$ if $z > 0$ or $2P(Z \leq z)$ if $z < 0$.

Step 4. State the conclusion and interpret results. We choose a significance level α before implementing a hypothesis test. The decision rule is to reject the null hypothesis when *p*-value $< \alpha$ and not reject the null hypothesis when *p*-value $\geq \alpha$.

EXAMPLE 9.7

A research analyst disputes a trade group's prediction that back-to-school spending will average \$606.40 per family this year. She believes that average back-to-school spending will significantly differ from this amount. She decides to conduct a test on the basis of a random sample of 30 households with school-age children. She calculates the sample mean as \$622.85. She also believes that back-to-school spending is normally distributed with a population standard deviation of \$65.

a. Specify the competing hypotheses in order to test the research analyst's claim.
b. Calculate the value of the test statistic.
c. Calculate the p-value and state the decision rule.
d. At the 5% significance level, does average back-to-school spending differ from \$606.40?

SOLUTION:

a. Since we want to determine if the average is different from the predicted value of \$606.40, we specify the hypotheses as

$$H_0: \mu = 606.40$$

$$H_A: \mu \neq 606.40$$

b. Note that $\overline{X}$ is normally distributed since it is computed from a random sample drawn from a normal population. Since σ is known, the test statistic follows the standard normal distribution, and its value is

$$z = \frac{\overline{x} - \mu_0}{\sigma/\sqrt{n}} = \frac{622.85 - 606.40}{65/\sqrt{30}} = 1.39.$$

c. For a two-tailed test with a positive value for the test statistic, we compute the p-value as $2P(Z \geq 1.39)$. From the z table, we first find $P(Z \geq 1.39) = 1 - 0.9177 = 0.0823$; so the p-value $= 2 \times 0.0823 = 0.1646$. The decision rule is to reject the null hypothesis if the p-value $= 0.1646$ is less than the chosen level of significance α.

d. We do not reject the null hypothesis since the p-value $> \alpha$ $(0.1646 > 0.05)$. Therefore, at the 5% significance level, we cannot conclude that average back-to-school spending differs from \$606.40 per family this year. The sample data do not support the research analyst's claim.

The Critical Value Approach

LO 9.4

Explain the steps of a hypothesis test using the critical value approach.

We always use sample evidence and the chosen significance level α to conduct hypothesis tests. The p-value approach makes the comparison in terms of probabilities. The value of the test statistic is used to compute the p-value, which is then compared with α in order to arrive at a decision. The critical value approach, on the other hand, makes the comparison directly in terms of the value of the test statistic. Both approaches always lead to the same conclusion.

Earlier, we had used the p-value approach to validate a sociologist's claim that the mean retirement age in the United States is greater than 67. In a random sample of 25 retirees, the average retirement age was 71. It was also assumed that retirement age is normally distributed with a population standard deviation σ of 9 years. The first two steps with the critical value approach remain the same as those with the p-value approach. In other words, the competing hypotheses are $H_0: \mu \leq 67$ versus $H_A: \mu > 67$ and the value of the test statistic is $z = \frac{\overline{x} - \mu_0}{\sigma/\sqrt{n}} = \frac{71 - 67}{9/\sqrt{25}} = 2.22$. Recall that the resulting p-value was 0.0132, and for $\alpha = 0.05$, we rejected the null hypothesis since $0.0132 < 0.05$.

The critical value approach specifies a region of values, also called the **rejection region**, such that if the test statistic falls into this region, then we reject the null hypothesis.

The **critical value** is a point that separates the rejection region from the nonrejection region. Once again we need to make distinctions between the three types of competing hypotheses. For a right-tailed test, the critical value is z_α, where $P(Z \geq z_\alpha) = \alpha$. The resulting rejection region includes values greater than z_α.

With α known, we can easily find the corresponding z_α from the z table. In the retirement age example with $\alpha = 0.05$, we evaluate $P(Z \geq z_\alpha) = 0.05$ to derive the critical value as $z_\alpha = z_{0.05} = 1.645$. Figure 9.3 shows the critical value as well as the corresponding rejection region of the test.

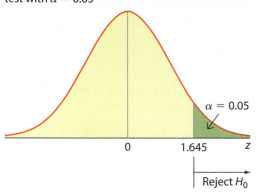

FIGURE 9.3 The critical value for a right-tailed test with $\alpha = 0.05$

As shown in Figure 9.3, the decision rule is to reject H_0 if $z > 1.645$. Since the value of the test statistic, $z = 2.22$, exceeds the critical value, $z_\alpha = 1.645$, we reject the null hypothesis and conclude that the mean age is significantly greater than 67. Thus, we confirm the conclusion reached with the p-value approach.

We would like to stress that we always arrive at the same statistical conclusion whether we use the p-value approach or the critical value approach. If z falls in the rejection region, then the p-value must be less than α. Similarly, if z does not fall in the rejection region, then the p-value must be greater than α. Figure 9.4 shows the equivalence of the two results in the retirement age example of a right-tailed test.

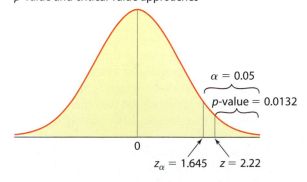

FIGURE 9.4 Equivalent conclusions resulting from the p-value and critical value approaches

We reject the null hypothesis because the p-value $= 0.0132$ is less than $\alpha = 0.05$, or equivalently, because $z = 2.22$ is greater than $z_\alpha = 1.645$.

The above example uses a right-tailed test to calculate the critical value as z_α. Given the symmetry of the z distribution around zero, the critical value for a left-tailed test is $-z_\alpha$. For a two-tailed test, we split the significance level in half to determine *two* critical values $-z_{\alpha/2}$ and $z_{\alpha/2}$ where $P(Z \geq z_{\alpha/2}) = \alpha/2$.

Figure 9.5 shows the three different scenarios of determining the critical value(s) depending on the specification of the competing hypotheses.

FIGURE 9.5 Critical values for one- and two-tailed tests

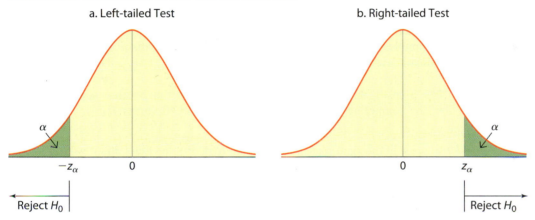

a. Left-tailed Test   b. Right-tailed Test

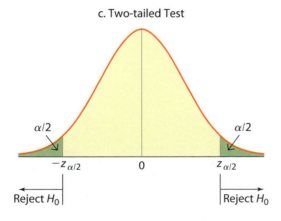

c. Two-tailed Test

Figure 9.5a shows a negative critical value for a left-tailed test where we reject the null hypothesis if $z < -z_\alpha$. Similarly, Figure 9.5b shows a positive critical value for a right-tailed test where we reject the null hypothesis if $z > z_\alpha$. There are two critical values for a two-tailed test, where we reject the null hypothesis when $z < -z_{\alpha/2}$ or when $z > z_{\alpha/2}$ (see Figure 9.5c).

We will now summarize the four-step procedure using the critical value approach.

EXAMPLE 9.8

Repeat Example 9.7 using the critical value approach. Recall that a research analyst wishes to determine if average back-to-school spending differs from $606.40. A random sample of 30 households, drawn from a normally distributed population with a standard deviation of $65, results in a sample mean of $622.85.

SOLUTION: Steps 1 and 2 remain the same as with the *p*-value approach. In particular, the competing hypotheses are H_0: $\mu = 606.40$ versus H_A: $\mu \neq 606.40$ and the value of the test statistic is $z = \frac{\bar{x} - \mu_0}{\sigma/\sqrt{n}} = \frac{622.85 - 606.40}{65/\sqrt{30}} = 1.39$. For a two-tailed test, we split the significance level in half to determine *two* critical values, one on each side of the distribution of the test statistic. Given a 5% level of significance, $\alpha/2 = 0.05/2 = 0.025$ is used to derive $z_{\alpha/2} = z_{0.025}$ as 1.96. Thus, the critical values are -1.96 and 1.96. As shown in Figure 9.6, the decision rule is to reject the H_0 if $z > 1.96$ or $z < -1.96$.

FIGURE 9.6 The critical values for a two-tailed test with $\alpha = 0.05$

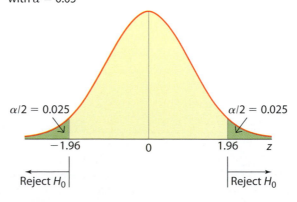

Since $z = 1.39$ does not fall in the rejection region ($-1.96 < 1.39 < 1.96$), we do not reject the null hypothesis. At the 5% significance level, we cannot conclude that average back-to-school spending differs from $606.40 per family. As always, our conclusion is consistent with that using the *p*-value approach.

Confidence Intervals and Two-Tailed Hypothesis Tests

For a two-tailed hypothesis test, we can also construct a confidence interval to arrive at the conclusion. Given that we conduct the hypothesis test at the α significance level, we can use the sample data to determine a corresponding $100(1 - \alpha)\%$ confidence interval for the population mean μ. If the confidence interval does not contain the value of the hypothesized mean μ_0, then we reject the null hypothesis. If the confidence interval contains μ_0, then we do not reject the null hypothesis.

> ### IMPLEMENTING A TWO-TAILED TEST USING A CONFIDENCE INTERVAL
>
> The general specification for a $100(1 - \alpha)\%$ confidence interval of the population mean μ when the population standard deviation σ is known is computed as
>
> $$\bar{x} \pm z_{\alpha/2}\frac{\sigma}{\sqrt{n}} \quad \text{or} \quad \left[\bar{x} - z_{\alpha/2}\frac{\sigma}{\sqrt{n}}, \bar{x} + z_{\alpha/2}\frac{\sigma}{\sqrt{n}}\right].$$
>
> Given a hypothesized mean value μ_0, the **decision rule** is
>
> $$\text{Reject } H_0 \text{ if } \mu_0 < \bar{x} - z_{\alpha/2}\frac{\sigma}{\sqrt{n}} \text{ or if } \mu_0 > \bar{x} + z_{\alpha/2}\frac{\sigma}{\sqrt{n}}.$$

EXAMPLE 9.9

Repeat Example 9.8 by constructing a confidence interval for μ.

SOLUTION: We are testing H_0: $\mu = 606.40$ versus H_A: $\mu \neq 606.40$ at the 5% significance level. We use $n = 30$, $\bar{x} = 622.85$, and $\sigma = 65$, along with $\alpha = 0.05$ to determine a 95% confidence interval. We find $z_{\alpha/2} = z_{0.025} = 1.96$ and compute

$$\bar{x} \pm z_{\alpha/2}\frac{\sigma}{\sqrt{n}} = 622.85 \pm 1.96\frac{65}{\sqrt{30}} = 622.85 \pm 23.26,$$

resulting in the interval [599.59, 646.11]. Since the hypothesized value of the population mean $\mu_0 = 606.40$ falls within the 95% confidence interval, we do not reject H_0. Thus, we arrive at the same conclusion as with the p-value and the critical value approaches; that is, the sample data do not support the research analyst's claim that average back-to-school spending differs from \$606.40 per family this year.

Using Excel to Solve Hypothesis Tests

Fortunately, Excel provides several functions that simplify the steps of a hypothesis test. Here we discuss one of these functions using the following example.

EXAMPLE 9.10

FILE

A recent report in *The New York Times* (August 7, 2010) suggests that consumers are spending less not only as a response to the economic downturn, but also due to a realization that excessive spending does not make them happier. A researcher wants to use debit card data to contradict the generally held view that the average amount spent annually on a debit card is at least \$8,000. She surveys 20 consumers and asks them how much they spend annually on their debit cards. The results are given below; the data, labeled **Debit Spending**, are also available on the text website.

7,960	7,700	7,727	7,704	8,543	7,661	7,767	8,761	7,530	8,128
7,938	7,771	7,272	8,113	7,727	7,697	7,690	8,000	8,079	7,547

Historical data show that the population standard deviation is $500 and that spending on debit cards is normally distributed. Test the claim at a 1% level of significance.

SOLUTION: The researcher would like to establish that average spending on debit cards is less than $8,000, or equivalently, $\mu < 8{,}000$. Thus, we formulate the two hypotheses as

$$H_0: \mu \geq 8{,}000$$
$$H_A: \mu < 8{,}000$$

The normality condition of $\overline{X}$ is satisfied since spending on debit cards is normally distributed. Also, since the population standard deviation is known, the test statistic is assumed to follow the z distribution. We know that the p-value for a left-tailed test is given by $P(Z \leq z)$. The Excel function Z.TEST produces $P(Z \geq z)$, which is the appropriate p-value for a right-tailed test. For a left-tailed test, as in this example, we simply subtract the value that Excel returns from one. (For a two-tailed test, if the value that Excel returns for $P(Z \geq z)$ is less than 0.50, we multiply this value by 2 to obtain the p-value; if the value for $P(Z \geq z)$ is greater than 0.50, we calculate the p-value as $2 \times (1 - P(Z \geq z))$.) We follow these steps.

A. Open the *Debit Spending* data file found on the text website.

B. Select **Formulas** > **Insert Function** > **Z.TEST**. This command returns the p-value associated with a right-tailed test.

C. See Figure 9.7. We supply the following three arguments in the dialog box:

- **Array** is the data set. We select the 20 observations.
- **X** is the hypothesized mean under the null hypothesis. We enter 8000.
- **Sigma** is the value of the population standard deviation. We enter 500.

FIGURE 9.7 Z.TEST dialog box

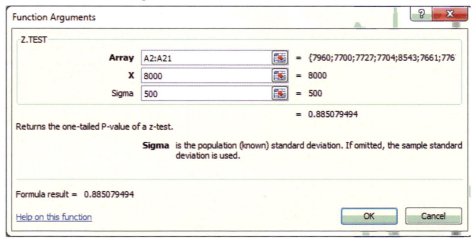

Excel returns the probability of 0.8851, which corresponds to a right-tailed p-value. Subtracting this value from one yields 0.1149, which is the p-value for the left-tailed test.

The hypothesis test is conducted at the 1% significance level. Thus, since 0.1149 is not less than $\alpha = 0.01$, we do not reject the null hypothesis. In other words, at a 1% level of significance, the researcher cannot conclude that annual spending on debit cards is less than $8,000. Perhaps these findings can be reconciled with a report that claims that individuals are shunning their credit cards and using debit cards to avoid incurring more debt (Businessweek.com, September 8, 2010).

One Last Remark

An important component of any well-executed statistical analysis is to clearly communicate the results. Thus, it is not sufficient to end the analysis with a conclusion that you reject the null hypothesis or you do not reject the null hypothesis. You must interpret the results, clearly reporting whether or not the claim regarding the population parameter of interest can be justified on the basis of the sample information.

Concepts

11. Consider the following hypotheses:

$$H_0: \mu \leq 12.6$$
$$H_A: \mu > 12.6$$

A sample of 25 observations yields a sample mean of 13.4. Assume that the sample is drawn from a normal population with a known population standard deviation of 3.2.

a. Calculate the p-value.
b. What is the conclusion if $\alpha = 0.10$?
c. Calculate the p-value if the above sample mean was based on a sample of 100 observations.
d. What is the conclusion if $\alpha = 0.10$?

12. Redo the preceding question using the critical value approach.

13. Consider the following hypotheses:

$$H_0: \mu \geq 150$$
$$H_A: \mu < 150$$

A sample of 80 observations results in a sample mean of 144. The population standard deviation is known to be 28.

a. What is the critical value for the test with $\alpha = 0.01$ and with $\alpha = 0.05$?
b. Does the above sample evidence enable us to reject the null hypothesis at $\alpha = 0.01$?
c. Does the above sample evidence enable us to reject the null hypothesis at $\alpha = 0.05$?

14. Redo the preceding question using the p-value approach.

15. Consider the following hypotheses:

$$H_0: \mu = 1,800$$
$$H_A: \mu \neq 1,800$$

The population is normally distributed with a population standard deviation of 440. Compute the value of the test statistic and the resulting p-value for each of the following sample results.

a. $\bar{x} = 1,850; n = 110$
b. $\bar{x} = 1,850; n = 280$
c. $\bar{x} = 1,650; n = 32$
d. $\bar{x} = 1,700; n = 32$

16. Consider the following hypotheses:

$$H_0: \mu = 120$$
$$H_A: \mu \neq 120$$

The population is normally distributed with a population standard deviation of 46.

a. Use a 5% level of significance to determine the critical value(s) of the test.
b. What is the conclusion with $\bar{x} = 132$ and $n = 50$?
c. Use a 10% level of significance to determine the critical value(s) of the test.
d. What is the conclusion with $\bar{x} = 108$ and $n = 50$?

Applications

17. Customers at Costco spend an average of $130 per trip (*The Wall Street Journal*, October 6, 2010). One of Costco's rivals would like to determine whether its customers spend more per trip. A survey of the receipts of 25 customers found that the sample mean was $135.25. Assume that the population standard deviation is $10.50 and that spending follows a normal distribution.

a. Specify the appropriate null and the alternative hypotheses to test whether average spending at the rival's store is more than $130.
b. Calculate the value of the test statistic. Calculate the p-value.
c. At the 5% significance level, what is the conclusion?
d. Repeat the test using the critical value approach.

18. It is advertised that the average braking distance for a small car traveling at 65 miles per hour equals 120 feet. A transportation researcher wants to determine if the statement made in the advertisement is false. She randomly test drives 36 small cars at 65 miles per hour and records the braking distance. The sample average braking distance is computed as 114 feet. Assume that the population standard deviation is 22 feet.

a. State the null and the alternative hypotheses for the test.
b. Calculate the value of the test statistic and the p-value.
c. Use $\alpha = 0.01$ to determine if the average breaking distance differs from 120 feet.
d. Repeat the test with the critical value approach.

19. An article in the *National Geographic News* (February 24, 2005) reports that Americans are increasingly skimping on their sleep. A researcher wants to determine if Americans are sleeping less than the recommended 7 hours of sleep on weekdays. He takes a random sample of 150 Americans and

computes the average sleep time of 6.7 hours on weekdays. Assume that the population is normally distributed with a known standard deviation of 2.1 hours.

a. Use the p-value approach to test the researcher's claim at $\alpha = 0.01$.

b. Use the critical value approach to test the researcher's claim at $\alpha = 0.01$.

20. In May 2008 CNN reported that Sports Utility Vehicles (SUVs) are plunging toward the "endangered" list. Due to soaring oil prices and environmental concerns, consumers are replacing gas-guzzling vehicles with fuel-efficient smaller cars. As a result, there has been a big drop in the demand for new as well as used SUVs. A sales manager of a used car dealership for SUVs believes that it takes more than 90 days, on average, to sell an SUV. In order to test his claim, he samples 40 recently sold SUVs and finds that it took an average of 95 days to sell an SUV. He believes that the population standard deviation is fairly stable at 20 days.

a. State the null and the alternative hypotheses for the test.

b. What is the p-value?

c. Is the sales manager's claim justifiable at $\alpha = 0.01$?

d. Repeat the above hypothesis test with the critical value approach.

21. A local bottler in Hawaii wishes to ensure that an average of 16 ounces of passion fruit juice is used to fill each bottle. In order to analyze the accuracy of the bottling process, he takes a random sample of 48 bottles. The mean weight of the passion fruit juice in the sample is 15.80 ounces. Assume that the population standard deviation is 0.8 ounce.

a. State the null and the alternative hypotheses for the test.

b. Use the critical value approach to test the bottler's concern at $\alpha = 0.05$.

c. Make a recommendation to the bottler.

22. **FILE** (Use Excel) A realtor in Mission Viejo, California, believes that the average price of a house is more than $500 thousand.

a. State the null and the alternative hypotheses for the test.

b. Open the **Mission Viejo (raw)** data from the text website into an Excel spreadsheet (data are in $1,000s). Use the function Z.TEST to calculate the p-value. Assume the population standard deviation is $100 (in $1,000s).

c. At $\alpha = 0.05$ what is the conclusion? Is the realtor's claim supported by the data?

23. **FILE** (Use Excel) Access the hourly wage data on the text website (**Hourly Wage**). An economist wants to test if the average hourly wage is less than $22.

a. State the null and the alternative hypotheses for the test.

b. Use the function Z.TEST to calculate the p-value. Assume that the population standard deviation is $6.

c. At $\alpha = 0.05$ what is the conclusion? Is the average hourly wage less than $22?

24. **FILE** (Use Excel) Access the weekly stock prices for Home Depot in the data file on the text website (**Home Depot**). Assume that returns are normally distributed with a population standard deviation of $3.

a. State the null and the alternative hypotheses in order to test whether or not the average weekly price differs from $30.

b. Use the function Z.TEST to calculate the p-value.

c. At $\alpha = 0.05$ can you conclude that the average weekly price does not equal $30?

9.3 Hypothesis Test of the Population Mean When σ Is Unknown

LO **9.5**

Differentiate between the test statistics for the population mean.

So far we have considered hypothesis tests of the population mean μ under the assumption that the population standard deviation σ is known. In most business applications, however, σ is not known and we have to replace σ with the sample standard deviation s to estimate the standard error of $\overline{X}$. Recall from Chapter 8, we can use the sample standard deviation to evaluate the t_{df} distribution with $(n - 1)$ degrees of freedom, df.

TEST STATISTIC FOR μ WHEN σ IS UNKNOWN

When the **population standard deviation σ is unknown**, the **test statistic** for testing **the population mean μ** is assumed to follow the t_{df} distribution with $n - 1$ degrees of freedom, and its value is computed as $t_{df} = \frac{\overline{x} - \mu_0}{s/\sqrt{n}}$.

The next two examples show how we use the four steps outlined in the previous section for hypothesis testing when we do not know the population standard deviation σ.

EXAMPLE 9.11

In the introductory case to this chapter, the dean at a large university in California wonders if students at her university study less than the 1961 national average of 24 hours per week. She randomly selects 35 students and asks their average study time per week (in hours). From their responses (see Table 9.1) she calculates a sample mean of 16.37 hours and a sample standard deviation of 7.22 hours.

a. Specify the competing hypotheses to test the dean's concern.

b. Calculate the value of the appropriate test statistic.

c. At a 5% significance level, specify the critical value(s) and the decision rule.

d. What is the conclusion to the hypothesis test?

SOLUTION:

a. This is an example of a one-tailed test where we would like to determine if the mean hours studied is less than 24, or $\mu < 24$. We formulate the competing hypotheses as

$$H_0: \mu \geq 24 \text{ hours}$$
$$H_A: \mu < 24 \text{ hours}$$

b. Recall that for any statistical inference regarding the population mean, it is essential that the sample mean $\overline{X}$ is normally distributed. This condition is satisfied because the sample size is greater than 30, specifically $n = 35$. Given $\overline{x} = 16.37$ and $s = 7.22$, we compute the value of the test statistic as

$$t_{34} = \frac{\overline{x} - \mu_0}{s/\sqrt{n}} = \frac{16.37 - 24}{7.22/\sqrt{35}} = -6.25.$$

c. Since we have a left-tailed test, the critical value is given by $-t_{\alpha,df}$ where $P(T_{df} \geq t_{\alpha,df}) = \alpha$. Referencing the t table with $\alpha = 0.05$ and $df = n - 1 = 34$, we first find $t_{\alpha,df} = t_{0.05,34} = 1.691$. Therefore, the critical value is $-t_{0.05,34} = -1.691$. As shown in Figure 9.8, the decision rule is to reject the null hypothesis if $t_{34} < -1.691$.

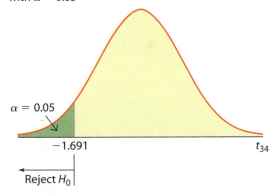

Figure 9.8 The critical value for a left-tailed test with $\alpha = 0.05$

$\alpha = 0.05$

-1.691

t_{34}

Reject H_0

d. We reject the null hypothesis since the value of the test statistic falls in the rejection region ($t_{34} = -6.25$ is less than $-t_{0.05,34} = -1.691$). At the 5% significance level, average study time at the university is less than the 1961 average of 24 hours per week.

EXAMPLE 9.12

As the introductory case to this chapter mentions, recent research finds that today's undergraduates study an average of 14 hours per week. Using the sample data from Table 9.1, the dean would also like to test if the mean study time of students at her university differs from today's national average of 14 hours per week.

a. How should the dean formulate the competing hypotheses for this test?
b. Calculate the value of the test statistic.
c. Approximate the p-value.
d. At the 5% significance level, what is the conclusion to this test?

SOLUTION:

a. The dean would like to test if the mean study time of students at her university differs from 14 hours per week. Therefore, we formulate the hypothesis for this two-tailed test as

$$H_0: \mu = 14 \text{ hours}$$
$$H_A: \mu \neq 14 \text{ hours}$$

b. Given $n = 35$, $\bar{x} = 16.37$, and $s = 7.22$, we calculate the value of the test statistic as

$$t_{34} = \frac{\bar{x} - \mu_0}{s/\sqrt{n}} = \frac{16.37 - 14}{7.22/\sqrt{35}} = 1.94.$$

c. Since $t_{34} = 1.94 > 0$, the p-value for a two-tailed test is $2P(T_{34} \geq t_{34})$. Referencing the t table for $df = 34$, we find that the exact probability $P(T_{34} \geq 1.94)$ cannot be determined. Table 9.3 shows a portion of the t table where we see that $t_{34} = 1.94$ lies between 1.691 and 2.032. This means that $P(T_{34} \geq 1.94)$ will lie between $P(T_{34} > 2.032) = 0.025$ and $P(T_{34} \geq 1.691) = 0.05$, that is $0.025 < P(T_{34} \geq 1.94) < 0.05$. Multiplying this probability by two results in a p-value between 0.05 and 0.10, that is, $0.05 < p\text{-value} < 0.10$. Shortly, we will use Excel to find the exact p-value.

TABLE 9.3 Portion of the t Table

df	Area in Upper Tail, α					
	0.20	0.10	0.05	0.025	0.01	0.005
1	1.376	3.078	6.341	12.706	31.821	63.657
⋮	⋮	⋮	⋮	⋮	⋮	⋮
34	0.852	1.307	1.691	2.032	2.441	2.728

d. Since the p-value satisfies $0.05 < p\text{-value} < 0.10$, it must be greater than $\alpha = 0.05$; we do not reject the null hypothesis. Therefore, the mean study time of students at the university is not statistically different from today's national average of 14 hours per week.

Using Excel to Calculate p-Values from the t_{df} Distribution

In Example 9.12, we used the t table to approximate the p-value for $P(T_{34} \geq 1.94)$. We can easily calculate exact probabilities with Excel. For instance, we can use the function option on Excel to determine the exact probability of $P(T_{34} \geq 1.94)$ by following these commands.

A. Select **Formulas** > **Insert Function** > **T.DIST.2T**. This command returns the p-value associated with the relevant t_{df} for a two-tailed test. (For a one-tailed test, we can simply divide this p-value by two. Alternatively, for a right-tailed test, we can use Formulas > Insert Function > T.DIST.RT. For a left-tailed test, we can use Formulas > Insert Function > T.DIST.)

B. See Figure 9.9. Supply the following two arguments in the dialog box:
- **X** is the absolute value of the test statistic, that is $|t_{df}|$. Since $t_{34} = 1.94$, we enter 1.94.
- **Deg_freedom** are the degrees of freedom associated with the test statistic. We enter 34.

FIGURE 9.9 T.DIST.2T dialog box

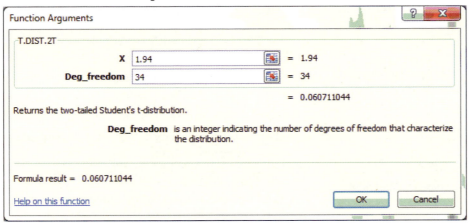

Excel returns the exact p-value of 0.0607, so $2 \times P(T_{34} \geq 1.94) = 0.0607$. Consistent with our conclusion in Example 9.12, we do not reject the null hypothesis since the p-value of 0.0607 is greater than the significance level of $\alpha = 0.05$.

SYNOPSIS OF INTRODUCTORY CASE

A recent report claims that undergraduates are studying far less today as compared to five decades ago (*The Boston Globe*, July 4, 2010). The report finds that in 1961 students invested 24 hours per week in their academic pursuits, whereas today's students study an average of 14 hours per week. In an attempt to determine whether or not this national trend is present at a large university in California, 35 students are randomly selected and asked their average study time per week (in hours). The sample produces a mean of 16.37 hours with a standard deviation of 7.22 hours. Two hypothesis tests are conducted. The first test examines whether the mean study time of students at this university is below the 1961 national average of 24 hours per week. At the

5% significance level, the sample data suggest that the mean is significantly less than 24 hours per week. The second test investigates whether the mean study time of students at this university differs from today's national average of 14 hours per week. At the 5% significance level, the results suggest that the mean study time is not significantly different from 14 hours per week. Thus, the sample results support the overall findings of the report: undergraduates study, on average, 14 hours per week, far below the 1961 average of 24 hours per week. Our analysis, however, does not explain why that might be the case. For instance, we cannot determine whether students have just become lazier or if with the advent of the computer, they can access information in less time.

EXERCISES 9.3

Concepts

25. Consider the following hypotheses:

$$H_0: \mu \leq 210$$
$$H_A: \mu > 210$$

Approximate the p-value for this test based on the following sample information.

a. $\bar{x} = 216; s = 26; n = 40$
b. $\bar{x} = 216; s = 26; n = 80$
c. $\bar{x} = 216; s = 16; n = 40$
d. $\bar{x} = 214; s = 16; n = 40$

26. Which of the sample information in the preceding question enables us to reject the null hypothesis at $\alpha = 0.01$ and at $\alpha = 0.10$?

27. Consider the following hypotheses:

$$H_0: \mu = 12$$
$$H_A: \mu \neq 12$$

Approximate the p-value for this test based on the following sample information.

a. $\bar{x} = 11; s = 3.2; n = 36$
b. $\bar{x} = 13; s = 3.2; n = 36$
c. $\bar{x} = 11; s = 2.8; n = 36$
d. $\bar{x} = 11; s = 2.8; n = 49$

28. Which of the sample information in the preceding question enables us to reject the null hypothesis at $\alpha = 0.01$ and at $\alpha = 0.10$?

29. Determine the critical values for the following tests of the population mean with an unknown population standard deviation. The analysis is based on 18 observations drawn from a normally distributed population at a 1% level of significance.

a. $H_0: \mu \leq 52$ versus $H_A: \mu > 52$
b. $H_0: \mu = 9.2$ versus $H_A: \mu \neq 9.2$
c. $H_0: \mu \geq 5.6$ versus $H_A: \mu < 5.6$
d. $H_0: \mu = 10$ versus $H_A: \mu \neq 10$

30. In order to conduct a hypothesis test of the population mean, a random sample of 24 observations is drawn from a normally distributed population. The resulting mean and the standard deviation are calculated as 4.8 and 0.8, respectively. Use the p-value approach to conduct the following tests at $\alpha = 0.05$.

a. $H_0: \mu \leq 4.5$ against $H_A: \mu > 4.5$
b. $H_0: \mu = 4.5$ against $H_A: \mu \neq 4.5$

31. Use the critical value approach to conduct the same two tests in the preceding question at $\alpha = 0.05$.

32. In order to test if the population mean differs from 16, you draw a random sample of 32 observations and compute the sample mean and the sample standard deviation as 15.2 and 0.6, respectively. Use (a) the p-value approach and (b) the

critical value approach to implement the test at a 1% level of significance.

33. Consider the following hypotheses:

$$H_0: \mu = 8$$
$$H_A: \mu \neq 8$$

The population is normally distributed. A sample produces the following observations:

6	9	8	7	7	11	10

Use the p-value approach to conduct the test at a 5% level of significance.

34. Consider the following hypotheses:

$$H_0: \mu \geq 100$$
$$H_A: \mu < 100$$

The population is normally distributed. A sample produces the following observations:

95	99	85	80	98	97

Use the critical value approach to conduct the test at a 1% level of significance.

Applications

35. A machine that is programmed to package 1.20 pounds of cereal is being tested for its accuracy. In a sample of 36 cereal boxes, the sample weight and standard deviation are calculated as 1.22 pounds and 0.06 pound, respectively.

a. Set up the null and the alternative hypotheses to determine if the machine is working improperly, that is, it is either underfilling or overfilling the cereal boxes.
b. Calculate the value of the test statistic.
c. Approximate the p-value. At a 5% level of significance, can you conclude that the machine is working improperly? Explain.
d. Repeat the exercise using the critical value approach.

36. The manager of a small convenience store does not want her customers standing in line for too long prior to a purchase. In particular, she is willing to hire an employee for another cash register if the average wait time of the customers is more than five minutes. She randomly observes the wait time (in minutes) of customers during the day as:

3.5	5.8	7.2	1.9	6.8	8.1	5.4

a. Set up the null and the alternative hypotheses to determine if the manager needs to hire another employee.
b. Calculate the value of the test statistic. What assumption regarding the population is necessary to implement this step?

c. Use the critical value approach to decide whether the manager needs to hire another employee at $\alpha = 0.10$.

d. Repeat the above analysis with the *p*-value approach.

37. Small, energy-efficient, Internet-centric, new computers are increasingly gaining popularity (*New York Times,* July 20, 2008). These computers, often called netbooks, have scant onboard memory and are intended largely for surfing websites and checking e-mail. Some of the biggest companies are wary of the new breed of computers because their low price could threaten PC makers' already thin profit margins. An analyst comments that the larger companies have a cause for concern since the mean price of these small computers has fallen below $350. She examines six popular brands of these small computers and records their retail price as:

| $322 | $269 | $373 | $412 | $299 | $389 |

a. What assumption regarding the distribution of the price of small computers is necessary to test the analyst's claim?

b. Specify the appropriate null and the alternative hypotheses to test the analyst's claim.

c. Calculate the value of the test statistic.

d. At the 5% significance level, what is the critical value(s)? What is the conclusion to the test? Should the larger computer companies be concerned?

38. A local brewery wishes to ensure that an average of 12 ounces of beer is used to fill each bottle. In order to analyze the accuracy of the bottling process, the bottler takes a random sample of 48 bottles. The sample mean weight and the sample standard deviation of the bottles are 11.80 ounces and 0.8 ounce, respectively.

a. State the null and the alternative hypotheses for the test.

b. Do you need to make any assumption regarding the population for testing?

c. At $\alpha = 0.05$ what is the critical value(s)? What is the decision rule?

d. Make a recommendation to the bottler.

39. Based on the average predictions of 47 members of the National Association of Business Economists (NABE), the U.S. gross domestic product (GDP) will expand by 3.2% in 2011 (*The Wall Street Journal,* May 23, 2010). Suppose the sample standard deviation of their predictions was 1%. At a 5% significance level, test if the mean forecast GDP of all NABE members is greater than 3%.

40. A car manufacturer is trying to develop a new sports car. Engineers are hoping that the average amount of time that the car takes to go from 0 to 60 miles per hour is below 6 seconds. The car company tested 12 of the cars and clocked their performance times. Three of the cars clocked in at 5.8 seconds, 5 cars at 5.9 seconds, 3 cars at 6.0 seconds, and 1 car at 6.1 seconds. At a 5% level of significance, test if the new sports car is meeting its goal to go from 0 to 60 miles per hour in less than 6 seconds. Assume a normal distribution for the analysis.

41. A mortgage specialist would like to analyze the average mortgage rates for Atlanta, Georgia. He studies the following sample APR quotes. These are the annual percentage rates (APR) for 30-year fixed loans. If he is willing to assume that these rates are randomly drawn from a normally distributed population, can he conclude that the mean mortgage rate for the population exceeds 4.2%? Test the hypothesis at a 10% level of significance using (a) the *p*-value approach and (b) the critical value approach.

Financial Institution	APR
G Squared Financial	4.125%
Best Possible Mortgage	4.250
Hersch Financial Group	4.250
Total Mortgages Services	4.375
Wells Fargo	4.375
Quicken Loans	4.500
Amerisave	4.750

Source: MSN Money.com; data retrieved October 1, 2010.

42. In September 2007, U.S. home prices continued to fall at a record pace, and price declines in Los Angeles and Orange counties in California outpaced other major metropolitan areas (*Los Angeles Times,* November 28, 2007). The report was based on the Standard & Poor's/Case-Shiller index that measures the value of single-family homes based on their sales histories. According to this index, the prices in San Diego dropped by an average of 9.6% from a year earlier. Assume that the survey was based on recent sales of 34 houses in San Diego that also resulted in a standard deviation of 5.2%. Can we conclude that the mean drop of all home prices in San Diego is greater than the 7% drop in Los Angeles? Use a 1% level of significance for the analysis.

43. (Use Excel) One of the consequences of the economic meltdown has been a free fall of the stock market's average price/earnings ratio, or P/E ratio (*The Wall Street Journal*, August 30, 2010). Generally, a high P/E ratio suggests that investors are expecting higher earnings growth in the future compared to companies with a lower P/E ratio. An analyst wants to determine if the P/E ratio of firms in the footwear industry is different from the overall average of 14.9. The table below shows the P/E ratios for a sample of seven firms in the footwear industry:

Firm	P/E Ratio
Brown Shoe Co., Inc.	20.54
Collective Brands, Inc.	9.33
Crocs, Inc.	22.63
DSW, Inc.	14.42
Nike, Inc.	18.68
Skechers USA, Inc.	9.35
Timberland Co.	14.93

Source: http://biz.yahoo.com; data retrieved August 23, 2010.

a. State the null and the alternative hypotheses in order to test whether the P/E ratio of firms in the footwear industry differs from the overall average of 14.9.

b. What assumption regarding the population is necessary?

c. Use Excel to calculate descriptive statistics for the data, then use the function T.DIST.2T to calculate the p-value.

d. At $\alpha = 0.10$ what is the conclusion?

44. **FILE** (Use Excel) Access the miles per gallon (MPG) data on the text website labeled **MPG**.

a. State the null and the alternative hypotheses in order to test whether the average MPG differs from 95.

b. Use Excel to calculate descriptive statistics for the data, then use the function T.DIST.2T to calculate the p-value.

c. At $\alpha = 0.05$ can you conclude that the MPG differs from 95?

45. **FILE** (Use Excel) A recent study found that consumers are making average monthly debt payments of $983 (Experian.com, November 11, 2010). The accompanying table shows a portion of average debt payments for 26 metropolitan areas.

The complete data set is on the text website and is labeled **Debt Payments**.

City	Debt Payments
Washington, D.C.	$1,285
Seattle	1,135
⋮	⋮
Pittsburgh	763

Source: www.Experian.com, November 11, 2010.

a. State the null and the alternative hypotheses in order to test whether average monthly debt payments are greater than $900.

b. What assumption regarding the population is necessary to implement this step?

c. Use Excel to calculate descriptive statistics for the data. Calculate the value of the test statistic.

d. Use Excel's function T.DIST.RT to calculate the p-value.

e. At $\alpha = 0.05$ what is your conclusion?

9.4 Hypothesis Test of the Population Proportion

LO 9.6

Specify the test statistic for the population proportion.

As discussed earlier, sometimes the variable of interest is *qualitative* rather than *quantitative*. While the population mean μ describes quantitative data, the population proportion p is the essential descriptive measure when the data type is qualitative. The parameter p represents the probability of success where success is defined by a particular outcome.

As in the case of the population mean, we estimate the population proportion on the basis of its sample counterpart. In particular, we use the sample proportion, $\bar{P} = X/n$, to estimate the population proportion p, where the random variable X represents the number of successes in n trials of the binomial experiment. Recall that although $\bar{P}$ is based on a binomial distribution, it can be approximated by a normal distribution in large samples. This approximation is considered valid when $np \geq 5$ and $n(1 - p) \geq 5$. Since p is not known, we typically test the sample size requirement under the hypothesized value of the population proportion p_0. In most applications, the sample size is large and the normal distribution approximation is justified. However, when the sample size is not deemed large enough, the statistical methods suggested here for inference regarding the population proportion are no longer valid.

Recall from Chapter 7 that the mean and standard deviation of the sample proportion $\bar{P}$ are given by $E(\bar{P}) = p$ and $SD(\bar{P}) = \sqrt{p(1 - p)/n}$, respectively. If $p = p_0$ and the normal approximation of the distribution of $\bar{P}$ is justified, the test statistic for p is defined as follows.

TEST STATISTIC FOR p

The **test statistic** for the hypothesis test of the **population proportion p** is assumed to follow the z distribution and its value is computed as $z = \dfrac{\bar{p} - p_0}{\sqrt{p_0(1 - p_0)/n}}$, where $\bar{p} = x/n$ and p_0 is the hypothesized value of the population proportion.

The following examples elaborate on the four-step procedure for a hypothesis test of the population proportion.

EXAMPLE 9.13

A popular weekly magazine asserts that fewer than 40% of households in the United States have changed their lifestyles because of escalating gas prices. A recent survey of 180 households finds that 67 households have made lifestyle changes due to escalating gas prices.

a. Specify the competing hypotheses to test the magazine's claim.

b. Calculate the value of the test statistic and the corresponding p-value.

c. At a 10% level of significance, what is the conclusion?

SOLUTION:

a. We wish to establish that the population proportion is less than 0.40, or $p < 0.40$. Thus, we construct the competing hypotheses as

$$H_0: p \geq 0.40$$
$$H_A: p < 0.40$$

b. We first ensure that we can use the normal distribution approximation for the test. Since both np_0 and $n(1 - p_0)$ exceed 5, the normal approximation is justified. We use the sample proportion, $\bar{p} = 67/180 = 0.3722$, to compute the value of the test statistic as

$$z = \frac{\bar{p} - p_0}{\sqrt{p_0(1 - p_0)/n}} = \frac{0.3722 - 0.40}{\sqrt{0.40(1 - 0.40)/180}} = -0.76.$$

Since this is a left-tailed test of the population proportion, we compute the p-value as $P(Z \leq z) = P(Z \leq -0.76) = 0.2236$. Figure 9.10 shows the value of the test and the corresponding p-value.

FIGURE 9.10 The p-value for a left-tailed test with $z = -0.76$

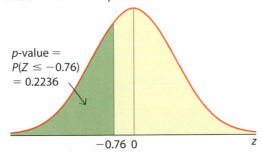

p-value =
$P(Z \leq -0.76)$
$= 0.2236$

-0.76 0

c. The p-value of 0.2236 is greater than the chosen significance level of $\alpha = 0.10$. Therefore, we do not reject the null hypothesis. This means that the magazine's claim that fewer than 40% of households in the United States have changed their lifestyles because of escalating gas prices is not justified by the sample data. This conclusion may be welcomed by firms that have invested in alternative energy.

EXAMPLE 9.14

Nearly one in three children and teens in the U.S. are obese or overweight (*Health*, October 2010). A health practitioner in the Midwest collects data on 200 children and teens and finds that 84 of them are either obese or overweight.

a. The health practitioner believes that the proportion of obese and overweight children in the Midwest is not representative of the national proportion. Specify the competing hypotheses to test her claim.

b. Calculate the value of the test statistic.

c. At the 1% significance level, specify the critical value(s) and the decision rule.

d. Do the sample data support the health practitioner's belief?

SOLUTION:

a. The parameter of interest is again the population proportion p. The health practitioner wants to test if the population proportion of obese or overweight children in the Midwest differs from the national proportion of $1/3 = 0.33$. We construct the hypotheses as

$$H_0: p = 0.33$$
$$H_A: p \neq 0.33$$

b. When evaluated at $p_0 = 0.33$ with $n = 200$, the normality requirement that $np \geq 5$ and $n(1 - p) \geq 5$ is easily satisfied. We use $\bar{p} = 84/200 = 0.42$ to calculate the value of the test statistic as

$$z = \frac{0.42 - 0.33}{\sqrt{0.33(1 - 0.33)/200}} = 2.71.$$

c. Given a 1% level of significance and a two-tailed test, $\alpha/2 = 0.01/2 = 0.005$ is used to find $z_{\alpha/2} = z_{0.005} = 2.575$. As shown in Figure 9.11, the critical values are -2.575 and 2.575. The decision rule is to reject H_0 if $z < -2.575$ or if $z > 2.575$.

FIGURE 9.11 The critical values for a two-tailed test with $\alpha = 0.01$

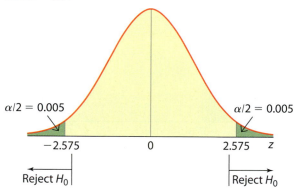

d. Since the value of the test statistic, $z = 2.71$, is greater than 2.575, the appropriate decision is to reject the null hypothesis. Therefore, at the 1% significance level, the practitioner concludes that the proportion of obese or overweight children in the Midwest is not the same as the national proportion of 0.33. Given that the test statistic fell in the right side of the distribution, the practitioner can conduct further analysis to determine whether or not the proportion of obese or overweight children in the Midwest is significantly greater than the national proportion. If this is the case, the obesity epidemic may be more problematic in the Midwest than elsewhere and may require more educational initiatives to curb its harmful ramifications.

Concepts

46. Consider the following hypotheses:

$$H_0: p \geq 0.38$$

$$H_A: p < 0.38$$

Compute the p-value based on the following sample information.

a. $x = 22; n = 74$

b. $x = 110; n = 300$

c. $\bar{p} = 0.34; n = 50$

d. $\bar{p} = 0.34; n = 400$

47. Which sample information in the preceding question enables us to reject the null hypothesis at $\alpha = 0.01$ and at $\alpha = 0.10$?

48. Consider the following hypotheses:

$$H_0: p = 0.32$$

$$H_A: p \neq 0.32$$

Compute the p-value based on the following sample information

a. $x = 20; n = 66$

b. $x = 100; n = 264$

c. $\bar{p} = 0.40; n = 40$

d. $\bar{p} = 0.40; n = 180$

49. Which sample information in the preceding question enables us to reject the null hypothesis at $\alpha = 0.05$ and at $\alpha = 0.10$?

50. Determine the critical value or values for the following tests of the population proportion. The analysis is conducted at a 5% level of significance.

a. $H_0: p \leq 0.22; H_A: p > 0.22$

b. $H_0: p = 0.69; H_A: p \neq 0.69$

c. $H_0: p \geq 0.56; H_A: p < 0.56$

51. In order to conduct a hypothesis test of the population proportion, you sample 320 observations that result in 128 successes. Use the p-value approach to conduct the following tests at $\alpha = 0.05$.

a. $H_0: p \geq 0.45; H_A: p < 0.45$

b. $H_0: p = 0.45; H_A: p \neq 0.45$

52. Repeat the preceding exercise using the critical value approach at $\alpha = 0.01$.

53. You would like to determine if the population probability of success differs from 0.70. You find 62 successes in 80 binomial trials. Implement the test at a 1% level of significance.

54. You would like to determine if more than 50% of the observations in a population are below 10. At $\alpha = 0.05$, conduct the test on the basis of the following 20 sample observations:

8	12	5	9	14	11	9	3	7	8
12	6	8	9	2	6	11	4	13	10

Applications

55. A recent study by Allstate Insurance Co. finds that 82% of teenagers have used cell phones while driving (*The Wall Street Journal*, May 5, 2010). In October 2010, Massachusetts enacted a law that forbids cell phone use by drivers under the age of 18. A policy analyst would like to determine whether the law has decreased the proportion of drivers under the age of 18 who use a cell phone.

a. State the null and the alternative hypotheses to test the policy analyst's objective.

b. Suppose a sample of 200 drivers under the age of 18 results in 150 who still use a cell phone while driving. What is the value of the test statistic? What is the p-value?

c. At $\alpha = 0.05$ has the law been effective?

d. Repeat this exercise using the critical value approach with $\alpha = 0.05$.

56. Due to the recent economic downturn, Americans have started raiding their already fragile retirement accounts to endure financial hardships such as unemployment, medical emergencies, and buying a home (*MSN Money*, July 16, 2008). It is reported that between 1998 and 2004, about 12% of families with 401(k) plans borrowed from them. An economist is concerned that this percentage now exceeds 20%. He randomly surveys 190 households with 401(k) plans and finds that 50 are borrowing against them.

a. Set up the null and the alternative hypotheses to test the economist's concern.

b. Compute the value of the appropriate test statistic.

c. Use the p-value approach to test if the economist's concern is justifiable at $\alpha = 0.05$.

57. The margarita is one of the most common tequila-based cocktails, made with tequila mixed with triple sec and lime or lemon juice, often served with salt on the glass rim. A common ratio for a margarita is 2:1:1, which includes 50% tequila, 25% Triple Sec, and 25% fresh lime or lemon juice. A manager at a local bar is concerned that the bartender does not use the correct proportions in more than 50% of margaritas. He secretly observes the bartender and finds that he used the correct proportions in only 10 out of 30 margaritas. Use the critical value approach to test if the manager's suspicion is justified at $\alpha = 0.05$.

58. A movie production company is releasing a movie with the hopes of many viewers returning to see the movie in the theater for a second time. Their target is to have 30 million viewers, and they want more than 30% of the viewers to return to see the movie again. They show the movie to a test audience of 200 people, and after the movie they asked them if they would see the movie in theaters again. Of the test audience, 68 people said they would see the movie again.

a. At a 5% level of significance, test if more than 30% of the viewers will return to see the movie again.

b. Repeat the analysis at a 10% level of significance.

c. Interpret your results.

59. Recent research commissioned by Vodafone suggests that older workers are the happiest employees (*BBC News,* July 21, 2008). The report documents that 70% of older workers in England feel fulfilled, compared with just 50% of younger workers. A demographer believes that an identical pattern does not exist in Asia. A survey of 120 older workers in Asia finds that 75 feel fulfilled. A similar survey finds that 58% of 210 younger workers feel fulfilled.

a. At a 5% level of significance, test if older workers in Asia feel less fulfilled than their British counterparts.

b. At a 5% level of significance, test if younger workers in Asia feel more fulfilled than their British counterparts.

60. A politician claims that he is supported by a clear majority of voters. In a recent survey, 24 out of 40 randomly selected voters indicated that they would vote for the politician. Is the politician's claim justifiable at a 5% level of significance?

61. New research shows that many banks are unwittingly training their online customers to take risks with their passwords and other sensitive account information, leaving them more vulnerable to fraud (Yahoo.com, July 23, 2008). Even web-savvy surfers could find themselves the victims of identity theft because they have been conditioned to ignore potential signs about whether the banking site they are visiting is real or a bogus site served up by hackers. Researchers at the University of Michigan found design flaws in 78% of the 214 U.S. financial institution websites they studied. Is the above sample evidence sufficient to conclude that more than three out of four financial institutions that offer online banking facilities are prone to fraud? Use a 5% significance level for the test.

62. The Social Security Administration is not expected to provide any increases in Social Security benefits for the second straight year (*US News & World Report*, October 4, 2010). With increasing medical prices, it is claimed that more than 60% of seniors are likely to make serious adjustments to their lifestyle. Test this claim at a 1% level of significance if in a survey of 140 seniors, 90 reported that they have made serious adjustments to their lifestyle.

WRITING WITH STATISTICS

The Associated Press reports that income inequality is at record levels in the United States (September 28, 2010). Over the years, the rich have become richer while working-class wages have stagnated. A local Latino politician has been vocal regarding his concern about the welfare of Latinos, especially given the recent downturn of the United States economy. In various speeches he has stated that the mean salary of Latinos in his county has fallen below the 2008 mean of $49,000. He has also stated that the proportion of Latino households making less than $30,000 has risen above the 2008 level of 20%. Both of his statements are based on income data for 36 Latino households in the county as shown in Table 9.4; the data set is also on the text website, labeled ***Latino Income***.

TABLE 9.4 Representative Sample of Latino Household Incomes in 2010

FILE

22	36	78	103	38	43
62	53	26	28	25	31
62	44	51	38	77	37
29	38	46	52	61	57
20	72	41	73	16	32
52	28	69	27	53	46

Incomes are measured in $1,000s and have been adjusted for inflation.

Trevor Jones is a newspaper reporter who is interested in verifying the concerns of the local politician.

Trevor wants to use the sample information to:

1. Determine if the mean income of Latino households has fallen below the 2008 level of $49,000.

2. Determine if the proportion of Latino households making less than $30,000 has risen above 20%.

Sample
Report—
Income
Inequality in
the United
States

One of the hotly debated topics in the United States is that of growing income inequality. Market forces such as increased trade and technological advances have made highly skilled and well-educated workers more productive, thus increasing their pay. Institutional forces, such as deregulation, the decline of unions, and the stagnation of the minimum wage, have contributed to income inequality. Arguably, this income inequality has been felt by minorities, especially African-Americans and Latinos, since a very high proportion of both groups is working class. The condition has been further exacerbated by the recent economic meltdown.

A sample of 36 Latino households resulted in a mean household income of $46,278 with a standard deviation of $19,524. The sample mean is below the 2008 level of $49,000. In addition, nine Latino households, or 25%, make less than $30,000; the corresponding percentage in 2008 was 20%. Based on these results, a politician concludes that current market conditions continue to negatively impact the welfare of Latinos. However, it is essential to provide statistically significant evidence to substantiate these claims. Toward this end, formal tests of hypotheses regarding the population mean and the population proportion are conducted. The results of the tests are summarized in Table 9.A.

TABLE 9.A Test Statistic Values and p-Values for Hypothesis Tests

Hypotheses	Test Statistic Value	p-Value
$H_0: \mu \geq 49,000$ $H_A: \mu < 49,000$	$t_{35} = \dfrac{46,278 - 49,000}{19,524/\sqrt{36}} = -0.84$	0.2033
$H_0: p \leq 0.20$ $H_A: p > 0.20$	$z = \dfrac{0.25 - 0.20}{\sqrt{\dfrac{(0.20)(0.80)}{36}}} = 0.75$	0.2266

When testing whether the mean income of Latino households has fallen below the 2008 level of $49,000, a test statistic value of -0.84 is obtained. Given a p-value of 0.2033, the null hypothesis regarding the population mean, specified in Table 9.A, cannot be rejected at any reasonable level of significance. Similarly, given a p-value of 0.2266, the null hypothesis regarding the population proportion cannot be rejected. Therefore, sample evidence does not support the claims that the mean income of Latino households has fallen below $49,000 or that the proportion of Latino households making less than $30,000 has risen above 20%. Perhaps the politician's remarks were based on a cursory look at the sample statistics and not on a thorough statistical analysis of the incomes.

Conceptual Review

LO 9.1 Define the null hypothesis and the alternative hypothesis.

Every hypothesis test contains two competing hypotheses: the **null hypothesis**, denoted H_0, and the **alternative hypothesis**, denoted H_A. We can think of the null hypothesis as corresponding to a presumed default state of nature or status quo, whereas the alternative hypothesis contradicts the default state or status quo.

On the basis of sample information, we either **reject H_0** or **do not reject H_0**.

As a general guideline, whatever we wish to establish is placed in the alternative hypothesis. If we reject the null hypothesis, we are able to conclude that the alternative hypothesis is true.

Hypothesis tests can be **one-tailed** or **two-tailed**. A one-tailed test allows the rejection of the null hypothesis only on one side of the hypothesized value of the population parameter. In a two-tailed test, the null hypothesis can be rejected on both sides of the hypothesized value of the population parameter.

Distinguish between Type I and Type II errors.

Since the statistical conclusion of a hypothesis test relies on sample data, there are two types of errors that may occur: a **Type I error** or a **Type II error**. A Type I error is committed when we reject the null hypothesis when it is actually true. On the other hand, a Type II error is made when we do not reject the null hypothesis when it is actually false. We denote the probability of a Type I error by α and the probability of a Type II error by β. For a given sample size n, a decrease (increase) in α will increase (decrease) β. However, both α and β will decrease if the sample size n increases.

Explain the steps of a hypothesis test using the *p*-value approach.

Every hypothesis test can be implemented by following a four-step procedure. There are two equivalent approaches, namely the ***p*-value approach** and the **critical value approach**. For the *p*-value approach, we follow these four steps:

Step 1. Specify the null and the alternative hypotheses. We identify the relevant population parameter of interest, determine whether it is a one- or a two-tailed test and, most importantly, include some form of the equality sign in the null hypothesis and place whatever we wish to establish in the alternative hypothesis.

Step 2. Specify the test statistic and compute its value. In this chapter, we derive the value of the test statistic by converting the estimate of the relevant population parameter into its corresponding standardized value, either z or t_{df}.

Step 3. Calculate the *p*-value. We find the probability that the test statistic is as extreme as its value computed from the given sample. If the test statistic is a standard normal random variable Z, then the *p*-value is calculated as

- $P(Z \geq z)$ for a right-tailed test,
- $P(Z \leq z)$ for a left-tailed test, or
- $2P(Z \geq z)$ if $z > 0$ or $2P(Z \leq z)$ if $z < 0$ for a two-tailed test.

Z and z are replaced by T_{df} and t_{df} if the assumed test statistic follows the t_{df} distribution with $n - 1$ degrees of freedom.

Step 4. State the conclusion and interpret results. The decision rule is to reject the null hypothesis if the *p*-value $< \alpha$, where α is the chosen significance level.

Explain the steps of a hypothesis test using the critical value approach.

For the critical value approach, we follow these four steps:

Step 1 and **Step 2** are the same as the *p*-value approach.

Step 3. Find the critical value *or* values. The critical value(s) defines the region of values of the test statistic for which the null hypothesis can be rejected. For a given α, the critical value(s) is found as:

- z_α where $P(Z \geq z_\alpha) = \alpha$ for a right-tailed test,
- $-z_\alpha$ where $P(Z \geq z_\alpha) = \alpha$ for a left-tailed test, or
- $-z_{\alpha/2}$ and $z_{\alpha/2}$ where $P(Z \geq z_{\alpha/2}) = \alpha/2$ for a two-tailed test.

Z and z_α are replaced by T_{df} and $t_{\alpha,df}$ if the assumed test statistic follows the t_{df} distribution with $n - 1$ degrees of freedom.

Step 4. State the conclusion and interpret results. The decision rule with the critical value approach is to reject the null hypothesis if the test statistic falls in the rejection region, or,

- For a right-tailed test, reject H_0 if $z > z_\alpha$,
- For a left-tailed test, reject H_0 if $z < -z_\alpha$, or
- For a two-tailed test, reject H_0 if $z < -z_{\alpha/2}$ or if $z > z_{\alpha/2}$.

z is replaced by t_{df} if the assumed test statistic follows the t_{df} distribution with $n - 1$ degrees of freedom.

LO **9.5**

Differentiate between the test statistics for the population mean.

The value of the test statistic for the hypothesis test of the **population mean** μ when the **population standard deviation** σ **is known** is computed as $z = \dfrac{\bar{x} - \mu_0}{\sigma/\sqrt{n}}$. The value of the test statistic for the hypothesis test of the **population mean** μ **when the population standard deviation** σ **is unknown** is computed as $t_{df} = \dfrac{\bar{x} - \mu_0}{s/\sqrt{n}}$ where $df = n - 1$.

LO **9.6**

Specify the test statistic for the population proportion.

The value of the test statistic for the hypothesis test of the **population proportion** p is computed as $z = \dfrac{\bar{p} - p_o}{\sqrt{p_0(1 - p_0)/n}}$, where $\bar{p} = x/n$.

Additional Exercises and Case Studies

63. A phone manufacturer wants to compete in the touch screen phone market. He understands that the lead product has a battery life of just 5 hours. The manufacturer claims that while the new touch phone is more expensive, its battery life is more than twice as long as that of the leading product. In order to test the claim, a researcher samples 45 units of the new phone and finds that the sample battery life averages 10.5 hours with a sample standard deviation of 1.8 hours.

    a. Set up the relevant null and the alternative hypotheses.

    b. Compute the value of the appropriate test statistic.

    c. Use the critical value approach to test the phone manufacturer's claim at $\alpha = 0.05$.

    d. Repeat the analysis with the p-value approach.

64. An advertisement for a popular weight loss clinic suggests that participants in its new diet program lose, on average, more than 10 pounds. A consumer activist decides to test the authenticity of the claim. She follows the progress of 18 women who recently joined the weight reduction program. She calculates the mean weight loss of these participants as 10.8 pounds with a standard deviation of 2.4 pounds.

    a. Set up the competing hypotheses to test the advertisement's claim.

    b. Calculate the value of the appropriate test statistic.

    c. At the 5% significance level, what is the critical value(s)? Specify the decision rule.

    d. What does the consumer activist conclude?

65. A city council is deciding whether or not to spend additional money to reduce the amount of traffic. The council decides that it will increase the transportation budget if the amount of waiting time for drivers exceeds 20 minutes. A sample of 32 main roads results in a mean waiting time of 22.08 minutes with a standard deviation of 5.42 minutes. Conduct a hypothesis test at a 1% level of significance to determine whether or not the city should increase its transportation budget.

66. Rates on 30-year fixed mortgages continue to be at historic lows (*Chron Business News*, September 23, 2010). According to Freddie Mac, the average rate for 30-year fixed loans for the week was 4.37%. An economist wants to test if there is any change in the mortgage rates in the following week. She searches for 30-year fixed loans on google.com in the following week and reports the rates offered by seven banks

as: 4.25%, 4.125%, 4.375%, 4.50%, 4.75%, 4.375%, and 4.875%. Assume that rates are normally distributed.

    a. State the hypotheses to test if the average mortgage rate differs from 4.37%.

    b. What is the value of the test statistic?

    c. Compute the critical value(s) of the test with $\alpha = 0.05$.

    d. State your conclusion.

67. **FILE** (Use Excel) An investor wants to test whether the average return of Vanguard's Precious Metals and Mining Fund is greater than 12% based on data over the past 25 years. Assume returns are normally distributed with a population standard deviation of 30%.

    a. State the null and the alternative hypotheses for the test.

    b. Open the **Metals** data from the text website into an Excel spreadsheet. Use the function Z.TEST to calculate the p-value.

    c. At $\alpha = 0.05$ what is the statistical conclusion?

    d. Is the return on Vanguard's Precious Metals and Mining Fund greater than 12%?

68. **FILE** (Use Excel) An entrepreneur examines monthly sales (in $1,000s) for 40 convenience stores in Rhode Island. Access the convenience store sales data on the text website (**Convenience Stores**).

    a. State the null and the alternative hypotheses in order to test whether average sales differ from $130,000.

    b. Use Excel to calculate descriptive statistics for the data; calculate the value of the test statistic.

    c. Use Excel's function T.DIST.2T to calculate the p-value.

    d. At $\alpha = 0.05$ what is your conclusion?

69. A retailer is looking to evaluate its customer service. Management has determined that if the retailer wants to stay competitive, then it will have to have at least a 90% satisfaction rate among its customers. Management will take corrective actions if the satisfaction rate falls below 90%. A survey of 1,200 customers showed that 1,068 were satisfied with their customer service.

    a. State the hypotheses to test if the retailer needs to improve its services.

    b. What is the value of the appropriate test statistic?

    c. Compute the p-value.

    d. Interpret the results at $\alpha = 0.05$.

70. The lingering economic crisis has cost America trillions of dollars in lost wealth and also has levied a heavy toll on the national psyche (*The Wall Street Journal*, December 21, 2009). According to a recent poll, just 33% of those surveyed said America was headed in the right direction. Suppose this poll was based on a sample of 1,000 people. Does the sample evidence suggest that the proportion of Americans who feel that America is headed in the right direction is below 35%? Use a 5% level of significance for the analysis. What if the sample size was 2,000?

71. A television network is deciding whether or not to give its newest television show a spot during prime viewing time at night. For this to happen, it will have to move one of its most viewed shows to another slot. The network conducts a survey asking its viewers which show they would rather watch. The network will keep its current lineup of shows unless the majority of the customers want to watch the new show. The network receives 827 responses, of which 428 indicate that they would like to see the new show in the lineup.

a. Set up the hypotheses to test if the television network should give its newest television show a spot during prime viewing time at night.

b. Compute the value of the test statistic.

c. Define the rejection region(s) at $\alpha = 0.01$.

d. What should the television network do?

72. A Pew Research study finds that 23% of Americans use only a cell phone, and no land line, for making phone calls (*The Wall Street Journal*, October 14, 2010). A year later, a researcher samples 200 Americans and finds that 51 of them use only cell phones for making phone calls.

a. Set up the hypotheses in order to determine whether the proportion of Americans who solely use cell phones to make phone calls differs from 23%.

b. Compute the value of the appropriate test statistic and the corresponding *p*-value.

c. At $\alpha = 0.05$, are the sample data inconsistent with Pew Research's findings of 2010? What do the sample data suggest?

CASE STUDIES

Case Study 9.1

Harvard University has recently revolutionized its financial aid policies, aimed at easing the financial strain on middle and upper-middle income families (*Newsweek*, August 18–25, 2008). The expected contribution of students who are admitted to Harvard has been greatly reduced. Many other elite private colleges are following suit to compete for top students. The motivation for these policy changes stems from the competition from public universities as well as political pressure.

A spokesman from an elite college claims that elite colleges have been very responsive to financial hardships faced by families due to rising costs of education. Now, he says, families with income of $40,000 will have to spend less than $6,500 to send their children to prestigious colleges. Similarly, families with incomes of $80,000 and $120,000 will have to spend less than $20,000 and $35,000, respectively, for their children's education.

Although in general, the cost of attendance has gone down at each family-income level, it still varies by thousands of dollars amongst prestigious schools. The accompanying table shows information on the cost of attendance by family income for 10 prestigious schools. (The data can be accessed from the text website and are labeled *Family Income*.)

Data for Case Study 9.1 Cost of Attendance to Schools by Family Income

School	Family Income		
	$40,000	$80,000	$120,000
Amherst College	$5,302	$19,731	$37,558
Bowdoin College	5,502	19,931	37,758
Columbia University	4,500	12,800	36,845
Davidson College	5,702	20,131	37,958
Harvard University	3,700	8,000	16,000
Northwestern University	6,311	26,120	44,146
Pomona College	5,516	19,655	37,283
Princeton University	3,887	11,055	17,792
Univ. of California system	10,306	19,828	25,039
Yale University	4,300	6,048	13,946

SOURCE: *Newsweek*, August 18–25, 2008.

In a report, use the sample information to:

1. Determine whether families with income of $40,000 will have to spend less than $6,500 to send their children to prestigious colleges. (Use $\alpha = 0.05$.)

2. Repeat the hypothesis test from part 1 by testing the spokesman's claims concerning college costs for families with incomes of $80,000 and $120,000, respectively. (Use $\alpha = 0.05$.)

3. Assess the validity of the spokesman's claims.

Case Study 9.2

The effort to reward city students for passing Advanced Placement tests is part of a growing trend nationally and internationally. Financial incentives are offered in order to lift attendance and achievement rates. One such program in Dallas, Texas, offers $100 for every Advanced Placement test on which a student scores a three or higher (Reuters, September 20, 2010). A wealthy entrepreneur decides to experiment with the same idea of rewarding students to enhance performance, but in Chicago. He offers monetary incentives to students at an inner-city high school. Due to this incentive, 122 students take the Advancement Placement tests. Twelve tests are scored at 5, the highest possible score. There are 49 tests with scores of 3 and 4, and 61 tests with failing scores of 1 and 2. Historically, about 100 of these tests are taken at this school each year, where 8% score 5, 38% score 3 and 4, and the remaining are failing scores of 1 and 2.
   In a report, use the sample information to:

1. Provide a descriptive analysis of student achievement on Advanced Placement before and after the monetary incentive is offered.

2. Conduct a hypothesis test that determines, at the 5% significance level, whether the monetary incentive has resulted in a higher proportion of scores of 5, the highest possible score.

3. At the 5% significance level, has the monetary incentive decreased the proportion of failing scores of 1 and 2?

4. Assess the effectiveness of monetary incentives in improving student achievement.

Case Study 9.3

The Gallup-Healthways Well-Being Index (http://www.well-beingindex.com) provides an assessment measure of health and well-being of U.S. residents. By collecting periodic data on life evaluation, physical health, emotional health, healthy behavior, work environment, and basic access, this assessment measure is of immense value to researchers in diverse fields such as business, medical sciences, and journalism. The overall composite score, as well as a score in each of the above six categories, is calculated on a scale from 0 to 100, where 100 represents fully realized well-being. In 2009, the overall well-being index score of American residents was reported as 65.9. Let the following table represent the overall well-being score of a random sample of 35 residents in Hawaii. (The data can be accessed from the text website and are labeled **Hawaiians**.)

Data for Case Study 9.3 Overall Well-being of Hawaiians, $n = 35$

20	40	40	100	60	20	40
90	90	60	60	90	90	90
80	100	90	80	80	80	100
70	90	80	100	20	70	90
80	30	80	90	90	80	30

In a report, use the sample information to:

1. Determine whether the well-being score of Hawaiians is more than the national average of 65.9 at the 5% significance level.

2. Determine if fewer than 40% of Hawaiians report a score below 50 at the 5% significance level.

10

Statistical Inference Concerning Two Populations

LEARNING OBJECTIVES

After reading this chapter you should be able to:

LO 10.1 Make inferences about the difference between two population means based on independent sampling.

LO 10.2 Make inferences about the mean difference based on matched-pairs sampling.

LO 10.3 Make inferences about the difference between two population proportions based on independent sampling.

In the preceding two chapters, we used estimation and hypothesis testing to analyze a single parameter, such as the population mean and the population proportion. In this chapter we extend our discussion from the analysis of a single population to the comparison of two populations. We first analyze differences between two population means. For instance, an economist may be interested in analyzing the salary difference between male and female employees. Similarly, a marketing researcher might want to compare the operating lives of two popular brands of batteries. In these examples, we use independent sampling for the analysis. We will also consider the mean difference of two populations based on matched-pairs sampling. An example of such a case would be a consumer group activist wanting to analyze the mean weight of customers before and after they enroll in a new diet program. Finally, we look at qualitative data and compare the difference between two population proportions. For instance, marketing executives and advertisers are often interested in the different preferences between males and females when determining where to target advertising dollars. In each of the statistical inferences concerning two populations, we first develop the procedure for estimation and then follow with hypothesis testing.

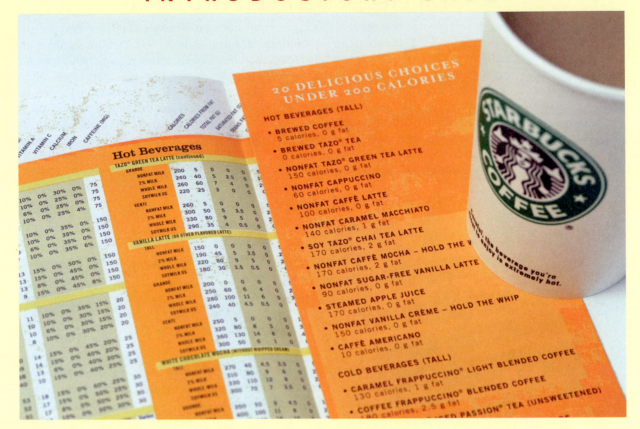

Effectiveness of Mandatory Caloric Postings

The federal health-care law enacted in March 2010 requires chain restaurants with 20 locations or more to post caloric information on their menus. The government wants calorie listings posted to make it easier for consumers to select healthier options. New York City pioneered the requirement of caloric information on menus in 2008, but research has shown mixed results on whether this requirement has prompted consumers to select healthier foods (*The Wall Street Journal*, August 31, 2010). Molly Hosler, a nutritionist in San Mateo, California, would like to study the effects of a recent local menu ordinance requiring caloric postings. She obtains transaction data for 40 Starbucks cardholders around the time that San Mateo implemented the ordinance. The average drink and food calories were recorded for each customer prior to the ordinance and then after the ordinance. Table 10.1 shows a portion of the data; the complete data, stored separately in files **Drink Calories** and **Food Calories**, are available on the text website.

TABLE 10.1 Average Caloric Intake Before and After Menu-Labeling Ordinance

Customer	Drink Calories		Food Calories	
	Before	**After**	**Before**	**After**
1	141	142	395	378
2	137	140	404	392
⋮	⋮	⋮	⋮	⋮
40	147	141	406	400

Molly wants to use the sample information to:

1. Determine whether average calories of purchased drinks declined after the passage of the ordinance.

2. Determine whether average calories of purchased food declined after the passage of the ordinance.

3. Assess the implications of caloric postings for Starbucks and other chains.

We provide a synopsis of this case at the end of Section 10.2.

10.1 Inference Concerning the Difference between Two Means

LO 10.1

Make inferences about the difference between two population means based on independent sampling.

In this section we consider statistical inference about the difference between two population means based on **independent random samples**. Independent random samples are samples that are completely unrelated to one another. Consider the example where we are interested in the difference between male and female salaries. For one sample, we collect data from the male population, while for the other sample we gather data from the female population. The two samples are considered to be independent because the selection of one is in no way influenced by the selection of the other. Similarly, in a comparison of battery lives between brand A and brand B, one sample comes from the brand A population, while the other sample stems from the brand B population. Again, both samples can be considered to be drawn independently.

INDEPENDENT RANDOM SAMPLES

Two (or more) random samples are considered independent if the process that generates one sample is completely separate from the process that generates the other sample. The samples are clearly delineated.

Confidence Interval for $\mu_1 - \mu_2$

In Chapter 8 we used sample statistics to estimate the population parameter of interest. For example, the sample mean $\overline{X}$ is the point estimator of the population mean μ. In a similar vein, the difference between the two sample means $\overline{X}_1 - \overline{X}_2$ is a point estimator of the difference between two population means $\mu_1 - \mu_2$, where μ_1 is the mean of the first population and μ_2 is the mean of the second population. The values of the sample means $\bar{x}_1$ and $\bar{x}_2$ are computed from two independent random samples with n_1 and n_2 observations, respectively.

Let's first discuss the sampling distribution of $\overline{X}_1 - \overline{X}_2$. As in the case of a single parameter, this estimator is unbiased, that is, $E(\overline{X}_1 - \overline{X}_2) = \mu_1 - \mu_2$. Moreover, recall that the statistical inference regarding the population mean μ is based on the condition that the sample mean $\overline{X}$ is normally distributed. Similarly, for statistical inference regarding $\mu_1 - \mu_2$, it is imperative that the sampling distribution of $\overline{X}_1 - \overline{X}_2$ is normally distributed. Therefore, we generally assume that the two sample means are derived from two independent, normally distributed populations because a linear combination of normally distributed random variables is also normally distributed. If the underlying populations cannot be assumed to be normal, then by the central limit theorem, the sampling distribution of $\overline{X}_1 - \overline{X}_2$ is approximately normal only if both sample sizes are sufficiently large, or when $n_1 \geq 30$ and $n_2 \geq 30$.

As in the case of a single population mean, we consider two scenarios. If we know the variances of the two populations σ_1^2 and σ_2^2 (or the standard deviations σ_1 and σ_2), we use the z distribution for the statistical inference. A more common case is to use the t_{df} distribution, where the sample variances, s_1^2 and s_2^2, are used in place of the unknown population variances. When σ_1^2 and σ_2^2 are not known, we will examine two cases: (a) they can be assumed equal ($\sigma_1^2 = \sigma_2^2$) or (b) they cannot be assumed equal ($\sigma_1^2 \neq \sigma_2^2$). With respect to these two cases where the population variances are unknown, we can conduct a formal test that allows us to conclude whether or not the population variances are equal. We cover this test in the next chapter; for ease of exposition here, we simply make assumptions regarding the unknown population variances.

The confidence interval for the difference in means is based on the same procedure outlined in Chapter 8. In particular, the formula for the confidence interval will follow the standard format given by: Point estimate $\pm$ Margin of error.

We use sample data to calculate the point estimate of $\mu_1 - \mu_2$ as the difference between the two sample means $\bar{x}_1 - \bar{x}_2$. The margin of error equals the standard deviation $SD(\bar{X}_1 - \bar{X}_2)$ multiplied by $z_{\alpha/2}$ or the standard error $SE(\bar{X}_1 - \bar{X}_2)$ multiplied by $t_{\alpha/2,df}$, depending on whether or not the population variances are known.

CONFIDENCE INTERVAL FOR $\mu_1 - \mu_2$

A $100(1-\alpha)\%$ confidence interval of the difference between two population means $\mu_1 - \mu_2$ is given by:

1. $(\bar{x}_1 - \bar{x}_2) \pm z_{\alpha/2}\sqrt{\dfrac{\sigma_1^2}{n_1} + \dfrac{\sigma_2^2}{n_2}}$, if the population variances, σ_1^2 and σ_2^2, are known.

2. $(\bar{x}_1 - \bar{x}_2) \pm t_{\alpha/2,df}\sqrt{s_p^2\left(\dfrac{1}{n_1} + \dfrac{1}{n_2}\right)}$, if σ_1^2 and σ_2^2 are unknown but assumed equal. A pooled estimate of the common variance is $s_p^2 = \dfrac{(n_1 - 1)s_1^2 + (n_2 - 1)s_2^2}{n_1 + n_2 - 2}$, where s_1^2 and s_2^2 are the corresponding sample variances, and the degrees of freedom are $df = n_1 + n_2 - 2$.

3. $(\bar{x}_1 - \bar{x}_2) \pm t_{\alpha/2,df}\sqrt{\dfrac{s_1^2}{n_1} + \dfrac{s_2^2}{n_2}}$, if σ_1^2 and σ_2^2 are unknown and cannot be assumed equal. The degrees of freedom are $df = \dfrac{(s_1^2/n_1 + s_2^2/n_2)^2}{(s_1^2/n_1)^2/(n_1 - 1) + (s_2^2/n_2)^2/(n_2 - 1)}$. Since the resultant value for df is rarely an integer, we generally round the value down to obtain the appropriate t value from the t table.

Note that in the case when we construct a confidence interval for $\mu_1 - \mu_2$ where σ_1^2 and σ_2^2 are unknown but assumed equal, we calculate a pooled estimate of the common variance s_p^2. In other words, because the two populations are assumed to have the same population variance, the two sample variances s_1^2 and s_2^2 are simply two separate estimates of this population variance. We estimate the population variance by a *weighted* average of s_1^2 and s_2^2, where the weights applied are their respective degrees of freedom relative to the total number of degrees of freedom. In the case when σ_1^2 and σ_2^2 are unknown and cannot be assumed equal, we cannot calculate a pooled estimate of the population variance because of different variabilities in the two populations.

EXAMPLE 10.1

A consumer advocate analyzes the nicotine content in two brands of cigarettes. A sample of 20 cigarettes of Brand A resulted in an average nicotine content of 1.68 milligrams with a standard deviation of 0.22 milligram; 25 cigarettes of Brand B yielded an average nicotine content of 1.95 milligrams with a standard deviation of 0.24 milligram.

Brand A	Brand B
$\bar{x}_1 = 1.68$ mg	$\bar{x}_2 = 1.95$ mg
$s_1 = 0.22$ mg	$s_2 = 0.24$ mg
$n_1 = 20$	$n_2 = 25$

Construct a 95% confidence interval for the difference between the two population means. Nicotine content is assumed to be normally distributed. In addition, the population variances are unknown but assumed equal.

SOLUTION: We wish to construct a confidence interval for $\mu_1 - \mu_2$ where μ_1 is the mean nicotine level for brand A and μ_2 is the mean nicotine level for brand B. Since the population variances are unknown but assumed equal, we use the formula

$$(\bar{x}_1 - \bar{x}_2) \pm t_{\alpha/2,df}\sqrt{s_p^2\left(\frac{1}{n_1} + \frac{1}{n_2}\right)}.$$

We calculate the point estimate $\bar{x}_1 - \bar{x}_2 = 1.68 - 1.95 = -0.27$. In order to find $t_{\alpha/2,df}$, we need $df = n_1 + n_2 - 2 = 20 + 25 - 2 = 43$. For a 95% confidence interval, $\alpha = 0.05$, so using the t table we find $t_{0.025,43} = 2.017$.

We then calculate the pooled estimate of the population variance as

$$s_p^2 = \frac{(n_1 - 1)s_1^2 + (n_2 - 1)s_2^2}{n_1 + n_2 - 2} = \frac{(20 - 1)(0.22)^2 + (25 - 1)(0.24)^2}{20 + 25 - 2} = 0.0535.$$

Inserting the appropriate values into the formula we have

$$-0.27 \pm 2.017\sqrt{0.0535\left(\frac{1}{20} + \frac{1}{25}\right)} = -0.27 \pm 0.14.$$

In other words, the 95% confidence interval for the difference between the two means ranges from -0.41 to -0.13. Shortly, we will see how to use this interval to conduct a two-tailed hypothesis test.

Hypothesis Test for $\mu_1 - \mu_2$

As always, when we specify the null hypothesis and the alternative hypothesis, it is important that we identify the relevant population parameter of interest, determine whether we conduct a one- or a two-tailed test, and finally include some form of the equality sign in the null hypothesis and use the alternative hypothesis to establish a claim. When conducting hypothesis tests concerning the parameter $\mu_1 - \mu_2$, the competing hypotheses will take one of the following general forms:

Two-tailed Test	Right-tailed Test	Left-tailed Test
$H_0: \mu_1 - \mu_2 = d_0$	$H_0: \mu_1 - \mu_2 \leq d_0$	$H_0: \mu_1 - \mu_2 \geq d_0$
$H_A: \mu_1 - \mu_2 \neq d_0$	$H_A: \mu_1 - \mu_2 > d_0$	$H_A: \mu_1 - \mu_2 < d_0$

In most applications, the hypothesized difference d_0 between two population means μ_1 and μ_2 is zero. In this scenario, a two-tailed test determines whether the two means differ from one another; a right-tailed test determines whether μ_1 is greater than μ_2; and a left-tailed test determines whether μ_1 is less than μ_2.

We can also construct hypotheses where the hypothesized difference d_0 is a value other than zero. For example, if we wish to determine if the mean return of an emerging market fund is more than 2% higher than that of a developed market fund, the resulting hypotheses are $H_0: \mu_1 - \mu_2 \leq 2$ versus $H_A: \mu_1 - \mu_2 > 2$.

EXAMPLE 10.2
Revisit Example 10.1.

a. Specify the competing hypotheses in order to determine whether the average nicotine levels differ between Brand A and Brand B.

b. Using the 95% confidence interval, what is the conclusion to the test?

SOLUTION:

a. We want to determine if the average nicotine levels differ between the two brands, or $\mu_1 \neq \mu_2$, so we formulate a two-tailed hypothesis test as

$$H_0: \mu_1 - \mu_2 = 0$$
$$H_A: \mu_1 - \mu_2 \neq 0$$

b. In Example 10.1, we calculated the 95% confidence interval for the difference between the two means as -0.27 ± 0.14; or equivalently, the confidence interval ranges from -0.41 to -0.13. This interval does not contain zero, the value hypothesized under the null hypothesis. This information allows us to reject H_0; the sample data support the conclusion that average nicotine levels between the two brands differ at the 5% significance level.

The Test Statistic

While it is true that we can use confidence intervals to conduct two-tailed hypothesis tests, the four-step procedure outlined in Chapter 9 can be implemented to conduct one- or two-tailed hypothesis tests. (It is possible to adjust the confidence interval to accommodate a one-tailed test, but we do not discuss this modification.) After we specify the competing hypotheses in the four-step procedure, we then specify the test statistic and calculate its value. We convert the point estimate $\bar{x}_1 - \bar{x}_2$ into its corresponding z or t_{df} test statistic by dividing the difference of $(\bar{x}_1 - \bar{x}_2) - d_0$ by either the standard deviation or the standard error of the estimator $(\bar{X}_1 - \bar{X}_2)$. (The choice of the denominator depends on whether or not the population variances are known.)

TEST STATISTIC FOR TESTING $\mu_1 - \mu_2$

1. If σ_1^2 and σ_2^2 are known, then the test statistic is assumed to follow the z distribution and its value is calculated as $z = \dfrac{(\bar{x}_1 - \bar{x}_2) - d_0}{\sqrt{\dfrac{\sigma_1^2}{n_1} + \dfrac{\sigma_2^2}{n_2}}}$.

2. If σ_1^2 and σ_2^2 are unknown but assumed equal, then the test statistic is assumed to follow the t_{df} distribution and its value is calculated as $t_{df} = \dfrac{(\bar{x}_1 - \bar{x}_2) - d_0}{\sqrt{s_p^2\left(\dfrac{1}{n_1} + \dfrac{1}{n_2}\right)}}$, where $s_p^2 = \dfrac{(n_1 - 1)s_1^2 + (n_2 - 1)s_2^2}{n_1 + n_2 - 2}$ and $df = n_1 + n_2 - 2$.

3. If σ_1^2 and σ_2^2 are unknown and cannot be assumed equal, then the test statistic is assumed to follow the t_{df} distribution and its value is calculated as $t_{df} = \dfrac{(\bar{x}_1 - \bar{x}_2) - d_0}{\sqrt{\left(\dfrac{s_1^2}{n_1} + \dfrac{s_2^2}{n_2}\right)}}$, where $df = \dfrac{(s_1^2/n_1 + s_2^2/n_2)^2}{(s_1^2/n_1)^2/(n_1 - 1) + (s_2^2/n_2)^2/(n_2 - 1)}$ is rounded down to the nearest integer.

We should note that these tests are valid only when the sampling distribution of $(\bar{X}_1 - \bar{X}_2)$ is normal.

EXAMPLE 10.3

An economist claims that average weekly food expenditure of households in City 1 is more than that of households in City 2. She surveys 35 households in City 1 and obtains an average weekly food expenditure of $164. A sample of 30 households in City 2 yields an average weekly food expenditure of $159. Historical data reveals that the population standard deviation for City 1 and City 2 are $12.50 and $9.25, respectively.

City 1	City 2
$\bar{x}_1 = \$164$	$\bar{x}_2 = \$159$
$\sigma_1 = \$12.50$	$\sigma_2 = \$9.25$
$n_1 = 35$	$n_2 = 30$

a. Specify the competing hypotheses to test the economist's claim.

b. Calculate the value of the test statistic and its associated p-value.

c. At the 5% significance level, is the economist's claim supported by the data?

SOLUTION:

a. The relevant parameter of interest is $\mu_1 - \mu_2$, where μ_1 is the mean weekly food expenditure for City 1 and μ_2 is the mean weekly food expenditure for City 2. The economist wishes to determine if the mean weekly food expenditure in City 1 is more than that of City 2, or $\mu_1 > \mu_2$. This is an example of a right-tailed test where the appropriate hypotheses are

$$H_0: \mu_1 - \mu_2 \leq 0$$
$$H_A: \mu_1 - \mu_2 > 0$$

b. Since the population standard deviations are known, we assume the Z test statistic whose value is

$$z = \frac{(\bar{x}_1 - \bar{x}_2) - d_0}{\sqrt{\dfrac{\sigma_1^2}{n_1} + \dfrac{\sigma_2^2}{n_2}}} = \frac{(164 - 159) - 0}{\sqrt{\dfrac{(12.50)^2}{35} + \dfrac{(9.25)^2}{30}}} = \frac{5}{2.70} = 1.85.$$

The p-value of the above right-tailed test is computed as p-value $= P(Z \geq 1.85) = 1 - 0.9678 = 0.0322$.

c. We reject the null hypothesis since the p-value of 0.0322 is less than the chosen significance level of $\alpha = 0.05$. Therefore, at the 5% significance level, the economist concludes that average weekly food expenditures in City 1 is more than that of City 2.

Using Excel to Solve Hypothesis Tests for $\mu_1 - \mu_2$

Fortunately, Excel again provides several options that simplify the steps when conducting a hypothesis test that compares two means. This is especially useful when we are given raw sample data and we first have to compute the sample means and the sample standard deviations for the test. Here, we discuss one of the options under the **Data** tab using the next example.

EXAMPLE 10.4

Table 10.2 shows annual return data for 10 firms in the gold industry and 10 firms in the oil industry; these data, labeled **Gold and Oil**, are also available on the text website. Can we conclude at the 5% significance level that the average returns in the two industries differ? Here we assume that we are sampling from two normal populations and that the population variances are unknown and not equal. The assumption concerning the population variances is reasonable since variance is a common measure of risk; we cannot assume that the risk from investing in the gold industry is the same as the risk from investing in the oil industry.

TABLE 10.2 Annual Returns (in percent)

FILE

Gold	Oil
6	−3
15	15
19	28
26	18
2	32
16	31
31	15
14	12
15	10
16	15

SOLUTION: We let μ_1 denote the mean return for the gold industry and μ_2 denote the mean return for the oil industry. Since we wish to test whether the mean returns differ, we set up the null and alternative hypotheses as

$$H_0: \mu_1 - \mu_2 = 0$$
$$H_A: \mu_1 - \mu_2 \neq 0$$

Given that we are testing the difference between two means when the population variances are unknown and not equal, we need to calculate $t_{df} = \dfrac{(\bar{x}_1 - \bar{x}_2) - d_0}{\sqrt{\left(\frac{s_1^2}{n_1} + \frac{s_2^2}{n_2}\right)}}$.

Recall that the calculation for the degrees of freedom for the corresponding test statistic is rather involved. Using one command on Excel, we are provided with the value of the test statistic, the degrees of freedom, and the p-value, as well as the relevant critical values. We follow these steps.

a. Open the *Gold and Oil* data found on the text website.

b. Choose **Data > Data Analysis > t-Test: Two-Sample Assuming Unequal Variances > OK.** (Note: Excel provides two other options when we want to test the difference between two population means and we have access to the raw data. If the population variances are known, we can use the option **z-Test: Two-Sample for Means**. If the population variances are unknown but assumed equal, we can use the option **t-Test: Two-Sample Assuming Equal Variances**.)

c. See Figure 10.1. In the *t-Test: Two-Sample Assuming Unequal Variances* dialog box, choose *Variable 1 Range* and select the gold data. Then, choose *Variable 2 Range* and select the oil data. Enter a *Hypothesized Mean Difference* of 0 since $d_0 = 0$, check the *Labels* box if you include Gold and Oil as headings, and enter an α value of 0.05 since the test is conducted at the 5% significance level. Choose an output range and click **OK**.

FIGURE 10.1 Excel's dialog box for *t* test with unequal variances

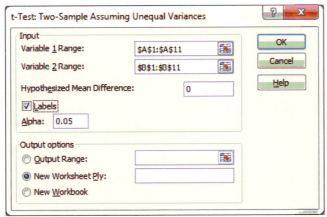

Table 10.3 shows the relevant output.

The output from Excel allows us to conduct the hypothesis test using either the p-value approach or the critical value approach. Given that we have a two-tailed hypothesis test, the relevant p-value is 0.7661 (see **P(T ≤ t) two-tail** in Table 10.3). At the 5% significance level, we cannot reject H_0, since the p-value is greater than 0.05. While average returns in the oil industry seem to slightly outperform average returns in the gold industry ($\bar{x}_2 = 17.3\% > \bar{x}_1 = 16.0\%$), the difference is not statistically significant.

TABLE 10.3 Excel's Output for t Test with Unequal Variances

	Gold	Oil
Mean	16	17.3
Variance	70.6667	114.2333
Observations	10	10
Hypothesized Mean Difference		0
Df		17
t Stat		**−0.3023**
P(T ≤ t) one-tail		0.3830
t Critical one-tail		1.7396
P(T ≤ t) two-tail		**0.7661**
t Critical two-tail		**2.1098**

We now show that we reach the same conclusion concerning the mean return of these two industries using the critical value approach as well as the confidence interval approach. Given $\alpha = 0.05$, the relevant critical values for this two-tailed test are -2.1098 and 2.1098 (see **t Critical two-tail** in Table 10.3). The decision rule is to reject H_0 if $t_{17} > 2.1098$ or $t_{17} < -2.1098$. The value of the test statistic is $t_{17} = -0.3023$ (see **t Stat** in Table 10.3). Since the value of the test statistic is between the two critical values, $-2.1098 < -0.3023 < 2.1098$, we cannot reject the null hypothesis. As always, our conclusion is consistent with that of the p-value approach.

Finally, given the information in Table 10.3, it is also possible to calculate the corresponding 95% confidence interval for $\mu_1 - \mu_2$ as

$$(\bar{x}_1 - \bar{x}_2) \pm t_{\alpha/2,df}\sqrt{\frac{s_1^2}{n_1} + \frac{s_2^2}{n_2}} = (16.0 - 17.3) \pm 2.110\sqrt{\frac{70.67}{10} + \frac{114.23}{10}}$$

$$= -1.3 \pm 9.07$$

That is, a 95% confidence interval for the difference between the two means ranges from -10.37 to 7.77. We note that this interval contains zero, the value hypothesized under the null hypothesis. Using a 95% confidence interval, we again see that the sample data support the conclusion that the population mean returns do not differ at the 5% significance level.

Caution

In Example 10.4, we may have made a strong assumption that the populations were normally distributed. We could not invoke the central limit theorem as we had small sample sizes. In Chapter 12, we will explore tests that check for normality. If we wish to draw inferences about $\mu_1 - \mu_2$ from nonnormal populations, we need to apply nonparametric techniques such as the Wilcoxon rank-sum test for independent samples, a test discussed in Chapter 20.

EXERCISES 10.1

Concepts

1. Consider the following data:

   $\bar{x}_1 = 25.7$ $\bar{x}_2 = 30.6$

   $\sigma_1^2 = 98.2$ $\sigma_2^2 = 87.4$

   $n_1 = 20$ $n_2 = 25$

a. Construct a 95% confidence interval for the difference between the population means.

b. Specify the competing hypotheses in order to determine whether or not the population means differ.

c. Using the confidence interval from part a, can you reject the null hypothesis? Explain.

2. Consider the following data:

$$\bar{x}_1 = -10.5 \qquad \bar{x}_2 = -16.8$$
$$s_1^2 = 7.9 \qquad s_2^2 = 9.3$$
$$n_1 = 15 \qquad n_2 = 20$$

   a. Construct a 95% confidence interval for the difference between the population means. Assume the population variances are unknown but equal.
   b. Specify the competing hypotheses in order to determine whether or not the population means differ.
   c. Using the confidence interval from part a, can you reject the null hypothesis? Explain.

3. Consider the following competing hypotheses and accompanying sample data drawn independently from normally distributed populations.

$$H_0: \mu_1 - \mu_2 = 0$$
$$H_A: \mu_1 - \mu_2 \neq 0$$

$$\bar{x}_1 = 57 \qquad \bar{x}_2 = 63$$
$$\sigma_1 = 11.5 \qquad \sigma_2 = 15.2$$
$$n_1 = 20 \qquad n_2 = 20$$

   a. Using the p-value approach, test whether the population means differ at the 5% significance level.
   b. Repeat the hypothesis test using the critical value approach.

4. Consider the following competing hypotheses and accompanying sample data. The two populations are known to be normally distributed.

$$H_0: \mu_1 - \mu_2 \leq 0$$
$$H_A: \mu_1 - \mu_2 > 0$$

$$\bar{x}_1 = 20.2 \qquad \bar{x}_2 = 17.5$$
$$s_1 = 2.5 \qquad s_2 = 4.4$$
$$n_1 = 10 \qquad n_2 = 12$$

   a. Implement the test at the 5% level under the assumption that the population variances are unknown but equal.
   b. Repeat the analysis at the 10% level.

5. Consider the following competing hypotheses and accompanying sample data drawn independently from normally distributed populations.

$$H_0: \mu_1 - \mu_2 \geq 0$$
$$H_A: \mu_1 - \mu_2 < 0$$

$$\bar{x}_1 = 249 \qquad \bar{x}_2 = 272$$
$$s_1 = 35 \qquad s_2 = 23$$
$$n_1 = 10 \qquad n_2 = 10$$

   a. Implement the test at the 5% level under the assumption that the population variances are unknown but equal.
   b. Implement the test at the 5% level under the assumption that the population variances are unknown and are not equal.

6. Consider the following competing hypotheses and accompanying sample data.

$$H_0: \mu_1 - \mu_2 = 5$$
$$H_A: \mu_1 - \mu_2 \neq 5$$

$$\bar{x}_1 = 57 \qquad \bar{x}_2 = 43$$
$$s_1 = 21.5 \qquad s_2 = 15.2$$
$$n_1 = 22 \qquad n_2 = 18$$

Assume that the populations are normally distributed with unknown but equal variances.
   a. Calculate the value of the test statistic.
   b. Using the p-value approach, test the above hypotheses at the 5% significance level.
   c. Repeat the analysis using the critical value approach.

7. Consider the following sample data drawn independently from normally distributed populations with equal population variances.

Sample 1	Sample 2
12.1	8.9
9.5	10.9
7.3	11.2
10.2	10.6
8.9	9.8
9.8	9.8
7.2	11.2
10.2	12.1

   a. Construct the relevant hypotheses to test if the mean of the second population is greater than the mean of the first population.
   b. What is the inference of the test at a 1% level of significance?
   c. What is the inference of the test at a 10% level of significance?

8. Consider the following sample data drawn independently from normally distributed populations with unequal population variances.

Sample 1	Sample 2
88	98
110	114
102	118
96	128
74	102
120	110

   a. Construct the relevant hypothesis to test if the means of the two populations differ.
   b. What is the value of the test statistic?
   c. Approximate the p-value of the test.
   d. What is the inference of the test at a 10% level of significance?

Applications

9. According to a new Health of Boston report, female residents in Boston have a higher average life expectancy as compared to male residents (*The Boston Globe*, August 16, 2010). You collect the following sample data to verify the results of the report. You also use the historical standard deviation of 8.2 years for females and 8.6 years for males.

Female	Male
$\bar{x}_1 = 81.1$ years	$\bar{x}_2 = 74.8$ years
$n_1 = 32$	$n_2 = 32$

   a. Set up the hypotheses to test whether the average life expectancy of female Bostonians is higher than that of male Bostonians.
   b. Calculate the value of the test statistic and its *p*-value.
   c. At the 10% significance level, what is the conclusion? On average, do female Bostonians live longer than male Bostonians?
   d. Repeat the hypothesis test using the critical value approach.

10. A joint project of the U.S. Census Bureau and the National Science Foundation shows that people with a bachelor's degree who transferred from a community college earn less than those who start at a four-year school (*USA Today*, March 17, 2009). Previous studies referred to this occurrence as a "community college penalty." Lucille Barnes uses the following information to determine if a similar pattern applies to her university. She believes that the population standard deviation is $4,400 for graduates with an associate degree and $1,500 for graduates with no associate degree.

Bachelor's Degree with Associate Degree	Bachelor's Degree with No Associate Degree
$\bar{x}_1 = \$52,000$	$\bar{x}_2 = \$54,700$
$n_1 = 100$	$n_2 = 100$

   a. Set up the hypotheses to test if the report's conclusion also applies to Lucille's university.
   b. Calculate the value of the test statistic and its *p*-value.
   c. At the 5% significance level, can we conclude that there is a "community college penalty" at Lucille's university?

11. The Chartered Financial Analyst (CFA®) designation is fast becoming a requirement for serious investment professionals. It is an attractive alternative to getting an MBA to students wanting a career in investment. A student of finance is curious to know if a CFA designation is a more lucrative option than an MBA. He collects data on 38 recent CFAs with a mean salary of $138,000 and a standard deviation of $34,000. A sample of 80 MBAs results in a mean salary of $130,000 with a standard deviation of $46,000.

   a. Use the *p*-value approach to test if a CFA designation is more lucrative than an MBA at the 5% significance level. Do not assume that the population variances are equal. Make sure to state the competing hypotheses.
   b. Repeat the analysis with the critical value approach.

12. David Anderson has been working as a lecturer at Michigan State University for the last three years. He teaches two large sections of introductory accounting every semester. While he uses the same lecture notes in both sections, his students in the first section outperform those in the second section. He believes that students in the first section not only tend to get higher scores, they also tend to have lower variability in scores. David decides to carry out a formal test to validate his hunch regarding the difference in average scores. In a random sample of 18 students in the first section, he computes a mean and a standard deviation of 77.4 and 10.8, respectively. In the second section, a random sample of 14 students results in a mean of 74.1 and a standard deviation of 12.2.

   a. Construct the null and the alternative hypotheses to test David's hunch.
   b. Compute the value of the test statistic. What assumption regarding the populations is necessary to implement this step?
   c. Implement the test at $\alpha = 0.01$ and interpret your results.

13. A phone manufacturer wants to compete in the touch screen phone market. Management understands that the leading product has a less than desirable battery life. They aim to compete with a new touch phone that is guaranteed to have a battery life more than two hours longer than the leading product. A recent sample of 120 units of the leading product provides a mean battery life of 5 hours and 40 minutes with a standard deviation of 30 minutes. A similar analysis of 100 units of the new product results in the mean battery life of 8 hours and 5 minutes and a standard deviation of 55 minutes. It is not reasonable to assume that the population variances of the two products are equal.

   a. Set up the hypotheses to test if the new product has a battery life more than two hours longer than the leading product.
   b. Implement the test at the 5% significance level using the critical value approach.

14. In May 2008, CNN reported that Sports Utility Vehicles (SUVs) are plunging toward the "endangered" list. Due to soaring oil prices and environmental concerns, consumers are replacing gas-guzzling vehicles with fuel-efficient smaller cars. As a result, there has been a big drop in the demand for new as well as used SUVs. A sales manager of a used car dealership believes that it takes 30 days longer to sell an SUV as compared to a small car. In the last two months, he sold 18 SUVs that took an average of 95 days to sell with a standard deviation of 32 days. He also sold 38 small cars with an average of 48 days to sell and a standard deviation of 24 days.

   a. Construct the null and the alternative hypotheses to contradict the manager's claim.
   b. Compute the value of the test statistic under the assumption that the variability of selling time for the SUVs and the small cars is the same.
   c. Implement the test at $\alpha = 0.10$ and interpret your results.

15. **FILE** (Use Excel) A consumer advocate researches the length of life between two brands of refrigerators, Brand A and Brand B. He collects data on the longevity of 40 refrigerators for Brand A and repeats the sampling for Brand B. These data are measured in years and can be found on the text website, labeled **Refrigerator Longevity**.

a. Specify the competing hypotheses to test whether the average length of life differs between the two brands.

b. Using the appropriate commands in Excel, find the value of the test statistic. Assume that $\sigma_A^2 = 4.4$ and $\sigma_B^2 = 5.2$. What is the p-value?

c. At the 5% significance level, what is the conclusion?

16. **FILE** (Use Excel) According to a study published in the *New England Journal of Medicine,* overweight people on low-carbohydrate and Mediterranean diets lost more weight and got greater cardiovascular benefits than people on a conventional low-fat diet (*The Boston Globe,* July 17, 2008). A nutritionist wishes to verify these results and follows 30 dieters on the low-carbohydrate and Mediterranean diets and 30 dieters on the low-fat diet. These data (measured in pounds) can be found on the text website, labeled **Different Diets**.

a. Set up the hypotheses to test the claim that the mean weight loss for those on low-carbohydrate or Mediterranean diets is greater than the mean weight loss for those on a conventional low-fat diet.

b. Using the appropriate commands in Excel, find the value of the test statistic. Assume that the population variances are equal and that the test is conducted at the 5% significance level. What are the critical value(s) and the rejection rule?

c. At the 5% significance level, can the nutritionist conclude that overweight people on low-carbohydrate or Mediterranean diets lost more weight than people on a conventional low-fat diet?

17. **FILE** (Use Excel) Baseball has always been a favorite pastime in America, and is rife with statistics and theories. While baseball purists may disagree, to an applied statistician no topic in baseball is too small or hypothesis too unlikely. In a recent paper, researchers at Wayne State University showed that major-league players who have nicknames live 2½ years longer than those without them (*The Wall Street Journal,* July 16, 2009). You do not believe in this result and decide to conduct a test to prove it wrong. Consider the following data on the lifespan of a player and the nickname variable, which equals 1 if the player had a nickname and 0 otherwise. These data can also be found on the text website, labeled **Nicknames**.

Years	Nickname	Years	Nickname	Years	Nickname
74	1	61	0	68	1
62	1	64	0	68	0
67	1	70	0	64	1
73	1	71	1	67	1
49	1	69	1	64	0
62	0	56	0	63	1
56	0	68	1	68	1
63	0	70	1	68	1
80	1	79	1	74	0
65	1	67	0	64	0

a. Create two subsamples consisting of players with and without nicknames. Calculate the average longevity for each subsample.

b. Specify the hypotheses to contradict the claim made by researchers at Wayne State University.

c. State the conclusion of the test using a 5% level of significance. Assume the population variances are unknown but equal.

d. What assumptions did you make regarding the populations?

10.2 Inference Concerning Mean Differences

LO **10.2**

Make inferences about the mean difference based on matched-pairs sampling.

One of the crucial assumptions in Section 10.1 concerning differences between two population means was that the samples were drawn independently. As mentioned earlier, two samples are independent if the selection of one is not influenced by the selection of the other. When we want to conduct tests on two population means based on samples that we believe are not independent, we need to employ a different methodology.

A common case of dependent sampling, commonly referred to as **matched-pairs sampling**, is when the samples are paired or matched in some way. Such samples are useful in evaluating strategies because the comparison is made between "apples" and "apples." For instance, an effective way to assess the benefits of a new medical treatment is by evaluating the same patients before and after the treatment. If, however, one group of people is given the treatment and another group is not, then it is not clear if the observed differences are due to the treatment or due to other important differences between the groups.

For matched-pairs sampling, the parameter of interest is referred to as the mean difference μ_D where $D = X_1 - X_2$, and the random variables X_1 and X_2 are matched in a pair. The statistical inference regarding μ_D requires that both X_1 and X_2 are normally distributed or the sample size $n \geq 30$.

Recognizing a Matched-Pairs Experiment

It is important to be able to determine whether a particular experiment uses independent or matched-pairs sampling. In general, two types of matched-pairs sampling occur:

1. The first type of matched-pairs sample is characterized by a measurement, an intervention of some type, and then another measurement. We generally refer to these experiments as "before" and "after" studies. For example, an operation manager of a production facility wants to determine whether a new workstation layout improves productivity at her plant. She first measures output of employees before the layout change. Then she measures output of the same employees after the change. Another classic before-and-after example concerns weight loss of clients at a diet center. In these examples, the same individual gets sampled before and after the experiment.

2. The second type of matched-pairs sample is characterized by a pairing of observations, where it is not the same individual that gets sampled twice. Suppose an agronomist wishes to switch to an organic fertilizer but is unsure what the effects might be on his crop yield. It is important to the agronomist that the yields be similar. He matches 20 adjacent plots of land using the nonorganic fertilizer on one half of the plot and the organic fertilizer on the other.

In order to recognize a matched-pairs experiment, we watch for a natural pairing between one observation in the first sample and one observation in the second sample. If a natural pairing exists, the experiment involves matched samples.

Confidence Interval for μ_D

When constructing a confidence interval for the mean difference μ_D, we follow the same general format of point estimate $\pm$ margin of error.

> **CONFIDENCE INTERVAL FOR μ_D**
>
> A $100(1 - \alpha)\%$ confidence interval of the mean difference μ_D is given by:
>
> $$\bar{d} \pm t_{\alpha/2,df} s_D/\sqrt{n}$$
>
> where $\bar{d}$ and s_D are the mean and the standard deviation, respectively, of the n sample differences, and $df = n - 1$.

In the next example, the values for $\bar{d}$ and s_D are explicitly given; we will outline the calculations when we discuss hypothesis testing.

EXAMPLE 10.5

A manager is interested in improving productivity at a plant by changing the layout of the workstation. She measures the productivity of 10 workers before the change and again after the change. She calculates the following summary statistics: $\bar{d} = 8.5$, $s_D = 11.38$, and $n = 10$. Construct a 95% confidence interval for the mean difference.

SOLUTION: In order to construct a 95% confidence interval for the mean difference, we use $\bar{d} \pm t_{\alpha/2,df} s_D/\sqrt{n}$. With $df = n - 1 = 10 - 1 = 9$ and $\alpha = 0.05$, we find $t_{\alpha/2,df} = t_{0.025,9} = 2.262$. Plugging the relevant values into the formula, we calculate $8.5 \pm 2.262(11.38/\sqrt{10}) = 8.5 \pm 8.14$. That is, a 95% confidence interval for the mean difference ranges from 0.36 to 16.64. This represents a fairly wide interval, caused by the high standard deviation s_D of the 10 sample differences.

Hypothesis Test for μ_D

As before, we generally want to test whether the mean difference μ_D is equal to, greater than, or less than a given hypothesized mean difference d_0, or:

Two-tailed Test	Right-tailed Test	Left-tailed Test
$H_0: \mu_D = d_0$	$H_0: \mu_D \leq d_0$	$H_0: \mu_D \geq d_0$
$H_A: \mu_D \neq d_0$	$H_A: \mu_D > d_0$	$H_A: \mu_D < d_0$

In practice, the competing hypotheses tend to be based on $d_0 = 0$.

EXAMPLE 10.6

Using the information from Example 10.5, can the manager conclude at the 5% significance level that there has been a change in productivity since the adoption of the new workstation?

SOLUTION: In order to determine whether or not there has been a change in the mean difference, we formulate the null and the alternative hypotheses as

$$H_0: \mu_D = 0$$
$$H_A: \mu_D \neq 0$$

In Example 10.5, we found that a 95% confidence interval for the mean difference ranges from 0.36 to 16.64. Although the interval is very wide, the entire range is above the hypothesized value of zero. Therefore, at the 5% significance level the sample data suggest that the mean difference differs from zero. In other words, there has been a change in productivity due to the different layout in the workstation.

The Test Statistic

We now examine the four-step procedure to conduct one- or two-tailed hypothesis tests concerning the mean difference. We again convert the sample mean difference into its corresponding t_{df} statistic by dividing the difference between the sample mean difference and the value of the hypothesized mean difference d_0 by the standard error of the estimator.

TEST STATISTIC FOR HYPOTHESIS TESTS ABOUT μ_D

The test statistic for hypothesis tests about μ_D is assumed to follow the t_{df} distribution with $df = n - 1$, and its value is

$$t_{df} = \frac{\bar{d} - d_0}{s_D/\sqrt{n}},$$

where $\bar{d}$ and s_D are the mean and standard deviation, respectively, of the n sample differences, and d_0 is a given hypothesized mean difference.

EXAMPLE 10.7

Let's revisit the chapter's introductory case. Recall that a local ordinance requires chain restaurants to post caloric information on their menus. A nutritionist wants to examine whether average drink calories declined at Starbucks after the passage of the ordinance. The nutritionist obtains transaction data for 40 Starbucks cardholders and records their average drink calories prior to the ordinance and then after the ordinance. A portion of the data is shown in Table 10.4. The entire data set can be found on the text website, labeled **Drink Calories**. Using the critical value approach, can she conclude at the 5% significance level that the ordinance reduced average drink calories?

SOLUTION: We first note that this is a matched-pairs experiment; specifically, it conforms to a "before" and "after" type of study. Moreover, we want to find out whether average drink calories consumed prior to the ordinance are significantly greater than average drink calories consumed after passage of the ordinance. Thus, we want to test if the mean difference μ_D is greater than zero, where $D = X_1 - X_2$, X_1 denotes drink calories before the ordinance, and X_2 denotes drink calories after the ordinance for a randomly selected Starbuck's customer. We specify the competing hypotheses as

$$H_0: \mu_D \leq 0$$
$$H_A: \mu_D > 0$$

The value of the test statistic is calculated as $t_{df} = \dfrac{\bar{d} - d_0}{s_D/\sqrt{n}}$ where d_0 equals 0. In order to determine $\bar{d}$ and s_D, we first calculate the difference d_i for each i-th consumer. For instance, consumer 1 consumes 141 calories prior to the ordinance and 142 calories after the ordinance, for a difference of $d_1 = 141 - 142 = -1$. The differences for a portion of the other consumers appear in the fourth column of Table 10.4.

TABLE 10.4 Data and Calculations for Example 10.7, $n = 40$

Customer	Drink Calories Before	Drink Calories After	d_i	$(d_i - \bar{d})^2$
1	141	142	-1	$(-1 - 2.1)^2 = 9.61$
2	137	140	-3	$(-3 - 2.1)^2 = 26.01$
$\vdots$	$\vdots$	$\vdots$	$\vdots$	$\vdots$
40	147	141	6	$(6 - 2.1)^2 = 15.21$
			$\Sigma d_i = 84$	$\Sigma(d_i - \bar{d})^2 = 2{,}593.60$

We obtain the sample mean as

$$\bar{d} = \frac{\Sigma d_i}{n} = \frac{84}{40} = 2.10.$$

Similarly, in the fifth column of Table 10.4, we square the differences between d_i and $\bar{d}$. Summing these squared differences yields the numerator in the formula for the sample variance s_D^2. The denominator is simply $n - 1$, so:

$$s_D^2 = \frac{\Sigma(d_i - \bar{d})^2}{n - 1} = \frac{2{,}593.60}{40 - 1} = 66.50.$$

As usual, the standard deviation is the positive square root of the sample variance, that is, $s_D = \sqrt{66.50} = 8.15$. We compute the value of the t_{df} test statistic with $df = n - 1 = 40 - 1 = 39$ as

$$t_{39} = \frac{\bar{d} - d_0}{s_D/\sqrt{n}} = \frac{2.10 - 0}{8.15/\sqrt{40}} = 1.63.$$

Given a right-tailed hypothesis test with $df = 39$, the relevant critical value with $\alpha = 0.05$ is found as $t_{\alpha,df} = t_{0.05,39} = 1.685$. Thus, the decision rule is to reject H_0 if $t_{39} > 1.685$. Since $t_{39} = 1.63$, we do not reject H_0. At the 5% significance level, we cannot conclude that the posting of nutritional information decreases average drink calories.

Using Excel to Solve Hypothesis Tests for μ_D

Excel provides an option that simplifies the calculations for a hypothesis test concerning μ_D. Example 10.8 illustrates the procedure.

EXAMPLE 10.8

The nutritionist from Example 10.7 also wants to use the data from the 40 Starbucks cardholders in order to determine if the posting of caloric information has reduced the intake of average food calories. This test is also conducted at the 5% significance level.

SOLUTION: We set up the same competing hypotheses as in Example 10.7, since we want to know if food caloric intake was greater before the ordinance as compared to after the ordinance.

$$H_0: \mu_D \leq 0$$
$$H_A: \mu_D > 0$$

Excel provides the sample value of the test statistic, the p-value, and the critical value(s), if we follow these steps.

a. Open the **Food Calories** data found on the text website.

b. Choose **Data > Data Analysis > t-Test: Paired Two Sample for Means > OK.**

c. See Figure 10.2. In the *t-Test: Paired Two Sample for Means* dialog box, choose *Variable 1 Range* and select food caloric intake before the ordinance. Choose *Variable 2 Range* and select food caloric intake after the ordinance. Enter a *Hypothesized Mean Difference* of 0 since $d_0 = 0$, check the *Labels* box if you include Before and After as headings, and enter an α value of 0.05 since the test is conducted at the 5% significance level. Choose an output range and click **OK.**

FIGURE 10.2 Excel's dialog box for *t* test with paired sample

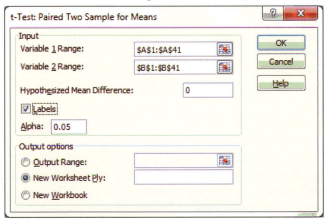

Table 10.5 shows the relevant output.

TABLE 10.5 Excel's Output for *t* Test with Paired Sample

	Before	After
Mean	400.275	391.475
Variance	49.94808	42.3583
Observations	40	40
Pearson Correlation	0.27080	
Hypothesized Mean Difference	0	
Df	39	
t Stat	**6.7795**	
P(T ≤ t) one-tail	**2.15E-08**	
t Critical one-tail	**1.6849**	
P(T ≤ t) two-tail	4.31E-08	
t Critical two-tail	2.0227	

The output from Excel allows us to conduct the hypothesis test using either the p-value approach or the critical value approach. Given that we have a one-tailed hypothesis test, the relevant p-value is 2.15E-08, that is, virtually zero. At the 5% significance level, we can reject H_0 because the p-value is less than 0.05.

Given degrees of freedom of 39 and $\alpha = 0.05$, the relevant critical value for this one-tailed test is $t_{\alpha,df} = t_{0.05,39} = 1.6849$ (see **t Critical one-tail** in Table 10.5). Since the value of the test statistic is greater than the critical value, $6.7795 > 1.6849$, we reject the null hypothesis. Thus, at the 5% significance level we can conclude that average food caloric intake has declined after the ordinance.

SYNOPSIS OF INTRODUCTORY CASE

In an effort to make it easier for consumers to select healthier options, the government wants chain restaurants to post caloric information on their menus. A nutritionist studies the effects of a recent local menu ordinance requiring caloric postings at a Starbucks in San Mateo, California. She obtains transaction data for 40 Starbucks cardholders and records their average drink and food calories prior to the ordinance and then after the ordinance. Two hypothesis tests are conducted. The first test examines whether drink caloric intake is less since the passage of the ordinance. After conducting a test on the mean difference at the 5% significance level, the nutritionist infers that the ordinance did not prompt consumers to reduce their drink caloric intake. The second test investigates whether food caloric intake is less since the passage of the ordinance. At the 5% significance level, the sample data suggest that consumers have reduced their food caloric intake since the passage of the ordinance. In sum, while the government is trying to ensure that customers process the calorie information as they are ordering, the results are consistent with research that has shown mixed results on whether mandatory caloric postings are prompting consumers to select healthier foods.

One Last Note on the Matched-Pairs Experiment

Similar to our remarks in the last section, when making inferences concerning μ_D, we require that the differences are normally distributed. If the differences are not normally distributed, we can use a nonparametric technique, such as the Wilcoxon signed-rank test for matched pairs, discussed in Chapter 20.

EXERCISES 10.2

Concepts

18. A sample of 20 paired observations generates the following data: $\bar{d} = 1.3$ and $s_D^2 = 2.6$. Assume a normal distribution.

   a. Construct a 90% confidence interval for the mean difference μ_D.

   b. Using the confidence interval, test whether the mean difference differs from zero. Explain.

19. The following table contains information on matched samples drawn from populations that are assumed to be normally distributed.

Number	Sample 1	Sample 2
1	18	21
2	12	11
3	21	23
4	22	20
5	16	20
6	14	17
7	17	17
8	18	22

a. Construct a 95% confidence interval for the mean difference μ_D.

b. Specify the competing hypotheses in order to test whether the mean difference differs from zero.

c. Using the confidence interval from part a, are you able to reject H_0? Explain.

20. Consider the following competing hypotheses and accompanying sample results.

Hypotheses: H_0: $\mu_D \geq 0$; H_A: $\mu_D < 0$

Sample results: $\bar{d} = -2.8$, $s_D = 5.7$, $n = 12$

a. Calculate the value of the test statistic under the assumption that the difference is normally distributed.

b. At the 5% significance level, what is the critical value?

c. What is the conclusion to the hypothesis test?

21. Consider the following competing hypotheses and accompanying sample results.

Hypotheses: H_0: $\mu_D \leq 2$; H_A: $\mu_D > 2$

Sample results: $\bar{d} = 5.6$, $s_D = 6.2$, $n = 10$

a. Calculate the value of the test statistic. Assume normality to approximate the p-value.

b. Use the 1% significance level to make a conclusion.

22. A sample of 35 paired observations generates the following results: $\bar{d} = 1.2$ and $s_D = 3.8$.

a. Specify the appropriate hypotheses to test if the mean difference is greater than zero.

b. Compute the value of the test statistic and approximate the p-value.

c. At the 5% significance level, can you conclude that the mean difference is greater than zero? Explain.

d. Repeat the hypothesis test using the critical value approach.

23. Consider the following matched samples representing observations before and after an experiment. Assume that sample data are drawn from two normally distributed populations.

Before	2.5	1.8	1.4	−2.9	1.2	−1.9	−3.1	2.5
After	2.9	3.1	3.9	−1.8	0.2	0.6	−2.5	2.9

a. Construct the competing hypotheses to determine if the experiment increases the magnitude of the observations.

b. Implement the test at a 5% significance level.

c. Do the results change if we implement the test at a 1% significance level?

Applications

24. A manager of an industrial plant asserts that workers on average do not complete a job using Method A in the same amount of time as they would using Method B. Seven workers are randomly selected. Each worker's completion time (in minutes) is recorded by the use of Method A and Method B.

Worker	Method A	Method B
1	15	16
2	21	25
3	16	18
4	18	22
5	19	23
6	22	20
7	20	20

a. Specify the null and alternative hypotheses to test the manager's assertion.

b. Assuming that completion times are normally distributed, calculate the value of the test statistic.

c. At the 10% significance level, what is the critical value(s)? What is the decision rule?

d. Is the manager's assertion supported by the data?

25. A diet center claims that it has the most effective weight loss program in the region. Its advertisements say "Participants in our program lose more than 5 pounds within a month." Six clients of this program are weighed on the first day of the diet and then one month later.

Client	Weight on First Day of Diet	Weight One Month Later
1	158	151
2	205	200
3	170	169
4	189	179
5	149	144
6	135	129

a. Specify the null and alternative hypotheses that test the diet center's claim.

b. Assuming that weight loss is normally distributed, calculate the value of the test statistic.

c. Approximate the p-value.

d. At the 5% significance level, do the data support the diet center's claim?

26. A bank employs two appraisers. When approving borrowers for mortgages, it is imperative that the appraisers value the same types of properties consistently. To make sure that this is the case, the bank evaluates six properties that the appraisers had valued recently.

Property	Value from Appraiser 1	Value from Appraiser 2
1	$235,000	$239,000
2	195,000	190,000
3	264,000	271,000
4	315,000	310,000
5	435,000	437,000
6	515,000	525,000

a. Specify the competing hypotheses that determine whether there is any difference between the average values estimated by appraiser 1 and appraiser 2.

b. Assuming that the difference is normally distributed, calculate the appropriate value of the test statistic.

c. Is there sufficient evidence to conclude at the 5% significance level that the appraisers are inconsistent in their estimates? Explain.

27. **FILE** (Use Excel) Researchers at The Wharton School of Business have found that men and women shop for different reasons (Knowledge@Wharton, November 28, 2007). While women enjoy the shopping experience, men are on a mission to get the job done. Men do not shop as frequently but when they do, they make big purchases like expensive electronics. Recently a large electronics store in Chicago has started making eye-catching ads aimed to attract men's attention. In order to test the effectiveness of the strategy, the store records the number of daily male customers for 10 days before and after the ads appeared. The data, shown in the accompanying table, can also be found on the text website, labeled **Men and Electronics**.

Day	Before	After
1	38	42
2	45	42
3	49	46
4	54	62
5	62	70
6	84	98
7	77	88
8	42	40
9	44	42
10	48	50

a. Specify the competing hypotheses to test the effectiveness of the strategy to attract more male customers.

b. Compute the value of the test statistic, assuming that the number of male customers follows a normal distribution.

c. Interpret the results of the test conducted at the 1% and the 10% levels of significance.

28. **FILE** (Use Excel) A recent report criticizes SAT-test-preparation providers for promising big score gains without any hard data to back up such claims (*The Wall Street Journal*, May 20, 2009). Suppose eight college-bound students take a mock SAT, complete a three-month test-prep course, and then take the real SAT. These scores can also be found on the text website, labeled **Mock SAT**.

Student	Score on Mock SAT	Score on Real SAT
1	1830	1840
2	1760	1800
3	2000	2010
4	2150	2190
5	1630	1620
6	1840	1960
7	1930	1890
8	1710	1780

a. Specify the competing hypotheses that determine whether completion of the test-prep course increases a student's score on the real SAT.

b. Assuming that SAT scores are normally distributed, calculate the value of the test statistic and its associated *p*-value.

c. At the 5% significance level, does the sample data support the test-prep providers' claims?

29. **FILE** (Use Excel) The following table shows the annual returns (in percent) for Fidelity's Select Electronic and Select Utilities mutual funds. These data can also be found on the text website, labeled **Electronic and Utilities**.

Year	Electronic	Utilities
2001	−14.23	−21.89
2002	−50.54	−30.40
2003	71.89	26.42
2004	−9.81	24.22
2005	15.75	9.36
2006	0.30	30.08
2007	4.67	18.13
2008	−49.87	−36.00
2009	84.99	14.39

Source: www.finance.yahoo.com

a. Set up the hypotheses to test the claim that the mean return for the Electronic mutual fund differs from the mean return for the Utilities mutual fund.

b. Using the appropriate commands in Excel, find the value of the test statistic. What is the *p*-value?

c. At the 5% significance level, do the mean returns differ?

10.3 Inference Concerning the Difference between Two Proportions

LO **10.3**

Make inferences about the difference between two population proportions based on independent sampling.

In the preceding two sections we focused on quantitative data, where we compared means of two populations. Now we turn our attention to qualitative data, where we provide statistical inference concerning the difference between two population proportions. This technique has many practical applications. For instance, an investor may want to determine whether the bankruptcy rate is the same for firms in the technology industry as compared to firms in the construction industry. The resulting analysis will help determine the relative risk of investing in these two industries. Or perhaps a marketing executive maintains that the proportion of women who buy a firm's product is significantly greater than the proportion of men who buy the product. If this claim is supported by the data, it provides information as to where the firm should advertise. In another case, a consumer advocacy group may state that the proportion of young adults (aged 18 to 35 years old) who carry health insurance is less than the proportion of older adults (aged 36 years or older). Health and government officials might be particularly interested in this type of information.

All of these examples deal with comparing two population proportions. Our parameter of interest is $p_1 - p_2$, where p_1 and p_2 denote the proportions in the first and second populations, respectively. As always, we estimate the unknown population parameter of interest on the basis of its sample counterpart. Here we use the difference between the sample proportions $\bar{P}_1 - \bar{P}_2$ as the point estimator of $p_1 - p_2$ where $\bar{P}_1$ and $\bar{P}_2$ are defined for two independent random samples with n_1 and n_2 observations, respectively. This estimator is unbiased, that is, $E(\bar{P}_1 - \bar{P}_2) = p_1 - p_2$. Also, recall from Chapter 7 that $SD(\bar{P}_1) = \sqrt{\frac{p_1(1 - p_1)}{n_1}}$ and $SD(\bar{P}_2) = \sqrt{\frac{p_2(1 - p_2)}{n_2}}$. Therefore, for two independently drawn samples, the standard deviation of $\bar{P}_1 - \bar{P}_2$ is calculated as $SD(\bar{P}_1 - \bar{P}_2) = \sqrt{\frac{p_1(1 - p_1)}{n_1} + \frac{p_2(1 - p_2)}{n_2}}$. Finally, when both n_1 and n_2 are sufficiently large, the sampling distribution of $\bar{P}_1 - \bar{P}_2$ can be approximated by the normal distribution with expected value $p_1 - p_2$ and standard deviation $\sqrt{\frac{p_1(1 - p_1)}{n_1} + \frac{p_2(1 - p_2)}{n_2}}$.

Confidence Interval for $p_1 - p_2$

Since the population proportions p_1 and p_2 are unknown, we estimate them by $\bar{p}_1$ and $\bar{p}_2$, respectively. The first sample proportion is computed as $\bar{p}_1 = x_1/n_1$ where x_1 denotes the number of successes in n_1 observations drawn from population 1. Similarly, $\bar{p}_2 = x_2/n_2$ is the sample proportion derived from population 2 where x_2 is the number of successes in n_2. The difference $\bar{p}_1 - \bar{p}_2$ is a point estimate of $p_1 - p_2$. In addition, we estimate the unknown $SD(\bar{P}_1 - \bar{P}_2) = \sqrt{\frac{p_1(1 - p_1)}{n_1} + \frac{p_2(1 - p_2)}{n_2}}$ by the standard error $SE(\bar{P}_1 - \bar{P}_2) = \sqrt{\frac{\bar{p}_1(1 - \bar{p}_1)}{n_1} + \frac{\bar{p}_2(1 - \bar{p}_2)}{n_2}}$, to compute the confidence interval.

> **CONFIDENCE INTERVAL FOR $p_1 - p_2$**
>
> A $100(1 - \alpha)\%$ confidence interval for the difference between two population proportions $p_1 - p_2$ is given by:
>
> $$(\bar{p}_1 - \bar{p}_2) \pm z_{\alpha/2}\sqrt{\frac{\bar{p}_1(1 - \bar{p}_1)}{n_1} + \frac{\bar{p}_2(1 - \bar{p}_2)}{n_2}}.$$

As mentioned earlier, the above formula is valid for large samples; the general guideline is that $n_1 p_1$, $n_1(1 - p_1)$, $n_2 p_2$, and $n_2(1 - p_2)$ must all be greater than or equal to 5, where p_1 and p_2 are evaluated at $\bar{p}_1$ and $\bar{p}_2$, respectively.

EXAMPLE 10.9

Despite his inexperience and some perception that he is a risky choice, candidate A appears to have gained support among the electorate. Three months ago, in a survey of 120 registered voters, 55 said that they would vote for Candidate A. Today, 41 registered voters in a sample of 80 said that they would vote for Candidate A. Construct a 95% confidence interval for the difference between the two population proportions.

SOLUTION: Let p_1 and p_2 represent the population proportion of the electorate who support the candidate today and three months ago, respectively. In order to calculate a 95% confidence interval for $p_1 - p_2$, we use the formula $(\bar{p}_1 - \bar{p}_2) \pm z_{\alpha/2} \sqrt{\frac{\bar{p}_1(1 - \bar{p}_1)}{n_1} + \frac{\bar{p}_2(1 - \bar{p}_2)}{n_2}}$. We compute the sample proportions as

$$\bar{p}_1 = x_1/n_1 = 41/80 = 0.5125 \quad \text{and} \quad \bar{p}_2 = x_2/n_2 = 55/120 = 0.4583.$$

Note that the normality condition is satisfied because $n_1\bar{p}_1$, $n_1(1 - \bar{p}_1)$, $n_2\bar{p}_2$, and $n_2(1 - \bar{p}_2)$ all exceed 5. For a 95% confidence interval we use the z table to find $z_{\alpha/2} = z_{0.05/2} = z_{0.025} = 1.96$. Substituting the values, we find

$$(0.5125 - 0.4583) \pm 1.96\sqrt{\frac{0.5125(1 - 0.5125)}{80} + \frac{0.4583(1 - 0.4583)}{120}}$$

$$= 0.0542 \pm 0.1412 \text{ or } [-0.0870, 0.1954].$$

With 95% confidence, we can report that the change in the proportion of support for the candidate is between -8.70% and 19.54%.

Hypothesis Test for $p_1 - p_2$

The null and alternative hypotheses for testing the difference between two population proportions under independent sampling will take one of the following forms:

Two-tailed Test	Right-tailed Test	Left-tailed Test
$H_0: p_1 - p_2 = d_0$	$H_0: p_1 - p_2 \leq d_0$	$H_0: p_1 - p_2 \geq d_0$
$H_A: p_1 - p_2 \neq d_0$	$H_A: p_1 - p_2 > d_0$	$H_A: p_1 - p_2 < d_0$

For notational simplicity, we again use the symbol d_0 to denote a given hypothesized difference, but now d_0 is not a hypothesized mean difference, but a hypothesized difference between the unknown population proportions p_1 and p_2. In most cases, d_0 is set to zero. For example, when testing if the population proportions differ—that is, if $p_1 \neq p_2$—we use a two-tailed test with the null hypothesis defined as $H_0: p_1 - p_2 = 0$. If, on the other hand, we wish to determine whether or not the proportions differ by some amount, say 20%, we set $d_0 = 0.20$ and define the null hypothesis as $H_0: p_1 - p_2 = 0.20$. One-tailed tests are defined similarly.

EXAMPLE 10.10

Let's revisit Example 10.9. Specify the competing hypotheses in order to determine whether the proportion of those who favor Candidate A has changed over the three-month period. Using the 95% confidence interval, what is the conclusion to the test? Explain.

SOLUTION: In essence, we would like to determine whether or not $p_1 = p_2$, where p_1 and p_2 represent the population proportion of the electorate who support the candidate today and three months ago, respectively. We formulate the competing hypotheses as:

$$H_0: p_1 - p_2 = 0$$
$$H_A: p_1 - p_2 \neq 0$$

In the previous example, we calculated a 95% confidence interval for the difference between the proportions as $[-0.0870, 0.1954]$. We note that the interval contains zero, the value hypothesized under the null hypothesis. Therefore, we are unable to reject the null hypothesis. In other words, from the given sample data, we cannot conclude at the 5% significance level that the support for candidate A has changed.

The Test Statistic

We now introduce the standard four-step procedure for conducting one- or two-tailed hypothesis tests concerning the difference between two proportions $p_1 - p_2$. We transform its estimator $\bar{P}_1 - \bar{P}_2$ into a corresponding z statistic by subtracting the hypothesized difference d_0 from this estimator and dividing by the standard error of the estimator $SE(\bar{P}_1 - \bar{P}_2)$. When we developed the confidence interval for $p_1 - p_2$ we assumed $SE(\bar{P}_1 - \bar{P}_2) = \sqrt{\frac{\bar{p}_1(1 - \bar{p}_1)}{n_1} + \frac{\bar{p}_2(1 - \bar{p}_2)}{n_2}}$. However, if d_0 is zero, that is $p_1 = p_2$, both $\bar{p}_1$ and $\bar{p}_2$ are essentially the estimates of the same unknown population proportion. For this reason, the standard error can be improved by computing the pooled estimate $\bar{p} = (x_1 + x_2)/(n_1 + n_2)$ of this proportion, based on a larger sample. This is analogous to using the pooled sample variance s_p^2 when making inferences about $\mu_1 - \mu_2$ under the assumption that σ_1^2 and σ_2^2 are unknown but equal.

TEST STATISTIC FOR TESTING $p_1 - p_2$

The test statistic is assumed to follow the z distribution.

1. If the hypothesized difference d_0 is zero, then the value of the test statistic is

$$z = \frac{\bar{p}_1 - \bar{p}_2}{\sqrt{\bar{p}(1 - \bar{p})\left(\frac{1}{n_1} + \frac{1}{n_2}\right)}},$$

where $\bar{p}_1 = \frac{x_1}{n_1}$, $\bar{p}_2 = \frac{x_2}{n_2}$, and $\bar{p} = \frac{x_1 + x_2}{n_1 + n_2}$.

2. If the hypothesized difference d_0 is not zero, then the value of the test statistic is

$$z = \frac{(\bar{p}_1 - \bar{p}_2) - d_0}{\sqrt{\frac{\bar{p}_1(1 - \bar{p}_1)}{n_1} + \frac{\bar{p}_2(1 - \bar{p}_2)}{n_2}}}.$$

EXAMPLE 10.11

Recent research by analysts and retailers claims significant gender differences when it comes to online shopping (*The Wall Street Journal*, March 13, 2008). A survey revealed that 5,400 of 6,000 men said they "regularly" or "occasionally" make purchases online, compared with 8,600 of 10,000 women surveyed. At the 5% significance level, test whether the proportion of all men who regularly or occasionally make purchases online is greater than the proportion of all women.

SOLUTION: We use the critical value approach to solve this example. Let p_1 and p_2 denote the population proportions of men and of women who make online purchases, respectively. We wish to test whether the proportion of men who make purchases online is greater than the proportion of women, or $p_1 - p_2 > 0$. Therefore, we construct the competing hypotheses as

$$H_0: p_1 - p_2 \leq 0$$
$$H_A: p_1 - p_2 > 0$$

Since the hypothesized difference is zero, or $d_0 = 0$, we compute the value of the test statistic as $z = \dfrac{\bar{p}_1 - \bar{p}_2}{\sqrt{\bar{p}(1 - \bar{p})\left(\frac{1}{n_1} + \frac{1}{n_2}\right)}}$. We first compute the sample proportions

$\bar{p}_1 = x_1/n_1 = 5{,}400/6{,}000 = 0.90$ and $\bar{p}_2 = x_2/n_2 = 8{,}600/10{,}000 = 0.86$. The normality condition is satisfied since $n_1\bar{p}_1$, $n_1(1 - \bar{p}_1)$, $n_2\bar{p}_2$, and $n_2(1 - \bar{p}_2)$ all exceed 5.

Next we calculate $\bar{p} = \dfrac{x_1 + x_2}{n_1 + n_2} = \dfrac{5{,}400 + 8{,}600}{6{,}000 + 10{,}000} = 0.875$. Thus,

$$z = \frac{(0.90 - 0.86)}{\sqrt{0.875(1 - 0.875)\left(\dfrac{1}{6{,}000} + \dfrac{1}{10{,}000}\right)}} = \frac{0.04}{0.0054} = 7.41.$$

For a right-tailed test with $\alpha = 0.05$, the appropriate critical value is $z_\alpha = z_{0.05} = 1.645$. The decision rule is to reject H_0 if $z > 1.645$. Since $7.41 > 1.645$, we reject H_0. The proportion of men who shop online either regularly or occasionally is greater than the proportion of women at the 5% significance level. Our results are consistent with the recent decision by so many retailers to redesign their websites to attract and keep male customers.

EXAMPLE 10.12

While we expect relatively expensive wines to have more desirable characteristics than relatively inexpensive wines, people are often confused in their assessment of the quality of wine in a blind test (*New York Times*, December 16, 2010). In a recent experiment at a local winery, the same wine is served to two groups of people but with different price information. In the first group, 60 people are told that they are tasting a $25 wine, of which 48 like the wine. In the second group, only 20 of 50 people like the wine when they are told that it is a $10 wine. The experiment is conducted to determine if the proportion of people who like the wine in the first group is more than 20 percentage points higher than those in the second group. Conduct this test at the 5% significance level using the *p*-value approach.

SOLUTION: Let p_1 and p_2 denote the proportions of people who like the wine in groups 1 and 2, respectively. We want to test if the proportion of people who like the wine in the first group is more than 20 percentage points higher than in the second group. Thus, we construct the competing hypotheses as

$$H_0: p_1 - p_2 \le 0.20$$
$$H_A: p_1 - p_2 > 0.20$$

We first compute the sample proportions as $\bar{p}_1 = x_1/n_1 = 48/60 = 0.80$ and $\bar{p}_2 = x_2/n_2 = 20/50 = 0.40$, and note that the normality condition is satisfied since $n_1\bar{p}_1$, $n_1(1 - \bar{p}_1)$, $n_2\bar{p}_2$, and $n_2(1 - \bar{p}_2)$ all exceed 5.

Since $d_0 = 0.20$, the value of the test statistic is computed as

$$z = \frac{(\bar{p}_1 - \bar{p}_2) - d_0}{\sqrt{\dfrac{\bar{p}_1(1 - \bar{p}_1)}{n_1} + \dfrac{\bar{p}_2(1 - \bar{p}_2)}{n_2}}} = \frac{(0.80 - 0.40) - 0.20}{\sqrt{\dfrac{0.80(1 - 0.80)}{60} + \dfrac{0.40(1 - 0.40)}{50}}} = 2.31.$$

For this right-tailed test, we compute the *p*-value as $P(Z \ge 2.31) = 1 - 0.9896 = 0.0104$. Since the *p*-value $< \alpha$, or $0.0104 < 0.05$, we reject the null hypothesis. At the 5% significance level, we conclude that the proportion of people who like the wine in the first group is more than 20 percentage points higher than in the second group. Overall, this result is consistent with scientific research, which has demonstrated the power of suggestion and expectations in wine tasting.

Concepts

30. Given $x_1 = 50, n_1 = 200, x_2 = 70, n_2 = 250$ construct a 95% confidence interval for the difference between the population proportions. Is there a statistical difference between the population proportions at the 5% significance level? Explain.

31. Given $\bar{p}_1 = 0.85, n_1 = 400, \bar{p}_2 = 0.90, n_2 = 350$ construct a 90% confidence interval for the difference between the population proportions. Is there a statistical difference between the population proportions at the 10% significance level? Explain.

32. Consider the following competing hypotheses and accompanying sample data.

$$H_0: p_1 - p_2 = 0$$
$$H_A: p_1 - p_2 \neq 0$$

$$x_1 = 100 \qquad x_2 = 172$$
$$n_1 = 250 \qquad n_2 = 400$$

   a. Calculate the value of the test statistic.
   b. Calculate the p-value.
   c. At the 5% significance level, what is the conclusion? Do the population proportions differ?
   d. Repeat the analysis with the critical value approach.

33. Consider the following competing hypotheses and accompanying sample data.

$$H_0: p_1 - p_2 \geq 0$$
$$H_A: p_1 - p_2 < 0$$

$$x_1 = 250 \qquad x_2 = 275$$
$$n_1 = 400 \qquad n_2 = 400$$

   a. Calculate the value of the test statistic.
   b. At the 5% significance level, calculate the critical value(s).
   c. What is the conclusion?

34. Consider the following competing hypotheses and accompanying sample data.

$$H_0: p_1 - p_2 = 0$$
$$H_A: p_1 - p_2 \neq 0$$

$$x_1 = 300 \qquad x_2 = 325$$
$$n_1 = 600 \qquad n_2 = 500$$

   a. Calculate the value of the test statistic.
   b. Calculate the p-value.
   c. At the 5% significance level, what is the conclusion?

35. Consider the following competing hypotheses and accompanying sample data.

$$H_0: p_1 - p_2 = 0.20$$
$$H_A: p_1 - p_2 \neq 0.20$$

$$x_1 = 150 \qquad x_2 = 130$$
$$n_1 = 250 \qquad n_2 = 400$$

   a. Calculate the value of the test statistic.
   b. Calculate the p-value.
   c. At the 5% significance level, what it the conclusion? Do the population proportions differ?
   d. Repeat the analysis with the critical value approach.

Applications

36. A recent study claims that girls and boys do not do equally well on math tests taken from the 2nd to 11th grades (*The Chicago Tribune*, July 25, 2008). Suppose in a representative sample, 344 of 430 girls and 369 of 450 boys score at proficient or advanced levels on a standardized math test.

   a. Construct a 95% confidence interval for the difference between the population proportions of boys and girls who score at proficient or advanced levels.
   b. Develop the appropriate null and alternative hypotheses to test whether the proportion of girls who score at proficient or advanced levels differs from the proportion of boys.
   c. At the 5% significance level, what is the conclusion? Do the results support the study's claim?

37. According to the Pew report, 14.6% of newly married couples in 2008 reported that their spouse was of another race or ethnicity (*CNNLiving*, June 7, 2010). In a similar survey in 1980, only 6.8% of newlywed couples reported marrying outside their race or ethnicity. Suppose both of these surveys were conducted on 120 newly married couples.

   a. Specify the competing hypotheses to test the claim that there is an increase in the proportion of people who marry outside their race or ethnicity.
   b. What is the value of the test statistic and the associated p-value?
   c. At the 5% level of significance, what is the conclusion?

38. Research by Harvard Medical School experts suggests that boys are more likely than girls to grow out of childhood asthma when they hit their teenage years (*BBC News*, August 15, 2008). Scientists followed over 1,000 children between the ages of 5 and 12, all of whom had mild to moderate asthma. By the age of 18, 14% of the girls and 27% of the boys seemed to have grown out of asthma. Suppose their analysis was based on 500 girls and 500 boys.

   a. Develop the hypotheses to test whether the proportion of boys who grow out of asthma in their teenage years is more than that of girls.
   b. Use the p-value approach to test the above assertion at the 5% significance level.
   c. Does the above experiment suggest that the proportion of boys who grow out of asthma in their teenage years is 0.10 or more than that of girls? Use the critical value approach to test this assertion at the 5% significance level.

39. More people are using social media to network, rather than phone calls or e-mails *(US News & World Report,* October 20, 2010). From an employment perspective, jobseekers are no longer calling up friends for help with job placement, as they can now get help online. In a recent survey of 150 jobseekers, 67 said they used LinkedIn to search for jobs. A similar survey of 140 jobseekers, conducted three years ago, had found that 58 jobseekers had used LinkedIn for their job search. Is there sufficient evidence to suggest that more people are now using LinkedIn to search for jobs as compared to three years ago? Use a 5% level of significance for the analysis.

40. According to a recent report, 32.2% of American adults (aged 20 and older) are obese *(The New York Times,* August 15, 2008). Among ethnic groups in general, African-American women are more overweight than Caucasian women, but African-American men are less obese than Caucasian men. Sarah Weber, a recent college graduate, is curious to determine if the same pattern also exists in her hometown on the west coast. She randomly selects 220 African-Americans and 300 Caucasian adults for the analysis. The following table contains the sample information.

Race	Gender	Obese	Not Obese
African-Americans	Males	36	94
	Females	35	55
Caucasians	Males	62	118
	Females	31	89

a. Use the *p*-value approach to test if the proportion of obese African-American men is less than the proportion of obese Caucasian men at $\alpha = 0.05$.

b. Use the critical value approach to test if the proportion of obese African-American women is more than the proportion of obese Caucasian women at $\alpha = 0.05$.

c. Use the critical value approach to test if the proportion of obese African-Americans differs from the proportion of obese Caucasian adults at the 5% significance level.

41. Only 26% of psychology majors are "satisfied" or "very satisfied" with their career paths as compared to 50% of accounting majors *(The Wall Street Journal,* October 11, 2010). Suppose these results were obtained from a survey of 300 psychology majors and 350 accounting majors.

a. Develop the appropriate null and alternative hypotheses to test whether the proportion of accounting majors satisfied with their career paths differs from psychology majors by more than 20%.

b. Calculate the value of the test statistic and *p*-value.

c. At the 5% significance level, what is the conclusion?

WRITING WITH STATISTICS

As college costs soar, costs of living rise, and student aid continues to drop, more and more college students rely on credit cards to pay for college expenses. A recent study reports a massive increase in credit card debt among college students over the last four years *(Money,* April 15, 2009). Timothy McKenna, dean of student affairs at a local university, has been studying this trend with his own undergraduates. In 2007, he surveyed 50 graduating seniors and found that their average credit card debt was $2,877 with a standard deviation of $375. The first column of Table 10.6 shows a portion of the data; the entire data set labeled ***Student Debt*** can be found on the text website. He also found that 28 out of 50 freshmen had substantial financial aid. Repeating the survey in 2011, Timothy surveys 50 graduating seniors and finds that these students have average credit card debt of $3,926 with a standard deviation of $471. A portion of these data is shown in the second column of Table 10.6. In addition, 12 out of 50 freshmen had substantial financial aid.

TABLE 10.6 Senior Credit Card Debt, 2007 versus 2011

FILE	Debt in 2007	Debt in 2011
	$2,939	$4,422
	2,812	4,266
	⋮	⋮
	2,856	3,718

Timothy wants to use the sample data to:

1. Determine whether average credit card debt was significantly lower for seniors in 2007 as compared to 2011.
2. Determine whether the proportion of freshmen with substantial financial aid was significantly greater in 2007 as compared to 2011.

Rising education costs, mounting loan debt, and a slumping student job market have combined to create a dim financial picture for undergraduates after graduation. More undergraduates are using their credit cards to pay for college expenses such as texts and fees (*USA Today*, April 13, 2009). This usage is resulting in higher and higher unpaid balances. A university dean wonders whether this trend is mirrored at his university. In 2007, he surveyed 50 graduating seniors and found that their average credit card debt was $2,877 with a standard deviation of $375. In 2011, he took another sample of 50 graduating seniors and found that their average credit card debt was $3,926 with a standard deviation of $471. A hypothesis test was conducted at the 5% significance level in order to determine whether average credit card debt in 2007, denoted μ_1, was significantly less than average credit card debt today, denoted μ_2. Given that undergraduate spending patterns may have changed over the last few years, the population variances are not assumed equal. The second row of Table 10.A shows the appropriate competing hypotheses, the value of the test statistic, and the p-value for this test. Since the p-value is approximately 0.0000, there is enough evidence to reject the null hypothesis and conclude that average credit card debt for graduating seniors in 2007 was less than it is in 2011.

TABLE 10.A Test Statistics and p-Values for Hypothesis Tests

Hypotheses	Test Statistic Value	p-Value
$H_0: \mu_1 - \mu_2 \geq 0$ $H_A: \mu_1 - \mu_2 < 0$	$t_{93} = \dfrac{2{,}877 - 3{,}926}{\sqrt{\dfrac{375^2}{50} + \dfrac{471^2}{50}}} = -12.32$	0.0000
$H_0: p_1 - p_2 \leq 0$ $H_A: p_1 - p_2 > 0$	$z = \dfrac{0.56 - 0.24}{\sqrt{0.40(1 - .40)\left(\dfrac{1}{50} + \dfrac{1}{50}\right)}} = 3.27$	0.0005

The dean then tested whether the proportion of freshmen with substantial financial aid in 2007, denoted p_1, is greater than the proportion of freshmen with substantial financial aid today, denoted p_2. The dean's survey found that 28 out of 50 freshmen had substantial financial aid in 2007, yielding a sample proportion $\bar{p}_1$ of $28/50 = 0.56$; in 2011, the survey showed that the sample proportion of freshmen with substantial financial aid was $\bar{p}_2 = 12/50 = 0.24$. The third row of Table 10.A shows the competing hypotheses, the value of the test statistic, and the p-value for this test. At the 5% significance level, the proportion of freshmen with substantial financial aid in 2007 was greater than the proportion in 2011. The results of both tests are consistent with the findings nationwide. In sum, there has been a substantial rise in credit card debt of undergraduates, much of it fueled by the rising cost of college and a financial aid system that cannot keep up.

Conceptual Review

LO **10.1**

Make inferences about the difference between two population means based on independent sampling.

Independent samples are samples that are completely unrelated to one another. A $100(1 - \alpha)\%$ **confidence interval for the difference between two population means** $\mu_1 - \mu_2$, based on independent samples, is

- $(\bar{x}_1 - \bar{x}_2) \pm z_{\alpha/2} \sqrt{\frac{\sigma_1^2}{n_1} + \frac{\sigma_2^2}{n_2}}$, if σ_1^2 and σ_2^2 are known.

- $(\bar{x}_1 - \bar{x}_2) \pm t_{\alpha/2,df} \sqrt{s_p^2\left(\frac{1}{n_1} + \frac{1}{n_2}\right)}$, if σ_1^2 and σ_2^2 are unknown but assumed equal. The pooled sample variance s_p^2 is $s_p^2 = \frac{(n_1 - 1)s_1^2 + (n_2 - 1)s_2^2}{n_1 + n_2 - 2}$, and $df = n_1 + n_2 - 2$.

- $(\bar{x}_1 - \bar{x}_2) \pm t_{\alpha/2,df} \sqrt{\left(\frac{s_1^2}{n_1} + \frac{s_2^2}{n_2}\right)}$, if σ_1^2 and σ_2^2 are unknown and assumed unequal. The degrees of freedom are calculated as $df = \frac{(s_1^2/n_1 + s_2^2/n_2)^2}{(s_1^2/n_1)^2/(n_1 - 1) + (s_2^2/n_2)^2/(n_2 - 1)}$, and are rounded down to the nearest integer.

When conducting **hypothesis tests about the difference between two means** $\mu_1 - \mu_2$, based on independent samples, the value of the **test statistic** is:

- $z = \dfrac{(\bar{x}_1 - \bar{x}_2) - d_0}{\sqrt{\frac{\sigma_1^2}{n_1} + \frac{\sigma_2^2}{n_2}}}$, if σ_1^2 and σ_2^2 are known.

- $t_{df} = \dfrac{(\bar{x}_1 - \bar{x}_2) - d_0}{\sqrt{s_p^2\left(\frac{1}{n_1} + \frac{1}{n_2}\right)}}$, if σ_1^2 and σ_2^2 are unknown but assumed equal.

- $t_{df} = \dfrac{(\bar{x}_1 - \bar{x}_2) - d_0}{\sqrt{\left(\frac{s_1^2}{n_1} + \frac{s_2^2}{n_2}\right)}}$, if σ_1^2 and σ_2^2 are unknown and assumed unequal.

The degrees of freedom for the last two tests are the same as the ones defined for the corresponding confidence intervals.

LO **10.2**

Make inferences about the mean difference based on matched-pairs sampling.

In general, two types of **matched-pairs sampling** occur. The first type of a matched-pairs sample is characterized by a measurement, an intervention of some type, and then another measurement. We generally refer to these experiments as "before" and "after" studies. The second type of a matched-pairs sample is characterized by a pairing of observations, where it is not the same individual that gets sampled twice.

For matched-pairs sampling, the population parameter of interest is referred to as the mean difference μ_D where $D = X_1 - X_2$, and the random variables X_1 and X_2 are matched in a pair. A $100(1 - \alpha)\%$ **confidence interval for the mean difference** μ_D, based on a matched-pairs sample, is given by $\bar{d} \pm t_{\alpha/2,df}s_D/\sqrt{n}$, where $\bar{d}$ and s_D are the mean and the standard deviation, respectively, of D, and $df = n - 1$. When conducting a **hypothesis test about** μ_D the value of the **test statistic** is calculated as $t_{df} = \dfrac{\bar{d} - d_0}{s_D/\sqrt{n}}$, where d_0 is a hypothesized mean difference.

LO **10.3**

Make inferences about the difference between two population proportions based on independent sampling.

A $100(1 - \alpha)\%$ **confidence interval for the difference between two population proportions** $p_1 - p_2$ is given by $(\bar{p}_1 - \bar{p}_2) \pm z_{\alpha/2} \sqrt{\frac{\bar{p}_1(1 - \bar{p}_1)}{n_1} + \frac{\bar{p}_2(1 - \bar{p}_2)}{n_2}}$.

When conducting **hypothesis tests about the difference between two proportions** $p_1 - p_2$, the value of the **test statistic** is calculated as:

- $z = \dfrac{\bar{p}_1 - \bar{p}_2}{\sqrt{\bar{p}(1 - \bar{p})\left(\frac{1}{n_1} + \frac{1}{n_2}\right)}}$, if the hypothesized difference d_0 between p_1 and p_2 is zero. The pooled sample proportion is $\bar{p} = \dfrac{x_1 + x_2}{n_1 + n_2}$.

- $z = \dfrac{(\bar{p}_1 - \bar{p}_2) - d_0}{\sqrt{\frac{\bar{p}_1(1 - \bar{p}_1)}{n_1} + \frac{\bar{p}_2(1 - \bar{p}_2)}{n_2}}}$, if the hypothesized difference d_0 between p_1 and p_2 is not zero.

42. Do men really spend more money on St. Patrick's Day as compared to women? A recent survey found that men spend an average of $43.87 while women spend an average of $29.54 (*USA Today*, March 17, 2009). Assume that these data were based on a sample of 100 men and 100 women and the population standard deviations of spending for men and women are $32 and $25, respectively.

    a. Specify the competing hypotheses to determine whether men spend more money than women spend on St. Patrick's Day.

    b. Calculate the value of the test statistic.

    c. Calculate the *p*-value.

    d. At the 1% significance level, do men spend more money than women spend on St. Patrick's day? Explain.

43. A new study has found that, on average, 6- to 12-year-old children are spending less time on household chores today compared to 1981 levels (*The Wall Street Journal*, August 27, 2008). Suppose two samples representative of the study's results report the following summary statistics for the two periods:

1981 Levels	2008 Levels
$\bar{x}_1 = 30$ minutes	$\bar{x}_2 = 24$ minutes
$s_1 = 4.2$ minutes	$s_1 = 3.9$ minutes
$n_1 = 30$	$n_2 = 30$

    a. Specify the competing hypotheses to test the study's claim that children today spend less time on household chores as compared to children in 1981.

    b. Calculate the value of the test statistic assuming that the unknown population variances are equal.

    c. Approximate the *p*-value.

    d. At the 5% significance level, do the data support the study's claim? Explain.

    e. Repeat the hypothesis test using the critical value approach.

44. A farmer is concerned that a change in fertilizer to an organic variant might change his crop yield. He subdivides 6 lots and uses the old fertilizer on one half of each lot and the new fertilizer on the other half. The following table shows the results.

Lot	Crop Yield Using Old Fertilizer	Crop Yield Using New Fertilizer
1	10	12
2	11	10
3	10	13
4	9	9
5	12	11
6	11	12

    a. Specify the competing hypotheses that determine whether there is any difference between the average crop yields from the use of the different fertilizers.

    b. Assuming that crop yields are normally distributed, calculate the value of the test statistic.

    c. At the 5% significance level, find the critical value(s).

    d. Is there sufficient evident to conclude that the crop yields are different? Should the farmer be concerned?

45. **FILE** (Use Excel) The accompanying table shows annual return data from 2001–2009 for Vanguard's Balanced Index and European Stock Index mutual funds. The data can also be accessed from the text website, labeled ***Vanguard Balanced and European Funds***.

Year	Balanced Index	European Stock Index
2001	−3.02%	−20.30%
2002	−9.52	−17.95
2003	19.87	38.70
2004	9.33	20.86
2005	4.65	9.26
2006	11.02	33.42
2007	6.16	13.82
2008	−22.21	−44.73
2009	20.05	31.91

Source: www.finance.yahoo.com

    a. Set up the hypotheses to test whether mean returns of the two funds differ.

    b. What is the value of the test statistic and its associated *p*-value given unequal population standard deviations?

    c. At the 5% significance level, what is the conclusion?

46. A recent Health of Boston report suggests that 14% of female residents suffer from asthma as opposed to 6% of males (*The Boston Globe*, August 16, 2010). Suppose 250 females and 200 males responded to the study.

    a. Develop the appropriate null and alternative hypotheses to test whether the proportion of females suffering from asthma is greater than the proportion of males.

    b. Calculate the value of the test statistic and its associated *p*-value.

    c. At the 5% significance level, what is the conclusion? Do the data suggest that females suffer more from asthma than males?

47. Depression engulfs millions of Americans every day. A new federal study reported that 10.9% of adults aged 18–24 identified with some level of depression versus 6.8% of adults aged 65 or older (*The Boston Globe*, October 18, 2010). Suppose 250 young adults (18–24 years old) and 200 older adults (65 years old and older) responded to the study.

    a. Develop the appropriate null and alternative hypotheses to test whether the proportion of young adults suffering from depression is greater than the proportion of older adults suffering from depression.

b. Calculate the value of the test statistic and the *p*-value.

c. At the 5% significance level, what is the conclusion? Do the sample data suggest that young adults suffer more from depression than older adults?

48. Fresh numbers from the U.S. Department of Transportation suggest that fewer flights in the U.S. arrive on time than before. The explanations offered for the lackluster performance are understaffed airlines, a high volume of travelers, and overtaxed air traffic control. A transportation analyst is interested in comparing the performance at two major international airports, namely Kennedy International (JFK) in New York and O'Hare International in Chicago. She finds that 70% of the flights were on time at JFK compared with 63% at O'Hare. Suppose these proportions were based on 200 flights at each of these two airports. The analyst believes that the proportion of on-time flights at JFK is more than 5 percentage points higher than that of O'Hare.

a. Develop the competing hypotheses to test the transportation analyst's belief.

b. Compute the value of the test statistic.

c. Use the *p*-value approach to test the above assertion.

d. Repeat the analysis with the critical value approach.

49. FILE (Use Excel) The SAT is required of most students applying for college admission in the United States. This standardized test has gone through many revisions over the years. In 2005, a new writing section was introduced that includes a direct writing measure in the form of an essay. People argue that female students generally do worse on math tests but better on writing tests. Therefore, the new section may help reduce the usual male lead on the overall average SAT score (*The Washington Post,* August 30, 2006). Consider the following scores on the writing component of the test of 8 male and 8 female students. The data can be found on the text website, labeled **SAT Writing Component**.

Males	620	570	540	580	590	580	480	620
Females	660	590	540	560	610	590	610	650

a. Construct the null and the alternative hypotheses to test if females outscore males on writing tests.

b. Compute the value of the test statistic. Do not assume that the population variances are equal.

c. Implement the test at $\alpha = 0.01$ and interpret your results.

50. FILE (Use Excel) An engineer wants to determine the effectiveness of a safety program. He collects annual loss of hours due to accidents in 12 plants "before and after" the program was put into operation. The data can be found on the text website, labeled **Safety Program**.

Plant	Before	After	Plant	Before	After
1	100	98	7	88	90
2	90	88	8	75	70
3	94	90	9	65	62
4	85	86	10	58	60
5	70	67	11	67	60
6	83	80	12	104	98

a. Specify the competing hypotheses that determine whether the safety program was effective.

b. Assuming that hours are normally distributed, calculate the value of the test statistic.

c. At the 5% significance level, calculate the critical value(s).

d. Is there sufficient evident to conclude that the safety program was effective? Explain.

CASE STUDIES

Case Study 10.1

Chad Perrone is a financial analyst in Boston studying the annual return data for the health and information technology industries. He randomly samples 20 firms in each industry and notes each firm's annual return. A portion of the data is shown in the accompanying table; the entire data set is found on the text website, labeled **Health and Info Tech**.

Data for Case Study 10.1 Annual Returns for
Firms in Health and Information Technology Industries

FILE

Health	Information Technology
10.29%	4.77%
32.17	1.14
⋮	⋮
13.21	22.61

In a report, use the sample information to:

1. Provide descriptive statistics and comment on the reward and risk in each industry.

2. Determine whether the average returns in each industry differ at the 5% significance level. Assume that the population variances are unequal.

Case Study 10.2

The Speedo LZR Racer Suit is a high-end, body-length swimsuit that was launched on February 13, 2008. When 17 world records fell at the December 2008 European Short Course Championships in Croatia, many believed a modification in the rules surrounding swimsuits was necessary. The FINA Congress, the international governing board for swimming, banned the LZR Racer and all other body-length swimsuits from competition effective January 2010. In a statement to the public, FINA defended its position with the following statement: "FINA wishes to recall the main and core principle that swimming is a sport essentially based on the physical performance of the athlete" (*BBC Sport*, March 14, 2009).

Luke Johnson, a freelance journalist, wonders if the decision made by FINA has statistical backing. He conducts an experiment with the local university's Division I swim team. He times 10 of the swimmers swimming the 50-meter breaststroke in his/her bathing suit and then retests them while wearing the LZR Racer. A portion of the results are shown in the accompanying table. The entire data set, labeled **LZR Racer**, can be accessed from the text website.

Data for Case Study 10.2 50-Meter Breaststroke Times (in seconds)

FILE

Swimmer	Time in Bathing Suit	Time in LZR Racer
1	27.64	27.45
2	27.97	28.06
⋮	⋮	⋮
10	38.08	37.93

In a report, use the sample information to:

1. Determine whether the LZR Racer significantly improves swimmers' times at the 5% significance level.

2. Comment on whether the data appear to support FINA's decision.

Case Study 10.3

Paige Thomsen is about to graduate from college at a local university in San Francisco. Her options are to look for a job in San Francisco or go home to Denver and search for work there. Recent data reports that average starting salaries for college graduates is $48,900 in San Francisco and $40,900 in Denver (*Forbes*, June 26, 2008). Suppose these data were based on 100 recent graduates in each city where the population standard deviation is $16,000 in San Francisco and $14,500 in Denver. For social reasons, Paige is also interested in the percent of the population who are in their 20s. The same report states that 20% of the population are in their 20s in San Francisco; the corresponding percentage in Denver is 22%.

In a report, use the sample information to:

1. Determine whether the average starting salary in San Francisco is greater than Denver's average starting salary at the 5% significance level.

2. Determine whether the proportion of the population in their 20s differs in these two cities at the 5% significance level.

11

Statistical Inference Concerning Variance

C H A P T E R

LEARNING OBJECTIVES

After reading this chapter you should be able to:

LO 11.1 Discuss features of the χ^2 distribution.

LO 11.2 Construct a confidence interval for the population variance.

LO 11.3 Conduct a hypothesis test for the population variance.

LO 11.4 Discuss features of the F distribution.

LO 11.5 Construct a confidence interval for the ratio of two population variances.

LO 11.6 Conduct a hypothesis test for the ratio of two population variances.

So far, when conducting statistical inference concerning quantitative data, we have restricted our attention to the population mean. The mean is a basic measure of central location, but in many instances we are also interested in making inferences about the data's variability or dispersion. For instance, quality-control studies use the population variance to measure the variability of the weight, size, or volume of the product. The population variance is also the most widely used quantitative measure of risk in investments. In this chapter we study statistical inference with respect to the population variance as well as the ratio of two population variances. In order to construct confidence intervals or conduct hypothesis tests regarding the population variance, we use a new distribution called the χ^2 (chi-square) distribution. We then turn our attention to analyzing the ratio of the two population variances. In order to construct confidence intervals or conduct hypothesis tests concerning this ratio, we use another new distribution called the F distribution.

Assessing the Risk of Mutual Fund Returns

In Chapter 3, investment counselor Rebecca Johnson examined annual return data for two top-performing mutual funds from the last decade: Vanguard's Precious Metals and Mining fund (henceforth, Metals) and Fidelity's Strategic Income fund (henceforth, Income). Table 11.1 shows relevant descriptive statistics for the two mutual funds for the years 2000–2009. Rebecca knows that the reward of investing is measured by its average return, while the standard deviation is the most widely used measure of risk. A client of Rebecca's has specific questions related to the risk of investing. He would like to invest a portion of his money in the Metals fund so long as the risk does not exceed 25%. He also wonders if the risk of investing in the Income fund differs from 8.5%, which is the risk inherent in similar funds. Rebecca is familiar with making statistical inference with respect to the population mean and a comparison of the population means; however, she is not clear on how to implement these techniques with respect to the population standard deviation.

TABLE 11.1 Descriptive Measures for the Metals and the Income Funds, $n = 10$

	Metals	Income
Mean	24.65%	8.51%
Standard Deviation	37.13%	11.07%

Rebecca would like to use the above sample information to:

1. Evaluate the investment risks of the Metals and the Income funds by constructing confidence intervals for the standard deviations.
2. Implement tests to verify if the investment risks of the Metals and Income funds deviate from specific values.
3. Determine if the risk of the Metals fund is significantly greater than the risk of the Income fund.

A synopsis of this case is provided at the end of Section 11.2.

11.1 Inference Concerning the Population Variance

The population variance is used in quality-control studies to measure the variability of the weight, size, or volume of the product. Consider, for example, a bottler who wishes its production line to fill a certain amount of beverage in each bottle. It is important not only to get the desired average amount filled in the bottles, but also to keep the variability of the amount filled below some tolerance limit. Similarly, with variance used as a quantitative measure of risk, an investor may want to evaluate his/her risk in a particular investment. Other examples for the relevance of making inference regarding the population variance include evaluating the consistency of an athlete or a team, the variability of speeds on a highway, and the variability of repair costs of a certain automobile.

Recall that we use the sample mean $\overline{X}$ as the estimator of the population mean μ. Similarly, we use the sample variance S^2 as an estimator of the population variance σ^2. Like $\overline{X}$, S^2 has the desirable properties of an estimator. In particular, it is unbiased ($E(S^2) = \sigma^2$), efficient, and consistent. Using a random sample of n observations drawn from the population, we compute $s^2 = \frac{\Sigma(x_i - \overline{x})^2}{n - 1}$ as an estimate of σ^2. In order to examine the techniques for statistical inferences regarding σ^2, we first need to analyze the sampling distribution of S^2.

Sampling Distribution of S^2

LO 11.1

Discuss features of the χ^2 distribution.

Statistical inferences regarding σ^2 are based on the χ^2 or **chi-square** distribution. Like the t distribution, the χ^2 distribution is characterized by a family of distributions, where each distribution depends on its particular degrees of freedom df. It is common, therefore, to refer to it as the χ^2_{df} distribution.

In general, the χ^2_{df} distribution is the probability distribution of the sum of several independent squared standard normal random variables. Here df is defined as the number of squared standard normal random variables included in the summation. Recall that the estimator S^2 of the population variance is based on the squared differences between the sample values and the sample mean. If S^2 is computed from a random sample of n observations drawn from an underlying normal population, then we can define the χ^2_{df} variable as $\frac{(n - 1)S^2}{\sigma^2}$.

> **THE SAMPLING DISTRIBUTION OF $\frac{(n-1)S^2}{\sigma^2}$**
>
> If a sample of size n is taken from a normal population with a finite variance, then the statistic $\chi^2_{df} = \frac{(n-1)S^2}{\sigma^2}$ follows the χ^2_{df} distribution with $df = n - 1$.

In earlier chapters, we denoted the random variables by upper-case letters and particular outcomes of the random variables by the corresponding lower-case letters. For instance, the statistics Z and T_{df} are random variables and their values are given by z and t_{df}, respectively. It is cumbersome to continue with the distinction between the random variable and its value in this chapter. Here we use the above statistic χ^2_{df} to represent a random variable as well as its value. Similarly, for the $F_{(df_1, df_2)}$ distribution introduced in Section 11.2, we will use $F_{(df_1, df_2)}$ to represent both a random variable and its value.

From Figure 11.1, we note that the χ^2_{df} distributions are positively skewed, where the extent of skewness depends on the degrees of freedom. As the df grow larger, the χ^2_{df} distribution tends to the normal distribution. For instance, in the figure, the χ^2_{20} distribution resembles the shape of the normal distribution.

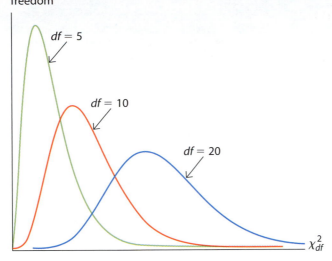

FIGURE 11.1 The χ^2_{df} distribution with various degrees of freedom

$df = 5$

$df = 10$

$df = 20$

χ^2_{df}

SUMMARY OF THE χ^2_{df} DISTRIBUTION

- The values of the χ^2_{df} distribution range from zero to infinity.
- The χ^2_{df} distribution is positively skewed.
- The family of χ^2_{df} distributions have shapes that depend on df. As the df grow larger, the χ^2_{df} distribution tends to the normal distribution.

Locating χ^2_{df}-Values and Probabilities

For a χ^2_{df} distributed random variable, we use the notation $\chi^2_{\alpha,df}$ to represent a value such that the area in the right (upper) tail of the distribution is α. In other words, $P(\chi^2_{df} \geq \chi^2_{\alpha,df}) = \alpha$. Figure 11.2 illustrates the notation $\chi^2_{\alpha,df}$, which we use to locate χ^2_{df}-values and probabilities from the χ^2 (chi-square) table.

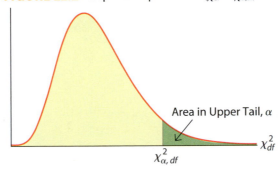

FIGURE 11.2 Graphical depiction of $P(\chi^2_{df} \geq \chi^2_{\alpha,df}) = \alpha$

Area in Upper Tail, α

$\chi^2_{\alpha,df}$

χ^2_{df}

A portion of the right-tail probabilities and the corresponding values of χ^2_{df} distributions are given in Table 11.2. Table 3 of Appendix A provides a more complete table.

Suppose we want to find the value $\chi^2_{\alpha,df}$ with $\alpha = 0.05$ and $df = 10$, that is, $\chi^2_{0.05,10}$. Using Table 11.2, we look at the first column labeled df and find the value 10. We then continue along this row until we reach the column $\chi^2_{0.050}$. Here we see the value $\chi^2_{0.05,10} = 18.307$ such that $P(\chi^2_{10} \geq 18.307) = 0.05$.

TABLE 11.2 Portion of the χ^2 table

df	\multicolumn{10}{c}{Area in Upper Tail, α}									
	0.995	0.990	0.975	0.950	0.900	0.100	0.050	0.025	0.010	0.005
1	0.000	0.000	0.001	0.004	0.016	2.706	3.841	5.024	6.635	7.879
⋮	⋮	⋮	⋮	⋮	⋮	⋮	⋮	⋮	⋮	⋮
10	2.156	2.558	3.247	**3.940**	4.865	15.987	**18.307**	20.483	23.209	25.188
⋮	⋮	⋮	⋮	⋮	⋮	⋮	⋮	⋮	⋮	⋮
100	67.328	70.065	74.222	77.929	82.358	118.342	124.342	129.561	135.807	140.170

Sometimes we need to derive values in the left (lower) tail of the distribution. Given that the area under any probability distribution equals one, if the area to the left of a given value equals α, then the area to the right must equal $1 - \alpha$. In other words, the relevant value on the left tail of the distribution is $\chi^2_{1-\alpha,df}$ where $P(\chi^2_{df} \geq \chi^2_{1-\alpha,df}) = 1 - \alpha$.

> ### LOCATING χ^2_{df}-VALUES ON THE LEFT TAIL
>
> For a χ^2_{df} distributed random variable, $\chi^2_{1-\alpha,df}$ represents a value such that $P(\chi^2_{df} < \chi^2_{1-\alpha,df}) = \alpha$, or equivalently, $P(\chi^2_{df} \geq \chi^2_{1-\alpha,df}) = 1 - \alpha$.

Suppose that we want to find the value such that the area to the left of the χ^2_{10} variable equals 0.05. Given that the area to the left of this value is 0.05, we know that the area to its right is $1 - 0.05 = 0.95$; thus, we need to find $\chi^2_{1-0.05,10} = \chi^2_{0.95,10}$. Again we find $df = 10$ in the first column and follow this row until we intersect the column $\chi^2_{0.95}$ and find the value 3.940. This is the value such that $P(\chi^2_{10} \geq 3.940) = 0.95$ or $P(\chi^2_{10} < 3.940) = 0.05$. Figure 11.3 graphically depicts the probability $\alpha = 0.05$ on both sides of the χ^2_{10} distribution and the corresponding χ^2_{10}-values.

FIGURE 11.3 Graph of the probability $\alpha = 0.05$ on both sides of χ^2_{10}

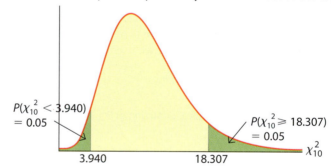

$P(\chi^2_{10} < 3.940) = 0.05$

$P(\chi^2_{10} \geq 18.307) = 0.05$

χ^2_{10}

3.940   18.307

EXAMPLE 11.1

Find the value x for which:

a. $P(\chi^2_5 \geq x) = 0.025$

b. $P(\chi^2_8 < x) = 0.025$

SOLUTION:

a. We find the value x such that the probability in the right tail of the distribution equals 0.025. Therefore, $x = 12.833$.

b. We find the value x such that the probability in the left tail of the distribution equals 0.025. We solve this problem as $P(\chi^2_8 \geq x) = 1 - 0.025 = 0.975$ where $x = 2.180$. This is equivalent to $P(\chi^2_8 < 2.180) = 0.025$.

Confidence Interval for the Population Variance

LO **11.2**

Construct a confidence interval for the population variance.

Consider a χ^2_{df} distributed random variable. Using the notation introduced above, we can make the following probability statement concerning this random variable:

$$P(\chi^2_{1-\alpha/2,df} \leq \chi^2_{df} \leq \chi^2_{\alpha/2,df}) = 1 - \alpha.$$

This indicates that the probability that χ^2_{df} falls between $\chi^2_{1-\alpha/2,df}$ and $\chi^2_{\alpha/2,df}$ is equal to $1 - \alpha$, where $1 - \alpha$ is the familiar confidence coefficient. For instance, for a 95% confidence level, $\alpha = 0.05$, $\chi^2_{\alpha/2,df} = \chi^2_{0.025,df}$ and $\chi^2_{1-\alpha/2,df} = \chi^2_{0.975,df}$. Substituting $\chi^2_{df} = \frac{(n-1)S^2}{\sigma^2}$ into the probability statement yields

$$P\left(\chi^2_{1-\alpha/2,df} \leq \frac{(n-1)S^2}{\sigma^2} \leq \chi^2_{\alpha/2,df}\right) = 1 - \alpha.$$

After manipulating this equation algebraically, we arrive at the formula for the confidence interval for σ^2.

CONFIDENCE INTERVAL FOR σ^2

A $100(1 - \alpha)\%$ confidence interval of the population variance σ^2 is computed as

$$\left[\frac{(n-1)s^2}{\chi^2_{\alpha/2,df}}, \frac{(n-1)s^2}{\chi^2_{1-\alpha/2,df}}\right],$$

where $df = n - 1$.

This formula is valid only when the random sample is drawn from a normally distributed population. Note that the confidence interval is not in the usual format of point estimate $\pm$ margin of error. Since the confidence intervals of the population mean and the population proportion are based on the z or the t_{df} distributions, the symmetry of these distributions leads to the same margin of error that is added to and subtracted from the point estimate. However, for a nonsymmetric χ^2_{df} distribution, what is added to the point estimate of the population variance is not the same as what is subtracted. Finally, since the standard deviation is just the positive square root of the variance, a $100(1 - \alpha)\%$ confidence interval for the population standard deviation is computed as

$$\left[\sqrt{\frac{(n-1)s^2}{\chi^2_{\alpha/2,df}}}, \sqrt{\frac{(n-1)s^2}{\chi^2_{1-\alpha/2,df}}}\right].$$

EXAMPLE 11.2

Compute 95% confidence intervals for the population standard deviation for the Metals fund as well as the Income fund using the data from Table 11.1 in the introductory case. Assume that returns are normally distributed.

SOLUTION: For the years 2000–2009 ($n = 10$), the sample standard deviation for the Metals fund is $s = 37.13\%$, while the sample standard deviation for the Income fund is $s = 11.07\%$.

We first determine the 95% confidence interval for the population variance of the Metals fund. Given $n = 10$, $df = 10 - 1 = 9$. For a 95% confidence interval, $\alpha = 0.05$ and $\alpha/2 = 0.025$. Thus, we find $\chi^2_{\alpha/2,df} = \chi^2_{0.025,9} = 19.023$ and $\chi^2_{1-\alpha/2,df} = \chi^2_{0.975,9} = 2.700$. The 95% confidence interval for the population variance is

$$\left[\frac{(n-1)s^2}{\chi^2_{\alpha/2,df}}, \frac{(n-1)s^2}{\chi^2_{1-\alpha/2,df}}\right] = \left[\frac{(10-1)(37.13)^2}{19.023}, \frac{(10-1)(37.13)^2}{2.700}\right]$$

$$= [652.25(\%)^2, 4{,}595.46(\%)^2].$$

Taking the positive square root of the limits of this interval, we find the corresponding 95% confidence interval for the population standard deviation as [25.54%, 67.79%]. With 95% confidence, we report that the standard deviation of the return for the Metals fund is between 25.54% and 67.79%. Similarly, for the Income fund, we compute the 95% confidence interval for the population standard deviation as [7.61%, 20.21%].

LO 11.3

Conduct a hypothesis test for the population variance.

Hypothesis Test for the Population Variance

Let's now develop the hypothesis test regarding the population variance. Following the methodology used in the last two chapters, we specify the null and the alternative hypotheses as:

Two-tailed Test	Right-tailed Test	Left-tailed Test
$H_0: \sigma^2 = \sigma_0^2$	$H_0: \sigma^2 \leq \sigma_0^2$	$H_0: \sigma^2 \geq \sigma_0^2$
$H_A: \sigma^2 \neq \sigma_0^2$	$H_A: \sigma^2 > \sigma_0^2$	$H_A: \sigma^2 < \sigma_0^2$

Here σ_0^2 is the hypothesized value of the population variance σ^2. As before, we can use the confidence intervals to implement two-tailed hypothesis tests; however, we apply the four-step procedure to conduct one-tailed hypothesis tests concerning the population variance.

We use the sample variance to conduct hypothesis tests regarding the population variance. As noted earlier, we use a χ^2 test if the underlying population is normally distributed.

TEST STATISTIC FOR σ^2

The value of the **test statistic** for the hypothesis test of the **population variance σ^2** is computed as

$$\chi_{df}^2 = \frac{(n-1)s^2}{\sigma_0^2},$$

where $df = n - 1$ and σ_0^2 is the hypothesized value of the population variance.

EXAMPLE 11.3

We again consider the introductory case. Rebecca Johnson's client asks if the standard deviation of returns for the Metals fund is significantly greater than 25%. This is equivalent to testing whether or not the variance is significantly greater than $625(\%)^2$. We conduct this test at the 5% significance level, based on the sample information provided in Table 11.1. We implement the four-step procedure using the critical value approach and assume that returns are normally distributed.

SOLUTION: In this example, the relevant parameter of interest is the population variance σ^2. Since we wish to determine whether the variance is greater than $625(\%)^2$, we specify the competing hypotheses as

$$H_0: \sigma^2 \leq 625$$
$$H_A: \sigma^2 > 625$$

The χ^2 test is valid because the underlying population is assumed to be normally distributed. Given that $n = 10$ and $s = 37.13$, we compute the value of the test statistic as

$$\chi_{df}^2 = \frac{(n-1)s^2}{\sigma_0^2} = \frac{(10-1)(37.13)^2}{625} = 19.85.$$

For the above right-tailed test, the critical value $\chi^2_{\alpha,df}$ is derived from $P(\chi^2_{df} \geq \chi^2_{\alpha,df}) = \alpha$.

Referencing the χ^2 (chi-square) table with $\alpha = 0.05$ and $df = n - 1 = 9$, we find the critical value $\chi^2_{0.05,9}$ as 16.919. The decision rule is to reject the null hypothesis if χ^2_9 exceeds 16.919.

We reject the null hypothesis because the value of the test statistic falls in the critical region ($\chi^2_9 = 19.85$ exceeds $\chi^2_{0.05,9} = 16.919$). At the 5% significance level, the variance of the Metals fund is significantly greater than $625(\%)^2$. Analogously, the standard deviation is significantly greater than 25%, implying that the risk associated with this investment is more than the client wants to accept.

EXAMPLE 11.4

Rebecca Johnson's client from the introductory case also wonders if the standard deviation of returns for the Income fund differs from 8.5%. This is equivalent to testing whether or not the variance differs from $72.25(\%)^2$. Use the p-value approach to conduct this test at the 5% significance level.

SOLUTION: This is an example of a two-tailed test of the population variance σ^2. We specify the competing hypotheses of the two-tailed test of the population variance as

$$H_0: \sigma^2 = 72.25$$
$$H_A: \sigma^2 \neq 72.25$$

Given that $n = 10$ and $s = 11.07$, we compute the value of the test statistic as

$$\chi^2_{df} = \frac{(n-1)s^2}{\sigma^2_o} = \frac{(10-1)(11.07)^2}{72.25} = 15.27.$$

Recall that the p-value is the probability of obtaining a value of the test statistic that is at least as extreme as the one that we actually observed, given that the null hypothesis is true as an equality. For a two-tailed test, we double the probability that is considered extreme. For example, for a two-tailed test of the population mean μ with a z statistic, the p-value is computed as $2P(Z \geq z)$ if $z > 0$ or $2P(Z \leq z)$ if $z < 0$. Note that $z > 0$ if $\bar{x} > \mu_0$ and $z < 0$ if $\bar{x} < \mu_0$. Similarly, for a two-tailed test of the population variance σ^2, the p-value is computed as two times the right-tail probability if $s^2 > \sigma^2_o$ or two times the left-tail probability if $s^2 < \sigma^2_o$.

For the Income fund, since $s^2 > \sigma^2_o$ (122.54 > 72.25), we compute the p-value as $2P(\chi^2_{df} \geq 15.27)$. For $df = 9$, since 15.27 lies between 14.684 and 16.919 (see χ^2 table), $P(\chi^2_9 \geq 15.27)$ lies between 0.05 and 0.10. Multiplying this probability by two results in a p-value between 0.10 and 0.20.

At the 5% significance level, we cannot reject H_0 because the p-value is greater than $\alpha = 0.05$. Therefore, we cannot conclude that the risk, measured by the variance of the return, differs from $72.25(\%)^2$; or equivalently, we cannot conclude that the standard deviation differs from 8.5%.

Using Excel to Calculate p-Values

We can easily find exact probabilities with Excel. For instance, with $df = 9$, we can use Excel to determine the exact probability of $P(\chi^2_{df} \geq 15.27)$ by following these commands.

A. From the menu select **Formulas** > **Insert Function** > **CHISQ.DIST.RT**. This command returns the right-tailed probability of the chi-squared distribution.

(If $s^2 < \sigma_0^2$ such that we need a left-tailed probability, we use **Formulas > Insert Function > CHISQ.DIST.**)

B. See Figure 11.4. Supply the following two arguments in the dialog box:
- **X** is the value of the test statistic. We enter 15.27.
- **Deg_freedom** are the degrees of freedom associated with the test statistic. We enter 9.

C. Click **OK**.

FIGURE 11.4 CHISQ.DIST.RT dialog box

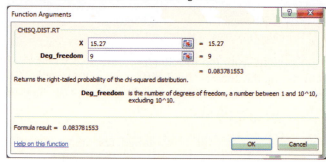

Excel returns the probability of 0.0838. The exact p-value for the two-tailed test is 2(0.0838) or 0.1676. Again, given a significance level of 5%, we are unable to reject the null hypothesis that the population variance equals 72.25(%)^2.

EXERCISES 11.1

Concepts

1. Find the value x for which:
   a. $P(\chi_8^2 \geq x) = 0.025$
   b. $P(\chi_8^2 \geq x) = 0.05$
   c. $P(\chi_8^2 < x) = 0.025$
   d. $P(\chi_8^2 < x) = 0.05$

2. Find the value x for which:
   a. $P(\chi_{20}^2 \geq x) = 0.005$
   b. $P(\chi_{20}^2 \geq x) = 0.01$
   c. $P(\chi_{20}^2 < x) = 0.005$
   d. $P(\chi_{20}^2 < x) = 0.01$

3. In order to derive a confidence interval of the population variance, a random sample of n observations is drawn from a normal population. Use this information to find $\chi_{\alpha/2,df}^2$ and $\chi_{1-\alpha/2,df}^2$ under the following scenarios.
   a. A 95% confidence level with $n = 18$.
   b. A 95% confidence level with $n = 30$.
   c. A 99% confidence level with $n = 18$.
   d. A 99% confidence level with $n = 30$.

4. A random sample of 25 observations is used to estimate the population variance. The sample mean and sample standard deviation are calculated as 52.5 and 3.8, respectively. Assume that the population is normally distributed.
   a. Construct a 90% interval estimate of the population variance.
   b. Construct a 99% interval estimate of the population variance.
   c. Use your answers to discuss the impact of the confidence level on the width of the interval.

5. The following values are drawn from a normal population.

20	29	32	27	34	25	30	31

   a. Calculate the point estimates of the population variance and the population standard deviation.
   b. Compute a 95% confidence interval for the population variance and the population standard deviation.

6. In order to conduct a hypothesis test of the population variance, you compute $s^2 = 75$ from a sample of 21 observations drawn from a normally distributed population. Use the critical value approach to conduct the following tests at $\alpha = 0.10$.
   a. $H_0: \sigma^2 \leq 50$; $H_A: \sigma^2 > 50$
   b. $H_0: \sigma^2 = 50$; $H_A: \sigma^2 \neq 50$

7. Consider the following hypotheses:

$$H_0: \sigma^2 = 200$$

$$H_A: \sigma^2 \neq 200$$

Approximate the p-value based on the following sample information, where the sample is drawn from a normally distributed population.

a. $s^2 = 300; n = 25$

b. $s^2 = 100; n = 25$

c. Which of the above sample information enables us to reject the null hypothesis at $\alpha = 0.05$?

8. You would like to test the claim that the variance of a normally distributed population is more than 2 squared units. You draw a random sample of 10 observations as 2, 4, 1, 3, 2, 5, 2, 6, 1, 4. At $\alpha = 0.10$, test the above claim using (a) the p-value approach and (b) the critical value approach.

Applications

9. A research analyst is examining a stock for possible inclusion in his client's portfolio. Over a 10-year period, the sample mean and the sample standard deviation of annual returns on the stock were 20% and 15%, respectively. The client wants to know if the risk, as measured by the standard deviation, differs from 18%.

a. Construct a 95% confidence interval of the population variance and then infer the 95% confidence interval of the population standard deviation.

b. What assumption did you make in constructing the confidence interval?

c. Based on the above confidence interval, does the risk differ from 18%?

10. A replacement part for a machine must be produced within close specifications in order for it to be acceptable to customers. Suppose the sample variance for 20 parts turns out to be $s^2 = 0.03$.

a. Construct a 95% confidence interval of the population variance.

b. Production specifications call for a variance in the lengths of the parts to be exactly 0.05. Comment on whether or not the specification is being violated.

11. A consumer advocacy group is concerned about the variability in the cost of prescription medication. The group surveys eight local pharmacies and obtains the following prices for a particular brand of medication:

| $25.50 | 32.00 | 33.50 | 28.75 | 29.50 | 35.00 | 27.00 | 29.00 |

a. Calculate the point estimate of the population variance.

b. The group assumes that the above prices represent a random sample drawn from a normally distributed population. Construct a 90% interval estimate of the population variance.

c. The group decides to begin a lobbying effort on its members' behalf if the variance in the price does not equal 4. What should the group do?

12. The following table shows the annual returns (in percent) for the Vanguard Energy Fund from 2005 through 2009.

Year	Energy
2005	44.60
2006	19.68
2007	37.00
2008	−42.87
2009	38.36

SOURCE: www.finance.yahoo.com.

a. Calculate the point estimate of σ.

b. Construct a 95% confidence interval of σ.

13. The manager of a supermarket would like the variance of the waiting times of the customers not to exceed 3 minutes-squared. She would add a new cash register if the variance exceeds this threshold. She regularly checks the waiting times of the customers to ensure that its variance does not rise above the allowed level. In a recent random sample of 28 customer waiting times, she computes the sample variance as 4.2 minutes-squared. She believes that the waiting times are normally distributed.

a. State the null and the alternative hypotheses to test if the threshold has been crossed.

b. Use the p-value approach to conduct the test at $\alpha = 0.05$.

c. Repeat the analysis with the critical value approach.

d. What should the manager do?

14. A restaurant owner is concerned about the consistency of business. He wants to determine if the standard deviation of the profits for each week is less than $300. The profits from last week are listed below (in dollars). Assume that profits are normally distributed.

| 1,825 | 1,642 | 1,675 | 1,553 | 1,925 | 2,037 | 1,902 |

a. State the appropriate null and alternative hypotheses for the test.

b. Compute the value of the test statistic.

c. Use the critical value approach to test the owner's concern at $\alpha = 0.01$.

d. Repeat the test at $\alpha = 0.10$.

15. India Fund, Inc. (IFN) is a close-ended equity mutual fund launched by the Blackstone Group, Asset Management Arm. Although it promises impressive returns, it does so at the cost of greater risk. An analyst would like to test if the variance of the returns for IFN is greater than $1,000(\%)^2$. He uses the following sample data to test his claim at a 5% level of significance.

2001	2002	2003	2004	2005	2006	2007
−28.33%	7.87%	140.63%	30.91%	63.35%	−2.78%	58.30%

a. State the competing hypotheses.

b. Compute the value of the test statistic. What assumption regarding the IFN returns did you make?

c. Given $\alpha = 0.05$, specify the critical value(s).

d. Is the variance of returns greater than $1,000(\%)^2$?

16. FILE (Use Excel) A realtor in Mission Viejo, California, believes that the standard deviation of house prices is more than 100 units, where each unit equals $1,000. Assume house prices are normally distributed.

a. State the null and the alternative hypotheses for the test.

b. Open the **Mission Viejo (raw)** data from the text website into an Excel spreadsheet (data are in $1,000s). Calculate the value of the test statistic.

c. Use Excel's function (either CHISQ.DIST.RT or CHISQ.DIST) to calculate the p-value.

d. At $\alpha = 0.05$ what is the conclusion? Is the realtor's claim supported by the data?

17. FILE (Use Excel) Access the miles per gallon (mpg) data on the text website labeled **MPG**.

a. State the null and the alternative hypotheses in order to test whether or not the variance of mpg differs from 62 mpg^2.

b. Calculate the relevant test statistic.

c. Use Excel's function (either CHISQ.DIST.RT or CHISQ.DIST) to calculate the p-value.

d. Make a conclusion at $\alpha = 0.01$.

18. FILE (Use Excel) While the housing market has not recovered, real estate investment in college towns continues to promise good returns (*The Wall Street Journal*, September 24, 2010). With rents holding up, this is good news for investors but the same cannot be said for students. There also tends to be significant variability in rents. Consider monthly rents of two bedroom apartments in two campus towns: Ann Arbor, Michigan, and Davis, California. A portion of the data is shown in the accompanying table; the complete data, labeled **Rentals**, can be found on the text website.

Ann Arbor Rent	Davis Rent
$850	$744
929	850
⋮	⋮
1450	1810

Source: www.zillow.com.

a. Use Excel to calculate the standard deviation of rent for Ann Arbor, Michigan, and Davis, California.

b. Construct and interpret 95% confidence intervals for the standard deviation of rent for both Ann Arbor, Michigan, and Davis, California.

c. For each campus town, determine if the standard deviation of rent differs from $200; use $\alpha = 0.05$.

11.2 Inference Concerning the Ratio of Two Population Variances

In this section we turn our attention to comparing two population variances σ_1^2 and σ_2^2. We may want to compare products on the basis of the relative variability of their weight, size, or volume. For example, a bottler may want to compare two production facilities based on the relative variability of the amount of beverage filled at each facility. Similarly, with variance used as a quantitative measure of risk in investments, an investor may want to compare the relative risk of two investment strategies. Other examples for the relevance of comparing two population variances include comparing the consistency of athletes or teams, the relative variability of speeds on highways, and the relative variability of repair costs of different makes of automobiles.

We specify the parameter of interest as the ratio of the population variances σ_1^2/σ_2^2 rather than their difference $\sigma_1^2 - \sigma_2^2$. Note that the condition $\sigma_1^2 = \sigma_2^2$ is equivalent to $\sigma_1^2 - \sigma_2^2 = 0$ as well as $\sigma_1^2/\sigma_2^2 = 1$. We use the ratio of the sample variances S_1^2/S_2^2 as an estimator of σ_1^2/σ_2^2, where the sample variances are computed from independent random samples drawn from two normally distributed populations. In order to examine the techniques for statistical inference, we first need to analyze the sampling distribution of S_1^2/S_2^2.

LO **11.4**

Discuss features of the *F* distribution.

Sampling Distribution of S_1^2/S_2^2

We use the sampling distribution of S_1^2/S_2^2 to define a new distribution, called the **F distribution**.[1] Like the t_{df} and χ_{df}^2 distributions, the F distribution is characterized by a family of distributions; however, each distribution depends on *two* degrees of freedom: the numerator degrees of freedom df_1 and the denominator degrees of freedom df_2. It is common to refer to it as the $F_{(df_1, df_2)}$ distribution. Like the χ_{df}^2 distribution, the $F_{(df_1, df_2)}$ distribution is

[1]The *F* distribution is named in honor of Sir Ronald Fisher, who discovered the distribution in 1922.

positively skewed with values ranging from zero to infinity, but becomes increasingly symmetric as df_1 and df_2 increase.

In general, the $F_{(df_1, df_2)}$ distribution is the probability distribution of the ratio of two independent chi-square variables, where each variable is divided by its own degrees of freedom, that is, $F_{(df_1, df_2)} = \dfrac{\chi^2_{df_1}/df_1}{\chi^2_{df_2}/df_2}$.

THE SAMPLING DISTRIBUTION OF S_1^2/S_2^2 WHEN $\sigma_1^2 = \sigma_2^2$

If independent samples of size n_1 and n_2 are drawn from normal populations with equal variances, then the statistic $F_{(df_1, df_2)} = S_1^2/S_2^2$ follows the $F_{(df_1, df_2)}$ distribution with $df_1 = n_1 - 1$ and $df_2 = n_2 - 1$.

As mentioned earlier, we will use $F_{(df_1, df_2)}$ to represent both a random variable and its value.

SUMMARY OF THE $F_{(df_1, df_2)}$ DISTRIBUTION

- The $F_{(df_1, df_2)}$ distribution is positively skewed.
- The values of the $F_{(df_1, df_2)}$ distribution range from zero to infinity.
- There is a family of $F_{(df_1, df_2)}$ distributions where the actual shape of each one depends on df_1 and df_2. As df_1 and df_2 grow larger, the $F_{(df_1, df_2)}$ distribution approaches the normal distribution.

FIGURE 11.5 The $F_{(df_1, df_2)}$ distribution with various degrees of freedom

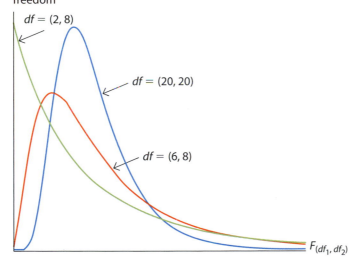

From Figure 11.5 we note that all $F_{(df_1, df_2)}$ distributions are positively skewed, where skewness depends on degrees of freedom, df_1 and df_2. As df_1 and df_2 grow larger, the $F_{(df_1, df_2)}$ distribution becomes less skewed and tends to the normal distribution. For instance, $F_{(20,20)}$ is relatively less skewed and more bell-shaped as compared to $F_{(2,8)}$ or $F_{(6,8)}$.

Locating $F_{(df_1, df_2)}$-Values and Probabilities

As with the χ^2_{df} distribution, we use the notation $F_{\alpha, (df_1, df_2)}$ to represent a value such that the area in the right- (upper) tail of the distribution is α. In other words, $P(F_{(df_1, df_2)} \geq F_{\alpha, (df_1, df_2)}) = \alpha$. Figure 11.6 illustrates the notation $F_{\alpha, (df_1, df_2)}$ used in the F table.

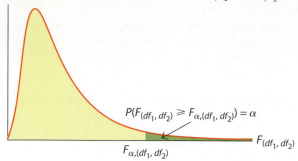

FIGURE 11.6 Graphical depiction of $P(F_{(df_1, df_2)} \geq F_{\alpha, (df_1, df_2)}) = \alpha$

$P(F_{(df_1, df_2)} \geq F_{\alpha, (df_1, df_2)}) = \alpha$

$F_{\alpha, (df_1, df_2)}$

$F_{(df_1, df_2)}$

A portion of the right-tail probabilities α and the corresponding $F_{(df_1, df_2)}$ values are given in Table 11.3. Table 4 of Appendix A provides a more complete table.

Table 11.3 Portion of the F Table

Denominator Degrees of Freedom, df_2	Area in Upper Tail, α	Numerator Degrees of Freedom, df_1		
		6	7	8
6	0.10	3.05	3.01	2.98
	0.05	4.28	4.21	4.15
	0.025	5.82	5.70	5.60
	0.01	8.47	8.26	8.10
7	0.10	2.83	2.78	2.75
	0.05	3.87	3.79	3.73
	0.025	5.12	4.99	4.90
	0.01	7.19	6.99	6.84
8	0.10	2.67	2.62	2.59
	0.05	**3.58**	3.50	3.44
	0.025	4.65	4.53	4.43
	0.01	**6.37**	6.18	6.03

Consider the degrees of freedom given by $df_1 = 6$ and $df_2 = 8$. With $df_1 = 6$ (read from the top row) and $df_2 = 8$ (read from the first column), we can easily determine the area in the right tail as $P(F_{(6,8)} \geq 3.58) = 0.05$ and $P(F_{(6,8)} \geq 6.37) = 0.01$. The F table is not very comprehensive and lists probabilities corresponding to a limited number of values in the right tail of the distribution. For instance, the exact probability $P(F_{(6,8)} \geq 3.92)$ cannot be determined from the table and we have to rely on approximate values. All we can say is the area to the right of 3.92 is between 0.025 and 0.05. Shortly, we will use Excel to find exact probabilities.

Sometimes we need to derive values such that the area to the left of a given value is equal to α. Given that the area under any distribution equals one, the area to the right of the given value must equal $1 - \alpha$. As in the case of the χ^2_{df} distribution, we let $F_{1-\alpha, (df_1, df_2)}$ denote the value such that the area to its right equals $1 - \alpha$ and thus the area to its left equals α. It is convenient, however, to find $F_{1-\alpha, (df_1, df_2)}$ using a simple rule that $F_{1-\alpha, (df_1, df_2)} = \dfrac{1}{F_{\alpha, (df_2, df_1)}}$. Note that the rule reverses the order of the numerator and the denominator degrees of freedom.

Suppose we need to find $F_{1-\alpha, (df_1, df_2)}$ where $\alpha = 0.05$, $df_1 = 6$, and $df_2 = 8$. We find $F_{0.95, (6,8)} = \frac{1}{F_{0.05, (8,6)}} = \frac{1}{4.15} = 0.24$. In other words, the left-tail probability is $P(F_{(6,8)} < 0.24) = 0.05$. Figure 11.7 graphically depicts $P(F_{(6,8)} \geq 3.58) = 0.05$ and $P(F_{(6,8)} < 0.24) = 0.05$.

FIGURE 11.7 Graph of the probability $\alpha = 0.05$ on both sides of $F_{(6,8)}$

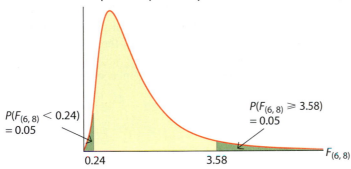

$P(F_{(6, 8)} < 0.24) = 0.05$

$P(F_{(6, 8)} \geq 3.58) = 0.05$

0.24   3.58 $F_{(6, 8)}$

EXAMPLE 11.5

Find the value x for which:

a. $P(F_{(7,10)} \geq x) = 0.025$

b. $P(F_{(7,10)} < x) = 0.05$

SOLUTION:

a. We find the value x such that the probability under the right tail of the distribution equals 0.025. Therefore, given $P(F_{(7,10)} \geq x) = 0.025$, we find $x = 3.95$.

b. We find the value x such that the probability under the left tail of the distribution equals 0.05, or equivalently, the probability in the right tail of the distribution equals 0.95. We have $F_{0.95, (7,10)} = \frac{1}{F_{0.05, (10,7)}} = \frac{1}{3.64} = 0.27$. In other words, $P(F_{(7,10)} < 0.27) = 0.05$.

Confidence Interval for the Ratio of Two Population Variances

The formula for a confidence interval for the ratio of the population variances σ_1^2 / σ_2^2 is derived in a manner analogous to previous confidence intervals. Here, we simply show the end result.

> ### CONFIDENCE INTERVAL FOR σ_1^2/σ_2^2
>
> A $100(1 - \alpha)\%$ confidence interval for the ratio of the population variances σ_1^2/σ_2^2 is computed as
>
> $$\left[\left(\frac{s_1^2}{s_2^2}\right)\frac{1}{F_{\alpha/2,(df_1,df_2)}}, \left(\frac{s_1^2}{s_2^2}\right)F_{\alpha/2,(df_2,df_1)}\right],$$
>
> where for samples of size n_1 and n_2, $df_1 = n_1 - 1$ and $df_2 = n_2 - 1$.

This specification is based on the assumption that the sample variances are computed from independently drawn samples from two normally distributed populations.

EXAMPLE 11.6

Students of two sections of a statistics course took a common final examination. A professor examines the variability in scores between the two sections. Random samples of $n_1 = 11$ and $n_2 = 16$ yield sample variances of $s_1^2 = 182.25$ and $s_2^2 = 457.96$. Construct a 95% confidence interval for the ratio of the population variances.

SOLUTION: In order to construct a 95% confidence interval for the ratio of the population variances, we determine $\left[\left(\frac{s_1^2}{s_2^2}\right)\frac{1}{F_{\alpha/2,(df_1,df_2)}}, \left(\frac{s_1^2}{s_2^2}\right)F_{\alpha/2,(df_2,df_1)}\right]$. The degrees of freedom in the numerator are $df_1 = n_1 - 1 = 11 - 1 = 10$ and the degrees of freedom in the denominator are $df_2 = n_2 - 1 = 16 - 1 = 15$. From the F table and given $\alpha = .05$, we find

$$F_{\alpha/2,(df_1,df_2)} = F_{0.025,(10,15)} = 3.06 \quad \text{and} \quad F_{\alpha/2,(df_2,df_1)} = F_{0.025,(15,10)} = 3.52.$$

The confidence interval is

$$\left[\left(\frac{182.25}{457.96}\right)\frac{1}{3.06}, \left(\frac{182.25}{457.96}\right)3.52\right] = [0.13, 1.40].$$

Therefore, a 95% confidence interval for the ratio of the population variances ranges from 0.13 to 1.40. In other words, the variance of scores in the first section is between 13% to 140% of the variance of scores in the second section.

As we have done in earlier chapters, we will be able to use this confidence interval to conduct a two-tailed hypothesis test.

LO 11.6

Conduct a hypothesis test for the ratio of two population variances.

Hypothesis Test for the Ratio of Two Population Variances

When comparing two population parameters σ_1^2 and σ_2^2, the competing hypotheses will take one of the following forms:

Two-tailed Test	Right-tailed Test	Left-tailed Test
$H_0: \sigma_1^2/\sigma_2^2 = 1$	$H_0: \sigma_1^2/\sigma_2^2 \leq 1$	$H_0: \sigma_1^2/\sigma_2^2 \geq 1$
$H_A: \sigma_1^2/\sigma_2^2 \neq 1$	$H_A: \sigma_1^2/\sigma_2^2 > 1$	$H_A: \sigma_1^2/\sigma_2^2 < 1$

A two-tailed test determines whether the two population variances are different. As noted earlier, the condition $\sigma_1^2 = \sigma_2^2$ is equivalent to $\sigma_1^2/\sigma_2^2 = 1$. A right-tailed test examines whether σ_1^2 is greater than σ_2^2, whereas a left-tailed test examines whether σ_1^2 is less than σ_2^2.

EXAMPLE 11.7

Let's revisit Example 11.6.

a. Specify the competing hypotheses in order to determine whether or not the variances in the two statistics sections differ.

b. Using the 95% confidence interval, what is the conclusion to the test?

SOLUTION:

a. Since we want to determine if the variances differ between the two sections, we formulate a two-tailed hypothesis test as

$$H_0: \sigma_1^2/\sigma_2^2 = 1$$
$$H_A: \sigma_1^2/\sigma_2^2 \neq 1$$

b. We calculated the 95% confidence interval for the ratio of the two variances ranging from 0.13 to 1.40. We note that this interval contains the value one; thus, we do not reject H_0. The sample data do not suggest that the variances between the two statistics sections differ at the 5% significance level.

Now we use the four-step procedure outlined in Chapter 9 to implement one- or two-tailed hypothesis tests. We use the ratio of the values of the sample variances s_1^2/s_2^2 to conduct hypothesis tests regarding the ratio of the population variances σ_1^2/σ_2^2. The resulting $F_{(df_1, df_2)}$ test is valid if the sample variances are computed from independently drawn samples from normally distributed populations.

TEST STATISTIC FOR σ_1^2/σ_2^2

The value of the **test statistic** for the hypothesis test of the **ratio of two population variances σ_1^2/σ_2^2** is computed as

$$F_{(df_1, df_2)} = s_1^2/s_2^2,$$

where for samples of size n_1 and n_2, $df_1 = n_1 - 1$ and $df_2 = n_2 - 1$.

We should point out that a left-tailed test can easily be converted into a right-tailed test by interchanging the variances of the two populations. For instance, we can convert H_0: $\sigma_1^2/\sigma_2^2 \geq 1$ versus H_A: $\sigma_1^2/\sigma_2^2 < 1$ into H_0: $\sigma_2^2/\sigma_1^2 \leq 1$ versus H_A: $\sigma_2^2/\sigma_1^2 > 1$.

PLACING THE LARGER SAMPLE VARIANCE IN THE NUMERATOR

It is preferable to place the larger sample variance in the numerator of the $F_{(df_1, df_2)}$ statistic. The resulting value allows us to focus only on the right tail of the distribution.

In other words, we define the hypotheses such that the resulting test statistic is computed as s_1^2/s_2^2 when $s_1^2 > s_2^2$ and as s_2^2/s_1^2 when $s_2^2 > s_1^2$; the degrees of freedom are adjusted accordingly. This saves us the additional work required to find the probability under the left tail of the $F_{(df_1, df_2)}$ distribution.

EXAMPLE 11.8

Let's again visit the case introduced at the beginning of this chapter. Investment counselor Rebecca Johnson wonders if the Metals fund is significantly riskier than the Income fund. We assume that returns are normally distributed to implement the test at the 5% significance level using the critical value approach. For reference, we repeat the sample descriptive measures of the two funds:

Metals fund: $\bar{x}_1 = 24.65\%$, $s_1 = 37.13\%$, and $n_1 = 10$

Income fund: $\bar{x}_2 = 8.51\%$, $s_2 = 11.07\%$, and $n_2 = 10$

SOLUTION: We define the population variance as the measure of risk and let σ_1^2 and σ_2^2 denote the population variances of the Metals and the Income funds, respectively. Since we wish to determine whether the variance of the Metals fund is greater than that of the Income fund, we specify the competing hypotheses as

$$H_0: \sigma_1^2/\sigma_2^2 \leq 1$$
$$H_A: \sigma_1^2/\sigma_2^2 > 1$$

Note that this specification is appropriate since $s_1 = 37.13\%$ is greater than $s_2 = 11.07\%$. Had s_2 been greater, we would have specified the hypotheses in terms of σ_2^2/σ_1^2 instead of σ_1^2/σ_2^2.

The F test is valid because the underlying populations are assumed to be normally distributed. We compute the value of the test statistic as

$$F_{(df_1, df_2)} = F_{(9,9)} = \frac{s_1^2}{s_2^2} = \frac{(37.13)^2}{(11.07)^2} = 11.25.$$

Using $\alpha = 0.05$, we find the critical value of this right-tailed test as $F_{\alpha,(df_1,df_2)} = F_{0.05,(9,9)} = 3.18$. The decision rule is to reject the null hypothesis if $F_{(df_1,df_2)} = F_{(9,9)}$ exceeds 3.18. (For a two-tailed test, the critical value would be $F_{\alpha/2,(df_1,df_2)} = F_{0.025,(9,9)} = 4.03$).

We reject the null hypothesis because the value of the test statistic falls in the rejection region ($F_{(9,9)} = 11.25$ exceeds the critical value $F_{0.05,(9,9)} = 3.18$). At the 5% significance level, the variance of the Metals fund is significantly greater than the variance of the Income fund. Therefore, we can conclude that the Metals fund is riskier than the Income fund.

Calculating the p-Value for the $F_{(df_1,df_2)}$ Statistic Using Excel

In Example 11.8 we calculated the value of the test statistic as $F_{(9,9)} = 11.25$. Therefore, the p-value of this right-tailed test is given by $P(F_{(9,9)} \geq 11.25)$. Since the value 11.25 is not listed in the F table, we can only state that this probability is less than 0.01.

As in the case of the t_{df} and the χ_{df}^2 distributions, we can easily get exact probabilities for the $F_{(df_1,df_2)}$ distribution with Excel. For instance, we can use the function option on Excel to determine the exact probability of $P(F_{(9,9)} > 11.25)$ by following these commands.

A. From the menu select **Formulas > Insert Function > F.DIST.RT**. This command returns the p-value for a right-tailed test. (For a two-tailed test, we would multiply this probability by two.)

B. See Figure 11.8. Supply the following three arguments in the dialog box:

- **X** is the value of the test statistic, or $F_{(df_1,df_2)}$. We enter 11.25.

- **Deg_freedom1** are the numerator degrees of freedom associated with the test statistic. We enter 9.

- **Deg_freedom2** are the denominator degrees of freedom associated with the test statistic. We enter 9.

C. Click **OK**.

FIGURE 11.8 F.DIST.RT dialog box

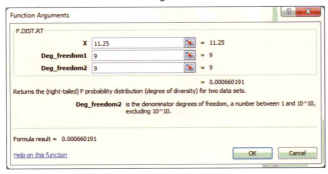

Excel returns the probability of 0.0007. Again, using the *p*-value approach and a significance level of 5%, we reject the null hypothesis and conclude that the variance of the Metals fund is greater than the variance of the Income fund.

Using the F.TEST Function on Excel

If we have access to the raw data, rather than summary statistics, then Excel's function F.TEST returns the *p*-value for a two-tailed test. Table 11.4 shows the annual total return data for the Metal and Income funds for the years 2000–2009; the data, labeled ***Fund Returns***, can also be found on the text website.

TABLE 11.4 Annual Total Returns (in percent) for Metals and Income Funds

Year	Metals	Income
2000	−7.34	4.07
2001	18.33	6.52
2002	33.35	9.38
2003	59.45	18.62
2004	8.09	9.44
2005	43.79	3.12
2006	34.30	8.15
2007	36.13	5.44
2008	−56.02	−11.37
2009	76.46	31.77

Source: www.finance.yahoo.com

A. **Open** the *Fund Returns* data from the text website into an Excel spreadsheet.

B. From the menu choose **Formulas > Insert Function > F.TEST**.

C. See Figure 11.9. In the FTEST dialog box, we select the data for the Metals fund for **Array1** and then select the data for the Income fund for **Array2**.

D. Click **OK**.

Excel returns 0.0013. This is the *p*-value for a two-tailed test. Since we conducted a one-tailed test, we divide this value by two (0.0013/2 = 0.0007), arriving at the *p*-value that we found earlier.

FIGURE 11.9 F.TEST dialog box

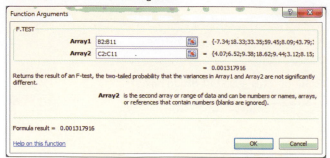

SYNOPSIS OF INTRODUCTORY CASE

Vanguard's Precious Metals and Mining fund (Metals) and Fidelity's Strategic Income fund (Income) were two top-performing mutual funds for the years 2000 through 2009. At first glance, the Metals fund seems attractive since its average return is greater than the average return for the Income fund (24.65% > 8.51%); however, the average return does not incorporate the risk of investing. Variance and standard deviation tend to be the most common measure of risk with financial data. An analysis of the variance and standard deviation of the returns for these funds provides additional relevant information. For the Metals fund, the 95% confidence interval for the population standard deviation of the return is between 25.54% and 67.79%, while the corresponding interval for the Income fund is between 7.61% and 20.21%. Since the intervals do not overlap, we may infer that the risk for the two funds is different with 95% confidence. Further testing reveals that the risk of the Metals fund is greater than the risk of the Income fund at the 5% significance level.

Two more hypothesis tests are also conducted. The first test examines whether the standard deviation of the Metals fund exceeds 25%. At the 5% significance level, the sample data suggest that the standard deviation is significantly greater than 25%. The second test investigates whether or not the standard deviation of the Income fund differs from 8.5%, the risk inherent in similar funds. At the 5% significance level, the results suggest that the standard deviation is not significantly different from 8.5%. These results stress the importance of analyzing the variance and standard deviation of the returns of an asset—an examination of only the average return of the two funds would be incomplete.

EXERCISES 11.2

Concepts

19. Find the value *x* for which:
    a. $P(F_{(4,8)} \geq x) = 0.025$
    b. $P(F_{(4,8)} \geq x) = 0.05$
    c. $P(F_{(4,8)} < x) = 0.025$
    d. $P(F_{(4,8)} < x) = 0.05$

20. Use the *F* table to approximate the following probabilities.
    a. $P(F_{(10,8)} \geq 3.35)$
    b. $P(F_{(10,8)} < 0.42)$
    c. $P(F_{(10,8)} \geq 4.30)$
    d. $P(F_{(10,8)} < 0.26)$

21. Construct a 90% interval estimate of the ratio of the population variances using the following results from two independently drawn samples from normally distributed populations.

    Sample 1: $\bar{x}_1 = 157$, $s_1^2 = 23.2$, and $n_1 = 9$

    Sample 2: $\bar{x}_2 = 148$, $s_2^2 = 19.9$, and $n_2 = 8$

22. Consider the following measures based on independently drawn samples from normally distributed populations:

    Sample 1: $s_1^2 = 220$, and $n_1 = 20$

    Sample 2: $s_2^2 = 196$, and $n_2 = 15$

a. Construct a 95% interval estimate of the ratio of the population variances.

b. Using the computed confidence interval, test if the ratio of the population variances differs from one at the 5% significance level. Explain.

23. Consider the following competing hypotheses and relevant summary statistics:

$$H_0: \sigma_1^2/\sigma_2^2 = 1$$
$$H_A: \sigma_1^2/\sigma_2^2 \neq 1$$

Sample 1: $\bar{x}_1 = 48.5$, $s_1^2 = 18.7$, and $n_1 = 10$

Sample 2: $\bar{x}_2 = 50.2$, $s_2^2 = 12.9$, and $n_2 = 8$

Assume that the two populations are normally distributed.

a. Using the p-value approach, conduct this hypothesis test at the 5% significance level.

b. Confirm your conclusions by using the critical value approach.

24. Consider the following competing hypotheses and relevant summary statistics:

$$H_0: \sigma_1^2/\sigma_2^2 \leq 1$$
$$H_A: \sigma_1^2/\sigma_2^2 > 1$$

Sample 1: $s_1^2 = 935$ and $n_1 = 14$

Sample 2: $s_2^2 = 812$ and $n_2 = 11$

Use the critical value approach to conduct this hypothesis test at the 5% significance level. State your assumptions.

25. Consider the following competing hypotheses and relevant summary statistics:

$$H_0: \sigma_1^2/\sigma_2^2 \geq 1$$
$$H_A: \sigma_1^2/\sigma_2^2 < 1$$

Sample 1: $s_1^2 = 1,315$ and $n_1 = 17$

Sample 2: $s_2^2 = 1,523$ and $n_2 = 19$

Conduct this left-tailed hypothesis test at the 5% significance level. You may want to first convert the above left-tailed test into a right-tailed test by switching the two variances. State your assumptions.

Applications

26. A firm has just developed a new cost-reducing technology for producing a certain replacement part for automobiles. Since a replacement part must be produced within close specifications in order for it to be acceptable to customers, the new technology's specifications must not deviate drastically from the older version. Suppose the sample variance for 15 parts produced using the older version is $s_1^2 = 0.35$, while the sample variance for 15 parts produced using the new technology is $s_2^2 = 0.48$. Assume that the two samples are drawn independently from normally distributed populations.

a. Develop the hypotheses to test whether the population variances differ.

b. Calculate the appropriate test statistic.

c. Using the critical value approach, determine the decision rule at the 5% significance level.

d. Can you conclude that the variances are different? Given that all other criteria are satisfied, should the company adopt the new technology?

27. Two basketball players on a school team are working hard on consistency of their performance. In particular, they are hoping to bring down the variance of their scores. The coach believes that the players are not equally consistent in their games. Over a 10-game period, the scores of these two players are shown below. Assume that the two samples are drawn independently from normally distributed populations.

| Player 1 | 13 | 15 | 12 | 18 | 14 | 15 | 11 | 13 | 11 | 16 |
| Player 2 | 11 | 21 | 18 | 9 | 20 | 11 | 13 | 11 | 19 | 8 |

a. Develop the hypotheses to test whether the players differ in consistency.

b. Use the critical value approach to test the coach's claim at $\alpha = 0.05$.

28. The following table shows the annual returns (in percent) for Fidelity's Electronic and Utilities funds.

Year	Electronic	Utilities
2005	13.23	9.36
2006	1.97	32.33
2007	2.77	21.03
2008	−50.00	−35.21
2009	81.65	14.71

Source: www.finance.yahoo.com.

Using the critical value approach, test if the population variances differ at the 5% significance level. State your assumptions.

29. (Use Excel) Nike's total revenues (in millions of $) for the Asian and Latin American regions for the years 2005 through 2009 are as follows:

	2005	2006	2007	2008	2009
Asia	1,897	2,054	2,296	2,888	3,322
Latin America	696	905	967	1,165	1,285

Source: Nike Online Annual Reports.

a. Specify the competing hypothesis in order to test whether the variance in revenues is greater in Asia than in Latin America.

b. Use Excel to calculate descriptive statistics and the relevant test statistic.

c. Use Excel's F.DIST function to calculate the p-value.

d. At $\alpha = 0.01$ what is your conclusion?

30. FILE (Use Excel) The monthly closing stock prices (rounded to the nearest dollar) for Starbucks Corp. and Panera Bread Co. for the first six months of 2010 are reported in the following table. The data are also available on the text website, labeled **Monthly Stock Prices**.

Month	Starbucks Corp.	Panera Bread Co.
January 2010	$22	$71
February 2010	23	73
March 2010	24	76
April 2010	26	78
May 2010	26	81
June 2010	24	75

Source: www.finance.yahoo.com.

a. State the null and the alternative hypotheses in order to determine if the variance of price differs for the two firms.

b. What assumption regarding the population is necessary to implement this step?

c. Use Excel's F.TEST function to calculate the *p*-value.

d. At $\alpha = 0.05$ what is your conclusion?

31. FILE (Use Excel) A variety of packaging solutions exist for products that must be kept within a specific temperature range. Cold chain distribution is particularly useful in the food and pharmaceutical industries. A packaging company is trying out a new packaging material that might reduce the variation of temperatures in the box. It is believed that the temperature in the box follows a normal distribution with both packaging materials. Inspectors randomly select 16 boxes of new and old packages, 24 hours after they

are sealed for shipment, and report the temperatures in degrees Celsius. We assume that the two samples are drawn independently from normally distributed populations. A portion of the data is shown below; the complete data, labeled **Packaging**, are available on the text website.

New Package	Old Package
3.98	5.79
4.99	6.42
⋮	⋮
4.95	5.95

a. State the appropriate hypotheses to test whether or not the new packaging material reduces the variation of temperatures in the box.

b. Use Excel's F.TEST function to calculate the *p*-value.

c. Make a conclusion at the 5% significance level.

32. FILE Access the data labeled **Rentals** on the text website that includes monthly rents of a two-bedroom apartment in two campus towns: Ann Arbor, Michigan, and Davis, California. Davis, California, is known to have higher rents than Ann Arbor, Michigan; however, it is not clear if it also has higher variability in rents. At a 5% significance level, determine if the variance of rent in Davis, California, is more than that of Ann Arbor, Michigan. State your assumptions clearly.

WRITING WITH STATISTICS

With the high cost of gasoline, many environmental groups and politicians are suggesting a return to the federal 55-mile-per-hour speed limit on America's highways. They argue that a lower national speed limit will improve traffic safety, save fuel, and reduce greenhouse emissions. Elizabeth Connolly believes that more focus should be put on the variability of speed limits as opposed to average speed limits. She points to recent research that suggests that increases in speed variability decrease overall safety. Specifically, Elizabeth feels that traffic accidents are more likely to occur when the standard deviation of speeds exceeds 5 mph. She records the speeds of 40 cars from a highway with a speed limit of 55 mph (Highway 1) and the speeds of 40 cars from a highway with a speed limit of 65 mph (Highway 2). A portion of the data are shown in Table 11.5; the complete data, labeled **Highway Speeds**, are available on the text website.

TABLE 11.5 Speed of Cars from Highway 1 and Highway 2

FILE Highway 1 (55-mph limit)	Highway 2 (65-mph limit)
60	70
55	65
⋮	⋮
52	65

Elizabeth would like to use the above sample information to:

1. Determine, at the 5% significance level, whether the standard deviation on the 55-mph highway exceeds 5 mph.

2. Determine, at the 5% significance level, whether the variability on the 55-mph highway is more than the variability on the 65-mph highway.

Increasing gas prices are prompting conservationists to lobby for a return to the federal 55-mile-per-hour (mph) speed limit on America's highways. Advocates point to potential money and fuel savings, noting that fuel efficiency worsens at speeds above 60 mph. It is not clear, however, if the return to 55 mph will increase traffic safety. Many believe that traffic safety is based on the variability of the speed rather than the average speed that people are driving—the more variation in speed, the more dangerous the roads.

In this report the variability of speeds on two highways is compared. The sample consists of the speeds of 40 cars recorded on a highway with a 55-mph speed limit (Highway 1) and the speeds of 40 cars recorded on a highway with a 65-mph speed limit (Highway 2). Table 11.A shows the most relevant descriptive measures for the analysis.

TABLE 11.A Summary Measures for Highway 1 and Highway 2

	Highway 1 (55-mph speed limit)	Highway 2 (65-mph speed limit)
Mean	56.60	66.00
Standard deviation	6.98	3.00
Number of cars	40	40

While it is true that cars travel at a slower speed, on average, on Highway 1 (56.60 mph < 66.00 mph), the variability of speeds is greater on Highway 1 as measured by standard deviation (6.98 mph > 3.00 mph).

Two hypothesis tests are conducted. The first test examines whether or not the standard deviation on Highway 1 is greater than 5 mph at the 5% significance level, or alternatively $\sigma^2 > 5^2$. The second test analyzes whether the standard deviation on Highway 1 is significantly greater than the standard deviation on Highway 2, or alternatively $\sigma_1^2/\sigma_2^2 > 1$. The results of the tests are summarized in Table 11.B.

TABLE 11.B Competing Hypotheses, Test Statistics, and p-Values

Hypotheses	Test Statistic	p-Value
$H_0: \sigma^2 \le 5^2$ $H_A: \sigma^2 > 5^2$	Highway 1: $\chi_{39}^2 = \dfrac{(n-1)s^2}{\sigma^2}, \dfrac{(40-1)(6.98)^2}{(5)^2} = 76.00$	0.00
$H_0: \sigma_1^2/\sigma_2^2 \le 1$ $H_A: \sigma_1^2/\sigma_2^2 > 1$	$F_{(39,39)} = \dfrac{s_1^2}{s_2^2} = \dfrac{(6.98)^2}{(3.00)^2} = 5.41$	0.00

When testing whether or not the standard deviation is greater than 5 mph on Highway 1, a test statistic of 76.00 is obtained. Given its p-value of 0.00, the null hypothesis regarding the population variance is rejected at any reasonable level of significance. In other words, the sample data suggest that the standard deviation is significantly greater than 5 mph on Highway 1. With a test statistic of 5.41 and a corresponding p-value of 0.00, the second hypothesis test reveals that the variance for Highway 1 is significantly greater than the variance for Highway 2.

American drivers love to drive fast, which explains why safety advocates and conservationists are losing the long-running debate over lowering highway speed limits. While a 55-mph limit will save fuel and reduce greenhouse emissions, it is still an open question as to whether it will also enhance safety. If traffic safety is based on the variability of the speeds that people are driving rather than the average speed, then the data suggest that a return to a federal 55-mph speed limit may not necessarily enhance safety.

Conceptual Review

LO 11.1   **Discuss features of the χ^2 distribution.**

The **χ^2 distribution** is characterized by a family of distributions, where each distribution depends on its particular degrees of freedom df. It is common, therefore, to refer to it as the χ^2_{df} distribution. It is positively skewed with values ranging from zero to infinity. As the df grow larger, the χ^2_{df} distribution tends to the normal distribution.

LO 11.2   **Construct a confidence interval for the population variance.**

The sample variance S^2 is a **point estimator** of the population variance σ^2. Statistical inferences regarding σ^2 are based on the χ^2_{df} distribution. A $100(1 - \alpha)\%$ **confidence interval** of σ^2 is computed as $\left[\frac{(n-1)s^2}{\chi^2_{\alpha/2,df}}, \frac{(n-1)s^2}{\chi^2_{1-\alpha/2,df}} \right]$. This formula is based on the requirement that s^2 is computed using a random sample drawn from a normally distributed population.

LO 11.3   **Conduct a hypothesis test for the population variance.**

The value of the **test statistic** for the **hypothesis test of σ^2** is computed as $\chi^2_{df} = \frac{(n-1)s^2}{\sigma_0^2}$, where σ_0^2 is the hypothesized value of the population variance. We apply the four-step procedure to conduct hypothesis tests using the p-value or the critical value approaches.

LO 11.4   **Discuss features of the F distribution.**

The **F distribution** is also characterized by a family of distributions; however, each distribution depends on *two* degrees of freedom: the numerator degrees of freedom df_1 and the denominator degrees of freedom df_2. It is common to refer to it as the $F_{(df_1,df_2)}$ distribution. The $F_{(df_1,df_2)}$ distribution is positively skewed with values ranging from zero to infinity, but becomes increasingly symmetric as df_1 and df_2 increase.

LO 11.5   **Construct a confidence interval for the ratio of two population variances.**

The ratio of the sample variances S_1^2/S_2^2 is a **point estimator** of the ratio of the population variances σ_1^2/σ_2^2.

Statistical inferences regarding σ_1^2/σ_2^2 are based on the $F_{(df_1,df_2)}$ distribution. A $100(1 - \alpha)\%$ **confidence interval** of σ_1^2/σ_2^2 is computed as $\left[\left(\frac{s_1^2}{s_2^2} \right) \frac{1}{F_{\alpha/2,(df_1,df_2)}}, \left(\frac{s_1^2}{s_2^2} \right) F_{\alpha/2,(df_2,df_1)} \right]$. This formula is based on the assumption that s_1^2 and s_2^2 are computed using independently drawn samples from two normally distributed populations.

LO 11.6   **Conduct a hypothesis test for the ratio of two population variances.**

The value of the **test statistic** for the **hypothesis test of σ_1^2/σ_2^2** is computed as $F_{(df_1,df_2)} = s_1^2/s_2^2$, with $df_1 = n_1 - 1$ and $df_2 = n_2 - 1$. It is assumed that s_1^2 and s_2^2 are based on independently drawn samples from two normally distributed populations with $\sigma_1^2/\sigma_2^2 = 1$. We apply the four-step procedure to conduct hypothesis tests using the p-value or the critical value approaches.

It is preferable to define the hypotheses such that the resulting test statistic is computed as $F_{(df_1,df_2)} = s_1^2/s_2^2$ when $s_1^2 > s_2^2$ and as $F_{(df_2,df_1)} = s_2^2/s_1^2$ when $s_2^2 > s_1^2$. This saves us the additional work required to calculate the probability in the left tail of the $F_{(df_1,df_2)}$ distribution.

33. A replacement part for a machine must be produced within close specifications in order for it to be acceptable to customers. A production process is considered to be working properly as long as the variance in the lengths of the parts does not exceed 0.05 squared-units. Suppose the sample variance computed from 30 parts turns out to be $s^2 = 0.07$. Use this sample evidence to test if the production specification is not being met at a 5% level of significance.

34. A consumer advocacy group is concerned about the variability in the cost of a generic drug. There is cause for concern if the variance of the cost exceeds 5 $(\$)^2$. The group surveys seven local pharmacies and obtains the following prices (in $) for a particular generic drug: 32, 36, 38, 32, 40, 31, 34.

    a. Use the p-value approach to test if there is a cause for concern for the consumer group at a 1% significance level.

    b. What assumption regarding the generic drug prices was made in this analysis?

35. A financial analyst maintains that the risk, measured by the variance, of investing in emerging markets is more than 280(%)^2. Data on 20 stocks from emerging markets revealed the following sample results: $\bar{x} = 12.1(\%)$ and $s^2 = 361(\%)^2$. Assume that the returns are normally distributed.

    a. Specify the competing hypotheses to test the analyst's claim.

    b. What is the value of the test statistic?

    c. At $\alpha = 0.01$ specify the critical value(s).

    d. Is the financial analyst's claim supported by the data?

36. **FILE** (Use Excel) The following table presents the returns of Fidelity's Select Automotive Fund; the data are also available on the text website, labeled **Automotive**. This mutual fund invests primarily in companies engaged in the manufacturing, the marketing, or the sales of automobiles, trucks, specialty vehicles, parts, tires, and related services.

Year	Fidelity Select Automotive Fund
2001	22.82%
2002	−6.48
2003	43.53
2004	7.11
2005	−1.75
2006	13.33
2007	0.01
2008	−61.20
2009	122.28

Source: http://biz.yahoo.com.

    a. State the null and the alternative hypotheses in order to test whether the standard deviation is greater than 35%.

    b. What assumption regarding the population is necessary to implement this step?

    c. Calculate the value of the relevant test statistic.

    d. Use Excel's function (either CHISQ.DIST.RT or CHISQ.DIST) to calculate the p-value.

    e. At $\alpha = 0.05$ what is your conclusion?

37. John Daum and Chris Yin are star swimmers at a local college. They are preparing to compete at the NCAA Division II national championship meet, where they both have a good shot at earning a medal in the men's 100-meter freestyle event. The coach feels that Chris is not as consistent as John, even though they clock about the same average time. In order to determine if the coach's concern is valid, you clock their time in the last 20 runs and compute a standard deviation of 0.85 second for John and 1.20 seconds for Chris. It is fair to assume that clock time is normally distributed for both John and Chris.

    a. Specify the hypotheses to test if the variance of time for John is smaller than that of Chris.

    b. Carry out the test at the 10% level of significance.

    c. Who has a better likelihood of breaking the record at the meet? Explain.

38. Annual growth rates for individual firms in the toy industry tend to fluctuate dramatically, depending on consumers' tastes and current fads. Consider the following growth rates (in percent) for two companies in this industry, Hasbro and Mattel.

Year	2005	2006	2007	2008	2009
Hasbro	3.0	2.1	21.8	4.8	1.2
Mattel	1.5	9.1	5.7	−0.1	−8.2

Source: Annual Reports for Hasbro, Inc. and Mattel, Inc.

    a. State the null and the alternative hypotheses in order to determine if the variance of growth rates differs for the two firms.

    b. What assumption regarding the population is necessary to implement this step?

    c. Specify the critical value(s) at $\alpha = 0.05$.

    d. What is your conclusion?

39. **FILE** (Use Excel) Barbara Dwyer, the manager at Lux Hotel, makes every effort to ensure that customers attempting to make phone reservations do not have to wait too long to speak with a reservation specialist. Since the hotel accepts phone reservations 24 hours a day, Barbara is especially interested in maintaining consistency in service. Barbara wants to determine if the variance of wait time in the early morning shift differs from that in the late morning shift. She uses the following independently drawn samples of wait time for phone reservations for both shifts for the analysis. The data can be found on the text website and are labeled **Wait Times**. Assume that wait times are normally distributed.

Shift	Wait Time (in seconds)							
Early Morning Shift: 12:00 am– 6:00 am	67	48	52	71	83	59	49	66
	57	68	60	66	82	63	64	83
	37	41	60	41	87	53	66	69
Late Morning Shift: 6:00 am– 12:00 pm	98	100	122	108	100	123	102	90
	125	121	120	128	123	94	128	113
	116	104	96	111	107	105	113	106

a. Specify the appropriate hypotheses to test if the variance of wait time in the early morning shift differs from that in the late morning shift.

b. Use Excel's F.TEST function to conduct the test at the 1% level of significance.

c. Does the variance of wait time in the early morning shift differ from that in the late afternoon shift?

40. **FILE** (Use Excel) Adidas revenues (in millions of €) in Asia and Latin America for the years 2005 through 2009 are shown in the accompanying table; the data, labeled **Adidas Revenues**, are also available on the text website.

	2005	2006	2007	2008	2009
Asia	1,523	2,020	2,254	2,662	2,614
Latin America	319	499	657	893	1,006

Source: *Adidas Online Annual Reports.*

a. Specify the competing hypothesis in order to test whether the variance in revenues is greater in Asia than in Latin America.

b. Use Excel to calculate the relevant test statistic.

c. Use Excel's F.TEST function to calculate the *p*-value.

d. At $\alpha = 0.05$ what is your conclusion?

CASE STUDIES

Case Study 11.1

Due to environmental concerns and the never-ending volatility of gas prices, drivers are becoming more concerned with their cars' gasoline consumption. Cameron White, a research analyst at a nonprofit organization, shares these concerns and wonders whether his car's gas consumption is as efficient as it was when he first bought the new car five years ago. Despite his best intentions, he has been a bit lax in his upkeep of the car and feels that this may adversely influence its performance. At the time he purchased the car, he was told that his car would average 29 miles per gallon (mpg) on highways with a standard deviation of 1 mpg. He records his car's mpg from the last 20 fill-ups and obtains the following values; these data labeled **Gasoline Consumption** are also available on the text website.

Data for Case Study 11.1 Gasoline Consumption: Miles per Gallon

26	28	25	29	27	28	30	27	29	28
26	28	29	27	26	27	28	25	28	27

In a report, use the above information to:

1. Construct a 95% confidence interval for the population standard deviation. Discuss any assumptions you made for the analysis.

2. Determine whether variability has significantly increased from the original standard deviation of 1 mpg at a 5% level of significance.

Case Study 11.2

Nicholas Grammas is an investment analyst examining the performance of two mutual funds with Janus Capital Group: The Janus Balanced Fund and the Janus Overseas Fund.

- The Janus Balanced Fund: This "core" fund consists of stocks and bonds and its goal is diversification. It has historically produced solid long-term returns through different market cycles.

- The Janus Overseas Fund: This fund invests in overseas companies based on their individual merits instead of their geography or industry sector.

The following table reports the annual returns (in percent) of these two funds over the past 10 years. These data, labeled **Janus Returns**, are also available on the text website.

Data for Case Study 11.2 Annual Total Return (%) History

FILE

Year	Janus Balanced Fund	Janus Overseas Fund
2000	−2.16	−18.57
2001	−5.04	−23.11
2002	−6.56	−23.89
2003	13.74	36.79
2004	8.71	18.58
2005	7.75	32.39
2006	10.56	47.21
2007	10.15	27.76
2008	−15.22	−52.75
2009	24.28	78.12

SOURCE: www.finance.yahoo.com.

In a report, use the above information to:

1. Describe the similarities and differences in these two funds' returns.
2. Examine whether the risk of one fund is different than the risk of the other fund at the 5% significance level. Discuss the assumptions made for the analysis.

Case Study 11.3

For decades, people have believed that boys are innately more capable than girls in math. In other words, due to the intrinsic differences in brains, boys are better suited for doing math than girls. Recent research challenges this stereotype, arguing that gender differences in math performance have more to do with culture than innate aptitude. In the U.S., for example, girls perform just as well on standardized math tests as boys. Others argue, however, that while the average may be the same, there is more variability in math ability for boys than girls, resulting in some boys with soaring math skills. A portion of representative data on math scores of boys and girls is shown below; the complete data, labeled **Math Scores**, are available on the text website.

Data for Case Study 11.3 Math Scores for Boys and Girls

FILE

Boys	Girls
74	83
89	76
⋮	⋮
66	74

In a report, use the above information to:

1. Construct and interpret 95% confidence intervals for the ratio of the variance of math scores for boys and for girls. Discuss the assumptions made for the analysis.
2. Determine at the 5% significance level if boys have more variability in math scores than girls.

12 Chi-Square Tests

CHAPTER

In this chapter we focus on the χ^2 (chi-square) distribution to develop statistical tests that compare observed data with what we would expect from a population with a specific distribution. Generally, the chi-square tests are used to assess two types of comparison. First, a *goodness-of-fit test* is commonly used with frequency data representing the various outcomes of a qualitative variable. For instance, we may want to substantiate a claim that market shares in the automotive industry have changed dramatically over the past 10 years. Whereas a goodness-of-fit test focuses on a single qualitative variable, a *test of independence* is used to compare two qualitative variables. For example, we may want to determine whether a person's gender influences his/her purchase of a product. We can also extend the goodness-of-fit test to determine whether it is reasonable to assume that sample data are drawn from a normal population. Since we use the normal distribution with quantitative data, we first convert the raw data into a frequency distribution, where each interval is now viewed as a category. Finally, we introduce the Jarque-Bera test, which allows us to test for normality using the data in their raw form.

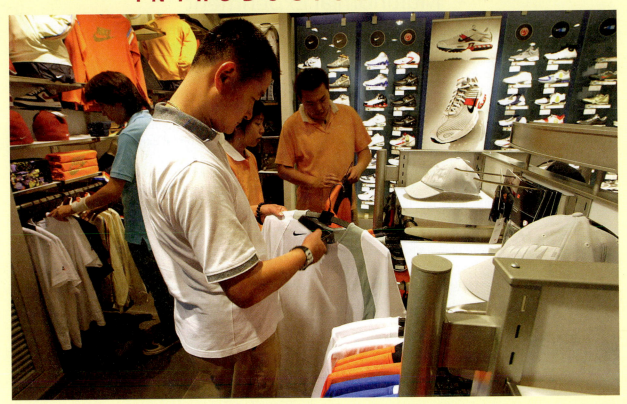

Sportswear Brands

In Chapter 4, we presented a case study in which Annabel Gonzalez, chief retail analyst at a marketing firm, studied the relationship between the brand name of compression garments in the sport-apparel industry and the age of the consumer. Specifically, she wanted to know whether the age of the consumer influenced the brand name purchased. She would like to conduct a formal test of independence between the age of the consumer and the brand name purchased.

Her initial feeling is that the Under Armour brand attracts a younger customer, whereas the more established companies, Nike and Adidas, draw an older clientele. She believes this information is relevant to advertisers and retailers in the sporting-goods industry, as well as to some in the financial community. Suppose she collects data on 600 recent purchases in the compression-gear market. The contingency table (cross-classified by age and brand name) from Chapter 4 is reproduced here as Table 12.1 for ease of exposition.

TABLE 12.1 Purchases of Compression Garments Based on Age and Brand Name

	Brand Name		
Age Group	Under Armour	Nike	Adidas
Under 35 years	174	132	90
35 years or older	54	72	78

Annabel wants to use the above sample information to:

1. Determine whether the two classifications (age and brand name) are dependent at the 5% significance level.
2. Discuss how the findings from the test for independence can be used.

A synopsis of this case will be provided at the end of Section 12.2.

12.1 Goodness-of-Fit Test for a Multinomial Experiment

LO 12.1

Conduct a goodness-of-fit test for a multinomial experiment.

The tests analyzed in this chapter are based on the χ^2 (chi-square) distribution that was discussed in Chapter 11. Recall that the distribution is characterized by a family of distributions, where each distribution depends on its particular degrees of freedom df. It is common to refer to it as the χ^2_{df} distribution.

In this section we examine whether two or more population proportions equal each other or any predetermined (hypothesized) set of values. Before conducting this test, we must first ensure that the random experiment satisfies the conditions of a **multinomial experiment**, which is simply a generalization of the binomial experiment first introduced in Chapter 5.

Recall that a binomial experiment, or a Bernoulli process, is a series of n identical trials of a random experiment, where each trial has only two possible outcomes, conventionally labeled "success" and "failure." For the binomial experiment, we generally denote the probability of success as p and the probability of failure as $1 - p$. Alternatively, we could let p_1 and p_2 represent these probabilities, where $p_1 + p_2 = 1$. Now let us denote the number of outcomes of an experiment by k. Essentially, the only difference between a binomial experiment and a multinomial experiment is that a multinomial experiment results in one of k possible outcomes, where $k \geq 3$; for a binomial experiment $k = 2$.

A MULTINOMIAL EXPERIMENT

A **multinomial experiment** consists of a series of n independent and identical trials of a random experiment, such that for each trial:

- There are k possible outcomes or categories, called cells.
- Each time we repeat the trial, the probability p_i that the outcome falls into a particular cell remains the same.
- The sum of the cell probabilities is one, that is, $p_1 + p_2 + \cdots + p_k = 1$.

Numerous random experiments fit the conditions of a multinomial experiment. For instance,

- As compared from the previous day, a stockbroker records whether the price of a stock rises, falls, or stays the same. This example has three possible outcomes ($k = 3$).
- A consumer rates service at a restaurant as excellent, good, fair, or poor ($k = 4$).
- The admissions office records which of the six business concentrations a student picks ($k = 6$).

When setting up the competing hypotheses for a multinomial experiment, we have essentially two choices. We can set all population proportions equal to the same specific value, or equivalently, equal to one another. For instance, if we want to judge on the basis of sample data whether the proportion of voters who favor four different candidates is the same, the competing hypotheses would take the following form:

$$H_0: p_1 = p_2 = p_3 = p_4 = 0.25$$
$$H_A: \text{Not all population proportions are equal to } 0.25.$$

Note that the hypothesized value under the null hypothesis is 0.25 because the population proportions must sum to one. We can also set each population proportion equal to a different predetermined (hypothesized) value. Suppose we want to determine whether 40% of the voters favor Candidate 1, 30% favor Candidate 2, 20% favor Candidate 3, and 10% favor Candidate 4. The competing hypotheses are formulated as

H_0: $p_1 = 0.40$, $p_2 = 0.30$, $p_3 = 0.20$, and $p_4 = 0.10$

H_A: At least one of the proportions is different from its hypothesized value.

When conducting a statistical test on a multinomial experiment, we take a random sample and determine whether the sample proportions are close enough to the hypothesized population proportions under the null hypothesis. For this reason, this type of test is called a **goodness-of-fit test**. Under the usual assumption that the null hypothesis is true, we derive the expected frequencies of the outcomes of a multinomial experiment and compare them with observed frequencies. The objective is to determine whether we can reject the null hypothesis in favor of the alternative hypothesis. To see how to conduct a goodness-of-fit test, consider the following example.

One year ago, the management at a restaurant chain surveyed its patrons to determine whether changes should be made in the menu. One question on the survey asked patrons to rate the quality of the restaurant's entrées. The percentages of the patrons responding Excellent, Good, Fair, or Poor are listed in the following table:

Excellent	Good	Fair	Poor
15%	30%	45%	10%

Based on responses to the overall survey, management decided to revamp the menu. Recently, the same question concerning the quality of entrées was asked of a random sample of 250 patrons. Their responses are shown below:

Excellent	Good	Fair	Poor
46	83	105	16

At the 5% significance level, we want to determine whether there has been any change in the population proportions calculated one year ago.

Since we want to determine whether the responses of the 250 patrons are consistent with the earlier proportions, we let the earlier population proportions denote the hypothesized probabilities for the test. Thus, we use p_1, p_2, p_3, and p_4 to denote the population proportions of those that responded Excellent, Good, Fair, or Poor, respectively, and construct the following competing hypotheses.

H_0: $p_1 = 0.15$, $p_2 = 0.30$, $p_3 = 0.45$, and $p_4 = 0.10$

H_A: At least one of the proportions is different from its hypothesized value.

The first step in calculating the test statistic is to calculate an expected frequency for each category. That is, we need to estimate the frequencies that we would expect to get if the null hypothesis is true. In general, in order to calculate the expected frequency e_i for category i we multiply the sample size n by the respective hypothesized value of the population proportion p_i. For example, consider the outcome Excellent. If H_0 is true, then we expect that 15% ($p_1 = 0.15$) of 250 patrons will find the quality of entrées to be excellent. Therefore, the expected frequency of Excellent responses is 37.5 ($= 250 \times 0.15$), whereas the corresponding observed frequency is 46. Expected frequencies for other responses are found similarly. Ultimately, when computing the value of the test statistic, we compare these expected frequencies to the frequencies we actually observe.

For a multinomial experiment with k categories, the test statistic follows the χ^2_{df} distribution with $k - 1$ degrees of freedom. The value of the test statistic is calculated as

$$\chi^2_{df} = \Sigma \frac{(o_i - e_i)^2}{e_i},$$

where o_i and $e_i = n \times p_i$ are the observed and expected frequency in the ith category, respectively.

Note: The test is valid so long as the expected frequencies in each category are five or more.

Table 12.2 shows the expected frequency e_i for each category. The condition that each expected frequency e_i must equal five or more is satisfied here. As we will see shortly, sometimes it is necessary to combine data from two or more categories to achieve this result.

TABLE 12.2 Calculation of Expected Frequency for Restaurant Example

	Hypothesized Proportion, p_i	Expected Frequency, $e_i = n \times p_i$
Excellent	0.15	$250 \times 0.15 = 37.5$
Good	0.30	$250 \times 0.30 = 75.0$
Fair	0.45	$250 \times 0.45 = 112.5$
Poor	0.10	$250 \times 0.10 = 25.0$
		$\Sigma e_i = 250$

As a check on the calculations, the sum of the expected frequencies Σe_i must equal the sample size n, which in this example equals 250. Once the expected frequencies are estimated, we are ready to compute the value of the test statistic.

The χ^2_{df} statistic measures how much the observed frequencies vary (or differ) from the expected frequencies. In particular, χ^2_{df} is computed as the sum of the standardized squared deviations. The smallest value that χ^2_{df} can assume is zero—this occurs when each observed frequency equals its expected frequency. Rejection of the null hypothesis occurs when χ^2_{df} is significantly greater than zero. As a result, these tests of hypotheses regarding multiple population proportions ($p_1, p_2, p_3, \ldots$) are always implemented as right-tailed tests. However, since the alternative hypothesis simply states that at least one of the proportions is not equal to its specified value in the null hypothesis, rejection of the null hypothesis does not indicate which proportion differs.

In this example, there are four categories ($k = 4$), so the degrees of freedom are equal to three. The value of the test statistic is calculated as

$$\chi^2_{df} = \chi^2_3 = \Sigma \frac{(o_i - e_i)^2}{e_i}$$

$$= \frac{(46 - 37.5)^2}{37.5} + \frac{(83 - 75)^2}{75} + \frac{(105 - 112.5)^2}{112.5} + \frac{(16 - 25)^2}{25}$$

$$= 1.93 + 0.85 + 0.50 + 3.24 = 6.52.$$

Since a goodness-of-fit test is a right-tailed test, the critical value with $\alpha = 0.05$ and $df = 3$ is found from the χ^2 (chi-square) table as $\chi^2_{\alpha,df} = \chi^2_{0.05,3} = 7.815$; we show a portion of the χ^2 table in Table 12.3 as a refresher. Hence, our decision rule is to reject H_0 if $\chi^2_3 > 7.815$.

Given that $\chi^2_3 = 6.52 < 7.815$, we decide not to reject H_0. We cannot conclude that the proportions differ from the ones from one year ago at the 5% significance level. Management may find this news disappointing in that the goal of the menu change was to improve

TABLE 12.3 Portion of the χ^2 table

df	Area in Upper Tail, α									
	0.995	0.990	0.975	0.950	0.900	0.100	0.050	0.025	0.010	0.005
1	0.000	0.000	0.001	0.004	0.016	2.706	3.841	5.024	6.635	7.879
2	0.010	0.020	0.051	0.103	0.211	4.605	5.991	7.378	9.210	10.597
3	0.072	0.115	0.216	0.352	0.584	6.251	**7.815**	9.348	11.345	12.838

customer satisfaction. Responses to other questions on the survey may shed more light on whether the goals of the menu change met or fell short of expectations.

Using Excel to Calculate *p*-values

As usual, we can conduct the above hypothesis test by using the *p*-value approach to hypothesis testing rather than the critical value approach, where the *p*-value is derived as $P(\chi_3^2 \geq 6.52)$. If we refer to Table 12.3, we see that 6.52 falls between 6.251 and 7.815 which allows us to conclude that the *p*-value is somewhere between 0.05 and 0.10. Using Excel, we can calculate an exact *p*-value by following these commands.

A. From the menu select **Formulas** > **Insert Function** > **CHISQ.DIST.RT**. This command returns the one-tailed probability of the χ_{df}^2 distribution.

B. See Figure 12.1. Supply the following two arguments in the dialog box:
  - **X** is the value of the test statistic, or χ_{df}^2. We enter 6.52.
  - **Deg_freedom** are the degrees of freedom associated with the test statistic. We enter 3.

C. Click **OK**.

FIGURE 12.1 CHISQ.DIST.RT dialog box for restaurant example

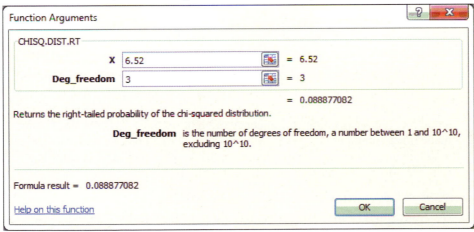

Excel returns the probability of 0.0889, which is equivalent to the *p*-value. Again, given a significance level of 5%, we are unable to reject the null hypothesis.

EXAMPLE 12.1

Table 12.4 lists the market share in 2010 of the five firms that manufacture a particular product. A marketing analyst wonders whether the market shares have changed since 2010. He surveys 200 customers. The last column of Table 12.4 shows the number of customers who recently purchased the product at each firm.

TABLE 12.4 Market Share of Five Firms

Firm	Market Share in 2010	Number of Recent Customers
1	0.40	70
2	0.32	60
3	0.24	54
4	0.02	10
5	0.02	6

a. Specify the competing hypotheses to test whether the market shares have changed since 2010.
b. Calculate the value of the test statistic.
c. At the 5% significance level, what is the critical value?
d. Have the market shares changed since 2010?

SOLUTION:

a. Let p_i denote the market share for the ith firm. In order to test whether the market shares have changed since 2010 we *initially* set up the competing hypotheses as

H_0: $p_1 = 0.40$, $p_2 = 0.32$, $p_3 = 0.24$, $p_4 = 0.02$, and $p_5 = 0.02$
H_A: At least one of the market shares is different from its hypothesized value.

b. The value of the test statistic is calculated as $\chi^2_{df} = \Sigma \frac{(o_i - e_i)^2}{e_i}$. The last column of Table 12.4 shows each firm's observed frequency o_i, so before applying the formula, we first calculate each firm's expected frequency e_i.

$$e_1 = 200 \times 0.40 = 80$$
$$e_2 = 200 \times 0.32 = 64$$
$$e_3 = 200 \times 0.24 = 48$$
$$e_4 = 200 \times 0.02 = 4 \Big\}$$
$$e_5 = 200 \times 0.02 = 4 \Big\} 8$$

We note that expected frequencies for firms 4 and 5 are less than five. The test is valid so long as the expected frequencies in each category are five or more. In order to achieve this result, we combine the expected frequencies for firms 4 and 5 to obtain a combined frequency of eight ($e_4 + e_5 = 8$). We could have made other combinations, say e_4 with e_1 and e_5 with e_2, but we preferred to maintain a category for the less dominant firms. After making this combination, we now re-specify the competing hypotheses as

H_0: $p_1 = 0.40$, $p_2 = 0.32$, $p_3 = 0.24$, and $p_4 = 0.04$
H_A: At least one of the market shares is different from its hypothesized value.

With $k = 4$ so that $df = 3$, we calculate the value of the test statistic as
$$\chi^2_3 = \Sigma \frac{(o_i - e_i)^2}{e_i} = \frac{(70 - 80)^2}{80} + \frac{(60 - 64)^2}{64} + \frac{(54 - 48)^2}{48} + \frac{(16 - 8)^2}{8}$$
$$= 1.25 + 0.25 + 0.75 + 8 = 10.25.$$

c. Given $\alpha = 0.05$, we find the critical value as $\chi^2_{0.05,3} = 7.815$; thus, the decision rule is to reject H_0 if $\chi^2_3 > 7.815$.

d. Since 10.25 is greater than 7.815, we reject the null hypothesis and conclude that at least one of the proportions (market shares) differs from its 2010 value.

As mentioned earlier, one limitation of this type of chi-square test is that we cannot tell which proportion differs. However, given the divergence between the observed and expected frequencies for the less dominant firms, it appears that they may be making some headway in this industry. Further testing can be conducted to see if this is the case.

Concepts

1. Consider a multinomial experiment with $n = 250$ and $k = 4$. The null hypothesis to be tested is $H_0: p_1 = p_2 = p_3 = p_4 = 0.25$. The observed frequencies resulting from the experiment are:

Category	1	2	3	4
Frequency	70	42	72	66

   a. Specify the alternative hypothesis.
   b. Calculate the value of the test statistic.
   c. What are the critical value and the decision rule at a 5% significance level?
   d. What is the conclusion to the hypothesis test?

2. Consider a multinomial experiment with $n = 400$ and $k = 3$. The null hypothesis is $H_0: p_1 = 0.60, p_2 = 0.25$, and $p_3 = 0.15$. The observed frequencies resulting from the experiment are:

Category	1	2	3
Frequency	250	94	56

   a. Define the alternative hypothesis.
   b. Calculate the value of the test statistic and approximate the p-value for the test.
   c. At the 5% significance level, what is the conclusion to the hypothesis test?

3. A multinomial experiment produced the following results:

Category	1	2	3	4	5
Frequency	57	63	70	55	55

   Can we conclude at the 1% significance level that the population proportions are not equal?

4. A multinomial experiment produced the following results:

Category	1	2	3
Frequency	128	87	185

   At the 1% significance level, can we reject $H_0: p_1 = 0.30$, $p_2 = 0.20$, and $p_3 = 0.50$?

Applications

5. You suspect that an unscrupulous employee at a casino has tampered with a die; that is, he is using a loaded die. In order to test this claim, you roll the die 200 times and obtain the following frequencies:

1	2	3	4	5	6
40	35	33	30	33	29

   a. Specify the null and alternative hypotheses in order to test your claim.
   b. Approximate the p-value.
   c. At a 10% significance level, can you conclude that the die is loaded?

6. A study conducted in September and October of 2010 found that fewer than half of employers who hired new college graduates last academic year plan to definitely do so again (*The Wall Street Journal*, November 29, 2010). Suppose the hiring intentions of the respondents were as follows:

Definitely hire	Likely to hire	Hire uncertain	Will not hire
37%	17%	28%	18%

   Six months later, a sample of 500 employers were asked their hiring intentions and gave the following responses:

Definitely hire	Likely to hire	Hire uncertain	Will not hire
170	100	120	110

   a. Specify the competing hypotheses to test whether the proportions from the initial study have changed.
   b. Calculate the value of the test statistic.
   c. At a 5% significance level, what is the critical value?
   d. What is the conclusion to the hypothesis test? Interpret your results.

7. A rent-to-own (RTO) agreement appeals to low-income and financially distressed consumers. It allows immediate access to merchandise, and by making all payments, the consumer acquires the merchandise. At the same time, goods can be returned at any point without penalty. Suppose a recent study documents that 65% of RTO contracts are returned, 30% are purchased, and the remaining 5% default. In order to test the validity of this claim, an RTO researcher looks at the transaction data of 420 RTO contracts, of which 283 are returned, 109 are purchased, and the rest defaulted.

   a. Set up the competing hypothesis to test whether the return, purchase, and default probabilities of RTO contracts differ from 0.65, 0.30, and 0.05, respectively.
   b. Compute the value of the test statistic.
   c. Conduct the test at the 5% level of significance and interpret the test results.

8. Despite Zimbabwe's shattered economy, with endemic poverty and widespread political strife and repression, thousands of people from overseas still head there every year (*BBC News*,

August 27, 2008). Main attractions include the magnificent Victoria Falls, the ruins of Great Zimbabwe, and herds of roaming wildlife. A tourism director claims that Zimbabwe visitors are equally represented by Europe, North America, and the rest of the world. Records show that of the 380 tourists who recently visited Zimbabwe, 135 were from Europe, 126 from North America, and 119 from the rest of the world.

a. A recent visitor to Zimbabwe believes that the tourism director's claim is wrong. Set up the competing hypotheses such that rejection of the null hypothesis supports the visitor's belief.

b. Use the critical value approach to conduct the test at a 5% level. Do the sample data support the visitor's belief?

c. Repeat the analysis with the p-value approach.

9. In 2003 *The World Wealth Report* first started publishing market shares of global millionaires (*The Wall Street Journal*, June 25, 2008). At this time, the distribution of the world's people worth $1 million or more was:

Region	Percentage of Millionaires
Europe	35.7%
North America	31.4%
Asia Pacific	22.9%
Latin America	4.3%
Middle East	4.3%
Africa	1.4%

Source: *The Wealth Report, 2003.*

A recent sample of 500 global millionaires produces the following results:

Region	Number of Millionaires
Europe	153
North America	163
Asia Pacific	139
Latin America	20
Middle East	20
Africa	5

a. Test whether the distribution of millionaires in 2011 is different from the distribution in 2003 at $\alpha = 0.05$.

b. Would the conclusion change if we tested it at $\alpha = 0.10$?

10. An Associated Press-GfK Poll shows that 38% of American drivers favor U.S. cars, while 33% prefer Asian brands, with the remaining 29% going for other foreign cars (www.msnbc.com, April 21, 2010). This highlights a significant improvement for U.S. automakers, especially when just a few years ago General Motors Co. and Chrysler LLC needed government help just to survive. Perhaps Americans are giving U.S. automakers a closer look due to their buffed-up offerings and Toyota's safety concerns. A researcher believes that the "buy American" sentiment may also be the result of watching an iconic American industry beaten down amid the Great Recession. He wonders whether the preferences for cars have changed since the Associated Press-GfK Poll. He surveys 200 Americans and finds that the number of respondents in the survey who prefer American, Asian, and other foreign cars are 66, 70, and 64, respectively. At the 5% significance level, can the researcher conclude that preferences have changed since the Associated Press-GfK Poll?

12.2 Chi-Square Test for Independence

LO **12.2**

Determine whether two classifications of a population are independent.

Recall from Chapter 4 that a contingency table is a useful tool when we want to examine or compare two qualitative variables.

CONTINGENCY TABLE

A **contingency table** generally shows frequencies for two qualitative or categorical variables, x and y, where each cell of the table represents a mutually exclusive combination of the pair of x and y values.

In this section, we use the data in a contingency table to conduct a hypothesis test that determines whether the classifications depend upon one another. Whereas a goodness-of-fit test examines a single qualitative variable, a **test of independence**—also called a **chi-square test of a contingency table**—analyzes the relationship between two qualitative variables. Many examples of the use of this test arise, especially in marketing, biomedical research, and the courts of law. For instance, a retailer may be trying to determine whether there is a relationship between the age of its clientele and where it chooses to advertise. Doctors might want to investigate whether or not losing weight through stomach surgery can extend the lives of severely obese patients. Or, one party in a discrimination lawsuit may be trying to show that gender and promotion are not independent events. All of these examples lend themselves to applications of the hypothesis test discussed in this section.

In the introductory case study, we are presented with a contingency table cross-classified by age and brand name. Specifically, we want to determine whether or not the age of a consumer influences his/her decision to buy a garment from Under Armour, Nike, or Adidas. We will conduct this test at the 5% significance level.

In general, the competing hypotheses for a statistical test of independence are formulated such that rejecting the null hypothesis leads to the conclusion that the two categories are dependent. Formally,

H_0: The two classifications are independent.

H_A: The two classifications are dependent.

Since the criteria upon which we classify the data are brand name and age, we write the competing hypotheses as

H_0: Age and brand name are independent.

H_A: Age and brand name are dependent.

Table 12.5 reproduces Table 12.1 of the introductory case. The category "age" has two possible outcomes: (1) under 35 years and (2) 35 years or older. The category "brand name" has three possible outcomes: (1) Under Armour, (2) Nike, and (3) Adidas. Each cell in this table represents an observed frequency o_{ij} where the subscript ij refers to the ith row and the jth column. Thus, o_{13} refers to the cell in the first row and the third column. Here, $o_{13} = 90$, or equivalently, 90 customers under 35 years of age purchased an Adidas product.

TABLE 12.5 Purchases of Compression Garments Based on Age and Brand Name

Age Group	Brand Name		
	Under Armour	Nike	Adidas
Under 35 years	174	132	90
35 years or older	54	72	78

Note that we have not specified a value under the null hypothesis. However, we will use the independence assumption postulated under the null hypothesis to derive an expected frequency for each cell from the sample data. In other words, we first estimate values in Table 12.5 as if no relationship exists between the age of a consumer and the brand name of the clothing purchased. Then we will compare these expected frequencies with the observed values to compute the value of the test statistic.

Calculating Expected Frequencies

For ease of exposition, we first denote each event or outcome of a classification using algebraic notation. We let events A_1 and A_2 represent the outcomes "under 35 years" and "35 years or older," respectively; events B_1, B_2, and B_3 stand for the outcomes Under Armour, Nike, and Adidas, respectively. We then determine the total values for each column and row in the contingency table. For instance, the total number of observations for Event A_1 is 396; this is obtained by summing the values in row A_1: 174, 132, and 90. Totals for the other rows and columns are shown in Table 12.6.

TABLE 12.6 Row and Column Totals

Age Group	Brand Name			Row Total
	B_1	B_2	B_3	
A_1	e_{11}	e_{12}	e_{13}	396
A_2	e_{21}	e_{22}	e_{23}	204
Column Total	228	204	168	600

Our goal is to calculate the expected frequency e_{ij} for each cell, where again the subscript ij refers to the ith row and the jth column. Thus, e_{13} refers to the cell in the first row and the third column, or the expected number of customers under 35 years of age who purchase an Adidas product.

Before we can arrive at the expected frequencies, we first calculate marginal row probabilities (the proportion of people under 35 years of age and those 35 years old or older) and marginal column probabilities (the proportion of people purchasing from each brand name). We calculate marginal row (column) probabilities by dividing the row (column) sum by the total sample size:

Marginal Row Probabilities:

$$P(A_1) = \frac{396}{600} \quad \text{and} \quad P(A_2) = \frac{204}{600}$$

Marginal Column Probabilities:

$$P(B_1) = \frac{228}{600}, P(B_2) = \frac{204}{600}, \text{and } P(B_3) = \frac{168}{600}$$

We can now calculate each cell probability by recalling from Chapter 4 the multiplication rule for independent events. That is, if two events are independent, say events A_1 and B_1 (our assumption under the null hypothesis), then their joint probability is

$$P(A_1 \cap B_1) = P(A_1)P(B_1) = \left(\frac{396}{600}\right)\left(\frac{228}{600}\right) = 0.2508.$$

Multiplying this joint probability by the sample size yields the expected frequency for cell e_{11}:

$$e_{11} = 600(0.2508) = 150.48.$$

CALCULATING EXPECTED FREQUENCIES FOR A TEST OF INDEPENDENCE

We use the following general formula to calculate the expected frequencies for each cell in a contingency table:

$$e_{ij} = \frac{(\text{Row } i \text{ total})(\text{Column } j \text{ total})}{\text{Sample Size}}$$

Applying the formula, we calculate all expected frequencies as

$$e_{11} = \frac{(396)(228)}{600} = 150.48 \quad e_{12} = \frac{(396)(204)}{600} = 134.64 \quad e_{13} = \frac{(396)(168)}{600} = 110.88$$

$$e_{21} = \frac{(204)(228)}{600} = 77.52 \quad e_{22} = \frac{(204)(204)}{600} = 69.36 \quad e_{23} = \frac{(204)(168)}{600} = 57.12$$

Table 12.7 shows the expected frequency e_{ij} of each cell. In order to satisfy subsequent assumptions, each expected frequency e_{ij} *must equal five or more*. This condition is satisfied here. As we saw in Example 12.1, it may be necessary to combine two or more rows or columns to achieve this result in other applications.

TABLE 12.7 Expected Frequencies for Contingency Table

Age Group	Brand Name			Row Total
	B_1	B_2	B_3	
A_1	150.48	134.64	110.88	396
A_2	77.52	69.36	57.12	204
Column Total	228	204	168	600

When conducting a test of independence, we apply the chi-square test statistic χ^2_{df}. Analogous to the discussion in Section 12.1, χ^2_{df} measures how much the observed frequencies vary (or differ) from the expected frequencies. The smallest value that χ^2_{df} can assume is zero—this occurs when each observed frequency equals its expected frequency. Thus, a test of independence is also implemented as *right-tailed test*.

TEST STATISTIC FOR A TEST OF INDEPENDENCE

For a contingency table with r rows and c columns, the test statistic follows the χ^2_{df} distribution with $df = (r - 1)(c - 1)$. The value of the test statistic is calculated as

$$\chi^2_{df} = \sum_i \sum_j \frac{(o_{ij} - e_{ij})^2}{e_{ij}},$$

where o_{ij} and e_{ij} are the observed and the expected frequencies in the ith row and the jth column, respectively.

Note: This test is valid only when the expected frequencies in each cell are five or more.

With two rows and three columns in the contingency table, degrees of freedom are calculated as $df = (r - 1)(c - 1) = (2 - 1)(3 - 1) = 2$. We apply the formula to compute the value of the test statistic as

$$\chi^2_2 = \frac{(174 - 150.48)^2}{150.48} + \frac{(132 - 134.64)^2}{134.64} + \frac{(90 - 110.88)^2}{110.88}$$
$$+ \frac{(54 - 77.52)^2}{77.52} + \frac{(72 - 69.36)^2}{69.36} + \frac{(78 - 57.12)^2}{57.12}$$
$$= 3.68 + 0.05 + 3.93 + 7.14 + 0.10 + 7.63 = 22.53.$$

Given a significance level of 5% and $df = 2$, we find the critical value as $\chi^2_{\alpha,df} = \chi^2_{0.05,2} = 5.991$. Hence, the decision rule is to reject H_0 if $\chi^2_2 > 5.991$. Since $\chi^2_2 = 22.53 > 5.991$, we reject H_0. At the 5% significance level, we conclude that the two qualitative variables are dependent; that is, there is a relationship between the age of a consumer and the brand name of the apparel purchased.

As usual, we can conduct the above hypothesis test by using the p-value approach to hypothesis testing rather than the critical value approach, where the p-value is derived as $P(\chi^2_2 \geq 22.53)$. As discussed earlier, we can calculate an exact p-value with Excel by selecting **Formulas > Insert Function > CHISQ.DIST.RT**. By inputting **X** = 22.53 and **Deg_freedom** = 2, Excel returns an almost zero p-value of 1.28×10^{-5}. Again, given a significance level of 5%, we reject the null hypothesis and conclude that age and brand name are not independent of one another.

EXAMPLE 12.2

A recent study of gender preferences among car shoppers found that men and women equally favor economy cars (www.cargurus.com, February 14, 2011). A marketing analyst doubts these results. He believes that a person's gender influences whether or not he/she purchases an economy car. He collects data on 400 recent car purchases cross-classified by gender and type of car (economy car versus noneconomy car). The results are shown in Table 12.8. At the 10% significance level, determine whether the sample data support the marketing analyst's claim.

TABLE 12.8 Car Preferences by Gender

	Economy Car	Noneconomy Car	Row Total
Female	50	60	110
Male	120	170	290
Column Totals	170	230	400

SOLUTION: In order to determine whether an economy car purchase depends on gender, we specify the competing hypotheses as

H_0: Gender and economy car purchase are independent.

H_A: Gender and economy car purchase are dependent.

The value of the test statistic for testing independence is calculated as $\chi^2_{df} = \sum_i \sum_j \frac{(o_{ij} - e_{ij})^2}{e_{ij}}$. Table 12.8 provides each cell's observed frequency o_{ij}, so before applying the formula, we first calculate each cell's expected frequency e_{ij}.

$$e_{11} = \frac{(110)(170)}{400} = 46.75 \qquad e_{12} = \frac{(110)(230)}{400} = 63.25$$

$$e_{21} = \frac{(290)(170)}{400} = 123.25 \qquad e_{22} = \frac{(290)(230)}{400} = 166.75$$

With two rows ($r = 2$) and two columns ($c = 2$) in the contingency table, we compute degrees of freedom as $df = (r - 1)(c - 1) = (2 - 1)(2 - 1) = 1$. The value of the test statistic is

$$\chi^2_1 = \frac{(50 - 46.75)^2}{46.75} + \frac{(60 - 63.25)^2}{63.25} + \frac{(120 - 123.25)^2}{123.25} + \frac{(170 - 166.75)^2}{166.75}$$
$$= 0.23 + 0.17 + 0.09 + 0.06 = 0.55.$$

Given $\alpha = 0.10$, we find the critical value as $\chi^2_{0.10,1} = 2.706$; Since $\chi^2_1 = 0.55 < 2.706$, we do not reject the null hypothesis. The sample data do not support the marketing analyst's claim that gender differences exist with respect to the purchase of an economy car.

SYNOPSIS OF INTRODUCTORY CASE

Under Armour pioneered clothing in the compression-gear market. Compression garments are meant to keep moisture away from a wearer's body during athletic activities in warm and cool weather. Under Armour has experienced exponential growth since the firm went public in November 2005 (*USA Today*, June 16, 2010); however, Nike and Adidas have aggressively entered the compression-gear market as well. An analysis is conducted to examine whether the age of the customer matters when making a purchase in the compression-gear market. This information is relevant not only for Under Armour and how the firm may focus its advertising efforts, but also to competitors and retailers in this market. Data were collected on 600 recent purchases in the compression-gear market; the data were then cross-classified by age group and brand name. A test of independence was conducted at the 5% significance level. The results suggest that a customer's age and the brand name purchased are dependent on one another. Given that age influences the brand name purchased, it is not surprising that Under Armour recently signed NFL quarterback Tom Brady (cnbc.com, October 6, 2010) to endorse its products, a move likely to attract a younger consumer. Brady had spent most of his career with Nike before breaking away to go with Under Armour.

EXERCISES 12.2

Concepts

11. Suppose you are conducting a test of independence. Specify the critical value under the following scenarios:

    a. rows = 3, columns = 3, and $\alpha = 0.10$.

    b. rows = 4, columns = 5, and $\alpha = 0.05$.

12. Suppose you are conducting a test of independence. Specify the critical value under the following scenarios:

    a. rows = 5, columns = 2, and $\alpha = 0.025$.

    b. rows = 3, columns = 5, and $\alpha = 0.01$.

13. Given the following contingency table, conduct a test of independence at the 5% significance level using (a) the critical value approach and (b) the *p*-value approach.

Category 2	Category 1	
	1	2
1	23	47
2	32	53

14. Given the following contingency table, conduct a test of independence at the 1% significance level using (a) the *p*-value approach and (b) the critical value approach.

Category 2	Category 1			
	1	2	3	4
1	120	112	100	110
2	127	115	120	124
3	118	115	110	124

Applications

15. According to an online survey by Harris Interactive for job site CareerBuilder.com (InformationWeek.com, September 27, 2007), more than half of IT workers say they have fallen asleep at work. Sixty-four percent of government workers admitted to falling asleep on the job. Assume that the following contingency table is representative of the survey results.

Slept on the Job?	Job Category	
	IT Professional	Government Professional
Yes	155	256
No	145	144

a. Specify the competing hypotheses to determine whether sleeping on the job is associated with job category.
b. Compute the value of the test statistic.
c. Approximate the *p*-value.
d. At the 5% significance level, can you conclude that sleeping on the job depends on job category?

16. A market researcher for an automobile company suspects differences in preferred color between male and female buyers. Advertisements targeted to different groups should take such differences into account, if they exist. The researcher examines the most recent sales information of a particular car that comes in three colors.

Color	Gender of Automobile Buyer	
	Male	Female
Silver	470	280
Black	535	285
Red	495	350

a. Specify the competing hypotheses to determine whether color preference depends on gender.
b. Compute the value of the test statistic.
c. Specify the critical value at the 1% significance level.
d. Does your conclusion suggest that the company should target advertisements differently for males versus females? Explain.

17. The following sample data reflect shipments received by a large firm from three different vendors.

Vendor	Defective	Acceptable
1	14	112
2	10	70
3	22	150

a. Specify the competing hypotheses to determine whether quality is associated with the source of the shipments.
b. Conduct the test at a 1% significance level using the critical value approach.
c. Should the firm be concerned about the source of the shipments? Explain.

18. According to a 2008 survey by the Pew Research Center, people in China are highly satisfied with their roaring economy and the direction of their nation (*USA Today*, July 22, 2008). Eighty-six percent of those who were surveyed expressed positive views of the way China is progressing and described the economic situation as good. A political analyst wants to know if this optimism among the Chinese depends on age. In an independent survey of 280 Chinese residents, the respondents are asked how happy they are with the direction that their country is taking. Their responses are tabulated below.

Age	Very Happy	Somewhat Happy	Not Happy
20 up to 40	23	50	18
40 up to 60	51	38	16
60 and above	19	45	20

a. Set up the appropriate hypotheses to test the claim that optimism regarding China's direction depends on the age of the respondent.
b. Use Excel to compute the *p*-value for the test.
c. At a 1% level of significance, can we infer that optimism among the Chinese is dependent on age?

19. A study by the Massachusetts Community & Banking Council found that blacks, and to a lesser extent, Latinos, remain largely unable to borrow money at the same interest rate as whites (*The Boston Globe*, February 28, 2008). The following contingency table shows representative data for the city

of Boston, cross-classified by race and type of interest rate received:

Race	Type of Interest Rate on Loan	
	High Interest Rate	Lower Interest Rate
Black	553	480
Latino	265	324
White	491	3701

At the 5% significance level, do the data indicate that the interest rate received on a loan is dependent on race? Provide the details.

20. Founded in February 2004, Facebook is a social utility that helps people communicate with their friends and family. In just six years, Facebook has acquired more than 500 million active users, of which 50% log on to Facebook in any given day. In a survey of 3,000 Facebook users, the designers looked at why Facebook users break up in a relationship (*The Wall Street Journal*, November 27–28, 2010).

Reasons for Breakup	Gender	
	Men	Women
Non-Approval	3%	4%
Distance	21%	16%
Cheating	18%	22%
Lost Interest	28%	26%
Other	30%	32%

Source: Internal survey of 3,000 Facebook users.

Suppose the survey consisted of 1,800 men and 1,200 women. Use the data to determine whether the reasons for breakup depend on gender at the 1% significance level. Provide the details.

12.3 Chi-Square Test for Normality

The goodness-of-fit test for a multinomial experiment can also be used to test the hypothesis that a population has a particular probability distribution. For instance, we can use this technique to determine whether the sample data fit the binomial or the Poisson distributions. However, due to its wide applicability, we focus on the normal distribution. We describe two chi-square tests for normality: the goodness-of-fit test and the Jarque-Bera test.

LO 12.3

Conduct a goodness-of-fit test for normality.

The Goodness-of-Fit Test for Normality

Suppose we want to test the claim that annual household income in a small Midwestern city is not normally distributed. We will use the representative data (in $1,000s) in Table 12.9 to test this claim at the 5% significance level; these data, labeled ***Household Income***, are also available on the text website.

TABLE 12.9 Household Income (in $1,000s)

FILE

90	15	85	54	62	38	38	55	62	210
19	38	57	78	98	42	19	62	66	90
25	38	14	65	77	110	22	18	180	52
44	17	45	99	250	78	58	35	57	45
37	58	62	44	35	78	35	82	94	58

We first use the sample data to compute the sample mean and the sample standard deviation as

$$\bar{x} = 63.80 \quad \text{and} \quad s = 45.78.$$

Since we want to determine whether or not the data may be looked upon as a random sample from a population having a normal distribution, we specify this in the null hypothesis, along with the above sample estimates of the population mean and the population standard deviation.

H_0: Income (in $1,000s) in a given small Midwestern city follows a normal distribution with mean $63.80 and standard deviation $45.78.

H_A: Income (in $1,000s) in a given small Midwestern city does not follow a normal distribution with mean $63.80 and standard deviation $45.78.

The null hypothesis implies that the underlying distribution is normal and also that the population mean and the population standard deviation equal their estimates. In other words, it uses $\mu = 63.80$ and $\sigma = 45.78$. As discussed in Section 12.1, the goodness-of-fit test for a multinomial experiment deals with a single population of qualitative data. Since observations that follow the normal distribution are quantitative, we essentially need to convert the data into a qualitative format. After computing the sample mean and the sample standard deviation, we subdivide the data into non-overlapping intervals (categories); in other words, we construct a frequency distribution. The first two columns of Table 12.10 show the frequency distribution for the raw data from Table 12.9.

TABLE 12.10 Calculations for the Normality Test Example

Income (in $1,000s)	Observed Frequency, o_i	p_i if Income Is Normally Distributed	Expected Frequency, $e_i = n \times p_i$	Standardized Squared Deviation, $\frac{(o_i - e_i)^2}{e_i}$
Income < 20	6	0.1685	$50 \times 0.1685 = 8.43$	$\frac{(6 - 8.43)^2}{8.43} = 0.70$
$20 \le$ Income < 40	10	0.1330	$50 \times 0.1330 = 6.65$	1.69
$40 \le$ Income < 60	13	0.1666	$50 \times 0.1666 = 8.33$	2.62
$60 \le$ Income < 80	10	0.1687	$50 \times 0.1687 = 8.44$	0.29
Income ≥ 80	11	0.3632	$50 \times 0.3632 = 18.16$	2.82
	$n = \Sigma o_i = 50$	$\Sigma p_i = 1$	$n = \Sigma e_i = 50$	$\chi_2^2 = \Sigma \frac{(o_i - e_i)^2}{e_i} = 8.12$

Note that we have six observations (15, 19, 19, 14, 18, and 17) that are less than 20. Other frequencies are found similarly. Earlier, we were able to calculate expected frequencies by multiplying the sample size n by the hypothesized probabilities (proportions) p_i under the null hypothesis. Here, we first calculate the probabilities under the assumption of a normal distribution and then use them to calculate expected frequencies. For example, under the null hypothesis that income is normally distributed with $\mu = 63.80$ and $\sigma = 45.78$, we reference the z table to find the probability that an individual's income is less than 20, or

$$P(X < 20) = P\left(\frac{X - \mu}{\sigma} < \frac{20 - 63.80}{45.78}\right) = P(Z < -0.96) = 0.1685.$$

We proceed with the other intervals in a like manner.

$$P(20 \le X < 40) = P\left(\frac{20 - 63.80}{45.78} \le \frac{X - \mu}{\sigma} < \frac{40 - 63.80}{45.78}\right)$$
$$= P(-0.96 \le Z < -0.52) = 0.1330$$

$$P(40 \le X < 60) = P\left(\frac{40 - 63.80}{45.78} \le \frac{X - \mu}{\sigma} < \frac{60 - 63.80}{45.78}\right)$$
$$= P(-0.52 \le Z < -0.08) = 0.1666$$

$$P(60 \le X < 80) = P\left(\frac{60 - 63.80}{45.78} \le \frac{X - \mu}{\sigma} < \frac{80 - 63.80}{45.78}\right)$$
$$= P(-0.08 \le Z < 0.35) = 0.1687$$

$$P(X \ge 80) = P\left(\frac{X - \mu}{\sigma} \ge \frac{80 - 63.80}{45.78}\right) = P(Z \ge 0.35) = 0.3632$$

The third column of Table 12.10 shows these probabilities. We are then able to compute the expected frequencies for each category as $n \times p_i$. The fourth column of Table 12.10 shows the values for the expected frequencies. As in Section 12.1, the appropriate test statistic follows the χ_{df}^2 distribution and its value is calculated as $\chi_{df}^2 = \Sigma \frac{(o_i - e_i)^2}{e_i}$. The only difference is that the degrees of freedom are equal to the number of categories minus one, minus the number of parameters estimated. Since we estimate two parameters—the mean and the standard deviation—from the sample data, the degrees of freedom for the chi-square test for normality are always $k - 1 - 2 = k - 3$.

Since in this example we formed five classes, that is, $k = 5$, we calculate $df = 5 - 3 = 2$. Then we sum the standardized squared deviations as shown in the last column of Table 12.10 to obtain the value of the chi-square test statistic as $\chi^2_{df} = \chi^2_2 = 8.12$.

The goodness-of-fit test for normality is again a right-tailed test. With a significance level of 5% and df of 2, we derive the critical value as $\chi^2_{\alpha,df} = \chi^2_{0.05,2} = 5.991$. Hence, our decision rule is to reject H_0 if $\chi^2_2 > 5.991$. Since $\chi^2_2 = 8.12 > 5.991$, we reject H_0. At the 5% significance level, we conclude that income in this Midwestern city does not follow a normal distribution with a mean of $63,800 and a standard deviation of $45,780. (Alternatively, we input **X** = 8.12 and **Deg_freedom** = 2 in Excel's **CHISQ.DIST.RT** command to obtain a p-value of 0.0172. At the 5% significance level, we again reject H_0.)

A criticism of this test of normality is that we first have to convert raw data into a frequency distribution by grouping them into a set of arbitrary class intervals or categories. The resulting value of the chi-square test statistic depends on how the data are grouped.

LO 12.4

Conduct the Jarque-Bera test for normality.

The Jarque-Bera Test for Normality

An alternative to the goodness-of-fit test for normality is the **Jarque-Bera test**. In this test it is not necessary to convert the quantitative data into a qualitative form. Instead, using the raw data, we calculate the **skewness coefficient** S and the (excess) **kurtosis coefficient** K of the sample data. A skewness coefficient of zero indicates that the data are symmetric about its mean. The kurtosis coefficient measures whether a distribution is more or less peaked than a normal distribution. The skewness coefficient and the kurtosis coefficient for the normal distribution are both equal to zero. We use Excel to calculate the skewness and the kurtosis coefficients.

When testing whether sample data are derived from the normal distribution, the null hypothesis consists of the joint hypothesis that both the skewness coefficient and the kurtosis coefficient are zero. It can be shown that the Jarque-Bera test statistic follows the χ^2_{df} distribution with two degrees of freedom.

EXAMPLE 12.3

Using the data from Table 12.9 and the Jarque-Bera test, determine whether or not annual household income is normally distributed at the 1% significance level.

SOLUTION:

The competing hypotheses take the following form:

$$H_0: S = 0 \text{ and } K = 0$$
$$H_A: S \neq 0 \text{ or } K \neq 0$$

In order to compute the value of the test statistic, we first need to compute the skewness and kurtosis coefficients, S and K. We can use the **SKEW** and **KURT** functions in Excel to approximate these values. Alternatively, we can choose **Data** > **Data Analysis** > **Descriptive Statistics** whereby Excel reports approximate S and K along with other descriptive measures. Using either method, we find that $S = 2.32$ and $K = 6.73$.

The value of the test statistic is calculated as

$$JB = \chi_2^2 = (n/6)[S^2 + K^2/4] = (50/6)[2.32^2 + 6.73^2/4] = 139.21.$$

With a significance level of 1% and $df = 2$, we find the critical value $\chi_{\alpha,df}^2 = \chi_{0.01,2}^2 = 9.210$. Since $\chi_2^2 > \chi_{0.01,2}^2$ (139.21 > 9.210), we reject H_0 and conclude that income in this Midwestern city does not follow a normal distribution.

In the above examples, the conclusion with the Jarque-Bera test and the goodness-of-fit test for normality is the same. This result is not surprising, as it is fairly well documented that income distribution, in general, is skewed to the right (not normally distributed), with a few households accounting for most of the total income. For this reason, we prefer to use the median rather than the mean to get a more accurate reflection of the typical income; hypothesis tests for the median will be discussed in Chapter 20.

EXERCISES 12.3

Concepts

21. Consider the following sample data with mean and standard deviation of 20.5 and 5.4, respectively.

Class	Frequency
Less than 10	25
10 up to 20	95
20 up to 30	65
30 or more	15
	$n = 200$

a. Using the goodness-of-fit test for normality, specify the competing hypotheses in order to determine whether or not the data are normally distributed.

b. Calculate the value of the test statistic.

c. At the 5% significance level, what is the critical value? What is the decision rule?

d. What is the conclusion?

22. The following frequency distribution has a sample mean of -3.5 and a sample standard deviation of 9.7.

Class	Frequency
Less than -10	70
-10 up to 0	40
0 up to 10	80
10 or more	10

At the 1% significance level, use the goodness-of-fit test for normality to determine whether or not the data are normally distributed.

23. You are given the following summary statistics from a sample of 50 observations:

Mean	77.25
Standard Deviation	11.36
Skewness	1.12
Kurtosis	1.63

a. Using the Jarque-Bera test, specify the null and alternative hypotheses to determine whether or not the data are normally distributed.

b. Calculate the value of the test statistic.

c. At the 5% significance level, what is the critical value?

d. What is the conclusion? Can you conclude that the data do not follow the normal distribution? Explain.

Applications

24. An economics professor states on her syllabus that final grades will be distributed using the normal distribution. The final averages of 300 students are calculated, and she groups the data into a frequency distribution as shown below. The mean and the standard deviation of the final averages are $\bar{x} = 72$ and $s = 10$.

Final Averages	Observed Frequency
F: Less than 50	5
D: 50 up to 70	135
C: 70 up to 80	105
B: 80 up to 90	45
A: 90 or above	10
	Total = 300

a. Using the goodness-of-fit test for normality, state the competing hypotheses in order to determine if we can reject the professor's normality claim.

b. Calculate the value of the test statistic.

c. At a 5% significance level, what is the critical value?

d. What is the conclusion to the test?

25. Fifty cities provided information on vacancy rates (in percent) in local apartments in the following frequency distribution. The sample mean and the sample standard deviation are 9% and 3.6%, respectively.

Vacancy Rate (in percent)	Frequency
Less than 6	10
6 up to 9	10
9 up to 12	20
12 or more	10

Apply the goodness-of-fit test for normality at the 5% significance level. Do the sample data suggest that vacancy rates do not follow the normal distribution?

26. Total 2005 CEO compensation for the largest U.S. companies by revenue is reported in the following frequency distribution, along with some summary statistics. Total compensation includes salary, bonuses, stock and incentives, the potential value of stock options, and gains from stock options exercised.

Total Compensation (in millions of $)	Observed Frequency
Less than 5	43
5 up to 10	65
10 up to 15	32
15 up to 20	38
20 or more	60
	$n = 238$

Other summary statistics for CEO compensation (in millions of $) are as follows:

Mean	Median	Standard Deviation	Skewness	Kurtosis
19.03	11.02	27.61	5.26	35.53

a. Conduct a goodness-of-fit test for normality of CEO compensation at the 1% significance level.

b. Conduct the Jarque-Bera test for normality at the 1% significance level.

c. Does total compensation of CEOs for the largest U.S. companies not follow the normal distribution?

27. The following frequency distribution shows the distribution of monthly returns for Starbucks Corp. for the years 2003 through 2007.

Class (in percent)	Observed Frequency
Less than −5	14
−5 up to 0	9
0 up to 5	18
5 up to 10	11
10 or more	8
	$n = 60$

Source: www.yahoo.finance.com.

Over this time period, the following summary statistics are provided:

Mean	Median	Standard Deviation	Skewness	Kurtosis
1.16%	1.79%	7.38%	−0.31	−0.65

a. Conduct a goodness-of-fit test for normality at the 5% significance level. Can you conclude that monthly returns do not follow the normal distribution?

b. Conduct the Jarque-Bera test at the 5% significance level. Can you conclude that monthly returns do not follow the normal distribution?

28. **FILE** (Use Excel) Access the weekly stock prices for Home Depot in the data file on the text website, labeled **Home Depot**.

a. Specify the competing hypotheses for the Jarque-Bera test of normality of Home Depot's stock prices.

b. Calculate the value of the Jarque-Bera test statistic. Use Excel to calculate the *p*-value.

c. At $\alpha = 0.05$ can you conclude that Home Depot's stock prices are not normally distributed?

29. **FILE** (Use Excel) Access the miles per gallon (MPG) data on the text website, labeled **MPG**.

a. Specify the competing hypotheses for the Jarque-Bera test of normality of MPG.

b. Calculate the value of the Jarque-Bera test statistic. Use Excel to calculate the *p*-value.

c. At $\alpha = 0.05$ can you conclude that MPG are not normally distributed?

WRITING WITH STATISTICS

Javier Gonzalez is in the process of writing a comprehensive analysis on the three-year returns of the 50 largest mutual funds. Before he makes any inferences concerning the return data, he would first like to determine whether or not the data follow a normal distribution. Table 12.11 shows a portion of the three-year return data for the 50 largest mutual funds; the complete data set can be found on the text website, labeled **50 Largest Funds**.

TABLE 12.11 Three-Year Returns for the 50 Largest Mutual Funds

Mutual Fund	Return (%)
American Growth	5.7
Pimco Total Return	4.7
⋮	⋮
Loomis Sayles Bond	5.4

SOURCE: *The Boston Sunday Globe*, August 17, 2008.

Javier wants to use the sample information to:

1. Conduct a goodness-of-fit test for normality that determines, at the 5% significance level, whether or not three-year returns follow a normal distribution.

2. Perform the Jarque-Bera test that determines, at the 5% significance level, whether or not three-year returns follow a normal distribution.

As part of a broader report concerning the mutual fund industry in general, three-year return data for the 50 largest mutual funds were collected with the objective of determining whether or not the data follow a normal distribution. Information of this sort is particularly useful because much statistical inference is based on the assumption of normality. If the assumption of normality is not supported by the data, it may be more appropriate to use nonparametric techniques to make valid inferences. Table 12.A shows relevant summary statistics for three-year returns for the 50 largest mutual funds.

Sample Report— Assessing Whether Data Follow the Normal Distribution

TABLE 12.A Three-Year Return Summary Measures for the 50 Largest Mutual Funds, August 2008

Mean	Median	Standard Deviation	Skewness	Kurtosis
5.96%	4.65%	3.39%	1.37	2.59

The average three-year return for the 50 largest mutual funds is 5.96%, with a median of 4.65%. When the mean is significantly greater than the median, it is often an indication of a positively skewed distribution. The skewness coefficient of 1.37 seems to support this claim. Moreover, the kurtosis coefficient of 2.59 suggests a distribution that is more peaked than the normal distribution. A formal test will determine whether the conclusion from the sample can be deemed real or due to chance.

The goodness-of-fit test is first applied to check for normality. The raw data is converted into a frequency distribution with five categories ($k = 5$). Expected frequencies are calculated by multiplying the sample size $n = 50$ by the hypothesized proportions p_i, under the null hypothesis that the data follow the normal distribution with mean 5.96% and standard deviation 3.39%. Finally, the value of the chi-square test statistic is computed by summing the standardized squared deviations. All of these calculations are shown in Table 12.B.

TABLE 12.B Calculations for the Normality Test Example

Return (in %)	Observed Frequency, o_i	p_i if Return Is Normally Distributed	Expected Frequency, $e_i = n \times p_i$	Standardized Squared Deviation, $\frac{(o_i - e_i)^2}{e_i}$
Return < 2.5	7	0.1539	$50 \times 0.1539 = 7.70$	$\frac{(7 - 7.70)^2}{7.70} = 0.06$
$2.5 \leq$ Return < 5.0	20	0.2359	$50 \times 0.2359 = 11.80$	5.70
$5.0 \leq$ Return < 7.5	6	0.2839	$50 \times 0.2839 = 14.20$	4.74
$7.5 \leq$ Return < 10	11	0.2093	$50 \times 0.2093 = 10.47$	0.03
Return $\geq$ 10	6	0.1170	$50 \times 0.1170 = 5.85$	0.00
	$n = \Sigma o_i = 50$	$\Sigma p_i = 1$	$n = \Sigma e_i = 50$	$\chi_2^2 = \Sigma \frac{(o_i - e_i)^2}{e_i} = 10.53$

Table 12.C shows the competing hypotheses, the value of the test statistic, and the p-value that result from applying the goodness-of-fit test for normality and the Jarque-Bera test for normality.

TABLE 12.C Test Statistics and p-Values for Hypothesis Tests

Hypotheses	Test Statistic	p-value
Goodness-of-fit Test: H_0: Returns are normally distributed. H_A: Returns are not normally distributed.	$\chi_2^2 = 10.53$	$P(\chi_2^2 \geq 10.53) = 0.0052$
Jarque-Bera Test: H_0: $S = 0$ and $K = 0$ H_A: $S = 0$ or $K = 0$	$\chi_2^2 = 29.62$	$P(\chi_2^2 \geq 29.62) = 0.0000$

At the 5% significance level, the p-value of 0.0052 from the goodness-of-fit test allows us to reject the null hypothesis. The three-year returns do not follow the normal distribution at the 5% significance level.

Under the Jarque-Bera (JB) test, the null hypothesis states that the skewness coefficient and the kurtosis coefficient are both zero. The value for the JB test statistic is 29.62 and its associated p-value is 0.0000; thus, at the 5% significance level, the null hypothesis that skewness and kurtosis are both zero is rejected. This result is consistent with the conclusion drawn from the goodness-of-fit test for normality. Both statistical tests reject the null hypothesis of normality—three-year returns do not follow the normal distribution. Statistical inference would best be conducted using nonparametric techniques.

Conceptual Review

LO 12.1 **Conduct a goodness-of-fit test for a multinomial experiment.**

A **multinomial experiment** consists of a series of n independent trials of a random experiment such that on each trial there are k possible outcomes or categories. We conduct a **goodness-of-fit test** on a multinomial experiment to test if the population proportions equal some predetermined (hypothesized) values.

For a multinomial experiment with k categories, the **test statistic** follows the χ^2_{df} (chi-square) distribution with $k - 1$ degrees of freedom and its value is calculated as $\chi^2_{df} = \Sigma \frac{(o_i - e_i)^2}{e_i}$, where o_i and $e_i = n \times p_i$ are the observed frequency and expected frequency, respectively, in the ith category. The test is valid when the expected frequencies in each category are five or more. This test is always implemented as a right-tailed test.

LO 12.2 **Determine whether two classifications of a population are independent.**

A goodness-of-fit test examines a single qualitative variable, whereas a **test of independence**, or equivalently, a **chi-square test of a contingency table**, analyzes the relationship between two qualitative variables. A contingency table shows frequencies for two qualitative variables, x and y, where each cell of the table represents a mutually exclusive combination of the pair of x and y values.

In order to determine whether or not the two variables are independent, we again compare observed frequencies with expected frequencies. The expected frequency for each cell is calculated as $e_{ij} = \frac{(\text{Row } i \text{ total})(\text{Column } j \text{ total})}{\text{Sample Size}}$.

The value of the chi-square **test statistic** is calculated as $\chi^2_{df} = \sum_i \sum_j \frac{(o_{ij} - e_{ij})^2}{e_{ij}}$, where o_{ij} and e_{ij} are the observed and expected frequencies in the ith row and the jth column, respectively. Degrees of freedom are calculated as $(r - 1)(c - 1)$ where r and c refer to the number of rows and columns, respectively, in the contingency table. The test of independence is also implemented as a right-tailed test and is valid when the expected frequencies in each cell are five or more.

LO 12.3 **Conduct a goodness-of-fit test for normality.**

We can use the **goodness-of-fit test** to test the hypothesis that a population follows the **normal distribution**. Since observations that follow the normal distribution are quantitative in nature and the goodness-of-fit test is applied to qualitative data, we must first convert the data into a qualitative format.

We construct a frequency distribution with k intervals. We then calculate the probability of observing the ith interval p_i under the assumption of a normal distribution and then use this probability to calculate the expected frequency as $e_i = n \times p_i$. As in the goodness-of-fit test for a multinomial experiment, the **test statistic** follows the χ^2_{df} distribution and its value is calculated as $\chi^2_{df} = \Sigma \frac{(o_i - e_i)^2}{e_i}$, with $df = k - 3$. Since it is a goodness-of-fit test, it is implemented as a right-tailed test and is valid only when the expected frequencies in each cell are five or more.

LO 12.4 **Conduct the Jarque-Bera test for normality.**

In the goodness-of-fit test for normality, we have to first convert raw data into a frequency distribution by grouping them into a set of arbitrary class intervals or categories. The resulting value of the chi-square test statistic depends on how the data are grouped. For the **Jarque-Bera test**, it is not necessary to convert the quantitative data into a qualitative form.

Using the raw data, we use the skewness coefficient S and the (excess) kurtosis coefficient K of the sample data to conduct the test. The **Jarque-Bera JB test statistic** for normality follows the χ^2_{df} distribution with $df = 2$ and its value is calculated as $JB = \chi^2_2 = (n/6)[S^2 + K^2/4]$ where n is the sample size.

Additional Exercises and Case Studies

30. The following table lists the market share of the four firms in a particular industry in 2010 and total sales for each firm in 2011.

Firm	Market Share in 2010	Total Sales in 2011 (in billions of $)
1	0.40	200
2	0.30	180
3	0.20	100
4	0.10	70

a. Specify the competing hypotheses to test whether the market shares in 2010 are not valid in 2011.

b. Calculate the value of the test statistic.

c. At the 1% significance level, what is the critical value?

d. Do the sample data suggest that the market shares changed from 2010 to 2011?

31. A study suggests that airlines have increased restrictions on cheap fares by raising overnight requirements (*The Wall Street Journal*, August 19, 2008). This would force business travelers to pay more for their flights, since they tend to need the most flexibility and want to be home on weekends. Eight months ago, the overnight stay requirements were as follows:

One night	Two nights	Three nights	Saturday night
37%	17%	28%	18%

A recent sample of 644 flights found the following restrictions:

One night	Two nights	Three nights	Saturday night
117	137	298	92

a. Specify the competing hypotheses to test whether the recent proportions differ from those cited in the study.

b. Calculate the value of the test statistic.

c. At a 5% significance level, what is the critical value?

d. What is the conclusion to the hypothesis test? Interpret your results.

32. A local TV station claims that 60% of people support Candidate A, 30% support Candidate B, and 10% support Candidate C. A survey of 500 registered voters is taken. The accompanying table indicates how they are likely to vote.

Candidate A	Candidate B	Candidate C
350	125	25

a. Specify the competing hypotheses to test whether the TV station's claim can be rejected by the data.

b. Use the *p*-value approach to test the hypothesis at a 1% significance level.

33. Although founded only in 2004, Facebook has more than 500 million active users, of which 50% log on to Facebook on any given day. In a recent survey by Facebook, young users (those born after 1984) were asked about their preference for delivering the news about breaking up a relationship (*The Wall Street Journal*, November 27–28, 2010). One of the shocking results was that only 47% of users preferred to break the news in person. A researcher decides to verify the survey results of Facebook by taking her own sample of 200 young Facebook users. The preference percentages from Facebook and the researcher's survey are presented in the following table.

Delivery Method	Facebook Results	Researcher's Results
In Person	47%	55%
Phone	30%	28%
Email	4%	8%
Facebook	5%	3%
Instant Message	14%	6%

At the 5% level of significance, test if the researcher's results are inconsistent with the survey results conducted by Facebook. Provide the details, using the *p*-value approach.

34. A recent study in the *Journal of the American Medical Association* (February 20, 2008) found that patients who go into cardiac arrest while in the hospital are more likely to die if it happens after 11 pm. The study investigated 58,593 cardiac arrests during the day or evening. Of those, 11,604 survived to leave the hospital. There were 28,155 cardiac arrests during the shift that began at 11 pm, commonly referred to as the graveyard shift. Of those, 4,139 survived for discharge. The following contingency table summarizes the results of the study:

Shift	Survived for Discharge	Did Not Survive for Discharge	Row Totals
Day or Evening Shift	11,604	46,989	58,593
Graveyard Shift	4,139	24,016	28,155
Column Totals	15,743	71,005	86,748

a. Specify the competing hypotheses to determine whether a patient's survival depends on the time at which he/she experiences cardiac arrest.

b. Calculate the value of the test statistic.

c. At a 1% significance level, what is the critical value?

d. What is the conclusion to the statistical test? Is the timing of when a cardiac arrest occurs independent of whether or not the patient survives for discharge? Given your answer, what type of recommendations might you give to hospitals?

35. An analyst is trying to determine whether the prices of certain stocks on the NASDAQ are independent of the industry to which they belong. She examines four industries and classifies the stock prices in these industries into one of three categories (high-priced, average-priced, low-priced).

Stock Price	Industry			
	I	II	III	IV
High	16	8	10	14
Average	18	16	10	12
Low	7	8	4	9

a. Specify the competing hypotheses to determine whether stock price depends on the industry.
b. Calculate the value of the test statistic. Approximate the p-value with the table or calculate its exact value with Excel.
c. At a 1% significance level, what can the analyst conclude?

36. Many parents have turned to St. John's wort, a herbal remedy, to treat their children with attention deficit hyperactivity disorder (ADHD). *The Journal of the American Medical Association* (June 11, 2008) recently published an article that explored the herb's effectiveness. Children with ADHD were randomly assigned to take either St. John's wort capsules or placebos. The contingency table below broadly reflects the results found in the study.

Treatment	Effect on ADHD	
	No Change in ADHD	Improvement in ADHD
St. John's wort	12	15
Placebo	14	13

At the 5% significance level, do the data indicate that St. John's wort affects children with ADHD?

37. A recent poll asked 3,228 Americans aged 16 to 21 whether they are likely to serve in the U.S. military. The following table, cross-classified by gender and race, reports those who responded that they are likely or very likely to serve in the active-duty military.

Gender	Race		
	Hispanic	Black	White
Male	1098	678	549
Female	484	355	64

Source: Defense Human Resources Activity telephone poll of 3,228 Americans conducted October through December 2005.

a. State the competing hypotheses to test whether race and gender are dependent when making a choice to serve in the military.
b. Conduct the test using the critical value approach at the 5% significance level.

38. Given a shaky economy and high heating costs, more and more households are struggling to pay utility bills (*The Wall Street Journal*, February, 14, 2008). Particularly hard hit are households with homes heated with propane or heating oil. Many of these households are spending twice as much to stay warm this winter compared to those who heat with natural gas or electricity. A representative sample of 500 households was taken to investigate if the type of heating influences whether or not a household is delinquent in paying its utility bill. The following table reports the results.

Delinquent in Payment?	Type of Heating			
	Natural Gas	Electricity	Heating Oil	Propane
Yes	50	20	15	10
No	240	130	20	15

At the 5% significance level, test whether the type of heating influences a household's delinquency in payment. Interpret your results.

39. The following frequency distribution shows the monthly stock returns for Home Depot for the years 2003 through 2007.

Class (in percent)	Observed Frequency
Less than −5	13
−5 up to 0	16
0 up to 5	20
5 or more	11
	$n = 60$

Source: www.yahoo.finance.com.

Over this time period, the following summary statistics are provided:

Mean	Median	Standard Deviation	Skewness	Kurtosis
0.31%	0.43%	6.49%	0.15	0.38

a. Conduct a goodness-of-fit test for normality at the 5% significance level. Can you conclude that monthly stock returns do not follow the normal distribution?
b. Conduct the Jarque-Bera test at the 5% significance level. Are your results consistent with your answer in part a?

40. **FILE** (Use Excel) Access the data file on the text website labeled ***Arlington Homes***. It contains data on various variables, including price and square footage, for 36 single-family homes in Arlington, Massachusetts, sold in the first quarter of 2009.
a. Use the Jarque-Bera test to test if house prices are not normally distributed at $\alpha = 0.05$.
b. Use the Jarque-Bera test to test if square footage is not normally distributed at $\alpha = 0.05$.

CASE STUDIES

Case Study 12.1

A detailed study of Americans' religious beliefs and practices by the Pew Forum on Religion & Public Life revealed that religion is quite important in an individual's life (*The Boston Globe*, June 24, 2008). The second column of the accompanying table reports the proportion of Americans who feel a certain way about religion. The study also concludes that Massachusetts residents are the least likely to say that they are religious. In order to test this claim, assume 400 randomly selected Massachusetts residents are asked about the importance of religion in his/her life. The results of this survey are shown in the last column of the accompanying table.

Data for Case Study 12.1 Importance of Religion, U.S. versus Massachusetts

Importance of Religion	U.S. Results	Responses of Massachusetts Residents
Very important	0.58	160
Somewhat important	0.25	140
Not too important	0.15	96
Don't know	0.02	4

In a report, use the sample information to:

1. Determine whether Massachusetts residents' religious beliefs differ from those based on the United States at a 5% significance level.

2. Discuss whether you would expect to find the same conclusions if you conducted a similar test for the state of Utah or states in the Southern Belt of the United States.

Case Study 12.2

A University of Utah study examined 7,925 severely obese adults who had gastric bypass surgery and an identical number of people who did not have the surgery (*The Boston Globe*, August 23, 2007). The study wanted to investigate whether losing weight through stomach surgery prolonged the lives of severely obese patients, thereby reducing their deaths from heart disease, cancer, and diabetes.

Over the course of the study, 534 of the participants died. Of those who died, the cause of death was classified as either a disease death (disease deaths include heart disease, cancer, and diabetes) or a nondisease death (nondisease deaths include suicide or accident). The following contingency table summarizes the study's findings:

Data for Case Study 12.2 Deaths Cross-Classified by Cause and Method of Losing Weight

Cause of Death	Method of Losing Weight	
	No Surgery	Surgery
Death from disease	285	150
Death from nondisease	36	63

In a report, use the sample information to:

1. Determine at the 5% significance level whether the cause of death depends on the method of losing weight.

2. Discuss how the findings of the statistical test used in question 1 might be used by those in the health industry.

Case Study 12.3

Matthew Jordon is a research analyst for a large investment firm. He is preparing a report on the stock performance of Nike, Inc. One aspect of his report will contain inferences concerning monthly stock returns. Before making valid inferences, Matthew first wants to determine whether the return data follow the normal distribution. To this end, he constructs the following frequency distribution on monthly stock returns for the years 2006 through 2010.

Class (in percent)	Observed Frequency
Less than −5	8
−5 up to 0	20
0 up to 5	14
5 or more	18

Source: www.yahoo.finance.com.

He also calculates the following summary statistics over this time period:

Mean	Median	Standard Deviation	Skewness	Kurtosis
1.50%	1.31%	6.98%	0.11	−0.33

In a report, use the sample information to:

1. Conduct a goodness-of-fit test in order to determine whether the monthly stock returns are not normally distributed at the 5% significance level.

2. Perform the Jarque-Bera test in order to determine whether the monthly stock returns are not normally distributed at the 5% significance level.

13

Analysis of Variance

LEARNING OBJECTIVES

After reading this chapter you should be able to:

LO 13.1 Provide a conceptual overview of ANOVA.

LO 13.2 Conduct and evaluate hypothesis tests based on one-way ANOVA.

LO 13.3 Use confidence intervals and Tukey's HSD method in order to determine which means differ.

LO 13.4 Conduct and evaluate hypothesis tests based on two-way ANOVA with no interaction.

LO 13.5 Conduct and evaluate hypothesis tests based on two-way ANOVA with interaction.

In this chapter, we study analysis of variance which is more commonly referred to as ANOVA. ANOVA is a statistical technique used to determine if differences exist between the means of three or more populations, thus generalizing the two-sample tests discussed in Chapter 10. For instance, we may want to determine whether all brands of small hybrid cars have the same average miles per gallon. Or we may wish to compare the effectiveness of different fertilizers on the average yield per acre. These are examples of one-way ANOVA, where we examine the effect of one categorical variable or one factor on the mean. We then move on to two-way ANOVA, where the mean may be influenced by two categorical variables or two factors. For instance, we may want to determine if average miles per gallon are affected by the brand of a hybrid and the octane level of gasoline. Or we may wish to determine if the average yield per acre is influenced by the fertilizer and the acidity level of the soil. Tests based on two-way ANOVA can be conducted *with* or *without* the interaction of the factors.

Public Transportation

Sean Cox, a research analyst at an environmental organization, believes that an upswing in the use of public transportation has taken place due to environmental concerns, the volatility of gas prices, and the general economic climate. He is especially pleased with a recent study, which highlights the average annual cost savings when commuters use public transportation (*The Boston Globe*, May 8, 2009). Commuters who use public transportation save on buying, maintaining, and operating their cars, which comprise the largest household expenditure after housing. The study finds that Boston leads 20 other American cities in the amount that commuters can save if they take public transportation. Sean wonders whether or not cost savings vary dramatically by city. He collects a representative sample of public transit riders in the top four cost-savings cities: Boston, New York, San Francisco, and Chicago. Table 13.1 shows each public transit rider's annual cost savings by city; the data are also available on the text website, labeled **Public Transportation**.

TABLE 13.1 Annual Cost Savings from Using Public Transportation

FILE

Boston	New York	San Francisco	Chicago
$12,500	$12,450	$11,800	$10,595
12,640	12,500	11,745	10,740
12,600	12,595	11,700	10,850
12,625	12,605	11,800	10,725
12,745	12,650	11,700	10,740
	12,620	11,575	
	12,560		
	12,700		
$\bar{x}_1 = \$12,622$	$\bar{x}_2 = \$12,585$	$\bar{x}_3 = \$11,720$	$\bar{x}_4 = \$10,730$
$s_1 = \$87.79$	$s_2 = \$80.40$	$s_3 = \$83.96$	$s_4 = \$90.62$
$n_1 = 5$	$n_2 = 8$	$n_3 = 6$	$n_4 = 5$

Sean wants to use the above sample information to:

1. Determine whether there are differences in mean cost savings among these four cities at the 5% significance level.

2. Establish where mean cost savings significantly differ.

We provide a synopsis of this case at the end of Section 13.2.

13.1 One-Way ANOVA

LO 13.1

Provide a conceptual
overview of ANOVA.

We use analysis of variance (ANOVA) tests to determine if differences exist between the means of three or more populations, thus generalizing the two-sample tests discussed in Chapter 10. These tests are based on the $F_{(df_1, df_2)}$ distribution that was introduced in Chapter 11. One-way ANOVA refers to comparing population means based on one categorical variable or factor. For instance, in the introductory case of this chapter we want to compare cost savings of using public transportation depending on where an individual resides. We thus delineate cost savings of using public transportation by city (the factor). We choose to collect sample data from four cities: Boston, New York, San Francisco, and Chicago. In general, when performing a one-way ANOVA test, our sample consists of c levels of the factor drawn from each of c populations. In our example c equals four. In addition, we make the following three assumptions:

1. The populations are normally distributed.
2. The population standard deviations are unknown but assumed equal.
3. The samples are selected independently.

In short, each population i, where $i = 1, 2, \ldots, c$, has mean μ_i and standard deviation σ where both parameters are unknown. From each population, we draw independent random samples where the selection of one sample does not affect the selection of another sample. In other words, the experiment has a **completely randomized design**. From each sample, we calculate the sample mean $\bar{x}_i$ and the sample standard deviation s_i to implement the test.

> **ONE-WAY ANOVA AND A COMPLETELY RANDOMIZED DESIGN**
>
> **ANOVA** is a statistical technique used to determine if differences exist between several population means. **One-Way ANOVA** analyzes the effect of one factor on the mean. It is based on a **completely randomized design** in which independent random samples are drawn from the c different levels of this factor (c populations), ignoring all other possible factors.

The term "treatment" is often used to identify the c populations being examined. The practice of referring to different populations as different treatments is due to the fact that many ANOVA techniques were originally developed in connection with agricultural experiments where different fertilizers were regarded as different treatments applied to soil.

Table 13.2 summarizes the notation of the completely randomized design of ANOVA. We define the notation as:

x_{ij} is the jth value in the ith sample,
$\bar{x}_i$ is the sample mean of the ith sample,
s_i is the sample standard deviation of the ith sample, and
n_i is the number of observations in the ith sample.

TABLE 13.2 Notation for the Completely Randomized Design of ANOVA

Treatments	1	2	...	c
Sample Values	x_{11}	x_{21}	...	x_{c1}
	x_{12}	x_{22}	...	x_{c2}
	$\vdots$	$\vdots$	$\vdots$	$\vdots$
	x_{1n_1}	x_{2n_2}	...	x_{cn_c}
Sample Mean	$\bar{x}_1$	$\bar{x}_2$	...	$\bar{x}_c$
Sample Standard Deviation	s_1	s_2	...	s_c
Sample Size	n_1	n_2	...	n_c

LO **13.2**

Conduct and evaluate hypothesis tests based on one-way ANOVA.

It is easiest to examine one-way ANOVA through an example. Recall from the introductory case that Sean wishes to determine whether the annual cost savings from using public transportation varies by city. He focuses on annual cost savings in Boston, New York, San Francisco, and Chicago. Table 13.3 reproduces the summary statistics from each city.

TABLE 13.3 Summary Statistics from Using Public Transportation in Four Cities

Boston	New York	San Francisco	Chicago
$\bar{x}_1 = \$12{,}622$	$\bar{x}_2 = \$12{,}585$	$\bar{x}_3 = \$11{,}720$	$\bar{x}_4 = \$10{,}730$
$s_1 = \$87.79$	$s_2 = \$80.40$	$s_3 = \$83.96$	$s_4 = \$90.62$
$n_1 = 5$	$n_2 = 8$	$n_3 = 6$	$n_4 = 5$

Since we wish to test whether or not the mean annual cost savings from using public transportation is the same in Boston, New York, San Francisco, and Chicago, we formulate the following competing hypotheses:

$$H_0: \mu_1 = \mu_2 = \mu_3 = \mu_4$$

$$H_A: \text{Not all population means are equal}$$

Note that H_A does not require that all means must differ from one another. In principle, the sample data may support the rejection of H_0 in favor of H_A even if only two means differ.

When conducting the equality of means test, you might be tempted to set up a series of hypothesis tests, comparing μ_1 and μ_2, then μ_1 and μ_3, and so on, and then use the two-sample t test discussed in Chapter 10. However, such an approach is not only cumbersome, but also flawed. In this example, where we evaluate the equality of four means, we would have to compare six combinations of two means at a time. This is based on the combination formula first encountered in Chapter 4 that yields $_4C_2 = \frac{4!}{2!2!} = 6$ combinations. Also, by conducting numerous pairwise comparisons, we inflate the risk of the Type I error α; that is, we increase the risk of incorrectly rejecting the null hypothesis. In other words, if we conduct all six pairwise tests at a 5% level of significance, the resulting α for the overall test will be greater than 5%. Later, we will discuss how we can modify the significance level of pairwise comparison tests for an accurate inference.

Fortunately, the ANOVA technique avoids this problem by providing one test that simultaneously evaluates the equality of several means. In the public transportation example, if the four population means are equal, we would expect the resulting sample means, $\bar{x}_1$, $\bar{x}_2$, $\bar{x}_3$, and $\bar{x}_4$, to be relatively close to one another. Figure 13.1a illustrates the distributions of the sample means if H_0 is true. Here, the relatively small variability in the sample means can be explained by chance. What if the population means differ? Figure 13.1b shows the distributions of the sample means if the sample data support H_A. In this scenario, the sample means are relatively far apart since each sample mean is

FIGURE 13.1 The logic of ANOVA

a. Distributions of sample means if H_0 is true

b. Distributions of sample means if H_0 is false

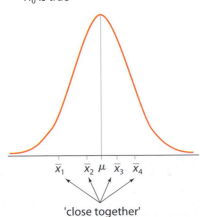

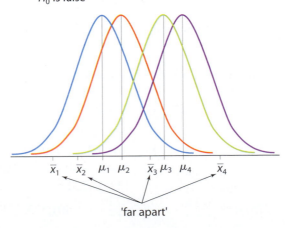

'close together'

'far apart'

calculated from a population with a different mean. The resulting variability in the sample means cannot be explained by chance alone.

We develop two independent estimates of the common population variance σ^2. One estimate can be attributed to inherent differences between the c populations, while the other estimate can be attributed to chance.

1. **Between-Treatments Estimate of σ^2.** One estimate of σ^2 is based on the variability *between* the sample means. This is referred to as **between-treatments variability**.
2. **Within-Treatments Estimate of σ^2.** The other estimate of σ^2 is based on the variability of the data *within* each sample, that is, the variability due to chance. This estimate is generally called **within-treatments variability**.

If we find that the variability of between-treatments is significantly greater than the variability within-treatments, then we are able to reject the null hypothesis of equal means; this is equivalent to concluding that the ratio of between-treatments variability to within-treatment variability is significantly greater than one.

> We use **ANOVA** to test for differences between population means by examining the amount of variability *between* the samples relative to the amount of variability *within* the samples. If the ratio of the *between* to *within* variabilities is significantly greater than one, then we reject the null hypothesis of equal means.

Between-Treatments Estimate of σ^2

Between-treatments variability is based on a weighted sum of squared differences between the sample means and the overall mean of the data set, referred to as the **grand mean** and denoted as $\bar{\bar{x}}$. We compute the grand mean by summing all observations in the data set and dividing by the total number of observations.

Each squared difference of a sample mean from the grand mean $(\bar{x}_i - \bar{\bar{x}})^2$ is multiplied by the respective sample size for each treatment n_i. After summing the weighted squared differences, we arrive at a value called the **sum of squares due to treatments** or *SSTR*. When we average a sum of squares over its respective degrees of freedom, we obtain the mean sum of squares. Dividing *SSTR* by $c - 1$ yields the **mean square for treatments** or *MSTR*.

> **CALCULATIONS FOR THE BETWEEN-TREATMENTS ESTIMATE OF σ^2**
>
> The **grand mean** $\bar{\bar{x}}$ is calculated as $\bar{\bar{x}} = \dfrac{\sum\limits_{i=1}^{c} \sum\limits_{j=1}^{n_i} x_{ij}}{n_T}$, where $n_T = \sum\limits_{i=1}^{c} n_i$ is the total sample size.
>
> The **sum of squares due to treatments** *SSTR* is calculated as $SSTR = \sum\limits_{i=1}^{c} n_i(\bar{x}_i - \bar{\bar{x}})^2$.
>
> The **mean square for treatments** *MSTR* is calculated as $MSTR = \dfrac{SSTR}{c - 1}$.

The calculations for $\bar{\bar{x}}$, *SSTR*, and *MSTR* for the public transportation example are as follows:

$$\bar{\bar{x}} = \frac{\sum\limits_{j=1}^{c} \sum\limits_{i=1}^{n_j} x_{ij}}{n_T} = \frac{12,500 + 12,640 + \cdots + 10,740}{24} = \$11,990.$$

$$\begin{aligned}
SSTR = \sum\limits_{i=1}^{c} n_i(\bar{x}_i - \bar{\bar{x}})^2 &= 5(12,622 - 11,990)^2 + 8(12,585 - 11,990)^2 \\
&\quad + 6(11,720 - 11,990)^2 + 5(10,730 - 11,990)^2 \\
&= 13,204,720.
\end{aligned}$$

$$MSTR = \frac{SSTR}{c - 1} = \frac{13,204,720}{4 - 1} = 4,401,573.$$

Within-Treatments Estimate of σ^2

We just calculated a value of $MSTR$ equal to 4,401,573. Is this value of $MSTR$ large enough to indicate that the population means differ? To answer this question we compare $MSTR$ to the variability that we expect due to the nature of sampling. We first calculate the **error sum of squares**, denoted as SSE. SSE provides a measure of the degree of variability that exists even if all population means are the same. We calculate SSE as a weighted sum of the sample variances of each treatment. We calculate the **mean square error** MSE by dividing SSE by its respective degrees of freedom, $df = n_T - c$.

CALCULATIONS FOR WITHIN-TREATMENTS ESTIMATE FOR σ^2

The **error sum of squares** SSE is calculated as $SSE = \sum_{i=1}^{c} (n_i - 1)s_i^2$.

The **mean square error** MSE is calculated as $MSE = \frac{SSE}{n_T - c}$.

The values of SSE and MSE for the public transportation example are calculated as follows:

$$SSE = \sum_{i=1}^{c} (n_i - 1)s_i^2$$
$$= (5 - 1)(87.79)^2 + (8 - 1)(80.40)^2 + (6 - 1)(83.96)^2 + (5 - 1)(90.62)^2$$
$$= 144,172.$$
$$MSE = \frac{SSE}{n_T - c} = \frac{144,172}{24 - 4} = 7,209.$$

The Test Statistic

Earlier, we noted that if the ratio of the two independent estimates of the assumed common population variance is close to one, then this is evidence in support of the null hypothesis of equal population means. We use this ratio to develop the ANOVA test. ANOVA tests are based on the $F_{(df_1, df_2)}$ distribution.

TEST STATISTIC FOR A ONE-WAY ANOVA TEST

The **test statistic** for the hypothesis test of the equality of the population means using one-way ANOVA is assumed to follow the $F_{(df_1, df_2)}$ distribution with $df_1 = c - 1$ and $df_2 = n_T - c$ and its sample value is

$$F_{(df_1, df_2)} = \frac{MSTR}{MSE},$$

where $MSTR$ and MSE are based on independent samples drawn from c normally distributed populations with a common variance σ^2.

When conducting an ANOVA test, we reject the null hypothesis when the numerator of the $F_{(df_1, df_2)}$ test statistic is significantly greater than the denominator. This result would imply that between-treatments variability is significantly greater than within-treatments variability, indicating that the population means are not all equal. This test is always a right-tailed test. We are now in a position to conduct a four-step hypothesis test for the public transportation example.

Given $MSTR = 4,401,573$, $MSE = 7,209$, $df_1 = c - 1 = 4 - 1 = 3$, and $df_2 = n_T - c = 24 - 4 = 20$, we compute the value of the test statistic as

$$F_{(3,20)} = \frac{MSTR}{MSE} = \frac{4,401,573}{7,209} = 610.57.$$

Since the ANOVA test is a right-tailed test, the critical value with $\alpha = 0.05$, $df_1 = 3$, and $df_2 = 20$ is found from the F table as $F_{\alpha,(df_1,df_2)} = F_{0.05,(3,20)} = 3.10$; we show a portion of the F table in Table 13.4 as a refresher. Hence, the decision rule is to reject H_0 if $F_{(3,20)} > 3.10$.

TABLE 13.4 Portion of the *F* table

Denominator Degrees of Freedom, df_2	Area in Upper Tail	Numerator Degrees of Freedom, df_1		
		1	2	3
20	0.10	2.97	2.59	2.38
	0.05	4.35	3.49	**3.10**
	0.025	5.87	4.46	3.86
	0.01	8.10	5.85	4.94

We reject the null hypothesis because the value of the test statistic falls in the rejection region (610.57 is greater than 3.10). Therefore, we conclude that the mean cost savings from using public transportation is not the same for each city.

The ANOVA Table

Most software packages summarize the ANOVA calculations in a table. The general format of the ANOVA table is presented in Table 13.5.

TABLE 13.5 General Format of a One-way ANOVA Table

Source of Variation	SS	df	MS	F
Between Groups	SSTR	$c - 1$	MSTR	$F_{(df_1, df_2)} = \dfrac{MSTR}{MSE}$
Within Groups	SSE	$n_T - c$	MSE	
Total	SST	$n_T - 1$		

We should also note that **total sum of squares** *SST* is equal to the sum of the squared differences of each observation from the grand mean. This is equivalent to summing *SSTR* with *SSE*; that is, $SST = SSTR + SSE$.

Using Excel to Solve One-Way ANOVA Problems

Fortunately, Excel provides the value of the $F_{(df_1, df_2)}$ test statistic, the critical value, as well as the precise *p*-value for a one-way ANOVA problem. In order to solve the public transportation example using Excel, we follow these steps.

A. **FILE** Open the **Public Transportation** data found on the text website.

B. Choose **Data > Data Analysis > ANOVA: Single Factor**.

C. In the *ANOVA: Single Factor* dialog box shown in Figure 13.2, choose the box next to *Input range* and then select all the data, including the city names. Check the *Labels* box. If testing at a significance level other than 5%, insert the relevant significance level in the box next to *Alpha*. Choose an output range and click **OK**.

FIGURE 13.2 Excel's ANOVA: Single Factor dialog box

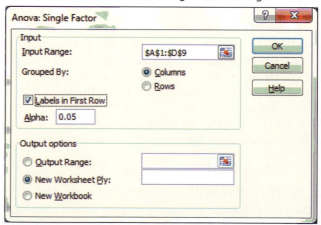

In addition to the ANOVA table, Excel provides descriptive statistics for the sample data. Table 13.6 shows the results. You should verify that all of the hand calculations match the values produced by Excel. Any differences between the hand calculations and the computer-generated results are due to rounding.

TABLE 13.6 Excel-Produced ANOVA Results for Public Transportation Example

SUMMARY					
Groups	**Count**	**Sum**	**Average**	**Variance**	
Boston	5	63110	12622	7707.5	
New York	8	100680	12585	6464.3	
San Francisco	6	70320	11720	7050	
Chicago	5	53650	10730	8212.5	

ANOVA						
Source of Variation	**SS**	**df**	**MS**	**F**	**p-value**	**F crit**
Between Groups	13204720	3	4401573	**610.57**	**7.96E-20**	3.098
Within Groups	144180	20	7209			
Total	13348900	23				

EXAMPLE 13.1

Using the information in Table 13.6, repeat the ANOVA test for the public transportation example using the p-value approach.

SOLUTION: In order to determine whether cost savings in public transportation differ between the four cities, we specify the same competing hypotheses as

$$H_0: \mu_1 = \mu_2 = \mu_3 = \mu_4$$
$$H_A: \text{Not all population means are equal}$$

From Table 13.6, we find that the value of the test statistic is $F_{3,20} = 610.57$. Its corresponding p-value is 7.96×10^{-20}, or equivalently, $P(F_{3,20} \geq 610.57) \approx 0.0000$. (See the value for the test statistic and the p-value in boldface in Table 13.6.) Since the p-value is less than $\alpha = 0.05$, we reject the null hypothesis and again conclude that the mean cost savings from using public transportation is not the same for each city.

EXERCISES 13.1

Concepts

1. A random sample of five observations from three treatments produced the following data:

Treatments		
A	**B**	**C**
22	20	19
25	25	22
27	21	24
24	26	21
22	23	19
$\bar{x}_A = 24$	$\bar{x}_B = 23$	$\bar{x}_C = 21$
$s_A^2 = 4.5$	$s_B^2 = 6.5$	$s_C^2 = 4.5$

a. Calculate the grand mean.
b. Calculate SSTR and MSTR.
c. Calculate SSE and MSE.
d. Specify the competing hypotheses in order to determine whether some differences exist between the population means.
e. Calculate the value of the $F_{(df_1, df_2)}$ test statistic.
f. Using the critical value approach at the 5% significance level, what is the conclusion to the test?

2. Random sampling from four treatments produced the following data:

Treatments			
A	**B**	**C**	**D**
−11	−8	−8	−12
−13	−13	−13	−13
−10	−15	−8	−15
	−12	−13	
		−10	
$\bar{x}_A = -11.3$	$\bar{x}_B = -12$	$\bar{x}_C = -10.4$	$\bar{x}_D = -13.3$
$s_A^2 = 2.33$	$s_B^2 = 8.7$	$s_C^2 = 6.3$	$s_D^2 = 2.3$

a. Calculate the grand mean.

b. Calculate SSTR and MSTR.

c. Calculate SSE and MSE.

d. Specify the competing hypotheses in order to determine whether some differences exist between the population means.

e. Calculate the value of the F test statistic.

f. Approximate the p-value.

g. At the 10% significance level, what is the conclusion to the test?

3. Given the following information, construct an ANOVA table and perform an ANOVA test of mean differences at the 1% significance level.

$SSTR = 220.7$; $SSE = 2{,}252.2$; $c = 3$; $n_1 = n_2 = n_3 = 8$

4. Given the following information, construct an ANOVA table and perform an ANOVA test of mean differences at the 5% significance level.

$SST = 70.47$; $SSTR = 11.34$; $c = 4$; $n_1 = n_2 = n_3 = n_4 = 15$

5. A completely randomized design of an analysis of variance experiment produced a portion of the accompanying ANOVA table.

Source of Variation	SS	df	MS	F	p-value	F crit
Between Groups	25.08	3	?	?	0.0004	2.725
Within Groups	92.64	76	?			
Total	117.72	79				

a. Fill in the missing statistics in the ANOVA table.

b. Specify the competing hypotheses in order to determine whether some differences exist between the population means.

c. At the 5% significance level, what is the conclusion to the test?

6. A completely randomized design of an analysis of variance experiment produced a portion of the following ANOVA table.

Source of Variation	SS	df	MS	F	p-value	F crit
Between Groups		5	?	?	?	?
Within Groups	4321.11	54	?			
Total	4869.48	59				

a. Fill in the missing statistics in the ANOVA table.

b. Specify the competing hypotheses in order to determine whether some differences exist between the population means.

c. At the 10% significance level, what is the conclusion to the test?

Applications

7. Asian residents in Boston have the highest average life expectancy of any racial or ethnic group—a decade longer than black residents (*The Boston Globe*, August 16, 2010). Suppose sample results indicative of the overall results are as follows.

Asian	Black	Latino	White
$\bar{x}_1 = 83.7$ years	$\bar{x}_2 = 73.5$ years	$\bar{x}_3 = 80.6$ years	$\bar{x}_4 = 79.0$ years
$s_1^2 = 26.3$	$s_2^2 = 27.5$	$s_3^2 = 28.2$	$s_4^2 = 24.8$
$n_1 = 20$	$n_2 = 20$	$n_3 = 20$	$n_4 = 20$

a. Construct an ANOVA table.

b. Specify the competing hypotheses to test whether there are some differences in average life expectancies between the four ethnic groups.

c. At the 5% significance level, what is the conclusion to the test?

8. A well-known conglomerate claims that its detergent "whitens and brightens better than all the rest." In order to compare the cleansing action of the top three brands of detergents, 24 swatches of white cloth were soiled with red wine and grass stains and then washed in front-loading machines with the respective detergents. The following whiteness readings were obtained:

Detergent		
1	**2**	**3**
84	78	87
79	74	80
87	81	91
85	86	77
94	86	78
89	89	79
89	69	77
83	79	78
$\bar{x}_1 = 86.3$	$\bar{x}_2 = 80.3$	$\bar{x}_3 = 80.9$
$s_1^2 = 20.8$	$s_2^2 = 45.1$	$s_3^2 = 27.3$
	$\bar{\bar{x}} = 82.5$	

a. Construct an ANOVA table.

b. Specify the competing hypotheses to test whether there are some differences in the average whitening effectiveness of the three detergents.

c. At the 5% significance level, what is the conclusion to the test?

9. A recent survey by Genworth Financial Inc., a financial-services company, concludes that the cost of long-term

care in the U.S. varies significantly, depending on where an individual lives (*The Wall Street Journal*, May 16, 2009). An economist collects data from the five states with the highest annual costs (Alaska, Massachusetts, New Jersey, Rhode Island, and Connecticut) in order to determine if his sample data are consistent with the survey's conclusions. The economist provides the following portion of an ANOVA table:

ANOVA					
Source of Variation	**SS**	**df**	**MS**	**F**	**p-value**
Between Groups	635.0542	4	?	?	?
Within Groups	253.2192	20	?		
Total	888.2734	24			

a. Complete the ANOVA table.
b. Specify the competing hypotheses to test whether some differences exist in the mean long-term care costs in these five states.
c. At the 5% significance level, do mean costs differ?

10. An online survey by the Sporting Goods Manufacturers Association, a trade group of sports retailers and marketers, claimed that household income of recreational athletes varies by sport (*The Wall Street Journal*, August 10, 2009). In order to verify this claim, an economist samples five sports enthusiasts participating in each of six different recreational sports and obtains each enthusiast's income (in $1,000s), as shown in the table below:

Snorkeling	Sailing	Boardsailing/ Windsurfing	Bowling	On-road triathlon	Off-road triathlon
90.9	87.6	75.9	79.3	64.5	47.7
86.0	95.0	75.6	75.8	67.2	59.6
93.6	94.6	83.1	79.6	62.8	68.0
98.8	87.2	74.4	78.5	59.2	60.9
98.4	82.5	80.5	73.2	66.5	50.9
$\bar{x}_1 = 93.5$	$\bar{x}_2 = 89.4$	$\bar{x}_3 = 77.9$	$\bar{x}_4 = 77.3$	$\bar{x}_5 = 64.0$	$\bar{x}_6 = 57.4$
$s_1^2 = 28.8$	$s_2^2 = 28.5$	$s_3^2 = 13.8$	$s_4^2 = 7.4$	$s_5^2 = 10.3$	$s_6^2 = 66.4$

$$\bar{\bar{x}} = 76.6$$

a. Specify the competing hypotheses in order to test the association's claim.
b. Create an ANOVA table.
c. At the 5% significance level, what is the critical value?
d. Do some average incomes differ depending on the recreational sport? Explain.

11. **FILE** (Use Excel) A statistics instructor wonders whether significant differences exist in her students' final exam scores in her three different sections. She randomly selects the scores from 10 different students in each section. A portion of the data is shown below; the complete data, labeled *Exam Scores*, are available on the text website.

Section 1	Section 2	Section 3
85	91	74
68	84	69
⋮	⋮	⋮
74	75	73

Do these data provide enough evidence at the 5% significance level to indicate that there are some differences in final exam scores among these three sections?

13.2 Multiple Comparison Methods

In the preceding section we used one-way ANOVA to determine whether differences exist between population means. Suppose that for a given sample, we reject the null hypothesis of equal means. While the ANOVA test determines that not all population means are equal, it does not indicate which ones differ. To find out which population means differ requires further analysis of the direction and the statistical significance of the difference between paired population means ($\mu_i - \mu_j$). By constructing confidence intervals for all pairwise differences of the population means, we can identify which means significantly differ from one another.

In this section we also introduce a more powerful method, developed by the renowned 20th century statistician John Tukey (1915–2000), that identifies "honestly significant differences" between population means. Note that there are no significant differences to find if the ANOVA test does not reject the null hypothesis of equal means.

LO 13.3

Use confidence intervals and Tukey's HSD method in order to determine which means differ.

Fisher's Least Difference (LSD) Method

In Chapter 10 we stated that, when σ_i and σ_j are unknown but assumed equal, the $100(1 - \alpha)\%$ confidence interval of the difference between two population means $\mu_i - \mu_j$ is

$$(\bar{x}_i - \bar{x}_j) \pm t_{\alpha/2, n_i + n_j - 2} \sqrt{s_p^2 \left(\frac{1}{n_i} + \frac{1}{n_j} \right)}.$$

Here s_p^2 is a pooled estimate of the common population variance, and is computed as

$$s_p^2 = \frac{(n_i - 1)s_i^2 + (n_j - 1)s_j^2}{n_i + n_j - 2}.$$

We can improve upon the precision of this estimate by substituting MSE from the ANOVA test for s_p^2. Recall that when we conduct an ANOVA test we assume that we are sampling from populations that have the same population variance σ^2. We still apply the t_{df} distribution, but we use the degrees of freedom corresponding to MSE, or $df = n_T - c$.

EXAMPLE 13.2

Using the sample means and the ANOVA results from the public transportation example of Section 13.1, calculate 95% confidence intervals for the difference between all possible pairings of the four population means. Comment on the direction and the significance of the differences at the 5% level.

SOLUTION: We are given the following descriptive statistics:

$$\bar{x}_{\text{Boston}} = 12{,}622 \qquad n_{\text{Boston}} = 5$$
$$\bar{x}_{\text{New York}} = 12{,}585 \qquad n_{\text{New York}} = 8$$
$$\bar{x}_{\text{San Francisco}} = 11{,}720 \qquad n_{\text{San Francisco}} = 6$$
$$\bar{x}_{\text{Chicago}} = 10{,}730 \qquad n_{\text{Chicago}} = 5$$

In addition, $MSE = 7{,}209$ (derived from the ANOVA test in Section 13.1), $n_T - c = 24 - 4 = 20$, and $t_{\alpha/2, n_T - c} = t_{0.025, 20} = 2.086$. Table 13.7 shows the 95% confidence intervals.

TABLE 13.7 Fisher's 95% Confidence Intervals for Example 13.2

Population Mean Differences	Confidence Interval
$\mu_{\text{Boston}} - \mu_{\text{New York}}$	$(12{,}622 - 12{,}585) \pm 2.086\sqrt{7{,}209\left(\frac{1}{5} + \frac{1}{8}\right)} = 37 \pm 100.97$ or $[-63.97, 137.97]$
$\mu_{\text{Boston}} - \mu_{\text{San Francisco}}$	$(12{,}622 - 11{,}720) \pm 2.086\sqrt{7{,}209\left(\frac{1}{5} + \frac{1}{6}\right)} = 902 \pm 107.25$ or $[794.75, 1{,}009.25]$
$\mu_{\text{Boston}} - \mu_{\text{Chicago}}$	$(12{,}622 - 10{,}730) \pm 2.086\sqrt{7{,}209\left(\frac{1}{5} + \frac{1}{5}\right)} = 1{,}892 \pm 112.02$ or $[1{,}779.98, 2{,}004.02]$
$\mu_{\text{New York}} - \mu_{\text{San Francisco}}$	$(12{,}585 - 11{,}720) \pm 2.086\sqrt{7{,}209\left(\frac{1}{8} + \frac{1}{6}\right)} = 865 \pm 95.65$ or $[769.35, 960.65]$
$\mu_{\text{New York}} - \mu_{\text{Chicago}}$	$(12{,}585 - 10{,}730) \pm 2.086\sqrt{7{,}209\left(\frac{1}{8} + \frac{1}{5}\right)} = 1{,}855 \pm 100.97$ or $[1{,}754.03, 1{,}955.97]$
$\mu_{\text{San Francisco}} - \mu_{\text{Chicago}}$	$(11{,}720 - 10{,}730) \pm 2.086\sqrt{7{,}209\left(\frac{1}{6} + \frac{1}{5}\right)} = 990 \pm 107.25$ or $[882.75, 1{,}097.25]$

The 95% confidence interval for $\mu_{\text{Boston}} - \mu_{\text{New York}}$ is given by 37 ± 100.97, which is $[-63.97, 137.97]$. Since this interval contains the value zero, we cannot reject the null hypothesis, given by H_0: $\mu_{\text{Boston}} - \mu_{\text{New York}} = 0$, at the 5% significance level. In other words, the average cost savings from using public transportation in Boston and in New York are not significantly different.

For $\mu_{\text{Boston}} - \mu_{\text{San Francisco}}$, the entire interval, ranging from 794.75 to 1,009.25, is above the value zero. We can therefore conclude at the 5% significance level that average cost savings from using public transportation in Boston are different from the average cost savings in San Francisco. In fact, the remaining intervals are all above zero, suggesting that average cost savings are different between the corresponding cities. In other words, we can conclude at the 5% significance level that average cost savings from using public transportation are different between Boston and Chicago, New York and San Francisco, New York and Chicago, and San Francisco and Chicago.

These pairwise comparisons of the means use **Fisher's least significant difference (LSD) method**, although the LSD tests are motivated within a hypothesis-testing framework. (Recall that we can conduct two-tailed tests with confidence intervals.) We can apply this method only if the ANOVA test has rejected the null hypothesis of equal means. However, as mentioned earlier, some problems are associated with inferring the equality of means by conducting paired tests. In Example 13.2, we have six paired tests. Therefore, if we use the 5% significance level for each test, the probability that we would make a Type I error (incorrectly rejecting a null hypothesis of equal means) on *at least* one of these individual tests will be greater than 5%. The more means we compare, the more the Type I error becomes inflated.

One way to avoid this problem is to perform each individual paired test at a reduced significance level, which ensures that the overall significance level for the equality of all means does not exceed α. The resulting confidence intervals are wider and hence reduce the probability of incorrectly rejecting the null hypothesis of equal means. However, this technique reduces the power of the test and thus results in an increased risk of a Type II error (incorrectly failing to reject a null hypothesis of equal means).

Tukey's Honestly Significant Differences (HSD) Method

A more powerful multiple comparison technique is **Tukey's honestly significant differences (HSD) method**. The original Tukey's HSD method was introduced with **balanced** data, but it was subsequently modified for **unbalanced** data. A completely randomized ANOVA design is said to be balanced if there is an equal number of observations in each sample, that is, when $n_1 = n_2 = \cdots = n_c$. An unbalanced design refers to situations where different numbers of observations occur in each sample, that is, when $n_i \neq n_j$. Tukey's method uses the studentized range distribution, which has broader, flatter, and thicker tails than the t_{df} distribution. In other words, for a given probability under the right tail of the distribution, the studentized range value will be larger than the corresponding t_{df} value. Therefore, Tukey's HSD method protects against an inflated risk of a Type I error.

The studentized range value $q_{\alpha,(c,n_T-c)}$ varies with the significance level α, the number of populations c, and $n_T - c$. Table 13.8 shows a portion of the studentized range table; Table 5 in Appendix A provides a more comprehensive table. For example, with $\alpha = 0.05$, $c = 6$, and $n_T - c = 19$, we find $q_{0.05,(6,19)} = 4.47$. With $\alpha = 0.01$, $c = 3$, and $n_T - c = 20$, we find $q_{0.01,(3,20)} = 4.64$. These values are in boldface in Table 13.8.

TABLE 13.8 Portion of Values for $q_{\alpha,(c,n_T - c)}$ in Tukey's HSD Method

$n_T - c$	α	\multicolumn{8}{c}{c = number of means}
		2	3	4	5	6	7	8	9
19	0.05	2.96	3.59	3.98	4.25	**4.47**	4.65	4.79	4.92
	0.01	4.05	4.67	5.05	5.33	5.55	5.73	5.89	6.02
20	0.05	2.95	3.58	3.96	4.23	4.45	4.62	4.77	4.90
	0.01	4.02	**4.64**	5.02	5.29	5.51	5.69	5.84	5.97

EXAMPLE 13.3

A consumer advocate in California is concerned with the price of a common generic drug. Specifically, he feels that one region of the state has significantly higher prices for the drug than two other regions. He divides the state into three regions and collects the generic drug's price from 10 pharmacies in each region. He produces the summary statistics and ANOVA results shown in Table 13.9

TABLE 13.9 Summary Statistics and ANOVA Results for Example 13.3

SUMMARY					
Groups	*Count*	*Sum*	*Average*	*Variance*	
Region 1	10	350	35.0	3.78	
Region 2	10	342	34.2	5.07	
Region 3	10	395	39.5	2.72	

ANOVA						
Source of Variation	**SS**	**df**	**MS**	**F**	**p-value**	**F crit**
Between Groups	163.27	2	81.63	21.17	2.95E-06	3.35
Within Groups	104.10	27	3.86			
Total	267.37	29				

a. At the 5% significance level, do differences exist between the mean drug prices in the three regions?

b. If significant differences exist, use Tukey's HSD method to determine which regions' means differ at the 5% significance level.

SOLUTION:

a. In order to test differences between the mean drug prices in the three regions, we specify the competing hypotheses as

$$H_0: \mu_{\text{Region1}} = \mu_{\text{Region2}} = \mu_{\text{Region3}}$$
$$H_A: \text{Not all mean drug prices are equal.}$$

The ANOVA table shows the value of the test statistic as $F_{(2,27)} = 21.17$ with a p-value of 2.95×10^{-6}, or $P(F_{2,27} \geq 21.17) \approx 0$. Since the p-value is less than the significance level of 0.05, we reject H_0 and conclude that not all mean drug prices are equal.

b. Since each sample size is the same ($n_1 = n_2 = n_3 = 10$ and $n_T = 30$), we can use Tukey's confidence intervals for balanced data. Given $\alpha = 0.05$, $c = 3$, and $n_T - c = 30 - 3 = 27$, we find $q_{\alpha,(c,n_T-c)} = q_{0.05,(3,27)} = 3.51$. We use $(\bar{x}_i - \bar{x}_j) \pm q_{\alpha,(c,n_T-c)} \sqrt{\frac{MSE}{n}}$ to compute 95% confidence intervals for all pairwise differences of the means. The results are shown in Table 13.10.

TABLE 13.10 Tukey's 95% Confidence Intervals for Example 13.3

Population Mean Differences	Confidence Interval	
$\mu_1 - \mu_2$	$(35.0 - 34.2) \pm 3.51\sqrt{\frac{3.86}{10}}$	or $[-1.38, 2.98]$
$\mu_1 - \mu_3$	$(35.0 - 39.5) \pm 3.51\sqrt{\frac{3.86}{10}}$	or $[-6.68, -2.32]^*$
$\mu_2 - \mu_3$	$(34.2 - 39.5) \pm 3.51\sqrt{\frac{3.86}{10}}$	or $[-7.48, -3.12]^*$

The asterisk * shows that the confidence interval does not include the value zero, thus indicating the corresponding means are different at the 5% significance level. The consumer advocate's claim is supported by the data. At the 5% significance level, the average price of generic drugs in region 3 is different from the average prices in regions 1 and 2. At the 5% significance level, the consumer advocate cannot conclude that average prices in regions 1 and 2 differ.

We also employed Tukey's method for unbalanced data using the ANOVA results from the public transportation example. While the resulting intervals (not reported) became wider than those reported in Table 13.7, the inference regarding the population means remains the same.

A recent report by the American Public Transportation Association suggests that commuters who use public transportation can save a substantial amount of money annually. Sean Cox, a research analyst at an environmental firm, conducts a survey to determine whether average cost savings differ depending on where the commuters reside. He collects data on public transit riders in the top four cost-savings cities: Boston, New York, San Francisco, and Chicago. Table 13.11 shows summary statistics and relevant ANOVA results.

TABLE 13.11 Summary Statistics and Relevant ANOVA Results

Boston	New York	San Francisco	Chicago
$\bar{x}_1 = \$12{,}622$	$\bar{x}_2 = \$12{,}585$	$\bar{x}_3 = \$11{,}720$	$\bar{x}_4 = \$10{,}730$
$s_1 = \$87.79$	$s_2 = \$80.40$	$s_3 = \$83.96$	$s_4 = \$90.62$
$n_1 = 5$	$n_2 = 8$	$n_3 = 6$	$n_4 = 5$
Mean Square Error (MSE): 7,209			
Calculated F-statistic and its p-value: 610.6 and 0.0000, respectively.			

Sean reports that in all four major cities the sample average cost savings are above $10,000. Also, since the p-value of the ANOVA test is close to zero, he concludes that there are differences in cost savings between the cities at the 5% significance level. Sean constructs confidence intervals for each pairing to summarize the order of cost savings and concludes that commuters in Chicago have the least cost savings of the four cities, followed by commuters in San Francisco. Commuters in Boston and New York have the highest cost savings; however, at the 5% significance level, their average cost savings do not differ from one another.

EXERCISES 13.2

Concepts

12. The following statistics are computed by sampling from three normal populations whose variances are equal:

$\bar{x}_1 = 25.3, n_1 = 8; \bar{x}_2 = 31.5, n_2 = 10; \bar{x}_3 = 32.3, n_3 = 6; MSE = 27.2$

a. Calculate 95% confidence intervals for $\mu_1 - \mu_2, \mu_1 - \mu_3,$ and $\mu_2 - \mu_3$ using Fisher's LSD approach.

b. Repeat the analysis with Tukey's HSD approach.

c. Which of these two approaches would you use to determine whether differences exist between the population means? Explain.

13. The following statistics are calculated by sampling from four normal populations whose variances are equal:

$\bar{x}_1 = 149, n_1 = 10; \bar{x}_2 = 154, n_2 = 10; \bar{x}_3 = 143, n_3 = 10;$
$\bar{x}_4 = 139, n_4 = 10; MSE = 51.3$

a. Use Fisher's LSD test to determine which population means differ at $\alpha = 0.01$.

b. Use Tukey's HSD test to determine which population means differ at $\alpha = 0.01$.

c. Do all population means differ? Explain.

14. A completely randomized design of an analysis of variance experiment produced a portion of the following ANOVA table.

SUMMARY		
Groups	**Count**	**Average**
Column 1	6	0.57
Column 2	6	1.38
Column 3	6	2.33

ANOVA						
Source of Variation	**SS**	**df**	**MS**	**F**	**p-value**	**F crit**
Between Groups	9.12	2	4.56	12.84	0.0006	3.68
Within Groups	5.33	15	0.36			
Total	14.46	17				

a. Conduct an ANOVA test at the 5% significance level to determine if some population means differ.

b. Calculate 95% confidence interval estimates of $\mu_1 - \mu_2$, $\mu_1 - \mu_3$, and $\mu_2 - \mu_3$ with Tukey's approach.

c. Given your response to part b, which means significantly differ?

15. A completely randomized design of an analysis of variance experiment produced a portion of the following ANOVA table.

SUMMARY

Groups	Count	Average
Column 1	10	349
Column 2	10	348
Column 3	10	366
Column 4	10	365

ANOVA

Source of Variation	SS	df	MS	F	p-value	F crit
Between Groups	2997.11	3	999.04	15.54	1.2E-06	2.866
Within Groups	2314.71	36	64.30			
Total	5311.82	39				

a. Use Fisher's LSD test to determine which means differ at the 5% level of significance.

b. Use Tukey's HSD test to determine which means differ at the 5% level of significance.

c. Given your responses to parts a and b, do the population means differ at the 5% significance level?

Applications

16. In an attempt to improve efficiency, Starbucks has implemented "lean" Japanese techniques at many of its 11,000 U.S. stores (*The Wall Street Journal*, August 4, 2009). By reducing the time baristas (employees) spend on bending, reaching, and walking, they will have more time to interact with customers and improve the Starbucks experience. Suppose Starbucks adopts the lean technique at Store 1, but makes no changes at Stores 2 and 3. On a recent Monday morning between the hours of 7:00 AM and 8:00 AM, the following statistics were obtained relating to average time per order (in seconds):

Store 1: $\bar{x}_1 = 56$, $n_1 = 18$
Store 2: $\bar{x}_2 = 66$, $n_2 = 12$
Store 3: $\bar{x}_3 = 63$, $n_3 = 14$

Excel produced the following ANOVA table:

Source of Variation	SS	df	MS	F	p-value	F crit
Between Groups	811.70	2	405.85	52.11	5.5E-12	3.226
Within Groups	319.30	41	7.79			
Total	1131.00	43				

a. Compute 95% confidence interval estimates of all paired differences of the means using Fisher's LSD approach.

b. Repeat the analysis with Tukey's HSD approach.

c. Which of these two approaches is more reliable? Explain.

d. Does the data suggest that the lean technique is improving efficiency? Explain.

17. The following Excel output summarizes the results for a completely randomized design of an analysis of variance experiment in which the treatments were three different hybrid cars and the variable measured was the miles per gallon (mpg) obtained while driving the same route.

Hybrid 1: $\bar{x}_1 = 38$, $n_1 = 20$
Hybrid 2: $\bar{x}_2 = 48$, $n_2 = 15$
Hybrid 3: $\bar{x}_3 = 39$, $n_3 = 18$

Source of Variation	SS	df	MS	F	p-value	F crit
Between Groups	1034.51	2	517.26	19.86	4.49E-07	3.182
Within Groups	1302.41	50	26.05			
Total	2336.92	52				

a. At the 5% significance level, can we conclude that average mpg differs between the hybrids?

b. If significant differences exist, use Tukey's HSD test at the 5% significance level to determine which hybrids' means differ.

18. Do energy bills vary dramatically depending on where you live in the United States? Suppose 25 households from four regions in the United States are sampled. The values for the average annual energy bill are shown below and are consistent with those found by The Department of Energy (*Money*, June 2009).

Region	West	Northeast	Midwest	South
Average Annual Energy Bill	$1,491	$2,319	$1,768	$1,758

A portion of the ANOVA calculations are below:

Source of Variation	SS	df	MS	F	p-value
Between Groups	7531769	3	?	?	7.13E-24
Within Groups	3492385	96	?		
Total	11024154	99			

a. Complete the ANOVA table.

b. At the 1% significance level, can we conclude that average annual energy bills vary by region?

c. If significant differences exist, use Tukey's method at the 1% significance level to determine which regions' means differ.

19. Producers of a new grass seed called Pearl's Premium claim that grass grown using its seed blend requires less maintenance as compared to other brands (*The Boston Globe*, July 4, 2009). For instance, grass grown using Pearl's

Premium needs mowing only once a month. Suppose an independent tester wants to test whether the average height of grass after one month's growth is the same between Pearl's Premium and the other two top-selling brands. The independent tester measures 25 grass blades using each of the three seeds (glass blades are measured in inches). Using Excel, he constructs the following ANOVA table with supporting descriptive statistics.

SUMMARY		
Groups	**Count**	**Average**
Pearl's Premium	25	4.83
Top Brand 1	25	6.50
Top Brand 2	25	6.99

ANOVA						
Source of Variation	**SS**	**df**	**MS**	**F**	**p-value**	**F crit**
Between Groups	64.43	2	32.21	121.67	8.09E-24	3.123
Within Groups	19.06	72	0.26			
Total	83.49	74				

a. At the 5% significance level, can we conclude that the average heights of grass blades differ by brand?

b. If significant differences exist, use Tukey's method at the 5% significance level to determine which brands differ.

20. **FILE** (Use Excel) The accompanying table shows a portion of quarterly data on Nike's revenue for the fiscal years 2001 through 2010. Data for a fiscal year refers to the time period from June 1 through May 31. The entire data set can be found on the text website, labeled **Nike Revenue**.

	Quarters Ended			
Year	**August 31**	**November 30**	**February 28**	**May 31**
2001	2,637	2,199	2,170	2,483
2002	2,614	2,337	2,260	2,682
⋮	⋮	⋮	⋮	⋮
2010	4,799	4,406	4,733	5,077

Source: Annual Reports for Nike, Inc.

a. Use one-way ANOVA to determine if the data provide enough evidence at the 5% significance level to indicate that there are quarterly differences in Nike's revenue.

b. Given your response to part a, does the construction of confidence intervals using Fisher's or Tukey's methods provide further information? Explain.

13.3 Two-Way ANOVA: No Interaction

LO **13.4**

Conduct and evaluate hypothesis tests based on two-way ANOVA with no interaction.

As we have seen, one-way ANOVA tests are used to compare population means based on one categorical variable or factor. For instance, we can use one-way ANOVA to determine whether differences exist in average miles per gallon depending on the brand name of hybrid cars. Two-way ANOVA tests extend the analysis by measuring the effects of two factors simultaneously. Suppose we want to determine if the brand of a hybrid car and the octane level of gasoline influence average miles per gallon. Whereas one-way ANOVA tests are able to assess either the brand effect or the octane-level effect in isolation, two-way ANOVA tests are able to assess the effect of a factor while controlling for the other factor. The additional factor explains some of the unexplained variation in miles per gallon, or equivalently, reduces the error sum of squares for a more discriminating $F_{(df_1, df_2)}$ test statistic.

Another feature of two-way ANOVA is that it can be extended to capture the interaction between the factors. In the above example, if we believe that some brands of a hybrid car react more positively to the octane levels than others, then we can include the interaction of these factors in examining miles per gallon. We use tests that help determine whether we can reject the null hypothesis that the factors are independent, and thus conclude that the factors do indeed interact.

> **Two-way ANOVA** tests are used to simultaneously examine the effect of two factors on the mean. These tests can be conducted with or without the interaction of the factors.

In the following example we initially apply one-way ANOVA and recognize its limitations. We then introduce two-way ANOVA without interaction. In Section 13.4 we discuss two-way ANOVA with interaction.

EXAMPLE 13.4

Julia Hayes is an undergraduate who is completely undecided as to what career she should pursue. To help in her decision process, she wants to determine whether or not there are significant differences in annual incomes depending on the field of employment. Initially, she confines her analysis to the following three fields: educational services, financial services, and medical services. As a preliminary experiment, she surveys four workers from each of these three fields and asks how much he/she earns annually. Table 13.12 shows the results (in $1,000s) from the experiment; the data are also available on the text website, labeled *One-Factor Income*.

TABLE 13.12 Data for Example 13.4

FILE	Educational Services	Financial Services	Medical Services
	35	58	110
	18	90	62
	75	25	26
	46	45	43

Use one-way ANOVA to determine if differences exist among the fields' average incomes at the 5% significance level.

SOLUTION: Table 13.13 shows the relevant results from implementing a one-way ANOVA test.

TABLE 13.13 ANOVA Results for Example 13.4

ANOVA						
Source of Variation	SS	df	MS	F	p-value	F crit
Between Groups	579.5	2	289.75	0.32998	0.727281	4.2565
Within Groups	7902.75	9	878.0833			
Total	8482.25	11				

In order to determine whether mean incomes differ by field of employment, we specify the following hypotheses:

$$H_0: \mu_{\text{Education}} = \mu_{\text{Financial}} = \mu_{\text{Medical}}$$
$$H_A: \text{Not all population means are equal}$$

The value of the test statistic is $F_{(2,9)} = 0.33$. Using the critical value approach, the decision rule is to reject H_0 if $F_{(2,9)} > 4.26$. We do not reject the null hypothesis since the value of the test statistic does not fall in the rejection region (0.33 is not greater than 4.26). At the 5% significance level, we cannot conclude that average incomes differ by field.

Julia is surprised by these results, since she feels that those in the educational services industry probably earn less than those in the other two fields. Julia is advised that she must interpret these results with caution because many other factors influence annual income—one of which is an individual's educational attainment. We can capture the true influence of field of employment on income only when educational attainment is held fixed.

As mentioned earlier, two-way ANOVA helps us find a more discriminating $F_{(df_1, df_2)}$ test statistic, since the additional factor reduces the resulting error sum of squares. An added requirement for two-way ANOVA tests is that all groups must have the same sample size.

To show how two-way ANOVA works, we redo the analysis from Example 13.4, but this time we allow the variation in income to be affected by field (the treatment or factor A) *and* educational attainment (the block or factor B). We match a worker from each field according to his or her highest educational attainment; that is, we delineate one worker whose highest educational attainment is a high school degree; we then select three other matched groups, or blocks, whose highest educational attainments are a bachelor's degree, a master's degree, and a Ph.D. or its equivalent. The outcomes in this experiment are **matched** or **blocked** according to their educational attainment, with one worker for each field of employment and level of educational attainment. In general, blocks are the levels at which we hold an extraneous factor fixed, so that we can measure its contribution to the total variation of the data. This experimental design is called a **randomized block design**. The experiment in this example is designed to eliminate the variability in income attributable to differences in educational attainment.

TWO-WAY ANOVA (WITHOUT INTERACTION) AND RANDOMIZED BLOCK DESIGN

In two-way ANOVA without interaction, the total variability of the data is partitioned into three components attributed to the treatment (factor A), the block (factor B), and chance, respectively. The term block refers to a matched group of observations from each population. If units within each block are randomly assigned to each of the treatments, then the design of the experiment is referred to as a **randomized block design**.

Table 13.14 shows the incomes (in $1,000s) for 12 workers according to their field of employment and highest educational attainment; these data labeled **Two-Factor Income** are also available on the text website. Also included in the table are the factor means.

TABLE 13.14 Data for Two-Factor Income Example (No Interaction)

Education Level (Factor B)	Field of Employment (Factor A)			Factor B Means
	Educational Services	Financial Services	Medical Services	
High School	18	25	26	$\bar{x}_{high\ school} = 23.00$
Bachelor's	35	45	43	$\bar{x}_{bachelor's} = 41.00$
Master's	46	58	62	$\bar{x}_{master's} = 55.33$
Ph.D.	75	90	110	$\bar{x}_{Ph.D.} = 91.67$
Factor A Means	$\bar{x}_{education} = 43.50$	$\bar{x}_{financial} = 54.50$	$\bar{x}_{medical} = 60.25$	$\bar{\bar{x}} = 52.75$

The goal of the analysis is to answer the following two questions:

a. At the 5% significance level, do average annual incomes differ by field of employment?

b. At the 5% significance level, do average annual incomes differ by level of educational attainment?

One-way ANOVA is based on one factor for which we used the notation "sum of squares due to treatments *SSTR*" to capture the variability *between* the levels of this factor. Since now we are examining two factors, we use the notation *SSA* to capture the variability *between* the levels of factor A and *SSB* to capture the variability *between* the levels of factor B. As mentioned earlier, with two-way ANOVA without replication, we partition the total sum of squares *SST* into three distinct components: the **sum of squares for factor A**, *SSA*; the **sum of squares for factor B**, *SSB*; and the **error sum of squares**, *SSE*. Thus,

$$SST = SSA + SSB + SSE.$$

The Sum of Squares for Factor A, SSA

We calculate the sum of squares for factor A as we did before; that is, we first calculate the sum of the squared differences between the mean for each level of factor A and the grand mean. Algebraically, $SSA = \sum_{i=1}^{c} (\bar{x}_i - \bar{\bar{x}})^2$. We then multiply this sum by the number of rows in the randomized block design r. For this example, r equals four. We calculate SSA as

$$SSA = r \sum_{i=1}^{c} (\bar{x}_i - \bar{\bar{x}})^2$$
$$= 4[(43.50 - 52.75)^2 + (54.50 - 52.75)^2 + (60.25 - 52.75)^2]$$
$$= 579.50.$$

Dividing SSA by the number of columns in the randomized block design minus one $(c - 1)$ yields the **mean square for factor A**, MSA. For this example, c equals three, so MSA is

$$MSA = \frac{SSA}{c - 1} = \frac{579.50}{3 - 1} = 289.75.$$

The Sum of Squares for Factor B, SSB

In order to obtain the sum of squares for factor B, we calculate the sum of the squared differences between the mean for each level of factor B and the grand mean. Algebraically, $SSB = \sum_{j=1}^{r} (\bar{x}_j - \bar{\bar{x}})^2$. We multiply this sum by the number of columns in the randomized block design c. Applying this formula to the sample data yields

$$SSB = c \sum_{j=1}^{r} (x_j - \bar{\bar{x}})^2$$
$$= 3[(23.00 - 52.75)^2 + (41.00 - 52.75)^2 + (55.33 - 52.75)^2 + (91.67 - 52.75)^2]$$
$$= 7,633.64.$$

Dividing SSB by the number of rows in the randomized block design minus one $(r - 1)$ yields the **mean square for factor B**, MSB, or

$$MSB = \frac{SSB}{r - 1} = \frac{7,633.64}{4 - 1} = 2,544.55.$$

The Error Sum of Squares, SSE

In two-way ANOVA we calculate the error sum of squares as the difference between SST and the sum of SSA and SSB. Since $SST = SSA + SSB + SSE$, we can rewrite this expression as $SSE = SST - (SSA + SSB)$. We calculate SST as the sum of squared differences between each data point and the grand mean, or equivalently, $SST = \sum_{i=1}^{c} \sum_{j=1}^{r} (x_{ij} - \bar{\bar{x}})^2$. For this example, we calculate SST as

$$SST = \sum_{i=1}^{c} \sum_{j=1}^{r} (x_{ij} - \bar{\bar{x}})^2$$
$$= (18 - 52.75)^2 + (35 - 52.75)^2 + \cdots + (110 - 52.75)^2$$
$$= 8,482.25.$$

We then compute SSE as

$$SSE = SST - (SSA + SSB) = 8,482.25 - (579.50 + 7,633.64) = 269.11.$$

We can make some generalizations about the difference in the magnitudes of the SSE values for the one-way ANOVA versus the two-way ANOVA examples. When we used one factor (field of employment) to explain annual incomes, the value of SSE was 7,902.75 (see Table 13.13). By ignoring the second factor (level of educational attainment), we could not establish that annual incomes were different by field of employment. However, once we include this second factor, the value of SSE declines dramatically to 269.11. We will show shortly that by accounting for the effect of educational attainment on income, an $F_{(df_1, df_2)}$ test statistic is produced that allows Julia to conclude that significant differences do exist among annual incomes by field of employment.

Dividing SSE by its degrees of freedom ($n_T - c - r + 1$) yields the **mean square error** MSE or

$$MSE = \frac{SSE}{n_T - c - r + 1} = \frac{269.11}{12 - 3 - 4 + 1} = 44.85.$$

Most software packages easily provide these statistics. Table 13.15 shows the general format of an ANOVA table for the randomized block design.

TABLE 13.15 General Format of ANOVA Table for Randomized Block Design

Source of Variation	SS	df	MS	F
Rows	SSB	$r - 1$	$MSB = \dfrac{SSB}{r - 1}$	$F_{(df_1, df_2)} = \dfrac{MSB}{MSE}$
Columns	SSA	$c - 1$	$MSA = \dfrac{SSA}{c - 1}$	$F_{(df_1, df_2)} = \dfrac{MSA}{MSE}$
Error	SSE	$n_T - c - r + 1$	$MSE = \dfrac{SSE}{n_T - c - r + 1}$	
Total	SST	$n_T - 1$		

Table 13.15 shows values for two $F_{(df_1, df_2)}$ test statistics. We use the first statistic $\left(F_{(df_1, df_2)} = \dfrac{MSB}{MSE}, \text{ where } df_1 = r - 1, df_2 = n_T - c - r + 1 \right)$ to test whether significant differences exist between the factor B means. We use the second statistic $\left(F_{(df_1, df_2)} = \dfrac{MSA}{MSE}, \text{ where } df_1 = c - 1, df_2 = n_T - c - r + 1 \right)$ to test whether significant differences exist between the factor A means.

Using Excel to Solve Two-Way ANOVA Problems (No Interaction)

In order to reproduce our manual calculations for the two-factor income example using Excel, we follow these steps.

A. **FILE** Open the *Two-factor Income* data found on the text website.

B. Choose **Data > Data Analysis > ANOVA: Two Factor Without Replication**.

C. In the *ANOVA: Two Factor Without Replication* dialog box shown in Figure 13.3, choose the box next to *Input range* and then select all the data, including the labels. Check the *Labels* box. If testing at a significance level other than 5%, insert the relevant significance level in the box next to *Alpha*. Choose an output range and click **OK**.

FIGURE 13.3 Excel's ANOVA: Two-Factor Without Replication dialog box

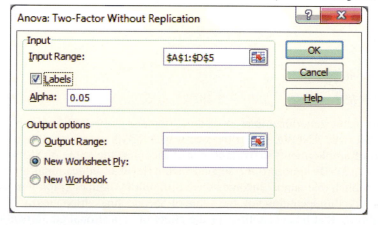

Table 13.16 shows a portion of the results. Any differences between our manual calculations and the values that appear in the table are due to rounding. Note that Excel provides

precise *p*-values for the calculated test statistics and critical values at the 5% significance level (this is the value of α specified in Excel's dialog box).

TABLE 13.16 Excel's ANOVA Output for the Two-Factor Income Example

ANOVA						
Source of Variation	SS	df	MS	F	p-value	F crit
Rows	7632.92	3	2544.31	56.58	8.6E-05	4.76
Columns	579.50	2	289.75	6.44	0.03207	5.14
Error	269.83	6	44.97			
Total	8482.25	11				

EXAMPLE 13.5

Use the Excel output from Table 13.16 to conduct the following hypothesis tests.

a. At the 5% significance level, do average annual incomes differ by field of employment?

b. At the 5% significance level, do average annual incomes differ by level of educational attainment?

SOLUTION:

a. Using the critical value approach, we determine whether average annual incomes differ by field of employment. The competing hypotheses are

$$H_0: \mu_{\text{Education}} = \mu_{\text{Financial}} = \mu_{\text{Medical}}$$
$$H_A: \text{Not all population means are equal}$$

When testing whether the factor A (column) means differ, the value of the test statistic is $F_{(df_1, df_2)} = \frac{MSA}{MSE} = \frac{289.75}{44.97} = 6.44$ where $df_1 = c - 1 = 3 - 1 = 2$ and $df_2 = n_T - c - r + 1 = 12 - 3 - 4 + 1 = 6$, that is, $F_{(2,6)} = 6.44$. At the 5% significance level, the critical value is $F_{0.05,(2,6)} = 5.14$. The decision rule is to reject H_0 if $F_{(2,6)} > 5.14$. We reject H_0 because the value of the test statistic is greater than the critical value. Therefore, contrary to the results derived earlier with one-way ANOVA, average annual salaries do differ by field of employment at the 5% significance level.

b. Using the *p*-value approach, we determine whether average annual incomes differ by level of educational attainment. The competing hypotheses are

$$H_0: \mu_{\text{High School}} = \mu_{\text{Bachelor's}} = \mu_{\text{Master's}} = \mu_{\text{Ph.D.}}$$
$$H_A: \text{Not all population means are equal}$$

When testing whether the factor B (row) means differ, the value of the test statistic is $F_{(df_1, df_2)} = \frac{MSB}{MSE} = \frac{2,544.31}{44.97} = 56.58$ where $df_1 = r - 1 = 4 - 1 = 3$ and $df_2 = n_T - c - r + 1 = 12 - 3 - 4 + 1 = 6$, that is, $F_{(3,6)} = 56.58$. From Table 13.16, the *p*-value associated with this test statistic is 8.6×10^{-5}, or $P(F_{(3,6)} \geq 56.58) \approx 0.0000$. We reject H_0 because the *p*-value is less than the significance level of 5%. We conclude at the 5% significance level that average annual salaries also differ by level of educational attainment. Since level of education attainment exerts a significant influence on salaries, it must be incorporated in ANOVA testing.

We would like to point out that, analogous to the last section, we can apply the *MSE* estimate from the two-way ANOVA test to construct useful confidence intervals for the paired differences in population means using Fisher's LSD method. The only significant modification to these confidence intervals is with respect to degrees of freedom, which are now given by $df = n_T - c - r + 1$. Similarly, we can also use Tukey's *HSD* method to determine which column means or row means are significantly different from one another. The value for the margin of error in the confidence interval will depend on whether we are assessing differences between the column means or the row means. When constructing the confidence interval for the difference between two column means, we calculate the margin of error as $q_{\alpha,(c,n_T-c)}\sqrt{\frac{MSE}{n}}$, where n is the number of observations in each column. When constructing the confidence interval for the difference between two row means, we calculate the margin of error as $q_{\alpha,(r,n_T-r)}\sqrt{\frac{MSE}{n}}$, where n is the number of observations in each row.

EXERCISES 13.3

Concepts

21. The observations shown in the accompanying table were drawn from a randomized block design with no interaction.

Factor B	Factor A				$\bar{x}_j$ for Factor B
	1	2	3	4	
1	2	3	2	4	2.8
2	6	5	7	6	6.0
3	8	10	9	10	9.3
$\bar{x}_i$ for Factor A	5.3	6.0	6.0	6.7	$\bar{x} = 6$

a. Calculate *SST*, *SSA*, *SSB*, and *SSE*.
b. Calculate *MSA*, *MSB*, and *MSE*.
c. Construct an ANOVA table.
d. At the 5% significance level, do the levels of Factor *B* differ?
e. At the 5% significance level, do the levels of Factor *A* differ?

22. The observations shown in the accompanying table were drawn from a randomized block design with no interaction.

Factor B	Factor A			$\bar{x}_j$ for Factor B
	1	2	3	
1	5	15	12	10.6
2	2	10	8	6.7
3	0	−9	−2	−3.7
4	−3	−14	−8	−8.3
$\bar{x}_i$ for Factor A	1.0	0.5	2.5	$\bar{x} = 1.33$

a. Calculate *SST*, *SSA*, *SSB*, and *SSE*.
b. Calculate *MSA*, *MSB*, and *MSE*.
c. Construct an ANOVA table.
d. At a 1% significance level, can you conclude that the column means differ?
e. At a 1% significance level, can you conclude that the row means differ? That is, is blocking necessary?

23. For a randomized block design having three treatments and five blocks, the results include the following sum of square terms:

$$SST = 311.7 \quad SSA = 201.6 \quad SSE = 69.3$$

a. Construct an ANOVA table.
b. At the 5% significance level, can you conclude that the row means differ?

c. At the 5% significance level, can you conclude that the column means differ?

24. For a randomized block design with no interaction having four levels of factor *A* and three levels of factor *B*, the results include the following sum of square terms:

$$SST = 1,630.7 \quad SSB = 532.3 \quad SSE = 374.5$$

a. Construct an ANOVA table.
b. At the 1% significance level, can you conclude that the factor *A* means differ?
c. At the 1% significance level, can you conclude that the factor *B* means differ?

25. The following table summarizes a portion of the results for a randomized block experiment with no interaction.

ANOVA						
Source of Variation	SS	df	MS	F	p-value	F crit
Rows	25.17	2	$MSB = ?$	$F_{Factor\ B} = ?$	0.0832	5.143
Columns	142.25	3	$MSA = ?$	$F_{Factor\ A} = ?$	0.0037	4.757
Error	19.50	6	$MSE = ?$			
Total	186.92	11				

a. Find the missing values in the ANOVA table.
b. At the 5% significance level, can you conclude that the column means differ?
c. At the 5% significance level, can you conclude that the row means differ?

26. The following table summarizes a portion of the results for a randomized block experiment with no interaction.

ANOVA						
Source of Variation	SS	df	MS	F	p-value	F crit
Rows	1057	5	$MSB = ?$	$F_{Factor\ B} = ?$	0.0064	3.326
Columns	7	2	$MSA = ?$	$F_{Factor\ A} = ?$	0.9004	4.103
Error	330	10	$MSE = ?$			
Total	1394	17				

a. Find the missing values in the ANOVA table.
b. At the 5% significance level, can you conclude that the column means differ?
c. At the 5% significance level, can you conclude that the row means differ?

Applications

27. The following output summarizes a portion of the results for a randomized block experiment with no interaction in which factor A consists of four different kinds of organic fertilizers, factor B consists of three different kinds of soil acidity levels, and the variable measured is the height (in inches) of a plant at the end of four weeks.

ANOVA

Source of Variation	SS	df	MS	F	p-value	F crit
Rows	0.13	2	$MSB = ?$	$F_{Factor B} = ?$	0.8182	5.143
Columns	44.25	3	$MSA = ?$	$F_{Factor A} = ?$	0.0001	4.757
Error	1.88	6	$MSE = ?$			
Total	46.25	11				

a. Find the missing values in the ANOVA table.
b. At the 5% significance level, can you conclude that average growth of the plant differs by organic fertilizer?
c. At the 5% significance level, can you conclude that the average growth of the plant differs by acidity level?

28. During a typical Professional Golf Association (PGA) tournament, the competing golfers play four rounds of golf, where the hole locations are changed for each round. Here are the scores for the top five finishers at the 2009 U.S. Open.

Golfer	Round 1	2	3	4
Lucas Glover	69	64	70	73
Phil Mickelson	69	70	69	70
David Duval	67	70	70	71
Ricky Barnes	67	65	70	76
Ross Fisher	70	78	79	72
Grand mean: $\bar{\bar{x}} = 70.45$				

The following statistics were computed:

$SST = 272.95$ $SSB = 93.2$ $SSE = 127.6$

a. Construct an ANOVA table.
b. At the 5% significance level, can you conclude that average scores produced by the four different rounds differ?
c. At the 5% significance level, can you conclude that the average scores produced by the five different players differ?

29. **FILE** Given a recent outbreak of illness caused by *E. coli* bacteria, the mayor in a large city is concerned that some of his restaurant inspectors are not consistent with their evaluations of a restaurant's cleanliness. In order to investigate this possibility, the mayor has five restaurant inspectors grade (scale of 0 to 100) the cleanliness of three restaurants. The results are shown in the accompanying table and can also be found on the text website, labeled **Restaurants**.

Inspector	Restaurant 1	2	3
1	72	54	84
2	68	55	85
3	73	59	80
4	69	60	82
5	75	56	84

a. Use Excel to generate the ANOVA table.
b. At the 5% significance level, can you conclude that average grades differ by restaurant?
c. If average grades differ by restaurant, use Tukey's HSD test at the 5% significance level to determine which averages differ.
d. At the 5% significance level, can you conclude that the average grades differ by inspector? Does the mayor have cause for concern?

30. **FILE** First National Bank employs three real estate appraisers whose job is to establish a property's market value before the bank offers a mortgage to a prospective buyer. It is imperative that each appraiser values a property with no bias. Suppose First National Bank wishes to check the consistency of the recent values that its appraisers have established. The bank asked the three appraisers to value (in $1,000s) three different types of homes: a cape, a colonial, and a ranch. The results are shown in the accompanying table and can also be found on the text website, labeled **Houses**.

House Type	Appraiser 1	2	3
Cape	$425	$415	$430
Colonial	530	550	540
Ranch	390	400	380

a. Use Excel to generate the appropriate ANOVA table.
b. At the 5% significance level, can you conclude that average values differ by appraiser? Should the bank be concerned with appraiser inconsistencies?
c. At the 5% significance level, can you conclude that average values differ by house type?
d. If average values differ by house type, use Tukey's HSD test at the 5% significance level to determine which averages differ.

13.4 Two-Way ANOVA: With Interaction

LO **13.5**

Conduct and evaluate hypothesis tests based on two-way ANOVA with interaction.

As mentioned in Section 13.3, we use a two-way ANOVA test with interaction to capture the possible relationship between factors A and B. Such tests allow the influence of factor A to change over levels of factor B and the influence of factor B to change over levels of factor A. In the annual income example from Section 13.3, field of employment may interact with educational attainment. In other words, the influence of field of employment may vary between levels of educational attainment. Similarly, the differences between educational attainment may not be the same for all fields of employment.

TWO-WAY ANOVA WITH INTERACTION

In **two-way ANOVA with interaction**, we partition the total sum of squares SST into four distinct components: the sum of squares for factor A, SSA; the sum of squares for factor B, SSB; the sum of squares for the interaction between the two factors, $SSAB$; and the error sum of squares, SSE. That is,

$$SST = SSA + SSB + SSAB + SSE.$$

While we still use a randomized block design, we need at least two observations for each combination of the ith level of factor A and the jth level of factor B. In other words, we need more than one observation per cell.

To illustrate two-way ANOVA with interaction, we reanalyze the income example, using new data with three incomes for each combination. Given the data in Table 13.17, we ultimately want to determine whether interaction is present between educational attainment and field of employment; these data, labeled *Two-Factor Income Interaction*, are also available on the text website.

TABLE 13.17 Data for Two-Factor Income Example with Interaction

Education Level (Factor *B*)	Field of Employment (Factor *A*)		
	Educational Services	**Financial Services**	**Medical Services**
High School	20	27	26
	25	25	24
	22	25	25
Bachelor's	30	44	42
	35	46	43
	34	48	45
Master's	46	50	62
	47	58	56
	50	56	60
Ph.D.	79	90	90
	78	92	100
	74	95	105

We are specifically interested in whether field of employment and education level interact with respect to average annual income. In order to find the relevant sum of squares for the test, we first compute the cell means and the factor means. For example, the cell mean for workers in educational services with a high school education is computed as $(20 + 25 + 22)/3 = 22.33$. Factor means are based on one row or one column of the data. Table 13.18 shows the cell means $\bar{x}_{ij}$, factor means $\bar{x}_i$ and $\bar{x}_j$, and the grand mean $\bar{\bar{x}}$ for the data.

TABLE 13.18 Cell and Factor Means for Two-Factor Income Example with Interaction

| Education Level (Factor B) | Field of Employment (Factor A) | | | Factor B Means |
	Educational Services	Financial Services	Medical Services	
High School	22.33	25.67	25.00	24.33
Bachelor's	33.00	46.00	43.33	40.78
Master's	47.67	54.67	59.33	53.89
Ph.D.	77.00	92.33	98.33	89.22
Factor A Means	45.00	54.67	56.50	$\bar{\bar{x}} = 52.06$

The Total Sum of Squares, SST

SST is computed as $SST = \sum_{i=1}^{c} \sum_{j=1}^{r} \sum_{k=1}^{w} (x_{ijk} - \bar{\bar{x}})^2$, where $w = 3$ is the number of observations per cell. Using all observations from Table 13.17 and the grand mean from Table 13.18, we calculate

$$SST = (20 - 52.06)^2 + (25 - 52.06)^2 + \cdots + (105 - 52.06)^2$$
$$= 22,008.$$

The Sum of Squares for Factor A, SSA, and the Sum of Squares for Factor B, SSB

The calculations of SSA and SSB are analogous to the earlier two-way ANOVA discussion, with one minor modification. For two-way ANOVA without interaction, SSA and SSB were calculated as $r\sum_{i=1}^{c} (\bar{x}_i - \bar{\bar{x}})^2$ and $c\sum_{j=1}^{r} (\bar{x}_j - \bar{\bar{x}})^2$, respectively. Now each formula is multiplied by the number of observations per cell w: $SSA = wr\sum_{i=1}^{c} (\bar{x}_i - \bar{\bar{x}})^2$ and $SSB = wc\sum_{j=1}^{r} (\bar{x}_j - \bar{\bar{x}})^2$. Given the means in Table 13.18 with $w = 3$, $c = 3$, and $r = 4$, we calculate

$$SSA = (3 \times 4)[(45 - 52.06)^2 + (54.67 - 52.06)^2 + (56.5 - 52.06)^2]$$
$$= 916,$$

and

$$SSB = (3 \times 3)[(24.33 - 52.06)^2 + (40.78 - 52.06)^2 + (53.89 - 52.06)^2$$
$$+ (89.22 - 52.06)^2]$$
$$= 20,524.$$

We divide by the respective degrees of freedom to obtain the **mean square for factor A**, *MSA* and the **mean square for factor B**, *MSB* as

$$MSA = \frac{SSA}{c - 1} = \frac{916}{3 - 1} = 458 \quad \text{and}$$

$$MSB = \frac{SSB}{r - 1} = \frac{20,524}{4 - 1} = 6,841.$$

The Sum of Squares for the Interaction of Factor A and Factor B, SSAB

When two factors interact, the effect of one factor on the mean depends upon the specific value or level present for the other factor. Interaction exists between these factors when two mathematical expressions, denoted Expression 1 and Expression 2, are significantly different from one another.

Expression 1 is defined as the difference of a cell mean from the grand mean, or equivalently, $(\bar{x}_{ij} - \bar{\bar{x}})$. Using the data from Table 13.18, one such difference would be $(\bar{x}_{11} - \bar{\bar{x}}) = (22.33 - 52.06)$.

Expression 2 is defined as the *combined* differences of the corresponding factor A mean from the grand mean and the corresponding factor B mean from the grand mean, or equivalently, $(\bar{x}_i - \bar{\bar{x}}) + (\bar{x}_j - \bar{\bar{x}})$. Again using the first cell in Table 13.18 as reference, the corresponding difference would be $(45 - 52.06) + (24.33 - 52.06)$.

If the difference between Expression 1 and Expression 2 is nonzero, then there is evidence of interaction. If we let I denote interaction, then we can measure I as

$$I = (\bar{x}_{ij} - \bar{\bar{x}}) - [(\bar{x}_i - \bar{\bar{x}}) + (\bar{x}_j - \bar{\bar{x}})].$$

This expression can be simplified to

$$I = \bar{x}_{ij} - \bar{x}_i - \bar{x}_j + \bar{\bar{x}}.$$

The sum of squares for the interaction between factor A and factor B, $SSAB$, is then based on a weighted sum of the squared interactions (I^2) where the weight equals the number of observations per cell w:

$$SSAB = w \sum_{i=1}^{c} \sum_{j=1}^{r} (\bar{x}_{ij} - \bar{x}_i - \bar{x}_j + \bar{\bar{x}})^2.$$

Using the means in Table 13.18, we calculate

$$SSAB = 3[(22.33 - 45 - 24.33 + 52.06)^2 + (33 - 45 - 40.78 + 52.06)^2$$
$$+ \cdots + (98.33 - 56.5 - 89.22 + 52.06)^2]$$
$$= 318.$$

We obtain the **mean square for interaction**, $MSAB$, by dividing $SSAB$ by the relevant degrees of freedom $(c - 1)(r - 1)$, or

$$MSAB = \frac{SSAB}{(c - 1)(r - 1)} = \frac{318}{(3 - 1)(4 - 1)} = 53.$$

The Error Sum of Squares, SSE

We solve for SSE by rearranging $SST = SSA + SSB + SSAB + SSE$, that is,

$$SSE = SST - (SSA + SSB + SSAB) = 22{,}008 - (916 + 20524 + 318) = 250.$$

Finally, we divide SSE by its degrees of freedom $rc(w - 1)$ and obtain the **mean square error** MSE as

$$MSE = \frac{SSE}{rc(w - 1)} = \frac{250}{(4 \times 3)(3 - 1)} = 10.4.$$

Using Excel to Solve Two-Way ANOVA Problems (with Interaction)

Fortunately, Excel easily calculates all of these statistics. We follow these steps.

A. **FILE** Open the *Two-Factor Income Interaction* data found on the text website.

B. Choose **Data** > **Data Analysis** > **ANOVA: Two Factor With Replication**.

C. In the *ANOVA: Two Factor With Replication* dialog box shown in Figure 13.4, choose the box next to *Input range* and then select all the data, including the labels. Enter 3

FIGURE 13.4 Excel's ANOVA: Two-Factor With Replication dialog box

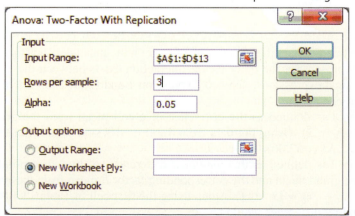

for *Rows Per Sample*. If testing at a significance level other than 5%, insert the relevant significance level in the box next to *Alpha*. Choose an output range and click **OK**.

Table 13.19 shows the relevant portion of the output. Any differences in our manual calculations and the values found in the table are due to rounding.

TABLE 13.19 Excel's ANOVA Output for the Two-Factor Income (with Interaction) Example

Source of Variation	SS	df	MS	F	p-value	F crit
Sample (Rows)	20524	3	6841	658.5	3.58E-23	3.009
Columns	916.2	2	458.1	44.1	9.18E-09	3.403
Interaction	318.4	6	53.07	5.109	0.001659	2.508
Within (Error)	249.3	24	10.39			
Total	22008	35				

Table 13.19 shows values for three $F_{(df_1, df_2)}$ test statistics. The first two test statistics are used to examine the **main effects**—potential differences in factor B or the row means $\left(F_{(df_1, df_2)} = \frac{MSB}{MSE}, \text{ where } df_1 = r - 1, df_2 = rc(w - 1) \right)$ and potential differences in factor A or the column means $\left(F_{(df_1, df_2)} = \frac{MSA}{MSE}, \text{ where } df_1 = c - 1, df_2 = rc(w - 1) \right)$. The third calculated test statistic $\left(F_{(df_1, df_2)} = \frac{MSAB}{MSE}, \text{ where } df_1 = (r - 1)(c - 1), df_2 = rc(w - 1) \right)$ is used to test whether there is interaction between factor A and factor B.

EXAMPLE 13.6

Use the Excel output from Table 13.19 to determine whether field of employment and education level interact with respect to the average annual income at the 5% significance level.

SOLUTION: We set up the following competing hypotheses:

H_0 : There is no interaction between factors A and B.

H_A: There is interaction between factors A and B.

The value of the test statistic is $F_{(df_1, df_2)} = \frac{MSAB}{MSE} = \frac{53.07}{10.39} = 5.11$ where $df_1 = (r - 1)$ $(c - 1) = (4 - 1)(3 - 1) = 6$ and $df_2 = rc(w - 1) = (4 \times 3)(3 - 1) = 24$, or $F_{(6,24)} = 5.11$ with a corresponding p-value of 0.0017. At the 5% significance level, we reject H_0 and conclude that sufficient evidence exists of an interaction effect between educational attainment and field of employment. This result implies that the average annual income for attaining an advanced degree is higher in some fields than in others.

Note that due to the interaction, the differences between educational attainment are not the same for all fields of employment. Such an outcome serves to complicate the interpretation of the main effects, since differences in one factor are not consistent across the other factor. This is why we should perform the interaction test before making any conclusions using the other two $F_{(df_1, df_2)}$ statistics. If the interaction effect is not significant, then we can proceed by focusing on the main effects: testing whether or not the row means or the column means differ. If the interaction effect is significant, as it is here, one option is to use another technique called regression analysis. Regression analysis is discussed in the next four chapters.

Concepts

31. A randomized block design has three levels of factor A and five levels of factor B where six replicates for each combination are examined. The results include the following sum of square terms:

    $SST = 1558 \quad SSA = 1008 \quad SSB = 400 \quad SSAB = 30$

    a. Construct an ANOVA table.
    b. At the 1% significance level, can you conclude that there is interaction between factor A and factor B?
    c. At the 1% significance level, can you conclude that the factor A means differ?
    d. At the 1% significance level, can you conclude that the factor B means differ?

32. A randomized block design has four levels of factor A and three levels of factor B. Five replicates for each combination are examined. The results include the following sum of square terms:

    $SST = 2500 \quad SSA = 1200 \quad SSB = 1000 \quad SSE = 280$

    a. Construct an ANOVA table
    b. At the 5% significance level, can you conclude that there is interaction between factor A and factor B?
    c. At the 5% significance level, can you conclude that the factor A means differ?
    d. At the 5% significance level, can you conclude that the factor B means differ?

33. A researcher conducts a randomized block experiment with interaction and provides the following ANOVA table.

ANOVA						
Source of Variation	SS	df	MS	F	p-value	F crit
Sample	752.78	2	$MSB=?$	$F_{\text{Factor B}} = ?$	0.0116	3.885
Columns	12012.50	1	$MSA=?$	$F_{\text{Factor A}} = ?$	5.62E-09	4.747
Interaction	58.33	2	$MSAB=?$	$F_{\text{Interaction}} = ?$	0.6117	3.885
Within	683.33	12	$MSE=?$			
Total	13506.94	17				

    a. Find the missing values in the ANOVA table.
    b. At the 5% significance level, can you conclude that there is an interaction effect?
    c. At the 5% significance level, can you conclude that the column means differ?
    d. At the 5% significance level, can you conclude that the row (sample) means differ?

34. A researcher conducts a randomized block experiment with interaction and provides the following ANOVA table.

ANOVA					
Source of Variation	SS	df	MS	F	p-value
Sample	30.827	1	30.827	11.690	0.0031
Columns	169.861	2	84.930	32.208	1.13E-06
Interaction	4.241	2	2.120	0.804	0.4629
Within	47.465	18	2.637		
Total	252.393	23			

    a. At the 1% significance level, can you conclude that there is interaction between the two factors?
    b. Are you able to conduct tests based on the main effects? If yes, conduct these tests at the 1% significance level. If no, explain.

Applications

35. The effects of detergent brand name (factor A) and the temperature of the water (factor B) on the brightness of washed fabrics are being studied. Four brand names and two temperature levels are used, and six replicates for each combination are examined. The following ANOVA table is produced.

ANOVA						
Source of Variation	SS	df	MS	F	p-value	F crit
Sample	75	1	75	63.38	8.92E-10	4.084
Columns	130.25	3	43.42	36.69	1.45E-11	2.839
Interaction	8.67	3	2.89	2.44	0.0783	2.839
Within	47.33	40	1.18			
Total	261.25	47				

    a. Can you conclude that there is interaction between detergent brand name and the temperature of the water at the 5% significance level?
    b. Are you able to conduct tests based on the main effects? If yes, conduct these tests at the 5% significance level. If no, explain.

36. **FILE** A consumer advocate examines whether the longevity of car batteries (measured in years) is affected by the brand name (factor A) and whether or not the car is kept in a garage (factor B). Interaction is suspected. The results are shown in the accompanying table and are also available on the text website, labeled **Brand and Garage**.

	Brand Name of Battery		
Kept in Garage?	A	B	C
Yes	7, 8, 8	6, 7, 7	8, 9, 9
No	5, 6, 6	4, 5, 4	6, 7, 7

    a. Use Excel to generate the appropriate ANOVA.

b. At the 5% significance level, is there interaction between brand name and whether a car is garaged?

c. At the 5% significance level, can you conclude that average battery lives differ by brand name?

d. At the 5% significance level, can you conclude that average battery lives differ depending on whether a car is garaged?

37. **FILE** (Use Excel) It is generally believed that a practical major such as business or engineering can really pay off for college graduates (CNNMoney.com, July 22, 2010). Other studies have shown that it is not just the major but also how students perform, as measured by their GPA, that influences their salaries. Henry Chen, an employee of PayScale.com, wants to measure the effect of major and GPA on starting salaries of graduates of the University of California at Irvine. He samples starting salaries of five graduates for a given GPA range from the schools of business, engineering, and social sciences. The sample data are shown in the following table; the data can also be found on the text website labeled **ANOVA-Salaries**.

GPA	Business	Engineering	Social Sciences
3.5–4.0	68	70	44
	54	66	52
	78	62	66
	80	56	42
	58	72	72
3.0–3.5	48	66	48
	76	54	48
	60	70	58
	48	52	56
	64	64	38
< 3.0	54	60	44
	42	42	38
	66	48	42
	58	59	52
	66	65	50

a. At the 5% significance level, is there interaction between major and GPA?

b. At the 5% significance level, can you conclude that starting salary differs between majors?

c. At the 5% significance level, can you conclude that starting salary depends on GPA?

38. **FILE** (Use Excel) A human resource specialist wants to determine whether the average job satisfaction score (on a scale of 0 to 100) is the same for three different industries and three types of work experience. A randomized block experiment with interaction is performed. The results are shown in the accompanying table and are also available on the text website, labeled **Job Satisfaction**.

| Work Experience | Industry | | |
	A	B	C
Less than 5 years	77	66	81
	67	58	59
	82	54	64
Five up to 10 years	93	65	57
	92	60	49
	97	68	72
10 years or more	58	75	60
	78	57	45
	91	47	59

a. Use Excel to generate the appropriate ANOVA table.

b. At the 5% significance level, is there interaction between industry and work experience?

c. At the 5% significance level, can you conclude that job satisfaction differs by industry?

d. At the 5% significance level, can you conclude that job satisfaction differs by work experience?

WRITING WITH STATISTICS

The Texas Transportation Institute, one of the finest higher-education-affiliated transportation research agencies in the nation, recently published its highly anticipated *2009 Annual Urban Mobility Report* (July 8, 2009). The study finds that the average U.S. driver languished in rush-hour traffic for 36.1 hours, as compared to 12 hours in 1982 when the records begin. This congestion also wasted approximately 2.81 billion gallons in fuel, or roughly three weeks' worth of gas per traveler. John Farnham, a research analyst at an environmental firm, is stunned by some of the report's conclusions. John is asked to conduct an independent study in order to see if differences exist in congestion depending

on the city where the traveler drives. He selects 25 travelers from each of the five cities that suffered from the worst congestion. He asks each traveler to approximate the time spent in traffic (in hours) over the last calendar year. Table 13.20 shows a portion of his sample results. The full data set can be found on the text website and is labeled *Congestion*.

TABLE 13.20 Annual Hours of Delay per Traveler in Five Cities

FILE

Los Angeles	Washington, DC	Atlanta	Houston	San Francisco
71	64	60	58	57
60	64	58	56	56
⋮	⋮	⋮	⋮	⋮
68	57	57	59	56

John wants to use the sample information to:

1. Determine whether significant differences exist in congestion, depending on the city where the traveler drives.

2. Use Tukey's method to establish in which of the five cities travelers experience the least and the worst delays.

Sample Report— Evaluating Traffic Congestion by City

Does traffic congestion vary by city? *The 2009 Annual Urban Mobility Report* found that traffic congestion, measured by annual hours of delay per traveler, was the worst in Los Angeles, followed by Washington, DC, Atlanta, Houston, and then San Francisco. An independent survey was conducted to verify some of the findings. Twenty-five travelers in each of these cities were asked how many hours they wasted in traffic over the past calendar year. Table 13.A reports the summary statistics. The sample data indicate that Los Angeles residents waste the most time sitting in traffic with an average of 69.2 hours per year. Washington, DC, residents rank a close second, spending an average of 62 hours per year in traffic. Residents in Atlanta, Houston, and San Francisco spend on average, 57.0, 56.5, and 55.6 hours per year in traffic. Houston had the highest and San Francisco the lowest variability of congestion as measured by their respective standard deviations.

TABLE 13.A Summary Statistics and Relevant ANOVA Results

Los Angeles	Washington, DC	Atlanta	Houston	San Francisco
$\bar{x}_1 = 69.2$	$\bar{x}_2 = 62.0$	$\bar{x}_3 = 57.0$	$\bar{x}_4 = 56.5$	$\bar{x}_5 = 55.6$
$s_1 = 4.6$	$s_2 = 4.7$	$s_3 = 4.8$	$s_4 = 5.4$	$s_5 = 3.7$
$n_1 = 25$	$n_2 = 25$	$n_3 = 25$	$n_4 = 25$	$n_5 = 25$

A one-way ANOVA test was conducted to test if significant differences in congestion exist in these five worst-congested cities. The value of the test statistic is $F_{4,120} = 37.3$ with a *p*-value of approximately zero. Therefore, at the 5% level of significance, we reject the null hypothesis of equal means and conclude that traffic congestion does vary by city.

In order to determine which cities had significantly different average delays per traveler, Tukey's *HSD* method was used. The 95% confidence interval for the difference between two population means $\mu_i - \mu_j$ was computed as $(\bar{x}_i - \bar{x}_j) \pm q_{\alpha,(c,n_T-c)} \sqrt{\frac{MSE}{n}}$. Referencing the studentized range table, the approximate value of $q_{0.05,(5,115)}$ is 3.92. The one-way ANOVA test produced an *MSE* of 21.82; thus, the margin of error for the confidence interval was $3.92 \sqrt{\frac{21.82}{25}}$, which equals 3.66. Therefore, we can conclude with 95% confidence that travelers in Los Angeles suffered the most hours of congestion followed by travelers in Washington, DC. Congestion was not significantly different in the cities of Atlanta, Houston, and San Francisco.

Conceptual Review

LO 13.1   **Provide a conceptual overview of ANOVA.**

Analysis of variance (ANOVA) tests are used to determine if differences exist between the means of three or more populations, thus generalizing the two-sample tests discussed in Chapter 10. The null hypothesis states that all population means are equal; thus, rejection of the null hypothesis indicates that not all population means are equal. ANOVA examines the amount of variability *between* the samples relative to the amount of variability *within* the samples. If the ratio of the *between* to *within* variabilities is significantly different from one, then we reject the null hypothesis of equal means. ANOVA tests are always specified as right-tailed tests and are based on the F distribution.

LO 13.2   **Conduct and evaluate hypothesis tests based on one-way ANOVA.**

One-way ANOVA analyzes the effect of one factor on the mean. It is based on a completely randomized design in which independent random samples are drawn from the c different levels of this factor (c populations), ignoring all other possible factors.

The **test statistic** for the hypothesis test of the equality of the population means using one-way ANOVA is assumed to follow the $F_{(df_1, df_2)}$ distribution with $df_1 = c - 1$ and $df_2 = n_T - c$, and its sample value is $F_{(df_1, df_2)} = \dfrac{MSTR}{MSE}$, where $MSTR$ and MSE are based on independent samples drawn from c normally distributed populations with a common variance σ^2.

LO 13.3   **Use confidence intervals and Tukey's HSD method in order to determine which means differ.**

The ANOVA test can determine whether significant differences exist between the population means. However, it cannot indicate which population means differ. By constructing confidence intervals for all pairwise differences of the population means, we can identify which means differ. Note that if the ANOVA test does not reject H_0, then there are no differences to find.

Fisher's LSD method is implemented by computing $100(1 - \alpha)\%$ confidence intervals for all mean differences $\mu_i - \mu_j$ as $(\bar{x}_i - \bar{x}_j) \pm t_{\alpha/2, n_T - c} \sqrt{MSE\left(\dfrac{1}{n_i} + \dfrac{1}{n_j}\right)}$ where the mean square error MSE is estimated from the ANOVA test. If the computed interval does not include the value zero, then we reject the null hypothesis $H_0: \mu_i - \mu_j = 0$.

When pairwise comparisons are made with Fisher's LSD method, we inflate the risk of the Type I error α; that is, we increase the risk of incorrectly rejecting the null hypothesis. In other words, if we conduct all pairwise tests at $\alpha = 0.05$, the resulting α for the overall test will be greater than 0.05.

A more powerful multiple comparison technique is **Tukey's HSD method**, which seeks out "honestly significant differences" between paired means. Tukey's method uses the **studentized range distribution**, which has broader, flatter, and thicker tails than the t_{df} distribution, and therefore, protects against an inflated risk of a Type I error. Tukey's $100(1 - \alpha)\%$ confidence interval for $\mu_i - \mu_j$ is computed as $(\bar{x}_i - \bar{x}_j) \pm q_{\alpha,(c, n_T - c)} \sqrt{\dfrac{MSE}{n}}$ for **balanced data** ($n = n_i = n_j$) and $(\bar{x}_i - \bar{x}_j) \pm q_{\alpha,(c, n_T - c)} \sqrt{\dfrac{MSE}{2}\left(\dfrac{1}{n_i} + \dfrac{1}{n_j}\right)}$ for **unbalanced data** ($n_i \neq n_j$), where $q_{\alpha,(c, n_T - c)}$ is the studentized range value.

LO 13.4   **Conduct and evaluate hypothesis tests based on two-way ANOVA with no interaction.**

Whereas one-way ANOVA tests are used to compare population means based on one factor, **two-way ANOVA** tests extend the analysis to measure the effects of two factors simultaneously. The additional factor explains some of the unexplained variation, or equivalently, reduces the error sum of squares for a more discriminating $F_{(df_1, df_2)}$ statistic. Two-way ANOVA tests can be conducted with or without interaction between the factors.

In **two-way ANOVA without interaction**, we partition the total variation SST into the sum of squares for factor A (SSA), the sum of squares for factor B (SSB), and the error sum of squares (SSE), that is, $SST = SSA + SSB + SSE$. We find two statistics. The value of the first statistic $F_{(df_1, df_2)} = \frac{MSB}{MSE}$, where $df_1 = r - 1$ and $df_2 = n_T - c - r + 1$ is used to test whether significant differences exist between the factor B means (the row means). The value of the second statistic $F_{(df_1, df_2)} = \frac{MSA}{MSE}$, where $df_1 = c - 1$ and $df_2 = n_T - c - r + 1$ is used to test whether significant differences exist between the factor A means (the column means).

LO 13.5   **Conduct and evaluate hypothesis tests based on two-way ANOVA with interaction.**

In **two-way ANOVA with interaction**, we partition the total variation SST into four components: the sum of squares for factor A (SSA), the sum of squares for factor B (SSB), the sum of squares for the interaction of the two factors ($SSAB$), and the error sum of squares (SSE), that is, $SST = SSA + SSB + SSAB + SSE$. Here we find the values of three $F_{(df_1, df_2)}$ test statistics. The first two statistics are used to examine the **main effects**—differences in the levels of factor B $\left(F_{(df_1, df_2)} = \frac{MSB}{MSE}, \text{ where } df_1 = r - 1 \text{ and } df_2 = rc(w - 1) \right)$ and differences in the levels of factor A $\left(F_{(df_1, df_2)} = \frac{MSA}{MSE}, \text{ where } df_1 = c - 1 \text{ and } df_2 = rc(w - 1) \right)$. The value of the third test statistic $F_{(df_1, df_2)} = \frac{MSAB}{MSE}$, where $df_1 = (r - 1)(c - 1)$ and $df_2 = rc(w - 1)$, is used to test whether there is interaction between factor A and factor B.

Interaction between the factors complicates the interpretation of the main effects. This is why we should perform the interaction test before testing the main effects. If the interaction effect is not significant, then we can proceed by focusing on the main effects. If the interaction effect is significant, one option is to use another technique called regression analysis. Regression analysis is discussed in the next four chapters.

Additional Exercises and Case Studies

39. A government agency wants to determine whether the average salaries of four various kinds of transportation operators differ. A random sample of five employees in each of the four categories yields the salary data given in the table below:

Average Salaries of Transportation Operators ($1,000s)			
Locomotive Engineer	**Truck Driver**	**Bus Driver**	**Taxi and Limousine Driver**
54.7	40.5	32.4	26.8
53.2	42.7	31.2	27.1
55.1	41.6	30.9	28.3
54.3	40.9	31.8	27.9
51.5	39.2	29.8	29.9
$\bar{x}_1 = 53.76$	$\bar{x}_2 = 40.98$	$\bar{x}_3 = 31.22$	$\bar{x}_4 = 28.00$
$s_1^2 = 2.10$	$s_2^2 = 1.69$	$s_3^2 = 0.96$	$s_4^2 = 1.49$
Grand mean: $\bar{\bar{x}} = 38.49$			

a. Construct an ANOVA table and estimate the p-value.

b. Specify the competing hypotheses in order to determine whether the average salaries of the transportation operators differ.

c. At the 5% significance level, can we conclude that the average salaries of the four transportation operators differ?

40. An economist wants to determine whether average Price/Earnings (P/E) ratios differ for firms in three industries. Independent samples of five firms in each industry show the following results:

Industry A	12.19	12.44	7.28	9.96	10.51	$\bar{x}_A = 10.48, s_A^2 = 4.32$
Industry B	14.34	17.80	9.32	14.90	9.41	$\bar{x}_B = 13.15, s_B^2 = 13.69$
Industry C	26.38	24.75	16.88	16.87	16.70	$\bar{x}_C = 20.32, s_C^2 = 23.30$
	Grand Mean: $\bar{\bar{x}} = 14.65$					

a. Construct an ANOVA table.

b. At the 5% significance level, determine whether average P/E ratios differ in the three industries.

c. If differences exist, use Tukey's test at the 5% significance level to determine which industries' mean P/E ratios differ.

41. An employee of a small software company in Minneapolis bikes to work during the summer months. He can travel to work using one of three routes and wonders whether the average commute

times (in minutes) differ between the three routes. He obtains the following data after traveling each route for one week.

Route 1	29	30	33	30	32
Route 2	27	32	28	30	29
Route 3	25	27	24	29	26

The following one-way ANOVA results were obtained for $\alpha = 0.01$:

ANOVA

Source of Variation	SS	df	MS	F	p-value	F crit
Between Groups	54.53	2	27.27	8.099	0.0059	6.93
Within Groups	40.40	12	3.37			
Total	94.93	14				

a. Determine at the 1% significance level whether the average commute times differ between the three routes.

b. If differences exist, use Tukey's *HSD* test at the 1% significance level to determine which routes' average times differ.

42. Before the recession, job-creating cities in the Sunbelt, like Las Vegas, Phoenix, and Orlando saw their populations, income levels, and housing prices surge. Las Vegas, however, offered something that often eluded these other cities: upward mobility for the working class. For example, hard-working hotel maids were able to prosper during the boom times. According to the Bureau of Labor Statistics (BLS), the average hourly rate for hotel maids was $14.25 in Las Vegas, versus $9.25 in Phoenix and $8.84 in Orlando (*The Wall Street Journal*, July 20, 2009). Suppose the following summary statistics and ANOVA table were produced for $\alpha = 0.05$ from a sample of hourly wages of 25 hotel maids in each city.

SUMMARY

Groups	Count	Average	
Las Vegas	25	13.91	
Phoenix	25	8.82	
Orlando	25	8.83	

ANOVA

Source of Variation	SS	df	MS	F	p-value	F crit
Between Groups	430.87	2	215.44	202.90	2.58E-30	3.124
Within Groups	76.44	72	1.06			
Total	507.31	74				

a. At the 5% significance level, do mean hourly rates for hotel maids differ between the three cities?

b. If differences exist, use Tukey's method to determine which cities' mean hourly rates differ at the 5% significance level.

43. An accounting professor wants to know if students perform the same on the departmental final exam irrespective of the accounting section they attend. The following Excel

output for $\alpha = 0.05$ summarizes a portion of the results for a completely randomized design in which the treatments were three different sections of an accounting course and the variable measured was the grade on the final exam.

ANOVA

Source of Variation	SS	df	MS	F	p-value	F crit
Between Groups	57.39	2	$MSTR = ?$	$F_{2,57} = ?$	0.3461	3.159
Within Groups	$SSE = ?$	57	$MSE = ?$			
Total	1570.19	59				

a. Find the missing values in the ANOVA table.

b. At the 5% significance level, can you conclude that average grades differ in the accounting sections?

44. The following Excel output for $\alpha = 0.05$ summarizes a portion of the results for a randomized block experiment without interaction where factor A (column) represents three income categories (low, medium, high), factor B (rows) consists of three different kinds of political parties (Democrat, Republican, Independent), and the variable measured was the amount (in $) contributed to the political party during the 2008 presidential election.

ANOVA

Source of Variation	SS	df	MS	F	p-value	F crit
Rows	25416.67	2	$MSB = ?$	$F_{Factor\ B} = ?$	0.0990	6.944
Columns	42916.67	2	$MSA = ?$	$F_{Factor\ A} = ?$	0.0457	6.944
Error	11666.67	4	$MSE = ?$			
Total	80000	8				

a. Find the missing values in the ANOVA table.

b. At the 5% significance level, can you conclude that average contributions differ by political party?

c. At the 5% significance level, can you conclude that average contributions differ by income level?

45. At a gymnastics meet, three judges evaluate the balance beam performances of five gymnasts. The judges use a scale of 1 to 10, where 10 is a perfect score.

Gymnast	Judge			Means
	1	**2**	**3**	
1	8.0	8.5	8.2	$\bar{x}_{Gymnast\ 1} = 8.2$
2	9.5	9.2	9.7	$\bar{x}_{Gymnast\ 2} = 9.5$
3	7.3	7.5	7.7	$\bar{x}_{Gymnast\ 3} = 7.5$
4	8.3	8.7	8.5	$\bar{x}_{Gymnast\ 4} = 8.5$
5	8.8	9.2	9.0	$\bar{x}_{Gymnast\ 5} = 9.0$
Means	$\bar{x}_{Judge\ 1} = 8.4$	$\bar{x}_{Judge\ 2} = 8.6$	$\bar{x}_{Judge\ 3} = 8.6$	

A statistician wants to examine the objectivity and consistency of the judges. She performs a two-way ANOVA analysis for $\alpha = 0.01$ and obtains the following results:

ANOVA

Source of Variation	SS	df	MS	F	p-value	F crit
Rows	6.742	4	1.686	44.75	1.62E-05	7.006
Columns	0.192	2	0.096	2.55	0.1392	8.649
Error	0.301	8	0.038			
Total	7.235	14				

a. At the 1% significance level, can you conclude that average scores differ by judge?

b. At the 1% significance level, can you conclude that average scores differ by gymnast?

c. If average scores differ by gymnast, use Tukey's HSD test at the 1% significance level to determine which gymnasts' performances differ.

46. FILE (Use Excel) An environmentalist wants to examine whether average fuel consumption (measured in miles per gallon) is affected by fuel type (factor A) and type of hybrid (factor B). A random block experiment with replication is performed. The results are shown in the accompanying table and are also available on the text website, labeled **ANOVA-fuel, hybrid**.

Car Type	Fuel A	Fuel B	Fuel C
	36	36	36
Hybrid I	43	43	43
	48	48	48
	36	36	36
Hybrid II	43	43	43
	48	48	48
	36	36	36
Hybrid III	43	43	43
	48	48	48

a. Use Excel to generate the appropriate ANOVA table.

b. At the 5% significance level, is there interaction between fuel type and hybrid type?

c. At the 5% significance level, can you conclude that average fuel consumption differs by fuel type?

d. At the 5% significance level, can you conclude that average fuel consumption differs by type of hybrid?

47. A management consultant wants to determine whether the age and gender of a restaurant's wait staff influence the size of the tip the customer leaves. Three age brackets (factor A in columns: young, middle-age, older) and gender (factor B in rows: male, female) are used to construct a random block experiment. For each combination, the percentage of the total bill left as a tip for 10 wait staff is examined. The following ANOVA table with $\alpha = 0.01$ is produced.

ANOVA

Source of Variation	SS	df	MS	F	p-value	F crit
Sample	0.04278	1	0.04278	16.5951	0.00015	7.129
Columns	0.01793	2	0.00897	3.47884	0.03792	5.021
Interaction	0.00561	2	0.00281	1.08872	0.34392	5.021
Within	0.1392	54	0.00258			
Total	0.20552	59				

a. Can you conclude that there is interaction between age and gender at the 1% significance level?

b. Are you able to conduct tests based on the main effects? If yes, conduct these tests at the 1% significance level. If no, explain.

CASE STUDIES

Case Study 13.1

Lisa Grattan, a financial analyst for a small investment firm, collects annual stock return data for 10 firms in the energy industry, 13 firms in the retail industry, and 16 firms in the utilities industry. A portion of the data is shown in the accompanying table; the entire data set is found on the text website, labeled **Industry Returns**.

Data for Case Study 13.1 Annual Stock Returns (in %)

Energy	Retail	Utilities
12.5	6.6	3.5
8.2	7.4	6.4
⋮	⋮	⋮
6.9	7.9	4.3

In a report, use the sample information to:

1. Determine whether significant differences exist in the annual returns for the three industries at the 5% significance level.

2. Construct 95% confidence intervals for the difference between annual returns for each pairing using Tukey's HSD method.

3. Evaluate which means (if any) significantly differ from one another using the results from part 2.

FILE Case Study 13.2

In 2007, the United States experienced the biggest jump in food prices in 17 years (*The Wall Street Journal*, April 1, 2008). A variety of reasons led to this result, including rising demand for meat and dairy products in emerging overseas markets, increased use of grains for alternative fuels, and bad weather in some parts of the world. A recent survey compared prices of selected products at grocery stores in the Boston area. The accompanying table shows the results; the data are also on the text website, labeled *Grocery Prices*.

Data for Case Study 13.2 Prices of Select Groceries at Three Stores

Item	Crosby's	Shaw's	Market Basket
Two-liter Coke	$1.79	$1.59	$1.50
Doritos chips	4.29	4.99	3.50
Cheerios cereal	3.69	2.99	3.00
Prince spaghetti	1.59	1.69	1.99
Skippy peanut butter	5.49	4.49	3.99
Cracker Barrel cheese	4.99	4.99	3.49
Pepperidge Farm white bread	3.99	3.99	3.99
Oreo cookies	4.69	3.39	3.00
One dozen eggs*	2.49	2.69	1.59
Coffee*	4.49	4.79	3.99
Gallon of milk*	3.69	3.19	1.59

*Store brand items; data collected October 5–6, 2011.

In a report, use the sample information to:

1. Determine whether differences exist in the average prices of products sold at the three stores at the 5% significance level.
2. Determine whether differences exist in the average prices of the 11 products at the 5% significance level.
3. If differences exist between the average prices of products sold at the three stores, use Tukey's HSD method to determine which stores' prices differ.

Case Study 13.3

The manager of an SAT review program wonders whether the ethnic background of a student and the program's instructor affect the student's performance on the SAT. Four ethnicities and three instructors are examined. Ten student scores for each combination are sampled. A portion of the data is shown in the following table; the full data set can be found on the text website, labeled *ANOVA-SAT*.

Data for Case Study 13.3 Ethnic Background and SAT Scores

	White	Black	Asian-American	Mexican-American
	1587	1300	1660	1366
Instructor A	1562	1255	1576	1531
	⋮	⋮	⋮	⋮
	1598	1296	1535	1345
Instructor B	1539	1286	1643	1357
	⋮	⋮	⋮	⋮
	1483	1289	1641	1400
Instructor C	1525	1272	1633	1421
	⋮	⋮	⋮	⋮

In a report, use the sample information and $\alpha = 0.05$ to:

1. Determine if there is any interaction between instructor and ethnicity.
2. Establish whether average SAT scores differ by instructor.
3. Establish whether average SAT scores differ by ethnicity.

14 Regression Analysis

LEARNING OBJECTIVES

After reading this chapter you should be able to:

LO 14.1 Conduct a hypothesis test for the population correlation coefficient.

LO 14.2 Discuss the limitations of correlation analysis.

LO 14.3 Estimate the simple linear regression model and interpret the coefficients.

LO 14.4 Estimate the multiple linear regression model and interpret the coefficients.

LO 14.5 Calculate and interpret the standard error of the estimate.

LO 14.6 Calculate and interpret the coefficient of determination R^2.

LO 14.7 Differentiate between R^2 and adjusted R^2.

As researchers or analysts, we often need to examine the relationship between two or more variables. We begin this chapter with a review of the correlation coefficient, first discussed in Chapter 3, and then conduct a hypothesis test to determine if two variables are significantly correlated. Although the correlation analysis may establish a linear relationship between two variables, it does not demonstrate that one variable causes change in the other variable. In this chapter we introduce a method called regression analysis that assumes that one or more variables influence another variable. We first explore the procedures for estimating a simple linear relationship between two variables, commonly referred to as the simple linear regression model. We then extend the simple linear regression model to the case involving several variables, called the multiple regression model. Finally, we discuss objective measures to assess how well the estimated model fits the data. These goodness-of-fit measures are used to select the best-fitting regression model.

Consumer Debt Payments

A recent study found that American consumers are making average monthly debt payments of $983 (Experian.com, November 11, 2010). However, the study of 26 metropolitan areas reveals quite a bit of variation in debt payments, depending on where the consumer lives. For instance, in Washington, DC, residents pay the most ($1,285 per month), while Pittsburghers pay the least ($763 per month). Madelyn Davis, an economist at a large bank, believes that income differences between cities are the primary reason for the disparate debt payments. For example, the Washington, DC, area's high incomes have likely contributed to its placement on the list. She is unsure about the likely effect of unemployment on consumer debt payments. On the one hand, higher unemployment rates may reduce consumer debt payments, as consumers forgo making major purchases such as homes and cars. On the other hand, higher unemployment rates may raise consumer debt payments as consumers struggle to pay their bills. In order to analyze the relationship between income, the unemployment rate, and consumer debt payments, Madelyn gathers data from the same 26 metropolitan areas used in the debt payment study. Specifically, she collects each area's 2010–2011 median household income as well as the monthly unemployment rate and average consumer debt for August 2010. Table 14.1 shows a portion of the data; the complete data set can be found on the text website, labeled **Debt Payments**.

TABLE 14.1   Income, the Unemployment Rate, and Consumer Debt Payments, 2010–2011

Metropolitan Area	Income (in $1,000s)	Unemployment	Debt
Washington, D.C.	$103.50	6.3%	$1,285
Seattle	81.70	8.5	1,135
⋮	⋮	⋮	⋮
Pittsburgh	63.00	8.3	763

SOURCE: eFannieMae.com reports 2010–2011 Area Median Household Incomes; bls.com gives monthly unemployment rates for August 2010; Experian.com collected average monthly consumer debt payments in August 2010 and published the data in November 2010.

Madelyn would like to use the sample information in Table 14.1 to:

1. Determine if debt payments and income are significantly correlated.

2. Use regression analysis to make predictions for debt payments for given values of income and the unemployment rate.

3. Use various goodness-of-fit measures to determine the regression model that best fits the data.

A synopsis of this case is provided at the end of Section 14.4.

14.1 The Covariance and the Correlation Coefficient

LO **14.1**

Conduct a
hypothesis test
for the population
correlation coefficient.

It will be useful in this section to review a scatterplot, as well as the calculation of the sample covariance and the sample correlation coefficient—these concepts were discussed in Chapters 2 and 3. A scatterplot graphically shows the relationship between two variables, while the covariance and the correlation coefficient quantify the direction and the strength of the linear relationship between two variables.

A SCATTERPLOT

A **scatterplot** is a graphical tool that helps in determining whether or not two variables are related in some systematic way. Each point in the diagram represents a pair of observed values of the two variables.

Using the data from the introductory case, Figure 14.1 shows a scatterplot depicting the relationship between income and debt payments. We may infer that the two variables have a positive relationship; as one increases, the other one tends to increase.

FIGURE 14.1 Scatterplot of debt payments against income

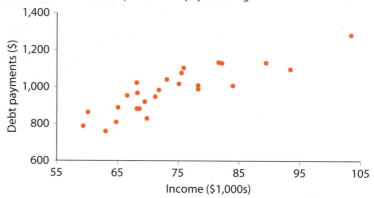

A numerical measure that reveals the direction of the linear relationship between two variables x and y is called the **covariance**. It assesses whether a positive or a negative linear relationship exists between x and y.

THE SAMPLE COVARIANCE

The **sample covariance** is a measure of the linear relationship between two variables x and y. We compute the sample covariance s_{xy} as

$$s_{xy} = \frac{\Sigma(x_i - \bar{x})(y_i - \bar{y})}{n - 1},$$

where $\bar{x}$ and $\bar{y}$ are the sample means of x and y, respectively, and n represents the number of observations.

A positive value of the sample covariance implies that, on average, when x is above its mean, y is also above its mean. Similarly, a negative value suggests when x is above its mean, y is below its mean, indicating a negative linear relationship exists. If the covariance is zero, then the two variables have no linear relationship. Further interpretation of the covariance is difficult because it is sensitive to the units of measurement. For instance, the covariance between two variables might be 100 and the covariance between two other variables might be 1,000, yet all we can conclude is that both sets of variables are positively related. In other words, we cannot comment on the strength of the relationships.

An easier measure to interpret is the **correlation coefficient**, which describes both the direction and strength of the relationship between x and y.

THE SAMPLE CORRELATION COEFFICIENT

The **sample correlation coefficient** gauges the strength of the linear relationship between two variables x and y. We calculate the sample correlation coefficient r_{xy} as

$$r_{xy} = \frac{s_{xy}}{s_x s_y},$$

where s_x and s_y are the sample standard deviations of x and y, respectively, and $-1 \leq r_{xy} \leq 1$.

In short, the sample correlation coefficient r_{xy} is unit-free and its value falls between -1 and 1. If r_{xy} equals 1, then a perfect positive linear relationship exists between x and y. Similarly, a perfect negative linear relationship exists if r_{xy} equals -1. If r_{xy} equals zero, then no linear relationship exists between x and y. Other values for r_{xy} must be interpreted with reference to -1, 0, and 1. As the absolute value of r_{xy} approaches 1, the stronger the linear relationship. For instance, $r_{xy} = -0.80$ indicates a strong negative relationship, whereas $r_{xy} = 0.12$ indicates a weak positive relationship. However, we should comment on the direction of the relationship only if the correlation coefficient is found to be statistically significant—a topic which we address shortly.

EXAMPLE 14.1

Calculate the sample covariance and the sample correlation coefficient between debt payments and income from the data in Table 14.1. Interpret these values.

SOLUTION: Let x denote income (in $1,000s) and y denote average monthly consumer debt payments (in $). We first compute the sample mean and the sample standard deviation of these variables as $\bar{x} = \$74.05$, $\bar{y} = \$983.46$, $s_x = \$10.35$, and $s_y = \$124.61$. We then calculate deviations from the mean for each variable. The first two columns in Table 14.2 show a portion of these calculations. Then we find the product of each pairing and sum these products. These calculations are shown in the third column.

TABLE 14.2 Calculations for Example 14.1

$x_i - \bar{x}$	$y_i - \bar{y}$	$(x_i - \bar{x})(y_i - \bar{y})$
$103.50 - 74.05 = 29.45$	$1{,}285 - 983.46 = 301.54$	$(29.45)(301.54) = 8{,}880.35$
$81.70 - 74.05 = 7.65$	$1{,}135 - 983.46 = 151.54$	$(7.65)(151.54) = 1{,}159.28$
$\vdots$	$\vdots$	$\vdots$
$63.00 - 74.05 = -11.05$	$763 - 983.46 = -220.46$	$(-11.05)(-220.46) = 2{,}436.08$
		$\Sigma(x_i - \bar{x})(y_i - \bar{y}) = 27{,}979.50$

Using the overall sum from the third column in Table 14.2 and $n = 26$, we calculate the covariance as

$$s_{xy} = \frac{\Sigma(x_i - \bar{x})(y_i - \bar{y})}{n - 1} = \frac{27{,}979.50}{26 - 1} = 1{,}119.18.$$

Given that $s_x = \$10.35$ and $s_y = \$124.61$, the correlation coefficient is calculated as

$$r_{xy} = \frac{s_{xy}}{s_x s_y} = \frac{1{,}119.18}{(10.35)(124.61)} = 0.87.$$

Thus, the covariance of 1,119.18 indicates that income and debt payments have a positive linear relationship. In addition, the correlation coefficient of 0.87 indicates that the strength of the positive linear relationship is strong. We will soon see that the correlation coefficient is statistically significant.

Using Excel to Calculate the Covariance and the Correlation Coefficient

As discussed in Chapter 3, Excel easily produces the covariance and the correlation coefficients. Consider the next example.

EXAMPLE 14.2 FILE

Use Excel to recalculate the sample covariance and the sample correlation coefficient between debt payments and income from the data in Table 14.1.

SOLUTION:

A. Open the data labeled ***Debt Payments*** found on the text website.

B. Choose **Formulas** > **Insert Function** > **COVARIANCE.S** from the menu.

C. In the *COVARIANCE.S* dialog box shown in Figure 14.2, click on the box to the right of *Array 1* and select the income data. Then click on the box to the right of *Array 2* and select the debt payments data. Excel returns a value of 1,119.18.

D. In order to calculate the correlation coefficient, choose **Formulas** > **Insert Function** > **CORREL**. Select the data as you did when calculating the covariance. Excel returns a value of 0.87.

FIGURE 14.2 Excel's dialog box for the covariance

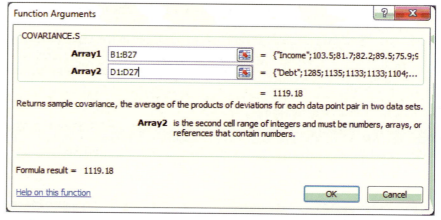

Testing the Correlation Coefficient

We conduct a hypothesis test to determine whether the apparent relationship between the two variables, implied by the sample correlation coefficient, is real or due to chance. Let ρ_{xy} denote the population correlation coefficient. A two-tailed test of whether the population correlation coefficient differs from zero takes the following form:

$$H_0: \rho_{xy} = 0$$
$$H_A: \rho_{xy} \neq 0$$

Note that we can easily modify the test to a one-tailed test. As in all hypothesis tests, the next step is to specify and calculate the value of the test statistic.

EXAMPLE 14.3

Using the critical value approach to hypothesis testing, determine whether the correlation coefficient between income and debt payments is significant at the 5% level.

SOLUTION: When testing whether the correlation coefficient between income x and debt payments y is significant, we set up the following competing hypotheses:

$$H_0: \rho_{xy} = 0$$
$$H_A: \rho_{xy} \neq 0$$

Using $r_{xy} = 0.87$ and $n = 26$ from Example 14.1 and $df = n - 2 = 24$, we calculate the value of the test statistic as

$$t_{24} = \frac{r_{xy}\sqrt{n - 2}}{\sqrt{1 - r_{xy}^2}} = \frac{0.87\sqrt{26 - 2}}{\sqrt{1 - (0.87)^2}} = 8.64.$$

With $\alpha = 0.05$, $t_{\alpha/2,df} = t_{0.025,24} = 2.064$. Thus, the decision rule is to reject H_0 if $t_{24} > 2.064$ or $t_{24} < -2.064$. Since $8.64 > 2.064$, we reject H_0. At the 5% significance level, the correlation coefficient between income and debt payments is significantly different from zero.

If we conduct the test with the p-value approach, we can use the t table to approximate $2P(T_{24} \geq 8.64)$. Alternatively, we can obtain the exact p-value as 0.0000 using the T.DIST.2T function in Excel (we input $X = 8.64$ and Deg_freedom $= 24$). Consistent with the critical value approach, we reject H_0 because the p-value $< \alpha$.

Limitations of Correlation Analysis

Several limitations apply to correlation analysis.

A. The correlation coefficient captures only a linear relationship. Two variables can have a very low correlation coefficient yet have a strong *nonlinear* relation. Consider the following sample data:

x	−20	−15	−10	−5	0	5	10	15	20
y	380	210	90	20	0	30	110	240	420

The sample correlation coefficient for these data is $r_{xy} = 0.09$, implying an extremely weak positive linear relationship. However, further analysis of the data would reveal a perfect nonlinear relationship given by $y_i = x_i + x_i^2$.

B. The correlation coefficient may not be a reliable measure when *outliers* are present in one or both of the variables. Recall that outliers are a small number of extreme high or low values in the data set. As a general rule, we must determine whether the sample correlation coefficient varies dramatically by removing a few outliers. However, we must use judgment to determine whether those outliers contain important information about the relationship between the two variables (and should be included in the correlation analysis) or do not contain important information (and should be excluded).

C. Correlation does not imply causation. Even if two variables are highly correlated, one does not necessarily cause the other. *Spurious correlation* can make two variables appear closely related when no causal relation exists. Spurious correlation between two variables is *not* based on any theoretical relationship, but rather on a relation that arises in the data solely because each of the two variables is related to some third variable. For example, Robert Matthews in his article "Storks Bring Babies" (*Teaching Statistics*, Summer 2000) finds that the correlation coefficient between stork breeding pairs and the human birth rate for 17 European countries is 0.62. Further, he finds that the correlation is significantly different from zero at the 5% significance level. He stresses that the most plausible explanation for this observed correlation—and absurd conclusion—is the existence of a confounding variable, namely land area. That is, we are likely to see higher human birth rates in more densely populated areas. More densely populated areas also provide more chimneys, where stork breeding pairs prefer to nest.

EXERCISES 14.1

Concepts

1. Consider the following sample data:

x	8	5	3	10	2
y	380	210	90	20	2

   a. Construct and interpret a scatterplot.
   b. Calculate and interpret the sample covariance.
   c. Calculate and interpret the sample correlation coefficient.

2. Consider the following sample data:

x	−30	10	0	23	16
y	44	−15	−10	−2	5

   a. Construct and interpret a scatterplot.
   b. Calculate and interpret s_{xy}.
   c. Calculate and interpret r_{xy}.

3. Consider the following competing hypotheses:

   $$H_0: \rho_{xy} = 0$$
   $$H_A: \rho_{xy} \neq 0$$

   The sample consists of 25 observations and the sample correlation coefficient is 0.15.

   a. Calculate the value of the test statistic.
   b. At the 5% significance level, specify the critical value(s) and the decision rule.
   c. What is the conclusion to the test? Explain.

4. Consider the following competing hypotheses:

   $$H_0: \rho_{xy} \geq 0$$
   $$H_A: \rho_{xy} < 0$$

   The sample consists of 30 observations and the sample correlation coefficient is −0.60.

   a. Calculate the value of the test statistic.
   b. Approximate the *p*-value.
   c. At the 5% significance level, what is the conclusion to the test? Explain.

5. A sample of 10 observations provides the following statistics:

   $$s_x = 13, \quad s_y = 18, \quad \text{and} \quad s_{xy} = 117.22$$

   a. Calculate and interpret the sample correlation coefficient r_{xy}.
   b. Specify the hypotheses to determine whether the population correlation coefficient is positive.
   c. Calculate the value of the test statistic. Approximate the *p*-value.
   d. At the 5% significance level, what is the conclusion to the test? Explain.

6. A sample of 25 observations provides the following statistics:

   $$s_x = 2, \quad s_y = 5, \quad \text{and} \quad s_{xy} = -1.75$$

   a. Calculate and interpret the sample correlation coefficient r_{xy}.
   b. Specify the competing hypotheses in order to determine whether the population correlation coefficient differs from zero.
   c. Make a conclusion at the 5% significance level.

Applications

7. In June 2009 an onslaught of miserable weather in New England played havoc with people's plans and psyches. However, the dreary weather brought a quiet benefit to many city neighborhoods. Police reported that the weather was a key factor in reducing fatal and nondeadly shootings (*The Boston Globe*, July 3, 2009). For instance, it rained in

Boston on 22 days in June, when 15 shootings occurred. In 2008, the city saw rain on only eight days and 38 shootings occurred. The table below shows the number of rainy days and the number of shootings that occurred in June from 2005 to 2009.

	Number of Rainy Days	Number of Shootings
June 2005	7	31
June 2006	15	46
June 2007	10	29
June 2008	8	38
June 2009	22	15

SOURCE: *The Boston Globe*, July 3, 2009.

a. Calculate and interpret the covariance and the correlation coefficient.

b. Specify the competing hypotheses in order to determine whether there is a negative population correlation between the number of rainy days and crime.

c. Calculate the value of the test statistic and approximate its *p*-value.

d. At the 5% significance level, what is the conclusion to the test? Does it appear that dreary weather and crime are negatively correlated?

8. FILE Diversification is considered important in finance because it allows investors to reduce risk by investing in a variety of assets. It is especially effective when the correlation between the assets is low. Consider the accompanying table, which shows a portion of monthly data on closing stock prices of four companies in 2010. The entire data can be found on the text website, labeled *2010 Stock Returns*.

Month	Microsoft	Coca Cola	Bank of America	General Electric
Jan	27.61	49.52	15.13	15.64
Feb	28.22	54.88	16.61	15.72
⋮	⋮	⋮	⋮	⋮
Dec	27.91	55.58	13.34	18.29

SOURCE: finance.yahoo.com.

a. Compute the correlation coefficients between all pairs of stock prices.

b. Suppose an investor already has a stake in Microsoft and would like to add another asset to her portfolio. Which of the remaining three assets will give her the maximum benefit of diversification? (*Hint*: Find the asset with the lowest correlation with Microsoft.)

c. Suppose an investor does not own any of the above four stocks. Pick two stocks so that she gets the maximum benefit of diversification.

9. A realtor studies the relationship between the size of a house (in square feet) and the property taxes owed by the owner. He collects the following data on six homes in an affluent suburb 60 miles outside of New York City.

	Square Feet	Property Taxes ($)
Home 1	4,182	12,540
Home 2	2,844	9,363
Home 3	5,293	22,717
Home 4	2,284	6,508
Home 5	1,586	5,355
Home 6	3,394	7,901

a. Construct and interpret a scatterplot.

b. Calculate and interpret s_{xy} and r_{xy}.

c. Specify the competing hypotheses in order to determine whether the population correlation between the size of a house and property taxes differs from zero.

d. Calculate the value of the test statistic and approximate its *p*-value.

e. At the 5% significance level, what is the conclusion to the test?

10. FILE Many attempts have been made to relate happiness with various factors. One such study relates happiness with age and finds that holding everything else constant, people are least happy when they are in their mid-40s (*The Economist*, December 16, 2010). The accompanying table shows a portion of data on a respondent's age and his/her perception of well-being on a scale from 0 to 100; the complete data are on the text website, labeled ***Happiness and Age***.

Age	Happiness
49	62
51	66
⋮	⋮
69	72

a. Calculate and interpret the sample correlation coefficient between age and happiness.

b. Is the population correlation coefficient statistically significant at the 1% level?

c. Construct a scatterplot to point out a flaw with the above correlation analysis.

11. FILE The following table lists the National Basketball Association's leading scorers, their average points per game (PPG), and their average minutes per game (MPG) for 2008; the data are also available on the text website, labeled ***Points***.

	PPG	MPG
D. Wade	30.2	38.6
L. James	28.4	37.7
K. Bryant	26.8	36.1
D. Nowitzki	25.9	37.3
D. Granger	25.8	36.2
K. Durant	25.3	39.0
C. Paul	22.8	38.5
C. Anthony	22.8	34.5
C. Bosh	22.7	38.0
B. Roy	22.6	37.2

SOURCE: www.espn.com.

a. Calculate and interpret the sample correlation coefficient between PPG and MPG.

b. Specify the competing hypotheses in order to determine whether the population correlation between PPG and MPG is positive.

c. Calculate the value of the test statistic and the corresponding *p*-value.

d. At the 5% significance level, what is the conclusion to the test? Is this result surprising? Explain.

14.2 The Simple Linear Regression Model

LO 14.3

Estimate the simple linear regression model and interpret the coefficients.

As mentioned earlier, the covariance and the correlation coefficient may establish a linear relationship between two variables, but the measures do not suggest that one variable causes change in the other variable. With **regression analysis**, we explicitly assume that one variable, called the **response variable**, is influenced by other variables, called the **explanatory variables**. Consequently, we use information on the explanatory variables to predict and/or describe changes in the response variable. Alternative names for the explanatory variables are independent variables, predictor variables, control variables, or regressors, while the response variable is often referred to as the dependent variable, the explained variable, the predicted variable, or the regressand.

Recall from the introductory case that Madelyn is interested in how income and the unemployment rate might influence debt payments. Similarly, using regression analysis, we can predict an individual's salary based on education and years of experience; estimate the selling price of a house on the basis of its size and location; or describe auto sales with respect to consumer income, interest rates, and price discounts.

In all of these examples, we cannot expect to predict the exact value of the relevant response variable because some omitted factors may also influence the response variable. If the value of the response variable is uniquely determined by the values of the explanatory variables, we say that the relationship between the variables is **deterministic**. This is often the case in the physical sciences. For example, momentum *p* is the product of the mass *m* and velocity *v* of an object, that is, $p = mv$. In most fields of research, however, we tend to find that the relationship between the explanatory variables and the response variable is inexact, or **stochastic**, due to the omission of relevant factors (sometimes not measurable) that influence the response variable. For instance, debt payments are likely to be influenced by housing costs—a variable that is not included in the introductory case. Similarly, when trying to predict an individual's salary, the individual's natural ability is often omitted since it is extremely difficult, if not impossible, to quantify.

DETERMINISTIC VERSUS STOCHASTIC RELATIONSHIPS

The relationship between the response variable and the explanatory variables is **deterministic** if the value of the response variable is uniquely determined by the explanatory variables; otherwise, the relationship is **stochastic**.

Our objective is to develop a mathematical model that accurately captures the relationship between the response variable *y* and the *k* explanatory variables $x_1, x_2, \ldots, x_k$. The model must also account for the randomness that is a part of real life. We start with a deterministic component that approximates the relationship we want to model, and then make it stochastic by adding a random error term to it.

In this section we focus on the **simple linear regression model**, which uses one explanatory variable, denoted x_1, to explain the variability in the response variable, denoted *y*. For ease of exposition when discussing the simple linear regression model, we often drop the subscript on the explanatory variable and refer to it solely as *x*. In the next section we extend the simple linear regression model to the **multiple regression model**, where more than one explanatory variable is linearly related with the response variable.

A fundamental assumption underlying the simple linear regression model is that the expected value of *y* lies on a straight line, denoted by $\beta_0 + \beta_1 x$, where β_0 and β_1 (the

Greek letters read as betas) are the unknown intercept and slope parameters, respectively. The expression $\beta_0 + \beta_1 x$ is the deterministic component of the regression model, which can be thought of as the expected value of y for a given value of x. In other words, conditional on x, $E(y) = \beta_0 + \beta_1 x$. The slope parameter β_1 determines whether the linear relationship between x and $E(y)$ is positive ($\beta_1 > 0$) or negative ($\beta_1 < 0$); $\beta_1 = 0$ indicates that there is no linear relationship. Figure 14.3 shows the deterministic portion of the regression model for various values of the intercept β_0 and the slope β_1 parameters.

FIGURE 14.3 Various examples of a simple linear regression model

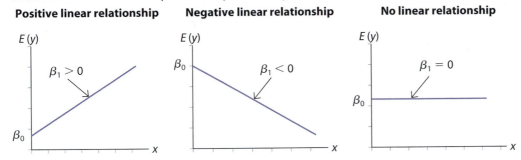

As noted earlier, the actual value y may differ from the expected value $E(y)$. Therefore, we add a random error term ε (the Greek letter read as epsilon) to develop a simple linear regression model.

> ### THE SIMPLE LINEAR REGRESSION MODEL
>
> The simple linear regression model is defined as
>
> $$y = \beta_0 + \beta_1 x + \varepsilon,$$
>
> where y and x are the response variable and the explanatory variable, respectively, and ε is the random error term. The coefficients β_0 and β_1 are the unknown parameters to be estimated.

Determining the Sample Regression Equation

The population parameters β_0 and β_1 used in the linear regression model are unknown, and therefore, must be estimated. As always, we use sample data to estimate the population parameters of interest. Here sample data consist of n pairs of observations on y and x; shortly we will see an application of a linear regression model.

Let b_0 and b_1 represent the estimates of β_0 and β_1, respectively. We form the **sample regression equation** or the **predicted regression equation** as $\hat{y} = b_0 + b_1 x$, where $\hat{y}$ (read as y-hat) is the predicted value of the response variable given a specified value of the explanatory variable x.

> The **sample regression equation** for the simple linear regression model is denoted as
>
> $$\hat{y} = b_0 + b_1 x,$$
>
> where b_0 and b_1 are the point estimates of β_0 and β_1, respectively.

We use this equation to make predictions for y for a given x. Since the predictions cannot be totally accurate, the difference between the predicted and the actual value represents the **residual** e; that is, $e = y - \hat{y}$.

Before estimating a simple linear regression model, it is extremely useful to visualize the relationship between y and x by constructing a scatterplot. Here, we explicitly place y on the vertical axis and x on the horizontal axis, implying that x influences the variability in y. In Figure 14.1, we used the data from the introductory case to show a scatterplot of debt payments plotted against income. In Figure 14.4, we superimpose a linear trend line through the points on the scatterplot. In this chapter we focus only on linear relationships; nonlinear relationships will be considered in Chapter 16.

The superimposed line in Figure 14.4 is the sample regression equation, $\hat{y} = b_0 + b_1 x$, where y and x represent debt payments and income, respectively. The upward slope of the line suggests that as income increases, the predicted debt payments also increase. Also, the vertical distance between any data point on the scatterplot and the corresponding point on the line, y and $\hat{y}$, represents the residual, $e = y - \hat{y}$.

FIGURE 14.4 Scatterplot with a superimposed trend line

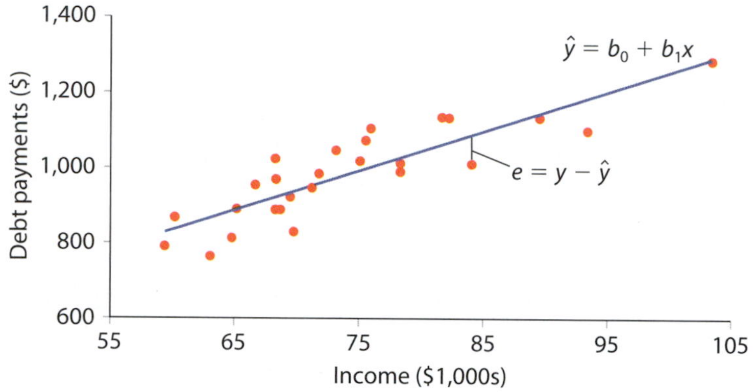

Using Excel to Construct a Scatterplot and a Trendline FILE

In order to replicate Figure 14.4 using Excel we follow these steps.

A. Open the **Debt Payments** data found on the text website. For the purpose of creating a scatterplot of debt payments to income, disregard the column with the unemployment data.

B. Simultaneously select the income and the debt data and choose **Insert > Scatter**. Select the graph on the top left.

C. Right click on the scatter points, choose **Add Trendline**, and then choose **Linear**.

D. Further formatting regarding colors, axes, etc. can be done by selecting **Layout** from the menu.

A common approach to fitting a line to the scatterplot is the **method of least squares**, also referred to as **ordinary least squares OLS**. In other words, we use OLS to estimate the parameters β_0 and β_1. This method chooses the line whereby the **error (or residual) sum of squares SSE** is minimized, where *SSE* is computed as $\Sigma(y_i - \hat{y}_i)^2 = \Sigma e_i^2$. Note that *SSE* is the sum of the squared distances from the regression equation. Thus, using this distance measure, we say that the OLS method produces the straight line that is "closest" to the data. In the context of Figure 14.4, the superimposed line has been estimated by OLS; note that this line provides a better fit than any other line fit to the scatter points.

Using calculus, equations have been developed for b_0 and b_1 that satisfy the OLS criterion.

In essence, b_1 is a ratio of the sample covariance s_{xy} between x and y to the variance s_x^2 of x. This becomes apparent when we rewrite the regression coefficient as $b_1 = \frac{\Sigma(x_i - \bar{x})(y_i - \bar{y})/(n-1)}{\Sigma(x_i - \bar{x})^2/(n-1)} = \frac{s_{xy}}{s_x^2}$. Since we calculate the sample correlation coefficient as $r_{xy} = \frac{s_{xy}}{s_x s_y}$, we can express b_1 and r_{xy} in terms of each other.

Recall that in earlier chapters we used the uppercase/lowercase convention to distinguish between an estimator and an estimate. It is cumbersome to continue with this distinction in regression models, since so many parameters are involved. Therefore, we will use b, for example, to denote both the estimator and the estimate of β. Similarly, we will use y to denote a random response variable and its value. We would also like to point out that under the assumptions of the classical linear regression model, OLS is the best linear unbiased estimator (BLUE). This result implies that the OLS estimator is not only unbiased ($E(b) = \beta$), it is also efficient, in that it has a smaller variance than other linear unbiased estimators. The assumptions underlying the OLS estimators are discussed in the next chapter.

It is important to be able to interpret the estimated regression coefficients. As we will see in the following example, it is not always possible to provide an economic interpretation of the intercept estimate b_0; mathematically, however, it represents the predicted value $\hat{y}$ when x has a value of zero. The slope estimate b_1 represents the change in $\hat{y}$ when x increases by one unit. Measurement units of the coefficients are the same as those of y.

EXAMPLE 14.4

Using the data from Table 14.1, let debt payments represent the response variable and income represent the explanatory variable.

a. Calculate and interpret b_1.

b. Calculate and interpret b_0.

c. What is the sample regression equation?

d. Predict debt payments if income is $80,000.

SOLUTION: We use the regression model, Debt $= \beta_0 + \beta_1$Income $+ \varepsilon$, or simply, $y = \beta_0 + \beta_1 x + \varepsilon$, where y and x represent debt payments and income, respectively.

a. We use the results from Example 14.1 that $\bar{x} = \$74.05$, $\bar{y} = \$983.46$, $s_x = \$10.35$, and $s_y = \$124.61$. The calculations for obtaining b_1 are shown in Table 14.3. We first calculate deviations from the mean for both x and y, as shown in the first two columns of the table. We then calculate the product of deviations from the mean, as shown in the third column. The sum of the products of the deviations from the mean is the numerator in the formula for b_1; this value is found in the last cell of the third column. The fourth column shows the calculations for the sum of the squared deviations for the explanatory variable. This value, found in the last cell of the fourth column, is the denominator in the formula for b_1.

TABLE 14.3 Calculations for Example 14.4

$x_i - \bar{x}$	$y_i - \bar{y}$	$(x_i - \bar{x})(y_i - \bar{y})$	$(x_i - \bar{x})^2$
$103.50 - 74.05 = 29.45$	$1{,}285 - 983.46 = 301.54$	$(29.45)(301.54) = 8{,}880.35$	$(29.45)^2 = 867.30$
$81.70 - 74.05 = 7.65$	$1{,}135 - 983.46 = 151.54$	$(7.65)(151.54) = 1{,}159.28$	$(7.65)^2 = 58.52$
$\vdots$	$\vdots$	$\vdots$	$\vdots$
$63.00 - 74.05 = -11.05$	$763 - 983.46 = -220.46$	$(-11.05)(-220.46) = 2{,}436.08$	$(-11.05)^2 = 122.10$
		$\Sigma(x_i - \bar{x})(y_i - \bar{y}) = 27{,}979.50$	$\Sigma(x_i - \bar{x})^2 = 2{,}679.75$

Using the summations from the last rows of the last two columns, we compute $b_1 = \frac{\Sigma(x_i - \bar{x})(y_i - \bar{y})}{\Sigma(x_i - x)^2} = \frac{27{,}979.50}{2{,}679.75} = 10.44$. Since we had earlier computed the sample correlation coefficient as $r_{xy} = 0.87$ (Example 14.1), we can also estimate the slope coefficient as $b_1 = r_{xy}\frac{s_y}{s_x} = 0.87 \times \frac{124.61}{10.35} = 10.47$ (slight difference due to rounding). As anticipated, the slope is positive, suggesting a positive relationship between income and debt payments. Since income is measured in \$1,000s, our interpretation is that if median household income increases by \$1,000, then on average, we predict consumer debt payments to increase by b_1, that is, by \$10.44.

b. Using $b_1 = 10.44$ and the sample means of $\bar{x} = 74.05$ and $\bar{y} = 983.46$, we obtain an estimate for b_0 as $b_0 = \bar{y} - b_1\bar{x} = 983.46 - 10.44 \times 74.05 = 210.38$. This estimated intercept coefficient of 210.38 suggests that if income equals zero, then predicted debt payments are \$210.38. In this particular application, this conclusion makes some sense, since a household with no income still needs to make debt payments for any credit card use, automobile loans, and/or a mortgage. However, we should be careful about predicting y when we use a value for x that is not included in the sample. In the *Debt Payments* data set, the lowest and highest values for income (in \$1,000s) are \$59.40 and \$103.50, respectively; plus the scatterplot suggests that a line fits the data well within this range of the explanatory variable. Unless we assume that income and debt payments will maintain the same linear relationship at income values less than \$59.40 and more than \$103.50, we should refrain from choosing values of the explanatory variable outside the sample range.

c. With $b_0 = 210.38$ and $b_1 = 10.44$, we write the sample regression equation as $\hat{y} = 210.38 + 10.44x$, or $\widehat{\text{Debt}} = 210.38 + 10.44\text{Income}$.

d. Note that income is measured in \$1,000s; therefore if income equals \$80,000, we input Income = 80 in the sample regression equation and find predicted debt payments as $\widehat{\text{Debt}} = 210.38 + 10.44(80) = \$1{,}045.58$.

Using Excel to Calculate the Sample Regression Equation

Fortunately, we rarely have to calculate a sample regression equation by hand. Virtually every statistical software package computes the necessary output to construct a sample regression equation. In addition, values of all relevant statistics for assessing the model are also included. Consider the following example.

EXAMPLE 14.5 FILE

Given the data from Table 14.1, use Excel to re-estimate the sample regression equation with debt payments as the response variable and income as the explanatory variable.

SOLUTION:

A. Open the data labeled **Debt Payments** found on the text website.
B. Choose **Data** > **Data Analysis** > **Regression** from the menu.
C. See Figure 14.5. In the *Regression* dialog box, click on the box next to *Input Y Range*, then select the debt data, including its heading. For *Input X Range*, select the income data, including its heading. Check *Labels*, since we are using Debt and Income as headings.
D. Click **OK**.

FIGURE 14.5 Regression dialog box for Example 14.5

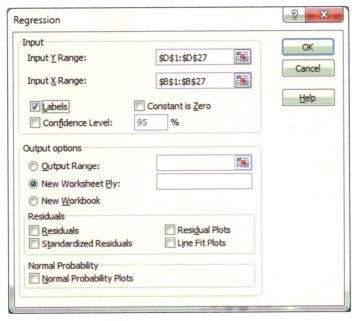

The Excel output is presented in Table 14.4.

TABLE 14.4 Regression Results for Example 14.5

Regression Statistics	
Multiple R	0.8675
R Square	0.7526
Adjusted R Square	0.7423
Standard Error	63.26
Observations	26

ANOVA					
	df	SS	MS	F	Significance F
Regression	1	292136.91	292136.9	73.00	1E-08
Residual	24	96045.55	4001.9		
Total	25	388182.46			

	Coefficients	Standard Error	t Stat	p-value	Lower 95%	Upper 95%
Intercept	**210.2977**	91.3387	2.3024	0.0303	21.78	398.81
Income	**10.4411**	1.2220	8.5440	0.0000	7.92	12.96

As Table 14.4 shows, Excel produces quite a bit of statistical information. In order to answer the questions in Example 14.5, we need only the boldface coefficients. We will address the remaining information later. The estimates for β_0 and β_1 are $b_0 = 210.2977$ and $b_1 = 10.4411$. The estimated sample regression, Debt = 210.30 + 10.44Income, is virtually the same as the one we calculated with the formulas; the intercept estimate is slightly off due to rounding.

EXERCISES 14.2

Concepts

12. In a simple linear regression, the following information is given:

$$\bar{x} = 34; \bar{y} = 44; \Sigma(x_i - \bar{x})(y_i - \bar{y}) = 1{,}250;$$
$$\Sigma(x_i - \bar{x})^2 = 925$$

  a. Calculate b_1.
  b. Calculate b_0.
  c. What is the sample regression equation? Predict y if x equals 40.

13. In a simple linear regression, the following information is given:

$$\bar{x} = -25; \bar{y} = 56; \Sigma(x_i - \bar{x})(y_i - \bar{y}) = -866;$$
$$\Sigma(x_i - \bar{x})^2 = 711$$

  a. Calculate b_1.
  b. Calculate b_0.
  c. What is the sample regression equation? Predict y if x equals −20.

14. Consider the following data:

$$\bar{x} = 32; s_x = 3.4; \bar{y} = 73; s_y = 7.2; r_{xy} = 0.34$$

  a. Calculate b_1.
  b. Calculate b_0.
  c. What is the sample regression equation? Predict y if x equals 25.

15. Consider the following data:

$$\bar{x} = -10; s_x = 2.5; \bar{y} = 24; s_y = 3.7; b_1 = -1.35$$

  a. Calculate r_{xy}.
  b. Calculate b_0.
  c. What is the sample regression equation? Predict y if x equals −5.

16. In a simple linear regression, the following sample regression equation is obtained:

$$\hat{y} = 15 + 2.5x.$$

  a. Predict y if x equals 10.
  b. What happens to this prediction if x doubles in value?

17. In a simple linear regression, the following sample regression equation is obtained:

$$\hat{y} = 436 - 17x.$$

  a. Interpret the slope coefficient.
  b. Predict y if x equals −15.

18. Consider the following sample data:

x	12	23	11	23	14	21	18	16
y	28	43	21	40	33	41	37	32

  a. Construct a scatterplot and verify that estimating a simple linear regression is appropriate in this problem.
  b. Calculate b_1 and b_0. What is the sample regression equation?
  c. Find the predicted value for y if x equals 10, 15, and 20.

19. Consider the following sample data:

x	22	24	27	21	23	14	14	15
y	101	139	250	88	87	14	16	20

  a. Construct a scatterplot and verify that estimating a simple linear regression is appropriate in this problem.
  b. Calculate b_0 and b_1. What is the sample regression equation?
  c. Find the predicted value for y if x equals 20, 100, and 200.

Applications

20. The director of graduate admissions at a large university is analyzing the relationship between scores on the math portion of the Graduate Record Examination (GRE) and subsequent performance in graduate school, as measured by a student's grade point average (GPA). She uses a sample of 8 students who graduated within the past five years. The data are as follows:

GRE	700	720	650	750	680	730	740	780
GPA	3.0	3.5	3.2	3.7	3.1	3.9	3.3	3.5

  a. Construct a scatterplot placing "GRE" on the horizontal axis.
  b. Find the sample regression equation for the model: $GPA = \beta_0 + \beta_1 GRE + \varepsilon$.
  c. What is a student's predicted GPA if he/she scored 710 on the math portion of the GRE?

21. A social scientist would like to analyze the relationship between educational attainment and salary. He collects the following sample data, where "Education" refers to years of higher education and "Salary" is the individual's annual salary in thousands of dollars:

Education	3	4	6	2	5	4	8	0
Salary	$40	53	80	42	70	50	110	38

a. Find the sample regression equation for the model: Salary $= \beta_0 + \beta_1$Education $+ \varepsilon$.
b. Interpret the coefficient of education.
c. What is the predicted salary for an individual who completed 7 years of higher education?

22. **FILE** The consumption function captures one of the key relationships in economics that was first developed by John Maynard Keynes. It expresses consumption as a function of disposable income, where disposable income is income after taxes. The table below shows a portion of average U.S. annual consumption and disposable income for the years 1985–2006. The complete data set can be found on the text website, labeled **Consumption Function**.

	Consumption	Disposable Income
1985	$23,490	$22,887
1986	23,866	23,172
⋮	⋮	⋮
2006	48,398	58,101

Source: The Statistical Abstract of the United States.

When estimating the model:

Consumption $= \beta_0 + \beta_1$Disposable Income $+ \varepsilon$,

the following output is produced.

	Coefficients	Standard Error	t Stat	p-value
Intercept	8550.675	593.925	14.397	5.12E-12
Disposable Income	0.686	0.015	44.332	1.9E-21

a. Use Excel to replicate the above regression output.
b. What is the sample regression equation?

c. In this model the slope coefficient is called the marginal propensity to consume. Interpret its meaning.
d. What is predicted consumption if disposable income is $57,000?

23. **FILE** The following table lists Major League Baseball's (MLB's) leading pitchers, their earned run average (ERA), and their salary (given in millions of dollars) for 2008. The data are also available on the text website, labeled **MLB Pitchers**.

	ERA	Salary (in $ millions)
J. Santana	2.53	17.0
C. Lee	2.54	4.0
T. Lincecum	2.62	0.4
C. Sabathia	2.70	11.0
R. Halladay	2.78	10.0
J. Peavy	2.85	6.5
D. Matsuzaka	2.90	8.3
R. Dempster	2.96	7.3
B. Sheets	3.09	12.1
C. Hamels	3.09	0.5

Source: www.ESPN.com.

a. Use Excel to estimate the model: Salary $= \beta_0 + \beta_1$ERA $+ \varepsilon$ and interpret the coefficient of ERA.
b. Use the estimated model to predict salary for each player, given his ERA. For example, use the sample regression equation to predict the salary for J. Santana with ERA $= 2.53$.
c. Derive the corresponding residuals and explain why the residuals might be so high.

24. **FILE** In order to answer the following questions, use the data labeled **Happiness and Age** on the text website.
a. Use Excel to estimate a simple regression model with happiness as the response variable and age as the explanatory variable.
b. Use the estimates to predict happiness when age equals 25, 50, and 75.
c. Construct a scatterplot of happiness against age. Discuss why your predictions might not be accurate.

14.3 The Multiple Regression Model

The simple linear regression model allows us to analyze the linear relationship between an explanatory variable and the response variable. However, by restricting the number of explanatory variables to one, we sometimes reduce the potential usefulness of the model. For instance, in the last section we analyzed how debt payments are influenced by income, ignoring the possible effect of the unemployment rate. It is possible that debt payments are influenced by *both* income and the unemployment rate. A **multiple regression model** allows us to study how the response variable is influenced by two or more

LO **14.4**

Estimate the multiple linear regression model and interpret the coefficients.

explanatory variables. The choices of the explanatory variables are based on economic theory, intuition, and/or prior research. The multiple regression model is a straightforward extension of the simple linear regression model.

> **THE MULTIPLE LINEAR REGRESSION MODEL**
>
> The multiple linear regression model is defined as
>
> $$y = \beta_0 + \beta_1 x_1 + \beta_2 x_2 + \cdots + \beta_k x_k + \varepsilon,$$
>
> where y is the response variable, $x_1, x_2, \ldots, x_k$ are the k explanatory variables, and ε is the random error term. The coefficients $\beta_0, \beta_1, \ldots, \beta_k$ are the unknown parameters to be estimated.

Determining the Sample Regression Equation

As in the case of the simple linear regression model, we apply the OLS method that minimizes the error sum of squares errors SSE. As before, $SSE = \Sigma(y_i - \hat{y}_i)^2 = \Sigma e_i^2$ where e_i is the residual.

> The **sample regression equation** for the multiple regression model is denoted as
>
> $$\hat{y} = b_0 + b_1 x_1 + b_2 x_2 + \cdots + b_k x_k,$$
>
> where $b_0, b_1, \ldots, b_k$ are the point estimates of $\beta_0, \beta_1, \ldots, \beta_k$.

For each explanatory variable x_j ($j = 1, \ldots, k$), the corresponding slope coefficient b_j is the point estimate of β_j. We slightly modify the interpretation of the slope coefficients in the context of a multiple regression model. Here b_j measures the change in the predicted value of the response variable $\hat{y}$ given a unit increase in the associated explanatory variable x_j, *holding all other explanatory variables constant*. In other words, it represents the partial influence of x_j on $\hat{y}$.

When we used formulas to estimate the simple linear regression model, we found that the calculations were quite cumbersome. As you might imagine, if we were to estimate the multiple regression model by hand, the calculations would become even more tedious. Thus, we rely solely on using statistical packages to estimate a multiple regression model.

EXAMPLE 14.6 `FILE`

a. Given the data from Table 14.1, estimate the multiple regression model with debt payments as the response variable and income and the unemployment rate as the explanatory variables.

b. Interpret the regression coefficients.

c. Predict debt payments if income is $80,000 and the unemployment rate is 7.5%.

SOLUTION:

a. We will use Excel to estimate the multiple regression model, Debt = β_0 + β_1Income + β_2Unemployment + ε. We follow similar steps as we did with the simple linear regression.

   • Open the data labeled ***Debt Payments*** found on the text website.

- Choose **Data** > **Data Analysis** > **Regression** from the menu.
- In the *Regression* dialog box, click on the box next to *Input Y Range*, then select the debt payments data. For *Input X Range*, *simultaneously* select income and the unemployment rate data. Check *Labels,* since we are using Debt, Income, and Unemployment as headings.
- Click **OK**.

We show the Excel output in Table 14.5.

TABLE 14.5 Regression Results for Example 14.6

Regression Statistics						
Multiple R	0.8676					
R Square	0.7527					
Adjusted R Square	0.7312					
Standard Error	64.61					
Observations	26					
ANOVA						
	df	SS	MS	F	Significance F	
Regression	2	292170.77	146085.39	35.00	1E-07	
Residual	23	96011.69	4174.42			
Total	25	388182.46				
	Coefficients	Standard Error	t Stat	p-value	Lower 95%	Upper 95%
Intercept	**198.9956**	156.3619	1.2727	0.2159	−124.46	522.45
Income	**10.5122**	1.4765	7.1195	0.0000	7.46	13.57
Unemployment	**0.6186**	6.8679	0.0901	0.9290	−13.59	14.83

Using the boldface estimates, $b_0 = 198.9956$, $b_1 = 10.5122$, and $b_2 = 0.6186$, we derive the sample regression equation as

$$\widehat{\text{Debt}} = 199.00 + 10.51\text{Income} + 0.62\text{Unemployment}.$$

b. The regression coefficient of income is 10.51. Since income is measured in $1,000s, the model suggests that if income increases by $1,000, then debt payments are predicted to increase by $10.51, holding the unemployment rate constant. Similarly, the regression coefficient of the unemployment rate is 0.62, implying that a one percentage point increase in the unemployment rate leads to a predicted increase in debt payments of $0.62, holding income constant. It seems that the predicted impact of unemployment, with income held constant, is rather small. In fact, the influence of the unemployment rate is not even statistically significant at any reasonable level; we will discuss such tests of significance in the next chapter.

c. If income is $80,000 and the unemployment rate is 7.5%, predicted debt payments are

$$\widehat{\text{Debt}} = 199.00 + 10.51(80) + 0.62(7.5) = \$1,044.45.$$

EXERCISES 14.3

Concepts

25. In a multiple regression, the following sample regression equation is obtained:

$$\hat{y} = 152 + 12.9x_1 + 2.7x_2.$$

   a. Predict y if x_1 equals 20 and x_2 equals 35.
   b. Interpret the slope coefficient of x_1.

26. In a multiple regression, the following sample regression equation is obtained:

$$\hat{y} = -8 + 2.6x_1 - 47.2x_2.$$

   a. Predict y if x_1 equals 40 and x_2 equals −10.
   b. Interpret the slope coefficient of x_2.

27. Consider the following sample data:

y	46	51	28	55	29	53	47	36
x_1	40	48	29	44	30	58	60	29
x_2	13	28	24	11	28	28	29	14

   a. Estimate a multiple linear regression model and interpret its coefficients.
   b. Find the predicted value for y if x_1 equals 50 and x_2 equals 20.

28. Consider the following sample data:

y	52	49	45	54	45	52	40	34
x_1	11	10	9	13	9	13	6	7
x_2	25	39	25	24	31	22	28	21

   a. Estimate a multiple linear regression model and interpret the coefficient for x_2.
   b. Find the predicted value for y if x_1 equals 12 and x_2 equals 30.

Applications

29. Osteoporosis is a degenerative disease that primarily affects women over the age of 60. A research analyst wants to forecast sales of StrongBones, a prescription drug for treating this debilitating disease. She uses the model Sales = $\beta_0 + \beta_1$Pop + β_2Inc + ε, where Sales refers to the sales of StrongBones ($ millions), Pop is the number of women over the age of 60 (in millions), and Inc is the average income of women over the age of 60 ($1,000s). She collects data on 38 cities across the United States and obtains the following relevant regression results:

	Coefficients	Standard Error	t Stat	p-value
Intercept	10.35	4.02	2.57	0.0199
Population	8.47	2.71	3.12	0.0062
Income	7.62	6.63	1.15	0.2661

   a. What is the sample regression equation?
   b. Interpret the slope coefficients.
   c. Predict sales if a city has 1.5 million women over the age of 60 and their average income is $44,000.

30. A sociologist believes that the crime rate in an area is significantly influenced by the area's poverty rate and median income. Specifically, she hypothesizes crime will increase with poverty and decrease with income. She collects data on the crime rate (crimes per 100,000 residents), the poverty rate (in %), and the median income (in $1,000s) from 41 New England cities. A portion of the regression results is shown below.

	Coefficients	Standard Error	t Stat	p-value
Intercept	−301.62	549.71	−0.55	0.5864
Poverty	53.16	14.22	3.74	0.0006
Income	4.95	8.26	0.60	0.5526

   a. Are the signs as expected on the slope coefficients?
   b. Interpret the slope coefficient for Poverty.
   c. Predict the crime rate in an area with a poverty rate of 20% and a median income of $50,000.

31. FILE A realtor in Arlington, Massachusetts, is analyzing the relationship between the sale price of a home (Price), its square footage (Sqft), the number of bedrooms (Beds), and the number of bathrooms (Baths). She collects data on 36 recent sales in Arlington in the first quarter of 2009 for the analysis. A portion of the data is shown below; the complete data set can be found on the text website, labeled **Arlington Homes**.

Price	Sqft	Beds	Baths
840000	2768	4	3.5
822000	2500	4	2.5
⋮	⋮	⋮	⋮
307500	850	1	1

Source: Newenglandmoves.com.

She estimates the model as Price = $\beta_0 + \beta_1$Sqft + β_2Beds + β_3Baths + ε and obtains the following output.

	Coefficients	Standard Error	t Stat	p-value
Intercept	153348.27	57141.79	2.6836	0.0114
Sqft	95.86	35.40	2.7078	0.0108
Beds	556.89	20280.31	0.0275	0.9783
Baths	92022.91	25012.30	3.6791	0.0009

   a. Replicate the above regression output.
   b. Interpret the slope coefficients.
   c. Predict the price of a 2,500 square-foot home with three bedrooms and two bathrooms.

32. FILE Education reform is one of the most hotly debated subjects on both state and national policy makers' list of socioeconomic topics. Consider a regression model that relates school expenditures and family background to student performance in Massachusetts using 224 school districts. The response variable is the mean score on the

MCAS (Massachusetts Comprehensive Assessment System) exam given in May 1998 to 10th-graders. Four explanatory variables are used: (1) STR is the student-to-teacher ratio, (2) TSAL is the average teacher's salary, (3) INC is the median household income, and (4) SGL is the percentage of single family households. A portion of the data is shown below; the complete data set can be found on the text website, labeled **MCAS**.

Score	STR (%)	TSAL (in $1,000)	INC (in $1,000)	SGL (%)
227.00	19.00	44.01	48.89	4.70
230.67	17.90	40.17	43.91	4.60
⋮	⋮	⋮	⋮	⋮
230.67	19.20	44.79	47.64	5.10

Source: Massachusetts Department of Education and the Census of Population and Housing.

a. For each explanatory variable, discuss whether it is likely to have a positive or negative causal effect on Score.

b. Estimate the sample regression equation. Are the signs on the coefficients as expected?

c. What is the predicted score if STR = 18, TSAL = 50, INC = 60, SGL = 5?

d. What is the predicted score if everything else is the same as above except INC = 80?

33. **FILE** American football is the highest paying sport on a per-game basis. The quarterback, considered the most important player on the team, is appropriately compensated. A sports statistician wants to use 2009 data to estimate a multiple regression model that links the quarterback's salary with his pass completion percentage (PCT), total touchdowns scored (TD), and his age. A portion of the data is shown below; the complete data set can be found on the text website, labeled **Quarterback Salaries**.

Name	Salary (in $ millions)	PCT	TD	Age
Philip Rivers	25.5566	65.2	28	27
Jay Cutler	22.0441	60.5	27	26
⋮	⋮	⋮	⋮	⋮
Tony Romo	0.6260	63.1	26	29

Source: USA Today database for salaries; NFL.com for other data.

a. Estimate the model defined as Salary $= \beta_0 + \beta_1 PCT + \beta_2 TD + \beta_2 Age + \varepsilon$.

b. Are you surprised by the estimated coefficients?

c. Drew Brees earned 12.9895 million dollars in 2009. According to the model, what is his predicted salary given his PCT, TD, and age of 70.6, 34, and 30, respectively?

d. Tom Brady earned 8.0073 million dollars in 2009. According to the model, what is his predicted salary given his PCT, TD, and age of 65.7, 28, and 32, respectively?

e. Compute and interpret the residual salary for Drew Brees and Tom Brady.

14.4 Goodness-of-Fit Measures

By simply observing the sample regression equation, we cannot assess how well the explanatory variables explain the variability of the response variable. However, several objective "goodness-of-fit" measures do exist that summarize how well the sample regression equation fits the data. If all the observations lie on the sample regression equation, then we have a perfect fit. Since that almost never happens, we evaluate the models on a relative basis.

We will study three goodness-of-fit measures: the standard error of the estimate, the coefficient of determination, and the adjusted coefficient of determination. The relevant formulas used to derive these measures are applicable for both simple and multiple regression models, as long as the model includes the intercept term.

In the introductory case study we were interested in predicting consumer debt payments. We analyzed two models. Let Model 1 represent the simple regression model, Debt $= \beta_0 + \beta_1 Income + \varepsilon$, and Model 2 represent the multiple regression model, Debt $= \beta_0 + \beta_1 Income + \beta_2 Unemployment + \varepsilon$. (For ease of exposition, we use the same notation to refer to the coefficients in Models 1 and 2. We note, however, that these coefficients and their estimates may have a different meaning depending on which model we are referencing.)

If you had to choose one of these models to predict debt payments, which model would you choose? It may be that by using more explanatory variables, you can better describe the response variable. However, for a given sample, more is not always better. In order to select the preferred model, you need to use goodness-of-fit measures.

The Standard Error of the Estimate

We first describe goodness-of-fit measures in the context of a simple linear regression model. Figure 14.6 reproduces the scatterplot of debt payments against income, as well as the sample regression equation. Recall that the residual e represents the difference $y - \hat{y}$ between an observed value and the predicted value of the response variable. If all the data points had fallen on the line, then each residual would be zero; in other words, there would be no dispersion between the observed and predicted values. Since in practice we rarely, if ever, obtain this result, we evaluate models on the basis of the relative magnitude of the residuals. The sample regression equation provides a good fit when the dispersion of the residuals is relatively small.

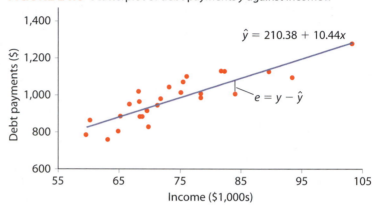

FIGURE 14.6 Scatterplot of debt payments y against income x

A numerical measure that gauges dispersion from the sample regression equation is the sample variance of the residual, denoted s_e^2. We generally report the standard deviation of the residual, denoted s_e, more commonly referred to as the **standard error of the estimate**. The variance s_e^2 is defined as the average squared difference between y_i and $\hat{y}_i$. The numerator of the formula is the error sum of squares $SSE = \Sigma(y_i - \hat{y}_i)^2 = \Sigma e_i^2$. Dividing SSE by its respective degrees of freedom $n - k - 1$ yields s_e^2, also referred to as the **mean square error MSE**. Recall that k denotes the number of explanatory variables in the regression model; thus, for a simple linear regression model, k equals one. The standard error of the estimate s_e is the positive square root of s_e^2. The less the dispersion, the smaller the s_e, which implies a better fit to the model. As mentioned earlier, if all points fall on the line, then no dispersion occurs, so s_e equals zero.

THE STANDARD ERROR OF THE ESTIMATE

The **standard error of the estimate** s_e is a point estimate of the standard deviation of the random error ε, and is calculated as

$$s_e = \sqrt{s_e^2} = \sqrt{MSE} = \sqrt{\frac{SSE}{n - k - 1}} = \sqrt{\frac{\Sigma e_i^2}{n - k - 1}} = \sqrt{\frac{\Sigma(y_i - \hat{y}_i)^2}{n - k - 1}}.$$

Theoretically, s_e can assume any value between zero and infinity, $0 \le s_e < \infty$. The closer s_e is to zero, the better the model fits.

EXAMPLE 14.7

Consider the sample data in Table 14.1 and the regression output for Model 1 in Table 14.4. Use the sample regression equation, $\widehat{Debt} = 210.30 + 10.44 Income$, to calculate and interpret the standard error of the estimate s_e.

SOLUTION: First, we calculate the variance of the residual s_e^2. Let y and x denote Debt and Income, respectively. The first two columns of Table 14.6 show the values of these variables. The third column shows the predicted values $\hat{y}$ and the fourth column shows the squared residuals, $e^2 = (y - \hat{y})^2$. The value in the last row of the last column is the error sum of the squares SSE and is the numerator in the formula for s_e^2.

TABLE 14.6 Calculations for Example 14.7

y	x	$\hat{y} = 210.30 + 10.44x$	$e^2 = (y - \hat{y})^2$
1285	103.50	$210.30 + 10.44 \times 103.50 = 1290.84$	$(1285 - 1290.84)^2 = 34.11$
1135	81.70	$210.30 + 10.44 \times 81.70 = 1063.25$	$(1135 - 1063.25)^2 = 5148.35$
⋮	⋮	⋮	⋮
763	63.00	$210.30 + 10.44 \times 63.00 = 868.02$	$(763 - 868.02)^2 = 11029.20$
			$\Sigma(y_i - \hat{y}_i)^2 = \Sigma e_i^2 = 96045.72$

Using $SSE = \Sigma e_i^2 = 96{,}045.72$, we determine the variance of the residual s_e^2 as

$$s_e^2 = \frac{\Sigma e_i^2}{n - k - 1} = \frac{96{,}045.72}{26 - 1 - 1} = 4{,}001.91.$$

Taking the square root of the variance, we obtain

$$s_e = \sqrt{s_e^2} = \sqrt{4{,}001.91} = 63.26.$$

The standard error of the estimate is measured in the same units of measurement as the response variable. Since debt payments are in dollars, we report s_e as $63.26.

We mentioned earlier that the closer s_e is to zero, the better the fit. Can we conclude that a value of $63.26 is close to zero? A general guideline is to evaluate the value of s_e with respect to the mean of the response variable. If we construct the ratio $s_e/\bar{y}$ and find that this ratio is less than 0.20, then we have some evidence that the model is an effective analytical and forecasting tool. Given that average debt payments are $983.46, we compute the ratio as $63.26/983.46 = 0.06$. Thus, Model 1 appears promising.

Most of the time we rely on statistical software packages to report s_e. (If s_e is not explicitly given, other statistics like SSE are generally provided, which then greatly facilitate the calculation of s_e.) Excel reports the value for s_e in the regression output section entitled *Regression Statistics*. It is simply referred to as Standard Error. In column 2 of Table 14.7, we report the Excel regression statistics for Model 1. Note that $s_e = 63.26$ is the same as the one calculated above.

TABLE 14.7 Regression Statistics for Model 1 and Model 2

	Model 1	Model 2
Multiple R	0.8675	0.8676
R Square	0.7526	0.7527
Adjusted R Square	0.7423	0.7312
Standard Error	63.26	64.61
Observations	26	26
Regression Equation	$\hat{y} = 210.30 + 10.44x$	$\hat{y} = 199 + 10.51x_1 + 0.62x_2$

Our objective in adding another explanatory variable to the regression model is to increase the model's usefulness. In Model 2 we use income x_1 and the unemployment rate x_2 to explain debt payments y. If Model 2 is an improvement over Model 1, then we would expect it to have a smaller standard error of the estimate. Table 14.7 also shows the relevant regression statistics for Model 2. We note that the standard error of the estimate for Model 2, $s_e = \$64.61$, is actually greater than that for Model 1 ($64.61 > 63.26$). In other words, there is less dispersion between the observed values of debt payments and the predicted values of debt payments when we include only one explanatory variable in the model. So far, this suggests that Model 1 provides a better fit for the sample data. In general, we use the standard error of the estimate in conjunction with other measures to judge the overall usefulness of a model.

LO **14.6**

Calculate and interpret the coefficient of determination R^2.

The Coefficient of Determination

The **coefficient of determination**, commonly referred to as R^2, is another goodness-of-fit measure that is easier to interpret than the standard error of the estimate. It too evaluates how well the sample regression equation fits the data. In particular, R^2 quantifies the sample variability in the response variable y that is explained by changes in the explanatory variable(s), that is, by the sample regression equation. It is computed as the ratio of the explained variation of the response variable to its total variation. We generally convert this ratio into a percent by multiplying it by 100. For example, if $R^2 = 0.72$, we say that 72% of the variation in the response variable is explained by the sample regression equation. Other factors, which have not been included in the model, account for the remaining 28% of the sample variation.

We use analysis of variance (ANOVA) to derive R^2. Recall from Chapter 13 that we denote the **total variation** in y as $\Sigma(y_i - \bar{y})^2$, which is the numerator in the formula for the variance of y. This value, called the **total sum of squares** *SST*, can be broken down into two components: **explained** variation and **unexplained** variation. Figure 14.7 illustrates the decomposition of the total variation in y into its two components.

FIGURE 14.7 Total, explained, and unexplained variations in y

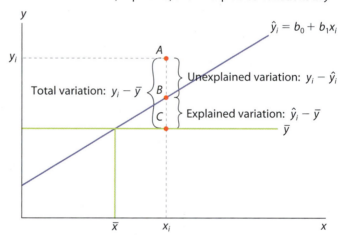

For ease of exposition, we show a scatterplot with all the points removed except one (point A). Point A refers to the observation (x_i, y_i). The blue line represents the estimated regression equation based on the entire sample data; the horizontal and vertical green lines represent the sample means $\bar{y}$ and $\bar{x}$, respectively. The vertical distance (difference) between the data point A and $\bar{y}$ (point C) is the total variation $y_i - \bar{y}$ (distance AC). For each data point, we square these differences and then find their sum—this amounts to $SST = \Sigma(y_i - \bar{y})^2$.

Now, we focus on the difference between the predicted value of the data point $\hat{y}_i$ (point B) and $\bar{y}$. This difference is the explained variation in y (distance BC). Explained variation indicates that the positive difference between $\hat{y}_i$ and $\bar{y}$ occurs because y rises with x and in this case x is above its mean. Squaring all such differences and summing them yields the **regression sum of squares**, $SSR = \Sigma(\hat{y}_i - \bar{y})^2$.

The difference between the particular observation and its predicted value (distance AB) is the unexplained variation in y. This is the portion of the variation in y that remains unexplained; it is the variation due to random error or chance. Squaring all such differences and summing them yields the familiar **error sum of squares**, $SSE = \Sigma(y_i - \hat{y}_i)^2$.

Thus, the total variation in y can be decomposed into explained and unexplained variation as follows:

$$SST = SSR + SSE$$

Dividing both sides by SST and rearranging yields:

$$\frac{SSR}{SST} = 1 - \frac{SSE}{SST}$$

The above equation represents the coefficient of determination R^2. The value of R^2 falls between zero and one, $0 \leq R^2 \leq 1$. The closer R^2 is to one, the stronger the fit; the closer it is to zero, the weaker the fit.

THE COEFFICIENT OF DETERMINATION R^2

The coefficient of determination $\boldsymbol{R^2}$ is the proportion of the variation in the response variable that is explained by the sample regression equation. We compute R^2 as

$$R^2 = 1 - \frac{SSE}{SST},$$

where $SSE = \Sigma(y_i - \hat{y}_i)^2$ and $SST = \Sigma(y_i - \bar{y})^2$.

Most statistical packages, including Excel, provide the ANOVA calculations for SST, SSR, and SSE.

EXAMPLE 14.8

Calculate and interpret the coefficient of determination R^2 given the sample data in Table 14.1 and the sample regression equation from Model 1: $\widehat{\text{Debt}} = 210.30 + 10.44\text{Income}$.

SOLUTION: In Example 14.7 we calculated SSE for Model 1 as 96,045.72. Using $R^2 = 1 - SSE/SST$, the only missing part is SST. Given $\bar{y} = 983.46$, we calculate SST as

$$\Sigma(y_i - \bar{y})^2 = (1285 - 983.46)^2 + (1135 - 983.46)^2 + \cdots + (763 - 983.46)^2$$
$$= 388,182.46.$$

Therefore,

$$R^2 = 1 - \frac{SSE}{SST} = 1 - \frac{96,045.72}{388,182.46} = 0.7526.$$

Note that this value matches the Excel estimate shown in Table 14.7. The coefficient of determination R^2 shows that 75.26% of the sample variation in debt payments is explained by changes in income.

Another interesting statistic in Table 14.7 is **Multiple R**. Using our earlier notation, this measure is simply the sample correlation between the response variable y and its predicted value $\hat{y}$, or $r_{y\hat{y}}$. In a simple linear regression model, Multiple R also represents the absolute value of the correlation between y and x, or $|r_{yx}|$. Moreover, the coefficient of determination is the square of Multiple R, that is, $R^2 = r_{y\hat{y}}^2$.

The coefficient of determination R^2 can also be computed as $R^2 = r_{y\hat{y}}^2$, where $r_{y\hat{y}}$ is the sample correlation between y and $\hat{y}$.

EXAMPLE 14.9

Using the regression statistics from Table 14.7, what is the sample correlation coefficient between y and $\hat{y}$ for Model 2? Square this value to compute R^2.

SOLUTION: The Multiple R in Table 14.7 implies that the sample correlation coefficient between y and $\hat{y}$ for Model 2 is $r_{y\hat{y}} = 0.8676$. Thus, $R^2 = r_{y\hat{y}}^2 = 0.8676^2 = 0.7527$.

Recall that the standard error of the estimate for Model 1 ($s_e = 63.26$) was smaller than that for Model 2 ($s_e = 64.61$), suggesting that Model 1 provides a better fit. Now, the coefficient of determination for Model 2 ($R^2 = 0.7527$) is slightly higher than that of Model 1 ($R^2 = 0.7526$), implying that Model 2 explains more of the variation in debt payments. How do we resolve these apparent conflicting results? It turns out that we cannot use R^2 for model comparison when the competing models do not include the same number of explanatory variables. This occurs because R^2 never decreases as we add more explanatory variables to the model. A popular model selection criterion in such situations is adjusted R^2.

LO **14.7**

Differentiate between R^2 and adjusted R^2.

The Adjusted R^2

Since R^2 never decreases as we add more explanatory variables to the regression model, it is possible to increase its value unintentionally by including a group of explanatory variables that may have no economic or intuitive foundation in the regression model. This is true especially when the number of explanatory variables k is large relative to the sample size n. In order to avoid the possibility of R^2 creating a false impression, virtually all software packages include **adjusted R^2**. Unlike R^2, adjusted R^2 explicitly accounts for the sample size n and the number of explanatory variables k. It is common to use adjusted R^2 for model selection because it imposes a penalty for any additional explanatory variable that is included in the analysis.

ADJUSTED R^2

The adjusted coefficient of determination, calculated as adjusted $R^2 = 1 - (1 - R^2)\left(\frac{n-1}{n-k-1}\right)$, is used to compare competing regression models with different numbers of explanatory variables; the higher the adjusted R^2, the better model.

If SSE is substantially greater than zero and k is large compared to n, then adjusted R^2 will differ substantially from R^2. Adjusted R^2 may be negative, if the correlation between the response variable and the explanatory variables is sufficiently low.

EXAMPLE 14.10

Using the regression statistics from Table 14.7, use the value of the adjusted R^2 for model comparison.

SOLUTION: We note from Table 14.7 that Model 1 has an adjusted R^2 of 0.7423, whereas Model 2's value is 0.7312. Therefore, given its higher adjusted R^2, we choose Model 1 to predict debt payments.

SYNOPSIS OF INTRODUCTORY CASE

A recent study shows substantial variability in consumer debt payments depending on where the consumer resides (Experian.com, November 11, 2010). A possible explanation is that a linear relationship exists between consumer debt payments and an area's median household income. In order to substantiate this claim, relevant data on 26 metropolitan areas are collected. The correlation coefficient between debt payments and income is computed as 0.87, suggesting a strong positive linear relationship between the two variables. A simple test confirms that the correlation coefficient is statistically significant at the 5% level.

Two regression models are also estimated for the analysis. A simple linear regression model (Model 1), using consumer debt payments as the response variable and median household income as the explanatory variable, is estimated as $\widehat{Debt} = 210.30 + 10.44\text{Income}$. For every $1,000 increase in median household income, consumer debt payments are predicted to increase by $10.44. In an attempt to improve upon the prediction, a multiple regression model (Model 2) is proposed, where median household income and the unemployment rate are used as explanatory variables. The sample regression line for Model 2 is $\widehat{Debt} = 199.00 + 10.51\text{Income} + 0.62\text{Unemployment}$. Given its slope coefficient of only 0.62, the economic impact of the unemployment rate on consumer debt payments, with median household income held fixed, seems extremely weak. Goodness-of-fit measures confirm that Model 1 provides a better fit than Model 2. The standard error of the estimate is smaller for Model 1, suggesting less dispersion of the data from the sample regression equation. In addition, the adjusted R^2 is higher for Model 1, implying that more of the variability in consumer debt payments is explained by the simple regression model. Using Model 1 and an area's median household income of $80,000, consumer debt payments are predicted to be $1,045.50.

EXERCISES 14.4

Concepts

34. In a simple linear regression based on 25 observations, the following intermediate data are given: $\Sigma(y_i - \hat{y})^2 = 1{,}250$ and $\Sigma(y_i - \bar{y})^2 = 1{,}500$.
    a. Calculate s_e^2 and s_e.
    b. Calculate R^2.

35. In a simple linear regression based on 30 observations, it is found that $SSE = 2{,}540$ and $SST = 13{,}870$.
    a. Calculate s_e^2 and s_e.
    b. Calculate R^2.

36. In a multiple regression with two explanatory variables, the following intermediate data are given: $n = 50$, $\Sigma(y_i - \hat{y})^2 = 35$, and $\Sigma(y_i - \bar{y})^2 = 90$.
    a. Calculate the standard error of the estimate.
    b. Calculate the coefficient of determination R^2.

37. In a multiple regression with four explanatory variables and 100 observations, it is found that $SSR = 4.75$ and $SST = 7.62$.
    a. Calculate the standard error of the estimate.
    b. Calculate the coefficient of determination R^2.
    c. Calculate adjusted R^2.

38. The following ANOVA table was obtained when estimating a multiple linear regression.

ANOVA	df	SS	MS	F	Significance F
Regression	2	161478.4	80739.19	11.5854	0.0002
Residual	27	188163.9	6969.03		
Total	29	349642.2			

   a. Calculate the standard error of the estimate. Given that the mean of the response variable is 557, does the model seem promising? Explain.

b. Calculate and interpret the coefficient of determination.

c. Compute adjusted R^2.

39. The following ANOVA table was obtained when estimating a multiple regression.

ANOVA	df	SS	MS	F	Significance F
Regression	2	188246.8	94123.4	35.2	9.04E-07
Residual	17	45457.32	2673.96		
Total	19	233704.1			

a. Calculate the standard error of the estimate. Given that the mean of the response variable is 345, does the model seem promising? Explain.

b. Calculate and interpret the coefficient of determination.

c. Calculate adjusted R^2.

Applications

40. The director of college admissions at a local university is trying to determine whether a student's high school GPA or SAT score is a better predictor of the student's subsequent college GPA. She formulates two models:

Model 1. College GPA $= \beta_0 + \beta_1$High School GPA $+ \varepsilon$

Model 2. College GPA $= \beta_0 + \beta_1$SAT Score $+ \varepsilon$

She estimates these models using data from a sample of 10 recent college graduates. A portion of the results are as follows:

ANOVA Results for Model 1					
	df	SS	MS	F	Significance F
Regression	1	1.4415	1.4415	11.5032	0.0095
Residual	8	1.0025	0.1253		
Total	9	2.4440			

ANOVA Results for Model 2					
	df	SS	MS	F	Significance F
Regression	1	1.0699	1.0699	6.2288	0.0372
Residual	8	1.3741	0.1718		
Total	9	2.4440			

a. Calculate the standard error of the estimate for Model 1 and Model 2.

b. Calculate the coefficient of determination for Model 1 and Model 2.

c. Given these two measures, which model is a better fit? Explain.

41. For a sample of 41 New England cities, a sociologist studies the crime rate in each city (crimes per 100,000 residents) as a function of its poverty rate (in %) and its median income (in $1,000s). A portion of the regression results are shown.

ANOVA	df	SS	MS	F	Significance F
Regression	2	3549788	1774894	16.12513	8.5E-06
Residual	38	4182663	110070.1		
Total	40	7732451			

a. Calculate the standard error of the estimate. Given that the mean crime rate for this sample is 597, calculate and interpret $s_e/\bar{y}$.

b. What proportion of the variability in crime rate is explained by the variability in the explanatory variables? What proportion is unexplained?

42. A financial analyst uses the following model to estimate a firm's stock return: Return $= \beta_0 + \beta_1 P/E + \beta_2 P/S + \varepsilon$, where P/E is a firm's price-to-earnings ratio and P/S is a firm's price-to-sales ratio. A portion of the regression results is shown.

ANOVA	df	SS	MS	F	Significance F
Regression	2	918.746	459.373	2.817	0.0774
Residual	27	4402.786	163.066		
Total	29	5321.532			

a. Calculate the standard error of the estimate. Given that the mean return for this sample is 1.31%, calculate and interpret $s_e/\bar{y}$.

b. Calculate and interpret the coefficient of determination.

c. Calculate the corresponding adjusted R^2.

43. FILE Is it defense or offense that wins football games? Consider the following data, which include a team's winning record (Win), the average number of yards made, and the average number of yards allowed during the 2009 NFL season. The complete data, labeled **Football**, can be found on the text website.

Team	Win (%)	Yards Made	Yards Allowed
Arizona Cardinals	62.50	344.40	346.40
Atlanta Falcons	56.30	340.40	348.90
⋮	⋮	⋮	⋮
Washington Redskins	25.00	312.50	319.70

Source: NFL website.

a. Compare two simple linear regression models, where Model 1 predicts winning percentage based on Yards Made and Model 2 uses Yards Allowed.

b. Estimate a multiple regression model, Model 3, that applies both Yards Made and Yards Allowed to forecast winning percentage. Is this model an improvement over the other two models? Explain.

44. FILE Executive compensation has risen dramatically beyond the rising levels of an average worker's wage over the years. This has been a hot topic for discussion, especially with the crisis in the financial sector and the controversy over the federal bailout. The government is even considering a cap on high-flying salaries for executives (*New York Times*, February 9, 2009). Consider the following data, which link total compensation of the 455 highest-paid CEOs in 2006 with two performance measures (industry-adjusted return on assets (Adj ROA) and industry-adjusted stock return (Adj Stock Return)) and the firm's size (Total Assets). The complete data, labeled **Executive Compensation**, are available on the text website.

Compensation (in $ millions)	Adj ROA	Adj Stock Return	Total Assets (in $ millions)
16.58	2.53	−0.15	20,917.5
26.92	1.27	0.57	32,659.5
⋮	⋮	⋮	⋮
2.3	0.45	0.75	44,875.0

Source: SEC website and Compustat.

a. Estimate three simple linear regression models that use compensation as the response variable with Adj ROA, Adj Stock Return, or Total Assets as the explanatory variable. Which model do you select? Explain.

b. Estimate multiple regression models that use various combinations of two, or all three explanatory variables. Which model do you select? Explain.

WRITING WITH STATISTICS

Matthew Farnham is an investment consultant who always recommends a well-diversified portfolio of mutual funds to his clients. He knows that a key concept in benefiting from diversification is correlation. Correlation is the extent to which assets perform in relation to one another. If all of an investor's assets move in lockstep, or are highly correlated, then the investor is either all right or all wrong. In order to reduce risk, it is considered good practice to invest in assets whose values rise and fall independently of one another. Matthew is approached by a client who has already invested in Vanguard's 500 Index Fund—a fund that mimics the Standard & Poor's 500 Index. She seeks advice for choosing her next investment from one of the following Vanguard funds:

- Inflation-Protected Securities Index
- Intermediate-Term Bond Index
- Real Estate Investment Trust Index
- Small Cap Index

Matthew collects 10 years of monthly return data for each mutual fund for the analysis. A portion of the data is shown in Table 14.8. The complete data set can be found on the text website, labeled **Vanguard Funds**.

TABLE 14.8 Monthly Return Data for Five Mutual Funds, January 2001–December 2010 FILE

	500 Index	Inflation-Protected Securities	Intermediate-Term Bond	Real Estate	Small Cap
January 2001	0.0342	0.0205	0.0181	0.0044	0.0527
February 2001	−0.1007	0.0161	0.0129	−0.0175	−0.0658
⋮	⋮	⋮	⋮	⋮	⋮
December 2010	0.0585	−0.0284	−0.0320	0.0355	0.0663

Source: finance.yahoo.com; data retrieved January 4, 2011.

Matthew would like to use the sample information in Table 14.8 to:

1. Calculate and interpret the sample correlation coefficient of each fund with Vanguard's 500 Index.

2. Make a recommendation for a mutual fund that is not correlated with Vanguard's 500 Index.

Sample
Report–
Making
Investment
Decisions by
Diversifying

In attempting to create a well-diversified portfolio, an analysis of the correlation between assets' returns is crucial. The correlation coefficient measures the direction and the strength of the linear relationship between assets' returns. This statistic can aid in the hunt for assets that form a portfolio. An investor has already chosen Vanguard's 500 Index mutual fund as part of her portfolio. When choosing to add to her portfolio, she considers these four mutual funds from the Vanguard family:

- Inflation-Protected Securities Index
- Intermediate-Term Bond Index
- Real Estate Investment Trust Index
- Small Cap Index

Ten years of monthly return data for each of these prospective funds, as well as the 500 Index, are collected. The first row of Table 14.A shows the sample correlation coefficients between the 500 Index and each mutual fund.

TABLE 14.A Analysis of Correlations between the 500 Index and Each Mutual Fund

	Inflation-Protected Securities	Intermediate-Term Bond	Real Estate	Small Cap
Correlation Coefficient	0.0796	−0.0408	0.6630	0.9030
Test Statistic	0.87	−0.44	9.62	22.83
p-value	0.39	0.66	0.00	0.00

The correlation coefficient always assumes a value between −1 and 1; an absolute value close to 1 implies that the two assets move in sync. In this sample, the highest sample correlation coefficient is between the 500 Index and the Small Cap Index, with a value of 0.9030. Next on the list is the correlation of 0.6630 between the 500 Index and the Real Estate Index. Sometimes investors choose assets that are negatively correlated in order to hedge risk; that is, one asset does well when the other does poorly. Such strategies are only recommended in the short term, since returns essentially cancel one another out. The investor wants to invest across a range of asset classes that earn respectable returns but are relatively uncorrelated. This way, if one asset in a portfolio suffers, the rest may be unaffected. Given that the Inflation-Protected Securities Index and the Intermediate-Term Bond Index have correlation coefficients close to zero, these may prove to be desirable additions to the investor's portfolio.

A hypothesis test is conducted in order to determine whether the population correlation coefficients are significantly different from zero at the 5% significance level. The null hypothesis is that the returns are uncorrelated and the alternative hypothesis suggests either a positive or a negative correlation. Rows 2 and 3 of Table 14.A show the value of the test statistics and the corresponding p-values. For instance, given a p-value of 0.39, the correlation coefficient between the 500 Index and the Inflation-Protected Securities Index is not significantly different from zero at the 5% significance level. This same conclusion holds for the correlation coefficient between the 500 Index and the Intermediate-Term Bond Index. On the other hand, given p-values of 0.00 for both of the test statistics associated with the correlation coefficient between the 500 Index and the Real Estate Index and the 500 Index and the Small Cap Index, we can conclude that these correlation coefficients are significantly different from zero.

Assuming that the correlation between assets is likely to remain stable in the future, then it appears that the investor should add either the Inflation-Protected Securities Index or the Intermediate Bond Index to her portfolio. Compared to the other two funds, these funds would offer the maximum benefit from diversification in the sense of reducing volatility.

Conceptual Review

Conduct a hypothesis test for the population correlation coefficient.

The **covariance** is a measure of the linear relationship between two variables x and y. We compute the sample covariance as $s_{xy} = \frac{\Sigma(x_i - \bar{x})(y_i - \bar{y})}{n - 1}$, where n represents the number of observations. The **correlation coefficient** is a unit-free measure that gauges the strength of the linear relationship between two variables x and y. We calculate the sample correlation coefficient as $r_{xy} = \frac{s_{xy}}{s_x s_y}$, where $-1 \leq r_{xy} \leq 1$.

When determining whether the correlation coefficient differs from zero, the null and alternative hypotheses are formulated as $H_0: \rho_{xy} = 0$ and $H_A: \rho_{xy} \neq 0$, where ρ_{xy} is the population correlation coefficient; one-tailed tests are constructed similarly. The corresponding test statistic for conducting the test follows the t distribution with $df = n - 2$, and its value is calculated as $t_{df} = \frac{r_{xy}\sqrt{n - 2}}{\sqrt{1 - r_{xy}^2}}$.

Discuss the limitations of correlation analysis.

There are several **limitations to correlation analysis**. These include: (1) two variables may have a very low correlation coefficient, yet a strong *nonlinear* relation; (2) the existence of *outliers* may blur the interpretation of the covariance and the correlation coefficient; and (3) *spurious correlation* can make two variables appear closely related when no causal relationship exists.

Estimate the simple linear regression model and interpret the coefficients.

Regression analysis explicitly assumes that one variable, called the **response variable**, is influenced by other variables, called the **explanatory variables**.

The **simple linear regression model** uses only one explanatory variable to predict and/or describe change in the response variable. The model is expressed as $y = \beta_0 + \beta_1 x + \varepsilon$, where y and x are the response variable and the explanatory variable, respectively, and ε is the random error term. The coefficients β_0 and β_1 are the unknown parameters to be estimated.

We apply the **ordinary least squares (OLS)** method to find a sample regression equation, $\hat{y} = b_0 + b_1 x$, where $\hat{y}$ is the predicted value of the response variable and b_0 and b_1 are the point estimates of β_0 and β_1, respectively. The estimated slope coefficient b_1 represents the change in $\hat{y}$ when x changes by one unit. The units of b_1 are the same as those of y.

Estimate the multiple linear regression model and interpret the coefficients.

The **multiple regression model** allows more than one explanatory variable to be linearly related with the response variable y. It is defined as $y = \beta_0 + \beta_1 x_1 + \beta_2 x_2 + \cdots + \beta_k x_k + \varepsilon$, where y is the response variable, $x_1, x_2, \ldots, x_k$ are the k explanatory variables and ε is the random error term. The coefficients $\beta_0, \beta_1, \ldots, \beta_k$ are the unknown parameters to be estimated. We again use the OLS method to arrive at the following sample regression equation: $\hat{y} = b_0 + b_1 x_1 + b_2 x_2 + \cdots + b_k x_k$, where $b_0, b_1, \ldots, b_k$ are the point estimates of $\beta_0, \beta_1, \ldots, \beta_k$, respectively.

For each explanatory variable x_j ($j = 1, \ldots, k$), the corresponding slope coefficient b_j is the estimated regression coefficient. It measures the change in the predicted value of the response variable $\hat{y}$ given a unit increase in the associated explanatory variable x_j, *holding all other explanatory variables constant*. In other words, it represents the partial influence of x_j on $\hat{y}$.

Calculate and interpret the standard error of the estimate.

The **standard error of the estimate** s_e is a point estimate of the standard deviation of the random error ε, and is calculated as $s_e = \sqrt{s_e^2} = \sqrt{MSE} = \sqrt{\frac{SSE}{n-k-1}} = \sqrt{\frac{\Sigma e_i^2}{n-k-1}} = \sqrt{\frac{\Sigma(y_i - \hat{y}_i)^2}{n-k-1}}$. Theoretically, s_e can assume any value between zero and infinity, $0 \le s_e < \infty$; the closer s_e is to zero, the better the model fits. Since s_e has no predetermined upper limit, it is difficult to interpret the standard error of the estimate in isolation; however, if the ratio $s_e/\bar{y}$ is less than 0.20, then this indicates that the model is an effective analytical and forecasting tool.

Calculate and interpret the coefficient of determination R^2.

The **coefficient of determination R^2** is the proportion of the variation in the response variable that is explained by the sample regression equation. It falls between 0 and 1; the closer the value is to 1, the better the model fits. For example, if $R^2 = 0.72$, we say that 72% of the sample variation in y is explained by the estimated model.

We compute the coefficient of determination as $R^2 = 1 - \frac{SSE}{SST}$ where $SSE = \Sigma(y_i - \hat{y}_i)^2$ and $SST = \Sigma(y_i - \bar{y})^2$. Alternatively, we can compute it as $R^2 = r_{y\hat{y}}^2$, where $r_{y\hat{y}}$ is the sample correlation between y and $\hat{y}$.

Differentiate between R^2 and adjusted R^2.

Adjusted R^2 adjusts R^2 by accounting for the sample size n and the number of explanatory variables k used in the regression. It is calculated as adjusted $R^2 = 1 - (1 - R^2)\left(\frac{n-1}{n-k-1}\right)$. In comparing competing models with different number of explanatory variables, the preferred model will have the highest adjusted R^2.

Additional Exercises and Case Studies

45. The following table shows the annual returns for two of Vanguard's mutual funds: the Vanguard Energy Fund and the Vanguard Healthcare Fund.

Annual Total Returns (in percent)		
Year	Energy x	Healthcare y
2004	36.65	9.51
2005	44.60	15.41
2006	19.68	10.87
2007	37.00	4.43
2008	−42.87	−18.45
	$\bar{x} = 19.01$	$\bar{y} = 4.35$
	$s_x = 35.77$	$s_y = 13.34$
	$s_{xy} = 447.68$	

SOURCE: www.finance.yahoo.com.

a. Calculate and interpret the sample correlation coefficient r_{xy}.
b. Specify the competing hypotheses in order to determine whether the population correlation coefficient is significantly different from zero.
c. At the 5% significance level, what is the conclusion to the test? Are the returns on the mutual funds significantly correlated?

46. In response to the global financial crisis, Federal Reserve leaders continue to keep the short-run target interest rate near zero. While the Fed controls short-term interest rates, long-term interest rates essentially depend on supply/demand dynamics, as well as longer-term interest rate expectations. Consider the following annualized rates for 3-month Treasury yields and 10-year Treasury yields.

Year	3-Month Yield (%)	10-Year Yield (%)
2001	3.47	5.02
2002	1.63	4.61
2003	1.03	4.02
2004	1.40	4.27
2005	3.21	4.29
2006	4.85	4.79
2007	4.47	4.63
2008	1.39	3.67
2009	0.15	3.26
2010	0.14	3.21

SOURCE: Federal Reserve Bank of Dallas.

a. Construct and interpret a scatterplot of a 10-year treasury yield against a 3-month yield.

b. Calculate and interpret the sample correlation coefficient. Use $\alpha = 0.05$ to test if the population correlation coefficient is significantly different from zero.

c. Estimate and interpret a sample regression equation using the 10-year yield as the response variable and the 3-month yield as the explanatory variable.

47. **FILE** The homeownership rate in the U.S. was 67.4% in 2009. In order to determine if homeownership is linked with income, 2009 state level data on homeownership rate (Ownership) and median household income (Income) were collected. A portion of the data is shown below; the complete data can be found on the text website, labeled **Home Ownership**.

State	Income	Ownership
Alabama	$39,980	74.1%
Alaska	$61,604	66.8%
⋮	⋮	⋮
Wyoming	$52,470	73.8%

Source: www.census.gov.

a. Estimate and interpret the model: Ownership $= \beta_0 + \beta_1$Income $+ \varepsilon$.

b. What is the standard error of the estimate? Calculate and interpret $s_e/\bar{y}$.

c. Interpret the coefficient of determination.

48. **FILE** A research analyst is trying to determine whether a firm's price-earnings (P/E) and price-sales (P/S) ratios can explain the firm's stock performance over the past year. A P/E ratio is calculated as a firm's share price compared to the income or profit earned by the firm per share. Generally, a high P/E ratio suggests that investors are expecting higher earnings growth in the future compared to companies with a lower P/E ratio. The P/S ratio is calculated by dividing a firm's share price by the firm's revenue per share for the trailing 12 months. In short, investors can use the P/S ratio to determine how much they are paying for a dollar of the firm's sales rather than a dollar of its earnings (P/E ratio). In general, the lower the P/S ratio, the more attractive the investment. The accompanying table shows the year-to-date (YTD) returns and the P/E and P/S ratios for a portion of the 30 firms included in the Dow Jones Industrial Average. The complete data set can be found on the text website, labeled **Dow 2010**.

	YTD return (in %)	P/E ratio	P/S ratio
1. 3M Co.	4.4	14.37	2.41
2. Alcoa Inc.	−4.5	11.01	0.78
⋮	⋮	⋮	⋮
30. Walt Disney Company	16.3	13.94	1.94

Source: The 2010 returns (January 1, 2010–December 31, 2010) were obtained from *The Wall Street Journal*, January 3, 2010; the P/E ratios and the P/S ratios were obtained from finance.yahoo.com on January 20, 2011.

a. Estimate: Return $= \beta_0 + \beta_1$P/E $+ \beta_2$P/S $+ \varepsilon$. Are the signs on the coefficients as expected? Explain.

b. Interpret the slope coefficient of the P/S ratio.

c. What is the predicted return for a firm with a P/E ratio of 10 and a P/S ratio of 2?

d. What is the standard error of the estimate? Calculate and interpret $s_e/\bar{y}$.

e. Interpret R^2.

49. **FILE** There has been a lot of discussion regarding the relationship between Scholastic Aptitude Test (SAT) scores and test-takers' family income (*New York Times,* August 27, 2009). It is generally believed that the wealthier a student's family, the higher the SAT score. Another commonly used predictor for SAT scores is the student's grade point average (GPA). Consider the following data collected on 24 students. The data can also be found on the text website, labeled **SAT**.

SAT	Income	GPA
1651	47,000	2.79
1581	34,000	2.97
⋮	⋮	⋮
1940	113,000	3.96

a. Estimate three models:
   (i) SAT $= \beta_0 + \beta_1$Income $+ \varepsilon$,
   (ii) SAT $= \beta_0 + \beta_1$GPA $+ \varepsilon$, and
   (iii) SAT $= \beta_0 + \beta_1$Income $+ \beta_2$GPA $+ \varepsilon$.

b. Use goodness-of-fit measures to select the best-fitting model.

c. Predict SAT given the mean value of the explanatory variable(s).

50. **FILE** Many of today's leading companies, including Google, Microsoft, and Facebook, are based on technologies developed within universities. Lisa Fisher is a business school professor who would like to analyze university factors that enhance innovation. She collects data on 143 universities in 2008 for a regression where the response variable is the number of startups (Startups), which is used as a measure for innovation. The explanatory variables include the university's research expenditure in $ millions (Research), the number of patents issued (Patents), and the age of its technology transfer office in years (Duration). A portion of the data is shown below; the complete data set can be found on the text website, labeled **Startups**.

Startups	Research ($ millions)	Patents	Duration
1	$145.52	8	23
1	$237.52	16	23
⋮	⋮	⋮	⋮
1	$154.38	3	9

Source: Association of University Managers and National Science Foundation.

a. Estimate: Startups $= \beta_0 + \beta_1$Research $+ \beta_2$Patents $+ \beta_3$Duration $+ \varepsilon$.

b. Predict the number of startups for a university that spent $120 million on research, issued 8 patents, and has had a technology transfer office for 20 years.

c. How much more research expenditure is needed for the university to have an additional predicted startup, with everything else being the same?

51. **FILE** A researcher interviews 50 employees of a large manufacturer and collects data on each worker's hourly wage (Wage), years of higher education (EDUC), experience (EXPER), and age (AGE). The data can be found on the text website, labeled *Hourly Wage*.

a. Estimate: Wage $= \beta_0 + \beta_1\text{EDUC} + \beta_2\text{EXPER} + \beta_3\text{AGE} + \varepsilon$.

b. Are the signs as expected?

c. Interpret the coefficient of EDUC.

d. Interpret the coefficient of determination.

e. Predict the hourly wage of a 40-year-old employee who has 5 years of higher education and 8 years of experience.

CASE STUDIES

Case Study 14.1

A local university offers its employees the following Fidelity investment products for their retirement plans:

- Fidelity Total Bond Fund
- Fidelity Short-Term Bond Fund
- Fidelity Magellan Fund
- Fidelity International Small Cap Fund
- Fidelity Freedom Income Fund

After working at the university for a year, Minori Vardan is now eligible to participate in the retirement plan. She has already decided to invest a portion of her retirement funds in the Magellan fund. She would like to choose one other fund that has the smallest correlation, preferably zero, with the Magellan fund. She collects 5 years of monthly return data for each mutual fund, a portion of which is shown in the accompanying table. The complete data set can be found on the text website, labeled *Fidelity Retirement*.

Data for Case Study 14.1 Monthly Return Data for Five Mutual Funds

	Magellan	Total Bond	Short-Term Bond	Int'l Small Cap	Freedom Income
January 2006	0.0477	0.0026	0.0013	0.0904	0.0107
February 2006	−0.0149	0.0026	0.0027	−0.0152	0.0000
⋮	⋮	⋮	⋮	⋮	⋮
December 2010	0.0586	−0.0183	−0.0035	0.0478	0.0036

SOURCE: finance.yahoo.com; data retrieved January 6, 2011.

In a report, use the sample information to:

1. Calculate and interpret the sample correlation coefficient of each fund with Magellan.
2. Discuss the statistical significance of the correlation coefficients.
3. Make an investment recommendation for Minori.

Case Study 14.2

Akiko Hamaguchi, the manager at a small sushi restaurant in Phoenix, Arizona, is concerned that the weak economic environment has hampered foot traffic in her area, thus causing a dramatic decline in sales. Her cousin in San Francisco, Hiroshi Sato, owns a similar restaurant, but he has seemed to prosper during these rough economic times. Hiroshi agrees that higher unemployment rates have likely forced some customers to dine out less frequently, but he maintains an aggressive marketing campaign to thwart this apparent trend. For instance, he advertises in local papers with valuable two-for-one coupons and promotes early-bird specials over the airwaves. Despite the fact that advertising increases overall costs, he believes that this campaign has positively affected sales at his restaurant. In order to support his claim, Hiroshi provides monthly sales data and advertising costs pertaining to his restaurant, as well as the monthly unemployment rate from San Francisco County. A portion of the data is shown in the accompanying table; the complete data can be found on the text website, labeled **Sushi Restaurant**.

Data for Case Study 14.2 Hiroshi's Sales, Advertising Costs, and Unemployment Data

Month	Year	Sales (in $1,000s)	Advertising Costs (in $)	Unemployment Rate* (in percent)
January	2008	27.0	550	4.6
February	2008	24.2	425	4.3
⋮	⋮	⋮	⋮	⋮
May	2009	27.4	550	9.1

SOURCE FOR THE UNEMPLOYMENT RATE DATA: Development Department, State of California, June 2009.

In a report, use the sample information to:

1. Estimate a simple regression model, $Sales = \beta_0 + \beta_1 Advertising + \varepsilon$ as well as a multiple regression model, $Sales = \beta_0 + \beta_1 Advertising + \beta_2 Unemployment + \varepsilon$.

2. Show that the multiple regression model is more appropriate for making predictions.

3. Make predictions for sales with an unemployment rate of 6% and advertising costs of $400 and $600.

Case Study 14.3

Megan Hanson, a realtor in Brownsburg, Indiana, would like to use estimates from a multiple regression model to help prospective sellers determine a reasonable asking price for their homes. She believes that the following four factors influence the asking price (Price) of a house: (1) the square footage of the house (SQFT); (2) the number of bedrooms (Bed); (3) the number of bathrooms (Bath); and (4) the lot size (LTSZ) in acres. She randomly collects online listings for 50 single-family homes. A portion of the data is presented in the accompanying table; the complete data can be found on the text website, labeled **Indiana Real Estate**.

Data for Case Study 14.3 Real Estate Data for Brownsburg, Indiana

Price	SQFT	Bed	Bath	LTSZ
399,900	5,026	4	4.5	0.3
375,000	3,200	4	3	5
⋮	⋮	⋮	⋮	⋮
102,900	1,938	3	1	0.1

SOURCE: *Indianapolis Star*, February 27, 2008.

In a report, use the sample information to:

1. Provide summary statistics on the asking price, square footage, the number of bedrooms, the number of bathrooms, and the lot size.

2. Estimate and interpret a multiple regression model where the asking price is the response variable and the above four factors are the explanatory variables.

3. Interpret the resulting coefficient of determination.

15

Inference with Regression Models

CHAPTER

LEARNING OBJECTIVES

After reading this chapter you should be able to:

LO **15.1** Conduct tests of individual significance.

LO **15.2** Conduct a test of joint significance.

LO **15.3** Conduct a general test of linear restrictions.

LO **15.4** Calculate and interpret interval estimates for predictions.

LO **15.5** Explain the role of the assumptions on the OLS estimators.

LO **15.6** Describe common violations of the assumptions and offer remedies.

In Chapter 14 we employed simple and multiple regression models to find a relationship between a response variable and one or more explanatory variables. We also studied objective goodness-of-fit measures that assess how well the sample regression equation fits the data. While the estimated regression models and goodness-of-fit measures are useful, it is not clear if the conclusions based on the estimated coefficients are real or due to chance. In this chapter we focus on statistical inference with regression models. In particular, we develop hypothesis tests that enable us to determine the individual and joint significance of the explanatory variables. We also develop interval estimates for a prediction from the sample regression equation. Finally, we examine the importance of the assumptions on the statistical properties of the OLS estimator, as well as the validity of the testing procedures. We address common violations to the model assumptions, the consequences when these assumptions are violated, and offer some remedial measures.

Analyzing the Winning Percentage in Baseball

On a recent radio talk show, two sports analysts quarreled over which statistic was a better predictor of a Major League Baseball team's winning percentage (Win). One argued that the team's batting average (BA) was a better predictor of a team's success since the team with the higher batting average has won approximately 75% of the World Series contests. The other insisted that a team's pitching is clearly the main factor in determining wins—the lower a team's earned run average (ERA), the higher the team's winning percentage. In order to determine if these claims are backed by the data, relevant information is collected for the 14 American League (AL) and 16 National League (NL) teams during the regular season of 2010. A portion of the data is shown in Table 15.1; the complete data set can be found on the text website, labeled **Baseball**.

TABLE 15.1   Winning Percentage, Batting Average, and Earned Run Average in Baseball

Team	League	Win	BA	ERA
Baltimore Orioles	AL	0.407	0.259	4.59
Boston Red Sox	AL	0.549	0.268	4.20
⋮	⋮	⋮	⋮	⋮
Washington Nationals	NL	0.426	0.250	4.13

Source: http://mlb.mlb.com.

Three regression models are estimated. Model 1 predicts winning percentage based on BA, whereas Model 2 uses ERA; Model 3 applies both BA and ERA to predict winning percentage.

   Use the sample information to:

1. Employ goodness-of-fit measures to determine which of the three models best fits the data.

2. Determine the individual and joint significance of BA and ERA at the 5% significance level.

A synopsis of this case is provided at the end of Section 15.1.

15.1 Tests of Significance

This section continues from Chapter 14 with the assessment of linear regression models. Here we turn our attention to hypothesis testing about the unknown parameters (coefficients) of the population regression model. In particular, we test the regression coefficients both individually and jointly in order to determine whether there is evidence of a linear relationship between the response and the explanatory variables. We must point out that these tests require that the OLS estimators be normally distributed. This condition is satisfied if the random error term of the model has a normal distribution. If we cannot assume that the random error is normal, then the tests are valid only for large sample sizes.

The objective outlined in the introductory case study is to predict a baseball team's winning percentage, denoted Win, either on the basis of its batting average BA or its earned run average ERA, or jointly by BA and ERA. For those readers who do not follow baseball, BA is a ratio of hits divided by times at bat, and ERA is the average number of earned runs given up by a pitcher per nine innings pitched. A priori, we expect that a large BA positively influences a team's winning percentage, while a large ERA negatively affects a team's winning percentage. We define

Model 1 as $\text{Win} = \beta_0 + \beta_1 \text{BA} + \varepsilon$,

Model 2 as $\text{Win} = \beta_0 + \beta_1 \text{ERA} + \varepsilon$, and

Model 3 as $\text{Win} = \beta_0 + \beta_1 \text{BA} + \beta_2 \text{ERA} + \varepsilon$.

Before we develop the tests of significance, we will use goodness-of-fit measures discussed in Chapter 14 to choose the appropriate model. Table 15.2 shows the relevant Excel output for the three models; we advise you to replicate these results using the sample data in Table 15.1.

TABLE 15.2 Relevant Regression Output to Compare the Models

	Model 1	Model 2	Model 3
Multiple R	0.4596	0.6823	0.8459
R Square	0.2112	0.4656	0.7156
Adjusted R Square	0.1830	0.4465	0.6945
Standard Error	0.0614	0.0505	0.0375
Observations	30	30	30

We choose Model 3 to predict winning percentage because it has the lowest standard error of the estimate and the highest adjusted R^2.

LO 15.1

Conduct tests of individual significance.

Tests of Individual Significance

Consider the following multiple regression model, which links the response variable y with k explanatory variables $x_1, x_2, \ldots, x_k$:

$$y = \beta_0 + \beta_1 x_1 + \beta_2 x_2 + \cdots + \beta_k x_k + \varepsilon.$$

We first determine the individual significance of x_j $(j = 1, \ldots, k)$ on y; later we will evaluate the joint significance of all explanatory variables. If the slope coefficient β_j equals zero, then the explanatory variable x_j basically drops out of the above model, implying that x_j does not influence y. In other words, if β_j equals zero, there is no linear relationship between x_j and y. Conversely, if β_j does not equal zero, then x_j influences y.

Following the methodology introduced in earlier chapters, we want to test whether the population coefficient β_j is different from, greater than, or less than β_{j0}, where β_{j0} is the hypothesized value of β_j. That is, the competing hypotheses take one of the following forms:

Two-tailed Test	Right-tailed Test	Left-tailed Test
$H_0: \beta_j = \beta_{j0}$	$H_0: \beta_j \leq \beta_{j0}$	$H_0: \beta_j \geq \beta_{j0}$
$H_A: \beta_j \neq \beta_{j0}$	$H_A: \beta_j > \beta_{j0}$	$H_A: \beta_j < \beta_{j0}$

When testing whether x_j significantly influences y, we set $\beta_{j0} = 0$ and specify a two-tailed test as $H_0: \beta_j = 0$ and $H_A: \beta_j \neq 0$. We could easily specify one-tailed competing hypotheses for a positive linear relationship ($H_0: \beta_j \leq 0$ and $H_A: \beta_j > 0$) or a negative linear relationship ($H_0: \beta_j \geq 0$ and $H_A: \beta_j < 0$).

Although most tests of significance are based on $\beta_{j0} = 0$, in some situations we might wish to determine whether the slope coefficient differs from a nonzero value. For instance, we may want to determine if an extra hour of review before the exam will increase a student's score by more than 5 points. Here we formulate the hypotheses as $H_0: \beta_j \leq 5$ and $H_A: \beta_j > 5$ where $\beta_{j0} = 5$. The procedure for conducting the test remains the same.

As in all hypothesis tests, the next step is to specify the test statistic and compute its value.

TEST STATISTIC FOR THE TEST OF INDIVIDUAL SIGNIFICANCE

The test statistic for a test of individual significance is assumed to follow the t_{df} distribution with $df = n - k - 1$ and its value is

$$t_{df} = \frac{b_j - \beta_{j0}}{s_{b_j}},$$

where n is the sample size, k is the number of explanatory variables, s_{b_j} is the standard error of the OLS estimator b_j, and β_{j0} is the hypothesized value of β_j. If $\beta_{j0} = 0$, the value of the test statistic reduces to $t_{df} = \frac{b_j}{s_{b_j}}$.

EXAMPLE 15.1

Let's revisit Model 3, $\text{Win} = \beta_0 + \beta_1 \text{BA} + \beta_2 \text{ERA} + \varepsilon$, estimated with the sample data in Table 15.1. Conduct a hypothesis test to determine whether batting average influences winning percentage at the 5% significance level.

SOLUTION: We will use the p-value approach for the test. We set up the following hypotheses in order to determine whether winning percentage and batting average have a linear relationship:

$$H_0: \beta_1 = 0$$
$$H_A: \beta_1 \neq 0$$

Table 15.3 shows a portion of the regression output that is needed to conduct the tests of individual significance.

TABLE 15.3 Portion of Regression Results for Model 3: $\text{Win} = \beta_0 + \beta_1\text{BA} + \beta_2\text{ERA} + \varepsilon$

	Coefficients	Standard Error	t Stat	p-value	Lower 95%	Upper 95%
Intercept	0.1269	0.1822	0.6964	0.4921	−0.25	0.50
BA	3.2754	0.6723	4.8719	0.0000	1.90	4.65
ERA	−0.1153	0.0167	−6.9197	0.0000	−0.15	−0.08

From Table 15.3, we find that $b_1 = 3.2754$ and $s_{b_1} = 0.6723$. In addition, given $n = 30$ and $k = 2$, we find $df = n - k - 1 = 30 - 2 - 1 = 27$. So we calculate the value of the test statistic as $t_{27} = \frac{b_1 - \beta_{10}}{s_{b_1}} = \frac{3.2754 - 0}{0.6723} = 4.8719$. From Table 15.3 we see that this calculation is not necessary since Excel automatically provides the value of the test statistic and its associated p-value.

We can use the results reported by Excel since we have a standard case where $\beta_{j0} = 0$; shortly, we will see an application with a nonstandard case. As usual, the decision rule is to reject H_0 if the p-value $< \alpha$. Since the p-value is approximately zero, we reject H_0. At the 5% significance level, there is a linear relationship between winning percentage and batting average; in other words, batting average is significant in explaining winning percentage.

COMPUTER-GENERATED TEST STATISTIC AND THE *P*-VALUE

Excel and virtually all other statistical packages report a value of the test statistic and its associated p-value for a two-tailed test that assesses whether the regression coefficient differs from zero.

- If we specify a one-tailed test, then we need to divide the computer-generated p-value in half.

- If we test whether the coefficient differs from a nonzero value, then we cannot use the value of the computer-generated test statistic and p-value.

Using a Confidence Interval to Determine Individual Significance

In earlier chapters we constructed a confidence interval to conduct a two-tailed hypothesis test. When assessing whether the regression coefficient differs from zero, we can apply the same methodology.

CONFIDENCE INTERVAL FOR β_j

A $100(1 - \alpha)\%$ confidence interval of the regression coefficient β_j is computed as

$$b_j \pm t_{\alpha/2,df}s_{b_j} \quad \text{or} \quad \left[b_j - t_{\alpha/2,df}s_{b_j}, \; b_j + t_{\alpha/2,df}s_{b_j} \right],$$

where s_{b_j} is the standard error of b_j and $df = n - k - 1$.

Excel automatically provides a 95% confidence interval for the regression coefficients; it will provide other levels if prompted. In general, if the confidence interval for the slope coefficient contains the value zero, then the explanatory variable associated with the regression coefficient is not significant. Conversely, if the confidence interval does not contain the value zero, then the explanatory variable associated with the regression coefficient is significant.

EXAMPLE 15.2

Use a confidence interval to determine whether earned run average is significant in explaining winning percentage at the 5% significance level.

SOLUTION: For testing whether earned run average is significant, we set up the following hypotheses:

$$H_0: \beta_2 = 0$$
$$H_A: \beta_2 \neq 0$$

For a 95% confidence interval, $\alpha = 0.05$ and $\alpha/2 = 0.025$. Given that $df = 30 - 2 - 1 = 27$, we reference the t table to find $t_{\alpha/2,df} = t_{0.025,27} = 2.052$. Given $b_2 = -0.1153$ and $s_{b_2} = 0.0167$ (from Table 15.3), the 95% confidence interval for the population coefficient β_2 is

$$b_j \pm t_{\alpha/2,df}s_{b_j} = -0.1153 \pm 2.052 \times 0.0167 = -0.1153 \pm 0.0343.$$

Thus, the lower and upper limits of the confidence interval are -0.1496 and -0.0810, respectively. Note that Table 15.3 also provides these limits. Since the 95% confidence interval does not contain the value zero, we can conclude that earned run average is significant in explaining winning percentage at $\alpha = 0.05$.

A Test for a Nonzero Slope Coefficient

In Examples 15.1 and 15.2, the null hypothesis included a zero value for the slope coefficient, that is, $\beta_{j0} = 0$. We now motivate a test where the hypothesized value is not zero by using a renowned financial application—the capital asset pricing model (CAPM).

Let R represent the return on a stock or portfolio of interest. Given the market return R_M and the risk-free return R_f, the CAPM expresses the risk-adjusted return of an asset, $R - R_f$, as a function of the risk-adjusted market return, $R_M - R_f$. It is common to use the return of the S&P 500 index for R_M and the return on a Treasury bill for R_f. For empirical estimation, the CAPM is specified as

$$R - R_f = \alpha + \beta(R_M - R_f) + \varepsilon.$$

We can rewrite the model as $y = \alpha + \beta x + \varepsilon$, where $y = R - R_f$ and $x = R_M - R_f$. Note that this is essentially a simple linear regression model that uses α and β, in place of the usual β_0 and β_1, to represent the intercept and the slope coefficients, respectively. The slope coefficient β, called the stock's **beta**, measures how sensitive the stock's return is to changes in the level of the overall market. When β equals 1, any change in the market return leads to an identical change in the given stock return. A stock for which β is greater than 1 is considered more "aggressive" or riskier than the market, whereas one for which the value is less than 1 is considered "conservative" or less risky. We also give importance to the intercept coefficient α, called the stock's **alpha**. The CAPM theory predicts α to be zero, and thus a nonzero estimate indicates abnormal returns. Abnormal returns are positive when $\alpha > 0$ and negative when $\alpha < 0$.

EXAMPLE 15.3

Johnson & Johnson (J&J) was founded more than 120 years ago on the premise that doctors and nurses should use sterile products to treat people's wounds. Since that time, J&J products have become staples in most people's homes. Consider the CAPM where the J&J risk-adjusted stock return $R - R_f$ is used as the response variable and the risk-adjusted market return $R_M - R_f$ is used as the explanatory variable. A portion of 60 months of data is shown in Table 15.4; the complete data can be found on the text website, labeled **Johnson & Johnson**.

TABLE 15.4 Risk-adjusted Stock Return of J&J and Market Return

FILE

Date	$R - R_f$	$R_M - R_f$
1/1/2006	−4.59	2.21
2/1/2006	0.39	−0.31
⋮	⋮	⋮
12/1/2010	0.48	2.15

Source: Finance.yahoo.com and U.S. Treasury.

a. Since consumer staples comprise many of the products sold by J&J, its stock is often considered less risky; that is, people need these products whether the economy is good or bad. At the 5% significance level, is the beta coefficient less than one?

b. At the 5% significance level, are there abnormal returns? In other words, is the alpha coefficient significantly different from zero?

SOLUTION: We use the critical value approach for the tests. Using the CAPM notation, we estimate the model, $R - R_f = \alpha + \beta(R_M - R_f) + \varepsilon$; the relevant portion of the Excel output is presented in Table 15.5.

TABLE 15.5 Portion of CAPM Regression Results for J&J

	Coefficients	Standard Error	t Stat	p-value
Intercept	0.2666	0.4051	0.6580	0.5131
$R_M - R_f$	0.5844	0.0803	7.2759	0.0000

a. The estimate for the beta coefficient is 0.5844 and its standard error is 0.0803. Interestingly, our estimate is identical to the beta reported in the popular press (www.dailyfinance.com, March 4, 2011). In order to determine whether the beta coefficient is significantly less than one, we formulate the hypotheses as

$$H_0: \beta \geq 1$$
$$H_A: \beta < 1$$

Given 60 data points, $df = n - k - 1 = 60 - 1 - 1 = 58$. We cannot use the test statistic value reported in Table 15.5, since the hypothesized value of β is not zero. We calculate the test statistic value as $t_{58} = \frac{b_j - \beta_{j0}}{s_{b_j}} = \frac{0.5844 - 1}{0.0803} = -5.18$. With $df = 58$ and $\alpha = 0.05$, the critical value for a left-tailed test is $-t_{0.05,58} = -1.672$. The decision rule is to reject H_0 if $t_{58} < -t_{0.05,58}$. Since $-5.18 < -1.672$, we reject H_0 and conclude that β is significantly less than one; that is, the return on J&J stock is less risky than the return on the market.

b. Abnormal returns exist when α is significantly different from zero. Thus, the competing hypotheses are $H_0: \alpha = 0$ versus $H_A: \alpha \neq 0$. Since it is a standard case, where the hypothesized value of the coefficient is zero, we can use the reported test statistic value of 0.6580 with an associated p-value of 0.5131. We cannot reject H_0 at any reasonable level of significance. Therefore, we cannot conclude that there are abnormal returns for J&J stock.

LO 15.2

Conduct a test of joint significance.

Test of Joint Significance

So far we considered tests of individual significance of explanatory variables. For instance, we used a t test to determine whether the batting average has a statistically significant influence on winning percentage. It is important to also conduct a test of joint significance when we assess a multiple regression model. A test of joint significance is often regarded as a test of the overall usefulness of a regression. This test determines whether the explanatory variables $x_1, x_2, \ldots, x_k$ have a joint statistical influence on y. In the null hypothesis of the test of joint significance, *all* of the slope coefficients are assumed zero. A more general test of restrictions is discussed in the next section.

The competing hypotheses for a test of joint significance are specified as

$$H_0: \beta_1 = \beta_2 = \cdots = \beta_k = 0$$
$$H_A: \text{At least one } \beta_j \neq 0.$$

You might be tempted to implement this test by performing a series of tests of individual significance with the t statistic. However, such an option is not appropriate. The test of joint significance determines if at least one of the explanatory variables is significant. Therefore, it is not clear if one or all of the explanatory variables must be significant in order to document a joint significance. In addition, recall from the ANOVA chapter that if we conduct many individual tests at a given α, the resulting significance level for the joint test will not be the same.

Testing a series of individual hypotheses is not equivalent to testing the same hypotheses jointly.

To conduct the test of joint significance, we employ a one-tailed F test. (Recall that the $F_{(df_1,df_2)}$ distribution introduced in Chapter 11 was used for hypothesis testing in Chapters 11 and 13.) The test statistic measures how well the regression equation explains the variability in the response variable. It is defined as the ratio of the mean regression sum of squares MSR to the mean error sum of squares MSE, where $MSR = SSR/k$ and $MSE = SSE/(n - k - 1)$. These values, including the $F_{(df_1,df_2)}$ test statistic, are provided in the ANOVA portion of the regression results.

TEST STATISTIC FOR THE TEST OF JOINT SIGNIFICANCE

The test statistic for a test of joint significance is assumed to follow the $F_{(df_1,df_2)}$ distribution with $df_1 = k$ and $df_2 = n - k - 1$ and its value is

$$F_{(df_1,df_2)} = \frac{SSR/k}{SSE/(n - k - 1)} = \frac{MSR}{MSE},$$

where MSR and MSE are the mean regression sum of squares and the mean error sum of squares, respectively.

In general, a large value of $F_{(df_1,df_2)}$ indicates that most of the variability in y is explained by the regression model; thus, the model is useful. A small value of $F_{(df_1,df_2)}$ implies that most of the variability in y remains unexplained. In fact, the test of joint significance is sometimes referred to as the test of the significance of R^2. Note that while the test of joint significance is important for a multiple regression model, it is redundant for a simple regression model. In fact, in a simple regression model, the p-value of the F test is identical to that of the t test; we advise you to verify this result.

EXAMPLE 15.4

Let's revisit Model 3, $\text{Win} = \beta_0 + \beta_1 \text{BA} + \beta_2 \text{ERA} + \varepsilon$, estimated with the sample data in Table 15.1. Conduct a test to determine if batting average and earned run average are jointly significant in explaining winning percentage at $\alpha = 0.05$.

SOLUTION: When testing whether the explanatory variables are jointly significant in explaining winning percentage, we set up the following hypotheses:

$$H_0: \beta_1 = \beta_2 = 0$$
$$H_A: \text{At least one } \beta_j \neq 0.$$

The relevant regression output needed to conduct the test of joint significance appears in Table 15.6.

TABLE 15.6 Portion of Regression Results for Model 3: $\text{Win} = \beta_0 + \beta_1\text{BA} + \beta_2\text{ERA} + \varepsilon$

ANOVA	df	SS	MS	F	Significance F
Regression	2	0.0958	0.0479	33.9663	0.0000
Residual	27	0.0381	0.0014		
Total	29	0.1338			

Given $n = 30$ and $k = 2$, we find that $df_1 = k = 2$ and $df_2 = n - k - 1 = 27$. From Table 15.6, we calculate the test statistic as

$$F_{(2,27)} = \frac{MSR}{MSE} = \frac{0.0479}{0.0014} = 34.21.$$

Note that Excel reports the test statistic value as 33.9663. The values are slightly different due to rounding.

Given the computer-generated regression output, the easiest way to conduct a test of joint significance is with the p-value approach, since the ANOVA table from the computer output provides both the value of the test statistic and its associated p-value. The value under the heading *Significance F* is the p-value, or $P(F_{(2,27)} > 33.9663) = 0.0000$. Since the p-value is less than $\alpha = 0.05$, we reject H_0. At the 5% significance level, the batting average and the earned run average variables are jointly significant in explaining winning percentage.

Reporting Regression Results

Regression results are often reported in a "user-friendly" table. Table 15.7 reports the regression results for the three models discussed in this section to explain a baseball team's winning percentage. The explanatory variables are batting average in Model 1, earned run average in Model 2, and both factors in Model 3. If we were supplied with only this table, we would be able to compare these models, construct the sample regression equation of the chosen model, and perform a respectable assessment of the model with the statistics provided. Many tables contain a Notes section at the bottom explaining some of the notation. We choose to put the p-values in parentheses under all estimated coefficients; however, some researchers place the standard errors of the coefficients or the values of the test statistics in parentheses. Whichever method is chosen must be made clear to the reader in the Notes section.

TABLE 15.7 Estimates of the Alternative Regression Models

Variable	Model 1	Model 2	Model 3
Intercept	−0.2731 (0.3421)	0.9504* (0.0000)	0.1269 (0.4921)
Batting Average	3.0054* (0.0106)	NA	3.2754* (0.0000)
Earned Run Average	NA	−0.1105* (0.0000)	−0.1153* (0.0000)
S_e	0.0614	0.0505	0.0375
R^2	0.2112	0.4656	0.7156
Adjusted R^2	0.1830	0.4465	0.6945
F-test (p-value)			33.9663*(0.0000)

NOTES: Parameter estimates are in the top half of the table with the p-values in parentheses; NA denotes not applicable; *represents significance at the 5% level. The lower part of the table contains goodness-of-fit measures.

SYNOPSIS OF INTRODUCTORY CASE

Two sports analysts have conflicting views over how best to predict a Major League Baseball team's winning percentage. One argues that the team's batting average is a better predictor of a team's success, since the team with the higher batting average has won approximately 75% of the World Series contests. The other analyst insists that a team's pitching is clearly the main factor in determining wins. Three regression models are used to analyze a baseball team's winning percentage (Win). The explanatory variables are batting average (BA) in Model 1, earned run average (ERA) in Model 2, and both BA and ERA in Model 3.

After estimating the models using data from 14 American League teams and 16 National League teams during the regular season of 2010, it is found that Model 2 has a lower standard error and a higher R^2 than Model 1. Therefore, if simply choosing between these two models, Model 2 appears better for prediction. However, Model 3 provides the best overall fit, as measured by its highest adjusted R^2 value. The sample regression equation for Model 3 is $\widehat{Win} = 0.13 + 3.28BA - 0.12ERA$. Further testing of this preferred model reveals that the two explanatory variables are jointly as well as individually significant in explaining winning percentage at the 5% significance level. It appears that neither analyst is totally right or totally wrong. Given $R^2 = 0.7156$, approximately 72% of the sample variability in winning percentage is explained by the estimated Model 3. However, 28% of the sample variability in winning percentage remains unexplained. This is not entirely surprising, since other factors, besides batting average and earned run average, influence a baseball team's winning percentage.

EXERCISES 15.1

Concepts

1. In a simple linear regression based on 30 observations, it is found that $b_1 = 3.25$ and $s_{b_1} = 1.36$. Consider the hypotheses:
$$H_0: \beta_1 = 0 \text{ and } H_A: \beta_1 \neq 0.$$
   a. Calculate the value of the appropriate test statistic.
   b. Approximate the p-value.
   c. At the 5% significance level, what is the conclusion? Is the explanatory variable significant?

2. In a simple linear regression based on 25 observations, it is found that $b_1 = 0.5$ and $s_{b_1} = 0.3$. Consider the hypotheses:
$$H_0: \beta_1 \leq 0 \text{ and } H_A: \beta_1 > 0.$$
   a. Calculate the value of the appropriate test statistic.
   b. At the 5% significance level, what is the critical value?
   c. What is the conclusion to the test?

3. In a simple linear regression based on 30 observations, it is found that $b_1 = 7.2$ and $s_{b_1} = 1.8$. Consider the hypotheses:
$$H_0: \beta_1 \geq 10 \text{ and } H_A: \beta_1 < 10.$$
   a. Calculate the value of the appropriate test statistic.
   b. At the 5% significance level, what is the critical value(s)?
   c. What is the conclusion to the test?

4. Consider the following regression results based on 20 observations.

	Coefficients	Standard Error	t Stat	p-value	Lower 95%	Upper 95%
Intercept	34.2123	4.5665	7.4920	0.0000	24.62	43.81
x_1	0.1223	0.1794	0.6817	0.5041	−0.25	0.50

   a. Specify the hypotheses to determine if the intercept differs from zero. Perform this test at the 5% significance level.
   b. Construct the 95% confidence interval for the slope coefficient. At the 5% significance level, does the slope differ from zero? Explain.

5. Consider the following regression results based on 40 observations.

	Coefficients	Standard Error	t Stat	p-value	Lower 95%	Upper 95%
Intercept	43.1802	12.6963	3.4010	0.0016	17.48	68.88
x_1	0.9178	0.9350	0.9816	0.3325	−0.97	2.81

   a. Specify the hypotheses to determine if the slope differs from minus one.
   b. Calculate the value of the test statistic.
   c. At the 5% significance level, find the critical value(s).
   d. Does the slope differ from minus one? Explain.

6. When estimating a multiple regression model based on 30 observations, the following results were obtained.

	Coefficients	Standard Error	t Stat	p-value	Lower 95%	Upper 95%
Intercept	152.27	119.70	1.27	0.2142	−93.34	397.87
x_1	12.91	2.68	4.81	5.06E-05	7.40	18.41
x_2	2.74	2.15	1.28	0.2128	−1.67	7.14

   a. Specify the hypotheses to determine whether x_1 is linearly related to y. At the 5% significance level, use the p-value approach to complete the test. Are x_1 and y linearly related?
   b. What is the 95% confidence interval for β_2? Using this confidence interval, is x_2 significant in explaining y? Explain.
   c. At the 5% significance level, can you conclude that β_1 is less than 20? Show the relevant steps of the appropriate hypothesis test.

7. The following ANOVA table was obtained when estimating a multiple regression model.

ANOVA	df	SS	MS	F	Significance F
Regression	2	22016.75	11008.38		0.0228
Residual	17	39286.93	2310.996		
Total	19	61303.68			

a. How many explanatory variables were specified in the model? How many observations were used?
b. Specify the hypotheses to determine whether the explanatory variables are jointly significant.
c. Compute the value of the test statistic.
d. At the 5% significant level, what is the conclusion to the test? Explain.

Applications

8. A recent study on the evolution of mankind shows that, with a few exceptions, world-record holders in the 100-meter dash have progressively gotten bigger over time (*The Wall Street Journal*, July 22, 2009). The following table shows runners who have held the record, along with their record-holding times and heights:

Record Holder/Year	Time (in seconds)	Height (in inches)
Eddie Tolan (1932)	10.30	67
Jesse Owens (1936)	10.20	70
Charles Greene (1968)	9.90	68
Eddie Hart (1972)	9.90	70
Carl Lewis (1991)	9.86	74
Asafa Powell (2007)	9.74	75
Usain Bolt (2008)	9.69	77

A portion of the Excel results from estimating Time = $\beta_0 + \beta_1$Height + ε are:

	Coefficients	Standard Error	t Stat	p-value	Lower 95%	Upper 95%
Intercept	13.353	1.1714	11.3990	9.1E-05	10.34	16.36
Height	−0.0477	0.0163		0.0332	−0.09	−0.01

a. Formulate the estimated regression equation.
b. Specify the hypotheses to determine whether Height is linearly related to Time.
c. Calculate the value of the appropriate test statistic.
d. At the 5% significance level, is Height significant? Explain.

9. For a sample of 20 New England cities, a sociologist studies the crime rate in each city (crimes per 100,000 residents) as a function of its poverty rate (in %) and its median income (in $1,000s). A portion of the regression results are as follows.

ANOVA	df	SS	MS	F	Significance F
Regression	2	188246.8	94123.4		9.04E-07
Residual	17	45457.32	2673.96		
Total	19	233704.1			

	Coefficients	Standard Error	t Stat	p-value	Lower 95%	Upper 95%
Intercept	−301.62	549.7135	−0.5487	0.5903	−1,461.52	858.28
Poverty	53.1597	14.2198	3.7384	0.0016	23.16	83.16
Income	4.9472	8.2566	0.5992	0.5569	−12.47	22.37

a. Specify the estimated regression equation.
b. At the 5% significance level, show whether the poverty rate and the crime rate are linearly related.
c. Construct a 95% confidence interval for the slope coefficient of income. Using the confidence interval, determine whether income is significant in explaining the crime rate at the 5% significance level.
d. At the 5% significance level, are the poverty rate and income jointly significant in explaining the crime rate?

10. A model relating the return on a firm's stock as a function of its price-to-earnings ratio and its price-to-sales ratio is estimated: Return = $\beta_0 + \beta_1$P/E + β_2P/S + ε. A portion of the regression results follows.

ANOVA	df	SS	MS	F	Significance F
Regression	2	918.7455	459.3728	2.817095	0.077415
Residual	27	4402.786	163.0661		
Total	29	5321.532			

	Coefficients	Standard Error	t Stat	p-value	Lower 95%	Upper 95%
Intercept	−12.0243	7.886858	−1.5246	0.1390	−28.21	4.16
P/E	0.1459	0.4322	0.3376	0.7383	−0.74	1.03
P/S	5.4417	2.2926	2.3736	0.0250	0.74	10.15

a. Specify the estimated regression equation.
b. At the 10% significant level, are P/E and P/S jointly significant? Show the relevant steps of the appropriate hypothesis test.
c. Are both explanatory variables individually significant at the 10% significance level? Show the relevant steps of the appropriate hypothesis tests.

11. Akiko Hamaguchi is a manager at a small sushi restaurant in Phoenix, Arizona. Akiko is concerned that the weak economic environment has hampered foot traffic in her area, thus causing a dramatic decline in sales. In order to offset the decline in sales, she has pursued a strong advertising campaign. She believes advertising expenditures have a positive influence on sales. To support her claim, Akiko estimates a regression model as Sales = $\beta_0 + \beta_1$Advertising + β_2Unemployment + ε. A portion of the regression results follows.

ANOVA	df	SS	MS	F	Significance F
Regression	2	72.6374	36.3187	8.760	0.0034
Residual	14	58.0438	4.1460		
Total	16	130.681			

	Coefficients	Standard Error	t Stat	p-value	Lower 95%	Upper 95%
Intercept	17.5060	3.9817	4.3966	0.0006	8.97	26.05
Unemployment	−0.6879	0.2997	−2.2955	0.0377	−1.33	−0.05
Advertising	0.0266	0.0068	3.9322	0.0015	0.01	0.04

a. At the 5% significance level, test whether the explanatory variables jointly influence sales.

b. At the 1% significance level, test whether the unemployment rate is negatively related with sales.

c. At the 1% significance level, test whether advertising expenditures are positively related with sales.

12. **FILE** A realtor examines the factors that influence the price of a house in Arlington, Massachusetts. He collects data on recent house sales (Price) and notes each house's square footage (Sqft) as well as its number of bedrooms (Beds) and number of bathrooms (Baths). A portion of the data is shown. The entire data set is found on the text website, labeled **Arlington Homes**.

Price	Sqft	Beds	Baths
840000	2768	4	3.5
822000	2500	4	2.5
⋮	⋮	⋮	⋮
307500	850	1	1

a. Estimate: Price $= \beta_0 + \beta_1$Sqft $+ \beta_2$Beds $+ \beta_3$Baths $+ \varepsilon$. Show the regression results in a well-formatted table.

b. At the 5% significance level, are the explanatory variables jointly significant in explaining Price?

c. At the 5% significance level, are all explanatory variables individually significant in explaining Price?

13. An economist examines the relationship between changes in short-term interest rates and long-term interest rates. He believes that changes in short-term rates are significant in explaining long-term interest rates. He estimates the model Dlong $= \beta_0 + \beta_1$Dshort $+ \varepsilon$, where Dlong is the change in the long-term interest rate (10-year Treasury bill) and Dshort is the change in the short-term interest rate (3-month Treasury bill). Monthly data from January 2006 through December 2010 were obtained from the St. Louis Federal Reserve's website. A portion of the regression results are shown below ($n = 60$):

	Coefficients	Standard Error	t Stat	p-value	Lower 95%	Upper 95%
Intercept	−0.0038	0.0088	−0.4273	0.6708	−0.02	0.01
Dshort	0.0473	0.0168	2.8125	0.0067	0.01	0.08

Use a 5% significance level in order to determine whether there is a linear relationship between Dshort and Dlong.

14. **FILE** Caterpillar, Inc. manufactures and sells heavy construction equipment worldwide. The performance of Caterpillar's stock is likely to be strongly influenced by the economy. For instance, during the subprime mortgage crisis, the value of Caterpillar's stock plunged dramatically. Monthly data for Caterpillar's risk-adjusted return and the risk-adjusted market return are collected for a five-year period ($n = 60$). A portion of the data is shown below. The entire data set is found on the text website, labeled **Caterpillar**.

Date	$R - R_f$	$R_M - R_f$
1/1/2006	17.66	2.21
2/1/2006	7.27	−0.31
⋮	⋮	⋮
11/1/2010	3.37	2.15

Source: Finance.yahoo.com and U.S. Treasury.

a. Estimate the CAPM model for Caterpillar, Inc. Show the regression results in a well-formatted table.

b. At the 5% significance level, determine if investment in Caterpillar is riskier than the market (beta significantly greater than 1).

c. At the 5% significance level, is there evidence of abnormal returns?

15.2 A General Test of Linear Restrictions

The significance tests discussed in the preceding section can also be labeled as tests of linear restrictions. For example, the t test is a test of one restriction that determines whether or not a slope coefficient is zero. Similarly, the F test is a test of k restrictions that determines whether or not all slope coefficients are zero. In this section we apply the F test for any number of linear restrictions; the resulting F test is often referred to as the **partial F test**. We can apply this test to any subset of the regression coefficients.

Consider a multiple regression model with three explanatory variables:

$$y = \beta_0 + \beta_1 x_1 + \beta_2 x_2 + \beta_3 x_3 + \varepsilon.$$

As mentioned earlier, we use a t test for a test of one restriction, $\beta_j = 0$, and an F test for a test of $k = 3$ restrictions, $\beta_1 = \beta_2 = \beta_3 = 0$. What if we wanted to test if x_2 and x_3 are jointly significant? This is an example of a test of two restrictions, $\beta_2 = \beta_3 = 0$. Similarly, we may wish to test if the influence of x_3 is identical to that of x_2. This would be a test of one restriction, $\beta_2 = \beta_3$. When conducting a partial F test, the null hypothesis implies that the restrictions are valid. In these two examples, the null hypothesis would be specified as

LO **15.3**

Conduct a general test of linear restrictions.

$H_0: \beta_2 = \beta_3 = 0$ and $H_0: \beta_2 = \beta_3$, respectively. As usual, the alternative hypothesis implies that the null hypothesis is not true. We conclude that the restrictions implied by the null hypothesis are not valid if we reject the null hypothesis.

In order to conduct the partial F test, we estimate the model with and without the restrictions. The **restricted model** is a reduced model where we do not estimate the coefficients that are restricted under the null hypothesis. The **unrestricted model** is a complete model that imposes no restrictions on the coefficients; therefore, all coefficients are estimated. If the restrictions are valid, that is, the null hypothesis is true, then the error sum of squares of the restricted model SSE_R will not be significantly larger than the error sum of squares of the unrestricted model SSE_U. With the partial F test, we basically analyze the ratio of $(SSE_R - SSE_U)$ to SSE_U. If this ratio, suitably adjusted for the degrees of freedom, is significantly large, then we reject the null hypothesis and conclude that the restrictions implied by the null hypothesis are not valid.

TEST STATISTIC FOR THE TEST OF LINEAR RESTRICTIONS

When testing linear restrictions, the test statistic is assumed to follow the $F_{(df_1, df_2)}$ distribution with df_1 equal to the number of linear restrictions and $df_2 = n - k - 1$, where k is the number of explanatory variables in the unrestricted model. Its value is calculated as

$$F_{(df_1, df_2)} = \frac{(SSE_R - SSE_U)/df_1}{SSE_U/df_2},$$

where SSE_R and SSE_U are the error sum of squares of the restricted and the unrestricted models, respectively.

We will consider two examples of the partial F test.

EXAMPLE 15.5

A manager at a car wash company in Missouri wants to measure the effectiveness of price discounts and various types of advertisement expenditures on sales. For the analysis, he uses varying price discounts (Discount) and advertisement expenditures on radio (Radio) and newspapers (Newspaper) in 40 counties in Missouri. A portion of the monthly data on sales (in $1,000s), price discounts (in percent), and advertisement expenditures (in $1,000s) on radio and newspapers are shown in Table 15.8; the complete data are available on the text website, labeled *Car wash*. At the 5% level, determine if the advertisement expenditures on radio and newspaper have a significant influence on sales.

TABLE 15.8 Sales, Price Discounts, and Advertising Expenditures, $n = 40$

County	Sales (in $1,000s)	Discount (in %)	Radio (in $1,000s)	Newspaper (in $1,000s)
1	62.72	40	2.27	3.00
2	49.65	20	3.78	1.78
⋮	⋮	⋮	⋮	⋮
40	49.95	40	3.57	1.57

FILE

SOLUTION: A test that determines whether advertisement expenditures on radio and newspaper have a significant influence on sales is equivalent to a test that determines whether the Radio and Newspaper variables are jointly significant. We formulate the hypotheses as

$$H_0: \beta_2 = \beta_3 = 0$$

$H_A:$ At least one of the coefficients is nonzero.

We estimate two regression models to implement the partial F test. The unrestricted model (U) does not impose restrictions on the coefficients and is specified as

(U) $Sales = \beta_0 + \beta_1 Discount + \beta_2 Radio + \beta_3 Newspaper + \varepsilon.$

In the restricted model (R), we do not estimate the coefficients that are restricted under the null hypothesis. Therefore, we exclude Radio and Newspaper and specify the model as

(R) $Sales = \beta_0 + \beta_1 Discount + \varepsilon.$

For ease of exposition, we use the same notation to refer to the coefficients in models U and R. We note, however, that these coefficients and their estimates have a different meaning depending on which model we are referencing. Table 15.9 shows the relevant regression output of the models.

TABLE 15.9 Relevant Regression Output for Example 15.5

Variable	Restricted	Unrestricted
Intercept	43.4541* (0.0000)	6.7025 (0.3559)
Discount	0.4016* (0.0001)	0.3417* (0.0000)
Radio	NA	6.0624* (0.0007)
Newspaper	NA	9.3968* (0.0001)
SSE	2182.5649	1208.1348

NOTES: Parameter estimates are in the main body of the table with the p-values in parentheses; NA denotes not applicable; *represents significance at 5% level. The last row presents the error sum of squares.

We will use the critical value approach to conduct the test. We use $df_1 = 2$, since we are testing for two restrictions, $\beta_2 = 0$ and $\beta_3 = 0$, and $df_2 = n - k - 1 = 40 - 3 - 1 = 36$. Taking the appropriate SSE values from Table 15.9, we calculate the value of the relevant test statistic as

$$F_{(2,36)} = \frac{(SSE_R - SSE_U)/df_1}{SSE_U/df_2} = \frac{(2182.5649 - 1208.1348)/2}{1208.1348/36} = 14.52.$$

With $\alpha = 0.05$, $df_1 = 2$, and $df_2 = 36$, we find the approximate critical value as $F_{0.05,(2,36)} = 3.26$, or equivalently, we use Excel's function F.INV.RT(0.05,2,36) and obtain 3.26. We reject H_0 since 14.52 is greater than 3.26. At the 5% level, we conclude that the advertisement expenditures on radio and newspaper have a significant influence on sales.

EXAMPLE 15.6 FILE

In Example 15.5, we used the data labeled *Car wash* to show that advertising has a significant influence on sales. The manager believes that the influence of the advertisement expenditures on radio and newspapers is not the same. Conduct the appropriate partial F test at the 5% level to verify the manager's belief.

SOLUTION: Since we want to determine whether the influence of money spent on radio advertising is different from that of newspaper advertising, we formulate the competing hypotheses as

$$H_0: \beta_2 = \beta_3$$
$$H_A: \beta_2 \neq \beta_3$$

We again specify the unrestricted model (U) as

(U) $\text{Sales} = \beta_0 + \beta_1 \text{Discount} + \beta_2 \text{Radio} + \beta_3 \text{Newspaper} + \varepsilon.$

In order to implement the partial F test, we then create the restricted (R) model. Note that under the restriction that $\beta_2 = \beta_3$, the unrestricted model simplifies to

$\text{Sales} = \beta_0 + \beta_1 \text{Discount} + \beta_2 \text{Radio} + \beta_2 \text{Newspaper} + \varepsilon,$ that is,

(R) $\text{Sales} = \beta_0 + \beta_1 \text{Discount} + \beta_2 (\text{Radio} + \text{Newspaper}) + \varepsilon.$

Thus, the restricted model uses only two explanatory variables, where the second variable is defined as the sum of Radio and Newspaper. The resulting estimated coefficient for this modified explanatory variable applies to both Radio and Newspaper. Note that the restricted model imposes one restriction, as there is one fewer coefficient to estimate. Table 15.10 presents the relevant portion of the regression results.

TABLE 15.10 Relevant Regression Output for Example 15.6

Variable	Restricted	Unrestricted
Intercept	7.9524 (0.2740)	6.7025 (0.3559)
Discount	0.3517* (0.0000)	0.3417* (0.0000)
Radio	7.1831* (0.0000)	6.0624* (0.0007)
Newspaper	Same as for Radio	9.3968* (0.0001)
SSE	1263.6243	1208.1348

NOTES: Parameter estimates are in the main body of the table with the p-values in parentheses; *represents significance at 5% level. The last row presents the error sum of squares.

We will use the p-value approach to conduct the test. We use $df_1 = 1$ since we are testing for only one restriction, $\beta_2 = \beta_3$, and $df_2 = n - k - 1 = 40 - 3 - 1 = 36$. Using the appropriate SSE values from Table 15.10, we calculate the value of the test statistic as

$$F_{(1,36)} = \frac{(SSE_R - SSE_U)/df_1}{SSE_U/df_2} = \frac{(1263.6243 - 1208.1348)/1}{1208.1348/36} = 1.65.$$

With $df_1 = 1$ and $df_2 = 36$, we use Excel to compute the p-value as 0.2072 (F.DIST.RT(1.65,1,36) = 0.2072). We do not reject H_0 since the p-value $> \alpha = 0.05$. At the 5% significance level, we cannot conclude that the influence of the advertisement expenditures on radio is different from the influence of the advertisement expenditures on newspapers.

EXERCISES 15.2

Concepts

15. Consider the multiple linear regression model, $y = \beta_0 + \beta_1 x_1 + \beta_2 x_2 + \beta_3 x_3 + \varepsilon.$ You wish to test whether the slope coefficients β_1 and β_3 are jointly significant. Define the restricted and the unrestricted models needed to conduct the test.

16. Consider the multiple linear regression model, $y = \beta_0 + \beta_1 x_1 + \beta_2 x_2 + \beta_3 x_3 + \varepsilon.$ You wish to test whether the slope coefficients β_1 and β_3 are statistically different from each another. Define the restricted and the unrestricted models needed to conduct the test.

17. Consider the multiple linear regression model, $y = \beta_0 + \beta_1 x_1 + \beta_2 x_2 + \varepsilon.$ Define the restricted and the unrestricted models if the hypotheses are

$H_0: \beta_1 + \beta_2 = 1$ and $H_A: \beta_1 + \beta_2 \neq 1.$

18. Consider a portion of simple linear regression results,

$$\hat{y} = 105.40 + 39.17x_1; \quad SSE = 407{,}308, n = 30$$

In an attempt to improve the results, two explanatory variables are added. A portion of the regression results are

$$\hat{y} = 4.87 + 19.47x_1 - 26.31x_2 + 7.31x_3;$$
$$SSE = 344{,}784, n = 30$$

a. Formulate the hypotheses to determine whether x_2 and x_3 are jointly significant in explaining y.

b. Calculate the value of the test statistic.

c. At the 5% significance level, find the critical value(s).

d. What is the conclusion to the test?

Applications

19. A real estate analyst estimates the following regression, relating a house price to its square footage (Sqft):

$$\widehat{Price} = 48.39 + 52.74Sqft; \quad SSE = 56{,}944, n = 50$$

In an attempt to improve the results, he adds two more explanatory variables: the number of bedrooms (Beds) and the number of bathrooms (Baths). The estimated regression equation is

$$\widehat{Price} = 28.11 + 40.17Sqft + 10.08Beds + 16.14Baths;$$
$$SSE = 48{,}074, n = 50$$

a. Formulate the hypotheses to determine whether Beds and Baths are jointly significant in explaining Price.

b. Calculate the value of the test statistic.

c. At the 5% significance level, find the critical value(s).

d. What is the conclusion to the test?

20. A financial analyst believes that the best way to predict a firm's returns is by using the firm's price-to-earnings ratio (P/E) and its price-to sales ratio (P/S) as explanatory variables. He estimates the following regression, using 30 large firms:

$$\widehat{Return} = -33.40 + 3.97P/E - 3.37P/S;$$
$$SSE = 5{,}021.63, n = 30$$

A colleague suggests that he can improve on his prediction if he also includes the P/E-to-growth ratio (PEG) and the dividend yield (DIV). He re-estimates the model by including these explanatory variables and obtains

$$\widehat{Return} = -31.84 + 4.26P/E - 2.16P/S - 11.49PEG$$
$$+ 3.82DIV; \quad SSE = 4{,}149.21, n = 30$$

At the 5% significance level, is the colleague's claim substantiated by the data? Explain.

21. Lisa Fisher is a business school professor who would like to analyze university factors that enhance innovation. She collects data on 143 universities in 2008 for a regression where the response variable is the number of startups (Startups), which is used as a measure for innovation. Lisa believes that the amount of money that a university directs towards research (Research) is the most important factor

influencing Startups. She estimates Startups as a function of Research and obtains

$$\widehat{Startups} = 0.21 + 0.01Research; \quad SSE = 1{,}434.78, n = 143$$

Two other explanatory variables are also likely to influence Startups: the number of patents issued (Patents), and the age of its technology transfer office in years (Duration). Lisa then includes these additional variables in the model and obtains

$$\widehat{Startups} = 0.42 + 0.01Research + 0.05Patents$$
$$- 0.02Duration; \quad SSE = 1{,}368.14, n = 143$$

At the 5% significance level, should Lisa include Patents and Duration in the model predicting Startups?

22. FILE A researcher interviews 50 employees of a large manufacturer and collects data on each worker's hourly wage (Wage), years of higher education (EDUC), experience (EXPER), and age (AGE). A portion of the data is shown below; the entire data set can be found on the text website; labeled **Hourly Wage**.

Wage	EDUC	EXPER	AGE
$37.85	11	2	40
21.72	4	1	39
⋮	⋮	⋮	⋮
24.18	8	11	64

a. Estimate: $Wage = \beta_0 + \beta_1EDUC + \beta_2EXPER + \beta_3AGE + \varepsilon$.

b. The researcher wonders if the influence of experience is different from that of age, or if $\beta_2 \neq \beta_3$. Specify the competing hypotheses for this test.

c. What is the restricted model given that the null hypothesis is true? Estimate this model.

d. At the 5% significance level, can you conclude that the influence of experience is different from that of age?

23. FILE A multiple regression model is used to predict an NFL team's winning record (Win). For the explanatory variables, the average rushing yards (Rush) and the average passing yards (Pass) are used to capture offense and the average yards allowed are used to capture defense. A portion of the data for the 2009 NFL season is given below; the complete data, labeled **Football**, can be found on the text website.

Team	Win (%)	Rush	Pass	Yards Allowed
Arizona Cardinals	62.50	93.40	251.00	346.40
Atlanta Falcons	56.30	117.21	223.19	348.90
⋮	⋮	⋮	⋮	⋮
Washington Redskins	25.00	94.38	218.13	319.70

Source: NFL website.

a. Estimate the model: $Win = \beta_0 + \beta_1Rush + \beta_2Pass + \beta_3Yards\ Allowed + \varepsilon$.

b. Conduct a test at the 10% significance level to determine whether the impact of Rush is different from that of Pass in explaining Win, or $\beta_1 \neq \beta_2$. Provide the relevant steps.

15.3 Interval Estimates for Predictions

LO 15.4

Calculate and interpret interval estimates for predictions.

Consider a multiple regression model $y = \beta_0 + \beta_1 x_1 + \beta_2 x_2 + \cdots + \beta_k x_k + \varepsilon$ with k explanatory variables, $x_1, x_2, \ldots, x_k$. We often estimate this model and use the sample regression equation, $\hat{y} = b_0 + b_1 x_1 + b_2 x_2 + \cdots + b_k x_k$, to make predictions. In the introductory case, we analyzed the winning percentage of a baseball team on the basis of its batting average (BA) and earned run average (ERA). We can use the estimated Model 3, $\widehat{\text{Win}} = 0.13 + 3.28\text{BA} - 0.12\text{ERA}$, to make predictions about a team's winning percentage. For example, for a team with BA = 0.25 and ERA = 4, we compute

$$\widehat{\text{Win}} = 0.13 + 3.28 \times 0.25 - 0.12 \times 4 = 0.47.$$

While such predictions can be useful, they are subject to sampling variations. In other words, the predicted value is a point estimate that ignores sampling error. In this section we focus on the interval estimates for a prediction from the OLS regression equation. As in the case of tests of significance, we assume that the OLS estimators are normally distributed.

We will construct two kinds of interval estimates regarding y:

1. A confidence interval for the expected value of y.

2. A prediction interval for an individual value of y.

It is common to call the first one a confidence interval and the second one a prediction interval. Consider the following multiple regression equation:

$$y^0 = \beta_0 + \beta_1 x_1^0 + \beta_2 x_2^0 + \cdots + \beta_k x_k^0 + \varepsilon^0,$$

where $x_1^0, x_2^0, \ldots, x_k^0$ denote specific values for $x_1, x_2, \ldots, x_k$ at which y^0 is evaluated. In the above example, we used $x_1^0 = 0.25$ and $x_2^0 = 4$. Alternatively, we can evaluate the expected value of the response variable at $x_1^0, x_2^0, \ldots, x_k^0$ as

$$E(y^0) = \beta_0 + \beta_1 x_1^0 + \beta_2 x_2^0 + \cdots + \beta_k x_k^0.$$

The expected value equation uses the fact that the expected value of the error term is assumed to be zero, that is, $E(\varepsilon^0) = 0$; we discuss this assumption in the next section. Note that the prediction interval will be wider than the confidence interval because it also incorporates the error term ε^0. Intuitively, it is easier to predict the average value for a response variable as compared to its individual value. We first derive a confidence interval for $E(y^0)$, followed by a prediction interval for y^0.

The predicted value, $\hat{y}^0 = b_0 + b_1 x_1^0 + b_2 x_2^0 + \cdots + b_k x_k^0$, is the point estimate for $E(y^0)$. In our earlier example, 0.47 is the point estimate of $E(y^0)$ when $x_1^0 = 0.25$ and $x_2^0 = 4$. We form a $100(1 - \alpha)\%$ confidence interval for $E(y^0)$ as $\hat{y}^0 \pm t_{\alpha/2,df}\, se(\hat{y}^0)$, where $se(\hat{y}^0)$ is the standard error of the prediction. While there is a simple formula to compute the standard error $se(\hat{y}^0)$ for a simple regression model, it is very cumbersome to do so for a multiple regression model. We describe a relatively easy way to construct a confidence interval that works for both simple and multiple regression models.

CONFIDENCE INTERVAL FOR THE EXPECTED VALUE OF y

For specific values of $x_1, x_2, \ldots, x_k$, denoted by $x_1^0, x_2^0, \ldots, x_k^0$, a $100(1 - \alpha)\%$ confidence interval of the expected value of y is computed as

$$\hat{y}^0 \pm t_{\alpha/2,df}\, se(\hat{y}^0),$$

where $\hat{y}^0 = b_0 + b_1 x_1^0 + b_2 x_2^0 + \cdots + b_k x_k^0$, $se(\hat{y}^0)$ is the standard error of $\hat{y}^0$, and $df = n - k - 1$.

To derive $\hat{y}^0$ and $se(\hat{y}^0)$ we first estimate a modified regression model where y is the response variable and the explanatory variables are defined as $x_1^* = x_1 - x_1^0$, $x_2^* = x_2 - x_2^0, \ldots, x_k^* = x_k - x_k^0$. The resulting estimate of the intercept and its standard error equal $\hat{y}^0$ and $se(\hat{y}^0)$, respectively.

EXAMPLE 15.7

We again reference the data from Table 15.1 and the regression model Win $= \beta_0 + \beta_1 BA + \beta_2 ERA + \varepsilon$. Construct a 95% confidence interval for expected winning percentage if BA is 0.25 and ERA is 4.

SOLUTION: Let y, x_1, and x_2 denote Win, BA, and ERA, respectively. In order to construct a confidence interval for $E(y^0)$, we follow the above-mentioned procedure to derive $\hat{y}^0$ as well as $se(\hat{y}^0)$. First, we define two modified explanatory variables as $x_1^* = x_1 - 0.25$ and $x_2^* = x_2 - 4$. Table 15.11 shows the computations of their values.

TABLE 15.11 Computing the Values of Modified Explanatory Variables (Example 15.7)

y	x_1	x_2	$x_1^* = x_1 - 0.25$	$x_2^* = x_2 - 4$
0.407	0.259	4.59	$0.259 - 0.25 = 0.009$	$4.59 - 4 = 0.59$
0.549	0.268	4.20	$0.268 - 0.25 = 0.018$	$4.20 - 4 = 0.20$
$\vdots$	$\vdots$	$\vdots$	$\vdots$	$\vdots$
0.426	0.250	4.13	$0.250 - 0.25 = 0.000$	$4.13 - 4 = 0.13$

The regression output with y as the response variable and x_1^* and x_2^* as the explanatory variables is presented in Table 15.12.

TABLE 15.12 Regression Results with Modified Explanatory Variables (Example 15.7)

Regression Statistics		
Multiple R	0.8459	
R Square	0.7156	
Adjusted R Square	0.6945	
Standard Error	**0.0375**	
Observations	30	

ANOVA					
	df	SS	MS	F	Significance F
Regression	2	0.0958	0.0479	33.9663	4.25E-08
Residual	27	0.0381	0.0014		
Total	29	0.1338			

	Coefficients	Standard Error	t Stat	p-value	Lower 95%	Upper 95%
Intercept	**0.4847**	**0.0085**	57.2582	0.0000	**0.4673**	**0.5021**
x_1^*	3.2754	0.6723	4.8719	0.0000	1.8960	4.6549
x_2^*	−0.1153	0.0167	−6.9197	0.0000	−0.1494	−0.0811

The modified regression output is identical to the original regression output (see the summarized results for Model 3 in Table 15.7) except for the estimates of the intercept term. The boldface intercept estimate is 0.4847 and its standard error is 0.0085. Therefore, we use $\hat{y}^0 = 0.4847$ and $se(\hat{y}^0) = 0.0085$ in constructing the confidence interval. Note that Excel's calculation for $\hat{y}^0$ is slightly different from our earlier estimate, $\hat{y}^0 = 0.13 + 3.28 \times 0.25 - 0.12 \times 4 = 0.47$; this is simply due to rounding.

For a 95% confidence level and $df = n - k - 1 = 30 - 2 - 1 = 27$, we find $t_{\alpha/2,df} = t_{0.025,27} = 2.052$. The 95% confidence interval for $E(y^0)$ is

$$\hat{y}^0 \pm t_{\alpha/2,df}\,se(\hat{y}^0) = 0.4847 \pm 2.052 \times 0.0085 = 0.4847 \pm 0.0174.$$

Or, with 95% confidence,

$$0.4673 \leq E(y^0) \leq 0.5021.$$

Given BA of 0.25 and ERA of 4, we have 95% confidence that the average winning percentage lies between 0.4673 and 0.5021. Note that these calculations are also provided in the boldface Lower 95% and Upper 95% values of Table 15.12.

As mentioned earlier, the prediction interval pertains to the individual value of the response variable defined for specific explanatory variables as $y^0 = \beta_0 + \beta_1 x_1^0 + \beta_2 x_2^0 + \cdots + \beta_k x_k^0 + \varepsilon^0$. The prediction interval is wider than the confidence interval because it incorporates the variability of the random error term ε^0.

PREDICTION INTERVAL FOR AN INDIVIDUAL VALUE OF y

For specific values of $x_1, x_2, \ldots, x_k$, denoted by $x_1^0, x_2^0, \ldots, x_k^0$, a $100(1 - \alpha)\%$ prediction interval for an individual value of y is computed as

$$\hat{y}^0 \pm t_{\alpha/2,df}\sqrt{(se(\hat{y}^0))^2 + s_e^2},$$

where $df = n - k - 1$, $se(\hat{y}^0)$ is the standard error of $\hat{y}^0$, and s_e is the standard error of the estimate.

EXAMPLE 15.8

Reconsider the estimated model, $\hat{y}^0 = 0.13 + 3.28x_1 - 0.12x_2$, where y, x_1, and x_2 denote Win, BA, and ERA, respectively.

a. Construct the 95% prediction interval for Win if BA is 0.25 and ERA is 4.

b. Comment on any differences between this prediction interval and the confidence interval constructed in Example 15.7.

SOLUTION:

a. As in the calculation of the confidence interval, we compute $\hat{y}^0 = 0.4847$, $se(\hat{y}^0) = 0.0085$, and $t_{\alpha/2,df} = t_{0.025,27} = 2.052$. The only thing missing from the prediction interval formula is the standard error of the estimate s_e. From Table 15.12, we extract the boldface value, $s_e = 0.0375$. The 95% prediction interval for y^0 is then

$$\hat{y}^0 \pm t_{\alpha/2,df}\sqrt{(se(\hat{y}^0))^2 + s_e^2} = 0.4847 \pm 2.052\sqrt{0.0085^2 + 0.0375^2}$$
$$= 0.4847 \pm 0.0789.$$

Or, with 95% confidence,

$$0.4058 \leq y^0 \leq 0.5636.$$

b. The prediction interval, 0.4847 ± 0.0789, is wider than the confidence interval, 0.4847 ± 0.0174, found in Example 15.7. As discussed earlier, in forming the prediction interval, we also have to account for a very important source of variability caused by the error term. The higher variability makes it more difficult to predict accurately, thus necessitating a wider interval. In these two examples, we have less uncertainty about the expected winning percentage than about a single value of the winning percentage when BA is 0.25 and ERA is 4.

Concepts

24. In a simple linear regression based on 30 observations, the following information is provided: $\hat{y} = -6.92 + 1.35x$ and $s_e = 2.78$. Also, $se(\hat{y}^0)$ evaluated at $x = 30$ is 1.02.

    a. Construct a 95% confidence interval for $E(y)$ if $x = 30$.

    b. Construct a 95% prediction interval for y if x equals 30.

    c. Which interval is narrower? Explain.

25. In a multiple regression with 40 observations, the following sample regression equation is obtained: $\hat{y} = 12.8 + 2.6x_1 - 1.2x_2$ with $s_e = 5.84$. Also, when x_1 equals 15 and x_2 equals 6, $se(\hat{y}^0) = 2.20$.

    a. Construct a 95% confidence interval for $E(y)$ if x_1 equals 15 and x_2 equals 6.

    b. Construct a 95% prediction interval for y if x_1 equals 15 and x_2 equals 6.

    c. Which interval is wider? Explain.

26. Consider the following sample data:

x	12	23	11	23	14	21	18	16
y	28	43	21	40	33	41	37	32

    a. Find the sample regression line, $\hat{y} = b_0 + b_1 x$.

    b. Construct a 95% confidence interval for $E(y)$ if $x = 15$.

    c. Construct a 95% prediction interval for y if $x = 15$.

27. Consider the following sample data:

y	46	51	28	55	29	53	47	36
x_1	40	48	29	44	30	58	60	29
x_2	13	28	24	11	28	28	29	14

    a. Find the sample regression equation, $\hat{y} = b_0 + b_1 x_1 + b_2 x_2$.

    b. Construct a 95% confidence interval for $E(y)$ if x_1 equals 50 and x_2 equals 20.

    c. Construct a 95% prediction interval for y if x_1 equals 50 and x_2 equals 20.

Applications

28. Using the data in the accompanying table, estimate the model: Salary $= \beta_0 + \beta_1$Education $+ \varepsilon$, where salary is measured in $1,000s and education refers to years of higher education.

Education	3	4	6	2	5	4	8	0
Salary	40	53	80	42	70	50	110	38

    a. Construct a 90% confidence interval for the expected salary for an individual who completed 6 years of higher education.

    b. Construct a 90% prediction interval for salary for an individual who completed 6 years of higher education.

    c. Comment on the difference in the widths of these intervals.

29. With the data in the accompanying table, estimate GPA $= \beta_0 + \beta_1$GRE $+ \varepsilon$, where GRE is a student's score on the math portion of the Graduate Record Examination score and GPA is the student's grade point average in graduate school.

GRE	700	720	650	750	680	730	740	780
GPA	3.0	3.5	3.2	3.7	3.1	3.9	3.3	3.5

    a. Construct a 90% confidence interval for the expected GPA for an individual who scored 710 on the math portion of the GRE.

    b. Construct a 90% prediction interval for the GPA for an individual who scored 710 on the math portion of the GRE.

30. **FILE** Access the data labeled **Debt Payments** from the text website and estimate Debt $= \beta_0 + \beta_1$Income $+ \varepsilon$, where Debt is the average debt payments for a household in a particular city (in $) and Income is the city's median income (in $1,000s).

    a. Construct a 95% confidence interval for expected debt payments if income is $80,000 (remember that income is measured in $1,000s).

    b. Construct a 95% prediction interval for debt payments if income is $80,000 (remember that income is measured in $1,000s).

31. **FILE** Access the data labeled **Arlington Homes** from the text website and estimate: Price $= \beta_0 + \beta_1$Sqft $+ \beta_2$Beds $+ \beta_3$Baths $+ \varepsilon$, where Price, Sqft, Beds, and Baths refer to home price, square footage, number of bedrooms, and number of bathrooms, respectively. Construct a 95% confidence interval for the expected price of a 2,500-square-foot home in Arlington, Massachusetts, with three bedrooms and two bathrooms. Construct the corresponding prediction interval for an individual home. Interpret both intervals.

15.4 Model Assumptions and Common Violations

So far we have focused on the estimation and the assessment of simple and multiple regression models. In particular, we used sample data to estimate and assess models. It is important to understand that the statistical properties of the OLS estimator, as well as the validity of the testing procedures, depend on the assumptions of the classical linear regression model. In this section we discuss these assumptions. We also address common

LO 15.5

Explain the role of the assumptions on the OLS estimators.

violations to the assumptions, discuss the consequences when the assumptions are violated, and where possible, offer some remedies.

REQUIRED ASSUMPTIONS OF REGRESSION ANALYSIS

1. The regression model given by $y = \beta_0 + \beta_1 x_1 + \beta_2 x_2 + \cdots + \beta_k x_k + \varepsilon$ is *linear in the parameters*, $\beta_0, \beta_1, \ldots, \beta_k$, with an additive error term ε.

2. Conditional on $x_1, x_2, \ldots, x_k$, the error term has a an *expected value of zero*, or $E(\varepsilon) = 0$. This implies that $E(y) = \beta_0 + \beta_1 x_1 + \beta_2 x_2 + \cdots + \beta_k x_k$.

3. There is no exact linear relationship among the explanatory variables; or in statistical terminology, there is *no perfect multicollinearity*.

4. Conditional on $x_1, x_2, \ldots, x_k$, the variance of the error term ε is the same for all observations. In other words, the error term is *homoskedastic*, which means equally scattered.

5. Conditional on $x_1, x_2, \ldots, x_k$, the error term ε is uncorrelated across observations. In other words, there is no *serial correlation* or *autocorrelation*.

6. The error term ε is not correlated with any of the explanatory variables $x_1, x_2, \ldots, x_k$. In other words, there is no *endogeneity*.

7. The error term ε is *normally distributed*. This assumption allows us to construct confidence intervals and conduct the tests of significance. If ε is not normally distributed, the hypothesis tests are valid only for large sample sizes.

Recall from Chapter 7 that desirable properties of an estimator include unbiasedness and efficiency. In the regression context, an estimator b_j is unbiased if $E(b_j) = \beta_j$, or in other words, the average value of the estimator equals the unknown population parameter. Efficiency is implied when an unbiased estimator also has the minimum variance among the class of all unbiased estimators; that is, the estimator estimates the parameter of interest in the best possible manner.

Under the assumptions of the classical linear regression model, OLS provides the best linear unbiased estimator (BLUE) in that it is unbiased and efficient. These desirable properties of the OLS estimator become compromised as one or more model assumptions are violated. Aside from parameter estimates, the validity of the significance tests is also influenced by the assumptions. For certain violations, the standard errors of the estimators are biased; in these cases it is not possible to make meaningful inferences from the t and the F test results.

The assumptions of the classical linear regression model are, for the most part, based on the error term ε. Since the residuals, or the observed error term, $e = y - \hat{y}$, contain useful information regarding ε, it is common to use the residuals to investigate the assumptions. In this section, we will rely on **residual plots** to detect common violations to the assumptions. These graphical plots are easy to use and provide informal analysis of the estimated regression models. Formal tests are beyond the scope of this book.

RESIDUAL PLOTS

For the regression model, $y = \beta_0 + \beta_1 x_1 + \beta_2 x_2 + \cdots + \beta_k x_k + \varepsilon$, the residuals are computed as $e = y - \hat{y}$, where $\hat{y} = b_0 + b_1 x_1 + b_2 x_2 + \cdots + b_k x_k$. These residuals can be plotted against variables such as x_j, $\hat{y}$, and even time periods to look for model inadequacies.

It is common to plot the residuals e on the vertical axis and the explanatory variable x_j on the horizontal axis. Such plots are useful for detecting deviations from linearity, discussed in the next chapter, as well as heteroskedasticity. For a multiple regression model, we can also plot the residuals against the predicted value $\hat{y}$ of the model. Finally, if the regression is based on time series data, we can plot the residuals against time to detect serial correlation.

In Figure 15.1, we present a residual plot when none of the assumptions has been violated. (Excel computes the residuals and also plots them against all explanatory variables. After choosing **Data** > **Data Analysis** > **Regression**, we select *Residuals* and *Residual Plots* in the regression dialog box.)

FIGURE 15.1 Residual plot of a correctly specified model

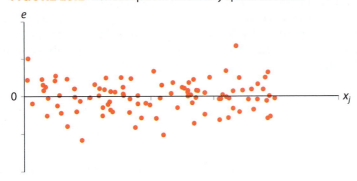

Note that all the points are randomly dispersed around the zero value of the residuals.

As we will see below, any discernible pattern of the residuals indicates that one or more assumptions have been violated.

Common Violation 1: The Model Suffers from Multicollinearity

LO 15.6

Describe common violations of the assumptions and offer remedies.

Perfect multicollinearity exists when two or more explanatory variables have an exact linear relationship. Consider the model $y = \beta_0 + \beta_1 x_1 + \beta_2 x_2 + \varepsilon$, where y is bonus, x_1 is the number of cars sold, and x_2 is the number of cars remaining in the lot. If all car salesmen started with the same inventory, we have a case of *perfect* multicollinearity and the model cannot be estimated. However, if x_2 represents the proportion of positive reviews from customers, we have *some* multicollinearity, since the number of cars sold and the proportion of positive reviews are likely to be correlated. In most applications, some degree of correlation exists between the explanatory variables. Models using time series data are especially susceptible to multicollinearity because explanatory variables often have a common underlying trend.

In the presence of multicollinearity, the OLS estimators are still BLUE in that they are unbiased and efficient. However, they have large standard errors, which increase with the level of multicollinearity. Multicollinearity makes it difficult to disentangle the separate influences of the explanatory variables on the response variable. If multicollinearity is severe, we find insignificance of the explanatory variables; some parameter estimates may even have wrong signs. In short, just because the OLS estimators are better than others in the presence of multicollinearity, they may not be "best" in an absolute sense.

Detection

The detection methods for multicollinearity are mostly informal. The presence of a high R^2 coupled with individually insignificant explanatory variables can be indicative of multicollinearity. Sometimes researchers examine the correlations between the explanatory variables to detect severe multicollinearity. One such guideline suggests that multicollinearity is severe if the sample correlation coefficient between any two explanatory variables is more than 0.80 or less than -0.80. Seemingly wrong signs of the estimated regression coefficients may also be indicative of multicollinearity.

Revisit the introductory case, where we used the data labeled **Baseball** to estimate a multiple regression model as $\widehat{\text{Win}} = 0.13 + 3.28\text{BA} - 0.12\text{ERA}$. Examine the multicollinearity issue in this model.

SOLUTION: We select the data on BA and ERA, and use the CORREL function in Excel to compute the sample correlation $r_{\text{BA,ERA}} = 0.0581$. The fact that the sample correlation is very weak is not surprising, since we do not expect a team's batting average to be correlated with its earned run average. After all, a team's pitching staff determines ERA, whereas the remaining players on the team predominantly influence BA. We conclude that multicollinearity is of no concern in this application.

Remedy

Inexperienced researchers tend to include too many explanatory variables in their quest not to omit anything important and in doing so may include redundant variables that essentially measure the same thing. When confronted with multicollinearity, a good remedy is to drop one of the collinear variables if we can justify its redundancy. Another option is to obtain more data, since the sample correlation may get weaker as we include more observations. Sometimes it helps to go back to the drawing board and reformulate a model with transformed variables that may not be collinear. At times, the best approach may be to *do nothing*, especially if the estimated model yields a high R^2, which implies that the estimated model is good for prediction as is.

Common Violation 2: The Error Term Is Heteroskedastic

Under the assumption of homoskedasticity (equal scatter), the variance of the error term, conditional on $x_1, x_2, \ldots, x_k$, is the same for all observations. When this assumption is violated, we say that the errors are heteroskedastic. This assumption often breaks down in studies with cross-sectional data. Consider the model, $y = \beta_0 + \beta_1 x + \varepsilon$, where y is the consumption expenditure and x is the disposable income of a household. It may be unreasonable to assume that the variability of consumption is the same across a cross-section of household incomes. For example, we would expect higher-income households to have a higher variability in consumption as compared to lower-income households. Similarly, home prices tend to vary more as homes get larger and sales tend to vary more as firm size increases.

In the presence of heteroskedasticity, the OLS estimators are still unbiased, though they are no longer efficient. In other words, they are not BLUE. Furthermore, the standard errors of the OLS estimators can be biased upward or downward. Consequently, we cannot put much faith in the confidence intervals, or the standard t or F tests, in the presence of heteroskedasticity.

Detection

We can use informal residual plots to gauge heteroskedasticity. The residuals of the estimated model are plotted against the explanatory variables or against the predicted values $\hat{y}$. There is no heteroskedasticity if the residuals are randomly dispersed across the values of x_j or $\hat{y}$. On the other hand, heteroskedasticity exists if the variability increases or decreases over the values of x_j or $\hat{y}$.

EXAMPLE 15.10

Consider a simple regression model that relates monthly sales (Sales) from a chain of convenience stores with the square footage (Sqft) of the store. A portion of the data used for the analysis is shown in Table 15.13; the complete data, labeled *Convenience Stores*, are available on the text website. Estimate the model and use a residual plot to determine if there is heteroskedasticity in the data.

TABLE 15.13 Sales and Square Footage of Convenience Stores

FILE

Sales (in $1,000)	Sqft
140	1810
160	2500
⋮	⋮
110	1470

SOLUTION: The sample regression is given by $\widehat{Sales} = 22.08 + 0.06Sqft$. A residual plot of the estimated model is shown in Figure 15.2.

FIGURE 15.2 Residual plot against square footage (Example 15.10)

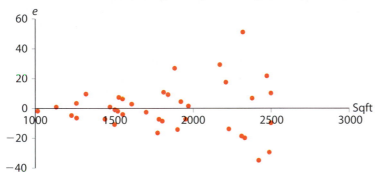

Note that the residuals seem to fan out across the horizontal axis. Therefore, we conclude that heteroskedasticity is a likely problem in our application relating sales to square footage. This result is not surprising, since you would expect sales to vary more as square footage increases. For instance, a small convenience store is likely to include only bare essentials for which there is a fairly stable demand. A larger store, on the other hand, may include specialty items resulting in more fluctuation in sales.

Remedy

As mentioned earlier, there are two problems associated with heteroskedasticity. First, while the estimators are unbiased, they are not efficient. Second, even if we ignore the issue of efficiency, we cannot conduct an important aspect of statistical analysis, namely the tests of significance. The t and F tests are no longer valid, since the standard errors of the estimators are biased. This has prompted some researchers to use the OLS estimates along with a correction for the standard errors, called White's correction. Many statistical computer packages routinely make this correction, thus enabling researchers to perform legitimate t and F tests. Unfortunately, the current version of Excel does not have the ability to make this correction. Other methods for correction are outside the scope of this book.

Common Violation 3: The Error Term Is Serially Correlated

When obtaining the OLS estimators, we assume that the error term is uncorrelated across observations; that is, there is no serial correlation. This assumption often breaks down in studies with time series data where the errors are likely to exhibit positive serial correlation. Variables such as GDP, employment, and asset returns exhibit business cycles. As a consequence, successive observations are not independent of each other. The omission of important explanatory variables can also cause serial correlation.

In the presence of serial correlation, the OLS estimators are generally unbiased, though not efficient. In other words, they are no longer BLUE. In addition, with positive serial correlation (the most common form of serial correlation), the standard errors are biased downward, making the model look better than it really is with a spuriously high R^2. Furthermore, the inflated values of the t_{df} and $F_{(df_1, df_2)}$ statistics may suggest that the explanatory variables are individually and jointly significant when this is not true.

Detection

We can plot the residuals against time to look for serial correlation. If the residuals show no pattern around the horizontal axis, then serial correlation is not likely a problem. Positive serial correlation is implied if a positive residual in one period is followed by positive residuals in the next few periods, followed by negative residuals for a few periods, then positive residuals, and so on. Regression models estimated using time series data often suffer from positive serial correlation. On the other hand, negative serial correlation is implied if a positive residual is followed by a negative residual, then a positive residual, and so on.

EXAMPLE 15.11

Consider $y = \beta_0 + \beta_1 x_1 + \beta_2 x_2 + \varepsilon$ where y represents sales at a sushi restaurant and x_1 and x_2 represent advertising costs and the unemployment rate, respectively. A portion of monthly data from January 2008 to June 2009 is given in Table 15.14; the complete data, labeled **Sushi Restaurant**, are on the text website. Inspect the behavior of the residuals in order to comment on serial correlation.

TABLE 15.14 Sales, Advertising Costs, and Unemployment Data for Example 15.11

Month	Year	Sales (in $1,000s)	Advertising Costs (in $)	Unemployment Rate (in percent)
January	2008	27.0	550	4.6
February	2008	24.2	425	4.3
⋮	⋮	⋮	⋮	⋮
May	2009	27.4	550	9.1

SOURCE FOR THE UNEMPLOYMENT RATE DATA: Development Department, State of California, June 2009.

SOLUTION: The model is estimated as $\hat{y} = 17.5060 + 0.0266x_1 - 0.6879x_2$. In order to detect serial correlation, we plot the residuals against time t, where t is given by 1, 2, . . . , 17 for the 17 months of time series data. (In order to construct this residual plot with Excel, we first estimate the model and choose *Residuals* from Excel's *Regression* dialog box. Given the regression output, we select the residual data. We then choose **Insert > Scatter** and choose the option on the top left.)

Figure 15.3 shows a wavelike movement in the residuals over time, first clustering below the horizontal axis, then above the horizontal axis, etc. Given this pattern around the horizontal axis, we conclude that positive serial correlation is a likely problem in this application.

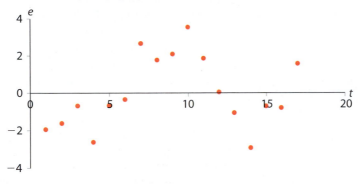

FIGURE 15.3 Scatterplot of residuals against time t

Remedy

Since the OLS estimators are unbiased under the presence of serial correlation, researchers often use the OLS estimates but correct the standard errors using the Newey-West procedure. As in the case of heteroskedasticity, many statistical computer packages have the capacity to make this correction; unfortunately, the current version of Excel does not have this capability. We can perform legitimate t and F tests once the standard errors have been corrected. Other methods for correction are outside the scope of this book.

Common Violation 4: The Explanatory Variable Is Endogenous

Another crucial assumption in a linear regression model is that the error term is not correlated with the explanatory variables. If this assumption is violated, then the regression model is said to suffer from **endogeneity**. If one or more of the explanatory variables are endogenous, then the resulting OLS estimators are biased. The extent of the bias depends on the degree of the correlation between the error term and the explanatory variables.

Endogeneity is often caused by omitted explanatory variables. Suppose we want to estimate $y = \beta_0 + \beta_1 x + \varepsilon$, where y is salary and x is years of education. This model excludes innate ability, which is an important ingredient for salary. Since ability is omitted, it gets incorporated in the error term and the resulting error term is likely to be correlated with years of education. This violates the OLS assumption that the error term is not correlated with any of the explanatory variables. Now consider someone who is highly educated and also commands a high salary. The model will associate high salary with education, when in fact, it may be the person's unobserved high level of ability that has raised both education and salary. Since ability is positively correlated with both education and salary, the OLS estimator b_1 will be biased upward.

Remedy

It is common to use the instrumental variable technique to address the endogeneity problem. We find an instrumental variable that is highly correlated with the endogenous explanatory variable but not with the error term. Further discussion of the instrumental variable approach is outside the scope of this text.

EXERCISES 15.4

Concepts

32. Using 20 observations, the multiple regression model $y = \beta_0 + \beta_1 x_1 + \beta_2 x_2 + \varepsilon$ was estimated. Excel produced the following relevant results.

	df	SS	MS	F	Significance F
Regression	2	2.12E + 12	1.06E + 12	56.5561	3.07E-08
Residual	17	3.19E + 11	1.88E + 10		
Total	19	2.44E + 12			

	Coefficients	Standard Error	t Stat	p-value	Lower 95%	Upper 95%
Intercept	−987557	131583	−7.5052	0.0000	−1265173	−709941
x_1	29233	32653	0.8952	0.3832	−39660	98125
x_2	30283	32645	0.9276	0.3666	−38592	99158

a. At the 5% significance level, are the explanatory variables jointly significant?

b. At the 5% significance level, is each explanatory variable individually significant?

c. What is the likely problem with this model?

33. A simple linear regression, $y = \beta_0 + \beta_1 x + \varepsilon$, is estimated with cross-sectional data. The resulting residuals e, along with the values of the explanatory variable x, are shown below.

x	1	2	5	7	10	14	15	20	24	30
e	−2	1	−3	2	4	−5	−6	8	11	−10

a. Graph the residuals e against the values of the explanatory variable x and look for any discernible pattern.

b. Which assumption is being violated? Discuss its consequences and suggest a possible remedy.

34. A simple linear regression, $y = \beta_0 + \beta_1 x + \varepsilon$, is estimated with time series data. The resulting residuals e and the time variable t are shown below.

t	1	2	3	4	5	6	7	8	9	10
e	−5	−4	−2	3	6	8	4	−5	−3	−2

a. Graph the residuals against time and look for any discernible pattern.

b. Which assumption is being violated? Discuss its consequences and suggest a possible remedy.

Applications

35. Consider the results of a survey where students were asked about their GPA and also to break down their typical 24-hour day into study, leisure (including work), and sleep. Consider the model GPA $= \beta_0 + \beta_1$Study $+ \beta_2$Leisure $+ \beta_3$Sleep $+ \varepsilon$.

a. What is wrong with this model?

b. Suggest a simple way to reformulate the model.

36. **FILE** Consider the monthly rent of a home in Ann Arbor, Michigan (Rent) as a function of the number of bedrooms (Beds), the number of bathrooms (Baths), and square footage (Sqft).

a. Access the data labeled **Ann Arbor Rental** from the text website and estimate Rent $= \beta_0 + \beta_1$Beds $+ \beta_2$Baths $+ \beta_3$Sqft $+ \varepsilon$.

b. Which of the explanatory variables might cause heteroskedasticity in the model? Explain.

c. Use residual plots to verify your economic intuition.

37. **FILE** Healthy living has always been an important goal for any society. In a recent ad campaign for Walt Disney, First Lady Michelle Obama shows parents and children that eating well and exercising can also be fun (*USA Today*, September 30, 2010). Consider a regression model that conjectures that fruits and vegetables and regular exercising have a positive effect on health and smoking has a negative effect on health. The sample consists of the percentage of these variables observed in various states in the U.S in 2009. A portion of the data is shown below; the complete data set can be found on the text website, labeled **Healthy Living**.

State	Healthy (%)	Fruits/Vegetables (%)	Exercise (%)	Smoke (%)
AK	88.7	23.3	60.6	14.6
AL	78.3	20.3	41	16.4
⋮	⋮	⋮	⋮	⋮
WY	87.5	23.3	57.2	15.2

Source: Centers for Disease Control and Prevention.

a. Estimate the model Healthy $= \beta_0 + \beta_1$Fruits/Vegetables $+ \beta_2$Exercise $+ \beta_3$Smoke $+ \varepsilon$.

b. Analyze the data to determine if multicollinearity and heteroskedasticity are present.

38. **FILE** A capital asset pricing model (CAPM) for Johnson & Johnson (J&J) was discussed in Example 15.3. The model uses the risk-adjusted stock return $R - R_f$ for J&J as the response variable and the risk-adjusted market return $R_M - R_f$ as the explanatory variable. The data for the model can be found on the text website, labeled **Johnson & Johnson**. Since serial correlation may occur with time series data, it is prudent to inspect the behavior of the residuals. Construct a scatterplot of the residuals against time to comment on serial correlation.

39. **FILE** In August 2010, the Department of Commerce reported that economic weakness continues across the country with consumer spending continuing to stagnate. The government is considering various tax benefits to stimulate consumer spending through increased disposable income. The consumption function is one of the key relationships in economics, where consumption y depends on disposable income x. Consider the quarterly data for these seasonally adjusted variables, measured in billions of dollars. A portion of the data is shown in the accompanying table; the complete data set is on the text website, labeled **Consumption Quarterly**.

Date	Consumption ($ billions)	Disposable Income ($ billions)
2006:01	9148.2	9705.2
2006:02	9266.6	9863.8
⋮	⋮	⋮
2010:04	10525.2	11514.7

Source: U.S. Department of Commerce.

a. Estimate Consumption $= \beta_0 + \beta_1$Disposable Income $+ \varepsilon$. Plot the residuals against time to determine if there is a possibility of serial correlation.

b. Discuss the consequences of serial correlation and suggest a possible remedy.

WRITING WITH STATISTICS

Ben Leach is a statistician for a Major League Baseball (MLB) team. One aspect of his job is to assess the value of various players. At the moment, Ben's team is in dire need of an outfielder. Management is ready to make an offer to a certain prospect, but asks Ben for some input concerning salary. Management believes that a player's batting average (BA), runs batted in (RBI), and years of experience playing professional baseball (Experience) are the most important factors that influence a player's salary. Management is focusing on a player who has played professional baseball for seven years and whose average BA and RBI over this time have been 266 and 50, respectively. Ben collects data on salary (in $1,000s), BA, RBI, and Experience for 138 outfielders in 2008. A portion of the data is found in Table 15.15; all data can be found on the text website, labeled **MLB Salary**.

TABLE 15.15 Major League Baseball Outfielder Data, $n = 138$

FILE

Player	Salary (in $1,000s)	BA	RBI	Experience
1. Nick Markakis	455	299	87	3
2. Adam Jones	390	261	23	3
⋮	⋮	⋮	⋮	⋮
138. Randy Winn	8,875	288	53	11

Notes: All data collected from usatoday.com or espn.com; BA and RBI are averages over the player's professional life through 2008. For exposition, BA has been multiplied by 1000.

Ben would like to use information in Table 15.15 to:

1. Summarize Salaries, BAs, RBIs, and Experience of current outfielders.

2. Address management's claim that BA, RBI, and Experience have a statistically significant influence on salary.

3. Evaluate the expected salary for the prospective player, given his values for BA, RBI, and Experience.

In an attempt to assess the factors that influence an outfielder's salary in MLB, data were collected from 138 current players. Management believes that an outfielder's salary is best predicted using the outfielder's overall batting average (BA), runs batted in (RBI), and years of experience (Experience) as an MLB player. Table 15.A provides some descriptive statistics on these relevant variables.

The average salary of an MLB outfielder in 2008 is a staggering $3,459,000; however, the minimum salary of $390,000 and the maximum salary of $18,623,000 suggest quite

Sample Report—Baseball Salaries

TABLE 15.A Descriptive Statistics on Salary, BA, RBI, and Experience, $n = 138$

	Salary (in $1,000s)	BA	RBI	Experience
Mean	3,459	271	43	6
Minimum	390	152	1	1
Maximum	18,623	331	102	20

a bit of variability in salary. The average outfielder has a BA of 271 with 43 RBIs in a season. Experience of outfielders in 2008 varied from only 1 year to 20 years, with an average of 6 years.

Table 15.B provides regression results from estimating a model where BA, RBI, and Experience are the explanatory variables and Salary is the response variable.

TABLE 15.B Analysis of Salary of Baseball Players

Variable	Coefficient
Intercept	−4769.40 (0.1301)
BA	4.76 (0.6984)
RBI	80.44* (0.0000)
Experience	539.67* (0.0000)
$R^2 = 0.58$	
$F_{(3,133)} = 61.54$ (associated p-value = 0.0000)	

NOTES: p-values are in parentheses; *denotes significance at the 5% level.

All slope coefficients are positive, suggesting a positive relationship between all three explanatory variables and Salary. For instance, the slope coefficient of Experience indicates that if an outfielder stays in the major leagues for one additional year, then on average, his salary will increase by $539,670, holding BA and RBI constant. The p-value associated with the value of the $F_{(3,133)}$ test statistic shows that the explanatory variables are jointly significant at the 5% level. Upon testing the explanatory variables individually, the extremely small p-values associated with RBI and Experience reveal that these variables have a significant linear relationship with Salary; surprisingly, BA is not significant at the 5% level. The coefficient of determination R^2 shows that 58% of Salary is explained by the estimated regression model, leaving 42% of the variability in Salary unexplained.

Lastly, for an MLB player with seven years' experience and an average BA and RBI of 266 and 50, respectively, the model predicts a salary of $4,295,320. With 95% confidence, expected salary will lie between $3,731,360 and $4,859,280. Perhaps before management makes an offer to the player, the model should consider including other factors that may significantly influence a player's salary. One possible explanatory variable for inclusion is a player's on-base percentage.

Conceptual Review

LO **15.1**

Conduct tests of individual significance.

A test of individual significance determines whether the explanatory variable x_j has an individual statistical influence on y. The test statistic is assumed to follow the t_{df} distribution with $df = n - k - 1$ and its value is $t_{df} = \frac{b_j - \beta_{j0}}{s_{b_j}}$, where s_{b_j} is the standard error of the OLS estimator b_j and β_{j0} is the hypothesized value of β_j. If $\beta_{j0} = 0$, the value of the test statistic reduces to $t_{df} = \frac{b_j}{s_{b_j}}$. If H_0 of a two-tailed test is rejected, we conclude that x_j has a statistically significant influence on y.

Excel reports a value of a test statistic and its associated p-value for a two-tailed test that assesses whether the regression coefficient differs from zero, or $\beta_{j0} \neq 0$. If we specify a one-tailed test, then we need to divide the computer-generated p-value in half. If we test whether the coefficient differs from a nonzero value, that is, $\beta_{j0} \neq 0$, then we cannot use the value of the computer-generated test statistic and p-value.

A $100(1 - \alpha)\%$ confidence interval of the regression coefficient β_j is given by $b_j \pm t_{\alpha/2,df}s_{b_j}$ or $[b_j - t_{\alpha/2,df}s_{b_j}, b_j + t_{\alpha/2,df}s_{b_j}]$, where $df = n - k - 1$. We can use this confidence interval to conduct a two-tailed hypothesis test.

LO 15.2 Conduct a test of joint significance.

A **test of joint significance** determines whether the explanatory variables $x_1, x_2, \ldots, x_k$ have a joint statistical influence on y. The test statistic is assumed to follow the $F_{(df_1,df_2)}$ distribution with $df_1 = k$ and $df_2 = n - k - 1$ and its value is $F_{(df_1,df_2)} = \frac{SSR/k}{SSE/(n - k - 1)} = \frac{MSR}{MSE}$, where MSR and MSE are the mean regression sum of squares and the mean error sum of squares, respectively.

It is implemented as a right-tailed test and if H_0 is rejected, we conclude that $x_1, x_2, \ldots, x_k$ have a statistically significant influence on y.

The ANOVA table from computer output provides both the value of the test statistic and its associated p-value.

LO 15.3 Conduct a general test of linear restrictions.

When **testing linear restrictions**, the test statistic is assumed to follow the $F_{(df_1,df_2)}$ distribution with df_1 equal to the number of linear restrictions and $df_2 = n - k - 1$, where k is the number of explanatory variables in the unrestricted model. Its value is calculated as $F_{(df_1,df_2)} = \frac{(SSE_R - SSE_U)/df_1}{SSE_U/df_2}$, where SSE_R and SSE_U are the error sum of squares of the restricted and the unrestricted models, respectively. If the null hypothesis is rejected, we conclude that the linear restrictions are not valid.

LO 15.4 Calculate and interpret interval estimates for predictions.

For specific values of $x_1, x_2, \ldots, x_k$, denoted by $x_1^0, x_2^0, \ldots, x_k^0$, a $100(1 - \alpha)\%$ **confidence interval of the expected value of y** is given by $\hat{y}^0 \pm t_{\alpha/2,df}se(\hat{y}^0)$ where $df = n - k - 1$ and $se(\hat{y}^0)$ is the standard error of $\hat{y}^0$. To derive $\hat{y}^0$ and $se(\hat{y}^0)$ we first estimate a modified regression model where y is the response variable and the explanatory variables are defined as $x_1^* = x_1 - x_1^0, x_2^* = x_2 - x_2^0, \ldots, x_k^* = x_k - x_k^0$. The resulting estimate of the intercept and its standard error equal $\hat{y}^0$ and $se(\hat{y}^0)$, respectively.

For specific values of $x_1, x_2, \ldots, x_k$, denoted by $x_1^0, x_2^0, \ldots, x_k^0$, a $100(1 - \alpha)\%$ **prediction interval for an individual value of y** is given by $\hat{y} \pm t_{\alpha/2,df}\sqrt{(se(\hat{y}^0))^2 + s_e^2}$, where $df = n - k - 1$, $se(\hat{y}^0)$ is the standard error of $\hat{y}^0$, and s_e is the standard error of the estimate.

LO 15.5 Explain the role of the assumptions on the OLS estimators.

Under the assumptions of the classical linear regression model, OLS provides the best linear unbiased estimator (BLUE) in that it is unbiased and efficient. These desirable properties of the OLS estimator become compromised as one or more model assumptions are violated. Aside from regression coefficient estimates, the validity of the tests of significance is also influenced by the assumptions. For certain violations, the standard errors of the estimators are biased; in these cases it is not possible to make meaningful inferences from the t and F test results.

Residual plots are used to capture model misspecifications. The model is adequate if the residuals are randomly dispersed around the zero value.

Some degree of **multicollinearity** is present in most applications. A high R^2 coupled with insignificant explanatory variables are often indicative of multicollinearity. Multicollinearity is considered serious if the sample correlation coefficient between any two explanatory variables is more than 0.80 or less than -0.80. We can drop one of the collinear variables if its omission can be justified. We can obtain more data, as that may weaken the correlation. Another option is to reformulate the model. At times the best approach may be to do nothing, especially if the estimated model yields a high R^2.

The assumption of no **heteroskedasticity** often breaks down in cross-sectional studies. The resulting OLS estimators are unbiased but not efficient. In addition, the standard errors of the OLS estimators are biased, making the standard t or F tests invalid. Heteroskedasticity is likely if the variability of the residuals increases or decreases over the value of an explanatory variable. Researchers often use the OLS estimates along with a correction for the standard errors, called White's correction.

The assumption of no **serial correlation** often breaks down in time series studies. The resulting OLS estimators are generally unbiased but not efficient. With positive serial correlation, the standard errors are biased downward, making the model look better than it really is with a spuriously high R^2. Furthermore, the inflated values of the t_{df} and $F_{(df_1, df_2)}$ statistics may incorrectly suggest significance of the explanatory variables. Serial correlation is likely if the residuals show a pattern around the horizontal time axis. Researchers often use the OLS estimates along with a correction for the standard errors, using the Newey-West procedure.

Additional Exercises and Case Studies

40. In an attempt to determine whether or not a linear relationship exists between the price of a home (in $1,000s) and the number of days it takes to sell the home, a real estate agent collected data from recent sales in his city and estimated the following model: Price $= \beta_0 + \beta_1$Days $+ \varepsilon$. A portion of the Excel results is shown in the accompanying table.

	Coefficients	Standard Error	t Stat	p-value
Intercept	−491.27	156.94	−3.13	0.0203
Days	6.17	1.19	5.19	0.0020

Specify the hypotheses to determine whether Days is significant in explaining a house's price. At the 5% significance level, what is the conclusion to the test? Explain.

41. **FILE** A sociologist wishes to study the relationship between happiness and age. He interviews 24 individuals and collects data on age and happiness, measured on a scale from 0 to 100. A portion of the data is shown; the entire data set is found on the text website, labeled **Happiness and Age**.

Age	Happiness
49	62
51	66
⋮	⋮
69	72

Estimate Happiness $= \beta_0 + \beta_1$Age $+ \varepsilon$. At the 1% significance level, is Age significant in explaining Happiness? Show the relevant steps of a hypothesis test using the critical value approach.

42. **FILE** The homeownership rate in the U.S. was 67.4% in 2009. In order to determine if homeownership is linked with income, 2009 state level data on the homeownership rate (Ownership) and median household income (Income) were collected. A portion of the data is shown below; the complete data can be found on the text website, labeled **Home Ownership**.

State	Income	Ownership
Alabama	$39,980	74.1%
Alaska	$61,604	66.8%
⋮	⋮	⋮
Wyoming	$52,470	73.8%

Source: www.census.gov.

a. Estimate: Ownership $= \beta_0 + \beta_1$Income $+ \varepsilon$.
b. At the 5% significance level, is Income linearly related to Ownership? Show the steps of a hypothesis test using the critical value approach.
c. Construct a 95% confidence interval for the expected value of Ownership if Income is $50,000.

d. Compare the above confidence interval with a 95% prediction interval for Ownership.

43. **FILE** A researcher studies the relationship between SAT scores, the test-taker's family income (Income), and his/her grade point average (GPA). Data are collected from 24 students. A portion of the data is shown; the entire data set can be found on the text website, labeled **SAT**.

SAT	Income	GPA
1651	47,000	2.79
1581	34,000	2.97
⋮	⋮	⋮
1940	113,000	3.96

Estimate: $SAT = \beta_0 + \beta_1 Income + \beta_2 GPA + \varepsilon$.

a. At the 5% significance level, are income and GPA individually significant? Show the relevant steps of each test, using the critical value approach.

b. At the 5% significance level, are income and GPA jointly significant? Show the relevant steps of the hypothesis test, using the critical value approach.

c. Predict SAT if Income is $80,000 and GPA is 3.5. Use these values for the explanatory variables to construct a 95% prediction interval for the individual SAT score.

44. **FILE** George believes that returns of mutual funds are influenced by annual turnover rates and annual expense ratios. In order to substantiate his claim, he randomly selects eight mutual funds and collects data on each fund's five-year annual return (Return), its annual holding turnover rate (Turnover), and its annual expense ratio (Expense). The data set can be found on the text website, labeled **Turnover and Expense**.

	Return (%)	Turnover (%)	Expense (%)
American Funds EuroPacific	6.06	41	0.83
Artisan International	2.94	54	1.22
⋮	⋮	⋮	⋮
Royce Value Plus	1.48	42	1.48

Source: All data as of July 31, 2009 from finance.yahoo.com.

a. Estimate $Return = \beta_0 + \beta_1 Turnover + \beta_2 Expense + \varepsilon$. Conduct appropriate tests to verify George's theory at the 5% significance level.

b. Discuss the potential problems of multicollinearity and heteroskedasticity.

45. **FILE** A government researcher examines the factors that influence a city's crime rate. For 41 cities, she collects the crime rate (crimes per 100,000 residents), the poverty rate (in %), the median income (in $1,000s), the percent of residents younger than 18, and the percent of residents older than 65. A portion of the data is shown; the entire data set can be obtained from the text website, labeled **Crime**.

Crime	Poverty	Income	Under 18	Over 65
710.6	3.8	58.422	18.3	23.4
1317.7	16.7	48.729	19.0	10.3
⋮	⋮	⋮	⋮	⋮
139.7	3.9	59.445	19.7	16

a. Estimate $Crime = \beta_0 + \beta_1 Poverty + \beta_2 Income + \beta_3 Under 18 + \beta_4 Over 65 + \varepsilon$. Discuss the individual and joint significance of the explanatory variables at the 5% significance level.

b. At the 5% level, conduct a partial F test to determine if the influence of Under 18 is different from that of Over 65.

c. Which explanatory variables are likely to be collinear? Find their sample correlation coefficients to confirm.

46. **FILE** A research analyst is trying to determine whether a firm's price-earnings (P/E) and price-sales (P/S) ratios can explain the firm's stock performance over the past year. Generally, a high P/E ratio suggests that investors are expecting higher earnings growth in the future compared to companies with a lower P/E ratio. Investors use the P/S ratio to determine how much they are paying for a dollar of the firm's sales rather than a dollar of its earnings (P/E ratio). In short, the higher the P/E ratio and the lower the P/S ratio, the more attractive the investment. The table below shows the 2010 annual returns, the P/E ratios, and the P/S ratios for a portion of the 30 firms included in the Dow Jones Industrial Average. The complete data set can be found on the text website, labeled **Dow 2010**.

DOW Components	Return (in %)	P/E ratio	P/S ratio
3M Co.	4.4	14.37	2.41
Alcoa Inc.	−4.5	11.01	0.78
⋮	⋮	⋮	⋮
Walt Disney Company	16.3	13.94	1.94

Source: The 2010 returns (January 1, 2010–December 31, 2010) were obtained from *The Wall Street Journal*, January 3, 2011; the P/E ratios and the P/S ratios were obtained from finance.yahoo.com on January 20, 2011.

a. Estimate $Return = \beta_0 + \beta_1 P/E + \beta_2 P/S + \varepsilon$. Show the regression results in a well-formatted table.

b. Determine whether P/E and P/S are jointly significant at the 5% significance level.

c. Establish whether the explanatory variables are individually significant at the 5% significance level.

d. What is the predicted return for a firm with a P/E ratio of 10 and a P/S ratio of 2? Use this value to construct a 95% confidence interval for the expected return.

47. **FILE** A nutritionist wants to understand the influence of income and healthy food on the incidence of smoking. He collects 2009 data on the percentage of smokers in each state in the U.S. and the corresponding median income and the percentage of the population that regularly eats fruits and vegetables. A portion of the data is shown in the

accompanying table; the complete data set can be found on the text website, labeled **Smoking**.

State	Smoke (%)	Fruits/Vegetables (%)	Median Income
AK	14.6	23.3	61,604
AL	16.4	20.3	39,980
⋮	⋮	⋮	⋮
WY	15.2	23.3	52,470

Source: Centers for Disease Control and Prevention and U.S. Census Bureau.

a. Estimate: Smoke $= \beta_0 + \beta_1$Fruits/Vegetables $+ \beta_2$Median Income $+ \varepsilon$.

b. At the 5% level of significance, are the explanatory variables individually and jointly significant? Explain.

c. Use the sample correlation coefficients to evaluate the potential problem of multicollinearity.

48. **FILE** A researcher examines the factors that influence student performance. She gathers data on 224 school districts in Massachusetts. The response variable is the students' mean score on a standardized test (Score). She uses four explanatory variables in her analysis: the student-to-teacher ratio (STR), the average teacher's salary (TSAL), the median household income (INC), and the percentage of single family households (SGL). A portion of the data is

shown in the accompanying table; the complete data set can be found on the text website, labeled **MCAS**.

Score	STR (%)	TSAL (in $1,000s)	INC (in $1,000s)	SGL (%)
227.00	19.00	44.01	48.89	4.70
230.67	17.90	40.17	43.91	4.60
⋮	⋮	⋮	⋮	⋮
230.67	19.20	44.79	47.64	5.10

Source: Massachusetts Department of Education and the Census of Population and Housing.

a. Estimate Score $= \beta_0 + \beta_1$STR $+ \beta_2$TSAL $+ \beta_3$INC $+ \beta_4$SGL $+ \varepsilon$ and show the regression results in a well-formatted table.

b. Suppose you want to test if school input factors, STR and TSAL, are significant in explaining Score. Specify the competing hypotheses. Estimate the restricted model. At the 5% significance level, can you conclude that STR and TSAL are jointly significant?

c. Suppose you want to test if socioeconomic factors, INC and SGL, are significant in explaining Score. Specify the competing hypotheses. Estimate the restricted model. At the 5% significance level, can you conclude that INC and SGL are jointly significant?

CASE STUDIES

Case Study 15.1

American football is the highest-paying sport on a per-game basis. Given that the quarterback is considered the most important player on the team, he is typically well-compensated. A sports statistician examines the factors that influence a quarterback's salary (Salary). He believes that a quarterback's pass completion rate (PC) is the most important variable affecting Salary. The statistician also wonders how total touchdowns scored (TD) and a quarterback's age (Age) might impact Salary. The statistician collects 2009 data on Salary, PC, TD, and Age. A portion of the data is shown in the accompanying table; the complete data set can be found on the text website, labeled **Quarterback Salaries**.

Data for Case Study 15.1 Quarterback Salary Data, 2009

Name	Salary (in $ millions)	PC	TD	Age
Philip Rivers	25.5566	65.2	28	27
Jay Cutler	22.0441	60.5	27	26
⋮	⋮	⋮	⋮	⋮
Tony Romo	0.6260	63.1	26	29

Source: USA Today database for salaries; NFL.com for other data.

In a report, use the sample information to:

1. Estimate and interpret the model: Salary $= \beta_0 + \beta_1$PC $+ \beta_2$TD $+ \beta_3$Age $+ \varepsilon$.

2. Discuss the individual and joint significance of the explanatory variables at the 5% level.

3. Determine whether TD and Age are jointly significant at the 5% significance level.

4. Construct a 95% confidence interval for the expected salary of a quarterback with average values of PCT, TD, and Age.

Case Study 15.2

Apple Inc. has established a unique reputation in the consumer electronics industry with its development of products such as the iPod, the iPhone, and the iPad. As of May 2010, Apple had surpassed Microsoft as the most valuable company in the world (*The New York Times*, May 26, 2010). Michael Gomez is a stock analyst and wonders if the return on Apple's stock is best modeled using the CAPM model. He collects five years of monthly data, a portion of which is shown. The full data set can be found on the text website, labeled *Apple*.

Data for Case Study 15.2 Apple Return Data, $n = 60$

Date	$R - R_f$	$R_M - R_f$
1/1/2006	4.70	2.21
2/1/2006	−9.65	−0.31
⋮	⋮	⋮
11/1/2010	1.68	2.15

Source: Finance.yahoo.com and U.S. Treasury.

In a report, use the sample information to:

1. Estimate and interpret CAPM: $R - R_f = \beta_0 + \beta_1(R_M - R_f) + \varepsilon$. Search for Apple's reported Beta on the Web and compare it with your estimate.

2. At the 5% significance level, is the stock return of Apple riskier than that of the market? At the 5% significance level, do abnormal returns exist? Explain.

3. Use a residual plot to analyze the potential problem of serial correlation.

Case Study 15.3

According to a recent report by the government, new home construction fell to an 18-month low in October, 2010 (CNNMoney.com, November 17, 2010). Housing starts, or the number of new homes being built, experienced an 11.7% drop in its seasonally adjusted annual rate. Urmil Singh works for a mortgage company in Madison, Wisconsin. She wants to better understand the quantitative relationship between housing starts, the mortgage rate, and the unemployment rate. She gathers seasonally adjusted monthly data on these variables from 2006:01–2010:12. A portion of the data is shown below; the complete data, labeled *Housing Starts*, are available on the text website.

Data for Case Study 15.3 Housing Starts and Other Factors, $n = 60$

Date	Housing Starts (in 1,000s)	Mortgage Rate (%)	Unemployment Rate (%)
2006–01	2273	6.15	4.7
2006–02	2119	6.25	4.8
⋮	⋮	⋮	⋮
2010–12	520	4.71	9.4

Source: Census Bureau and Board of Governors.

In a report, use the sample information to:

1. Estimate a multiple regression model for housing starts using the mortgage rate and the unemployment rate as the explanatory variables.

2. At the 5% significance level, evaluate the individual and joint significance of the explanatory variables.

3. Discuss the potential problems of multicollinearity and serial correlation in this time series data application.

16 Regression Models for Nonlinear Relationships

CHAPTER

Regression analysis is one of the most widely used statistical techniques in business, engineering, and the social sciences. It empirically validates not only whether a relationship exists between variables, but also quantifies the strength of the relationship. So far, we have considered only linear regression models, whether single- or multiple-variable. There are numerous applications where the relationship between the explanatory variable and the response variable cannot be represented by a straight line and, therefore, must be captured by an appropriate curve. In fact, the choice of a functional form is a crucial part of specifying a regression model. In this chapter, we discuss some common nonlinear regression models by making simple transformations of the variables. These transformations include squares and natural logarithms, which capture interesting nonlinear relationships while still allowing easy estimation within the framework of a linear regression model. We will use numerical measures to choose between alternative model specifications.

Rental Market in Ann Arbor, Michigan

While the housing market is in recession and is not likely to emerge anytime soon, real estate investment in college towns continues to promise good returns (*The Wall Street Journal*, September 24, 2010). First, students offer a steady stream of rental demand as cash-strapped public universities are unable to house their students beyond freshman year. Second, this demand is projected to grow as more children of baby boomers head to college. Marcela Treisman works for an investment firm in Michigan. Her assignment is to analyze the rental market in Ann Arbor, which is home to the main campus of the University of Michigan. She knows that with a third of its population consisting of university students, Ann Arbor is consistently rated as one of the best places to live in the United States. Marcela wants to understand what kind of off-campus homes promise good rental income. She gathers data on monthly rent (Rent, in $) for 2011, along with three characteristics of the home: number of bedrooms (Beds), number of bathrooms (Baths), and square footage (Sqft). A portion of the data is shown in Table 16.1; the complete data, labeled ***Ann Arbor Rental***, can be found on the text website.

TABLE 16.1   Rental Data for Ann Arbor, Michigan; $n = 40$

FILE

Rent (in $)	Beds	Baths	Sqft
645	1	1	500
675	1	1	648
⋮	⋮	⋮	⋮
2400	3	2.5	2700

Source: www.zillow.com.

Marcela would like to use the information in Table 16.1 to:

1. Evaluate various models that quantify the relationship between rent and home characteristics.

2. Use model selection criteria to select the most appropriate model.

3. Make predictions for rental income for specific values of home characteristics.

A synopsis of this case is provided at the end of Section 16.2.

16.1 Polynomial Regression Models

LO **16.1**

Use and evaluate
polynomial
regression models.

Linear regression models are often justified on the basis of their computational simplicity. An implication of a simple linear regression model, $y = \beta_0 + \beta_1 x + \varepsilon$, is that if x goes up by one unit, we expect y to change by β_1, irrespective of the value of x. However, in many applications, the relationship cannot be represented by a straight line and, therefore, must be captured by an appropriate curve. We note that the linearity assumption discussed in Chapter 15 places the restriction of linearity on the parameters and not on the variables. Consequently, we can capture many interesting nonlinear relationships, within the framework of a linear regression model, by simple transformations of the response and/or the explanatory variables.

If you ever studied microeconomics, you may have learned that a firm's (or industry's) average cost curve tends to be "U-shaped." Due to economies of scale, the average cost y of a firm initially decreases as output x increases. However, as x increases beyond a certain point, its impact on y turns positive. Other applications show the influence of the explanatory variable initially positive but then turning negative, leading to an "inverted U shape." (Mathematically, U-shaped means concave, whereas inverted U-shaped means convex.) The **quadratic regression model** is appropriate when the slope, capturing the influence of x on y, changes in magnitude as well as sign.

A quadratic regression model with one explanatory variable is specified as $y = \beta_0 + \beta_1 x + \beta_2 x^2 + \varepsilon$; we can easily extend it to include multiple explanatory variables. The expression $\beta_0 + \beta_1 x + \beta_2 x^2$ is the deterministic component of a quadratic regression model. In other words, conditional on x, $E(y) = \beta_0 + \beta_1 x + \beta_2 x^2$. This model can easily be estimated as a regression of y on x and x^2.

THE QUADRATIC REGRESSION MODEL

In a **quadratic regression model** $y = \beta_0 + \beta_1 x + \beta_2 x^2 + \varepsilon$, the coefficient $\boldsymbol{\beta_2}$ determines whether the relationship between x and y is U-shaped ($\beta_2 > 0$) or inverted U-shaped ($\beta_2 < 0$).

Predictions with this model are made by $\hat{y} = b_0 + b_1 x + b_2 x^2$.

As mentioned above, the coefficient β_2 determines the shape of the relationship; Figure 16.1 highlights some representative shapes of a quadratic regression model.

FIGURE 16.1 Representative shapes of a quadratic regression model: $y = \beta_0 + \beta_1 x + \beta_2 x^2 + \varepsilon$

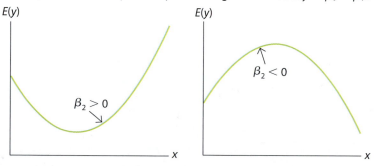

It is important to be able to determine whether a quadratic regression model provides a better fit than the linear regression model. As we learned in Chapter 14, we cannot compare these models on the basis of their respective R^2 values because the quadratic regression model uses one extra parameter than the linear regression model. For comparison purposes, we use adjusted R^2, which imposes a penalty for the extra parameter.

EXAMPLE 16.1

Table 16.2 shows a portion of the average cost (in $) for 20 manufacturing firms and their annual output (in millions of units); the complete data set can be found on the text website, labeled **Cost Functions**. We also include a column of Output² which will be used for the estimation of the quadratic regression model.

TABLE 16.2 Average Cost and Output Data for 20 Manufacturing Firms

FILE	Average Cost ($)	Output (millions of units)	Output²
	9.61	4	16
	9.55	5	25
	⋮	⋮	⋮
	9.62	11	121

a. Plot average cost (AC) against output.

b. Estimate the linear and the quadratic regression models. Determine which model fits the data best.

c. Use the best-fitting model to predict the average cost for a firm that produces 7 million units.

SOLUTION:

a. It is always informative to begin with a scatterplot of the response variable against the explanatory variable. Make sure that the response variable is on the vertical axis. Figure 16.2 shows average cost against output. We also superimpose linear and quadratic trends on the scatterplot (in Excel, right click on the scatterpoints, add Trendline, and choose Linear and Polynomial with Order 2). At lower and higher levels of output, average costs are highest. It appears that the average cost in this industry would best be estimated using a quadratic regression model.

FIGURE 16.2 Scatterplot of average cost versus output

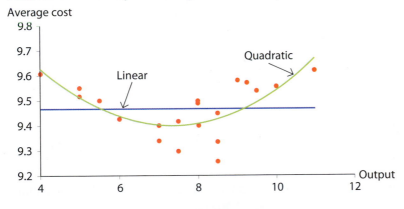

b. The second column of Table 16.3 shows the regression results for the linear regression model: $AC = \beta_0 + \beta_1 Output + \varepsilon$. The linear regression model provides a poor fit, which is not surprising given the scatterplot in Figure 16.2. Not only is Output statistically insignificant, the adjusted R^2 is negative. In order to estimate a quadratic regression model, we have to first create data on the squared Output variable. A portion of these data, computed by squaring Output, are shown in Table 16.2. The third column of Table 16.3 shows the regression results for the quadratic regression model: $AC = \beta_0 + \beta_1 Output + \beta_2 Output^2 + \varepsilon$. In the quadratic regression model, Output is now significant. In addition, the slope coefficient of $Output^2$ is positive and significant, indicating a U-shaped relationship between average cost and output.

TABLE 16.3 Estimates of the Linear and the Quadratic Regression Models for Example 16.1

Variable	Linear Regression Model	Quadratic Regression Model
Intercept	9.4461* (0.00)	10.5225* (0.00)
Output	0.0029 (0.84)	−0.3073* (0.00)
$Output^2$	NA	0.0210* (0.00)
Adjusted R^2	−0.0531	0.4540

NOTES: Parameter estimates are in the main body of the table with the p-values in parentheses; NA denotes not applicable; *represents significance at the 5% level. The last row presents adjusted R^2 for model comparison.

Given an adjusted R^2 of 0.4540, the quadratic regression model is clearly better than the linear regression model in explaining average cost.

c. Using the quadratic regression model, the predicted average cost for a firm that produces 7 million units is

$$\widehat{AC} = 10.5225 - 0.3073(7) + 0.0210(7^2) = \$9.40.$$

It is important to evaluate the estimated marginal effect of the explanatory variable x on the predicted value of the response variable $\hat{y}$, or equivalently, evaluate the change in $\hat{y}$ due to a one unit increase in x. In a linear regression model, $y = \beta_0 + \beta_1 x + \varepsilon$, the marginal effect is constant, estimated by the slope coefficient b_1. In a quadratic regression model, it can be shown with calculus that the marginal effect of x on $\hat{y}$ can be approximated by $b_1 + 2b_2 x$. This marginal effect, unlike in the case of a linear regression model, depends on the value of x at which it is evaluated. It is common to use the sample mean $\bar{x}$ when interpreting the marginal effect. In addition, $\hat{y}$ reaches a maximum ($b_2 < 0$) or minimum ($b_2 > 0$) when the marginal effect equals zero. The value of x at which this happens is obtained from solving the equation $b_1 + 2b_2 x = 0$ as $x = \dfrac{-b_1}{2b_2}$.

EXAMPLE 16.2

Use the quadratic regression model from Example 16.1 to find the output level that minimizes costs.

SOLUTION: Given $b_1 = -0.3073$ and $b_2 = 0.0210$, the output level that minimizes the average cost is $x = \dfrac{-b_1}{2b_2} = \dfrac{-(-0.3073)}{2(0.0210)} = 7.32$ million units. Looking back at Figure 16.2, this amount closely approximates what we would have estimated using the graph.

Let's now turn to an example with an inverted U-shaped relationship.

EXAMPLE 16.3

In the U.S., age discrimination is illegal, but its occurrence is very hard to prove (*Newsweek*, March 17, 2010). Even without discrimination, it is widely believed that wages of workers decline as they get older. A young worker can expect wages to rise with age only up to a certain point, beyond which wages begin to fall. Ioannes Papadopoulos works in the human resources department of a large manufacturing firm and is examining the relationship between wages (in $), education, and age. Specifically, he wants to verify the quadratic effect of age on wages. He gathers data on 80 workers in his firm with information on their hourly wage, education, and age. A portion of the data is shown in Table 16.4; the complete data, labeled **Wages**, can be found on the text website.

TABLE 16.4 Data for Example 16.3 on Hourly Wage, Education, and Age; $n = 80$

Wage ($)	Education	Age
17.54	12	76
20.93	10	61
⋮	⋮	⋮
23.66	12	49

a. Plot hourly wage against age and evaluate whether a linear or quadratic regression model better captures the relationship. Verify your choice by using the appropriate numerical measure.

b. Use the appropriate model to predict hourly wages for someone with 16 years of education and age equal to 30, 50, or 70.

c. According to the model, at what age will someone with 16 years of education attain the highest wages?

SOLUTION:

a. Figure 16.3 shows a scatterplot of Age against Wage. We superimpose linear and quadratic trends on the scatterplot. It seems that the quadratic regression model provides a better fit for the data as compared to the linear regression model.

FIGURE 16.3 Scatterplot of wages versus age

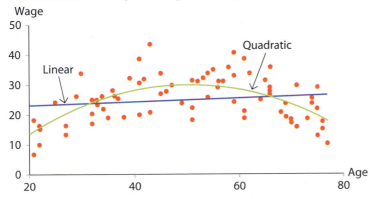

In order to estimate a quadratic regression model, we first create data on Age². The relevant portions of the output of the linear regression model, Wage = $\beta_0 + \beta_1$Education + β_2Age + ε, and the quadratic regression model, Wage = $\beta_0 + \beta_1$Education + β_2Age + β_3Age² + ε, are presented in Table 16.5.

TABLE 16.5 Estimates of the Linear and the Quadratic Regression Models for Example 16.3

Variable	Linear Regression Model	Quadratic Regression Model
Intercept	2.6381 (0.27)	−22.7219* (0.00)
Education	1.4410* (0.00)	1.2540* (0.00)
Age	0.0472 (0.13)	1.3500* (0.00)
Age^2	NA	−0.0133* (0.00)
Adjusted R^2	0.6088	0.8257

NOTES: Parameter estimates are in the main body of the table with the p-values in parentheses; NA denotes not applicable; *represents significance at the 5% level. The last row presents adjusted R^2 for model comparison.

Regression results highlight an interesting result. In the linear regression model, Age has an estimated coefficient of only 0.0472, which is not statistically significant (p-value $= 0.13$) even at the 10% significance level. However, results change dramatically when Age^2 is included along with Age. In the quadratic regression model, both of these variables, with p-values about zero, are statistically significant at any reasonable level. Also, the adjusted R^2 is higher for the quadratic regression model ($0.8257 > 0.6088$), making it a better choice for prediction. This conclusion is consistent with our visual impression from the scatterplot in Figure 16.3, which suggested a weak linear but strong quadratic relationship between age and hourly wage.

b. From Table 16.5, the estimated regression equation for the quadratic regression model is

$$\widehat{\text{Wage}} = -22.7219 + 1.2540\text{Education} + 1.3500\text{Age} - 0.0133\text{Age}^2.$$

Therefore, the predicted hourly wage for a 30-year-old person with 16 years of education is

$$\widehat{\text{Wage}} = -22.7219 + 1.2540(16) + 1.3500(30) - 0.0133(30^2) = \$25.87.$$

Similarly, the predicted hourly wage for a 50- and a 70-year-old person is $31.59 and $26.67, respectively. Note that, consistent with the estimates, the hourly wage increases as a person ages from 30 to 50, but then decreases as a person ages from 50 to 70.

c. In part b, we predicted the hourly wage for a 30-, 50-, and 70-year-old person with 16 years of education. Therefore, of the three ages considered, a 50-year-old person earns the highest wage. In Figure 16.4, we plot the predicted wage with 16 years of education and vary age from 20 to 80 with increments of 1. In order to determine the optimal age at which wage is maximized, we also solve

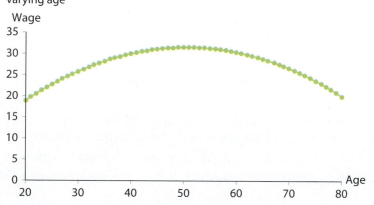

FIGURE 16.4 Predicted wages with 16 years of education and varying age

$x = \frac{-b_2}{2b_3} = \frac{-(1.3500)}{2(-0.0133)} = 50.75$. The optimal age at which the wage is maximized is about 51 years, with a wage of about \$31.60. It is worth noting that at a different education level, predicted wages will not be the same, yet the highest wage will still be achieved at the same 51 years of age. We advise you to plot a similar graph with 12 years of education and varying age levels.

The quadratic regression model allows one sign change of the slope capturing the influence of x on y. It is a special case of a **polynomial regression model**. Polynomial regression models describe various numbers of sign changes. Sometimes a quadratic regression model with one sign change is referred to as a polynomial regression model of order 2. In fact, a linear regression model is a polynomial regression model of order 1, which, with a constant slope coefficient, does not allow any sign change.

The linear and the quadratic regression models are the most common polynomial regression models. Sometimes, researchers use a polynomial regression model of order 3, also called the **cubic regression model**. The cubic regression model allows for two changes in slope.

THE CUBIC REGRESSION MODEL

A **cubic regression model**, $y = \beta_0 + \beta_1 x + \beta_2 x^2 + \beta_3 x^3 + \varepsilon$, allows two sign changes of the slope capturing the influence of x on y.

Predictions with this model are made by $\hat{y} = b_0 + b_1 x + b_2 x^2 + b_3 x^3$.

The expression $\beta_0 + \beta_1 x + \beta_2 x^2 + \beta_3 x^3$ is the deterministic component of a cubic regression model; equivalently, conditional on x, $E(y) = \beta_0 + \beta_1 x + \beta_2 x^2 + \beta_3 x^3$. The shape of a cubic relationship depends on the coefficients. Figure 16.5 highlights a representative shape of a cubic regression model when $\beta_1 > 0$, $\beta_2 < 0$, and $\beta_3 > 0$.

FIGURE 16.5 Representative shape of a cubic regression model: $y = \beta_0 + \beta_1 x + \beta_2 x^2 + \beta_3 x^3 + \varepsilon$

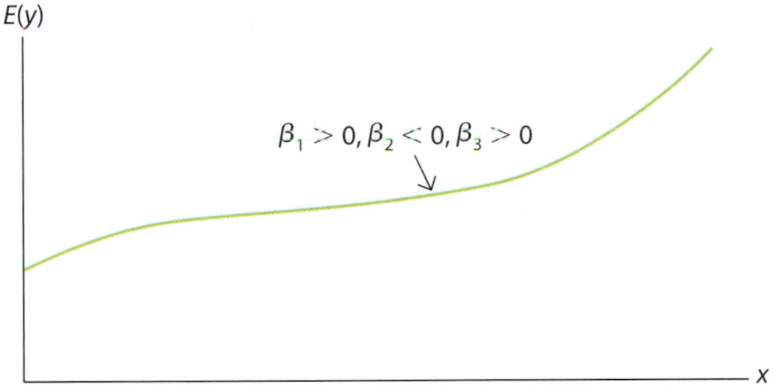

We often apply the cubic regression model when estimating the total cost curve of a firm. Generally, total costs of a firm increase gradually and then rapidly, as predicted by the law of diminishing returns. In general, the law of diminishing returns states that when increasing amounts of one factor of production (generally labor) are employed in a production process along with a fixed amount of another factor (generally capital), then after some point, the resulting increases in output of the product become smaller and smaller. A common example is adding more workers to a job, such as assembling a car in a factory. At some point, adding more workers will result in inefficiency as workers get in each other's way or wait for access to a machine. Producing one more unit of output will eventually cost increasingly more, due to inputs being used less and less effectively. We can think of Figure 16.5 as a firm's typical total cost curve where x and y represent a firm's output and total cost, respectively.

A cubic regression model can easily be estimated within the framework of a linear regression model where we use y as the response variable and x, x^2, and x^3 as the explanatory variables. It is easy to estimate a cubic regression model after we have created data on x^2 and x^3. As before, we can compare polynomial models of various orders on the basis of adjusted R^2.

EXAMPLE 16.4

Table 16.6 shows a portion of data on the total cost (in $1,000s) and output for producing a particular product; the entire data set can be found on the text website, labeled **Total Cost**. We also include a portion of the squared output and cubed output variables; these variables will be used in the estimation process.

a. Use a cubic regression model to estimate total cost (TC).
b. Predict the total cost if a firm produces 11 units of the product.

TABLE 16.6 Data for Example 16.4 on Total Cost y and Output x, $n = 40$

FILE	Total Cost (in $1,000s)	Output	Output²	Output³
	37.49	9	81	729
	37.06	7	49	343
	⋮	⋮	⋮	⋮
	33.92	4	16	64

SOLUTION:

a. In order to estimate a cubic regression model, we first create data on the squared output and the cubed output variables (see Table 16.6). We then estimate $TC = \beta_0 + \beta_1 Output + \beta_2 Output^2 + \beta_3 Output^3 + \varepsilon$. Table 16.7 shows the relevant regression results. All variables are significant at the 5% level. In addition, the adjusted R^2 (not shown) is 0.8551, which is higher than the adjusted R^2 of 0.6452 and 0.8289 for the linear and the quadratic regression models, respectively. We advise you to verify these results.

TABLE 16.7 Estimates of the Cubic Regression Model for Example 16.4

Variable	Cubic Regression Model
Intercept	17.1836* (0.00)
Output	6.4570* (0.00)
Output²	−0.7321* (0.00)
Output³	0.0291* (0.01)

NOTES: p-values are in parentheses; *represents significance at the 5% level.

b. We calculate the total cost of production to a firm that produces 11 units of the product as $\widehat{TC} = 17.1836 + 6.4570(11) - 0.7321(11^2) + 0.0291(11^3) = 38.37$, or $38,370.

EXERCISES 16.1

Concepts

1. Consider the following two estimated models:

$$\hat{y} = 25 + 1.2x$$
$$\hat{y} = 30 + 1.4x - 0.12x^2$$

For each of the estimated models, predict y when x equals 5 and 10.

2. Consider the following three models:

$$\hat{y} = 80 + 1.2x$$
$$\hat{y} = 200 + 2.1x - 0.6x^2$$
$$\hat{y} = 100 + 16x - 2.2x^2 + 0.08x^3$$

For each of the estimated models, predict y when x equals 10 and 15.

3. Consider the following 10 observations on the response variable y and the explanatory variable x.

y	13.82	19.06	16.67	13.30	11.77	13.64	18.30	20.78	13.02	16.13
x	6	6	5	3	3	12	10	8	5	11

   a. Plot the above data and then estimate the linear and the quadratic regression models.
   b. Use the appropriate numerical measure to justify which model fits the data best.
   c. Given the best-fitting model, predict y for $x = 4, 8$, and 12.
   d. Find x at which the quadratic equation reaches a minimum or maximum.

4. Consider the following 10 observations on the response variable y and the explanatory variable x.

y	9.42	4.88	3.36	3.28	1.67	7.35	6.30	4.67	9.33	5.04
x	11	9	5	5	4	10	3	10	11	8

   a. Plot the above data and estimate the linear and the quadratic regression models.
   b. Use the appropriate numerical measure to justify which model fits the data best.
   c. Given the best-fitting model, predict y for $x = 4, 6$, and 12.
   d. Find x at which the quadratic equation reaches a minimum or maximum.

5. Consider the following sample regressions for the linear, the quadratic, and the cubic models along with their respective R^2 and adjusted R^2.

	Linear	Quadratic	Cubic
Intercept	9.66	10.00	10.06
x	2.66	2.75	1.83
x^2	NA	−0.31	−0.33
x^3	NA	NA	0.26
R^2	0.810	0.836	0.896
Adjusted R^2	0.809	0.833	0.895

   a. Predict y for $x = 1$ and 2 with each of the estimated models.
   b. Select the most appropriate model. Explain.

6. Consider the following sample regressions for the linear, the quadratic, and the cubic models along with their respective R^2 and adjusted R^2.

	Linear	Quadratic	Cubic
Intercept	19.80	20.08	20.07
x	1.35	1.50	1.58
x^2	NA	−0.31	−0.27
x^3	NA	NA	−0.03
R^2	0.640	0.697	0.698
Adjusted R^2	0.636	0.691	0.689

   a. Predict y for $x = 2$ and 3 with each of the estimated models.
   b. Select the most appropriate model. Explain.

Applications

7. **FILE** Numerous studies have shown that watching too much television hurts school grades. Others have argued that television is not necessarily a bad thing for children (*Mail Online*, July 18, 2009). Like books and stories, television not only entertains, it also exposes a child to new information about the world. While watching too much TV is harmful, a little bit may actually help. Researcher Matt Castle gathers information on the grade point average (GPA) of 28 middle school children and the number of hours of TV they watched per week. A portion of the data is shown in the accompanying table; the complete data, labeled **Television**, is found on the text website.

GPA	Hours TV
3.24	19
3.10	21
⋮	⋮
3.31	4

   a. Estimate a quadratic regression model where the GPA of middle school children is regressed on hours and hours-squared.
   b. Is the quadratic term in this model justified? Explain.
   c. Find the optimal number of weekly hours of TV for middle school children.

8. **FILE** Consider a sample comprised of firms that were targets of tender offers during the period 1978–1985. Conduct an analysis where the response variable represents the number of bids (Bids) received prior to the takeover of the firm. The explanatory variables include the bid premium (Premium) and firm size (Size). It is generally believed that a high initial bid premium, defined as the percentage excess of the firm's stock price, would deter subsequent bids. Moreover, while tender offers for large firms are likely to receive more media coverage and thereby attract the attention of opportunistic bidders, it also is a wealth constraint to potential bidders. A portion of the data is shown in the accompanying table; see the text website for the complete data set, labeled **Bids**.

Bids	Premium	Size (in $ billions)
3	1.1905	0.7668
1	1.0360	0.1625
⋮	⋮	⋮
2	1.0329	3.4751

Source: Compustat and *The Wall Street Journal* Index.

   a. Estimate the model, Bids $= \beta_0 + \beta_1 \text{Premium} + \beta_2 \text{Size} + \beta_2 \text{Size}^2 + \varepsilon$.
   b. Justify the inclusion of the quadratic term in the model.
   c. Find the predicted number of bids for a firm that has a bid premium of 1.2 and firm size of $4, 8, 12$, and 16 billion, respectively. What firm size is likely to get the highest number of bids?

9. **FILE** You collect data on 26 metropolitan areas to analyze average monthly debt payments in terms of income and the unemployment rate. A portion of the data is shown in the

accompanying table; the complete data set can be found on the text website, labeled **Debt Payments**.

Metropolitan Area	Income (in $1,000s)	Unemployment	Debt
Washington, D.C.	$103.50	6.3%	$1,285
Seattle	81.70	8.5	1,135
⋮	⋮	⋮	⋮
Pittsburgh	63.00	8.3	763

Source: eFannieMae.com; bls.com; and Experian.com.

a. Estimate the model $Debt = \beta_0 + \beta_1 Inc + \beta_2 Unemp + \varepsilon$. Is unemployment significant at the 5% level?

b. You are told that the unemployment rate might have a quadratic influence on monthly debt payments. Provide an intuitive justification for this claim.

c. Estimate $Debt = \beta_0 + \beta_1 Inc + \beta_2 Unemp + \beta_3 Unemp^2 + \varepsilon$ to determine if Unemp and $Unemp^2$ are jointly significant at the 5% level.

16.2 Regression Models with Logarithms

LO **16.2**

Use and evaluate log transformed models.

In the preceding section, we squared and/or cubed the explanatory variable in order to capture nonlinearities between the response variable and the explanatory variables. Another commonly used transformation is based on the natural logarithm. You may recall from your math courses that the natural logarithmic function is the inverse of the exponential function. It is useful to briefly review exponential and logarithmic functions before using them in regression models.

The exponential function is defined as

$$y = \exp(x) = e^x,$$

where $e \approx 2.718$ is a constant and x is the function argument. We can use Excel or a calculator to compute, for example, $e^2 = 7.39$, or $e^5 = 148.41$.

The inverse of the exponential function is the natural logarithm (or simply, log), that is, the logarithm with the base $e \approx 2.718$. In other words,

$$\text{if } y = e^x, \quad \text{then} \quad \ln(y) = x,$$

where $\ln(y)$ is the natural log of y. For example, if $y = e^2 = 7.39$, then $\ln(y) = \ln(7.39) = 2$. Similarly, if $y = e^5 = 148.41$, then $\ln(y) = \ln(148.41) = 5$. Since $\exp(\ln(x)) = x$, the exponential function is sometimes referred to as the anti-log function. Finally, the log of a negative or zero value is not defined. Therefore, we can log-transform only those values that are positive.

As mentioned earlier, in many applications, linearity is not justifiable. For instance, consider an estimated linear regression of annual food expenditure y on annual income x: $\hat{y} = 9000 + 0.20x$. An estimated slope coefficient value of $b_1 = 0.20$ implies that a $1,000 increase in annual income would lead to a $200 increase in annual food expenditure, irrespective of whether the income increase is from $20,000 to $21,000 or from $520,000 to $521,000. Since we would expect the impact to be smaller at high income levels, it may be more meaningful to analyze what happens to food expenditure as income increases by a certain percentage rather than by some dollar amount.

It is common to log-transform variables that are naturally expressed in percentages, such as incomes, house prices, and sales. On the other hand, variables such as age, experience, and scores are generally expressed in their original form. We rely both on economic intuition as well as statistical measures to find the appropriate form for the variables.

We first illustrate log models with only one explanatory variable, which we later extend to a multiple regression model.

A Log-Log Model

In a log-log model, both the response variable and the explanatory variable are transformed into natural logs. We can write this model as

$$\ln(y) = \beta_0 + \beta_1 \ln(x) + \varepsilon,$$

where $\ln(y)$ is the log-transformed response variable and $\ln(x)$ is the log-transformed explanatory variable. With these transformations, the relationship between y and x is captured by a curve whose shape depends on the sign and magnitude of the slope coefficient β_1. Figure 16.6 shows a couple of representative shapes of a log-log regression model.

FIGURE 16.6 Representative shapes of a log-log model: $\ln(y) = \beta_0 + \beta_1 \ln(x) + \varepsilon$

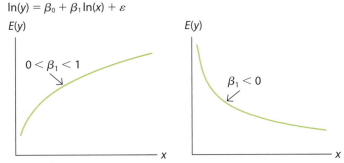

For $0 < \beta_1 < 1$, the log-log model implies a positive relationship between x and $E(y)$; as x increases, $E(y)$ increases at a slower rate. This may be appropriate in the earlier example, where we expect food expenditure to react positively to changes in income, but with the impact diminishing at higher income levels. If $\beta_1 < 0$, it suggests a negative relationship between x and $E(y)$; as x increases, $E(y)$ decreases at a slower rate. Finally, $\beta_1 > 1$ implies a positive and increasing relationship between x and y; this case is less common in a log-log application and is not shown in Figure 16.6. For any application, the estimated value of β_1 is determined by the data.

Note that while the log-log regression model is nonlinear in the variables, it is still linear in the coefficients, thus satisfying the requirement of the linear regression model. The only requirement is that we have to first transform both variables into logs before running the regression. We should also point out that in a log-log regression model, the slope coefficient β_1 measures the percentage change in y for a given (small) percentage change in x. In other words, β_1 is a measure of elasticity. For instance, if y represents the quantity demanded of a particular good and x is its unit price, then β_1 measures the price elasticity of demand, a parameter of considerable economic interest. Suppose $\beta_1 = -1.2$; then a 1% increase in the price of this good is expected to lead to a 1.2% decrease in its quantity demanded.

Finally, even though the response variable is transformed into logs, we still make predictions in regular units. Given $\widehat{\ln(y)} = b_0 + b_1\ln(x)$, you may be tempted to use the antilog function, to make predictions in regular units as $\hat{y} = \exp(\widehat{\ln(y)}) = \exp(b_0 + b_1\ln(x))$, where b_0 and b_1 are the coefficient estimates. However, this transformation is known to systematically underestimate the expected value of y. One relatively simple correction is to make predictions as $\hat{y} = \exp(b_0 + b_1\ln(x) + s_e^2/2)$, where s_e is the standard error of the estimate from the log-log model. This correction is easy to implement since virtually all statistical packages report s_e.

THE LOG-LOG REGRESSION MODEL

In a **log-log model**, $\ln(y) = \beta_0 + \beta_1\ln(x) + \varepsilon$, and β_1 measures the approximate percentage change in $E(y)$ when x increases by one percent.

Predictions with this model are made by $\hat{y} = \exp(b_0 + b_1\ln(x) + s_e^2/2)$, where b_0 and b_1 are the coefficient estimates and s_e is the standard error of the estimate.

EXAMPLE 16.5

Refer back to the food expenditure example where y represents expenditure on food and x represents income. Let the sample regression be $\widehat{\ln(y)} = 3.64 + 0.50\ln(x)$ with the standard error of the estimate $s_e = 0.18$.

a. What is the predicted food expenditure for an individual whose income is $20,000?

b. What is the predicted value if income increases to $21,000?

c. Interpret the slope coefficient, $b_1 = 0.50$.

SOLUTION: For this log-log model, we make predictions as $\hat{y} = \exp(b_0 + b_1\ln(x) + s_e^2/2)$.

a. For income equal to $20,000, we predict food expenditure as $\hat{y} = \exp(3.64 + 0.50 \times \ln(20{,}000) + 0.18^2/2) = \$5{,}475$.

b. For $x = 21{,}000$, we find $\hat{y} = \exp(3.64 + 0.50 \times \ln(21{,}000) + 0.18^2/2) = \$5{,}610$.

c. As income increases from $20,000 to $21,000, or by 5%, $\hat{y}$ increases from $5,475 to $5,610, or by about 2.5%. This is consistent with the elasticity interpretation of the slope coefficient; that is, $b_1 = 0.5$ implies that a 5% increase in income will lead to approximately a 2.5% ($= 5 \times 0.5$) increase in predicted food expenditure.

The Logarithmic Model

A log-log specification transforms all variables into logs. It is also common to employ a **semi-log** model, in which not all variables are transformed into logs. We will discuss two types of semi-log models in the context of simple regression. A semi-log model that transforms only the explanatory variable is called the **logarithmic model** and a semi-log model that transforms only the response variable is called the **exponential model**. We can have many variants of semi-log models when we extend the analysis to include multiple explanatory variables.

The logarithmic model is defined as

$$y = \beta_0 + \beta_1 \ln(x) + \varepsilon.$$

Like the log-log model, this model implies that an increase in x will lead to an increase ($\beta_1 > 0$) or decrease ($\beta_1 < 0$) in $E(y)$ at a decreasing rate. These models are especially attractive when only the explanatory variable is better captured in percentages. Figure 16.7 highlights some representative shapes of this model. Since the log-log and the logarithmic model can allow similar shapes, the choice between the two models can be tricky. We will compare models later in this section.

FIGURE 16.7 Representative shapes of a logarithmic model: $y = \beta_0 + \beta_1 \ln(x) + \varepsilon$

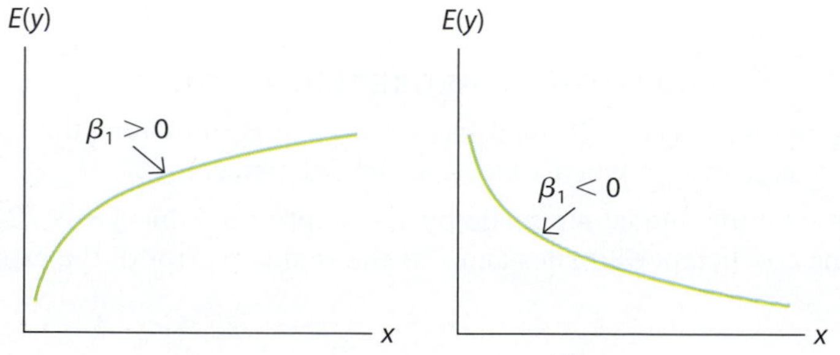

In the logarithmic model, the response variable is specified in regular units but the explanatory variable is transformed into logs. Therefore, $\beta_1/100$ measures the approximate unit change in $E(y)$ when x increases by one percent. For example, if $\beta_1 = 5000$, then a 1% increase in x leads to a 50 unit ($= 5000/100$) increase in $E(y)$. Since the response variable is already specified in regular units, no further transformation is necessary when making predictions.

> **THE LOGARITHMIC MODEL**
>
> In a **logarithmic model**, $y = \beta_0 + \beta_1 \ln(x) + \varepsilon$, and $\beta_1/100$ measures the approximate change in $E(y)$ when x increases by one percent.
>
> **Predictions** with this model are made by $\hat{y} = b_0 + b_1 \ln(x)$, where b_0 and b_1 are the coefficient estimates.

EXAMPLE 16.6

Continuing with the earlier example of food expenditure, let the estimated regression be $\hat{y} = 12 + 566 \ln(x)$.

a. What is the predicted food expenditure for an individual whose income is $20,000?

b. What is the predicted value if income increases to $21,000?

c. Interpret the slope coefficient, $b_1 = 566$.

SOLUTION: For this logarithmic model, we make predictions as $\hat{y} = b_0 + b_1 \ln(x)$.

a. The predicted food expenditure for an income of $20,000 is calculated as $\hat{y} = 12 + 566 \times \ln(20{,}000) = \$5{,}617$.

b. For $x = 21{,}000$, we find $\hat{y} = 12 + 566 \times \ln(21{,}000) = \$5{,}645$.

c. With a 5% increase in income from $20,000 to $21,000, $\hat{y}$ increases from $5,617 to $5,645, or by about $28. This is consistent with the interpretation of the slope coefficient; that is, $b_1 = 566$ implies that a 5% increase in income will lead to approximately a $28 $\left(= \frac{5 \times 566}{100} \right)$ increase in predicted food expenditure.

The Exponential Model

Unlike the logarithmic model just discussed, in which we were interested in finding the unit change in $E(y)$ for a 1% increase in x, the **exponential model** allows us to estimate the percent change in $E(y)$ when x increases by one unit. The exponential model is defined as

$$\ln(y) = \beta_0 + \beta_1 x + \varepsilon.$$

Figure 16.8 shows some representative shapes of this model.

FIGURE 16.8 Representative shapes of an exponential model: $\ln(y) = \beta_0 + \beta_1 x + \varepsilon$

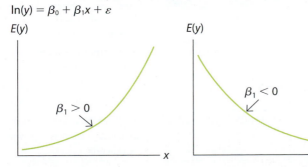

For an exponential model, $\beta_1 \times 100$ measures the approximate percentage change in $E(y)$ when x increases by one unit. For example, a value of $\beta_1 = 0.05$ implies that a one-unit increase in x leads to a 5% ($= 0.05 \times 100$) increase in $E(y)$. In applied work, we often see this model used to describe the rate of growth of certain economic variables, such as population, employment, wages, productivity, and the gross national product (GNP). As in the case of a log-log model, we make a correction for making predictions, since the response variable is measured in logs.

THE EXPONENTIAL MODEL

In an **exponential model**, $\ln(y) = \beta_0 + \beta_1 x + \varepsilon$, and $\beta_1 \times 100$ measures the approximate percentage change in $E(y)$ when x increases by one unit.

Predictions with this model are made by $\hat{y} = \exp(b_0 + b_1 x + s_e^2/2)$, where b_0 and b_1 are the coefficient estimates and s_e is the standard error of the estimate.

EXAMPLE 16.7

Continuing again with the example of expenditure on food, let the estimated regression be $\widehat{\ln(y)} = 7.60 + 0.00005x$ with the standard error of the estimate, $s_e = 0.20$.

a. What is the predicted expenditure on food for an individual whose income is $20,000?

b. What is the predicted value if income increases to $21,000?

c. Interpret the slope coefficient, $b_1 = 0.00005$.

SOLUTION: For this exponential model, we make predictions as $\hat{y} = \exp(b_0 + b_1 x + s_e^2/2)$.

a. The predicted food expenditure for an income of $20,000 is calculated as
$\hat{y} = \exp(7.60 + 0.00005 \times 20000 + 0.20^2/2) = \$5,541$.

b. For $x = 21,000$, we find $\hat{y} = \exp(7.60 + 0.00005 \times 21000 + 0.20^2/2) = \$5,825$.

c. With a $1,000 increase in income, $\hat{y}$ increases from $5,541 to $5,825, or by about 5%. This result is consistent with the interpretation of the slope coefficient; that is, $b_1 = 0.00005$ implies that a $1,000 increase in income, will lead to approximately a 5% ($= 1000 \times 0.00005 \times 100$) increase in predicted food expenditure.

While these log models are easily estimated within the framework of a linear regression model, care must be exercised in making predictions and interpreting the estimated slope coefficient. When interpreting the slope coefficient, keep in mind that logs essentially convert changes in variables into percentage changes. Table 16.8 summarizes the results.

TABLE 16.8 Summary of the Linear, Log-Log, Logarithmic, and Exponential Models

Model	Predicted Value	Estimated Slope Coefficient
$y = \beta_0 + \beta_1 x + \varepsilon$	$\hat{y} = b_0 + b_1 x$	b_1 measures the change in $\hat{y}$ when x increases by one unit.
$\ln(y) = \beta_0 + \beta_1 \ln(x) + \varepsilon$	$\hat{y} = \exp(b_0 + b_1 \ln(x) + s_e^2/2)$	b_1 measures the approximate percentage change in $\hat{y}$ when x increases by 1%.
$y = \beta_0 + \beta_1 \ln(x) + \varepsilon$	$\hat{y} = b_0 + b_1 \ln(x)$	$b_1/100$ measures the approximate change in $\hat{y}$ when x increases by 1%.
$\ln(y) = \beta_0 + \beta_1 x + \varepsilon$	$\hat{y} = \exp(b_0 + b_1 x + s_e^2/2)$	$b_1 \times 100$ measures the approximate percentage change in $\hat{y}$ when x increases by one unit.

EXAMPLE 16.8

The objective outlined in the introductory case was to evaluate the influence of the number of bedrooms (Beds), the number of bathrooms (Baths), and the square footage (Sqft) on monthly rent (Rent). Use the Ann Arbor rental data in Table 16.1 to answer the following questions.

a. Plot rent against each of the three explanatory variables and evaluate whether the relationship is best captured by a line or a curve. Identify variables that may require a log-transformation.

b. Estimate the linear and the relevant log models to predict rent for a 1,600-square-foot home with three bedrooms and two bathrooms.

SOLUTION: Given the nature of Beds and Baths, we will specify these variables only in regular units. We will, however, consider log-transformations for Rent and Sqft, since their changes are often expressed in percentages.

a. In Figure 16.9, we plot Rent against (a) Beds and (b) Baths and superimpose linear and exponential curves (recall that an exponential model log-transforms only the response variable).

FIGURE 16.9 Comparing Rent against (a) Beds and (b) Baths

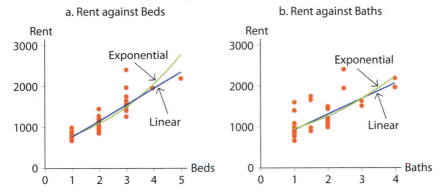

It is hard to tell from Figure 16.9 whether the relationship between Rent and Beds or Rent and Baths is better captured by a line or a curve. We will use formal numerical measures for the selection.

We now plot Rent against Sqft in Figure 16.10.

FIGURE 16.10 Comparing Rent against Square Footage

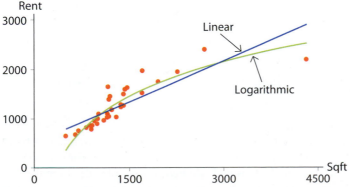

Here it appears that the relationship between Rent and Sqft is better captured by a curve than a line. Figure 16.10 shows that a logarithmic model that log-transforms Sqft fits the data better than the linear model, suggesting that as

square footage increases, rent increases at a decreasing rate. In other words, the increase in Rent is higher when Sqft increases from 1,000 to 2,000 than from 2,000 to 3,000. Two other models worth considering are the exponential model, where only Rent is log-transformed, and a log-log model, where both Rent and Sqft are log-transformed. In order to avoid a "cluttered" figure, these curves are not superimposed on the scatterplot; however, we will formally evaluate all models.

b. While the above visual tools are instructive, we evaluate four models and use numerical measures to select the most appropriate model for prediction.

$$\text{Model 1: Rent} = \beta_0 + \beta_1\text{Beds} + \beta_2\text{Baths} + \beta_3\text{Sqft} + \varepsilon$$

$$\text{Model 2: Rent} = \beta_0 + \beta_1\text{Beds} + \beta_2\text{Baths} + \beta_3\ln(\text{Sqft}) + \varepsilon$$

$$\text{Model 3: } \ln(\text{Rent}) = \beta_0 + \beta_1\text{Beds} + \beta_2\text{Baths} + \beta_3\text{Sqft} + \varepsilon$$

$$\text{Model 4: } \ln(\text{Rent}) = \beta_0 + \beta_1\text{Beds} + \beta_2\text{Baths} + \beta_3\ln(\text{Sqft}) + \varepsilon$$

In order to estimate these models, we first log-transform Rent and Sqft; see the last two columns of Table 16.9.

TABLE 16.9 Transforming Rent and Sqft into Logs

Rent	Beds	Baths	Sqft	ln(Rent)	ln(Sqft)
645	1	1	500	6.4693	6.2146
675	1	1	648	6.5147	6.4739
⋮	⋮	⋮	⋮	⋮	⋮
2400	3	2.5	2700	7.7832	7.9010

In Models 1 and 2, we use Rent as the response variable with Beds and Baths, along with Sqft in Model 1 and ln(Sqft) in Model 2, as the explanatory variables. Similarly, in Models 3 and 4, we use ln(Rent) as the response variable with Beds and Baths, along with Sqft in Model 3 and ln(Sqft) in Model 4, as the explanatory variables. Model estimates are summarized in Table 16.10.

TABLE 16.10 Regression Results for Example 16.8

	Response Variable: Rent		Response Variable: ln(Rent)	
	Model 1	**Model 2**	**Model 3**	**Model 4**
Intercept	300.4116* (0.00)	−3,909.7415* (0.00)	6.3294* (0.00)	3.3808* (0.00)
Beds	225.8100* (0.00)	131.7781* (0.04)	0.2262* (0.00)	0.1246* (0.01)
Baths	89.2661 (0.12)	36.4255 (0.49)	0.0831 (0.06)	0.0254 (0.51)
Sqft	0.2096* (0.03)	NA	0.0001 (0.36)	NA
ln(Sqft)	NA	675.2648* (0.00)	NA	0.4742* (0.00)
s_e	193.1591	172.2711	0.1479	0.1262
R^2	0.8092	0.8482	0.8095	0.8613

Notes: Parameter estimates are followed with the *p*-values in parentheses; NA denotes not applicable; *represents significance at the 5% level.

For the most part, the number of bedrooms and the square footage of the house are statistically significant at the 5% level, while the number of bathrooms is insignificant. We use the model results to predict rent for a 1,600-square-foot home with three bedrooms and two bathrooms. In order to make a prediction with Models 3 and 4, which are both based on ln(Rent), we must add the correction term $s_e^2/2$.

$$\text{Model 1: } \widehat{\text{Rent}} = 300.4116 + 225.8100(3) + 89.2661(2) + 0.2096(1600)$$
$$= \$1,492$$

Model 2: $\widehat{\text{Rent}} = -3909.7415 + 131.7781(3) + 36.4255(2) + 675.2648$
$\times \ln(1600) = \$1,540$

Model 3: $\widehat{\text{Rent}} = \exp(6.3294 + 0.2262(3) + 0.0831(2) + 0.0001(1600)$
$+ 0.1479^2/2) = \$1,549$

Model 4: $\widehat{\text{Rent}} = \exp(3.3808 + 0.1246(3) + 0.0254(2) + 0.4742$
$\times \ln(1600) + 0.1262^2/2) = \$1,498$

The predicted rent ranges from $1,492 in Model 1 to $1,549 in Model 3. We would like to know which model provides the best prediction, as we discuss next.

Comparing Linear and Log-Transformed Models

LO **16.3**

Describe the method used to compare linear with log transformed models.

As seen in Example 16.8, it is often not clear which regression model is best suited for an application. While we can use economic intuition and scatterplots for direction, we also justify our selection on the basis of numerical measures. In Chapter 14, we introduced R^2 to compare models based on the same number of explanatory variables; we compared adjusted R^2 if the number of explanatory variables was different. Such comparisons are valid only when the response variable of the competing models is the same. Since R^2 measures the percentage of sample variations of the response variable explained by the model, we cannot compare the percentage of explained variations of y with that of $\ln(y)$. Comparing models based on the computer-generated R^2 is like comparing apples with oranges. For a valid comparison, we need to compute the percentage of explained variations of y even though the estimated model uses $\ln(y)$ as the response variable. To do this, it will help to revisit the formula for calculating R^2. Recall that an easy way to compute R^2 is by squaring the sample correlation coefficient of y and $\hat{y}$.

REVISITING THE CALCULATION OF THE COEFFICIENT OF DETERMINATION R^2

The coefficient of determination R^2 can be computed as $R^2 = (r_{y\hat{y}})^2$ where $r_{y\hat{y}}$ is the sample correlation coefficient between y and $\hat{y}$.

Example 16.9 elaborates on the method.

EXAMPLE 16.9

Revisit the four regression models in Example 16.8 and determine which model is best suited for making predictions.

SOLUTION: From Table 16.10, Model 4 has the highest computer-generated R^2 value of 0.8613. However, this does not mean that Model 4 is necessarily the best, since R^2 is based on Rent for Models 1 and 2 and on $\ln(\text{Rent})$ for Models 3 and 4. Therefore, while we can infer that Model 2 is superior to Model 1 (0.8482 > 0.8092) and Model 4 is superior to Model 3 (0.8613 > 0.8095), we cannot directly compare Models 2 and 4 based on the computer-generated R^2. For a valid comparison, we compute R^2 for Model 4 from scratch; that is, R^2 is based on y, even though it uses $\ln(y)$ for estimation.

For Model 4, we can compute $\widehat{\text{Rent}} = \exp(b_0 + b_1\text{Beds} + b_2\text{Baths} + b_3\ln(\text{Sqft}) + s_e^2/2)$ for the given sample values of the explanatory variables. For example, for the first sample observation, with Beds = 1, Baths = 1, and Sqft = 500, the predicted rent is computed as

$$\widehat{Rent} = \exp(3.3808 + 0.1246(1) + 0.0254(1) + 0.4742 \times \ln(500) + 0.1262^2/2)$$
$$= \$656.$$

Excel is useful in performing these calculations—it provides the predicted values for the ln(Rent) if we check *Residuals* in the *Regression* dialog box. Since Excel provides $\widehat{\ln(Rent)}$ for Model 4, we can easily compute the predicted rent as $\widehat{Rent} = \exp(\widehat{\ln(Rent)} + s_e^2/2)$. In Table 16.11, we present a portion of these calculations, using y to represent Rent; we used unrounded values in these calculations.

TABLE 16.11 Predicted Rent for Model 4

y	$\widehat{\ln(y)}$	$\hat{y} = \exp(\widehat{\ln(y)} + 0.1262^2/2)$
645	6.4778	655.7334
675	6.6007	742.5210
⋮	⋮	⋮
2400	7.5648	1,944.5760

We use the Correlation function in Excel (select **Formulas > Insert Function > CORREL**) to derive the correlation between y and $\hat{y}$, in columns 1 and 3 of Table 16.11, as $r_{y\hat{y}} = 0.8691$. We square this value to compute the coefficient of determination, $R^2 = (0.8691)^2 = 0.7553$. We can now compare this value with the computer-generated value for Model 2. We conclude that Model 2 is better suited for making predictions, since $0.8482 > 0.7553$.

SYNOPSIS OF INTRODUCTORY CASE

The recession-resistance of campus towns has prompted many analysts to call investment in off-campus student housing a smart choice (*The Wall Street Journal*, September 24, 2010). First, there is a stable source of demand in college towns, as cash-strapped public universities are unable to house all students. Second, this demand may actually improve due to a projected increase in college enrollment. In this study, Ann Arbor, which is home to the main campus of the University of Michigan, is used to study rental opportunities. Four regression models analyze the monthly rent (Rent) on the basis of the number of bedrooms (Beds), the number of bathrooms (Baths), and the square footage (Sqft) of off-campus houses. Nonlinearities between the variables are captured by transforming Rent and/or Sqft into natural logs. The coefficient of determination R^2, computed in the original units, is used to select the best model. The selected model is estimated as $\widehat{Rent} = -3{,}909.74 + 131.78Beds + 36.43Baths + 675.26\ln(Sqft)$. The bedroom coefficient implies that for every additional bedroom, the monthly rent is predicted to go up by about \$132, holding other factors constant. Similarly, for every one percent increase in square footage, the monthly rent is predicted to increase by about \$6.75 (675/100). This sample regression model can also be used to make predictions for rent. For example, a 1,000-square-foot house with two bedrooms and one bathroom is predicted to rent for \$1,055. Similarly, a 1,600-square-foot house with three bedrooms and two bathrooms is predicted to rent for \$1,540. These results are useful to any investor interested in off-campus housing in Ann Arbor.

Concepts

10. Consider the following four estimated models:

$$\hat{y} = 500 - 4.2x$$

$$\hat{y} = 1370 - 280\ln(x)$$

$$\widehat{\ln(y)} = 8.4 - 0.04x;\ s_e = 0.13$$

$$\widehat{\ln(y)} = 8 - 0.8\ln(x);\ s_e = 0.11$$

a. Interpret the slope coefficient in each of these estimated models.

b. For each model, what is the predicted change in y when x increases by 1%, from 100 to 101?

11. Consider the following estimated models:

$$\hat{y} = 10 + 4.4x$$

$$\hat{y} = 2 + 23\ln(x)$$

$$\widehat{\ln(y)} = 3.0 + 0.1x;\ s_e = 0.07$$

$$\widehat{\ln(y)} = 2.6 + 0.6\ln(x);\ s_e = 0.05$$

a. Interpret the slope coefficient in each of these estimated models.

b. For each model, what is the predicted change in y when x increases by 5%, from 10 to 10.5?

12. Consider the sample regressions for the linear, the logarithmic, the exponential, and the log-log models. For each of the estimated models, predict y when x equals 100.

	Response Variable: y		Response Variable: $\ln(y)$	
	Model 1	Model 2	Model 3	Model 4
Intercept	240.42	−69.75	1.58	0.77
x	4.68	NA	0.05	NA
$\ln(x)$	NA	162.51	NA	1.25
s_e	83.19	90.71	0.12	0.09

13. Consider the sample regressions for the linear, the logarithmic, the exponential, and the log-log models. For each of the estimated models, predict y when x equals 50.

	Response Variable: y		Response Variable: $\ln(y)$	
	Model 1	Model 2	Model 3	Model 4
Intercept	18.52	−6.74	1.48	1.02
x	1.68	NA	0.06	NA
$\ln(x)$	NA	29.96	NA	0.96
s_e	23.92	19.71	0.12	0.10

14. Consider the following 10 observations of y and x.

y	22.21	21.94	22.83	22.66	21.44	22.51	22.87	22.50	22.88	23.16
x	12	5	15	16	4	8	11	12	18	16

a. Plot the above data to choose between the linear and the logarithmic models.

b. Justify your choice using the appropriate numerical measure.

c. Use the selected model to predict y for $x = 10$.

15. Consider the following 10 observations of y and x.

y	34.62	8.06	12.67	23.02	11.82	27.23	18.23	11.23	11.00	21.07
x	22	2	11	19	2	21	18	11	19	20

a. Plot the above data to choose between the linear and the exponential model.

b. Justify your choice using R^2 defined in terms of y.

c. With the best-fitting model, predict y for $x = 20$.

Applications

16. **FILE** According to the *World Health Organization*, obesity has reached epidemic proportions globally. While obesity has generally been linked with chronic disease and disability, researchers argue that it may also affect wages. Body Mass Index (BMI) is a widely used weight measure that also adjusts for height. A person is considered normal weight if BMI is between 18.5 to 25, overweight if BMI is between 25 to 30, and obese if BMI is over 30. The accompanying table shows a portion of data on the salary of 30 college-educated men with their respective BMI; the complete data, labeled **BMI**, are available on the text website.

Salary (in $1,000s)	BMI
34	33
43	26
⋮	⋮
45	21

a. Estimate a linear model with salary as the response variable and BMI as the explanatory variable. What is the estimated salary of a college-educated man with a BMI of 25? With a BMI of 30?

b. Estimate an exponential model using log of salary as the response variable and BMI as the explanatory variable. What is the estimated salary of a college-educated man with a BMI of 25? With a BMI of 30?

c. Which of the above two models is more appropriate for this application? Use R^2 for comparison.

17. **FILE** Professor Orley Ashenfelter of Princeton University is a pioneer in the field of wine economics. He claims that, contrary to old orthodoxy, the quality of wine can be explained mostly in terms of weather conditions. Wine romantics accuse him of undermining the whole wine-tasting culture. In an interesting co-authored paper that appeared in *Chance* magazine in 1995, he ran a multiple regression model where quality, measured by the prices that wines fetch at auctions, is used as the response variable y. The explanatory variables used in the analysis were the average temperature in Celsius x_1, the amount of winter rain x_2, the amount of harvest rain x_3, and the years since vintage x_4. A portion of the data is shown in the accompanying table; the complete data, labeled **Wine Pricing**, is available on the text website.

Price	Temperature	Winter Rain	Harvest Rain	Vintage
1.4448	17.12	600	160	31
1.8870	16.73	690	80	30
⋮	⋮	⋮	⋮	⋮
1.1457	16.00	578	74	3

SOURCE: http://www.liquidasset.com.

Country	Male Life Expectancy	Female Life Expectancy	People/Physician
Argentina	67	74	370
Bangladesh	54	53	6,166
⋮	⋮	⋮	⋮
Zaire	52	56	23,193

SOURCE: *The World Almanac and Book Facts*, 1993.

a. Use the above data to estimate a linear model, $y = \beta_0 + \beta_1 x_1 + \beta_2 x_2 + \beta_3 x_3 + \beta_4 x_4 + \varepsilon$. What is the predicted price if $x_1 = 16$, $x_2 = 600$, $x_3 = 120$, and $x_4 = 20$?

b. Use the above data to estimate an exponential model, $\ln(y) = \beta_0 + \beta_1 x_1 + \beta_2 x_2 + \beta_3 x_3 + \beta_4 x_4 + \varepsilon$. What is the predicted price if $x_1 = 16$, $x_2 = 600$, $x_3 = 120$, and $x_4 = 20$?

c. Use R^2 to select the appropriate model for prediction.

18. **FILE** Chad Dobson has heard about the positive outlook for real estate investment in college towns. He is interested in investing in Davis, California, which houses one of the University of California campuses. He uses zillow.com to access data on 2011 monthly rent for 27 houses, along with three characteristics of the home: number of bedrooms (Beds), number of bathrooms (Baths), and square footage (Sqft). A portion of the data is shown in the accompanying table; the complete data, labeled **Davis Rental**, are available on the text website.

Rent	Beds	Baths	Sqft
2950	4	4	1453
2400	4	2	1476
⋮	⋮	⋮	⋮
744	2	1	930

SOURCE: www.zillow.com.

a. Estimate a linear model that uses rent and an exponential model that uses log of rent as the response variable.

b. Compute the predicted rent for a 1,500-square-foot house with three bedrooms and two bathrooms for the linear and the exponential models (ignore the significance tests).

c. Use R^2 to select the appropriate model for prediction.

19. **FILE** Life expectancy at birth is the average number of years that a person is expected to live. There is a huge variation in life expectancies between countries with the highest being in Japan, and the lowest in some African countries. An important factor for such variability is the availability of suitable health care. One measure of a person's access to health care is the people-to-physician ratio. We expect life expectancy to be lower for countries where this ratio is high. The accompanying table lists a portion of life expectancy of males and females in 40 countries and their corresponding people-to-physician ratio; the complete data, labeled **Life Expectancy**, are available on the text website.

a. Construct a scatterplot of female life expectancy against the people-to-physician ratio. Superimpose a linear trend and a logarithmic trend to determine the appropriate model.

b. Estimate a simple linear regression model with life expectancy of females as the response variable and the people-to-physician ratio as the explanatory variable. What happens to life expectancy of females as the people-to-physician ratio decreases from 1,000 to 500?

c. Estimate a logarithmic regression model with the natural log of the people-to-physician ratio as the explanatory variable. What happens to life expectancy of females as the people-to-physician ratio decreases from 1,000 to 500?

d. Use R^2 to determine which of the above two models is more appropriate.

20. **FILE** Use the data in Exercise 19 to answer the same four questions regarding life expectancy of males. Who is more likely to benefit from adding more physicians to the population? Explain.

21. **FILE** Economists often examine the relationship between the inputs of a production function and the resulting output. A common way of modeling this relationship is referred to as the Cobb-Douglas production function. This function can be expressed as $\ln(Q) = \beta_0 + \beta_1 \ln(L) + \beta_2 \ln(K) + \varepsilon$, where Q stands for output, L for labor, and K for capital. The following table lists a portion of data relating to the U.S. agricultural industry in the year 2004; the complete data, labeled **Production Function**, are available on the text website.

State	Output	Labor	Capital
AL	3.1973	2.7682	3.1315
AR	7.7006	4.9278	4.7961
⋮	⋮	⋮	⋮
WY	1.2993	1.6525	1.5206

SOURCE: www.ers.usda.gov/Data/AgProductivity; see Tables 3, 8, 10. Values in table are indices.

Estimate $\ln(Q) = \beta_0 + \beta_1 \ln(L) + \beta_2 \ln(K) + \varepsilon$.

a. What is the predicted change in output if labor increases by 1%, holding capital constant?

b. Holding capital constant, can we conclude at the 5% level that a 1% increase in labor will increase the output by more than 0.5%?

WRITING WITH STATISTICS

Numerous attempts have been made to relate happiness to various factors. Since there is no unique way to quantify happiness, researchers generally rely on surveys to capture a subjective assessment of well-being. One recent study relates happiness with age and finds that holding everything else constant, people seem to be least happy when they are in their mid- to upper-40s (*The Economist*, December 16, 2010). Perhaps with greater age comes maturity that contributes to a better sense of overall well-being. With regards to the influence of money, a study from Princeton University's Woodrow Wilson School suggests that money does buy happiness, but its effect diminishes as incomes rise above $75,000 a year (*Time Magazine*, September 6, 2010). Perhaps people do not need

more than $75,000 to do what matters most to their emotional well-being, such as spending time with friends and family and meeting their basic food, health, and leisure needs. Nick Fisher is a young business school graduate who is fascinated by these reports. He decides to collect his own data to better comprehend and also verify the results of these studies. He surveys working adults in his hometown and inputs information on the respondent's self-assessed happiness on a scale of 0 to 100, along with age and family income. A portion of the data is shown in Table 16.12; the complete data set is found on the text website, labeled *Happiness*.

TABLE 16.12 Happiness, Age, and Income Data, $n = 100$.

FILE Respondent	Happiness	Age	Family Income
1	69	49	$52,000
2	83	47	$123,000
⋮	⋮	⋮	⋮
100	79	31	$105,000

Nick would like to use the above sample information to:

1. Find the appropriate functional form to capture the influence of age and family income on happiness.

2. With a family income of $80,000, calculate happiness associated with varying levels of age.

3. For a 60-year-old working adult, compute happiness associated with varying levels of family income.

Sample Report— Understanding Happiness

In a survey of 100 working adults, respondents were asked to report their age and family income, as well as rate their happiness on a scale of 0 to 100. This report summarizes the analysis of several regression models that examine the influence of age and income on the perceived happiness of respondents. The models used various transformations to capture interesting nonlinearities suggested by recent research reports. For example, one such report shows that people get happier as they get older, despite the fact that old age is associated with a loss of hearing, vision, and muscle tone (*The New York Times*, May 31, 2010). In addition, while people start out feeling pretty good about themselves in their 20s, their self-assessed happiness deteriorates until around age 50 and then improves steadily thereafter. In order to quantify this possible quadratic effect, both age and age-squared variables are used for the regression. Also, the natural log of income is considered in order to capture the possible diminishing effect on happiness of incomes above $75,000 (*Time Magazine*, September 6, 2010). The results of the various regression models are summarized in Table 16.A.

TABLE 16.A Regression Results

	Model 1	Model 2	Model 3	Model 4
Intercept	49.1938* (0.00)	118.5285* (0.00)	−81.0939* (0.00)	−13.3021 (0.39)
Age	0.2212* (0.00)	−2.4859* (0.00)	0.2309* (0.00)	−2.4296* (0.00)
Age-squared	NA	0.0245* (0.00)	NA	0.0241* (0.00)
Income	0.0001* (0.00)	0.0001* (0.00)	NA	NA
ln(Income)	NA	NA	12.6761* (0.00)	12.7210* (0.00)
Adjusted R^2	0.4863	0.6638	0.5191	0.6907

NOTES: Parameter estimates are in the top portion of the table with the *p*-values in parentheses; NA denotes not applicable; *represents significance at the 5% level. The last row presents the adjusted R^2 values for model comparison.

Model 4 was selected as the most appropriate model because it has the highest adjusted R^2 value of 0.6907. The estimated parameters of this model were used to make predictions. For instance, with family income equal to $80,000, the predicted happiness for a 30-, 50-, and 70-year-old is 79.09, 69.00, and 78.17, respectively. Note that these results are consistent with those suggesting that happiness first decreases and then increases with age. Specifically, using the estimated coefficients for Age, a person is least happy at 50.4 years of age. These results are shown graphically in Figure 16.A(a) where Happiness is plotted against Age, holding Income fixed at $80,000.

The regression results were also used to analyze the income effect. For instance, for a 60-year-old, the predicted happiness with family income of $50,000, $75,000, and $100,000 is 65.20, 70.36, and 74.02, respectively. Note that there is a greater increase in Happiness when income increases from $50,000 to $75,000 than when it increases from $75,000 to $100,000. These results are shown in Figure 16.A(b) where happiness is plotted against Income, holding Age fixed at 60 years. Overall, the results support recent research findings.

FIGURE 16.A Predicted happiness using Model 4 regression results

a. Happiness against Age with $80,000 in Income

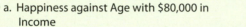
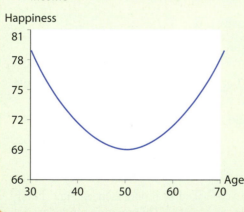

b. Happiness against Income at 60 years of Age

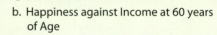
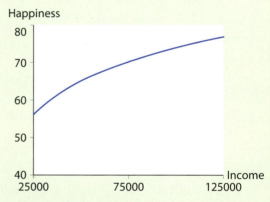

Conceptual Review

LO 16.1 Use and evaluate polynomial regression models.

In a **quadratic regression model**, $y = \beta_0 + \beta_1 x + \beta_2 x^2 + \varepsilon$, the sign of the coefficient β_2 determines whether the relationship between x and $E(y)$ is U-shaped ($\beta_2 > 0$) or inverted U-shaped ($\beta_2 < 0$). **Predictions** are made by $\hat{y} = b_0 + b_1 x + b_2 x^2$.

In a quadratic regression model, the marginal effect of x on $\hat{y}$ is approximated by $b_1 + 2b_2 x$; so this effect depends on the value of x. It is common to use $\bar{x}$ when interpreting the marginal effect. The quadratic equation reaches a maximum (if $b_2 < 0$) or minimum (if $b_2 > 0$) at $x = \frac{-b_1}{2b_2}$.

A **cubic regression model**, $y = \beta_0 + \beta_1 x + \beta_2 x^2 + \beta_3 x^3 + \varepsilon$, allows two sign changes of the slope capturing the influence of x on $E(y)$. **Predictions** are made by $\hat{y} = b_0 + b_1 x + b_2 x^2 + b_3 x^3$.

We compare polynomial regression models of various orders on the basis of adjusted R^2.

LO 16.2 | Use and evaluate log transformed models.

Many interesting nonlinear relationships can be captured by transforming the response and/or the explanatory variables into natural logs. These regression models are summarized as follows:

In a **log-log model**, $\ln(y) = \beta_0 + \beta_1 \ln(x) + \varepsilon$, and the slope coefficient β_1 measures the approximate percentage change in $E(y)$ when x increases by one percent. **Predictions** are made by $\hat{y} = \exp(b_0 + b_1 \ln(x) + s_e^2/2)$, where b_0 and b_1 are the coefficient estimates and s_e is the standard error of the estimate.

In a **logarithmic model**, $y = \beta_0 + \beta_1 \ln(x) + \varepsilon$, and $\beta_1/100$ measures the approximate change in $E(y)$ when x increases by one percent. **Predictions** are made by $\hat{y} = b_0 + b_1 \ln(x)$ where b_0 and b_1 are the coefficient estimates.

In an **exponential model**, $\ln(y) = \beta_0 + \beta_1 x + \varepsilon$, and $\beta_1 \times 100$ measures the approximate percentage change in $E(y)$ when x increases by one unit. **Predictions** are made by $\hat{y} = \exp(b_0 + b_1 x + s_e^2/2)$, where b_0 and b_1 are the coefficient estimates and s_e is the standard error of the estimate.

LO 16.3 | Describe the method used to compare linear with log transformed models.

We use the coefficient of determination R^2 to compare models that employ the same number of explanatory variables and use adjusted R^2 if the number differs. Such comparisons are valid only when the response variable of the competing models is the same. In other words, we cannot compare the percentage explained variations of y with that of $\ln(y)$. For a valid comparison, for any model that uses $\ln(y)$ as the response variable, we compute R^2 as $R^2 = (r_{y\hat{y}})^2$, where $r_{y\hat{y}}$ is the sample correlation coefficient between y and $\hat{y}$.

Additional Exercises and Case Studies

Exercises

22. **FILE** A sports enthusiast wants to examine the factors that influence a quarterback's salary (Salary). In particular, he wants to assess the influence of the pass completion rate (PC), the total touchdowns scored (TD), and a quarterback's age (Age) on Salary. He uses 2009 data, a portion of which is shown in the accompanying table; the complete data set can be found on the text website, labeled **Quarterback Salaries**.

Name	Salary (in $ millions)	PC	TD	Age
Philip Rivers	25.5566	65.2	28	27
Jay Cutler	22.0441	60.5	27	26
⋮	⋮	⋮	⋮	⋮
Tony Romo	0.6260	63.1	26	29

Source: *USA Today* database for salaries; NFL.com for other data.

a. Estimate and interpret the model: Salary $= \beta_0 + \beta_1 PC + \beta_2 TD + \beta_3 Age + \varepsilon$. Show that this model is preferable to a model that uses log of salary as the response variable.

b. Consider the quadratic effect of Age by adding Age^2 in the regression. Use a partial F test to determine the joint statistical significance of Age and Age^2.

23. **FILE** A realtor examines the factors that influence the price of a house. He collects data on the prices for 36 single-family homes in Arlington, Massachusetts sold in the first quarter of 2009. For explanatory variables, he uses the house's square footage (Sqft), as well as its number of bedrooms (Beds) and bathrooms (Baths). A portion of the data is shown in the accompanying table; the complete data are found on the text website, labeled **Arlington Homes**.

Price	Sqft	Beds	Baths
840000	2768	4	3.5
822000	2500	4	2.5
⋮	⋮	⋮	⋮
307500	850	1	1

Source: NewEnglandMoves.com.

a. Estimate the linear model, Price $= \beta_0 + \beta_1 Sqft + \beta_2 Beds + \beta_3 Baths + \varepsilon$, and the exponential model, $\ln(Price) = \beta_0 + \beta_1 Sqft + \beta_2 Beds + \beta_3 Baths + \varepsilon$.

b. Interpret the slope coefficients of the estimated models.

c. Use the coefficient of determination to choose the preferred model.

24. A nutritionist wants to understand the influence of income and healthy food on the incidence of smoking. He collects 2009 data on the percentage of smokers in each state in the U.S. and the corresponding median income and the percentage of the population that regularly eats fruits and vegetables. A portion of the data is shown below; the complete data set can be found on the text website, labeled **Smoking**.

State	Smoke (%)	Fruits/ Vegetables (%)	Median Income
AK	14.6	23.3	61,604
AL	16.4	20.3	39,980
⋮	⋮	⋮	⋮
WY	15.2	23.3	52,470

SOURCE: Centers for Disease Control and Prevention and U.S. Census Bureau.

a. Estimate: Smoke $= \beta_0 + \beta_1$Fruits/Vegetables $+ \beta_2$Median Income $+ \varepsilon$.

b. Compare this model with a model that log-transforms the median income variable.

25. The savings rate has declined dramatically over the past few decades (CNNMoney.com, June 30, 2010). While some economists are extremely concerned about this decline, others believe that it is a nonissue. Consider the following monthly data on the personal savings rate (Savings) and the personal disposable income (Income) in the U.S. from January 2007 to November 2010; the complete dataset, labeled **Savings Rate**, can be found on the text website.

Date	Savings (%)	Income ($ billions)
2007–01	2.2	10198.2
2007–02	2.3	10252.9
⋮	⋮	⋮
2010–11	5.5	11511.9

SOURCE: Bureau of Economic Analysis.

a. Compare the linear model, Savings $= \beta_0 + \beta_1$Income $+ \varepsilon$, with a log-log model, ln (Savings) $= \beta_0 + \beta_1$ln (Income) $+ \varepsilon$.

b. Interpret the estimated slope coefficient of both models.

c. Which is the preferred model? Explain.

CASE STUDIES

Case Study 16.1

Executive compensation has risen dramatically beyond the rising levels of an average worker's wage over the years. This has been a hot topic for discussion, especially with the crisis in the financial sector and the controversy over the federal bailout. The government is even considering a cap on high-flying salaries for executives (*The New York Times*, February 9, 2009). Consider the following data that link total compensation of the 455 highest-paid CEOs in 2006 with two performance measures (industry-adjusted return on assets, ROA, and industry-adjusted stock return) and the firm's size (Total Assets). The complete data, labeled **Executive Compensation**, are on the text website.

Data for Case Study 16.1 Executive Compensation and Other Factors, $n = 455$

Compensation (in $ million)	Adj ROA	Adj Return	Total Assets (in $ millions)
16.58	2.53	−0.15	20,917.5
26.92	1.27	0.57	32,659.5
⋮	⋮	⋮	⋮
2.30	0.45	0.75	44,875.0

SOURCE: SEC website and Compustat.

In a report, use the sample information to:

1. Estimate two models where each model uses Compensation as the response variable and Adj ROA and Adj Return as the explanatory variables along with Total Assets in Model 1 and natural log of Total Assets in Model 2.

2. Use the preferred model to predict compensation given the average values of the explanatory variables.

Case Study 16.2

A British survey just revealed that the New York Yankees baseball team pays their players, on average, more than any other team in the world (http://sportsillustrated.cnn.com, April 7, 2010). Brendan Connolly, a statistician for a Major League Baseball (MLB) team, wants to elaborate on the salary of baseball players. Excluding pitchers from his analysis, he believes that a baseball player's batting average (BA), runs batted in (RBI), and years of experience playing professional baseball (Experience) are the most important factors that influence a player's salary. Further, he believes that salaries rise with experience only up to a point, beyond which they begin to fall; in other words, experience has a quadratic effect on salaries. Brendan collects data on salary (in $1,000s), BA, RBI, and experience for 138 outfielders in 2008. A portion of the data is shown in the accompanying table; all data can be found on the text website, labeled **MLB Salary**.

Data for Case Study 16.2 Major League Baseball Outfielder Data, $n = 138$

FILE

Player	Salary (in $1,000s)	BA	RBI	Experience
1. Nick Markakis	455	299	87	3
2. Adam Jones	390	261	23	3
⋮	⋮	⋮	⋮	⋮
138. Randy Winn	8,875	288	53	11

NOTES: All data collected from usatoday.com or espn.com; BA and RBI are averages over the player's professional life through 2008. For exposition, BA has been multiplied by 1000.

In a report, use the sample information to:

1. Estimate a quadratic regression model using Salary as the response variable and BA, RBI, Experience, and Experience^2 as the explanatory variables.
2. Compare the above quadratic regression model with a linear model that uses BA, RBI, and Experience as the explanatory variables.

Case Study 16.3

According to a recent report by the government, new home construction fell to an 18-month low in October, 2010 (CNNMoney.com, November 17, 2010). Housing starts, or the number of new homes being built, experienced an 11.7% drop in the seasonally adjusted annual rate. Beena Singh works for a mortgage company in Madison, Wisconsin. She wants to better understand the quantitative relationship between housing starts, the mortgage rate, and the unemployment rate. She gathers monthly data on these variables from 2006:01–2010:12. A portion of the data is shown in the following table; the complete data, labeled **Housing Starts**, are available on the text website.

Data for Case Study 16.3 Housing Starts and Other Factors, $n = 60$

FILE

Date	Housing Starts (in 1,000s)	Mortgage Rate (%)	Unemployment Rate (%)
2006–01	2273	6.15	4.7
2006–02	2119	6.25	4.8
⋮	⋮	⋮	⋮
2010–12	520	4.71	9.4

SOURCE: Census Bureau and Board of Governors.

In a report, use the sample information to:

1. Construct scatterplots to quantify the relationship of housing starts with the mortgage rate and the unemployment rate.
2. Estimate a linear and an exponential regression model and use numerical measures to select the most appropriate model for prediction.
3. Discuss the potential problems of serial correlation in this time series data application.

17 Regression Models with Dummy Variables

LEARNING OBJECTIVES

After reading this chapter you should be able to:

LO 17.1 Use dummy variables to capture a shift of the intercept.

LO 17.2 Test for differences between the categories of a qualitative variable.

LO 17.3 Use dummy variables to capture a shift of the intercept and/or slope.

LO 17.4 Use a linear probability model to estimate a binary response variable.

LO 17.5 Interpret the results from a logit model.

Up until now, regression analysis has allowed us to answer questions such as: What is the contribution of advertisement expenditures to the firm's sales? Can we improve elementary education by reducing class size? How much will an additional hour of review before the final exam contribute to the score? All of these questions use response and explanatory variables that are quantitative in nature. There are other important applications that use qualitative variables representing two or more categories. For instance, we may want answers to questions such as: Do women get paid as much as men for the same work? Are sales of electronic goods higher in the 4th quarter than in the other quarters? What is the influence of family income on the probability of buying a house? In order to answer these questions, the regression analysis must incorporate qualitative response and/or explanatory variables. This chapter examines these kinds of situations, using methods called dummy variable models and binary choice probability models.

Is There Evidence of Wage Discrimination?

Three female Seton Hall professors recently learned in a court decision that they could pursue their lawsuit alleging that the university paid better salaries to younger instructors and male professors (www.nj.com, November 23, 2010). Numerous studies have focused on salary differences between men and women, whites and blacks, and young and old. Mary Schweitzer works in the human resources department at a large liberal arts college. After the Seton Hall news, the college asked her to test for both gender and age discrimination in salaries. Mary gathered information on the annual salaries (in $1,000s) of 42 professors, along with their experience (in years), gender (male or female), and age (under 60 years old or at least 60 years old). A portion of the data is shown in Table 17.1; the complete data set can be found on the text website, labeled **Professor Salary**.

TABLE 17.1 Salary and Other Information on 42 Professors

Individual	Salary (in $1,000s)	Experience (in years)	Gender	Age
1	67.50	14	Male	Under
2	53.51	6	Male	Under
⋮	⋮	⋮	⋮	⋮
42	73.06	35	Female	Over

Mary would like to use the sample information in Table 17.1 to:

1. Test whether salary differs by a fixed amount between males and females.

2. Determine whether there is evidence of age discrimination in salaries.

3. Determine if the salary difference between males and females increases with experience.

A synopsis of this case is provided at the end of Section 17.2.

17.1 Dummy Variables

In the previous chapters, all the variables used in the regression applications have been **quantitative**; in other words, they assume some numerical values. For instance, the variables used earlier in the regression describing monthly rents based on the square footage and the number of bedrooms and bathrooms are all quantitative. In empirical work, however, it is very common to have some variables that are **qualitative** in nature. Although qualitative variables can be described by several categories, they are often binary, meaning that they represent one of only two possible categories. Examples include gender (male or female), home ownership (own or do not own), Internet connection (yes or no), and college choice (public or private).

> **QUANTITATIVE VERSUS QUALITATIVE VARIABLES IN REGRESSION**
>
> Variables employed in a regression can be **quantitative** or **qualitative**. Quantitative variables assume meaningful numerical values, whereas qualitative variables represent categories.

In a regression model, qualitative variables can be used as explanatory variables as well as response variables. In the first two sections of this chapter, we focus on explanatory qualitative variables. Binary response variables will be discussed in Section 17.3.

Qualitative Variables with Two Categories

A qualitative variable with two categories can be associated with a **dummy variable**, also referred to as an **indicator variable**, or simply a **dummy**. A dummy d is defined as a variable that assumes a value of 1 for one of the categories and 0 for the other. For example, in the case of gender, we can define 1 for males and 0 for females. Alternatively, we can define 1 for females and 0 for males, with no change in inference. Sometimes we define a dummy from a variable that is not necessarily qualitative. For instance, in studying teen behavior, we may have access to quantitative information on age, but we can generate a dummy variable that equals 1 for ages between 13 and 19 and 0 otherwise. Here, we convert the quantitative variable to a qualitative variable with two categories.

> **A DUMMY VARIABLE**
>
> A **dummy variable** d is defined as a variable that takes on values of 0 or 1. It is commonly used to describe a qualitative variable with two categories.

LO 17.1
Use dummy variables to capture a shift of the intercept.

For the sake of simplicity, we will begin this section with a model containing one quantitative explanatory variable and one dummy variable. As we will see shortly, the model can easily be extended to include additional variables.

Consider the following model:

$$y = \beta_0 + \beta_1 x + \beta_2 d + \varepsilon,$$

where x is a quantitative variable and d is a dummy variable with values of 0 or 1. We can use sample data to estimate the model as

$$\hat{y} = b_0 + b_1 x + b_2 d.$$

For a given x and $d = 1$, we can compute the predicted values as

$$\hat{y} = b_0 + b_1 x + b_2 = (b_0 + b_2) + b_1 x.$$

Similarly, for $d = 0$,

$$\hat{y} = b_0 + b_1 x.$$

The dummy variable d used as an explanatory variable allows a shift in the intercept of the estimated regression line. Note that the estimated intercept b_0 when $d = 0$ shifts to $(b_0 + b_2)$ when $d = 1$. In other words, the dummy variable enables us to use a single regression equation to represent both categories of the qualitative variable. All we need to do is to use d along with the other explanatory variable x in the regression. Figure 17.1 shows a shift in the intercept of the estimated regression line when $d = 0$ changes to $d = 1$, given $b_2 > 0$.

FIGURE 17.1 Using d for an intercept shift

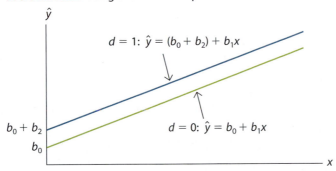

Note that the dummy variable d affects the intercept, but not the slope, of the linear regression line. Sometimes, d is referred to as the **intercept dummy**. Shortly, we will consider an interaction variable, xd, that affects the slope of the regression line.

EXAMPLE 17.1

The objective outlined in the introductory case is to determine if there is any gender or age discrimination at a large liberal arts college. Use the data in Table 17.1 to answer the following questions.

a. Estimate $y = \beta_0 + \beta_1 x + \beta_2 d_1 + \beta_3 d_2 + \varepsilon$, where y is the annual salary (in $1,000s) of a professor, x is the number of years of experience, d_1 is a dummy variable that equals 1 if the professor is male and 0 otherwise, and d_2 is a dummy variable that equals 1 if the professor is 60 years of age or older and 0 otherwise.

b. Compute the predicted salary of a 50-year-old male professor with 10 years of experience. Compute the predicted salary of a 50-year-old female professor with 10 years of experience. Discuss the impact of gender on predicted salary.

c. Compute the predicted salary of a 65-year-old female professor with 10 years of experience. Discuss the impact of age on predicted salary.

SOLUTION:

a. To estimate the above model, we first convert the qualitative variables in Table 17.1 to their respective gender and age dummy variables, d_1 and d_2, in Table 17.2.

TABLE 17.2 Generating d_1 and d_2 from the Data in Table 17.1

y	x	Gender Dummy d_1	Age Dummy d_2
67.50	14	1	0
53.51	6	1	0
⋮	⋮	⋮	⋮
73.06	35	0	1

Table 17.3 shows the relevant regression results.

TABLE 17.3 Regression Results for $y = \beta_0 + \beta_1 x + \beta_2 d_1 + \beta_3 d_2 + \varepsilon$

	Coefficients	Standard Error	t Stat	p-value
Intercept	40.61	3.69	11.00	0.00
x	1.13	0.18	6.30	0.00
d_1	13.92	2.87	4.86	0.00
d_2	4.34	4.64	0.94	0.36

The estimated model is $\hat{y} = 40.61 + 1.13x + 13.92d_1 + 4.34d_2$.

b. The predicted salary of a 50-year old male professor ($d_1 = 1$ and $d_2 = 0$) with 10 years of experience ($x = 10$) is

$$\hat{y} = 40.61 + 1.13(10) + 13.92(1) + 4.34(0) = 65.83, \text{ or } \$65,830.$$

The corresponding salary of a 50-year-old female ($d_1 = 0$ and $d_2 = 0$) is

$$\hat{y} = 40.61 + 1.13(10) + 13.92(0) + 4.34(0) = 51.91, \text{ or } \$51,910.$$

The predicted difference in salary between a male and a female professor with 10 years of experience is $13,920 (65,830 − 51,910). This difference can also be inferred from the estimated coefficient 13.92 of the gender dummy variable d_1. Note that the salary difference does not change with experience. For instance, the predicted salary of a 50-year-old male with 20 years of experience is $77,130. The corresponding salary of a 50-year-old female is $63,210, for the same difference of $13,920.

c. For a 65-year-old female professor with 10 years of experience, the predicted salary is

$$\hat{y} = 40.61 + 1.13(10) + 13.92(0) + 4.34(1) = 56.25, \text{ or } 56,250.$$

Prior to any statistical testing, it appears that an older female professor earns, on average, $4,340 (56,250 − 51,910) more than a younger female professor with the same experience.

LO **17.2**

Test for differences between the categories of a qualitative variable.

Dummy variables are treated just like other explanatory variables; that is, all statistical tests discussed in Chapter 15 remain valid. In particular, using the t test we can examine whether a particular dummy is statistically significant. This allows us to determine if the response variable depends on the two categories represented by this dummy. An F test can be conducted similarly.

TESTING THE SIGNIFICANCE OF DUMMY VARIABLES

In a model, $y = \beta_0 + \beta_1 x + \beta_2 d_1 + \beta_3 d_2 + \varepsilon$, we can perform the t test to determine the significance of each dummy variable. We can also conduct the partial F test for joint significance of the dummy variables.

EXAMPLE 17.2

Refer to the regression results in Table 17.3.

a. Determine whether there is a difference in salary depending on gender at the 5% significance level.

b. Determine whether an older professor's salary differs from a younger professor's salary at the 5% significance level.

SOLUTION:

a. In order to test for a salary difference between male and female professors, we set up the hypotheses as $H_0: \beta_2 = 0$ against $H_A: \beta_2 \neq 0$. Given a value of the t_{df} test statistic of 4.86 with a p-value ≈ 0.00, we reject the null hypothesis and conclude that the gender dummy variable is statistically significant at the 5% level. We conclude that male and female professors do not make the same salary, holding other variables constant.

b. Here the hypotheses take the form $H_0: \beta_3 = 0$ against $H_A: \beta_3 \neq 0$. Given a value of the t_{df} test statistic of 0.94 with a p-value $= 0.36$, we cannot reject the null hypothesis. At the 5% significance level, we cannot conclude age discrimination with respect to a professor's salary. We should bear in mind that some of the age effect is captured by experience. In the next section, we will consider a scenario where males get a higher compensation for experience than females, making their salaries diverge over time.

Qualitative Variables with Multiple Categories

So far we have used dummy variables when a given qualitative variable has only two categories, such as male and female. Sometimes, a qualitative variable may be described by more than two categories. For example, the mode of transportation used to commute may be described by three categories: public transportation, driving alone, and car pooling. In such cases we use multiple dummy variables to capture the effect of the qualitative variable. For instance, we can define two dummy variables d_1 and d_2, where d_1 equals 1 to denote public transportation, 0 otherwise, and d_2 equals 1 to denote driving alone, 0 otherwise. For this three-category case, we need to define only two dummies; car pooling is indicated when $d_1 = d_2 = 0$.

Consider the following regression model:

$$y = \beta_0 + \beta_1 x + \beta_2 d_1 + \beta_3 d_2 + \varepsilon,$$

where y denotes commuting expenditure, x denotes distance to work, and d_1 and d_2 represent the public transportation and driving alone dummy variables. We can use sample data to estimate the model as

$$\hat{y} = b_0 + b_1 x + b_2 d_1 + b_3 d_2.$$

For $d_1 = 1, d_2 = 0$ (public transportation), $\hat{y} = b_0 + b_1 x + b_2 = (b_0 + b_2) + b_1 x.$
For $d_1 = 0, d_2 = 1$ (driving alone), $\hat{y} = b_0 + b_1 x + b_3 = (b_0 + b_3) + b_1 x.$
For $d_1 = d_2 = 0$ (car pooling), $\hat{y} = b_0 + b_1 x.$

Here we use car pooling as the reference category in the estimated regression line with the intercept b_0. The intercept changes to $(b_0 + b_2)$ for public transportation and $(b_0 + b_3)$ for driving alone. Therefore, we account for all three categories with just two dummy variables.

Given the intercept term, we exclude one of the dummy variables from the regression, where the excluded variable represents the reference category against which the others are assessed. If we include as many dummy variables as there are categories, then their sum will equal one. For instance, if we add a third dummy d_3 that equals 1 to denote car pooling, then for all observations, $d_1 + d_2 + d_3 = 1$. This creates a problem of perfect multicollinearity. Such a model cannot be estimated. This situation is referred to as the **dummy variable trap**.

> **AVOIDING THE DUMMY VARIABLE TRAP**
>
> Assuming that the linear regression model includes an intercept, the number of dummy variables representing a qualitative variable should be **one less than the number of categories** of the variable.

EXAMPLE 17.3

A recent article suggests that Asian-Americans face serious discrimination in the college admissions process (*The Boston Globe*, February 8, 2010). Specifically, Asian applicants typically need an *extra* 140 points on the SAT to compete with white students. Another report suggests that colleges are eager to recruit Hispanic students who are generally underrepresented in applicant pools (*USA Today*, February 8, 2010). In an attempt to corroborate these claims, a sociologist first wants to determine if SAT scores differ by ethnic background. She collects data on 200 individuals from her city with their recent SAT scores and ethnic background. A portion of the data is shown in Table 17.4; the complete data, labeled **SAT and Ethnicity**, can be found on the text website.

TABLE 17.4 SAT Scores and Ethnic Background; $n = 200$

Individual	SAT	White	Black	Asian
1	1515	1	0	0
2	1530	0	0	0
⋮	⋮	⋮	⋮	⋮
200	1614	1	0	0

a. Estimate the model $y = \beta_0 + \beta_1 d_1 + \beta_2 d_2 + \beta_3 d_3 + \varepsilon$, where y is an individual's SAT score; d_1 equals 1 if the individual is white, 0 otherwise; d_2 equals 1 if the individual is black, 0 otherwise; and d_3 equals 1 if the individual is Asian, 0 otherwise. Note that Hispanics represent the reference category.

b. What is the predicted SAT score for an Asian individual? For a Hispanic individual?

c. Do SAT scores vary by ethnic background at the 5% significance level? Explain.

SOLUTION:

a. We report the regression results of this model in Table 17.5.

TABLE 17.5 Regression Results for SAT $= \beta_0 + \beta_1 d_1 + \beta_2 d_2 + \beta_3 d_3 + \varepsilon$

	Coefficients	Standard Error	t Stat	p-value
Intercept	1388.89	9.36	148.44	0.00
d_1	201.14	12.91	15.59	0.00
d_2	−31.45	22.19	−1.42	0.16
d_3	264.86	17.86	14.83	0.00

b. For an Asian individual, we set $d_1 = 0$, $d_2 = 0$, $d_3 = 1$ and calculate $\hat{y} = 1388.89 + 264.86 = 1653.75$. Thus, the predicted SAT score for an Asian individual is approximately 1654. The predicted SAT score for a Hispanic individual ($d_1 = d_2 = d_3 = 0$) is $\hat{y} = 1388.89$, or approximately 1389.

c. Since the *p*-values corresponding to d_1 and d_3 are approximately zero, we conclude at the 5% level that the SAT scores of White and Asian students are different from those of Hispanic students. However, with a *p*-value of 0.16, we cannot conclude that the SAT scores of Black and Hispanic students are statistically different.

Concepts

1. Consider a linear regression model where y represents the response variable and x and d are the explanatory variables; d is a dummy variable assuming values 0 or 1. The model is estimated as

$$\hat{y} = 14.8 + 4.4x - 3.8d.$$

   a. Interpret the dummy variable coefficient.
   b. Compute $\hat{y}$ for $x = 3$ and $d = 1$.
   c. Compute $\hat{y}$ for $x = 3$ and $d = 0$.

2. Consider a linear regression model where y represents the response variable, d_1 is a dummy variable assuming values of 0 or 1, and d_2 is another dummy variable assuming values of 0 or 1. The model is estimated as $\hat{y} = 160 + 15d_1 + 32d_2$.

   a. Compute $\hat{y}$ for $d_1 = 1$ and $d_2 = 1$.
   b. Compute $\hat{y}$ for $d_1 = 0$ and $d_2 = 0$.

3. Using 50 observations, the following regression output is obtained from estimating $y = \beta_0 + \beta_1 x + \beta_2 d_1 + \beta_3 d_2 + \varepsilon$.

	Coefficients	Standard Error	t Stat	p-value
Intercept	−0.61	0.23	−2.75	0.0074
x	3.12	1.04	3.01	0.0034
d_1	−13.22	15.65	−0.85	0.4006
d_2	5.35	1.25	4.27	0.0000

   a. Compute $\hat{y}$ for $x = 250$, $d_1 = 1$, and $d_2 = 0$; then compute $\hat{y}$ for $x = 250$, $d_1 = 0$, and $d_2 = 1$.
   b. Interpret d_1 and d_2. Are both dummy variables individually significant at the 5% level? Explain.

4. Using 30 observations, the following regression output is obtained from estimating $\ln(y) = \beta_0 + \beta_1 x + \beta_2 d + \varepsilon$, where $\ln(y)$ is the natural log of y.

	Coefficients	Standard Error	t Stat	p-value
Intercept	1.56	0.73	2.14	0.0415
x	0.21	0.08	2.63	0.0139
d	0.15	0.04	3.75	0.0008
The standard error of the estimate is $s_e = 0.35$.				

   a. Interpret the estimated coefficient for the dummy variable d.
   b. Compute $\hat{y}$ for $x = 20$ and $d = 0$, then compute $\hat{y}$ for $x = 20$ and $d = 1$.
   c. Is d significant at the 5% level? Explain.

Applications

5. In an attempt to "time the market," a financial analyst studies the quarterly returns of a stock. He uses the model $y = \beta_0 + \beta_1 d_1 + \beta_2 d_2 + \beta_3 d_3 + \varepsilon$ where y is the quarterly return of a stock, d_1 is a dummy variable that equals 1 if quarter 1 and 0 otherwise, d_2 is a dummy variable that equals 1 if quarter 2

and 0 otherwise, and d_3 is a dummy variable that equals 1 if quarter 3 and 0 otherwise. The following table is a portion of the regression results.

	Coefficients	Standard Error	t Stat	p-value
Intercept	10.62	5.81	1.83	0.08
d_1	−7.26	8.21	−0.88	0.38
d_2	−1.87	8.21	−0.23	0.82
d_3	−9.31	8.21	−1.13	0.27

   a. Given that there are four quarters in a year, why doesn't the analyst include a fourth dummy variable in his model?
   b. At the 5% significance level, are the dummy variables individually significant? Explain. Is the analyst able to obtain higher returns depending on the quarter?

6. **FILE** In the United States, baseball has always been a favorite pastime and is rife with statistics and theories. While baseball purists may disagree, to an applied statistician no topic in baseball is too small or hypothesis too unlikely. In a recent paper, researchers at Wayne State University showed that major-league players who have nicknames live 2½ years longer than those without them (*The Wall Street Journal,* July 16, 2009). Perhaps nicknames add to the self-esteem of a player. Consider the following portion of data on the lifespan (years) of a player and a nickname dummy that equals 1 if the player had a nickname and 0 otherwise; the complete data set can be found on the text website, labeled **Nicknames**.

Years	Nickname
74	1
62	1
⋮	⋮
64	0

   a. Create two subsamples, with one consisting of players with a nickname and the other one without a nickname. Calculate the average longevity for each subsample.
   b. Estimate a linear regression model of Years on the Nickname dummy variable. Compute the predicted longevity of players with and without a nickname.
   c. Conduct a one-tailed test at a 5% level to determine if players with a nickname live longer.

7. **FILE** The SAT has gone through many revisions over the years. In 2005, a new writing section was introduced that includes a direct writing measure in the form of an essay. People argue that female students generally do worse on math tests but better on writing tests. Therefore, the new section may help reduce the usual male lead on the overall average SAT score (*The Washington Post,* August 30, 2006). Consider the following portion of data on 20 students who took the SAT test last year; the complete data set can be

found on the text website, labeled **SATdummy**. Information includes each student's score on the math and writing sections of the exam. Also included are the student's GPA and a dummy that equals 1 for female and 0 for male.

Writing	Math	GPA	Female
620	600	3.44	0
570	550	3.04	0
⋮	⋮	⋮	⋮
540	520	2.84	0

a. Estimate a linear regression model with writing score as the response variable and GPA and the female dummy variable as the explanatory variables.

b. Compute the predicted score for a male student with a GPA of 3.5. Repeat the analysis for a female student.

c. Perform a test to determine if there is a statistically significant gender difference in writing scores at a 5% level.

8. **FILE** Use the data described in Exercise 7 to estimate a linear regression model with math score as the response variable and GPA and the female dummy variable as the explanatory variables.

a. Compute the predicted score for a male student with a GPA of 3.5. Repeat the analysis for a female student.

b. Perform a test to determine if there is a statistically significant gender difference in math scores at the 5% level.

9. **FILE** A manager at an ice cream store is trying to determine how many customers to expect on any given day. Overall business has been relatively steady over the past several years, but the customer count seems to have ups and downs. He collects data over 30 days and records the number of customers, the high temperature (degrees Fahrenheit), and whether the day fell on a weekend (1 equals weekend, 0 otherwise). A portion of the data is shown; the entire data set can be found on the text website, labeled **Ice Cream**.

Customers	Temperature	Weekend
376	75	0
433	78	0
⋮	⋮	⋮
401	68	0

a. Estimate: Customers $= \beta_0 + \beta_1$Temperature $+ \beta_2$Weekend $+ \varepsilon$.

b. How many customers should the manager expect on a Sunday with a forecasted high temperature of 80°?

c. Interpret the weekend coefficient. Is it significant at the 5% level? How might this affect the store's staffing needs?

10. **FILE** A researcher wonders whether males get paid more, on average, than females at a large firm. She interviews 50 employees and collects data on each worker's hourly wage (Wage), years of higher education (EDUC), experience

(EXPER), age (AGE), and gender of the employee (d equals 1 if male). A portion of the data is shown; the entire data set can be found on the text website, labeled **Hourly Wage**.

Wage	EDUC	EXPER	AGE	d
$37.85	11	2	40	1
21.72	4	1	39	0
⋮	⋮	⋮	⋮	⋮
24.18	8	11	64	0

a. Estimate: Wage $= \beta_0 + \beta_1$EDUC $+ \beta_2$EXPER $+ \beta_3$AGE $+ \beta_4 d + \varepsilon$.

b. Predict the hourly wage of a 40-year-old male employee with 10 years of higher education and 5 years experience. Predict the hourly wage of a 40-year-old female employee with the same qualifications.

c. Interpret the gender coefficient. Is the gender variable significant at the 5% level? Does the data suggest that gender discrimination exists at this firm?

11. **FILE** A government researcher is analyzing the relationship between retail sales and the gross national product (GNP). He also wonders whether there are significant differences in retail sales related to the quarters of the year. He collects ten years of quarterly data. A portion is shown in the accompanying table; the complete data set can be found on the text website, labeled **Retail Sales**.

Year	Quarter	Retail Sales (in $ millions)	GNP (in $ billions)	d_1	d_2	d_3
2001	1	696,048	9,740.5	1	0	0
	2	753,211	9,983.5	0	1	0
⋮	⋮	⋮	⋮	⋮	⋮	⋮
2009	4	985,649	14,442.8	0	0	0

Source: Retail sales obtained from www.census.gov; GNP obtained from research. stlouisfed.org.

a. Estimate $y = \beta_0 + \beta_1 x + \beta_2 d_1 + \beta_3 d_2 + \beta_4 d_3 + \varepsilon$ where y is retail sales, x is GNP, d_1 is a dummy variable that equals 1 if quarter 1 and 0 otherwise, d_2 is a dummy variable that equals 1 if quarter 2 and 0 otherwise, and d_3 is a dummy variable that equals 1 if quarter 3 and 0 otherwise.

b. Predict retail sales in quarters 2 and 4 if GNP equals $13,000 billion.

c. Which of the quarterly sales are significantly different from those of the 4th quarter at the 5% level?

d. Use the partial F test to determine if the three seasonal dummy variables used in the model are jointly significant at the 5% level.

12. **FILE** The issues regarding executive compensation have received extensive media attention. The government is even considering a cap on high-flying salaries for executives (*New York Times*, February 9, 2009). Consider a regression model that links executive compensation with the total assets of the firm and the firm's industry. Dummy variables are used to represent four industries: Manufacturing

Technology d_1, Manufacturing Other d_2, Financial Services d_3, and Nonfinancial Services d_4. A portion of the data for 455 highest-paid CEOs in 2006 is given in the accompanying table; the complete data, labeled **Industry Compensation**, are available on the text website.

Compensation (in $ million)	Assets (in $ millions)	d_1	d_2	d_3	d_4
16.58	20,917.5	1	0	0	0
26.92	32,659.5	1	0	0	0
⋮	⋮	⋮	⋮	⋮	⋮
2.30	44,875.0	0	0	1	0

Source: SEC website and Compustat.

a. Estimate the model: $\ln(y) = \beta_0 + \beta_1 \ln(x) + \beta_2 d_1 + \beta_3 d_2 + \beta_4 d_3 + \varepsilon$, where $\ln(y)$ and $\ln(x)$ denote the log of compensation and the log of total assets, respectively. The nonfinancial services industry dummy d_4 is used for reference.

b. Interpret the estimated coefficients.

c. Use a 5% level of significance to determine which industries, relative to the nonfinancial services industry, have a different executive compensation.

d. Use the partial F test to determine if the three industry dummy variables used in the model are jointly significant at the 5% level.

17.2 Interactions with Dummy Variables

So far we have used a dummy variable d to allow for a shift in the intercept. In other words, d allows a constant change in the estimated y for all values of x. We can also use d to create an **interaction variable**, which allows the estimated change in y to vary across the values of x. The interaction variable is a product term xd that captures the interaction between a quantitative variable x and a dummy variable d. Together, the variables d and xd allow the intercept as well as the slope of the estimated linear regression line to vary between the categories of a qualitative variable.

LO **17.3**

Use dummy variables to capture a shift of the intercept and/or slope.

Consider the following regression model:

$$y = \beta_0 + \beta_1 x + \beta_2 d + \beta_3 xd + \varepsilon.$$

We can use sample data to estimate the model as

$$\hat{y} = b_0 + b_1 x + b_2 d + b_3 xd.$$

For a given x and $d = 1$, we can compute the predicted value as

$$\hat{y} = b_0 + b_1 x + b_2 + b_3 x = (b_0 + b_2) + (b_1 + b_3)x.$$

Similarly, for $d = 0$,

$$\hat{y} = b_0 + b_1 x.$$

The use of the dummy variable d along with the interaction variable xd produces a shift in the intercept as well as the slope of the estimated regression line. Note that the estimated intercept b_0 and slope b_1 when $d = 0$ shift to $(b_0 + b_2)$ and $(b_1 + b_3)$, respectively, when $d = 1$. Figure 17.2 shows a shift in the intercept and the slope of the estimated regression line when $d = 0$ changes to $d = 1$, given $b_2 > 0$ and $b_3 > 0$.

FIGURE 17.2 Using d and xd for intercept and slope shifts

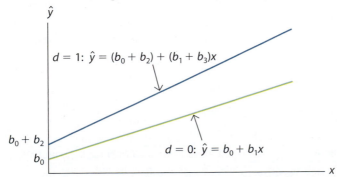

$d = 1$: $\hat{y} = (b_0 + b_2) + (b_1 + b_3)x$

$b_0 + b_2$
b_0

$d = 0$: $\hat{y} = b_0 + b_1 x$

Note that we have to use sample data to generate two variables, d and xd, to capture the change in the intercept and the slope, respectively. We simply use these variables along with other explanatory variables in the regression. Tests of significance are performed as before.

> ### TESTING THE SIGNIFICANCE OF DUMMY AND INTERACTION VARIABLES
>
> In a model $y = \beta_0 + \beta_1 x + \beta_2 d + \beta_3 xd + \varepsilon$, we can perform t tests for the individual significance of the dummy d and the interaction xd. Similarly, we can perform the partial F test for the joint significance of d and xd.

EXAMPLE 17.4

In Section 17.1 we estimated a regression model that tested for gender and age discrimination in salaries. We found that the number of years of experience x and the gender dummy d_1 were significant in explaining salary differences; however, the age dummy d_2 was insignificant. In an attempt to refine the model explaining salary, we drop d_2 and estimate three models using the data from Table 17.1, where y represents annual salary (in \$1,000s).

$$\text{Model 1. } y = \beta_0 + \beta_1 x + \beta_2 d_1 + \varepsilon$$
$$\text{Model 2. } y = \beta_0 + \beta_1 x + \beta_2 xd_1 + \varepsilon$$
$$\text{Model 3. } y = \beta_0 + \beta_1 x + \beta_2 d_1 + \beta_3 xd_1 + \varepsilon$$

a. Estimate and interpret each of the above three models.

b. Select the most appropriate model, based on an objective model selection criterion.

c. Use the selected model to predict salaries for males and females over various years of experience.

SOLUTION:

a. In order to estimate the three models, we first generate data on both d_1 and xd_1; Table 17.6 shows a portion of the data.

TABLE 17.6 Generating d_1 and xd_1 from the Data in Table 17.1

y	x	d_1	xd_1
67.50	14	1	$14 \times 1 = 14$
53.51	6	1	$6 \times 1 = 6$
⋮	⋮	⋮	⋮
73.06	35	0	$35 \times 0 = 0$

The relevant portion of the regression results is shown in Table 17.7.

TABLE 17.7 Summary of Model Estimates

	Model 1	Model 2	Model 3
Intercept	39.43*	47.07*	49.42*
	(0.00)	(0.00)	(0.00)
Experience x	1.24*	0.85*	0.76*
	(0.00)	(0.00)	(0.00)
Gender Dummy d_1	13.89*	NA	−4.00
	(0.01)		(0.42)
Interaction Variable xd_1	NA	0.77*	0.93*
		(0.00)	(0.00)
Adjusted R^2	0.7031	0.7923	0.7905

NOTES: The top portion of the table contains parameter estimates with p-values in parentheses; NA denotes not applicable; * represents significance at the 5% level; Adjusted R^2, reported in the last row, is used for model selection.

Model 1 uses a gender dummy variable d_1 to allow salaries between males and females to differ by a fixed amount, irrespective of experience. It is estimated as $\hat{y} = 39.43 + 1.24x + 13.89d_1$. Since d_1 is associated with a p-value of 0.01, we conclude at the 5% level that d_1 has a statistically significant influence on salary. The estimated model implies that, on average, males earn \$13,890 ($13.89 \times 1,000$) more than females at all levels of experience.

Model 2 uses an interaction variable xd_1 to allow the difference in salaries between males and females to change with experience. It is estimated as $\hat{y} = 47.07 + 0.85x + 0.77xd_1$. Since xd_1 is associated with a p-value ≈ 0.00, we conclude that it is statistically significant at the 5% level. With every extra year of experience, the estimated difference in salaries between males and females increases by \$770 ($0.77 \times 1,000$).

Model 3 uses d_1 along with xd_1 to allow a fixed as well as a changing difference in salaries between males and females. The estimated regression equation is $\hat{y} = 49.42 + 0.76x - 4.00d_1 + 0.93xd_1$. Interestingly, the variable d_1 is no longer statistically significant at the 5% level with a p-value of 0.42. However, the variable xd_1 is significant, suggesting that with every extra year of experience, the estimated difference in salaries between males and females increases by \$930 ($0.93 \times 1,000$).

b. While Model 1 shows that the gender variable d_1 is significant and Model 2 shows that the interaction variable xd_1 is significant, Model 3 provides somewhat conflicting results. This raises an important question: which model should we trust? It is not uncommon to contend with such scenarios in business applications. As discussed in Chapter 14, we usually rely on adjusted R^2 to compare models that have a different number of explanatory variables. Based on the adjusted R^2 values of the models, reported in the last row of Table 17.7, we select Model 2 as the preferred model because it has the highest value of 0.7923.

c. In order to interpret the results further, we use Model 2 to estimate salaries with varying levels of experience, for both males and females. For example, with 10 years of experience, the predicted salary for males ($d_1 = 1$) is

$$\hat{y} = 47.07 + 0.85(10) + 0.77(10 \times 1) = 63.27, \text{ or } \$63,270.$$

The corresponding predicted salary for females ($d_1 = 0$) is

$$\hat{y} = 47.07 + 0.85(10) + 0.77(10 \times 0) = 55.57, \text{ or } \$55,570.$$

Therefore, with 10 years of experience, the salary difference between males and females is about \$7,700. Predicted salaries at other levels of experience are presented in Table 17.8.

TABLE 17.8 Estimated Salaries at Various Levels of Experience

Experience	Males	Females	Difference
1	\$48,690	\$47,920	\$770
2	50,310	48,770	1,540
3	51,930	49,620	2,310
4	53,550	50,470	3,080
5	55,170	51,320	3,850
10	63,270	55,570	7,700
15	71,370	59,820	11,550
20	79,470	64,070	15,400
25	87,570	68,320	19,250
30	95,670	72,570	23,100

Note that as experience increases, the salary difference between males and females becomes wider. For instance, the difference is $7,700 with 10 years of experience, which increases to $19,250 with 25 years of experience. This is consistent with the inclusion of the interaction variable in Model 2.

The shift in the slope, implied by the predicted salaries in Table 17.8, is shown in Figure 17.3.

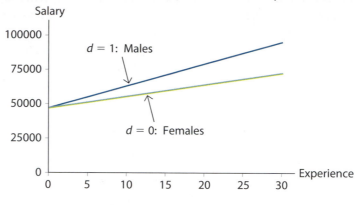

FIGURE 17.3 Predicted salaries of male and female professors

SYNOPSIS OF INTRODUCTORY CASE

A recent lawsuit brought against Seton Hall University by three female professors alleges that the university engages in both age and gender discrimination with respect to salaries (www.nj.com, November 23, 2010). Another large university wonders if the same can be said about its practices. Information is collected on the annual salaries (in $1,000s) of 42 professors, along with their experience (in years), gender (male or female), and age (whether he/she is 60 years old or older). A regression of salary against experience, a gender dummy variable, and an age dummy variable reveals that gender discrimination exists, while age discrimination does not seem to be a problem.

In an attempt to refine the model describing salary, various models are estimated that remove the age dummy variable, but use the gender dummy variable to allow both fixed and changing effects on salary. The sample regression line that best fits the data does not include the gender dummy for a fixed effect. However, the interaction variable, defined as a product of gender and experience, is significant at any reasonable level, implying that males make about $770 more than females for every year of experience. While the estimated difference in salaries between males and females is only $770 with 1 year of experience, the difference increases to $19,250 with 25 years of experience. In sum, the findings suggest that there is gender discrimination with the salary difference between males and females increasing with experience.

Concepts

13. Consider a linear regression model where y represents the response variable and x and d are the explanatory variables; d is a dummy variable assuming values 0 or 1. A model with the dummy d and the interaction xd variables is estimated as $\hat{y} = 5.2 + 0.9x + 1.4d + 0.2xd$.

   a. Compute $\hat{y}$ for $x = 10$ and $d = 1$.

   b. Compute $\hat{y}$ for $x = 10$ and $d = 0$.

14. Using 20 observations, the following regression output is obtained from estimating $y = \beta_0 + \beta_1 x + \beta_2 d + \beta_3 xd + \varepsilon$.

	Coefficients	Standard Error	t Stat	p-value
Intercept	13.56	3.31	4.09	0.0009
x	4.62	0.56	8.31	0.0000
d	−5.15	4.97	−1.04	0.3156
xd	2.09	0.79	2.64	0.0178

   a. Compute $\hat{y}$ for $x = 10$ and $d = 1$; then compute $\hat{y}$ for $x = 10$ and $d = 0$.

   b. Are the dummy d and the interaction xd variables individually significant at the 5% level? Explain.

Applications

15. House price y is estimated as a function of the square footage of a house x; a dummy variable d that equals 1 if the house has ocean views and 0 otherwise; and a product of this dummy and the square footage xd. The estimated house price, measured in $1,000s, is given by $\hat{y} = 80 + 0.12x + 40d + 0.01xd$.

   a. Compute the predicted price of a house with ocean views and square footage of 2,000 and 3,000, respectively.

   b. Compute the predicted price of a house without ocean views and square footage of 2,000 and 3,000, respectively.

   c. Discuss the impact of ocean views on the house price.

16. **FILE** A sociologist is looking at the relationship between consumption expenditures y of families in the United States, family income x, and whether or not the family lives in an urban or rural community (Urban = 1 if urban, 0 otherwise). She collects data on 50 families across the United States, a portion of which is shown in the accompanying table. The full data set can be found on the text website, labeled **Urban**.

Consumption ($)	Income ($)	Urban
62336	87534	0
60076	94796	1
⋮	⋮	⋮
59055	100908	1

   a. Estimate a linear model without a dummy, $y = \beta_0 + \beta_1 x + \varepsilon$. Compute the predicted consumption expenditures of a family with income of $75,000.

   b. Include a dummy d to predict consumption for Income = $75,000 in urban and rural communities.

   c. Include a dummy d and an interaction xd variable to predict consumption for Income = $75,000 in urban and rural communities.

   d. Which of the above models is most suitable for the data? Explain.

17. **FILE** According to the *World Health Organization,* obesity has reached epidemic proportions globally. While obesity has generally been linked with chronic disease and disability, researchers argue that it may also affect wages. In other words, the body mass index (BMI) of an employee is a predictor for salary. (A person is considered overweight if his/her BMI is at least 25 and obese if BMI exceeds 30.) Consider salary data (in $1,000s) of 30 college-educated men with their respective BMI and a race dummy that represents 1 for white and 0 otherwise. A portion of the data is shown in the accompanying table; the complete data set can be found on the text website, labeled **BMI**.

Salary	BMI	White
34	33	1
43	26	1
⋮	⋮	⋮
45	21	1

   a. Estimate a model for Salary with BMI and White as the explanatory variables. What is the estimated salary of a white college-educated worker with a BMI of 30? Compute the corresponding salary of a nonwhite worker.

   b. Re-estimate the model with BMI, White, and a product of BMI and White as the explanatory variables. What is the estimated salary of a white college-educated worker with a BMI of 30? Compute the corresponding salary of a nonwhite worker.

18. **FILE** One of the theories regarding initial public offering (IPO) pricing is that the initial return (change from offer to open price) on an IPO depends on the price revision (change from pre-offer to offer price). Another factor that may influence the initial return is a high-tech dummy that equals 1 for high-tech firms and 0 otherwise. Consider the data on 264 IPO firms from January 2001 through September 2004; the complete data, labeled **IPO**, is available on the text website.

Initial Return (%)	Price Revision (%)	High-tech Dummy
33.93	7.14	0
18.68	−26.39	0
⋮	⋮	⋮
0.08	−29.41	1

SOURCE: www.ipohome.com, www.nasdaq.com.

a. Estimate a model with the initial return as the response variable and the price revision and the high-tech dummy as the explanatory variables.

b. Re-estimate the model with price revision along with the dummy and the product of the dummy and price revision.

c. Which of these models is the preferred model? Explain.

19. **FILE** The savings rate has declined dramatically over the past few decades (CNNMoney.com, June 30, 2010). While some economists are extremely concerned about this decline, others believe that it is a nonissue. Consider the following monthly data on the personal savings rate (Savings) and the personal disposable income (Income) in the U.S. from January 2007 to November 2010; the complete data set, labeled **Savings Rate**, can be found on the text website.

Date	Savings (%)	Income ($ billions)
2007–01	2.2	10198.2
2007–02	2.3	10252.9
⋮	⋮	⋮
2010–11	5.5	11511.9

SOURCE: Bureau of Economic Analysis.

a. Estimate and interpret a log-log model, $\ln(\text{Savings}) = \beta_0 + \beta_1 \ln(\text{Income}) + \varepsilon$. What is the predicted percentage change in savings when personal disposable income increases by 1%?

b. Suppose we want to test whether or not there has been a structural shift due to the financial crisis that erupted in the fall of 2008. Consider a dummy variable d that assumes a value 0 before August 2008 and a value of 1 starting August 2008 onwards. Estimate: $\ln(\text{Savings}) = \beta_0 + \beta_1 \ln(\text{Income}) + \beta_2 d + \beta_3 \ln(\text{Income}) \times d + \varepsilon$. What is the predicted percentage change in savings when personal disposable income increases by 1% prior to August 2008? What is the predicted percentage change starting in August 2008 onward?

c. At the 5% significance level, conduct the partial F test to determine whether or not β_2 and β_3 are jointly significant. Has there been a structural shift?

17.3 Binary Choice Models

We have been considering models where dummy (binary) variables are used as explanatory variables. In numerous applications, however, the variable of interest—the response variable—is binary. The consumer choice literature is replete with applications such as whether or not to buy a house, join a health club, or go to graduate school. At the firm level, managers make decisions such as whether or not to distribute dividends, hire people, or launch a new product. In all such applications the response variable is binary, where one of the choices can be designated as 1 and the other as 0. Usually, this choice can be related to a host of factors—the explanatory variables. For instance, whether or not a family buys a house depends on variables such as household income, mortgage rates, and so on.

> **BINARY CHOICE MODELS**
>
> Regression models that use a dummy (binary) variable as the response variable are called **binary choice** models. They are also referred to as **discrete choice** models or **qualitative response** models.

LO 17.4

Use a linear probability model to estimate a binary response variable.

The Linear Probability Model

Consider a simple linear regression model $y = \beta_0 + \beta_1 x + \varepsilon$ where y is a binary variable; we can easily extend it to include multiple explanatory variables. A linear regression model applied to a binary response variable is called a **linear probability model (LPM)**. While we know that the relationship implied by this model is linear, it may not be obvious why it is also called a probability model. Recall that in the above simple linear regression model, the expression $\beta_0 + \beta_1 x$ is its deterministic component, which is the expected value of y for a given value of x. In other words, conditional on x, $E(y) = \beta_0 + \beta_1 x$. Here, since y is a discrete random variable with possible values 0 and 1, its expected value conditional on x can also be computed as $E(y) = 0 \times P(y = 0) + 1 \times P(y = 1) = P(y = 1)$, where $P(y = 1)$ is often referred to as the probability of success. Therefore, $E(y) = P(y = 1) = \beta_0 + \beta_1 x$.

In other words, we can write $y = \beta_0 + \beta_1 x + \varepsilon = P(y = 1) + \varepsilon$, where $P(y = 1)$, or simply P, is a linear function of the explanatory variable.

> ### A LINEAR PROBABILITY MODEL
>
> A **linear probability model** (**LPM**) is formulated as $y = \beta_0 + \beta_1 x + \varepsilon = P(y = 1) + \varepsilon$, where y assumes a 0 or 1 value and $P(y = 1)$ is the probability of success. Predictions with this model are made by $\hat{P} = \hat{y} = b_0 + b_1 x$ where b_0 and b_1 are the estimates of the population parameters β_0 and β_1.

EXAMPLE 17.5

The subprime mortgage crisis has forced financial institutions to be extra stringent in granting mortgage loans. Many seemingly creditworthy applicants are having their loan requests denied. Thirty recent mortgage applications were obtained to analyze the mortgage approval rate. The response variable y equals 1 if the mortgage loan is approved, 0 otherwise. It is believed that approval depends on the percentage of the down payment x_1 and the percentage of income-to-loan amount x_2. Table 17.9 shows a portion of the data; the complete data set can be found on the text website, labeled **Mortgage Applications**. Estimate and interpret the linear probability model, $y = \beta_0 + \beta_1 x_1 + \beta_2 x_2 + \varepsilon$. Make predictions of the approval probability for representative applicants.

TABLE 17.9 Mortgage Application Data (Example 17.5)

FILE

Approval	Down Payment (%)	Income-to-Loan (%)
1	16.35	49.94
1	34.43	56.16
⋮	⋮	⋮
0	17.85	26.86

SOLUTION: Table 17.10 shows the relevant regression results. The estimated regression equation is $\hat{P} = \hat{y} = -0.8682 + 0.0188 x_1 + 0.0258 x_2$. Note that both explanatory variables exert a positive and statistically significant influence on loan approval at a 5% level, with p-values of 0.0120 and 0.0003, respectively. Also, $b_1 = 0.0188$ implies that a 1-percentage-point increase in down payment increases the approval probability by 0.0188, or by 1.88%. Similarly, a 1-percentage-point increase in the income-to-loan ratio increases the approval probability by 0.0258.

TABLE 17.10 LPM Model Results for Example 17.5

	Coefficients	Standard Error	t Stat	p-value
Intercept	−0.8682	0.2811	−3.0889	0.0046
Down Payment (%)	0.0188	0.0070	2.6945	0.0120
Income-to-Loan (%)	0.0258	0.0063	4.1070	0.0003

We can use this estimated model to predict the approval probability for any applicant. Consider an applicant who puts 20% down ($x_1 = 20$), has an income of $60,000 and a loan amount of $200,000 ($x_2 = (60/200) \times 100 = 30$). The predicted approval probability for this applicant is $\hat{P} = -0.8682 + 0.0188(20) + 0.0258(30) = 0.2818$. Similarly, with 30% down, $\hat{P} = -0.8682 + 0.0188(30) + 0.0258(30) = 0.4698$. In other words, as down payment increases by 10 percentage points, the predicted probability of approval increases by 0.1880 (= 0.4698 − 0.2818), which is essentially the estimated slope, 0.0188, multiplied by 10. The estimated slope coefficient for the percentage of income-to-loan variable can be analyzed similarly.

Although it is easy to estimate and interpret a linear probability model, it also has some shortcomings. The major shortcoming is that it can produce predicted probabilities that are greater than 1 or less than 0. For instance, for a down payment of 60%, with the same income-to-loan ratio of 30%, we get a predicted mortgage approval rate of $\hat{P} = -0.8682 + 0.0188(60) + 0.0258(30) = 1.0338$, a probability greater than one! Similarly, for a down payment of 5%, the model predicts a negative probability, $\hat{P} = -0.8682 + 0.0188(5) + 0.0258(30) = -0.0002$. Furthermore, the linearity of the relationship may also be questionable. For instance, we would expect a big increase in the probability of loan approval if the applicant makes a down payment of 30% instead of 20%. This increase in probability is likely to be much smaller if the same 10-percentage-point increase in down payment is from 60 to 70 percent. An LPM cannot differentiate between these two scenarios. For these reasons, we introduce a more appropriate probability model for binary choice variables.

LO **17.5**

Interpret the results from a logit model.

The Logit Model

Let's again consider a model with a single explanatory variable, which we will later extend to include multiple variables. An LPM, $y = \beta_0 + \beta_1 x + \varepsilon$, uses $P = \beta_0 + \beta_1 x$. Here, the marginal contribution of x on P, denoted by the slope β_1, is constant. In addition, there is always some value of the explanatory variable x for which the predicted probability is outside the $[0,1]$ interval. We basically want a nonlinear specification that also ensures that the predicted probability is constrained between 0 and 1.

Consider the specification

$$P = \frac{\exp(\beta_0 + \beta_1 x)}{1 + \exp(\beta_0 + \beta_1 x)},$$

where $\exp(\beta_0 + \beta_1 x) = e^{\beta_0 + \beta_1 x}$ and $e \approx 2.718$. This nonlinear specification ensures that the probability is between 0 and 1, for all values of x. The above function is the cumulative distribution function of the so-called logistic distribution. Thus, the resulting regression model is called a logistic model, or simply a **logit model**.

The logit model cannot be estimated with standard OLS procedures. Instead, we rely on the method of **maximum likelihood estimation (MLE)** to estimate a logit model. While the MLE of the logit model is not supported by Excel, it can easily be estimated with most statistical packages, including Minitab, JMP, and SPSS. The theory of MLE is beyond the scope of this book; however, given the relevance of the logit model in numerous business applications, it is important to be able to estimate and interpret it.

> **THE LOGIT MODEL**
>
> The **logit model** is estimated with the method of maximum likelihood estimation (MLE). Predictions with this model are made by
>
> $$\hat{P} = \frac{\exp(b_0 + b_1 x)}{1 + \exp(b_0 + b_1 x)},$$
>
> where b_0 and b_1 are the MLE estimates of the population parameters β_0 and β_1.

Figure 17.4 highlights the relationship between the predicted probability $\hat{P}$ and the explanatory variable x for an LPM and a logit probability model, given $b_1 > 0$. Note that in an LPM, the probability falls below 0 for small values of x and exceeds 1 for large values of x. The probabilities implied by a logit model, however, are always constrained in the $[0,1]$ interval. (For ease of exposition, we use the same notation to refer to the coefficients in the LPM and logit model. We note, however, that these coefficients and their estimates have a different meaning depending on which model we are referencing.)

FIGURE 17.4 Predicted probabilities with an LPM and a logit model

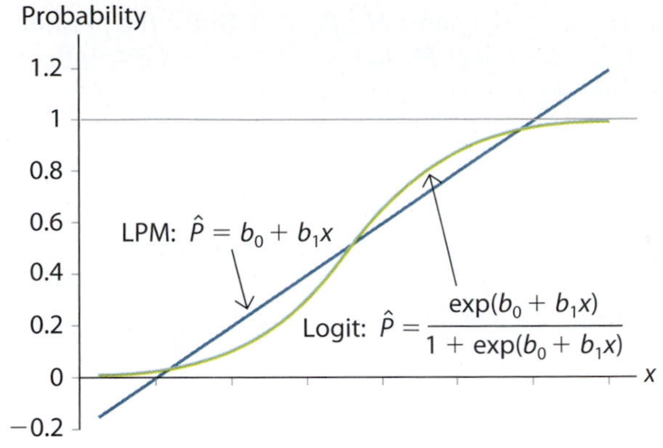

It is important to be able to interpret the regression coefficients of a logit model. In an LPM, the interpretation of a regression coefficient is obvious. For instance, if the estimated LPM is $\hat{P} = -0.20 + 0.03x$, it implies that for every 1-unit increase in x, the predicted probability $\hat{P}$ increases by 0.03. We note that $\hat{P}$ increases by 0.03, whether x increases from 10 to 11 or from 20 to 21.

Now consider the estimated logit model, $\hat{P} = \dfrac{\exp(-2.10 + 0.18x)}{1 + \exp(-2.10 + 0.18x)}$. Since the regression coefficient $b_1 = 0.18$ is positive, we can infer that x exerts a positive influence on $\hat{P}$. However, the exact impact based on the estimated regression coefficient is not obvious. A useful method to interpret the regression coefficient of the estimated logit model is to highlight the changing impact of x on $\hat{P}$. For instance, given $x = 10$, we can compute the predicted probability as $\hat{P} = \dfrac{\exp(-2.10 + 0.18 \times 10)}{1 + \exp(-2.10 + 0.18 \times 10)} = 0.43$. Similarly, for $x = 11$, the predicted probability is $\hat{P} = 0.47$. Therefore, as x increases by one unit from 10 to 11, the predicted probability increases by 0.04. However, the increase in $\hat{P}$ will not be the same if x increases from 20 to 21. We can show that $\hat{P}$ increases from 0.82 when $x = 20$ to 0.84 when $x = 21$, for a smaller increase of 0.02.

EXAMPLE 17.6

There is a declining interest among teenagers in pursuing a career in science and health care (*US News and World Report*, May 23, 2011). In a recent survey, 50% of high school students showed no interest in the sciences. An educator wants to determine if a student's interest in the sciences is linked with the student's GPA. She estimates a logit model where the choice of field (1 for choosing science, 0 otherwise) depends on the student's GPA. She uses Minitab to produce the logit regression results shown in Table 17.11. (Instructions for Minitab as well as other software packages can be found on the text website.)

TABLE 17.11 Logit Regression Results for Example 17.6

Predictor	Coef	SE	z	P
Constant	−4.4836	1.5258	−2.938	0.0033
GPA	1.5448	0.4774	3.236	0.0012

a. Use a 5% level of significance to determine if GPA has a statistically significant influence on the probability of pursuing a career in science and health care.

b. Compute and interpret the probability that a student will pursue a career in science and health care given a GPA of 3.0, 3.5, and 4.0.

SOLUTION:

a. In order to determine the significance of GPA, we specify the competing hypotheses as $H_0: \beta_1 = 0$ against $H_A: \beta_1 \neq 0$. Since the p-value $= 0.0012$ is less than $\alpha = 0.05$, we reject H_0 and conclude that GPA influences the probability that a student pursues a career in science and health care. (In maximum likelihood estimation, the significance tests are valid only with large samples. Consequently, we conduct the z test, in place of the usual t test, to evaluate the statistical significance of a coefficient.)

b. Since the estimated regression coefficient for GPA is positive ($b_1 = 1.5448$), it suggests that GPA exerts a positive influence on the predicted probability of pursuing a career in science and health care. For a student with a GPA $= 3.0$, we compute the predicted probability as

$$\hat{P} = \frac{\exp(-4.4836 + 1.5448 \times 3.0)}{1 + \exp(-4.4836 + 1.5448 \times 3.0)} = 0.54.$$

Similarly, we compute the predicted probabilities for a student with GPA $= 3.5$ and GPA $= 4.0$ as 0.72 and 0.84, respectively. Note that the predicted probability increases by $0.18 (= 0.72 - 0.54)$ as GPA increases from 3.0 to 3.5. The increase is only $0.12 (= 0.84 - 0.72)$ when GPA increases from 3.5 and 4.0.

FILE EXAMPLE 17.7

Let us revisit Example 17.5, based on the **Mortgage Applications** data, a portion of which was presented in Table 17.9. Estimate and interpret a logit model for mortgage approval y based on the applicant's percentage of down payment x_1 and the applicant's percentage of income-to-loan ratio x_2. Make predictions of the approval probability for representative applicants. Compare the results of the logit model with those of the LPM.

SOLUTION: We again use Minitab to estimate the logit model; Table 17.12 shows a portion of the output.

TABLE 17.12 Logit Regression Results for Example 17.7

Predictor	Coef	SE	z	P
Constant	−9.3671	3.1960	−2.9309	0.0034
Down Payment (%)	0.1349	0.0640	2.1074	0.0351
Income to Loan (%)	0.1782	0.0646	2.7577	0.0058

The estimated probability equation is computed as

$$\hat{P} = \frac{\exp(-9.3671 + 0.1349x_1 + 0.1782x_2)}{1 + \exp(-9.3671 + 0.1349x_1 + 0.1782x_2)}.$$

As in the case of the linear probability model, both variables exert a positive and statistically significant influence on loan approval at a 5% level, with positive estimated coefficients and p-values of 0.0351 and 0.0058, respectively.

We can use the estimated model to predict approval probabilities for any applicant. For instance, for an individual with $x_1 = 20$ and $x_2 = 30$, the predicted approval probability is

$$\hat{P} = \frac{\exp(-9.3671 + 0.1349 \times 20 + 0.1782 \times 30)}{1 + \exp(-9.3671 + 0.1349 \times 20 + 0.1782 \times 30)} = 0.2103.$$

Table 17.13 provides predicted probabilities based on the LPM, estimated in Example 17.5, and the above logit model for selected values of x_1 given $x_2 = 30$.

TABLE 17.13 Predicted Probabilities with a LPM versus a Logit Model

Down Payment (%) x_1	Income to Loan Amount (%) x_2	LPM	Logit Model
5	30	−0.0002	0.0340
20	30	0.2818	0.2103
30	30	0.4698	0.5065
60	30	1.0338	0.9833

As discussed earlier, with a linear probability model, the predicted probabilities can be negative or greater than one. The probabilities based on a logit model always stay between zero and one for all possible values of the explanatory variables. Therefore, whenever possible, it is preferable to use the logit model over the LPM for binary choice models.

EXERCISES 17.3

Concepts

20. Consider a binary response variable y and an explanatory variable x that varies between 0 to 50. The linear probability model is estimated as $\hat{y} = 0.92 - 0.02x$.

a. Compute the estimated probability for $x = 25$ and $x = 40$.

b. For what values of x is the estimated probability negative?

21. Consider a binary response variable y and an explanatory variable x. The following table contains the parameter estimates of the linear probability model (LPM) and the logit model, with the associated p-values shown in parentheses.

Variable	LPM	Logit
Constant	−0.72 (0.04)	−6.2 (0.04)
x	0.05 (0.06)	0.26 (0.02)

a. Test for the significance of the intercept and the slope coefficients at a 5% level in both models.

b. What is the predicted probability implied by the linear probability model for $x = 20$ and $x = 30$?

c. What is the predicted probability implied by the logit model for $x = 20$ and $x = 30$?

22. Consider a binary response variable y and an explanatory variable x. The following table contains the parameter estimates of the linear probability model (LPM) and the logit model, with the associated p-values shown in parentheses.

Variable	LPM	Logit
Constant	−0.40 (0.03)	−4.50 (0.01)
x	0.32 (0.04)	1.54 (0.03)

a. Use both models to predict the probability of success as x varies from 1 to 5 with increments of 1.

b. Comment on the suitability of the linear probability model in modeling binary outcomes.

23. Consider a binary response variable y and two explanatory variables x_1 and x_2. The following table contains the parameter estimates of the linear probability model (LPM) and the logit model, with the associated p-values shown in parentheses.

Variable	LPM	Logit
Constant	−0.40 (0.03)	−2.20 (0.01)
x_1	0.32 (0.04)	0.98 (0.06)
x_2	−0.04 (0.01)	−0.20 (0.01)

a. Comment on the significance of the variables.

b. What is the predicted probability implied by the linear probability model for $x_1 = 4$ with x_2 equal to 10 and 20?

c. What is the predicted probability implied by the logit model for $x_1 = 4$ with x_2 equal to 10 and 20?

24. Using 30 observations, the following regression output is obtained from estimating the linear probability model $y = \beta_0 + \beta_1 x + \varepsilon$.

	Coefficients	Standard Error	t Stat	p-value
Intercept	1.31	0.31	4.17	0.0002
x	−0.04	0.01	−2.67	0.0125

a. What is the predicted probability when $x = 20$?

b. Is x significant at the 5% level?

25. Using 30 observations, the following output was obtained when estimating the logit model.

Predictor	Coef	SE	Z	P
Constant	−0.188	0.083	2.27	0.024
x	3.852	1.771	2.18	0.030

a. What is the predicted probability when $x = 0.40$?

b. Is x significant at the 5% level?

26. Using 40 observations, the following output was obtained when estimating the logit model.

Predictor	Coef	SE	Z	P
Constant	1.609	1.405	1.145	0.252
x_1	−0.194	0.143	−1.357	0.177
x_2	0.202	0.215	0.940	0.348
x_3	0.223	0.086	2.593	0.010

a. What is the predicted probability when $x_1 = 15$, $x_2 = 10$, and $x_3 = -2$?

b. At the 5% significance level, which of the explanatory variables are significant?

Applications

27. **FILE** Annabel, a retail analyst, has been following Under Armour, Inc., the pioneer in the compression-gear market. Compression garments are meant to keep moisture away from a wearer's body during athletic activities in warm and cool weather. Annabel believes that the Under Armour brand attracts a younger customer, whereas the more established companies, Nike and Adidas, draw an older clientele. In order to test her belief, she collects data on the age of the customers and whether or not they purchased Under Armour (1 for Under Armour, 0 otherwise). A portion of the data is shown in the accompanying table; the complete data set is found on the text website, labeled **Purchase**.

Under Armour	Age
1	30
0	19
⋮	⋮
1	24

a. Estimate a linear probability model using Under Armour as the response variable and age as the explanatory variable.

b. Compute the predicted probability of an Under Armour purchase for a 20-year-old customer and a 30-year-old customer.

c. Test Annabel's belief that the Under Armour brand attracts a younger customer at the 5% level.

28. **FILE** Use the above data labeled **Purchase** to estimate a logit model.

a. Compute the predicted probability of an Under Armour purchase for a 20-year-old customer and a 30-year-old customer.

b. Test Annabel's belief that the Under Armour brand attracts a younger customer at the 5% level.

29. **FILE** According to the National Coalition on Health Care, there has been a steady decline in the proportion of Americans who have health insurance. The rising insurance premiums have made it difficult for small employers to offer insurance and those that do offer insurance are contributing a smaller share of the premium. As a result, an increasing number of Americans do not have health insurance because they cannot afford it. Consider a portion of data in the following table relating to insurance coverage (1 for coverage, 0 for no coverage) for 30 working individuals in Atlanta, Georgia. Also included in the table is the percentage of the premium paid by the employer

and the individual's income (in $1,000s). The complete data set can be found on the text website, labeled **Health Insurance**.

Insurance	Premium Percentage (in %)	Income (in $1,000s)
1	0	88
0	0	60
⋮	⋮	⋮
0	60	60

a. Analyze a linear probability model for insurance coverage with premium percentage and income used as the explanatory variables.

b. Consider an individual with an income of $60,000. What is the probability that she has insurance coverage if her employer contributes 50% of the premium? What if the employer contributes 75% of the premium?

30. **FILE** Analyze a logit model with the above **Health Insurance** data. Consider an individual with an income of $60,000. What is the probability that she has insurance coverage if her employer contributes 50% of the premium? What if the employer contributes 75% of the premium?

31. **FILE** According to a recent estimate, the divorce rate in England has fallen to a 26-year low (*The Guardian*, August 29, 2008). However, it is documented that the rate of divorce is more than twice as high for men and women aged 25 to 29. John Haddock is a sociologist from Sussex University who wants to analyze the divorce rate based on the individual's age, family income, and the number of children that the couple has. He collects data on 30 individuals in a small town near Brighton, a portion of which is shown in the accompanying table; the complete data set can be found on the text website, labeled **Divorce**.

Divorce	Age	Income (in £1,000s)	Children
0	1	19	3
0	0	46	3
⋮	⋮	⋮	⋮
0	0	26	0

a. Estimate and interpret a linear probability model where divorce (1 for divorce; 0 otherwise) depends on age (1 if 25–29 years old; 0 otherwise), family income (in £1,000s), and the number of children.

b. Do the data support the article's claim that the divorce rate is higher for those aged 25–29 years old? Explain.

c. Use the above estimates to predict the probability of divorce for an individual who is 27 years old, has £60,000 of family income and one child. Recalculate the probability with three children.

32. **FILE** Estimate and interpret the logit model with the above **Divorce** data.

a. Do the data support the article's claim that the divorce rate is higher for those aged 25–29 years old? Explain.

b. Use the above estimates to predict the probability of divorce for an individual who is 27 years old, has £60,000 of family income, and one child. Recalculate the probability with three children.

WRITING WITH STATISTICS

During the 2009–2010 NBA season, the Los Angeles Lakers had the highest offensive production throughout the league. Led by Kobe Bryant, the Lakers beat the Boston Celtics in game seven of the championships for the 2010 NBA title. Jaqueline Thomsen, an amateur statistician, would like to examine the factors that led to the Lakers' success. Specifically, Jaqueline wishes to predict the likelihood of a Lakers' win as a function of field goal percentage (FG), rebounds (Rebounds), and turnovers (Turnovers). The probability of winning should be positively influenced by FG and Rebounds, but negatively affected by Turnovers. In addition, she wonders whether playing at home significantly influences the team's chances of winning. Table 17.14 shows a portion of data on the Lakers' 82-game regular season; the complete data set can be found on the text website, labeled **Lakers**.

TABLE 17.14 Statistics on the Los Angeles Lakers 2009–2010 Regular Season

Game	Win/Loss	FG %	Rebounds	Turnovers	Home/Away	FILE
1	Win	41.2	47	16	Home	
2	Loss	39.5	40	19	Home	
⋮	⋮	⋮	⋮	⋮	⋮	
82	Loss	39.5	49	14	Away	

Source: www.nba.com.

Jaqueline would like to use the above sample information to:

1. Choose an appropriate model to predict the probability of winning.
2. Determine whether there is a home court advantage.
3. Predict the probability of winning if the Lakers are playing at home or away, with average values of FG, Rebounds, and Turnovers.

Sample Report— Predicting the Probability of Winning

With the highest offensive production throughout the league during the 2009–2010 season, it is not surprising that the Los Angeles Lakers won the 2010 NBA championship. Other teams might benefit if they could unravel the factors that led to the Lakers' success. In an attempt to examine the factors that influence a team's chances of winning, regression analysis is conducted on the Lakers' 82-game regular season. The response variable is Win (equals 1 for a win, 0 otherwise) and the explanatory variables include:

- The team's field goal percentage (FG),
- The number of rebounds,
- The number of turnovers, and
- A "home" dummy that equals 1 for a home game and 0 otherwise.

The probability of winning should be positively influenced by FG and rebounds, but negatively affected by turnovers. In addition, if there truly is a home court advantage, then playing at home should positively influence the team's chances of winning.

Two models are evaluated that link the probability of winning with the explanatory variables: the linear probability model and the logit model. The parameter estimates of both models are shown in Table 17.A.

TABLE 17.A Regression Results of the Linear Probability Model and the Logit Model

Response Variable: Win (equals 1 if Lakers win, 0 otherwise)		
	LPM	Logit
Constant	−2.391*	−28.76*
	(0.00)	(0.00)
FG	0.047*	0.49*
	(0.00)	(0.00)
Rebounds	0.019*	0.17*
	(0.00)	(0.02)
Turnovers	−0.004	−0.04
	(0.68)	(0.71)
Home	0.232*	1.82*
	(0.01)	(0.02)

NOTES: Parameter estimates of both models are presented with *p*-values in parentheses; *represents significance at the 5% level.

Estimation of the linear probability model generated a sample regression line of $\widehat{Win} = -2.391 + 0.047FG + 0.019Rebounds - 0.004Turnovers + 0.232Home$. All signs on the slope coefficients are as expected; that is, the field goal percentage, the number of rebounds, and playing at home all appear to exert a positive influence on the chances of winning; the number of turnovers suggests a negative relationship with the response variable. Upon testing the explanatory variables individually, the extremely small *p*-values associated with FG, Rebounds, and Home reveal that these variables have a significant relationship with the probability of winning; Turnovers is not significant at the 5% level. The slope coefficient of Home indicates that the likelihood of winning increases by approximately 23% if the Lakers play at home. While the results of the linear probability model seem reasonable, some values of the explanatory variables may yield predicted probabilities that are either negative or greater than one. In order to avoid this possibility, the logit model is preferred.

The estimated probability equation for the logit model is computed as

$$\widehat{Win} = \frac{\exp(-28.76 + 0.49FG + 0.17Rebounds - 0.04Turnovers + 1.82Home)}{1 + \exp(-28.76 + 0.49FG + 0.17Rebounds - 0.04Turnovers + 1.82Home)}.$$

As in the case of the linear probability model, FG, Rebounds, and Home are again individually significant at the 5% level; thus, the significance of Home supports the belief of a home field advantage. Over the 82-game season, the averages for field goal percentage, the number of rebounds, and the number of turnovers were 45%, 44, and 13, respectively. If the Lakers are playing an "average" game away from home, then the model predicts a 56.2% probability of winning. However, if they are playing an "average" game at home, then their probability of winning jumps to 88.8%. In sum, the home court advantage overwhelmingly puts the likelihood of success in their favor.

Conceptual Review

LO 17.1

Use dummy variables to capture a shift of the intercept.

A **dummy variable** *d* is defined as a variable that takes on values of 0 or 1. It is used to represent two (or more) categories of a qualitative variable. The number of dummy variables for a multi-category qualitative variable should be one less than the number of categories of the variable.

A regression model with a dummy variable d, representing two categories of a qualitative variable, and a quantitative variable x is specified by $y = \beta_0 + \beta_1 x + \beta_2 d + \varepsilon$. We estimate this model to make predictions as $\hat{y} = (b_0 + b_2) + b_1 x$ for $d = 1$ and as $\hat{y} = b_0 + b_1 x$ for $d = 0$.

LO 17.2 **Test for differences between the categories of a qualitative variable.**

Using $y = \beta_0 + \beta_1 x + \beta_2 d + \varepsilon$, we can perform a standard t test to determine whether difference exists between two categories.

LO 17.3 **Use dummy variables to capture a shift of the intercept and/or slope.**

A regression model with a dummy variable d, a quantitative variable x, and an interaction variable xd is specified by $y = \beta_0 + \beta_1 x + \beta_2 d + \beta_3 xd + \varepsilon$. We estimate this model to make predictions as $\hat{y} = (b_0 + b_2) + (b_1 + b_3)x$ for $d = 1$, and as $\hat{y} = b_0 + b_1 x$ for $d = 0$. In addition, we can perform the t test to determine the significance of d or xd. Similarly, we can implement the partial F test to determine the joint significance of d and xd.

LO 17.4 **Use a linear probability model to estimate a binary response variable.**

Models that use a dummy (binary) variable as the response variable are called binary choice models. A **linear probability model** (**LPM**) is formulated as $y = \beta_0 + \beta_1 x_1 + \beta_2 x_2 + \cdots + \beta_k x_k + \varepsilon = P(y = 1) + \varepsilon$, where y assumes values of 0 or 1 and $P(y = 1)$ is the probability of success.

Predictions with this model are made by $\hat{P} = \hat{y} = b_0 + b_1 x + b_2 x_2 + \cdots + b_k x_k$, where $b_0, b_1, b_2, \ldots, b_k$ are the estimates.

The major shortcoming of the LPM is that it can produce predicted probabilities that are greater than one or less than zero.

LO 17.5 **Interpret the results from a logit model.**

A **logit model** ensures that the predicted probability of the binary response variable falls between zero and one. A logit model is estimated with the method of maximum likelihood estimation (MLE). Predictions with this model are made by $\hat{P} = \dfrac{\exp(b_0 + b_1 x_1 + b_2 x_2 + \cdots + b_k x_k)}{1 + \exp(b_0 + b_1 x_1 + b_2 x_2 + \cdots + b_k x_k)}$, where $b_0, b_1, b_2, \ldots, b_k$ are the MLE estimates.

Additional Exercises and Case Studies

Exercises

33. **FILE** A financial analyst would like to determine whether the return on Fidelity's Magellan mutual fund varies depending on the quarter; that is, if there is a seasonal component describing return. He collects 10 years of quarterly return data. A portion is shown in the accompanying table; the complete data set can be found on the text website, labeled **Magellan dummy**.

Year	Quarter	Return	d_1	d_2	d_3
2000	1	4.85	1	0	0
2000	2	−3.96	0	1	0
⋮	⋮	⋮	⋮	⋮	⋮
2009	4	4.06	0	0	0

Source: http://finance.yahoo.com.

a. Estimate $y = \beta_0 + \beta_1 d_1 + \beta_2 d_2 + \beta_3 d_3 + \varepsilon$, where y is Magellan's quarterly return, d_1 is a dummy variable that equals 1 if quarter 1 and 0 otherwise, d_2 is a dummy variable that equals 1 if quarter 2 and 0 otherwise, and d_3 is a dummy variable that equals 1 if quarter 3 and 0 otherwise.
b. Interpret the slope coefficients of the dummy variables.
c. Predict Magellan's stock return in quarters 2 and 4.

34. **FILE** In a seminal study, researchers documented race-based hiring in the Boston and Chicago labor markets (*American Economic Review*, September 2004). They sent out identical resumes to employers, half with traditionally African-American names and the other half with traditionally Caucasian names. Interestingly, there was a 53% difference in call-back rates between the two groups of people. A research fellow at

an institute in Santa Barbara decides to repeat the same experiment with names along with age in the Los Angeles labor market. She repeatedly sends out resumes for sales positions in the city that are identical except for the difference in the names and ages of the applicants. She also records the call-back rate for each candidate. The accompanying table shows a portion of data on call-back rate (%), age, and a Caucasian dummy that equals 1 for a Caucasian-sounding name; the complete data set can be found on the text website, labeled **Hiring**.

Call-back	Age	Caucasian
12	60	1
9	56	0
⋮	⋮	⋮
15	38	0

a. Estimate a linear regression model with call-back as the response variable, and age and the Caucasian dummy as the explanatory variables.
b. Compute the call-back rate for a 30-year-old applicant with a Caucasian-sounding name. What is the corresponding call-back rate for a non-Caucasian?
c. Conduct a test for race discrimination at the 5% significance level.

35. An analyst studies quarterly data on the relationship between retail sales (y, in $ millions), gross national product (x, in $ billions), and a quarterly dummy d that equals 1 if the sales are for the 4th quarter; 0 otherwise. He estimates the model $y = \beta_0 + \beta_1 x + \beta_2 d + \beta_3 xd + \varepsilon$. Relevant regression results are shown in the accompanying table.

	Coefficients	Standard Error	t Stat	p-value
Intercept	186553.3	56421.1	3.31	0.0021
x	55.0	4.6	12.08	0.0000
d	112605.8	117053.0	0.96	0.3424
xd	−4.7	9.3	−0.50	0.6178

a. Interpret the intercept dummy. Is it significant at the 5% level?
b. Interpret the interaction variable. Is it significant at the 5% level?

36. **FILE** According to the U.S. Department of Health and Human Services, African-American women have the highest rates of being overweight compared to other groups in the U.S. Individuals are considered overweight if their body mass index (BMI) is 25 or greater. Consider the following data on BMI of 120 individuals and the corresponding gender and race dummies. The complete data, labeled **Overweight**, can be found on the text website.

BMI	Female	Black
28.70	0	1
28.31	0	0
⋮	⋮	⋮
24.90	0	1

NOTE: Female = 1 for females and 0 for males; Black = 1 for African Americans and 0 otherwise.

a. Estimate the model, BMI $= \beta_0 + \beta_1$Female $+ \beta_2$Black $+ \beta_3$(Female $\times$ Black) $+ \varepsilon$, to predict the BMI for white males, white females, black males, and black females.
b. Is the difference between white females and white males statistically significant at the 5% level?
c. Is the difference between white males and black males statistically significant at the 5% level?

37. **FILE** According to the Center for Disease Control and Prevention, life expectancy at age 65 in America is about 18.7 years. Medical researchers have argued that while excessive drinking is detrimental to health, drinking a little alcohol every day, especially wine, may be associated with an increase in life expectancy. Others have also linked longevity with income and gender. The accompanying table shows a portion of data relating to the length of life after 65, average income (in $1,000s) at a retirement age of 65, a "woman" dummy, and the average number of alcoholic drinks consumed per day. The full data set can be found on the text website, labeled **Longevity**.

Life	Income (in $1,000)	Woman	Drinks
19.00	64	0	1
19.30	43	1	3
⋮	⋮	⋮	⋮
20.24	36	1	0

a. Use the data to model life expectancy at 65 on the basis of Income, Woman, and Drinks.
b. Conduct a one-tailed test at $\alpha = 0.01$ to determine if women live longer than men.
c. Estimate the life expectancy at 65 of a man with an income of $40,000 and an alcoholic consumption of two drinks per day; repeat the prediction for a woman.

38. **FILE** Seton Hall University is a Roman Catholic university situated in New Jersey, with easy access to New York City. Like most universities, it uses SAT scores and high school GPA as primary criteria for admission. The accompanying table shows a portion of data concerning information on admission (1 for admission and 0 otherwise), SAT score, and GPA for 30 students who had recently applied to Seton Hall; the full data set can be found on the text website, labeled **Seton Hall**.

Admission	SAT	GPA
1	1700	3.39
1	2020	2.65
⋮	⋮	⋮
0	1300	2.47

a. Estimate the linear probability model where admission depends on the SAT score and high school GPA. Analyze the significance of the variables at the 5% level.
b. Use these estimates to predict the probability of admission for an individual with a GPA of 3.5 and a SAT score of 1700.
c. Re-estimate the probabilities with a SAT score of 1800.

39. FILE Use the **Seton Hall** data to estimate the logit model.

   a. Analyze the significance of the variables at the 5% level.

   b. Use the above estimates to predict the probability of admission for an individual with a GPA of 3.5 and a SAT score of 1700.

   c. Re-estimate the probabilities with a SAT score of 1800.

40. FILE More and more parole boards are using risk assessment tools when trying to determine an individual's likelihood of returning to crime (*The Boston Globe*, February 20, 2011). Most of these models are based on a range of character traits and biographical facts about an individual. Many studies have found that older people are less likely to re-offend than younger ones. In addition, once released on parole, women are not likely to re-offend. A sociologist collects data on 20 individuals who were released on parole two years ago. She notes if he/she committed another crime over the last two years (crime equals 1 if crime committed, 0 otherwise), the individual's age at the time of release, and the gender of the individual (gender equals 1 if male, 0 otherwise). The accompanying table shows a portion of data; the full data set can be found on the text website, labeled **Parole**.

Crime	Age	Gender
1	25	1
0	42	1
⋮	⋮	⋮
0	30	1

   a. Estimate the linear probability model where crime depends on age and gender.

   b. Are the results consistent with the claims of other studies with respect to age and gender?

   c. Predict the probability of a 25-year-old male parolee committing another crime; repeat the prediction for a 25-year-old female parolee.

41. FILE Estimate the logit model with the above **Parole** data.

   a. Are the results consistent with the claims of other studies with respect to age and gender?

   b. Predict the probability of a 25-year-old male parolee committing another crime; repeat the prediction for a 25-year-old female parolee.

CASE STUDIES

Case Study 17.1

A recent study examined "sidewalk rage" in an attempt to find insight into anger's origins and offer suggestions for anger-management treatments (*The Wall Street Journal*, February 15, 2011). "Sidewalk ragers" tend to believe that pedestrians should behave in a certain way. For instance, slower pedestrians should keep to the right or should step aside to take a picture. If pedestrians violate these "norms," then ragers feel that the "violaters" are breaking the rules of civility. Since anger is associated with a host of negative health consequences, psychologists suggest developing strategies to quell the rage. One possible strategy is to avoid slow walkers. A portion of the study looked at the average speed of walkers (feet per second) in Lower Manhattan and found that average speeds differ when the pedestrian is distracted by other activities (smoking, talking on a cell phone, tourism, etc.) or exhibits other traits (elderly, obese, etc.). Sample data were obtained from 50 pedestrians in Lower Manhattan. Each pedestrian's speed was calculated (feet per second). In addition, it was noted if the pedestrian was smoking (equaled 1 if smoking, 0 otherwise), was a tourist (equaled 1 if tourist, 0 otherwise), was elderly (equaled 1 if over 65 years old, 0 otherwise), and/or was obese (equaled 1 if obese, 0 otherwise). Each pedestrian is associated with no more than one of these four characteristics/traits. The accompanying table shows a portion of the data; the complete data set can be found on the text website, labeled **Pedestrian Speeds**.

Data for Case Study 17.1 Pedestrian Speeds with Defining Characteristics/Traits

Speed	Smoking	Tourist	Elderly	Obese	FILE
3.76	0	1	0	0	
3.82	0	1	0	0	
⋮	⋮	⋮	⋮	⋮	
5.02	0	0	0	0	

In a report, use the sample information to:

1. Estimate $Speed = \beta_0 + \beta_1 Smoking + \beta_2 Tourist + \beta_3 Elderly + \beta_4 Obese + \varepsilon$.

2. Interpret the slope coefficient of tourist. Interpret the intercept. Predict the speed of an elderly pedestrian. Predict the speed of an obese pedestrian.

3. Are the explanatory variables jointly significant in explaining speed at the 5% significance level? Are all explanatory variables individually significant at the 5% level? What type of pedestrian should a "sidewalk rager" avoid?

Case Study 17.2

Jack Sprague is the relocation specialist for a real estate firm in the town of Arlington, Massachusetts. He has been working with a client who wishes to purchase a single-family home in Arlington. After seeing the information that Jack provided, the client is perplexed by the variability of home prices in Arlington. She is especially puzzled by the premium that a colonial house commands. (A colonial house is a style dating back to the time of the American colonies, with a simple rectangular structure and a peaked roof.) Despite Jack's eloquent explanations, it seems that the client will not be satisfied until she understands the quantitative relationship between house prices and house characteristics. Jack decides to use a multiple regression model to provide the client with the necessary information. He collects data on the prices for 36 single-family homes in Arlington sold in the first quarter of 2009. Also included in the data is the information on square footage, the number of bedrooms, the number of bathrooms, and whether or not the house is a colonial (1 for colonial; 0 otherwise). A portion of the data is shown in the accompanying table; the complete data set is on the text website, labeled **Arlington Homes**.

Data for Case Study 17.2 Sales Information of Single-Family Homes in Arlington, MA

FILE

Price	Square feet	Bedrooms	Baths	Colonial
$840,000	2,768	4	3.5	1
822,000	2,500	4	2.5	1
⋮	⋮	⋮	⋮	⋮
307,500	850	1	1	0

Source: NewEnglandMoves.com.

In a report, use the sample information to:

1. Estimate and interpret three models, using d as the colonial dummy:

Model 1: Price $= \beta_0 + \beta_1$Sqft $+ \beta_2$Beds $+ \beta_3$Baths $+ \beta_4 d + \varepsilon$.

Model 2: Price $= \beta_0 + \beta_1$Sqft $+ \beta_2$Beds $+ \beta_3$Baths $+ \beta_4$(Sqft $\times d$) $+ \varepsilon$.

Model 3: Price $= \beta_0 + \beta_1$Sqft $+ \beta_2$Beds $+ \beta_3$Baths $+ \beta_4 d + \beta_5$(Sqft $\times d$) $+ \varepsilon$.

2. Choose which model is more reliable in predicting the price of a house. Provide at least one reason for your choice. Are price differences between colonial homes versus other styles fixed and/or changing at the 5% significance level?

3. Use this model to make predictions for a colonial home versus other styles, given the average values of the explanatory variables.

Case Study 17.3

The Chartered Financial Analyst (CFA®) designation is fast becoming a requirement for serious investment professionals. Although it requires a successful completion of three levels of grueling exams, it also promises great careers with lucrative salaries. Susan Wayne works as a research analyst at Fidelity Investments. She is thinking about taking the CFA exam in the summer and wants to understand why the recent pass rate for Level I has been under 40%. She firmly believes that those who were good students in college have a better chance of passing. She has also been told that work experience helps. She has access to the information on 30 Fidelity employees who took the test last year, including their success on the exam (1 for pass, 0 for fail), their college GPA, and years of work experience. A portion of the data is shown in the accompanying table; the full data set is on the text website, labeled **CFA**.

Data for Case Study 17.3 Information on Individuals Who Took CFA Exam

Pass	GPA	Experience	
1	3.64	12	FILE
0	3.16	5	
⋮	⋮	⋮	
0	2.64	4	

In a report, use the sample information to:

1. Analyze a linear probability model to explain the probability of success. Predict the probability of passing the CFA exam for a candidate with various values of college GPA and years of experience.

2. Analyze a logit model to explain the probability of success. Predict the probability of passing the CFA exam for a candidate with various values of college GPA and years of experience.

3. Choose which model is more reliable in predicting the probability of passing the CFA exam. Provide at least one reason for your choice.

18 Time Series and Forecasting

CHAPTER

LEARNING OBJECTIVES

After reading this chapter you should be able to:

LO 18.1 Distinguish among the various models used in forecasting.

LO 18.2 Use smoothing techniques to make forecasts.

LO 18.3 Use trend regression models to make forecasts.

LO 18.4 Calculate and interpret seasonal indices and use them to seasonally adjust a time series.

LO 18.5 Use decomposition analysis to make forecasts.

LO 18.6 Use trend regression models with seasonal dummy variables to make forecasts.

LO 18.7 Use causal forecasting models to make forecasts.

Forecasting is an important aspect of statistical analysis, providing guidance for decisions in all areas of business. Examples are abundant and include forecasting product sales, the inflation rate, the price of a financial asset, or a company's cash flows. In fact, the success of any business or government agency depends on the ability to accurately forecast many vital variables. Sound forecasts not only improve the quality of business plans, but also help identify and evaluate potential risks. The field of forecasting has developed rapidly over the last few decades, with some approaches requiring highly sophisticated techniques. In this chapter we focus on some of the easier approaches, which nevertheless provide a flavor and insight into this fascinating field. In particular, we use simple smoothing techniques for making forecasts when short-term fluctuations in the data represent random departures from the overall pattern with no discernible trend or seasonal fluctuations. Special forecasting methods are introduced when trend and seasonal fluctuations are present in the data. We will also explain a regression approach for forecasting.

Nike Revenue Forecast

Chad Moriarty, a research analyst at a small investment firm, is evaluating Nike Inc.'s performance by analyzing the firm's revenues. Some analysts argue that Nike's revenue may slow down due to the global economic crisis and increased competition from emerging brands. Others believe that with a strong and free cash flow, Nike will likely survive this current environment and emerge stronger as some of the weaker competitors get squeezed. Chad fully understands that nobody really knows how well this Oregon-based sportswear company will perform in a softening global economy. However, he believes that Nike's past performance will aid in predicting its future performance. He collects quarterly data on Nike's revenue for the fiscal years 1999 through 2008; for instance, data for fiscal year 1999 refers to the time period from June 1, 1998 through May 31, 1999. A portion of the data is shown in Table 18.1; the full data set can be found on the text website, labeled **Nike Revenues**.

TABLE 18.1 Quarterly Revenue for Nike, Inc. (in millions $)

Year	Quarters Ended			
	August 31	November 30	February 28	May 31
1999	2,505	1,913	2,177	2,182
2000	2,501	2,060	2,162	2,273
⋮	⋮	⋮	⋮	⋮
2008	4,655	4,340	4,544	5,088

NOTES: All data retrieved from Annual Reports for Nike, Inc.

Chad would like to use the information in Table 18.1 to:

1. Determine whether revenue exhibits any sort of trend.
2. Determine whether revenue exhibits a significant seasonal component.
3. Forecast revenue for fiscal year 2009.

A synopsis of this case is provided at the end of Section 18.4.

18.1 Choosing a Forecasting Model

In this chapter we focus our attention on **time series** data. Observations of any variable recorded over time in sequential order are considered a time series. The time period can be expressed in terms of a year, a quarter, a month, a week, a day, or even an hour. Examples of time series include the *hourly* volume of stocks traded on the New York Stock Exchange (NYSE) on four consecutive days; the number of *daily* visitors that frequent the Statue of Liberty over the month of June; the *monthly* sales for a retailer over a five-year period; and the growth rate of a country over the past 15 *years*.

> A **time series** is a set of sequential observations of a variable over time.

Let $y_1, y_2, \ldots, y_T$ represent a sample of T observations of a variable of interest y with y_t denoting the value of y at time t. With time series data, it is customary to use the notation T, instead of n, to represent the number of sample observations and to use a subscript to identify time. For instance, if the number of daily visitors (in 1,000s) to the Statue of Liberty over five days are 100, 94, 98, 110, 102, then $y_1 = 100, \ldots, y_5 = 102$.

Forecasting Methods

Forecasting methods are broadly classified as **quantitative** or **qualitative**. Qualitative forecasting procedures are based on the judgment of the forecaster, who uses prior experience and expertise to make forecasts. On the other hand, quantitative forecasting uses a formal model along with historical data for the variable of interest.

Qualitative forecasting is especially attractive when past data are either not available or are misleading. For instance, a manager may use qualitative forecasts when she attempts to project sales for a brand new product, or when a major structural change in market conditions has rendered previous data obsolete. Similarly, an economist may use qualitative forecasts of credit flow resulting from a newly introduced stimulus package by the federal government.

Although attractive in certain scenarios, qualitative forecasts are often criticized on the ground that they are prone to some well-documented biases such as optimism and overconfidence. Decisions based on the judgment of an overly optimistic manager may prove costly to the business. Also, qualitative forecasting is difficult to document and its quality is totally dependent on the judgment and skill of the forecaster. Two people with access to similar information may offer different qualitative forecasts.

In this chapter we focus on quantitative forecasting. Formal quantitative models have been used extensively to forecast variables such as sales, inflation, and housing starts. These models are further split up into **causal** and **noncausal** models. Causal methods are based on a regression framework, where the variable of interest is related to a single or multiple explanatory variables. In other words, forecasts are "caused" by the known values of the explanatory variables. Noncausal models, also referred to as purely time series models, do not present any explanation of the mechanism generating the variable of interest and simply provide a method for projecting historical data. Despite the lack of theory, noncausal models can provide sound forecasts. However, they provide no guidance on the likely effects of changes in policy (explanatory) variables. Both types of quantitative forecasting methods are discussed in this chapter, although the emphasis is on noncausal methods.

> **TYPES OF FORECASTING METHODS**
>
> Forecasting methods are broadly classified as **quantitative** or **qualitative**. Quantitative forecasting models are further divided into **causal** and **noncausal** models. Noncausal models are also referred to as purely time series models.

Model Selection Criteria

Numerous models can be used to make a forecast, with each model well-suited to capture a particular feature of the time series. It would be easy to choose the right model if we knew which feature truly describes the given series. Unfortunately, the truth is almost never known. Because we do not know *a priori* which of the competing models is likely to provide the best forecast, it is common to consider various models. **Model selection** is one of the most important steps in forecasting. Therefore, it is important to understand model selection criteria before we even introduce any of the formal models.

Two types of model selection criteria are used to compare the performance of competing models. These are broadly defined as **in-sample criteria** and **out-of-sample criteria**. These criteria give rise to two important questions: How well does a model explain the given sample data? And how well does a model make out-of-sample forecasts? Ideally, the chosen model is best in terms of its in-sample predictability *and* its out-of-sample forecasting ability. In this chapter we will focus on in-sample criteria.

Let y_t denote the value of the series at time t and let $\hat{y}_t$ represent its forecast. This in-sample forecast is also referred to as the **predicted** or **fitted value**. For every forecasting model, the sample forecast is likely to differ from the actual series. In other words, $\hat{y}_t$ will not equal y_t. Recall that we define $e_t = y_t - \hat{y}_t$ as the residual. All in-sample model selection criteria compare competing models on the basis of these residuals.

> The in-sample forecast $\hat{y}_t$ is also called the **predicted** or **fitted** value of y_t. As always, the **residuals** are computed as $e_t = y_t - \hat{y}_t$.

In the earlier chapters on regression, we used the coefficient of determination R^2 as a goodness-of-fit measure. We cannot use R^2 in noncausal models because many of them do not use a regression model framework. Instead, a commonly used measure for the comparison of competing forecasting models is the **mean square error** (**MSE**), which is the error (residual) sum of squares divided by the number of observations n for which the residuals are available.[1] As we will see shortly, it is not uncommon for n to be less than the number of observations T in the series. Another measure is the **mean absolute deviation** (**MAD**), which is the mean of the absolute residuals. The preferred model will have the lowest *MSE* and *MAD*.

> ### MODEL SELECTION CRITERIA
>
> The **mean square error** (**MSE**) and the **mean absolute deviation** (**MAD**) are computed as
>
> $$MSE = \frac{\Sigma(y_t - \hat{y}_t)^2}{n} = \frac{\Sigma e_t^2}{n} \quad \text{and}$$
>
> $$MAD = \frac{\Sigma|y_t - \hat{y}_t|}{n} = \frac{\Sigma|e_t|}{n},$$
>
> where n is the number of residuals used in the computation. We choose the model with the lowest *MSE* and *MAD*.

In the following sections we employ various forecasting models and compare them on the basis of these goodness-of-fit measures.

---

[1] Here the *MSE* formula is different from the one defined in Chapter 14, where the error sum of squares was divided by the appropriate degrees of freedom.

18.2 Smoothing Techniques

LO 18.2

Use smoothing techniques to make forecasts.

Time series generally consist of **systematic** and **unsystematic** patterns. Systematic patterns are caused by a set of identifiable components, whereas unsystematic patterns by definition are difficult to identify. Three identifiable components occur in systematic patterns: the trend, the seasonal, and the cyclical components. In this section we focus on applications where the time series is described primarily by unsystematic patterns. In the following sections we discuss systematic patterns.

Unsystematic patterns are caused by the presence of a **random (irregular) error** term. As mentioned earlier, a time series is a sequence of observations that are ordered in time. Inherently, any data collected over time is likely to exhibit some form of random variation. For instance, the checkout time at a campus bookstore or weekly sales at a convenience store encounter random variations for no apparent reason.

> ### TIME SERIES PATTERNS
> Time series consist of **systematic** and **unsystematic** patterns. Systematic patterns are caused by the **trend**, the **seasonal**, and the **cyclical** components. Unsystematic patterns are difficult to identify and are caused by the presence of a **random (irregular) error** term.

A simple plot of the time series provides insights into its components. A jagged appearance, caused by abrupt changes in the series, indicates random variations. Smoothing techniques are often employed to reduce the effect of random fluctuations. These techniques can also be used to provide forecasts if short-term fluctuations represent random departures from the structure, with no discernible systematic patterns. These techniques are especially attractive when forecasts of multiple variables need to be updated frequently. For example, consider a manager of a convenience store who has to update the inventories of numerous items on a weekly basis. It is not practical in such situations to develop complex forecasting models. We discuss two distinct smoothing techniques: the **moving average** and the **exponential smoothing** techniques.

Moving Average Methods

Due to its simplicity, the moving average method ranks among the most popular techniques for processing time series. The method is based on computing the average from a fixed number m of the most recent observations. For instance, a 3-period moving average is formed by averaging the three most recent observations. The term "moving" is used because as a new observation becomes available, the average is updated by including the newest and dropping the oldest observation.

> ### CALCULATING A MOVING AVERAGE
> An m-**period moving average** is computed as
> $$\text{Moving Average} = \frac{\text{Sum of the } m \text{ most recent observations}}{m}.$$

Here we focus on the calculation of odd-numbered moving averages, such as 3-period, 5-period, and so on. Later, we will use even-numbered moving averages to extract the seasonal component of a time series.

> ### EXAMPLE 18.1
> According to the Energy Information Administration, the United States consumes about 21 million barrels (882 million gallons) of petroleum each day. About half of this consumption is in the form of gasoline. Table 18.2 shows a portion of weekly

U.S. finished motor gasoline production, measured in thousands of barrels per day; the full data set can be found on the text website, labeled **Gas Production**.

a. Construct a 3-period moving average series for the data.

b. Plot production and its corresponding 3-period moving average and comment on any differences.

c. Using the 3-period moving average series, forecast gasoline production on May 29, 2009 (week 22).

d. Calculate the mean square error *MSE* and the mean absolute deviation *MAD*.

TABLE 18.2 Weekly U.S. Finished Motor Gasoline Production

FILE	Date	Week	Production (1,000s of barrels/day)
	January 2, 2009	1	9,115
	January 9, 2009	2	8,813
	January 16, 2009	3	8,729
	January 23, 2009	4	8,660
	January 30, 2009	5	8,679
	⋮	⋮	⋮
	May 8, 2009	19	8,710
	May 15, 2009	20	8,735
	May 22, 2009	21	9,378

Source: Energy Information Administration.

SOLUTION:

a. For notational simplicity, let production be denoted by y_t and the corresponding moving average be denoted by $\bar{y}_t$. We form a 3-period moving average series by averaging all sets of three consecutive values of the original series. The first value of a 3-period moving average is calculated as

$$\bar{y}_2 = \frac{y_1 + y_2 + y_3}{3} = \frac{9,115 + 8,813 + 8,729}{3} = 8,885.67.$$

We designate this value $\bar{y}_2$ because it represents the average in weeks 1 through 3. The next moving average, representing the average in weeks 2 through 4, is

$$\bar{y}_3 = \frac{y_2 + y_3 + y_4}{3} = \frac{8,813 + 8,729 + 8,660}{3} = 8,734.00.$$

Other values of $\bar{y}_t$ are calculated similarly and are presented in column 3 of Table 18.3. Note that we lose one observation at the beginning and one at the end of the 3-period moving average series $\bar{y}_t$. (If it were a 5-period moving average, we would lose two observations at the beginning and two at the end.)

TABLE 18.3 3-Period Moving Averages, Forecasts, and Residuals

Week (1)	y (2)	$\bar{y}$ (3)	$\hat{y}$ (4)	$e = y - \hat{y}$ (5)	e^2 (6)	$\lvert e \rvert$ (7)
1	9,115	—	—	—	—	—
2	8,813	8,885.67	—	—	—	—
3	8,729	8,734.00	—	—	—	—
4	8,660	8,689.33	8,885.67	−225.67	50,925.44	225.67
5	8,679	8,610.33	8,734.00	−55.00	3,025.00	55.00
⋮	⋮	⋮	⋮	⋮	⋮	⋮
19	8710	8787.67	8932.00	−222.00	49,284.00	222.00
20	8,735	8,941.00	8,806.00	−71.00	5,041.00	71.00
21	9,378	—	8,787.67	590.33	348,493.44	590.33
Total					953,509.78	3,312.67

b. In Figure 18.1, we plot production and its corresponding 3-period moving average against weeks. Note that the original production series has a jagged appearance, suggesting the presence of an important random component of the series. The series of moving averages, on the other hand, presents a much smoother picture.

FIGURE 18.1 Weekly production and 3-period moving average

c. As mentioned earlier, if the primary component of the series is random variations, we can use moving averages to generate forecasts. Since $\bar{y}_2$ represents the average in weeks 1 through 3, it is the most updated estimate of the series prior to period 4. Therefore, with a 3-period moving average, $\hat{y}_4 = \bar{y}_2$ where $\hat{y}_4$ is the in-sample forecast for period 4. Similarly, $\hat{y}_5 = \bar{y}_3$ is the forecast for period 5, where $\bar{y}_3$ is the average in weeks 2 through 4, and so on. These forecasts, derived as $\hat{y}_t = \frac{y_{t-3} + y_{t-2} + y_{t-1}}{3}$, are shown in column 4 of Table 18.3. Following this simple process, we compute the out-of-sample forecast in week 22 as

$$\hat{y}_{22} = \bar{y}_{20} = \frac{y_{19} + y_{20} + y_{21}}{3} = \frac{8,710 + 8,735 + 9,378}{3} = 8,941.$$

Therefore, our forecast for gasoline production on May 29, 2009 (week 22) is 8,941 thousand barrels. One potential weakness when using the moving average technique is that all future forecasts take on the same value as the first out-of-sample forecast; that is, the forecast for week 23 is also 8,941 thousand barrels.

d. In order to calculate the mean square error *MSE* and the mean absolute deviation *MAD*, we first compute the residuals as $e_t = y_t - \hat{y}_t$, shown in column 5 of Table 18.3. These residuals are squared (see column 6) and then summed to compute *MSE* as

$$MSE = \frac{\Sigma e_t^2}{n} = \frac{953,509.78}{18} = 52,973.$$

The absolute values of the residuals, presented in column 7, are used to compute *MAD* as

$$MAD = \frac{\Sigma |e_t|}{n} = \frac{3,312.67}{18} = 184.$$

While it is difficult to interpret the numerical values of *MSE* and *MAD*, they are useful in comparing alternative models.

Exponential Smoothing Methods

Although the moving average approach is popular, it has some shortcomings. First, the choice of the order *m* is arbitrary, although we can use trial and error to choose the value of *m* that results in the smallest *MSE* and *MAD*. Second, it may not be appropriate to give equal weight to all recent *m* observations. Whereas the moving average method weighs all recent observations equally, the method called exponential smoothing assigns exponentially decreasing weights as the observations get older. As in the case of moving averages, exponential smoothing is a procedure for continually revising a forecast in the light of more recent observations.

Let A_t denote the estimated level of the series at time t, where A_t is defined as

$$A_t = \alpha y_t + \alpha(1 - \alpha)y_{t-1} + \alpha(1 - \alpha)^2 y_{t-2} + \alpha(1 - \alpha)^3 y_{t-3} + \cdots, \text{ where } 0 \le \alpha \le 1.$$

That is, A_t is simply a weighted average of exponentially declining weights, with α dictating the speed of decline. For example, with $\alpha = 0.8$,

$$A_t = 0.8y_t + 0.16y_{t-1} + 0.032y_{t-2} + 0.0064y_{t-3} + \cdots.$$

Similarly, with $\alpha = 0.2$,

$$A_t = 0.2y_t + 0.16y_{t-1} + 0.128y_{t-2} + 0.1024y_{t-3} + \cdots.$$

Note that the speed of decline is higher when $\alpha = 0.8$ as compared to when $\alpha = 0.2$.

Using algebra, it can be shown that the initial equation simplifies to

$$A_t = \alpha y_t + (1 - \alpha)A_{t-1}.$$

We generally use this representation to define the formula for exponential smoothing. Because A_t represents the most updated level at time t, we can use it to make a one-period-ahead forecast as $\hat{y}_{t+1} = A_t$.

CALCULATING AN EXPONENTIALLY SMOOTHED SERIES

The **exponential smoothing** procedure continually updates the level of the series as

$$A_t = \alpha y_t + (1 - \alpha)A_{t-1},$$

where α represents the speed of decline. **Forecasts** are made as $\hat{y}_{t+1} = A_t$.

In order to implement this method, we need to determine α and the initial value of the series A_1. Typically, the initial value is set equal to the first value of the time series, that is, $A_1 = y_1$; the choice of the initial value is less important if the number of observations is large. The optimal value for α is determined by a trial-and-error method. We evaluate various values of α and choose the one that results in the smallest *MSE* and *MAD*.

FILE EXAMPLE 18.2

Revisit the **Gas Production** data on weekly U.S. finished motor gasoline production, measured in thousands of barrels per day.

a. Construct the exponentially smoothed series with $\alpha = 0.20$ and $A_1 = y_1$.

b. Plot production and its corresponding exponentially smoothed series against weeks. Comment on any differences.

c. Using the exponentially smoothed series, forecast gasoline production on May 29, 2009 (week 22).

d. Calculate *MSE* and *MAD*. Compare these values with those obtained using the 3-period moving average method.

SOLUTION:

a. In Column 3 of Table 18.4, we present sequential estimates of A_t with the initial value $A_1 = y_1 = 9,115$. We use $A_t = \alpha y_t + (1 - \alpha)A_{t-1}$ to continuously update the level with $\alpha = 0.2$. For instance, for periods 2 and 3 we calculate:

$$A_2 = 0.20(8,813) + 0.80(9,115) = 9,054.60, \text{ and}$$
$$A_3 = 0.20(8,729) + 0.80(9,054.60) = 8,989.48.$$

All other estimates of A_t are found in a like manner.

TABLE 18.4 Exponentially Smoothed Series with $\alpha = 0.20$, Forecasts, and Residuals

Week (1)	y (2)	A_t (3)	$\hat{y}$ (4)	$e = y - \hat{y}$ (5)	e^2 (6)	$\lvert e \rvert$ (7)
1	9,115	9,115.00	—	—	—	—
2	8,813	9,054.60	9,115.00	−302.00	91,204.00	302.00
3	8,729	8,989.48	9,054.60	−325.60	106,015.36	325.60
⋮	⋮	⋮	⋮	⋮	⋮	⋮
21	9,378	8,933.29	8,822.11	555.89	309,011.71	555.89
Total					1,153,160.28	3,995.40

b. In Figure 18.2, we plot production and its corresponding exponentially smoothed series against weeks. As mentioned earlier, while the original series has the jagged appearance, the exponentially smoothed series removes most of the sharp points and, much like the moving average series, presents a much smoother picture.

FIGURE 18.2 Weekly production and exponentially smoothed series

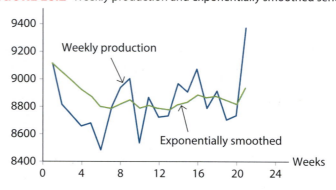

c. Forecasts given by $\hat{y}_{t+1} = A_t$ are presented in column 4 of Table 18.4. For instance, for period 2, $\hat{y}_2 = A_1 = 9,115$. Similarly, $A_2 = 9,054.60$ is the forecast for $\hat{y}_3$. Therefore, the forecast for gasoline production on May 29, 2009, computed as $\hat{y}_{22} = A_{21}$, equals 8,933.29 thousand barrels. As with the moving average method, any further out-of-sample forecasts also assume this same value; for instance, $\hat{y}_{23} = 8,933.29$ thousand barrels.

d. In columns 5, 6, and 7 we present the residuals, their squares, and their absolute values, respectively. We compute model selection measures as

$$MSE = \frac{\sum e_t^2}{n} = \frac{1,153,160.28}{20} = 57,658 \quad \text{and}$$

$$MAD = \frac{\sum \lvert e_t \rvert}{n} = \frac{3,995.40}{20} = 200.$$

The moving average model employed in Example 18.1 outperforms, as it yields a lower *MSE* of 52,973 and a lower *MAD* of 184 than the exponential model. Note that we used the residuals from Weeks 4–21 with moving averages and Weeks 2–21 with exponential smoothing. For a fair comparison, we recalculated *MSE* = 53,108 and *MAD* = 187 with exponential smoothing, using the residuals only from Weeks 4–21. The moving average method still outperforms.

There is nothing sacrosanct about $\alpha = 0.2$; we used this value primarily to illustrate the exponential smoothing procedure. As we noted earlier, it is common to evaluate various values of α and choose the one that produces the smallest *MSE* and *MAD* for forecasting. In order to illustrate how α is chosen, we generate the *MSE* and *MAD* with α values ranging from 0.1 to 0.9 with increments of 0.1. The results are summarized in Table 18.5.

TABLE 18.5 Various Values of α and the Resulting *MSE* and *MAD*

α	0.1	0.2	0.3	0.4	0.5	0.6	0.7	0.8	0.9
MSE	66,906	57,658	54,368	53,364	53,470	54,200	55,394	57,047	59,235
MAD	209	200	196	194	191	188	185	184	188

Here, the choice of α depends on whether we employ *MSE* or *MAD* for comparison with *MSE* suggesting $\alpha = 0.4$ and *MAD* suggesting $\alpha = 0.8$. In instances where *MSE* and *MAD* give conflicting results, we choose the procedure with the smallest *MSE*; we make this choice because *MSE* penalizes larger deviations more harshly due to squaring. Therefore, we choose α equal to 0.4 since it has the smallest *MSE* of 53,364. In this application, the moving average model still outperforms the exponential smoothing model, as measured by its lower *MSE* and *MAD*.

Using Excel for Moving Averages and Exponential Smoothing

Excel easily calculates moving averages. From the menu choose **Data > Data Analysis > Moving Average > OK** in order to activate the *Moving Average* dialog box. Click on the box next to *Input Range* and select the relevant time series y_t. Next to *Interval*, enter the value for *m*; for example, if you want to calculate a 3-period moving average, enter 3. Then click **OK**.

Excel also calculates an exponentially smoothed series. From the menu choose **Data > Data Analysis > Exponential Smoothing > OK** in order to activate the *Exponential Smoothing* dialog box. Click on the box next to *Input Range* and select the relevant time series y_t. Select the box next to *Damping Factor*. If we want to construct an exponentially smoothed series with $\alpha = 0.2$, then for *Damping Factor* we enter $1 - \alpha = 1 - 0.2 = 0.8$. Then click **OK**.

EXERCISES 18.2

Concepts

1. **FILE** Consider the following sample data, consisting of 10 observations. The data are also on the text website, labeled *Exercise 18.1*.

t	1	2	3	4	5	6	7	8	9	10
y_t	11	12	9	12	10	8	11	12	10	9

  a. Construct a 3-period moving average and plot it along with the actual series. Comment on smoothing.
  b. Use the 3-period moving average to make forecasts and compute the resulting *MSE* and *MAD*.
  c. Make a forecast for period 11.

2. **FILE** Consider the following sample data, consisting of 20 observations. The data are also on the text website, labeled *Exercise 18.2*.

t	1	2	3	4	5	6	7	8	9	10
y_t	27	35	38	33	34	39	40	38	48	35
t	11	12	13	14	15	16	17	18	19	20
y_t	37	38	35	44	40	37	30	39	34	45

  a. Construct a 5-period moving average and plot it along with the actual series. Comment on smoothing.
  b. Use the 5-period moving average to make forecasts and compute the resulting *MSE* and *MAD*.
  c. Make a forecast for period 21.

3. **FILE** Consider the following sample data, consisting of 20 observations. The data are also on the text website, labeled *Exercise 18.3*.

t	1	2	3	4	5	6	7	8	9	10
y_t	12.9	12.6	11.1	14.8	11.9	12.9	12.1	13.6	11.9	9.0
t	11	12	13	14	15	16	17	18	19	20
y_t	8.9	9.3	13.3	10.7	13.5	15.1	11.3	13.6	12.4	13.0

  a. Plot the above series and discuss the presence of random variations.
  b. Use the exponential smoothing method to make forecasts with $\alpha = 0.2$. Compute the resulting *MSE* and *MAD*.
  c. Repeat the process with $\alpha = 0.4$.
  d. Use the appropriate value of α to make a forecast for period 21.

4. **FILE** Consider the following sample data, consisting of 20 observations. The data are also on the text website, labeled *Exercise 18.4*.

t	1	2	3	4	5	6	7	8	9	10
y_t	14	17	12	16	18	16	15	19	23	23
t	11	12	13	14	15	16	17	18	19	20
y_t	18	19	19	21	21	25	23	26	23	20

a. Use the 3-period moving average to make forecasts and compute the resulting *MSE* and *MAD*.

b. Use the exponential smoothing method to make forecasts with $\alpha = 0.4$. Compute the resulting *MSE* and *MAD*.

c. Use the preferred method to make a forecast for period 21.

Applications

5. **FILE** Rock 'n' roll is a form of music that evolved in the United States and very quickly spread to the rest of the world. The interest in rock music, like any other genre, has gone through ups and downs over the years. The Recording Industry Association of America (RIAA) reports consumer trends on the basis of annual data on genre, format, age, and gender of purchasers and place of purchase. The accompanying table lists a portion of the percentage (share) of total shipment of music that falls in the category of rock music from 1990–2008. The full data set can be found on the text website, labeled *Rock Music*.

Year	Share
1991	34.8
1992	31.6
⋮	⋮
2008	31.8

SOURCE: www.riaa.com.

a. Plot the above series and discuss the presence of random variations.

b. Use a 3-period moving average to make a forecast for the share of rock music in 2009.

c. Use a 5-period moving average to make a forecast for the share of rock music in 2009.

d. Use the *MSE* to pick the appropriate moving average for making a forecast for the share of rock 'n' roll music in 2009.

6. **FILE** Use the data from the preceding question for the share of total shipment of music that falls in the category of rock music from 1990–2008.

a. Make a forecast for the share of rock music in 2009 using the exponential smoothing method with $\alpha = 0.4$.

b. Make a forecast for the share of rock music in 2009 using the exponential smoothing method with $\alpha = 0.6$.

c. Use the *MSE* to pick the appropriate speed of decline for making a forecast for the share of rock music in 2009.

7. **FILE** According to the Census Bureau, the number of people below the poverty level has been steadily increasing (CNN, September 16, 2010). This means many families are finding themselves there for the first time. The following table shows a portion of the percent of families in the United States who are below the poverty level from 1986–2009. The full data set can be found on the text website, labeled *Poverty Rate*.

Year	Poverty Rate
1986	10.9
1987	10.7
⋮	⋮
2009	11.1

SOURCE: U.S. Census Bureau.

a. Plot the above series and comment on its shape.

b. Use a 3-period moving average to make in-sample forecasts. Compute the resulting *MSE* and *MAD*.

c. Use the exponential smoothing method to make in-sample forecasts with $\alpha = 0.6$. Compute the resulting *MSE* and *MAD*.

d. Choose the appropriate model to make a forecast of the poverty rate in 2010.

8. **FILE** Consider the following table, which shows a portion of the closing prices of the S&P 500 Index for 21 trading days in November 2010. The complete data set can be found on the text website, labeled *S&P Price*.

Date	S&P Price
1-Nov	1184.38
2-Nov	1193.57
⋮	⋮
30-Nov	1180.55

SOURCE: finance.yahoo.com.

a. Use a 3-period moving average to make a price forecast for December 1, 2010.

b. Use the exponential smoothing method to make a price forecast for December 1, 2010. Use $\alpha = 0.4$.

c. Which of the above smoothing methods results in a lower *MSE*?

d. You find out that the actual S&P 500 closing price on December 1, 2010 was 1,206.07. Was the forecast performance of the two methods consistent with their in-sample performance in part c?

9. **FILE** The accompanying table shows a portion of monthly data on seasonally adjusted inflation and unemployment rates in the United States from January 2009 to November

2010; the entire data set is on the text website, labeled **Unemployment and Inflation**.

Year	Month	Unemployment	Inflation
2009	Jan	7.7	0.3
⋮	⋮	⋮	⋮
2010	Nov	9.8	0.1

Source: Bureau of Labor Statistics.

a. Use a 3-period moving average and exponential smoothing with $\alpha = 0.6$ to make in-sample forecasts for unemployment. Use the more appropriate smoothing method to forecast unemployment for December 2010.

b. Use a 3-period moving average and exponential smoothing with $\alpha = 0.6$ to make in-sample forecasts for inflation. Use the more appropriate smoothing method to forecast inflation for December 2010.

18.3 Trend Forecasting Models

LO **18.3**

Use trend regression models to make forecasts.

The smoothing techniques discussed in the preceding section are used when the time series represent random fluctuations with no discernible trend or seasonal fluctuations. When trend and seasonal variations *are* present in the time series, we need to use special models for analysis. In this section we focus on trend analysis, which extracts long-term upward or downward movements of the series.

The Linear Trend

We can estimate a linear trend using the regression techniques described in earlier chapters. Let y_t be the value of the response variable at time t. Here we use t as the explanatory variable corresponding to consecutive time periods, such as 1, 2, 3, and so on. Example 18.3 shows how to use this model to make forecasts.

> ### THE LINEAR TREND MODEL
>
> A **linear trend model** is specified as $y_t = \beta_0 + \beta_1 t + \varepsilon_t$, where y_t is the value of the series at time t. The estimated model is used to make **forecasts** as $\hat{y}_t = b_0 + b_1 t$, where b_0 and b_1 are the coefficient estimates.

EXAMPLE 18.3

The United States continues to increase diversity, with more than a third of its population belonging to a minority group (CNN.com, May 14, 2009). Hispanics are the fastest-growing minority segment, comprising one out of six residents in the country. Table 18.6 shows a portion of data relating to the number as well as the median income of Hispanic households from 1975 through 2007. The full data set is on the text website, labeled **Hispanic Characteristics**.

TABLE 18.6 Number and Median Income of Hispanics, 1975–2007

Year	Number (in 1,000s)	Median Income
1975	2,948	$8,865
1976	3,081	9,569
⋮	⋮	⋮
2007	13,339	38,679

Source: United States Census Bureau.

a. Use the sample data to estimate the linear trend model for the number (regression 1) and the median income (regression 2) of Hispanic households. Interpret the slope coefficients.

b. Forecast the number and the median income of Hispanic households in 2008.

SOLUTION: In order to estimate the above trend models, we first relabel the 33 years of observations from 1 to 33. In other words, we make the explanatory variable t assume values 1, 2, . . . , 33 rather than 1975, 1976, . . . , 2007. Table 18.7 uses a portion of the data to show how t is created.

TABLE 18.7 Generating the Time Variable t

Year	t	Number (in 1,000s)	Median Income
1975	1	2,948	$8,865
1976	2	3,081	9,569
⋮	⋮	⋮	⋮
2007	33	13,339	38,679

Relevant portions of the Excel output for the linear regression models are presented in Table 18.8.

TABLE 18.8 Regression Results for Example 18.3

	Response Variable: Number (Regression 1)	Response Variable: Income (Regression 2)
	Coefficients	Coefficients
Intercept	1657.8428*	7796.9186*
	(0.00)	(0.00)
t	327.4709*	887.7249*
	(0.00)	(0.00)

NOTES: Parameter estimates are followed with the p-values in parentheses; *represents significance at 5%.

a. The slope coefficient in regression 1 implies that the number of Hispanic households has grown, on average, by approximately 327 (thousand) each year. Regression 2 shows that the median income for Hispanic households has grown, on average, by approximately $888 each year. The slope coefficients in both regressions are significant at any level, since the p-values approximate zero in each case.

b. Using the estimates from regression 1, we forecast the number of Hispanic households in 2008 ($t = 34$) as 1,657.8428 + 327.4709(34) = 12,792 (in 1,000s). Similarly, the forecast for the median income of Hispanic households in 2008 is 7,796.9186 + 887.7249(34) = $37,980. Forecasts for other years can be computed similarly.

The Exponential Trend

A linear trend model by definition uses a straight line to capture the trend, thus implying that for each period, the value of the series changes by a fixed amount. For example, in Example 18.3 we concluded that the median income of Hispanic households grows by approximately $888 each year. The **exponential trend model** is attractive when the increase in the series gets larger over time. Figure 18.3 compares linear and exponential trends.

While both graphs have positive slopes, the exponential trend, unlike the linear trend, allows the series to grow by an increasing amount for each time period.

Recall from Chapter 16 that we estimate an exponential model as $\ln(y_t) = \beta_0 + \beta_1 t + \varepsilon_t$. In order to estimate this model, we first generate the series in logs, $\ln(y_t)$, and then run a regression of $\ln(y_t)$ on t. Since the response variable is measured in logs, we make forecasts in regular units as $\hat{y}_t = \exp(b_0 + b_1 t + s_e^2/2)$ where s_e is the standard error of the estimate. As discussed in Chapter 16, if we make the forecast using $\exp(b_0 + b_1 t)$, then $\hat{y}$ systematically underestimates the expected value of y; the inclusion of $s_e^2/2$ in the forecast equation resolves this problem.

FIGURE 18.3 Linear and exponential trends

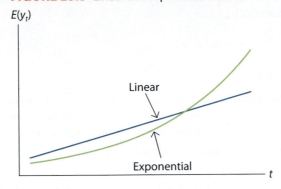

THE EXPONENTIAL TREND MODEL

An **exponential trend model** is specified as $\ln(y_t) = \beta_0 + \beta_1 t + \varepsilon_t$, where $\ln(y_t)$ is the natural log of the series y_t. The estimated model is used to make **forecasts** as $\hat{y}_t = \exp(b_0 + b_1 t + s_e^2/2)$, where b_0 and b_1 are the coefficient estimates and s_e is the standard error of the estimate.

It is always advisable to inspect the data visually as a first step. Graphs offer an informal way to gauge whether a linear or an exponential trend provides a better fit. Figures 18.4 and 18.5 are scatterplots of the number and the median income of Hispanic households from 1975 through 2007. We relabel the 33 years of annual observations from 1 to 33 and also superimpose the linear and the exponential trends to the data.

FIGURE 18.4 Number of Hispanic households with superimposed trends

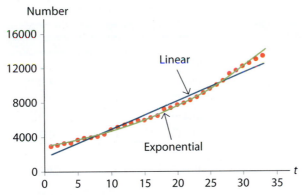

FIGURE 18.5 Median income of Hispanic households with superimposed trends

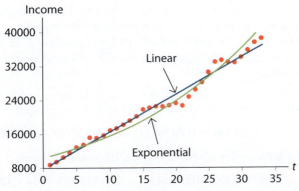

It appears that while the median income follows a linear trend, the number of Hispanics seems to grow exponentially.

FILE **EXAMPLE 18.4**

a. Revisit the *Hispanic Characteristics* data to estimate the exponential trend model for both the number (regression 1) and the median income (regression 2) of Hispanic households. Interpret the slope coefficients.

b. Forecast the number as well as the median income of Hispanic households in 2008.

c. Use formal model selection criteria to decide whether the linear or the exponential model is more appropriate for the series.

SOLUTION: In order to estimate the exponential model, we first transform both series to natural logs. Table 18.9 shows a portion of the data where the variables (number and income) are log-transformed.

TABLE 18.9 Generating the Natural Log of the Series (Example 18.4)

Year	t	Number	Income	ln (Number)	ln (Income)
1975	1	2,948	$8,865	7.9889	9.0899
1976	2	3,081	$9,569	8.0330	9.1663
⋮	⋮	⋮	⋮	⋮	⋮
2007	33	13,339	38,679	9.4984	10.5631

Relevant portions of the Excel output for the exponential regression models are presented in Table 18.10.

TABLE 18.10 Regression Results for Example 18.4

	Response Variable: Log of Number (Regression 1)	Response Variable: Log of Income (Regression 2)
	Coefficients	Coefficients
Intercept	7.9706* (0.00)	9.2517* (0.00)
t	0.0479* (0.00)	0.0418* (0.00)
s_e	0.0311	0.0775

NOTES: Parameter estimates are followed with the *p*-values in parentheses; *represents significance at the 5% level. The last row shows the standard error of the estimate s_e.

a. Consistent with the results of the linear trend models, the exponential trend models suggest that the number and the median income of Hispanic households are trending upward, since both regressions show positive slope coefficients: 0.0479 for regression 1 and 0.0418 for regression 2. In addition, the slope coefficients are highly significant, with the *p*-values approximately zero in both regressions.

b. We make forecasts as $\hat{y}_t = \exp(b_0 + b_1 t + s_e^2/2)$. In order to forecast the number of Hispanic households for 2008 ($t = 34$), we compute

$$\hat{y}_{34} = \exp(7.9706 + 0.0479(34) + 0.0311^2/2) = 14,760.$$

Similarly, the forecast for Hispanic median income is computed as

$$\hat{y}_{34} = \exp(9.2517 + 0.0418(34) + 0.0775^2/2) = \$43,300.$$

Forecasts for other years can be computed similarly. Note that 2008 forecasts with the exponential trend model are higher than those with the linear trend model.

It is important to point out that whenever possible, it is preferred to use unrounded values for making forecasts in an exponential model because even a small difference, when exponentiated, can make a big difference in the forecast.

c. We compute $\hat{y}$ for the exponential model in regular units and not in logs. The resulting $\hat{y}$ also enables us to compare the linear and the exponential models in terms of MSE and MAD or in terms of R^2. In Table 18.11, we present a portion of the series $\hat{y}_t$, along with y_t, for both models; we did these calculations in Excel with unrounded values for the estimates. We then compute $MSE = \frac{\Sigma e_t^2}{n}$ and $MAD = \frac{\Sigma |e_t|}{n}$ where $e_t = y_t - \hat{y}_t$. While these calculations are not reported, the MSE and MAD values for the linear and the exponential models are shown in the last two rows of Table 18.11.

TABLE 18.11 Analysis of Linear and Exponential Trend Models

t	Number of Hispanics y			Income of Hispanics y		
	y	ŷ (Linear)	ŷ (Exponential)	y	ŷ (Linear)	ŷ (Exponential)
1	2,948	1,985.31	3,037.97	8,865	8,684.64	10,899.65
2	3,081	2,312.79	3,186.97	9,569	9,572.37	11,364.43
⋮	⋮	⋮	⋮	⋮	⋮	⋮
33	13,339	12,464.38	14,061.05	38,679	37,091.84	41,471.14
MSE		281,255	45,939		1,508,369	2,210,693
MAD		460	155		881	1,289

The exponential trend model appears to be better suited to describe the number of Hispanic households, since it has a lower MSE and MAD than the linear trend model. On the other hand, median income is better described by the linear trend model. These findings are consistent with our earlier analysis with Figures 18.4 and 18.5. Therefore, we use the exponential trend model to forecast the number of Hispanic households in 2008 as 14,760. The linear trend model is used to forecast the median income of Hispanic households in 2008 as $37,980.

Polynomial Trends

Sometimes a time series reverses direction, due to any number of circumstances. A common polynomial function that allows for curvature in the series is a **quadratic trend model**. This model describes one change in the direction of a series and is estimated as

$$y_t = \beta_0 + \beta_1 t + \beta_2 t^2 + \varepsilon_t.$$

The coefficient β_2 determines whether the trend is U-shaped or inverted U-shaped. Figure 18.6 depicts possible trends of a quadratic model.

In order to estimate the quadratic trend model, we generate t^2, which is simply the square of t. Then we run a multiple regression model that uses y as the response variable and both t and t^2 as the explanatory variables. The estimated model is used to make forecasts as

$$\hat{y}_t = b_0 + b_1 t + b_2 t^2.$$

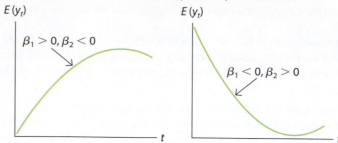

FIGURE 18.6 Representative shapes of a quadratic trend

Higher-order polynomial functions can be estimated similarly. For instance, consider a cubic trend model specified as

$$y_t = \beta_0 + \beta_1 t + \beta_2 t^2 + \beta_3 t^3 + \varepsilon_t.$$

The cubic trend model allows for two changes in the direction of a series. Figure 18.7 presents possible shapes of a cubic model.

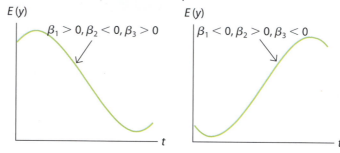

FIGURE 18.7 Representative shapes of a cubic trend

In the cubic trend model we basically generate two additional variables, t^2 and t^3, for the regression. A multiple regression model is run that uses y as the response variable and t, t^2, and t^3 as the explanatory variables. The estimated model is used to make forecasts as $\hat{y}_t = b_0 + b_1 t + b_2 t^2 + b_3 t^3$.

While we use the *MSE* and the *MAD* of in-sample forecast errors to compare the linear and the exponential models, we cannot use them to compare the linear, quadratic, and cubic trend models. The reason is that the values of *MSE* and *MAD* are always lowest for the highest-order polynomial trend model, since the values decrease as we estimate additional parameters. The problem is similar to that of the coefficient of determination R^2 discussed in earlier chapters. When comparing polynomial trend models, we use adjusted R^2, which imposes a penalty for over-parameterization.

THE POLYNOMIAL TREND MODEL

A polynomial trend model of order q is estimated as

$$y_t = \beta_0 + \beta_1 t + \beta_2 t^2 + \beta_3 t^3 + \cdots + \beta_q t^q + \varepsilon_t.$$

This model specializes to a linear trend model, quadratic trend model, and cubic trend model for $q = 1$, 2, and 3, respectively. The estimated model is used to make forecasts as $\hat{y}_t = b_0 + b_1 t + b_2 t^2 + b_3 t^3 + \cdots + b_q t^q$, where $b_0, b_1, \ldots, b_q$ are the coefficient estimates. We use **adjusted R^2** to compare polynomial trend models with different orders.

A good application of the polynomial trend model is used in the Writing with Statistics section later in this chapter.

Concepts

10. Consider the following estimated trend models. Use them to make a forecast for $t = 21$.
    a. Linear Trend: $\hat{y} = 13.54 + 1.08t$
    b. Quadratic Trend: $\hat{y} = 18.28 + 0.92t - 0.01t^2$
    c. Exponential Trend: $\widehat{\ln(y)} = 1.8 + 0.09t; s_e = 0.01$

11. **FILE** Consider the following table, consisting of 20 observations of the variable y and time t. The data are also on the text website, labeled **Exercise 18.11**.

t	y	t	y	t	y	t	y
1	3.01	6	4.94	11	7.28	16	14.16
2	3.13	7	6.10	12	9.04	17	14.85
3	4.19	8	5.91	13	9.49	18	16.77
4	5.07	9	6.56	14	12.12	19	18.07
5	4.46	10	7.29	15	13.15	20	19.99

    a. Plot the series along with the superimposed linear and exponential trends. Which trend model do you think describes the data well?
    b. Estimate a linear trend model and an exponential trend model for the sample. Validate your guess from the graphs by comparing the MSE and MAD.

12. **FILE** Consider the following table, consisting of 20 observations of the variable y and time t. The data are also on the text website, labeled **Exercise 18.12**.

t	y	t	y	t	y	t	y
1	10.32	6	13.84	11	16.95	16	16.26
2	12.25	7	14.39	12	16.18	17	16.77
3	12.31	8	14.40	13	17.22	18	17.10
4	13.00	9	15.05	14	16.71	19	16.91
5	13.15	10	14.99	15	16.64	20	16.79

    a. Plot the series along with the superimposed linear and quadratic trends. Which trend model do you think describes the data well?
    b. Estimate a linear trend model and a quadratic trend model. Validate your guess from the graphs by comparing their adjusted R^2.

Applications

13. Despite the growth in digital entertainment, the nation's 400 amusement parks have managed to hold on to visitors, as the following data show:

Year	Visitors (in millions)
2000	317
2001	319
2002	324
2003	322
2004	328
2005	335
2006	335
2007	341

Source: International Association of Amusement Parks and Attractions.

a. Plot the series. Does the linear trend model or the exponential trend model fit the series best?
b. Estimate both models. Verify your answer in part a by comparing the MSE of the models.
c. Given the model of best fit, make a forecast for visitors to amusement parks in 2008 and 2009.

14. The potentially deadly 2009 Swine Flu outbreak was due to a new flu strain of subtype H1N1 not previously reported in pigs. When the World Health Organization declared a pandemic, the virus continued to spread in the United States, causing illness along with regular seasonal influenza viruses. Consider the following 2009 weekly data on total Swine Flu cases in the United States, reported by the Centers for Disease Control and Prevention (CDC).

Week	Total	Week	Total
17	1,190	22	2,904
18	2,012	23	3,024
19	1,459	24	3,206
20	2,247	25	1,829
21	2,280	26	1,093

Source: www.cdc.gov.

a. Plot the series. Estimate the linear and the quadratic trend models. Use their adjusted R^2 to choose the preferred model.
b. Given the preferred model, make a forecast for the number of Swine Flu cases in the U.S. for week 27.

15. **FILE** Rapid advances in technology have had a profound impact on the United States recording industry (*The New York Times*, July 28, 2008). While cassette tapes gave vinyl records strong competition, they were subsequently eclipsed by the introduction of the compact disc (CD) in the early 1980s. Lately, the CD, too, has been in rapid decline, primarily because of Internet music stores. The following data show a portion of year-end shipment statistics on the three formats of the United States recording industry, in particular, the manufacturers' unit shipments, in millions, of vinyl, cassettes, and CDs from 1991 to 2008. The full data set can be found on the text website, labeled **Recording Industry**.

Year	Vinyl	Cassettes	CDs
1991	4.8	360.1	333.3
1992	2.3	366.4	407.5
⋮	⋮	⋮	⋮
2008	2.9	0.1	384.7

Source: www.riaa.com.

a. Plot the series for cassettes. Estimate the quadratic and the cubic trend models for this series. Make a forecast with the chosen model for 2009.

b. Plot the series for CDs. Estimate the linear and the quadratic trend models for this series. Make a forecast with the chosen model for 2009.

16. **FILE** While the national unemployment rate may have ticked up slightly in 2010, in states such as California, Nevada, and Michigan the employment picture continues to look grim (CNNMoney, September 21, 2010). Consider the following table, which lists a portion of the monthly unemployment rates (seasonally adjusted) in California from 2007–2010. The full data set can be found on the text website, labeled **California Unemployment**.

Year	Month	Unemployment Rate (%)
2007	Jan	4.9
2007	Feb	5.0
⋮	⋮	⋮
2010	Dec	12.5

Source: Bureau of Labor Statistics.

a. Plot the above series. Which polynomial trend model do you think is most appropriate?

b. Verify your answer by formally comparing the linear, the quadratic, and the cubic trend models.

c. Forecast the unemployment rate in California for January 2011.

18.4 Trend and Seasonality

As mentioned earlier, time series generally consist of systematic and unsystematic patterns. Smoothing methods prove useful for forecasting a series that is described primarily by an unsystematic component. Systematic patterns are identified by the trend, seasonal, and cyclical components. In the preceding section we focused on trend. We now turn our attention to the seasonal and the cyclical components of systematic time series.

The **seasonal** component typically represents repetitions over a one-year period. Time series consisting of weekly, monthly, or quarterly observations tend to exhibit seasonal variations that repeat year after year. For instance, every year, sales of retail goods increase during the Christmas season, and the number of vacation packages goes up during the summer. The **cyclical** component represents wavelike fluctuations or business cycles, often caused by expansion and contraction of the economy. Unlike the well-defined seasons, the length of a business cycle varies, as fluctuations may last for several months or years. In addition, even the magnitude of business cycles varies over time. Because cycles vary in length and amplitude, they are difficult to capture with historical data. For these reasons, we ignore the cyclical component in this text and refer the reader to advanced books for further details.

In this section we will make forecasts based on the seasonal as well as the trend components of a series. Note that some economic series are available in a seasonally adjusted format. In such instances, we only have to focus on trend.

Decomposition Analysis

Let T, S, and I represent the trend, the seasonal, and the random components, respectively, of the time series y_t. With seasonal data, it is necessary to model seasonality along with trend. Consider the following multiplicative model, which relates sample observations to T, S, and I:

$$y_t = T_t \times S_t \times I_t.$$

We can use sample information to extract the trend and the seasonal components of the series and then project them into the future. Let $\hat{T}_t$ and $\hat{S}_t$ denote the estimated trend and seasonal components, respectively. Note that by their very nature, random variations cannot be identified. Therefore, we set $\hat{I}_t = 1$ and make forecasts as $\hat{y}_t = \hat{T}_t \times \hat{S}_t$. This process is often referred to as **decomposition analysis**. Alternatively, we can use a multiple regression model to simultaneously estimate trend along with **seasonal dummy variables**. We first elaborate on decomposition analysis, then discuss the use of seasonal dummy variables.

In the introductory case to this chapter, we considered the **Nike Revenues** data on Nike's quarterly revenue from 1999 through 2008. Figure 18.8 is a scatterplot of the data, where we have relabeled the 10 years of quarterly observations from 1 to 40. The graph highlights some important characteristics of Nike's revenue. First, there is a persistent upward movement in the data. Second, the trend does not seem to be linear and is likely to be better captured by an exponential model. Third, a seasonal pattern repeats itself year after year. For instance, revenue is consistently higher in the first and fourth quarters as compared to the second and third quarters.

FIGURE 18.8 Scatterplot of Nike's quarterly revenue (in millions $)

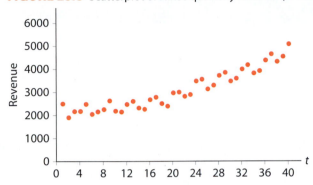

Extracting Seasonality

Moving averages are often employed to separate the effect of trend from seasonality. Given quarterly data, we use a 4-period moving average by averaging all sets of four consecutive quarterly values of the series. Using the earlier notation, let y_t denote revenue at time t and let $\bar{y}_t$ represent its corresponding 4-period moving average. We calculate the first moving average as

$$\bar{y}_{2.5} = \frac{y_1 + y_2 + y_3 + y_4}{4} = \frac{2{,}505 + 1{,}913 + 2{,}177 + 2{,}182}{4} = 2{,}194.25.$$

We designate the first moving average $\bar{y}_{2.5}$ because it represents the average in quarters 1 through 4. The next two moving averages, representing the average in quarters 2 through 5, and quarters 3 through 6, respectively, are

$$\bar{y}_{3.5} = \frac{y_2 + y_3 + y_4 + y_5}{4} = \frac{1{,}913 + 2{,}177 + 2{,}182 + 2{,}501}{4} = 2{,}193.25, \text{ and}$$

$$\bar{y}_{4.5} = \frac{y_3 + y_4 + y_5 + y_6}{4} = \frac{2{,}177 + 2{,}182 + 2{,}501 + 2{,}060}{4} = 2{,}230.00.$$

Other moving averages are calculated similarly.

We note two important points at the outset. First, a 4-period moving average basically represents a quarterly average in one year. The first moving average uses all four quarters of 1999, the second uses three quarters of 1999 and one of 2000, and so on. Since all four quarters are represented in every 4-period moving average, it eliminates seasonal fluctuations in the series. Second, while it is appropriate to designate a moving average in the middle quarter, there is no middle quarter in the original series. For instance, the moving average is represented by $\bar{y}_{2.5}, \bar{y}_{3.5}, \bar{y}_{4.5}$, etc. when the original series is y_1, y_2, y_3, etc.

In order to represent an even-period moving average, we rely on the **centered moving average CMA**, which is essentially the average of two consecutive moving averages. In the above example, the first 4-period centered moving average is formed as an average of the first two 4-period moving averages. In other words,

$$\bar{y}_3 = \frac{\bar{y}_{2.5} + \bar{y}_{3.5}}{2} = \frac{2{,}194.25 + 2{,}193.25}{2} = 2{,}193.75.$$

LO **18.4**

Calculate and interpret seasonal indices and use them to seasonally adjust a time series.

Note that this centered moving average $\bar{y}_3$ is not designated in the middle quarter and corresponds with y_3 of the actual series. Similarly,

$$\bar{y}_4 = \frac{\bar{y}_{3.5} + \bar{y}_{4.5}}{2} = \frac{2{,}193.25 + 2{,}230.00}{2} = 2{,}211.63.$$

The *CMA* series, $\bar{y}_t$, is shown in column 4 of Table 18.12. (We should mention here that Excel calculates $\bar{y}_{2.5}, \bar{y}_{3.5}, \bar{y}_{4.5}, \ldots$, when calculating a 4-quarter moving average. We then need to prompt Excel to "center" the values by creating another column that calculates the average between each pairing.)

TABLE 18.12 Analysis of Seasonal Data

Period	t	y	Centered Moving Average: $\bar{y}$	Ratio-to-Moving Average: $y/\bar{y}$
1999:01	1	2,505	—	—
1999:02	2	1,913	—	—
1999:03	3	2,177	2,193.75	0.9924
1999:04	4	2,182	2,211.63	0.9866
⋮	⋮	⋮	⋮	⋮
2008:01	37	4,655	4,403.38	1.0571
2008:02	38	4,340	4,568.63	0.9500
2008:03	39	4,544	—	—
2008:04	40	5,088	—	—

We note that $\bar{y}_t$ eliminates seasonal variations and also some random variations, that is, $\bar{y}_t$ represents a series that only includes the trend component T_t. Heuristically, since $y_t = T_t \times S_t \times I_t$ and $\bar{y}_t = T_t$, when we divide y_t by $\bar{y}_t$, we are left with $S_t \times I_t$. This series, $y_t/\bar{y}_t$ is called the **ratio-to-moving average** and is presented in column 5 of Table 18.12.

In Table 18.13, we rearrange $y_t/\bar{y}_t$ by quarter from 1999–2008. Note that each quarter has multiple ratios, where each ratio corresponds to a different year. For instance, $y_t/\bar{y}_t$ for the third quarter is 0.9924 in 1999, 0.9541 in 2000, and so on. In this example, each quarter has nine ratios. We use the arithmetic average (sometimes statisticians prefer to use the median) to determine a common value for each quarter. By averaging, we basically cancel out the random component and extract the seasonal component of the series. We refer to this summary measure as the **unadjusted seasonal index** for the quarter. For instance, the average of the ratios for the first quarter is calculated as $(1.1225 + \cdots + 1.0571)/9 = 1.0815$.

TABLE 18.13 Computation of Seasonal Indices

Year	Quarter 1	Quarter 2	Quarter 3	Quarter 4
1999	—	—	0.9924	0.9866
2000	1.1225	0.9206	0.9541	0.9881
⋮	⋮	⋮	⋮	⋮
2008	1.0571	0.9500	—	—
Unadjusted Seasonal Index	1.0815	0.9413	0.9379	1.0377
Adjusted Seasonal Index	1.0819	0.9417	0.9383	1.0381

For quarterly data, the seasonal indices must add up to 4 (the number of seasons or m) so that the average is one. In order to ensure this requirement, we multiply each unadjusted seasonal index by 4 and divide by the sum of the four unadjusted seasonal indices. In this case, the "multiplier" equals

$$\text{Multiplier} = \frac{4}{1.0815 + 0.9413 + 0.9379 + 1.0377} = 1.0004.$$

Therefore, the adjusted seasonal index for quarter 1 is calculated as 1.0815(1.0004) = 1.0819. This is our final estimate of the seasonal index rounded to the 4th decimal place—it is referred to as the **adjusted seasonal index**. Table 18.13 shows adjusted seasonal indices for each quarter. Note that the average of the adjusted seasonal indices equals one.

Let us interpret these adjusted seasonal indices. There is no seasonality if all indices equal their average of one. On the other hand, if the seasonal index for a quarter is greater (less) than one, it implies that the observations in the given quarter are greater (less) than the average quarterly values. In the above example, the adjusted seasonal index of 1.0819 for quarter 1 implies that Nike's revenue is about 8.19% higher in the first quarter as compared to the average quarterly revenue. The adjusted seasonal index for the second quarter is 0.9417, suggesting that revenues are about 5.83% lower than the average quarterly revenue. Other adjusted seasonal indices are interpreted similarly.

CALCULATING A SEASONAL INDEX

- Calculate the **moving average MA** (if m is odd) or the **centered moving average CMA** (if m is even) of the series. We represent MA or CMA by $\bar{y}_t$.
- Compute the **ratio-to-moving average** as $y_t/\bar{y}_t$.
- Find the average of $y_t/\bar{y}_t$ for each season. This average is referred to as the **unadjusted seasonal index**.
- Multiply each unadjusted seasonal index by $m/$(Sum of the unadjusted seasonal indices), where m is the number of seasons. The resulting value, referred to as the **adjusted seasonal index**, is the final estimate for the seasonal index.

Extracting Trend

In order to extract the trend from a time series, we first eliminate seasonal variations by dividing the original series y_t by its corresponding adjusted seasonal index $\hat{S}_t$. Here $\hat{S}_t$ represents four quarters of adjusted seasonal indices, repeated over the years. The seasonally adjusted series, $y_t/\hat{S}_t$, is shown in column 5 of Table 18.14.

LO **18.5**

Use decomposition analysis to make forecasts.

TABLE 18.14 Creating Seasonally Adjusted Series

Period	t	Unadjusted Series: y	Seasonal Index: S	Seasonally Adjusted Series: $y/\hat{S}$
1999:01	1	2,505	1.0819	2,315.29
1999:02	2	1,913	0.9417	2,031.39
1999:03	3	2,177	0.9383	2,320.24
1999:04	4	2,182	1.0381	2,101.97
2000:01	5	2,501	1.0819	2,311.59
⋮	⋮	⋮	⋮	⋮
2008:04	40	5,088	1.0381	4,901.38

As noted earlier, the adjusted seasonal index of 1.0819 implies that Nike's revenue in the first quarter is about 8.19% higher than average quarterly revenue. Therefore, without the seasonal effect, the revenue would be lower. For instance, the revenue of 2,505 million in 1999:01 is only 2,315.29 million once it has been seasonally adjusted (we used unrounded values in the calculations). In Figure 18.9, we plot revenue along with seasonally adjusted revenue.

Note that the seasonally adjusted series is free of seasonal variations, thus highlighting the long-term movement (trend) of the series. Figure 18.9 also confirms that the exponential trend model is better suited for the data than is the linear trend model.

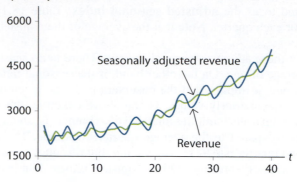

FIGURE 18.9 Regular and seasonally adjusted quarterly revenue

In order to obtain the **seasonally adjusted series**, we divide the original series by its corresponding seasonal index ($y_t/\hat{S}_t$). We use the appropriate trend model on the seasonally adjusted series to extract the trend component $\hat{T}_t$.

We estimate the exponential trend model where the response variable is the natural log of the seasonally adjusted revenues $\ln(y_t/\hat{S}_t)$ and the explanatory variable t assumes values 1, 2, . . . , 40, representing 10 years of quarterly data from 1999 to 2008. The relevant portion of the regression output is given in Table 18.15. We encourage you to compare the results of this model with the linear trend model, using model selection criteria.

TABLE 18.15 Exponential Regression Results on Seasonally Adjusted Data

	Coefficients	Standard Error	t Stat	p-value
Intercept	7.5571	0.0185	407.52	0.00
t	0.0218	0.0008	27.63	0.00
Standard error of the estimate s_e equals 0.0575.				

Note that the slope coefficient is positive and highly significant (p-value $\approx$ 0). We forecast trend for the seasonally adjusted revenue as $\hat{T}_t = \exp(b_0 + b_1 t + s_e^2/2)$. Therefore, a trend forecast for the seasonally adjusted revenue in the first quarter of 2009 is computed as

$$\hat{T}_{2009:01} = \hat{T}_{41} = \exp(7.5571 + 0.0218(41) + 0.0575^2/2) = 4{,}687.02.$$

Similarly, the seasonally adjusted trend for other quarters is computed as

$$\hat{T}_{2009:02} = \hat{T}_{42} = \exp(7.5571 + 0.0218(42) + 0.0575^2/2) = 4{,}790.32,$$
$$\hat{T}_{2009:03} = \hat{T}_{43} = \exp(7.5571 + 0.0218(43) + 0.0575^2/2) = 4{,}895.90, \text{ and}$$
$$\hat{T}_{2009:04} = \hat{T}_{44} = \exp(7.5571 + 0.0218(44) + 0.0575^2/2) = 5{,}003.80.$$

As mentioned earlier, whenever possible, it is preferable to use unrounded estimates in deriving forecasts with an exponential trend model.

Forecasting with Decomposition Analysis

Now that we have estimated the trend and the seasonal components, we recompose them to make forecasts for Nike's quarterly revenue in 2009. We basically multiply the trend forecast of the seasonally adjusted series with the appropriate seasonal index. This gives us the forecast as $\hat{y}_t = \hat{T}_t \times \hat{S}_t$. The trend forecast of Nike's seasonally adjusted revenue in the first quarter of 2009 is $\hat{T}_{41} = 4{,}687.02$. We also have $\hat{S}_{41} = 1.0819$ since $t = 41$ represents the first quarter for which we expect the revenue to be 8.19% higher. Therefore, we derive the forecast as

$$\hat{y}_{2009:01} = \hat{y}_{41} = \hat{T}_{41} \times \hat{S}_{41} = 4{,}687.02 \times 1.0819 = \$5{,}070.89 \text{ million.}$$

Similarly, the forecast of Nike's revenue for the remaining quarters of 2009 is computed as

$$\hat{y}_{2009:02} = \hat{y}_{42} = \hat{T}_{42} \times \hat{S}_{42} = 4{,}790.32 \times 0.9417 = \$4{,}511.04 \text{ million,}$$

$$\hat{y}_{2009:03} = \hat{y}_{43} = \hat{T}_{43} \times \hat{S}_{43} = 4{,}895.90 \times 0.9383 = \$4{,}593.82 \text{ million, and}$$

$$\hat{y}_{2009:04} = \hat{y}_{44} = \hat{T}_{44} \times \hat{S}_{44} = 5{,}003.80 \times 1.0381 = \$5{,}194.44 \text{ million.}$$

EXAMPLE 18.5

A tourism specialist uses decomposition analysis to examine hotel occupancy rates for Bar Harbor, Maine. She collects quarterly data for the past five years ($n = 20$) and finds that the linear trend model best captures the trend of the seasonally adjusted series: $\hat{T}_t = 0.60 + 0.0049t$. In addition, she calculates quarterly indices as $\hat{S}_1 = 0.53$, $\hat{S}_2 = 0.90$, $\hat{S}_3 = 1.40$, and $\hat{S}_4 = 1.17$.

a. Interpret the first and third quarterly indices.

b. Forecast next year's occupancy rates.

SOLUTION:

a. The first quarter's index of 0.53 implies that the occupancy rate in the first quarter is 47% below the average quarterly occupancy rate, whereas the occupancy rate in the third quarter is 40% above the average quarterly occupancy rate.

b. We calculate the next year's quarterly occupancy rates as $\hat{y}_t = \hat{T}_t \times \hat{S}_t$, or

Year 6, Quarter 1: $\hat{y}_{21} = (0.60 + 0.0049(21)) \times 0.53 = 0.3725$.

Year 6, Quarter 2: $\hat{y}_{22} = (0.60 + 0.0049(22)) \times 0.90 = 0.6370$.

Year 6, Quarter 3: $\hat{y}_{23} = (0.60 + 0.0049(23)) \times 1.40 = 0.9978$.

Year 6, Quarter 4: $\hat{y}_{24} = (0.60 + 0.0049(24)) \times 1.17 = 0.8396$.

Seasonal Dummy Variables

LO 18.6

Use trend regression models with seasonal dummy variables to make forecasts.

With the method of **seasonal dummy variables**, we estimate a trend forecasting model that includes seasonal dummies. In Chapter 17, we studied that a dummy variable is a binary variable that equals either 0 or 1. Dummy variables are used to describe a qualitative variable with two or more categories. Here we use them to describe seasons. For quarterly data, we need to define only three dummy variables. Let d_1, d_2, and d_3 be the dummy variables for the first three quarters, using the fourth quarter as reference. Therefore for quarter 1, we use $d_1 = 1$, $d_2 = 0$, and $d_3 = 0$. Similarly, for quarter 2, $d_1 = 0$, $d_2 = 1$, and $d_3 = 0$, for quarter 3, $d_1 = 0$, $d_2 = 0$, and $d_3 = 1$, and for quarter 4, $d_1 = 0$, $d_2 = 0$, and $d_3 = 0$.

The linear and the exponential trend models with seasonal dummy variables are summarized below; here we remove the t subscript to simplify the notation.

TREND MODELS WITH SEASONAL DUMMY VARIABLES

A **linear trend model with seasonal dummy variables** is specified as

$$y = \beta_0 + \beta_1 d_1 + \beta_2 d_2 + \beta_3 d_3 + \beta_4 t + \varepsilon.$$

Forecasts based on the estimated model are as follows:

Quarter 1 ($d_1 = 1, d_2 = 0, d_3 = 0$): $\hat{y}_t = (b_0 + b_1) + b_4 t$

Quarter 2 ($d_1 = 0, d_2 = 1, d_3 = 0$): $\hat{y}_t = (b_0 + b_2) + b_4 t$

Quarter 3 ($d_1 = 0, d_2 = 0, d_3 = 1$): $\hat{y}_t = (b_0 + b_3) + b_4 t$

Quarter 4 ($d_1 = 0, d_2 = 0, d_3 = 0$): $\hat{y}_t = b_0 + b_4 t$

An **exponential trend model with seasonal dummy variables** is specified as

$$\ln(y) = \beta_0 + \beta_1 d_1 + \beta_2 d_2 + \beta_3 d_3 + \beta_4 t + \varepsilon.$$

Forecasts based on the estimated model are as follows:

$$\text{Quarter 1 } (d_1 = 1, d_2 = 0, d_3 = 0): \hat{y}_t = \exp((b_0 + b_1) + b_4 t + s_e^2/2)$$
$$\text{Quarter 2 } (d_1 = 0, d_2 = 1, d_3 = 0): \hat{y}_t = \exp((b_0 + b_2) + b_4 t + s_e^2/2)$$
$$\text{Quarter 3 } (d_1 = 0, d_2 = 0, d_3 = 1): \hat{y}_t = \exp((b_0 + b_3) + b_4 t + s_e^2/2)$$
$$\text{Quarter 4 } (d_1 = 0, d_2 = 0, d_3 = 0): \hat{y}_t = \exp(b_0 + b_4 t + s_e^2/2)$$

FILE **EXAMPLE 18.6**

Revisit the *Nike Revenues* data considered in the introductory case. Use the seasonal dummy variable model to make a forecast for Nike's quarterly revenue in 2009.

SOLUTION: Given quarterly data, we first construct relevant variables for the regression. Table 18.16 specifies seasonal dummy variables, along with the time variable t.

TABLE 18.16 Constructing Seasonal Dummy Variables (Example 18.6)

Period	y	$\ln(y)$	t	d_1	d_2	d_3
1999:01	2,505	7.8260	1	1	0	0
1999:02	1,913	7.5564	2	0	1	0
1999:03	2,177	7.6857	3	0	0	1
1999:04	2,182	7.6880	4	0	0	0
2000:01	2,501	7.8245	5	1	0	0
2000:02	2,060	7.6305	6	0	1	0
2000:03	2,162	7.6788	7	0	0	1
2000:04	2,273	7.7289	8	0	0	0
⋮	⋮	⋮	⋮	⋮	⋮	⋮
2008:03	4544	8.4216	39	0	0	1
2008:04	5,088	8.5346	40	0	0	0

As in the case of decomposition analysis, we use the exponential model to capture trend: $\ln(y) = \beta_0 + \beta_1 d_1 + \beta_2 d_2 + \beta_3 d_3 + \beta_4 t + \varepsilon$. Relevant estimates of the regression model are presented in Table 18.17.

TABLE 18.17 Regression Results for Example 18.6

	Coefficients	Standard Error	t Stat	p-value
Intercept	7.5929	0.0261	290.57	0.00
d_1	0.0501	0.0268	1.87	0.07
d_2	−0.1036	0.0267	−3.87	0.00
d_3	−0.0985	0.0267	−3.69	0.00
t	0.0218	0.0008	26.53	0.00
The standard error of the estimate s_e equals 0.0597.				

The estimated equation, with values rounded to the 4th decimal place, is $\hat{y} = \exp(7.5929 + 0.0501 d_1 - 0.1036 d_2 - 0.0985 d_3 + 0.0218 t + 0.0597^2/2)$. The coefficients for seasonal dummy variables indicate that the revenue is about 5% higher in the first quarter and about 10% lower in the second and third quarters as compared to the fourth quarter. The trend coefficient suggests that the quarterly increase in revenue is about 2.18%.

For 2009:01, we use $d_1 = 1$, $d_2 = 0$, $d_3 = 0$, $t = 41$ to forecast Nike's revenue as $\hat{y}_{41} = \exp(7.5929 + 0.0501 + 0.0218(41) + 0.0597^2/2) = \$5,108.10$ million. Similarly, for 2009:02, we use $d_1 = 0$, $d_2 = 1$, $d_3 = 0$, $t = 42$ to determine $\hat{y}_{42} = \exp(7.5929 - 0.1036 + 0.0218(42) + 0.0597^2/2) = \$4,476.88$ million.

Forecasts for 2009:03 and 2009:04 yield \$4,598.94 million and \$5,186.85 million, respectively. As before, whenever possible, it is advisable to make forecasts with unrounded values.

As emphasized earlier, we always use model selection criteria to choose the appropriate forecasting model. In Table 18.18 we present the *MSE* and *MAD* based on the residuals, $e_t = y_t - \hat{y}_t$, with decomposition analysis and seasonal dummy variables; we did these calculations in Excel with unrounded values for the estimates. We encourage you to replicate these results.

TABLE 18.18 In-Sample Model Selection Criteria

Model	MSE	MAD
Decomposition Analysis	24,353.95	118.10
Seasonal Dummy Variables	24,843.48	121.32

We select the decomposition analysis method to make forecasts because it has the lower *MSE* and *MAD* of in-sample forecast errors. Therefore, the quarterly forecasts for 2009, as derived earlier, are \$5,070.89, \$4,511.04, \$4,593.82, and \$5,194.44 million, respectively. This results in a sum of \$19,370.19 million or \$19.37 billion for fiscal year 2009.

SYNOPSIS OF INTRODUCTORY CASE

Nike, Inc., is the world's leading supplier and manufacturer of athletic shoes, apparel, and sports equipment. Its revenue in the fiscal year ending May 31, 2008, was \$18.627 billion. While some analysts argue that a slowdown of Nike's revenue may occur due to the global economic crisis and increased competition from emerging brands, others believe that with its strong cash flow, Nike will emerge even stronger than before as its competitors get squeezed. This report analyzes the quarterly revenue of Nike from 1999–2008 to make a forecast for fiscal year 2009.

The detailed analysis of the data suggests significant trend and seasonal components in Nike's revenue. For each fiscal year, the revenue is generally higher in the first quarter (June 1–August 31) and the fourth quarter (March 1–May 31). This result is not surprising given that these quarters cover summer and spring seasons, when people most often participate in outdoor activities. Based on various model selection criteria, the decomposition method is chosen as the preferred forecasting technique. It provides forecasts by multiplying the exponential trend estimate with the corresponding seasonal index. The quarterly revenue forecasts for 2009 are \$5,070.89, \$4,511.04, \$4,593.82, and \$5,194.44 million, respectively, resulting in \$19.37 billion for fiscal year 2009. Interestingly, this forecast, based on a time series analysis of revenue, is extremely close to the actual revenue of \$19.20 billion reported by Nike.

EXERCISES 18.4

Concepts

17. Six years of quarterly data of a seasonally adjusted series are used to estimate a linear trend model as $\hat{T}_t = 128.20 + 1.06t$. In addition, quarterly seasonal indices are calculated as $\hat{S}_1 = 0.93$, $\hat{S}_2 = 0.88$, $\hat{S}_3 = 1.14$, and $\hat{S}_4 = 1.05$.

    a. Interpret the first and fourth quarterly indices.

    b. Make a forecast for all four quarters of next year.

18. Eight years of quarterly data of a seasonally adjusted series are used to estimate an exponential trend model as $\widehat{\ln(T_t)} = 2.80 + 0.03t$ with a standard error of the estimate, $s_e = 0.08$. In addition, quarterly seasonal indices are calculated as $\hat{S}_1 = 0.94$, $\hat{S}_2 = 1.08$, $\hat{S}_3 = 0.86$, and $\hat{S}_4 = 1.12$.

    a. Interpret the third and fourth quarterly indices.

    b. Make a forecast for all four quarters of next year.

19. Ten years of monthly data of a seasonally adjusted series are used to estimate a linear trend model as $\hat{T}_t = 24.50 + 0.48t$. In addition, seasonal indices for January and February are calculated as 1.04 and 0.92, respectively. Make a forecast for the first two months of next year.

20. **FILE** Consider the following 20 observations, representing quarterly information for 5 years. The data are also on the text website, labeled **Exercise 18.20**.

Year	Quarter 1	Quarter 2	Quarter 3	Quarter 4
1	8.37	12.78	8.84	15.93
2	10.03	12.48	8.91	24.81
3	9.61	9.65	15.93	22.00
4	8.80	11.45	6.79	10.16
5	7.46	10.58	13.35	19.77

    a. Calculate the 4-quarter centered moving average.

    b. Calculate the ratio-to-moving average.

    c. Calculate and interpret the seasonal indices for quarters 1 and 4.

21. **FILE** Consider the following monthly observations for 5 years. The data are also on the text website, labeled **Exercise 18.21**.

Year	Jan	Feb	Mar	Apr	May	Jun	Jul	Aug	Sep	Oct	Nov	Dec
1	13	17	15	12	32	15	21	17	33	15	34	21
2	26	10	14	19	17	14	27	30	25	15	18	27
3	24	11	19	23	19	18	31	18	15	31	34	27
4	23	22	17	24	17	24	15	19	33	19	16	39
5	17	19	25	30	18	17	19	36	19	26	21	35

    a. Calculate the 12-month centered moving average.

    b. Calculate the ratio-to-moving average.

    c. Calculate and interpret the seasonal indices for April and November.

22. **FILE** Consider the following 20 observations, representing quarterly information for 5 years. The data are also on the text website, labeled **Exercise 18.22**.

Year	Q1	Q2	Q3	Q4
1	6.49	7.34	7.11	10.82
2	7.04	7.92	7.69	11.71
3	7.62	8.58	8.34	12.68
4	8.25	9.29	9.02	13.74
5	8.94	10.08	9.78	14.88

    a. Plot the above series and discuss its trend and seasonal components.

    b. Use decomposition analysis to make forecasts with the exponential trend and seasonal indices. Compute the mean square errors of in-sample forecast errors.

    c. Estimate an exponential trend with seasonal dummies model. Compute the mean square errors of in-sample forecast errors.

    d. Use the appropriate model to make forecasts for all four quarters of the next year.

23. **FILE** Consider a portion of monthly sales data for 5 years for a growing firm. The full data set can be found on the text website, labeled **Exercise 18.23**.

Year	Month	Sales
1	Jan	345
1	Feb	322
⋮	⋮	⋮
5	Dec	10,745

    a. Construct the seasonal indices for the data.

    b. Plot the seasonally adjusted series to recommend the appropriate trend model.

    c. Use the trend and seasonal estimates to make forecasts for the next two months.

24. **FILE** Revisit the **Exercise 18.23** data to estimate (a) a linear trend model with seasonal dummies, (b) an exponential trend model with seasonal dummies. Which of the two models has a lower *MSE* and *MAD*? Use the appropriate model to make forecasts for the next two months.

Applications

25. **FILE** Hybrid cars have gained popularity because of their fuel economy and the uncertainty regarding the price of gasoline. All automakers, including the Ford Motor Co., have planned to significantly expand their hybrid vehicle lineup (CNN.com, November 9, 2005). The following table contains quarterly sales of Ford and Mercury hybrid cars. The data are also on the text website, labeled **Sales Data**.

Year	Q1	Q2	Q3	Q4
2006	6,192	5,663	4,626	5,645
2007	5,149	6,272	5,196	6,545
2008	5,467	5,235	3,160	7,007
2009	5,337			

Source: Internal Revenue Service, United States Department of Treasury.

a. Plot the above series. Comment on the trend and seasonal variation in the sales of hybrid cars.

b. Compute and interpret the seasonal indices.

26. **FILE** Consider a portion of monthly return data on 20-year Treasury Bonds from 2006–2010. The full data set can be found on the text website, labeled **Treasury Bonds**.

Year	Month	Return (%)
2006	Jan	4.65
2006	Feb	4.73
⋮	⋮	⋮
2010	Dec	4.16

Source: Federal Reserve Bank of Dallas.

a. Plot the above series and discuss its seasonal variations.

b. Construct the seasonal indices for the data.

c. Estimate a linear trend model to the seasonally adjusted series.

d. Use the trend and seasonal estimates to make forecasts for the first three months of 2011.

27. **FILE** Revisit the **Treasury Bonds** data to estimate a linear trend model with seasonal dummy variables to make forecasts for the first three months of 2011.

28. **FILE** The controller of a small construction company is attempting to forecast expenses for the next year. He collects quarterly data on expenses (in $1,000s) over the past 5 years, a portion of which is shown in the accompanying table. The full data set is on the text website, labeled **Expenses**.

Year	Quarter	Expenses
2006	1	$2,136
2006	2	2,253
⋮	⋮	⋮
2010	4	3,109

a. Estimate a linear trend model with seasonal dummy variables and compute the *MSE* and *MAD* of in-sample forecast errors.

b. Estimate an exponential trend model with seasonal dummy variables and compute the resulting *MSE* and *MAD*.

c. Which model is more appropriate? With this model, forecast expenses for year 2011.

29. **FILE** Blockbuster Inc. has lately faced challenges by the growing online market (CNNMoney.com, March 3, 2009). Its revenue from rental stores has been sagging as customers are increasingly getting their movies through the mail or high-speed Internet connections. The following table contains a portion of the total revenue from rentals of all formats of movies at Blockbuster Inc. (in millions of dollars). The full data set can be found on the text website, labeled **Blockbuster**.

Year	Quarter	Revenue
2001	1	$1.403683
2001	2	1.287625
⋮	⋮	⋮
2008	4	1.097712

a. Compute seasonal indices.

b. Fit linear and quadratic trend models to the seasonally adjusted data. Which model do you prefer?

c. Use decomposition analysis to make quarterly forecasts for 2009.

30. **FILE** Revisit the **Blockbuster** data to:

a. Estimate a linear trend model with seasonal dummies.

b. Estimate a quadratic trend model with seasonal dummies.

c. Use the appropriate model to make quarterly forecasts for 2009.

31. **FILE** While there is still an overwhelmingly gloomy outlook, Americans are growing more upbeat about the economy (CNNMoney.com, October 26, 2010). The following table lists a portion of the University of Michigan's Consumer Sentiment Index. This index is normalized to have a value of 100 in 1965 and is used to record changes in consumer morale. The full data set can be found on the text website, labeled **Consumer Sentiment**.

Year	Month	Consumer Sentiment
2005	Jan	95.5
2005	Feb	91.2
⋮	⋮	⋮
2010	Oct	67.7

Source: Federal Reserve Bank of St. Louis.

a. Plot and interpret the series.

b. Construct and interpret seasonal indices for the series.

c. Estimate linear, quadratic and cubic trend models to the seasonally adjusted data. Select the best fitting model.

d. Use decomposition analysis to make a forecast for November and December of 2010.

32. **FILE** Use the **Consumer Sentiment** data from the preceding question. Fit an appropriate polynomial trend model along with seasonal dummies to make a forecast for November and December of 2010.

18.5 Causal Forecasting Methods

LO 18.7

Use causal forecasting models to make forecasts.

So far we have discussed noncausal, or purely time series, models. These models do not offer any explanation of the mechanism generating the variable of interest and simply provide a method for projecting historical data. Although this method can be effective, it provides no guidance on the likely effects of changes in policy (explanatory) variables. **Causal forecasting models** are based on a regression framework, where the explanatory variables influence the outcome of the response variable. For instance, consider the following simple linear regression model:

$$y_t = \beta_0 + \beta_1 x_t + \varepsilon_t.$$

Here y is the response variable caused by the explanatory variable x. Let the sample observations be denoted by $y_1, y_2, \ldots, y_T$ and $x_1, x_2, \ldots, x_T$, respectively. Once we have estimated this model, we can make a one-step-ahead forecast as

$$\hat{y}_{T+1} = b_0 + b_1 x_{T+1}.$$

Multi-step-ahead forecasts can be made similarly. This causal approach works only if we know, or can predict, the future value of the explanatory variable x_{T+1}. For instance, let sales y be related to expenditure on advertisement x. We can forecast sales $\hat{y}_{T+1}$ only if we know the advertisement budget, x_{T+1}, for the next period.

Lagged Regression Models

For forecasting, sometimes we use a causal approach with lagged values of x and y as explanatory variables. For instance, consider the model,

$$y_t = \beta_0 + \beta_1 x_{t-1} + \varepsilon_t,$$

where β_1 represents the slope of the lagged explanatory variable x. Note that if we have T sample observations, the estimable sample will consist of $T - 1$ observations, where $y_2, y_3, \ldots, y_T$ are matched with $x_1, x_2, \ldots, x_{T-1}$. Here a one-step-ahead forecast is easily made as

$$\hat{y}_{T+1} = b_0 + b_1 x_T.$$

This forecast is not conditional on any predicted value of the explanatory variables, since x_T is its last known sample value. We can generalize this model to include more lags of x. For example, we can specify a two-period lagged regression model as $y_t = \beta_0 + \beta_1 x_{t-1} + \beta_2 x_{t-2} + \varepsilon_t$. A one-step-ahead forecast is now made as $\hat{y}_{T+1} = b_0 + b_1 x_T + b_2 x_{T-1}$.

Another popular specification for causal forecasting uses lagged values of the response variable as an explanatory variable. For instance, consider the model

$$y_t = \beta_0 + \beta_1 y_{t-1} + \varepsilon_t,$$

where the parameter β_1 represents the slope of the lagged response variable y. This regression is also referred to as an **autoregressive model** of order one, or simply an AR(1). Higher-order autoregressive models can be constructed similarly. A one-period-ahead forecast is made as

$$\hat{y}_{T+1} = b_0 + b_1 y_T.$$

Finally, we can also use lagged values of both x and y as the explanatory variables. For instance, consider

$$y_t = \beta_0 + \beta_1 x_{t-1} + \beta_2 y_{t-1} + \varepsilon_t.$$

Here, a one-period-ahead forecast is made as

$$\hat{y}_{T+1} = b_0 + b_1 x_T + b_2 y_T.$$

EXAMPLE 18.7

Table 18.19 shows a portion of data on net private housing units sold (in 1,000s), and real per-capita gross domestic product (in $1,000s); the entire data set is on the text website, labeled ***Housing Units***. Let Housing denote housing units sold and GDP denote real per-capita gross domestic product. Estimate the following three models and use the most suitable model to make a forecast for housing units sold in 2009.

Model 1: $\text{Housing}_t = \beta_0 + \beta_1 \text{GDP}_{t-1} + \varepsilon_t$.

Model 2: $\text{Housing}_t = \beta_0 + \beta_1 \text{Housing}_{t-1} + \varepsilon_t$.

Model 3: $\text{Housing}_t = \beta_0 + \beta_1 \text{GDP}_{t-1} + \beta_2 \text{Housing}_{t-1} + \varepsilon_t$.

TABLE 18.19 Housing and GDP Data

Year	Housing Units Sold	Real Per-Capita GDP
1981	436	23.007
1982	412	22.346
1983	623	23.146
⋮	⋮	⋮
2008	509	38.399

Source: The Department of Commerce.

SOLUTION: In order to estimate these models, we first have to lag Housing and GDP. Table 18.20 uses a portion of the data to show lagged values.

TABLE 18.20 Generating Lagged Values

Year	Housing$_t$	GDP$_t$	GDP$_{t-1}$	Housing$_{t-1}$
1981	436	23.007	—	—
1982	412	22.346	23.007	436
1983	623	23.146	22.346	412
⋮	⋮	⋮	⋮	⋮
2008	509	38,399	38.148	776

Note that we lose one observation for the regression, since we do not have information on the lagged values for 1981. Table 18.21 summarizes the regression results of the three models.

TABLE 18.21 Model Evaluation with Causal Forecasting

Parameters	Model 1	Model 2	Model 3
Constant	−112.9093	122.7884	300.0187
	(0.59)	(0.14)	(0.07)
GDP$_{t-1}$	29.0599*	NA	−10.9084
	(0.00)		(0.20)
Housing$_{t-1}$	NA	0.8433*	1.0439*
		(0.00)	(0.00)
Adjusted R^2	0.3974	0.7264	0.7340

NOTES: The top portion of the table contains parameter estimates with p-values in parentheses; NA denotes not applicable; the symbol * denotes significance at the 5% level.

As discussed earlier, it is preferable to compare competing multiple regression models in terms of adjusted R^2 since it appropriately penalizes for the excessive use of explanatory variables. We choose Model 3 because it has the highest adjusted R^2 of 0.7340. In particular,

$$\widehat{\text{Housing}}_{2009} = b_0 + b_1 \text{GDP}_{2008} + b_2 \text{Housing}_{2008}$$
$$= 300.0187 - 10.9084(38.399) + 1.0439(509) = 412.49.$$

Therefore, we forecast that about 412,490 net private housing units will be sold in 2009.

EXERCISES 18.5

Concepts

33. **FILE** Consider the following portion of data on the response variable y and the explanatory variable x. The data are on the text website, labeled **Exercise 18.33**.

t	y	x
1	27.96	29.88
2	30.15	21.07
⋮	⋮	⋮
12	24.47	26.41

a. Estimate $y_t = \beta_0 + \beta_1 x_{t-1} + \varepsilon_t$ and $y_t = \beta_0 + \beta_1 x_{t-1} + \beta_2 x_{t-2} + \varepsilon_t$.

b. Use the appropriate model to make a one-step-ahead forecast ($t = 13$) for y.

34. **FILE** Consider the following portion of data on the variable y. The data are on the text website, labeled **Exercise 18.34**.

t	y
1	29.32
2	30.96
⋮	⋮
24	48.58

a. Estimate an autoregressive model of order 1, $y_t = \beta_0 + \beta_1 y_{t-1} + \varepsilon_t$, to make a one-step-ahead forecast ($t = 25$) for y.

b. Estimate an autoregressive model of order 2, $y_t = \beta_0 + \beta_1 y_{t-1} + \beta_2 y_{t-2} + \varepsilon_t$, to make a one-step-ahead forecast ($t = 25$) for y.

c. Which of the above models is more appropriate for forecasts? Explain.

35. **FILE** Consider the following portion of data on y and x that appears on the text website, labeled **Exercise 18.35**.

t	y	x
1	18.23	17.30
2	19.82	16.05
⋮	⋮	⋮
12	22.75	13.66

a. Estimate $y_t = \beta_0 + \beta_1 x_{t-1} + \varepsilon_t$, to make a one-step-ahead forecast for period 13.

b. Estimate $y_t = \beta_0 + \beta_1 y_{t-1} + \varepsilon_t$, to make a one-step-ahead forecast for period 13.

c. Which of the above models is more appropriate for forecasts? Explain.

36. **FILE** Consider the following portion of data on y and x that appears on the text website, labeled **Exercise 18.36**.

t	y	x
1	56.96	9,171.61
2	57.28	9,286.56
⋮	⋮	⋮
12	51.99	9,217.94

a. Estimate $y_t = \beta_0 + \beta_1 x_{t-1} + \varepsilon_t$.

b. Estimate $y_t = \beta_0 + \beta_1 y_{t-1} + \varepsilon_t$.

c. Estimate $y_t = \beta_0 + \beta_1 x_{t-1} + \beta_2 y_{t-1} + \varepsilon_t$.

d. Use the most suitable model to make a one-step-ahead forecast ($t = 13$) for y.

Applications

37. Hiroshi Sato, an owner of a sushi restaurant in San Francisco, has been following an aggressive marketing campaign to thwart the effect of rising unemployment rates on business. He used monthly data on sales ($1,000s), advertising costs ($), and the unemployment rate (%) from January 2008 to May 2009 to estimate the following sample regression equation:

$$\widehat{Sales}_t = 17.51 + 0.03\text{Advertising Costs}_{t-1} - 0.69\text{Unemployment Rate}_{t-1}.$$

a. Hiroshi had budgeted $620 toward advertising costs in May 2009. Make a forecast for Sales for June 2009 if the unemployment rate in May 2009 was 9.1%.

b. What will be the forecast if he raises his advertisement budget to $700?

c. Reevaluate the above forecasts if the unemployment rate was 9.5% in May 2009.

38. **FILE** The Phillips curve is regarded as a reliable tool for forecasting inflation. It captures the inverse relation between the rate of unemployment and the rate of inflation; the lower the unemployment in an economy, the higher is the inflation rate. Consider the following portion of monthly data on seasonally adjusted inflation and unemployment rates in the United States from January 2009 to November 2010. The full data set can be found on the text website, labeled **Phillips Curve**.

Year	Month	Unemployment	Inflation
2009	Jan	7.7	0.3
2009	Feb	8.2	0.4
⋮	⋮	⋮	⋮
2010	Nov	9.8	0.1

Source: Bureau of Labor Statistics.

a. Estimate two models, of order 1 and 2, using unemployment as the response variable and lagged inflation as the explanatory variable(s). Should you use either model for forecasting unemployment? Explain.

b. Estimate autoregressive models of order 1 and 2 on unemployment. Choose the appropriate model to make a forecast of unemployment for December 2010.

39. **FILE** A research analyst at an investment firm is attempting to forecast the daily stock price of Home Depot, using causal models. The following table shows a portion of the daily adjusted closing prices of Home Depot y and the Dow Jones Industrial Average x from August 14, 2009, to August 31, 2009. The full data set is on the text website, labeled **HD and DOW**.

t	y	x
August 14	26.92	9,321.40
August 17	25.89	9,135.34
⋮	⋮	⋮
August 31	27.07	9,496.28

Source: www.finance.yahoo.

Estimate three models: (a) $y_t = \beta_0 + \beta_1 x_{t-1} + \varepsilon_t$, (b) $y_t = \beta_0 + \beta_1 y_{t-1} + \varepsilon_t$, and (c) $y_t = \beta_0 + \beta_1 x_{t-1} + \beta_2 y_{t-1} + \varepsilon_t$. Use the most suitable model to forecast Home Depot's daily stock price for September 1, 2009.

WRITING WITH STATISTICS

An important indicator of an economy is its inflation rate, which is generally defined as the percentage change in the consumer price index over a specific period of time. It is well documented that high inflation rates lead to a decline in the real value of money, which in turn can discourage investment and saving. The task of keeping the inflation rate within desired limits is entrusted to monetary authorities who use various policy instruments to control it. However, their actions depend primarily on their ability to gauge inflationary pressures accurately, or in other words, to correctly forecast the inflation rate.

Pooja Nanda is an economist working for *Creative Thinking*, a well-regarded policy institute based in Washington, DC. She has been given the challenging task of forecasting inflation for June 2009. She has access to seasonally adjusted monthly inflation rates in the United States from January 2007 to May 2009, a portion of which is shown in Table 18.22. The full data set can be found on the text website, labeled ***Inflation Rates***.

TABLE 18.22 Seasonally Adjusted Monthly Inflation Rates

FILE

Date	Inflation Rate
Jan-07	0.1
Feb-07	0.4
⋮	⋮
May-09	0.1

Source: Bureau of Labor Statistics.

Pooja would like to use the sample information to:

1. Evaluate various polynomial trend models for the inflation rate.
2. Use the best-fitting trend model to forecast the inflation rate for June 2009.

Economists generally agree that high levels of inflation are caused by the money supply growing faster than the rate of economic growth. During high inflationary pressures, monetary authorities decrease the money supply, thereby raising short-term interest rates. Sometimes they also have to contend with deflation, or a prolonged reduction in the level of prices. As prices fall, consumers tend to delay purchases until prices fall further, which in turn can depress overall economic activity.

The global economic crisis that began in the summer/fall of 2008 raised deflationary fears, with rapidly rising unemployment rates and capital markets in turmoil. An increase in price levels in 2007 was followed by a decrease in 2008 with a slight hint of price stability in the second quarter of 2009. This report does not focus on the effectiveness of monetary policy. Instead, a forecast of the inflation rate is made from a noncausal perspective by simply projecting historical data. Seasonality is not a concern, since the inflation data are already seasonally adjusted.

A simple plot of the inflation rate from January 2007 to May 2009 is shown in Figure 18.A. In order to gauge whether a linear or nonlinear trend is appropriate, various trend models are superimposed on the inflation rate scatterplot. The exponential trend is not included, since the log of the inflation rate is not defined for nonpositive inflation rates.

FIGURE 18.A Scatterplot of inflation (in percent) and superimposed trends

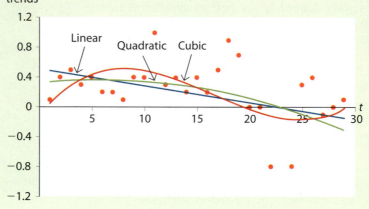

Interestingly, the implied forecasts seem to vary widely between competing models. Although Figure 18.A suggests that the cubic model accurately captures the changing trend of the inflation rate over the last 29 months, this finding must be supplemented with formal model selection criteria.

Three trend models were estimated, where y_t represents the inflation rate and t represents the relabeled monthly observations from 1 (January 2007) through 29 (May 2009).

$$\text{Linear Model: } y_t = \beta_0 + \beta_1 t + \varepsilon_t$$
$$\text{Quadratic Model: } y_t = \beta_0 + \beta_1 t + \beta_2 t^2 + \varepsilon_t$$
$$\text{Cubic Model: } y_t = \beta_0 + \beta_1 t + \beta_2 t^2 + \beta_3 t^3 + \varepsilon_t$$

Table 18.A presents parameter estimates of the three models. Also included in the table are the adjusted R^2 for model comparison, which suitably penalizes over parameterization.

TABLE 18.A Analysis of the Linear, Quadratic, and Cubic Trend Models

Variable	Linear	Quadratic	Cubic
Constant	0.5153*	NA	NA
	(0.011)		
t	−0.0229*	0.0583*	0.1472*
	(0.047)	(0.012)	(0.009)
t^2	NA	−0.0025*	−0.0125*
		(0.014)	(0.029)
t^3	NA	NA	0.0003*
			(0.072)
Adjusted R^2	0.1058	0.1463	0.2143

NOTES: The top portion of the table contains parameter estimates with p-values in parentheses; NA denotes not applicable; the constant is removed from the quadratic and cubic trend models since it is found to be insignificant; the symbol * represents significance at the 10% level; the last row of the table contains adjusted R^2 for model comparison.

Consistent with the informal graphical analysis, the cubic trend provides the best sample fit, as it has the highest adjusted R^2 of 0.2143. Therefore, the estimated cubic trend model is used with unrounded estimates to derive the forecast for June 2009 as

$$\hat{y}_{30} = 0.14724265(30) - 0.01253915(30^2) + 0.00025575(30^3) = 0.0372.$$

Inflation forecasts are widely regarded as key inputs for implementing monetary policy. Whether or not it can be forecasted accurately is an open empirical question. In this report, an attempt is made to forecast inflation, despite market turbulence.

Conceptual Review

LO 18.1 Distinguish among the various models used in forecasting.

Observations of any variable recorded over time in sequential order are considered a **time series**. The purpose of any forecasting model is to forecast the outcome of a time series at time t, or $\hat{y}_t$. Forecasting methods are broadly classified as **quantitative** or **qualitative**. While qualitative forecasts are based on prior experience and the expertise of the forecaster, quantitative forecasts use a formal model, along with historical data for the variable of interest. Quantitative forecasting models are further divided into **causal** and **noncausal models**. Causal methods are based on a regression framework, where the variable of interest is related to a single or multiple explanatory variables. Noncausal models, also referred to as purely time series models, do not present any explanation of the mechanism generating the variable of interest and simply provide a method for projecting historical data.

The in-sample forecast $\hat{y}_t$ is also called the **predicted** or **fitted** value of y_t. The in-sample forecast errors or the **residuals** are computed as $e_t = y_t - \hat{y}_t$. We use the residuals, computed as $e_t = y_t - \hat{y}_t$, to compute $MSE = \frac{\Sigma e_t^2}{n}$ and $MAD = \frac{\Sigma |e_t|}{n}$. When selecting among various models, we choose the one with the smallest MSE and MAD. If MSE and MAD provide conflicting results, then we choose the model with the smallest MSE.

LO 18.2 Use smoothing techniques to make forecasts.

Time series consist of **systematic** and **unsystematic** patterns. Systematic patterns are caused by the **trend**, the **seasonal**, and the **cyclical** components. Unsystematic patterns are difficult to identify and are caused by the presence of a **random (irregular) error** term. **Smoothing techniques** are employed to provide forecasts if short-term fluctuations represent random departures from the structure with no discernible systematic patterns.

A **moving average** is the average from a fixed number of the m most recent observations. We use moving averages to make forecasts as $\hat{y}_t = \frac{y_{t-m} + y_{t-m+1} + \cdots + y_{t-1}}{m}$.

Exponential smoothing is a weighted average approach where the weights decline exponentially as they become more distant. The exponential smoothing procedure continually updates the level of the series as $A_t = \alpha y_t + (1 - \alpha)A_{t-1}$, where α represents the speed of decline. Forecasts are made as $\hat{y}_{t+1} = A_t$.

LO **18.3**

Use trend regression models to make forecasts.

For a time series that grows by a fixed amount for each time period, we use the **linear trend model**, $y_t = \beta_0 + \beta_1 t + \varepsilon_t$. We estimate this model to make forecasts as $\hat{y}_t = b_0 + b_1 t$, where b_0 and b_1 are the coefficient estimates.

For a time series that grows by an increasing amount for each time period, we use the **exponential trend model**, $\ln(y_t) = \beta_0 + \beta_1 t + \varepsilon_t$, where $\ln(y_t)$ is the natural log of the series. We estimate this model to make forecasts as $\hat{y}_t = \exp(b_0 + b_1 t + s_e^2/2)$, where b_0 and b_1 are the coefficient estimates and s_e is the standard error of the estimate.

A **polynomial trend model** of order q is estimated as $y_t = \beta_0 + \beta_1 t + \beta_2 t^2 + \beta_3 t^3 + \cdots + \beta_q t^q + \varepsilon_t$. This model specializes to a linear trend model for $q = 1$, to a quadratic trend model for $q = 2$, and to a cubic trend model for $q = 3$. We estimate this model to make forecasts as $\hat{y}_t = b_0 + b_1 t + b_2 t^2 + b_3 t^3 + \cdots + b_q t^q$, where $b_0, b_1, \ldots, b_q$ are the coefficient estimates.

It is always informative to start a trend analysis with a scatterplot of the series. We compare the linear and the exponential trend models on the basis of their *MSE* and *MAD*. We use adjusted R^2 to compare various orders of the polynomial trend model.

LO **18.4**

Calculate and interpret seasonal indices and use them to seasonally adjust a time series.

Centered Moving Averages *CMA* are often employed to separate the effect of trend from seasonality. We use a centered 4-period moving average for quarterly data and a centered 12-period moving average for monthly data. The **ratio-to-moving average** is calculated as $y_t/\bar{y}_t$, where $\bar{y}_t = CMA_t$. For each season, there are many estimates of the ratio-to-moving average. The **unadjusted seasonal index** is computed by averaging these ratios over the years. A minor adjustment ensures that the average of **adjusted seasonal indices** $\hat{S}$ equals one. A **seasonally adjusted** series is computed as $y_t/\hat{S}_t$. We use the appropriate trend model on the seasonally adjusted series to extract $\hat{T}_t$.

LO **18.5**

Use decomposition analysis to make forecasts.

We let T, S, and I represent the trend, the seasonal, and the random (irregular) components, respectively, of the series y_t. Using **decomposition analysis**, we decompose or isolate the individual components of the time series to make forecasts. Forecasts are made as $\hat{y}_t = \hat{T}_t \times \hat{S}_t$, where $\hat{T}_t$ and $\hat{S}_t$ represent the estimated trend and the seasonal index, respectively.

LO **18.6**

Use trend regression models with seasonal dummy variables to make forecasts.

As an alternative to decomposition analysis, we use a multiple regression model to simultaneously estimate trend along with **seasonal dummy variables**. With quarterly data, a **linear** trend model with seasonal dummy variables is specified as $y = \beta_0 + \beta_1 d_1 + \beta_2 d_2 + \beta_3 d_3 + \beta_4 t + \varepsilon$. Forecasts based on the estimated model are $\hat{y}_t = (b_0 + b_1) + b_4 t$ (Quarter 1), $\hat{y}_t = (b_0 + b_2) + b_4 t$ (Quarter 2), $\hat{y}_t = (b_0 + b_3) + b_4 t$ (Quarter 3), and $\hat{y}_t = b_0 + b_4 t$ (Quarter 4). An **exponential** trend model with seasonal dummy variables is specified as $\ln(y) = \beta_0 + \beta_1 d_1 + \beta_2 d_2 + \beta_3 d_3 + \beta_4 t + \varepsilon$. Forecasts based on the estimated model are $\hat{y}_t = \exp((b_0 + b_1) + b_4 t + s_e^2/2)$ (Quarter 1), $\hat{y}_t = \exp((b_0 + b_2) + b_4 t + s_e^2/2)$ (Quarter 2), $\hat{y}_t = \exp((b_0 + b_3) + b_4 t + s_e^2/2)$ (Quarter 3), and $\hat{y}_t = \exp(b_0 + b_4 t + s_e^2/2)$ (Quarter 4). Forecasts with monthly data can be made similarly.

LO 18.7 | **Use causal forecasting models to make forecasts.**

Causal forecasting models are based on a regression framework. A forecast with a simple regression model, $y_t = \beta_0 + \beta_1 x_t + \varepsilon_t$, can be made as $\hat{y}_{T+1} = b_0 + b_1 x_{T+1}$ only if the future value of the explanatory variable x_{T+1} is known. Sometimes researchers use a causal approach with lagged values of x and y for making forecasts. For instance, we can estimate $y_t = \beta_0 + \beta_1 x_{t-1} + \varepsilon_t$ to make a forecast as $\hat{y}_{T+1} = b_0 + b_1 x_T$. Similarly, we can estimate $y_t = \beta_0 + \beta_1 y_{t-1} + \varepsilon_t$ to make a forecast as $\hat{y}_{T+1} = b_0 + b_1 y_T$. We can also estimate a combined model $y_t = \beta_0 + \beta_1 x_{t-1} + \beta_2 y_{t-1} + \varepsilon_t$ to make a forecast as $\hat{y}_{T+1} = b_0 + b_1 x_T + b_2 y_T$.

Additional Exercises and Case Studies

40. **FILE** The U.S. housing market remains fragile despite historically low mortgage rates (AARP, July 2, 2010). Since the rate on 30-year mortgages is tied to the 10-year yield on Treasury bonds, it is important to be able to predict this yield accurately. The accompanying table shows a portion of the 10-year yield on Treasury bonds (in %) for 21 trading days in November 2010; the complete data set can be found on the text website, labeled **Yields**.

Date	Yield (in %)
1-Nov	2.63
2-Nov	2.59
⋮	⋮
30-Nov	2.80

Source: finance.yahoo.com.

a. Use a 3-period moving average to make a forecast for December 1, 2010.
b. Use the exponential smoothing method to make a forecast for December 1, 2010. Use $\alpha = 0.5$.
c. Which of these smoothing methods has a better in-sample performance?
d. The actual 10-year yield on December 1, 2010 was 2.96. Was the forecast performance of the two methods consistent with their in-sample performance in part c?

41. **FILE** The following table lists a portion of the percentage (share) of total shipment of music that falls in the category of country and rap/hip-hop rock music from 1990–2008. The complete data set is on the text website, labeled **Country and Rap**.

Year	Country (in %)	Rap/Hip-hop (in %)
1990	9.6	8.5
1991	12.8	10.0
⋮	⋮	⋮
2008	11.9	10.7

Source: www.riaa.com.

a. Plot each of the above series and comment on the respective trend.
b. Estimate a linear, a quadratic, and a cubic trend model for the share of country music in the United States. Use their adjusted R^2 to choose the preferred model and with this model make a forecast for 2009.
c. Estimate a linear, a quadratic, and a cubic trend model for the share of rap/hip-hop music in the United States. Use their adjusted R^2 to choose the preferred model and with this model make a forecast for 2009.

42. **FILE** Tourism was hit hard by the international financial crisis that began in the fall of 2008. According to the Bureau of Economic Analysis (December 20, 2010), tourism spending has picked up, but it still remains below its peak, which occurred in 2007. The accompanying table shows a portion of seasonally adjusted data on real tourism spending (in millions of $); the full data set is on the text website, labeled **Tourism Spending**.

Year	Quarter 1	Quarter 2	Quarter 3	Quarter 4
2004	664,924	672,678	675,262	679,410
2005	683,989	690,226	695,753	700,037
⋮	⋮	⋮	⋮	⋮
2010	676,929	682,681	695,917	NA

Source: U.S. Bureau of Economic Analysis.

a. Construct seasonal indices for the data.
b. Plot the seasonally adjusted series. Estimate the cubic trend model on the seasonally adjusted series.
c. Use the seasonal and trend components to forecast tourism spending for the fourth quarter of 2010 and the first three quarters of 2011.

43. FILE Prices of crude oil have been steadily rising over the last two years (*The Wall Street Journal*, December 14, 2010). Consider the following portion of monthly data on price per gallon of unleaded regular gasoline in the U.S from January 2009 to December 2010; the full data set can be found on the text website, labeled **Gas Price Forecast**.

Year	Month	Price Per Gallon
2009	Jan	$1.79
2009	Feb	1.92
⋮	⋮	⋮
2010	Dec	2.99

Source: U.S. Energy Information Administration.

a. Plot the above series to identify an appropriate polynomial trend model. You may ignore seasonality.
b. Compare the adjusted R^2 of the linear, the quadratic, and the cubic trend models.
c. Use the appropriate model to make a forecast for the price of regular unleaded gasoline for January and February of 2011.

44. FILE Consider the following portion of data on real estate loans granted by FDIC-insured Commercial Banks in the United States (in billions of U.S. dollars, base = 2007) from 1972 to 2007; the full data set can be found on the text website, labeled **Loans**.

Year	Loans
1972	489.27
1973	567.26
⋮	⋮
2007	3,604.03

Source: www2.fdic.gov.

a. Plot the above series and comment on the growth of real estate loans.
b. Estimate the linear and exponential trend models for real estate loans. Compare the models in terms of their mean square errors. Use the preferred model to make a forecast for real estate loans in year 2008.
c. Compare the in-sample performance of the preferred model used in part b with an autoregressive model of order one, AR(1). Make a forecast for real estate loans in year 2008 with this model.

45. FILE While U.S. inventory levels remain low, there is a slight indication of an increase in the U.S. business inventory-to-sales ratio, due to higher sales (*The Wall Street Journal*, December 15, 2010). The accompanying table shows a portion of seasonally adjusted inventory-to-sales ratios from January 2008 to October 2010; the full data set can be found on the text website, labeled **Inventory-to-Sales**.

Year	Month	Inventory-to-Sales
2008	Jan	1.28
2008	Feb	1.30
⋮	⋮	⋮
2010	Oct	1.27

Source: U.S. Department of Commerce.

a. Plot the above series. Which polynomial trend model do you think is most appropriate?
b. Verify your answer by formally comparing the linear, quadratic, and cubic trend models.
c. Make a forecast for the inventory-to-sales ratio for November and December of 2010.

46. FILE Revenue passenger-miles are calculated by multiplying the number of paying passengers by the distance flown in thousands. The accompanying table shows a portion of monthly data on revenue passenger-miles (in millions) from January 2006 through September 2010; the full data set can be found on the text website, labeled **Revenue Passenger-Miles**.

Year	Month	Revenue Passenger-Miles
2006	Jan	43.1652
2006	Feb	44.0447
⋮	⋮	⋮
2010	Sep	43.7704

Source: Bureau of Transportation Statistics.

a. Plot the above series and comment on its trend and seasonal variations.
b. Compute seasonal indices and use them to seasonally adjust the series.
c. Fit the appropriate trend model to the seasonally adjusted series.
d. Use decomposition analysis to make monthly forecasts for the last three months of 2010.

47. FILE Use the data in the preceding question to:
a. Estimate a linear trend model with seasonal dummies.
b. Estimate an exponential trend model with seasonal dummies.
c. Use the *MSE* and *MAD* to compare these models.
d. Use the appropriate model to make monthly forecasts for the last three months of 2010.

48. FILE The following data represent a portion of quarterly net sales (in millions of dollars) of Lowe's Companies, Inc., over the past five years; the full data set can be found on the text website, labeled **Lowe's Net Sales**.

Year	Quarter 1	Quarter 2	Quarter 3	Quarter 4
2004	$8,861	$10,169	$9,064	$8,550
2005	9,913	11,929	10,592	10,808
⋮	⋮	⋮	⋮	⋮
2008	12,009	14,509	11,728	9,984

Source: All data retrieved from Annual Reports for Lowe's Companies, Inc.

a. Estimate a linear trend model with seasonal dummy variables and compute the MSE and MAD.

b. Estimate an exponential trend model with seasonal dummy variables and compute the MSE and MAD.

c. Which model is more appropriate? Use this model to forecast net sales for Lowe's Companies, Inc., for fiscal year 2009.

49. **FILE** The S&P 500 Index is a value-weighted index of prices of 500 large-cap common stocks actively traded in the United States. A research analyst at an investment firm is attempting to forecast the daily stock price of Genzyme Corporation, one of the world's leading biotech companies, using both the S&P 500 Index as well as Genzyme's past stock prices. The following table shows a portion of the daily adjusted closing prices of Genzyme (y) and the S&P 500 Index (x) from December 1, 2010, to December 22, 2010; the full data set is on the text website, labeled **Genzyme**.

Date	y	x
12/1/2010	71.14	1206.07
12/2/2010	70.97	1221.53
⋮	⋮	⋮
12/22/2010	71.52	1258.84

Source: www.finance.yahoo.

Estimate three models: (a) $y_t = \beta_0 + \beta_1 x_{t-1} + \varepsilon_t$, (b) $y_t = \beta_0 + \beta_1 y_{t-1} + \varepsilon_t$, and (c) $y_t = \beta_0 + \beta_1 x_{t-1} + \beta_2 y_{t-1} + \varepsilon_t$. Use the most suitable model to forecast the Genzyme daily stock price for December 23, 2010.

50. **FILE** In August 2010, the Department of Commerce reported that economic weakness continues across the country, with consumer spending continuing to stagnate. The government is considering various tax benefits to stimulate consumer spending through increased disposable income. The consumption function is one of the key relationships in economics, where consumption (y) depends on disposable income (x). Consider the following table, which presents a portion of quarterly data on disposable income and personal consumption expenditure for the U.S. Both variables are measured in billions of dollars and are seasonally adjusted. The full data set is on the text website, labeled **Income and Consumption**.

Year	Quarter	Income (x)	Consumption (y)
2006	1	9705.2	9148.2
2006	2	9863.8	9266.6
⋮	⋮	⋮	⋮
2010	4	11514.7	10525.2

Source: U.S. Department of Commerce.

a. Plot the consumption series. Estimate the appropriate polynomial trend model to forecast consumption expenditure for the 1st quarter of 2011.

b. Estimate $y_t = \beta_0 + \beta_1 x_{t-1} + \varepsilon_t$ to forecast consumption expenditure for the 1st quarter of 2011.

c. Which of these two models is more appropriate for making forecasts? Explain.

CASE STUDIES

Case Study 18.1

Fried dough is a popular North American food associated with outdoor food stands at carnivals, amusement parks, fairs, and festivals, etc. Usually dusted with powdered sugar and drenched in oil, it is not particularly good for you but it sure is tasty! Jose Sanchez owns a small stall at Boston Commons in Boston, Massachusetts, where he sells fried dough and soft drinks. Although business is good, he is apprehensive about the variation in sales for no apparent reason. He asks a friend to help him make a forecast for fried dough as well as soft drinks. The accompanying table shows a portion of data on the number of plates of fried dough and soft drinks that he sold over the last 20 days; the full data set is on the text website, labeled **Fried Dough**.

Data for Case Study 18.1 Data on Fried Dough and Soft Drinks

Day	Fried Dough	Soft Drinks
1	70	150
2	69	145
⋮	⋮	⋮
20	61	153

In a report, use the sample information to:

1. Construct the exponentially smoothed series for fried dough and soft drinks using $\alpha = 0.30$ and $\alpha = 0.70$.

2. Calculate *MSE* and *MAD* for each series.

3. Forecast sales of fried dough and soft drinks for day 21 with the best-fitting series.

Case Study 18.2

Madelyn Davis is a research analyst for a large investment firm. She has been assigned the task of forecasting sales for Wal-Mart Stores, Inc., for fiscal year 2011. She collects quarterly sales for Wal-Mart Stores, Inc. (in millions $) for the 10-year period 2001 through 2010, a portion of which is shown in the accompanying table. The full data set is on the text website, labeled *Wal-Mart Sales*.

Data for Case Study 18.2 Wal-Mart Quarterly Sales (in millions $)

Year	Quarters Ended			
	April 30	July 31	October 31	January 31
2001	42,985	46,112	45,676	56,556
2002	48,052	52,799	52,738	64,210
⋮	⋮	⋮	⋮	⋮
2010	93,471	100,082	98,667	112,826

SOURCE: All data retrieved from Annual Reports for Wal-Mart Stores, Inc.

In a report, use the sample information to:

1. Use a scatterplot to determine which model best depicts trend for Wal-Mart's sales.

2. Determine whether or not a seasonal component exists in the series, using the seasonal dummy variable approach.

3. Given the conclusions on trend and the seasonal component, provide forecast values for the four quarters of 2011 as well as total projected sales for fiscal year 2011.

Case Study 18.3

Gary Martin is a research analyst at an investment firm in Chicago. He follows the oil industry and has developed a pretty sophisticated model that forecasts an oil company's stock price. However, given the recent strife in the Middle East, he wonders if simpler causal models might do a better job at predicting stock prices in the near future. He collects data on the daily adjusted closing price of Exxon Mobil Corporation (XOM) as well as the Dow Jones Industrial Average (DJIA) for February 2011. A portion of the data is shown in the accompanying table; the full data set is on the text website, labeled *XOM*.

Data for Case Study 18.3 XOM and DJIA Adjusted Closing Prices, February 2011

t	DJIA	XOM	
February 1	12,040.16	83.47	FILE
February 2	12,041.97	82.97	
⋮	⋮	⋮	
February 28	12,226.34	85.53	

Source: www.finance.yahoo.

In a report, use the sample information to:

1. Estimate three models: (a) $XOM_t = \beta_0 + \beta_1 DJIA_{t-1} + \varepsilon_t$, (b) $XOM_t = \beta_0 + \beta_1 XOM_{t-1} + \varepsilon_t$, and (c) $XOM_t = \beta_0 + \beta_1 DJIA_{t-1} + \beta_2 XOM_{t-1} + \varepsilon_t$.

2. Determine which model best fits the data.

3. Use the most appropriate model to forecast daily stock price for March 1, 2011.

19 Returns, Index Numbers, and Inflation

CHAPTER

LEARNING OBJECTIVES

After reading this chapter you should be able to:

LO **19.1** Define and compute investment returns.

LO **19.2** Use the Fisher equation to convert nominal returns into real returns and vice versa.

LO **19.3** Calculate and interpret a simple price index.

LO **19.4** Calculate and interpret the unweighted aggregate price index.

LO **19.5** Compare the Laspeyres and the Paasche methods for computing the weighted aggregate price index.

LO **19.6** Use price indices to deflate economic time series and derive the inflation rate.

In Chapter 18 we derived seasonal indices to adjust time series for seasonal changes. Policy makers often analyze time series in this format, as they are not particularly interested in its seasonal variations. Other transformations of time series also facilitate interpretation and statistical analysis. For example, financial analysts are interested in the analysis of investment returns. The underlying data may consist of asset prices and income distributions, but these can easily be transformed into investment returns. Similarly, economists are often interested in measuring the magnitude of economic changes over time. They can create index numbers that transform the original data into figures representing percentage changes. Finally, many time series are reported both in nominal as well as real terms. While the nominal values represent dollar amounts, the corresponding real values incorporate inflation to represent the purchasing power of money. In this chapter we will compute and interpret all such transformed time series.

Analyzing Beer and Wine Price Changes

Jehanne-Marie Roche is the owner of a convenience store in Mt. Angel, a cozy little town in Oregon, nestled between foothills and farmland. Although Jehanne-Marie sells selected grocery and household items, the major source of revenue is from the sale of liquor. However, a significant decline in consumer demand for liquor has occurred, due to the economic crisis that began in the fall of 2008. Jehanne-Marie has been forced to offer numerous price discounts to sell beer and wine at the store. Recently, she asked her nephew to help her understand the price movement of liquor at her store during the 2007–2009 time period. She gives him the average price and quantity information for red wine, white wine, and beer listed in Table 19.1.

TABLE 19.1   Average Price and Quantity of Wine and Beer

Year		Red Wine	White Wine	6-pack of Beer
2007	Price	$12.30	$11.90	$8.10
	Quantity	1,560	1,410	2,240
2008	Price	$12.10	$11.05	$8.25
	Quantity	1,490	1,390	2,310
2009	Price	$9.95	$10.60	$7.95
	Quantity	1,280	1,010	2,190

Jehanne-Marie wants to use the above information to:

1. Determine the percentage price change of red wine, white wine, and beer from 2007 to 2009.
2. Derive and interpret the aggregate price index of liquor.

A synopsis of this case is provided at the end of Section 19.2.

19.1 Investment Return

LO **19.1**

Define and compute investment returns.

In earlier chapters, the focus of many examples was on the analysis of **investment returns**. Here we describe a simple method to compute them. The time period used for computing an investment return may be a day, a week, a month, a year, or multiple years, and the investment may be in assets such as stocks, bonds, currencies, Treasury bills, or real estate. The investment may be in an individual asset or a portfolio of assets (for example, a mutual fund). An investment return consists of two components. The income component is the direct cash payments from the underlying asset, such as dividends, interest, or rental income. The price change component is the capital gain or loss resulting from an increase or decrease in the value of the asset.

Consider a share of Microsoft Corporation stock that an investor purchased a year ago for $25. If the price of this share jumps to $28 in a year, then $3 ($28 − $25) is the annual capital gain from this stock. In percentage terms, it is computed as $(3/25) \times 100 = 12\%$. If Microsoft has also paid a dividend of $1 per share during the year, the income component, in percentage terms, is $(1/25) \times 100 = 4\%$. Therefore, the total annual return from investing in Microsoft is 16% (12% + 4%).

CALCULATING AN INVESTMENT RETURN

An **investment return** R_t at the end of time t is calculated as

$$R_t = \frac{P_t - P_{t-1} + I_t}{P_{t-1}},$$

where P_t and P_{t-1} are the price of the asset at times t (current) and $t - 1$ (prior), respectively, and I_t is the income distributed during the investment period. The ratios $\frac{P_t - P_{t-1}}{P_{t-1}}$ and $\frac{I_t}{P_{t-1}}$ are the **capital gains yield** and the **income yield** components, respectively.

The process for computing an investment return is the same for all assets. The income component is dividends for stocks, interest for bonds, and rental income for a real estate investment. For some assets, like Treasury bills, there is no income component and the investment return consists entirely of a capital gain or loss.

EXAMPLE 19.1

Helen Watson purchased a corporate bond for $950 a year ago. She received a coupon payment (interest) of $60 during the year. The bond is currently selling for $975. Compute Helen's (a) capital gains yield, (b) income yield, and (c) investment return.

SOLUTION:

a. We calculate the capital gains yield as $\frac{P_t - P_{t-1}}{P_{t-1}} = \frac{975 - 950}{950} = 0.0263$ or 2.63%.

b. Given the interest payment of $60, we calculate the income yield as $\frac{I_t}{P_{t-1}} = \frac{60}{950} = 0.0632$ or 6.32%.

c. The investment return is the sum of the capital gains yield and the income yield, that is, $0.0263 + 0.0632 = 0.0895$ or 8.95%. We can also compute it directly as $R_t = \frac{P_t - P_{t-1} + I_t}{P_{t-1}} = \frac{975 - 950 + 60}{950} = \frac{85}{950} = 0.0895$ or 8.95%.

EXAMPLE 19.2

Last year Jim Hamilton bought a stock for \$35 and recently received a dividend of \$1.25. The stock is now selling for \$31. Find Jim's (a) capital gains yield, (b) income yield, and (c) investment return.

SOLUTION:

a. The capital gains yield is $\frac{P_t - P_{t-1}}{P_{t-1}} = \frac{31 - 35}{35} = -0.1143$ or -11.43%.

b. The income yield is $\frac{I_t}{P_{t-1}} = \frac{1.25}{35} = 0.0357$ or 3.57%.

c. The investment return is $-0.1143 + 0.0357 = -0.0786$ or -7.86%.
   Equivalently, we can compute the investment return as

$$R_t = \frac{P_t - P_{t-1} + I_t}{P_{t-1}} = \frac{31 - 35 + 1.25}{35} = \frac{-2.75}{35} = -0.0786 \text{ or } -7.86\%.$$

Note that the investment return is unaffected by the decision to sell or hold assets. A common misconception is that if you do not sell an asset, there is no capital gain or loss involved, as a given price increase or decrease leads only to paper gain or loss. This misconception often leads an investor to hold a "loser" asset longer than necessary because of the reluctance to admit a bad investment decision. The nonrecognition of the loss is relevant for tax purposes, since only realized income must be reported in tax returns. However, whether or not you have liquidated an asset is irrelevant when measuring its performance.

The Adjusted Close Price

Historical returns are often used by investors, analysts, and other researchers to assess past performance of a stock. In Example 19.2, we saw that dividend payments also influence stock returns. Therefore, we need the dividend data along with the price data to compute historical returns. Similarly, we need information on stock splits and reverse stock splits in computing returns. Tabulating corporate decisions such as the announcement of dividends, stock splits, and reverse stock splits can be very cumbersome. For these reasons, most data sources for stock price information, such as http://finance.yahoo .com, also include data on the **adjusted close price**. Here, price data are adjusted using appropriate dividend and split multipliers; we recommend an introductory finance book for further details.

Given that the adjustment has been made for all applicable splits and dividend distributions, we can compute the total investment return on the basis of the price appreciation or depreciation of the adjusted close prices.

USING ADJUSTED CLOSE PRICES TO CALCULATE AN INVESTMENT RETURN

Let P_t^* and P_{t-1}^* represent the **adjusted close price** of a stock at times t (current) and $t - 1$ (prior), respectively. The investment return R_t at the end of time t is calculated as

$$R_t = \frac{P_t^* - P_{t-1}^*}{P_{t-1}^*}.$$

EXAMPLE 19.3

Consider the adjusted close stock prices of Microsoft Corporation in Table 19.2. Find the monthly returns for November and December of 2010.

TABLE 19.2 Monthly Stock Prices for Microsoft Corporation

Date	Adjusted Close Price
December 2010	$26.04
November 2010	$25.11
October 2010	$26.35

Source: Data obtained from finance.yahoo.com on December 2010.

SOLUTION: We compute the monthly return for November 2010 as $R_t = \frac{25.11 - 26.35}{26.35} = -0.0471$, or -4.71%. Similarly, the monthly return for December 2010 is $R_t = \frac{26.04 - 25.11}{25.11} = 0.0370$ or 3.70%.

LO 19.2

Use the Fisher equation to convert nominal returns into real returns and vice versa.

Nominal versus Real Rates of Return

So far we have focused on **nominal returns**, which make no allowance for inflation. Financial rates such as interest rates, discount rates, and rates of return are generally reported in nominal terms. However, the nominal return does not represent a true picture because it does not capture the erosion of the purchasing power of money due to inflation. Consider, for example, an investment of $100 that becomes $105 after one year. While the nominal return on this investment is 5%, the purchasing power of the money is likely to have increased by less than 5%. Once the effects of inflation have been factored in, investors can determine the real, or true, return on their investment. In sum, the **real return** captures the change in the purchasing power, whereas the nominal return simply reflects the change in the number of dollars.

The relationship between the nominal and the real return was developed by Irving Fisher (1867–1947), a prominent economist. The **Fisher equation** is a theoretical relationship between nominal returns, real returns, and the expected inflation rate.

THE FISHER EQUATION

Let R be the nominal rate of return, r the real rate of return, and i the expected inflation rate. The **Fisher equation** is defined as

$$1 + r = \frac{1 + R}{1 + i}.$$

When the expected inflation rate is relatively low, a reasonable approximation to the Fisher equation is $r = R - i$; we will not be using this approximation in this chapter.

EXAMPLE 19.4

The quoted rate of return on a one-year U.S. Treasury bill in January 2010 is 0.45% (www.ustreas.gov). Compute and interpret the real rate of return that investors can earn if the inflation rate is expected to be 1.6%.

SOLUTION: Using the Fisher equation, $1 + r = \frac{1 + R}{1 + i} = \frac{1.0045}{1.0160} = 0.9887$; we derive the real rate of return as $r = 0.9887 - 1 = -0.0113$, or -1.13%. The negative real rate of return implies that investors were extremely cautious and were even willing to accept a small drop in their purchasing power during the financial crisis period.

EXAMPLE 19.5

A bond produces a real rate of return of 5.30% for a time period when the inflation rate is expected to be 3%. What is the nominal rate of return on the bond?

SOLUTION: The Fisher equation can be rewritten as $1 + R = (1 + r)(1 + i)$. Therefore, given the real rate of return of 5.30% and the inflation rate of 3%, we can easily compute, $1 + R = (1.053)(1.03) = 1.0846$ giving us the nominal return of $R = 1.0846 - 1 = 0.0846$, or 8.46%.

EXERCISES 19.1

1. You borrowed $2,000 to take a vacation in the Caribbean islands. At the end of the year, you had to pay back $2,200. What is the annual interest that you paid on your loan?

2. You bought a corporate bond last year for $980. You received a coupon payment (interest) of $60 and the bond is currently selling for $990. What is the (a) income yield, (b) capital gains yield, and (c) total return on the investment?

3. The price of a stock has gone up from $24 to $35 in one year. It also paid a year-end dividend of $1.20. What is the stock's (a) income yield, (b) capital gains yield, and (c) total return?

4. The year-end price and dividend information on a stock is given in the following table.

Year	Price	Dividend
1	$23.50	NA
2	24.80	$0.18
3	22.90	0.12

   a. What is the nominal return of the stock in years 2 and 3?
   b. What is the corresponding real return if the inflation rates for years 2 and 3 were 2.8% and 1.6%, respectively?

5. A portfolio manager invested $1,500,000 in bonds in 2007. In one year the market value of the bonds dropped to $1,485,000. The interest payments during the year totaled $105,000.
   a. What was the manager's total rate of return for the year?
   b. What was the manager's real rate of return if the inflation rate during the year was 2.3%?

6. Bill Anderson purchased 1,000 shares of Microsoft Corporation stock for $17,100 at the beginning of 2009. At the end of the year, he sold all of his Microsoft shares at $30.48 a share. He also earned a dividend of $0.52 per share during the year.
   a. What is Bill's total return on the investment?
   b. What is the dollar gain from the investment?

7. You would like to invest $20,000 for a year in a risk-free investment. A conventional CD offers a 4.6% annual rate of return. You are also considering an "Inflation-Plus" CD which offers a real rate of return of 2.2% regardless of the inflation rate.
   a. What is the implied (expected) inflation rate?
   b. You decide to invest $10,000 in the conventional and $10,000 in the "Inflation-Plus" CD. What is your expected dollar value at the end of the year?
   c. Which of the two CDs is a better investment if the actual inflation rate for the year turns out to be 2.2%?

8. Consider the following adjusted close stock prices of Intel Corporation. Find the monthly returns for November and December of 2010.

Date	Adjusted Close Price
December 2010	$21.48
November 2010	$20.98
October 2010	$19.73

Source: Data obtained from http://finance.yahoo.com on December 2010.

9. Consider the following adjusted close stock prices of Johnson and Johnson (J&J) and Caterpillar, Inc. Compute and compare the monthly returns for both companies.

Date	Johnson and Johnson	Caterpillar
March 2011	60.70	99.86
February 2011	61.44	102.93
January 2011	59.23	97.01
December 2010	61.30	93.22
November 2010	61.00	84.20
October 2010	62.63	78.23

Source: Data obtained from http://finance.yahoo.com on March 2011.

19.2 Index Numbers

An **index number** is an easy-to-interpret numerical value that reflects a percentage change in price or quantity from a base value. In this chapter, we focus on price indices. The base value for a price index is set equal to 100 for the selected base period, and values in other periods are adjusted in proportion to the base. Thus, if the price index for a given year is 125, it implies that the price has grown by 25% from the base year. Similarly, a price index of 90 implies that the price has dropped by 10% from the base year. By working in a manner similar to percentages, index numbers make changes over time easier to compare. Index numbers enable policy makers and analysts to focus on the movements in variables rather than on their raw absolute values.

LO **19.3**

Calculate and interpret a simple price index.

Simple Price Indices

Consider the price of a hamburger that increases from $3.25 in 1995 to $4.75 in 2010. We can easily determine that the price of a hamburger has increased by $\frac{4.75 - 3.25}{3.25} = 0.46$, or 46%. Alternatively, if we use 1995 as the base year with an index value of 100, then the corresponding index value for 2010 is 146, implying a 46% increase in price. This is an example of a **simple price index**.

> ### A SIMPLE PRICE INDEX
>
> A **simple price index** for any item is the ratio of the price in period t, p_t, and the price in the base period, p_0, expressed as a percentage. It is calculated as $\frac{p_t}{p_0} \times 100$.

EXAMPLE 19.6

Consider the data presented in the introductory case of this chapter in Table 19.1. Use the base year of 2007 to compute and interpret the 2008 and 2009 simple price indices for:

a. red wine

b. white wine

c. 6-pack of beer

SOLUTION: Since 2007 is the base year, we set the corresponding index value equal to 100. The index values for other years are computed below.

a. For red wine, the simple price index for 2008 is

$$\frac{\text{Price in 2008}}{\text{Price in 2007}} \times 100 = \frac{12.10}{12.30} \times 100 = 98.37.$$

Similarly, for 2009, it is

$$\frac{\text{Price in 2009}}{\text{Price in 2007}} \times 100 = \frac{9.95}{12.30} \times 100 = 80.89.$$

Therefore, the average price of red wine in 2008 and 2009 was 98.37% and 80.89%, respectively, of what it was in 2007. In other words, as compared to 2007, the price of red wine dropped by 1.63% in 2008 and 19.11% in 2009.

b. For white wine, the simple price index for 2008 is $(11.05/11.90) \times 100 = 92.86$ for 2008 and $(10.60/11.90) \times 100 = 89.08$ for 2009. Therefore, relative to 2007, the average price of white wine dropped by 7.14% in 2008 and 10.92% in 2009.

c. The simple price index for a six-pack of beer is $(8.25/8.10) \times 100 = 101.85$ for 2008 and $(7.95/8.10) \times 100 = 98.15$ for 2009. Interestingly, while the prices of both red and white wines experienced substantial declines, the price of beer stayed fairly stable. Relative to the base year of 2007, there was a 1.85% increase in the price of beer in 2008 and a 1.85% decline in 2009.

EXAMPLE 19.7

Table 19.3 shows the average price and corresponding price index for gasoline from 2000 to 2008. Interpret the price indices for 2001 and 2008.

TABLE 19.3 Price and Corresponding Price Index for Unleaded Gasoline in U.S., Base Year 2000

Year	2000	2001	2002	2003	2004	2005	2006	2007	2008
Price	1.51	1.46	1.36	1.59	1.88	2.30	2.59	2.80	3.27
Price Index (Base = 2000)	100	96.69	90.07	105.30	124.50	152.32	171.52	185.43	216.56

Source: Bureau of Labor Statistics.

SOLUTION: Since 2000 is treated as the base year, the index number for 2000 is 100. The index number for 2001 is calculated as $(1.46/1.51) \times 100 = 96.69$. Thus, the gasoline price in 2001 was 96.69% of what it was in 2000, or 3.31% lower. Given a price index of 216.56 in 2008, the gasoline price in 2008 was 116.56% higher relative to 2000.

In Figure 19.1, we plot the raw price and price indices for gasoline from 2000 to 2008. Note that although the units of the gasoline price and index number graphs are different, the basic shape of the two graphs is similar. This shows that the main purpose of index numbers is to provide an easy interpretation of the changes of the series over time.

FIGURE 19.1 Price of gasoline and the corresponding index numbers for 2000–2008

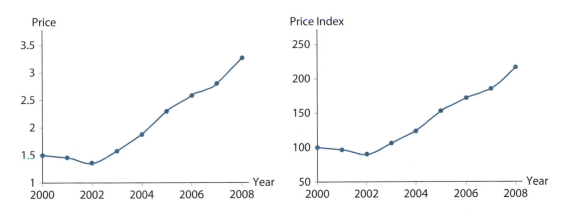

It is important to note that index numbers provide direct comparisons only with respect to the base year. Similar direct comparisons cannot be made between non–base years. For instance, based on the index numbers for 2005 and 2008, we cannot say that prices rose by 64.24% (216.56% − 152.32%) from 2005 to 2008. The actual percentage change from 2005 and 2008 is $\frac{216.56 - 152.32}{152.32} \times 100 = 42.17$, implying that prices rose by 42.17% from 2005 to 2008.

Alternatively, we can use index numbers directly to compare prices between 2005 and 2008 by making 2005 the base year. It may be more meaningful to compare 2008 values with those in 2005 rather than the values in 2000. In fact, federal agencies routinely update the base year used in their calculations of statistical indices. For example, the reported imports and exports price indices in 2008 have been updated from the base year of 1995 to a revised base year of 2000.

It is fairly simple to revise the base period of an index. We basically transform the index of the newly chosen base period as 100 and values in other periods are adjusted by the same proportion.

EXAMPLE 19.8

Update the index numbers in Table 19.3 with a base year revised from 2000 to 2005.

SOLUTION: With a revised base of 2005, the index number for 2005 is updated from 152.32 to 100. Other indices are adjusted according to the revision rule. For instance, the index number for 2006 is updated as $(171.52/152.32) \times 100 = 112.61$. Table 19.4 contains index numbers that have been similarly updated.

TABLE 19.4 Price Index for Gasoline Using Base Year of 2000 and 2005

Year	2000	2001	2002	2003	2004	2005	2006	2007	2008
Price	1.51	1.46	1.36	1.59	1.88	2.30	2.59	2.80	3.27
Price Index (Base = 2000)	100	96.69	90.07	105.30	124.50	152.32	171.52	185.43	216.56
Price Index (Base = 2005)	65.65	63.48	59.13	69.13	81.74	100.00	112.61	121.74	142.17

With the revised base of 2005, we can directly deduce that the gasoline price in 2008 was 142.17% of what it was in 2005, or 42.17% higher.

LO **19.4**

Calculate and interpret the unweighted aggregate price index.

Unweighted Aggregate Price Index

The **aggregate price index** is used to represent relative price movements for a group of items. Examples include the closely watched consumer price index (CPI) and the producer price index (PPI). The aggregate price index can be weighted or unweighted. The **unweighted aggregate price index** is based entirely on aggregate prices with no emphasis placed on quantity. In other words, it does not incorporate the information that consumers may not be consuming equal quantities over the years of the items comprising the index. Weighted methods, on the other hand, use quantity as weights in the calculations.

CALCULATION OF AN UNWEIGHTED AGGREGATE PRICE INDEX

Let p_{it} represent the price of item i in period t and let p_{i0} be the corresponding price in the base period ($t = 0$). The **unweighted aggregate price index** in period t is

$\frac{\Sigma p_{it}}{\Sigma p_{i0}} \times 100.$

EXAMPLE 19.9

A real estate firm based in Florida collects data on the average selling price of condominiums, single-family homes, and multifamily homes that it sold over the last three years. Table 19.5 shows the results. Compute the unweighted price index for the properties, using 2007 as the base year.

TABLE 19.5 Average Price (in $1,000s) of Properties Sold in Florida (Example 19.9)

Year	Condominiums	Single-family	Multifamily
2007	225	375	440
2008	148	250	390
2009	130	235	400

SOLUTION: In order to find the unweighted aggregate price index, we first aggregate prices for each year by adding up the prices of condominiums, single-family homes, and multifamily homes. For 2007, the aggregate price is computed as $\Sigma p_{0i} = 225 + 375 + 440 = 1{,}040$. Similarly, the aggregate prices are $\Sigma p_{ti} = 148 + 250 + 390 = 788$ for 2008 and $\Sigma p_{ti} = 130 + 235 + 400 = 765$ for 2009. Then, using 2007 as the base year, the unweighted aggregate price indices are computed as

$$\text{Price Index for 2008} = \frac{788}{1{,}040} \times 100 = 75.77, \text{ and}$$

$$\text{Price Index for 2009} = \frac{765}{1{,}040} \times 100 = 73.56.$$

Thus, according to the unweighted aggregate price index, property values in 2008 were 75.77% of what they were in 2007, or equivalently, they were 24.23% lower. Similarly, relative to 2007, property values in 2009 were 26.44% lower. Although the unweighted aggregate price index captures the overall drop in property values in Florida, the drop seems slightly lower than what has been reported in the popular press. A possible explanation is that the unweighted index unfairly treats all property prices equally. The drop in property values would be greater if we take into account the fact that most properties in Florida consisted of condominiums and single-family homes, which witnessed a steeper price decline than multifamily homes.

Weighted Aggregate Price Index

LO **19.5**

Compare the Laspeyres and the Paasche methods for computing the weighted aggregate price index.

The **weighted aggregate price index** does not treat prices of different items equally. A higher weight is given to the items that are sold in higher quantities. However, there is no unique way to determine the weights, as they depend on the period in which the quantities are evaluated. One option is to evaluate the changing quantities over the years to derive the weighted average. However, in many applications, the quantity information is not readily available and we have to rely on its evaluation in a single time period. Two popular choices for weights are based on the quantities evaluated in the base period and in the current period. The **Laspeyres price index** uses the quantities evaluated in the base period to compute the weighted aggregate price index.

> **CALCULATION OF A WEIGHTED AGGREGATE PRICE INDEX: THE LASPEYRES PRICE INDEX**
>
> Let p_{it} and q_{it} represent the price and quantity of item i in period t and let p_{i0} and q_{i0} be the corresponding values in the base period ($t = 0$). Using only the base period quantities q_{i0}, the **Laspeyres price index** for period t is
>
> $$\frac{\Sigma p_{it} q_{i0}}{\Sigma p_{i0} q_{i0}} \times 100.$$

EXAMPLE 19.10

Table 19.6 shows the number of condominiums, single-family homes, and multi-family homes sold in Florida. Use these quantities, along with the price information from Table 19.5, to compute the Laspeyres price index for real estate, given a base year of 2007.

TABLE 19.6 Number of Properties Sold in Florida

Year	Condominiums	Single-family	Multifamily
2007	42	104	20
2008	28	76	16
2009	32	82	10

SOLUTION: Since the Laspeyres price index evaluates the quantities in the base period, we will only use the number of properties sold in 2007 in the calculation. Table 19.7 aids in the calculation of the Laspeyres index.

TABLE 19.7 Calculations for Example 19.10

Year	Weighted Price $= \Sigma p_{it} q_{i0}$	The Laspeyres Index
2007	$225 \times 42 + 375 \times 104 + 440 \times 20 = 57{,}250$	100
2008	$148 \times 42 + 250 \times 104 + 390 \times 20 = 40{,}016$	$(40{,}016/57{,}250) \times 100 = 69.90$
2009	$130 \times 42 + 235 \times 104 + 400 \times 20 = 37{,}900$	$(37{,}900/57{,}250) \times 100 = 66.20$

Based on the above Laspeyres index, the real estate prices in 2008 were 69.90% of what they were in 2007, or equivalently they were 30.10% lower. Similarly, the real estate prices in 2009 were 33.80% lower. Note that the computed drop in property values based on the Laspeyres price index is sharper than the one inferred from the unweighted aggregate price index.

As mentioned earlier, the choice of weights for the weighted aggregate price index depends on the quantity evaluated in a given period. Whereas the Laspeyres index uses the base period quantities as weights, the **Paasche index** uses the current period quantities in deriving the weights. Since the choice of weights for the two methods are different, the Laspeyres and Paasche indices differ for the period under evaluation.

> ### CALCULATION OF A WEIGHTED AGGREGATE PRICE INDEX: THE PAASCHE PRICE INDEX
>
> Let p_{it} and q_{it} represent the price and quantity of item i in period t and let p_{i0} and q_{i0} be the corresponding values in the base period ($t = 0$). Using only the current period ($t = n$) quantities q_{in}, the **Paasche price index** for period t is
>
> $$\frac{\Sigma p_{it} q_{in}}{\Sigma p_{i0} q_{in}} \times 100.$$

EXAMPLE 19.11

Consider Tables 19.5 and 19.6, representing the price and quantity data for properties sold in Florida. Use this information to compute the Paasche price index for real estate, given a base year of 2007.

SOLUTION: Since the Paasche price index uses the quantities evaluated in the current period, we use only the numbers of properties sold in 2009 in the calculations. Table 19.8 aids in the calculation of the Paasche index.

TABLE 19.8 Calculations for Example 19.11

Year	Weighted Price $= \Sigma p_{it} q_{in}$	The Paasche Index
2007	$225 \times 32 + 375 \times 82 + 440 \times 10 = 42{,}350$	100
2008	$148 \times 32 + 250 \times 82 + 390 \times 10 = 29{,}136$	$(29{,}136/42{,}350) \times 100 = 68.80$
2009	$130 \times 32 + 235 \times 82 + 400 \times 10 = 27{,}430$	$(27{,}430/42{,}350) \times 100 = 64.77$

The Paasche index is calculated as 68.80 for 2008 and 64.77 for 2009. Therefore, according to the Paasche index with a base year of 2007, property values dropped by 31.20% in 2008 and 35.23% in 2009.

In general, the Laspeyres and Paasche indices provide similar results if the periods being compared are not too far apart. The two indices tend to differ when the length of time between the periods increases since the relative quantities of items (weights) adjust to the changes in consumer demand over time. Consumers tend to adjust their consumption patterns by decreasing (increasing) the quantity of items that undergo a larger relative price increase (decrease). For instance, a sharp increase in the price of an item is typically accompanied by a decrease in the quantity demanded, making its relative weight go down in value. Similarly, a sharp decrease in the price of an item will make its relative weight go up. Therefore, a Paasche index that uses the updated weights theoretically produces a lower estimate than a Laspeyres index when prices are increasing and a higher estimate when prices are decreasing. Our results regarding property values are consistent with this reasoning. During the period of price decline, the Laspeyres index suggests that relative to 2007, property values have dropped by 30.10% and 33.80% in 2008 and 2009, respectively. According to the Paasche index for the same period, property values had larger drops of 31.20% and 35.23%, respectively.

The Paasche index is attractive because it incorporates current expenditure patterns. However, its data requirements are more stringent than those of the Laspeyres index. The Paasche index requires that the weights be updated each year and the index numbers be recomputed for all of the previous years. The additional cost required to process current expenditure data, needed to revise the weights, can be substantial. It may not always be possible to produce a timely Paasche index. Therefore, the Laspeyres index is a more widely used weighted aggregate price index. The base period is changed periodically to ensure that the Laspeyres index does not become outdated. Here the base period revision involves updated calculations using quantity weights of the new base period.

EXAMPLE 19.12

Let us revisit the introductory case with the data presented in Table 19.1. Using 2007 as the base year, compute and interpret the weighted aggregate price indices for liquor using

a. The Laspeyres method
b. The Paasche method

SOLUTION: Since 2007 is used as the base year, its value for both indices is set equal to 100.

a. For the Laspeyres price index, the prices are weighted by the quantities evaluated in the base period of 2007. Therefore, the weighted price for 2007 is computed as

$$\Sigma p_{it} q_{i0} = 12.30 \times 1,560 + 11.90 \times 1,410 + 8.10 \times 2,240 = \$54,111.$$

Similarly, the weighted price equals

$$12.10 \times 1,560 + 11.05 \times 1,410 + 8.25 \times 2,240 = \$52,936.5 \text{ for 2008 and}$$
$$9.95 \times 1,560 + 10.60 \times 1,410 + 7.95 \times 2,240 = \$48,276 \text{ for 2009.}$$

The corresponding price index is $(52,936.5/54,111) \times 100 = 97.83$ for 2008 and $(48,276/54,111) \times 100 = 89.22$ for 2009. Therefore, based on the Laspeyres index, liquor prices are 97.83% in 2008 and 89.22% in 2009 of what they were in 2007. In other words, relative to 2007, overall liquor prices dropped by 2.17% in 2008 and by 10.78% in 2009.

b. For the Paasche price index, the prices are weighted by the quantities evaluated in the current period, which in our example is 2009. Therefore, the weighted price for 2007 is computed as

$$\Sigma p_{it} q_{in} = 12.30 \times 1,280 + 11.90 \times 1,010 + 8.10 \times 2,190 = \$45,502.$$

Similarly, the weighted prices equal

$$12.10 \times 1,280 + 11.05 \times 1,010 + 8.25 \times 2,190 = \$44,716 \text{ for 2008 and}$$
$$9.95 \times 1,280 + 10.60 \times 1,010 + 7.95 \times 2,190 = \$40,852.5 \text{ for 2009.}$$

The corresponding price index is $(44,716/45,502) \times 100 = 98.27$ for 2008 and $(40,852.5/45,502) \times 100 = 89.78$ for 2009. Therefore, based on the Paasche index, liquor prices are 98.27% in 2008 and 89.78% in 2009 of what they were in 2007. In other words, relative to 2007, overall liquor prices dropped by 1.73 percent in 2008 and by 10.22 percent in 2009.

SYNOPSIS OF INTRODUCTORY CASE

The global financial crisis that began in 2008 has had major consequences in all aspects of the American economy. The staggering number of layoffs highlights the effects of the financial crisis being passed on to the real economy. Jehanne-Marie, the owner of a small convenience store in Oregon, has not been spared the effects of the crisis. She has been forced to offer numerous price discounts to counter the plummeting demand for liquor. Interestingly, the cutbacks by consumers have not been uniform across red wine, white wine, and beer. While the price of red wine has dropped by 19.11% from 2007 to 2009, the corresponding drop in price has been 10.92% for white wine and only 1.85% for beer. In order to capture the overall price movement of liquor, two weighted aggregate price indices are also computed. These indices devote a higher weight to the price of items that are sold in higher quantities. The weights are defined by the base period quantities for the Laspeyres index and the current period quantities for the Paasche index. Both indices suggest that relative to 2007, Jehanne-Marie has experienced an overall price decline of about 2% in 2008 and a larger 10.50% in 2009. In sum, Jehanne-Marie is advised to focus more on beer sales, rather than wine, during harsh economic times. A comprehensive analysis that includes other grocery items like bread, cheese, and soda would better describe the full impact of the economic crisis on her total sales.

Concepts

10. Consider the following price data from 1994 to 2002.

Year	1994	1995	1996	1997	1998	1999	2000	2001	2002
Price	62	60	64	67	66	70	74	72	70

   a. Compute the simple price index using 1994 as the base year.
   b. Determine the percentage change in prices from 1994 to 1998.

11. Consider the following simple price index created with a base year of 2004.

Year	2004	2005	2006	2007	2008	2009	2010	2011	2012
Price Index	100	102.2	106.3	110.8	109.4	107.2	108.9	110.5	114.7

   a. Update the index numbers using a revised base year of 2008.
   b. Determine the percentage change in price from 2004 to 2012.
   c. Determine the percentage change in price from 2008 to 2012.

12. Consider the following price and quantity data of three products from 2008 to 2010.

Year		Product 1	Product 2	Product 3
2008	Price	$14.30	$13.90	$18.10
	Quantity	992	1,110	800
2009	Price	$14.90	$13.70	$18.50
	Quantity	980	1220	790
2010	Price	$15.50	$13.80	$17.90
	Quantity	140	1290	810

   a. Compute the simple price index for each product, using 2008 as the base year.
   b. Compare the relative price movements of the three products.

13. Use the price and quantity information in the previous exercise to compute the following aggregate price indices, given a base year of 2008:
   a. The unweighted aggregate price index
   b. The Laspeyres price index
   c. The Paasche price index

Applications

14. Consider the following average monthly prices for regular gasoline in California in 2008.

Month	Jan	Feb	Mar	Apr	May	Jun	Jul	Aug	Sep	Oct	Nov	Dec
Price	3.25	3.18	3.56	3.82	3.97	4.48	4.46	4.16	3.79	3.39	2.46	1.82

Source: http://www.energyalmanac.ca.gov.

   a. Construct a simple price index with January 2008 as the base.
   b. Determine the percentage change in the average gasoline price in California from January to June.

15. The following table shows the monthly adjusted close price per share of Microsoft Corporation for 2009.

Month	Jan	Feb	Mar	Apr	May	Jun	Jul	Aug	Sep	Oct	Nov	Dec
Price	16.6	15.8	18.0	19.8	20.6	23.4	23.2	24.4	25.5	27.5	29.2	30.3

Source: http://finance.yahoo.com.

   a. Construct a simple price index with January 2009 as the base.
   b. What is the percentage price change in July relative to January?
   c. What is the percentage price change in December relative to January?

16. The MIT Sloan School of Management is one of the leading business schools in the U.S. The following table contains the tuition data for the masters program in the Sloan School of Management.

Year	2004	2005	2006	2007	2008	2009
Tuition	$36,850	$39,844	$42,634	$44,556	$46,784	$48,650

Source: http://web.mit.edu/ir/financial/tuition.html.

   a. Use 2004 as the base year to form a simple price index for tuition.
   b. Use 2007 as the base year to form a simple price index for tuition.
   c. Compare the percentage tuition increase from 2004 through 2007 and 2007 through 2009.

17. **FILE** According to dollar cost averaging, a fixed amount of money is invested periodically in a portfolio. Consequently, more units of a financial asset are purchased when prices are low and fewer units are purchased when prices are high. Robert Dudek follows dollar cost averaging by making a monthly investment of $500 toward retirement. His monthly investment is divided equally among two T. Rowe Price mutual funds: Equity Income and Short-term Bond funds. The following table represents the monthly adjusted close price of the funds in 2009. The data set can also be found on the text website, labeled ***Returns 2009***.

Month	EqInc	Bond	Month	EqInc	Bond
January	14.77	4.47	July	18.4	4.72
February	12.93	4.49	August	19.45	4.75
March	14.14	4.53	September	19.92	4.78
April	16.04	4.58	October	19.53	4.80
May	16.87	4.64	November	20.60	4.85
June	16.89	4.66	December	20.99	4.82

Source: http://finance.yahoo.com.

   a. Compute and interpret the Laspeyres price index.
   b. Compute and interpret the Paasche price index.
   c. Why are the results of the two indices different?

18. JJ Diner is a small mom and pop restaurant in Lincoln, Nebraska. They offer three choices for breakfast: omelets, pancakes, or cereal. The average prices (in dollars) for

these options for 2007, 2008, and 2009 are shown in the accompanying table.

Year	Omelet	Pancakes	Cereal
2007	4.75	3.50	3.50
2008	5.25	4.25	4.00
2009	5.00	4.50	4.25

a. Compute and interpret the simple price index for each breakfast, using 2007 as the base year.

b. Compute and interpret the unweighted aggregate price index for breakfast, using 2007 as the base year.

19. The following table shows the number (in 1,000s) of breakfasts sold at JJ Diner.

Year	Omelet	Pancakes	Cereal
2007	9.26	7.98	2.44
2008	11.82	9.20	2.62
2009	10.48	8.50	2.12

Use this information, along with the price data provided in the previous exercise, to

a. Compute and interpret the Laspeyres price index.

b. Compute and interpret the Paasche price index.

20. With the collapse of house prices that started in 2006, the American Dream has become a nightmare for many of the 75 million Americans who own a home (*CBS Evening News*, February 2, 2010). However, the drop in house prices has not been uniform across the country. The accompanying table represents median home prices (in $1,000s) by region for 2007, 2008, and 2009.

Region	2007	2008	2009
Northeast	288.1	271.5	240.7
Midwest	161.4	150.5	142.5
South	178.8	169.4	154.6
West	342.5	276.1	224.2

Source: http://www.realtor.org.

a. Use 2007 as the base year to construct a simple price index for each region.

b. Use the percentage decline in home values to discuss regional differences in price drops.

21. Consider the following table, which reports the sale (quantity in 1,000s) of homes by region for 2007, 2008, and 2009.

Region	2007	2008	2009
Northeast	1,006	849	868
Midwest	1,327	1,129	1,165
South	2,235	1,865	1,913
West	1,084	1,070	1,210

Source: http://www.realtor.org.

Use this information, along with the price data provided in the previous exercise, to

a. Compute and interpret the Laspeyres aggregate home price index for the U.S.

b. Compute and interpret the Paasche aggregate home price index for the U.S.

c. Comment on the differences between the two indices.

19.3 Using Price Indices to Deflate a Time Series

LO 19.6

Use price indices to deflate economic time series and derive the inflation rate.

Most business and economic time series are generally reported in nominal terms, implying that they are measured in dollar amounts. Since inflation erodes the value of money over time, the dollar differences over time do not quite tell the whole story. For instance, we cannot directly compare the starting salary of a recent college graduate with that of a college graduate five years ago. Due to price increases, the purchasing power of recent graduates may be lower even if they make more money than their predecessors. Similarly, a hardware store may have doubled its revenue over 20 years, but the true increase in value may be much smaller once it has been adjusted for inflation.

An important function of the price indices, mentioned in the previous section, is to serve as deflators. A **deflated** series is obtained by adjusting the given time series for changes in prices, or inflation. We use the price indices to remove the effect of inflation so that we can evaluate business and economic time series in a more meaningful way.

NOMINAL VERSUS REAL VALUES

A time series that has been deflated is said to be represented in **real terms**. The unadjusted time series is said to be represented in **nominal terms**. We use a price index to convert the nominal value of a time series into its real value as

$$\text{Real Value} = \frac{\text{Nominal Value}}{\text{Price Index}} \times 100.$$

Consider the following example. Lisa Redford has worked in a small marketing firm in Florida for the last three years. Due to the recent economic crisis, her salary has dropped from $80,000 in 2007 to $64,000 in 2009. While her salary has dropped by 20%, a larger drop in property values for the same time period may have made it easier for Lisa to own a home in Florida. In Example 19.10, we used the base year of 2007 to derive the Laspeyres price index of property values for 2009 as 66.20, implying that real estate prices were 33.80% lower in 2009 than in 2007. It is more meaningful to compare Lisa's salary of $80,000 in 2007 (the base year) with the price-adjusted (real) salary of ($64,000/66.20) × 100 = $96,677 in 2009. Using the Laspeyres price index of property values for adjustment, Lisa is actually slightly better off in 2009 than she was in 2007, despite the salary cut. However, it is not reasonable to adjust Lisa's salary solely on the basis of the price index of property values in Florida. Since her expenditure is not limited to mortgage payments, a more comprehensive price index is needed to make the price adjustment to the salary. In fact, when we say that a series has been deflated, we imply that the series has been adjusted on the basis of the price of a comprehensive basket of goods and services.

The two most commonly used price indices used to deflate economic time series are the **Consumer Price Index**, **CPI**, and the **Producer Price Index**, **PPI**. While both the CPI and PPI measure the percentage price change over time for a fixed basket of goods and services, they differ in the composition of the basket and in the types of prices used in the analysis. The general process of computing the CPI and PPI is similar to the method outlined in the preceding section. However, we will not elaborate on their composition in this chapter.

The CPI is perhaps the best-known weighted aggregate price index. The U.S. Bureau of Labor Statistics computes a monthly CPI based on the prices paid by urban consumers for a representative basket of goods and services. As of 2010, the CPI uses 1982 as the base year. The prices of several hundred consumption items are included in the index. In addition, randomly selected consumers help determine the expenditure for the representative basket of goods and services. The corresponding quantities of items in the base year are used for computing the weights for the index.

The PPI is a weighted aggregate price index of prices measured at the wholesale, or producer level. Prior to 1978, the PPI was called the Wholesale Price Index, WPI. The U.S. Bureau of Labor Statistics computes a monthly PPI based on the selling prices received by domestic producers for their entire marketed output. The target set includes purchases of goods and services by consumers—directly from the producer or indirectly from a retailer—and by other producers as inputs to their production or as capital investment.

Note that the CPI is based on out-of-pocket expenditures of an urban consumer and the PPI is based on the portion that is actually received by the producer. Therefore, although sales and excise taxes are included in the CPI, they are not included in the PPI because they do not represent revenue to the producer. The differences between the PPI and CPI are consistent with the way these indices are used for deflation. It is common to use the CPI to adjust wages for changes in the cost of living. The PPI, on the other hand, is useful to deflate revenue in order to obtain real growth in output.

It is often assumed that the direction and magnitude of a price change in the PPI for finished goods anticipates a similar change in the CPI for all items. This is not always the case. In Figure 19.2, we plot the annual CPI and PPI from 1960–2010, with a base of 1982–1984 (Source: Bureau of Labor Statistics); the relevant data, labeled **CPI & PPI**, are available on the text website. Interestingly, the two indices moved in sync until the early 1980s. Beyond that, changes in prices that consumers paid far exceeded those received by producers, with the difference peaking in 2002. Also, noteworthy is the fact that while there was a significant dip in the PPI, the CPI showed a very slight decline during the peak of the financial crisis in 2009.

FIGURE 19.2 CPI and PPI for 1960–2010; base period 1982–1984 FILE

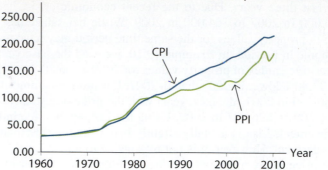

EXAMPLE 19.13

Tom Denio has been a project manager in a small construction firm in Atlanta since 2000. He started with a salary of $52,000, which grew to $84,000 in 2008. The revenue of the construction firm also grew over the years, increasing from $13 million in 2000 to $18 million in 2008. According to the Bureau of Labor Statistics, the values of the consumer price index with a base of 1982–1984 for 2000 and 2008 are 172.20 and 215.30, respectively. The corresponding values of the producer price index are 132.70 and 189.60, respectively.

a. Compute and analyze the nominal and real increase in Tom's salary.

b. Compute and analyze the nominal and real revenue growth of the construction firm.

SOLUTION:

a. Tom's nominal salary grew by $\frac{84,000 - 52,000}{52,000} = 0.62$, or by 62% from 2000 to 2008. This nominal salary makes no cost of living adjustment. We use the CPI to compute his real salary as ($52,000/172.20) × 100 = $30,197 in 2000 and ($84,000/215.30) × 100 = $39,015 in 2008. These are Tom's real salaries based on 1982–1984 prices. Thus, while Tom's salary increased by 62% in dollar amounts, his purchasing power increased by only $\frac{39,015 - 30,197}{30,197} = 0.29$, or 29%.

b. The nominal revenue of the construction firm grew by $\frac{18 - 13}{13} = 0.38$, or by 38% from 2000 to 2008. We use the producer price index to compute the revenue growth in real terms. The real revenue is ($13/132.70) × 100 = $9.80 million in 2000 and ($18/189.60) × 100 = $9.49 million in 2008. Therefore, the real growth in revenue for the construction firm has been $\frac{9.49 - 9.80}{9.80} = -0.03$, or −3%.

Inflation Rate

The **inflation rate** is the percentage rate of change of a price index over time. We generally use the CPI to compute the inflation rate in the U.S. Also, although it is common to quote the inflation rate in annual terms, the CPI can be used to calculate the inflation rate for any time period.

CALCULATING THE INFLATION RATE

The reported **inflation rate** i_t for a given period is generally based on the consumer price index, CPI. It is computed as $i_t = \frac{CPI_t - CPI_{t-1}}{CPI_{t-1}}$.

EXAMPLE 19.14

The consumer price indices for the years 2006, 2007, and 2008 are reported as 201.59, 207.34, and 215.30, respectively (Source: Bureau of Labor Statistics). Use this information to compute the annual inflation rate for 2007 and 2008.

SOLUTION: The inflation rates for 2007 and 2008 are computed as:

$$i_{2007} = \frac{CPI_{2007} - CPI_{2006}}{CPI_{2006}} = \frac{207.34 - 201.59}{201.59} = 0.0285 \text{ or } 2.85\%.$$

$$i_{2008} = \frac{CPI_{2008} - CPI_{2007}}{CPI_{2007}} = \frac{215.30 - 207.34}{207.34} = 0.0384 \text{ or } 3.84\%.$$

Therefore, the inflation rate increased from 2.85% in 2007 to 3.84% in 2008.

EXAMPLE 19.15

At the beginning of 2007, Joe Gonzales invested $1,000 in a mutual fund, which grew to $1,050 in a year. The consumer price index, with a base of 1982–1984, is 203.37 for January 2007 and 212.23 for January 2008. Compute the real annual rate of return for Joe.

SOLUTION: The real rate of return is based on the deflated investment values, which for the two years are computed as $\frac{1,000}{203.37} \times 100 = \$491.71$ and $\frac{1,050}{212.23} \times 100 = \$494.75$, respectively. The resulting real return of investment is derived as $\frac{494.75 - 491.71}{491.71} = 0.0062$, or 0.62%.

In Section 19.1, we used the Fisher equation to convert the nominal return into the real return. The Fisher equation will give us this same value for the real return on the investment. The nominal return for Joe is $\frac{1,050 - 1,000}{1,000} = 0.05$ and the corresponding inflation rate is $\frac{212.23 - 203.37}{203.37} = 0.0436$. Therefore, using the Fisher equation, we can compute $1 + r = \frac{1 + R}{1 + i} = \frac{1.05}{1.0436} = 1.0061$ to get the real rate of return $r = 0.0061$, which varies slightly from the previous calculation for the real rate of return due to rounding.

EXERCISES 19.3

Concepts

22. The nominal values for four years are given by 32, 37, 39, and 42. Convert these values to real terms if the price index values for the corresponding years are given by 100, 102, 103, 108.

23. An item increases in value from 240 to 280 in one year. What is the percentage change in the value of this item? Compute the percentage change in real terms if overall prices have increased by 5% for the same period.

24. Let revenues increase by 10% from $100,000 to $110,000. Calculate the percentage change in real terms if the relevant price index increases by 4% from 100 to 104.

25. The following table represents the nominal values of an item and the corresponding price index for 2007 and 2008.

Year	Nominal Value	Price Index
2007	38	112
2008	40	120

a. Compute the inflation rate for 2008.

b. Compute the annual percentage change of the item in real terms.

26. The following table represents the nominal values of an item and the corresponding price index from 2009 to 2011.

Year	Nominal Value	Price Index
2009	38	100
2010	40	103
2011	42	112

a. Compare the percentage change in the nominal values with the corresponding real values from 2009 to 2010.

b. Compare the percentage change in the nominal values with the corresponding real values from 2010 to 2011.

c. Use the price data to compute the inflation rate for 2010 and 2011.

Applications

27. **FILE** Economists often look at retail sales data to gauge the state of the economy. This is especially so in a recession year, when consumer spending has decreased. Consider the following table, which shows U.S. monthly nominal retail sales for 2009. Sales are measured in millions of dollars and have been seasonally adjusted. Also included in the table is the corresponding producer price index (PPI) for 2009. The data set can also be found on the text website, labeled **Sales 2009**.

Month	Sales	PPI	Month	Sales	PPI
January	340,439	171.2	July	342,489	171.6
February	342,356	170.9	August	350,800	174.1
March	339,228	169.6	September	343,687	173.3
April	338,344	170.6	October	347,641	174.0
May	339,873	170.6	November	354,467	176.6
June	342,912	173.7	December	353,817	177.3

Source: Federal Reserve Bank of Dallas.

a. How many times were nominal sales below that of the previous month?

b. Use the PPI to compute the sales in real terms. How many times were real sales below that of the previous month?

c. Compute the total percentage increase in nominal as well as real retail sales in 2009.

d. Can economists feel optimistic about the economy based on the retail sales data?

28. Japan was the first Asian country to challenge the dominance of the U.S. in 1980s. However, since then, its economy has been in a slow but relentless decline (*The New York Times*, October 16, 2010). This country has been trapped in low growth and a downward spiral of prices, known as deflation. Consider the following CPI of Japan for the years 2001 through 2009. Compute and interpret the annual inflation rates in Japan in the 2000s.

Year	2001	2002	2003	2004	2005	2006	2007	2008	2009
CPI	120.1	119.0	118.7	118.7	118.3	118.7	118.7	120.3	118.7

Source: Bureau of Labor Statistics.

29. **FILE** Each month the Current Employment Statistics (CES) program surveys numerous businesses and government agencies in order to obtain detailed data on earnings of workers. Consider the following data on the national average of hourly earnings for 2008. Also included is the corresponding consumer price index for 2008. The data set can also be found on the text website, labeled **Earnings 2008**.

Month	Earnings	CPI	Month	Earnings	CPI
January	21.25	173.3	July	21.66	183.7
February	21.29	173.9	August	21.74	181.9
March	21.43	175.8	September	21.80	182.0
April	21.43	176.5	October	21.84	177.3
May	21.52	178.8	November	21.93	172.3
June	21.60	181.5	December	21.96	169.4

Source: Bureau of Labor Statistics.

a. Use the CPI to deflate the national average of hourly earnings.

b. Compute the percentage change in the nominal as well as real hourly earnings in 2008.

c. Were consumers getting better off over 2008? Explain.

Use the following information on CPI and PPI for the next three exercises.

Year	CPI (1982–84 = 100)	PPI (1982 = 100)
2006	201.59	164.80
2007	207.34	172.70
2008	215.30	189.60
2009	214.54	172.90

Source: Bureau of Labor Statistics.

30. The total revenue for The Walt Disney Company was $35,510,000 for 2007, $37,843,000 for 2008, and $36,149,000 for 2009 (Source: http://finance.yahoo.com).

a. Deflate the total revenue with the relevant price index.

b. Discuss the revenue trend during the 2007–2009 period using nominal as well as real values.

31. According to the New Hampshire Department of Education, the average teacher salary in public school districts in New Hampshire was $46,797 in 2006, $48,310 in 2007, and $46,797 in 2008. Comment on the percentage change in the dollar value (nominal) as well as the purchasing power (real) of salaries.

32. According to Fisher College of Business at the Ohio State University, the starting salary of their graduates in the MBA program in 2008 was $89,156. What must be the starting salary of the MBAs in 2009 if the salary increase makes the exact cost of living adjustment?

WRITING WITH STATISTICS

Valerie Barnes is a graduate student in the department of political science at Michigan State University. She has been asked to write a brief report on the changes in the economic climate during the presidency of Ronald Reagan from 1981–1989. Valerie collects information on various economic indicators at the beginning and the end of President Reagan's term, as shown in Table 19.9.

TABLE 19.9 Select Economic Indicators during the Reagan Presidency

Economic Indicators	1981	1989
Federal Debt ($ billions)	$994.8	$2,868.0
Median Household Income	$19,074	$28,906
Cost of a New Home	$83,000	$148,800
Dow Jones Industrial Average High	1,024	2,791
Cost of a Gallon of Regular Gasoline	$1.38	$1.12
Consumer Price Index (1982–1984 = 100)	90.9	124

Source: http://www.1980sflashback.com.

Valerie would like to use the above information to:

1. Evaluate the change in prices over the Reagan Era, including the annual inflation rate.
2. Calculate and interpret corresponding deflated economic indicators for 1981 and 1989.
3. Comment on changes in select economic indicators during Reagan's presidency.

Sample Report— Economic Indicators during Reagan's Presidency

Ronald Wilson Reagan became the 40th President of the United States in 1981, after serving eight years as governor of California. He took office at a time when the U.S. was experiencing economic stagnation and inflation. As president, Reagan advocated reduced business regulation and extensive tax cuts to boost economic growth. Arguably, the Reagan era signifies a period of significant growth as the economy recovered from the recession.

Crucial economic indicators were analyzed during Reagan's presidency. The consumer price index (CPI) values imply that prices were 9.1% lower in 1981 and 24% higher in 1989 than during the base years of 1982–1984. The percentage price increase during Reagan's term is calculated as 36.41%, resulting in an annualized inflation rate of $(1 + 0.3641)^{1/8} - 1 = 3.96\%$. The CPI is also used to deflate crucial economic indicators. For instance, while the median household income increased from $19,074 to $28,906, or by 51.55%, the corresponding deflated incomes increased from $20,984 to $23,311, or by 11.09%. Other similarly deflated economic indicators are presented in Table 19.A.

TABLE 19.A Deflated Economic Indicators

Economic Indicators	1981	1989
Federal Debt ($ billions)	$1,094.4	$2,312.9
Median Household Income	$20,984	$23,311
Cost of a New Home	$91,309	$120,000
Dow Jones Industrial Average High	1,127	2,251
Cost of a Gallon of Regular Gasoline	$1.52	$0.90

The significant increase in the federal debt during the Reagan era is noteworthy. When Reagan took office, he used deficit spending through tax cuts to stimulate the economy.

However, the debt continued to grow throughout the boom years. The resulting deflated federal debt rose sharply from \$1,094.4 billion in 1981 to \$2,312.9 billion in 1989, or by 111%. The deflated cost of a new home grew from \$91,309 to \$120,000, or by 31.42%. Therefore, despite the 11.09% growth in real income, a higher percentage increase in home values made owning a new home more difficult. Interestingly, the deflated Dow Jones Industrial Average High grew by a whopping 99.73% from 1,127 in 1981 to 2,251 in 1989. Finally, there was a steep decline of 40.79% in the deflated price of gasoline from \$1.52 per gallon to \$0.90 per gallon. Perhaps the price decline was the consequence of the falling demand as consumers reacted to the energy crisis of the 70s.

President Reagan's policies reflected his personal belief in individual freedom. According to Reagan supporters, his policies resulted in the largest peacetime economic boom in American history. His critics, on the other hand, argue that the Reagan era is associated with a widening of inequality, where the rich got richer with little economic gains for most Americans. This argument is partly reflected by a meager 11.09% real increase in the median household income during the supposedly good years.

Conceptual Review

LO 19.1

Define and compute investment returns.

The **investment return** R_t is calculated as $R_t = \dfrac{P_t - P_{t-1} + I_t}{P_{t-1}}$, where $\dfrac{P_t - P_{t-1}}{P_{t-1}}$ and $\dfrac{I_t}{P_{t-1}}$ are the **capital gains yield** and the **income yield** components, respectively.

The **adjusted close prices** make appropriate adjustments for dividend distributions, stock splits and reverse stock splits. Let P_t^* and P_{t-1}^* represent the adjusted close price of a stock at times t (current) and $t - 1$ (prior), respectively. Using adjusted close prices, the investment return R_t at the end of time t is calculated as $R_t = \dfrac{P_t^* - P_{t-1}^*}{P_{t-1}^*}$.

LO 19.2

Use the Fisher equation to convert nominal returns into real returns and vice versa.

The **Fisher equation**, $1 + r = \dfrac{1 + R}{1 + i}$, represents the relationship between the nominal return R, the real return r, and the expected inflation rate i.

LO 19.3

Calculate and interpret a simple price index.

An **index number** is an easy-to-interpret numerical value that reflects a percentage change in price or quantity from a base value. A **simple price index** is a ratio of the price in period t, p_t, and the price in the base period, p_0, expressed as a percentage. It is calculated as $\dfrac{p_t}{p_0} \times 100$. It is common to update the base period over time. We update a simple index, with a revised base period, as Updated Index $= \dfrac{\text{Old Index Value}}{\text{Old Index Value of New Base}} \times 100$.

LO 19.4

Calculate and interpret the unweighted aggregate price index.

Let p_{it} represent the price of item i in period t and let p_{i0} be the corresponding price in the base period ($t = 0$). The **unweighted aggregate price index** in period t is $\dfrac{\Sigma p_{it}}{\Sigma p_{i0}} \times 100$.

LO 19.5

Compare the Laspeyres and the Paasche methods for computing the weighted aggregate price index.

Let p_{it} and q_{it} represent the price and quantity of item i in period t and let p_{i0} and q_{i0} be the corresponding values in the base period ($t = 0$). Using only the base period quantities q_{i0}, the **Laspeyres price index** for period t is $\dfrac{\Sigma p_{it} q_{i0}}{\Sigma p_{i0} q_{i0}} \times 100$.

Using only the current period ($t = n$) quantities q_{in}, the **Paasche price index** for period t is $\frac{\sum p_{it}q_{in}}{\sum p_{i0}q_{in}} \times 100$.

LO **19.6** **Use price indices to deflate economic time series and derive the inflation rate.**

A **deflated** time series is obtained by adjusting it for changes in prices, or inflation. A time series that has been deflated is said to be represented in **real terms**. The unadjusted time series is said to be represented in **nominal terms**. We use a price index to convert the nominal value of a time series into its real value as Real Value $= \frac{\text{Nominal Value}}{\text{Price Index}} \times 100$.

Two commonly used price indices used to deflate economic time series are the **Consumer Price Index (CPI)** and the **Producer Price Index (PPI)**. It is common to use the CPI to adjust wages for changes in the cost of living. On the other hand, the PPI is useful to deflate revenue in order to obtain real growth in output. The reported **inflation rate** i_t for a given period is generally based on the CPI and is computed as $i_t = \frac{CPI_t - CPI_{t-1}}{CPI_{t-1}}$.

Additional Exercises and Case Studies

33. Kim Baek invested $20,000 for a year in corporate bonds. Each bond sold for $1,000 and earned a coupon payment of $80 each during the year. The price of the bond at the end of the year has dropped to $980.

    a. Calculate Kim's investment return.

    b. Calculate Kim's total dollar gain or loss on his investment.

34. Toyota Motor Corp., once considered a company synonymous with reliability and customer satisfaction, has been engulfed in a perfect storm with millions of cars recalled (*BBC News*, March 19, 2010). The following table shows the monthly adjusted close price per share of Toyota from October 2009 to March 2010.

Date	Adjusted Close Price	Date	Adjusted Close Price
October 2009	78.89	January 2010	77.00
November 2009	78.54	February 2010	74.83
December 2009	84.16	March 2010	79.56

Source: http://finance.yahoo.com.

    a. Form a simple price index with October 2009 as the base.

    b. Update the simple price index, using January 2010 as the base.

    c. What is the percentage price change from October 2009 to December 2009?

    d. What is the percentage price change from January 2010 to March 2010?

35. Consider the following price data from 2002 to 2010.

Year	2002	2003	2004	2005	2006	2007	2008	2009	2010
Price	3.20	3.46	3.51	4.02	4.18	4.30	4.59	4.50	4.70

    a. Compute the simple price index using 2002 as the base year.

    b. Update the index numbers with a base year revised from 2002 to 2005.

    c. Plot the index numbers with a base year of 2002 and a base year of 2005. Compare the two plots.

36. Consider the following price data from 2009 to 2011.

Year	Product 1	Product 2	Product 3
2009	38	94	45
2010	40	92	48
2011	42	98	56

    a. Compute and interpret the simple price index for each product, using 2009 as the base year.

    b. Compute and interpret the unweighted aggregate price index, using 2009 as the base year.

37. Let the quantities corresponding to the prices in the previous exercise be given by the following table.

Year	Product 1	Product 2	Product 3
2009	90	32	48
2010	82	34	46
2011	76	30	36

    a. Compute the Laspeyres price index, using 2009 as the base year.

    b. Compute the Paasche price index, using 2009 as the base year.

    c. Comment on the differences between the two indices.

38. Lindsay Kelly bought 100 shares of Google, 300 shares of Microsoft, and 500 shares of Nokia in January 2005. The adjusted close prices of these stocks over the next three years are shown in the accompanying table.

Year	Google	Microsoft	Nokia
2005	195.62	24.11	13.36
2006	432.66	26.14	16.54
2007	505.00	28.83	19.83

Source: http://finance.yahoo.com.

    a. Compute and interpret the unweighted aggregate price index for Lindsay's portfolio, using 2005 as the base year.

b. Compute and interpret the corresponding weighted price index using the Laspeyres approach.

c. Why are the results from parts a and b so different?

39. Citigroup, Inc., is a major financial services company based in New York. It suffered huge losses during the global financial crisis and was rescued in November 2008 in a massive bailout by the U.S. government. Consider the following table, representing the net revenue and net income of Citigroup for 2006 to 2009. Both variables are measured in billions of dollars.

Year	Net Revenue	Net Income
2006	146.6	21.2
2007	159.2	3.6
2008	105.8	−27.7
2009	111.0	−1.6

Source: http://money.cnn.com.

a. Compute and interpret the simple price index for net revenue, using 2006 as the base year.

b. Compute and interpret the simple price index for net income, using 2006 as the base year.

40. Consider the following consumer price index and producer price index for 2006–2009.

Year	CPI (1982–84 = 100)	PPI (1982 = 100)
2006	201.59	164.80
2007	207.34	172.70
2008	215.30	189.60
2009	214.54	172.90

Source: Bureau of Labor Statistics.

a. Use the relevant price index to deflate the data on net revenue of Citigroup, given in the previous exercise.

b. Use the relevant price index to deflate the data on net income of Citigroup, given in the previous exercise.

41. An investor bought 1,000 shares of Citigroup in January 2009 for $3.55 a share. She sold all of her shares in December 2009 for $3.31 a share.

a. What annual rate of return did the investor earn?

b. Use the CPI information from the previous exercise to compute the inflation rate for 2009.

c. What is the investor's real rate of return?

42. The adjusted close prices of Wendy's/Arby's Group, Inc., for the first three months of 2008 are presented in the following table. Also included in the table is the corresponding consumer price index (CPI).

Date	Adjusted Close Price	CPI (Base 1982–1984)
January, 2008	8.94	212.225
February, 2008	8.29	212.703
March, 2008	6.01	213.543

Source: http://finance.yahoo.com; and Bureau of Labor Statistics.

a. Find the real rate of return for the three months by first using the CPI to deflate the adjusted close price.

b. Replicate the above result with Fisher's equation, based on the nominal rate of return and the inflation rate.

CASE STUDIES

Case Study 19.1

The dot-com period, roughly between 1995–2000, was characterized by extreme investor optimism for Internet-based businesses. This period was also marked by young, bold managers, who made a good deal of money by reaching consumers only over the Internet. Arguably, the dot-com boom was a case of too much too fast and was consequently followed by a crash in March 2000. Jose Menges is a business student at a California State University. For his senior seminar course, he has been asked to compare the stock performance of Internet-based companies with non-Internet-based companies during the dot-com boom-bust period. He collects monthly data on the adjusted close prices from 1999 to 2000 for four companies. Amazon (AMZN) and eBay (EBAY) are chosen to represent the Internet-based companies, whereas Coca-Cola (COKE) and Johnson and Johnson (JNJ) reflect non-Internet companies. A portion of the data is shown below; the complete data set can be found on the text website, labeled **Dotcom**.

Data for Case Study 19.1 Monthly Adjusted Close Prices for Four Firms, 1999–2000

FILE	Month	AMZN	EBAY	COKE	JNJ
	January, 1999	58.47	11.57	44.00	33.93
	February, 1999	64.06	13.92	43.80	34.13
	⋮	⋮	⋮	⋮	⋮
	December, 2000	15.56	8.25	30.84	41.86

Source: http://finance.yahoo.com; data obtained in July 2010.

In a report, use the sample information to:

1. Compute monthly returns for all companies for 1999 and 2000.

2. Compare the stock performance of the Internet-based companies with non-Internet based companies in the dot-com boom-bust period.

Case Study 19.2

The U.S. is often blamed for triggering the 2008 global financial crisis because many of the excesses and bad practices originated in the U.S. The crisis has had consequences on all aspects of the global economy. According to a recent report by Brookings Institute, the U.S. economic crisis is linked to a huge drop in world trade. Since U.S. imports have been an important component of world demand, a drop in imports has had repercussions in its exports. Rami Horowitz is a young economist working for a trade policy institute. He wishes to analyze the changes in U.S. imports and exports based on the data in the accompanying table. Both real exports and imports represent quarterly, seasonally adjusted values, measured in billions of 2005 dollars. A portion of the data is shown below; the complete data set can be found on the text website, labeled **World Trade**.

Data for Case Study 19.2 U.S. Real Exports and Imports

FILE	Period	Real Exports	Real Imports
	2007: Quarter 1	1485.9	2190.8
	2007: Quarter 2	1504.8	2188.1
	⋮	⋮	⋮
	2009: Quarter 4	1555.5	1902.7

Source: Federal Reserve Bank of Dallas.

In a report, use the sample information to:

1. Create simple indices for real exports and real imports with Quarter 1, 2007, used as the base period.

2. Interpret the percentage changes in real exports and real imports over the three-year period.

Case Study 19.3

The Cheesecake Factory, Inc., is a popular restaurant chain in the U.S. Although it started as a small restaurant in 1978, it currently has over 140 branches all over the country. The restaurants are characterized by extensive menus, custom décor, and large portions of food. Jeff Watson works as the Kitchen Manager in one of their regional branches. He is responsible for managing the operations as well as food and labor costs. He constantly monitors market conditions and, in his annual reports, analyzes the changing retail cost of the ingredients used in cooking. In his current report, he decides to analyze meat prices. He collects data on monthly average retail prices of three varieties of ground beef. This information is important, as the restaurant purchases about 1,400 pounds of regular, 800 pounds of ground chuck, and 500 pounds of lean ground beef each month. A portion of the data is shown below; the complete data set can be found on the text website, labeled **Ground Beef**.

Data for Case Study 19.3 2009 Monthly Retail Cost of Ground Beef (in $ per pound)

FILE	Month	Regular Beef	Ground Chuck	Lean Ground Beef
	January	2.357	2.961	3.426
	February	2.436	3.019	3.440
	⋮	⋮	⋮	⋮
	December	2.186	2.828	3.391

Source: United States Department of Agriculture.

In a report, use the sample information to:

1. Compute and interpret simple indices for each variety of meat, using January 2009 as the base period.

2. Compute and interpret the weighted aggregate price index, using January 2009 as the base period.

3. Compare the above indices.

20 Nonparametric Tests

LEARNING OBJECTIVES

After reading this chapter you should be able to:

LO 20.1 Distinguish between parametric and nonparametric tests.

LO 20.2 Conduct a hypothesis test concerning a single population median.

LO 20.3 Determine whether the population median difference differs from zero under matched-pairs sampling.

LO 20.4 Determine whether two population medians differ under independent sampling.

LO 20.5 Determine whether the medians of more than two populations differ.

LO 20.6 Analyze the correlation between two variables.

LO 20.7 Determine whether two populations differ under matched-pairs sampling with ordinal data.

LO 20.8 Determine whether the elements of a sequence appear in a random order.

The hypothesis tests presented in earlier chapters make certain assumptions about the underlying population. We refer to these tests as parametric tests. A t or an F test, for example, requires that the observations come from a normal distribution. These tests are quite "robust," in the sense that they are still useful when the assumptions are not exactly fulfilled, especially when the sample size is large. However, in situations when the underlying population is markedly nonnormal, we apply distribution-free alternative techniques called nonparametric methods. In addition to not needing to fulfill a given distribution requirement, another benefit of nonparametric methods is that they do not require a level of measurement as strong as that necessary for parametric tests. For instance, we cannot calculate means and variances with ordinal data (required calculations for parametric tests) because the numbers on an ordinal scale have no meaning except to indicate rank order. In this chapter we explore a variety of nonparametric tests that make fewer assumptions about the distribution of the underlying population and/or treat data of a weaker scale.

Analyzing Mutual Fund Returns

In Chapter 3 we were introduced to Rebecca Johnson, an investment counselor at a large bank. One of her clients has narrowed his investment options to two top-performing mutual funds from the last decade: Vanguard's Precious Metals and Mining fund (henceforth, Metals) and Fidelity's Strategic Income fund (henceforth, Income). He has some final questions for Rebecca with respect to each fund's return data. Rebecca explains that her analysis will use techniques that do not rely on stringent assumptions concerning the distribution of the underlying population, since return data often diverge from the normal distribution. Table 20.1 shows a portion of the annual return data for each fund and some relevant descriptive statistics over the last decade; the full data set, labeled **Fund Returns**, can be found on the text website.

TABLE 20.1 Annual Returns (in percent) for Metals and Income Funds, 2000–2009

Year	Metals	Income
2000	−7.34	4.07
2001	18.33	6.52
⋮	⋮	⋮
2009	76.46	31.77
	$\bar{x} = 24.65\%$	$\bar{x} = 8.51\%$
	median $= 33.83\%$	median $= 7.34\%$
	$s = 37.13\%$	$s = 11.07\%$

Source: http://finance.yahoo.com.

Rebecca would like to use the above sample information to:

1. Determine whether the median return for the Metals fund is greater than 5%.

2. Determine whether the median difference between the returns of the Metals and the Income funds differs from zero.

3. Examine whether the funds are correlated.

A synopsis of this case is provided at the end of Section 20.4.

20.1 Testing a Population Median

LO 20.1

Distinguish between parametric and nonparametric tests.

The parametric tests presented in earlier chapters make certain assumptions about the underlying population. These conventional tests can be misleading if the underlying assumptions are not met. **Nonparametric tests**, also referred to as distribution-free tests, are attractive when the parametric assumptions seem unreasonable. Nonparametric tests use fewer and weaker assumptions than those associated with parametric tests. For instance, these tests do not assume that the sample data originate from a normal distribution. Nonparametric tests are especially useful when sample sizes are small. Finally, while parametric tests require data of interval or ratio scale, nonparametric tests can be performed on data of nominal or ordinal scale. (For a review of these data concepts, see Section 3 in Chapter 1.)

Nonparametric tests have disadvantages, too. If the parametric assumptions are valid yet we choose to use a nonparametric test, the nonparametric test is less powerful (more prone to Type II error) than its parametric counterpart. The reason for less power is that a nonparametric test uses the data less efficiently. As we will see shortly, nonparametric tests often focus on the rank of the data rather than the magnitude of the sample values, thus possibly ignoring useful information.

Table 20.2 summarizes some of the parametric tests that we examined in earlier chapters. The first column shows the parametric test of interest, the second column states the underlying assumptions of the test, and the third column lists where the test was covered in the text. Each one of these parametric tests has a nonparametric counterpart. At the end of Section 20.4 we will present a table that lists the corresponding nonparametric test for each parametric test.

TABLE 20.2 Summary of Select Parametric Tests

Parametric Test	Population Characteristics and Other Description	Reference Section
t test concerning the population mean	Sampling from a normal population or large sample; σ unknown	9.3
t test to determine whether the population mean difference differs from zero under matched-pairs sampling	Sampling from a normal population or large sample	10.2
t test to determine whether two population means differ under independent sampling	Sampling from normal populations or large samples; σ_1 and σ_2 unknown	10.1
F test to determine whether the means of more than two populations differ	Sampling from normal populations or large samples; $\sigma_1, \sigma_2, \sigma_3, \ldots$ unknown but assumed equal	13.1
t test to determine whether two variables are correlated	Sampling from a normal population or large sample	14.1

LO 20.2

Conduct a hypothesis test concerning a single population median.

Wilcoxon Signed-Rank Test for a Population Median

In Chapter 9 we used a t test to determine whether the population mean μ (σ unknown) differs from some assumed value. However, as shown in Table 20.2, a t test requires that we sample from a normal distribution. If we cannot assume that the data are normally distributed and/or we want to test whether the population *median* differs from some hypothesized value, we can apply the **Wilcoxon signed-rank test**. The Wilcoxon signed-rank test makes no assumptions concerning the distribution of the population except that it is continuous and symmetric.

Let's revisit the introductory case. Here we learn that Rebecca's analysis of the fund return data will use nonparametric techniques. She chooses these methods because the distribution of return data often has "fatter tails" as compared to the normal distribution;

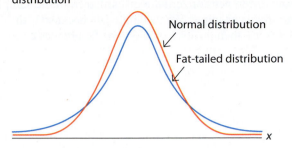

FIGURE 20.1 Normal distribution versus "fat-tailed" distribution

that is, the likelihood of extreme returns (area under the tail) is higher for a fatter-tailed distribution than for a normal distribution. Figure 20.1 shows a normal distribution versus a distribution with fatter tails. If Rebecca were to rely on tests that incorrectly assume that the data are normally distributed, then there is a chance that she may make erroneous conclusions. She chooses to use the Wilcoxon signed-rank test for the population median.

Following the methodology outlined in earlier chapters, when conducting a hypothesis test for the population median m, we want to test whether m is not equal to, greater than, or less than m_0, the value of the population median postulated in the null hypothesis. The null and alternative hypotheses will assume one of the following forms:

Two-tailed Test	Right-tailed Test	Left-tailed Test
$H_0: m = m_0$	$H_0: m \leq m_0$	$H_0: m \geq m_0$
$H_A: m \neq m_0$	$H_A: m > m_0$	$H_A: m < m_0$

For the Metals fund return data in Table 20.1, we would like to determine whether the median return for this fund is greater than 5%. We formulate the one-tailed test as

$$H_0: m \leq 5$$
$$H_A: m > 5$$

In order to arrive at the sample value for the Wilcoxon signed-rank test statistic T, several calculations are necessary.

a. We first calculate the difference d_i between each observed value and the hypothesized median. In this case, $d_i = x_i - 5$, as shown in the second column of Table 20.3.

TABLE 20.3 Calculations for the Wilcoxon Signed-Rank Test Statistic

Return, x (1)	$d = x - m_0$ (2)	$\lvert d \rvert$ (3)	Rank (4)	Ranks of Negative Differences (5)	Ranks of Positive Differences (6)
-7.34	$-7.34 - 5 = -12.34$	12.34	2	2	
18.33	13.33	13.33	3		3
33.35	28.35	28.35	4		4
59.45	54.45	54.45	8		8
8.09	3.09	3.09	1		1
43.79	38.79	38.79	7		7
34.30	29.30	29.30	5		5
36.13	31.13	31.13	6		6
-56.02	-61.02	61.02	9	9	
76.46	71.46	71.46	10		10
				$T^- = 11$	$T^+ = 44$

b. We then take the absolute value of each difference, $|d_i|$. See the third column of Table 20.3. Any differences of zero are discarded from the sample; no zero-differences occur in this example. We calculate $|d_i|$ because if the median is 5 (the null hypothesis is true), then positive or negative differences of a given magnitude are equally likely.

c. Next we rank the absolute value of each difference, assigning 1 to the smallest $|d_i|$ and n to the largest $|d_i|$. Note that n would be smaller than the original sample size if there were some zero-difference observations, which we discarded; here, n equals the original sample size of 10. Any ties in the ranks of differences are assigned the average of the tied ranks. For instance, if two observations have the rank of 5 (occupying the 5th and 6th positions), each is assigned the rank of $(5 + 6)/2 = 5.5$. Or, if three observations have a ranking of 1, each is assigned a rank of $(1 + 2 + 3)/3 = 2$. In the Metals fund return example, there are no ties. The rankings for the differences are shown in the fourth column of Table 20.3.

d. We then sum the ranks of the negative differences (denoted T^-) and sum the ranks of the positive differences (denoted T^+). In this example we find two negative differences, whose rank sum is $T^- = 11$, and eight positive differences, whose rank sum is $T^+ = 44$. These calculations are shown in the fifth and sixth columns of Table 20.3.

The sum of T^- and T^+ should equal $n(n + 1)/2$, which is the formula for the sum of consecutive integers from 1 to n. In our example, $T^- + T^+ = 11 + 44 = 55$. Also, $n(n + 1)/2 = 10(10 + 1)/2 = 55$. As we will see shortly, the value of T^- is not used in the actual analysis, but its calculation can help us avoid errors.

Values of T^- and T^+ relatively close to one another indicate that the rank sums more or less offset one another and provide evidence in support of the null hypothesis. However, a small value of T^- relative to T^+, for example, implies larger positive deviations from the hypothesized median value of 5. This would suggest that the median is greater than 5. We can view a small value of T^+ relative to T^- in a like manner.

THE TEST STATISTIC T FOR THE WILCOXON SIGNED-RANK TEST

The **test statistic T** is defined as $T = T^+$, where T^+ denotes the sum of the ranks of the positive differences from the hypothesized median m_0.

The statistic T has a distribution whose critical values are shown in Table 6 of Appendix A for $n \le 10$.

If $n \ge 10$, T can be assumed normally distributed with mean $\mu_T = \dfrac{n(n + 1)}{4}$ and standard deviation $\sigma_T = \sqrt{\dfrac{n(n + 1)(2n + 1)}{24}}$, and hence the value of the resulting test statistic is computed as $z = \dfrac{T - \mu_T}{\sigma_T}$.

For ease of exposition, we do not make a distinction between the random variable and the particular outcomes of the random variable in this chapter. For example, we use the statistic T to represent a random variable as well as its sample value. We adopt this same practice for the statistics W, H, r_S, and R that we introduce in later sections.

The critical value(s) for the Wilcoxon signed-rank test is found in Table 6 of Appendix A; a portion of this table is shown in Table 20.4. A lower critical value T_L is used for a left-tailed test, an upper critical value T_U is used for a right-tailed test, and both lower and upper critical values are used for a two-tailed test.

TABLE 20.4 Portion of the Lower T_L and Upper T_U Critical Values for the Wilcoxon Signed-Rank Test

Two-tailed Test: One-tailed Test:	$\alpha = 0.10$ $\alpha = 0.05$	$\alpha = 0.05$ $\alpha = 0.025$	$\alpha = 0.02$ $\alpha = 0.01$	$\alpha = 0.01$ $\alpha = 0.005$
$n = 8$	5, 31	3, 33	0, 36	—
9	8, 37	5, 40	1, 44	0, 45
10	10, **45**	8, 47	3, 52	1, 54

EXAMPLE 20.1

Given the return data in Table 20.1, determine whether the median return for the Metals fund is significantly greater than 5% with $\alpha = 0.05$.

SOLUTION: As discussed above, the competing hypotheses for the test are $H_0: m \le 5$ versus $H_A: m > 5$. We already calculated the value of the test statistic as $T = T^+ = 44$. For a right-tailed test with $\alpha = 0.05$ and $n = 10$, the decision rule is to reject the null hypothesis if the value of the test statistic T is *greater than or equal to* $T_U = 45$ (see the boldface value in Table 20.4). Since $T = 44 < 45 = T_U$, we do not reject H_0. At the 5% significance level, we cannot conclude that the median return is greater than 5% for the Metals fund.

Using a Normal Distribution Approximation for T

The sampling distribution of T can be approximated by the normal distribution if n has at least 10 observations.[1] We can then easily implement a z test with this approximation.

EXAMPLE 20.2

Redo the test specified in Example 20.1 assuming that T is normally distributed.

SOLUTION: Again we use the competing hypotheses, $H_0: m \le 5$ versus $H_A: m > 5$, and the value of the test statistic, $T = T^+ = 44$. Since there are 10 years of return data ($n = 10$), we calculate the mean and standard deviation of the sampling distribution of T as

$$\mu_T = \frac{n(n + 1)}{4} = \frac{10(10 + 1)}{4} = 27.5 \text{ and}$$

$$\sigma_T = \sqrt{\frac{n(n + 1)(2n + 1)}{24}} = \sqrt{\frac{10(10 + 1)(2 \cdot 10 + 1)}{24}} = 9.81.$$

The corresponding value of the test statistic is

$$z = \frac{T - \mu_T}{\sigma_T} = \frac{44 - 27.5}{9.81} = 1.68.$$

Therefore, with the normal distribution approximation, we find the corresponding p-value as $P(Z \ge 1.68) = 0.0465$. Since the p-value is slightly lower than $\alpha = 0.05$, we reject H_0. This conclusion differs from that made in Example 20.1. We note that the reliability of this test improves with sample size.

We suggest that you take the time to show that a similar test employed on the Income fund results in a test statistic value of $T = T^+ = 40$. Then, for $\alpha = 0.05$, using the tests with and without the normal distribution approximation, we cannot conclude that the median return for the Income fund is greater than 5%.

[1]Since the normality assumption for parametric tests becomes less stringent in large samples, the main appeal of rank-based tests tends to be with relatively small samples.

EXERCISES 20.1

Concepts

1. Consider the following competing hypotheses and sample data.

   $H_0: m = 20$ $n = 7$ $T^- = 2$ $T^+ = 26$
   $H_A: m \neq 20$

   a. Specify the decision rule at the 5% significance level.
   b. What is the conclusion? Explain.

2. Consider the following competing hypotheses and sample data.

   $H_0: m \geq 150$ $n = 9$ $T^- = 42$ $T^+ = 3$
   $H_A: m < 150$

   a. Specify the decision rule at the 1% significance level.
   b. What is the conclusion? Explain.

3. Consider the following competing hypotheses and sample data.

   $H_0: m \leq 150$ $n = 30$ $T^- = 200$ $T^+ = 265$
   $H_A: m > 150$

   a. Assuming that the sampling distribution of T is normally distributed, determine the value of the test statistic.
   b. Calculate the p-value.
   c. At the 5% significance level, what is the conclusion? Explain.

4. Consider the following sample data.

8	5	11	7	6	5

   a. Specify the competing hypotheses that determine whether the median is less than 10.
   b. Calculate the value of the test statistic T.
   c. With $\alpha = 0.05$, what is the decision rule?
   d. Is the median less than 10? Explain.

5. Consider the following sample data.

105	90	110	80	85	85	103	70	115	75

   a. Specify the competing hypotheses that determine whether the median differs from 100.
   b. Calculate the value of the test statistic. Assume that the sampling distribution of T is normally distributed.
   c. Determine the critical value(s) of the test at $\alpha = 0.10$.
   d. Is the median different from 100? Explain.

Applications

6. During the fourth quarter of 2009, rents declined in almost all major cities in the United States. The largest fall was in New York, where average rents fell nearly 20% to $44.69 per square foot annually (*The Wall Street Journal*, January 8, 2010). The following table lists the average rent per square foot for 10 cities during the fourth quarter of 2009.

City	Rent	City	Rent
New York	$45	Miami	$24
Washington, D.C.	42	Seattle	24
San Francisco	30	Chicago	21
Boston	30	Houston	20
Los Angeles	27	Philadelphia	20

   a. Specify the competing hypotheses in order to determine whether the median rent is greater than $25 per square foot.
   b. Calculate the value of the test statistic. Assume the normal approximation for T.
   c. Calculate the p-value.
   d. At the 1% significance level, can you conclude that the median rent exceeds $25 per square foot?

7. The following table lists the annual returns (in percent) for a top-performing mutual fund, ING Russia, over the last decade.

Year	Return	Year	Return
2000	−17.80	2005	70.94
2001	80.32	2006	67.52
2002	24.72	2007	30.69
2003	75.88	2008	−71.51
2004	5.91	2009	129.97

   SOURCE: www.finance.yahoo.com

   a. Specify the competing hypotheses in order to determine whether the median return differs from 8%.
   b. Calculate the value of the test statistic. Do not assume the normal approximation for T.
   c. At the 10% significance level, what is the decision rule?
   d. Does the median return differ from 8%?

20.2 Testing Two Population Medians

In Chapter 10 we presented t tests to determine whether significant differences existed between means from matched-pairs and independent samples. When using a t test, we assume that we are sampling from normal populations. If we wish to compare central tendencies from nonnormal populations, then the **Wilcoxon signed-rank test** serves as the nonparametric counterpart to the matched-pairs t test. The **Wilcoxon rank-sum test**, also referred to as the **Mann-Whitney test**, is used for independent samples. We again note that if the normality assumption is not unreasonable, then these tests are less powerful than the standard t tests. We begin this section by examining the Wilcoxon signed-rank test for a matched-pairs experiment followed by the Wilcoxon rank-sum test for independent samples.

Wilcoxon Signed-Rank Test for a Matched-Pairs Sample

LO **20.3**

In this application of matched-pairs sampling, the parameter of interest is referred to as the median difference m_D where $D = X - Y$, and the random variables X and Y are matched in a pair. We refer you to Chapter 10 for details on matched-pairs sampling. When we wish to test whether m_D is not equal to, greater than, or less than 0, we set up the competing hypotheses as follows.

Determine whether the population median difference differs from zero under matched-pairs sampling.

Two-tailed Test	Right-tailed Test	Left-tailed Test
$H_0: m_D = 0$	$H_0: m_D \leq 0$	$H_0: m_D \geq 0$
$H_A: m_D \neq 0$	$H_A: m_D > 0$	$H_A: m_D < 0$

Since applying the Wilcoxon signed-rank test to a matched-pairs sample is nearly identical to its use for a single sample, we describe its use with an example and computer output.

EXAMPLE 20.3

We again use the *Fund Returns* data from the introductory case. At the 5% significance level, determine whether the median difference between the returns of the Metals fund and the Income fund differs from zero.

SOLUTION: We must first recognize that these samples are dependent, in that each return observation is blocked by year. We apply the Wilcoxon signed-rank test to determine whether significant differences exist between the median difference of the returns and formulate the two-tailed test as

$$H_0: m_D = 0$$
$$H_A: m_D \neq 0$$

Table 20.5 summarizes the method of calculating the value of the T statistic; that is, we first calculate differences between the returns (column 4), find absolute

---

TABLE 20.5 Calculations for Wilcoxon Signed-Rank Test

Year (1)	Metals x (2)	Income y (3)	$d = x - y$ (4)	$\lvert d \rvert$ (5)	Rank (6)	Ranks of Negative Differences (7)	Ranks of Positive Differences (8)
2000	−7.34	4.07	$-7.34 - 4.07 = -11.41$	11.41	2	2	
2001	18.33	6.52	11.81	11.81	3		3
2002	33.35	9.38	23.97	23.97	4		4
2003	59.45	18.62	40.83	40.83	8		8
2004	8.09	9.44	−1.35	1.35	1	1	
2005	43.79	3.12	40.67	40.67	7		7
2006	34.30	8.15	26.15	26.15	5		5
2007	36.13	5.44	30.69	30.69	6		6
2008	−56.02	−11.37	−44.65	44.65	9	9	
2009	76.46	31.77	44.69	44.69	10		10
						$T^- = 12$	$T^+ = 43$

differences (column 5), and determine rankings (column 6). Then we compute the sum of the ranks of negative differences (column 7, $T^- = 12$), and the sum of the ranks of positive differences (column 8, $T^+ = 43$). The value of the test statistic T is $T = T^+ = 43$. Given the critical values in Table 20.4, the decision rule is to reject H_0 if $T \leq 8$ or $T \geq 47$. Since $8 < T = 43 < 47$, we do not reject H_0; at the 5% significance level we cannot conclude that the median difference of the returns differs from zero.

Using the Computer for the Wilcoxon Signed-Rank Test

These calculations become extremely cumbersome with larger data sets. Excel does not include nonparametric methods in its standard data analysis package, but fortunately, most other statistical software packages provide a nonparametric option. Here, we use Minitab to complement the results that we obtained manually. (Directions on how to use Minitab and other software packages can be found on the text website.) Table 20.6 reports a portion of the Minitab output when testing whether the median difference between the Metals fund and the Income fund differs from zero. Minitab reports a Wilcoxon Statistic of 43, which is the same value that we calculated manually. The p-value corresponding to this test statistic is 0.126. At the 5% significance level, we do not reject the null hypothesis and again do not conclude that the median difference of the returns differs from zero.

TABLE 20.6 Minitab Output for Example 20.3

Test of median = 0.000 versus median not = 0.000				
	N	N for Test	Wilcoxon Statistic	P
Metals-Income	10	10	43.0	0.126

Determine whether two population medians differ under independent sampling.

Wilcoxon Rank-Sum Test for Independent Samples

Now we discuss whether significant differences exist between two population medians when the underlying populations are nonnormal and the samples are independent. In this situation, we use the Wilcoxon rank-sum test; this test is based completely on the order of the observations from the two independent samples. The parameter of interest is the difference between two population medians $m_1 - m_2$. When we wish to test whether $m_1 - m_2$ is not equal to, greater than, or less than 0, we set up the competing hypotheses as follows.

Two-tailed Test	Right-tailed Test	Left-tailed Test
$H_0: m_1 - m_2 = 0$	$H_0: m_1 - m_2 \leq 0$	$H_0: m_1 - m_2 \geq 0$
$H_A: m_1 - m_2 \neq 0$	$H_A: m_1 - m_2 > 0$	$H_A: m_1 - m_2 < 0$

Consider the next example.

An undergraduate at a local university has narrowed her choice of major to computer science or finance. She wonders whether her choice will significantly influence her salary upon graduation. She gathers salary data (in $1,000s) on 10 recent graduates who majored in computer science and 10 recent graduates who majored in finance. The data are shown in Table 20.7 and are available on the text website, labeled *Undergraduate Salaries*.

TABLE 20.7 Salary Information on Computer Science and Finance Graduates (in $1,000s)

FILE

Computer Science		Finance	
66	59	61	55
60	67	52	52
58	64	54	52
65	68	50	47
70	69	62	46

In order to determine whether salaries are significantly different depending on major, we apply the Wilcoxon rank-sum test. Let m_1 and m_2 denote the population median salary for computer science and finance majors, respectively. We formulate the two-tailed test as

$$H_0: m_1 - m_2 = 0$$
$$H_A: m_1 - m_2 \neq 0$$

In order to arrive at the value of the test statistic for the Wilcoxon rank-sum test W, several steps are necessary.

a. We first pool the data from sample 1 (computer science) and sample 2 (finance), with n_1 and n_2 observations, and arrange **all** the data in ascending order of magnitude. That is, we treat the independent samples as if they are one large sample of size $n_1 + n_2 = n$. See column 1 of Table 20.8.

b. We then rank the observations from lowest to highest, assigning the numbers 1 to n. Since we have a multiple tie at ranks 4, 5, and 6, we assign to each of the tied observations the mean of the ranks which they jointly occupy, or $(4 + 5 + 6)/3 = 5$. See columns 2 and 3 of Table 20.8. We note that the finance salaries occupy the lower ranks, whereas the computer science salaries occupy the higher ranks.

c. We then sum the ranks of the computer science salaries (denoted W_1) and sum the ranks of the finance salaries (denoted W_2). Here we find that $W_1 = 149$ and $W_2 = 61$; see columns 4 and 5 of Table 20.8. In order to check that we have performed the calculations properly, we confirm that the sum of the rank sums, $W_1 + W_2$, equals $\frac{(n_1 + n_2)(n_1 + n_2 + 1)}{2}$, which is equivalent to the sum of the integers from 1 to $n_1 + n_2$. We first find that $W_1 + W_2 = 149 + 61 = 210$. Since $n_1 = 10$ and $n_2 = 10$, we then find that $\frac{(n_1 + n_2)(n_1 + n_2 + 1)}{2} = \frac{(10 + 10)(10 + 10 + 1)}{2} = 210$.

TABLE 20.8 Calculations for Wilcoxon Rank-Sum Test

Salary (1)	Sample of Origin (2)	Rank (3)	Computer Science Ranks (4)	Finance Ranks (5)
46	Finance	1		1
47	Finance	2		2
50	Finance	3		3
52	Finance	5		5
52	Finance	5		5
52	Finance	5		5
54	Finance	7		7
55	Finance	8		8
58	Computer Science	9	9	
59	Computer Science	10	10	
60	Computer Science	11	11	
61	Finance	12		12
62	Finance	13		13
64	Computer Science	14	14	
65	Computer Science	15	15	
66	Computer Science	16	16	
67	Computer Science	17	17	
68	Computer Science	18	18	
69	Computer Science	19	19	
70	Computer Science	20	20	
			$W_1 = 149$	$W_2 = 61$

If the median salary of computer science majors is equal to the median salary of finance majors, then we would expect each major to produce about as many low ranks as high ranks, so that W_1 is relatively close to W_2. However, if the median salaries are significantly different, then most of the higher ranks will be occupied by one major and most of the lower ranks will be occupied by the other major, so that W_1 will significantly differ from W_2. We determine whether W_1 is close to or far from W_2 by comparing one of these values to the appropriate critical value.

THE TEST STATISTIC W FOR THE WILCOXON RANK-SUM TEST

The **test statistic** W is the value associated with the minimum of n_1 and n_2, $\min(n_1, n_2)$:

a. If $n_1 \leq n_2$, then $W = W_1$, or

b. If $n_1 > n_2$, then $W = W_2$,

where W_1 and W_2 denote the sums of the ranks of the values in samples 1 and 2.

The statistic W has a distribution whose critical values are shown in Table 7 of Appendix A for $n_1 \leq 10$ and $n_2 \leq 10$.

If $n_1 \geq 10$ and $n_2 \geq 10$, W can be assumed normally distributed with mean $\mu_W = \dfrac{(n_1 + n_2 + 1) \times \min(n_1, n_2)}{2}$ and standard deviation $\sigma_W = \sqrt{\dfrac{n_1 n_2 (n_1 + n_2 + 1)}{12}}$, and hence the value of the resulting test statistic is computed as $z = \dfrac{W - \mu_W}{\sigma_W}$.

In the above example, since $n_1 = n_2 = 10$, we select the value of the test statistic as the rank sum of sample 1, so $W = W_1 = 149$.

Table 20.9 shows a portion of lower W_L and upper W_U critical values for the Wilcoxon rank-sum test with n_1 and n_2 as the number of observations in the respective samples. (A more complete version is found in Table 7 of Appendix A.) Based on the specification of the hypothesis test, the rejection region will be in either one or both sides.

TABLE 20.9 Lower W_L and Upper W_U Critical Values for the Wilcoxon Rank-Sum Test

	$\alpha = 0.025$ for one-tailed test and $\alpha = 0.05$ for a two-tailed test							
	n_1: 3	4	5	6	7	8	9	10
n_2: 8	8, 28	14, 38	21, 49	29, 61	39, 73	49, 87	51, 93	54, 98
9	8, 31	15, 41	22, 53	31, 65	41, 78	51, 93	63, 108	66, 114
10	9, 33	16, 44	24, 56	32, 70	43, 83	54, 98	66, 114	**79, 131**

EXAMPLE 20.4

Use the salary data in Table 20.7 to determine whether the median computer science salary differs from the median finance salary at the 5% significance level.

SOLUTION: As discussed earlier, the competing hypotheses for the test are H_0: $m_1 - m_2 = 0$ versus H_A: $m_1 - m_2 \neq 0$ and the value of the test statistic is $W = W_1 = 149$. For a two-tailed test with $\alpha = 0.05$ and $n_1 = n_2 = 10$, the decision rule is to reject the null hypothesis if $W \leq 79$ or $W \geq 131$ (see the boldface values in Table 20.9).

Since the value of the test statistic $W = 149$ is greater than 131, we can reject H_0. At the 5% significance level, we conclude that the median computer science salary differs from the median finance salary.

Using a Normal Distribution Approximation for W

When n_1 and n_2 both have at least 10 observations, we can use the normal distribution approximation to implement a z test.

EXAMPLE 20.5

Assuming that the distribution of W is approximately normal, let's again determine whether the median computer science salary differs from the median finance salary at the 5% significance level.

SOLUTION: We specify the same competing hypotheses, $H_0: m_1 - m_2 = 0$ versus $H_A: m_1 - m_2 \neq 0$, and compute the value of the test statistic as $W = W_1 = 149$. We now compute the mean and standard deviation as

$$\mu_W = \frac{n_1(n_1 + n_2 + 1)}{2} = \frac{10(10 + 10 + 1)}{2} = 105, \text{ and}$$

$$\sigma_W = \sqrt{\frac{n_1 n_2 (n_1 + n_2 + 1)}{12}} = \sqrt{\frac{(10 \cdot 10)(10 + 10 + 1)}{12}} = 13.23.$$

The value of the test statistic is calculated as

$$z = \frac{W - \mu_W}{\sigma_W} = \frac{149 - 105}{13.23} = 3.33.$$

Using the z table, we find the p-value as $2 \times P(Z \geq 3.33) = 0.0009$. Since the p-value is less than the significance level of $\alpha = 0.05$, we reject H_0 and conclude, as before, that the median computer science salary differs from the median finance salary.

Using the Computer for the Wilcoxon Rank-Sum Test

Table 20.10 shows a portion of the Minitab output for Example 20.5. (Minitab references the test as the Mann-Whitney Test.) The value of the test statistic W matches the value that we calculated by hand. Minitab refers to m_1 and m_2 as ETA1 and ETA2, respectively, and provides a p-value of 0.0010. At the 5% significance level, we again conclude that the median salaries between the two majors differ.

TABLE 20.10 Minitab Output for Example 20.5

$W = 149.0$
Test of ETA1 = ETA2 vs ETA1 not = ETA2 is significant at 0.0010.
The test is significant at 0.0010 (adjusted for ties).

EXERCISES 20.2

Concepts

8. Consider the following competing hypotheses and accompanying sample data drawn from a matched-pairs sample.

$H_0: m_D \geq 0$

$H_A: m_D < 0$ $\quad n = 9 \quad\quad T^- = 40 \quad\quad T^+ = 5$

a. Specify the decision rule at the 5% significance level.

b. What is the conclusion?

9. Consider the following competing hypotheses and accompanying sample data drawn from a matched-pairs sample.

$H_0: m_D = 0$

$H_A: m_D \neq 0$ $\quad n = 50 \quad\quad T^- = 400 \quad\quad T^+ = 875$

a. Determine the value of the test statistic using a normal approximation for T.

b. Calculate the p-value.

c. At the 5% significance level, what is the conclusion?

10. **FILE** The following table contains information on a matched-pairs sample. The data are also available on the text website, labeled **Exercise 20.10**.

Number	Sample 1	Sample 2
1	18	21
2	12	11
3	21	23
4	22	20
5	16	20
6	14	17
7	17	17
8	18	22

a. Specify the competing hypotheses that determine whether the median difference between Population 1 and Population 2 is less than zero.

b. Calculate the value of the test statistic T.

c. With $\alpha = 0.05$, what is the decision rule?

d. Is the median difference between Population 1 and Population 2 less than zero? Explain.

11. **FILE** The following data are derived from a matched-pairs sample. The data are also available on the text website, labeled **Exercise 20.11**.

Observation	Sample 1	Sample 2
1	120	125
2	156	160
3	143	140
4	100	90
5	115	132
6	140	124
7	111	112
8	142	144
9	175	200
10	190	182

a. Specify the competing hypotheses that determine whether the population median difference differs from zero.

b. Assuming that T is normally distributed, determine the value of the test statistic.

c. Calculate the p-value.

d. At the 1% significance level, what is the conclusion?

12. Consider the following competing hypotheses and accompanying sample data drawn independently.

$H_0: m_1 - m_2 = 0$ $W_1 = 80$ $W_2 = 40$
$H_A: m_1 - m_2 \neq 0$ $n_1 = 7$ $n_2 = 8$

a. Determine the value of the test statistic.

b. Specify the decision rule at the 5% significance level.

c. What is the conclusion?

13. Consider the following competing hypotheses and accompanying sample data drawn independently.

$H_0: m_1 - m_2 \geq 0$ $W_1 = 20$ $W_2 = 35$
$H_A: m_1 - m_2 < 0$ $n_1 = 5$ $n_2 = 5$

a. Determine the value of the test statistic.

b. Specify the decision rule at the 5% significance level.

c. What is the conclusion?

14. The following two samples represent independent random samples.

Sample 1	15	23	19	34	30	
Sample 2	28	25	34	35	37	40

a. Specify the competing hypotheses to determine whether the median of Population 1 is less than the median of Population 2.

b. Calculate the value of the test statistic W.

c. With $\alpha = 0.05$, what is the decision rule?

d. Is the median of Population 1 less than the median of Population 2? Explain.

15. The following two samples represent independent random samples.

Sample 1	-2	0	4	-5	2	
Sample 2	-3	-8	-1	0	-10	3

a. Specify the competing hypotheses to determine whether the median of Population 1 is greater than the median of Population 2.

b. Calculate the value of the test statistic W.

c. With $\alpha = 0.05$, what is the decision rule?

d. Is the median of Population 1 greater than the median of Population 2? Explain.

16. The following data are provided for two independent samples: $W = 700$, $n_1 = 25$, and $n_2 = 20$. Suppose the distribution of W is approximately normal.

a. Calculate the mean and standard deviation of the distribution of W.

b. Specify the competing hypotheses to determine whether the median of Population 1 is greater than the median of Population 2.

c. Calculate the value of the test statistic Z.

d. What is the decision rule with $\alpha = 0.05$?

e. What is the conclusion?

17. The following data are provided for two independent samples: $W = 545$, $n_1 = 25$, and $n_2 = 25$. Suppose the distribution of W is approximately normal.

a. Calculate the mean and standard deviation of the distribution of W.

b. Specify the competing hypotheses to determine whether the median of Population 1 differs from the median of Population 2.

c. Calculate the value of the test statistic Z.

d. Calculate the p-value.

e. At the 10% significance level, what is the conclusion?

Applications

18. **FILE** A bank employs two appraisers. When approving borrowers for mortgages, it is imperative that the appraisers value the same types of properties consistently. To make sure that this is the case, the bank asks the appraisers to value 10

different properties. The following data are also available on the text website, labeled **Appraisals**.

Property	Value from Appraiser 1	Value from Appraiser 2
1	$235,000	$239,000
2	195,000	190,000
3	264,000	271,000
4	315,000	310,000
5	435,000	437,000
6	515,000	525,000
7	350,000	352,000
8	225,000	224,000
9	437,000	440,000
10	575,000	583,000

a. Specify the competing hypotheses to determine whether the median difference between the values from appraiser 1 and appraiser 2 differs from zero.

b. Calculate the value of the test statistic T. Assume the normal approximation for T.

c. At the 5% significance level, what is the decision rule?

d. Is there sufficient evidence to conclude that the appraisers are not consistent in their appraisals? Explain.

19. A diet center claims that it has the most effective weight loss program in the region. Its advertisement says "Participants in our program really lose weight." Five clients of this program are weighed on the first day of the diet and then three months later.

Client	Weight on First Day of Diet	Weight Three Months Later
1	155	151
2	205	203
3	167	168
4	186	183
5	194	195

a. Specify the null and alternative hypotheses to test the diet center's claim.

b. Calculate the value of the test statistic T.

c. At the 5% significance level, what is the decision rule?

d. Do the data support the diet center's claim? Explain.

20. A recent analysis of census data suggests that married men have a higher median income than unmarried men

(*The Boston Globe*, January 19, 2010). Suppose the incomes (in $1,000s) of six married men and seven unmarried men produce the following representative results:

Married	84	75	83	67	70	76	
Unmarried	67	63	62	66	71	64	68

a. Set up the hypotheses to test the claim that the median income of married men is greater than the median income of unmarried men.

b. Calculate the value of the test statistic W.

c. With $\alpha = 0.05$, what is the decision rule?

d. Is the claim supported by the data? Explain.

21. A professor teaches two sections of an introductory statistics course. He gives each section the same final and wonders if any significant differences exist between the medians of these sections. He randomly draws a sample of seven scores from Section A and six scores from Section B.

Section A	75	62	87	93	74	77	65
Section B	64	95	72	78	85	80	

a. Set up the hypotheses to test the claim that the median test score in Section A differs from the median test score in Section B.

b. Calculate the value of the test statistic W.

c. With $\alpha = 0.05$, what is the decision rule?

d. Do the median test scores differ? Explain.

22. **FILE** According to the Organization of Economic Cooperation and Development, South Koreans spend more hours per year on the job than people in any other developed country (*The Wall Street Journal*, March 1, 2010). Suppose 10 workers in South Korea and 10 workers in the United States are asked to report the number of hours worked in the last year. The results are shown in the accompanying table and also appear on the text website, labeled **South Koreans**.

South Korea	2624	1560	2698	2730	2879	3215	1753	2457	2669	2259
United States	2132	1432	1718	1456	2323	1795	2861	1600	1104	1041

a. Set up the hypotheses to test the claim that the median annual hours worked in South Korea are greater than the median annual hours worked in the United States.

b. Calculate the value of the test statistic W.

c. Assume that the distribution of W is approximately normal. With $\alpha = 0.05$, is the claim supported by the data? Explain.

20.3 Testing More Than Two Population Medians

LO 20.5

Determine whether the medians of more than two populations differ.

In Chapter 13 we applied the one-way ANOVA F test to compare more than two population means. In order to implement this test, we assumed that for each population the variable of interest was normally distributed with the same variance. The **Kruskal-Wallis test** is a nonparametric alternative to the one-way ANOVA test that can be used when the assumptions of normality and/or equal population variances cannot be validated. It is based on ranks and is used for testing the equality of three or more population medians.

Since the Kruskal-Wallis test is essentially an extension of the Wilcoxon rank-sum test, we discuss its application through an example.

Kruskal-Wallis Test

An undergraduate admissions officer would like to examine whether SAT scores differ by ethnic background. She collects a representative sample of SAT scores from Blacks, Hispanics, Whites, and Asians. Her results are shown in Table 20.11. (The data are also available on the text website, labeled **KW-SAT**.) She decides not to pursue the one-way ANOVA F test because she does not believe that the population variances are equal. Instead she chooses to apply the Kruskal-Wallis test.

TABLE 20.11 SAT Scores by Ethnic Background

Blacks	1246	1148	1300	1404	1396	1450	
Hispanics	1267	1228	1450	1351	1280		
Whites	1581	1649	981	1877	1629	1800	1423
Asians	1623	1550	1936	1800	1750		

Let m_1, m_2, m_3, and m_4 denote the median SAT scores for Blacks, Hispanics, Whites, and Asians, respectively. We formulate the competing hypotheses as

$$H_0: m_1 = m_2 = m_3 = m_4$$

$$H_A: \text{Not all population medians are equal}$$

As in the Wilcoxon rank-sum test, we follow several steps to arrive at the Kruskal-Wallis test statistic H.

a. First, we pool the k independent samples (here, $k = 4$) and then rank the observations from 1 to n. Since the total number of observations is 23, we rank the scores from 1 to 23. As before, if there are any ties, then we assign to each of the tied observations the mean of the ranks which they jointly occupy. In this sample, two individuals score 1450 and each is assigned the rank of 12.5, since the values jointly occupy the 12th and 13th ranks. Also, two individuals score 1800 and each is assigned the rank of 20.5. Table 20.12 shows the rank for each SAT score.

b. We then calculate a ranked sum, denoted R_i, for each of the k samples. For instance, the ranked sum for Blacks is calculated as $4 + 2 + 7 + 10 + 9 + 12.5 = 44.5$. These sums are shown in the second-to-last row of Table 20.12.

TABLE 20.12 Calculations for Kruskal-Wallis Test

Blacks	Rank	Hispanics	Rank	Whites	Rank	Asians	Rank
1246	4	1267	5	1581	15	1623	16
1148	2	1228	3	1649	18	1550	14
1300	7	1450	12.5	981	1	1936	23
1404	10	1351	8	1877	22	1800	20.5
1396	9	1280	6	1629	17	1750	19
1450	12.5			1800	20.5		
				1423	11		
$R_1 = 44.5$		$R_2 = 34.5$		$R_3 = 104.5$		$R_4 = 92.5$	
$\frac{R_1^2}{n_1} = 330.0$		$\frac{R_2^2}{n_2} = 238.1$		$\frac{R_3^2}{n_3} = 1560.0$		$\frac{R_4^2}{n_4} = 1711.3$	

If median SAT scores across ethnic groups are the same, we expect the ranked sums R_i to be relatively close to one another. However, if these sums deviate substantially from one another, then this is evidence that not all population medians are the same. We determine whether the variability of the ranked sums significantly differs from one another by first calculating the value of the test statistic H.

For small sample values ($n_i < 5$), the test may be based on special tables; however, we will not pursue that case. The Kruskal-Wallis test is always a right-tailed test.

EXAMPLE 20.6

Use the data in Table 20.12 to conduct the Kruskal-Wallis test to determine if median SAT scores differ by ethnic background at the 5% significance level.

SOLUTION: As discussed earlier, the appropriate hypotheses for the test are

$$H_0: m_1 = m_2 = m_3 = m_4$$
$$H_A: \text{Not all population medians are equal}$$

We compute the value of the test statistic *H* as

$$
\begin{aligned}
H &= \left(\frac{12}{n(n+1)} \sum_{i=1}^{k} \frac{R_i^2}{n_i} \right) - 3(n+1) \\
&= \left(\frac{12}{23(23+1)} (330.0 + 238.1 + 1560.0 + 1711.3) \right) - 3(23+1) \\
&= 83.5 - 72 = 11.5
\end{aligned}
$$

With $\alpha = 0.05$ and $k = 4$, so that degrees of freedom equal $df = k - 1 = 3$, we reference the chi-square table and find a critical value of $\chi^2_{0.05,3} = 7.815$. Since the value of the test statistic, $H = 11.5$, is greater than the critical value of 7.815, we reject H_0. At the 5% significance level, not all median SAT scores across ethnicity are the same.

Using the Computer for the Kruskal-Wallis Test

Table 20.13 shows a portion of the Minitab output as applied to the SAT example. The value of the test statistic computed by Minitab is the same value as the one that we calculated by hand ($H = 11.48$). In addition, Minitab reports the *p*-value as 0.009; thus, given that 0.009 is less than the significance level of 0.05, we again reject H_0 and conclude that not all scores are the same.

TABLE 20.13 Minitab Output for SAT Example

Kruskal-Wallis Test on SAT		
$H = 11.48$	DF $= 3$	P $= 0.009$ (adjusted for ties)

EXAMPLE 20.7

A sociologist suspects differences in median incomes in three major eastern cities. He randomly samples 100 workers from each city. The top of Table 20.14 shows a portion of the data; the full data set can be found on the text website, labeled *City Income*. Unsure that the median income is the same in each city, he uses Minitab to conduct a

Kruskal-Wallis test and produces the results shown at the bottom of Table 20.14. Can he conclude that median incomes differ at the 5% significance level?

TABLE 20.14 Data and Minitab Output for City Income Example

City 1	City 2	City 3
86.5	88.1	102.4
76.7	73.3	127.9
⋮	⋮	⋮
85	63.3	80.1

Kruskal-Wallis Test on Income

$H = 85.50 \quad DF = 2 \quad P = 0.000$ (adjusted for ties)

SOLUTION: We let m_1, m_2, and m_3 denote the population median incomes for City 1, City 2, and City 3, respectively, and formulate the competing hypotheses as

$$H_0: m_1 = m_2 = m_3$$
$$H_A: \text{Not all population median incomes are equal}$$

The value of the test statistic computed by Minitab is $H = 85.50$ with an associated p-value ≈ 0. Since the p-value is less than the significance level of 0.05, we reject H_0 and conclude that not all median incomes across cities are the same.

EXERCISES 20.3

Concepts

23. Consider the following sample information: $k = 3$ and $H = 4.5$.
    a. Specify the competing hypotheses in order to test whether differences exist between the medians.
    b. At the 10% significance level, what are the critical value and the decision rule?
    c. Do the medians differ? Explain.

24. Consider the following sample information: $k = 5$ and $H = 12.4$.
    a. Specify the competing hypotheses in order to test whether differences exist between the medians.
    b. Approximate the p-value.
    c. At the 5% significance level, do the medians differ? Explain.

25. FILE Three independent samples produced the results in the accompanying table. The data are also available on the text website, labeled *Exercise 20.25*.

Sample 1	120	95	115	110	90
Sample 2	100	85	105	80	75	90
Sample 3	72	65	100	76	66	55

   a. Specify the competing hypotheses in order to test whether differences exist between the medians.
   b. What is the value of the test statistic H?
   c. At the 10% significance level, what is the critical value?
   d. Do the medians differ? Explain.

26. FILE Four independent samples produced the results in the accompanying table. The data are also available on the text website, labeled *Exercise 20.26*.

Sample 1	−10	−15	0	5	10
Sample 2	−2	−3	−4	−5	−6
Sample 3	2	4	6	8	10
Sample 4	5	7	9	11	13

   a. Specify the competing hypotheses in order to test whether differences exist between the medians.
   b. What is the value of the test statistic H?
   c. Approximate the p-value.
   d. At the 1% significance level, do the medians differ? Explain.

Applications

27. FILE A research analyst wants to test whether the unemployment rate differs from one region of the country to another. She collects the unemployment rate (in percent) of similar-sized cities in three regions of the United States. The results are shown in the accompanying table, and are also available on the text website, labeled *Regional Unemployment*.

Region A	12.5	13.0	8.5	10.7	9.3
Region B	9.0	9.5	7.0	6.7	8.2
Region C	8.2	7.4	10.9	11.1	10.4

   a. Specify the competing hypotheses in order to test whether differences exist in the median unemployment rate between the three regions.

b. Calculate the value of the test statistic H.

c. At the 10% significance level, what is the critical value?

d. Does the unemployment rate differ by region? Explain.

28. **FILE** A quality-control manager wants to test whether there is any difference in the length of life of three brands of light bulbs. Random samples of new light bulbs installed in the firm's office light fixtures yield the expiration data (in hours) in the following table. The data are also available on the text website, labeled **Bulb Longevity**.

Brand 1	Brand 2	Brand 3
375	280	350
400	290	415
425	300	425
410	325	380
420	350	405

a. Specify the competing hypotheses in order to test whether differences exist in the median length of life of the three brands of light bulbs.

b. Calculate the value of the test statistic H.

c. Approximate the p-value.

d. At the 10% significance level, do differences exist between the median length of life of the three brands? Explain.

29. **FILE** A research analyst examines annual returns (in percent) from Industry A, Industry B, and Industry C. The table below summarizes the relevant data which are also available on the text website, labeled **Industry Returns**.

Industry A	Industry B	Industry C
16.86	15.41	13.53
5.11	10.87	9.58
12.45	4.43	18.75
−32.44	−18.45	−28.77
32.11	20.96	32.17

a. Specify the competing hypotheses in order to test whether differences exist in the median returns of the three industries.

b. Calculate the value of the test statistic H.

c. At the 10% significance level, what is the critical value?

d. Do differences exist between the returns of the three industries? Explain.

30. **FILE** A well-known conglomerate claims that its detergent "whitens and brightens better than all the rest." In order to compare the cleansing action of the top three detergents, 15 swatches of white cloth were soiled with red wine and grass stains and then washed in front-loading machines with the respective detergents. The following whiteness readings are shown in the accompanying table. The data are also on the text website, labeled **Detergents**.

Detergent 1	Detergent 2	Detergent 3
84	78	87
79	74	80
87	81	91
85	86	77
94	86	78

a. Specify the competing hypotheses in order to test whether differences exist in the cleansing action of the three detergents.

b. Calculate the value of the test statistic H.

c. Approximate the p-value.

d. At the 1% significance level, does cleansing action differ by detergent? Explain.

20.4 Testing the Correlation between Two Variables

LO 20.6

Analyze the correlation between two variables.

In earlier chapters we used the correlation coefficient, also referred to as the Pearson correlation coefficient, to measure the strength and direction of the linear relationship between two random variables. Recall that the value of this correlation coefficient falls between −1 and +1; as its absolute value approaches one, the linear relationship becomes stronger. We used a t test to determine whether the population correlation coefficient differs from zero, which assumes that we sample from normal populations. Since this assumption breaks down in some situations, we need a nonparametric alternative. The **Spearman rank correlation test** serves as this option. The Spearman rank correlation coefficient measures the correlation between two random variables based on rank orderings. Its value also falls between −1 and +1 and is interpreted in the same way as the Pearson correlation coefficient.

Figure 20.2 shows a scatterplot of the return data for the Metals and Income funds from the introductory case. Each point in the scatterplot represents a pairing of each fund's return for a given year. It appears that the two funds are positively related.

FIGURE 20.2 Scatterplot of return data for the Metals and Income funds

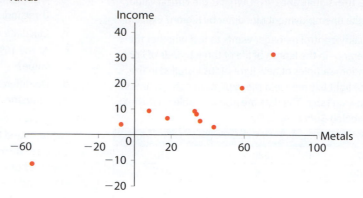

Suppose we want to determine whether the observed relationship is real or due to chance. As we noted before, return data often do not follow the normal distribution. Therefore, using the t test to analyze the Pearson correlation coefficient is not appropriate. Instead, we let ρ_s denote the population Spearman rank correlation coefficient, and we formulate a two-tailed test as

$$H_0: \rho_s = 0$$
$$H_A: \rho_s \neq 0$$

In order to conduct the test, we first calculate the sample Spearman rank correlation coefficient r_S using the following steps.

a. We rank the observations from the Metals fund from smallest to largest. In the case of ties, we assign to each tied observation the average of the ranks that they jointly occupy. We perform the same procedure for the Income fund. Columns 2 and 3 of Table 20.15 show the original return data, and columns 4 and 5 show the funds' ranked values.

TABLE 20.15 Calculations of the Spearman Rank Correlation Coefficient

Year (1)	Metals x (2)	Income y (3)	Rank for Metals (4)	Rank for Income (5)	Difference d (6)	Difference Squared d² (7)
2000	−7.34	4.07	2	3	−1	1
2001	18.33	6.52	4	5	−1	1
2002	33.35	9.38	5	7	−2	4
2003	59.45	18.62	9	9	0	0
2004	8.09	9.44	3	8	−5	25
2005	43.79	3.12	8	2	6	36
2006	34.30	8.15	6	6	0	0
2007	36.13	5.44	7	4	3	9
2008	−56.02	−11.37	1	1	0	0
2009	76.46	31.77	10	10	0	0
					$\Sigma d_i = 0$	$\Sigma d_i^2 = 76$

b. We calculate the difference d_i between the ranks of each pair of observations. See column 6 of Table 20.15. As a check, when we sum the differences, Σd_i, we should obtain zero.

c. We then sum the squared differences. The resulting value is shown in the last cell of column 7 in Table 20.15: $\Sigma d_i^2 = 76$.

THE SPEARMAN RANK CORRELATION TEST

The sample **Spearman rank correlation coefficient** r_S between two variables x and y is defined as

$$r_S = 1 - \frac{6\sum d_i^2}{n(n^2 - 1)},$$

where d_i is the difference between the ranks of observations x_i and y_i. If $n \leq 10$, we conduct the hypothesis test by comparing $|r_s|$ with positive critical values shown in Table 8 of Appendix A.

If $n \geq 10$, r_S can be assumed normally distributed with zero mean and standard deviation of $\sqrt{\frac{1}{n-1}}$, and hence the value of the resulting test statistic is computed as $z = r_S\sqrt{n-1}$.

We calculate r_S as

$$r_S = 1 - \frac{6\sum d_i^2}{n(n^2-1)} = 1 - \frac{6 \times 76}{10 \times (10^2 - 1)} = 1 - 0.46 = 0.54.$$

A value of $r_S = 0.54$ implies that the Metals and Income funds have a positive, rather moderate, relationship.

For $n \leq 10$, the rank correlation tests are based on special tables determined from the exact distribution of r_S. Table 20.16 shows a portion of upper critical values for one- and two-tailed tests concerning ρ_S at various α values. (A more complete version is found in Table 8 of Appendix A.) For a two-tailed test with $\alpha = 0.05$ and $n = 10$, the decision rule is to reject the null hypothesis if $|r_S| > 0.648$. See the relevant critical value in boldface in Table 20.16.

TABLE 20.16 Upper Critical Values for the Spearman Rank Correlation Coefficient

Two-tailed Test:	$\alpha = 0.10$	$\alpha = 0.05$	$\alpha = 0.02$	$\alpha = 0.01$
One-tailed Test:	$\alpha = 0.05$	$\alpha = 0.025$	$\alpha = 0.01$	$\alpha = 0.005$
$n = 8$	0.643	0.738	0.833	0.881
9	0.600	0.683	0.783	0.833
10	0.564	**0.648**	0.745	0.794

Since the value of the test statistic, $r_S = 0.54$, is not greater than 0.648, we cannot reject H_0. At the 5% significance level, we cannot conclude that the rank correlation between the Metals fund and the Income fund differs from zero.

Using a Normal Distribution Approximation for r_S

As mentioned above, when $n \geq 10$, we can also use the normal distribution approximation to implement a z test.

EXAMPLE 20.8

A sports statistician would like to analyze the relationship between a quarterback's salary (in $ millions) and his age. He collects data on 32 quarterbacks. The top of Table 20.17 shows a portion of the data; the full data set can be found on the text website, labeled **Quarterback Salary**. He uses Minitab to calculate the Spearman rank correlation coefficient and produces the result shown at the bottom of Table 20.17. Can he conclude that salary and age are correlated at the 5% significance level?

TABLE 20.17 Data and Minitab Output for Example 20.8

FILE	Salary	Age
	25.5566	27
	22.0441	26
	⋮	⋮
	0.6260	29
	Spearman's rho = 0.375	

> **SOLUTION:** In order to determine whether salary and age are correlated, we formulate the competing hypotheses as
>
> $$H_0: \rho_s = 0$$
> $$H_A: \rho_s \neq 0$$
>
> Referencing Table 20.17, we find that $r_S = 0.375$. Under normality, the value of the corresponding test statistic is calculated as $z = 0.375\sqrt{32-1} = 2.09$, which yields a p-value of $2 \times P(Z \geq 2.09) = 0.037$. Since the p-value is less than the significance level of 5%, we reject H_0 and conclude that salary and age are correlated.

Summary of Parametric and Nonparametric Tests

Table 20.18 summarizes the select parametric tests referenced in Section 20.1 and their nonparametric counterparts. Nonparametric tests use fewer and weaker assumptions than those associated with parametric tests and are especially attractive when the underlying population is markedly nonnormal. However, a nonparametric test ignores useful information since it focuses on the rank rather than the magnitude of sample values. Therefore, in situations when the parametric assumptions are valid, the nonparametric test is less powerful than its parametric counterpart. In general, when the assumptions for a parametric test are met, it is preferable to use a parametric test rather than a nonparametric test. Since the normality assumption for parametric tests is less stringent in large samples, the main appeal of nonparametric tests tends to be with relatively small samples.

TABLE 20.18 Parametric Test versus Nonparametric Alternative

Parametric Test	Nonparametric Alternative
t test concerning the population mean	Wilcoxon signed-rank test concerning the population median
t test to determine whether the population mean difference differs from zero under matched-pairs sampling	Wilcoxon signed-rank test to determine whether the population median difference differs from zero under matched-pairs sampling
t test to determine whether two population means differ under independent sampling	Wilcoxon rank-sum test to determine whether two population medians differ under independent sampling
F test to determine whether the means of more than two populations differ	Kruskal-Wallis test to determine whether the medians of more than two populations differ
t test to determine whether two variables are correlated	Spearman rank correlation test to determine whether two variables are correlated

SYNOPSIS OF INTRODUCTORY CASE

Vanguard's Precious Metals and Mining fund (referred to as Metals) and Fidelity's Strategic Income fund (referred to as Income) were two top-performing mutual funds from 2000–2009. Annual return data for the funds were obtained from http://finance.yahoo.com for the analysis of their returns. Given that return data often have "fatter tails" than the normal distribution, the analysis focuses on nonparametric techniques. These techniques do not rely on the normality assumption concerning the underlying population. When applying the Wilcoxon signed-rank test at the 5% significance level, it is found that the median return for the Metals fund is not significantly greater than 5%. The same test is also used to conclude that the median difference between the Metals and Income returns does not differ from zero at the 5% significance level. Finally,

Spearman's rank correlation coefficient is calculated as 0.54, implying a moderate, positive relationship between the returns of the two funds. However, a test conducted at the 5% significance level finds that the population Spearman's rank correlation coefficient is not significantly different from zero. Interestingly, the Metals and the Income fund are not related, despite the fact that they are both influenced by underlying market conditions.

Concepts

31. Consider the following competing hypotheses and accompanying sample data.

$H_0: \rho_S = 0$ $r_S = 0.92$ and $n = 8$
$H_A: \rho_S \neq 0$

a. What is the value of the test statistic?
b. Specify the decision rule at the 1% significance level.
c. What is the conclusion?

32. Consider the following competing hypotheses and accompanying sample data.

$H_0: \rho_S \geq 0$ $r_S = -0.64$ and $n = 9$
$H_A: \rho_S < 0$

a. What is the value of the test statistic?
b. Specify the decision rule at the 5% significance level.
c. What is the conclusion?

33. Consider the following sample data:

x	12	18	20	22	25	15
y	15	20	25	22	27	19

a. Calculate and interpret r_S.
b. Specify the competing hypotheses in order to determine whether the Spearman population correlation coefficient differs from zero.
c. At the 5% significance level, what is the decision rule?
d. What is the conclusion?

34. Consider the following sample data:

x	−2	0	3	−1	4	7
y	−4	−3	−8	−5	−9	−10

a. Calculate and interpret r_S.
b. Specify the competing hypotheses in order to determine whether the Spearman population correlation coefficient is less than zero.
c. At the 1% significance level, what is the decision rule?
d. What is the conclusion?

35. Consider the following competing hypotheses and accompanying sample data.

$H_0: \rho_S = 0$ $r_S = -0.85$ and $n = 65$
$H_A: \rho_S \neq 0$

a. What is the value of the test statistic and its associated p-value? Assume the normal approximation for r_S.
b. At the 10% significance level, what is the conclusion?

36. Consider the following competing hypotheses and accompanying sample data.

$H_0: \rho_S \leq 0$ $r_S = 0.64$ and $n = 50$
$H_A: \rho_S > 0$

a. What is the value of the test statistic and its associated p-value? Assume the normal approximation for r_S.
b. At the 1% significance level, what is the conclusion?

Applications

37. The following table shows the ranks given by two judges to the performance of six finalists in a men's figure skating competition:

Skater	A	B	C	D	E	F
Judge 1	6	5	4	3	2	1
Judge 2	5	6	4	3	1	2

a. Calculate and interpret the Spearman rank correlation coefficient r_S.
b. Specify the competing hypotheses in order to determine whether the correlation coefficient is significantly different from zero.
c. At the 10% significance level, specify the critical value and the decision rule.
d. What is the conclusion to the test? Are the ranks significantly related?

38. **FILE** The following table shows the World Bank's 2008 ranking of the richest countries, as measured by per capita GNP. The data are also available on the text website, labeled **WB ranking**. In addition, it gives each country's respective rank with respect to infant mortality according to the Central Intelligence Agency. A higher rank indicates a lower mortality rate.

Country	Per Capita GNP Rank	Infant Mortality Rank
Luxembourg	1	7
Norway	2	4
Singapore	3	1
United States	4	10
Ireland	5	9
Switzerland	6	5
Netherlands	7	8
Austria	8	6
Sweden	9	2
Iceland	10	3

a. Calculate and interpret the Spearman rank correlation coefficient r_S.

b. Specify the competing hypotheses in order to determine whether the correlation coefficient is significantly different from zero.

c. At the 5% significance level, specify the critical value and the decision rule.

d. Are GNP and the infant mortality rate correlated? Explain.

39. You are interested in whether the returns on Asset A are negatively correlated with the returns on Asset B. Consider the following annual return data on the two assets:

	Asset A	Asset B
Year 1	−20%	8%
Year 2	−5	5
Year 3	18	−1
Year 4	15	−2
Year 5	4	3
Year 6	−12	2

a. Calculate and interpret the Spearman rank correlation coefficient r_S.

b. Specify the competing hypotheses in order to determine whether the asset returns are negatively correlated.

c. At the 1% significance level, specify the critical value.

d. What is the conclusion to the test? Are the returns negatively correlated?

40. FILE In an attempt to determine whether a relationship exists between the price of a home and the number of days it takes to sell the home, a real estate agent collected the following data from recent sales in his city (the data are also available on the text website, labeled **Price/Days**):

Price (in $1,000s)	Days to Sell Home
265	136
225	125
160	120
325	140
430	145
515	121
180	122
423	145

a. Calculate and interpret the Spearman rank correlation coefficient r_S.

b. Specify the competing hypotheses in order to determine whether the price of a home and the number of days it takes to sell are related.

c. At the 5% significance level, specify the critical value and the decision rule.

d. Are these variables related? Explain.

41. FILE The director of graduate admissions at a local university is analyzing the relationship between scores on the Graduate Record Examination (GRE) and subsequent performance in graduate school, as measured by a student's grade point average (GPA). She uses a sample of 7 students who graduated within the past five years. The data are in the accompanying table and on the text website, labeled **GRE/GPA**.

Student	1	2	3	4	5	6	7
GRE	1500	1400	1000	1050	1100	1250	800
GPA	3.4	3.5	3.0	2.9	3.0	3.3	2.7

a. Calculate and interpret the Spearman rank correlation coefficient r_S.

b. Specify the competing hypotheses in order to determine whether GRE and GPA are positively related.

c. At the 5% significance level, specify the critical value and the decision rule.

d. Are GRE and GPA positively related? Explain.

42. A social scientist analyzes the relationship between educational attainment and salary. For 65 individuals he collects data on each individual's educational attainment (in years) and his/her salary (in $1,000s). He then calculates a Spearman rank correlation coefficient of 0.85.

a. Specify the competing hypotheses in order to determine whether educational attainment and salary are related.

b. Assume that the distribution of r_S is approximately normal. Calculate the value of the test statistic and the p-value of the test.

c. At the 5% significance level, are educational attainment and salary related?

43. An engineer examines the relationship between the weight of a car and its average miles per gallon (MPG). For a sample of 100 cars, he calculates a Spearman rank correlation coefficient of −0.60.

a. Specify the competing hypotheses in order to determine whether a negative relationship exists between a car's weight and its average MPG.

b. Assume that the distribution of r_S is approximately normal. Calculate the value of the test statistic and the p-value.

c. At the 5% significance level, are the variables negatively related? Explain.

20.5 The Sign Test

In some applications, a matched-pairs sample originates from ordinal data rather than from interval- or ratio-scaled data. Let's review the definition of ordinal data first introduced in Chapter 1. With ordinal data we are able to categorize and rank the data with respect to some characteristic or trait. The weakness with ordinal-scaled data is that we cannot interpret the difference between the ranked values because the actual numbers used are arbitrary. For example, suppose you are asked to classify the service at a particular hotel as excellent, good, fair, or poor. A standard way to record the ratings is

Excellent	4	Fair	2
Good	3	Poor	1

Here the value attached to excellent (4) is higher than the value attached to good (3), indicating that the response of excellent is preferred to good. However, another representation of the ratings might be

Excellent	100	Fair	70
Good	80	Poor	40

Excellent still receives a higher value than good, but now the difference between the two categories is 20 (100–80), as compared to a difference of 1 (4–3) when we use the first classification. In other words, differences between categories are meaningless with ordinal data.

We use the **sign test** on a matched-pairs sample of ordinal data to determine whether there are significant ordinal differences in the population. When applying the sign test, we are only interested in whether the difference between two values in a pair is greater than, equal to, or less than zero. The difference between each pairing is replaced by a plus sign (+) if the difference is positive (that is, the first value exceeds the second value) or by a minus sign (−) if the difference between the pair is negative. If the difference between the pair is zero, we discard that particular observation from the sample.

If significant differences do not exist between the two populations, then we expect just as many plus signs as minus signs. Equivalently, we should observe plus signs 50% of the time and minus signs 50% of the time. Suppose we let p denote the population proportion of plus signs. (We could just as easily allow p to represent the population proportion of minus signs without loss of generality.) The competing hypotheses for the sign test take one of the following forms.

Two-tailed Test	Right-tailed Test	Left-tailed Test
$H_0: p = 0.50$	$H_0: p \leq 0.50$	$H_0: p \geq 0.50$
$H_A: p \neq 0.50$	$H_A: p > 0.50$	$H_A: p < 0.50$

A two-tailed test allows us to determine whether the proportion of plus signs differs from the proportion of minus signs. A right-tailed (left-tailed) test allows us to determine whether the proportion of plus signs is greater than (less than) the proportion of minus signs.

Let $\overline{P} = X/n$ be the estimator of the population proportion of plus signs. As discussed in Chapter 7, if np and $n(1 - p)$ are both 5 or more, then the distribution of $\overline{P}$ is approximately normal, with mean $E(\overline{P}) = p$ and standard deviation $SD(\overline{P}) = \sqrt{p(1 - p)/n}$. Assuming a probability of success $p = 0.50$, the approximation is satisfactory as long as $n \geq 10$. When $n < 10$, we rely on the binomial distribution to conduct the sign test; we will not consider such cases.

LO **20.7**

Determine whether two populations differ under matched-pairs sampling with ordinal data.

The **test statistic** is assumed to follow the z distribution, and its value is computed as $z = \frac{\bar{p} - 0.5}{0.5/\sqrt{n}}$, where $\bar{p} = x/n$ is the sample proportion of plus signs. The test is valid when $n \geq 10$.

EXAMPLE 20.9

In December 2009, Domino's Pizza, Inc. released untraditional ads citing that its old recipe for pizza produced crust that tasted like cardboard and sauce that tasted like ketchup. Domino's Pizza claims that its reformulated pizza is a vast improvement over the old recipe; for instance, garlic and parsley are now baked into the crust and a new sweeter, bolder tomato sauce is used. Suppose 20 customers are asked to sample the old recipe and then sample the new recipe. Each person is asked to rate the pizzas on a 5-point scale, where 1 = inedible and 5 = very tasty. The ratings are shown in Table 20.19; the data labeled ***Domino's Pizza*** can also be found on the text website. Do these data provide sufficient evidence to allow us to conclude that the new recipe is preferred to the old recipe? Use $\alpha = 0.05$.

TABLE 20.19 Calculations for Sign Test in Example 20.9

FILE

Customer	Old Recipe	New Recipe	Sign	Customer	Old Recipe	New Recipe	Sign
1	3	4	−	11	3	4	−
2	3	2	+	12	4	5	−
3	2	5	−	13	1	2	−
4	4	4	0	14	3	3	0
5	2	5	−	15	5	3	+
6	1	3	−	16	3	4	−
7	3	2	+	17	1	5	−
8	1	2	−	18	4	2	+
9	2	4	−	19	3	4	−
10	4	5	−	20	2	5	−

SOLUTION: If customers feel that there is no difference between the old recipe and the new recipe, then we expect 50% of the customers to prefer the old recipe and 50% to prefer the new recipe. Let p denote the population proportion of consumers that prefer the old recipe. We want to specify the competing hypotheses such that rejection of the null hypothesis provides evidence that customers prefer the new recipe (implying that p is significantly less than 0.50). We set up the competing hypotheses as

$$H_0: p \geq 0.50$$
$$H_A: p < 0.50$$

Table 20.19 shows the signs for each customer. For example, customer 1 ranks the old recipe with the value 3 and the new recipe with the value 4, which yields a minus sign: $3 - 4 = -1$. This difference implies that this customer prefers the new recipe. We find 4 positive signs, 14 negative signs, and 2 ties (ranks of zero). We then let n denote the number of matched-paired observations such that the sign between the rankings is nonzero; thus, n equals 18. We denote $\bar{p}$ as the sample proportion of plus signs. Given that there are four plus signs, the sample proportion is calculated as $\bar{p} = 4/18 = 0.22$. (Note that if we had calculated the sample proportion of minus signs, then $\bar{p} = 0.78$; the resulting value of the test statistic only differs in its sign. In this instance, we would conduct a right-tailed hypothesis test.) We calculate the value of the test statistic as

$$z = \frac{\bar{p} - 0.5}{0.5/\sqrt{n}} = \frac{0.22 - 0.5}{0.5/\sqrt{18}} = \frac{-0.28}{0.118} = -2.37.$$

Using the z table, we find the p-value for a left-tailed test as $P(Z \leq -2.37) = 0.0089$. Since the p-value is less than the significance level of $\alpha = 0.05$, we reject H_0 and conclude that consumers prefer the reformulated version as compared to the old recipe at the 5% significance level.

The sign test can be used with quantitative as well as ordinal data. However, since the sign test ignores the magnitude in the difference between two observations, it is advisable to use the Wilcoxon signed-rank test if quantitative data are available.

EXERCISES 20.5

Concepts

44. Consider the following competing hypotheses and sample data.

$H_0: p = 0.50$ $\quad n = 40 \quad \bar{p} = 0.30$
$H_A: p \neq 0.50$

   a. Determine the value of the test statistic.
   b. Calculate the p-value.
   c. At the 5% significance level, what is the conclusion? Explain.

45. Consider the following competing hypotheses and sample data.

$H_0: p \leq 0.50$ $\quad n = 25 \quad \bar{p} = 0.64$
$H_A: p > 0.50$

   a. Determine the value of the test statistic.
   b. At the 1% significance level, what is the decision rule?
   c. What is the conclusion? Explain.

46. Consider the following sign data, produced from a matched-pairs sample of ordinal data.

+	+	+	−	+	+	−	+	+	+	+	−	+	+	−	−	+	+	+	+

   a. Specify the competing hypotheses to determine whether the proportion of negative signs differs from the proportion of positive signs.
   b. Calculate the value of the test statistic.
   c. Calculate the p-value.
   d. At the 5% significance level, what is the conclusion? Explain.

47. Consider the following sign data, produced from a matched-pairs sample of ordinal data.

+	−	−	+	−	−	+	−	+	−	+	−	−	−	+	−

   a. Specify the competing hypotheses to determine whether the proportion of negative signs is significantly greater than the proportion of positive signs.
   b. Calculate the value of the test statistic.
   c. What is the decision rule with a 1% level of significance?
   d. What is the conclusion? Explain.

Applications

48. **FILE** Concerned with the increase of plastic water bottles in landfills, a leading environmentalist wants to determine whether there is any difference in taste between the local tap water and the leading bottled water. She randomly selects 14 consumers and conducts a blind taste test. She asks the consumers to rank the taste on a scale of one to five (with "five" indicating excellent taste). The sample results are shown in the accompanying table and are also available on the text website, labeled **Water**.

Consumer	Tap Water	Bottled Water	Consumer	Tap Water	Bottled Water
1	4	5	8	5	2
2	3	2	9	3	4
3	5	4	10	2	4
4	4	3	11	5	4
5	3	5	12	4	3
6	5	3	13	5	2
7	2	1	14	3	4

   a. Specify the competing hypotheses to determine whether there are significant differences in preferences between tap water and bottled water.
   b. Calculate the value of the test statistic.
   c. Calculate the p-value.
   d. At the 5% significance level, what is the conclusion? Do the results indicate that significant differences exist in preferences?

49. In March 2009, 100 registered voters were asked to rate the "effectiveness" of President Obama. In March 2010, these same people were again asked to make the same assessment. Seventy percent of the second ratings were lower than the first ratings and 30% were higher.

   a. Specify the competing hypotheses to determine whether the President's rating has significantly declined.
   b. Calculate the value of the test statistic.

c. Calculate the *p*-value.

d. At the 5% significance level, do the data suggest that the President's rating has significantly declined?

50. **FILE** For scholarship purposes, two graduate faculty members rate 12 applicants to the PhD program on a scale of 1 to 10 (with 10 indicating an excellent candidate). These ratings are shown in the following table and are also available on the text website, labeled ***PhD Rating***.

Candidate	Faculty A's Rating	Faculty B's Rating	Candidate	Faculty A's Rating	Faculty B's Rating
1	5	6	7	2	2
2	7	8	8	8	9
3	8	5	9	9	10
4	7	7	10	6	4
5	9	10	11	8	9
6	4	3	12	6	8

a. Specify the competing hypotheses to determine whether the ratings are significantly different between the two faculty members.

b. Calculate the value of the test statistic.

c. Determine the critical values at the 10% significance level.

d. Do the data suggest significantly different faculty ratings?

51. A new diet and exercise program claims that it significantly lowers a participant's cholesterol level. In order to test this claim, a sample of 60 participants is taken. Their cholesterol levels are measured before and after the three-month program. Forty of the participants recorded lower cholesterol levels at the end of the program, 18 participants recorded higher cholesterol levels, and 2 participants recorded no change.

a. Specify the competing hypotheses to test the program's claim.

b. Calculate the value of the test statistic.

c. Calculate the *p*-value.

d. At the 5% significance level, do the data support the program's claim? Explain.

20.6 Tests Based on Runs

LO 20.8

Determine whether the elements of a sequence appear in a random order.

In many applications we wish to determine whether some observed values occur in a truly random fashion or whether some form of a nonrandom pattern exists. In other words, we want to test if the elements of the sequence are mutually independent. The **Wald-Wolfowitz runs test** is a procedure used to examine whether the elements in a sequence appear in a random order. It can be applied to either quantitative or qualitative data so long as we can separate the sample data into two categories.

Suppose we observe a machine filling 16-ounce cereal boxes. Since a machine is unlikely to dispense exactly 16 ounces in each box, we expect the weight of each box to deviate from 16 ounces. We might conjecture that a machine is operating properly if the deviations from 16 ounces occur in a random order. Let's sample 30 cereal boxes and denote those boxes that are overfilled with the letter O and those that are underfilled with the letter U. The following sequence of Os and Us is produced:

Sequence: OOOOUUUOOOOUOOOUUUUOOOOUUOOOOO

One possible way to test whether or not a machine is operating properly is to determine if the elements of a particular sequence of Os and Us occur randomly. If we observe a long series of consecutive Os (or Us), then the machine may be significantly overfilling (or underfilling) the cereal boxes. Adjustment of the machine is likely necessary if this is the case. Given the observed sequence, can we conclude that the machine is operating properly in the sense that the series of Os and Us occur randomly?

In general, when applying the runs test, we specify the competing hypotheses as

H_0: The elements occur randomly.

H_A: The elements do not occur randomly.

In this particular application, the null hypothesis implies that the machine properly fills the boxes and the alternative hypothesis implies that it does not. Before deriving the test statistic, it is first necessary to introduce some terminology. We define a **run** as an uninterrupted sequence of one letter, symbol, or attribute, such as O or U. We rewrite the observed sequence, but now include single horizontal lines below the letter O. The five single lines indicate that we observe five runs of O, or $R_O = 5$. Similarly, the double horizontal lines below the letter U show that we have four runs of U, or $R_U = 4$. Thus, the total number of runs R is equal to nine: $R = R_O + R_U = 5 + 4 = 9$. Also, note that we have a total of 30 observations, of which 20 are Os and 10 are Us, or $n = n_O + n_U = 20 + 10 = 30$.

Sequence: <u>OOOO</u> <u>UUU</u> <u>OOOO</u> <u>U</u> <u>OOO</u> <u>UUUU</u> <u>OOOO</u> <u>UU</u> <u>OOOOO</u>

We then ask: "Are nine runs consisting of 30 observations too few or too many compared with the number of runs expected in a strictly random sequence of 30 observations?"

In general, the runs test is a two-tailed test; that is, too many runs are deemed just as unlikely as too few runs. For example, consider the following two sequences:

Sequence A: <u>OOOOOOOOOOOOO</u> <u>UUUUUU</u> <u>OOOOOOOOOOOOO</u>

Sequence B: <u>O</u> <u>U</u> <u>O</u> <u>U</u> <u>O</u> <u>U</u> <u>O</u> <u>U</u> <u>O</u> <u>U</u> <u>O</u> <u>U</u> <u>O</u> <u>U</u> <u>O</u> <u>U</u> <u>O</u> <u>U</u> <u>O</u> <u>U</u> <u>O</u> <u>U</u> <u>O</u> <u>U</u> <u>O</u> <u>U</u> <u>O</u> <u>U</u> <u>O</u> <u>U</u>

If the null hypothesis of randomness is true, Sequence A seems unlikely in the sense that there appear to be too few runs given a sample of 30 observations. Sequence B also seems unlikely since O and U alternate systematically, or equivalently, there appear to be too many runs. It is more readily apparent in the machine-filling application that a sequence that produces too few runs indicates a machine that is not operating properly; that is, the machine has a pattern of consistently overfilling and/or underfilling the cereal boxes. However, a machine that exhibits a perfect regularity of overfilling, underfilling, overfilling, underfilling, etc. (too many runs) may be just as problematic. If there are too many runs, then this may indicate some sort of repeated alternating pattern.

Let n_1 and n_2 denote the numbers of Os and Us in an n-element sequence. In general, the sampling distribution of R (the distribution for the runs test) is quite complex and its critical values are provided in specially constructed tables. However, if n_1 and n_2 are at least 10, then the distribution of R is approximately normal.

THE TEST STATISTIC R FOR THE WALD-WOLFOWITZ RUNS TEST

The **test statistic** is assumed to follow the z distribution, and its value is computed as $z = \dfrac{R - \mu_R}{\sigma_R}$ where R represents the number of runs with mean $\mu_R = \dfrac{2n_1n_2}{n} + 1$ and standard deviation $\sigma_R = \sqrt{\dfrac{2n_1n_2(2n_1n_2 - n)}{n^2(n - 1)}}$; n_1 and n_2 are the number of elements in a sequence possessing and not possessing a certain attribute and $n = n_1 + n_2$. The test is valid when $n_1 \geq 10$ and $n_2 \geq 10$.

For the machine example, we found that $R = 9$; in addition, we have $n_1 = n_O = 20$ and $n_2 = n_U = 10$. We calculate the mean and the standard deviation of the distribution of R as

$$\mu_R = \frac{2n_1n_2}{n} + 1 = \frac{2(20)(10)}{30} + 1 = 14.33 \text{ and}$$

$$\sigma_R = \sqrt{\frac{2n_1n_2(2n_1n_2 - n)}{n^2(n - 1)}} = \sqrt{\frac{(2 \times 20 \times 10)(2 \times 20 \times 10 - 30)}{30^2(30 - 1)}} = \sqrt{\frac{148,000}{26,100}} = 2.38.$$

Thus, the expected number of runs in a sample with 30 observations is 14.33 and the standard deviation is 2.38. We calculate the value of the test statistic as $z = \dfrac{R - \mu_R}{\sigma_R} = \dfrac{9 - 14.33}{2.38} = -2.24$. We find the p-value for a two-tailed test as $2 \times P(Z \leq -2.24) = 0.0250$. Since the p-value is less than $\alpha = 0.05$, we reject H_0 and conclude that the machine does not properly fill the boxes. At the 5% significance level, adjustment of the machine is necessary.

The Method of Runs Above and Below the Median

As mentioned earlier, the runs test can be applied to both qualitative and quantitative data. Any sample with numerical values can be treated similarly by using letters, say A and B, to denote values falling above and below the median of the sample, respectively. We omit values that are equal to the median. The resulting As and Bs can be tested for randomness by applying the **method of runs above and below the median**. This test is especially useful in detecting trends and cyclical patterns in economic data. A finding of too few runs is suggestive of a trend; that is, we first observe mostly As and later mostly Bs (or vice versa). In computing the value of the test statistic, we omit values that are equal to the median. A systematic alternation of As and Bs—that is, too many runs—implies a cyclical pattern. Consider the following example.

EXAMPLE 20.10

Table 20.20 shows the growth rate in the gross domestic product (GDP) for the United States from 1980 through 2009; the data labeled *US GDP* can also be found on the text website. Use the method of runs above and below the median with a significance level of 10% to test the null hypothesis of randomness against the alternative that a trend or cyclical pattern occurs.

TABLE 20.20 GDP Growth Rates (in percent) for the United States, 1980–2009

FILE

Year	GDP	Year	GDP	Year	GDP
1980	−0.24	1990	1.86	2000	3.69
1981	2.52	1991	−0.19	2001	0.76
1982	−1.97	1992	3.34	2002	1.61
1983	4.52	1993	2.69	2003	2.52
1984	7.20	1994	4.06	2004	3.65
1985	4.10	1995	2.54	2005	3.08
1986	3.43	1996	3.75	2006	2.87
1987	3.34	1997	4.55	2007	2.00
1988	4.12	1998	4.22	2008	1.10
1989	3.53	1999	4.49	2009	−2.40

Source: http://data.worldbank.org/indicator

SOLUTION: Since we are testing the null hypothesis of randomness against the alternative that there is a trend or cyclical pattern, we formulate the competing hypotheses as

H_0: The GDP growth rate is random.

H_A: The GDP growth rate is not random.

We first calculate the median GDP growth rate as 3.21%. Letting A and B denote an observation that falls above the median and below the median, respectively, we rewrite the data using the following sequence of As and Bs:

Sequence: BBB AAAAAAA BB A B A B AAAAA BBB A BBBBB

We see that the number of runs below the median R_B is 6, while the number of runs above the median R_A is 5, so the total number of runs R is 11. Also, since no values were discarded (no value was equal to the median), the total number of observations are $n = 30$, where the number of observations below the median and the number of

---

observations above the median are $n_B = 15$ and $n_A = 15$, respectively. Using this information, we compute the mean and the standard deviation of the distribution of R as

$$\mu_R = \frac{2n_A n_B}{n} + 1 = \frac{2(15)(15)}{30} + 1 = 16 \text{ and}$$

$$\sigma_R = \sqrt{\frac{2n_A n_B(2n_A n_B - n)}{n^2(n-1)}} = \sqrt{\frac{(2 \times 15 \times 15)(2 \times 15 \times 15 - 30)}{30^2(30-1)}} = \sqrt{\frac{189{,}000}{26{,}100}}$$

$$= 2.69.$$

Thus, the value of the test statistic is $z = \frac{R - \mu_R}{\sigma_R} = \frac{11 - 16}{2.69} = -1.86$. Using the z table, we find the p-value for a two-tailed test as $2 \times P(Z \le -1.86) = 0.0628$. Since the p-value is less than $\alpha = 0.10$, we reject H_0 and conclude that the sample is not random. In fact, since the observed number of runs ($R = 11$) is significantly less than the expected number of runs ($\mu_R = 16$), there is evidence of a trend. In order to determine whether there is an upward or downward trend in the data, we must reference the actual values. During most of the Reagan and Clinton administrations (the early observations), the GDP growth rates were above the median, while during the majority of the George W. Bush administration (the later observations), the GDP growth rates were below the median. This type of finding suggests a downward trend in GDP growth rates.

Using the Computer for the Runs Test

Table 20.21 shows a portion of Minitab output for the GDP example. The letter K denotes the median growth rate of 3.21%. Note that the observed number of runs and the expected number of runs of 11 and 16, respectively, match those that we calculated by hand. In addition, the p-value also matches our hand-calculated value, allowing us to reject the null hypothesis of randomness at the 10% significance level.

TABLE 20.21 Minitab Output for the GDP Example

Runs Test for GDP
Runs above and below K = 3.21
The observed number of runs = 11
The expected number of runs = 16
15 observations above K, 15 below
P-value = 0.063

EXERCISES 20.6

Concepts

52. Consider the following information: $n_1 = 24$, $n_2 = 28$ and $R = 18$, where R is the number of runs, n_1 and n_2 are the number of elements in a sequence possessing and not possessing a certain attribute, and $n_1 + n_2 = n$.
    a. Specify the competing hypotheses in order to test for nonrandomness.
    b. What is the value of the test statistic?
    c. Calculate the p-value.
    d. At the 5% significance level, are the observations nonrandom?

53. Consider the following information: $n_1 = 10$, $n_2 = 13$ and $R = 8$, where R is the number of runs, n_1 and n_2 are the number of elements in a sequence possessing and not possessing a certain attribute, and $n_1 + n_2 = n$.
    a. Specify the competing hypotheses in order to test for nonrandomness.
    b. What is the value of the test statistic?
    c. Calculate the p-value.
    d. At the 5% significance level, are the observations nonrandom?

54. Let A and B be two possible outcomes of a single experiment. The sequence of the outcomes is as follows:

BBAABAABBABABBBABBAAABABBABBABA

At the 5% significance level, conduct a hypothesis test in order to determine if the outcomes are nonrandom.

55. Let D denote a desirable outcome and U denote an undesirable outcome. The sequence of the outcomes is as follows:

DDDUUDUUUUUDDDUUDUUUDDDUUUUDDD

At the 1% significance level, conduct a hypothesis test in order to determine if the outcomes are nonrandom.

Applications

56. Given the digits zero through nine, a computer program is supposed to generate even and odd numbers randomly. The computer produced the following sequence of numbers:

5 3 4 6 8 0 2 9 7 7 1 6 8 3 1 5 2 4 3 3 9 2

a. Specify the competing hypotheses in order to test for nonrandomness.

b. What is the value of the test statistic?

c. What is the decision rule with a 1% level of significance?

d. Is the program operating properly? Explain.

57. A gambler suspects that a coin may be weighted more heavily toward the outcome of tails (T) over heads (H). He flips the coin 25 times and notes the following sequence:

TTHTTTHHTHTTHTTTHHTHTHTTH

a. Specify the competing hypotheses in order to test the gambler's belief on nonrandomness.

b. What is the value of the test statistic?

c. Calculate the p-value.

d. At the 5% significance level, is the gambler's belief supported by the data?

58. **FILE** The following table shows a portion of the growth rate in the gross domestic product (GDP) for India from 1980 through 2008; the full data set can be found on the text website, labeled **India GDP**. Use the method of runs above and below the median with a significance level of 5% to test the null hypothesis of randomness against the alternative that there is a trend or cyclical pattern.

Year	GDP
1980	6.74
1981	6.00
⋮	⋮
2008	6.07

Source: http://data.worldbank.org/indicator.

59. **FILE** The superintendent of a large suburban high school must decide whether to close the school for at least two days due to the spread of flu. If she can confirm a trend in absenteeism, then she will close the high school. The following are the number of students absent from the high school on 25 consecutive school days (the data are also available on the text website labeled **Absenteeism**):

44, 56, 55, 40, 42, 51, 50, 59, 58, 45, 44, 52, 52, 43, 48, 58, 57, 42, 60, 65, 69, 75, 70, 72, 72

Use the method of runs above and below the median and $\alpha = 0.05$ to test the null hypothesis of randomness against the alternative that there is a trend.

60. **FILE** A research analyst follows the biotechnology industry and examines the daily stock price of Amgen, Inc. over the past year. The table below shows a portion of the daily stock price of Amgen for the 252 trading days in 2010; the full data set can be found on the text website, labeled **Amgen**. The research analyst wants to test the random-walk hypothesis that suggests that stock prices move randomly over time with no discernible pattern.

Date	Adjusted Stock Price
1/4/2010	$57.72
1/5/2010	57.22
⋮	⋮
12/31/2010	54.9

a. Use the method of runs above and below the median to test the null hypothesis of randomness against the alternative that there is a trend at the 5% significance level.

b. Can the research analyst conclude that the movement of Amgen's stock price is consistent with the random-walk hypothesis?

WRITING WITH STATISTICS

Meg Suzuki manages a trendy sushi restaurant in Chicago, Illinois. She is planning an aggressive advertising campaign to offset the loss of business due to competition from other restaurants. She knows advertising costs increase overall costs, but she hopes this effort will positively affect sales, as it has done in the past under her tenure. She collects monthly data on sales (in $1,000s) and advertising costs (in $) over the past two years and produces the following regression equation:

$$\text{Estimated Sales} = 17.77 + 0.03\text{Advertising Costs}$$
$$t\text{-statistics} = (17.77) \ (21.07)$$

At the 5% significance level, Meg initially concludes that advertising is significant in explaining sales. However, to estimate this regression model, she had to make certain assumptions that might not be valid. Specifically, with a time series analysis, the assumption maintaining the independence of the error terms often breaks down. In other words, the regression model often suffers from serial correlation. Table 20.22 shows a portion of the values of the residuals; the full data set can be found on the text website, labeled **Residuals**.

TABLE 20.22 Values of Residuals

FILE

Observation	Residual
1	−0.31
2	−0.80
⋮	⋮
24	0.12

Meg would like to use the runs test to determine whether the positive and negative residuals occur randomly at the 5% significance level.

Sample Report— Testing the Independence of Residuals

One of the underlying assumptions of a linear regression model is that the error term is uncorrelated across observations; that is, there is no serial correlation. In a regression model relating sales to advertising costs, there is reason to believe that serial correlation may be a problem because the data are time series. Figure 20.A is a scatterplot of the residuals against time. If the residuals show no pattern around the horizontal axis, then serial correlation is not likely a problem. Given the wavelike movement in the residuals over time (clustering below the horizontal axis, then above the horizontal axis, etc.), positive serial correlation is likely a problem in this application.

FIGURE 20.A Scatterplot of Residuals against Time

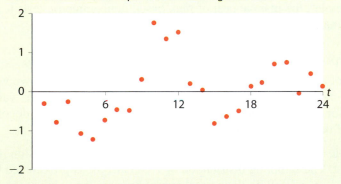

The above graphical analysis is supplemented with a runs test to determine if the residuals fail to follow a random pattern. A residual is given a + symbol if the residual is positive and a − symbol if the residual is negative. There are 12 positive residuals and 12 negative residuals, or $n_+ = 12$ and $n_- = 12$, respectively. A run is then defined as an uninterrupted sequence of a + or a − sign. The sample data exhibits three positive runs, $R_+ = 3$, and three negative runs, $R_- = 3$, for a total number of runs equal to six, $R = 6$.

Are six runs consisting of 24 observations too few or too many compared with the number of runs expected in a strictly random sequence of 24 observations? In order to answer this question, the mean and the standard deviation for the distribution of R are calculated. The mean number of runs in a sample of 24 observations is 13 with a standard deviation of 2.4. Table 20.A provides summary data to conduct the runs test.

TABLE 20.A Data for Runs Test, $n = 24$

- Mean number of runs, $\mu_R = 13$, versus actual number of runs, $R = 6$.
- Standard deviation of the sampling distribution of R: $\sigma_R = 2.4$.
- z-statistic $= -2.92$; the p-value (two-tailed) $= 0.0036$.

The sample value of the test statistic is $z = -2.92$ with an associated p-value of 0.0036. The null hypothesis of the randomness of the residuals is rejected at the 5% level; the pattern of the residuals is nonrandom. Moreover, given that the actual number of runs is significantly less than the expected number of runs, or too few runs, positive serial correlation is likely to be the problem. Corrective measures should be taken before statistical inference is conducted on the estimated model.

Conceptual Review

LO 20.1

Distinguish between parametric and nonparametric tests.

Nonparametric tests, also referred to as distribution-free tests, do not require stringent assumptions of parametric tests and are especially attractive when the underlying population is markedly nonnormal. Also, while parametric tests require data of interval or ratio scale, nonparametric tests can be performed on data of nominal or ordinal scale.

However, a nonparametric test ignores useful information since it often focuses on the rank rather than the magnitude of sample values. Therefore, in situations when the parametric assumptions are valid, the nonparametric test is less powerful (more prone to Type II error) than its parametric counterpart. In general, when the assumptions for a parametric test are met, it is preferable to use a parametric test rather than a nonparametric test. Since the normality assumption for parametric tests is less stringent in large samples, the main appeal of rank-based nonparametric tests tends to be with relatively small samples.

LO 20.2

Conduct a hypothesis test concerning a single population median.

If we cannot assume that the data are normally distributed and/or we want to test the population median, we apply the **Wilcoxon signed-rank test**. The value of the test statistic T for the Wilcoxon signed-rank test is $T = T^+$, where T^+ denotes the sum of the ranks of the positive differences from the hypothesized median m_0.

If the sample size $n \leq 10$, we use a special table to derive the decision rule for the hypothesis test. The sampling distribution of T can also be approximated by the normal distribution if $n \geq 10$. With the normal approximation, the value of the test statistic is calculated as $z = \frac{T - \mu_T}{\sigma_T}$, where $\mu_T = \frac{n(n+1)}{4}$ and $\sigma_T = \sqrt{\frac{n(n+1)(2n+1)}{24}}$.

LO 20.3

Determine whether the population median difference differs from zero under matched-pairs sampling.

We can also apply the **Wilcoxon signed-rank test** as the nonparametric counterpart to the t test that was used to determine whether two population means differ under matched-pairs sampling. The measurement of interest is the difference between paired observations, or $d_i = x_i - y_i$. We conduct the test by following analogous steps to those applied for a one-sample Wilcoxon signed-rank test.

LO 20.4 **Determine whether two population medians differ under independent sampling.**

We use the **Wilcoxon rank-sum test** to determine whether two populations have different medians under independent sampling. We pool the data and calculate the rank sum of sample 1, W_1, and the rank sum of sample 2, W_2. If the two sample sizes satisfy $n_1 \leq n_2$, then the test statistic W is $W = W_1$. Otherwise, we set $W = W_2$.

If either sample is less than or equal to 10, we use a special table to obtain the critical value(s) for the hypothesis test. The sampling distribution of W can be approximated by the normal distribution if both sample sizes are greater than or equal to 10. The value of the test statistic is calculated as $z = \frac{W - \mu_W}{\sigma_W}$, where $\mu_W = \frac{(n_1 + n_2 + 1) \times \min(n_1, n_2)}{2}$ and $\sigma_W = \sqrt{\frac{n_1 n_2 (n_1 + n_2 + 1)}{12}}$.

LO 20.5 **Determine whether the medians of more than two populations differ.**

We employ the **Kruskal-Wallis test** as the nonparametric alternative to the one-way ANOVA F test. It is based on ranks and is used for testing the differences between the medians of k populations. The value of the test statistic for the Kruskal-Wallis test is $H = \frac{12}{n(n+1)} \sum_{i=1}^{k} \frac{R_i^2}{n_i} - 3(n+1)$, where R_i and n_i are the rank sum and the size of the ith sample, $n = \sum_{i=1}^{k} n_i$, and k is the number of populations (independent samples). So long as $n_i \geq 5$, the test statistic H follows the χ^2 distribution with $k - 1$ degrees of freedom.

LO 20.6 **Analyze the correlation between two variables.**

The **Spearman rank correlation coefficient** r_S measures the sample correlation between two random variables. We compute it as $r_S = 1 - \frac{6 \Sigma d_i^2}{n(n^2 - 1)}$, where d_i is the difference between the ranks assigned to the variables. When the sample size is small ($n \leq 10$), we use a special table to determine the significance of the population Spearman rank correlation coefficient ρ_s. When n has at least 10 observations, it is also reasonable to assume that the distribution of r_S is approximately normal. The resulting value of the test statistic is calculated as $z = r_S \sqrt{n - 1}$.

LO 20.7 **Determine whether two populations differ under matched-pairs sampling with ordinal data.**

We use the **sign test** to determine whether significant differences exist between two matched-pairs populations of ordinal data. The value of the test statistic is computed as $z = \frac{\bar{p} - 0.5}{0.5/\sqrt{n}}$, where $\bar{p}$ is the sample proportion of positive signs. The test is valid when $n \geq 10$.

LO 20.8 **Determine whether the elements of a sequence appear in a random order.**

We apply the **Wald-Wolfowitz runs test** to examine whether or not the attributes in a sequence appear in a random order. The test statistic is assumed to follow the z distribution, and its value is computed as $z = \frac{R - \mu_R}{\sigma_R}$ where $\mu_R = \frac{2n_1 n_2}{n} + 1$ and $\sigma_R = \sqrt{\frac{2n_1 n_2 (2n_1 n_2 - n)}{n^2 (n - 1)}}$. The test is valid when $n_1 \geq 10$ and $n_2 \geq 10$. We can use the runs test with quantitative data to investigate whether the values randomly fall above and below the sample's median. This test is especially useful in detecting trends and cyclical patterns in economic data.

Additional Exercises and Case Studies

Exercises

61. The following are the closing stock prices for a pharmaceutical firm over the past two weeks.

Day	1	2	3	4	5	6	7	8	9	10
Price ($)	61.22	60.99	61.91	61.59	61.76	61.91	61.30	61.37	61.95	62.82

a. Specify the competing hypotheses in order to determine whether the median stock price is greater than $61.25.
b. Calculate the value of the Wilcoxon signed-rank test statistic T. Do not assume that the sampling distribution of T is normally distributed.
c. At the 5% significance level, what is the decision rule?
d. Is the median stock price greater than $61.25? Explain.

62. A farmer is concerned that a change in fertilizer to an organic variant might change his crop yield. He subdivides 6 lots and uses the old fertilizer on one half of each lot and the new fertilizer on the other half. The following table shows the results.

Lot	Crop Yield Using Old Fertilizer	Crop Yield Using New Fertilizer
1	10	12
2	11	10
3	10	13
4	12	9
5	12	11
6	11	12

a. Specify the competing hypotheses to determine whether the median difference between the crop yields differs from zero.
b. Calculate the value of the Wilcoxon signed-rank test statistic T. Do not assume that the sampling distribution of T is normally distributed.
c. At the 5% significance level, what is the decision rule?
d. Is there sufficient evidence to conclude that the median difference between the crop yields differs from zero? Should the farmer be concerned? Explain.

63. **FILE** The table below shows a portion of the returns for Fidelity's Equity Income mutual fund and Vanguard's Equity Income mutual fund from 2000 through 2010; the full data set is on the text website, labeled **Fund Comparison**.

Year	Fidelity	Vanguard
2000	3.88	13.57
2001	−5.02	−2.34
⋮	⋮	⋮
2010	15.13	14.88

Source: http://finance.yahoo.com.

a. Specify the competing hypotheses to determine whether the median difference between the returns differs from zero.
b. Calculate the value of the Wilcoxon signed-rank test statistic T. Assume normality of T.
c. At the 5% significance level, what is the decision rule?
d. Does the median difference between the returns differ from zero? Explain.

64. **FILE** A consumer advocate researches the length of life between two brands of refrigerators, Brand A and Brand B. He collects data on the longevity of 40 refrigerators for Brand A and repeats the sampling for Brand B. A portion of the data is shown in the accompanying table; the full data set is on the text website, labeled **Refrigerator Longevity**.

Brand A	Brand B
16	16
14	20
⋮	⋮
18	17

a. Specify the competing hypotheses to test whether the median length of life differs between the two brands.
b. Calculate the value of the Wilcoxon rank-sum statistic W.
c. Assume that the sampling distribution of W is approximately normal; calculate the value of the test statistic Z.
d. With $\alpha = 0.05$, does median longevity differ between the two brands? Explain.

65. **FILE** A psychiatrist believes that the location of a test center may influence a test taker's performance. In order to test his claim, he collects SAT scores from four different locations (the data are also available on the text website, labeled **Test Centers**).

Location 1	Location 2	Location 3	Location 4
1350	1300	1000	1450
1275	1320	1350	1700
1200	1260	1100	1600
1450	1400	1050	1325
1150	1425	1025	1200

a. Specify the competing hypotheses to test whether the median test scores differ by location.
b. Calculate the value of the test statistic H.
c. At the 5% significance level, what is the critical value?
d. Do the data support the psychiatrist's belief? Explain.

66. **FILE** An economist wants to determine whether the Price/Earnings (P/E) ratio is the same for firms in three industries. Independent samples of five firms in each industry show the following results. The data are also available on the text website, labeled **Industry P/E**.

Industry A	12.19	12.44	7.28	9.96	10.51
Industry B	14.34	17.80	9.32	14.90	9.41
Industry C	26.38	24.75	16.88	16.87	16.70

a. Specify the competing hypotheses to test whether the median P/E ratios differ by industry.

b. Calculate the value of the test statistic H.

c. At the 5% significance level, what is the critical value?

d. Do P/E ratios differ by industry? Explain.

67. **FILE** The following table shows a portion of the annual returns (in percent) for two of Fidelity's mutual funds: the Fidelity Advisor's Electronic Fund and the Fidelity Advisor's Utilities Fund; the full data set is on the text website, labeled **Electronics and Utilities**.

Year	Electronics	Utilities
2001	47.41	−15.28
2002	20.74	−29.48
⋮	⋮	⋮
2010	16.84	11.08

Source: http://finance.yahoo.com.

a. Calculate and interpret the Spearman rank correlation coefficient r_S.

b. Specify the competing hypotheses to determine whether the mutual fund returns are related.

c. At the 5% significance level, specify the critical value and the decision rule. Assume that the sampling distribution of r_S is approximately normal.

d. What is the conclusion to the test? Are the returns correlated?

68. A research analyst believes that a positive relationship exists between a firm's advertising expenditures and its sales. For 65 firms, she collects data on each firm's yearly advertising expenditures and subsequent sales. She calculates a Spearman rank correlation coefficient of 0.45.

a. Specify the competing hypotheses to determine whether advertising and sales are correlated.

b. Assume that the sampling distribution of r_S is approximately normal. Calculate the value of the test statistic and the p-value.

c. At the 5% significance level, are advertising and sales correlated? Explain.

69. **FILE** In order to ensure the public's health and safety, state health inspectors are required to rate the cleanliness and quality of all restaurants in the state. Restaurants that consistently score below a certain level often lose their licenses to operate. From a sample of 10 restaurants, two health inspectors give the ratings shown in the accompanying table, where a score of 10 denotes excellence in cleanliness and quality. The data are also on the text website, labeled **Inspectors**.

Restaurant	Inspector A's Rating	Inspector B's Rating
1	9	8
2	5	6
3	10	8
4	5	4
5	2	3
6	7	5
7	8	6
8	4	1
9	3	2
10	8	9

a. Using the sign test, specify the competing hypotheses to determine whether the ratings are significantly different between the two health inspectors.

b. Calculate the value of the test statistic.

c. Calculate the p-value.

d. At the 5% significance level, do the data suggest that the ratings significantly differ?

70. **FILE** The following table shows a portion of the growth rate in the gross domestic product (GDP) for China from 1980 through 2008; the full data set is on the text website, labeled **China GDP**. Use the method of runs above and below the median with a significance level of 5% to test the null hypothesis of randomness against the alternative that there is a trend or cyclical pattern.

Year	GDP
1980	7.8
1981	5.2
⋮	⋮
2008	9.0

Source: http://data.worldbank.org/indicator.

71. **FILE** A research analyst follows the monthly price data for the Dow Jones Industrial Average for the years 2008–2010. The accompanying table shows a portion of the price data; the full data set, labeled **Dow Jones**, can be found on the text website. The analyst wants to test the random-walk hypothesis that suggests that prices move randomly over time with no discernible pattern.

Date	Adjusted Close Price
1/2/2008	12,650.36
2/1/2008	12,266.39
⋮	⋮
12/1/2010	11,577.51

Source: http://finance.yahoo.com.

a. Use the method-of-runs above and below the median to test the null hypothesis of randomness against the alternative that there is a trend at the 5% significance level.

b. Can the research analyst conclude that the movement of the Dow Jones Industrial Average is consistent with the random-walk hypothesis?

72. **FILE** The following table shows a portion of the percent change in the consumer price index (CPI) for the United States from 1980 through 2008; the full data set can be found on the text website, labeled **US CPI**. Use the method of runs above and below the median with a significance level of 5% to test the null hypothesis of randomness against the alternative that there is a trend or cyclical pattern.

Year	CPI
1980	12.5
1981	8.9
⋮	⋮
2008	0.1

Source: http://data.worldbank.org/indicator.

CASE STUDIES

Case Study 20.1

The economic recovery in California has become increasingly divided between coastal and inland areas (*The Wall Street Journal*, February 2, 2010). For instance, the median home price in Southern California increased 7.5% in December 2009 from a year earlier to $360,000; however, the median home price declined by 10% to $180,000 over the same time period in the Inland Empire counties of San Bernardino and Riverside. An economist gathers 10 recent home sales (in $1,000s) in Southern California and 10 recent home sales (in $1,000s) in the Inland Empire counties. A portion of the results are shown in the accompanying table; the complete data set can be found on the text website, labeled *California Homes*.

Data for Case Study 20.1 California Home Prices

Home	Southern California	Inland Empire
1	418	167
2	491	186
⋮	⋮	⋮
10	885	262

In a report, use the sample information to:

1. Calculate and interpret relevant summary measures for California home prices in these two regions.

2. Explain why the *t* test for comparing means from independent samples might be inappropriate in this case.

3. Use the Wilcoxon rank-sum method to determine whether the median home price in Southern California is greater than the median home price in the Inland Empire.

Case Study 20.2

There has been a lot of discussion lately surrounding the levels and structure of executive compensation. It is well documented that in general, compensation received by senior executives has risen steeply in recent years. The accompanying table lists a portion of total compensation of the top 10 CEOs in four industry classifications: Manufacturing (technology); Manufacturing (other); Services (financial); Services (other). Total compensation for 2006 is measured in $ millions; the full data set is on the text website, labeled *Compensation by Industry*.

Data for Case Study 20.2 Top Executive Compensation (in $ millions), 2006

Manufacturing (Technology)	Manufacturing (Other)	Services (Financial)	Services (Other)
39.82	64.63	91.38	24.02
32.85	60.73	48.13	21.51
⋮	⋮	⋮	⋮
24.08	30.80	25.75	13.04

Source: Compustat.

In a report, use the sample information to:

1. Calculate and interpret relevant summary measures for executive compensation in these four industries.
2. Explain why the one-way ANOVA F test for comparing more than two means may be inappropriate in this case.
3. At the 5% significance level, use the Kruskal-Wallis test to determine whether total executive compensation varies across classifications.

Case Study 20.3

The consumption function, developed by John Maynard Keynes, captures one of the key relationships in economics. It expresses consumption as a function of disposable income, where disposable income is defined as income after taxes. The accompanying table shows a portion of average U.S. annual consumption and disposable income for the years 1985–2006. The complete data, labeled ***Consumption Function***, can be found on the text website.

Data for Case Study 20.3 Consumption and Disposable Income, 1985–2006

Year	Consumption	Disposable Income
1985	$23,490	$22,887
1986	23,866	23,172
⋮	⋮	⋮
2006	48,398	58,101

Source: The Statistical Abstract of the United States.

In a report, use the sample information to:

1. Estimate and interpret the model: Consumption $= \beta_0 + \beta_1$Disposable Income $+ \varepsilon$.
2. Indicate which assumption might be violated, given that the analysis uses time series data.
3. Use the runs test to determine whether the positive and negative residuals occur randomly at the 5% significance level.

APPENDIX A

Tables

TABLE 1 Standard Normal Curve Areas

Entries in this table provide cumulative probabilities, that is, the area under the curve to the left of $-z$. For example, $P(Z \leq -1.52) = 0.0643$.

z	0.00	0.01	0.02	0.03	0.04	0.05	0.06	0.07	0.08	0.09
−3.9	0.0000	0.0000	0.0000	0.0000	0.0000	0.0000	0.0000	0.0000	0.0000	0.0000
−3.8	0.0001	0.0001	0.0001	0.0001	0.0001	0.0001	0.0001	0.0001	0.0001	0.0001
−3.7	0.0001	0.0001	0.0001	0.0001	0.0001	0.0001	0.0001	0.0001	0.0001	0.0001
−3.6	0.0002	0.0002	0.0001	0.0001	0.0001	0.0001	0.0001	0.0001	0.0001	0.0001
−3.5	0.0002	0.0002	0.0002	0.0002	0.0002	0.0002	0.0002	0.0002	0.0002	0.0002
−3.4	0.0003	0.0003	0.0003	0.0003	0.0003	0.0003	0.0003	0.0003	0.0003	0.0002
−3.3	0.0005	0.0005	0.0005	0.0004	0.0004	0.0004	0.0004	0.0004	0.0004	0.0003
−3.2	0.0007	0.0007	0.0006	0.0006	0.0006	0.0006	0.0006	0.0005	0.0005	0.0005
−3.1	0.0010	0.0009	0.0009	0.0009	0.0008	0.0008	0.0008	0.0008	0.0007	0.0007
−3.0	0.0013	0.0013	0.0013	0.0012	0.0012	0.0011	0.0011	0.0011	0.0010	0.0010
−2.9	0.0019	0.0018	0.0018	0.0017	0.0016	0.0016	0.0015	0.0015	0.0014	0.0014
−2.8	0.0026	0.0025	0.0024	0.0023	0.0023	0.0022	0.0021	0.0021	0.0020	0.0019
−2.7	0.0035	0.0034	0.0033	0.0032	0.0031	0.0030	0.0029	0.0028	0.0027	0.0026
−2.6	0.0047	0.0045	0.0044	0.0043	0.0041	0.0040	0.0039	0.0038	0.0037	0.0036
−2.5	0.0062	0.0060	0.0059	0.0057	0.0055	0.0054	0.0052	0.0051	0.0049	0.0048
−2.4	0.0082	0.0080	0.0078	0.0075	0.0073	0.0071	0.0069	0.0068	0.0066	0.0064
−2.3	0.0107	0.0104	0.0102	0.0099	0.0096	0.0094	0.0091	0.0089	0.0087	0.0084
−2.2	0.0139	0.0136	0.0132	0.0129	0.0125	0.0122	0.0119	0.0116	0.0113	0.0110
−2.1	0.0179	0.0174	0.0170	0.0166	0.0162	0.0158	0.0154	0.0150	0.0146	0.0143
−2.0	0.0228	0.0222	0.0217	0.0212	0.0207	0.0202	0.0197	0.0192	0.0188	0.0183
−1.9	0.0287	0.0281	0.0274	0.0268	0.0262	0.0256	0.0250	0.0244	0.0239	0.0233
−1.8	0.0359	0.0351	0.0344	0.0336	0.0329	0.0322	0.0314	0.0307	0.0301	0.0294
−1.7	0.0446	0.0436	0.0427	0.0418	0.0409	0.0401	0.0392	0.0384	0.0375	0.0367
−1.6	0.0548	0.0537	0.0526	0.0516	0.0505	0.0495	0.0485	0.0475	0.0465	0.0455
−1.5	0.0668	0.0655	0.0643	0.0630	0.0618	0.0606	0.0594	0.0582	0.0571	0.0559
−1.4	0.0808	0.0793	0.0778	0.0764	0.0749	0.0735	0.0721	0.0708	0.0694	0.0681
−1.3	0.0968	0.0951	0.0934	0.0918	0.0901	0.0885	0.0869	0.0853	0.0838	0.0823
−1.2	0.1151	0.1131	0.1112	0.1093	0.1075	0.1056	0.1038	0.1020	0.1003	0.0985
−1.1	0.1357	0.1335	0.1314	0.1292	0.1271	0.1251	0.1230	0.1210	0.1190	0.1170
−1.0	0.1587	0.1562	0.1539	0.1515	0.1492	0.1469	0.1446	0.1423	0.1401	0.1379
−0.9	0.1841	0.1814	0.1788	0.1762	0.1736	0.1711	0.1685	0.1660	0.1635	0.1611
−0.8	0.2119	0.2090	0.2061	0.2033	0.2005	0.1977	0.1949	0.1922	0.1894	0.1867
−0.7	0.2420	0.2389	0.2358	0.2327	0.2296	0.2266	0.2236	0.2206	0.2177	0.2148
−0.6	0.2743	0.2709	0.2676	0.2643	0.2611	0.2578	0.2546	0.2514	0.2483	0.2451
−0.5	0.3085	0.3050	0.3015	0.2981	0.2946	0.2912	0.2877	0.2843	0.2810	0.2776
−0.4	0.3446	0.3409	0.3372	0.3336	0.3300	0.3264	0.3228	0.3192	0.3156	0.3121
−0.3	0.3821	0.3783	0.3745	0.3707	0.3669	0.3632	0.3594	0.3557	0.3520	0.3483
−0.2	0.4207	0.4168	0.4129	0.4090	0.4052	0.4013	0.3974	0.3936	0.3897	0.3859
−0.1	0.4602	0.4562	0.4522	0.4483	0.4443	0.4404	0.4364	0.4325	0.4286	0.4247
−0.0	0.5000	0.4960	0.4920	0.4880	0.4840	0.4801	0.4761	0.4721	0.4681	0.4641

SOURCE: Probabilities calculated with Excel.

TABLE 1 (Continued)

Entries in this table provide cumulative probabilities, that is, the area under the curve to the left of z. For example, $P(Z \leq 1.52) = 0.9357$.

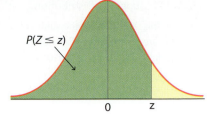

$P(Z \leq z)$

z	0.00	0.01	0.02	0.03	0.04	0.05	0.06	0.07	0.08	0.09
0.0	0.5000	0.5040	0.5080	0.5120	0.5160	0.5199	0.5239	0.5279	0.5319	0.5359
0.1	0.5398	0.5438	0.5478	0.5517	0.5557	0.5596	0.5636	0.5675	0.5714	0.5753
0.2	0.5793	0.5832	0.5871	0.5910	0.5948	0.5987	0.6026	0.6064	0.6103	0.6141
0.3	0.6179	0.6217	0.6255	0.6293	0.6331	0.6368	0.6406	0.6443	0.6480	0.6517
0.4	0.6554	0.6591	0.6628	0.6664	0.6700	0.6736	0.6772	0.6808	0.6844	0.6879
0.5	0.6915	0.6950	0.6985	0.7019	0.7054	0.7088	0.7123	0.7157	0.7190	0.7224
0.6	0.7257	0.7291	0.7324	0.7357	0.7389	0.7422	0.7454	0.7486	0.7517	0.7549
0.7	0.7580	0.7611	0.7642	0.7673	0.7704	0.7734	0.7764	0.7794	0.7823	0.7852
0.8	0.7881	0.7910	0.7939	0.7967	0.7995	0.8023	0.8051	0.8078	0.8106	0.8133
0.9	0.8159	0.8186	0.8212	0.8238	0.8264	0.8289	0.8315	0.8340	0.8365	0.8389
1.0	0.8413	0.8438	0.8461	0.8485	0.8508	0.8531	0.8554	0.8577	0.8599	0.8621
1.1	0.8643	0.8665	0.8686	0.8708	0.8729	0.8749	0.8770	0.8790	0.8810	0.8830
1.2	0.8849	0.8869	0.8888	0.8907	0.8925	0.8944	0.8962	0.8980	0.8997	0.9015
1.3	0.9032	0.9049	0.9066	0.9082	0.9099	0.9115	0.9131	0.9147	0.9162	0.9177
1.4	0.9192	0.9207	0.9222	0.9236	0.9251	0.9265	0.9279	0.9292	0.9306	0.9319
1.5	0.9332	0.9345	0.9357	0.9370	0.9382	0.9394	0.9406	0.9418	0.9429	0.9441
1.6	0.9452	0.9463	0.9474	0.9484	0.9495	0.9505	0.9515	0.9525	0.9535	0.9545
1.7	0.9554	0.9564	0.9573	0.9582	0.9591	0.9599	0.9608	0.9616	0.9625	0.9633
1.8	0.9641	0.9649	0.9656	0.9664	0.9671	0.9678	0.9686	0.9693	0.9699	0.9706
1.9	0.9713	0.9719	0.9726	0.9732	0.9738	0.9744	0.9750	0.9756	0.9761	0.9767
2.0	0.9772	0.9778	0.9783	0.9788	0.9793	0.9798	0.9803	0.9808	0.9812	0.9817
2.1	0.9821	0.9826	0.9830	0.9834	0.9838	0.9842	0.9846	0.9850	0.9854	0.9857
2.2	0.9861	0.9864	0.9868	0.9871	0.9875	0.9878	0.9881	0.9884	0.9887	0.9890
2.3	0.9893	0.9896	0.9898	0.9901	0.9904	0.9906	0.9909	0.9911	0.9913	0.9916
2.4	0.9918	0.9920	0.9922	0.9925	0.9927	0.9929	0.9931	0.9932	0.9934	0.9936
2.5	0.9938	0.9940	0.9941	0.9943	0.9945	0.9946	0.9948	0.9949	0.9951	0.9952
2.6	0.9953	0.9955	0.9956	0.9957	0.9959	0.9960	0.9961	0.9962	0.9963	0.9964
2.7	0.9965	0.9966	0.9967	0.9968	0.9969	0.9970	0.9971	0.9972	0.9973	0.9974
2.8	0.9974	0.9975	0.9976	0.9977	0.9977	0.9978	0.9979	0.9979	0.9980	0.9981
2.9	0.9981	0.9982	0.9982	0.9983	0.9984	0.9984	0.9985	0.9985	0.9986	0.9986
3.0	0.9987	0.9987	0.9987	0.9988	0.9988	0.9989	0.9989	0.9989	0.9990	0.9990
3.1	0.9990	0.9991	0.9991	0.9991	0.9992	0.9992	0.9992	0.9992	0.9993	0.9993
3.2	0.9993	0.9993	0.9994	0.9994	0.9994	0.9994	0.9994	0.9995	0.9995	0.9995
3.3	0.9995	0.9995	0.9995	0.9996	0.9996	0.9996	0.9996	0.9996	0.9996	0.9997
3.4	0.9997	0.9997	0.9997	0.9997	0.9997	0.9997	0.9997	0.9997	0.9997	0.9998
3.5	0.9998	0.9998	0.9998	0.9998	0.9998	0.9998	0.9998	0.9998	0.9998	0.9998
3.6	0.9998	0.9998	0.9999	0.9999	0.9999	0.9999	0.9999	0.9999	0.9999	0.9999
3.7	0.9999	0.9999	0.9999	0.9999	0.9999	0.9999	0.9999	0.9999	0.9999	0.9999
3.8	0.9999	0.9999	0.9999	0.9999	0.9999	0.9999	0.9999	0.9999	0.9999	0.9999
3.9	0.9999	0.9999	0.9999	0.9999	0.9999	0.9999	0.9999	0.9999	0.9999	0.9999

Source: Probabilities calculated with Excel.

TABLE 2 Student's *t* Distribution

Entries in this table provide the values of $t_{\alpha, df}$ that correspond to a given upper-tail area α and a specified number of degrees of freedom *df*. For example, for $\alpha = 0.05$ and $df = 10$, $P(T_{10} \geq 1.812) = 0.05$.

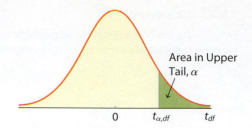

Area in Upper Tail, α

			α			
df	0.20	0.10	0.05	0.025	0.01	0.005
1	1.376	3.078	6.314	12.706	31.821	63.657
2	1.061	1.886	2.920	4.303	6.965	9.925
3	0.978	1.638	2.353	3.182	4.541	5.841
4	0.941	1.533	2.132	2.776	3.747	4.604
5	0.920	1.476	2.015	2.571	3.365	4.032
6	0.906	1.440	1.943	2.447	3.143	3.707
7	0.896	1.415	1.895	2.365	2.998	3.499
8	0.889	1.397	1.860	2.306	2.896	3.355
9	0.883	1.383	1.833	2.262	2.821	3.250
10	0.879	1.372	1.812	2.228	2.764	3.169
11	0.876	1.363	1.796	2.201	2.718	3.106
12	0.873	1.356	1.782	2.179	2.681	3.055
13	0.870	1.350	1.771	2.160	2.650	3.012
14	0.868	1.345	1.761	2.145	2.624	2.977
15	0.866	1.341	1.753	2.131	2.602	2.947
16	0.865	1.337	1.746	2.120	2.583	2.921
17	0.863	1.333	1.740	2.110	2.567	2.898
18	0.862	1.330	1.734	2.101	2.552	2.878
19	0.861	1.328	1.729	2.093	2.539	2.861
20	0.860	1.325	1.725	2.086	2.528	2.845
21	0.859	1.323	1.721	2.080	2.518	2.831
22	0.858	1.321	1.717	2.074	2.508	2.819
23	0.858	1.319	1.714	2.069	2.500	2.807
24	0.857	1.318	1.711	2.064	2.492	2.797
25	0.856	1.316	1.708	2.060	2.485	2.787
26	0.856	1.315	1.706	2.056	2.479	2.779
27	0.855	1.314	1.703	2.052	2.473	2.771
28	0.855	1.313	1.701	2.048	2.467	2.763
29	0.854	1.311	1.699	2.045	2.462	2.756
30	0.854	1.310	1.697	2.042	2.457	2.750

TABLE 2 (*Continued*)

df	0.20	0.10	0.05	0.025	0.01	0.005
31	0.853	1.309	1.696	2.040	2.453	2.744
32	0.853	1.309	1.694	2.037	2.449	2.738
33	0.853	1.308	1.692	2.035	2.445	2.733
34	0.852	1.307	1.691	2.032	2.441	2.728
35	0.852	1.306	1.690	2.030	2.438	2.724
36	0.852	1.306	1.688	2.028	2.434	2.719
37	0.851	1.305	1.687	2.026	2.431	2.715
38	0.851	1.304	1.686	2.024	2.429	2.712
39	0.851	1.304	1.685	2.023	2.426	2.708
40	0.851	1.303	1.684	2.021	2.423	2.704
41	0.850	1.303	1.683	2.020	2.421	2.701
42	0.850	1.302	1.682	2.018	2.418	2.698
43	0.850	1.302	1.681	2.017	2.416	2.695
44	0.850	1.301	1.680	2.015	2.414	2.692
45	0.850	1.301	1.679	2.014	2.412	2.690
46	0.850	1.300	1.679	2.013	2.410	2.687
47	0.849	1.300	1.678	2.012	2.408	2.685
48	0.849	1.299	1.677	2.011	2.407	2.682
49	0.849	1.299	1.677	2.010	2.405	2.680
50	0.849	1.299	1.676	2.009	2.403	2.678
51	0.849	1.298	1.675	2.008	2.402	2.676
52	0.849	1.298	1.675	2.007	2.400	2.674
53	0.848	1.298	1.674	2.006	2.399	2.672
54	0.848	1.297	1.674	2.005	2.397	2.670
55	0.848	1.297	1.673	2.004	2.396	2.668
56	0.848	1.297	1.673	2.003	2.395	2.667
57	0.848	1.297	1.672	2.002	2.394	2.665
58	0.848	1.296	1.672	2.002	2.392	2.663
59	0.848	1.296	1.671	2.001	2.391	2.662
60	0.848	1.296	1.671	2.000	2.390	2.660
80	0.846	1.292	1.664	1.990	2.374	2.639
100	0.845	1.290	1.660	1.984	2.364	2.626
150	0.844	1.287	1.655	1.976	2.351	2.609
200	0.843	1.286	1.653	1.972	2.345	2.601
500	0.842	1.283	1.648	1.965	2.334	2.586
1000	0.842	1.282	1.646	1.962	2.330	2.581
∞	0.842	1.282	1.645	1.960	2.326	2.576

SOURCE: *t* values calculated with Excel.

TABLE 3 χ^2 (Chi-Square) Distribution

Entries in this table provide the values of $\chi^2_{\alpha,df}$ that correspond to a given upper-tail area α and a specified number of degrees of freedom df. For example, for $\alpha = 0.05$ and $df = 10$, $P(\chi^2_{10} \geq 18.307) = 0.05$.

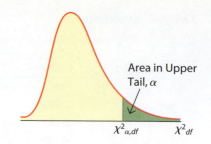

Area in Upper Tail, α

$\chi^2_{\alpha,df}$ χ^2_{df}

df	0.995	0.990	0.975	0.950	0.900	0.100	0.050	0.025	0.010	0.005
1	0.000	0.000	0.001	0.004	0.016	2.706	3.841	5.024	6.635	7.879
2	0.010	0.020	0.051	0.103	0.211	4.605	5.991	7.378	9.210	10.597
3	0.072	0.115	0.216	0.352	0.584	6.251	7.815	9.348	11.345	12.838
4	0.207	0.297	0.484	0.711	1.064	7.779	9.488	11.143	13.277	14.860
5	0.412	0.554	0.831	1.145	1.610	9.236	11.070	12.833	15.086	16.750
6	0.676	0.872	1.237	1.635	2.204	10.645	12.592	14.449	16.812	18.548
7	0.989	1.239	1.690	2.167	2.833	12.017	14.067	16.013	18.475	20.278
8	1.344	1.646	2.180	2.733	3.490	13.362	15.507	17.535	20.090	21.955
9	1.735	2.088	2.700	3.325	4.168	14.684	16.919	19.023	21.666	23.589
10	2.156	2.558	3.247	3.940	4.865	15.987	18.307	20.483	23.209	25.188
11	2.603	3.053	3.816	4.575	5.578	17.275	19.675	21.920	24.725	26.757
12	3.074	3.571	4.404	5.226	6.304	18.549	21.026	23.337	26.217	28.300
13	3.565	4.107	5.009	5.892	7.042	19.812	22.362	24.736	27.688	29.819
14	4.075	4.660	5.629	6.571	7.790	21.064	23.685	26.119	29.141	31.319
15	4.601	5.229	6.262	7.261	8.547	22.307	24.996	27.488	30.578	32.801
16	5.142	5.812	6.908	7.962	9.312	23.542	26.296	28.845	32.000	34.267
17	5.697	6.408	7.564	8.672	10.085	24.769	27.587	30.191	33.409	35.718
18	6.265	7.015	8.231	9.390	10.865	25.989	28.869	31.526	34.805	37.156
19	6.844	7.633	8.907	10.117	11.651	27.204	30.144	32.852	36.191	38.582
20	7.434	8.260	9.591	10.851	12.443	28.412	31.410	34.170	37.566	39.997
21	8.034	8.897	10.283	11.591	13.240	29.615	32.671	35.479	38.932	41.401
22	8.643	9.542	10.982	12.338	14.041	30.813	33.924	36.781	40.289	42.796
23	9.260	10.196	11.689	13.091	14.848	32.007	35.172	38.076	41.638	44.181
24	9.886	10.856	12.401	13.848	15.659	33.196	36.415	39.364	42.980	45.559
25	10.520	11.524	13.120	14.611	16.473	34.382	37.652	40.646	44.314	46.928
26	11.160	12.198	13.844	15.379	17.292	35.563	38.885	41.923	45.642	48.290
27	11.808	12.879	14.573	16.151	18.114	36.741	40.113	43.195	46.963	49.645
28	12.461	13.565	15.308	16.928	18.939	37.916	41.337	44.461	48.278	50.993
29	13.121	14.256	16.047	17.708	19.768	39.087	42.557	45.722	49.588	52.336
30	13.787	14.953	16.791	18.493	20.599	40.256	43.773	46.979	50.892	53.672

TABLE 3 (*Continued*)

					α					
df	0.995	0.990	0.975	0.950	0.900	0.100	0.050	0.025	0.010	0.005
31	14.458	15.655	17.539	19.281	21.434	41.422	44.985	48.232	52.191	55.003
32	15.134	16.362	18.291	20.072	22.271	42.585	46.194	49.480	53.486	56.328
33	15.815	17.074	19.047	20.867	23.110	43.745	47.400	50.725	54.776	57.648
34	16.501	17.789	19.806	21.664	23.952	44.903	48.602	51.966	56.061	58.964
35	17.192	18.509	20.569	22.465	24.797	46.059	49.802	53.203	57.342	60.275
36	17.887	19.233	21.336	23.269	25.643	47.212	50.998	54.437	58.619	61.581
37	18.586	19.960	22.106	24.075	26.492	48.363	52.192	55.668	59.893	62.883
38	19.289	20.691	22.878	24.884	27.343	49.513	53.384	56.896	61.162	64.181
39	19.996	21.426	23.654	25.695	28.196	50.660	54.572	58.120	62.428	65.476
40	20.707	22.164	24.433	26.509	29.051	51.805	55.758	59.342	63.691	66.766
41	21.421	22.906	25.215	27.326	29.907	52.949	56.942	60.561	64.950	68.053
42	22.138	23.650	25.999	28.144	30.765	54.090	58.124	61.777	66.206	69.336
43	22.859	24.398	26.785	28.965	31.625	55.230	59.304	62.990	67.459	70.616
44	23.584	25.148	27.575	29.787	32.487	56.369	60.481	64.201	68.710	71.893
45	24.311	25.901	28.366	30.612	33.350	57.505	61.656	65.410	69.957	73.166
46	25.041	26.657	29.160	31.439	34.215	58.641	62.830	66.617	71.201	74.437
47	25.775	27.416	29.956	32.268	35.081	59.774	64.001	67.821	72.443	75.704
48	26.511	28.177	30.755	33.098	35.949	60.907	65.171	69.023	73.683	76.969
49	27.249	28.941	31.555	33.930	36.818	62.038	66.339	70.222	74.919	78.231
50	27.991	29.707	32.357	34.764	37.689	63.167	67.505	71.420	76.154	79.490
55	31.735	33.570	36.398	38.958	42.060	68.796	73.311	77.380	82.292	85.749
60	35.534	37.485	40.482	43.188	46.459	74.397	79.082	83.298	88.379	91.952
65	39.383	41.444	44.603	47.450	50.883	79.973	84.821	89.177	94.422	98.105
70	43.275	45.442	48.758	51.739	55.329	85.527	90.531	95.023	100.425	104.215
75	47.206	49.475	52.942	56.054	59.795	91.061	96.217	100.839	106.393	110.286
80	51.172	53.540	57.153	60.391	64.278	96.578	101.879	106.629	112.329	116.321
85	55.170	57.634	61.389	64.749	68.777	102.079	107.522	112.393	118.236	122.325
90	59.196	61.754	65.647	69.126	73.291	107.565	113.145	118.136	124.116	128.299
95	63.250	65.898	69.925	73.520	77.818	113.038	118.752	123.858	129.973	134.247
100	67.328	70.065	74.222	77.929	82.358	118.498	124.342	129.561	135.807	140.169

SOURCE: χ^2 values calculated with Excel.

TABLE 4 F Distribution

Entries in this table provide the values of $F_{\alpha,(df_1,df_2)}$ that correspond to a given upper-tail area α and a specified number of degrees of freedom in the numerator df_1 and degrees of freedom in the denominator df_2. For example, for $\alpha = 0.05$, $df_1 = 8$, and $df_2 = 6$, $P(F_{(8,6)} \leq 4.15) = 0.05$.

df_2	α	df_1 1	2	3	4	5	6	7	8	9	10	15	25	50	100	500
1	0.10	39.86	49.5	53.59	55.83	57.24	58.2	58.91	59.44	59.86	60.19	61.22	62.05	62.69	63.01	63.26
	0.05	161.45	199.50	215.71	224.58	230.16	233.99	236.77	238.88	240.54	241.88	245.95	249.26	251.77	253.04	254.06
	0.025	647.79	799.50	864.16	899.58	921.85	937.11	948.22	956.66	963.28	968.63	984.87	998.08	1008.12	1013.17	1017.24
	0.01	4052.18	4999.50	5403.35	5624.58	5763.65	5858.99	5928.36	5981.07	6022.47	6055.85	6157.28	6239.83	6302.52	6334.11	6359.50
2	0.10	8.53	9.00	9.16	9.24	9.29	9.33	9.35	9.37	9.38	9.39	9.42	9.45	9.47	9.48	9.49
	0.05	18.51	19.00	19.16	19.25	19.30	19.33	19.35	19.37	19.38	19.40	19.43	19.46	19.48	19.49	19.49
	0.025	38.51	39.00	39.17	39.25	39.30	39.33	39.36	39.37	39.39	39.40	39.43	39.46	39.48	39.49	39.50
	0.01	98.50	99.00	99.17	99.25	99.30	99.33	99.36	99.37	99.39	99.40	99.43	99.46	99.48	99.49	99.50
3	0.10	5.54	5.46	5.39	5.34	5.31	5.28	5.27	5.25	5.24	5.23	5.20	5.17	5.15	5.14	5.14
	0.05	10.13	9.55	9.28	9.12	9.01	8.94	8.89	8.85	8.81	8.79	8.70	8.63	8.58	8.55	8.53
	0.025	17.44	16.04	15.44	15.10	14.88	14.73	14.62	14.54	14.47	14.42	14.25	14.12	14.01	13.96	13.91
	0.01	34.12	30.82	29.46	28.71	28.24	27.91	27.67	27.49	27.35	27.23	26.87	26.58	26.35	26.24	26.15
4	0.10	4.54	4.32	4.19	4.11	4.05	4.01	3.98	3.95	3.94	3.92	3.87	3.83	3.80	3.78	3.76
	0.05	7.71	6.94	6.59	6.39	6.26	6.16	6.09	6.04	6.00	5.96	5.86	5.77	5.70	5.66	5.64
	0.025	12.22	10.65	9.98	9.60	9.36	9.20	9.07	8.98	8.90	8.84	8.66	8.5	8.38	8.32	8.27
	0.01	21.20	18.00	16.69	15.98	15.52	15.21	14.98	14.80	14.66	14.55	14.20	13.91	13.69	13.58	13.49
5	0.10	4.06	3.78	3.62	3.52	3.45	3.4	3.37	3.34	3.32	3.30	3.24	3.19	3.15	3.13	3.11
	0.05	6.61	5.79	5.41	5.19	5.05	4.95	4.88	4.82	4.77	4.74	4.62	4.52	4.44	4.41	4.37
	0.025	10.01	8.43	7.76	7.39	7.15	6.98	6.85	6.76	6.68	6.62	6.43	6.27	6.14	6.08	6.03
	0.01	16.26	13.27	12.06	11.39	10.97	10.67	10.46	10.29	10.16	10.05	9.72	9.45	9.24	9.13	9.04
6	0.10	3.78	3.46	3.29	3.18	3.11	3.05	3.01	2.98	2.96	2.94	2.87	2.81	2.77	2.75	2.73
	0.05	5.99	5.14	4.76	4.53	4.39	4.28	4.21	4.15	4.10	4.06	3.94	3.83	3.75	3.71	3.68
	0.025	8.81	7.26	6.60	6.23	5.99	5.82	5.70	5.6	5.52	5.46	5.27	5.11	4.98	4.92	4.86
	0.01	13.75	10.92	9.78	9.15	8.75	8.47	8.26	8.10	7.98	7.87	7.56	7.30	7.09	6.99	6.90
7	0.10	3.59	3.26	3.07	2.96	2.88	2.83	2.78	2.75	2.72	2.70	2.63	2.57	2.52	2.50	2.48
	0.05	5.59	4.74	4.35	4.12	3.97	3.87	3.79	3.73	3.68	3.64	3.51	3.4	3.32	3.27	3.24
	0.025	8.07	6.54	5.89	5.52	5.29	5.12	4.99	4.90	4.82	4.76	4.57	4.4	4.28	4.21	4.16
	0.01	12.25	9.55	8.45	7.85	7.46	7.19	6.99	6.84	6.72	6.62	6.31	6.06	5.86	5.75	5.67

	df_1															
df_2	α	1	2	3	4	5	6	7	8	9	10	15	25	50	100	500
8	0.10	3.46	3.11	2.92	2.81	2.73	2.67	2.62	2.59	2.56	2.54	2.46	2.40	2.35	2.32	2.30
	0.05	5.32	4.46	4.07	3.84	3.69	3.58	3.50	3.44	3.39	3.35	3.22	3.11	3.02	2.97	2.94
	0.025	7.57	6.06	5.42	5.05	4.82	4.65	4.53	4.43	4.36	4.30	4.1	3.94	3.81	3.74	3.68
	0.01	11.26	8.65	7.59	7.01	6.63	6.37	6.18	6.03	5.91	5.81	5.52	5.26	5.07	4.96	4.88
9	0.10	3.36	3.01	2.81	2.69	2.61	2.55	2.51	2.47	2.44	2.42	2.34	2.27	2.22	2.19	2.17
	0.05	5.12	4.26	3.86	3.63	3.48	3.37	3.29	3.23	3.18	3.14	3.01	2.89	2.80	2.76	2.72
	0.025	7.21	5.71	5.08	4.72	4.48	4.32	4.20	4.10	4.03	3.96	3.77	3.6	3.47	3.40	3.35
	0.01	10.56	8.02	6.99	6.42	6.06	5.8	5.61	5.47	5.35	5.26	4.96	4.71	4.52	4.41	4.33
10	0.10	3.29	2.92	2.73	2.61	2.52	2.46	2.41	2.38	2.35	2.32	2.24	2.17	2.12	2.09	2.06
	0.05	4.96	4.1	3.71	3.48	3.33	3.22	3.14	3.07	3.02	2.98	2.85	2.73	2.64	2.59	2.55
	0.025	6.94	5.46	4.83	4.47	4.24	4.07	3.95	3.85	3.78	3.72	3.52	3.35	3.22	3.15	3.09
	0.01	10.04	7.56	6.55	5.99	5.64	5.39	5.20	5.06	4.94	4.85	4.56	4.31	4.12	4.01	3.93
11	0.10	3.23	2.86	2.66	2.54	2.45	2.39	2.34	2.30	2.27	2.25	2.17	2.10	2.04	2.01	1.98
	0.05	4.84	3.98	3.59	3.36	3.20	3.09	3.01	2.95	2.90	2.85	2.72	2.60	2.51	2.46	2.42
	0.025	6.72	5.26	4.63	4.28	4.04	3.88	3.76	3.66	3.59	3.53	3.33	3.16	3.03	2.96	2.90
	0.01	9.65	7.21	6.22	5.67	5.32	5.07	4.89	4.74	4.63	4.54	4.25	4.01	3.81	3.71	3.62
12	0.10	3.18	2.81	2.61	2.48	2.39	2.33	2.28	2.24	2.21	2.19	2.10	2.03	1.97	1.94	1.91
	0.05	4.75	3.89	3.49	3.26	3.11	3.00	2.91	2.85	2.80	2.75	2.62	2.50	2.40	2.35	2.31
	0.025	6.55	5.10	4.47	4.12	3.89	3.73	3.61	3.51	3.44	3.37	3.18	3.01	2.87	2.80	2.74
	0.01	9.33	6.93	5.95	5.41	5.06	4.82	4.64	4.50	4.39	4.30	4.01	3.76	3.57	3.47	3.38
13	0.10	3.14	2.76	2.56	2.43	2.35	2.28	2.23	2.20	2.16	2.14	2.05	1.98	1.92	1.88	1.85
	0.05	4.67	3.81	3.41	3.18	3.03	2.92	2.83	2.77	2.71	2.67	2.53	2.41	2.31	2.26	2.22
	0.025	6.41	4.97	4.35	4.00	3.77	3.60	3.48	3.39	3.31	3.25	3.05	2.88	2.74	2.67	2.61
	0.01	9.07	6.70	5.74	5.21	4.86	4.62	4.44	4.30	4.19	4.10	3.82	3.57	3.38	3.27	3.19
14	0.10	3.10	2.73	2.52	2.39	2.31	2.24	2.19	2.15	2.12	2.10	2.01	1.93	1.87	1.83	1.80
	0.05	4.60	3.74	3.34	3.11	2.96	2.85	2.76	2.70	2.65	2.60	2.46	2.34	2.24	2.19	2.14
	0.025	6.30	4.86	4.24	3.89	3.66	3.50	3.38	3.29	3.21	3.15	2.95	2.78	2.64	2.56	2.50
	0.01	8.86	6.51	5.56	5.04	4.69	4.46	4.28	4.14	4.03	3.94	3.66	3.41	3.22	3.11	3.03
15	0.10	3.07	2.7	2.49	2.36	2.27	2.21	2.16	2.12	2.09	2.06	1.97	1.89	1.83	1.79	1.76
	0.05	4.54	3.68	3.29	3.06	2.90	2.79	2.71	2.64	2.59	2.54	2.40	2.28	2.18	2.12	2.08
	0.025	6.20	4.77	4.15	3.80	3.58	3.41	3.29	3.20	3.12	3.06	2.86	2.69	2.55	2.47	2.41
	0.01	8.68	6.36	5.42	4.89	4.56	4.32	4.14	4.00	3.89	3.80	3.52	3.28	3.08	2.98	2.89
16	0.10	3.05	2.67	2.46	2.33	2.24	2.18	2.13	2.09	2.06	2.03	1.94	1.86	1.79	1.76	1.73
	0.05	4.49	3.63	3.24	3.01	2.85	2.74	2.66	2.59	2.54	2.49	2.35	2.23	2.12	2.07	2.02
	0.025	6.12	4.69	4.08	3.73	3.50	3.34	3.22	3.12	3.05	2.99	2.79	2.61	2.47	2.40	2.33
	0.01	8.53	6.23	5.29	4.77	4.44	4.20	4.03	3.89	3.78	3.69	3.41	3.16	2.97	2.86	2.78

TABLE 4 (*Continued*)

df_2	α	df_1 1	2	3	4	5	6	7	8	9	10	15	25	50	100	500
17	0.10	3.03	2.64	2.44	2.31	2.22	2.15	2.10	2.06	2.03	2.00	1.91	1.83	1.76	1.73	1.69
	0.05	4.45	3.59	3.20	2.96	2.81	2.70	2.61	2.55	2.49	2.45	2.31	2.18	2.08	2.02	1.97
	0.025	6.04	4.62	4.01	3.66	3.44	3.28	3.16	3.06	2.98	2.92	2.72	2.55	2.41	2.33	2.26
	0.01	8.40	6.11	5.18	4.67	4.34	4.10	3.93	3.79	3.68	3.59	3.31	3.07	2.87	2.76	2.68
18	0.10	3.01	2.62	2.42	2.29	2.20	2.13	2.08	2.04	2.00	1.98	1.89	1.80	1.74	1.70	1.67
	0.05	4.41	3.55	3.16	2.93	2.77	2.66	2.58	2.51	2.46	2.41	2.27	2.14	2.04	1.98	1.93
	0.025	5.98	4.56	3.95	3.61	3.38	3.22	3.10	3.01	2.93	2.87	2.67	2.49	2.35	2.27	2.20
	0.01	8.29	6.01	5.09	4.58	4.25	4.01	3.84	3.71	3.60	3.51	3.23	2.98	2.78	2.68	2.59
19	0.10	2.99	2.61	2.40	2.27	2.18	2.11	2.06	2.02	1.98	1.96	1.86	1.78	1.71	1.67	1.64
	0.05	4.38	3.52	3.13	2.90	2.74	2.63	2.54	2.48	2.42	2.38	2.23	2.11	2.00	1.94	1.89
	0.025	5.92	4.51	3.90	3.56	3.33	3.17	3.05	2.96	2.88	2.82	2.62	2.44	2.30	2.22	2.15
	0.01	8.18	5.93	5.01	4.50	4.17	3.94	3.77	3.63	3.52	3.43	3.15	2.91	2.71	2.60	2.51
20	0.10	2.97	2.59	2.38	2.25	2.16	2.09	2.04	2.00	1.96	1.94	1.84	1.76	1.69	1.65	1.62
	0.05	4.35	3.49	3.10	2.87	2.71	2.60	2.51	2.45	2.39	2.35	2.20	2.07	1.97	1.91	1.86
	0.025	5.87	4.46	3.86	3.51	3.29	3.13	3.01	2.91	2.84	2.77	2.57	2.40	2.25	2.17	2.10
	0.01	8.10	5.85	4.94	4.43	4.10	3.87	3.70	3.56	3.46	3.37	3.09	2.84	2.64	2.54	2.44
21	0.10	2.96	2.57	2.36	2.23	2.14	2.08	2.02	1.98	1.95	1.92	1.83	1.74	1.67	1.63	1.60
	0.05	4.32	3.47	3.07	2.84	2.68	2.57	2.49	2.42	2.37	2.32	2.18	2.05	1.94	1.88	1.83
	0.025	5.83	4.42	3.82	3.48	3.25	3.09	2.97	2.87	2.80	2.73	2.53	2.36	2.21	2.13	2.06
	0.01	8.02	5.78	4.87	4.37	4.04	3.81	3.64	3.51	3.40	3.31	3.03	2.79	2.58	2.48	2.38
22	0.10	2.95	2.56	2.35	2.22	2.13	2.06	2.01	1.97	1.93	1.90	1.81	1.73	1.65	1.61	1.58
	0.05	4.30	3.44	3.05	2.82	2.66	2.55	2.46	2.40	2.34	2.30	2.15	2.02	1.91	1.85	1.80
	0.025	5.79	4.38	3.78	3.44	3.22	3.05	2.93	2.84	2.76	2.70	2.50	2.32	2.17	2.09	2.02
	0.01	7.95	5.72	4.82	4.31	3.99	3.76	3.59	3.45	3.35	3.26	2.98	2.73	2.53	2.42	2.33
23	0.10	2.94	2.55	2.34	2.21	2.11	2.05	1.99	1.95	1.92	1.89	1.80	1.71	1.64	1.59	1.56
	0.05	4.28	3.42	3.03	2.80	2.64	2.53	2.44	2.37	2.32	2.27	2.13	2.00	1.88	1.82	1.77
	0.025	5.75	4.35	3.75	3.41	3.18	3.02	2.90	2.81	2.73	2.67	2.47	2.29	2.14	2.06	1.99
	0.01	7.88	5.66	4.76	4.26	3.94	3.71	3.54	3.41	3.30	3.21	2.93	2.69	2.48	2.37	2.28
24	0.10	2.93	2.54	2.33	2.19	2.10	2.04	1.98	1.94	1.91	1.88	1.78	1.70	1.62	1.58	1.54
	0.05	4.26	3.40	3.01	2.78	2.62	2.51	2.42	2.36	2.30	2.25	2.11	1.97	1.86	1.80	1.75
	0.025	5.72	4.32	3.72	3.38	3.15	2.99	2.87	2.78	2.70	2.64	2.44	2.26	2.11	2.02	1.95
	0.01	7.82	5.61	4.72	4.22	3.90	3.67	3.50	3.36	3.26	3.17	2.89	2.64	2.44	2.33	2.24

df_2	α	1	2	3	4	5	6	7	8	9	10	15	25	50	100	500
25	0.10	2.92	2.53	2.32	2.18	2.09	2.02	1.97	1.93	1.89	1.87	1.77	1.68	1.61	1.56	1.53
	0.05	4.24	3.39	2.99	2.76	2.60	2.49	2.40	2.34	2.28	2.24	2.09	1.96	1.84	1.78	1.73
	0.025	5.69	4.29	3.69	3.35	3.13	2.97	2.85	2.75	2.68	2.61	2.41	2.23	2.08	2.00	1.92
	0.01	7.77	5.57	4.68	4.18	3.85	3.63	3.46	3.32	3.22	3.13	2.85	2.60	2.40	2.29	2.19
26	0.10	2.91	2.52	2.31	2.17	2.08	2.01	1.96	1.92	1.88	1.86	1.76	1.67	1.59	1.55	1.51
	0.05	4.23	3.37	2.98	2.74	2.59	2.47	2.39	2.32	2.27	2.22	2.07	1.94	1.82	1.76	1.71
	0.025	5.66	4.27	3.67	3.33	3.10	2.94	2.82	2.73	2.65	2.59	2.39	2.21	2.05	1.97	1.90
	0.01	7.72	5.53	4.64	4.14	3.82	3.59	3.42	3.29	3.18	3.09	2.81	2.57	2.36	2.25	2.16
27	0.10	2.90	2.51	2.30	2.17	2.07	2.00	1.95	1.91	1.87	1.85	1.75	1.66	1.58	1.54	1.50
	0.05	4.21	3.35	2.96	2.73	2.57	2.46	2.37	2.31	2.25	2.20	2.06	1.92	1.81	1.74	1.69
	0.025	5.63	4.24	3.65	3.31	3.08	2.92	2.80	2.71	2.63	2.57	2.36	2.18	2.03	1.94	1.87
	0.01	7.68	5.49	4.60	4.11	3.78	3.56	3.39	3.26	3.15	3.06	2.78	2.54	2.33	2.22	2.12
28	0.10	2.89	2.50	2.29	2.16	2.06	2.00	1.94	1.90	1.87	1.84	1.74	1.65	1.57	1.53	1.49
	0.05	4.20	3.34	2.95	2.71	2.56	2.45	2.36	2.29	2.24	2.19	2.04	1.91	1.79	1.73	1.67
	0.025	5.61	4.22	3.63	3.29	3.06	2.90	2.78	2.69	2.61	2.55	2.34	2.16	2.01	1.92	1.85
	0.01	7.64	5.45	4.57	4.07	3.75	3.53	3.36	3.23	3.12	3.03	2.75	2.51	2.30	2.19	2.09
29	0.10	2.89	2.50	2.28	2.15	2.06	1.99	1.93	1.89	1.86	1.83	1.73	1.64	1.56	1.52	1.48
	0.05	4.18	3.33	2.93	2.70	2.55	2.43	2.35	2.28	2.22	2.18	2.03	1.89	1.77	1.71	1.65
	0.025	5.59	4.20	3.61	3.27	3.04	2.88	2.76	2.67	2.59	2.53	2.32	2.14	1.99	1.90	1.83
	0.01	7.60	5.42	4.54	4.04	3.73	3.50	3.33	3.20	3.09	3.00	2.73	2.48	2.27	2.16	2.06
30	0.10	2.88	2.49	2.28	2.14	2.05	1.98	1.93	1.88	1.85	1.82	1.72	1.63	1.55	1.51	1.47
	0.05	4.17	3.32	2.92	2.69	2.53	2.42	2.33	2.27	2.21	2.16	2.01	1.88	1.76	1.70	1.64
	0.025	5.57	4.18	3.59	3.25	3.03	2.87	2.75	2.65	2.57	2.51	2.31	2.12	1.97	1.88	1.81
	0.01	7.56	5.39	4.51	4.02	3.70	3.47	3.30	3.17	3.07	2.98	2.70	2.45	2.25	2.13	2.03
50	0.10	2.81	2.41	2.20	2.06	1.97	1.90	1.84	1.80	1.76	1.73	1.63	1.53	1.44	1.39	1.34
	0.05	4.03	3.18	2.79	2.56	2.40	2.29	2.20	2.13	2.07	2.03	1.87	1.73	1.60	1.52	1.46
	0.025	5.34	3.97	3.39	3.05	2.83	2.67	2.55	2.46	2.38	2.32	2.11	1.92	1.75	1.66	1.57
	0.01	7.17	5.06	4.20	3.72	3.41	3.19	3.02	2.89	2.78	2.70	2.42	2.17	1.95	1.82	1.71
100	0.10	2.76	2.36	2.14	2.00	1.91	1.83	1.78	1.73	1.69	1.66	1.56	1.45	1.35	1.29	1.23
	0.05	3.94	3.09	2.70	2.46	2.31	2.19	2.10	2.03	1.97	1.93	1.77	1.62	1.48	1.39	1.31
	0.025	5.18	3.83	3.25	2.92	2.70	2.54	2.42	2.32	2.24	2.18	1.97	1.77	1.59	1.48	1.38
	0.01	6.90	4.82	3.98	3.51	3.21	2.99	2.82	2.69	2.59	2.50	2.22	1.97	1.74	1.60	1.47
500	0.10	2.72	2.31	2.09	1.96	1.86	1.79	1.73	1.68	1.64	1.61	1.5	1.39	1.28	1.21	1.12
	0.05	3.86	3.01	2.62	2.39	2.23	2.12	2.03	1.96	1.9	1.85	1.69	1.53	1.38	1.28	1.16
	0.025	5.05	3.72	3.14	2.81	2.59	2.43	2.31	2.22	2.14	2.07	1.86	1.65	1.46	1.34	1.19
	0.01	6.69	4.65	3.82	3.36	3.05	2.84	2.68	2.55	2.44	2.36	2.07	1.81	1.57	1.41	1.23

df_1

Source: F-values calculated with Excel.

TABLE 5 Studentized Range Values $q_{\alpha,(c, n_T - c)}$ for Tukey's HSD Method

$n_T - c$	α	2	3	4	5	6	7	8	9	10	11	12
5	0.05	3.64	4.60	5.22	5.67	6.03	6.33	6.58	6.80	6.99	7.17	7.32
	0.01	5.70	6.98	7.80	8.42	8.91	9.32	9.67	9.97	10.24	10.48	10.70
6	0.05	3.46	4.34	4.90	5.30	5.63	5.90	6.12	6.32	6.49	6.65	6.79
	0.01	5.24	6.33	7.03	7.56	7.97	8.32	8.61	8.87	9.10	9.30	9.48
7	0.05	3.34	4.16	4.68	5.06	5.36	5.61	5.82	6.00	6.16	6.30	6.43
	0.01	4.95	5.92	6.54	7.01	7.37	7.68	7.94	8.17	8.37	8.55	8.71
8	0.05	3.26	4.04	4.53	4.89	5.17	5.40	5.60	5.77	5.92	6.05	6.18
	0.01	4.75	5.64	6.20	6.62	6.96	7.24	7.47	7.68	7.86	8.03	8.18
9	0.05	3.20	3.95	4.41	4.76	5.02	5.24	5.43	5.59	5.74	5.87	5.98
	0.01	4.60	5.43	5.96	6.35	6.66	6.91	7.13	7.33	7.49	7.65	7.78
10	0.05	3.15	3.88	4.33	4.65	4.91	5.12	5.30	5.46	5.60	5.72	5.83
	0.01	4.48	5.27	5.77	6.14	6.43	6.67	6.87	7.05	7.21	7.36	7.49
11	0.05	3.11	3.82	4.26	4.57	4.82	5.03	5.20	5.35	5.49	5.61	5.71
	0.01	4.39	5.15	5.62	5.97	6.25	6.48	6.67	6.84	6.99	7.13	7.25
12	0.05	3.08	3.77	4.20	4.51	4.75	4.95	5.12	5.27	5.39	5.51	5.61
	0.01	4.32	5.05	5.50	5.84	6.10	6.32	6.51	6.67	6.81	6.94	7.06
13	0.05	3.06	3.73	4.15	4.45	4.69	4.88	5.05	5.19	5.32	5.43	5.53
	0.01	4.26	4.96	5.40	5.73	5.98	6.19	6.37	6.53	6.67	6.79	6.90
14	0.05	3.03	3.70	4.11	4.41	4.64	4.83	4.99	5.13	5.25	5.36	5.46
	0.01	4.21	4.89	5.32	5.63	5.88	6.08	6.26	6.41	6.54	6.66	6.77
15	0.05	3.01	3.67	4.08	4.37	4.59	4.78	4.94	5.08	5.20	5.31	5.40
	0.01	4.17	4.84	5.25	5.56	5.80	5.99	6.16	6.31	6.44	6.55	6.66
16	0.05	3.00	3.65	4.05	4.33	4.56	4.74	4.90	5.03	5.15	5.26	5.35
	0.01	4.13	4.79	5.19	5.49	5.72	5.92	6.08	6.22	6.35	6.46	6.56
17	0.05	2.98	3.63	4.02	4.30	4.52	4.70	4.86	4.99	5.11	5.21	5.31
	0.01	4.10	4.74	5.14	5.43	5.66	5.85	6.01	6.15	6.27	6.38	6.48
18	0.05	2.97	3.61	4.00	4.28	4.49	4.67	4.82	4.96	5.07	5.17	5.27
	0.01	4.07	4.70	5.09	5.38	5.60	5.79	5.94	6.08	6.20	6.31	6.41
19	0.05	2.96	3.59	3.98	4.25	4.47	4.65	4.79	4.92	5.04	5.14	5.23
	0.01	4.05	4.67	5.05	5.33	5.55	5.73	5.89	6.02	6.14	6.25	6.34
20	0.05	2.95	3.58	3.96	4.23	4.45	4.62	4.77	4.90	5.01	5.11	5.20
	0.01	4.02	4.64	5.02	5.29	5.51	5.69	5.84	5.97	6.09	6.19	6.28

The number of means, c

TABLE 5 (Continued)

$n_T - c$	α	The number of means, c										
		2	3	4	5	6	7	8	9	10	11	12
24	0.05	2.92	3.53	3.90	4.17	4.37	4.54	4.68	4.81	4.92	5.01	5.10
	0.01	3.96	4.55	4.91	5.17	5.37	5.54	5.69	5.81	5.92	6.02	6.11
30	0.05	2.89	3.49	3.85	4.10	4.30	4.46	4.60	4.72	4.82	4.92	5.00
	0.01	3.89	4.45	4.80	5.05	5.24	5.40	5.54	5.65	5.76	5.85	5.93
40	0.05	2.86	3.44	3.79	4.04	4.23	4.39	4.52	4.63	4.73	4.82	4.90
	0.01	3.82	4.37	4.70	4.93	5.11	5.26	5.39	5.50	5.60	5.69	5.76
60	0.05	2.83	3.40	3.74	3.98	4.16	4.31	4.44	4.55	4.65	4.73	4.81
	0.01	3.76	4.28	4.59	4.82	4.99	5.13	5.25	5.36	5.45	5.53	5.60
120	0.05	2.80	3.36	3.68	3.92	4.10	4.24	4.36	4.47	4.56	4.64	4.71
	0.01	3.70	4.20	4.50	4.71	4.87	5.01	5.12	5.21	5.30	5.37	5.44
∞	0.05	2.77	3.31	3.63	3.86	4.03	4.17	4.29	4.39	4.47	4.55	4.62
	0.01	3.64	4.12	4.40	4.60	4.76	4.88	4.99	5.08	5.16	5.23	5.29

Source: E. S. Pearson and H. O. Hartley, *Biometrika Tables for Statisticians,* vol. 1 (Cambridge: Cambridge University Press, 1966).

TABLE 6 Lower (T_L) and Upper (T_U) Critical Values for the Wilcoxon Signed-Rank Test

Two-Tail Test:	$\alpha = 0.10$	$\alpha = 0.05$	$\alpha = 0.02$	$\alpha = 0.01$
One-Tail Test:	$\alpha = 0.05$	$\alpha = 0.025$	$\alpha = 0.01$	$\alpha = 0.005$
$n = 5$	0, 15	—, —	—, —	—, —
6	2, 19	0, 21	—, —	—, —
7	3, 25	2, 26	0, 28	—, —
8	5, 31	3, 33	1, 35	0, 36
9	8, 37	5, 40	3, 42	1, 44
10	10, 45	8, 47	5, 50	3, 52

Source: Adapted from "Extended Tables of the Wilcoxon Matched Pairs Signed Rank Statistics," *Journal of the American Statistical Association* 60 (1965), 864–71.

TABLE 7 Lower (W_L) and Upper (W_U) Critical Values for the Wilcoxon Rank-Sum Test

		$\alpha = 0.025$ for one-tailed test and $\alpha = 0.05$ for a two-tailed test							
	n_1:	3	4	5	6	7	8	9	10
n_2:	3	5, 16	6, 18	6, 21	7, 23	7, 26	8, 28	8, 31	9, 33
	4	6, 18	11, 25	12, 28	12, 32	13, 35	14, 38	15, 41	16, 44
	5	6, 21	12, 28	18, 37	19, 41	20, 45	21, 49	22, 53	24, 56
	6	7, 23	12, 32	19, 41	26, 52	28, 56	29, 61	31, 65	32, 70
	7	7, 26	13, 35	20, 45	28, 56	37, 68	39, 73	41, 78	43, 83
	8	8, 28	14, 38	21, 49	29, 61	39, 73	49, 87	51, 93	54, 98
	9	8, 31	15, 41	22, 53	31, 65	41, 78	51, 93	63, 108	66, 114
	10	9, 33	16, 44	24, 56	32, 70	43, 83	54, 98	66, 114	79, 131
		$\alpha = 0.05$ for one-tailed test and $\alpha = 0.10$ for a two-tailed test							
	n_1:	3	4	5	6	7	8	9	10
n_2:	3	6, 15	7, 17	7, 20	8, 22	9, 24	9, 27	10, 29	11, 31
	4	7, 17	12, 24	13, 27	14, 30	15, 33	16, 36	17, 39	18, 42
	5	7, 20	13, 27	19, 36	20, 40	22, 43	24, 46	25, 50	26, 54
	6	8, 22	14, 30	20, 40	28, 50	30, 54	32, 58	33, 63	35, 67
	7	9, 24	15, 33	22, 43	30, 54	39, 66	41, 71	43, 76	46, 80
	8	9, 27	16, 36	24, 46	32, 58	41, 71	52, 84	54, 90	57, 95
	9	10, 29	17, 39	25, 50	33, 63	43, 76	54, 90	66, 105	69, 111
	10	11, 31	18, 42	26, 54	35, 67	46, 80	57, 95	69, 111	83, 127

Source: F. Wilcoxon and R. A. Wilcox, *Some Rapid Approximate Statistical Procedures* (New York: American Cyanamid Company, 1964).

TABLE 8 Upper Critical Values for the Spearman Rank-Correlation Coefficient

Two-Tail Test:	$\alpha = 0.10$	$\alpha = 0.05$	$\alpha = 0.02$	$\alpha = 0.01$
One-Tail Test:	$\alpha = 0.05$	$\alpha = 0.025$	$\alpha = 0.01$	$\alpha = 0.005$
$n = 5$	0.900	—	—	—
6	0.829	0.886	0.943	—
7	0.714	0.786	0.893	—
8	0.643	0.738	0.833	0.881
9	0.600	0.683	0.783	0.833
10	0.564	0.648	0.745	0.794

Source: E. G. Olds, "Distribution of Sums of Squares of Rank Differences for Small Samples," *Annals of Mathematical Statistics* 9 (1938).

Answers to Even-Numbered Exercises

Chapter 1

1.2 35 is likely the estimated average age. It would be rather impossible to reach all video game players.

1.4 a. The population is all marketing managers.

b. No, the average salary was likely computed from a sample in order to save time and money.

1.6 Answers will vary depending on when data are retrieved. The numbers represent time series data.

1.8 Answers will vary depending on when data are retrieved. The numbers represent cross-sectional data.

1.10 Answers will vary depending on when data are retrieved. The numbers represent cross-sectional data.

1.12 a. Qualitative

b. Quantitative, continuous

c. Quantitative, discrete

1.14 a. Ratio

b. Ordinal

c. Nominal

1.16 a. Nominal

b.

Major	Number of Students
Accounting	5
Economics	7
Finance	5
Marketing	4
Management	5
Undecided	4

c. Economics (Marketing) has the highest (lowest) number of students.

Chapter 2

2.2 a.

Rating	Frequency	Relative Frequency
Excellent	5	0.208
Good	12	0.500
Fair	4	0.167
Poor	3	0.125

b. The most common response is Good. Over 70 percent of the patients reveal that they are in either good or excellent health, suggesting overall health of first-time patients is strong.

2.4 a.

Delays	Frequency	Relative Frequency
PM Delays	1	0.056
All Day Delays	6	0.333
AM Delays	4	0.222
None	7	0.389

b.

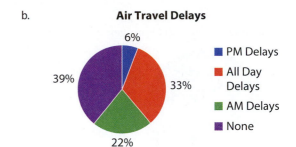

Air Travel Delays

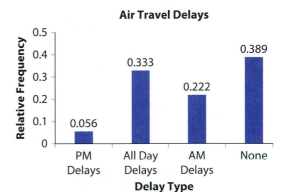

Air Travel Delays

2.6 a.

Response	Frequency
Good jobs	1970
Affordable homes	799
Top schools	586
Low crime	1225
Things to do	745

b.

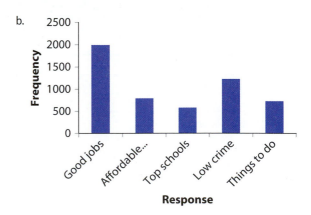

2.8   a.

Company	Relative Frequency
Enterprise	0.489
Hertz	0.215
Avis Budget	0.183
Dollar Thrifty	0.068
Other	0.046

b. Hertz accounted for 21.5% of sales.

c.

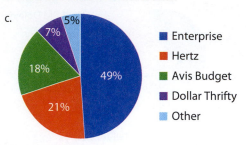

- Enterprise
- Hertz
- Avis Budget
- Dollar Thrifty
- Other

2.10   a. 5584

b. 0.052

c.

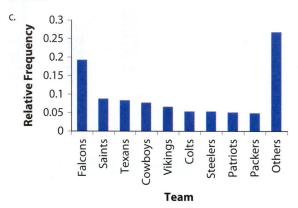

2.12 This graph does not correctly depict the data. The vertical axis has been stretched so that the increase in sales appears more pronounced than warranted.

2.14

Class	Frequency	Relative Frequency	Cumulative Relative Frequency
−10 up to 0	9	0.129	0.129
0 up to 10	31	0.443	0.572
10 up to 20	19	0.271	0.843
20 up to 30	8	0.114	0.957
30 up to 40	3	0.043	1

a. 19 observations

b. 27.1%; 84.3%

c.

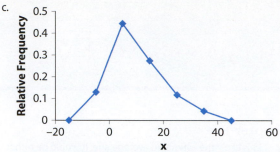

2.16   a.

Class	Relative Frequency
1,000 up to 1100	0.1250
1,100 up to 1200	0.4375
1,200 up to 1300	0.1875
1,300 up to 1400	0.2500

43.75% of observations are at least 1,100 but less than 1200.

b.

Class	Cumulative Frequency	Cumulative Relative Frequency
1,000 up to 1100	2	0.125
1,100 up to 1200	9	0.562
1,200 up to 1300	12	0.750
1,300 up to 1400	16	1

12 observations are less than 1300.

c.

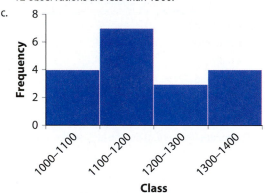

2.18   a.

Class	Frequency
−20 up to −10	2
−10 up to 0	14
0 up to 10	13
10 up to 20	11
20 up to 30	10

14 observations are at least −10 but less than 0.

b.

Class	Cumulative Frequency
−20 up to −10	2
−10 up to 0	16
0 up to 10	29
10 up to 20	40
20 up to 30	50

40 observations are less than 20.

c.

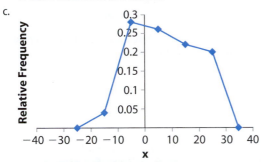

2.20 a.

Assets (in billions USD)	Frequency
40 up to 70	9
70 up to 100	8
100 up to 130	2
130 up to 160	0
160 up to 190	1

b.

Assets (in billions USD)	Relative Frequency	Cumulative Frequency	Cumulative Relative Frequency
40 up to 70	0.45	9	0.45
70 up to 100	0.40	17	0.85
100 up to 130	0.10	19	0.95
130 up to 160	0	19	0.95
160 up to 190	0.05	20	1

c. 2 funds; 19 funds

d. 40%; 95%

e.

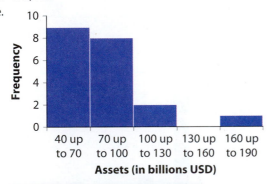

2.22 a.

Temperature (°F)	Frequency
60 up to 70	2
70 up to 80	7
80 up to 90	14
90 up to 100	10

b.

Temperature (°F)	Relative Frequency	Cumulative Frequency	Cumulative Relative Frequency
60 up to 70	0.061	2	0.061
70 up to 80	0.212	9	0.273
80 up to 90	0.424	23	0.697
90 up to 100	0.303	33	1

c. 9 cities

d. 42.4%; 69.7%

e.

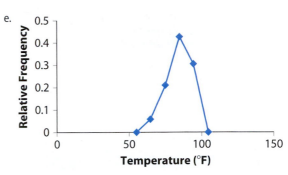

The distribution is slightly negatively skewed.

2.24 a.

Vacancy Rate (%)	Relative Frequency	Cumulative Frequency	Cumulative Relative Frequency
0 up to 3	0.10	5	0.1
3 up to 6	0.20	15	0.3
6 up to 9	0.40	35	0.7
9 up to 12	0.20	45	0.9
12 up to 15	0.10	50	1

b. 45 cities; 40%; 70%

c.

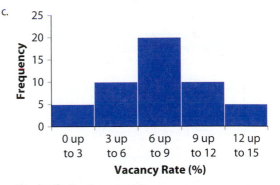

The distribution is symmetric.

2.26 a.

Age	Frequency	Relative Frequency	Cumulative Relative Frequency
18 up to 22	45	0.45	0.45
22 up to 26	25	0.25	0.70
26 up to 30	15	0.15	0.85
30 up to 34	11	0.11	0.96
34 up to 38	4	0.04	1

b. 15 guests; 25%; 96%; 4%

c.

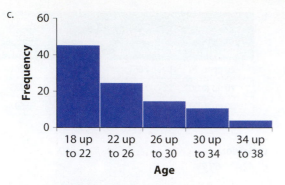

The distribution is positively skewed.

2.28

Stem	Leaf
−8	7 5 5 3 2 0 0 0
−7	9 7 5 3 3 2 1
−6	5 5 4
−5	2 0

The distribution is not symmetric.

2.30

Stem	Leaf
7	3 4 6 7 8 8
8	0 1 2 3 4 4 4 4 7 8
9	0 0 0 1 1 2 2 2 3 3 4 4 4 4 4 5 6 6 6 8 8 9
10	6 7

Temperatures ranged from 73 to 107. Temperatures in the 90s were most frequent.

2.32 Spain

Stem	Leaf
2	1 1 1 2 3 3 4 4 5 5 5 6 7 8 9 9 9
3	0 0 2

Netherlands

Stem	Leaf
2	2 3 3 4 5 5 5 6 6 6 7 7 7 7 9
3	0 3 5 5 9

Spain has a relatively younger team. Spain's ages range from 21 to 32 while the Netherlands' ages range from 22 to 39. Most players on both teams are in their 20s.

2.34

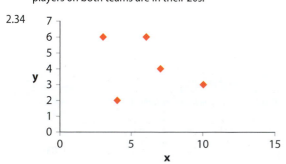

There is no relationship between x and y.

2.36

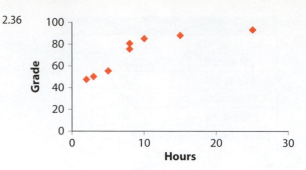

There is a positive relationship; the more hours spent studying, the higher the grade on average.

2.38

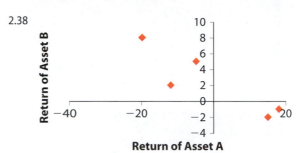

The returns of the assets are negatively correlated. The investor would be wise to include these in her portfolio.

2.40 a.

Response	Utah Relative Frequency	Kentucky Relative Frequency
Yes	0.10	0.45
No	0.90	0.55

45% of households in Kentucky allow smoking at home whereas only 10% do in Utah.

b.

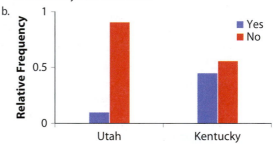

The bar chart shows that smoking at home is much more common in Kentucky.

2.42

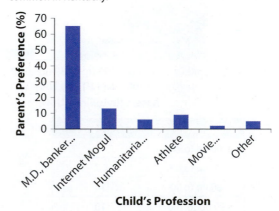

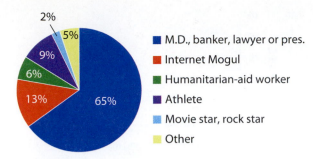

2% 5%

- M.D., banker, lawyer or pres. (65%)
- Internet Mogul (13%)
- Humanitarian-aid worker (6%)
- Athlete (9%)
- Movie star, rock star (2%)
- Other (5%)

b. $(0.09)(550) \approx 50$ parents.

2.44 a.

Region	Relative Frequency
Northeast	0.165
Midwest	0.194
South	0.416
West	0.225

19.4% of people living below the poverty line live in the Midwest.

b.

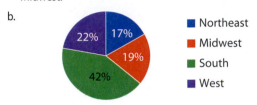

- Northeast (17%)
- Midwest (19%)
- South (42%)
- West (22%)

2.46 a.

Response	Frequency
A few days	642
A few long weekends	550
One week	1101
Two weeks	764

b.

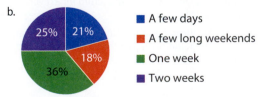

- A few days (21%)
- A few long weekends (18%)
- One week (36%)
- Two weeks (25%)

2.48 a.

Drug	Relative Frequency
Topamax	0.319
Lamictal	0.295
Depakote	0.135
Lyrica	0.127
Keppra	0.124

b. Lamictal accounted for 29.5% of sales.

c.

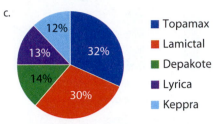

- Topamax (32%)
- Lamictal (30%)
- Depakote (14%)
- Lyrica (13%)
- Keppra (12%)

2.50 a.

Average MPG	Relative Frequency	Cumulative Frequency	Cumulative Relative Frequency
15 up to 20	0.1875	15	0.1875
20 up to 25	0.3750	45	0.5625
25 up to 30	0.1875	60	0.75
30 up to 35	0.1250	70	0.875
35 up to 40	0.0875	77	0.9625
40 up to 45	0.0375	80	1

b. 60 cars; 37.5%; 87.5%; 12.5%

c.

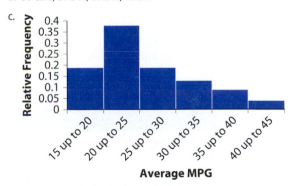

2.52 a. 16%

b. 76%

c.

Stem	Leaf
3	6 6
4	4 7
5	3 3 4 6
6	0 1 5 5 6 7 7 9
7	0 1 3 3 3 7 8 9 9

The distribution is negatively skewed.

2.54 a.

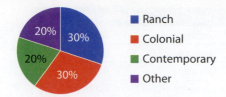

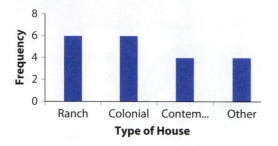

60% of homes sold are either Ranch or Colonial; remaining 40% split between Contemporary or Other.

b.

Price ($)	Frequency
300,000 up to 350,000	4
350,000 up to 400,000	6
400,000 up to 450,000	4
450,000 up to 500,000	2
500,000 up to 550,000	3
550,000 up to 600,000	1

c.

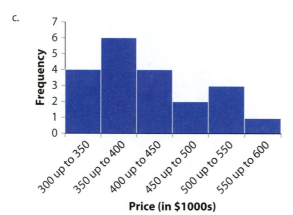

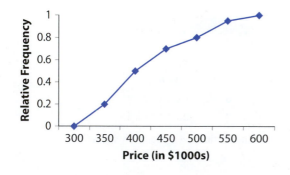

2.56

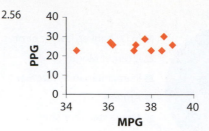

No relationship between PPG and MPG.

Chapter 3

3.2 Mean $= -2.67$; Median $= -3.5$; Mode $= -4$

3.4 Mean $= 18.33$; Median $= 20$; Mode $= 15, 20$

3.6 a. Mean $= 763.97$

  b. Median $= 548.55$. The mean does not reflect the typical compensation because it is affected by outliers.

3.8 The mode.

3.10 a. Mean $= 516.03$; Median $= 523$; Mode $= 430$

  b. The mean and median are close in value. However, the median is a better measure of central location because it is less influenced by outliers.

3.12 $P_{20} = -339.8$;
  $P_{40} = -299.4$;
  $P_{70} = -255.8$

3.14 a. $P_{25} = -0.05$;
  $P_{50} = 0.04$;
  $P_{75} = 0.10$

  b. $IQR = Q_3 - Q_1 = 0.15$; Since no observations are less than $Q_1 - 1.5 \times IQR = -0.275$ or greater than $Q_3 + 1.5 \times IQR = 0.325$, there are no outliers.

3.16 a. $P_{25} = 3.83$; $P_{50} = 7.34$; $P_{75} = 11.74$.

  b. $IQR = 7.91$; Lower limit $= Q_1 - 1.5 \times IQR = -8.035$; Upper limit $= Q_3 + 1.5 \times IQR = 23.605$. Therefore, -11.37 and 31.77 are outliers.

  c. The median is slightly closer to Q_3 than Q_1, suggesting a positively skewed distribution.

3.18 $G_g = 0.0313$

3.20 $G_g = -0.006$

3.22 $G_g = 0.0647$

3.24 a.

Time Period	Growth Rate
Year 1 to Year 2	0.0667
Year 2 to Year 3	0.0781
Year 3 to Year 4	0.1014

  b. $G_g = 0.082$

3.26 a. Arithmetic mean $= 8.605\%$. The return for a given year is on average 8.61%.

  b. $G_g = 0.0258$; the geometric return indicates that if an asset was invested in the stock over the entire time period, it would have earned an annualized return of 2.58%.

  c. $(1000)(1 + 0.0258)^4 = 1107.26$

3.28 a.

Time Period	Home Depot Growth Rate	Lowe's Growth Rate
2008 to 2009	−0.0783	−0.001
2009 to 2010	−0.0717	−0.0209

    b. $G_{HD} = -0.075$; $G_{Lowe's} = -0.011$

3.30 a. $G_g = 0.0869$

    b. $G_g = \sqrt[4]{\dfrac{19{,}176}{13{,}470}} - 1 = 0.0869$

3.32 a. Range $= 10 - (-8) = 18$

    b. $\mu = 0$; $MAD = \dfrac{\Sigma|x_i - \mu|}{N} = \dfrac{24}{5} = 4.8$

    c. $\sigma^2 = \dfrac{\Sigma(x_i - \mu)^2}{N} = \dfrac{184}{5} = 36.8$

    d. $\sigma = 6.07$

3.34 a. Range $= 12 - (-10) = 22$

    b. $\bar{x} = 0.67$; $MAD = \dfrac{\Sigma|x_i - \bar{x}|}{n} = \dfrac{44}{6} = 7.33$

    c. $s^2 = \dfrac{\Sigma(x_i - \bar{x})^2}{n-1} = \dfrac{389.33}{5} = 77.87$; $s = 8.82$

    d. $CV = 13.16$

3.36 a. $s^2_{Starbucks} = 2.57$; $s_{Starbucks} = 1.6$; $s^2_{Panera} = 12.67$; $s_{Panera} = 3.56$;

    b. Starbucks has lower variability than Panera.

    c. $CV_{Panera} = 0.05$; $CV_{Starbucks} = 0.07$; Starbucks

3.38 a. $\bar{x}_{MKT} = 164.1$; $s_{MKT} = 74.01$; $CV_{MKT} = 0.45$

    b. $\bar{x}_R = 40.71$; $s_R = 105.07$; $CV_R = 2.58$

    c. Total return

3.40 a. Investment B (higher mean); Investment A (smaller standard deviation)

    b. $Sharpe_A = 1.72$; $Sharpe_B = 1.36$

    Investment A provides a higher reward per unit of risk as $Sharpe_A$ is larger.

3.42 a. Vanguard Energy Fund

    b. Vanguard Energy Fund

    c. $Sharpe_{Energy} = 0.45$; $Sharpe_{Health} = 0.24$

    The Energy Fund has a higher Sharpe ratio, meaning it offers a higher return per unit of risk.

3.44 a. at least 75%

    b. at least 89%

3.46 a. at least 75%

    b. at least 89%

3.48 a. 16%

    b. 80 observations

3.50 a. $s = \dfrac{Range}{4} = 2.5$

    b. 97.5%

    c. 2.5%

3.52 a. at least 75%

    b. at least 89%

3.54 a. 68%

    b. 2.5%

    c. 16%

3.56 a. at least 75%

    b. 95%

3.58 a. $\bar{x} = \dfrac{\Sigma m_i f_i}{n} = \dfrac{2305}{35} = 65.86$

    b. $s^2 = \dfrac{\Sigma(m_i - \bar{x})^2 f_i}{n-1} = \dfrac{3024.3}{34} = 88.95$; $s = 9.4$

3.60 a. $\bar{x} = \dfrac{\Sigma m_i f_i}{n} = \dfrac{168}{50} = 3.36$

    b. $s^2 = \dfrac{\Sigma(m_i - \bar{x})^2 f_i}{n-1} = \dfrac{189.52}{49} = 3.87$; $s = 1.97$

3.62 a. $\bar{x} = \dfrac{\Sigma m_i f_i}{n} = \dfrac{538}{70} = 7.69$

    b. $s^2 = \dfrac{\Sigma(m_i - \bar{x})^2 f_i}{n-1} = \dfrac{231.01}{69} = 3.35$; $s = 1.83$

3.64 a. $\bar{x} = \dfrac{\Sigma m_i f_i}{n} = \dfrac{2065}{80} = 25.81$

    b. $s^2 = \dfrac{\Sigma(m_i - \bar{x})^2 f_i}{n-1} = \dfrac{3647.19}{79} = 46.17$; $s = 6.79$

3.66 a. $\bar{x} = \dfrac{\Sigma m_i f_i}{n} = \dfrac{3767}{100} = 37.67$

    b. $s^2 = \dfrac{\Sigma(m_i - \bar{x})^2 f_i}{n-1} = \dfrac{46{,}386.61}{99} = 468.55$; $s = 21.65$

3.68 a. $\bar{x} = \$12.17$

    b. $\bar{x} = \$13.27$

3.70 a. $s_{xy} = \dfrac{\Sigma(x_i - \bar{x})(y_i - \bar{y})}{n-1} = -\dfrac{49.2}{4} = -12.3$

    b. $r_{xy} = \dfrac{s_{xy}}{s_x s_y} = -0.96$; strong negative relationship between x and y

3.72 a. $s_{xy} = \dfrac{\Sigma(x_i - \bar{x})(y_i - \bar{y})}{n-1} = \dfrac{4419.75}{7} = 631.39$; positive relationship

    b. $r_{xy} = \dfrac{s_{xy}}{s_x s_y} = 0.45$; moderately strong relationship

3.74 a. $s_{xy} = \dfrac{\Sigma(x_i - \bar{x})(y_i - \bar{y})}{n-1} = \dfrac{245}{7} = 35$; positive relationship

    b. $r_{xy} = \dfrac{s_{xy}}{s_x s_y} = 0.95$; very strong relationship

3.76 Mean $= 809.14$; Median $= 366$; No mode. The median best reflects typical sales since Olive Garden is clearly an outlier that pulls the mean up.

3.78 a. $G_{Gap} = -0.050$; $G_{AE} = -0.012$

    b. American Eagle

3.80 a. $\bar{x} = \dfrac{\Sigma m_i f_i}{n} = \dfrac{109{,}000}{60} = 1{,}816.67$

    b. $s^2 = \dfrac{\Sigma(m_i - \bar{x})^2 f_i}{n-1} = \dfrac{6{,}670{,}840}{59} = 113{,}065.1$; $s = 336.25$

3.82 a. $s_{xy} = \dfrac{\Sigma(x_i - \bar{x})(y_i - \bar{y})}{n-1} = \dfrac{685.9}{4} = 171.5$

    b. $r_{xy} = \dfrac{s_{xy}}{s_x s_y} = 0.95$; There is a strong, positive relationship between returns.

3.84

Statistic	Income	Unemployment	Debt
Mean	74.05	9.77	983.46
Median	71.5	9.3	987.5
Mode	78.3	9.3	1133
Standard Deviation	10.35	2.23	124.61
Range	44.1	9.4	522
Minimum	59.4	6.3	763
Maximum	103.5	15.7	1285

Chapter 4

4.2 a. 1 to 1

    b. 9 to 1

    c. 0.67 to 1

4.4 a. $A \cup B = \{1, 2, 3, 5, 6\} \neq S$. Thus A and B are not exhaustive. $A \cap B = A \neq \emptyset$. Thus A and B are not mutually exclusive.

b. $A \cup C = \{1, 2, 3, 4, 6\} \neq S$. Thus A and C are not exhaustive. $A \cap C \neq \emptyset$. Thus A and C are mutually exclusive.

c. $A \cup D = \{1, 2, 3, 4, 5, 6\} = S$. Thus A and D are exhaustive. $A \cap D = \emptyset$. Thus A and D are mutually exclusive.

d. $B \cup C = \{1, 2, 3, 4, 5, 6\} = S$. Thus B and C are exhaustive. $B \cap C = \{6\} \neq \emptyset$. Thus B and C are not mutually exclusive.

4.6 a. A and B are not exhaustive since one may not get an offer from either firm.

b. A and B are not mutually exclusive since one may get an offer from both firms.

4.8 a. In 1971, $P(\text{Age} \leq 40) = 0.71$. In 2006, $P(\text{Age} \leq 40) = 0.13$.

b. In 1971, $P(\text{Age} \geq 51) = 0.08$. In 2006, $P(\text{Age} \geq 51) = 0.59$.

c. Municipal managers tend to be older in 2006 compared to 1971.

4.10 a. Net gain = \$533.33. Net loss would have been \$1,000.

b. $P(\text{Spain wins}) = 0.652$.

4.12 a. $P(A \cap B) = P(A|B)P(B) = 0.135$

b. $P(A \cup B) = P(A) + P(B) - P(A \cap B) = 0.815$

c. $P(B|A) = P(A \cap B)/P(A) = 0.208$

4.14 a. $P(A \cap B) = 0$, since A and B are mutually exclusive.

b. $P(A \cup B) = P(A) + P(B) = 0.55$

c. $P(A|B) = P(A \cap B)/P(B) = 0$

4.16 a. No, since $P(A|B) \neq P(A)$.

b. No, since $P(A \cap B) = P(A|B)P(B) = 0.135 \neq 0$.

c. $P((A \cup B)^c) = 1 - P(A \cup B) = 0.185$

4.18 a. $P(B) = 1 - P(B^c) = 0.6$

b. $P(A|B) = P(A \cap B)/P(B) = 0.133$

c. $P(B|A) = P(A \cap B)/P(A) = 0.32$

4.20 a. $P(A^c|B^c) = P(A^c \cap B^c)/P(B^c) = 0.48$

b. $P(A^c \cup B^c) = P(A^c) + P(B^c) - P(A^c \cap B^c) = 0.86$

c. $P(A \cup B) = 1 - P(A^c \cap B^c) = 0.76$

4.22 R = Reduction in unemployment; E = Recession in Europe

a. $P(R^c) = 1 - P(R) = 0.82$

b. $P(R^c \cap E) = P(R^c|E)P(E) = 0.0752$

4.24 F = Foreign student; S = Smoker
$P(S|F) = P(F \cap S)/P(F)$. Thus $P(F) = P(F \cap S)/P(S|F) = 0.10$

4.26 A = Experienced problems shopping online; B = abandoned transaction or switched to a competitor's website; C = contacted customer-service representatives

a. $P(A^c) = 0.13$

b. $P(A \cap B) = P(B|A)P(A) = 0.37$

c. $P(A \cap C) = P(C|A)P(A) = 0.46$

4.28 S = Women face sexual harassment; T = Women use public transportation

a. $P(S \cap T) = P(S|T)P(T) = 0.23$

b. $P(T|S) = P(S \cap T)/P(S) = 0.34$

4.30 F = Foreclosed; H = centered in Arizona, California, Florida, or Nevada
$P(F \cap H) = P(H|F)P(F) = 0.0049$

4.32 a.

	B	B^c	Total
A	0.26	0.34	0.60
A^c	0.14	0.26	0.40
Total	0.40	0.60	1.00

b. $P(A) = 0.60$

c. $P(A \cap B) = 0.26$

d. $P(A|B) = P(A \cap B)/P(B) = 0.65$

e. $P(B|A^c) = P(A^c \cap B)/P(A^c) = 0.35$

f. No, since $P(A \cap B) = 0.26 \neq 0$.

g. No, since $P(A|B) \neq P(A)$.

4.34 a.

	IT	G	Total
Yes	0.2214	0.3657	0.5871
No	0.2071	0.2057	0.4129
Total	0.4286	0.5714	1

b. $P(\text{IT}) = 0.4286$

c. $P(\text{Yes}) = 0.5871$

d. $P(\text{IT}|\text{Yes}) = P(\text{Yes} \cap \text{IT})/P(\text{Yes}) = 0.3771$

e. $P(\text{Yes}|G) = P(\text{Yes} \cap G)/P(G) = 0.64$

f. No, since $P(\text{IT}|\text{Yes}) \neq P(\text{IT})$.

4.36 a.

	Vaccinated (V)	Dummy Shot (D)	Total
Infected (I)	0.016	0.014	0.030
Not Infected	0.477	0.493	0.970
Total	0.493	0.507	1

b. $P(V) = 0.493$

c. $P(I) = 0.03$

d. $P(I|V) = 0.03$

e. Yes, since $P(I|V) = P(I) = 0.03$.

4.38 L = Like it, M = man, W = woman, A = American, B = European, C = Asian

a. $P(L|M) = 480/(480 + 520) = 0.48$

b. $P(L|C) = (120 + 180)/500 = 0.60$

c. BW = European woman; $P(L^c|BW) = 190/(310 + 190) = 0.38$

d. AM = American man; $P(L^c|AM) = 290/(210 + 290) = 0.58$

e. i. America: $P(L|M) = 210/(210 + 290) = 0.42 \neq P(L) = (210 + 370)/1200 = 0.48$; not independent

ii. Europe: $P(L|M) = 150/(150 + 150) = 0.50 \neq P(L) = (150 + 310)/800 = 0.58$; not independent

iii. Asia: $P(L|M) = 120/(120 + 80) = 0.60 = P(L) = (120 + 180)/500$; independent

f. $P(L|M) = 480/(480 + 520) = 0.48 \neq P(L) = (480 + 860)/2,500 = 0.54$; not independent. Women tend to like the perfume more than men.

4.40 a. $P(B^c) = 0.40$

b. $P(A \cap B) = P(A|B)P(B) = 0.48$
$P(A \cap B^c) = P(A|B^c)P(B^c) = 0.04$

c. $P(A) = P(A \cap B) + P(A \cap B^c) = 0.52$

d. $P(B|A) = P(A \cap B)/P(A) = 0.9231$

4.42

Prior Probabilities	Conditional Probabilities	Joint Probabilities	Posterior Probabilities
$P(B_1) = 0.1$	$P(A|B_1) = 0.4$	$P(A \cap B_1) = 0.04$	$P(B_1|A) = 0.06$
$P(B_2) = 0.6$	$P(A|B_2) = 0.6$	$P(A \cap B_2) = 0.36$	$P(B_2|A) = 0.56$
$P(B_3) = 0.3$	$P(A|B_3) = 0.8$	$P(A \cap B_3) = 0.24$	$P(B_3|A) = 0.38$
Total = 1		$P(A) = 0.64$	Total = 1

4.44 D = Experience a decline; N = Ratio is negative
$P(N) = P(N \cap D) + P(N \cap D^c) = P(N|D)P(D) + P(N|D^c)P(D^c) = 0.26$. Then, $P(D|N) = P(N \cap D)/P(N) = 0.54$

4.46 F = Fit to play; N = Not fit to play; S = Somewhat fit to play
   a. $P(W) = P(W|F)P(F) + P(W|S)P(S) + P(W|N)P(N)$
      $= 0.62$
   b. $P(F|W) = P(W \cap F)/P(W) = 0.52$

4.48 a. $8! = 40{,}320$; $6! = 720$
   b. $8!/(2! \, 6!) = 28$
   c. $8!/2! = 20{,}160$

4.50 $8! = 40{,}320$

4.52 a. $10!/(5!5!) = 252$
   b. $10!/5! = 30{,}240$

4.54 U = US equity; F = Foreign equity
   a. $P(U|F) = P(U \cap F)/P(F) = 0.8$
   b. $P((U \cup F)^c) = 1 - P(U \cup F) = 0.2$

4.56 The odds for a fight occurring during the game are 5.25 to 1.

4.58 U = Unemployed eligible worker; F = Female eligible worker; M = Male eligible worker
   a. $P(M|U) = P(M \cap U)/P(U) = P(U|M)P(M)/P(U) = 0.538$
   b. $P(F|U) = P(F \cap U)/P(U) = P(U|F)P(F)/P(U) = 0.395$

4.60

	Survived (S)	Did not Survive (S^c)	Total
Day or Evening (D)	0.1338	0.5417	0.6755
Graveyard Shift (G)	0.0477	0.2768	0.3245
Total	0.1815	0.8185	1.00

   a. $P(G) = 0.3245$
   b. $P(S) = 0.1815$
   c. $P(S|G) = P(S \cap G)/P(G) = 0.1470$
   d. $P(G|S) = P(S \cap G)/P(S) = 0.2628$
   e. No, since $P(S|G) \neq P(S)$

4.62 W = US economy performs well; P = US economy performs poorly; A = Asian countries perform well
   a. $P(W \cap A) = P(A|W)P(A) = 0.32$
   b. $P(A) = P(A \cap W) + P(A \cap P) = P(A \cap W) + P(A|P) \times P(P)$
      $= 0.50$
   c. $P(W|A) = P(A \cap W)/P(A) = 0.64$

Chapter 5

5.2 a. $P(X = 10) = 0.45$
   b.

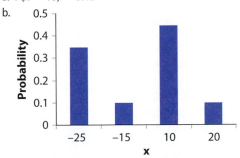

   The distribution is not symmetric.
   c. $P(X < 0) = 0.45$
   d. $P(X > -20) = 0.65$
   e. $P(X < 20) = 0.90$

5.4 a. $P(X \leq 0) = 0.5$
   b. $P(X = 50) = 0.25$
   c. Yes. The distribution has a finite number of values, each with an equal probability of occurring.

5.6 a.

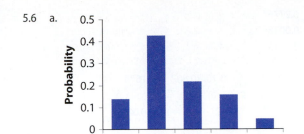

The analyst has a pessimistic view of this equity fund.

   b.

Performance	Cumulative Probability
1 (Very poor)	0.14
2 (Poor)	0.57
3 (Neutral)	0.79
4 (Good)	0.95
5 (Very good)	1

   c. $P(X \geq 4) = 0.21$

5.8 a. $P(62 \leq X \leq 65) = 0.40$
   b. $P(X \geq 62) = 0.65$

5.10 $E(X) = 10.75$;
   $\sigma^2 = 28.19$; $\sigma = 5.31$

5.12 a. $E(X) = 1$
   b. $\sigma^2 = 31.5$; $\sigma = 5.61$

5.14 $E(X) = 2.2$

5.16 a. $E(X) = \$3{,}150$
   b. If Victor is risk neutral, he should not buy the warranty. The decision is not clear-cut if he is risk averse.

5.18 a. $E(R) = 6\%$;
   $\sigma^2 = 124$; $\sigma = 11.14$
   b. $E(R) = 6\%$;
   $\sigma^2 = 964$; $\sigma = 31.05$
   c. Pick Fund 1; while both have the same expected return, Fund 1 has a smaller standard deviation.

5.20 $w_X = 0.45$; $w_Y = 0.55$

5.22 a. $w_X = 0.4$; $w_Y = 0.6$
   b. $E(R) = 10.4$
   c. $\sigma^2 = 213.12$; $\sigma = 14.60$

5.24 a. $E(R) = 11.6$;
   $\sigma^2 = 309.66$
   b. $E(R) = 10$;
   $\sigma^2 = 243.36$
   c. Both portfolios offer higher expected returns, but both also have a higher variance than the bond fund (with a variance of $14^2 = 196$).

5.26 a. $\frac{5!}{0!5!} (0.35)^0 (0.65)^5 = 0.1160$
   b. $\frac{5!}{1!4!} (0.35)^1 (0.65)^4 = 0.3124$
   c. $P(X = 0) + P(X = 1) = 0.4284$

5.28 a. $P(X = 4) = \frac{8!}{4!4!} (0.32)^4 (0.68)^4 = 0.1569$
   b. $P(X = 4) + P(X = 5) = 0.2160$
   c. $P(X = 3) + P(X = 4) + P(X = 5) = 0.4828$

5.30 a. 0.2776
   b. 0.0038
   c. 0.1348
   d. 0.4630

5.32 a. $P(X = 0) = \frac{8!}{0!8!}(0.20)^0(0.80)^8 = 0.1678$
   b. $P(X \leq 2) = P(X = 0) + P(X = 1) + P(X = 2) = 0.7969$
   c. $P(X \geq 7) = P(X = 7) + P(X = 8) = 0.0001$
   d. $E(X) = np = 1.6$
   e. $\sigma^2 = npq = 1.28; \sigma = 1.13$

5.34 a. $P(X < 5) = P(X = 0) + P(X = 1) + P(X = 2) + P(X = 3) + P(X = 4) = 0.9431$
   b. 0.6078

5.36 a. $P(X = 1) = \frac{6!}{1!5!}(0.76)^1(0.24)^5 = 0.0036$
   b. $P(X \geq 5) = P(X = 5) + P(X = 6) = 0.5578$
   c. $P(X < 2) = P(X = 0) + P(X = 1) = 0.0038$
   d. $E(X) = np = 4.56; P(X \geq 5) = 0.5578$ (from b.)

5.38 a. $p = 0.50; P(X > 2) = 0.3125$
   b. $p = 0.63; P(X > 2) = 0.5276$
   c. $p = 0.36; P(X > 2) = 0.1362$

5.40 a. $P(X = 10) = 0.1171$
   b. $P(X \leq 10) = 0.8725$
   c. $P(X \geq 15) = 0.0016$

5.42 a. $\frac{e^{-1.5}1.5^1}{1!} = 0.3347$
   b. $\frac{e^{-1.5}1.5^2}{2!} = 0.2510$
   c. $1 - [P(X = 0) + P(X = 1)] = 0.4422$

5.44 a. $\mu = \frac{8}{2} = 4$
   b. $P(X \geq 2) = 1 - [P(X = 0) + P(X = 1)] = 0.9084$
   c. $\mu = 16$
   d. $P(X = 10) = 0.0341$

5.46 a. 0.0661
   b. 0.5297
   c. 0.0446
   d. 0.4905

5.48 a. $\mu = 6; P(X = 2) = 0.0446$
   b. $\mu = 6; P(X \geq 2) = 1 - [P(X = 0) + P(X = 1)] = 0.9826$
   c. $\mu = 60; P(X = 40) = 0.0014$

5.50 a. $\mu = 2; P(X > 2) = 1 - [P(X = 0) + P(X = 1) + P(X = 2)] = 0.3233$
   b. $\mu = 10; P(X = 6) = 0.0631$
   c. $\mu = 360$

5.52 a. $P(X \leq 425) = 0.8980$
   b. $P(X \geq 375) = 0.8998$

5.54 a. $\frac{\frac{3!}{0!3!} \times \frac{22!}{4!18!}}{\frac{25!}{4!21!}} = 0.5783$
   b. $\frac{\frac{3!}{1!2!} \times \frac{22!}{3!19!}}{\frac{25!}{4!21!}} = 0.3652$
   c. $P(X = 0) + P(X = 1) = 0.9435$

5.56 $P(X = 0) = \frac{\frac{2!}{0!2!} \times \frac{10!}{3!7!}}{\frac{12!}{3!9!}} = 0.5455; \mu = 0.5; \sigma = 0.5839$

5.58 $P(X \geq 8) = 0.0777; \mu = 5; \sigma = 1.74$

5.60 a. $P(X = 3) = \frac{\frac{12!}{3!9!} \times \frac{6!}{0!6!}}{\frac{18!}{3!15!}} = 0.2696$
   b. $P(X \geq 2) = 1 - [P(X = 0) + P(X = 1)] = 0.7549$

5.62 $P(X = 2) = \frac{\frac{4!}{2!2!} \times \frac{16!}{0!16!}}{\frac{20!}{2!18!}} = 0.0316$

5.64 a. $P(X = 2) = 0.0495$
   b. $P(X = 5) = 0.0000002$
   c. $P(X = 1) = 0.0256$
   d. 0.00000000512

5.66 a. $E(R) = 2$
   b. $\sigma^2 = 101; \sigma = 10.05$

5.68 a. $E(R) = 6.75$
   b. $\sigma^2 = 33; \sigma = 5.74$

5.70 a. $P(X = 5) = 0.0014$
   b. $P(X = 0) = 0.2073$

5.72 a. $P(X = 10) = 0.0272$
   b. $P(10 \leq X \leq 20) = 0.0451$
   c. $P(X \leq 8) = 0.8996$

5.74 a. $P(X \geq 5) = 0.5595$
   b. $P(X \leq 4) = 0.4405$

5.76 a. $P(X = 6) = 0.0115$
   b. $P(X \geq 5) = 0.0647$
   c. $P(X \leq 2) = 0.5206$
   d. $E(X) = 2.5$

Chapter 6

6.2 a. 0.30
   b. 0.16
   c. 0.70

6.4 a. $f(x) = 0.0333$
   b. $\mu = 20; \sigma^2 = 75; \sigma = 8.66$
   c. $P(X > 10) = 0.8325$

6.6 a. $\mu = 20; \sigma^2 = 33.33; \sigma = 5.77$
   b. $f(x) = 0.05; P(X > 22) = 0.4$
   c. $P(15 \leq X \leq 23) = 0.4$

6.8 a. $\mu = 16$
   b. $f(x) = 0.125; P(X < 15.5) = 0.4375$
   c. $P(X > 14) = 0.75$

6.10 $f(x) = 0.11; P(X > 10) = 0.67$

6.12 a. $1 - 0.9066 = 0.0934$
   b. 0.0934
   c. $0.9911 - 0.9066 = 0.0845$
   d. $0.9911 - 0.0934 = 0.8977$

6.14 a. $0.4090 - 0.2514 = 0.1576$
   b. $0.9750 - 0.5 = 0.4750$
   c. $0.5 - 0.1003 = 0.3997$
   d. $\approx 1 - 1 = 0$

6.16 a. $z = -1.27$
   b. $0.5 - 0.1772 = 0.3228; z = -0.46$
   c. $1 - 0.9929 = 0.0071; z = -2.45$
   d. $0.3368 + 0.6554 = 0.9922; z = 2.42$

6.18 a. About 68%
   b. About 2.5%

6.20 a. About 95%

    b. About 2.5%; $(82)(0.025) = 2.05$; approx. 2 games

6.22 a. $P(X \leq 0) = P(Z \leq -2.5) = 0.0062$

    b. $P(X > 2) = P(Z > -2) = 1 - 0.0228 = 0.9772$

    c. $P(4 \leq X \leq 10) = P(-1.5 \leq Z \leq 0) = 0.5 - 0.0668 = 0.4332$

    d. $P(6 \leq X \leq 14) = P(-1 \leq Z \leq 1) = 0.8413 - 0.1587 = 0.6826$

6.24 a. $P(X > 7.6) = P(Z > 2.55) = 1 - 0.9946 = 0.0054$

    b. $P(7.4 \leq X \leq 10.6) = P(2.45 \leq Z \leq 4.05)$
                             $= 1 - 0.9929 = 0.0071$

    c. $z = 1.96; x = 6.42$

    d. $P(X < x) = 0.0057; z = -2.53; x = -2.56$

6.26 a. $z = 1.28; \mu = 130.8$

    b. $\mu = 118$

    c. $\sigma = 10.94$

    d. $\sigma = 17.19$

6.28 a. $P(X > 8) = P(Z > 1.5) = 1 - 0.9332 = 0.0668$

    b. $P(X < 6) = P(Z < -0.17) = 0.4325$

    c. $P(6 \leq X \leq 8) = P(-0.17 \leq Z \leq 1.5) = 0.9332 - 0.4325$
                             $= 0.5007$

6.30 a. $P(X > 19) = P(Z > -1.5) = 1 - 0.0668 = 0.9332$

    b. $P(X > 19) = P(Z > 1.5) = 1 - 0.9332 = 0.0668$

    c. $P(23 \leq X \leq 25) = P(0.5 \leq Z \leq 1.5) = 0.9332 - 0.6915$
                             $= 0.2417$

    d. $P(23 \leq X \leq 25) = P(3.5 \leq Z \leq 4.5) \approx 1 - 0.9998 = 0.0002$

6.32 a. $P(10 \leq X \leq 20) = P(-0.75 \leq Z \leq 0.5) = 0.6915 - 0.2266$
                             $= 0.4649$

    b. $P(X > 24) + P(X < 6) = P(Z > 1) + P(Z < -1.25)$
                             $= 0.1587 + 0.1056 = 0.2643$

6.34 $P(X \leq 28) = P(Z \leq z) = 0.975; z = 1.96; \sigma = 1.53$

6.36 a. $P(50 \leq X \leq 80) = P(-0.5 \leq Z \leq 1) = 0.8413 - 0.3085$
                             $= 0.5328$

    b. $P(20 \leq X \leq 40) = P(-2 \leq Z \leq -1) = 0.1587 - 0.0228$
                             $= 0.1359$

    c. $P(X < x) = 0.85; z = 1.04; x = 80.8$

    d. $P(X < x) = 0.10; z = -1.28; x = 34.4$

6.38 $P(X \leq 0) = 0.10; z = -1.28; \sigma = 4.375$

6.40 a. Risky fund: $P(X < 0) = P(Z < -0.57) = 0.2843$; Less risky fund: $P(X < 0) = P(Z < -0.8) = 0.2119$; Pick the less risky fund.

    b. Risky fund: $P(X > 8) = P(Z > 0) = 0.5$; Less risky fund: $P(X > 8) = P(Z > 0.8) = 1 - 0.7881 = 0.2119$; Pick the riskier fund.

6.42 a. $\lambda = 0.04; SD(X) = 25$

    b. $(1 - e^{-0.04(30)}) - (1 - e^{-0.04(20)}) = 0.1481$

    c. $(1 - e^{-0.04(35)}) - (1 - e^{-0.04(15)}) = 0.3022$

6.44 a. $\mu_Y = 55; \sigma_Y^2 = 19,046$

    b. $\mu_Y = 403; \sigma_Y^2 = 1,039,849$

    c. $\mu_Y = 665; \sigma_Y^2 = 8,443,697$

6.46 a. $P(Y \leq 7.5) = P(X \leq 2.01) = P(Z \leq 0.26) = 0.6026$

    b. $P(8 < Y < 9) = P(2.08 < X < 2.20) = P(0.35 < Z < 0.50)$
             $= 0.0547$

    c. $P(Y < y) = 0.9; z = 1.28; x = 2.824; y = 16.84$

6.48 a. $\lambda = 0.1667; SD(X) = 6$

    b. No, the prob. of each customer arriving is independent of other customers

    c. $P(X \leq 5) = 1 - e^{-0.1667(5)} = 0.5655$

    d. $P(X > 30) = 1 - (1 - e^{-0.1667(30)}) = 0.0067$

6.50 a. $\mu = 10.5564; \sigma^2 = 0.0617; \sigma = 0.2485$

    b. $P(Y > 39,626) = P(X > 10.5872) = P(Z > 0.12)$
         $= 0.4522$

    c. $P(Y < 20,000) = P(X < 9.9035) = P(Z < -2.63)$
         $= 0.0043$

    d. $z = 0.67; x = 10.7230; y = 45,388$

6.52 a. $\mu = 3; Var(X) = 1.33$

    b. $f(x) = 0.25; P(X > 4) = 0.25; 25\%$

    c. $P(X < 2.5) = 0.375; 37.5\%$

6.54 a. $P(80 \leq X \leq 90) = P(0.1 \leq Z \leq 1.1) = 0.8643 - 0.5398$
         $= 0.3245$

    b. $P(120 \leq X \leq 139) = P(-0.29 \leq Z \leq 0.82) = 0.7939 -$
         $0.3859 = 0.4080$

6.56 a. $P(X > 50) = P(Z > 2.04) = 0.0207$

    b. $P(X > 50) = P(Z > 1.86) = 0.0314$

    c. Women

6.58 a. $E(X) = 15, \lambda = 0.0667$

    b. $P(X < 10) = 1 - e^{-0.0667(10)} = 0.4868$

    c. $P(X > 25) = 1 - (1 - e^{-0.0667(25)}) = 0.1887$

6.60 a. $P(X < 4) = P(Z < -1) = 0.1587$

    b. $P(Y < 4) = P(X < 1.3863) = P(Z < -1.09) = 0.1379$

    c. The probability is higher if the relief time is normally distributed.

Chapter 7

7.2 Nonresponse bias if some people are less likely to stop at the booth. Selection bias since the booth is only open on the weekend.

7.4 a. Nonresponse bias if the people who respond are systematically different from those who do not respond.

    b. Selection bias since those who frequent the store in the morning are likely to prefer an earlier opening time.

    c. Selection bias since not everyone reads a newspaper. Nonresponse bias since people who respond may be systematically different.

7.6 a. Both sample means will be normally distributed since the population is normally distributed.

    b. Yes

    c. $n = 20: P(\overline{X} < 12.5) = P(Z < 1.49) = 0.9319$
        $n = 40: P(\overline{X} < 12.5) = P(Z < 2.11) = 0.9826$

7.8 a. $E(\overline{X}) = 80; SD(\overline{X}) = \frac{14}{\sqrt{100}} = 1.4$

    b. $P(77 \leq \overline{X} \leq 85) = P(-2.14 \leq Z \leq 3.57) = 0.9998 - 0.0162$
        $= 0.9836$

    c. $P(\overline{X} > 84) = P(Z > 2.86) = 1 - 0.9979 = 0.0021$

7.10 a. $P(\overline{X} > 105) = P(Z > 1.77) = 1 - 0.9616 = 0.0384$

    b. $P(\overline{X} < 95) = P(Z < -1.77) = 0.0384$

    c. $P(95 \leq \overline{X} \leq 105) = 0.9616 - 0.0384 = 0.9232$

7.12 a. $P(\overline{X} \geq 18) = P(Z \geq 1.85) = 1 - 0.9678 = 0.0322$

    b. $P(\overline{X} \geq 17.5) = P(Z \geq 2.03) = 1 - 0.9788 = 0.0212$

    c. Janice; her findings are more likely if a representative sample is used.

7.14. a. The sample mean has a normal distribution because the population is normally distributed.

b. $P(\overline{X} > 25) = P(Z > 2.4) = 1 - 0.9918 = 0.0082$

c. $P(18 \le \overline{X} \le 24) = P(-3.20 \le Z \le 1.60) = 0.9452 - 0.0007$
$= 0.9445$

7.16. a. $E(\overline{P}) = 0.68$; $SD(\overline{P}) = \sqrt{\dfrac{0.68(1 - 0.68)}{20}} = 0.1043$; Yes, since
$np = 13.6 > 5$ and $n(1 - p) = 6.4 > 5$.

b. $E(\overline{P}) = 0.68$; $SD(\overline{P}) = \sqrt{\dfrac{0.68(1 - 0.68)}{50}} = 0.066$; Yes, since
$np = 34 > 5$ and $n(1 - p) = 16 > 5$.

7.18. a. $E(\overline{P}) = 0.75$; $SD(\overline{P}) = \sqrt{\dfrac{0.75(1 - 0.75)}{200}} = 0.0306$

b. $P(0.7 \le \overline{P} \le 0.8) = P(-1.63 \le Z \le 1.63)$
$= 0.9484 - 0.0516 = 0.8968$

c. $P(\overline{P} < 0.7) = P(Z < -1.63) = 0.0516$

7.20. a. Yes, since $np = 34 > 5$ and $n(1 - p) = 166 > 5$.

b. $P(\overline{P} > 0.2) = P(Z > 1.13) = 1 - 0.8708 = 0.1292$

7.22. a. $P(\overline{P} < 0.3) = P(Z < 1.29) = 0.9015$

b. $P(\overline{P} > 0.75) = P(Z > 0.32) = 1 - 0.6255 = 0.3745$

7.24. a. $P(\overline{P} > 0.20) = P(Z > -0.50) = 1 - 0.3085 = 0.6915$

b. $P(\overline{P} > 0.20) = P(Z > -1.01) = 1 - 0.1562 = 0.8438$

c. The higher sample size makes less extreme sample statistics more likely.

7.26. a. $E(\overline{X}) = 220$; $SD(\overline{X}) = \sqrt{\dfrac{324}{70}} \sqrt{\dfrac{500 - 70}{500 - 1}} = 1.997$; Yes, since
$70 > 500(0.05) = 25$.

b. $P(\overline{X} < 210) = P(Z < -5.01) \approx 0$

c. $P(215 \le \overline{X} \le 230) = P(-2.50 \le Z \le 5.01) \approx 1 - 0.0062$
$= 0.9938$

7.28. a. $E(\overline{P}) = 0.46$; $SD(\overline{P}) = \sqrt{\dfrac{0.46(1 - 0.46)}{80}} \sqrt{\dfrac{600 - 80}{600 - 1}} = 0.0519$;
Yes, since $80 > 600(0.05) = 30$.

b. $P(\overline{P} < 0.40) = P(Z < -1.16) = 0.1230$

7.30. a. No, since $12 < 500(0.005) = 25$.

b. No, since $n < 30$ and the population is not necessarily normally distributed.

c. $E(\overline{X}) = 10.32$; $SD(\overline{X}) = \dfrac{9.78}{\sqrt{12}} = 2.823$

d. No, since the sample mean is not normally distributed (see part b).

7.32 $P(\overline{P} > 0.625) = P(Z > -1.12) = 1 - 0.1314 = 0.8686$

7.34. a.

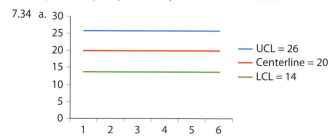

b.

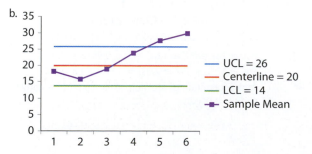

c. The last two points are outside the control limits. The upward trend suggests the process is becoming out of control and should be adjusted.

7.36. a.

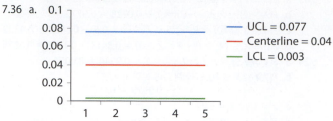

b.

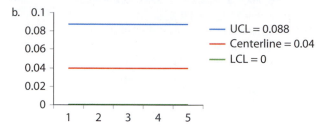

c. The control limits have a larger spread with smaller sample sizes.

7.38. a.

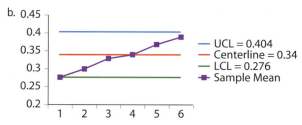

b.

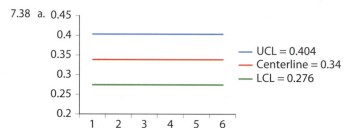

c. No points outside the control limits. The upward trend, however, suggests the process may become out of control.

7.40. a.

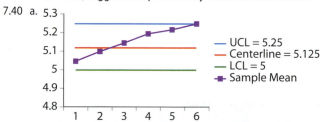

b. There are no points outside the control limits. The upward trend, however, suggests the process may become out of control

7.42. a.

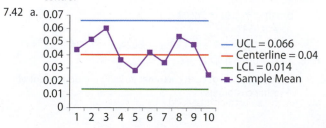

b. Yes. No points outside the control limits and no apparent trend.

7.44 a.
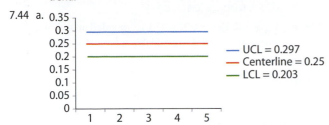

b. Yes, since $240/750 = 0.32$, which is outside the control limits.

7.46 a. Selection bias could occur if beachgoers tend to walk more.

b. Nonresponse bias due to differences in people who respond to mail.

c. Selection bias because it excludes those without Internet access or computer savvy. Also, some nonresponse bias.

d. Selection bias occurs since those in hospitals probably have different walking behavior than those outside hospitals.

7.48 a. $P(\overline{X} > 20) = P(Z > -2.83) = 1 - 0.0023 = 0.9977$

b. $P(\overline{X} < 15) = P(Z < -2.24) = 0.0125$

7.50 a. $P(X < 79) = P(Z < -0.5) = 0.3085$

b. $P(\overline{X} < 79) = P(Z < -1.58) = 0.0571$

c. $P(\overline{X} < 79) = P(Z < -2.74) = 0.0031$

7.52 a. $P(\overline{X} > 25{,}000) = P(Z > 2.57) = 1 - 0.9949 = 0.0051$

b. $P(\overline{X} < 22{,}000) = P(Z < -1.68) = 0.0465$

c. $P(20{,}686 \le \overline{X} \le 25{,}686) = P(-3.54 \le Z \le 3.54)$
$= 0.9998 - 0.0002 = 0.9996$

7.54 a. $P(\overline{P} > 0.8) = P(Z > 0.87) = 1 - 0.8078 = 0.1922$

b. $P(\overline{P} < 0.7) = P(Z < -2.04) = 0.0207$

7.56 a. $P(\overline{P} > 0.5) = P(Z > 0.71) = 1 - 0.7611 = 0.2389$

b. $P(\overline{P} > 0.5) = P(Z > 0.28) = 1 - 0.6103 = 0.3897$

7.58 a.
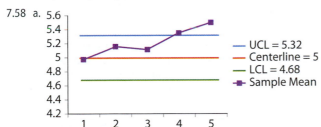

b. The last two points are outside the control limits. The upward trend suggests the process is out of control and needs to be adjusted.

7.60 a.
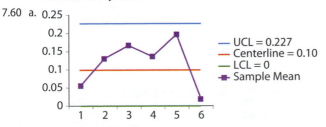

No adjustments needed.

b.
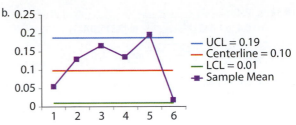

Week 5 is slightly above the control limit. The firm may want to inspect the machine.

Chapter 8

8.2 $\overline{x} = -2.33$

8.4 a. $\overline{p} = 0.75$

b. $\overline{p} = 0.25$

8.6 $\overline{x} = 7.89$

8.8 a. $\overline{p} = 0.30$

b. $\overline{p} = 0.10$

8.10 a. $\alpha/2 = 0.055; z_{0.055} = 1.60$

b. $\alpha/2 = 0.04; z_{0.04} = 1.75$

c. $\alpha/2 = 0.02; z_{0.02} = 2.05$

8.12 a. Yes, $n = 64 > 30$.

b. $1.96\left(\frac{26.8}{\sqrt{64}}\right) = 6.57$

c. $1.96\left(\frac{26.8}{\sqrt{225}}\right) = 3.50$

d. The one with the smaller sample size.

8.14 a. $\overline{x} = 78.1$

b. $1.645\left(\frac{4.5}{\sqrt{50}}\right) = 1.05$

c. 78.1 ± 1.05, or $[77.05, 79.15]$

8.16 a. $6.4 \pm 1.96 \frac{1.8}{\sqrt{80}}$, or $[6.01, 6.79]$

b. Yes, because the value 7 does not fall in the interval.

8.18 a. $2.575\left(\frac{500}{\sqrt{100}}\right) = 128.75$

b. 7790 ± 128.75, or $[7661.25, 7918.75]$

8.20 a. $t_{0.05,27} = 1.703$

b. $t_{0.025,27} = 2.052$

c. $t_{0.05,14} = 1.761$

d. $t_{0.025,14} = 2.145$

8.22 a. $48.68 \pm 2.131 \frac{5.8}{\sqrt{16}}$, or $[45.59, 51.77]$

b. $48.68 \pm 2.064 \frac{5.8}{\sqrt{16}}$, or $[46.29, 51.07]$

c. A larger sample size leads to a smaller, more precise, interval.

8.24 a. Yes, since the population is normally distributed.

b. $2.110 \frac{9.2}{\sqrt{18}} = 4.58$

c. 12.5 ± 4.58, or $[7.92, 17.08]$

8.26 a. $2.724 \frac{10}{\sqrt{36}} = 4.54$

b. 100 ± 4.54, or $[95.46, 104.54]$

8.28 a. $17.25 \pm 3.499 \frac{5.95}{\sqrt{8}}$, or $[9.89, 24.61]$

b. We must assume the population is normally distributed.

8.30 a. $15.70 \pm 1.943 \frac{5.22}{\sqrt{7}}$, or $[11.87, 19.53]$

8.32 a. Electronic: $9.81 \pm 4.604 \frac{47.24}{\sqrt{5}}$, or $[-87.5, 107.1]$

Utilities: $8.44 \pm 4.604 \frac{25.86}{\sqrt{5}}$, or $[-44.8, 61.7]$

b. The annual returns of both funds follow normal distributions.

8.34 a. 0.4

b. $0.4 \pm 1.645\sqrt{\frac{0.4(1-0.4)}{100}}$, or $[0.319, 0.481]$

c. $0.4 \pm 2.575\sqrt{\frac{0.4(1-0.4)}{100}}$, or $[0.274, 0.526]$

8.36 a. $0.6 \pm 1.96\sqrt{\frac{0.6(1-0.6)}{50}}$, or $[0.46, 0.74]$

b. $0.6 \pm 1.96\sqrt{\frac{0.6(1-0.6)}{200}}$, or $[0.53, 0.67]$; The margin of error falls as the sample size increases.

8.38 a. $0.6 \pm 1.555\sqrt{\frac{0.6(1-0.6)}{30}}$, or $[0.46, 0.74]$

b. $0.6 \pm 2.33\sqrt{\frac{0.6(1-0.6)}{30}}$, or $[0.39, 0.81]$

c. The margin of error rises as the confidence level increases.

8.40 The population parameter of interest is the proportion of Americans who support Arizona's immigration law;

$0.51 \pm 1.96\sqrt{\frac{0.51(1-0.51)}{1079}}$, or $[0.48, 0.54]$

8.42 a. $0.37 \pm 1.645\sqrt{\frac{0.37(1-0.37)}{5324}}$, or $[0.36, 0.38]$

b. $0.37 \pm 2.575\sqrt{\frac{0.37(1-0.37)}{5324}}$, or $[0.35, 0.39]$

c. The margin of error in b. is higher since the confidence level is higher.

8.44 a. $0.44 \pm 1.645\sqrt{\frac{0.44(1-0.44)}{1000}}$, or $[0.41, 0.47]$

b. 0.03

c. $2.575\sqrt{\frac{0.44(1-0.44)}{1000}} = 0.04$

8.46 $0.28 \pm 1.96\sqrt{\frac{0.28(1-0.28)}{140}}$, or $[0.21, 0.35]$

8.48 $n = \left(\frac{1.645 \times 3.5}{1.2}\right)^2 = 23.02$, rounded up to 24

$n = \left(\frac{1.645 \times 3.5}{0.7}\right)^2 = 67.65$, rounded up to 68

8.50 $n = \left(\frac{1.96 \times 40}{10}\right)^2 = 61.47$, rounded up to 62

8.52 $n = \left(\frac{1.96}{0.08}\right)^2 (0.36)(1-0.36) = 138.3$, rounded up to 139. If $D = 0.12$, the required sample size is 62.

8.54 $n = \left(\frac{1.96}{0.06}\right)^2 (0.5)(1-0.5) = 266.78$, rounded up to 267

8.56 a. $n = \left(\frac{1.96 \times 0.206}{0.04}\right)^2 = 101.89$, rounded up to 102

b. $n = \left(\frac{1.96 \times 0.128}{0.04}\right)^2 = 39.34$, rounded up to 40

c. Fund A has a higher standard deviation, thus requiring a larger sample, for the same margin of error.

8.58 $n = \left(\frac{1.96 \times 137.5}{20}\right)^2 = 181.57$, rounded up to 182

8.60 $n = \left(\frac{1.96}{0.06}\right)^2 (0.4)(1-0.4) = 135.42$, rounded up to 136

8.62 $10 \pm 2.262\left(\frac{15}{\sqrt{10}}\right)$, or $[-0.73, 20.73]$

8.64 a. $31.71 \pm 1.943\frac{11.4}{\sqrt{7}}$, or $[23.34, 40.08]$

b. $31.71 \pm 3.707\frac{11.4}{\sqrt{7}}$, or $[15.74, 47.68]$

c. As the confidence level increase, the interval becomes wider and less precise.

8.66 a. $16 \pm 1.96\frac{12}{\sqrt{225}}$, or $[14.43, 17.57]$

b. Yes, since the interval does not include 14.

8.68 $n = \left(\frac{1.645 \times 150}{15}\right)^2 = 270.6$, rounded up to 271

8.70 a. $\bar{x} = 19.35$

b. $19.35 \pm 2.776\frac{36}{\sqrt{5}}$, or $[-25.34, 64.04]$

c. You must assume that the annual returns follow a normal distribution.

8.72 a. $1.96\sqrt{\frac{0.121(1-0.121)}{1235}} = 0.018$

b. 0.121 ± 0.018, or $[0.103, 0.139]$

8.74 $n = \left(\frac{1.645}{0.05}\right)^2 (0.2)(1-0.2) = 173.19$, rounded up to 174. This assumes that $\hat{p} = 0.2$ is a reasonable estimate of p.

Chapter 9

9.2 a. Invalid. The test is about the population parameter μ.

b. Valid

c. Valid

d. Invalid. The null hypothesis must include some form of the equality sign.

9.4 a. Incorrect. We never accept the null hypothesis.

b. Correct.

c. Incorrect. We cannot establish a claim because the null hypothesis is not rejected.

d. Correct.

9.6 a. Type I error is to incorrectly conclude the mean weight is different from 18 ounces. Type II error is to incorrectly conclude the mean weight does not differ from 18 ounces.

b. Type I error is to incorrectly conclude that the stock price increases on more than 60 percent of trading days. Type II error is to incorrectly conclude that the price does not increase on more than 60 percent of trading days.

c. Type I error is to incorrectly conclude that Americans sleep less than 7 hours a day. Type II error is to incorrectly conclude that Americans do not sleep less than 7 hours a day.

9.8 a. Type I error is to incorrectly conclude that the majority of voters support the candidate. Type II error is to incorrectly conclude that the majority of the voters do not support the candidate.

b. Type I error is to incorrectly conclude that the average pizza is less than 10 inches. Type II error is to incorrectly conclude that the average pizza is not less than 10 inches.

c. Type I error is to incorrectly conclude that the average tablet does not contain 250 mg. Type II error is to incorrectly conclude that an average tablet contains 250 mg.

9.10 a. 3%

b. 2%

c. Type I error is to incorrectly conclude that an individual has the disease. Type II error is to incorrectly conclude that an individual does not have the disease.

d. We do not prove that the individual is free of disease if we do not reject the null hypothesis.

9.12 a and b. $z = \frac{13.4 - 12.6}{3.2/\sqrt{25}} = 1.25$; $1.25 < 1.28 = z_{0.10}$; do not reject H_0

c and d. $z = \frac{13.4 - 12.6}{3.2/\sqrt{100}} = 2.5$; $2.5 > 1.28 = z_{0.10}$; reject H_0

9.14 $z = \frac{144 - 150}{28/\sqrt{80}} = -1.92$; p-value $= 0.0274 > 0.01 = \alpha$; do not reject H_0; $0.0274 < 0.05 = \alpha$; reject H_0

9.16 a. ± 1.96

b. $z = \frac{132 - 120}{46/\sqrt{50}} = 1.84$; do not reject H_0

c. ± 1.645

d. Reject H_0.

9.18 a. $H_0: \mu = 120$; $H_A: \mu \neq 120$

b. $z = \frac{114 - 120}{22/\sqrt{36}} = -1.64$, p-value $= 0.101$

c. p-value $= 0.101 > 0.01 = \alpha$; do not reject H_0; cannot conclude that the average breaking distance differs from 120 feet.

d. The critical values are ± 2.575; do not reject H_0.

9.20 a. $H_0: \mu \leq 90$; $H_A: \mu > 90$

b. $z = \frac{95 - 90}{20/\sqrt{40}} = 1.58$; p-value $= 0.0571$

c. No, since we do not reject H_0.

d. $z = 1.58 < 2.33 = z_{0.01}$; we do not reject H_0.

9.22 a. $H_0: \mu \leq 500{,}000$; $H_A: \mu > 500{,}000$

b. p-value $= 0.1681$

c. No, since we do not reject H_0.

9.24 a. $H_0: \mu = 30$; $H_A: \mu \neq 30$

b. p-value $= 0.0164$

c. p-value $= 0.0164 < 0.05 = \alpha$; reject H_0. Yes.

9.26 a. Reject H_0 at $\alpha = 0.10$; do not reject H_0 at $\alpha = 0.01$
b. Reject H_0 at $\alpha = 0.10$; do not reject H_0 at $\alpha = 0.01$
c. Reject H_0 at $\alpha = 0.10$; do not reject H_0 at $\alpha = 0.01$
d. Reject H_0 at $\alpha = 0.10$; do not reject H_0 at $\alpha = 0.01$

9.28 a. Reject H_0 at $\alpha = 0.10$; do not reject H_0 at $\alpha = 0.01$
b. Reject H_0 at $\alpha = 0.10$; do not reject H_0 at $\alpha = 0.01$
c. Reject H_0 at $\alpha = 0.10$; do not reject H_0 at $\alpha = 0.01$
d. Reject H_0 at $\alpha = 0.10$; do not reject H_0 at $\alpha = 0.01$

9.30 a. $t_{23} = \frac{4.8 - 4.5}{0.8/\sqrt{24}} = 1.84$; $0.025 < p$-value < 0.05; reject H_0

b. $t_{23} = 1.84$; $0.05 < p$-value < 0.10; do not reject H_0

9.32 $H_0: \mu = 16$; $H_A: \mu \neq 16$; $t_{31} = \frac{15.2 - 16}{0.6/\sqrt{32}} = -7.54$

a. p-value $< \alpha = 0.01$; reject H_0.

b. $t_{31} = 7.54 > t_{0.005,31} = 2.744$; reject H_0.

9.34 $t_5 = \frac{92.33 - 100}{7.89/\sqrt{6}} = -2.38 > -3.365 = -t_{0.01,5}$; do not reject H_0.

9.36 a. $H_0: \mu \leq 5$; $H_A: \mu > 5$

b. $t_6 = \frac{5.53 - 5}{2.18/\sqrt{7}} = 0.64$; normal population

c. $t_6 = 0.64 < 1.440 = t_{0.10,6}$; do not reject H_0. Do not hire another employee.

d. p-value $> \alpha = 0.10$; do not reject H_0.

9.38 a. $H_0: \mu = 12$; $H_A: \mu \neq 12$

b. No, $n = 48 > 30$.

c. $t_{0.025,47} = 2.012$; reject H_0 if $t_{47} < -2.012$ or $t_{47} > 2.012$

d. $t_{47} = \frac{11.8 - 12}{0.8/\sqrt{48}} = -1.73$; do not reject H_0. Process seems to work fine.

9.40 $H_0: \mu \geq 6$; $H_A: \mu < 6$; $t_{11} = \frac{5.92 - 6}{0.09/\sqrt{12}} = -3.08$;

$0.005 < p$-value < 0.001; reject H_0. The carmaker's goal has been achieved.

9.42 $H_0: \mu \leq 7$; $H_A: \mu > 7$; $t_{33} = \frac{9.6 - 7}{5.2/\sqrt{34}} = 2.92$;

$0.001 < p$-value < 0.005; reject H_0. The mean drop of home prices is greater than 7% in San Diego.

9.44 a. $H_0: \mu = 95$; $H_A: \mu \neq 95$

b. $t_{24} = \frac{96.52 - 95}{10.70/\sqrt{25}} = 0.71$, p-value $= 0.48$

c. p-value $= 0.48 > 0.05 = \alpha$; do not reject H_0. MPG does not significantly differ from 95.

9.46 a. $z = \frac{0.3 - 0.38}{\sqrt{\frac{0.38(1 - 0.38)}{74}}} = -1.42$; p-value $= 0.0778$

b. $z = \frac{0.37 - 0.38}{\sqrt{\frac{0.38(1 - 0.38)}{300}}} = -0.36$; p-value $= 0.3594$

c. $z = \frac{0.34 - 0.38}{\sqrt{\frac{0.38(1 - 0.38)}{50}}} = -0.58$; p-value $= 0.2810$

d. $z = \frac{0.34 - 0.38}{\sqrt{\frac{0.38(1 - 0.38)}{400}}} = -1.65$; p-value $= 0.0495$

9.48 a. $z = \frac{\bar{p} - p_0}{\sqrt{\frac{p_0(1 - p_0)}{n}}} = \frac{0.3 - 0.32}{\sqrt{\frac{0.32(1 - 0.32)}{66}}} = -0.35$;

p-value $= 0.7264$

b. $z = \frac{0.38 - 0.32}{\sqrt{\frac{0.32(1 - 0.32)}{264}}} = 2.09$;

p-value $= 0.0366$

c. $z = \frac{0.40 - 0.32}{\sqrt{\frac{0.32(1 - 0.32)}{40}}} = 1.08$;

p-value $= 0.2802$

d. $z = \frac{0.40 - 0.32}{\sqrt{\frac{0.32(1 - 0.32)}{180}}} = 2.30$;

p-value $= 0.0214$

9.50 a. $z_{0.05} = 1.645$

b. $-z_{0.025} = -1.96$ and $z_{0.025} = 1.96$

c. $-z_{0.05} = -1.645$

9.52 a. $z = \frac{0.4 - 0.45}{\sqrt{\frac{0.45(1 - 0.45)}{320}}} = -1.80 > -2.33 = -z_{0.01}$; do not reject H_0.

b. $-2.575 < z = -1.80 < 2.575$; do not reject H_0.

9.54 $H_0: p \leq 0.5$; $H_A: p > 0.5$; $z = \frac{0.65 - 0.5}{\sqrt{\frac{0.5(1 - 0.5)}{20}}} = 1.34$;

p-value $= 0.0901 > 0.05 = \alpha$; do not reject H_0. Cannot conclude that more than 50% of the observations in a population are below 10.

9.56 a. $H_0: p \leq 0.2$; $H_A: p > 0.2$

b. $z = \frac{0.263 - 0.2}{\sqrt{\frac{0.2(1 - 0.2)}{190}}} = 2.17$

c. p-value $= 0.015 < 0.05 = \alpha$; reject H_0. The concern is supported.

9.58 a. $H_0: p \leq 0.3$; $H_A: p > 0.3$; $z = \frac{0.34 - 0.3}{\sqrt{\frac{0.3(1 - 0.3)}{200}}} = 1.23$;

p-value $= 0.1093 > 0.05 = \alpha$. Do not reject H_0.

b. p-value $= 0.1093 > 0.10 = \alpha$. Do not reject H_0.

c. Cannot conclude that more than 30% of moviegoers return to see movie for a second time.

9.60 $H_0: p \leq 0.5$; $H_A: p > 0.5$; $z = \frac{0.6 - 0.5}{\sqrt{\frac{0.5(1 - 0.5)}{40}}} = 1.26$;

p-value $= 0.1038 > 0.05 = \alpha$; do not reject H_0. The claim is not justified.

9.62 $H_0: p \leq 0.6$; $H_A: p > 0.6$; $z = \frac{\bar{p} - p_0}{\sqrt{\frac{p_0(1 - p_0)}{n}}} = \frac{0.64 - 0.6}{\sqrt{\frac{0.6(1 - 0.6)}{140}}} = 0.97$;

p-value $= 0.166 > 0.01 = \alpha$; do not reject H_0. The claim is not supported.

9.64 a. $H_0: \mu \leq 10$; $H_A: \mu > 10$

b. $t_{17} = \frac{10.8 - 10}{2.4/\sqrt{18}} = 1.41$

c. $t_{0.05,17} = 1.740$

d. $t_{17} = 1.41 < 1.740$; do not reject H_0. The claim is not supported.

9.66 a. $H_0: \mu = 4.37$; $H_A: \mu \neq 4.37$

b. $t_6 = \frac{4.46 - 4.37}{0.27/\sqrt{7}} = 0.88$

c. ± 2.447

d. $-2.447 < t_6 < 2.447$; do not reject H_0. Cannot conclude that rates have changed from the previous week.

9.68 a. $H_0: \mu = 130$; $H_A: \mu \neq 130$

b. $t_{39} = \frac{128.25 - 130}{30.88/\sqrt{40}} = -0.358$

c. p-value $= 0.7222$

d. p-value $= 0.7222 > 0.05 = \alpha$; do not reject H_0. Cannot conclude that average sales differ from \$130 (thousand).

9.70 $H_0: p \geq 0.35$; $H_A: p < 0.35$; $z = \frac{0.33 - 0.35}{\sqrt{\frac{0.35(1 - 0.35)}{1000}}} = -1.33$;

p-value $= 0.0918 > 0.05 = \alpha$; do not reject H_0. The evidence does not support the claim. If $n = 2000$,

$z = \frac{0.33 - 0.35}{\sqrt{\frac{0.35(1 - 0.35)}{2000}}} = -1.88$; p-value $= 0.03 < 0.05 = \alpha$;

reject H_0. The evidence supports the claim.

9.72 a. $H_0: p = 0.23$; $H_A: p \neq 0.23$

b. $z = \frac{0.26 - 0.23}{\sqrt{\frac{0.23(1 - 0.23)}{200}}} = 1.01$; p-value $= 0.3124$

c. p-value $> 0.05 = \alpha$; do not reject H_0. The data are not consistent with Pew Research's findings.

Chapter 10

10.2 a. $t_{0.025,33} = 2.035$; $s_p^2 = 8.71$; 6.3 ± 2.05, or [4.25 to 8.35]

b. $H_0: \mu_1 - \mu_2 = 0$; $H_A: \mu_1 - \mu_2 \neq 0$

c. The interval does not contain 0; reject H_0.

10.4 a. $t_{0.05,20} = 1.725$; $s_p^2 = 13.46$;

$t_{20} = \frac{(\bar{x}_1 - \bar{x}_2) - d_0}{\sqrt{s_p^2\left(\frac{1}{n_1} + \frac{1}{n_2}\right)}} = 1.72$; $t_{20} = 1.72 < 1.725 = t_{0.05,20}$;

do not reject H_0.

b. $t_{20} = 1.72 > 1.356 = t_{0.10,20}$; reject H_0.

10.6 a. $s_p^2 = 358.81$; $t_{38} = \frac{(\bar{x}_1 - \bar{x}_2) - d_0}{\sqrt{s_p^2\left(\frac{1}{n_1} + \frac{1}{n_2}\right)}} = 1.49$

b. $0.10 < p$-value < 0.20; do not reject H_0.

c. $-2.024 < t_{38} < 2.024$; do not reject H_0.

10.8 a. $H_0: \mu_1 - \mu_2 = 0$; $H_A: \mu_1 - \mu_2 \neq 0$

b. $t_{df} = \frac{(\bar{x}_1 - \bar{x}_2) - d_0}{\sqrt{\frac{s_1^2}{n_1} + \frac{s_2^2}{n_2}}} = -1.67$

c. $df = \frac{\left(\frac{s_1^2}{n_1} + \frac{s_2^2}{n_2}\right)^2}{\frac{\left(\frac{s_1^2}{n_1}\right)^2}{n_1 - 1} + \frac{\left(\frac{s_2^2}{n_2}\right)^2}{n_2 - 1}} = 8.74$,

which is rounded down to 8; $0.10 < p$-value < 0.20.

d. Since p-value $> 0.10 = \alpha$, do not reject H_0. Cannot conclude that the population means differ.

10.10 a. $H_0: \mu_1 - \mu_2 \geq 0$; $H_A: \mu_1 - \mu_2 < 0$

b. $z = \frac{(\bar{x}_1 - \bar{x}_2) - d_0}{\sqrt{\frac{\sigma_1^2}{n_1} + \frac{\sigma_2^2}{n_2}}} = -5.81$;

p-value ≈ 0

c. Reject H_0 since p-value $< \alpha = 0.05$; yes

10.12 a. $H_0: \mu_1 - \mu_2 \leq 0$; $H_A: \mu_1 - \mu_2 > 0$

b. $t_{df} = \frac{(\bar{x}_1 - \bar{x}_2) - d_0}{\sqrt{\frac{s_1^2}{n_1} + \frac{s_2^2}{n_2}}} = 0.80$; normal population.

c. $t_{df} = 0.80$; regardless of the value of the degrees of freedom, H_0 will not be rejected. No evidence that the first class outperforms the second.

10.14 a. $H_0: \mu_1 - \mu_2 = 30$; $H_A: \mu_1 - \mu_2 \neq 30$

b. $s_p^2 = 717.04$; $t_{54} = \frac{(\bar{x}_1 - \bar{x}_2) - d_0}{\sqrt{s_p^2\left(\frac{1}{n_1} + \frac{1}{n_2}\right)}} = 2.22$

c. $t_{54} = 2.22 > 1.674 = t_{0.05,54}$; reject H_0. Belief supported.

10.16 a. $H_0: \mu_1 - \mu_2 \leq 0$; $H_A: \mu_1 - \mu_2 > 0$

b. $t_{0.05,58} = 1.672$. Reject H_0 if $t_{58} > 1.672$.

c. $t_{58} = 7.58 > 1.672$; reject H_0. Low-carb dieters lost more weight.

10.18 a. $1.3 \pm 1.729\left(\frac{1.61}{\sqrt{20}}\right) = 1.3 \pm 0.62$, or [0.68, 1.92]

b. Since 0 is not included in the interval, reject H_0. The mean difference is not equal to zero.

10.20 a. $t_{df} = \frac{\bar{d} - d_0}{s_D/\sqrt{n}} = -1.702$

b. $-t_{0.05,11} = -1.796$

c. $t_{11} = -1.702 > -1.796 = -t_{0.05,11}$; do not reject H_0. Cannot conclude that the mean difference is less than 0.

10.22 a. $H_0: \mu_D \leq 0$; $H_A: \mu_D > 0$

b. $t_{34} = \frac{\bar{d} - d_0}{s_D/\sqrt{n}} = 1.87$; $0.025 < p$-value < 0.05

c. p-value $< 0.05 = \alpha$; reject H_0. The mean difference is greater than 0.

d. $t_{0.05,34} = 1.691$, $t_{34} = 1.87 > 1.691$; reject H_0.

10.24 a. $H_0: \mu_D = 0$; $H_A: \mu_D \neq 0$

b. $\bar{d} = -1.86$; $s_D = 2.34$; $t_6 = \frac{\bar{d} - d_0}{s_D/\sqrt{n}} = -2.10$

c. Reject H_0 if $t_6 > 1.943$ or $t_6 < -1.943$.

d. $t_6 = -2.10 < -1.943$, reject H_0. Assertion is supported.

10.26 a. $H_0: \mu_D = 0$; $H_A: \mu_D \neq 0$

b. $\bar{d} = -2166.67$; $s_D = 6177.92$;

$t_5 = \frac{\bar{d} - d_0}{s_D/\sqrt{n}} = -0.86$

c. Critical values are ± 2.571; $-2.571 < t_5 = -0.86 < 2.571$; do not reject H_0. Cannot conclude that appraisers are inconsistent in their estimates.

10.28 a. $H_0: \mu_D \geq 0$; $H_A: \mu_D < 0$

b. $t_7 = -1.71$, p-value $= 0.0653$

c. p-value $> 0.05 = \alpha$; do not reject H_0. Claims not supported.

10.30 $(\bar{p}_1 - \bar{p}_2) \pm z_{\alpha/2}\sqrt{\frac{\bar{p}_1(1 - \bar{p}_1)}{n_1} + \frac{\bar{p}_2(1 - \bar{p}_2)}{n_2}}$

$= 0.03 \pm 0.0818$, or $[-0.1118, 0.0518]$. Since 0 is in the interval, cannot conclude that proportions differ.

10.32 a. $\bar{p}_1 = 0.40$; $\bar{p}_2 = 0.43$; $\bar{p} = \frac{x_1 + x_2}{n_1 + n_2} = 0.4185$;

$z = \frac{\bar{p}_1 - \bar{p}_2}{\sqrt{\bar{p}(1 - \bar{p})\left(\frac{1}{n_1} + \frac{1}{n_2}\right)}} = -0.75$

b. p-value $= 0.4532$

c. p-value $= 0.4532 > 0.05 = \alpha$; do not reject H_0. Cannot conclude that the population proportions differ.

d. $z_{0.025} = 1.96$; $-1.96 < z = -0.75 < 1.96$; do not reject H_0.

10.34 a. $\bar{p}_1 = 0.50$; $\bar{p}_2 = 0.65$; $\bar{p} = \frac{x_1 + x_2}{n_1 + n_2} = 0.5682$;

$z = \frac{\bar{p}_1 - \bar{p}_2}{\sqrt{\bar{p}(1 - \bar{p})\left(\frac{1}{n_1} + \frac{1}{n_2}\right)}} = -5.00$

b. p-value ≈ 0

c. p-value $\approx 0 < 0.05 = \alpha$; reject H_0. Population proportions differ.

10.36 a. $\bar{p}_1 = 0.80; \bar{p}_2 = 0.82; z_{0.025} = 1.96$

$(\bar{p}_1 - \bar{p}_2) \pm z_{\alpha/2} \sqrt{\frac{\bar{p}_1(1-\bar{p}_1)}{n_1} + \frac{\bar{p}_2(1-\bar{p}_2)}{n_2}} = -0.02 \pm 0.0519,$
or $[-0.0719, 0.0319]$

b. $H_0: p_1 - p_2 = 0; H_A: p_1 - p_2 \neq 0$

c. Zero is included in the interval; do not reject H_0. Results do not support study's claim.

10.38 a. $H_0: p_1 - p_2 \leq 0; H_A: p_1 - p_2 > 0$

b. $\bar{p}_1 = 0.27, n_1 = 500; \bar{p}_2 = 0.14, n_2 = 500; \bar{p} = \frac{n_1\bar{p}_1 + n_2\bar{p}_2}{n_1 + n_2} =$

$0.205; z = \frac{\bar{p}_1 - \bar{p}_2}{\sqrt{\bar{p}(1-\bar{p})\left(\frac{1}{n_1} + \frac{1}{n_2}\right)}} = 5.10$

p-value $\approx 0 < 0.05 = \alpha$; reject H_0. The proportion of boys growing out of asthma is more than the corresponding proportion of girls.

c. $H_0: p_1 - p_2 \leq 0.10; H_A: p_1 - p_2 > 0.10$

$z = \frac{(\bar{p}_1 - \bar{p}_2) - d_o}{\sqrt{\frac{\bar{p}_1(1-\bar{p}_1)}{n_1} + \frac{\bar{p}_2(1-\bar{p}_2)}{n_2}}} = 1.19$

$z = 1.19 < 1.645 = z_{0.05}$; do not reject H_0. Cannot conclude that the proportion of boys who grow out of asthma exceeds by more than 0.10 that of girls.

10.40 a. $H_0: p_1 - p_2 \geq 0; H_A: p_1 - p_2 < 0$

$\bar{p}_1 = 0.2769; \bar{p}_2 = 0.3444; \bar{p} = \frac{x_1 + x_2}{n_1 + n_2} = 0.3161;$

$z = \frac{\bar{p}_1 - \bar{p}_2}{\sqrt{\bar{p}(1-\bar{p})\left(\frac{1}{n_1} + \frac{1}{n_2}\right)}} = -1.26$

p-value $= 0.1038 > 0.05 = \alpha$; do not reject H_0. Cannot conclude that the proportion of obese African-American men is less than the proportion of their Caucasian counterparts.

b. $H_0: p_1 - p_2 \leq 0; H_A: p_1 - p_2 > 0$

$\bar{p}_1 = 0.3889; \bar{p}_2 = 0.2583; \bar{p} = \frac{x_1 + x_2}{n_1 + n_2} = 0.3143;$

$z = \frac{\bar{p}_1 - \bar{p}_2}{\sqrt{\bar{p}(1-\bar{p})\left(\frac{1}{n_1} + \frac{1}{n_2}\right)}} = 2.02$

$z = 2.02 > 1.645 = z_{0.05}$; reject H_0. The proportion of obese African-American women is greater than the proportion of their Caucasian counterparts.

c. $H_0: p_1 - p_2 = 0; H_A: p_1 - p_2 \neq 0$

$\bar{p}_1 = 0.3227; \bar{p}_2 = 0.3100; \bar{p} = \frac{x_1 + x_2}{n_1 + n_2} = 0.3154;$

$z = \frac{\bar{p}_1 - \bar{p}_2}{\sqrt{\bar{p}(1-\bar{p})\left(\frac{1}{n_1} + \frac{1}{n_2}\right)}} = 0.31$

$-1.96 < z = 0.31 < 1.96$; do not reject H_0. Cannot conclude that the proportion of obese African-American adults differs from the proportion of their Caucasian counterparts.

10.42 a. $H_0: \mu_1 - \mu_2 \leq 0; H_A: \mu_1 - \mu_2 > 0$

b. $z = \frac{\bar{x}_1 - \bar{x}_2}{\sqrt{\frac{\sigma_1^2}{n_1} + \frac{\sigma_1^2}{n_1}}} = 3.53$

c. p-value $= 0.0002$

d. Since p-value $= 0.0002 < 0.01 = \alpha$, reject H_0. The claim is supported.

10.44 a. $H_0: \mu_D = 0; H_A: \mu_D \neq 0$

b. $\bar{d} = -0.67; s_D = 1.63; t_5 = \frac{\bar{d} - d_o}{s_D/\sqrt{n}} = -1.01$

c. ± 2.571

d. $-2.571 < t_5 = -1.01 < 2.571$; do not reject H_0. Cannot conclude that crop yield with new fertilizer differs from crop yield with old fertilizer.

10.46 a. $H_0: p_1 - p_2 \leq 0; H_A: p_1 - p_2 > 0$

b. $\bar{p}_1 = 0.14, n_1 = 250; \bar{p}_2 = 0.06, n_2 = 200; \bar{p} = \frac{n_1\bar{p}_1 + n_2\bar{p}_2}{n_1 + n_2}$
$= 0.1044$

$z = \frac{\bar{p}_1 - \bar{p}_2}{\sqrt{\bar{p}(1-\bar{p})\left(\frac{1}{n_1} + \frac{1}{n_2}\right)}} = 2.76$

p-value $= 0.0029$.

c. p-value $= 0.0029 < 0.05 = \alpha$; reject H_0. The proportion of females that suffer from asthma is greater than the proportion of males.

10.48 a. $H_0: p_1 - p_2 \leq 0.05; H_A: p_1 - p_2 > 0.05$

b. $z = \frac{\bar{p}_1 - \bar{p}_2 - 0.05}{\sqrt{\frac{\bar{p}_1(1-\bar{p}_1)}{n_1} + \frac{\bar{p}_2(1-\bar{p}_2)}{n_2}}} = 0.42$

c. p-value $= 0.3372 > 0.05 = \alpha$; do not reject H_0. Cannot conclude that the proportion of on-time flights at JFK is more than 5 percentage points higher than that of O'Hare.

d. $z = 0.42 < 1.645 = z_{0.05}$; do not reject H_0.

10.50 a. $H_0: \mu_D \leq 0; H_A: \mu_D > 0$

b. $t_{11} = 2.95$

c. $t_{0.05,11} = 1.80$

d. $t_{11} = 2.95 > 1.80$; reject H_0. Safety program is effective.

Chapter 11

11.2 a. 39.997

b. 37.556

c. 7.434

d. 8.260

11.4 a. $\left[\frac{(25-1)14.44}{36.415}, \frac{(25-1)14.44}{13.848}\right] = [9.52, 25.03]$

b. $\left[\frac{(25-1)14.44}{45.558}, \frac{(25-1)14.44}{9.886}\right] = [7.61, 35.06]$

c. The width of the interval increases with the confidence level.

11.6 a. $\chi_{20}^2 = \frac{(21-1)75}{50} = 30 > 28.412 = \chi_{0.10,20}^2$; reject H_0

b. $\chi_{0.05,20}^2 = 31.410, \chi_{0.95,20}^2 = 10.851; 10.851 < \chi_{20}^2 = 30 < 31.410$; do not reject H_0

11.8 a. $H_0: \sigma^2 \leq 2; H_A: \sigma^2 > 2; s^2 = 2.89;$

$\chi_9^2 = \frac{(10-1)2.89}{2} = 13$; using Excel p-value $=$

$0.16 > 0.10 = \alpha$; do not reject H_0. Cannot conclude that variance is greater than 2.

b. $\chi_9^2 = 13 < 14.684 = \chi_{0.10,9}^2$; do not reject H_0

11.10 a. $\left[\frac{(20-1)0.03}{32.852}, \frac{(20-1)0.03}{8.907}\right] = [0.02, 0.06]$

b. 0.05 is included in interval; cannot conclude that specification is being violated.

11.12 a. $s^2 = 1295.48, s = 35.99$

b. $\left[\frac{(5-1)1295.48}{11.143}, \frac{(5-1)1295.48}{0.484}\right]$

$= [465.04, 10,706.45]$; the interval for the population standard deviation is $[21.56, 103.47]$.

11.14 a. $H_0: \sigma^2 \geq 90,000; H_A: \sigma^2 < 90,000$

b. $s^2 = 30,697; \chi_6^2 = \frac{(7-1)30,967}{90,000} = 2.05$

c. $\chi_6^2 = 2.05 > 0.872 = \chi_{0.99,6}^2$; do not reject H_0. Cannot conclude that the standard deviation is less than 300.

d. $\chi_6^2 = 2.05 < 2.204 = \chi_{0.90,6}^2$; reject H_0. The standard deviation is less than 300.

11.16 a. $H_0: \sigma^2 \leq 10,000; H_A: \sigma^2 > 10,000$

b. $s^2 = 10,527.97; \chi_{35}^2 = \frac{(36-1)10,527.91}{10,000} = 36.85$

c. p-value $= 0.38$

d. p-value $= 0.38 > 0.05 = \alpha$; do not reject H_0. The realtor's claim is not supported.

11.18 a. $s_{Ann Arbor} = 176.11, s_{Davis} = 297.64$

b. Ann Arbor: $\left[\sqrt{\frac{(10-1)176.11^2}{19.023}}, \sqrt{\frac{(10-1)176.11^2}{2.700}}\right] = [121, 322]$

Davis: $\left[\sqrt{\frac{(10-1)297.64^2}{19.023}}, \sqrt{\frac{(10-1)297.64^2}{2.700}}\right] = [205, 543]$

c. Cannot conclude that the standard deviation differs from $200 for Ann Arbor; conclude that it differs from $200 for Davis.

11.20 a. 0.05

b. 0.10

c. 0.025

d. 0.025

11.22 a. $\left[\frac{220}{196}\left(\frac{1}{2.86}\right), \frac{220}{196}(2.65)\right] = [0.39, 2.97]$

b. The interval contains 1, so we cannot conclude that the ratio differs from 1.

11.24 $F_{(13,10)} = \frac{935}{812} = 1.15 < 2.85 = F_{0.05,(13,10)}$; do not reject H_0. Assume sampling from normal populations.

11.26 a. $H_0: \frac{\sigma_2^2}{\sigma_1^2} = 1; H_A: \frac{\sigma_2^2}{\sigma_1^2} \neq 1$

b. $F_{(14,14)} = \frac{0.48}{0.35} = 1.37$

c. $F_{(14,14)} = 1.37 < 2.86 = F_{0.025,(14,14)}$; do not reject H_0

d. We cannot conclude the variances are different. Yes.

11.28 $F_{(4,4)} = \frac{2215.22}{668.68} = 3.31 < 9.6 = F_{0.025,(4,4)}$; do not reject H_0

11.30 a. $H_0: \frac{\sigma_2^2}{\sigma_1^2} = 1; H_A: \frac{\sigma_2^2}{\sigma_1^2} \neq 1$

b. Monthly closing prices are normally distributed.

c. p-value $= 0.1045$

d. p-value $> \alpha = 0.05$; do not reject H_0. Cannot conclude that the variances differ.

11.32 Assume sampling from normal populations. $F_{(9,9)} = \frac{297.64^2}{176.11^2} = 2.86$; p-value $= 0.067 > 0.05 = \alpha$; do not reject H_0. Cannot conclude that the variability in rents in Davis is greater than in Ann Arbor.

11.34 a. $H_0: \sigma^2 \leq 5; H_A: \sigma^2 > 5; \chi_6^2 = \frac{(7-1)11.57}{5} = 13.88$; $0.025 < p$-value < 0.05; p-value $> 0.01 = \alpha$; do not reject H_0. Cannot conclude that the variance exceeds 5.

b. The generic drug prices are normally distributed.

11.36 a. $H_0: \sigma^2 \leq 1,225; H_A: \sigma^2 > 1,225$

b. The population of returns is normally distributed.

c. $\chi_8^2 = \frac{(9-1)2402.48}{1225} = 15.69$

d. 0.047

e. Reject H_0; can conclude that standard deviation is greater than 35.

11.38 a. $H_0: \frac{\sigma_{Hasbro}^2}{\sigma_{Mattel}^2} = 1; H_A: \frac{\sigma_{Hasbro}^2}{\sigma_{Mattel}^2} \neq 1$

b. The growth rates are normally distributed.

c. $F_{0.025,(4,4)} = 9.6; \frac{1}{F_{0.025,(4,4)}} = 0.10$

d. $F_{(4,4)} = \frac{74.16}{43.00} = 1.72$; since $0.10 < F_{(4,4)} < 9.6$; do not reject H_0. Cannot conclude that the standard deviations of growth rates differ.

11.40 a. $H_0: \sigma_1^2/\sigma_2^2 \leq 1, H_A: \sigma_1^2/\sigma_2^2 > 1$

b. $F_{(df_1,df_2)} = F_{(4,4)} = \frac{s_1^2}{s_2^2} = \frac{219,354.8}{78,780.2} = 2.78$

---

c. p-value $= 0.173$

d. p-value $= 0.173 > 0.05 = \alpha$; do not reject H_0. Cannot conclude that variance in revenues is greater in Asia as compared to Latin America.

Chapter 12

12.2 a. H_A: At least one of the $p_i (i = 1, 2, 3)$ differs from its hypothesized value.

b. $\chi_2^2 = 1.043$; p-value > 0.10.

c. p-value $> \alpha = 0.05$; do not reject H_0. Cannot conclude that some proportions differ from hypothesized values.

12.4 $\chi_2^2 = 2.271$; p-value $> \alpha = 0.01$; do not reject H_0.

12.6 a. $H_0: p_1 = 0.37, p_2 = 0.17, p_3 = 0.28, p_4 = 0.18$

H_A: At least one of the $p_i (i = 1, 2, 3, 4)$ differs from its hypothesized value.

b. $\chi_3^2 = 11.16$

c. $\chi_{0.05,3}^2 = 7.815$

d. Reject H_0 since $\chi_3^2 = 11.16 > 7.815$. Can conclude that the proportions from the initial study have changed.

12.8 a. $H_0: p_1 = p_2 = p_3 = 1/3$; H_A: At least one of the $p_i (i = 1, 2, 3)$ differs from $1/3$.

b. $\chi_2^2 = 1.02 < 5.991 = \chi_{0.05,2}^2$; do not reject H_0. No.

c. p-value $> \alpha = 0.05$; do not reject H_0.

12.10 $\chi_2^2 = 2.18$; p-value $> \alpha = 0.05$; do not reject H_0. No.

12.12 a. $\chi_{0.025,4}^2 = 11.143$

b. $\chi_{0.01,8}^2 = 20.090$

12.14 H_0: The two categories are independent; H_A: The two categories are dependent; $\chi_6^2 = 1.25$

a. p-value $> \alpha = 0.01$; do not reject H_0.

b. $\chi_6^2 = 1.25 < 16.812 = \chi_{0.01,6}^2$; do not reject H_0.

12.16 a. H_0: Color preference is independent of gender; H_A: Color preference is dependent on gender

b. $\chi_2^2 = 8.00$

c. $\chi_{0.01,2}^2 = 9.210$

d. $\chi_2^2 = 8.00 < 9.210$; do not reject H_0. No need for targeted ads.

12.18 a. H_0: Optimism among Chinese and age are independent

H_A: Optimism among Chinese and age are dependent

b. $\chi_4^2 = 18.36$; p-value $= 0.001$

c. p-value $< \alpha = 0.01$; reject H_0. Optimism is dependent on age.

12.20 H_0: Breakup reasons and gender are independent

H_A: Breakup reasons and gender are dependent

$\chi_4^2 = 19.46 > 13.277 = \chi_{0.01,4}^2$; reject H_0. Breakup reason is dependent on gender.

12.22 H_0: The data are normally distributed with $\mu = -3.5$ and $\sigma = 9.7$

H_A: The data are not normally distributed with $\mu = -3.5$ and $\sigma = 9.7$

Class	o_i	p_i if normal	e_i
Less than -10	70	0.2514	50.28
-10 up to 0	40	0.3892	77.84
0 up to 10	80	0.2771	55.42
10 or more	10	0.0823	16.46

$\chi_1^2 = 39.57$; p-value $< \alpha = 0.01$; reject H_0.

12.24 a. H_0: The final grades are normally distributed with $\mu = 72$ and $\sigma = 10$

H_A: The final grades are not normally distributed with $\mu = 72$ and $\sigma = 10$

b. $\chi_2^2 = 3.00$

Class	o_i	p_i if normal	e_i
Less than 50	5	0.0139	4.17
50 up to 70	135	0.4068	122.04
70 up to 80	105	0.3674	110.22
80 up to 90	45	0.1760	52.80
90 or above	10	0.0359	10.77

c. $\chi_{0.05,2}^2 = 5.991$

d. $\chi_2^2 = 3.00 < 5.991$; do not reject H_0

12.26 a. H_0: CEO compensation is normally distributed with a mean of \$19.03 million and a standard deviation of \$27.61 million; H_A: CEO compensation is not normally distributed with a mean of \$19.03 million and a standard deviation of \$27.61 million; $\chi_2^2 = 230.91$; p-value $< \alpha = 0.01$; reject H_0

Class	Observed (o_i)	p_i if normal	Expected (e_i)
Less than 5	43	0.3050	72.59
5 up to 10	65	0.0657	15.64
10 up to 15	32	0.0697	16.59
15 up to 20	38	0.0756	17.99
20 or more	60	0.4840	115.19

b. H_0: $S = 0$ and $K = 0$; H_A: $S \neq 0$ or $K \neq 0$; $JB = \chi_2^2 = (n/6)[S^2 + K^2/4] = 13616.09$; p-value ≈ 0; reject H_0

c. Both tests indicate that CEO compensation is not normally distributed.

12.28 a. H_0: $S = 0$ and $K = 0$; H_A: $S \neq 0$ or $K \neq 0$

b. $JB = \chi_2^2 = (n/6)[S^2 + K^2/4] = 1.03$; p-value $= 0.60$

c. p-value $> \alpha = 0.05$; do not reject H_0. Cannot conclude that Home Depot stock prices are not normally distributed.

12.30 a. H_0: $p_1 = 0.40, p_2 = 0.30, p_3 = 0.20, p_4 = 0.10$
H_A: At least one of the p_i ($i = 1, 2, 3, 4$) differs from its hypothesized value

b. $\chi_3^2 = 8.182$

c. $\chi_{0.01,3}^2 = 11.345$

d. $\chi_3^2 = 8.18 < 11.345$; do not reject H_0. Cannot conclude that at least one of the proportions differs from its hypothesized value.

12.32 a. H_0: $p_A = 0.60, p_B = 0.30, p_C = 0.10$
H_A: At least one of the p_i ($i = A, B, C$) differs from its hypothesized value

b. $\chi_2^2 = 25.0$; p-value $\approx 0 < 0.01 = \alpha$; reject H_0. T.V. station's claim is not supported.

12.34 a. H_0: Surviving for discharge is independent of time of cardiac arrest
H_A: Surviving for discharge is dependent of time of cardiac arrest

b. $\chi_1^2 = 333.46$

c. $\chi_{0.01,1}^2 = 6.635$

d. $\chi_1^2 = 333.46 > 6.635$; reject H_0. Surviving for discharge is dependent of the time of the cardiac arrest.

12.36 H_0: Effect on ADHD is independent of treatment
H_A: Effect on ADHD is dependent on treatment
$\chi_1^2 = 0.297 < 3.841 = \chi_{0.05,1}^2$; do not reject H_0.
Cannot conclude that the effect of ADHD depends on treatment.

12.38 H_0: Household's delinquency in payment is independent of type of heating
H_A: Household's delinquency in payment is dependent of type of heating
$\chi_3^2 = 23.82 > 7.815 = \chi_{0.05,3}^2$; reject H_0. Household's delinquency in payment is dependent on type of heating.

12.40 a. H_0: $S = 0$ and $K = 0$; H_A: $S \neq 0$ or $K \neq 0$
$\chi_2^2 = (n/6)[S^2 + K^2/4] = 2.78$; p-value $= 0.2491 > 0.05 = \alpha$; do not reject H_0. Cannot conclude that house prices are not normally distributed.

b. H_0: $S = 0$ and $K = 0$; H_A: $S \neq 0$ or $K \neq 0$
$JB = \chi_2^2 = (n/6)[S^2 + K^2/4] = 1.69$; p-value $= 0.4305 > 0.05 = \alpha$; do not reject H_0. Cannot conclude that square footage is not normally distributed.

Chapter 13

13.2 a. $\bar{\bar{x}} = \frac{-174}{15} = -11.6$

b. $SSTR = \sum_{i=1}^{c} n_i(\bar{x}_i - \bar{\bar{x}})^2 = 16.78$; $MSTR = \frac{16.78}{4-1} = 5.59$

c. $SSE = \sum_{i=1}^{c} (n_i - 1)s_i^2 = 60.56$; $MSE = \frac{60.56}{15-4} = 5.51$

d. H_0: $\mu_A = \mu_B = \mu_C = \mu_D$; H_A: Not all population means are equal

e. $F_{(3,11)} = \frac{MSTR}{MSE} = \frac{5.59}{5.51} = 1.01$

f. p-value > 0.10

g. p-value $> \alpha = 0.10$; do not reject H_0; No significant differences in population means.

13.4

Source of Variation	SS	df	MS	F	F crit at 5%
Between Groups	11.34	3	3.78	3.58	2.77
Within Groups	59.13	56	1.06		
Total	70.47	59			

$F_{(3,56)} = 3.58 > 2.77 = F_{0.05,(3,56)}$; reject H_0. Some population means differ.

13.6 a.

Source of Variation	SS	df	MS	F	p-value	F crit at 10%
Between Groups	548.37	5	109.67	1.37	0.250	1.96
Within Groups	4,321.11	54	80.02			
Total	4,869.48	59				

b. H_0: $\mu_1 = \mu_2 = \mu_3 = \mu_4 = \mu_5 = \mu_6$; H_A: Not all populations means are equal

c. p-value $= 0.250 > 0.10 = \alpha$, do not reject H_0. No significant differences in population means.

13.8 a.

Source of Variation	SS	df	MS	F	p-value	F crit at 5%
Between Groups	174.72	2	87.36	2.81	0.083	3.47
Within Groups	652.40	21	31.07			
Total	827.12	23				

b. $H_0: \mu_1 = \mu_2 = \mu_3$; H_A: Not all populations means are equal

c. p-value $= 0.083 > 0.05 = \alpha$; do not reject H_0. No significant differences in the average whitening effectiveness of the detergents.

13.10 a. $H_0: \mu_{Snork.} = \mu_{Sail} = \mu_{NBoard/Windsurf} = \mu_{Bowl} = \mu_{On-road\ tri} = \mu_{Off-road\ tri}$

H_A: Not all population mean incomes are equal.

b.

Source of Variation	SS	df	MS	F	p-value	F crit at 5%
Between Groups	4,895.15	5	979.03	37.85	0.000	2.62
Within Groups	620.80	24	25.87			
Total	5,515.95	29				

c. $F_{0.05,(5,24)} = 2.62$

d. $F_{(5,24)} = 37.85 > 2.62 = F_{0.05,(5,24)}$; reject H_0. Some mean incomes differ.

13.12 a. $(\bar{x}_i - \bar{x}_j) \pm t_{\alpha/2, n_T - c} \sqrt{MSE\left(\frac{1}{n_i} + \frac{1}{n_j}\right)}$

$\mu_1 - \mu_2$: $[-11.35, -1.05]$

$\mu_1 - \mu_3$: $[-12.86, -1.14]$

$\mu_2 - \mu_3$: $[-6.40, 4.80]$

b. $(\bar{x}_i - \bar{x}_j) \pm q_{\alpha,(c, n_T - c)} \sqrt{\left(\frac{MSE}{2}\right)\left(\frac{1}{n_i} + \frac{1}{n_j}\right)}$

$\mu_1 - \mu_2$: $[-12.46, 0.06]$

$\mu_1 - \mu_3$: $[-14.13, 0.13]$

$\mu_2 - \mu_3$: $[-7.62, 6.02]$

c. The Tukey's HSD approach is preferred because it reduces the probability of Type I error.

13.14 a. $H_0: \mu_1 = \mu_2 = \mu_3$; H_A: Not all population means are equal
p-value $= 0.0006 < 0.05 = \alpha$; reject H_0

b. $(\bar{x}_i - \bar{x}_j) \pm q_{\alpha,(c, n_T - c)} \sqrt{\frac{MSE}{n}}$

$\mu_1 - \mu_2$: $[-1.71, 0.09]$

$\mu_1 - \mu_3$: $[-2.66, -0.86]$*

$\mu_2 - \mu_3$: $[-1.85, -0.05]$*

*indicates a difference between the two corresponding population means

c. μ_1 differs from μ_3; μ_2 differs from μ_3; μ_1 and μ_2 do not significantly differ

13.16 a. $(\bar{x}_i - \bar{x}_j) \pm t_{\alpha/2, n_T - c} \sqrt{MSE\left(\frac{1}{n_i} + \frac{1}{n_j}\right)}$;

$\mu_1 - \mu_2$: $[-12.10, -7.90]$*

$\mu_1 - \mu_3$: $[-9.01, -4.99]$*

$\mu_2 - \mu_3$: $[0.78, 5.22]$*

*indicates a difference between the two corresponding population means

b. $(\bar{x}_i - \bar{x}_j) \pm q_{\alpha,(c, n_T - c)} \sqrt{\left(\frac{MSE}{2}\right)\left(\frac{1}{n_i} + \frac{1}{n_j}\right)}$

$\mu_1 - \mu_2$: $[-12.53, -7.47]$*

$\mu_1 - \mu_3$: $[-9.42, -4.58]$*

$\mu_2 - \mu_3$: $[0.33, 5.67]$*

*indicates a difference between the two corresponding population means

c. The Tukey's HSD approach is preferred because it reduces the probability of Type I error.

d. Store 1 has significantly lower mean time spent on bending, etc. However, more research should be conducted since significant differences exist even in stores where no change in technique occurred.

13.18 a.

Source of Variation	SS	df	MS	F	p-value
Between Groups	7,531,769.00	3	2,510,589.67	69.01	0.000
Within Groups	3,492,385.00	96	36,379.01		
Total	11,024,154.00	99			

b. p-value $\approx 0 < 0.01 = \alpha$; reject H_0. The average annual energy bills are not all the same by region.

c. $(\bar{x}_i - \bar{x}_j) \pm q_{\alpha,(c, n_T - c)} \sqrt{\frac{MSE}{n}}$

$\mu_1 - \mu_2$: $[-999.66, -656.34]$*

$\mu_1 - \mu_3$: $[-448.66, -105.34]$*

$\mu_1 - \mu_4$: $[-438.66, -95.34]$*

$\mu_2 - \mu_3$: $[379.34, 722.66]$*

$\mu_2 - \mu_4$: $[389.34, 732.66]$*

$\mu_3 - \mu_4$: $[-161.66, 181.66]$

*indicates a difference between the two corresponding population means

13.20 a. $H_0: \mu_1 = \mu_2 = \mu_3 = \mu_4$; H_A: Not all of the mean quarterly revenues are the same; $F_{(3,36)} = 0.644 < 2.866 = F_{0.05,(3,36)}$; do not reject H_0

b. No, because H_0 was not rejected in part a.

13.22 a. $SST = \sum_{i=1}^{c} \sum_{j=1}^{r} (x_{ij} - \bar{\bar{x}})^2 = 894.67$; $SSA = r \sum_{i=1}^{c} (\bar{x}_i - \bar{\bar{x}})^2 = 8.67$;

$SSB = c \sum_{j=1}^{r} (\bar{x}_j - \bar{\bar{x}})^2 = 702$; $SSE = SST - (SSA + SSB) = 184$.

b. $MSA = \frac{8.67}{3 - 1} = 4.33$; $MSB = \frac{702}{4 - 1} = 234$;

$MSE = \frac{184.0}{12 - 3 - 4 + 1} = 30.67$

c.

Source of Variation	SS	df	MS	F	F crit at 1%
Rows	702.00	3	234.00	7.63	9.78
Columns	8.67	2	4.33	0.14	10.92
Error	184.00	6	30.67		
Total	894.67	11			

d. $F_{(2,6)} = 0.14 < 10.92 = F_{0.01,(2,6)}$; do not reject H_0. Column means do not significantly differ.

e. $F_{(3,6)} = 7.63 < 9.78 = F_{0.01,(3,6)}$; do not reject H_0. Row means do not significantly differ.

13.24 a.

Source of Variation	SS	df	MS	F	F crit at 1%
Rows	532.3	2	266.15	4.26	10.92
Columns	723.9	3	241.30	3.87	9.78
Error	374.5	6	62.42		
Total	1,630.7	11			

b. $F_{(3,6)} = 3.87 < 9.78 = F_{0.01,(3,6)}$; do not reject H_0. Factor A means do not significantly differ.

c. $F_{(2,6)} = 4.26 < 10.92 = F_{0.01,(2,6)}$; do not reject H_0. Factor B means do not significantly differ.

13.26 a.

Source of Variation	SS	df	MS	F	p-value	F crit at 1%
Rows	1057	5	211.43	6.40	0.0064	3.326
Columns	7	2	3.50	0.11	0.9004	4.103
Error	330	10	33.03			
Total	1,394	17				

b. p-value $= 0.9004 > 0.05 = \alpha$; do not reject H_0. Column means do not significantly differ.

c. p-value $= 0.0064 < 0.05 = \alpha$; reject H_0. Some row means differ.

13.28 a.

Source of Variation	SS	df	MS	F	p-value	F crit
Rows	93.2	4	23.3	2.19	0.1316	3.26
Columns	52.15	3	17.4	1.63	0.2335	3.49
Error	127.6	12	10.6			
Total	272.95	19				

b. p-value $= 0.2335 > 0.05 = \alpha$; do not reject H_0. Average round scores do not significantly differ.

c. p-value $= 0.1316 > 0.05 = \alpha$; do not reject H_0. Average player scores do not significantly differ.

13.30 a.

Source of Variation	SS	df	MS	F	p-value	F crit
Rows	37222.22	2	18611.11	167.50	0.0001	6.944
Columns	72.22	2	36.11	0.32	0.7400	6.944
Error	444.44	4	111.11			
Total	37738.89	8				

b. p-value $= 0.74 > 0.05 = \alpha$; do not reject H_0. Average values by appraisers do not significantly differ.

c. p-value $= 0.0001 < 0.05 = \alpha$; reject H_0. Some average values by house type differ.

d. $(\bar{x}_i - \bar{x}_j) \pm q_{\alpha,(c, n_T - c)} \sqrt{\dfrac{MSE}{n}}$

$\mu_1 - \mu_2$: $[-143.08, -90.26]^*$

$\mu_1 - \mu_3$: $[6.92, 59.74]^*$

$\mu_2 - \mu_3$: $[123.59, 176.41]^*$

*indicates a difference between the two corresponding population means

13.32 a.

Source of Variation	SS	df	MS	F	p-value
Sample (Rows)	1,000	2	500	85.71	0.000
Columns	1,200	3	400	68.57	0.000
Interaction	20	6	3.33	0.57	0.751
Within (Error)	280	48	5.83		
Total	2,500	59			

b. p-value $= 0.751 > 0.05 = \alpha$; do not reject H_0. No significant interaction.

c. p-value $\approx 0 < 0.05 = \alpha$; reject H_0. Some Factor A means differ.

d. p-value $\approx 0 < 0.05 = \alpha$; reject H_0. Some Factor B means differ.

13.34 a. p-value $= 0.4629 > 0.01 = \alpha$, do not reject H_0. No significant interaction.

b. Yes, because there is no significant interaction. Factor A: p-value $\approx 0 < 0.01 = \alpha$; reject H_0. Some Factor A means differ. Factor B: p-value $= 0.0031 < 0.01 = \alpha$; reject H_0. Some Factor B means differ.

13.36 a.

Source of Variation	SS	df	MS	F	p-value
Sample	20.056	1	20.056	60.167	0.000
Columns	14.111	2	7.056	21.167	0.000
Interaction	0.111	2	0.056	0.167	0.848
Within	4.000	12	0.333		
Total	38.278	17			

b. p-value $= 0.848 > 0.05 = \alpha$; do not reject H_0. No significant interaction.

c. p-value $\approx 0 < 0.05 = \alpha$; reject H_0. Average battery lives differ by brand name.

d. p-value $\approx 0 < 0.05 = \alpha$; reject H_0. Average battery lives depend on whether the car is garaged.

13.38 a.

Source of Variation	SS	df	MS	F	p-value
Sample	383.63	2	191.815	1.844	0.187
Columns	2591.19	2	1295.593	12.453	0.000
Interaction	622.59	4	155.648	1.496	0.245
Within	1872.67	18	104.037		
Total	5470.07	26			

b. p-value $= 0.245 > 0.05 = \alpha$; do not reject H_0. No significant interaction.

c. p-value $\approx 0 < 0.05 = \alpha$; reject H_0. Job satisfaction differs by industry.

d. p-value $= 0.187 > 0.05 = \alpha$; do not reject H_0. Job satisfaction does not significantly differ by work experience.

13.40 a.

Source of Variation	SS	df	MS	F	p-value	F crit at 5%
Between Groups	258.82	2	129.41	9.40	0.0035	3.89
Within Groups	165.22	12	13.77			
Total	424.04	14				

b. p-value $= 0.0035 < 0.05 = \alpha$; reject H_0. Not all average P/E ratios are the same.

c. $(\bar{x}_i - \bar{x}_j) \pm q_{\alpha,(c, n_T - c)} \sqrt{\dfrac{MSE}{n}}$

$\mu_A - \mu_B$: $[-8.93, 3.59]$

$\mu_A - \mu_C$: $[-16.10, -3.58]^*$

$\mu_B - \mu_C$: $[-13.43, -0.91]^*$

*indicates a difference between the two corresponding population means

13.42 a. p-value $\approx 0 < 0.05 = \alpha$; reject H_0. Average hourly rates are not the same in the three cities.

b. $(\bar{x}_i - \bar{x}_j) \pm q_{\alpha,(c, n_T - c)} \sqrt{\dfrac{MSE}{n}}$

$\mu_{\text{Las Vegas}} - \mu_{\text{Phoenix}}$: $[4.39, 5.79]^*$

$\mu_{\text{Las Vegas}} - \mu_{\text{Orlando}}$: $[4.38, 5.78]^*$

$\mu_{\text{Phoenix}} - \mu_{\text{Orlando}}$: $= [-0.71, 0.69]$

*indicates a difference between the two corresponding population means

13.44 a.

Source of Variation	SS	df	MS	F	p-value	F crit at 5%
Rows	25,416.67	2	12,708.34	4.36	0.099	6.944
Columns	42,916.67	2	21,458.34	7.36	0.046	6.944
Error	11,666.67	4	2,916.67			
Total	80,000	8				

b. p-value $= 0.099 > 0.05 = \alpha$; do not reject H_0. Average contributions do not significantly differ by political affiliation.

c. p-value $= 0.046 < 0.05 = \alpha$; reject H_0. Average contributions differ by income level.

13.46 a.

Source of Variation	SS	df	MS	F	p-value	F crit
Sample	98.296	2	49.148	2.035	0.160	3.555
Columns	289.852	2	144.926	6.002	0.010	3.555
Interaction	153.037	4	38.259	1.584	0.221	2.928
Within	434.667	18	24.148			
Total	975.852	26				

b. p-value $= 0.221 > 0.05 = \alpha$; do not reject H_0. No significant interaction.

c. p-value $= 0.010 < 0.05 = \alpha$; reject H_0. Average fuel consumption differs by fuel type.

d. p-value $= 0.160 > 0.05 = \alpha$; do not reject H_0. Average fuel consumption does not significantly differ by type of hybrid.

Chapter 14

14.2 a.

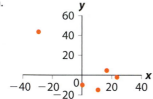

x and y appear to have a negative relationship.

b. $s_{xy} = \frac{-1519.6}{5-1} = -379.9$; negative linear relationship

c. $r_{xy} = \frac{-379.9}{(20.69)(23.42)} = -0.78$; strong negative linear relationship

14.4 a. $t_{28} = \frac{-0.60\sqrt{30-2}}{\sqrt{1-(-0.60)^2}} = -3.97$

b. p-value < 0.005

c. p-value $< \alpha = 0.05$; reject H_0; variables significantly, negatively correlated

14.6 a. $r_{xy} = \frac{-1.75}{(2)(5)} = -0.175$; weak negative linear relationship

b. H_0: $\rho_{xy} = 0$; H_A: $\rho_{xy} \neq 0$

c. $t_{23} = \frac{-0.175\sqrt{25-2}}{\sqrt{1-(-0.175)^2}} = -0.85$; $-2.069 < t_{23} < 2.069$; do not reject H_0; not significantly correlated.

14.8 a. $r_{mc} = 0.57$; $r_{mb} = 0.63$; $r_{mg} = 0.82$; $r_{cb} = 0.04$; $r_{cg} = 0.63$; $r_{bg} = 0.46$

b. Coca-Cola

c. Coca-Cola and Bank of America ($r_{cb} = 0.04$)

14.10 a. $r_{xy} = \frac{146.30}{(22.68)(11.29)} = 0.57$; positive relationship

b. H_0: $\rho_{xy} = 0$; H_A: $\rho_{xy} \neq 0$; $t_{22} = \frac{0.57\sqrt{24-2}}{\sqrt{1-(0.57)^2}} = 3.25$; p-value $< 0.01 = \alpha$, reject H_0; variables significantly correlated.

c. Relationship is nonlinear.

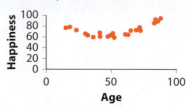

14.12 a. $b_1 = \frac{1250}{925} = 1.35$

b. $b_0 = 44 - (1.35)(34) = -1.90$

c. $\hat{y} = -1.90 + 1.35x$; $\hat{y} = -1.90 + (1.35)(40) = 52.10$

14.14 a. $b_1 = 0.34\left(\frac{7.2}{3.4}\right) = 0.72$

b. $b_0 = 73 - (0.72)(32) = 49.96$

c. $\hat{y} = 49.96 + 0.72x$; $\hat{y} = 49.96 + (0.72)(25) = 67.96$

14.16 a. $\hat{y} = 15 + (2.5)(10) = 40$

b. When x doubles from 10 to 20, $\hat{y}$ increases by 25 from 40 to 65.

14.18 a. Linear regression appears appropriate.

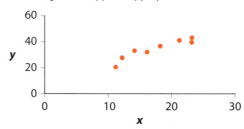

b. $b_1 = \frac{233.25}{159.5} = 1.46$;

$b_0 = 34.375 - (1.46)(17.25) = 9.19$

$\hat{y} = 9.19 + 1.46x$

c. $x = 10$, $\hat{y} = 23.79$; $x = 15$, $\hat{y} = 31.09$; $x = 20$, $\hat{y} = 38.39$

14.20 a.

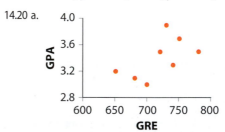

b. $b_1 = \frac{52}{11887.5} = 0.0044$;

$b_0 = 3.4 - (0.0044)(718.75) = 0.24$;

$\widehat{GPA} = 0.24 + 0.0044 GRE$

c. $\widehat{GPA} = 3.36$

14.22 a. Using Excel, choose Data > Data Analysis > Regression from the menu. Choose Consumption data as Input Y range, and Disposable Income as Input X range.

b. $\widehat{Consumption} = 8550.675 + 0.686 Disposable\ Income$

c. For each extra dollar in disposable income, 68.6 cents are spent on consumption goods.

d. 47,652.68

14.24 a. Using H for happiness, $\hat{H} = 56.18 + 0.28\text{Age}$

b. Age = 25, $\hat{H} = 63.18$; Age = 50, $\hat{H} = 70.18$; Age = 75, $\hat{H} = 77.18$

c. Relationship is nonlinear; see the graph in Exercise 14.10.

14.26 a. 568

b. As x_2 increases by one unit, $\hat{y}$ decreases by 47.2 units, holding x_1 constant.

14.28 a. $\hat{y} = 13.83 + 2.53x_1 + 0.29x_2$; As x_2 increases by one unit, $\hat{y}$ increases by 0.29 unit, holding x_1 constant.

b. $\hat{y} = 52.89$

14.30 a. The positive sign on Poverty is expected, but the positive sign on Income is unexpected.

b. As the poverty rate increases by 1%, the crime rate rises by 53.16 crimes per 100,000 residents, holding Income constant.

c. 1009.08 crimes per 100,000 residents

14.32 a. STR: negative; TSAL: positive; INC: positive; SGL: negative

b. $\widehat{\text{Score}} = 231.89 - 0.50\text{STR} - 0.02\text{TSAL} + 0.29\text{INC} - 0.88\text{SGL}$

The signs on the coefficients are all as expected except for TSAL, which has a slightly negative effect on score, holding all other variables constant.

c. 234.89

d. 240.69

14.34 a. $s_e^2 = \frac{1250}{25 - 1 - 1} = 54.35$; $s_e = 7.37$

b. $R^2 = 1 - \frac{1250}{1500} = 0.1667$

14.36 a. $s_e = \sqrt{\frac{35}{50 - 2 - 1}} = \sqrt{0.74} = 0.86$

b. $R^2 = 1 - \frac{35}{90} = 0.6111$

14.38 a. $s_e = \sqrt{6969.03} = 83.48$

$\frac{s_e}{\bar{y}} = \frac{83.48}{557} = 0.15 < 0.20$; the model seems promising.

b. $R^2 = \frac{161478.4}{349642.2} = 0.4618$

c. Adjusted $R^2 = 1 - (1 - 0.4618)\left(\frac{30 - 1}{30 - 2 - 1}\right) = 0.4219$

14.40 a. M1: $s_e = \sqrt{0.1253} = 0.3540$;

M2: $s_e = \sqrt{0.1718} = 0.4145$

b. M1: $R^2 = \frac{1.4415}{2.4440} = 0.5898$;

M2: $R^2 = \frac{1.0699}{2.4440} = 0.4378$

c. Model 1; the standard error is closer to 0 and the R^2 closer to 1.

14.42 a. $s_e = \sqrt{163.066} = 12.77$; $\frac{s_e}{\bar{y}} = \frac{12.77}{1.31} = 9.75 > 0.20$; the model is highly unpromising

b. $R^2 = \frac{918.746}{5321.532} = 0.1726$

c. Adjusted $R^2 = 1 - (1 - 0.1726)\left(\frac{30 - 1}{30 - 2 - 1}\right) = 0.1113$

14.44 a.

Explanatory Variables	Adj ROA (Model 1)	Adj Return (Model 2)	Total Assets (Model 3)
s_e	9.79	9.78	9.00
R^2	0.0004	0.0024	0.1560

Based on the lowest s_e and the highest R^2, Model 3 is the best.

b.

Explanatory Variables	Adj. ROA & Adj Return	Adj. ROA & Total Assets	Adj. Return & Total Assets	All 3 Variables
s_e	9.79	8.99	8.99	8.98
Adjusted R^2	−0.0018	0.1567	0.1567	0.1585

Based on the lowest s_e and the highest Adjusted R^2, the model using all 3 explanatory variables is the best.

14.46 a.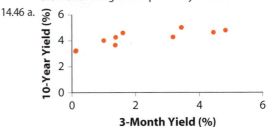

The scatterplot suggests a positive correlation.

b. $s_{xy} = \frac{7.98}{10 - 1} = 0.89$; $r_{xy} = \frac{0.89}{(1.71)(0.63)} = 0.81$; $H_0: \rho_{xy} = 0$;

$H_A: \rho_{xy} \neq 0$; $t_8 = \frac{0.81\sqrt{10 - 2}}{\sqrt{1 - (0.81)^2}} = 3.91 > 2.306 = t_{0.025,8}$;

reject H_0; x and y are significantly correlated.

c. $b_1 = \frac{7.98}{26.24} = 0.3$; $b_0 = 4.18 - 0.3(2.17) = 3.53$; $\hat{y} = 3.53 + 0.3x$

14.48 a. The signs of the estimated coefficients are as expected.

b. As the P/S ratio increases by 1 unit, the predicted return decreases by 3.37%, holding P/E constant.

c. $\widehat{\text{Return}} = -33.40 + 3.97(10) - 3.37(2) = -0.44\%$

d. $\frac{s_e}{\bar{y}} = \frac{13.64}{9.46} = 1.44 > 0.20$; model does not seem promising.

e. $R^2 = 0.4028$; 40.28% of the sample variation in y is explained by the regression equation.

14.50 a. $\widehat{\text{Startups}} = 0.4190 + 0.0087\text{Research} + 0.0517\text{Patents} - 0.0194\text{Duration}$

b. 1.49 startups

c. Approximately \$114.94 million $\left(\frac{1}{0.0087} = 114.94\right)$.

Chapter 15

15.2 a. $t_{23} = \frac{0.5 - 0}{0.3} = 1.67$

b. $t_{0.05,23} = 1.714$

c. $t_{23} = 1.67 < 1.714$, we do not reject H_0; β_1 not positive

15.4 a. $H_0: \beta_0 = 0$; $H_A: \beta_0 \neq 0$; p-value $\approx 0 < 0.05 = \alpha$; reject H_0; the intercept differs from zero

b. $0.1223 \pm (2.101)(0.1794)$; $[-0.2546, 0.4992]$; not significant since the interval contains 0

15.6 a. $H_0: \beta_1 = 0$; $H_A: \beta_1 \neq 0$; p-value $\approx 0 < 0.05 = \alpha$; reject H_0; x_1 and y are related

b. reported as $[-1.67, 7.14]$; no, since the interval contains 0

c. $H_0: \beta_1 \geq 20$; $H_A: \beta_1 < 20$; $t_{27} = \frac{12.91 - 20}{2.68} = -2.65 < -1.703 = -t_{0.05,27}$; reject H_0; yes, the slope is less than 20

15.8 a. $\widehat{\text{Time}} = 13.353 - 0.0477\text{Height}$

b. $H_0: \beta_1 = 0$; $H_A: \beta_1 \neq 0$

c. $t_5 = \frac{-0.0477 - 0}{0.0163} = -2.93$

d. p-value $= 0.0332 < 0.05 = \alpha$; reject H_0; Height significant

15.10 a. $\widehat{\text{Return}} = -12.0243 + 0.1459\text{P/E} + 5.4417\text{P/S}$

b. $H_0: \beta_1 = \beta_2 = 0$; H_A: At least one $\beta_j \neq 0$; $F_{(2,27)} = 2.8171$; p-value $= 0.0774 < 0.10 = \alpha$, reject H_0; P/E and P/S jointly significant

c. P/E: H_0: $\beta_1 = 0$; H_A: $\beta_1 \neq 0$; p-value $= 0.7383 > 0.10 = \alpha$; do not reject H_0; P/E not significant

P/S: H_0: $\beta_2 = 0$; H_A: $\beta_2 \neq 0$; p-value $= 0.0250 < 0.10 = \alpha$; reject H_0; P/S significant

15.12 a. $\widehat{Price} = 153348.27 + 95.86Sqft + 556.89Beds + 92022.91Baths$

Variables	Coefficients
Intercept	153348.27*
	(0.0114)
Sqft	95.86*
	(0.0108)
Beds	556.89
	(0.9783)
Baths	92022.91*
	(0.0009)
s_e	74984.98
R^2	0.7237
F	27.9348
(p-value)	(0.0000)

Notes: Parameter estimates are at the top with the p-values in parentheses; *represents significance at 5% level. Goodness-of-fit measures are at the bottom.

b. H_0: $\beta_1 = \beta_2 = 0$; H_A: At least one $\beta_j \neq 0$; p-value $\approx 0 < 0.05 = \alpha$; reject H_0; explanatory variables jointly significant

c. H_0: $\beta_j = 0$; H_A: $\beta_j \neq 0$; All coefficients have an associated p-value $< \alpha = 0.05$, except for β_2; only Beds not significant

15.14 a. $\widehat{R - R_f} = 1.5804 + 1.7584(R_M - R_f)$

	Coefficients	Standard Error	t Stat	p-value
Intercept	1.5804	0.9296	1.7002	0.0945
$R_M - R_f$	1.7584	0.1843	9.5412	0.0000

b. H_0: $\beta_1 \leq 1$; H_A: $\beta_1 > 1$; $t_{58} = \dfrac{1.7584 - 1}{0.1843} = 4.1150 > 1.672 = t_{0.05,58}$; reject H_0; Caterpillar is riskier than the market.

c. H_0: $\alpha = 0$; H_A: $\alpha \neq 0$; p-value $= 0.0945 > 0.05 = \alpha$; do not reject H_0; cannot conclude abnormal returns

15.16 H_0: $\beta_1 = \beta_3$; H_A: $\beta_1 \neq \beta_3$

Restricted Model: $y = \beta_0 + \beta_1(x_1 + x_3) + \beta_2x_2 + \varepsilon$

Unrestricted Model: $y = \beta_0 + \beta_1x_1 + \beta_2x_2 + \beta_3x_3 + \varepsilon$

15.18 a. H_0: $\beta_2 = \beta_3 = 0$; H_A: At least one $\beta_j \neq 0$

b. $F_{(2,26)} = \dfrac{(407{,}308 - 344{,}784)/2}{344{,}784/26} = 2.36$

c. $F_{0.05,(2,26)} = 3.37$

d. $F_{(2,26)} = 2.36 < 3.37$, do not reject H_0; x_2 and x_3 not jointly significant

15.20 H_0: $\beta_3 = \beta_4 = 0$; H_A: At least one $\beta_j \neq 0$

$F_{(2,25)} = \dfrac{(5021.63 - 4149.21)/2}{4149.21/25} = 2.63 < 3.385 = F_{0.05,(2,25)}$; do not reject H_0; colleague's claim not supported.

15.22 a. $\widehat{Wage} = 7.87 + 1.44Educ + 0.45Exper - 0.01Age$

b. H_0: $\beta_2 = \beta_3$; H_A: $\beta_2 \neq \beta_3$

c. $\widehat{Wage} = 5.16 + 1.31Educ + 0.14(Exper + Age)$

d. $F_{(1,46)} = \dfrac{(1516.01 - 1347.60)/1}{1347.60/46} = 5.75 > 4.05 = F_{0.05,(1,46)}$; reject H_0; the influence of Experience different from Age

15.24 a. $33.58 \pm (2.048)(1.02)$; [31.49, 35.67]

b. $33.58 \pm 2.048\sqrt{1.02^2 + 2.78^2}$; [27.52, 39.64]

c. The confidence interval is narrower because it assumes that the expected value of the error term is zero, whereas the prediction interval incorporates the nonzero error term.

15.26 a. $\hat{y} = 9.15 + 1.46x$

b. Regress y on $x^* = x - 15$ to get $\hat{y}^0 = 31.0846$, $s_e(\hat{y}^0) = 1.0571$ and $s_e = 2.67$; $31.0846 \pm (2.447)(1.0571)$; [28.50, 33.67]

c. $31.0846 \pm 2.447\sqrt{1.0571^2 + 2.67^2}$; [24.06, 38.11]

15.28 a. Regress y on $x^* = x - 6$ to get $\hat{y}^0 = 79.1369$, $s_e(\hat{y}^0) = 4.9212$ and $s_e = 10.4863$; $79.1369 \pm (1.943)(4.9212)$; [69.58, 88.70]

b. $79.1369 \pm 1.943\sqrt{4.9212^2 + 10.4863^2}$; [56.63, 101.64]

c. The confidence interval is narrower because it assumes that the expected value of the error term is zero, whereas the prediction interval incorporates the nonzero error term.

15.30 a. Regress y on $x^* = x - 80$ to get $\hat{y}^0 = 1045.5861$, $s_e(\hat{y}^0) = 14.3802$, and $s_e = 63.2606$; $1045.5861 \pm (2.064)(14.3802)$; [1015.91, 1075.27]

b. $1045.5861 \pm 2.064\sqrt{14.3802^2 + 63.2606^2}$; [911.69, 1179.49]

15.32 a. H_0: $\beta_1 = \beta_2 = 0$; H_A: At least one $\beta_j \neq 0$; p-value $\approx 0 < 0.05 = \alpha$; x_1 and x_2 jointly significant

b. H_0: $\beta_j = 0$; H_A: $\beta_j \neq 0$; p-value $= 0.3832 > 0.05 = \alpha$; do not reject H_0; x_1 not significant p-value $= 0.3666 > 0.05 = \alpha$; so do not reject H_0; x_2 not significant

c. Multicollinearity is likely since both explanatory variables are individually insignificant even though they are jointly significant. (Also, $R^2 = \dfrac{2.12}{2.44} = 0.87$ is high).

15.34 a.

b. Positive serial correlation since the residuals follow a wavelike pattern over time; the estimators are unbiased but not efficient; the standard errors are biased downwards, making the model look better than it really is; use the Newey-West procedure.

15.36 a. $\widehat{Rent} = 300.41 + 225.81Bed + 89.27Bath + 0.21Sqft$

b. Home prices and, therefore, Rent tend to vary more as they get larger; square footage variable may cause heteroskedasticity.

c. The residuals fan out when plotted against Sqft; the residuals are randomly dispersed when plotted against Bed and Bath (plots not shown).

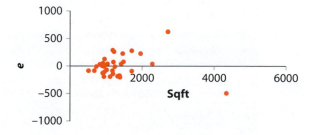

15.38 There does not appear to be any serial correlation, as the residuals do not show any pattern around the horizontal axis.

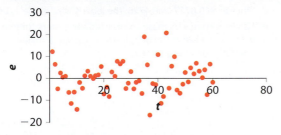

15.40 $H_0: \beta_1 = 0$; $H_A: \beta_1 \neq 0$; p-value $= 0.002 < 0.05 = \alpha$; reject H_0; Days significant

15.42 a. $\widehat{Ownership} = 78.98 - 0.0001Income$

b. $H_0: \beta_1 = 0$; $H_A: \beta_1 \neq 0$; $t_{49} = -1.7973$; $t_{0.025,49} = 2.010$; $-2.010 < t_{49} = -1.7973 < 2.010$; do not reject H_0; Income not significant

c. Regress y on $x^* = x - 50000$ to get $\hat{y}^0 = 69.1995$, $se(\hat{y}^0) = 0.8079$, and $s_e = 5.7685$; $69.1995 \pm (2.010)(0.8079)$; [67.58, 70.82]

d. $69.1995 \pm 2.010\sqrt{0.8079^2 + 5.7685^2}$; [57.49, 80.91]

15.44 a. $\widehat{Return} = 2.5364 + 0.1047Turnover - 3.6056Expense$

Neither Turnover nor Expense is individually significant because the corresponding p-values, 0.0717 and 0.1189, are greater than $\alpha = 0.05$. Also, the variables are not jointly significant because the corresponding p-value $= 0.1603 > 0.05$. George's theory is not supported.

b. The sample correlation coefficient of 0.6782 between Turnover and Expense is less than 0.80; serious multicollinearity unlikely; the residuals seem to vary more with larger Turnover; possible heteroskedasticity.

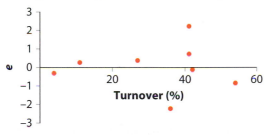

15.46 a. $\widehat{Return} = -33.40 + 3.97P/E - 3.37P/S$

Variable	Coefficients
Intercept	−33.40*
	(0.01)
P/E	3.97*
	(0.00)
P/S	−3.37
	(0.21)
s_e	13.64
R^2	0.40
F	9.10
(*p*-value)	(0.00)

NOTES: Parameter estimates are at the top with the *p*-values in parentheses; *represents significance at 5% level. Goodness-of-fit measures are at the bottom.

b. $H_0: \beta_1 = \beta_2 = 0$; $H_A:$ At least one $\beta_j \neq 0$; p-value $\approx 0 < 0.05 = \alpha$; reject H_0; P/E and P/S jointly significant

c. P/E: p-value $\approx 0 < 0.05 = \alpha$; reject H_0; P/E significant
P/S: p-value $= 0.21 > 0.05 = \alpha$; do not reject H_0, P/S not significant

d. Regress y on $x_1^* = x_1 - 10$ and $x_2^* = x_2 - 2$ to get $\hat{y}^0 = -0.4591$, and $s_e(\hat{y}^0) = 3.4099$; $-0.4591 \pm (2.052)(3.4099)$; [−7.46, 6.54]

15.48 a. $\widehat{Score} = 231.89 - 0.50STR - 0.02TSAL + 0.30INC - 0.88SGL$ (unrestricted model for both tests)

Variable	Unrestricted	Restricted ($\beta_1 = \beta_2 = 0$)	Restricted ($\beta_3 = \beta_4 = 0$)
Intercept	231.89*	223.62*	228.67*
	(0.00)	(0.00)	(0.00)
STR	−0.50*	NA	−1.07*
	(0.00)		(0.00)
TSAL	−0.02	NA	0.52*
	(0.75)		(0.00)
INC	0.30*	0.29*	NA
	(0.00)	(0.00)	
SGL	−0.88*	−1.04*	NA
	(0.00)	(0.00)	
SSE	4057.28	4342.27	8050.13

NOTES: Parameter estimates with the *p*-values in parentheses; NA denotes not applicable; *represents significance at 5% level. The last row shows SSE for the partial *F* test.

b. $H_0: \beta_1 = \beta_2 = 0$; $H_A:$ At least one $\beta_j \neq 0$; $F_{(2,219)} = \frac{(4342.27 - 4057.28)/2}{4057.28/219} = 7.69 > 3.04 = F_{0.05,(2,219)}$; reject H_0; STR and TSAL jointly significant

c. $H_0: \beta_3 = \beta_4 = 0$; $H_A:$ At least one $\beta_j \neq 0$; $F_{(2,219)} = \frac{(8050.13 - 4057.28)/2}{4057.28/219} = 107 > 3.04 = F_{0.05,(2,219)}$; reject H_0; INC and SGL jointly significant.

Chapter 16

16.2 $x = 10, 15$: $\hat{y} = 92, 98$ (linear); $\hat{y} = 161, 96.5$ (quadratic); $\hat{y} = 120, 115$ (cubic)

16.4 a.

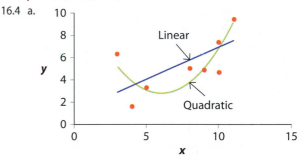

$\hat{y} = 1.1006 + 0.5828x$; $\hat{y} = 12.1338 - 3.1034x + 0.2565x^2$

b. The quadratic regression is better because of the higher adjusted R^2 (0.78 > 0.42)

c. $x = 4$, $\hat{y} = 3.82$; $x = 6$, $\hat{y} = 2.75$; $x = 12$, $\hat{y} = 11.83$

d. minimum at $x = \frac{-(-3.1034)}{2(0.2565)} = 6.05$

16.6 a. $x = 2, 3$: $\hat{y} = 22.5, 23.85$ (linear); $\hat{y} = 21.84, 21.79$ (quadratic); $\hat{y} = 21.91, 21.57$ (cubic)

b. The quadratic model is the best (highest adjusted R^2)

16.8 a. $\widehat{Bids} = 3.8129 - 1.0077Premium + 0.3747Size - 0.0159Size^2$

b. $Size^2$ is significant (p-value $= 0.01 < 0.05 = \alpha$), and sample regression with $Size^2$ has greater adjusted R^2 (0.0959 > 0.0490)

c. Size = 4, $\widehat{\text{Bids}}$ = 3.85; Size = 8, $\widehat{\text{Bids}}$ = 4.58; Size = 12, $\widehat{\text{Bids}}$ = 4.81; Size = 16, $\widehat{\text{Bids}}$ = 4.53; maximum at Size = $\frac{-0.3747}{2(-0.0159)}$ = $11.78 billion.

16.10 a. Model 1: As x increases by one unit, $\hat{y}$ decreases by 4.2 units.

Model 2: As x increases by one percent, $\hat{y}$ decreases by about 2.8 units.

Model 3: As x increases by one unit, $\hat{y}$ decreases by 4%.

Model 4: As x increases by one percent, $\hat{y}$ decreases by 0.8 %.

b. $\hat{y}$ decreases by 4.2 (model 1); $\hat{y}$ decreases by 2.8 (Model 2); $\hat{y}$ decreases by 3.22, or 3.92% (Model 3); $\hat{y}$ decreases by 0.59, or 0.78% (Model 4).

16.12 Model 1: $\hat{y} = 240.42 + 4.68(100) = 708.42$;

Model 2: $\hat{y} = -69.75 + 162.51\ln(100) = 678.64$;

Model 3: $\hat{y} = \exp\left(1.58 + 0.05(100) + \frac{0.12^2}{2}\right) = 725.74$;

Model 4: $\hat{y} = \exp\left(0.77 + 1.25\ln(100) + \frac{0.09^2}{2}\right) = 685.75$.

16.14 a.

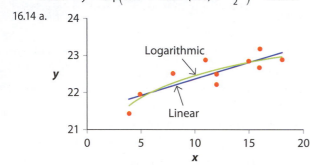

The logarithmic model seems slightly better.

b. Logarithmic model is better because of the higher R^2 (0.7723 > 0.7029).

c. $\hat{y} = 20.42 + 0.88\ln(10) = 22.45$

16.16 a. BMI = 25, $\widehat{\text{Salary}}$ = 66.1852 − 0.9931(25) = 41.358, or $41,358;

BMI = 30, $\widehat{\text{Salary}}$ = 36.392, or $36,392.

b. BMI = 25, $\widehat{\text{Salary}}$ = $\exp\left(4.3277 - 0.0248(25) + \frac{0.1111^2}{2}\right)$ = 41.012, or $41,012;

BMI = 30, $\widehat{\text{Salary}}$ = 36.229, or $36,229.

c. For the exponential model, we compute R^2 in terms of y for comparison with the linear model. Using the predicted $\widehat{\ln(y)}$ reported by Excel, we transform it into $\hat{y}$ and then compute $r_{y\hat{y}} = 0.7974$. Therefore, $R^2 = 0.7974^2 = 0.6358 > 0.6260$ (R^2 for the linear model); the exponential model is better.

16.18 a. $\widehat{\text{Rent}}$ = 65.8255 + 237.8506Beds + 389.3673Baths + 0.1831Sqft

$\widehat{\ln(\text{Rent})}$ = 6.2925 + 0.1326Beds + 0.2191Baths + 0.0002Sqft; s_e = 0.2067

b. $\widehat{\text{Rent}}$ = 65.8255 + 237.8506(3) + 389.3673(2) + 0.1831(1500) = $1832.76;

$\widehat{\text{Rent}}$ = $\exp\left(6.2925 + 0.1326(3) + 0.2181(2) + 0.0002(1500) + \frac{0.2067^2}{2}\right)$ = $1719.63.

c. For the exponential model, we compute R^2 in terms of y for comparison with the linear model. Using the predicted $\widehat{\ln(y)}$ reported by Excel, we transform it into $\hat{y}$ and then compute $r_{y\hat{y}} = 0.9001$. Therefore, $R^2 = 0.9001^2 = 0.8102 > 0.7936$ (R^2 for the linear model); the exponential model is better.

16.20 a. Although not obvious from the scatterplot (not shown), the exponential model seems slightly better.

b $\hat{y} = 67.1605 - 0.0006x$; if x decreases from 1000 to 500, $\hat{y}$ increases from 66.56 to 66.86, that is, by 0.30 year.

c. $\hat{y} = 96.2515 - 4.4075\ln(x)$; if x decreases from 1000 to 500, $\hat{y}$ increases from 65.81 to 68.86, that is, by 3.05 years.

d. Since $R^2 = 0.6717 > 0.4726$, the logarithmic model is better.

e. Life expectancy increases proportionally more for females with a decrease in the people-to-physician ratio; females are likely to benefit more.

16.22 a. $\widehat{\text{Salary}}$ = 32.77 − 0.83PCT + 0.79TF + 0.39Age with $R^2 = 0.3931$. For the exponential model, we compute R^2 in terms of y for comparison with the linear model. Using the predicted $\widehat{\ln(y)}$ reported by Excel, we transform it into $\hat{y}$ and then compute $r_{y\hat{y}} = 0.5147$. Thus, $R^2 = 0.5147^2 = 0.2649$. The linear model is better because of a higher R^2 (0.3931 > 0.2649).

b. $H_0: \beta_3 = \beta_4 = 0$; H_A: At least one $\beta_j \neq 0$

c. $F_{(2,27)} = \frac{(916.9832 - 819.8520)/2}{819.9520/27} = 1.60 < 3.35 = F_{0.05,(2,27)}$; do not reject H_0; Age and Age^2 not jointly significant

16.24 a. $\widehat{\text{Smoke}}$ = 27.4116 − 0.3547Fruits/Veggies − 0.0001Median Income; $R^2 = 0.4613$

b. $\widehat{\text{Smoke}}$ = 87.8631 − 0.3484Fruits/Veggies − 6.1512 ln(Median Income); $R^2 = 0.4663$; the logarithmic regression with a slightly higher R^2 is better.

Chapter 17

17.2 a. $\hat{y} = 160 + 15(1) + 32(1) = 207$

b. $\hat{y} = 160 + 15(0) + 32(0) = 160$

17.4 a. If d changes from 0 to 1, with x held constant, $\hat{y}$ increases by about 15%

b. $d = 0$, $\hat{y} = \exp\left(1.56 + 0.21(20) + 0.15(0) + \frac{0.35^2}{2}\right) = 337.39$;

$d = 1$, $\hat{y} = \exp\left(1.56 + 0.21(20) + 0.15(1) + \frac{0.35^2}{2}\right) = 392.00$

c. p-value = 0.0008 < 0.05 = α; d significant

17.6 a. With nicknames, $\bar{y} = 68.05$; without nicknames, $\bar{y} = 64.08$

b. $\hat{y} = 64.08 + 3.97$Nickname; predicted longevity same as in a.

c. $H_0: \beta_1 \leq 0$; $H_0: \beta_1 > 0$; p-value = 0.0494 < 0.05 = α; reject H_0; players with nicknames live longer

17.8 a. $\hat{y} = 274.12 + 98.71x - 21.10d$; $\hat{y} = 619.60$ (male); $\hat{y} = 598.50$ (female)

b. $H_0: \beta_2 = 0$, $H_A: \beta_2 \neq 0$; p-value = 0.0618 > 0.05 = α; do not reject H_0; insignificant gender differences

17.10 a. $\widehat{\text{Wage}}$ = 8.68 + 1.23EDUC + 0.42EXPER − 0.02AGE + 2.29d

b. $\widehat{\text{Wage}}$ = $24.57 (male); $\widehat{\text{Wage}}$ = $22.28 (female)

c. Male workers make on average $2.29 per hour more, holding everything else the same; p-value = 0.1787 > 0.05 = α; no discrimination

17.12 a. $\widehat{\ln(y)} = -1.44 + 0.40\ln(x) - 0.08d_1 - 0.29d_2 - 0.83d_3$

b. In any industry, for a 1% increase in Total Assets, the predicted compensation increases by about 0.40%; for given assets, relative to Nonfinancial Services, the predicted compensation is about: 8% lower in Manufacturing Technology; 29% lower in Manufacturing Other; 83% lower in Financial Services.

c. p-value = 0.59 > 0.05 = α; d_1 not significant; p-value = 0.0459 < 0.05 = α; d_2 significant; p-value ≈ 0 < 0.05 = α; d_3 significant. The significance of a particular industry dummy is interpreted relative to Nonfinancial Services.

d. $H_0: \beta_2 = \beta_3 = \beta_4 = 0$; H_A: At least one $\beta_j \neq 0$; $F_{(3,450)} = \frac{(387.81 - 355.28)/3}{355.28/450} = 13.72 > 2.62 = F_{0.05,(3,450)}$; reject H_0; industry dummy variables jointly significant

17.14 a. $\hat{y} = 75.51$ ($d = 1$); $\hat{y} = 59.76$ ($d = 0$)

b. p-value = 0.32 > 0.05 = α; d not significant; p-value = 0.02 < 0.05 = α; xd significant

17.16 a. $\hat{y} = 8160.34 + 0.55(75000) = \$49,410.34$

b. $\hat{y} = 13007.26 + 0.44x + 6544.43d$; $\hat{y} = \$52,551.69$ (Urban); $\hat{y} = \$46,007.26$ (Rural)

c. $\hat{y} = -1676.58 + 0.66x + 36361.71d - 0.38xd$; $\hat{y} = \$55,685.13$ (Urban); $\hat{y} = \$47,823.42$ (Rural)

d. The model estimated in part c. is the best because of the highest adjusted R^2 of 0.6332.

17.18 a. $\hat{y} = 8.42 + 0.22x + 3.68d$; adj. $R^2 = 0.1585$

b. $\hat{y} = 8.34 + 0.20x + 4.01d + 0.05xd$; adj. $R^2 = 0.1571$

c. The model in part a. is preferred.

17.20 a. $x = 25$, $\hat{y} = 0.42$; $x = 40$, $\hat{y} = 0.12$

b. $\hat{y} = 0.92 - 0.02x < 0$ is equivalent to $x > 46$.

17.22 a. $\hat{y} = -0.40 + 0.32x$ (LPM); $\hat{y} = \dfrac{\exp(-4.5 + 1.54x)}{1 + \exp(-4.5 + 1.54x)}$ (logit)

x	LPM	Logit
1	−0.08	0.05
2	0.24	0.19
3	0.56	0.53
4	0.88	0.84
5	1.20	0.96

b. LPM predicts a negative value when $x = 1$; not appropriate

17.24 a. $\hat{y} = 1.31 - 0.04(20) = 0.51$

b. p-value $= 0.0125 < 0.05 = \alpha$; reject H_0; x significant

17.26 a. $\hat{y} = \dfrac{\exp(1.609 - 0.194 \times 15 + 0.202 \times 10 + 0.223 \times (-2))}{1 + \exp(1.609 - 0.194 \times 15 + 0.202 \times 10 + 0.223 \times (-2))} = 0.57$

b. Only x_3 with a p-value of 0.01 is significant at $\alpha = 0.05$.

17.28 a. $\hat{y} = \dfrac{\exp(2.3069 - 0.1215\text{Age})}{1 + \exp(2.3069 - 0.1215\text{Age})}$; Age $= 20$, $\hat{y} = 0.47$;

Age $= 30$, $\hat{y} = 0.21$

b. $H_0: \beta_1 \geq 0$, $H_A: \beta_1 < 0$; p-value $= 0.0230 < 0.05 = \alpha$; reject H_0; Annabel's belief supported

17.30 $\hat{y} = \dfrac{\exp(-9.6504 + 0.0654x_1 + 0.1291x_2)}{1 + \exp(-9.6504 + 0.0654x_1 + 0.1291x_2)}$; $x_1 = 50$, $\hat{y} = 0.80$;

$x_1 = 75$, $\hat{y} = 0.95$

17.32 Relevant regression results from Minitab:

Predictor	Coef	SE	Z	P
Constant	−0.8103	1.1594	−0.70	0.485
Age	2.5615	1.1783	2.17	0.030
Income	0.0094	0.0184	0.51	0.608
Children	−1.2436	0.5964	−2.09	0.037

$\hat{y} = \dfrac{\exp(-0.8103 + 2.5615x_1 + 0.0094x_2 - 1.2436x_3)}{1 + \exp(-0.8103 + 2.5615x_1 + 0.0094x_2 - 1.2436x_3)}$

a. $H_0: \beta_1 \leq 0$, $H_A: \beta_1 > 0$; p-value $= 0.030/2 = 0.015 < 0.05 = \alpha$; reject H_0; divorce rate is higher for this age group

b. If $x_1 = 1$, $x_2 = 60$, $x_3 = 1$, then $\hat{y} = 0.74$; if $x_1 = 1$, $x_2 = 60$, $x_3 = 3$, then $\hat{y} = 0.20$

17.34 a. $\hat{y} = 25.15 - 0.32\text{Age} + 9.45d$

b. $d = 1$, $\hat{y} = 25\%$; $d = 0$, $\hat{y} = 15.55\%$

c. $H_0: \beta_2 = 0$, and $H_A: \beta_2 \neq 0$; p-value $\approx 0 < 0.05 = \alpha$; reject H_0; race discrimination

17.36 a. $\widehat{\text{BMI}} = 28.26 - 3.45\text{Female} - 1.31\text{Black} + 6.66\text{Female} \times \text{Black}$

$\widehat{\text{BMI}} = 28.26$ for white male; $\widehat{\text{BMI}} = 24.81$ for white female; $\widehat{\text{BMI}} = 26.95$ for black male; $\widehat{\text{BMI}} = 30.16$ for black female

b. $H_0: \beta_1 = 0$, $H_A: \beta_1 \neq 0$; p-value $\approx 0 < 0.05 = \alpha$; reject H_0; significant difference

c. $H_0: \beta_2 = 0$, $H_A: \beta_2 \neq 0$; p-value $= 0.003 < 0.05 = \alpha$; reject H_0; significant difference

17.38 a. $\hat{y} = -2.2461 + 0.0010\text{SAT} + 0.3780\text{GPA}$; both p-values $< \alpha = 0.05$; SAT and GPA individually significant.

b. $\hat{y} = 0.78$

c. $\hat{y} = 0.88$

17.40 a. $\hat{y} = 1.3863 - 0.0360\text{Age} + 0.2511\text{Gender}$

b. Age significant (p-value $= 0.002 < 0.05 = \alpha$); Gender not significant (p-value $= 0.1658 > 0.05 = \alpha$). The claim that women are less likely to re-offend is not supported.

c. $\hat{y} = 0.74$ (male); $\hat{y} = 0.49$ (female)

Chapter 18

18.2 a. The graph displays a jagged appearance, indicative of a significant random component in the series. The 5-period MA is much smoother.

b. 5-period MA

t	y_t	$\bar{y}$	$\hat{y}_t$	$e_t = y_t - \hat{y}_t$
1	27	—	—	—
2	35	—	—	—
3	38	33.4	—	—
⋮	⋮	⋮	⋮	⋮
6	39	36.8	33.4	5.6
⋮	⋮	⋮	⋮	⋮
20	45	—	36.00	9.0
21			**37**	

$MSE = \dfrac{443.04}{15} = 29.54$; $MAD = \dfrac{68.80}{15} = 4.59$

c. $\hat{y}_{21} = 37$

18.4 a. 3-period MA

t	y_t	$\bar{y}$	$\hat{y}_t$	$e_t = y_t - \hat{y}_t$
1	14	—	—	—
2	17	14.33	—	—
3	12	15	—	—
4	16	15.33	14.33	1.67
⋮	⋮	⋮	⋮	⋮
20	20	—	24	−4.00
21			**23**	

$MSE = \dfrac{155.33}{17} = 9.14$; $MAD = \dfrac{44.67}{17} = 2.63$

b. Exponential smoothing with $\alpha = 0.4$

t	y_t	A_t	$\hat{y}_t$	$e_t = y_t - \hat{y}_t$
1	14	14.00	—	—
2	17	15.20	14.00	3.00
⋮	⋮	⋮	⋮	⋮
20	20	22.13	23.55	−3.55
21			**22.13**	

$MSE = \dfrac{156.4}{19} = 8.23$; $MAD = \dfrac{45.73}{19} = 2.41$

c. The exponential smoothing method has lower MSE and a lower MAD; $\hat{y}_{21} = 22.13$.

18.6 a. Exponential smoothing with $\alpha = 0.4$

t	y_t	A_t	$\hat{y}_t$	$e_t = y_t - \hat{y}_t$
1991	34.8	34.80	—	—
1992	31.6	33.52	34.80	−3.20
⋮	⋮	⋮	⋮	⋮
2008	31.8	31.32	31.00	0.80
2009			**31.32**	

$MSE = \dfrac{219.16}{17} = 12.89$; $\hat{y}_{2009} = 31.32$

b. Exponential smoothing with $\alpha = 0.6$

t	y_t	A_t	$\hat{y}_t$	$e_t = y_t - \hat{y}_t$
1991	34.8	34.80	—	—
1992	31.6	32.88	34.80	−3.20
⋮	⋮	⋮	⋮	⋮
2008	31.8	31.95	32.18	−0.38
2009			**31.95**	

$MSE = \dfrac{178.79}{17} = 10.52$; $\hat{y}_{2009} = 31.95$

c. Exponential smoothing with $\alpha = 0.6$ since its MSE is smaller.

18.8 a. 3-period MA

t	y_t	$\bar{y}$	$\hat{y}_t$	$e_t = y_t - \hat{y}_t$
1-Nov	1184.38	—	—	—
2-Nov	1193.57	1191.97	—	—
3-Nov	1197.96	1204.2	—	—
4-Nov	1221.06	1214.96	1191.97	29.09
⋮	⋮	⋮	⋮	⋮
30-Nov	1180.55	—	1191.84	−11.29
1-Dec			**1185.90**	

$MSE = \dfrac{3616.579}{18} = 200.92$; $\hat{y}_{\text{December 1}} = 1185.90$

b. Exponential smoothing with $\alpha = 0.4$

t	y_t	A_t	$\hat{y}_t$	$e_t = y_t - \hat{y}_t$
1-Nov	1184.38	1184.38		
2-Nov	1193.57	1188.06	1184.38	9.19
⋮	⋮	⋮	⋮	⋮
30-Nov	1180.55	1186.30	1190.14	−9.59
1-Dec			**1186.30**	

$MSE = \dfrac{3562.81}{20} = 178.14$; $\hat{y}_{\text{December 1}} = 1186.30$.

c. Exponential smoothing method

d. Yes, the December 1 absolute errors induced by the methods are 20.17 and 19.77, respectively.

18.10 a. $\hat{y}_{21} = 13.54 + 1.08(21) = 36.22$

b. $\hat{y}_{21} = 18.26 + 0.92(21) - 0.01(21)^2 = 33.19$

c. $\hat{y}_t = \exp\left(1.8 + 0.09(21) + \dfrac{0.01^2}{2}\right) = 40.05$

18.12 a. From the graph, a quadratic trend model seems to be appropriate.

b. $\hat{y}_t = 11.7606 + 0.3144t$; adjusted $R^2 = 0.8356$
$\hat{y}_t = 10.0651 + 0.7768t - 0.0220t^2$; adjusted $R^2 = 0.9481$
Quadratic trend model is preferred since its adjusted R^2 is higher.

18.14 a. From the graph, a quadratic trend model seems to be appropriate.

b. $\hat{y}_t = 1806.5333 + 57.7939t$; adjusted $R^2 = -0.0643$
$\hat{y}_t = 153.7000 + 884.2106t - 75.1288t^2$; adjusted $R^2 = 0.5342$
Quadratic trend model is preferred since its adjusted R^2 is higher.

c. $\hat{y}_{11} = 153.7000 + 884.2106(11) - 75.1288(11)^2 = 789.43$

18.16 a. From the graph, a cubic trend model seems to be appropriate.

b. $\hat{y}_t = 3.9919 + 0.2087t$; adjusted $R^2 = 0.9242$
$\hat{y}_t = 3.3808 + 0.2820t - 0.0015t^2$; adjusted $R^2 = 0.9302$
$\hat{y}_t = 5.5027 - 0.2123t + 0.0235t^2 - 0.0003t^3$; adjusted $R^2 = 0.9879$
Cubic trend model is preferred since it has the highest adjusted R^2.

c. $\hat{y}_{49} = 11.48\%$.

18.18 a. Third and fourth quarter series are 14% below and 12% above the average quarterly level, respectively.

b. Q1: $\hat{y}_{33} = \exp(2.80 + 0.03(33) + 0.08^2/2) \times 0.94 = 41.73$
Q2: $\hat{y}_{34} = \exp(2.80 + 0.03(34) + 0.08^2/2) \times 1.08 = 49.41$
Q3: $\hat{y}_{35} = \exp(2.80 + 0.03(35) + 0.08^2/2) \times 0.86 = 40.54$
Q4: $\hat{y}_{36} = \exp(2.80 + 0.03(36) + 0.08^2/2) \times 1.12 = 54.41$

18.20 a–b. Calculating the ratio-to-moving averages:

Year	Quarter	t	y	$\bar{y}$	$y/\bar{y}$
1	1	1	8.37	—	—
1	2	2	12.78	—	—
1	3	3	8.84	11.69	0.7564
⋮	⋮	⋮	⋮	⋮	⋮
5	2	18	10.58	11.59	0.9130
5	3	19	13.35	—	—
5	4	20	19.77	—	—

c. Seasonal indices:

Quarter	Quarter 1	Quarter 2	Quarter 3	Quarter 4
Unadjusted	0.7412	0.8995	0.8145	1.4629
Adjusted	0.7567	0.9183	0.8315	1.4935

First quarter series is 24.33% below its average quarterly level; fourth quarter series is 49.35% above its average quarterly level.

18.22 b. Calculating the ratio-to-moving averages:

Year	Quarter	t	y	$\bar{y}$	$y/\bar{y}$
Year 1	Quarter 1	1	6.49	—	—
Year 1	Quarter 2	2	7.34	—	—
Year 1	Quarter 3	3	7.11	8.01	0.8878
⋮	⋮	⋮	⋮	⋮	⋮
Year 5	Quarter 2	18	10.08	10.78	0.9353
Year 5	Quarter 3	19	9.78	—	—
Year 5	Quarter 4	20	14.88	—	—

Seasonal indices:

Quarter	Quarter 1	Quarter 2	Quarter 3	Quarter 4
Unadjusted	0.8484	0.9345	0.8880	1.3278
Adjusted	0.8487	0.9348	0.8883	1.3282

Estimated exponential trend model with seasonal indices:

$\hat{y}_t = \exp(2.017531 + 0.019950t + s_e^2/2) \times \hat{S}_t$, where

$s_e = 0.0018867$; $MSE = \frac{0.0041}{20} = 0.0002$

c. Estimated exponential trend model with seasonal dummies:

$\hat{y}_t = \exp(2.301381 - 0.449995d_1 - 0.350265d_2$
$- 0.400063d_3 + 0.019921t + s_e^2/2)$, where $s_e = 0.000971$;

$MSE = \frac{0.00093}{20} = 0.00005$

d. The estimated exponential trend model with dummies has a lower MSE. Forecasts:

Year	Quarter	d_1	d_2	d_3	t	$\hat{y}_t$
6	1	1	0	0	21	9.68
6	2	0	1	0	22	10.91
6	3	0	0	1	23	10.59
6	4	0	0	0	24	16.11

18.24 a. Estimated linear trend model with seasonal dummies:

$\hat{y}_t = 390.6250 - 1683.9410d_1 - 1967.4736d_2 - 1743.4063d_3$
$- 1590.5389d_4 - 1400.8715d_5 - 1616.2042d_6$
$- 1480.5368d_7 - 1071.6694d_8 - 1506.0021d_9$
$- 995.1347d_{10} - 505.2674d_{11} + 118.9326t$;

$MSE = \frac{59373548.39}{60} = 989559.14$;

$MAD = \frac{46905.90}{60} = 781.77$

b. Estimated exponential trend model with seasonal dummies:

$\hat{y}_t = \exp(6.3047 - 0.4901d_1 - 0.6134d_2 - 0.4474d_3$
$- 0.3839d_4 - 0.3035d_5 - 0.3803d_6 - 0.3195d_7$
$- 0.2112d_8 - 0.3568d_9 - 0.2304d_{10} - 0.1188d_{11}$
$+ 0.0502t + s_e^2/2)$, where $s_e = 0.042759$;

$MSE = \frac{1594844.55}{60} = 26580.74$;

$MAD = \frac{5573.33}{60} = 92.89$

The exponential model has lower MSE. Forecasts:

Year	Month	d_1	d_2	t	$\hat{y}_t$
6	Jan	1	0	61	7186.15
6	Feb	0	1	62	6679.55

18.26 b. Calculating the ratio-to-moving averages:

Year	Month	t	y	$\bar{y}$	$y/\bar{y}$
2006	Jan	1	4.65	—	—
⋮	⋮	⋮	⋮	—	—
2006	Jul	7	5.25	5.01	1.0490
⋮	⋮	⋮	⋮	—	—
2010	Jun	54	3.95	4.04	0.9779
⋮	⋮	⋮	⋮	—	—
2010	Dec	60	4.16	—	—

Seasonal indices:

Month	Jan	Feb	Mar	Apr	May	Jun
Unadjusted	0.9582	0.9935	0.9852	1.0100	1.0243	1.0595
Adjusted	0.9550	0.9902	0.9819	1.0066	1.0209	1.0559

Month	Jul	Aug	Sep	Oct	Nov	Dec
Unadjusted	1.0588	1.0332	0.9955	1.0071	0.9831	0.9322
Adjusted	1.0552	1.0297	0.9921	1.0037	0.9798	0.9290

c. $\hat{T}_t = 5.160547 - 0.02228t$

d.

Year	Month	t	$\hat{S}_t$	$\hat{T}_t$	$\hat{y}_t = \hat{T}_t \times \hat{S}_t$
2011	Jan	61	0.9550	3.8017	3.6306
2011	Feb	62	0.9902	3.7794	3.7422
2011	Mar	63	0.9819	3.7572	3.6892

18.28 a. Estimated linear trend model with seasonal dummies:

$\hat{y}_t = 1947.5250 + 196.9188d_1 + 324.6125d_2 + 55.7063d_3$
$+ 64.9063t$;

$MSE = \frac{115438.38}{20} = 5771.92$;

$MAD = \frac{1164.85}{20} = 58.24$

b. Estimated exponential trend model with seasonal dummies:

$\hat{y}_t = \exp(7.615911 + 0.069376d_1 + 0.112936d_2 + 0.020109d_3$
$+ 0.023939t + s_e^2/2)$, where $s_e = 0.037138$;

$MSE = \frac{147176.96}{20} = 7358.85$;

$MAD = \frac{1372.20}{20} = 68.61$

c. The linear trend model outperforms the exponential model.

18.30 a. Estimated linear trend model with seasonal dummies:

$\hat{y}_t = 1.4702 + 0.0174d_1 - 0.0729d_2 - 0.0630d_3 - 0.0137t$;
adjusted $R^2 = 0.8560$;

b. Estimated quadratic trend model with seasonal dummies:

$\hat{y}_t = 1.4155 + 0.0174d_1 - 0.0734d_2 - 0.0636d_3 - 0.0040t$
$- 0.0003t^2$; adjusted $R^2 = 0.8800$

c. The quadratic model is used for 2009 forecasts as it has greater adjusted R^2.

Year	Quarter	$\hat{y}_t$
2009	1	0.9802
2009	2	0.8656
2009	3	0.8511
2009	4	0.8898

18.32 a. $\hat{y}_t = 86.071 + 1.1413t - 0.0630t^2 + 0.0006t^3 - 3.3372d_1$
$- 0.7017d_2 - 1.0219d_3 - 2.2938d_4 - 3.1546d_5$
$- 0.9083d_6 - 1.3086d_7 - 3.6762d_8 - 2.7149d_9$
$- 4.8952d_{10} - 4.0952d_{11}$.

Year	Month	$\hat{y}_t$
2010	Nov	77.055
2010	Dec	83.178

18.34 a. $\hat{y}_t = 11.4715 + 0.7569y_{t-1}$; adjusted $R^2 = 0.8506$; $\hat{y}_{25} = 48.24$

b. $\hat{y}_t = 18.1852 + 0.3321y_{t-1} + 0.2819y_{t-2}$; adjusted $R^2 = 0.7958$; $\hat{y}_{25} = 47.88$

c. Model estimated in a. has greater adjusted R^2

18.36 a. $\hat{y}_t = 113.6048 - 0.0064x_{t-1}$; adjusted $R^2 = -0.0371$

b. $\hat{y}_t = 3.9326 + 0.9201y_{t-1}$; adjusted $R^2 = 0.7930$

c. $\hat{y}_t = 56.8010 - 0.0057x_{t-1} + 0.9124y_{t-1}$; adjusted $R^2 = 0.8324$

d. Model in c. yields $\hat{y}_{13} = 52.18$

18.38 a. Let $y =$ Inflation: $\hat{y}_t = 9.5846 - 0.2671y_{t-1}$; adjusted $R^2 = -0.0351$

$\hat{y}_t = 9.6169 - 0.0381y_{t-1} - 0.0379y_{t-2}$; adjusted $R^2 = -0.1098$

Given the negative adjusted R^2 in both models, neither should be considered.

b. Let $y =$ Unemployment: $\hat{y}_t = 2.7465 + 0.7193y_{t-1}$; adjusted $R^2 = 0.8902$

$\hat{y}_t = 3.0236 + 0.7224y_{t-1} - 0.0320y_{t-2}$; adjusted $R^2 = 0.7987$

The estimated model with greater R^2 yields $\hat{y}_{24} = 9.80$.

18.40 a. $\hat{y}_{22} = 2.827$; $MSE = \frac{0.141}{18} = 0.008$; $MAD = \frac{1.241}{18} = 0.069$

b. $\hat{y}_{22} = 2.819$; $MSE = \frac{0.126}{20} = 0.006$; $MAD = \frac{1.196}{20} = 0.060$

c. The exponential smoothing method has slightly lower MSE and MAD.

d. For $t = 22$, $|y_t - \hat{y}_t|$ are 0.133 and 0.141, respectively. Thus, rather surprisingly, the error induced by the 3-period MA method is smaller.

18.42 a. Seasonal indices found by the ratio-to-moving average method:

Quarter	Q1	Q2	Q3	Q4
Unadjusted	0.997561	1.000594	1.00194	0.999119
Adjusted	0.9978	1.0008	1.0021	0.9993

b. $\hat{T}_t = 636544.16 + 16324.26t - 1052.97t^2 + 18.60t^3$

c.

Year	Quarter	t	$\hat{T}_t$	$\hat{S}_t$	$\hat{y}_t = \hat{T}_t \times \hat{S}_t$
2010	4	28	676354.7	0.9993	675892.8
2011	1	29	677982.8	0.9978	676463.1
2011	2	30	680740.9	1.0008	681279.6
2011	3	31	684740.7	1.0021	686201.3

18.44 a. The graph shows that loans were rising exponentially.

b. $\hat{y}_t = -3.1320 + 74.5887t$; $MSE = \frac{4080839.12}{36} = 113,356.64$

$\hat{y}_t = \exp(6.0545 + 0.0543t + s_e^2/2)$, where $s_e = 0.1082$;

$MSE = \frac{\Sigma e_t^2}{n} = \frac{1275107.37}{36} = 35,419.65$. The estimated exponential trend model has lower MSE, and it yields the forecast $\hat{y}_{37} = 3,189.63$ billion.

c. $\hat{y}_t = -37.2161 + 1.0961y_{t-1}$; $MSE = 4104.42$. The estimated AR(1) model has the lowest MSE, and it yields the forecast $\hat{y}_{37} = 3,913.21$ billion.

18.46 a. The graph shows a relatively flat trend with a succession of almost identical spikes in July of each year, indicative of the presence of a strong seasonality in the series.

b. Seasonal indices found by the ratio-to-moving average method:

Month	Jan	Feb	Mar	Apr	May	Jun
Unadjusted	0.8924	0.8471	1.0514	1.0065	1.0368	1.0998
Adjusted	0.8933	0.8480	1.0525	1.0075	1.0379	1.1009

Month	Jul	Aug	Sep	Oct	Nov	Dec
Unadjusted	1.1528	1.1138	0.9049	0.9858	0.9303	0.9657
Adjusted	1.1540	1.1150	0.9058	0.9869	0.9313	0.9667

c. The cubic trend model is chosen to fit the seasonally adjusted series: $\hat{T}_t = 45.8490 + 0.5940t - 0.0271t^2 + 0.0003t^3$; adjusted $R^2 = 0.6924$

d.

Year	Month	t	$\hat{T}_t$	$\hat{S}_t$	$\hat{y}_t = \hat{T}_t \times \hat{S}_t$
2010	Oct	58	47.4182	0.9869	46.7951
2010	Nov	59	47.9089	0.9313	44.6154
2010	Dec	60	48.4509	0.9667	46.8383

18.48 a. $\hat{y}_t = 7909.4250 + 1478.7938d_1 + 3159.8625d_2 + 982.9313d_3 + 176.3313t$

$MSE = \frac{9,634,206.98}{20} = 481,710.35$; $MAD = \frac{11,258.05}{20} = 562.90$

b. $\hat{y}_t = \exp(9.0170 + 0.1340d_1 + 0.2739d_2 + 0.0924d_3 + 0.0161t + s_e^2/2)$, where $s_e = 0.07293$;

$MSE = \frac{9099121.4346}{20} = 454,956.07$;

$MAD = \frac{10,953.9391}{20} = 547.70$

c. Exponential model; smaller MSE and MAD

Year	Quarter	Lowe's Net Sales
2009	1	13237.42
2009	2	15471.72
2009	3	13112.69
2009	4	12148.44
Total		53970.26

18.50 a. The cubic trend model chosen to fit the series: $\hat{y}_t = 8773.5228 + 287.3408t - 23.0026t^2 + 0.6474t^3$; adjusted $R^2 = 0.9236$; $\hat{y}_{21} = 10,659.50$

b. $\hat{y}_t = 3564.9344 + 0.5974x_{t-1}$; adjusted $R^2 = 0.8718$; $\hat{y}_{21} = 10,444.34$

c. The cubic model has greater adjusted R^2.

Chapter 19

19.2 a. $\frac{\$60}{\$980} = 0.0612$, or 6.12%

b. $\frac{\$990 - \$980}{\$980} = 0.0102$, or 1.02%

c. $R_t = 7.14\%$

19.4 a. Year 2: $\frac{\$24.80 - \$23.50 + \$0.18}{\$23.50} = 0.0630$;

Year 3: $\frac{\$22.90 - \$24.80 + \$0.12}{\$24.80} = -0.0718$

b. Year 2: $r = \frac{1 + 0.0630}{1 + 0.028} - 1 = 0.034$;

Year 3: $r = (1 - 0.0718)/(1 + 0.016) - 1 = -0.0864$

19.6 a. $R_t = \frac{\$30,480 - \$17,100 + \$520}{\$17,100} = 0.8129$, or 81.29%

   b. $13,901

19.8

Date	Adjusted Close Price	Monthly Return
Dec-10	$21.48	0.0238
Nov-10	$20.98	0.0634
Oct-10	$19.73	—

19.10 a.

Year	Price	Price Index
1994	62	100.00
1995	60	96.77
1996	64	103.23
1997	67	108.06
1998	66	106.45
1999	70	112.90
2000	74	119.35
2001	72	116.13
2002	70	112.90

   b. Increase of 6.45 percent.

19.12 a.

	Simple Price Index		
Year	Product 1	Product 2	Product 3
2008	100.00	100.00	100.00
2009	104.20	98.56	102.21
2010	108.39	99.28	98.90

   b. Product 1's price increased each year, while product 2's price decreased each year. Product 3's price increased in 2009, but then decreased in 2010.

19.14 a.

Month	Jan	Feb	Mar	Apr	May	Jun
Price	3.25	3.18	3.56	3.82	3.97	4.48
Simple Price Index	100.00	97.85	109.54	117.54	122.15	137.85

Month	Jul	Aug	Sep	Oct	Nov	Dec
Price	4.46	4.16	3.79	3.39	2.46	1.82
Simple Price Index	137.23	128.00	116.62	104.31	75.69	56.00

   b. The price rose by 37.85 percent.

19.16 a.

Year	Tuition	Simple Price Index (Base = 2004)
2004	$36,850	100.00
2005	$39,844	108.12
2006	$42,634	115.70
2007	$44,556	120.91
2008	$46,784	126.96
2009	$48,650	132.02

b.

Year	Simple Price index (Base = 2004)	Updated Price Index (Base = 2007)
2004	100.00	82.70
2005	108.12	89.42
2006	115.70	95.69
2007	120.91	100.00
2008	126.96	105.00
2009	132.02	109.19

   c. Tuition increased by 20.91 percent from 2004 through 2007, but only 9.19 percent from 2007 through 2009.

19.18 a. Relative to 2007, the 2009 prices of omelet, pancake, and cereal increased by 5.26%, 28.57%, and 21.43%, respectively.

	Simple Price Index		
Year	Omelet	Pancakes	Cereal
2007	100.00	100.00	100.00
2008	110.53	121.43	114.29
2009	105.26	128.57	121.43

   b. Relative to 2007, the prices of the three breakfast items increased by 14.89% and 17.02% in 2008 and 2009, respectively.

Year	$\sum p_{it}$	Unweighted Aggregate Price Index
2007	11.75	100.00
2008	13.50	114.89
2009	13.75	117.02

19.20 a.

	Simple Price Index		
Region	2007	2008	2009
Northeast	100.00	94.24	83.55
Midwest	100.00	93.25	88.29
South	100.00	94.74	86.47
West	100.00	80.61	65.46

   b. Home prices dropped significantly; more drastically in the West.

19.22

Nominal Value	Price Index	Real Value
32	100	32.00
37	102	36.27
39	103	37.86
42	108	38.89

19.24 Real revenue increases to $\frac{\$110,000}{104} \times 100 = \$105,769$, resulting in an increase of $\frac{105,769 - 100,000}{100,000} \times 100 = 5.77\%$.

19.26 a-b.

Year	Nominal Value	Price Index	Real Value
2009	38	100	38.00
2010	40	103	38.83
2011	42	112	37.50

2009–2010: Nominal values increase by 5.26 percent. Real values increase by 2.18 percent.

2010–2011: Nominal values increase by 5 percent. Real values decrease by 3.43 percent.

c. 2010: $\frac{103 - 100}{100} \times 100 = 3.00\%$; 2011: $\frac{112 - 103}{103} \times 100 = 8.74\%$

19.28

Year	CPI	Inflation Rate (%)
2001	120.1	—
2002	119.0	−0.92
2003	118.7	−0.25
2004	118.7	0.00
2005	118.3	−0.34
2006	118.7	0.34
2007	118.7	0.00
2008	120.3	1.35
2009	118.7	−1.33

Inflation in Japan has been negative four times, which supports the deflation claim.

19.30 a.

Year	Revenue	PPI (1982 = 100)	Real Revenue
2007	$35,510,000	172.7	$20,561,667.63
2008	$37,843,000	189.6	$19,959,388.19
2009	$36,149,000	172.9	$20,907,460.96

b. Nominal revenue increases in 2008, but decreases in 2009. Real revenue decreases in 2008, but increases in 2009.

19.32 The inflation rate in 2009 is $\left(\frac{214.54 - 215.3}{215.3}\right) \times 100 = -0.35\%$. The 2009 starting salary must be reduced to $89,156(0.9965) = $88,844$.

19.34 a.

Date	Adjusted Close Price	Simple Price Index (Base = Oct 09)
Oct-09	78.89	100.00
Nov-09	78.54	99.56
Dec-09	84.16	106.68
Jan-10	77.00	97.60
Feb-10	74.83	94.85
Mar-10	79.56	100.85

b.

Date	Adjusted Close Price	Updated Index (Base = Jan 2010)
Oct-09	78.89	102.46
Nov-09	78.54	102.00
Dec-09	84.16	109.30
Jan-10	77.00	100.00
Feb-10	74.83	97.19
Mar-10	79.56	103.33

c. Increase by 6.68 percent.

d. Increase by 3.33 percent.

19.36 a.

	Simple Price Index (Base = 2009)		
Year	Product 1	Product 2	Product 3
2009	100.00	100.00	100.00
2010	105.26	97.87	106.67
2011	110.53	104.26	124.44

b.

Year	Σp_{it}	Unweighted Aggregate Price Index
2009	177	100.00
2010	180	101.69
2011	196	110.73

19.38 a.

Year	Σp_{it}	Unweighted Aggregate Price Index
2005	233.09	100.00
2006	475.34	203.93
2007	553.66	237.53

b.

Year	$\Sigma p_{it} q_{i0}$	Laspeyres Price Index
2005	33475	100.00
2006	59378	177.38
2007	69064	206.32

c. The unweighted index shows higher increases due primarily to Google's rise, but since Lindsay did not buy as much Google stock as the others, the weighted index shows smaller increases.

19.40 a.

Year	Net Revenue	PPI (1982 = 100)	Real Net Revenue
2006	146.6	164.8	88.96
2007	159.2	172.7	92.18
2008	105.8	189.6	55.80
2009	111.0	172.9	64.20

b.

Year	Net Income	CPI (1982–84 = 100)	Real Net Income
2006	21.2	201.59	10.52
2007	3.6	207.34	1.74
2008	−27.7	215.30	−12.87
2009	−1.6	214.54	−0.75

19.42 a.

Date	Adjusted Price	CPI (Base 1982–1984)	Real Adjusted Price	Real Return
January, 2008	8.94	212.23	4.21	—
February, 2008	8.29	212.70	3.90	−0.0748
March, 2008	6.01	213.54	2.81	−0.2779

b.

Date	Adjusted Price	Nominal Return	CPI (Base 1982–1984)	Inflation	Real Interest with Fisher (%)
January, 2008	8.94	—	212.23	—	—
February, 2008	8.29	−0.0727	212.70	0.0023	−0.0748
March, 2008	6.01	−0.2750	213.54	0.0039	−0.2779

Chapter 20

20.2 a. Reject H_0 if $T \leq T_L = 1$

b. $T = T^+ = 3 > 1 = T_L$; do not reject H_0. Cannot conclude that population median is less than 150.

20.4 a. $H_0: m \geq 10; H_A: m < 10$
   b. $T = T^+ = 1$
   c. Reject H_0 if $T \leq T_L = 2$
   d. $T = 1 < 2 = T_L$; reject H_0. Population median is less than 10.

20.6 a. $H_0: m \leq 25; H_A: m > 25$
   b. $T = T^+ = 35$; T is assumed normally distributed with
   $$\mu_T = \frac{n(n+1)}{4} = 27.5 \text{ and}$$
   $$\sigma_T = \sqrt{\frac{n(n+1)(2n+1)}{24}} = 9.81; z = \frac{T - \mu_T}{\sigma_T} = 0.76$$
   c. p-value $= 0.2236$
   d. p-value $= 0.2236 > 0.01 = \alpha$; do not reject H_0. Cannot conclude that population median is greater than 5.

20.8 a. Reject H_0 if $T \leq T_L = 8$.
   b. $T = T^+ = 5 < 8 = T_L$; reject H_0. Population median difference is less than 0.

20.10 a. $H_0: m_D \geq 0; H_A: m_D < 0$
   b. $T = T^+ = 3.5$
   c. Reject H_0 if $T \leq T_L = 5$
   d. $T = 3.5 < 5 = T_L$; reject H_0. Population median difference is less than 0.

20.12 a. Given that $n_1 = 7 < 8 = n_2$, $W = W_1 = 80$
   b. Reject H_0 if $W \leq W_L = 39$ or $W \geq W_U = 73$
   c. $W = 80 > 73 = W_U$; reject H_0. Medians of Populations 1 and 2 differ.

20.14 a. $H_0: m_1 - m_2 \geq 0; H_A: m_1 - m_2 < 0$
   b. Given that $n_1 = 5 < 6 = n_2$, $W = W_1 = 19.5$
   c. Reject H_0 if $W \leq W_L = 20$
   d. $W = 19.5 < 20$; reject H_0. Median of Population 1 is less than median of Population 2.

20.16 a. Given $n_1 = 25 > 20 = n_2$, $W = W_2 = 700$. W is approximately normally distributed with $\mu_W = \frac{n_2(n_1 + n_2 + 1)}{2}$
   $= 460$ and $\sigma_W = \sqrt{\frac{n_1 n_2(n_1 + n_2 + 1)}{12}} = 43.78$.
   b. $H_0: m_1 - m_2 \leq 0; H_A: m_1 - m_2 > 0$
   c. $z = \frac{W - \mu_W}{\sigma_W} = 5.48$
   d. $z_{0.05} = 1.645$
   e. $z = 5.48 > 1.645 = z_{0.05}$; reject H_0. Median of Population 1 is greater than median of Population 2.

20.18 a. $H_0: m_D = 0; H_A: m_D \neq 0$
   b. $T = T^+ = 14; \mu_T = \frac{n(n+1)}{4} = 27.5, \sigma_T = \sqrt{\frac{n(n+1)(2n+1)}{24}}$
   $= 9.81; z = \frac{T - \mu_T}{\sigma_T} = -1.38$
   c. $z_{\alpha/2} = z_{0.025} = 1.96$; reject H_0 if $z < -1.96$ or $z > 1.96$.
   d. $-1.96 < z = -1.38 < 1.96$; do not reject H_0. No.

20.20 a. $H_0: m_1 - m_2 \leq 0; H_A: m_1 - m_2 > 0$
   b. Given $n_1 = 6 < 7 = n_2$, $W = W_1 = 59.5$
   c. Reject H_0 if $W \geq W_U = 54$
   d. $W = 59.5 > 54 = W_U$; reject H_0. Yes.

20.22 a. $H_0: m_1 - m_2 \leq 0; H_A: m_1 - m_2 > 0$
   b. Given $n_1 = n_2 = 10$, $W = W_1 = 138$
   c. $\mu_W = \frac{n_1(n_2 + n_1 + 1)}{2} = 105, \sigma_W = \sqrt{\frac{n_1 n_2(n_1 + n_2 + 1)}{12}} = 13.23$
   $z = \frac{W - \mu_W}{\sigma_W} = 2.49 > 1.645 = z_{0.05}$; reject H_0. The claim is supported.

20.24 a. $H_0: m_1 = m_2 = m_3 = m_4 = m_5; H_A:$ Not all population medians are equal.
   b. With $df = 4$, p-value is strictly between 0.01 and 0.025.
   c. p-value $< 0.05 = \alpha$; reject H_0. Some population medians differ.

20.26 a. $H_0: m_1 = m_2 = m_3 = m_4; H_A:$ Not all population medians are equal
   b. $H = \frac{12}{n(n+1)} \Sigma \frac{R_i^2}{n_i} - 3(n+1) = 10.52$
   c. With $df = 3$, p-value is strictly between 0.01 and 0.025.
   d. p-value $> \alpha = 0.01$; do not reject H_0. Cannot conclude that some population medians differ.

20.28 a. $H_0: m_1 = m_2 = m_3; H_A:$ Not all population medians are equal
   b. $H = \frac{12}{n(n+1)} \Sigma \frac{R_i^2}{n_i} - 3(n+1) = 9.11$
   c. With $df = 2$, p-value is strictly between 0.01 and 0.025.
   d. p-value $< \alpha = 0.10$; reject H_0. Some population medians differ.

20.30 a. $H_0: m_1 = m_2 = m_3; H_A:$ Not all population medians are equal
   b. $H = \frac{12}{n(n+1)} \Sigma \frac{R_i^2}{n_i} - 3(n+1) = 1.51$
   c. p-value is greater than 0.10.
   d. p-value $> \alpha = 0.01$; do not reject H_0. No.

20.32 a. $r_S = -0.64$
   b. Reject H_0 if $|r_S| >$ Critical-Value $= 0.600$
   c. $|r_S| = 0.64 > 0.600 =$ Critical-Value; reject H_0. Spearman rank correlation coefficient is less than zero.

20.34 a. $r_S = 1 - \frac{6\Sigma d_i^2}{n(n^2 - 1)} = -0.83$; strong, negative relationship
   b. $H_0: \rho_S \geq 0; H_A: \rho_S < 0$
   c. Reject H_0 if $|r_S| >$ Critical-Value $= 0.943$
   d. $|r_S| = 0.83 < 0.943 =$ Critical-Value; do not reject H_0. Cannot conclude that variables are negatively related.

20.36 a. $z = r_S \sqrt{n - 1} = 4.48$; p-value ≈ 0.
   b. p-value $\approx 0 < 0.01 = \alpha$; reject H_0. Variables are positively related.

20.38 a. $r_S = 1 - \frac{6\Sigma d_i^2}{n(n^2 - 1)} = -0.21$; weak, negative relationship
   b. $H_0: \rho_S = 0; H_A: \rho_S \neq 0$
   c. Reject H_0 if $|r_S| >$ Critical-Value $= 0.648$
   d. $|r_S| = 0.21 < 0.648 =$ Critical-Value; do not reject H_0. No.

20.40 a. $r_S = 1 - \frac{6\Sigma d_i^2}{n(n^2 - 1)} = 0.49$; moderate, positive relationship
   b. $H_0: \rho_S = 0; H_A: \rho_S \neq 0$
   c. Reject H_0 if $|r_S| >$ Critical-Value $= 0.738$
   d. $|r_S| = 0.49 < 0.738 =$ Critical-Value; do not reject H_0. No.

20.42 a. $H_0: \rho_S = 0; H_A: \rho_S \neq 0$
   b. $z = r_S \sqrt{n - 1} = 6.8$; p-value ≈ 0
   c. p-value $\approx 0 < 0.05 = \alpha$; reject H_0. Yes.

20.44 a. $z = \frac{\bar{p} - 0.50}{0.5/\sqrt{n}} = -2.53$
   b. p-value $= 0.0114$
   c. p-value $= 0.0114 < 0.05 = \alpha$; reject H_0. Population proportion differs from 0.50.

20.46 a. $H_0: p = 0.50; H_A: p \neq 0.50$
   b. $\bar{p} = \frac{15}{20} = 0.75; z = \frac{\bar{p} - 0.50}{0.5/\sqrt{n}} = 2.24$
   c. p-value $= 0.0250$
   d. p-value $= 0.0250 < 0.05 = \alpha$; reject H_0. Proportion of positive signs differs from proportion of negative signs.

20.48 a. $H_0: p = 0.50; H_A: p \neq 0.50$
   b. $\bar{p} = \frac{9}{14} = 0.64; z = \frac{\bar{p} - 0.50}{0.5/\sqrt{n}} = 1.05$
   c. p-value $= 0.2938$
   d. p-value $= 0.2938 > 0.05 = \alpha$; do not reject H_0. No.

20.50 a. $H_0: p = 0.50; H_A: p \neq 0.50$
   b. $\bar{p} = \frac{3}{12 - 2} = 0.70; z = \frac{\bar{p} - 0.50}{0.5/\sqrt{n}} = -1.26$

c. Reject H_0 if $z < -1.645$ or $z > 1.645$.

d. $-1.645 < z = -1.26 < 1.645$; do not reject H_0. No.

20.52 a. H_0: The elements occur randomly; H_A: The elements do not occur randomly.

b. $\mu_R = \frac{2n_1n_2}{n} + 1 = 26.85$, $\sigma_R = \sqrt{\frac{2n_1n_2(2n_1n_2 - n)}{n^2(n-1)}} = 3.55$; $z = \frac{R - \mu_R}{\sigma_R} = -2.49$

c. p-value $= 0.0128$

d. p-value $= 0.0128 < 0.05 = \alpha$; reject H_0. Yes.

20.54 a. H_0: outcomes occur randomly; H_A: Outcomes do not occur randomly

$R = 10 + 10 = 20$, $n_1 = 17$, $n_2 = 14$, $n = n_1 + n_2 = 31$;

$\mu_R = \frac{2n_1n_2}{n} + 1 = 16.35$, $\sigma_R = \sqrt{\frac{2n_1n_2(2n_1n_2 - n)}{n^2(n-1)}} = 2.71$;

$z = \frac{R - \mu_R}{\sigma_R} = 1.35$; p-value $= 0.1770 > 0.05 = \alpha$; do not reject H_0. Cannot conclude that outcomes are non-random.

20.56 a. H_0: Even and odd numbers occur randomly.
H_A: Even and odd numbers do not occur randomly.

b. $R = 4 + 4 = 8$, $n_1 = 12$, $n_2 = 10$, $n = n_1 + n_2 = 22$;

$\mu_R = \frac{2n_1n_2}{n} + 1 = 11.91$, $\sigma_R = \sqrt{\frac{2n_1n_2(2n_1n_2 - n)}{n^2(n-1)}} = 2.27$;

$z = \frac{R - \mu_R}{\sigma_R} = -1.72$

c. Reject H_0 if $z < -2.58$ or $z > 2.58$

d. $-2.58 < z = -1.72 < 2.58$; do not reject H_0. Yes.

20.58 H_0: GDP growth rate is random; H_A: GDP growth rate is not random.

$R = 6 + 5 = 11$, $n_1 = 14$, $n_2 = 14$, $n = n_1 + n_2 = 28$

$\mu_R = \frac{2n_1n_2}{n} + 1 = 15.0$, $\sigma_R = \sqrt{\frac{2n_1n_2(2n_1n_2 - n)}{n^2(n-1)}} = 2.60$;

$z = \frac{R - \mu_R}{\sigma_R} = -1.54$;

p-value $= 0.1236 > 0.05 = \alpha$; do not reject H_0. Cannot conclude that Indian GDP growth rate is non-random.

20.60 a. H_0: Amgen stock price follows a random walk.

H_A: Amgen stock price does not follow a random walk.

b. Using Minitab: p-value $\approx 0 < 0.05 = \alpha$; reject H_0. Amgen stock price does not follow a random walk.

20.62 a. H_0: $m_D = 0$; H_A: $m_D \neq 0$

b. $T = T^+ = 9.5$

c. Reject H_0 if $T \leq T_L = 0$ or $T \geq T_U = 21$

d. $0 < T = 9.5 < 21$; do not reject H_0. Population median difference is not significantly different from 0. Farmer should not be concerned.

20.64 a. H_0: $m_A - m_B = 0$; H_A: $m_A - m_B \neq 0$

b. Given $n_1 = n_2 = 40$, $W = W_1 = 1492$

c. $\mu_W = \frac{n_1(n_1 + n_2 + 1)}{2} = 1620$, $\sigma_W = \sqrt{\frac{n_1n_2(n_1 + n_2 + 1)}{12}} = 103.92$;

$z = \frac{W - \mu_W}{\sigma_W} = \frac{1492 - 1620}{103.92} = -1.23$.

d. p-value $= 0.2186 > 0.05 = \alpha$; do not reject H_0. Cannot conclude that median longevities of Brands A and B differ.

20.66 a. H_0: $m_1 = m_2 = m_3$; H_A: Not all population medians are equal.

b. $H = \frac{12}{n(n+1)} \sum \frac{R_i^2}{n_i} - 3(n+1) = 7.98$

c. $\chi^2_{0.05,2} = 5.991$

d. $H = 7.98 > 5.991$; reject H_0. Some population median P/E ratios differ.

20.68 a. H_0: $\rho_S = 0$; H_A: $\rho_S \neq 0$

b. $z = r_S \sqrt{n-1} = 0.45 \sqrt{65 - 1} = 3.60$; p-value ≈ 0

c. p-value $\approx 0 < 0.05 = \alpha$; reject H_0. Yes.

20.70 H_0: GDP growth rate is random; H_A: GDP growth rate is not random.

$R = 5 + 4 = 9$, $n_1 = 14$, $n_2 = 14$, and $n = n_1 + n_2 = 28$

$\mu_R = \frac{2n_1n_2}{n} + 1 = 15.0$, $\sigma_R = \sqrt{\frac{2n_1n_2(2n_1n_2 - n)}{n^2(n-1)}} = 2.6$; $z = \frac{R - \mu_R}{\sigma_R} = -2.31$;

p-value $= 0.0208 < 0.05 = \alpha$; reject H_0. China GDP growth rate is not random.

20.72 H_0: US CPI is random; H_A: US CPI is not random.

$R = 5 + 5 = 10$, $n_1 = 13$, $n_2 = 14$, $n = n_1 + n_2 = 27$

$\mu_R = \frac{2n_1n_2}{n} + 1 = 14.48$, $\sigma_R = \sqrt{\frac{2n_1n_2(2n_1n_2 - n)}{n^2(n-1)}} = 2.54$;

$z = \frac{R - \mu_R}{\sigma_R} = -1.76$;

p-value $= 0.0784 > 0.05 = \alpha$; do not reject H_0. Cannot conclude that CPI index in U.S. is non-random.

Addition rule   The probability that *A* or *B* occurs, or that at least one of these events occurs, is equal to the probability that *A* occurs, plus the probability that *B* occurs, minus the probability that both *A* and *B* occur, or equivalently,

$$P(A \cup B) = P(A) + P(B) - P(A \cap B).$$

Adjusted close price   Stock price data adjusted using appropriate dividend and split multipliers.

Adjusted R^2   A modification of the coefficient of determination that explicitly accounts for the sample size *n* and the number of explanatory variables *k* in regression analysis; often used as a criterion for selecting among regression models with different numbers of explanatory variables.

Aggregate price index   A representation of relative price movements for a group of items.

Alternative hypothesis (H_A)   In a hypothesis text, the alternative hypothesis contradicts the default state or status quo specified in the null hypothesis. Generally, whatever we wish to establish is placed in the alternative hypothesis.

Analysis of variance (ANOVA)   A statistical technique used to determine if differences exist between several population means.

Annualized return   A measure equivalent to the geometric mean return.

A priori probability   A probability value based on logical analysis rather than on observation or personal judgment.

Arithmetic mean   The arithmetic mean is the primary measure of central location. It is calculated by adding up the values of all the data points and dividing by the number of data points in the population or sample.

Autoregressive model   In forecasting, a model where lagged values of the response variable are used as explanatory variables.

Average growth rate   For growth rates $g_1, g_2, \ldots, g_n$, the average growth rate G_g is computed as

$$G_g = \sqrt[n]{(1 + g_1)(1 + g_2) \cdots (1 + g_n)} - 1,$$

where *n* is the number of multi-period growth rates.

Balanced data   A completely randomized ANOVA design with an equal number of observations in each sample.

Bar chart   A graph that depicts the frequency or relative frequency of each category of qualitative data as a bar rising vertically from the horizontal axis.

Bayes' theorem   The rule for updating probabilities is

$$P(B|A) = \frac{P(A|B)P(B)}{P(A|B)P(B) + P(A|B^c)P(B^c)},$$

where $P(B)$ is the prior probability and $P(B|A)$ is the posterior probability.

Bernoulli process   A series of *n* independent and identical trials of an experiment such that each trial has only two possible outcomes, conventionally labeled success and failure, and each time we repeat the trial, the probabilities of success and failure remain the same.

Between-treatments variability   In ANOVA, a measure of the variability between sample means.

Bias   The tendency of a sample statistic to systematically over- or underestimate a population parameter.

Binary choice models   Regression models that use a dummy (binary) variable as the response variable. Also called discrete choice or qualitative response models.

Binomial probability distribution   A description of the probabilities associated with the possible values of a binomial random variable.

Binomial random variable   The number of successes achieved in the *n* trials of a Bernoulli process.

Block   In ANOVA, a matched group of observations from each population. In general, blocks are the levels at which the extraneous factor is held fixed, so that its contribution to the total variation of the data can be measured.

Box plot   A graphical display of the smallest value, quartiles, and the largest value of a data set.

Capital gains yield   The gain or loss resulting from the increase or decrease in the value of an asset.

Causal forecasting models   Quantitative forecasts based on a regression framework, where the variable of interest is related to a single or multiple explanatory variables.

Central limit theorem (CLT)   The CLT states that the sum or mean of a large number of independent observations from the same underlying distribution has an approximate normal distribution. The approximation steadily improves as the number of observations increases.

Chebyshev's theorem   For any data set, the percentage of observations that lie within *k* standard deviations from the mean will be at least $1 - 1/k^2$, where *k* is any number greater than 1.

Chi-square (χ^2) distribution   A family of distributions where each distribution depends on its particular degrees of freedom *df*. It is positively skewed, but becomes increasingly symmetric as *df* increase.

Classes   Intervals of quantitative data.

Cluster sampling   A population is first divided up into mutually exclusive and collectively exhaustive groups of observations, called clusters. A cluster sample includes observations from randomly selected clusters.

Coefficient of determination (R^2)   The proportion of the sample variation in the response variable that is explained by the sample regression equation; used as a goodness-of-fit measure in regression analysis.

Coefficient of variation (CV)   The ratio of the standard deviation of a data set to its mean; a relative measure of dispersion.

Combination formula   The number of ways to choose *x* objects from a total of *n* objects, where the order in which the *x* objects is listed *does not matter*, is

$$_nC_x = \binom{n}{x} = \frac{n!}{(n - x)!x!}.$$

Complement rule   The probability of the complement of an event is one minus the probability of the event, or equivalently, $P(A^c) = 1 - P(A)$.

Completely randomized design   An experiment in which independent random samples are drawn from the *c* different levels of a given factor (*c* populations), ignoring all other possible factors.

Conditional probability   The probability of an event given that another event has already occurred.

Confidence coefficient   The probability that a given confidence interval will contain the population parameter of interest.

Confidence interval   A range of values that, with a certain measure of confidence, contains the population parameter of interest.

Consistency   An estimator is consistent if it approaches the unknown population parameter being estimated as the sample size grows larger.

Consumer price index (CPI)   A monthly weighted aggregate price index, computed by the U.S. Bureau of Labor Statistics, based on the prices paid by urban consumers for a representative basket of goods and services.

Contingency table   A table that shows frequencies for two qualitative or categorical variables, x and y, where each cell represents a mutually exclusive combination of the pair of x and y values.

Continuous (random) variable   A variable that assumes (infinitely) uncountable values and can take on any value within an interval.

Continuous uniform distribution   A distribution describing a continuous random variable that has an equally likely chance of assuming a value within a specified range.

Control chart   A plot of statistics of a production process over time. If the statistics randomly fall in an expected range, then the production process is in control. If the statistics reveal an undesirable trend, then adjustment of the production process is likely necessary.

Correlation coefficient   A measure that describes the direction and strength of the linear relationship between two variables.

Covariance   A measure that reveals the direction of the linear relationship between two variables.

Critical value   In a hypothesis test, the critical value is a point that separates the rejection region from the non-rejection region.

Cross-sectional data   Values of a characteristic of many subjects at the same point in time or without regard to differences in time.

Cubic regression model   In regression analysis, the relationship between the explanatory variable and the response variable is modeled as a polynomial of order 3; it is used when the influence of that explanatory variable on the response variable has two changes of sign.

Cumulative distribution function   A description of the probability that the value of a random variable X is less than or equal to a particular value x, $P(X \leq x)$.

Cumulative frequency distribution   A distribution of quantitative data recording the number of observations that falls below the upper limit of each class.

Cumulative relative frequency distribution   A distribution of quantitative data recording the fraction or proportion of observations that falls below the upper limit of each class.

Cyclical component   Wave-like fluctuations or business cycles of a time series, often caused by expansion and contraction of the economy.

Decomposition analysis   A method of estimating trend and seasonal components from a time series and then recomposing them to make forecasts.

Deflated time series   A series obtained by adjusting a given series for changes in prices, or inflation. The two most commonly used price indices for deflating economic time series are the Consumer Price Index, CPI, and the Producer Price Index, PPI.

Degrees of freedom   The number of independent pieces of information that go into the calculation of a given statistic. Many probability distributions are identified by the degrees of freedom.

Dependent events   The occurrence of one event is related to the probability of the occurrence of the other event.

Descriptive statistics   The summary of a data set in the form of tables, graphs, or the calculation of numerical measures.

Deterministic relationship   In regression analysis, a relationship in which the value of the response variable is uniquely determined by the values of the explanatory variables.

Discrete (random) variable   A variable that assumes either a finite number of values or an infinite sequence of values.

Discrete uniform distribution   A symmetric distribution where the random variable assumes a finite number of values and each value is equally likely.

Dummy variable   A variable that takes on values of 0 or 1. It is commonly used to describe a qualitative variable with two categories.

Dummy variable trap   A linear regression model where the number of dummy variables equals the number of categories of a qualitative variable; in a correctly specified model, the number of dummy variables is one less than the number of categories.

Efficiency   An unbiased estimator is efficient if its standard deviation or standard error is lower than that of other unbiased estimators.

Empirical probability   A probability value based on observing the relative frequency with which an event occurs.

Empirical rule   Given a sample mean $\bar{x}$, a sample standard deviation s, and a relatively symmetric and bell-shaped distribution:

- Approximately 68% of all observations fall in the interval $\bar{x} \pm s$,
- Approximately 95% of all observations fall in the interval $\bar{x} \pm 2s$, and
- Almost all observations fall in the interval $\bar{x} \pm 3s$.

Endogeneity   In regression analysis, a situation where the error term is correlated with the explanatory variables.

Error sum of squares (SSE)   In ANOVA, a measure of the degree of variability that exists even if all population means are the same. Also known as within-sample variation. In regression analysis, it is the sum of the squared residuals.

Estimate   A particular value of an estimator.

Estimator   A statistic used to estimate a population parameter.

Event   A subset of the sample space.

Exhaustive events   When all possible outcomes of a random experiment are included in the events.

Expected return of a portfolio   A weighted average of the expected returns of the individual assets in the portfolio.

Expected value   A weighted average of all possible values of a random variable.

Experiment   A trial that results in any one of several possible outcomes.

Explanatory variables   In regression analysis, the variables that we assume affect the response variable. They are also called the independent variables, predictor variables, control variables, or regressors.

Exponential probability distribution   A continuous probability distribution used to model lifetimes or failure times. It is based on one parameter that is referred to as the rate parameter.

Exponential regression model   A semi-log regression model in which only the response variable is transformed into natural logs.

Exponential smoothing   In time series analysis, a smoothing technique that assigns exponentially decreasing weights as the observations get older.

Exponential trend model   A model used for a time series that grows by an increasing amount each time period.

Factorial formula   The number of ways to assign every member of a group of size n to n slots is $n! = n \times (n - 1) \times (n - 2) \times (n - 3) \times \cdots \times 1$.

F distribution   A family of distributions where each distribution depends on two degrees of freedom: the numerator degrees of freedom df_1 and the denominator degrees of freedom df_2. It is positively skewed, but becomes increasingly symmetric as df_1 and df_2 increase.

Finite population correction factor   A correction factor that accounts for the added precision gained by sampling a larger percentage of the population. It is recommended when the sample constitutes at least 5% of the population.

Fisher equation   A theoretical relationship between nominal returns, real returns, and the expected inflation rate.

Fisher's least difference (LSD) method   In ANOVA, a test that determines which means significantly differ by computing all pairwise differences of the means.

Frequency distribution   A grouping of qualitative data into categories, or quantitative data into intervals called classes, recording the number of observations that fall into each category or class.

Geometric mean return   For multiperiod returns $R_1, R_2, \ldots, R_n$, the geometric mean return G_R is computed as

$$G_R = \sqrt[n]{(1 + R_1)(1 + R_2) \cdots (1 + R_n)} - 1,$$

where n is the number of multiperiod returns.

Goodness-of-fit test   A test, using the chi-square statistic, to determine if the sample proportions resulting from a multinomial experiment differ from the hypothesized population proportions specified in the null hypothesis.

Goodness-of-fit test for normality   A test, using the chi-square statistic, to determine if sample data are derived from the normally distributed population.

Grand mean   In ANOVA, the sum of all observations in a data set divided by the total number of observations.

Heteroskedasticity   In regression analysis, a violation of the assumption where the variance of the error term is not the same for all observations.

Histogram   A graphical depiction of a frequency or relative frequency distribution; it is a series of rectangles where the width and height of each rectangle represents the class width and frequency (or relative frequency) of the respective class.

Hypergeometric probability distribution   A description of the probabilities associated with the possible values of a hypergeometric random variable.

Hypergeometric random variable   The number of successes achieved in the n trials of a Bernoulli-type process in which the trials cannot be assumed to be independent.

Hypothesis test   A statistical procedure to resolve conflicts between two competing opinions (hypotheses) on a particular population parameter of interest.

Income yield   The direct cash payments from an underlying asset, such as dividends, interest, or rental income.

Independent events   The occurrence of one event does not affect the probability of the occurrence of the other event.

Independent random samples   Two (or more) random samples are considered independent if the process that generates one sample is completely separate from the process that generates the other sample.

Index number   An easy-to-interpret numerical value that reflects a percentage change in price or quantity from a base value. The most common example is a price index.

Inferential statistics   The practice of extracting useful information from a sample to draw conclusions about a population.

Inflation rate   The percentage rate of change of a price index over time.

In-sample criteria   Calculations showing how well a forecasting model predicts values within a sample of data.

Interquartile range (IQR)   The difference between the quartile values Q3 and Q1.

Interval estimate   See *Confidence interval*.

Interval-scaled data   Values of a quantitative variable that can be categorized and ranked, and in which differences between values are meaningful.

Inverse transformation   A standard normal variable Z can be transformed to the normally distributed random variable X with mean μ and standard deviation σ as $X = \mu + Z\sigma$.

Investment return   The net gain or loss in value of an investment over a time period.

Jarque-Bera test   A test, using the chi-square statistic, to determine if sample data are derived from the normally distributed population.

Joint probability   The probability of the occurrence of two events, A and B.

Joint probability table   A contingency table whose frequencies have been converted to relative frequencies.

Kruskal-Wallis test   A nonparametric test to determine whether differences exist between several population medians.

Kurtosis coefficient   A measure of whether data is more or less peaked than a normal distribution.

Laspeyres price index   A weighted aggregate price index based on quantities evaluated in the base period.

Linear probability model (LPM)   A linear regression model applied to a binary response variable.

Linear trend model   A regression model used for a time series that grows by a fixed amount each time period.

Logarithmic regression model   A semi-log regression model in which only the explanatory variable is transformed into natural logs.

Logit model   A regression model that ensures that the predicted probability of the binary response variable falls between zero and one.

Log-log regression model   A regression model in which both the response variable and the explanatory variable are transformed into natural logs.

Lognormal probability distribution   A positively skewed continuous probability distribution used to model variables that are known to be positively skewed.

Marginal (unconditional) probability   The probability of an event without any restriction.

Margin of error   A value that accounts for the variability of the estimator and the desired confidence level of the interval. Often the confidence interval is specified as: Point Estimate ± Margin of Error.

Matched-pairs sample   When samples are matched or paired in some way. The first type of matched-pairs sample is characterized by a measurement, an intervention of some type, and then another measurement. The second type of matched-pairs sample is characterized by a pairing of observations, where it is not the same individual or item that gets sampled twice.

Mean   Often used as a short form for the arithmetic average. It is calculated by adding up the values of all the data points and dividing by the number of data points in the population or sample.

Mean absolute deviation (MAD)   In forecasting, the mean of the absolute residuals; it is used for model selection.

Mean square error (MSE)   In forecasting, the residual sum of squares divided by the number of observations; it is used for model selection.

Mean-variance analysis   The idea that we measure the performance of an asset by its rate of return and evaluate this rate of return in terms of its reward (mean) and risk (variance).

Median   The middle value of a data set.

Mode   The most frequently occurring value in a data set.

Moving average method   In time series analysis, a smoothing technique based on computing the average from a fixed number m of the most recent observations.

Multicollinearity   In regression analysis, a situation where two or more explanatory variables are linearly related.

Multinomial experiment   A series of n identical trials of a random experiment, such that for each trial: there are k possible outcomes or categories, called cells; each time the trial is repeated, the probability that the outcome falls into a particular

cell p_i remains the same; the sum of the cell probabilities is one, $p_1 + p_2 + \cdots + p_k = 1$.

Multiple regression model   In regression analysis, more than one explanatory variable is used to explain the variability in the response variable.

Multiplication rule   The probability that A and B both occur, or a joint probability, is equal to the probability that A occurs given that B has occurred times the probability that B occurs, that is,

$$P(A \cap B) = P(A \mid B)P(B).$$

Mutually exclusive events   Events that do not share any common outcome of a random experiment.

Negatively skewed (left-skewed) distribution   A distribution in which extreme values are concentrated in the left tail of the distribution.

Nominal data   Values of a qualitative variable that differ merely by name or label.

Nominal return   Investment return that makes no allowance for inflation.

Non-causal forecasting models   Quantitative forecasts that do not present any explanation of the mechanism generating the variable of interest and simply provide a method for projecting historical data. Also called purely time-series models.

Nonparametric tests   Statistical tests that rely on fewer assumptions concerning the distribution of the underlying population. Often used when the underlying distribution is not normal and the sample size is small.

Nonresponse bias   A systematic difference in preferences between respondents and nonrespondents of a survey or a poll.

Normal curve   A graph depicting the normal probability density function.

Normal distribution   The most extensively used probability distribution in statistical work and the cornerstone of statistical inference. Also called the symmetric or bell-shaped distribution.

Normal transformation   Any normally distributed random variable X with mean μ and standard deviation σ can be transformed into the standard normal random variable Z as

$$Z = \frac{X - \mu}{\sigma}.$$

Null hypothesis (H_0)   In a hypothesis test, the null hypothesis corresponds to a presumed default state of nature or status quo.

Ogive   A graph of the cumulative frequency or cumulative relative frequency distribution in which lines connect a series of neighboring points, where each point represents the upper limit of each class and its corresponding cumulative frequency or cumulative relative frequency.

One-tailed hypothesis test   A test in which the null hypothesis is rejected only on one side of the hypothesized value of the population parameter.

One-way ANOVA   A statistical technique that analyzes the effect of one categorical variable or factor on the mean.

Ordinal data   Values of a qualitative variable that can be categorized and ranked.

Ordinary least squares (OLS) method   A regression technique for fitting a straight line that is "closest" to the data. Also known as the method of least squares.

Outliers   Extreme small or large values.

$\bar{p}$ bar chart   A control chart that monitors the proportion of defectives (or some other characteristic) of a production process.

Paasche price index   A weighted aggregate price index based on quantities evaluated in the current period.

Parameter   A constant characteristic of a population.

Partial F test   See *test of linear restrictions*.

Percentiles   The pth percentile divides a data set into two parts: Approximately p percent of the observations have values less than the pth percentile; approximately $(100 - p)$ percent of the observations have values greater than the pth percentile.

Permutation formula   The number of ways to choose x objects from a total of n objects, where the order in which the x objects is listed *does matter*, is $_nP_x = \dfrac{n!}{(n - x)!}$

Pie chart   A segmented circle portraying the categories and relative sizes of some qualitative variable.

Point estimate   The value of the point estimator derived from a given sample.

Point estimator   A function of the random sample used to make inferences about the value of an unknown population parameter.

Poisson process   A random experiment in which the number of successes within a specified time or space interval equals any integer between zero and infinity; the numbers of successes counted in nonoverlapping intervals are independent from one another; and the probability that success occurs in any interval is the same for all intervals of equal size and is proportional to the size of the interval.

Poisson probability distribution   A description of the probabilities associated with the possible values of a Poisson random variable.

Poisson random variable   The number of successes over a given interval of time or space in a Poisson process.

Polygon   A graph of a frequency or relative frequency distribution in which lines connect a series of neighboring points, where each point represents the midpoint of a particular class and its associated frequency or relative frequency.

Polynomial regression models   Regression models that describe various numbers of sign changes in the influence of an explanatory variable on a response variable.

Polynomial trend models   Models used for time series that reverse direction. A quadratic trend model is used for one change of direction, a cubic trend model is used for two changes of direction, etc.

Population   The complete collection of items with the characteristic we wish to understand; all items of interest in a statistical problem.

Portfolio   A collection of assets.

Portfolio variance   A measure reflecting a portfolio's risk that depends on the variance of the individual assets in the portfolio and on the covariance between the assets.

Positively skewed (right-skewed) distribution   A distribution in which extreme values are concentrated in the right tail of the distribution.

Prediction interval   In regression analysis, an interval that pertains to the individual value of the response variable defined for specific explanatory variables.

Probability   A numerical value between 0 and 1 that measures the likelihood that an uncertain outcome occurs.

Probability distribution   Every random variable is associated with a probability distribution that describes the variable completely. It is common to define discrete random variables in terms of their probability mass function and continuous random variables in terms of their probability density function.

Producer price index (PPI)   A monthly weighted aggregate price index, computed by the U.S. Bureau of Labor Statistics, based on prices measured at the wholesale or producer level.

p-Value   In a hypothesis test, the likelihood of observing a sample mean that is at least as extreme as the one derived from the given sample, under the assumption that the null hypothesis is true.

Quadratic regression model   In regression analysis, the relationship between the explanatory variable and the response variable is modeled as a polynomial of order 2; it is used when the influence of that explanatory variable on the response variable changes sign (U-shaped or inverted U-shaped curve).

Qualitative forecasting   Forecasts based on the judgment of the forecaster, using prior experience and expertise.

Qualitative variable   A variable normally described in words rather than numerically; it is often denoted by a binary outcome.

Quantitative forecasts   Forecasts based on a formal model, along with historical data for the variable of interest.

Quantitative variable   A variable that assumes meaningful numerical values.

Quartiles   Any of the three values that divide the ordered data into four equal parts, so that each part represents ¼ of the sample or population.

Randomized block design   In ANOVA, the design of an experiment in which units within each block are randomly assigned to each of the treatments.

Random variable   A function that summarizes outcomes of an experiment with numerical values.

Range   The difference between the maximum and the minimum values in a data set.

Ratio-scaled data   Values of a quantitative variable that can be categorized and ranked, and in which differences between values are meaningful; in addition, a true zero point (origin) exists.

Real return   Investment return that is adjusted for the change in purchasing power due to inflation.

Regression analysis   A statistical method for analyzing the relationship between variables. The method assumes that one variable, called the response variable, is influenced by other variables, called the explanatory variables.

Rejection region   In a hypothesis test, a range of values such that if the value of the test statistic falls into this range, then the decision is to reject the null hypothesis.

Relative frequency distribution A frequency distribution that shows the fraction or proportion of observations in each category of qualitative data or class of quantitative data.

Residual (e) In regression analysis, the difference between the predicted and the actual value, that is, $e = y - \hat{y}$.

Residual plots In regression analysis, graphs of residuals against variables and time to check for model inadequacies.

Response variable In regression analysis, the variable that we assume is affected by other variables. It is also called the dependent variable, the explained variable, the predicted variable, or the regressand.

Risk averse consumer Someone who may decline a risky prospect even if it offers a positive expected gain.

Risk loving consumer Someone who may accept a risky prospect even if the expected gain is negative.

Risk neutral consumer Someone who completely ignores risk and always accepts a prospect that offers a positive expected gain.

Runs test A procedure used to examine whether the elements in a sequence appear in random order.

Sample A subset of a population of interest.

Sample space (S) A record of all possible outcomes of an experiment.

Sampling distribution The probability distribution of an estimator.

Scatterplot A graphical tool that helps in determining whether or not two variables are related in some systematic way. Each point in the diagram represents a pair of known or observed values of the two variables.

Seasonal component Repetitions of a time series over a one-year period.

Seasonal dummy variables Dummy variables used to capture the seasonal component from a time series.

Seasonal index A measure of the seasonal variation within a time series; used to deseasonalize data.

Selection bias A systematic exclusion of certain groups from consideration for a sample.

Semi-log regression models Regression models in which some but not all variables are transformed into natural logs.

Serial correlation In regression analysis, a situation where the error term is correlated across observations.

Sharpe ratio The ratio of reward to risk, with the reward specified in terms of the mean and the risk specified in terms of the standard deviation.

Sign test A nonparametric test to determine whether significant differences exist between two populations using matched-pairs sampling with ordinal data.

Simple linear regression model In regression analysis, one explanatory variable is used to explain the variability in the response variable.

Simple price index For any item, the ratio of the price in a given time period to the price in the base period, expressed as a percentage.

Simple random sample A sample of n observations that has the same probability of being selected from the population as any other sample of n observations.

Skewness coefficient A measure of how symmetric data are about the mean. Symmetric data have a skewness coefficient of zero.

Smoothing techniques In time series analysis, methods to provide forecasts if short-term fluctuations represent random departures from the structure with no discernible systematic patterns.

Spearman rank correlation test A nonparametric test to determine whether two variables are correlated.

Standard deviation The positive square root of the variance; a common measure of dispersion.

Standard error An estimate of the standard deviation of an estimator.

Standard error of the estimate The standard deviation of the residual, used as a goodness-of-fit measure for regression analysis.

Standard normal distribution A special case of the normal distribution with a mean equal to zero and a standard deviation (or variance) equal to one.

Statistic A characteristic of a sample used to make inferences about an unknown population parameter; a statistic is a random variable whose value depends on the chosen random sample.

Statistical Quality Control Statistical techniques used to develop and maintain a firm's ability to produce high-quality goods and services.

Stem-and-leaf diagram A visual method of displaying quantitative data where each value of a data set is separated into two parts: a stem, which consists of the leftmost digits, and a leaf, which consists of the last digit.

Stochastic relationship In regression analysis, a relationship in which the explanatory variables do not exactly predict the response variable.

Stratified random sampling A population is first divided up into mutually exclusive and collectively exhaustive groups, called strata. A stratified sample includes randomly selected observations from each stratum, which are proportional to the stratum's size.

Subjective probability A probability value based on personal and subjective judgment.

Symmetric distribution A distribution that is a mirror image of itself about its mean.

Systematic patterns In time series, patterns caused by a set of identifiable components: the trend, seasonal, and the cyclical components.

t Distribution A family of distributions that are similar to the z distribution except that they have broader tails. They are identified by their degrees of freedom that determine the extent of broadness.

Test of independence A goodness-of-fit test analyzing the relationship between two qualitative variables. Also called a chi-square test of a contingency table.

Test of individual significance In regression analysis, a test that determines whether an explanatory variable has an individual statistical influence on the response variable.

Test of joint significance In regression analysis, a test to determine whether the explanatory variables have a joint statistical influence on the response variable; it is often regarded as a test of the overall usefulness of a regression model.

Test of linear restrictions   In regression analysis, a test to determine if the restrictions specified in the null hypothesis are invalid.

Time series   A set of sequential observations of a variable over time.

Total probability rule   A rule that expresses the unconditional probability of an event, $P(A)$, in terms of probabilities conditional on various mutually exclusive and exhaustive events. The total probability rule conditional on two events B and B^c is

$$P(A) = P(A \cap B) + P(A \cap B^c) = P(A|B)P(B) + P(A|B^c)P(B^c).$$

Tukey's honestly significant differences (HSD) method   In ANOVA, a test that determines which means significantly differ by comparing all pairwise differences of the means.

Two-tailed hypothesis test   A test in which we can reject the null hypothesis on either side of the hypothesized value of the population parameter.

Two-way ANOVA   A statistical technique used to examine simultaneously the effect of two factors on the mean. These tests can be conducted with or without the interaction of the factors.

Type I error   In a hypothesis test, this error occurs when the decision is to reject the null hypothesis, but the null hypothesis is actually true.

Type II error   In a hypothesis test, this error occurs when the decision is to not reject the null hypothesis, but the null hypothesis is actually false.

Unbalanced data   A completely randomized ANOVA design where the number of observations are not the same for each sample.

Unbiasedness   An estimator is unbiased if its expected value equals the unknown population parameter being estimated.

Unconditional probability   See *Marginal probability*.

Unsystematic patterns   In time series, patterns caused by the presence of an irregular or random error term.

Unweighted aggregate price index   An aggregate price index based entirely on aggregate prices with no emphasis placed on quantity.

Variable   A general characteristic being observed on a set of people, objects, or events, where each observation varies in kind or degree.

Variance   The average of the squared differences from the mean; a common measure of dispersion.

Weighted aggregate price index   An aggregate price index that gives higher weight to the items sold in higher quantities.

Wilcoxon rank-sum test   A nonparametric test to determine whether two population medians differ under independent sampling. Also known as the Mann-Whitney test.

Wilcoxon signed-rank test   A nonparametric test to determine whether a sample could have been drawn from a population having a hypothesized value as its median; this test can also be used to determine whether the median difference differs from zero under matched-pairs sampling.

Within-treatments variability   In ANOVA, a measure of the variability within each sample.

$\bar{x}$ bar chart   A control chart that monitors the central tendency of a production process.

z table   A table providing cumulative probabilities for positive or negative values of the standard normal random variable Z.

Jarque-Bera, 376
for Kruskal-Wallis test, 623
for mean difference, 317–318
for one-way ANOVA, 391–393
for population correlation coefficient, 426–427
for population mean, with known standard deviation, 278
for population proportion, 294
for population variance, 340
for population variance ratio, 349
for proportion differences, 325
for sign test, 632
for test of independence, 371
for Wald-Wolfowitz runs test, 635
for Wilcoxon rank-sum test, 618–619
for Wilcoxon signed-rank test, 611–612
Time series data; *see also* Forecasting; Returns; Smoothing techniques
defined, 6, 546
deflated, 598–600
nominal terms, 598
real terms, 598–600
serial correlation, 480–481
systematic patterns, 548, 562
unsystematic patterns, 548
Total probability rule, 118–121, 123
Total sum of squares (*SST*), 392, 411, 444
Toyota Motor Corp., 230
Transformations; *see also* Logarithms; Polynomial regression models
inverse, 189–191
normal, 187–189
Trend models
exponential, 556–559, 567–568
linear, 555–556, 567
polynomial, 559–560
quadratic, 559–560
seasonal dummy variables, 567–569
Trendlines, 432
Trends
extracting, 565–566
systematic patterns, 548
Tukey, John, 39, 395
Tukey's honestly significant differences (HSD) method, 397–399, 408
Two-tailed hypothesis tests, 273–274, 285
Two-tailed *t* test, 458–461, 467
Two-way ANOVA
defined, 402
example, 402–403
with interaction, 410–413
without interaction, 402–408
randomized block designs, 404–406
sample sizes, 403
uses of, 402
Type I errors, 275–276
Type II errors, 275–276

U

UCL; *see* Upper control limit
Unadjusted seasonal index, 564

Unbalanced data, 397–398
Unbiasedness, 242–243
Unconditional probability, 108, 119
Unexplained variation, 444
Union, of events, 97, 98, 105–106
U.S. Bureau of Labor Statistics, 6, 7, 599
U.S. Census Bureau, 7, 56
University of Pennsylvania Medical Center, 4
Unrestricted models, 468
Unsystematic patterns, 548
Unweighted aggregate price indices, 592–593
Upper control limit (UCL), 228–229, 230
USA TODAY, 5

V

Vanguard, 53, 73, 335, 352, 449, 450, 609, 628
Variability measures; *see* Dispersion measures
Variables; *see also* Dummy variables; Explanatory variables; Qualitative variables; Quantitative variables; Random variables
continuous, 9
defined, 8
discrete, 9
response, 430–431, 437–438
Variance; *see also* Analysis of variance; Population variance; Sample variance
defined, 70
of discrete random variable, 142–143
for frequency distribution, 80–81
mean-variance analysis, 74–75
of portfolio returns, 146–148
shortcut formula, 71, 81
Venn, John, 97
Venn diagrams, 97

W

Wald-Wolfowitz runs test, 634–637
Wall Street Journal, 7
Websites, data sources, 7
Weighted aggregate price indices, 593–596
Weighted mean, 81
Wilcox, R. A., 657, 658
Wilcoxon, F., 657, 658
Wilcoxon rank-sum test
critical values, 618, 658
for independent samples, 614, 616–619
software, 619
test statistic, 618–619
uses of, 312, 614–615
Wilcoxon signed-rank test
critical values, 612, 657
for matched-pairs sample, 615–616
for population median, 610–613
software, 616
test statistic, 611–612
uses of, 320, 614–615
Within-treatments estimate of population variance, 390, 391
Within-treatments variability, 390